NEWNES FAMILY LAWYER

Judges in their robes of office in procession from Westminster Abbey
to the House of Lords after the annual service at the Abbey at the
beginning of the Michaelmas Term.

NEWNES
FAMILY LAWYER

Edited by

DUDLEY PERKINS MA, (Cantab)

Solicitor of the Supreme Court of Judicature

General Editor

PETER FINCH MA, (Oxon)

GEORGE NEWNES LIMITED
15–17 Long Acre, London WC2

© George Newnes Limited

MADE AND PRINTED IN GREAT BRITAIN BY
MORRISON AND GIBB LIMITED, LONDON AND EDINBURGH

215264

CONTENTS

CONTENTS

SECTION 4: IN TROUBLE

CONTENTS

vii

CONTRIBUTORS

JOHN M. BULL, MA, LL.B, (*Barrister-at-Law*)

GERSHON ELLENBOGEN, MA (Cantab), (*Barrister-at-Law*)

C. GLYN HARDWICKE, (*Solicitor of the Supreme Court of Judicature*)

DESMOND HEAP, LL.M, (*Past President of the Town Planning Institute; Comptroller and City Solicitor to the Corporation of London*)

ESYR LEWIS, MA, LL.B (Cantab), (*Barrister-at-Law*)

MICHAEL LEWIS, MA (Oxon), (*Barrister-at-Law*)

JOSEPH M. MORAN, MA, LL.B, (*Advocate*)

GUY NAYLOR, MA (Cantab), (*Barrister-at-Law*)

MICHAEL UNDERHILL, (*Barrister-at-Law*)

G. B. WRIGHT, MA (Cantab), (*Solicitor of the Supreme Court of Judicature*)

Illustrations by BERNARD RICHARDSON, FRSA

Cover design 'Family Group' by A. BOOTH

Index by G. NORMAN KNIGHT, MA, MS Ind, (*Barrister-at-Law*) and PAMELA COLSTON-TURNER

viii

PREFACE

THERE IS an old legal maxim 'Ignorance of the law is no excuse' In other words, it is presumed that everyone knows what the law is. However fallacious this presumption may be, it is obviously necessary in a civilized society that everyone shall be bound by the law, and that no one shall be able to plead ignorance of it as an excuse for his acts or omissions.

The law is a living thing which guides and protects us all at all times, and the more we know about it the better we shall be able to steer a safe course through the difficulties and dangers of our complex modern life. Today, a work which will tell us in simple language something of the nature of the law and which will act as a signpost in the legal maze, is most welcome.

This book is intended to be just that, and, edited as it is by one who for so many years has himself explained in simple language to countless radio audiences how the law works, it would be surprising indeed if it did not fulfil that purpose admirably.

ARTHUR DRIVER

President of The Law Society, 1961-2

WHILE EVERY care has been taken to make this book accurate
and up to date, it must be emphasized that it is in no sense a
substitute for a solicitor's advice. The object of those who
have written it has been to try to show how and when the law
may affect any of us in our daily lives, *not* to provide a ready-
made answer to every legal problem.

The difference between the advice given by a solicitor,
and the interpretation of the law in this book is that a solicitor
advises on the facts of a particular case, and even a slight
variation in facts may affect his advice as to the law.

No reader therefore should attempt to act as his own lawyer
on the strength of the information contained herein, and for
that reason the Editor, Contributors, and Publishers cannot
accept responsibility.

Neither the Editor and Contributors, nor the Publishers
are prepared to enter into any personal correspondence.

The law as stated, in this revised impression of the First
Edition is, in general, as at 1st January 1962. It has, however,
been found possible to include references to later legislation,
e.g. legislation arising from the Budget of 1963, and to changes
in rates of interest on National Savings, and the Addendum on
pages 858–9 includes references to three recent Acts of
Parliament dealing with Husbands and Wives, the Nationalized
British Transport Industry and Weekly Tenants.

BUYING AND SELLING A HOUSE

BUYING A HOUSE

BUYING A HOUSE is one of the most important, perhaps the most important single transaction into which the average citizen will enter throughout the whole course of his life. And yet it is one in respect of which he probably knows a good deal less than many of the other comparatively minor transactions into which he enters in the course of his daily life.

The offer to purchase

Let us suppose that he has found the house which he would like to buy, that he has the means to buy it either out of his own resources or out of his own resources plus the money he reckons that he can borrow on mortgage. At this stage he may very likely be asked to sign something to show that his intentions are genuine. This is a moment of considerable risk not for the vendor but for him. Under English law if he signs a simple statement that he agrees to buy a specified house for a specified price and signs it, he is then legally committed to complete the purchase. If he fails to do so he may be liable for heavy damages, not merely for the sacrifice of any deposit which he has paid but for damages over and above the deposit. They might be high. They would have to represent the loss the vendor suffers if he has to sell at a lower price to someone else, or the loss he is suffering if he cannot sell to anyone for a considerable time.

The purchaser may say that he has no objection to committing himself in this way because he wants the house and is anxious to be legally bound so that the vendor may also be legally bound.

But two points arise. First of all, a statement which he signs may not bind the vendor. Secondly, that statement may bind him to go on with the purchase although, before it is completed, he may discover a whole lot of things about the house which, if he had known before, would have led him to call the whole thing off.

A typical statement which he may be asked to sign runs something like this: 'I, John Brown, of No. 1 Acacia Avenue, Anytown, agree to buy No. 5, Black Road from Mr Jones-Smith for the sum of £3,000.

Signed: John Brown.'

That very simple short statement is a binding legal contract which identifies

1

the purchaser, identifies the property, and states the price. Mr Brown is there and then under a legal obligation to buy the property at that price.

The risks of the unqualified offer

The dangers at this point are that there are a good many things about that house which he does not know, which in the nature of things he cannot know. What about the condition of the house itself? It may appear to be superficially sound as the result of recent redecoration. But what of the faults which are not obvious to the eye of anyone who is not an experienced surveyor or builder? There may be dry rot which is rather difficult to find unless you go in for extensive exploration; wood-worm in the timbers; no damp course, defective drains, etc. All these are things which are hidden from the eye of the ordinary observer. Suppose those defects are discovered after he has signed that simple contract. It is essential to realize that they do not give the would-be purchaser the right to cancel his agreement to buy. It would make no difference at all even if he could show that the vendor knew about some of these defects but said nothing about them. The law is that the vendor has no legal responsibility in this respect toward the purchaser. It is not for him to give warnings, it is for the purchaser to find out.

The second risk that the purchaser may run has nothing to do with physical defects of the house but concerns the future development of the neighbourhood. For instance, it may already have been decided by the local authority that that house and many others too should be pulled down for road widening, a very common thing in these days when large new roads are being built through towns and cities. There may be other reasons which would enable the local authority to exercise compulsory powers of purchase to take over the house and the land. Nowadays the price the local authority may pay on compulsory purchase is better than it used to be and is much nearer the market value of the house. But it may still not be equal to the price that the purchaser has paid—he may have paid too much—or equal to the price he could have got if he were selling it privately. In any case there is considerable interruption and upheaval.

Another risk is unknown legal liabilities of which there may be a good many. There may be obligations about the maintenance of party walls or boundary fences. There may be a system of sharing drains and sewers or water supplies involving a purchaser in financial outlay. There may be restrictive covenants affecting his use of the house, local authority requirements affecting outside walls or outbuildings and many other things which may involve a purchaser in expense, or restrict him in some way in his free use of the property.

The point to which all these rather sinister warnings is leading is this. It is always risky, even on a brand new house, to sign such a binding legal promise to buy until these questions have been investigated on the purchaser's behalf by two professional people who are thinking only of his interests. They are his solicitor and surveyor.

Meaning of 'subject to contract'

What then should the would-be purchaser do when, as mentioned above, he has found the house he wants, is anxious to buy it and is asked to sign

Faults not obvious to the eye of the ordinary purchaser.

something to prove the sincerity of his intention? The only safe answer that can be given is that in signing any kind of promise like that set out above, he should add the words, 'subject to contract'. These words mean that the promise to buy is genuine but that it is not to be legally binding until the vendor's solicitor has prepared a full and detailed contract disclosing all the possible legal liabilities and until *that* contract has been signed. The interval of time gives the purchaser's solicitor a chance to look into these possible liabilities and ask a variety of questions so that he may be able to say to his client either that the whole situation is completely clear or that there are certain snags which need to be investigated. When all inquiries are complete the solicitor can tell his client where he stands. The client can say that he will accept such risks or doubts as are left or that they are so serious that he must cancel his offer. As his signature to buy was 'subject to contract' he is not legally bound and he can cancel.

It is perfectly true that just as he is free to back out, so is the vendor, whose acceptance of the offer is also subject to contract, and during the time that these inquiries are being made the vendor may be tempted to sell to someone who offers a higher price. That is a risk. The purchaser may very much regret ultimately that he did not clinch the bargain straight away without troubling about these inquiries. On the other hand, the story they tell can be so serious that the only safe course for him to take is to sign subject to contract and allow a period which may amount to three to four weeks during which his solicitor and his surveyor can carry out these essential investigations for him.

The solicitor's inquiries

The problems with which the solicitor is concerned have already been mentioned, There are some thirty to forty questions which he will. as a matter of course, ask on almost any house purchase. Some of them he will put to the owner's solicitor. Others he will put to the County Council or the Urban or Rural District Council. His questions to the owner's solicitor will be directed to finding out mainly whether there are any restrictive covenants which affect the use of the property; whether there are any rights of way or rights of light; and other questions of this sort which are directed to finding out whether a new owner of the property is likely to find himself saddled with unusual expenses or unusual obligations toward other people. The questions to various local authorities, quite apart from the questions on town planning which have already been mentioned, will be concerned with local building by-laws or charges for making up a road, public health notices, etc. Their object, like the others, is to find out whether the client is buying a house which will be a burden to him.

The survey

Now we must come to the work of the other professional adviser which every would-be purchaser needs, the surveyor. There is a common impression that if the purchaser is borrowing money on mortgage whether from a building society or a private lender—and this will be dealt with later—then because the lender will certainly have the property surveyed, there is no need for the purchaser to have an independent survey. This is not a safe assumption. The lender's surveyor is not required to make a thorough, complete, and detailed

"... a full structural survey is what the purchaser needs. ..."

structural survey. His job is merely to make such a survey as will enable him to form a reasonable estimate of value. If the purchaser—the borrower—fails to keep up his payments and the lender has to exercise his legal remedies of taking over the property and expelling the purchaser from the house, would he be able to sell it for the amount of the loan?

The amount of the loan is certainly in most cases substantially less than the price which the purchaser is paying, and the mortgagee's surveyor is only concerned to be reasonably certain that on a sale the house would fetch that figure. In other words he may not be in the least concerned with defects which might cause a great deal of expense to a purchaser. For instance, a surveyor carrying out a thorough structural survey might advise that some of the roof should be re-tiled, that some of the drains should be renewed, that the electrical wiring is not adequate—matters which the purchaser would want to know before he commits himself to the expense of buying the house. The mortgagee's surveyor may not worry about these. His is only a *value* survey and these matters may not affect value. But a full *structural* survey, which is what the purchaser needs, is going to tell him everything that is wrong. It may affect his estimate of the price, it may lead him to go back to the vendor and try to negotiate a lower price, or it may lead him to say that he is not going to embark on that deal at all.

While these two sets of inquiries are going on, the vendor's solicitor will be preparing a draft of a full detailed contract which he will send to the purchaser's solicitor. The most important matters with which this contract will deal are first the nature of the title,—*i.e.* the proof of ownership—which the vendor is able to offer; secondly whether there are any restrictive covenants affecting the future use of the property; thirdly whether there are any encumbrances, a word which covers a variety of possible burdens. At this stage the vendor and his solicitor are not expected actually to prove the title but only to indicate the kind of title which can be offered, *e.g.* whether it is freehold or leasehold and how far back they are prepared to go to show that there is a good history of unimpeached ownership over a period long enough to carry the conviction that the title would not be successfully challenged today, and that once the purchaser has paid his money he can be confident that he is absolutely secure in what he has got. Equally important, that he can be absolutely sure that if he ever wants to sell the property, no future purchaser's solicitor will find defects in his title.

Finding the money

It will be useful at this point to say something about financing the purchase. If the would-be purchaser is not able or willing to provide the whole of the purchase money out of his own resources, he will want to borrow. The question of where to borrow is a matter on which he ought to get his solicitor's advice. Indeed this is one of the advantages of having a solicitor acting very early on in the purchase. Many a would-be purchaser starts wondering about financing before he has obtained advice and may indeed not get the best possible finance to meet his circumstances. If he has gone to a solicitor straight away the solicitor will help him not only to find a good surveyor to do the surveying work, but also to find the lender who will give him the best terms to meet his particular

Finding the money to finance the purchase of a house.

circumstances. The lender may be a building society. Another possible source of finance is a local authority. Another is a bank, although banks are not enthusiastic about lending on long loans for the purchase of property. Nevertheless they will do so occasionally. Another source of finance is the private lender, who may very well be a client of the solicitor, for instance, trustees who have funds to invest and who like to invest on the security of real property (*i.e.* land and houses).

The main difference between these different types of mortgages is in the method of repayment. The building society and the local authority will want to be repaid by instalments, usually monthly instalments, part of which will represent interest on the loan and part of which will be a repayment of the capital advanced. The result is that over a period of, say, twenty years the borrower will have not only paid a regular amount of interest but also repaid the whole of the capital advanced. The private lender, on the other hand, does not want his capital repaid. All he wants is a permanent loan on good security and he only asks for quarterly or half-yearly payments of interest. These payments, of course, will be very much less than the payments which include an element of capital. On the other hand, the capital loan always remains outstanding. The question of which to choose is a matter on which no general rules can possibly be laid down. It depends very much on the particular financial circumstances of every individual. Whichever method is chosen, however, it is generally regarded as sound advice to tell the borrower to take out a life policy or an endowment policy to cover the amount of the loan, so that if he dies before it has been repaid money is available to pay it off: a great advantage to his heirs.

Incidentally it is thought by many borrowers that as long as money is outstanding on mortgage the house does not 'belong' to the borrower, *i.e.* the mortgagor. That is nonsense. The house certainly belongs to him and he is free to sell it at any time. In law the house is HIS subject to a debt. The fact that the debt exists does not affect his legal ownership nor his complete freedom to dispose of the house as and when he pleases. He is merely under an obligation to pay off the debt with the proceeds of sale. He may even come to other arrangements such as transferring the debt to a future purchaser.

Another point of difference between the building society type of mortgage and the private lender's type of mortgage is that the building society will usually lend a higher proportion of their valuation of the property than the private lender will. The private lender as a rule is not willing to lend more than two-thirds of his valuation of the property. The reason for the difference, of course, is the point already made that under the building society type of loan a proportion of capital is being paid back month by month whereas under the private type of mortgage no capital is being repaid.

So far as rates of interest are concerned there is seldom any difference; as a rule the private lender and the building society charge much the same.

For houses built before 1919 a new scheme was introduced by the Government under the Housing and House Purchase Act of 1959 to help buyers who had difficulty in getting finance. Under this scheme building societies are able to get certain guarantees from the Treasury which enable them to lend fairly substantial sums on houses built before 1919. They will lend up to 95 per cent.

of the value of the house if its price is under £2,500 (or under £3,000 if it is in London). The scheme was necessary because there is such demand on building society funds that they were very naturally tending to give preference to loans on more modern houses where the security was greater, *i.e.* the possibility of resale was better if the borrower defaulted on his loan.

Occasionally a local authority will lend up to 100 per cent. of their valuation of the house, but this is not to be taken as a general rule and is subject to restriction in times of national economic difficulty.

Finally, on this question of finance, it has become apparent from the writer's personal experience that it can save a lot of worry and time if those who have decided that they want to buy a house would look into the question of finding the money *before* they start looking for the house. This may seem the wrong way round. In fact it is very much the right way round, because at the moment when the right house is found there may be very little time left in which to find a mortgagee, *i.e.* a lender, who is willing to move quickly enough to survey the house and say that he's willing to lend the desired amount of money. The lender may take weeks about this at a time when the would-be purchaser can scarcely afford that time. It is best to start exploring the means of finding the money before you look for the house. Here, too, a solicitor can help and it is not a bad idea to have him interested before you actually find the house. If you do not go to a solicitor at that stage but have decided that you would like to borrow through a building society it is very easy to go and see the society and to discover the kind of conditions which they are likely to lay down. For instance, one matter which plays a very important part in influencing a society whether to lend or not, is not just the kind of house which it is proposed to buy, but the kind of *person* the would-be borrower is. What are his or her earnings. What are his prospects. In short, is he the kind of person to whom the society would like to lend. It is all very well to say that the ultimate security is the house. The building society would prefer to lend with a reasonable assurance that the money will always be paid. They do not want to exercise their legal remedies of foreclosure and selling the house if they can avoid it. Naturally, therefore, they prefer to lend to people on whose personal character they can rely. So there is sense and purpose in exploring future finance before the actual house has been found.

One last warning. Even if the purchaser can borrow a large proportion of the price he will have to find a substantial proportion for himself. For instance, on a house costing £4,000 the purchaser might be able to borrow 80 per cent., that is £3,200, from a building society, but the deposit, the stamp duties which are a tax payable to the Inland Revenue, the legal fees payable to the solicitor, the fees payable to the surveyor, and the fees payable to a building society will add up to at least £950. That is a sum which the purchaser will have to find for himself. On a £3,000 house the purchaser would need to find rather less, probably about £700. On a conveyance of a £3,000 house there is no stamp duty for him to pay and the fees are correspondingly lower. But those two examples provide a sort of guide to the amounts which have to be found out of the purchaser's own pocket, even if he borrows from a building society which, as stated above, lends a higher proportion of the valuation of the house than the private lender.

The contract

Let us come back to the actual purchase of the house. We have reached the stage where assuming that the solicitor's preliminary inquiries and the surveyor's report are all satisfactory, and assuming that the draft contract meets with the purchaser's solicitor's approval, the contract is ready for signature. This detailed contract is the contract to which the original promise was subject. Once the purchaser signs one part of the contract and the vendor signs an exact duplicate part of the contract and the two parts are exchanged, there is a binding legal contract. At this stage neither vendor nor purchaser can back out (save for one important qualification mentioned in the next paragraph).

The substantial difference between this document and the simple little promise which Mr John Brown signed in the example given in the beginning is that the purchaser now knows that the house is structurally sound, that the mortgagees have valued it and will lend the sum that he needs and that so far as is forseeable he is likely to be able to live in his house undisturbed. Moreover, he knows that the vendor has undertaken to prove his title over a period of years going back to some definite landmark in the history of the house. This is the one factor which would enable the *purchaser* to break off his contract. If the vendor is unable to prove his title and can only produce something weaker or poorer than he has promised to do, the purchaser can break off the deal if he is so minded. In other words the purchaser is now in a very strong position.

After the contract

The sale and purchase of a house or land is usually effected by two documents: the first is the contract which has just been described, and the second is a deed of conveyance or transfer. The contract contains the mutual promises to buy and sell on certain terms and conditions; the deed of conveyance and transfer is the legal document which actually effects the transfer of ownership from vendor to purchaser. Between the date of the contract and the date of the final deed of transfer the purchaser and vendor have special rights and special obligations with regard to the house.

The vendor becomes in a sense the trustee of his property for the benefit of the purchaser. For instance, he must keep it in reasonable condition. He need not carry out any major works of repair or redecoration, but if, for example, windows are broken by the carelessness of himself or his family it is his duty to repair them. If a storm causes damage he must at his own expense carry out emergency repairs to stop further deterioration. The broad general principle which the law applies is that the vendor must take all reasonable care of the house for the benefit of the purchaser until the day arrives when the deed of transfer is signed and it belongs to the purchaser.

The purchaser also has certain obligations toward the vendor. One of the most important is that he has to take the risk of fire damaging the property before the sale is completed. Even if the house is totally destroyed by fire so that nothing but an empty shell is left for him to buy, he would still have to go on with the purchase and pay the price agreed upon in the contract. This is not so serious as it sounds, at least from the financial point of view, because a purchaser who has signed a binding contract is legally entitled to insure the house, and it is one of the matters on which his solicitor would be certain to advise him.

A point which sometimes crops up during this stage between the signing of the contract and the final deed of transfer is what fixtures and fittings have been included in the sale of the house. The general rule is that anything attached to the house or to the land is regarded as being included in the sale. But there can so easily be argument and misunderstanding about such fixtures and fittings as a free-standing kitchen range, or a water softener, or fitted cupboards. To avoid disputes of this kind it is desirable that a list of the most important

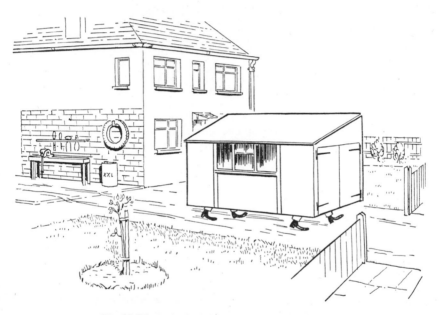

Would this be included in the sale of the house?

fixtures and fittings should be drawn up and actually included in the contract. It is a point very much for the purchaser personally to watch, because he will probably have been over the house several times, whereas his solicitor may not have seen it.

Proof of the vendor's title

The one remaining legal matter for the purchaser's solicitor to attend to is the proof of the title, that is, proof of the ownership of the vendor. This is a somewhat technical matter and very much one for the purchaser's solicitor to

11

deal with. At this stage he is given by the vendor's solicitor an abstract of the history of the recent title of the house. This means simply a record of the ways in which and the times at which the ownership of the house has changed hands.

Title is established by a chain of linked documents: each link must be legally valid. All the original documents which indicate that link must be examined by the purchaser's solicitor so that he may satisfy himself that not only do they contain the essential words necessary to pass on whatever legal estate was being dealt with but also that they're properly stamped, properly signed or executed, and so on.

". . . proof of the vendor's title. . . ."

This is the second important stage of the solicitor's functions in acting for a purchaser. The first stage, as we have seen, is the inquiries which he has to make before he can advise his client that he can safely put his signature to a legally binding contract. The second is to ensure that when the deed of transfer of the house is signed the purchaser is getting a document which is legally unassailable and which will establish his ownership of the house in times to come. It would, of course, be pointless to do the work of investigating the title before the legally binding contract had been signed, and that is why this work is done in two stages.

Registration of title

Another method of establishing title to property and land is the registration of title at the Land Registry in London. Registration of title simplifies the work of the purchaser's solicitor because instead of having to examine all the documents going back over a period of many years, he need only examine the Land Certificate and the entries therein. It is true that the Land Certificate may refer him to other documents which have a bearing on the title. The Land Certificate is not simply and solely a short document saying that No. 1 Acacia Avenue belongs to Mr John Jones. There are perhaps some Land Certificates which are nearly as simple as that, but most of them contain a good deal more information and indications of matters which the solicitor ought to look into. To mention only one—restrictive covenants. Moreover, there are matters which are not registered and he has to find out about them.

So registration is not a magic way to the utmost simplicity, but it is a simplification, and this fact is indicated by the lower fees which the solicitors are entitled to charge when they are dealing with registered land.

Registration of title to land is compulsory on all new dealings, that is, a sale and purchase, and on the granting of certain leases, on all property in the areas which are described in the appendix to this chapter. Elsewhere, registration is voluntary. The areas of compulsory registration are likely to be extended gradually, as the Land Registry can cope with the work.

A Land Certificate proving title to property in land is not in the least like a registration book of a motor-car. The registration book of a motor-car is not a document of title at all. It proves nothing except that the car has been registered in the name of a certain person. It does not prove that he is the owner. The Land Certificate is in quite a different category. It is not issued until the Land Registry have examined all the deeds and documents of title of the property just as the purchaser's solicitor would on a purchase, and it is a proof of ownership.

One reason why these questions of title to land are so important is that land by reason of its permanence has for hundreds, if not thousands, of years been regarded as a valuable heritable asset, and one which is capable of being used and enjoyed by people who have an interest in it which is something less than complete ownership. An obvious example is a tenant who merely has a right to occupy a part of the land for a period of time. Another example is a tenant for life, who may have the property for his or her life and, by law, is given certain very unusual rights not available to a tenant for a term of years. Another example is someone who has only a right to walk over a piece of land or a right to drive a car or other vehicle over that land. Then there is land which is held in trust for the benefit of other people. Land may be mortgaged and sub-mortgaged and sub-mortgaged again. Rights of light, rights of support, rights to have water, electricity, etc., carried through the land may be legal burdens on the land. Ownership of minerals under the land may be in different hands from ownership of the surface of the land. Equally, ownership of the trees on the land may be vested in someone other than the owner of the land. By reason of its permanence and its intrinsic value, land can be subject to an almost infinite division of rights and interests from the absolute owner of the whole down to the squatter who is busy trying to acquire squatter's title to a part of it. That, briefly, is why it is so important that the vendor's title should be expertly examined.

When the title is proved to the purchaser's solicitor's satisfaction, he prepares a draft of the conveyance or deed of transfer and sends it to the vendor's solicitor for approval. The draft may go back and forth with various amendments, but when agreed between the two solicitors it is ready to be signed, sealed, and delivered.

Completion of the purchase

To round off the picture, the final transaction will usually take place in the office of the vendor's solicitor where in return for money paid to him by the purchaser's solicitor, the vendor's solicitor will hand over the deed of transfer duly executed and all the documents of title or the Land Certificate.

If there is a mortgage the mortgagee's solicitor will also be there and he has a right to take the deeds of the property and the deed of transfer himself, because he will keep those on behalf of his client so long as the mortgage exists. When the mortgage is paid off he will return the deeds to the purchaser.

Costs and expenses

Every intending purchaser wants, of course, to know what all this is going to cost him in terms of stamp duty, solicitor's fees, surveyor's fees, and so on. The surveyor's fees for carrying out a structural survey are not fixed by any

SPECIMEN COSTS OF VENDOR AND PURCHASER

PRICE	£2,000	£3,000	£4,000	£5,000
SOLICITOR'S COSTS (Unregistered Land)	£37 10 0	£52 10 0	£60 0 0	£67 10 0
SOLICITOR'S COSTS (Registered Land)	£25 0 0	£35 0 0	£40 0 0	£43 15 0
STAMP DUTY* (Paid by Purchaser)	Nil	Nil	Nil	£25 0 0
ESTATE AGENT'S COMMISSION (Payable by Vendor)	£62 10 0	£87 10 0	£112 10 0	£137 10 0

THE ABOVE ARE THE BASIC CHARGES. *If there is a mortgage both parties' solicitors will charge a fee for preparation and approval of the mortgage deed. This is less than the fees quoted above but cannot easily be included in a table because it varies with the type of mortgage. On dealings in registered land the Land Registry charge a fee for registering the dealing, but it is not substantial,* e.g. *on a* £3,000 *house the fee is* £7 10s, *on a* £4,000 *house* £10, *etc.*

* As changed by the 1963 Finance Act.

scale laid down by a professional organization. They are a matter for negotiation and much will depend on how thorough the purchaser wants the survey to
be. As a very rough guide, on a house costing £4/5,000 a complete structural
survey would probably cost 20–25 guineas. On a smaller house it would be less.

The fees which a solicitor may charge are set out in detail in a very useful
little pamphlet published by the Law Society of Chancery Lane, London,
W.C.2, called *A Short Guide to Solicitors' Costs in Conveyancing Matters*.
There you will find the tables which will show not only the fees but also the
stamp duty which has to be paid to the Revenue.

It is true that a solicitor is entitled to make a bargain with his client before
the transaction begins that he will not charge according to these scales but may

"Free conveyance."

charge a fee which is reasonable having regard to all the circumstances, but it
is very seldom that a solicitor exercises this right. He prefers to let his fee be
determined by the scale, which, incidentally, is not drawn up by the solicitors'
profession but is laid down by a Statutory Committee.

A few examples of typical charges might be helpful and they are set out
on the opposite page.

The usual practice is for the purchaser to pay his own solicitor and the
vendor to pay his solicitor and that is what will happen if nothing is settled
about it at the time of the contract. Nothing is saved by having one solicitor
to act for both parties. At one time it was possible for the solicitor acting for
both parties legally to make a reduction in his fee. Now he is forbidden to do so,
because it is felt that, generally speaking, it is undesirable for one solicitor to
act for both parties. On a transaction as important as this it is really essential
that the solicitors engaged in the matter should be free of conflict of interest.
One solicitor should act exclusively for one client and think only of his interests.

Many builders who develop large housing estates offer what is called a
free conveyance to the purchasers of any of their houses. This means that when
the purchaser pays for the house he will receive a properly signed and executed
deed of transfer of the house to him. Any purchaser who likes to accept this

15

offer is, of course, free to do so, but in our view it is such a grave risk that it should never be accepted. There is no suggestion, of course, that anything wrong or deceitful would have been done. The point is that of the matters that have been described above, none have been investigated on the purchaser's behalf. The builder's solicitor owes him no duty; he has a duty to his client and to no one else.

Freehold or leasehold

One very important point for a purchaser to watch is whether the property for sale is freehold or leasehold. In simple terms, freehold means that the house is the absolute property of the owner, whereas a leasehold house will only remain his property for the term of years laid down in the lease. For example, if a house is offered for sale with a leasehold term of sixty years at a price of, say, £5,000, the purchaser who buys that house or his successor will have his right to occupy terminated at the end of sixty years. During that sixty years he and his successor or successors will probably have paid a small ground rent, but the capital sum will not have bought anything more than the right of occupation for the term of the lease.

It is true that the Landlord and Tenant Act of 1954, which is described elsewhere in this work under the heading 'Long Leaseholds', has given such a purchaser some new rights, and if he is able to take advantage of the provisions of the Act he may be able to remain in occupation on new terms. These matters are fully dealt with in the section on 'Long Leaseholds', and the only point it is desired to make here is that it is essential for the purchaser to realize that although he has paid a capital sum he has not bought a permanent ownership of the house but only ownership and right of occupation for a definite period of years.

Probably the best way to look at the transaction is to regard the capital sum as a payment of rent in advance—sixty years' rent in advance, or whatever the period of years may be.

However, a purchaser can always ensure that at the end of the term of years the money originally spent to buy the lease will come back to him with interest if he takes out an insurance policy known as a 'sinking fund policy', under which he pays a yearly premium which accumulates at compound interest to bring in an agreed sum of money at the end of a stated period.

He himself during the period of the lease will usually be able to sell it if he wishes to; for example, if he wants to move after ten years, he can offer for sale the remaining fifty years of the lease and the benefit of a sinking fund policy can be assigned to the purchaser.

The purchaser should also note carefully the provisions in the lease for repair. There are certain to be some quite strict provisions about keeping the house in repair.

It is naturally more difficult to obtain a mortgage on a leasehold than on a freehold property, although most mortgagees are willing to consider lending on leasehold property when the lease still has more than, say, sixty years left to run. It is possible to borrow on a shorter term, but the terms of the mortgage would probably be more severe than a mortgage of a freehold or a very long leasehold.

SELLING A HOUSE

Let us assume that you are a house-owner who has decided to sell his house. How will you set about it? There are three usual ways of doing so. First, to tell your friends and ask them to tell others that you are anxious to sell; in other words, a private chain of communication from friend to friend and from acquaintance to acquaintance. Secondly, you will put your own advertisement into a newspaper, a local or national or both. Thirdly, you will go to an estate agent and tell him that you want to sell your house and ask him to find a purchaser.

With regard to the first two methods there is nothing special to say. One of the main problems of anyone wanting to sell his house is what price to fix. He may, however, have a very good idea about this when he thinks of the prices at which similar houses in his neighbourhood have changed hands. He knows, moreover, what he has paid for the house, what he has spent on it, what has happened to the value of money during the period between the year when he bought it and the year in which he wants to sell, and taking those factors into account he should have no difficulty in fixing the price which he thinks he ought to get. Mark you, a man in this position may be wildly pessimistic or wildly optimistic. He may not be aware of such factors as scarcity of houses which has increased prices beyond what might be mathematically reasonable; alternatively he may not be aware of other factors like changes in the character of the neighbourhood or future planned changes in the character of the neighbourhood which will put off prospective purchasers. For example, when he bought his house it may have been, to use estate agents' jargon, a most 'desirable' neighbourhood. When he comes to sell it the desirability from the estate agents' point of view may have been negatived by new planning proposals leading to the establishment of, say, an industrial estate or an aerodrome or something of that sort in or near the immediate neighbourhood. He may, perhaps, not know of these plans but they will be a factor which will influence any future purchaser, at least if he is well advised. An experienced agent may help in this sort of case, because although if he is asked to give a valuation he is entitled to a special fee, he will usually give informal advice about the 'asking price' without charging an extra fee.

The first two methods, telling your friends or putting in your own advertisement, raise no particular difficulties but we must consider carefully the situation which arises when the house-owner instructs an estate agent.

Instructing an agent

How exactly will he instruct an agent? This is not just a simple matter of calling at the agent's office and saying, "Find me a buyer for my house". The agent will almost certainly want to know whether he is to be the only agent the owner is going to see or whether the house-owner is going to call on other agents in the town. Is he to have the sole agency or is the house-owner going to instruct other agents and set up competition between them?

This idea of competition between the agents may sound attractive. But there is at least one possible disadvantage. All the prospective buyers who are looking for a house in your district probably write to several agents. Perhaps all those agents have your house on their books. One of these potential purchasers agrees with you to buy. Then comes the question: who introduced that purchaser; to whom should you pay the commission? There is a risk of argument and disagreement, especially if the purchaser, unaware of the trouble he may be causing, has discussed the possibility of buying your house with more than one of the agents.

So to avoid this kind of complication, if you do decide to instruct several agents, it is very advisable to tell them all in writing that you have done this, that you will pay only one commission, and that to the agent who actually introduces the purchaser to you. This should go some way to obviate the risk of having to pay two commissions.

Another way of avoiding this risk is to appoint one firm of agents to be your sole agent, at any rate for a time. It is quite a sensible and common practice to appoint one agent, or one firm of agents, to be your sole agents for a period, let us say three months, and to inform them that if they have not found a purchaser by the end of three months you reserve the right to instruct other agents. This may be a far better spur to immediate activity on the part of those agents than the sort of competition which you may create by instructing several agents at the same time. There is much to be said in favour of giving one good agent whom you may have selected on the advice of your solicitor or bank manager or anyone else who advises you on your practical affairs, the sole agency for a period of time, and, in general, two to three months is reasonable.

Another method is to tell the agent you choose that you want him to instruct sub-agents. This means that he will give the details of your house to other firms of agents which he will select and then if one of these others finds the buyer, the agents, that is the head agent and the sub-agent, will divide the commission between them. You will not be concerned with any arguments between the agents as you might be if you instruct others direct. You will pay one commission on the recognized scale which has been drawn up by the leading professional associations of estate agents and there is a well-settled understanding among agents as to how that is to be divided between them in circumstances such as this. The scale for negotiating a sale by Private Treaty or introducing a person able, ready, and willing to purchase on terms authorized by the vendor is: 5 per cent. on the first £500; $2\frac{1}{2}$ per cent. on the next £4,500; and $1\frac{1}{2}$ per cent. on the residue. (Minimum fee, £7 10s 0d.) The same scale applies to a sale by Auction, including the preparation of particulars and advising as to reserves.

There is one other method. This is to instruct two agents and tell them to co-operate with each other. This is useful when you want to sell a house which is rather large or may be difficult to sell in the sense that it is only of interest to a few people: for instance, a large country house. In this sort of situation it is quite common to instruct one agent in the locality and one agent in the capital which may be London or Cardiff or Edinburgh—a firm with a national or international reputation. When you instruct two firms on this basis of equal co-operation and either of them finds a buyer, you have to pay a little more than the standard commission; you have to pay one and a half times ordinary commission and this is divided between them.

So, to sum up, these are the three most usual ways of instructing agents:

(1) free competition;
(2) sole agency, with the possible addition of sub-agents;
(3) two equal chief agents.

Whichever you choose, it is most important to get a clear understanding in writing, and to exchange letters with the agents which make it clear what you expect of them and what they agree to do.

Liability to pay commission

The situation may arise where you have asked one or more firms of estate agents to sell your house for you but before they find a purchaser, *you* succeed in doing so. It may be someone you already know; it may be someone introduced by a friend, it may even be a complete stranger who has heard from local gossip that your house is for sale and calls to see you. No agent has come into the picture at all.

The vital question in this sort of situation is: are you liable to pay commission to any agent? If any agent can establish that it was his publicity which led to the stranger coming to see you, then, of course, he would have a very strong case for your paying his commission. One can imagine a variety of circumstances where this question may be very difficult, but assuming that the purchaser has come *without any conceivable influence from any agent at all*, then there can be no question of commission being payable. The fact that an agent has been instructed on any of the three bases mentioned above does not mean that the house-owner is debarred from either making personal efforts to sell his house or from accepting an overture from a stranger *via* a friend, or *via* any other means, and if he does so he is not thereby making himself liable to pay commission. Even if he has given an agent the sole agency this does not mean that he is thereby prevented from making any personal effort to sell the house himself, or prevented from accepting any overtures coming *via* a friend or acquaintance from any would-be purchaser.

He is completely free to negotiate privately unless he has given an agent what are called 'the sole selling rights'. This is an unusual contract for any owner of property to enter into but it does exist and it is important to get it clear. It is more than a sole agency, it is an agreement to give the agent the 'sole selling rights'. Once that is done the owner must not negotiate privately; if any prospective purchaser comes to him he must send him to the agent. This is an exceptional contract but it does occur, particularly where the property may be rather difficult to sell; it may be rather large or rather special in some way. But in every other case when 'sole selling rights' are not given, the owner is free to arrange his own private sale without being liable to pay commission unless the agent had something to do with the introduction directly or indirectly. It is very important, of course, that if the owner does succeed in his private negotiations he must tell the agent at once. It would be most unfair to let them go on looking for purchasers when he has already found one.

We must come now to the question of commission. When does an agent earn his commission? Obviously if the sale which is accomplished is a result of his introduction. But suppose he introduces a purchaser and the sale goes off. When in those circumstances is he entitled to any commission?

The answer depends upon what the seller agrees with the agent at the time when he asks him to find a purchaser. The standard form of contract between house-owner and agent provides that the agent will undertake to try to find a buyer who is 'able, ready and willing' to buy the house on terms which are acceptable to the owner. Those words 'able, ready and willing' are taken from the official publication of the leading estate agents' societies which sets out the rates of commission and which is generally accepted by the majority of agents.

What do these words mean? There has been a good deal of litigation about them and it is not altogether easy to say in straightforward and simple language when a commission is payable under such a contract. Generally speaking, it seems that the words 'able, ready and willing to buy' mean that the agent has found a buyer who first signs a binding legal contract, and secondly pays over his money when the seller signs the Deed of Transfer. Those words carry the implication that the buyer not only signs a binding contract but also completes the transaction by paying the whole purchase price.

Suppose, however, that although he is legally bound he does not complete the transaction, although the house-owner is in no way to blame. There is nothing wrong with the title and no justification for the buyer backing out. The house-owner may very well be able to sue the defaulting purchaser for damages, to sue him for breach of contract. But he is not obliged to do this; he may prefer to let the matter drop and start again. The agent cannot make him embark on legal proceedings so that he may get his commission.

So the general rule is that an agent who undertakes to find a purchaser on these terms is entitled to his commission only when the sale is completed.

The situation may arise, however, where the house-*owner* changes his mind, and although the agent introduces a purchaser who is able, ready, and willing to buy, the seller decides that after all he will not sell. Whatever his reasons may be, *e.g.* that another house he wanted to buy is withdrawn, or that he has simply changed his mind, is he then liable for commission?

The answer is that the seller is free to break off at any moment up to the time when he exchanges a legally binding contract with the proposed purchaser. If he breaks off before that point he is not liable to pay commission even though the would-be purchaser introduced by the agent is anxious to go on. If, however, he breaks off negotiations after that contract has been signed he is liable to pay commission to the agent and probably liable to pay damages to the would-be purchaser as well.

It is understandable that agents have tried from time to time to protect themselves from a potential seller's late change of mind. For instance, one agent devised a contract under which commission was payable by his client, the potential seller, if he introduced someone who was '*prepared* to enter into a contract to purchase': *i.e.* he was genuine, but before the question of signing a binding contract to buy arose, the vendor had changed his mind.

This makes the vendor liable to pay commission even though he changes his mind. And there are other forms of agreement with the agent which similarly tie the vendor down. Clearly a vendor should read and understand what his agent asks him to sign, and as he will need a solicitor to act for him on a sale of his house, it would be intelligent to get his solicitor's advice on any unusual agreement an agent asks him to sign so that he can understand exactly what he is undertaking.

BUYING A HOUSE BY AUCTION

There is a fundamental difference between buying by auction and buying by private negotiation, which was described in the previous chapter—'by private treaty' as it is generally known in the estate agent's business. The difference is that when you buy at an auction you cannot make a bid 'subject to contract' as you can when you are buying by private negotiation. Such a bid, if it were possible, would indicate your serious interest in the property, but also that an acceptance of your offer is not going to convert it into a legally binding contract until you have made the kind of inquiries described in the section on 'Buying a House', and until you have signed a formal detailed contract. None of that is possible at an auction, because if your bid is accepted by the auctioneer, you are committed.

Preliminary inquiries

It follows from this that no buyer should go to an auction sale hoping to bid for a house until he already knows everything that he should and could know if all the inquiries described in that section had been made before he went to the auction. In short, at the stage matters have then reached he is in the position of a person who is prepared to sign a binding legal contract if only the price is acceptable and his bid is accepted by the auctioneer.

So if a house is advertised for sale by auction, the first step for the would-be buyer is to obtain from the auctioneer the detailed particulars of the property which the auctioneer will have prepared. They are usually printed; they contain a comprehensive description of the property and everything about it which the auctioneer feels that he ought to disclose and which will be of interest to a potential buyer.

Attached to these particulars there will usually be a list of the conditions of sale which have been prepared by the vendor's solicitor, together with a short memorandum of agreement which will be used as the form of contract between the vendor and the successful buyer. These conditions of sale are in fact very similar to the full formal detailed contract which will be prepared by the vendor's solicitor for a sale by private negotiation.

Armed with these particulars and conditions of sale, the would-be purchaser should go straight off to the solicitor he proposes to instruct to act for him, and the surveyor whom he proposes to instruct, so that they can then carry out exactly the same kind of inquiries as they would on a sale by private treaty.

The ideal state of affairs is that when the date of the auction comes along and the potential buyer, or someone acting on his behalf, goes to the auction ready to bid, he does so in the knowledge that all the essential preliminary inquiries have been made, the survey has proved to be satisfactory, and, provided only that he can buy the house at the price he is prepared to pay, he knows that he is getting a house which neither in its structure or physical condition nor in the legal encumbrances or hostile interests which may have become attached to it, will be a burden to him.

Method of conducting the sale

The auctioneer opens the sale by drawing attention to the particulars of sale and the conditions of sale, and saying that he assumes that all those interested have received copies so that he need not read them. If there are any amendments or alterations he will make them then. He will invite questions, but at this stage it is rather late for a potential buyer to ask important questions, either about the condition of the property or legal questions arising from the conditions of sale. Those are matters which should be got out of the way well before the day of the auction.

Once the auctioneer starts the sale by inviting bids, it goes on until the sale is completed by the fall of the hammer. The purchaser whose bid has been successful should wait until the end of the sale so that he can sign a memorandum of contract and pay the usual 10 per cent. deposit to the auctioneer. When he has done this he will receive from the auctioneer a copy of the contract, signed by the auctioneer as agent for the vendor.

On the fall of the hammer the auctioneer becomes by law the agent for both the vendor and the purchaser. He can sign both contracts in the absence of the parties, so even if the successful purchaser leaves the sale without waiting to sign the memorandum of contract, the auctioneer is legally entitled to sign on his behalf, and it will be just as binding on him as if he had signed it himself.

Reserve price

A sale by auction is very often subject to a reserve price, and the law is that the particulars of sale should state quite clearly whether there is a reserve price or not. If the property is to be sold 'without reserve' the auctioneer is bound to accept the highest bid, however small it is. Obviously very few houses are sold 'without reserve'.

If the bids do not reach the reserve price the property will be withdrawn from the sale. The auctioneer is not to disclose the precise reserve price to the bidders, but he is allowed to tell them whether the bids have reached the reserve or not. Sometimes during the course of an auction the auctioneer is actually asked this specific question. He will answer it; he may even volunteer the information, so that bidders then know that when they go on, in competition with each other, at least the reserve price has been passed.

The vendor is not allowed to bid himself or by his agent at an auction, with a view to stimulating interest in running up the price, unless there is a condition that the sale is 'subject to a reserved right to bid'. In that case the vendor or an agent engaged by him is allowed to bid in order to stimulate the bidding.

Expenses

The expenses of the sale and the auctioneer's commission are, in general, payable by the vendor. In some parts of the country, however, there is a custom whereby the purchaser pays part of the auctioneer's fees. This is not a common custom, but it is a question which the potential buyer would be well advised to put to his solicitor before the auction so that he may know beforehand whether he is likely to be involved in some additional expense.

The vital point which must be repeated, re-emphasized, is that the successful bidder at such an auction is absolutely committed when the hammer falls on his bid, and that all the important preliminary inquiries described in detail in the section on 'Buying a House' must be made before he sets foot in the auction rooms.

SELLING A HOUSE BY AUCTION

Advantages and disadvantages

What are the advantages and disadvantages of selling by auction? The advantages are the considerable publicity which is given to the proposed sale. A house which is likely to fetch a reasonable price will probably be extensively advertised by the auctioneer, both by newspaper advertisement and by posters. There is a reasonable certainty that, at least within the locality of the house, there will be wide general publicity and that both potential private buyers, and others who may be buying for investment, will become aware of the sale in a way which they might not if it is arranged privately.

A second advantage is that if there are two or three or more keen buyers at the auction, a considerable spirit of competition is generated and a much higher price may be obtained than otherwise. If there is merely one bidder the vendor may do very badly. It is something of a gamble. But if he gets two or three and is helped by a skilful auctioneer who can stimulate the bidding, it is probable that the price will be higher than might have been achieved by private negotiation. Bidders at an auction are probably freer with their bids than prospective purchasers by private treaty, because they have this great advantage that they know the bids of their competitors, and sometimes they can sense the atmosphere; sometimes they can judge how far they may have to go to beat their competitors.

There are, however, some disadvantages. First of all, it is more expensive than a sale by private negotiation, whether the vendor employs an agent or not. For instance, an auction inevitably means money to pay for advertising, bill-posting, and printing. These costs are not included in the auctioneer's commission, and so they have to be paid even if no sale results from the auction. They can be quite heavy—a sum of £20 to £30 on only a small property—and it is very advisable to get some estimate of what they might amount to before a decision to sell by auction is taken.

It is quite impossible to give any general advice whether it is better to sell by auction or better to sell by private treaty. Much depends upon the kind of house, the kind of neighbourhood, and sometimes even upon the time of year. It is a matter on which the vendor would be well advised to consult both his solicitor and the auctioneer whom he is proposing to instruct.

The vendor can, of course, ensure that if the auction is a failure and so few bidders attend that no spirit of competition is stimulated, the property nevertheless will not be knocked down at an absurd price because, as described above, in the section on buying at an auction, he can fix a reserve price below which the auctioneer is not to sell. The vendor is entitled to the auctioneer's advice on the figure to be fixed as a reserve without further fee, because his commission on the auction includes valuation for reserve. This is in contrast with the situation where the sale is to be negotiated privately. In that case the vendor is not entitled to get his agent's advice on the value unless he pays a valuation fee. In practice, of course, he very often does get indirect advice, because, between them, they fix the asking price for the property, and this may arise in course of conversation. But the agent is not legally obliged to fix a value for the property to be sold privately unless he is expressly asked to do so, and then he can charge a fee. On an auction sale, however, his commission includes advice on the right reserve price to fix.

Arrangements to be made with the auctioneer

The vendor must naturally come to a clear and explicit arrangement with the auctioneer as to the amount of his commission and his fee if there is no sale. At the same time he should come to some clear arrangement about the additional cost of printing and advertising which has already been mentioned.

Between the time of receiving instructions to prepare for an auction and the auction itself, the auctioneer will expect to be given a sole agency for the sale of the property, and it is customary to agree to this. In fact, it would be unwise not to; if the auctioneer is to act exclusively in your interests from then on, it is only fair and reasonable that he should have a sole agency, the terms of which have already been described in the section on selling a house by private treaty. This means that quite possibly, as a result of the publicity given to the forthcoming auction, some potential buyer will come along with an offer which is so good that the vendor might be advised in his own interests to accept it and not let the property go to auction where, perhaps, not such a good price would be obtained. After all, that potential buyer is not going to the auction to offer the same price as he offered in the private negotiations. He will start much lower, hoping to get the property at a lesser price, and if there is no competition and his price is at least above the reserve, he is bound to be successful.

The situation might arise that, when the sale by auction is advertised, and a buyer makes an offer before the sale which is accepted, the auctioneer's commission is payable, even though he has not been given the sole agency, and even though he did not actually introduce the buyer. He is entitled to his commission because, even though that buyer perhaps came along direct to the vendor privately and not through anyone else's introduction, it is almost certain that he came because of the publicity attendant on the forthcoming sale by auction. However, whatever the reason, the fact is that it is well established that the auctioneer is entitled to his commission.

If the auction fails to produce a buyer, because the reserve price is not reached, but a buyer comes along within three months afterwards, enters into a binding contract and completes the purchase of the house, the auctioneer is still entitled to his commission, even though that buyer may not have been introduced by him. He is as entitled to his commission as if he had sold at the auction.

Sometimes a buyer who comes along after an auction fails goes direct to the auctioneer whom he knows is connected with the property, and negotiates with him. In that event the auctioneer is even more clearly entitled to his commission, but to cover that kind of contingency an auctioneer will often ask for a sole agency to be granted to him for a period of, say, three months after the auction, and it is customary to accede to this request. It does not really matter whether the vendor accedes or not, because of the auctioneer's right to his commission on a sale effected within three months, but if he does, he may well find that the auctioneer through his many contacts will continue to do his very best to find a purchaser.

APPENDIX

Areas of compulsory registration

County of London.
County Borough of Eastbourne.
County Borough of Hastings.
County of Middlesex.
County Borough of Croydon.
County of Surrey.
County Borough of City of Oxford.
County Borough of Oldham.
County Borough of City of Leicester.
County Borough of City of Canterbury.
County of Kent:
> The municipal boroughs of Chatham, Gillingham, Gravesend, and Rochester;
> The urban districts of Swanscombe and Northfleet; and the rural district of Strood.
> The municipal boroughs of Deal, Dover, Margate, Ramsgate, and Sandwich;
> The urban district of Broadstairs and St Peters; and the rural districts of Bridge-Blean, Dover, and Eastry.
> The municipal boroughs of Faversham, Folkestone, Hythe, Lydd, Maidstone, New Romney, Queenborough, and Tenterden;
> The urban districts of Ashford, Herne Bay, Sheerness, Sittingbourne and Milton, and Whitstable; and the rural districts of Cranbrook, East Ashford, Elham, Hollingbourne, Maidstone, Malling, Romney Marsh, Sheppey, Swale, Tenterden, and West Ashford.
> The municipal boroughs of Beckenham, Bexley, Bromley, Dartford Erith, and Royal Tunbridge Wells;
> The urban districts of Chislehurst and Sidcup, Crayford, Orpington, Penge, Sevenoaks, Southborough, and Tonbridge; and the rural districts of Dartford, Sevenoaks, and Tonbridge.

County Borough of the Cities of Manchester and Salford.
County Boroughs of Huddersfield, Blackburn, Reading and Rochdale.
County of Berkshire.

FINANCIAL PROBLEMS OF HOME OWNERSHIP

SCHEDULE A TAX

IF YOU OWN a house and let it to a tenant, you will find it understandable and no doubt acceptable that you have to pay income tax on the rent which you receive. It is much more difficult to follow the reasoning which says that if you occupy the house yourself you must still pay tax—Schedule A tax, as it is called—on the amount which you would have received if you had chosen to let it instead. The difficulty of justifying this tax on 'notional income' has been pointed out to more than one Chancellor of the Exchequer, and its proposed abolition in 1963 or later, so far as it affects owner-occupiers, was announced in the Budget speech on April 9th, 1962.

In the meantime, for the householder, four factors lighten the load of Schedule A tax. In the first place, and most important of all, the present assessments (*i.e.* the estimated rental values upon which the tax must be paid) were made as long long ago as 1936–37 on the basis of rents payable in 1935 and they have never been brought up to date, notwithstanding the very great increases in rents which have taken place since that time. In the case of newly erected houses, the Inland Revenue could follow the rating re-valuations which were made in 1956 (these were based on 1939 rental values), but by concession they are still using the same basis as for existing houses. In 1963, all houses in England and Wales are due to be re-rated on the basis of their then current rental values, but even if Schedule A assessments follow suit, owner-occupiers will not be affected, because of the proposed abolition of the tax, so far as it relates to them.

Secondly, the Schedule A assessment is unearned 'income'. This means that any payments which can be set against the householder's total income for taxation purposes such as mortgage interest, bank overdraft interest, or payments under a seven-year deed of covenant, will obtain relief at the full standard rate of tax (or at the highest rate of tax for which the householder is liable if he is not liable at the standard rate) to the extent that such payments do not exceed the Schedule A assessment. Householders sometimes do not realize that if such payments have to be set against earned income, the effective saving of tax is not quite at the standard rate because Earned Income Relief (at present upon two-ninths of earned income) is thereby lost.

Thirdly, the basic assessment, called the Gross Annual Value, is automatically reduced by a statutory Repairs Allowance which varies in amount according to the amount of the Gross Annual Value which is hereafter abbreviated to its initial letters: G.A.V. The reduced assessment is known as the Net Annual Value, and it is upon this figure that Schedule A tax is actually payable.

The Repairs Allowance is given whether or not the householder actually does any repairs and it is at the rate of one-fourth of the G.A.V. where the G.A.V. does not exceed £40; or one-fifth of the G.A.V. where the G.A.V. falls between £50 and £100. If the G.A.V. is between £40 and £50, the allowance is £10, and if the G.A V. is over £100 the allowance is £20 plus one-sixth of any excess over £100.

Lastly, if the householder regularly spends more each year on repairs than the amount of his Repairs Allowance, he may be able to make what is known as a Maintenance Claim. (The proposed abolition of Schedule A tax will presumably not affect his right to make a claim for the years 1962–63 and earlier.) To do this, he must be able to prove to the Inland Revenue that the actual cost to him of maintenance, repairs, and insurance (taken as an annual average over the previous five years) has exceeded the statutory Repairs Allowance. He will then be able to claim repayment of the Schedule A tax upon the amount by which his average annual expenditure exceeds the Repairs Allowance. It should be noted that this is a claim for repayment of Schedule A tax only: therefore, the householder should ideally try to arrange his programme of repairs so that his annual average expenditure never exceeds the G.A.V., since the excess cannot possibly bring him any tax relief. However that is impossible very often.

The expenditure in support of a Maintenance Claim must be proved by production of the builder's receipted bills, or, in the case of insurance, by production of the premium receipt. If the work is done by the householder himself, he cannot charge for his own time, but if his wife does the work there is no reason why he should not pay her a reasonable wage, although there will be no advantage in this unless the wife's total income from all sources, including this one, attracts no tax or attracts tax at a lower rate than her husband's income. Even if the householder does the work himself, he can charge the cost of the materials which he uses and he can also charge the cost of replacing worn-out equipment such as paint brushes, etc.

Redecoration of the house itself and general repairs, both inside and out, are doubtless the most common types of expenditure leading to a maintenance claim, but there are many others which are also eligible. Some instances are the repair of boundary fences and entrance gates; the re-metalling or re-scarifying of entrance drives and paths; the lopping of branches which overhang the highway; the destruction of vermin; the repair of garages, greenhouses, and coal bunkers; householder's comprehensive insurance (but not insurance of the contents); and the fees of the accountant (if any) who prepares the claim.

Anything which can fairly be described as an alteration or an improvement is not allowable, but by concession the Inland Revenue will admit expenditure even on alterations to the extent of the estimated cost of any repairs which may have been obviated by the alterations.

To obtain a five-year average a new owner can utilize the previous owner's expenditure, if the previous owner is able and willing to supply him with the necessary details and receipts. But if this is impossible, the Inland Revenue, again by concession, will permit the new owner to make a claim based on his actual expenditure in the year of claim if the new owner undertakes in return to accept the 'actual year' basis for five complete years, *i.e.* until a five-year average is available. Clearly, anyone who wishes to obtain the best advantage from this concession must work out his programme of repairs so that they are spread out as evenly as possible over this initial five year period.

A maintenance claim must be made within six years of the year of assessment to which it relates. If it is rejected either in whole or in part, the householder may appeal to the General Commissioners, from whose decision there is a further right of appeal to the High Court on a question of law. If the claimant is still not satisfied he may next take the matter to the Court of Appeal, but

An alteration or an improvement is not allowable for tax concession.

from there he cannot go to the House of Lords unless he obtains leave to do so either from the Court of Appeal or from the House of Lords.

Schedule A tax is handled by the Inspector of Taxes in whose district the property is situated, so that the householder who lives in one town but works in another will usually find that he has two Inspectors to deal with. The tax is payable in full on January 1st in each year, *i.e.* partly in arrear and partly in advance (since the tax year runs from April 6th), but this method of payment may not apply to a P.A.Y.E. taxpayer whose Schedule A liability will usually be taken into account in arriving at his Code Number. The tax does not have to be paid for any period (however short) during which the house is empty both of people and of furniture.

LAND TAX

Schedule A tax is sometimes referred to as 'Property Tax' and as such it may be confused with Land Tax with which, in fact, it has no connection at all. Land Tax originated in the eighteenth century with a system under which a fixed 'quota' of tax was required from each district. As areas became more and more built-up, the Land Tax payable in respect of individual properties became smaller and smaller, until in 1949 it was provided in the Finance Act of that year that properties for which the tax was less than 10s per year should be wholly exonerated from payment of future tax. At the same time, the tax for those properties which were paying more than 10s per year was fixed for all future years at the amount which they actually paid in the tax year 1948–49.

Prior to 1949, it was possible to redeem Land Tax voluntarily (*i.e.* to free the land by a once-and-for-all capital payment equal to twenty-five times the annual charge) and many people did in fact do so: since 1949, redemption (also by payment of twenty-five times the annual charge) has been compulsory in certain circumstances, notably when a house is sold or when a householder dies leaving an estate worth not less than £2,000. (*N.B.*—If the estate is less than £2,000, the property is automatically exonerated.) When a house which is subject to Land Tax is sold, the law requires that the purchaser should be responsible for payment of the redemption money, which thereupon becomes a charge on the property. It sometimes happens that the necessity for redemption is overlooked, and it is therefore wise for a purchaser to establish the exact Land Tax position before he signs a contract. Otherwise he may find himself having to satisfy a charge which was really a previous owner's responsibility. Solicitors are, of course, well aware of this problem and it is one of the matters about which they automatically make pre-contract inquiries when they are acting for a purchaser.

The right to redeem Land Tax voluntarily has not been taken away by the new provisions for compulsory redemption and the combined effect of these various provisions is that it is becoming more and more unusual to find a house which is still subject to Land Tax. The intention is that it should eventually disappear altogether, but this is bound to be a lengthy process.

Exemption from Land Tax can be claimed by those whose income is less than £160 p.a.; while those whose income falls between that figure and £400 p.a. need only pay at half the normal rate.

Note: the Finance Act, 1963, provides for the abolition of Land Tax.

TITHE REDEMPTION ANNUITY

Tithe redemption annuity is not really a tax but it is convenient to bracket it with Schedule A tax and Land Tax, since it is also payable to the Crown. Such annuities replaced the old tithe rent-charges as from October 2nd, 1936, and they are payable for sixty years, the annual instalments being due on October 1st in each year from the owner for the time being of the property upon which the annuity is charged. (Tithe Act, 1936.) Those householders who have to shoulder this additional burden should take comfort in the fact that five-sixths of each instalment is a deductible allowance from the Gross Annual Value of the house for Schedule A tax purposes.

In the Budget Speech on April 9th, 1962, it was announced that provision is to be made for the compulsory redemption of tithe redemption annuity upon the first sale of any relevant property after October 1st, 1962. This provision now appears in the Finance Act, 1962, s. 32.

REPAIRS

Arguments between landlord and tenant about what repairs the tenant must do and when he should do them are, unfortunately, very common. In such circumstances the tenant may look forward to the day when he will buy a house of his own. Then, he may think, nobody will be able to tell him to do this repair or that repair, although to be sure he is a prudent fellow and will probably have the best maintained house in the road. But, and this is the point which he is making, if he does not want to do any repairs or feels that he cannot afford to do any, then nobody will be able to do anything about it.

To what extent does this view represent the law? Substantially it may seem to be correct for most, if not all, practical purposes, but the average householder would probably be surprised to know how many other people are entitled by law to have a say, directly or indirectly, in the way in which he looks after his own property.

First, there is the mortgagee. The vast majority of people nowadays buy their homes with the aid of a mortgage, and most standard forms of mortgage deed contain an express covenant by the borrower to keep the property in repair until the loan has been repaid. Even where there is no express covenant, a covenant to repair is implied in every mortgage which is made by deed. In practice this means that almost all mortgagees, be they building society, insurance company, local authority, or whoever, have the right to insist upon any necessary repairs being carried out by the borrower, and, if he refuses, they could in the last resort exercise their right under the mortgage to evict the borrower from the property and to sell it for the purpose of paying off the mortgage out of the proceeds of sale. Needless to say, it is seldom necessary for a mortgagee to take this drastic course, and a borrower will usually find that if his payments to the mortgagee are regularly kept up, the mortgagee will not even take the trouble to find out whether or not the property is in need of repair.

Secondly, when the house was bought, the householder may have entered into a covenant with the seller to carry out repairs of some sort, e.g. to a boundary fence, a party wall, or an access way used in common with a neighbour. Such covenants are very common and they are called Positive Covenants to distinguish them from Restrictive Covenants which, as their name implies, operate to restrict the householder from doing certain things on his own land, such as, e.g. keeping poultry. If you have entered into a positive covenant, you can be sued for damages even after you have sold the house, if the person who buys from you fails to carry out the covenant. This is the reason why in such circumstances, the solicitor who acts for you on the sale of the house would normally insist that the purchaser should give you a covenant of indemnity

Repairs

Where dangerous premises border upon a neighbour's land . . .

. . . the owner will be liable for the tort of nuisance . . .

. . . if the neighbour's use and enjoyment of his land . . .

. . . is materially disturbed!

against any damages you might be called upon to pay. In this roundabout way, a positive covenant to do repairs can often be enforced even against a person who was not the original covenantor. Indeed, sometimes a householder can be made to do or pay for repairs of this sort, although neither he nor any previous owner has entered into any covenant to do so. An example would be where the householder has been given the right to use a joint access way, subject to his contributing toward the cost of keeping it in repair. In such a case, the law says that he cannot take the benefit of the right unless he also accepts the burden to which it is made subject.

A third type of case occurs where the householder has improved or converted his house with the aid of an Improvement Grant from his local authority. Such a grant automatically carries with it an obligation for the householder to take all reasonable steps during the succeeding ten years to secure the maintenance of the house so that it is fit for human habitation.

Our final example relates to those who own property—it may be a house, a large tree, or perhaps an old wall—which borders upon a highway. If, through lack of repair or proper maintenance, a tile, for instance, falls from the roof, or a bough breaks from the tree, or the wall collapses, and in any of these cases a passer-by is injured, the householder may well be liable in damages for the tort of negligence, because the law imposes a duty upon an occupier of premises which adjoin a highway or other public place to take reasonable care not to injure members of the public. Indeed, if the danger is obvious and imminent, the householder will have committed an indictable misdemeanour known as a common nuisance, which is, of course, a criminal offence: and the local authority can exercise their right under the Highways Act, 1959, to obtain a court order requiring the householder to execute such works as will obviate the danger. Where dangerous premises border upon a neighbour's land, as opposed to a highway, this is not a criminal offence, but their owner will be liable for the tort of nuisance if the neighbour's use and enjoyment of his land is materially disturbed. (The meaning of 'tort' is explained elsewhere.)

The examples set out above do not constitute an exhaustive list, but they do cover some of the more common cases where even the most responsible of householders may find himself in the position of having to do repairs to his property at another's bidding. If the householder is not a responsible person and he permits his property to deteriorate grossly, very much more serious consequences may ensue, for public health and local amenities may be thereby put in peril. Deterioration of this order is, of course, unusual in an owner-occupied property, but if it does occur, the owner may find that action is taken against him under one or more of the following Acts:

(1) The Public Health Acts, 1936 and 1961

A local authority has power to take action under these Acts where a building appears to be in such condition as to be dangerous to persons who are in it or who are in any adjoining building, or where a building appears to be seriously detrimental to the amenities of the neighbourhood by reason of its ruinous or dilapidated condition. In such circumstances they can apply for a court order requiring the owner to execute any necessary repairs, or, if he so elects, to demolish the building. Failure to comply with the order renders the owner liable to a fine not exceeding £10 and also enables the local authority to carry out the work themselves at the owner's expense.

These Acts do not apply to London but there are similar provisions in the special legislation which relates to London.

(2) The Highways Act, 1959

The provisions of this Act in relation to dangerous property which borders upon a highway have already been mentioned.

(3) The Housing Act, 1957

This Act imposes a duty upon local authorities to ensure that houses which are unfit for human habitation are either made fit, if this can be done at a reasonable cost, or, if this is impossible, are no longer used for human habitation. Ample powers are bestowed upon local authorities for this purpose, enabling them to compel an owner to carry out any necessary repairs or, in extreme cases, to demolish the premises or not to use the premises for any purpose which has not been approved by themselves. Naturally, in such a case the local authority will not approve use as a 'human habitation'.

(4) The Weeds Act, 1959

If your neighbour, carelessly but without malice, permits thistles, docks, and other weeds to overrun his garden with the result that weed seeds are blown or carried into your garden, the Common Law gives you no remedy. Your neighbour may, however, attract the attention of the Minister of Agriculture, Fisheries, and Food, particularly if there is agricultural land nearby, and a farmer has complained. The Minister, whose powers in this respect may be delegated to the local county or borough council, may serve a notice on the offending occupier requiring him to take such action as may be necessary to prevent the weeds from spreading. If the occupier ignores this notice, he is guilty of an offence, and the Minister may have the work done at the occupier's expense.

(5) The Town and Country Planning Act, 1962

The principal object of Section 26 of this Act is to give local planning authorities a measure of control over waste land which has been neglected to such a degree that it has become a serious injury to local amenities. However, the section specifically refers to 'the condition of any *garden*, vacant site or other open land', so that the ordinary householder could, if the circumstances warranted it, be served with a notice under this section requiring him to abate the injury caused by the state of his garden by taking such remedial measures as are specified in the notice. Failure to comply with the notice within the time mentioned in it can lead to the service of an 'enforcement notice', and if this also is ignored the local planning authority can enter upon the land and do the work at the owner's expense.

It may well seem to the average householder that when he is counting the cost of home-ownership he need hardly concern himself with the rather exceptional situations described in the foregoing paragraphs. Nevertheless, cases can occur when even the most conscientious property-owner finds himself in difficulty: for instance, a man buys a house and after a few years the foundations begin to subside. He may not be able to afford the heavy cost of underpinning and in the meantime he has a 'dangerous structure' on his hands. Or again, a keen gardener who has bought a house with a large garden may suffer a protracted illness and neither be able to look after the garden himself nor have

The Weeds Act

If weed seeds are blown into your garden you have no remedy.

But if agricultural land is affected . . .

. . . notice may be served on the offender to prevent the weeds from spreading.

Failure to comply may lead to the local authority doing the work at the owner's expense.

sufficient means to employ a gardener. Local and other authorities can no doubt be relied upon to look sympathetically at such cases, but their duties to the public at large may force them to take action.

The information set out above may also be useful to householders whose property is being adversely affected by the dilapidated state of a neighbour's property. If the neighbour, or his landlord, refuses to mend his ways, the only practicable remedy may be to ask the local or other appropriate authority to take action against him.

Two final points are worth mentioning in relation to repairs to owner-occupied houses. The first is that if your expenditure on repairs is consistently heavy, you will probably be able to obtain repayment of part or all of your Schedule A tax by way of a Maintenance Claim. This is dealt with in greater detail under the heading of Schedule A tax. Secondly, if you own a house which is of outstanding architectural or historic interest, you may be able to get a grant from the Ministry of Works to help towards the cost of essential repairs.

"If you own a house of outstanding architectural or historical interest. . . ."

RATES

General rates

The assessment for General Rates proceeds by way of a Gross Annual Value based on rental values current in 1963 (replacing the former 1939 values), to a Net Annual Value, which is ascertained by deducting from the Gross Annual Value a Repairs Allowance. The amount of this Net Annual Value may be the Rateable Value, but sometimes a further deduction has to be made from the Net Annual Value to find the Rateable Value, e.g. one-third of the average annual amount of any Drainage Rate is deducted in a district where Drainage Rates are payable; and the actual amount of rates payable in any year is then found by multiplying the Rateable Value of the property by the rate in the pound which has been fixed by the local authority for that year. The latter rate must be sufficiently high to produce not less than the sum which the local authority will need in that year to cover its own expenditure and a proportionate part of the expenditure of the county council as well; and by the Rate-Demands Rules, 1958, the local authority's Demand Note for rates must contain a detailed statement showing how the rate in the pound is made up. The reverse page of the Demand Note usually shows this: so much for police, so much for education, so much for street lighting, refuse collection, and so on. The rate can be, and indeed often is, more than 20s in the £1. The 1963 revaluations have resulted in a steep rise in the general level of rates payable for houses, especially new houses, but the Minister of Housing and Local Government has power under the Rating and Valuation Act, 1961, to fix a temporarily higher deduction to be made from Net Annual Values in order to arrive at Rateable Values if he is convinced that in any particular district it would be equitable for him to do so.

General rates become due and payable as soon as the local authority have fixed the rate for the year, but local authorities usually exercise the discretion which they possess to make the rates payable by quarterly or half-yearly instalments. If a householder fails to pay his rates, the only remedy available to the local authority is to obtain the issue of a summons against the defaulter, with a view to securing a distress warrant if he cannot satisfy the justices that he has any lawful excuse for his failure to pay. Under the distress warrant the goods of the defaulter can be seized and sold for the purpose of paying the outstanding rates. By law, the local authority need only wait seven days after they have sent out a Demand Note before setting this drastic procedure in motion, but in practice they give ample warning of their intention to do so.

As with Schedule A tax, General Rates do not usually have to be paid for any period during which a house is empty of people and furniture, but the exemption is not automatic and may not apply, for instance, in the case of a seaside house which is only used during the summer, even if the furniture is removed for the winter. The test is whether occupation has ceased: a mere interruption may not be enough.

A householder may at any time make a proposal for the rateable value of his house to be altered, but he is hardly likely to be successful unless there has been some substantial change which has affected its rental value. Similarly, the Inland Revenue valuation officer who is in charge of the valuation list can make proposals for its alteration at any time, but he does not in practice do so unless, e.g. structural alterations have been made, or additional buildings have been erected. In proceedings of this sort it is useful to know how similar properties in the same district have been rated—the 'tone of the list' as it is called—and for this purpose it is possible to consult the Rate Book which the local authority are bound to keep available for inspection by ratepayers and by others who are liable to be assessed for rating purposes, e.g. the owners of newly erected houses.

If objections are duly lodged against a proposal for alteration of the list the householder or the valuation officer, as the case may be, may appeal to the local Valuation Court and thence to the Lands Tribunal, Court of Appeal and, with the leave of the Court of Appeal or the House of Lords, to the House of Lords itself.

If a householder has no complaint about his Rateable Value, but is dissatisfied in some way with a demand which has been made upon him, *e.g.* because he considers that he is entitled to exemption, then his proper course is to appeal to Quarter Sessions.

Water rates

A supply of water for domestic purposes is normally made available on a flat rate basis, regardless of the amount of water consumed, and it is both reasonable and convenient that the annual charge, or Water Rate, should be calculated by reference to the rateable value of the property. Legislation affecting water suppliers is still somewhat diverse in cases where the new water-works code set out in the Third Schedule of the Water Act, 1945, has not yet been applied, but in general the position is that if a supply of water is required for other than ordinary domestic purposes, *e.g.* for a private swimming pool, the water company is entitled to insist upon a meter being installed and the water used is then paid for at so much per 1,000 gallons.

Water Rates are payable whether or not the house is occupied, unless the water company have been asked to cut off the supply.

Other rates

Apart from General and Water Rates, other special rates are occasionally found, but these are usually local in character and small in amount. An example is the Common Rate which householders in the vicinity of a common some-times have to pay under the Commons Act, 1876, in order to provide funds for the improvement and management of the common. The principle here is that those who get the most benefit should foot the bill.

This principle need not be so closely observed in the case of Drainage Rates. Such rates, it is true, are payable only by householders who live in a 'drainage district' (*i.e.* a district from which water drains to a nearby river), but within this limitation, the drainage board does not have to consider whether or not the householder will actually derive any benefit from the works for which he is helping to pay. However, if they think that one area will in fact benefit more than another, they can levy differential rates to take account of this, and under the Land Drainage Act, 1961, it is now possible in certain circumstances for owners and occupiers in a drainage district to petition the drainage board for a differential levy, with a right of appeal, if their petition is rejected, to the local river board, or if the drainage board is in fact the river board, to the Minister of Agriculture, Fisheries, and Food. It is also possible under the same Act for an individual householder to apply for exemption from drainage rates by reason of the height of his property above sea-level, or for any other reason which he thinks is worthy of their consideration. Here again there is a right of appeal to the local river board, or the Minister, as the case may be.

A rate levied by a drainage board may be either an 'owner's drainage rate', which is, broadly speaking, raised for the purpose of paying for new drainage works or the improvement of existing works; or an 'occupier's drainage rate', which is used for the payment of any other expenses incurred by the board. The distinction, however, is of academic interest only to an owner-occupier of property, who is equally liable for both.

The drainage rates were formerly assessed on one-third of the Gross

Annual Value of the property for Schedule A tax purposes, but after the end of March 1963, they will be assessed instead on one-third of the Net Annual Value for General Rate purposes.

ROAD CHARGES

General

Once a street has been made up by the local authority, it normally becomes maintainable at the public expense, which means that the local authority are under a duty to keep it in repair out of the income which they receive in the form of General Rates. If you look at the Statement of Expenses which is set out on the back of your current Demand Note for General Rates, you will be able to calculate how much your local authority are expecting to spend this year on repairs of this sort. The actual process of making up, however, that is to say the sewering, levelling, paving, metalling, flagging, channelling, making good, and lighting of the street, must usually be paid for, in the form of road charges, by those who own the land and buildings which front upon the street.

Purchasers

Making up a street today is a costly business, so that it is more than ever necessary for the prospective purchaser of house property to find out the exact position with regard to road charges. If the property has a front, side, or rear boundary which abuts upon an unmade road, this fact will usually be obvious from inspection, but appearances are sometimes deceptive so that it is always safer to make inquiry of the local authority as to the exact status of any particular road or street. Such inquiries are made as a matter of course by solicitors who are acting for purchasers and they also find out whether the local authority have passed any resolution to make up any such road at the expense of the frontagers. Armed with this information, the prospective purchaser may be able to negotiate a reduction in the price which he is being asked to pay, but even if he cannot do this, he will at least know what liabilities he has to face if he decides to go ahead with his purchase.

Another danger which faces the prospective purchaser, even where the road has been made up, arises out of the fact that road charges are, as their name implies, a charge upon the property. This means that the local authority can enforce the payment of unpaid road charges against the owner of the property for the time being. Thus, if a vendor has not paid outstanding road charges at the date when he contracts to sell his house, or if, as is more likely, he has not paid all the outstanding instalments of road charges in a case where the local authority have agreed to accept payment by instalments, the unlucky purchaser may find himself saddled with the bill unless there is a specific provision in the contract of sale either requiring the vendor to pay the outstanding charges, or enabling the purchaser to deduct the appropriate sum from the purchase price so that he can discharge the obligation at the vendor's expense.

Where a purchaser is buying land upon which he wishes to build a house and the land fronts upon an unmade road, he may find that under the Advance Payments Code (Highways Act, 1959) he is not permitted to start building until he has first deposited with the local authority a sum which is equivalent, in their estimation, to what the road charges would be, if the road were to be made up at that time. He is then deemed to have discharged any future road charges which may become payable to the extent of the payment he has made plus simple interest thereon at a rate fixed from time to time by H.M. Treasury. If the road charges turn out to be less than the estimate, he is entitled to receive a refund which again takes into account simple interest on the basis mentioned above, but if they turn out to be more, any balance is payable by him.

"Making up a street is a costly business. . . ."

The Advance Payments Code was introduced in 1951 with the primary object of ensuring that developers of new housing estates should make adequate financial provision for new roads to serve the houses they were building. The Code applies in all boroughs and urban districts, but not in all rural districts, and even in the areas where it applies, a particular property may not be subject to it for any one of about a dozen reasons, the most common of which is that the developer of an estate has entered into an agreement with the local authority under Section 40, Highways Act, 1959, to make up the road to the satisfaction of the local authority. The performance of such an agreement is usually secured by an insurance bond, and for the purchaser of an individual house on such an estate, this is clearly more satisfactory than a mere covenant by the developer to indemnify the purchaser against road charges, a covenant which may or may not be effective according to the developer's financial position when the time comes for the road to be made up.

Once a payment under the Code has been made, a majority of the frontagers can prevent dawdling on the part of the local authority by formally requesting them to make up the road. The local authority cannot refuse to implement such a request.

Owners

Local authorities who are proposing to make up a road may do so under one of the two sets of provisions now contained in the Highways Act, 1959, and known as 'the code of 1875' and 'the code of 1892', or in some cases they may act under local legislation. The ultimate effect upon the owners of properties in the street is much the same, whichever method is used, but the diversity of the methods makes it difficult to give a general answer to the question whether an owner can take any effective steps against the local authority if he considers that the road ought not to be made up at the frontager's expense, or if he considers that the amount which he has been asked to pay is excessive. For the great majority of owners and streets, the answer will be that the charges must be paid and the benefit of a made-up road accepted gratefully in return. In some cases, however, this will not be so. An example is where the frontagers can prove that the street is an 'ancient' highway over which the public exercised rights of way prior to the passing of the Highway Act, 1835: in such a case, the street would already be maintainable at the public expense. And there may also be cases where an individual owner can show that the amount of road charges apportioned to him is unreasonable; e.g. because the degree of benefit to be derived by him from the proposed works is less than that to be derived by other owners. Where only a flank or rear frontage is involved, a local authority (except in London) can resolve to reduce or discharge entirely the liability of the owner for road charges, and where the street, when made up, is likely to be used, for example, as an important link road or as access to a council housing estate, the local authority can resolve to bear the whole or a portion of the expenses of making it up.

If, in the end, road charges have to be paid, most local authorities will, as has already been mentioned, agree to accept payment by instalments over a period which must not exceed thirty years. In that case, interest will normally be charged on the outstanding instalments, the prescribed rate being at present $5\frac{3}{4}$ per cent.

GRANTS FOR IMPROVEMENTS TO YOUR HOUSE

This section is concerned with the kind of work for which a house-owner may obtain an Improvement Grant, and the conditions which have to be satisfied before the grant can be made.

The grants are available to house-owners, either owner-occupiers or land-lords who have let their houses to tenants. Broadly speaking, grants are intended to help the owners of old houses, which still have a reasonably long useful life ahead of them, to bring them up to date by installing modern amenities and so turn them into comfortable homes by modern standards. Grants are also available for converting large houses into two or more flats, and also for making living accommodation out of buildings originally built for other purposes, such as old stables, coach-houses, and barns.

The scheme for Improvement Grants has been in force for some little time. It was first introduced by a Housing Act of 1949. It was, however, considerably changed and developed by a later Housing Act called the House Purchase and Housing Act of 1959, which, together with an Act concerned with housing finance which was passed in 1958, made such a number of changes that this section will not be concerned at all with the original scheme but only with the new one. This point must be emphasized because many readers may possibly have applied for a grant under the original scheme and been refused. They may not be aware that some of the important conditions on which grants are given have been changed, and that in the light of the new scheme it might be worth while their applying again.

All the grants are made by local authorities who naturally receive assistance from the Exchequer toward the grants. Application for a grant must therefore be made to your own local authority and it is vital to know that an application for a grant must be made before any work is actually begun. A good many people have been disappointed because, although the work they have done would have complied with all the necessary conditions, and although they might well have been given a grant if they had applied at the right time, the local authority has had to refuse the grant because they did not apply until after the work had been begun, or in some cases after it had been completed. This is not a piece of niggling bureaucracy. The Act lays it down, and this was only done after the most careful consideration, that the approval of the local authority must be obtained *before* any work is started. There is no need to go into the reasons for this here. It is a fact. The essential point is that if it is hoped to obtain a grant, no work of improvement or conversion should be started before the application for a grant has been approved by the local council.

One of the most important changes made by the new Act was to divide the grants into two kinds:

(1) Standard Grants.
(2) Discretionary Grants.

The significance of this is that the standard grants *must* be made, provided certain basic conditions are satisfied. The council has no discretion to give or to refuse, as it had under the former Act. This is a particularly important change, because under the former conditions where the council had discretion over the making of all grants, it was very marked that some councils refused to make any grants at all under any circumstances, presumably because they were against the whole policy of the grants, and other councils refused to make grants to owner-occupiers, and would only make them if the house was available for letting. These kinds of consideration are now completely swept away. The standard grant is a grant as of right.

Standard grants

Dealing first with standard grants, we will consider on what conditions they may be given:

(a) You must either own the freehold of your house, or hold a lease of the property with at least fifteen years left to run. If you do not occupy the premises yourself you must also have the written consent of the tenant to your making an application for a grant.

(b) Your house must as a general rule have been built before the end of 1944. But if it was produced by the conversion of another house or building, you can still get a grant provided that the original building was built before the end of 1944, and the conversions completed before the end of 1958.

(c) You must be able to satisfy the council that, after you have made the improvements which you propose, your house will be reasonably fit to live in, reasonably fit for human habitation, and likely to remain so for at least fifteen years. They must also consider and be satisfied that the house is likely to remain available for use as a dwelling for at least fifteen years, *i.e.* that it is not likely to be pulled down as a result of proposals, *e.g.* for road widening.

If you fulfil these three basic conditions, you can claim the standard grant toward the cost of installing five essential or 'standard' amenities. You may have some of them already, in which case it is only necessary for you to put in the balance to make up the five. The point is that you can get a grant either for putting in all five or for putting in those that are lacking and needed to make up the five standard amenities.

These are:

(a) a fixed bath or shower in a bathroom;
(b) a wash-hand basin;
(c) a hot water supply which must be connected to a sink as well as to the bath or shower and wash-hand basin;
(d) a water closet in, or contiguous to, the house;
(e) satisfactory larders or other facilities for storing food.

How much is the grant? It is half the cost of doing the work up to a maximum grant of £155 if you put in all five of the above, or less if you only put in some of them. The maximum of £155 will ordinarily be reduced by a specified amount for each amenity which is already in the house. For instance, if the house already has a bath or shower in the bathroom, £25 is deducted. If it already has a hot water supply £75 is deducted, and there are other figures for the other standard amenities which may already be there. The local council will give you precise details.

Sometimes it may be necessary to remove and replace an existing amenity in order to equip the house with all five. For example, conversion of a scullery into a bathroom might mean that the food store has to be moved somewhere else. In such cases no reduction is made in the maximum amount of the grant payable. You still get the same grant as you would if the amenity which has to be removed and put somewhere else had not already been in the house.

The grant is paid when the work is completed to the satisfaction of the council. In order to work out the amount of the grant, the council will require evidence of the cost of the work, and the best evidence of course is the bill that you have had to pay. The council can pay the grants only on the cost of the work necessary to install actual improvements, so if you have incidentally done work of repair or maintenance which does not qualify for a grant, that will have to be taken out of the bill to arrive at the amount which qualifies in the

"If the new work causes damage to the rest of the house, the cost of putting that right is obviously part of the work of carrying out the improvements. . . ."

sense that it is new work of improvement. But if the new work causes damage to the rest of the house, the cost of putting that right is obviously part of the work of carrying out the improvements.

Discretionary grants

Next, the grants which are called discretionary grants because they are not given as of right like the standard grants which we have just been discussing, but are still a matter for the discretion of the local council: discretionary grants are available for a wide range of improvements which will enable houses built before 1945 to be thoroughly modernized. Grants can only be paid for works of improvement or conversion, not ordinary repairs or maintenance, but the word improvement in this sense would include the work of repair involved in eliminating structural defects, such as the provision of a damp course in a house originally built without one; or the elimination of dry rot where that is reasonably practicable. Those are really rather extraordinary repairs and can be better described as improvements. Ordinary repairs do not qualify.

It is also possible to get a grant for such structural alterations as the fitting of additional windows and the raising of ceilings where this work is necessary to secure adequate lighting and ventilation.

If it is not possible to connect the house to the main drains it may be very desirable to install a septic tank. This is another kind of work for which an improvement grant may be made.

Passing on from structural work or essential sanitary work, it may be possible to get a grant for installing electric wiring or gas in a house without it— although not just for renewing old electric wiring or old pipes. It is also possible to get a grant for replacing an obsolete type of solid fuel burning stove by a modern and more efficient one.

As mentioned at the beginning, it is also possible to get a grant for converting one large house into flats or maisonettes, or a number of houses into smaller self-contained dwellings. A grant may also be made for converting buildings originally intended for some other purpose, like a barn or stable, into a dwelling-house.

Although, as previously stated, ordinary repair and maintenance work is not included in expenditure qualifying for a grant as a general rule, the work can be admitted where it results as a direct consequence of work of improvement or conversion. For example, major structural alterations inevitably damage the existing decorations; the cost of putting those right, although coming under the general heading of repair, is such a direct consequence of the work of improvement that it would qualify for inclusion in the work to be considered for a grant.

Qualifying conditions for discretionary grants

What are the conditions which must be satisfied before one of these discretionary grants may be given?

(a) Each dwelling provided by way of conversion, or improved with the help of a grant, must be self-contained.

(b) Save in exceptional circumstances, the council must be satisfied that when the work has been done, the house will conform to what is known as the twelve-point standard. This is as follows:

After improvement the house must:

(1) be in a good state of repair and substantially free from damp;
(2) have each room properly lighted and ventilated;
(3) have an adequate supply of drinking water laid on inside the dwelling;
(4) be provided with adequate means of supplying hot water;
(5) have an internal or readily accessible water closet;
(6) have a fixed bath or shower in a bathroom;
(7) be provided with at least one sink and proper drainage for getting rid of waste water;

(8) have a proper drainage system;

(9) be provided in each room with adequate points for gas or electric lighting;

(10) be provided with adequate facilities for heating;

(11) have satisfactory facilities for storing, preparing, and cooking food;

(12) have proper provision for the storage of fuel, where that is necessary.

It is possible that where one or other of these twelve points cannot be complied with, the condition may be waived by the council with the consent of the Minister of Housing and Local Government.

(c) Just as for the standard grant, you must either own the freehold of your house or have a lease with at least fifteen years to run.

(d) After improvement your house must have a useful life of at least 30 years. This is higher than the minimum required for a standard grant, which is 15 years. For this grant there must be a life of not less than 30 years, although the council has power to give a grant when the useful anticipated life is between 15 and 30 years.

(e) That for this period the house will provide reasonable accommodation up to the twelve-point standard set out above.

How much is the grant? The discretionary grant is half the cost of the work, but up to a higher maximum than the standard grant; it is up to a maximum of £400.

Although the maximum is, as a rule, half the cost up to a maximum of £400, it is possible that certain expenditure may justify a higher grant, for example, if you are converting a large house into three flats, where the approved expenditure on each flat amounts to at least £800, you could get a grant of £400 per flat, *i.e.* £1,200 in all, because the result of the expenditure is to produce three separate dwelling-houses where only one existed before. There are certain other special cases too. For instance, where the building had special architectural or historic interest, the council can, with the Minister's consent, pay a higher grant.

As a rule, the improvement grant is not given unless the estimated expenditure on improvement is at least £100.

The amount of a discretionary grant is fixed on the basis of an estimate of what the work will cost. This is necessary because the council have to decide whether to give a grant, and how much it should be, before the work is actually done. The grant cannot afterwards be altered, even if the actual cost of the work exceeds the estimate. The amount of grant approved is payable in one lump sum when the work has been completed to the council's satisfaction, but they have power to pay the grant by instalments as the work proceeds.

The terms on which a grant is given

Both the standard and discretionary grants have certain strings attached to them, certain conditions on which they are granted. These conditions are less stringent now than they were under the original Act of 1949. The first important point to note is that the conditions must be observed for a period of ten years after the improvements are completed and the house is fit to live in, and the conditions are binding not only on you, but on anyone who buys the house or leases the house from you.

One of the most important of these conditions is that if neither you nor a member of your family lives in the house, you must let it, or keep it available for letting at a rent which does not exceed a certain maximum. The maximum is fixed differently according to whether the grant given you is a standard grant or a discretionary grant. It is the kind of point on which detailed advice should be obtained from the council, who will be able to state the precise figure applicable to the house.

However, this condition will come to an end if the house is sold by you *after three years* from the date when the conditions described began to operate, and the house is occupied by the new owner or a member of his family.

If you sell *within three years* after receiving the grant, you must repay it, or a proportion of it. The exact proportion, of course, depends upon how near to the end of the three-year period you are at the date of the sale. You need no one's permission to make a sale. It is only necessary to repay a proportion of the grant, which you do out of the proceeds of sale.

If you sell *after* three years to someone buying for his own occupation or that of a member of his family, you repay nothing.

Obviously the reasoning behind this restriction is that if a grant of money is given toward the cost of improving a man's home, it is reasonable that there should be some brake on his immediately selling or renting at a high profit which may be due to the grant. The old restrictions lasted for very much longer. The new ones are a considerable relaxation, and you can get rid of them at any time by paying back the grant, or a proportion, out of the proceeds of sale.

Two other conditions which must be observed either by you or a new owner are that during the period of ten years from the grant the house must be used only as a private dwelling, unless the council agree otherwise in writing, and that it is kept up to a reasonable state of habitable repair.

So long as these conditions are observed, the grant is not repayable. If the conditions are broken, the local council will require you, or whoever is the owner at the time, to repay a proportion of the grant plus compound interest. Briefly, the proportion to be repaid is roughly equivalent to one-tenth of the grant for each year remaining of the ten-year period. But you can always free your house from the conditions of grant by repaying the amount then outstanding, calculated in the same way as the penalty for a breach of conditions.

Application for and payment of grant

As stated above, the standard grant is paid for on the basis of the cost of work done, and therefore bills have to be provided. If you do the work yourself you cannot charge for your own labour; only for materials bought. The discretionary grant is assessed on an estimate of the cost of the work to be done, and therefore it is very necessary to provide an accurate estimate.

When applying for a standard grant it is not necessary to provide plans, but it *is* necessary to provide a statement of the nature of the work to be done. An application for a discretionary grant probably will involve plans as well as estimates. As, however, a discretionary grant may be refused, it would be unwise to incur the expense of professionally drawn plans before you know whether there is some likelihood that the council will consider a grant for the work you propose. It is therefore very advisable to discuss your proposals in broad outline with one of the officers of the council who is engaged, among other things, in advising on the nature of works which might qualify for these grants. He will not be able to tell you for certain whether or not the work you propose will qualify for a grant from the council, but he can give you a very good idea whether it is worth your while to go to the expense of instructing a builder or a surveyor to provide the detailed plans and specifications which the council are likely to require. He can also advise on the extent to which those plans and specifications need go into detail. Incidentally, it is worth knowing that the cost of instructing an architect or a surveyor to prepare plans and estimates can be included in the cost of the work qualifying for the grant.

If the council refuse your application for a discretionary grant, they must, at your request, state their reason for refusal, *in writing*. This was one of the new provisions of the 1959 Act and was inserted because it was known that some councils had been refusing grants on grounds which were quite unconnected with the nature of the work to be done.

As the maximum grant in either case is half the cost of the work to be done, you may not be able to carry it out without further financial help. However, the balance of the cost may be advanced to you *on loan* by the council. They have power to make loans for this work. Apart from a loan from the council it may be possible to obtain an increase on any mortgage which you may have outstanding on the house. The improvement of the house is in the mortgagee's interest as well as in yours, and he may be willing to increase the amount of his loan to assist you in carrying out the work.

Building by-laws and planning permission

A good deal of the work of the kind described previously might require approval of the local authority under the building by-laws, or the approval of the local planning authority. In general, planning permission is not required for purely internal alterations, but an application may be necessary if an addition is to be made to the house. Moreover, all conversions need planning permission, whether it's dividing a house into flats or turning an old stable into living accommodation.

Approval under the by-laws is likely to be needed both for internal and external alterations. For example, such approval is needed for (a) any addition to the building; (b) the demolition and rebuilding of outer walls; (c) alteration to drainage systems; (d) installing of new sanitary works and certain heating appliances. Other works may need building by-law permission and it is a simple matter to find out this at the same time as you make your original approaches to the officer of the council to find out whether a grant may be payable.

The fact that approval is given under the by-laws, or that planning approval is given, does not mean that the *grant* will be given. Therefore, even after approval is obtained under these two headings, it is still necessary, as was emphasized at the beginning of this section, to get the council's acceptance of the work as qualifying for a grant before the work is actually begun.

TOWN AND COUNTRY PLANNING AND COMPULSORY PURCHASE OF LAND

THE LAW of town and country planning is an increasingly important branch of the law, controlling, as it does, the whole matter of the development of land. The statutory provisions are now rooted in the principal Act—the Town and Country Planning Act, 1962.

THE MINISTER: THE LOCAL PLANNING AUTHORITIES

The central authority for town planning is the Minister of Housing and Local Government and he is charged by Statute (of 1943) with 'the duty of securing consistency and continuity in the framing and execution of a national policy with respect to the use and development of land throughout England and Wales'.

The Minister is given wide powers under the 1962 Act to make Orders and Regulations (several of which will be referred to later) for supplementing the effect of the statutory provisions relating to town planning.

Local government authorities play a vital part in this matter of town planning control. There are 145 local planning authorities comprising all the county councils and county borough councils in England and Wales. The county borough council is the sole authority for all local government purposes (including town planning) within its own area. In the counties the county council may (and in some cases must) delegate certain of its powers relating to the day-to-day control of land development to the urban or rural district councils or non-county borough councils within its area.

DEVELOPMENT PLANS

Under the 1962 Act each one of the 145 local planning authorities had the responsibility (which has now been discharged) of making a development plan for its own area. This was a responsibility which could not be delegated. Once made these plans must be kept up to date by means of an obligatory quinquennial review. Thus a development plan never achieves finality. It is under constant review and in this way is the better calculated to represent what, at any given moment, are the latest concepts of good town and country planning. It is a sort of 'blueprint' for the future. It sets out in some detail the sort of development which is to be permitted in the future within the area covered by

48

TOWN AND COUNTRY PLANNING!

the plan. It does not of itself grant planning permission for development (this is an entirely separate matter) but acts as a guide to those who have this responsibility. It shows the kind of development for which planning permission for development might reasonably be expected to be forthcoming if applied for.

A development plan will indicate:

(a) the manner in which land is to be used (whether by the carrying out of development or not), and

(b) the stages by which the development is to be carried out.

Amongst other things a development plan may:

(a) define the sites of proposed roads, buildings, airfields, parks, pleasure grounds, nature reserves, and other open spaces;

(b) allocate areas for agricultural, residential, or industrial purposes; and

(c) designate land as subject to compulsory purchase.

Details as to the form and content of a development plan are contained in the Town and Country Planning (Development Plans) Regulations, 1948, as amended.

Before a development plan can come into operation it must be approved by the Minister, with or without modifications. Public advertisement of the making of a plan by the local planning authority must be given. Any person may object to the plan by notice in writing to the Minister, who will then hold either a public inquiry or a private hearing into the objections. This procedure applies also to any amendment of a development plan made upon the occasion of any subsequent review of the plan.

DEVELOPMENT

Under the 1962 Act no development of land may take place without planning permission being first obtained for it. Development is defined in the Act in the most comprehensive fashion but briefly it means either:

(a) carrying out some operation (*e.g.* building, engineering, or mining) in, on, over, or under land; or

(b) making some material change in the use of land or buildings.

Certain things are specifically defined as constituting development of land and these are:

(a) the use of a single dwelling-house for the purpose of two or more dwellings (*e.g.* flats);

(b) the depositing in certain circumstances of waste material on an existing dump; and

(c) the display of advertisements on the outside of a building not normally used for such display

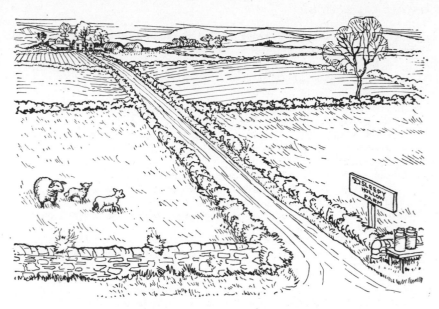

". . . it is not essential that any land or building should be subjected . . .

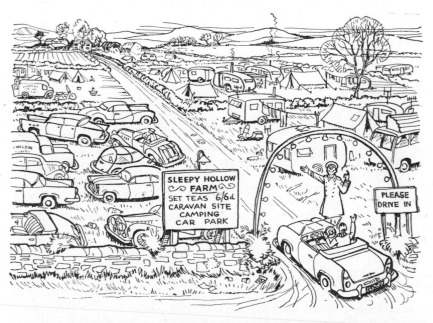

. . to a positive building or engineering operation before its 'development' may be said to have occurred."

On the other hand, the following matters do not constitute development and, accordingly, no planning permission for these is required:

(a) internal or external improvements, alterations or maintenance works, none of which materially affect the external appearance of the building so treated;

(b) maintenance or improvement works carried out by a local highway authority to, and within the boundaries of, a road;

(c) the breaking open of streets, etc., for the inspection, repair, or renewal of sewers, mains, pipes, cables, etc., by a local authority or a statutory undertaker;

(d) the use of any buildings or land within the curtilage of a dwelling-house for any purpose incidental to the enjoyment of the dwelling-house as a dwelling-house;

(e) the use of land for agriculture or forestry and the use for such purposes of any building occupied with land so used;

(f) in the case of buildings or other land used for a purpose of any class specified in the Town and Country Planning (Use Classes) Order, 1963, made by the Minister, the use thereof for any purpose in the same class.

It is to be noted that in the case of sub-paragraphs (d) and (e), by virtue of the definition of 'use' in the 1962 Act, the erection of new buildings for any of the purposes mentioned in those sub-paragraphs *will* constitute development.

The display of any outdoor advertisement constitutes development but, provided the display is in accordance with the Town and Country Planning (Control of Advertisement) Regulations, 1960, planning permission for such display is deemed by the Act to be granted.

It will be observed that it is not essential that any land or building should be subjected to a positive building or engineering operation before its 'development' may be said to have occurred. On the contrary, a mere *change in the use* of such land or building constitutes development, provided it is a 'material change' of use. The 1962 Act contains no definition of the expression 'material change', but the Minister has taken the view that to be a material change of use the new use must be *substantially* different from the old use.

Changes of use referred to in the Town and Country Planning (Use Classes) Order, 1963, do *not* constitute development and thus the need for planning permission in such cases does not arise.

If, in any case, there is difficulty about knowing whether that which a person seeks to do is, or is not, development, he may apply for the determination of this question to the local planning authority from whose decision there is an appeal to the Minister.

PERMITTED DEVELOPMENT

Even though planning permission is required before development may be carried out, it is not always necessary to make a formal application for such permission to the local planning authority. This is because the Town and

Country Planning General Development Order, 1963, as amended, itself grants planning permission, automatically as it were, over a large field of development. Twenty-three classes of permitted development are specified in this order.

Class I gives automatic planning permission for much development carried out within the curtilage of a dwelling-house, including the enlargement, improvement, or other alteration of the dwelling-house so long as the external cubic content of the original dwelling-house is not exceeded by more than 1,750 cubic feet or one-tenth, whichever is the greater, subject to a maximum of 4,000 cubic feet. It is to be noted that a garage, stable, loosebox, or coach-house erected within the curtilage is to count as an enlargement of the house, and no part of the enlargement (*e.g.* the garage) is to extend above, or project beyond the front of, the original house.

Under Class I are also authorized a number of other outbuildings frequently to be found within the curtilage of a house, *e.g.* summerhouses, greenhouses, tool-sheds, beehives, dog kennels, dovecotes, poultry-houses, provided that any such buildings or shelters do not exceed certain limitations in height.

Under Class II, gates, fences, walls, and other means of enclosure are authorized, provided they do not exceed 4 feet in height when abutting on a road used by vehicles or 7 feet in height in any other case. External painting of a building is also authorized, provided it is not in the nature of an advertisement.

Certain changes of use from one type of shop to another are permitted under Class III, whilst certain temporary uses of land and buildings are permitted under Class IV. Class V covers many uses of land by recreational organizations (*e.g.* the Boy Scouts Association), and Class VI will be of particular interest to farmers, relating, as it does, to agricultural buildings. Other kinds of permitted development relate to forestry buildings and works (Class VII), development for certain i ndustrial purposes (Class VIII), repairs by owners to unadopted streets (Class IX), repairs to sewers and similar services (Class X), repairs to war-damaged buildings (Class XI) unless in this case the Minister has by Order required express planning permission to be obtained, and a great deal of development by local authorities and statutory undertakers (Classes XII to XXII). Certain development on licensed caravan sites is permitted under Class XXIII.

APPLICATIONS FOR PLANNING PERMISSION

If any proposed development does not come within the ambit of 'permitted development' then formal application for planning permission for the development must be made to the local planning authority, or to the delegate authority acting on behalf of the local planning authority. The method of applying is dealt with in the Town and Country Planning General Development Order, 1963.

The application is made on a form issued by the authority and must include such particulars as the application form requires and must be accompanied by a plan sufficient to identify the land together with such other plans and drawings as are necessary to describe the development. There must also be lodged such additional copies (not exceeding three) of the application, plans, and drawings, as may be required by the directions printed on the application form, and the local planning authority may require such further information as is requisite to enable them to determine the application.

Either before he buys his land or before he incurs the cost of preparing detailed plans, a developer may wish to know whether his proposed development will be likely to get planning permission if he applies for it. In these circumstances a developer may make an 'outline application' for planning permission which can be granted subject to subsequent approval by the local planning authority of any matters relating to siting, design, and external appearance of buildings. The developer thus gets to know, before he incurs too much expense, whether in principle his proposed development is acceptable to the local planning authority. Once an outline application is granted the local planning authority are committed to allowing the proposed development in some form or other, the only matters requiring subsequent approval by the authority being such as are specifically reserved in the permission granted on the outline application.

An applicant for planning permission does not need to have a legal interest in the land to which the application relates; the application may be made (and frequently is—especially in the case of an 'outline application' as referred to in the previous paragraph) by a prospective purchaser or lessee. Formerly the application could be made without the knowledge of the owner of the land, but this is no longer the case. Notification of an application for planning permission must be given to the owner of the land affected and to any agricultural tenant of the land. To ensure that this is done the application must be accompanied by one or other of four kinds of certificate set out in the Town and Country Planning General Development Order, 1963. In addition to this, general publicity by Press advertisement must be given in respect of certain kinds of development which might be considered 'bad neighbours' and which are set out in the General Development Order, 1963. Any owner of land or agricultural tenant, and any person reading the advertisement may make representations about the proposed development to the local planning authority, who must consider them before arriving at a decision on the application.

If the proposed development is an industrial building of more than 5,000 square feet the certificate of the Board of Trade that the erection of the building is consistent with the proper distribution of industry must be obtained before the application for planning permission can be dealt with.

Once the application is properly made the local planning authority must (generally speaking) give a decision on the application within two months unless this time is extended. If they fail to do so the applicant may take the next step open to him as if the application had been refused (see below *re* refusal). In dealing with applications for planning permission a local planning authority must have regard to the provisions of its development plan but is not confined solely to the plan and may have regard to any other material considerations. Moreover, a local planning authority is authorized by the General Development Order, 1963, and subject to the directions of the Minister, to ignore, in such cases and subject to such conditions as may be prescribed by the directions aforesaid, the provisions of their development plan and grant permission for development which is contrary thereto.

DECISION OF THE
LOCAL PLANNING AUTHORITY

On receipt of an application for planning permission a local planning authority may:

(a) grant permission unconditionally, or
(b) grant permission subject to conditions, or
(c) refuse permission.

A register of all applications for planning permission and of the local planning authority's decisions is to be kept and to be open for public inspection.

In attaching conditions to planning permissions local planning authorities (and also the Minister) have wide discretionary powers which must, of course, be exercised reasonably. If they are to be exercised reasonably, the conditions must be related to, and dictated by, the requirements of proper planning and not otherwise.

If a local planning authority decide to grant permission for development subject to conditions, the conditions may restrict the development to a specified period, *i.e.* may grant permission for development for a temporary period only, or may regulate the development or use of any land controlled by the applicant, *i.e.* land not necessarily covered by the application.

Permission for development once granted will continue in being, unless revoked or modified, for the benefit of any person for the time being interested in the land in respect of which the permission was originally granted, and any person acquiring land may ascertain exactly what permissions for development have in fact been granted by searching the local register to be kept under the 1962 Act. Any such search will be additional to the usual conveyancing searches made by solicitors acting for prospective purchasers in registers of local land charges. (See the chapter on 'Buying a House'.)

APPEAL TO THE MINISTER

There is a right of appeal to the Minister against the decision of a local planning authority and notice of appeal must be given to the Minister within one month of the receipt of the local planning authority's decision or, in a case where no decision is given, of the expiry of the appropriate period of time within which such decision ought to be given.

On an appeal to him against the decision of a local planning authority the Minister may allow or dismiss the appeal or may reverse or vary any part of the local planning authority's decision. It is provided that 'the decision of the Minister . . . shall be final', but an aggrieved developer may yet challenge the Minister's decision by making the appropriate application to the High Court under the provisions of the Town and Country Planning Act, 1962.

Developers will bear in mind that by appealing to the Minister they put before him the whole of their application for planning permission and not merely that part of the local planning authority's decision in respect of which they feel aggrieved. Accordingly, in exercising his right to reverse or vary the local planning authority's decision the Minister may himself add more onerous conditions than were imposed by the local planning authority in the first place. Indeed, he may go to the extent of refusing planning permission altogether in a case where, in his view, the local planning authority were wrong in granting the permission.

SERVICE OF A PURCHASE NOTICE

On a refusal, either by a local planning authority or by the Minister, of planning permission or on the grant thereof subject to conditions, an aggrieved applicant, if an 'owner' as defined in the 1962 Act (and a freeholder who has let his land for less than a rack-rent is excluded by the definition), may in certain cases require his interest in the land to be purchased by the council of the county borough or county district (*i.e.* not necessarily the local planning authority) for the area where the land is situated. The requirement must be by notice in writing (called a 'purchase notice') served within six months of the decision on which the service of the notice is based.

Except when the council on whom a purchase notice is served are, of their own accord, willing to comply with it and purchase the land referred to in it, a purchase notice needs confirmation by the Minister before it can become effective and before confirming it the Minister must be satisfied:

(a) that the land to which it relates has become incapable of reasonably beneficial use in its existing state; and

(b) in a case where permission to develop the land has been granted subject to conditions, that the land cannot be rendered capable of reasonable beneficial use if the development is undertaken in accordance with those conditions, and

(c) in any case, that the land cannot be rendered capable of reasonably beneficial use by the carrying out of any other development for which permission:

(i) has been granted, or

(ii) is deemed to be granted under the 1962 Act, or

(iii) has been undertaken to be granted by the local planning authority or by the Minister.

It will be noted that the 1962 Act requires it to be shown that 'the land has become incapable of reasonably beneficial use in its existing state'. The words 'in its existing state' are of importance both to the landowner and to the local authority, because they narrow down the cases in which the landowner can 'unload' his land on to the local authority.

Before confirming a purchase notice or taking any other action open to him under the 1962 Act in lieu of confirming the notice, the Minister must give notice of his proposed action to the person who served the notice, to the local authority on whom it was served, to the local planning authority, and to any other local authority who might be substituted for the authority on whom the notice was served. The Minister must afford to any of these persons or authorities which require it an opportunity of being heard before he takes action in the matter.

REVOCATION OR MODIFICATION
OF PLANNING PERMISSION

It has already been stated that planning permission once given enures and continues in being for the benefit of all persons for the time being interested in the land affected, but this, of course, is subject to the right of a local planning authority to revoke or modify the planning permission by means of an order made by the authority and confirmed by the Minister. But a local planning authority desirous of revoking or modifying a planning permission previously granted by them must do so either:

(a) before building operations authorized by the permission have been completed, in which case the revocation or modification is not to affect so much of the building operations as have been carried out; or

(b) before any change in use of land authorized by the planning permission has taken place.

Compensation may become payable on revocation or modification of a planning permission.

ENFORCEMENT OF PLANNING CONTROL

(1) In respect of unauthorized development

Development carried out without planning permission is unauthorized development and a local planning authority may serve an 'enforcement notice' with respect to such development requiring the owner and the occupier of the affected land to restore the land to its condition before the development took place. No form of enforcement notice is prescribed. An appeal against the notice may be made in writing (stating the grounds of the appeal) to the Minister. The appeal must be made before the date when the notice takes effect, which date must be mentioned in the notice itself. Once an appeal has been made and dealt with, it will not be possible, in any subsequent proceedings arising out of the enforcement notice, to challenge the validity of the notice itself.

If an enforcement notice is not obeyed the local planning authority may enter on the land and carry out the requirements of the notice, recovering their expenses from the landowner who, in a case where the unauthorized development was carried out by some other person, may recover from that person whatever sum he, the landowner, has to pay to the local planning authority. Moreover, any person who uses land or carries out operation on land in defiance of an enforcement notice, may be fined a maximum of £100 with a daily penalty of £20.

(2) In respect of authorized development

The overall requirements of planning control may require the removal of an authorized building or the discontinuance of an authorized use of land. This can be secured by an order made under the 1962 Act by a local planning authority and confirmed by the Minister. Any landowner suffering loss as a

57

"The overall requirements of . . .

. . . planning control may require . . .

. . . the removal of an authorized building."

THE HOME

result of such an order may, within six months of the order, claim compensation from the local planning authority.

(3) Caravan sites

A separate system of control over caravan sites (outside the County of London) is provided for under Part I of the Caravan Sites and Control of Development Act, 1960. A site licence, issued by the local authority, must be held by the occupier of any land used as a caravan site except in certain circumstances specified in the 1960 Act. Any occupier using land as a caravan site without a site licence is liable to a maximum penalty of £100 for a first offence and £250 for any subsequent offence. This liability is separate from any to which he may be liable consequent upon the service of an enforcement notice under the 1962 Act.

Application for a site licence for caravans must be made by the occupier of land in accordance with the Caravan Sites (Licence Applications) Order, 1960. Planning permission for use of the land as a caravan site is additionally required. Before granting such planning permission the local planning authority must consult the site licensing authority unless, of course, the two authorities are the same. A site licence can be issued only if the requisite planning permission is in operation. If the latter is in operation and has been granted as a result of an express application for planning permission, then the site licence must be granted unless the applicant has had such a site licence revoked within the previous three years.

A site licence is transferrable to another person with the consent of the local authority, who must keep a public register of all such licences. A site licence must be for unlimited duration (except when associated with a planning permission which is for a limited period only) and may be subject to a large variety of conditions. Appeal (within twenty-eight days of the issue of the licence) against a condition in a licence may be made to a Magistrates' Court (whose decision is final) and the Court may vary or cancel any condition thought by the Court to be 'unduly burdensome'. Failure to comply with a condition renders an offender liable to a maximum penalty of £100 for a first offence and £250 for a subsequent offence. On a third or subsequent offence the Court may revoke the site licence. Conditions attached to a site licence may be varied by the local authority after consultation with the licence-holder, who may himself apply for such a variation. There is an appeal (within twenty-eight days) to the Magistrates' Court against any alteration of conditions or any refusal to make such an alteration. The Minister has issued Model Standards for the laying out of caravan sites and these are to be used by local authorities when considering the kind of conditions to be attached to a site licence.

COMPENSATION FOR PLANNING RESTRICTIONS

Compensation for planning restrictions on development (that is, for refusals of planning permission or for the grant of planning permission subject to conditions) may in certain, but by no means all, cases give rise to the payment of

59

compensation. A distinction must be drawn between development falling within the ambit of the 'existing use' of land or buildings and development which is 'new development', *i.e.* development of a kind which goes beyond the ambit of existing use.

Compensation for planning restrictions on 'existing use development' is dealt with under Part VII of the 1962 Act. It is payable by the local planning authority and is limited to those six cases of development set out in Part II of the Third Schedule to the 1962 Act relating to:

(i) The enlargement, improvement, or other alteration as often as required of (a) any building in existence on July 1st, 1948, or (b) any building substituted for a building which was in existence before July 1st, 1948, but which has been destroyed or demolished since January 7th, 1937, provided the cubic content of the original building is not increased in the case of a dwelling-house by more than one-tenth or 1,750 cubic feet (whichever is the greater), and in any other case by more than one-tenth;

(ii) The carrying out of building or other operations for agricultural or forestry purposes (but not dwelling-houses or market garden or nursery buildings) on land which was agricultural or forestry land on July 1st, 1948;

(iii) The working of minerals on land occupied along with agricultural land, provided such minerals are reasonably required for use on the agricultural land, *e.g.* for fertilization or the repair of agricultural buildings;

(iv) Where a building or land was used on July 1st, 1948, or, if unoccupied on and at all times since that day, was last used on or after January 7th, 1937, for a purpose falling within any of the twenty-two general classes specified in the Town and Country Planning (Use Classes for Third Schedule Purposes) Order, 1948, the use of that building for any other purpose falling within the same general class;

(v) Where part of a building or land was, on July 1st, 1948, used for a particular purpose, the use for the same purpose of an additional part not exceeding one-tenth of the cubic content of the first part;

(vi) Where the site of any land was, on July 1st, 1948, used for the deposit of waste materials or refuse in connection with the working of minerals, the use for the same purpose of any additional part of the site reasonably required in connection with the working of such minerals.

It is a condition precedent to the recovery of any compensation, even in the limited cases above mentioned, that the applicant shall challenge the decision of the local planning authority in refusing planning permission or in granting the same subject to conditions, by appealing against such decision to the Minister.

Compensation for planning restrictions on 'existing use development' will be assessed in accordance with the rules set out in the Land Compensation Act, 1961, s. 5. Under the Town and Country Planning (General) Regulations, 1948, claims for compensation must be in writing and must be made within six months of the refusal of planning permission or, as the case may be, the grant thereof subject to conditions.

For a planning restriction on 'new development' compensation may be payable under Part VII of the Town and Country Planning Act, 1962. It is a condition precedent to the getting of any compensation under Part VI of the

1962 Act for planning restrictions that there shall be an unexpended balance of established development value for the time being attaching to the land in question. Whether there is such a balance depends primarily on whether a claim in respect of the land was duly made on the £300 m. Fund formerly created under the Town and Country Planning Act, 1947, and was formally accepted and established under that Act by the Central Land Board. If no such claim was ever made, then no compensation for any planning restrictions on the land can ever be paid under Part VI of the 1962 Act.

The amount of the compensation (if any) will depend on how far the affected land is depreciated by the planning restriction, but will not exceed the amount of the unexpended balance of established development value for the time being attaching to the land. Any compensation paid will go in reduction or complete extinguishment, as the case may be, of the unexpended balance attaching to the land.

The right to compensation vests in any person having an interest in the affected land, and whether or not he was the applicant for planning permission subject to certain exceptions.

Compensation for planning restrictions on 'new development' is, however, excluded in many cases under the 1962 Act.

First, there is no compensation payable on a refusal of planning permission for any development which consists of or includes the making of any material change in the use of land or buildings. As most applications for planning permission in built-up areas are for change of use, it follows that compensation will not often be payable in connection with such applications.

Secondly, there is no compensation on refusal of planning permission for the display of advertisements or on the grant of such permission subject to conditions.

Thirdly, compensation is excluded where one of the reasons for the refusal of planning permission is because the application for permission is premature, having regard to either one or both of the following matters, namely:

(a) the order of priority, if any, indicated in the development plan for the area in which the land is situated for development in that area;

(b) any existing deficiency in the provision of water supplies or sewerage services, and the period within which any such deficiency may reasonably be expected to be made good.

These two grounds are the only two on which prematureness of application can be used as a basis of refusal and compensation can, at the same time, be avoided. The first ground may not always be available, because development is not always staged (or programmed) in all parts of a development plan. Moreover, a planning application cannot in any case be 'stood down' on the ground of prematureness for more than seven years from the date when it was first refused on this ground.

Fourthly, there is no compensation on a refusal of planning permission to develop land liable to flooding or subsidence.

Fifthly, there is a wide exclusion of compensation in respect of planning permissions which are granted but which have conditions (some of them severe) attaching to them. These conditions relate to:

(a) the number or disposition of the buildings on the plot of land affected by the planning application;
(b) the dimensions, design, structure, and external appearance of a building and the materials of which it may be constructed;
(c) the layout of land, including provision of facilities for the parking, loading, unloading, or fuelling of vehicles;
(d) the use of buildings or of land without buildings;
(e) the location or the design of a means of access to a highway or the materials of which it may be constructed;
(f) the mining or working of minerals.

In addition to the foregoing exclusions of compensation, it is further provided that no compensation is to be paid on a refusal of planning permission if, notwithstanding that refusal, planning permission *is* available for any development of a residential, commercial, or industrial character, being development which consists wholly or mainly of the construction of houses, flats, shop or office premises, or industrial buildings (including warehouses), or any combination thereof.

The object behind this is to secure that compensation is not to be payable for refusal to allow one kind of development, say industrial, if another kind, say, commercial or residential, is allowed. The principle is that, provided some reasonably remunerative development is allowed, the owner is not entitled to compensation because he is prevented from exploiting his land to the most remunerative development position.

Compensation under Part VI of the 1962 Act for planning restrictions is paid not by the local planning authority but by the Minister, and the Minister can review any planning decision and, if he so desires, vary it so as to avoid having to pay compensation.

Claims for compensation under the 1954 Act must be made within six months of the relevant decision, but the Minister may extend this period in a particular case. A claim must be in the form prescribed in the Town and Country Planning (Compensation) Regulations, 1963, and must be sent to the local planning authority for transmission to the Minister.

In default of agreement all claims for compensation for planning restrictions will, generally speaking, be settled by arbitration before the Lands Tribunal.

COMPULSORY PURCHASE OF LAND

The compulsory purchase of land is closely associated with town planning control over the development of land, if only by reason of the fact that the principles of town planning are ever calculated to look at development comprehensively. Thus, to get development going in the fashion outlined in a development plan will frequently require the reduction of a number of separate ownerships of land into one large ownership when the land will then be ripe for comprehensive development *as a whole*.

Accordingly, one of the many things which can be provided for in a development plan is the designation of land as liable to compulsory purchase by

Ministers, by local authorities and by statutory undertakers. The Minister may not approve a provision in a development plan designating land as liable to compulsory purchase if in his view the land is not likely to be required within ten years (or seven years in the case of agricultural land).

Land may be designated in a development plan as liable to compulsory purchase by a Minister, a local authority, or a statutory undertaker, for the purposes of any of their functions. It may be further designated for compulsory purchase by the 'appropriate local authority' if it is:

(1) land comprised in, or contiguous or adjacent to, an area of comprehensive development; or

(2) land which, in the opinion of the local planning authority, ought to be compulsorily acquired in order to secure that it will be used in the manner proposed by the development plan.

An 'area of comprehensive development' means any area to be developed or redeveloped as a whole for any one or more of the following purposes:

(1) for dealing satisfactorily with extensive war damage (blitzed land); or

(2) for dealing satisfactorily with conditions of bad layout or obsolete development (blighted land); or

(3) for the relocation of population or industry or the replacement of open space in the course of the development or redevelopment of any other area (*e.g.* an area of blitzed land or an area of blighted land); or

(4) for any other purpose specified in the development plan.

The unqualified scope of this last provision, *i.e.* number (4), is worthy of special note, as also is the provision that land may be included in an area of comprehensive development whether or not provision is made for the development or redevelopment of that particular land in the development plan.

Designation is a first step toward compulsory purchase. After designation has become operative (on the coming into force of the development plan) the acquiring authority must next make a compulsory purchase order under the procedure of the Acquisition of Land (Authorization Procedure) Act, 1946, authorizing the authority to buy the land compulsorily. Objection to the making of the compulsory purchase order may be made and, if not withdrawn, the Minister responsible for confirming the order must hold a public inquiry or a private hearing at which the objection can be investigated.

REMEDIES AVAILABLE TO AN OWNER ADVERSELY AFFECTED BY TOWN-PLANNING PROPOSALS

Part VIII (s. 138–152) of the Town and Country Planning Act, 1962, provides for a sort of compulsory purchase procedure in reverse. Thus, if a resident owner-occupier of a dwelling-house can show that his property is adversely affected (or 'blighted') by planning proposals (such as a proposal indicated in a development plan that the property will become the site of a new highway, or a new housing estate, or a new school, and will therefore need to be compulsorily acquired at some future date), and if the resident owner-occupier can show that in view of the foregoing he is unable, after making a reasonable endeavour, to sell his residential property except at a price substantially below what it might reasonably have been expected to fetch had there been no such planning proposals, he may, by notice under the Town and Country Planning (Prescribed Forms of Notices) Regulations, 1959, require his residential property to be purchased by the 'appropriate authority'.

The foregoing provisions relating to *resident* owner-occupiers are extended to a person who is the owner-occupier of a hereditament (other than a dwelling-house), provided the annual value of the hereditament does not exceed the prescribed limit (which, for the time being, and under the Town and Country Planning (Limit of Annual Value) Order, 1963, stands at £750), or who is the owner-occupier of an 'agricultural unit' (*i.e.* a farm, market garden, etc.) wholly or partly contained in the blighted land.

To be an 'owner-occupier' a person must be either the freeholder of the property or a tenant thereof under a tenancy which has at least three years still to run at the date of the service of the notice requiring the purchase of the property.

The authority which receives such a notice to purchase may dispute its validity by serving a counter-notice of objection and the matter will then be dealt with by the Lands Tribunal.

If the notice to purchase is upheld by the Lands Tribunal, or if no counter-notice is served, the authority on whom the notice to purchase was served are deemed to be authorized to acquire the 'blighted' property and to have served a notice to treat so to do. The purchase price will, of course, be the 'unblighted' value of the property.

COMPENSATION FOR COMPULSORY PURCHASE OF LAND

Compensation for compulsory purchase of land is dealt with under the Land Compensation Act, 1961. In default of agreement the compensation will be settled by arbitration before the Lands Tribunal. Compensation is basically the value of the land if sold in the open market by a willing seller, but this simple basic principle is subject to five important modifications which are as follows:

(a) No account is to be taken of any increase (or decrease) in the market value of the acquired land if the alteration in value has been brought about by the scheme of development which gave rise to the compulsory purchase. For this purpose the scheme of development covers any development carried out as part of an area of comprehensive development (as demarcated in a development plan made under the 1962 Act) or in any part of an area delineated as the site of a new town (under the New Towns Act, 1946) or in any part of an area delineated in a development plan as an area of town development (under the Town Development Act, 1952).

(b) The second modification secures that if on a compulsory purchase of land the scheme of development causes an increase in value of other 'contiguous or adjacent' land belonging to the same owner, such increase shall be set off against the price paid for the land compulsorily acquired.

(c) The third modification operates in favour of the vendor whose land has been taken compulsorily and ensures that any diminuation of the value of the land caused by the threat of compulsory purchase shall be ignored. This provision is important in connection with the provisions (already mentioned) of the 1962 Act under which certain property which has become unsaleable due to the provisions of a development plan (that is to say, property suffering from 'planning blight') can be required by the owner to be purchased by a local authority, but at an 'unblighted price'.

(d) The fourth modification is also in favour of the vendor whose property is acquired compulsorily. The 1961 Act provides that if, within five years of the completion of a compulsory purchase, it is found that the acquired land comes to be used for a more remunerative purpose than was thought possible under planning control at the date of the purchase, then the vendor can reopen the formerly completed sale of the land and claim additional compensation from the acquiring authority. But it is important to note, however, that this particular procedure does not apply in the case of land in an area of comprehensive development nor in a new town area nor in an area of town development.

(e) The fifth modification makes general what was already lawful under certain Acts, namely, the payment on any compulsory purchase of land of discretionary allowances to cover costs of removal and trade losses sustained as a result of the compulsory purchase by the 'little man' whose interest in the land acquired is not such as to entitle him to receive a notice to treat. These allowances, which cannot be claimed as a right, are without prejudice to any other payments claimed by law.

In these days of regulatory town planning control backed by legal sanctions the calculation of the market value of land will, in a case of compulsory purchase, depend very much on the kind of planning permission for development which might have been forthcoming had application therefor been made and had the land in question not been the subject of compulsory purchase. Accordingly, the 1961 Act provides for the making of certain assumptions (three general and four specially associated with the relevant development plan) as to the kind of planning permission which it would be reasonable to expect might have been obtained. But notwithstanding these statutory assumptions which, in so far as they are relevant to any given case, *must* be made, the 1961 Act does not exclude the taking into account of other matters to which the market in land might conceivably have regard.

If, in spite of the making of the foregoing assumptions, or such of them as are relevant, it still remains difficult to see what sort of planning permission would have been forthcoming had it been applied for, application may, in certain cases, be formally made to the local planning authority to issue a certificate stating what, in all the circumstances, is the kind of development for which the authority would have granted planning permission. There is an appeal to the Minister by any person aggrieved by the kind of certificate which is issued. By way of guidance to authorities called upon to give a certificate of 'appropriate alternative development', the Minister has stated that 'a certificate is not a planning permission but a statement to be used in ascertaining the fair market value of land' and that the Minister 'would expect the local planning authority to determine the question in the light of the character of the development in the surrounding area and the general policy of the development plan'. —Ministry of Housing and Local Government Circular 48/59.

SLUM CLEARANCE

THE HOUSING ACT, 1957, is the principal Act dealing with the removal of slums and the provision of new housing accommodation. The councils of boroughs, urban districts, and rural districts, and also the Common Council of the City of London, are housing authorities for each of these purposes. The London County Council and the metropolitan borough councils in their respective areas have concurrent jurisdiction in these two matters.

DEFINITION OF UNFIT HOUSES

Parts II and III of the 1957 Act deal with unfit dwelling-houses and their treatment. A statutory guide as to what constitutes unfitness for human habitation is now available. A house may be regarded as unfit for human habitation if, and only if, it is defective in one or more of the following eight matters to such an extent as to make it not reasonably suitable for occupation in its existing condition. The eight matters to which attention must be directed in deciding the question of unfitness are as follows: repairs, stability; freedom from damp; natural lighting; ventilation; water supply; drainage and sanitary conveniences; and facilities for the storage, preparation, and cooking of food, and for the disposal of waste water.

Houses which, on the foregoing test, are unfit fall into one or other of two categories, that is to say, being unfit they must be either: (a) capable of being made fit at reasonable expense; or (b) not so capable.

REPAIR ORDER FOR UNFIT HOUSE

The individual treatment of unfit houses is dealt with in Part II of the 1957 Act.

If a house is unfit for human habitation but is still capable of being made fit at reasonable expense, the local authority may serve on the person having control of the house a notice requiring him to carry out the repairs specified in the notice. In this context 'house' includes a hut, tent, caravan, or other temporary or movable form of shelter used for human habitation and which has been in the same inclosure for a period of two years next before the service of the notice. There is an appeal against this notice to the County Court. In default the local authority may do the repairs and recoup the cost thereof from the defaulting person. The person who has control of the house is the person who receives the rack-rent of the house (whether on his own account or as agent or trustee for another) or who would receive the rack-rent if the house were let at one. 'Rack-rent' means a rent which is not less than two-thirds of the full net annual value of the house.

"... unfit for human habitation ..."

DEMOLITION ORDER FOR UNFIT HOUSE

When an unfit house (again as above defined) is beyond repair, except at an expense which, in the local authority's opinion, is unreasonable, the authority may serve on the person having control of the house, on the owner and on every mortgagee of the house, a notice of the time and place when the state of repair of the house will be considered by the authority and giving any of the aforementioned persons an opportunity of appearing before the authority to make representations about the house.

If an undertaking not to use the house as a dwelling-house is offered and is accepted by the local authority, then nothing in the Rent Acts is to prevent the owner getting possession of the house. Any person using a house in breach of such an undertaking is liable to a fine or £20 and a daily penalty of £5.

An undertaking to repair the house at any cost may be offered and accepted by the local authority. If it is offered details of the proposed repairs must be given.

Unless one or other of the foregoing undertakings is accepted by the local authority, the authority must, except in special circumstances, make a demolition order in respect of the house. A demolition order, as its name suggests, requires the owner to pull down the house within a prescribed time, and if he fails to do so the authority may themselves demolish the house, sell the materials, and recoup from the owner any outstanding expenses. A demolition order may be temporarily held in abeyance to allow an owner to carry out repair works.

In the case of a house forming part of a larger building and where, accordingly, the making of a demolition order would be inappropriate, a closing order is to be made forbidding the use of the house for human habitation. The penalty for breach of a closing order is a fine of £20 and a daily penalty of £5.

Nothing in the Rent Acts is to prevent obtaining possession of a house which is the subject of a demolition order or a closing order.

In lieu of making a demolition order the authority may buy the unfit house, either by agreement or compulsorily in a case where the house can be rendered capable of providing housing accommodation of a standard which is adequate for the time being.

There is a right of appeal to the County Court against a demolition order, a closing order, or a notice of intention to purchase in lieu of making a demolition order.

CLEARANCE AREAS

Where a large area of unfit houses needs to be dealt with as a whole, the local authority will have recourse to Part III of the 1957 Act under which an area may be declared, by resolution of the authority, to be a clearance area provided the authority are satisfied that:

(a) the houses in the area are unfit for human habitation, or are, by reason of their bad arrangement, or the narrowness or bad arrangement of the streets, dangerous or injurious to the health of the inhabitants of the area, and that the other buildings (if any) in the area are for the same reason dangerous or injurious to the health of the inhabitants; and

(b) the most satisfactory way of dealing with the area is by the demolition of all the buildings in it; and

(c) alternative accommodation for displaced persons will be available; and

(d) the resources of the authority are sufficient.

Having declared the area to be a clearance area the local authority may then deal with the area in one of two ways, i.e. by making a clearance order requiring the owners to pull down their respective properties, or by making a compulsory purchase order authorizing the local authority to purchase all the land in the area with a view to demolishing the buildings in it themselves.

If a clearance order is made, the land in the area remains the property of the owners who must demolish the buildings; if they fail, the local authority may do the demolishing, sell the materials, and recoup any outstanding expenses from persons in default. Nothing in the Rent Acts is to prevent possession being obtained of a house included in a clearance order. If land subject to a clearance order is not redeveloped within eighteen months, the land may be acquired compulsorily by the local authority. The demolition of an unfit house in a clearance area may be postponed if in the meantime the house, on being purchased by the authority, can be rendered capable of providing housing accommodation of a standard adequate for the time being.

If, in lieu of a clearance order, a compulsory purchase order is made by the local authority, the authority may include in the order not only all the land in the clearance area but also other land surrounded by or adjoining the clearance area. This additional land will be purchased in order to get a cleared site suitable for redevelopment as a whole.

Copies of any clearance order or compulsory purchase order must be served on every owner, mortgagee, lessee, and occupier (except tenants for a month or less) of land affected by the order and public notice of the order must be advertised in the local Press. The order cannot come into operation unless it is confirmed by the Minister of Housing and Local Government who, if any objection to an order is made to him, must hold either a public local inquiry or a private hearing before confirming the order. The Minister may confirm an order with or without modification. If it is confirmed, the local authority must serve notice of this upon all those who appeared at the public inquiry and must also advertise the Minister's decision in the local Press. The order may be challenged by application in the High Court, which may quash the order if satisfied that it is not within the powers of the 1957 Act or that some requirement of the Act has not been complied with and the interests of the applicant have thereby been substantially prejudiced. If not so challenged the order becomes operative six weeks after publication of the advertisement that the Minister has confirmed it.

REDEVELOPMENT AREAS

Another way of dealing with a large area of unfit houses is for the local authority of an urban area (*i.e.* a local authority other than a rural district council), by resolution, to declare the area to be a redevelopment area. This can be done if the authority are satisfied that:

(a) the area contains fifty or more working-class houses;

(b) at least one-third of them are overcrowded or unfit for human habitation and not capable at reasonable expense of being made fit, or are so arranged as to be congested;

(c) the industrial and social conditions of the district are such that the area should be used substantially for working-class houses; and

(d) that it is expedient that the area should be redeveloped as a whole in connection with the provision of working-class housing accommodation.

The local authority make a redevelopment plan for the area showing how it is to be laid out for housing, streets, and open spaces. The plan cannot come into operation until confirmed by the Minister, who may approve, reject, or modify it. Notice that the plan is to be submitted to the Minister must be given to all owners, lessees, and occupiers (except tenants for a month or less) of land in the area and public notice must also be given in the local Press. If objection to the plan is made, the Minister may not confirm the plan without holding a public local inquiry. The provisions as to challenging, and as to the coming into operation of, a redevelopment plan are similar to those (already mentioned) relating to clearance orders and compulsory purchase orders made in connection with a clearance area.

When the redevelopment plan becomes operative the local authority may make arrangements for the redevelopment of the area by third parties in accordance with the plan. If this is not done, the authority must themselves purchase all the land in the area by agreement or compulsorily so as to secure its redevelopment in accordance with the plan. Nothing in the Rent Acts is to prevent possession being obtained of a house in order to enable redevelopment in accordance with a redevelopment plan to take place.

COMPENSATION ON COMPULSORY PURCHASE OF LAND IN CONNECTION WITH SLUM CLEARANCE

In the case of individual unfit houses compensation on compulsory purchase is to be the site value of the house but, under the Land Compensation Act, 1961, this may not exceed the market value of the site with the unfit house standing upon it. (The value of the site with the house upon it may be *less* than the value of the cleared site.) An additional sum, bringing the total compensation up to full market value, may, however, be paid in certain circumstances to an *owner-occupier* of an unfit house.

Compensation for the compulsory purchase in connection with slum clearance of any land and buildings other than unfit houses will follow the market value principle established by the Land Compensation Act, 1961, subject to the rules set out in Part III of the Third Schedule to the Housing Act, 1957.

When an unfit house is compulsorily acquired by a local authority at site value or is included in a clearance order, the Minister, if satisfied after an inspection that it has been well maintained, may authorize the additional payment of a well-maintained allowance. This discretionary allowance is paid to the owner if the house is occupied by him; if it is not so occupied the allowance is paid to the person who is responsible for the house being well maintained. The well-maintained allowance is not paid in a case where the compensation for the acquisition of the house is its full market value.

PROBLEMS OF LAND OWNERSHIP

RESTRICTIVE COVENANTS

LAWYERS divide covenants which affect land into two classes—positive and restrictive. Under a positive covenant, one owner of land (the covenantor) undertakes to perform some act for the benefit of another (the covenantee), a very common example being a covenant to keep a fence in repair. A restrictive covenant on the other hand is, for instance, an agreement whereby an owner agrees to restrict the use of his own land in some way, either for the benefit of the covenantee's land, or, in the case of land which is being developed as an estate, for the benefit of other houses on the estate. Usually, he only agrees to this restriction on land he retains because he sells other land at a good price and the price depends to some extent on the restriction on the land he retains. Examples of this type of covenant are not to use his land for any trade or business; not to erect any building other than one private dwelling-house; not to exhibit advertisements; not to keep poultry or other livestock; not to erect any buildings except in accordance with plans which have been approved by the vendor; and not to make any additions or alterations to existing buildings. Or, you may find the reverse case, where an owner of land selling part of it, makes the purchaser of that part enter into a restrictive covenant for the benefit of the land which the vendor retains.

From the legal point of view, the essential difference between these two types of covenant lies in the fact that a positive covenant can only be directly enforced against the original covenantor, the man who actually signed the document containing the covenant, whereas a restrictive covenant can in certain circumstances be enforced not only against the original covenantor, but also against any person to whom the affected land, or any part of the affected land, may subsequently be sold. Thus, it is not uncommon today to come across enforceable restrictive covenants which were originally imposed upon the land forty, fifty, or sixty years ago.

Restrictive covenants can accordingly provide a most effective means of maintaining the value of properties on a residential estate for an indefinite period of time by ensuring that all plots are of a minimum size and by rigorously excluding commercial activities of every sort. What may be more difficult is to free land of a restrictive covenant which with the passage of time has become oppressive, or perhaps merely inconvenient, to its owner. It may be, for instance, that upon the sale of an acre of land in 1920, the vendor exacted a covenant that the purchaser would erect no buildings other than one dwelling-house upon the land, this covenant being for the benefit of the vendor's adjoining house. In the course of time the adjoining house may have been demolished and several smaller houses or a block of flats may have been erected in its place. The purchaser of this one acre, however, or his successor in title if he has resold, will still be restricted to the erection of a single dwelling-house on the land to which the covenant applies. In such a case, it may be possible to secure a release of the covenant from all the persons who are entitled to the benefit of it, but this is not usually a practicable solution unless the number of persons who are so entitled is very small and their identity can be established beyond doubt. Even then it may be both difficult and costly to secure their co-operation.

Fortunately, however, the law has provided another remedy for land-owners who find themselves in this position. The Law of Property Act, 1925, s. 84, confers upon the Lands Tribunal power to modify or discharge a restrictive covenant upon the application of any person who is subject to it. The Tribunal must be satisfied either that changes in the neighbourhood have rendered the restriction obsolete; or that the continued existence of the restriction would impede the reasonable use of the land without being of any real benefit to other persons; or that the discharge or modification of the restriction would not injure the persons who are entitled to the benefit of it.

These grounds may appear to give the Lands Tribunal a fair amount of latitude in favour of the oppressed applicant, but in practice a very clear case for discharge or modification has to be made out before them, particularly if the persons who are entitled to the benefit of the restriction go to the trouble of opposing the application. Such proceedings can also be very expensive even for a successful applicant, because in addition to paying his own legal costs he may well be ordered to pay the legal costs of anyone who opposes his application.

Enough has now been said to indicate that even restrictive covenants entered into many years ago must be treated with the greatest respect. A prospective purchaser will normally be told by his solicitor before he signs a contract exactly what covenants affect the property, and he should consider these very carefully to make quite sure that they will not conflict with the use to which he proposes to put the property. It is a common mistake to suppose that if the local planning authority will give planning permission for a particular use or development, then those who are entitled to the benefit of a restriction which prohibits that use or development will have to fall into line. This is not so, and a planning permission is in fact useless in such circumstances. On the other hand, it is also true that a restrictive covenant is, as lawyers say, construed restrictively, and this means that if there is any ambiguity in the way in which a restriction is worded, it will usually be construed in favour of the person who is subject to it. Thus, a covenant not to erect more than two dwelling-houses was held in one case not to constitute any restriction at all upon the erection of buildings other than dwelling-houses; what the covenant should have said was 'not to erect any buildings other than two dwelling-houses'.

Let us now suppose that the boot is on the other foot and that you are the person who is entitled to the benefit of a restrictive covenant. If the person who is subject to the covenant fails to comply with it, what action can you take to bring him to heel? The usual remedy is to ask the Court for an 'injunction' and you can ask for this even though the breach of covenant may not have caused you any loss or damage. An injunction means that the Court is ordering the wrongdoer to comply with his covenant: if he disobeys this order, severe consequences will follow, because he is then guilty of 'contempt of Court' and, if need be, he can be sent to prison to 'purge his contempt'. However, an injunction will not be granted in every case: if, for instance, the character of the neighbourhood has changed to such an extent that the original purpose of the covenant has been defeated, you may find that the Court will not assist you in any way. Or again, if you stand by and permit the wrongdoer to break his covenant without taking prompt action against him, the Court may say that you have acquiesced in the breach and are entitled to nothing more than damages to compensate you for any loss which you can prove that you have suffered as a result of the breach. These are reasonable and sensible restraints which the law rightly imposes upon the use of one of its most powerful and effective weapons, and they leave substantially intact the fact that the person who is entitled to the benefit of a restrictive covenant is in a very strong legal position indeed.

Finally, it is very important to note that there are certain requirements for the registration of post-1926 restrictive covenants at H.M. Land Charges Registry or, in the case of registered land, at H.M. Land Registry. Failure to comply with these requirements will render a covenant ineffective against subsequent purchasers of the covenantor's land.

EASEMENTS, NATURAL RIGHTS, AND LICENCES AFFECTING LAND

E.G. RIGHTS OF LIGHT, AIR, SUPPORT, ETC.

Introduction

Easements, natural rights, and licences affecting land share one attribute in common—they are all legal 'rights'. Therein lies their similarity, but to distinguish between them may not be so simple. For instance, a 'right of way' is capable of being either an easement or a licence, and the difference, as we shall shortly see, may be of vital importance.

Natural rights are perhaps the easiest to define. These are the rights which automatically accompany the ownership of land; their existence is not the result of any agreement made between one person and another, but is an ordinary and inseparable incident of land ownership. Thus they pass inevitably from one owner to the next, and it is neither necessary nor customary to mention them in any deed which transfers the land which they benefit. Examples of natural rights are the *right to support* for land, from the land of a neighbour, and, in the case of riverside property, the right to receive an *unobstructed flow of unpolluted water*.

Easements, on the other hand, are essentially man-made rights. They come into being either as the result of an agreement made between one landowner and another, or, like a squatter's title to land, because one landowner has for many years exercised the right in question, openly and as of right, over the land of another. Easements can be of freehold or of leasehold tenure: and usually they follow the tenure of the land which they benefit, although this is neither necessarily nor invariably so. It is customary for easements to be specifically

73

mentioned in any deed which transfers the land they benefit, and they can, of course, be exercised by the person who is for the time being the owner of that land. Once created, they cannot be revoked or repudiated by the person over whose land they are exercisable. Examples of easements are *a right of way; a right of light; a right of air; a right to discharge rainwater from eaves on to another's land; a right of support for buildings from the land or buildings of a neighbour;* and there are many others.

A licence affecting land is also a man-made affair and every right which can be the subject of an easement is also capable of being the subject of a licence.

"... the right to receive an unobstructed flow of unpolluted water ..."

There are, however, two vital distinctions between a licence and an easement. In the first place, a licence is not an interest in land, but is merely a personal right. This means that only the person to whom the licence is granted (*i.e.* the licensee) can exercise the right which is the subject of the licence, and he cannot pass on the benefit of it to another person, unless he is first able to secure the permission of the person who granted the licence (*i.e.* the licensor). It also means that the licensee need not himself be a landowner, although he very often is.

In the second place, a licence can usually be revoked or repudiated at any time by the licensor, although it is true that if he does this without giving any notice which the licence or the law requires he may have to pay the licensee for any loss which the licensee suffers as a result. In practice, however, giving notice is not a serious hardship for the licensor, because most contractual licences (*i.e.* those under which the licensee pays for the benefit which he receives) contain a provision for their termination by the licensor upon fairly short notice; and if the licence is gratuitous (*i.e.* if the licensee gives nothing in return for the right which he receives) then the law implies a term that the licence can be terminated upon reasonable notice.

An example may help to illustrate the importance of these rather technical points. A householder had insufficient room at the side of his house to build an entrance drive for his car. His neighbour, who was the freehold owner of the house next door, gave him verbal permission, and indeed encouragement, to build the drive so that part of it was on her land. Nine years later she gave him two months' notice that she wished the arrangement to cease. The Court held that the arrangement was nothing more than a gratuitous licence which could accordingly be revoked on reasonable notice, and it was also decided that in the circumstances the notice given was, in fact, reasonable.

These are the actual facts of a case which was decided in 1958 in New Zealand where the law on this subject is the same as it is in England, and it shows very clearly the danger of relying on a casual arrangement with a neighbour. In the example given, it was the licensor herself who changed her mind, but a much more serious and common hazard in this sort of case is that the licensor may sell his or her property to a purchaser who will not feel even morally bound to keep the licence in being. What the householder in the New Zealand case should have done was to ask his neighbour to grant him a perpetual (*i.e.* a freehold) easement for the right which he required. This would no doubt have involved him in some legal costs in connection with the preparation of the necessary deed, but it would have been an effective insurance against the trouble which ensued. Incidentally, it would also have protected him if the licensor had sold her property because a legal easement binds a subsequent purchaser of the land over which the easement is exercisable, even though that purchaser knew nothing about the easement when he bought the property.

We have so far dealt with two types of licence only—contractual and gratuitous. There is, in fact, a third sort which is called a 'licence coupled with an interest'. This occurs only where the right granted by the licence is a right to do something in connection with an 'interest' which the licensee has already acquired in or on the licensor's land. Thus, if a man buys the standing timber in another's wood and he is given a licence to enter the wood for the purpose of felling the timber and carrying it away, that licence is a licence coupled with an interest. Such licences differ from ordinary licences, because they are both assignable and irrevocable. They are thus very similar in their effect to easements, but it will be apparent that by their nature they tend to be something of a rarity.

The acquisition of easements

Natural rights, as has already been explained, arise automatically as the result of adjoining areas of land being held by different owners. Licences, on the other hand, must be created, but as they are usually temporary affairs and as they are only personal rights, the law is not very fussy about the way in which this should be done. Licences can be, and often are, created in writing, sometimes even by deed: but at the other end of the scale is the licence which comes into being as the result of a friendly chat between neighbours over the garden fence, whilst occasionally the law will presume that a licence has been granted even though the 'licensor' and the 'licensee' have never spoken a word to each other in their lives. This could occur, for instance, where small children are in the habit of playing in a wood and the owner of the wood takes no steps to warn them off, even though he is well aware of what is going on.

With easements, however, it is different. They are 'interests in land' and the normal intention is that they should last indefinitely: therefore the law is very rigid and strict as to the methods by which they can be acquired.

The first of such methods is by *express grant*, and the Law of Property Act, 1925, requires that the grant should be made in the form of a deed. This is probably the most common method by which easements are acquired and it is certainly the most satisfactory, because both parties know exactly where they stand.

Secondly, there can be an *implied grant* of an easement where an owner of land sells part of that land to another person. Suppose, for instance, that a man with a house standing in a large garden sells the house, but retains part of the garden as a building plot. Unless he is careful to provide otherwise in the deed which conveys the house, he will find that the new owner of the house has acquired by implication a right to enjoy the continued flow of light to those windows of the house which overlook the building plot, and he will not be able to build on the plot in such a way that that flow of light is obstructed. It was upon facts just such as these that this point of law was established as long ago as 1663, although the modern law on the subject is now to be found in Section 62, Law of Property Act, 1925.

It is to be noted that implied grants arise only in favour of a purchaser: thus in the example mentioned above, if the seller had retained the house and sold the plot, he himself would not have acquired an easement of light for the house windows unless he had expressly provided for the reservation of such an easement in the deed of conveyance, and the moral of this is that the seller in such circumstances should always be careful to set out in the conveyance all the rights which he requires.

There is, however, one exception to this rather harsh rule, although it seldom arises in practice. This is where the land which the seller retains is entirely surrounded by the land which he has sold off. In such circumstances, the law will rather grudgingly imply for the benefit of the seller a 'way of necessity' over the sold-off land: *i.e.* that he must have a right of way to get to his own property.

The third method of acquiring an easement is by 'prescription'. This is a legal term meaning the acquisition of a right by long and continuous enjoyment, the underlying principle being that if enjoyment of a 'right' has lasted for a very long time, the law will presume that it had a lawful origin.

There are in fact three types of prescription, but the one which is most commonly used is that provided for by the Prescription Act, 1832. Under this Act, continuous and open enjoyment of the right in question for not less than twenty years immediately preceding any challenge of that right in the Courts is sufficient to establish an easement which the Courts will uphold. The enjoyment has to be 'as of right', *i.e.* the person against whom the easement is claimed must not have given verbal or written permission for the right to be enjoyed. However, in the case of a right to light, or in any case where there has been forty years' enjoyment, a mere verbal permission will not defeat the claim. Convincing proof of actual and continuous enjoyment must, of course, be available; and in totting up the twenty years, you cannot count any period during which the person against whom the easement is claimed was under a legal disability, *i.e.* was under twenty-one years old, or was of unsound mind, or was tenant for life under a settlement. An interruption in the enjoyment of the right will be fatal to the claim if it has lasted for not less than one year, and there are other complications and difficulties which may arise in special cases. All in all, it may be said that the law does not readily permit rights to be claimed in this way against another's land and it must be accepted that prescription is likely to be an uncertain and hazardous procedure, except possibly in the case of rights of light and of support, about which more details will shortly be given. A further grave disadvantage of prescription is that you cannot establish an easement in this way until your right to it has been challenged in the Courts; thus a prescriptive easement necessarily involves litigation, which most people want to avoid, especially where neighbours are concerned.

The extinguishment of easements

It is hardly necessary to say that there is nothing to prevent the owner of an easement from giving up his right either voluntarily or as the result of a bargain, whenever he wishes to. Strictly speaking, this should be done by deed, and although in certain circumstances the law will uphold even a verbal agreement, if the person who is subject to the easement has prejudiced his position in reliance upon the agreement, it is safer and more satisfactory to insist upon a deed in every case.

It will also be obvious that an easement will come to an end if the person who is entitled to the benefit of it buys the land over which it can be exercised, or vice versa. In such cases, the easement, whatever it may be, may continue to be exercised but it will no longer be exercised as an easement. It will simply be an action performed by an owner upon his own land.

Much more difficult questions arise where the properties are in separate ownership but the easement is not in fact used. Thus, a man may have a right of way over his neighbour's land but he may never once have exercised his right. It is possible in such a case for the benefit of an easement to be lost altogether, but very clear evidence would have to be available to show that the owner of the easement definitely intended to abandon his rights, and this would obviously be an extremely difficult thing to do if the owner himself were alleging the contrary.

Some particular easements

(1) *Rights of light.* The difficulty of acquiring easements by prescription has already been mentioned, but to acquire an easement of light in this way is nevertheless very common. This is partly due to the fact, as has already been said, that nothing short of a written permission will suffice to defeat a claim to

light based on twenty years' continuous enjoyment, and partly, no doubt, to the fact that a flow of light from across a neighbour's land can be enjoyed almost unnoticed. If the neighbour saw a man taking a short cut across his garden, he would stop him soon enough, but if he looks up and sees only a window in the next-door house overlooking his garden, he may well not appreciate that, minute by minute, an easement of light is being acquired which in due course may restrict the way in which he can build on his own land.

Suppose that the neighbour does realize what is happening; what can he do to prevent the easement from being acquired? His first task should be to look at the title deeds of his own land, since these may indicate that the flow of light to the next-door house from across his land is deemed to be enjoyed by his permission. This would constitute a written permission, which as we have seen, would be effective to defeat the prescriptive claim. If there is nothing in his deeds, he may be able to persuade the owner of the house to sign a written acknowledgement that he enjoys the flow of light by his permission, but if this too fails, then his best course will be to apply to the local authority for the registration of a notice under the Rights of Light Act, 1959.

Before he can make his application, he must tell the owner of the house of his intention, and he must get a certificate from the Lands Tribunal to say that he has done this in the way which they require. Once registered, the notice has the same effect as if the flow of light were being physically interrupted by an opaque structure in a position and of a size which have to be specified in the notice itself; and registration, unless successfully challenged by the owner of the house, lasts for one year, so that at the end of the year, the owner of the house will have to start all over again on a fresh twenty-year period of enjoyment, if he wants to establish a prescriptive easement. But in fact his position is really hopeless once a notice has been registered, because in due course, say in eighteen years' time, a new notice can be registered and he will be back on the starting line once more.

We have been speaking of twenty years' enjoyment in relation to a claim for an easement of light, but in fact the Rights of Light Act, 1959, has temporarily extended this period to twenty-seven years in the case of any Court proceedings started between July 14th, 1958, and January 1st, 1963, in which a right to light is brought into question. This extended period of twenty-seven years also applies in the case of any proceedings started after January 1st, 1963, in which a question arises whether any act, *e.g.* the registration of an 'obstruction' notice under the Act, done or begun *before* January 1st, 1963, constitutes an infringement of an alleged right to light.

These provisions are designed primarily to assist owners of vacant sites or war-damaged properties the development or redevelopment of which has been delayed because of the various building and planning controls imposed during and after the 1939–45 war. A typical example of such an owner would be a man whose house was demolished by enemy action in 1940. Neighbours with windows overlooking the site would, but for the 1959 Act, have acquired a potential easement of light in 1960, but under that Act the owner could have defeated any such claim by registering an 'obstruction' notice before December 31st, 1962, even though the registration would have been effected after the ordinary period of twenty years had expired.

78

One sometimes sees a notice-board bearing the words 'Ancient Lights' attached to the side of a house or other building. This is not really a lawyer's phrase nor does the notice have any legal effect. It is simply an indication that the owner of that house or building considers that he is entitled to a prescriptive right to light on that side of the house or building.

You will never see an 'Ancient Lights' notice except on a building, because it is not legally possible to acquire a right of light in respect of a garden or any other open or undeveloped land. Similarly, it is also not legally possible to acquire a right to a view or prospect from your house or garden, no matter how long you may have enjoyed it. Geographical circumstances, town planning restrictions, and restrictive covenants may in practice enable you to keep your view, but apart from such factors as these, if you buy a house with—perhaps because of—a view, you must always face the possibility that it may one day be spoiled, or even obliterated.

Where a right of light exists, it is not every obstruction of that right which will enable the injured party to ask for the Court's intervention. The test is not 'How much light has been taken?' but 'How much light is left?', and if what is left is enough 'for the comfortable use and enjoyment of the house according to the ordinary requirements of mankind', then the Court will not order the obstruction to be removed. Generally speaking, if a person has 45 degrees of unobstructed light, he will have no grounds at law for complaint, but this is by no means a hard and fast rule, and every case must really be separately considered so as to ascertain whether by reasonable standards there is a reasonable amount of light left, taking into account all the circumstances of the case, which would, of course, include the amount of light coming from other quarters.

(2) *Rights of air.* An express grant of a right to air is rarely, if ever, found in practice, and if the circumstances are such that a right to air might be implied for the benefit of a purchaser, *e.g.* where a vendor is selling only part of his land, then it is very common to find a declaration in the deed of conveyance that the flow of air to that part is deemed to be enjoyed by the vendor's consent and that the vendor may build on his remaining land notwithstanding that in so doing he may diminish the flow of air coming to the purchaser's land. Nevertheless, it is possible to acquire such a right by prescription, *i.e.* by long and continuous enjoyment, assuming, of course, that the conveyance does not contain a declaration of the type just mentioned. The usual requirements for prescriptive rights apply, but the law does not recognize any right to a general flow of air: the flow must be to a definite aperture in the building, or it must come through a defined channel. A good example of such an easement would be a right to receive an adequate flow of air to a ventilator intake, and this was in fact successfully claimed in one case.

It is important not to confuse this very limited easement with the natural right which all landowners possess to receive such air as does come to them in a reasonably unpolluted state. If pollution does take place, the polluter may well have committed the tort of nuisance, and this subject is dealt with in more detail in a later section of this book.

(3) *Rights of way.* Rights of way are no doubt the best known and are certainly the most important of all easements. Perhaps it is just because of their importance to those who are concerned with them that they have also given

Rights of Light

The term 'Ancient Lights' has no legal effect in itself.

There is also no legal right to a view or prospect from your house.

The test for obstruction of light is 'how much light is left?'

For instance, 45 degrees of unobstructed light would generally give no grounds for complaint.

rise to more legal difficulties and disputes than any other class of easement. To illustrate some of these difficulties and to see how they arise in practice, it is convenient to take the very common case of a passageway which provides access to the back gardens of the houses in a built-up road. The householder in such circumstances is likely to discover, if he reads his title deeds, that he is owner of the section of passageway which is co-extensive with his rear boundary fence, subject to the rights of his neighbours to use that section as a passageway, while he, in his turn, is given the right to use their sections in the same way.

This type of passageway seldom has a metalled surface, and in the course of time it will develop puddles and potholes. Whose liability is it to repair and who must pay the cost? On a modern, well-planned, private residential estate, there might well be a Residents' Society with adequate powers to deal with problems of this sort, backed by elaborate provisions for the payment of contributions by each of the residents, but such arrangements are still the exception rather than the rule. What is more likely is that the title deeds either say nothing about repair, or simply require each householder to contribute a fair proportion of the cost of repair, without saying who is to do the actual work. In neither of such cases is there any legal obligation on the individual householders to repair their own sections, although if they did in fact do so and there was an obligation upon other users to contribute, it is probable that the Court would assist them by preventing those who refused to contribute from continuing to use the passageway. Nor is there any legal obligation upon the individual householders to repair sections other than their own, but they do get an implied right to repair other sections, which they can exercise or not as they choose. If a particular owner flatly declines to do any repairs to his own section, the rather unsatisfactory answer may be that the other owners will have to do his repairs for him and at their own expense, if it is important to them that the repairs should be done.

The best practical solution to this rather difficult problem of repairing a common road or passageway is for all the owners to get together and agree upon some combined action, but there is again no legal obligation upon them to do this and it may not be easy to arrange, particularly if some owners make little or no use of the road or passageway.

Difficulties may also arise in connection with the way in which people use the passageway, but here the law is, fortunately, both clear and definite. For instance, if the title deeds grant a right of way 'on foot only', nobody can claim to be entitled to drive a car along it, even if it is amply wide enough for that purpose. Private rights of way can be effectively limited not only in this way, but also as to the times during which they may be used, and as to the purposes for which they may be used. The possibilities in this respect are endless.

Let us assume, however, that the right granted over our passageway is in fact a general one 'for all purposes and at all times with or without vehicles'. One of the persons who is entitled to use the right now obtains planning permission to convert his house into a school, and his pupils ride their bicycles along the passageway in substantial numbers to the irritation of the other householders. Assuming that the children are using the passageway for a proper purpose, e.g. for coming to and going from school, and are not misbehaving in the process, the other householders will have no legal grounds for complaint unless there is something in the title deeds which indicates either expressly or by inference that the right of way is only to be used for the purposes of an ordinary private dwelling-house such as existed at the time when the right was granted. Subject to this, the general rule is that a right of way may be used to whatever extent is necessary for the enjoyment from time to time of the property which it benefits.

Our passageway is clearly intended to be used only by the householders in the road, but if both ends of it link up with public highways, it may be that members of the public will start to use it as a short cut. They may do so hesitantly at first, but if nobody does stop them, they will gradually come to assume that nobody can stop them, and in the end they will be right, because the law presumes that there is a public right of way over land if the public have in fact used the land as a way without interruption for twenty years as though they were entitled to do so. However, this presumption does not arise if evidence is available that the owner of the land did not intend the public to have any such right, and in our case such evidence could easily be provided in one of two very common ways. The householders could either physically close the passageway to members of the public on one day in every year, or they could erect notices at the ends of the passageway informing the public that the passageway is not for their use. Most existing notices of this type are headed 'Rights of Way Act, 1932', which, except in London, is strictly speaking out of date, because the provisions of this Act have recently been repealed and re-enacted in the Highways Act, 1959. However, if you have a notice on your land which was erected under the old Act, there is no need to go to the trouble of changing it, because it will still fulfil its essential purpose of showing that you do not intend to let the public acquire a right of way over your land. Indeed, provided the wording of it is unambiguous, it is not strictly necessary for the notice to refer to either Act.

(4) *Wayleaves.* By strict legal definition, a right of way and a wayleave mean one and the same thing, namely, a right to cross over another person's land, but the term 'wayleave' is nowadays often loosely used to describe rights which are granted for the placing and maintaining of electric cables, telephone wires, gas pipes, water pipes, drains, sewers, railways, and other similar conduits and apparatus across private land. These rights can be true easements, as in the case of a householder who has a right to use a combined drainage system which may pass under several of his neighbours' gardens before it finally links up with the public sewer: but more usually they are nothing more than licences granted to the local gas, water, or electricity board, or, in the case of telephone and telegraph wires, to the Postmaster-General. In most cases, rights of this sort cannot be granted as legal easements, because the licensee possesses no land which could be benefited by an easement. It is usual for the licensee to pay an annual 'rent' for the privilege which he receives, and it is also usual for the licence to contain a provision for either party to bring the arrangement to an end by giving notice of a fixed length to the other party.

In every case, the householder who grants such a licence would do well to ensure that his licensee gives him in return an indemnity against any loss, damage, or injury which would not have occurred but for the granting of the licence.

82

Rights of Way

The general rule is that a right of way may be used to whatever extent . . .

. . . is necessary for the enjoyment of the property which it benefits.

(5) *Rights of support.* If your neighbour digs a hole in his garden which is so large and so close to your boundary that part of your garden collapses, he will be liable for the damage which he causes. This is because a landowner has a *natural right* to the *support of his land by adjoining land.* Buildings, however, are another matter. A landowner cannot claim to have these supported either by adjoining land or by adjoining buildings unless he has acquired the right to do so as an easement. The theory behind this distinction is that if you put an artificial weight on your land, you cannot reasonably expect your neighbour to shoulder the additional burden.

An easement of support for buildings can be acquired in the same way as other easements, *i.e.* by express or implied grant, or by prescription, and this means that in practice many, if not most, buildings erected more than twenty years ago are now protected by prescriptive rights.

The obligation which the law imposes upon a person against whom a right of support exists, is the same whether it is a natural right or an easement. He does not need to take any steps to maintain the land or buildings which provide support, but he must not do any act which would take that support away.

LEASES AND TENANCY AGREEMENTS

TENANCY AND LICENCE

IF THE OWNER of a house gives exclusive possession of it to someone else that person becomes the tenant. If, on the other hand, someone is allowed to store goods in a yard over which the owner retains general control, the man who stores the goods is only a licensee. The borderline is a difficult one but the distinction is important: a tenant has an interest in the property which the Courts will protect, while a licensee's position is generally in the hands of the person giving him the licence.

KINDS OF TENANCY

There are two important kinds of tenancy. On the one hand are those, of which weekly tenancies are a good example, which continue indefinitely from period to period until they are ended by either party. On the other hand, there are tenancies which run for a fixed term and which come to an end at a pre-arranged date. It is important that both parties to a tenancy should understand at the outset which type they are embarking upon.

The law classifies tenancies according to how long the tenancy is certain to last. Weekly, monthly, and quarterly tenancies—*periodic tenancies*—are self-explanatory. They often come into being as the result of an oral agreement and the type of tenancy may be inferred from the intervals at which it is fixed that rent shall be paid. Of course, if there is express agreement that the tenancy shall be a weekly one, a further provision, for the parties' convenience, that rent shall be paid monthly does not alter the fact that a weekly tenancy has been created.

A yearly tenancy, when it is expressly created, requires some precision of language if it is intended to make it possible for either party to withdraw at the end of the first year. This tenancy is described as a *tenancy from year to year* and if these words are used the term lasts in the first instance for only one year and may be ended by six months' notice on either side expiring at the end of the first year. The parties may in fact make their own modifications as to

Tenancy for life.

length of notice or time of termination. If the tenancy does not end after the first year it continues on a yearly basis until it is ended according to the terms of the agreement. However, if the parties agree at the outset on a *tenancy for a year and thereafter from year to year*, then the tenancy will last two years at least, with the same requirements as to notice. If the type of tenancy is expressly established it makes no difference if the rent is paid in instalments each month or each quarter. A common way in which tenancies from year to year arise is where the tenant stays on after the end of a fixed term of years, with the landlord's approval, and no agreement is made for a new fixed term. The tenant occupies the premises thereafter as a tenant from year to year, subject to all the provisions of the original agreement which are not inconsistent with such a tenancy.

The above tenancies are most often created when neither party has decided precisely how long the tenancy is to last. When the tenancy is to run for a fixed length of time it is called a *tenancy for a term of years*. Such tenancies may be created for a fixed term ending at any specified time, not necessarily at the end of a year measured from the beginning of the tenancy.

It is still possible for a *tenancy for life* to be created although, for te:hnical reasons, the Law of Property Act, 1925, has provided that such terms shall take effect as grant of a term of ninety years. This conversion into a fixed term makes no difficulties as regards the termination of the tenancy, as it provides that one month's notice to quit may be given after the death of the person for whose life the term was granted (whether that person was the tenant or not) or the survivor where more than one person is named. These same provisions apply to the grant of a tenancy until the tenant marries.

Where a right of occupancy of land is given for an unlimited period of time a *tenancy at will* comes into operation. Tenancies at will often occur where someone permits a member of his family to occupy a house rent free and without any agreement as to the length of time the occupant is permitted to remain. Or they can occur where the owner of a house allows an intending buyer to occupy it until the sale is concluded. Often the tenant pays nothing for occupying the property. The tenancy can be brought to an end by a demand for possession—for which written notice need not be given—or by the death or either party.

If a tenant stays on after the end of the term of his tenancy, of whatever type it may be, and the landlord does not actively object, he is called a *tenant on sufferance*. He is really hardly a tenant at all and the landlord can go to the Court to obtain possession without even demanding it beforehand.

NOTICES TO QUIT

Except in tenancies of *dwelling-houses* where the Rent Act, 1957, requires *a minimum of four weeks' notice*, the parties to a tenancy agreement are free to agree on any length of notice. If they make no agreement, the length of notice required is measured by the duration of the tenancy, so that a quarterly tenant must be given, or give, a full quarter's notice. If a date of determination is named it must be the date on which a complete period of tenancy ends so that, in a weekly tenancy beginning on a Saturday, notice must be given so as to end the tenancy either at midnight on the Friday or on the Saturday itself. Usually, to overcome any possible doubt as to the day or date on which the tenancy began, notice will be given that the tenancy is determined at the end of the next complete period of the tenancy after the date of the notice (or complete period of four weeks in the case of a dwelling-house). A tenancy from year to year requires six months' notice of determination, expiring at the end of a complete year of the tenancy unless the parties have agreed on a different length of notice.

No notice to quit is needed in the case of a tenancy of a term of years, for the tenancy automatically comes to an end when the term expires (unless the Rent Acts, Agricultural Holdings Acts, or the Landlord and Tenant Acts apply).

An unexpected and not generally known provision of the Rent Act of 1957, which was mentioned above, is that no notice to quit any premises which are let as a *dwelling*, whether they consist of a house, flat, maisonette or rooms, or whatever they might be, is to be valid unless it is given not less than four weeks before the notice is to take effect.

This new provision is not dependent upon the premises having at some time been subject to the Rent Acts. It has nothing whatever to do with the Rent Acts, although it is contained in a Rent Act. It is a new rule laying it down in clear and precise terms that the minimum length of notice to quit any premises let as a dwelling, even a single room (and it does not matter whether it is a furnished room or an unfurnished room), are to be subject to a minimum notice on either side by tenant or landlord of four weeks. This completely changes the old Common Law rule that a weekly tenancy should be terminable by a week's notice. It also overrides anything in the tenancy agreement. The agreement may provide in express terms for a week's notice. But since the Rent Act of 1957 that provision is overruled and a minimum period of notice of four weeks is to be given in every case. Apart from this, the parties to a tenancy agreement of premises let as a dwelling are free to agree on any length of notice they please. If, however, they agree on a longer notice in express terms then that notice is the proper notice to be given.

LEASES AND AGREEMENTS

For most practical purposes there is no need for elaborate formalities in creating a tenancy and many weekly and monthly tenancies, in particular, are the result of oral agreement. It is always preferable, however, to draw up a simple written agreement signed by the parties to set out the landlord's and the tenant's obligations.

When a term of three years or more is granted the tenant does not acquire a 'legal estate' in the property unless the grant is made by deed—that is, a document signed and sealed by the landlord and delivered to the tenant. (When there is a deed the tenant generally signs a copy, called the counterpart, which is kept by the landlord.) If no deed is executed the tenant acquires an 'equitable interest' in the property. The importance of the distinction may be shown in this way. If the tenant has only an equitable interest and his landlord—mistakenly or fraudulently—grants a legal estate by deed to a third party, and if that third party does not know of the tenant's equitable interest when the second grant is made, the legal estate takes precedence and the third party's right to the property would prevail. The tenant would then in fact have a claim in damages against the landlord, if he was worth suing, but that would be cold comfort against the loss of the property.

In spite of this, terms of three years or more are, in practice, frequently granted without the execution of a deed. This is usually done by drawing up a document, called an agreement for a lease, which will probably contain all the detailed provisions which one would expect in a formal lease (for the different words used see below). The prudent tenant can protect himself against the danger of the legal estate's being granted to a third party by registering the agreement at the Land Registry. If the agreement is registered the third party is presumed to have knowledge of the agreement whether he actually knows of it or not.

An agreement to grant a lease may be made in this detailed form or it may be a bare record of the essential terms of the tenancy (the name of the parties, a description of the property, the beginning and length of the tenancy and the rent). Such a record of agreement need not be contained in one document but may be found, for example, in an exchange of letters between the parties. If there is an agreement—or even if the tenant goes into occupation in reliance on an oral agreement—both the landlord and the tenant have an important remedy open to them, called 'specific performance'. This is an order of the Court, compelling the party who has agreed to do so to grant or accept a lease. If there is no agreement about the detailed provisions the Court will order that the usually accepted provisions, appropriate to the length of the tenancy, should be contained in the lease. Because of the existence of this remedy and of the right to register agreements in the Land Registry, the parties will often rely on an agreement to grant a lease throughout the tenancy and never trouble to create a formal lease.

The lease and agreement require to be stamped. The value of the stamp will vary with the rent. Where an agreement is made and is followed by the execution of the lease only one of the documents needs to be fully stamped and a nominal stamp duty only is due on the other. A document which is not duly stamped is not admissible in Court as evidence until it has been stamped and the penalties for failure to stamp at the proper time have been paid.

CONTENTS OF LEASES AND AGREEMENTS

Leases and detailed agreements for leases will commonly be drawn up in the way shown below. Technical legal names are given to the parts of the document but these will not actually appear in the document itself.

(1) 'The premises.' These comprise the following:

(a) The date. The document will begin by setting out the date when it was made. This is followed by the date from which the tenancy will run which may be at a date in the future (but not more than twenty-one years ahead) or a date earlier than the date of the agreement.

(b) Description of the landlord and tenant (*i.e.* their names, addresses, and occupations will be set out).

(c) The recitals (*e.g.* brief particulars of the contract to grant the lease).

(d) The consideration: *e.g.* the lump sum, if any, which the tenant has agreed to pay for the grant of the lease.

(e) The operative words. (In a lease the landlord will usually 'demise' the property to the tenant; in an agreement he will 'agree to grant a lease'.)

(f) A description of the property by a house-number in a street, or by reference to a plan, or otherwise, and of any rights which the landlord is granting in connection with it—*e.g.* a right of way.

(g) The exceptions and reservations. (A description of any part of the property which the landlord is retaining—*e.g.* a garage—and of any rights which he is reserving—*e.g.* a right to drainage across the property and to enter and to carry out necessary repairs. Unless the landlord expressly excludes them from his grant, the tenant is entitled to any rights which have been previously enjoyed in connection with the property.)

(2) The commencement and duration of the tenancy.

(3) The rent payable, the dates when the instalments of the rent fall due and the date of the first payment.

(4) 'The covenants.' There will be two groups of these, which are promises made by the landlord and tenant respectively. The tenant's covenants will commonly cover the following matters:

(a) To pay the rent on the dates and in the manner required.

(b) To pay all taxes (*e.g.* rates) except the landlord's property tax (*i.e.* Schedule A tax).

(c) To keep (and often to put) the property in good and substantial repair and condition (or in good and tenantable repair), fair wear and tear excepted. The respective rights and liabilities of landlords and tenants with regard to repairs in tenancies beginning on and after October 24th, 1961, are governed by a new and revolutionary provision in the Housing Act of 1961 which is described in detail elsewhere under the general heading of Repairs.

(d) To paint the interior and exterior at stated intervals.

(e) To permit the landlord or his agent and workmen to enter the premises at any reasonable time to inspect the premises and make good any breach of the tenant's repairing covenants at the tenant's expense.

(*N.B.*—The duty to repair laid on the tenant will of course vary. Broadly speaking, the longer the term of the tenancy, the heavier will be the tenant's obligations. In building leases for ninety-nine or nine hundred and ninety-nine years the whole burden of repair will usually be the tenant's.)

(f) Not to carry on a trade or business but to use the premises as a private residence. (Sub-letting part of the premises or taking in friends as paying guests may be in breach of this covenant. In certain circumstances in long leases the Lands Tribunal may release land from covenants restricting use and such covenants may become unenforceable where the character of the property has changed.)

(g) Not to do or permit anything to be done on the premises which may be or become a nuisance or annoyance or cause damage to the landlord, his other tenants or the occupiers of neighbouring houses. (This covers acts falling short of 'nuisance' in its technical legal sense.)

(h) Not to under-let or assign the premises without the previous consent in writing of the landlord, which consent shall not be unreasonably withheld. (See separate section below.)

(i) Not to make any alteration in the premises without the landlord's consent.

(j) To insure the premises against fire and, in the case of fire, lay out insurance moneys received in rebuilding, repairing, and reinstating the premises to the satisfaction of the landlord. But on any letting for less than seven years it is quite common for this obligation to be borne by the landlord.

(k) At the end of the term of the lease to yield up the premises in good and substantial repair in accordance with the repairing covenants.

The landlord's covenants will usually be less numerous. They will set out any repairing obligations which the landlord agrees to bear. In addition, the landlord will probably covenant to the effect that, as long as the tenant observes his covenants he shall 'peaceably hold and enjoy the demised premises without any interruption by the landlord or any person rightfully claiming under him'. This is known as the covenant for quiet possession. It gives the tenant a claim for damages if the landlord, or anyone to whom the landlord's interest has been transferred, unjustifiably evicts him or interferes with his enjoyment of the property.

THE MOST IMPORTANT CONDITIONS

After that list of the general conditions which you would find in a well-drawn-up lease or tenancy agreement, what are the ones to which special attention ought to be paid?

Sub-letting and assignment

First, the clause about sub-letting and assignment. Obviously it is reasonable that the landlord, the owner of the house, should keep some control over sub-letting. In the absence of any clause about it the general law is that a tenant has complete freedom to sub-let his house or flat or any part of it and complete freedom to assign his whole tenancy. If the landlord is indifferent as to what his tenant does, no clause may be put in the agreement. Most landlords, on the other hand, are very far from being indifferent about this and therefore some clause is put into the agreement to control sub-letting and assignment. A landlord has two choices. He may either forbid any sub-letting or assigning absolutely, or he may forbid it unless his consent is first obtained.

The important point for both landlord and tenant to watch is that if the clause says in effect: 'no sub-letting or assignment without the landlord's consent' then the general law steps in. An Act of Parliament of 1927 laid it down that when the agreement provides for no sub-letting or assignment without consent, the landlord must not refuse his consent unreasonably. He can inquire into the sub-tenant's character, he can ask for financial references, he can therefore refuse consent if, as a result of his inquiries he comes to the conclusion, reasonably, that the proposed sub-tenant is likely to be unreliable. But he cannot refuse arbitrarily or unreasonably.

So to sum up on this question of sub-letting or assigning, if the agreement is silent about the point, the tenant is legally free to sub-let or assign his tenancy as and when he pleases. If the landlord does not want this situation to arise he can either:

(a) forbid sub-letting or assigning absolutely, or
(b) forbid it without his consent.

If it is forbidden absolutely then there is nothing the tenant can do about it;

he cannot require the landlord to give his consent and the general law, the Act of Parliament which was referred to above, does not apply. The consent can be refused without any reason given. If, on the other hand, the clause uses words to the effect of no sub-letting or assigning without consent, then that consent must not be refused unreasonably. Clearly it is to the advantage of any tenant taking premises for some time to endeavour to get in his agreement the right to sub-let or assign with consent, because then he knows that the consent must not be unreasonably withheld.

The distinction between sub-letting and assigning, which is explained in more detail in another section, is that on the sub-letting the tenant remains primarily responsible to the landlord for the payment of his rent and the observance of conditions of the tenancy, he in turn collecting rent from his sub-tenant. On an assignment, however, it is possible for the assignee, the person who has taken over the whole of the rest of the term of the tenancy, to step completely into the shoes of the tenant and then to become directly responsible to the landlord.

Lodgers

No clause dealing with sub-letting or assignment can stop the tenant from taking lodgers. As is explained elsewhere, a lodger is not a tenant or a sub-tenant, so if the landlord wants to stop his tenant from taking lodgers, that must be stated expressly in the agreement. Furthermore, a clause which prohibits the sub-letting of a house would not prevent a *part* of the house being sub-let. So a properly drawn clause from the landlord's point of view would deal with the sub-letting of not merely the whole of the premises but any part thereof.

It is perhaps worth mentioning here that a statutory tenant, that is one statutorily protected by the Rent Acts, must never sub-let the whole of the premises comprised in his tenancy without his landlord's consent, even though his rent book or agreement says nothing about it. The reason for this is that if he does so, he may lose the protection of the Rent Acts.

Damage by fire

Another very important clause is that dealing with damage by fire. This is really important from the tenant's point of view. There should be a clause in the agreement allowing him to stop paying the rent or a proportion of the rent if his house, flat, or rooms are damaged by fire. The reason is that unless there is such a clause the tenant is obliged to go on paying rent even though the premises may be totally destroyed.

This rule may appear superficially to be unreasonable. Yet there is no good reason why the owner of a house should suffer rather than the tenant because of a fire, against which the tenant may possibly have insured. However, whether the rule is reasonable or unreasonable, it exists. The way for the tenant to avoid this hardship is for him to ask and do his best to obtain a clause which requires the landlord to insure and suspends payment of the rent either altogether or in proportion to the damage if the premises are wholly or partly destroyed or damaged. As a further protection, a tenant who takes out a comprehensive insurance policy on his furniture will be covered against many of the other

"No clause dealing only with sub-letting or assignment can stop the tenant from taking lodgers."

expenses which will fall on him as a result of the fire. For instance, paying rent to live somewhere else while the place is being repaired.

A clause on this topic frequently contains an obligation on the landlord to rebuild or reinstate the premises as soon as possible. This may be a fairly common clause where the tenancy or lease is for a long term of years. That, however, is an addition which is not so obviously important from the tenant's point of view as the clause enabling the rent to be suspended or a proportion of the rent to be suspended when the premises are either totally or partly destroyed.

Alterations

Another important clause is that dealing with alterations, additions, and improvements to the property. A landlord would be wise to insist on the clause which absolutely prohibits any alterations, additions, or improvements to be made without his consent. This does not mean that he has got to be extremely rigid and to refuse his consent to anything the tenant might want to do. Many additions and alterations could be for the general benefit of the property and for the ultimate benefit of the landlord. Many are such that they could easily be removed when the tenant goes and the landlord could have no reasonable objection, particularly as he can make it a condition of his consent that the tenant shall completely reinstate the property to its former condition. But if he has no such clause in the agreement, there is a good deal that the tenant can do, at least to the interior of the property, to the landlord's possible disadvantage.

PROVISO FOR RE-ENTRY

If the tenant breaks the promises made in the lease, what can the landlord do about it? He may go to Court and claim damages; or he can ask for an injunction to prevent the tenant continuing to break those promises. He may not bring the tenancy to an end unless the lease contains a specific provision to enable him to do so. Leases therefore usually conclude with the proviso that if the rent falls in arrear, or if the tenant fails to observe any of his covenants, the landlord shall be at liberty to re-enter and thereby bring the tenancy to an end. And if the tenancy is terminated the landlord can still claim damages in respect of the tenant's breach of agreement. In practice, however, the Court will sometimes give the tenant relief from the forfeiture of the lease. Relief from forfeiture is considered elsewhere.

REMEDIES FOR BREACH OF COVENANT

What can the landlord or the tenant do if either breaks any of the provisions of their agreement? The landlord's remedy, if the tenant does not pay his rent, is discussed elsewhere. For other breaches of the agreement there are three remedies open equally to both the landlord and the tenant. They can sue for damages; they can sue for an injunction to prevent the other party from doing something which the agreement forbids; and they can sue for specific performance to compel the other party to perform some act which he has undertaken to do.

For example, if a tenant has undertaken not to sub-let without the consent of his landlord and then threatens to do so without seeking that consent, his landlord may be able to restrain him by injunction. Again, if a tenant has undertaken to build on land comprised in his tenancy, a Court may order him to carry out his obligation. A landlord has a further right. He is in certain circumstances entitled to determine a tenancy before the term for which it was granted has expired. This is the right of forfeiture. These remedies are not exclusive of each other. Damages and an order for an injunction can, for example, be sought in the same action. These matters must now be looked at in more detail.

Damages

Damages can be sought for any breach of any term in a tenancy. Will the Court order damages if the tenant, for instance, fails to carry out his obligations about repairs? There are some restrictions on the landlord's right to recover damages for this.

First, there is a limit to the amount of damages which he is entitled to recover. The damages must not be more than the amount by which the value of the premises to the landlord is diminished as a result of the tenant's breach of covenant. This means that the landlord may not be able to recover from the tenant the cost of carrying out the repairs which the tenant should have done. To give an illustration, suppose when a lease expires the tenant fails to hand over the premises in good repair as he has undertaken to do and the landlord is intending to sell. If, as may well be, the evidence shows that the price which the landlord will get is reduced only a very little owing to the lack of repair, his damages will be limited to this small amount by which the selling price is reduced.

Secondly, where a tenant has undertaken to keep or put in repair during the currency of his lease any of the property comprised in it, a landlord cannot in certain circumstances bring an action for damages against him for a breach of this obligation without obtaining the leave of a Court, which will usually be the local County Court. This provision does not apply to any breach of an agreement by the tenant to carry out repairs when first taking possession of premises or within a reasonable time afterwards; neither does it apply to any agreement to leave the premises in repair at the end of the term. This restriction on the landlord's rights, which was brought into being by the Leasehold Property (Repairs) Act, 1938, has been extended to a wide range of tenancies by the Landlord and Tenant Act, 1954, and applies to tenancies which were originally granted for a fixed term of at least seven years and are not agricultural holdings, and arises if the landlord wishes to claim damages when at least three years of the term of the tenancy remain to run. Where this restriction applies, the landlord is obliged to serve on the tenant a notice specifying the particular breach of covenant of which he complains and requiring him to remedy it if it is capable of remedy. This notice must also inform the tenant that he is entitled to serve a counter-notice on the landlord within twenty-eight days of receiving the landlord's notice claiming the benefit of the 1938 Act. If the tenant serves a counter-notice, the landlord must obtain the leave of the Court before he begins proceedings for damages.

The landlord can only obtain leave to bring his action for damages if he proves that special circumstances exist which in the opinion of the Court render it just and equitable that leave should be given, or if he proves that one of several other circumstances provided for in the 1938 Act exist. Even then the Court has the power, in granting or refusing leave, to impose such terms and conditions on the landlord or the tenant as it may think fit, which, of course, enables the Court to strike a fair balance between the landlord and the tenant.

Forfeiture

As already pointed out in an earlier section, most tenancy agreements or leases contain a provision entitling a landlord to forfeit the tenancy before its term has expired in the event of a breach of one of the obligations which the tenant has undertaken. However, restrictions have been placed on the exercise of this right by landlords and provisions have been made which enable a tenant to continue to enjoy his tenancy even though the agreement itself entitles the landlord to end it, since it was considered by the Courts to be unfair that a landlord should be able to end a tenancy in every case where a tenant was in breach of his obligations, and later Parliament intervened.

It is now provided by Section 146 of the Law of Property Act, 1925, that before a landlord can enforce a right of re-entry, whether by trying to eject the tenant without resorting to the Courts or by bringing an action to remove him, he must serve a notice on the tenant specifying the same matters which have to be specified in the notice already considered above in relation to an action for damages to which the Leasehold Property (Repairs) Act, 1938, applies. Then, if the breach of which the landlord complains is one which is capable of being remedied by the tenant and he fails to remedy it within a reasonable time after receiving his landlord's notice and to pay his landlord reasonable compensation for the breach, the landlord can start an action to eject his tenant. It is now extremely rare for a landlord to attempt to eject a tenant without resorting to the Courts for the practical reason that it is extremely difficult to do so. It is sometimes difficult to determine whether a particular breach is of a type which is incapable of remedy. In one case where a tenant used his premises as a brothel in breach of a covenant in his tenancy, it was held that the breach was incapable of remedy, although it might be thought that he could have remedied it by desisting from using the premises for such purposes.

There is a further restriction on the landlord's right of re-entry in the case of tenancies to which the Leasehold Property (Repairs) Act, 1938, as extended by the Landlord and Tenant Act, 1954, applies. If at least three years of the term remain and the landlord wishes to forfeit it because the tenant has broken a provision to put or keep the premises in repair during the currency of the term, the landlord is obliged to inform the tenant in the notice which he serves under Section 146 of the Law of Property Act, 1925, that he is entitled to serve a counter-notice on the landlord within twenty-eight days of receiving his landlord's notice, claiming the benefit of the 1938 Act. If the tenant serves this counter-notice, the landlord cannot bring an action to enforce his right of re-entry without obtaining the leave of the Court even though the tenant has failed to comply with the requirements of the landlord's notice. Leave will only be given to the landlord to proceed with an action if he proves that one of the same special circumstances exist as in the case of an application for leave to bring an action for damages against a tenant whose tenancy is within the scope of the 1938 Act.

If a landlord serves a notice on his tenant under Section 146 of the 1925 Act requiring him to remedy decorative repairs as a preliminary to taking proceedings to forfeit the tenancy, the tenant may be able to prevent him from doing so. Provided that the tenant's liability does not arise out of an undertaking to put the premises into decorative repair which he has never carried out, or the decorative repairs are not necessary to put or keep the premises in a sanitary condition, or to maintain or preserve the structure, or to comply with a statutory liability to keep a house reasonably fit for human habitation, or to comply with an obligation to put the premises in a specified state of repair at the end of the term, the tenant can apply to the Court for relief after receiving the notice from his landlord. The Court then has power, if it is satisfied that the notice is unreasonable particularly having regard to the length of the tenancy which remains unexpired, to relieve the tenant either wholly or in part from his liability to do the decorative repairs specified in the notice. The longer the term has to run and the smaller the amount of decorative repair the tenant has failed to do, the more likely it is that he will obtain some measure of relief.

In almost every case where a landlord is seeking to enforce his right to forfeit the tenancy, the tenant is given the right under Section 146 of the Law of Property Act, 1925, to ask the Court to give him relief, that is, to permit him to retain his tenancy. Usually he will make his application by way of counter-claim in the landlord's action for forfeiture. The 1925 Act gives the Court an absolute discretion whether to grant or refuse relief and requires the Court to have regard to the conduct of the parties in relation to the events which have brought about the forfeiture and to all the other circumstances of the case. In general, a tenant will not obtain relief unless he has remedied or undertakes to remedy the breach of his agreement which has occasioned the forfeiture in so far as the breach can be remedied, and often the Court will allow relief subject to a condition that the breach is remedied by a certain date. Relief is not usually given where the tenancy has become liable to forfeiture owing to immoral use. The tenant will usually, too, have to pay the costs incurred by the landlord in bringing his action. In any event, the landlord is entitled under the 1925 Act to recover any reasonable expenses which he may have incurred by employing a surveyor to ascertain, for example, the extent of the needful repairs which the tenant has failed to carry out and a solicitor in preparing the necessary notice under Section 146 of the Act.

The right to relief under Section 146 is expressly excluded where the landlord is entitled to determine the tenancy on the grounds of the tenant's bankruptcy in the case of leases or agreements for the letting of agricultural land or mines, tenancies of public houses, furnished tenancies, and tenancies with respect to which the personal qualifications of the tenant are important for the preservation of the value or character of the property.

Section 146 of the 1925 Act also protects the interests of a sub-tenant whose immediate landlord's tenancy is forfeited. He can intervene in any action for forfeiture against his own landlord and the Court has power to vest the whole or any part of the property comprised in his own landlord's lease in him for a period not exceeding the length of the term granted to him by his sub-tenancy. The Court has a wide discretion as to the conditions which it can make in giving the sub-tenant relief and he may, for example, be required to pay any damages and costs for which his own landlord has become liable.

A landlord who has knowledge of any matter which would entitle him to forfeit the tenancy loses his right if he does anything which acknowledges the continued existence of the tenancy. This is called waiver. Thus, for example, if a tenant sub-lets in breach of a covenant not to do so without his landlord's consent and the landlord demands rent from him knowing that he is in breach of covenant, the landlord cannot afterwards enforce a right of re-entry in respect of the breach. However, where a tenant is under an obligation to keep premises in repair his duty to do so is a continuing one, so that until he puts the premises into repair the landlord is always entitled to forfeit the lease even though he has demanded and accepted rent since first becoming aware of his right to forfeit.

DISTRESS FOR RENT

What it means

Distress is the name given to the landlord's right of self-help to ensure that arrears of rent are paid, without the need of having to go to Court. He may seize any movable property he finds on the tenant's premises. Formerly, the landlord could only keep control of the property as a kind of pledge, but for many years now he has had the power to sell the property which he seizes or 'distrains'.

The right to distrain for rent is only open when there is an existing landlord and tenant relationship. This means that the right ceases when the tenancy ceases. Someone who takes in lodgers (who are usually only licensees, not tenants) cannot seize the lodgers' goods although he is commonly described as the 'landlord' and the payment due from the lodger is called 'rent'. Furthermore, the right can only be exercised to recover rent from the tenant and does not extend to other payments due. For example, where a landlord and a tenant agree, without making a new tenancy, that the tenant shall pay more than he agreed to pay originally, the difference is not strictly 'rent' and cannot be distrained for. Where the Rent Acts apply to a tenancy the landlord cannot distrain unless he obtains a Court order authorizing him to do so.

There is an exception to the rule that there must be a landlord and tenant relationship. Where a tenant remains in occupation after the end of the tenancy, so that he has ceased to be a tenant, the landlord may distrain for arrears of rent within six months of the end of the tenancy.

The landlord loses the right to distrain for arrears if he assigns his interest in the property to someone else. If he goes to Court and obtains a judgment for the sum due he cannot distrain afterwards for the same arrears. If the tenant, before the goods are sold, offers the amount of the rent and the expenses which the landlord has incurred in distraining the goods, the landlord's right of distress comes to an end. The landlord may also lose the right if he agrees with the tenant that he will not distrain. However, the fact that the landlord has frequently taken no action to recover arrears in the past does not prevent him from distraining at a later date during the tenancy.

What property may be seized

In general, any movable goods found on the premises which are the subject of the tenancy may be seized. It does not matter who is in actual possession of the premises. If a tenant assigns his tenancy and leaves goods on the premises the landlord may seize them if the assignee falls in arrear with his rent. Whether the goods are movable is decided on common-sense principles, so that carpets are movable, even though nailed to the floor. As an exception, growing crops are treated as movables.

There are, however, many restrictions on the general rule. Some goods may not be taken in distress in any circumstances. These include goods which a tradesman has on his premises which are not his own but which are there for the purposes of his trade. Thus, cloth which has been left in a tailor's shop by a third party to be made up into a suit may not be taken. The tools of a man's trade which he ordinarily uses, up to a value of £20—the plumber's mate's capacious bag and its contents, for example—cannot be taken, nor the clothes which he is wearing, nor his bedstead and bedding. As distress was in origin a seizure of a pledge which the landlord retained, and was obliged to return unspoiled, perishable goods (*e.g.* vegetables) may not be taken. By statute, fires, cookers, and appliances belonging to electricity, gas, and water boards, which are marked so as to indicate that they are only hired, are exempt from distress.

Other classes of goods may only be taken where there are insufficient goods apart from them to satisfy the claim to arrears of rent. These include, for example, a student's library or a farmer's ploughing horses and other implements of the tenant's trade or occupation which are not in actual use by him.

There is also a very important statutory restriction on distress. Formerly, goods on the premises which were owned by lodgers or other persons could be seized, though, of course, the lodger could reclaim their value from the tenant. If such goods are taken, the lodger can give written notice to the person distraining that the goods are not the tenant's and that they are not excluded from protection by the statute. He must also set out any rent due from him to the tenant and the times when he pays rent. He must undertake to pay his rent to the distrainor, *i.e.* the landlord asserting his right to distrain, until the tenant's arrears are met and attach to the notice a signed list of the property which belongs to him. If the landlord ignores the notice, the lodger can compel restoration of the goods to him by taking proceedings in the Magistrates' Court or in a County Court. Instead of distraining, the landlord may serve notice on a lodger (or sub-tenant) that the tenant's rent is in arrear by a stated amount and that he requires the lodger to pay future rent direct to him. Payments made after such a notice may be deducted from rent due to the tenant by the lodger.

These statutory restrictions do not protect goods on hire purchase, or goods belonging to the tenant's husband or wife. So, H.P. goods, or goods which

When a landlord resorts to his right of distress for recovery of arrears of rent—

—he may seize any movable property he finds on the tenant's premises.

have been transferred to the tenant's wife, may be seized by the landlord, and sold.

Only goods on the premises in respect of which the arrears are due may be taken. There is an exception to this. If a tenant removes the goods fraudulently and secretly to avoid their being taken by the landlord, the landlord may seize them within thirty days wherever they may be. However, if they have been genuinely sold to a buyer who does not know what the tenant has done the landlord cannot take them.

How 'Distress' is carried out

A landlord exercises his right of levying distress by entering the property and actually laying hands on the goods or, preferably, by written notice informing the occupier what goods are being seized. The landlord may do this himself or give written authority to a bailiff to do it as his agent. (Bailiffs are appointed by a certificate from the County Court Judge or Registrar.) The landlord (or bailiff) cannot break in, but he can open an unlocked door, go through an open window or over a wall. Once he has entered, if the tenant drives him out by violence or threats, the distrainor may call a policeman and actually break in. On the premises the distrainor may break open interior doors or cupboards in order to seize goods. A memorandum must be left on the premises. This should state the amount of rent distrained for and the expenses of doing so, give a list of goods seized, where they are impounded and where they are to be sold. (This must not be less than five clear days after the seizure.)

Public pounds used to exist where goods could be impounded after distress. There are still pounds in old towns, but they are generally not used. Impounded goods are often left on the premises where they have been seized or are taken to public auction rooms.

The landlord may have the goods sold (preferably by auction) if the tenant does not recover the right to them by offering payment of the arrears of rent and the expenses the landlord has incurred before they are sold. The landlord himself may not buy any of the goods at the sale. The tenant is entitled to any surplus of the money realized by the sale after the arrears of rent and proper expenses of the distress have been met.

The landlord can only seize enough property to satisfy the arrears. This is a matter of degree and he will not be guilty of excessive distress if there is only a small surplus. If the premises are empty except for one piece of valuable furniture the landlord may seize it even though it is worth very much more than the arrears of rent.

If the tenant retakes possession or removes goods which have been taken as distress he may commit an offence. On the other hand, if the landlord distrains when he has no right to distrain, or if he takes more than is due as rent, or if he sells before the proper time, he will be liable to pay damages to the tenant.

The remedy of distress is not so much used as it once was, chiefly because of the many technical rules which must be observed and the availability of other remedies in the County Court. No one should attempt to distrain for rent without taking proper legal advice. Nevertheless, in some cases distress may be the landlord's best remedy, especially when a tenant who has some valuable goods is unlikely to pay in cash after judgment has been given against him.

OTHER REMEDIES
FOR NON-PAYMENT OF RENT

If a tenant repeatedly falls in arrears with his rent the landlord will probably wish to get rid of him and find another tenant who will be less troublesome. Even in tenancies protected by the Rent Acts non-payment of rent is a ground on which the Court may make an order for possession. In the case of periodic tenancies which are not protected there is no difficulty. The landlord simply gives the tenant proper notice to quit and enforces it, if necessary, by getting an order for possession from the Court. If the rent remains unpaid the landlord can claim it by a Court action. (The County Court can deal with claims for possession where the rateable value of the property is not more than £100 and can deal with money claims up to £400.)

It may sometimes happen that the rent has not been paid for many years. The landlord may then only recover rent which fell due not more than six years before the date when he began the action. If the tenant, however, has acknowledged in writing within the six-year-period that he owes rent due more than six years before the landlord may also claim this.

Where the premises have been let to the tenant for a fixed number of years and the tenant fails to pay his rent, can the landlord evict him before the lease expires? He can do so only if there is a clause in the agreement which gives him the right to bring the tenancy to an end (see 'proviso for re-entry'). He must first formally demand the rent (unless the agreement dispenses with this, as it often does). Strictly speaking, if the tenant still does not pay the rent the landlord may literally re-enter and resume possession of the property. It is much safer, however, to ask the Court for an order that he is entitled to possession.

A landlord who wishes to recover possession in this way must be careful not to do anything which may be regarded as an acknowledgement by him that the tenancy still continues. Thus, he must not demand payment or accept rent after the right to re-enter has arisen. He must not distrain for arrears. If he does any of these things he loses the right, which does not revive unless the tenant fails to pay rent due at a later date.

Although the landlord does all the law requires of him the Courts may refuse an order for possession in certain circumstances. Thus, if the tenant offers, or pays into Court, the whole of the rent due plus the costs of the action before judgment is given against him for possession the landlord will not be permitted to continue the action and the tenant will be allowed to remain in possession under the terms of the lease. Even after judgment has been given in favour of the landlord the tenant may apply to the Court within six months. If it thinks fit, the Court may allow the tenant to go back into possession. The Court may impose any conditions which it thinks proper. The tenant will certainly have to pay all arrears of rent and will probably have to bear all costs of the proceedings.

Relief may also be obtained by a sub-tenant. If a tenant grants a sub-lease of premises and later fails to pay the landlord the rent due under the main lease it is obviously unfair that a sub-tenant who is not in default should be dispossessed because the tenant has failed to pay rent to the landlord. In these circumstances the sub-tenant can ask the Court not to allow the landlord to re-enter. If he does so the Court will frequently give him relief and order that he shall be put in the position, for the duration of his sub-lease, of direct tenant to the landlord.

A landlord whose tenant remains in occupation after his right to do so has come to an end can claim double rent for the period of the wrongful occupation. To be able to do so he must demand possession and serve written notice requiring the tenant to leave. The demand and notice may be given before or after the end of his tenancy. Alternatively, he may merely claim payment for the tenant's occupation during the same period. If he brings an action to recover this he should not claim the sum due as 'rent', for the tenant has become a trespasser. Instead he claims what are called 'mesne profits' from the end of the tenancy until the date on which he actually recovers possession. In practice, the landlord will often claim payment at the same rate as the rent under the tenancy. However, if he can show, for example, that he could have let the premises at a higher rent than he received under the tenancy agreement he may claim to be paid at this higher rate by his old tenant.

REPAIRS

OBLIGATIONS OF LANDLORD AND TENANT

THE RESPONSIBILITY of a landlord for repairs to property which he has rented has been changed in a very remarkable way by the Housing Act of 1961. But the Act, in this respect, affects only *new* lettings of less than seven years, beginning *on or after* October 24th, 1961.

The repairing obligations of a landlord and a tenant on a letting for seven years or more have almost always been set down in detail in the actual lease, and those terms settle the matter, and still do so. The terms of the lease are final and decisive.

But many a lease or agreement entered into for less than seven years has not dealt comprehensively with the respective obligations of landlord and tenant for work of repair or decoration. This is particularly true of thousands of monthly and weekly tenancies where neither rent book nor agreement has dealt fully with this problem.

The general legal principles applying to all lettings beginning before October 24th, 1961, are as follows:

(a) In the absence of any express agreement the landlord need do no work of repair, redecoration, or renewal of any kind;

(b) In the absence of express agreement the tenant need not do any such work described under paragraph (a) except that he must put right damage deliberately or negligently caused by himself, his family, or his visitors.

As will be described in more detail below, the landlord's exemption from responsibility has long been subject to two statutory exceptions:

(a) He is responsible for ensuring that houses let at a rent below a certain figure shall at least be reasonably fit for human habitation.

(b) Certain serious defects could expose him to proceedings by the local authority to avoid or remedy a nuisance under the provisions of the Acts of Parliament dealing with Public Health.

Subject, however, to these exceptions, a landlord had no responsibility—apart from work he had expressly agreed with the particular tenant to undertake.

This section will deal first with the law as it affects landlords and tenants under agreements or leases which came into force up to October 24th, 1961, and then with the law on and after that date.

THE LAW BEFORE OCTOBER 24th, 1961

As a general rule, if the tenancy agreement or lease does not contain specific obligations about repairs, neither the landlord nor the tenant is obliged by law to do any repairs to the property. This is the basic rule of English Law. It is often a shock, particularly to tenants, to realize that in general the law does not lay down any obligations, particularly that it does not place any obligations upon the landlord. There is a very general assumption, for instance, among tenants of flats in a block of flats or in parts of a house which have been converted into separate dwellings, that the landlord has some legal obligation for the repair of the roof, of the outside walls, of the main drains, and of other essential parts of the structure. There is also a very general assumption among tenants whether of a flat or of a house that a landlord is responsible for the repair or replacement of certain essential fixtures like the water tank in the roof which contains the water supply for the whole house, or for the calorifier which supplies the hot water, or for other basic and essential fixtures, like the bath, the water closet, the wash-hand basin, and so on. It is very generally assumed that a landlord has some automatic responsibility, both for the structure and for the main services like the drains, the cold water supply, the hot water supply, and so on.

The general rule under English Law is that this is not so. In fact, the general rule is that the landlord is responsible for nothing except for those repairs, if any, which he has expressly undertaken in the tenancy agreement. If he has not accepted certain specific responsibilities in the tenancy agreement, he is not responsible for any repairs or any decorations whatever.

This situation, whereby the landlord is completely exempt from all repairing obligations, except those he has expressly undertaken to do, has been varied by Acts of Parliament, putting certain obligations upon him in respect of houses let at a low rent. However, before we come to those particular obligations, let us now consider the position of the tenant under the general basic law, apart from the obligations set down in the tenancy agreement.

The position as regards the tenant is not unlike that of the landlord in that, apart from specific obligations in the tenancy agreement, he is not obliged to do any repairs. When the tenancy agreement places no specific obligations as

... the tenant can choose either to suffer the inconvenience—

—or do the necessary work himself!

to repair or redecoration on either landlord or tenant, what is to be done about repairs? For example, the hot water system breaks down. The banisters begin to break and the stairs become unsafe. The sash cords in a number of windows are broken and it is risky to open the windows. The roof begins to leak. The tenant who, in such a situation, asks, "What am I to do about this?" must be told that, whereas the landlord cannot *compel him* to do anything about these defects, yet he cannot *compel the landlord* to put them right. The answer is a stalemate if neither is willing to move. And if the tenant wants the hot water system put right, the sash cords repaired, the banisters mended, the roof renewed, and so on, under that situation the tenant must either do the work himself, or suffer the consequent inconvenience. Many a tenant in this situation says, in effect: "Why should I spend a good deal of money in work of repair or redecoration to a house or a flat of which I am only a weekly or monthly tenant, and which I may leave or have to leave at short notice?" The answer to that is: "Indeed why should you? But if you don't do the work of repair, you cannot compel your landlord to do it." Another tenant might say that he feels very disinclined to spend money on work of permanent benefit to a property when the value of that work will enure for the benefit of the landlord or for future tenants. That is a very understandable point of view. Under the general rule, however, which has been described, unless the tenancy agreement prescribes exactly who shall do what, then work of repair, renewal, or redecoration either has to be done by the tenant, or not done at all. The tenant can choose whether he will do it and spend the money for his greater comfort and convenience so long as his tenancy lasts, or not do it at all. No one can make him do it, it is entirely a matter for his choice; but equally he cannot make the landlord do it.

That is the law, where there is nothing in the tenancy agreement specifically prescribing who is to be responsible for repairs. It is surprising how many tenancy agreements, and how many rent books say nothing about this problem whatever. They deal simply with the problem of letting, and the amount of the rent, and when it is to be paid, and say nothing about repairs on either side.

The general law on this matter, however, does say something about a tenant's responsibility. While it does not require a landlord specifically to undertake any repairs or redecorations or replacements of any kind, it does require a tenant to avoid doing damage or at least to repair damage. The general rule is that he must use the premises in a 'tenant-like manner'. This means that he will have to make good any damage which is done by himself, or his family, or his friends, or his visitors by deliberate or careless acts. If one of his children breaks a window, or if he allows a bath to overflow and cause damage, he must carry out the necessary repairs. He must repair the window, he must put right the damage caused by the overflowing bath. The tenant's general responsibility was summed up by a Judge in a case in the Court of Appeal. The Judge said:

"Apart from express contract, a tenant owes no duty to the landlord to keep the premises in repair. The only duty of the tenant is to use the premises in a husband-like or tenant-like manner. What does this mean? I think it can best be shown by some illustrations. The tenant must take proper care of the premises. For example, if he leaves the house for a period during the

FAMILY LAWYER

winter, he must turn off the water and empty the tank. He must clean the chimneys and the windows. He must mend the electric light when it fuses. He must unstop the sink when it is blocked by waste. In short, he must do the little jobs about the place which a reasonable tenant would do. In addition, he must not damage the house wilfully or negligently—nor his family, nor his friends. If he does damage, he must repair it, or if they do damage he must repair it. But apart from such things, if the house falls into disrepair, through fair wear and tear or lapse of time or for any reason not caused by him or by people for whom he is responsible, the tenant is not liable to the landlord to repair it."

So there is the general rule. In the absence of express agreement a landlord has no responsibility whatever to do any repairs or redecorations of any kind, however major or minor they might be. A tenant has no such obligation either, except that he must use the premises in a tenant-like manner, and must not be careless or indifferent, and if damage is caused by his friends, his family, and so on, he has got to put it right. By and large, however, that is a small obligation, and, broadly speaking, it is true to say that neither landlord nor tenant has any obligation to the other to do repairs or redecoration. This general rule, of course, makes it vitally important that proper terms should be laid down and agreed in the tenancy agreement. From both points of view it is extremely important.

Nevertheless, there are certain statutory exceptions to this general rule.

The first exception applies to what are generally called 'low rent houses'.

This exception about 'low rent houses' derives from various Housing Acts and it applies to all houses including parts of houses let as separate dwellings, which are let at small rents. The important date which determines the rent limit at which these provisions of the Acts apply is July 6th, 1957. If the tenancy began before this date the Acts apply if the rent is not more than £40 in London, and not more than £26 elsewhere. If the tenancy began on or after this date, the Acts apply if the rent is not more than £80 in London, or £52 elsewhere—in other words, double the figures for the older tenancies.

The *rent* means the amount of money actually paid by the tenant. If he pays the rates, these are included for the purpose of finding if the house is within the limit.

So, if the money in rent and rates paid by the tenant is within these figures, then the landlord is under an obligation to do all essential repairs to make and keep the house (or part of the house) or flat, reasonably fit for habitation.

It should be emphasized that the landlord cannot escape this obligation even if he has persuaded the tenant to enter into an agreement which makes the tenant responsible for such repairs. Whatever the agreement says, the landlord of a house let at a rent within these limits is responsible for ensuring that it is at least reasonably fit for habitation, whatever the terms of the agreement may be.

What kind of disrepair can the tenant of such a house complain of? What is the standard of 'reasonably fit for human habitation'? It is not easy to give a precise answer, but clearly the landlord would be responsible for repairing leaking roofs, damp walls, broken drains, cracked walls or chimney stacks, and all such serious matters which would tend to make the place not reasonably fit to live in. Clearly he would not usually be responsible for mere decorative

106

disrepair, for this will only very rarely affect the *habitability* of the house. The Act is aimed at serious matters like defective roofs, structures, inadequate ventilation, inadequate water supply, defective drains, kitchens or larders where food may be exposed to contamination, and so on. The tenant must give

It is the landlord's responsibility for ensuring that the house is 'reasonably fit for human habitation', when the rent is below a certain figure (see text).

the landlord notice of the defects, and this is so even if the agreement allows the landlord to inspect the premises, so that a diligent landlord might be expected to know what was wrong.

If the landlord does not put these things right, what can the tenant do to compel him to do so. First of all, the tenant who has given reasonable notice to a landlord to put these things right where the landlord is statutorily obliged to do so, can leave the premises without being liable for further rent. In these days this perhaps is not a very realistic remedy, because with the acute shortage of housing accommodation, a tenant may have nowhere else to go, and he may be much more concerned about putting positive pressure on a landlord to put things right.

Therefore, he can take proceedings in the local County Court, compel the landlord to honour his obligations under the Housing Acts, and he would be well advised to ask a solicitor to act for him. Another way in which the tenant may compel the landlord to do something is by enlisting the help of the local authority. If he can satisfy the local authority that the house is unfit for human habitation, the authority can serve notice on the person who has control of the house, that is the person who receives the rent, and require him to do the work specified in the notice within twenty-one days.

The local authority will not serve this notice, however, if they consider that the house cannot be made reasonably fit for human habitation at reasonable cost. Moreover, the landlord can appeal to the County Court against the notice. However, if the local authority decide that by reasonable expenditure the house can be made reasonably fit for human habitation, and if the landlord does not do the work, they can serve a further notice on him informing him that it is their intention to do the work themselves. If they then do the work they can recover the cost of the work as a debt due to them by the landlord.

There is a right of appeal to the County Court against orders made and notices given by local authority under the Housing Acts. An owner or tenant, or anyone else who wishes to appeal, must act quickly, as the time for appeal is usually only twenty-one days.

Public Health Act, 1936

The provisions of the Housing Acts which have been considered above directly affect the position of landlord and tenant where repairs are concerned. They also give local authorities powers over houses which are unfit for habitation whether they are tenant- or owner-occupied. These latter powers overlap to some extent the powers given to local authorities by the Public Health Act, 1936. Under this Act the powers cover all houses, even those which are owner-occupied. In practice, however, a high proportion of the houses which have defects offending against the Act are occupied by tenants. This is often because the owner-occupier will take more care of his house than a tenant—or a landlord who is only receiving a small rent. The Act, therefore, may provide an indirect means by which a tenant may get his landlord to do important work to the house where the Housing Acts, the Rent Acts, or the tenancy agreement do not help him.

The Act declares that certain things shall be treated as 'statutory nuisances'. These include foul drains and gutters, smells emitted from premises, the accumulation of garbage, smoking chimneys, and, in general, 'premises in such a state as to be prejudicial to health or a nuisance'. Dampness in rooms, rotten floors, broken rain-water channels and the like may come within this general description. The authority, or a private individual (the tenant himself, for example), may serve a notice, called an 'abatement notice', on the person responsible for the nuisance or, if he cannot be found, on the owner or occupier of the premises. The notice must require him to put an end to the nuisance and do any work

108

necessary for that purpose. If the nuisance consists of a structural defect the notice must be served on the owner. If the nuisance is not abated after the notice the local Magistrates' Court will make an order that the nuisance should be abated. If the person against whom the Court's order has been made still does not comply the local authority may do the work itself and recover the cost from the defaulter. There is a right of appeal from the Magistrates to Quarter Sessions.

It may be that a house becomes defective because the tenant has failed to do the repairs which the tenancy agreement requires him to do. If this is so and the landlord is compelled to do the repairs or to pay for those which have been done he can sue the tenant for the expense to which he has been put. This does not apply, however, when a 'low rent' house becomes unfit for habitation. As we have seen, the law implies a condition in tenancy agreements for these houses that the landlord will put them in a fit state at the beginning of the tenancy and keep them so afterwards. This is so even if the tenancy agreement itself provides the contrary. If the landlord has to do work on a 'low rent' house to make it fit to live in, he cannot say that the unfitness has occurred because of the tenant's breach of the agreement.

Special powers are given to local authorities to deal with dangerous structures. They may direct the owners to take steps to make them safe or demolish them. If the owners take no action the authority may do any necessary work themselves and look to the owner to repay the cost. If buildings become derelict and ruinous so as to threaten to spoil the amenity of the area where they stand the local authority has similar powers to order the owners to restore or demolish them. Again, if the owners do nothing the authority may do the work and sue the owner for the cost if he fails to repay.

Agreements to repair

As we have seen, landlord and tenant are generally under no obligation to repair unless they have agreed differently. The law leaves them free to make any agreement they like on this subject—or not to make any agreement at all. The kind of agreement which is made depends very much on the length of tenancy which is being taken and the scarcity of accommodation at the time when the agreement is made.

Bearing in mind that the landlord will often be able to demand more of his tenant when rented property is scarce and less when the supply exceeds the demand, it is possible to make some general remarks about the repairing obligations which are to be expected in various kinds of tenancy.

In weekly tenancies, because the tenant has only very limited interest in the property—he need be given only a month's notice to quit—it may sometimes happen that the landlord does not ask the tenant to do any repairs. If he does not do so he will probably rely on getting sufficient rent from the tenant to do essential repairs himself, as well as getting a reasonable return on his investment in the property. In this way, too, he will be relieved of the trouble of compelling the tenant to repair or of taking legal action if he fails to do so. On the other hand, many weekly tenancy agreements will be based on the terms in a printed rent book, or contain a written provision in much the same words, by which the tenant promises to keep in repair all landlord's fixtures and fittings, all pipes and sanitary apparatus, and all windows. This kind of agreement makes the tenant responsible for the repair of things like fitted cupboards, fireplaces and stoves, baths, wash basins and plumbing, window panes and sash cords and catches. The agreement may go further so that the tenant promises to keep the interior of the premises in good and tenantable repair. This means that the tenant is obliged to see to the general state of the inside of the premises— including decorative repair—so that it is kept in reasonable condition when the age of the house, its location, and character are considered. In other words, the house must be kept in such a condition that a reasonable tenant of the class who would be expected to take a house in the area concerned would be willing to live in it. If the tenant promises to put and keep the premises in repair (or even only to keep them so) he will be compelled to do so even if their state is poor at the beginning of his tenancy and the effect of doing so is to leave his landlord with better-kept premises than he had before.

A weekly tenancy agreement will seldom require the landlord to do any repairs. It must be emphasized that an agreement by the tenant which excludes, for example, external repairs does not mean that the landlord is deemed to be responsible for them. He is not, unless he expressly agrees to do them.

In longer tenancy agreements, the tenant's obligations will usually be precise. Almost always, there will be a formal lease, or agreement for a lease, drawn up by a solicitor and there may be several clauses dealing with repairs. For example, in addition to a promise (which will generally be termed a 'covenant' in a formal lease) by the tenant in general terms to keep the premises in good and tenantable repair, he may specifically undertake to paint the premises and re-paper at fixed intervals. The extent and burden of the covenant which the tenant will have to accept will depend on the rent, the market, and the length of the tenancy. The tenant should try to secure a promise by the landlord in return to do any repairs not included in the tenant's obligations. This will often cover external repairs.

In long leases—for periods of, say, seven years or more—the landlord's liability for repairs will usually be little or nothing. The tenant may be obliged to accept what is called a full repairing lease and this will almost always be the case where a lease of new property—property developers often grant leases of ninety-nine or nine hundred and ninety-nine years—is sold at a substantial figure and where only a relatively small ground rent is payable to the landlord. A full repairing lease will usually contain covenants by the tenant to keep the premises in good and substantial repair and condition (which probably imports a rather higher standard than 'tenantable repair'); to paint with a specified number of coats the exterior of the premises, say, in every third year; to paint the interior every seventh year; and to yield up the premises at the end of the lease in good and substantial repair. The painting and repairing obligations will usually expressly extend to any additions made to the property. Thus, a brick-built garage which the tenant has erected will probably become a land- lord's fixture and will have to be cared for in the same way as the rest of the premises. These covenants, and particularly the last, may involve the tenant in considerable expense. It cannot be too strongly emphasized that no one should ever take a long lease of premises without having the advice of a solicitor—a different one from the landlord's—who will help the tenant to get the best possible bargain. He will be able to question unusually demanding covenants which the landlord puts forward and perhaps arrange some adjustment of rent in return for the burdens which the tenant is taking on.

Landlord's right of entry

Unless there is a term in the agreement which permits the landlord to enter to inspect or do repairs, for example, he cannot compel the tenant to let him. This is so even if he has expressly agreed to do some or all of the repairs himself. The agreement should therefore be framed to allow him, or anyone authorized by him, to enter at reasonable times, with or without workmen, to do any necessary work on the premises. The tenant is entitled to have reasonable notice of the landlord's intention.

Liability to third parties

Even if the tenancy agreement imposes no duties to repair, prudent tenants will take steps to see that the premises are reasonably safe so that their visitors are not injured because of defects in them. When the landlord has repairing obligations he will be held responsible for injury to the tenant or anyone on the premises who is injured because of his failure to carry them out. This is only so where the landlord has notice of the want of repair. Further, when the landlord retains some parts of the premises (for example, in a block of flats where he keeps control of staircases, lifts, and hall-ways) he will be liable to persons injured if he fails to take reasonable care to keep those parts in a safe state. This is by reason of the Occupiers Liability Act 1957.

The law from October 24th, 1961
for lettings of less than seven years

The Housing Act, 1961, has radically altered the former rule that a landlord has not been obliged to do any repairs to his property—except those he has agreed to do. The Act states that on every lease or tenancy for less than seven years entered into on or after October 24th, 1961, the landlord *must* accept certain basic repairing obligations. And it does not matter what the agreement or lease says to the contrary. The Act is paramount. The landlord must keep in repair the structure and the outside of the house (including drains, gutters, and external pipes). He must also keep in repair and proper working order the installations in the house for the supply of water, gas, and electricity; sanitary fittings (including baths, sinks, and lavatories); fireplaces (or other fixed means of heating); and any means provided for water-heating.

The tenant, for his part, still has a general duty to use the premises in a reasonable, tenant-like way, so that if he, his family, or his friends, damage the kitchen sink or the gas meter, either deliberately or by some careless act, the landlord not only isn't obliged to do the repairs, he can make the tenant do them. The tenant is also expected to do small odd jobs about the house such as replacing washers and mending fuses.

The landlord's obligations don't extend to apparatus such as electric and gas cookers or light fittings, nor to any fixtures which the tenant is entitled to remove from the house.

What is meant by keeping in repair? The Act says that it is necessary to look

"The tenant is expected to do small jobs about the house such as replacing washers—

—and mending fuses!"

at the age, character, and likely prospective life of the house, as well as the area it stands in, in order to judge the standard of repair to be demanded of the landlord. Obviously, he will be expected to keep a block of flats built since the war in a pleasant suburb, in a better state than a converted Victorian house which has seen better days.

To help the landlord to carry out his obligations only one promise is required of the tenant in return. He must allow the landlord, or anyone with his written permission, to inspect the condition of the house at reasonable times a day, provided the landlord has given at least twenty-four hours' notice, in writing, that he intends to make this inspection. The landlord also has a right to come into the house to carry out any repairs which he is obliged to do.

There is only one way in which the heavy repairing obligations put on the landlord by the Act can be excluded or modified. This is by an application to the County Court with the support of both parties. Then, if the County Court Judge thinks that it is reasonable to do so, in the light of the other provisions of the agreement and all the circumstances, he can order that the tenancy agreement should leave out or alter the promises that the Act ordinarily obliges the landlord to make.

Unless the County Court Judge makes an order to this effect, an agreement which tries to exclude or alter these provisions of the Act is ineffective. Even if the tenant has been persuaded to accept an agreement which relieves the landlord of these duties, this agreement can't be enforced against him.

These new duties to repair imposed on landlords only apply to dwelling-houses, though this includes, of course, flats, and each part of a house which is let under a separate tenancy agreement. The Act doesn't apply to agricultural holdings. It doesn't apply to leases of seven years or more. Nor when a new lease for a period of less than seven years is taken by someone already holding one for a period of more than seven years. A tenancy of business premises which include living accommodation is usually covered by the Landlord and Tenant Act of 1954. If it is, a new tenancy also covered by that Act will fall outside the scope of the Housing Act and again the provisions I have mentioned will not apply.

If there is any dispute about whether the tenancy is one which carries these obligations with it, the Act supplies a quick method of solving the problem— the County Court Judge decides.

To sum up this new Act: in nearly all new tenancies for less than seven years which begin on or after October 24th, 1961, the landlord will be responsible for all structural and external repairs, and for the repair and maintenance of essential amenities inside the house as well. And the tenant can't validly agree to release the landlord from these responsibilities without the approval of the County Court.

What are the practical results going to be? The people most likely to be affected in considerable numbers at first are those who took three- or four-year leases of decontrolled houses in 1958 and afterwards. When their leases come to an end, their landlords may be expected to do one of two things: either they will offer leases for seven years or more so that the Act does not apply, or they will offer shorter leases at greater rents, to offset the new burdens which the landlords will have to bear under the Act.

FIXTURES

FIXTURES are chattels or, in other words, movable articles, which have been attached to land or buildings. The problem that arises with regard to fixtures between a landlord and his tenant is whether the tenant can remove fixtures which he himself has installed during his tenancy when it comes to an end. Fixtures which the tenant is entitled to remove are generally called tenant's fixtures and those which he is not entitled to remove landlord's fixtures.

The *general rule* of English Law is that whatever is attached to land or the buildings on it becomes a part of the land and belongs to the landowner. But the difficult question is: has the fixture been so attached that it *is* part of the structure or the land? The test which the Courts apply to determine that question is to ask *to what extent* the chattel is attached to the land and *for what purpose* it is so attached. A chattel which is not attached to land at all, but is merely *resting* on it, cannot usually become a fixture. For example, a Dutch barn resting on wooden uprights which in turn lay on brick columns let into the ground has been held not to be a fixture and consequently removable by a tenant. On the other hand, stones laid upon each other without mortar by a tenant in order to make a wall have been held to have become fixtures.

Purpose for which fixture installed

If a chattel is attached to land or a building in order to be *more conveniently used as a chattel*, *i.e.* for what it is, and not in order to improve the land or the building, it will not become a fixture, unless it cannot be removed without causing irreparable damage to itself or to the land or buildings to which it is attached.

For example, in one case it was held that a switchback railway was not a fixture, since its attachment to the land on which it was erected was only for the purpose of its convenient use as a piece of machinery. Again, where a tenant who owned some valuable tapestry nailed strips of wood to a drawing-room wall to which he tacked the tapestry, it was held that the tapestry had not become a fixture, since the tenant's purpose in fixing it to the wall was to see it, and let his friends see it, which he could scarcely have done without hanging it up.

However, even if the immediate object of attaching a chattel to land or a building is to make its use more convenient, the fact that the chattel is essential for the use of the land or a building for its intended purpose will make the chattel a fixture. Thus it has been held that retorts, boilers, and gasholders in a gasworks are all fixtures. Similarly the plant in a steelworks would undoubtedly be held to be fixtures.

Trade fixtures

There are a number of important exceptions to the general rule that fixtures are irremovable by a tenant. The first exception relates to trade fixtures. Where

114

a tenant has fastened chattels, such as machinery, to land or buildings comprised in his tenancy in such a way that they have become fixtures he can remove them if he so fastened them for the purposes of the trade he carries on, provided that they can be moved without irreparable injury to the land or buildings and without losing their own character or value. For example, the tenant of a garage has been held to be entitled to remove a petrol pump which he had erected and which was fastened to a tank embedded in the ground, although the tank itself could not be removed. Again, a market gardener can remove trees or shrubs which he has planted as part of his stock-in-trade. The reason for the relaxation of the general rule in favour of trade fixtures has been to encourage and promote the growth of industry, since tenants who might lose valuable and expensive fixtures at the end of their tenancies would obviously hesitate to install them.

Ornamental fixtures

A second exception to the general rule relates to ornamental fixtures and fixtures installed for domestic convenience, which is of great importance to tenants of residential premises, since it was recognized very early by the Courts that it would be unfair that tenants should lose at the end of their tenancies chattels which might have a very great value and which they had installed in order to enjoy their beauty. Examples of fixtures which tenants have been allowed to remove under this principle are: marble chimney pieces, pier glasses, ornamental panelling, grates and stoves, beds fastened to walls, bookcases fastened by brackets to walls.

However, ornamental fixtures cannot be removed if irreparable injury would be done to the land or the building to which they are attached or if they have been installed with the intention of effecting a permanent improvement. They *can* be removed if the damage caused by their removal can be made good, and it is, of course, the tenant's responsibility to see to this.

Agricultural fixtures

A third exception to the general rule has been created by statute with reference to agricultural fixtures. At Common Law, a tenant has no right to remove fixtures attached to land or buildings by him for agricultural purposes. By Section 13 of the Agricultural Holdings Act, 1948, the tenant of agricultural land may remove 'any engine, machinery, fencing or other fixture or any building' erected by him on the holding (other than buildings in respect of which the 1948 Act entitles the tenant to compensation) at any time during the continuation of his tenancy or within two months of its termination, provided that he was not obliged to install the building or fixture under an agreement with his landlord or that the building or fixture was not installed in place of one belonging to his landlord. The tenant can only remove such buildings or fixtures, however, if he has paid all rent owing by him and has performed or satisfied all his other obligations to his landlord and if he gives his landlord notice in writing of his intention to remove the fixtures or building at least six months before he exercises his right of removal and before the termination of the tenancy. Even then, the landlord can stop the tenant from removing a building or fixture by giving the tenant a counter-notice in writing before the

115

Ornamental fixtures may be removed if the damage caused by their removal—

—is made good by the tenant.

tenant's notice expires, electing to buy any fixture or building referred to in the tenant's notice. The landlord is obliged to pay the tenant 'the fair value' of the fixture which he elects to buy 'to an incoming tenant'. It should be noted that the landlord and tenant of an agricultural holding can by agreement provide that Section 13 of the 1948 Act shall not apply to their relationship.

The fourth exception to the general rule that fixtures are irremovable arises when the landlord and tenant make an express agreement to the contrary. It is also open to them to agree if they wish that trade and ornamental fixtures shall not be removable by the tenant.

Finally, some kinds of fixtures may be removable by the tenant by local custom.

A tenant must remove fixtures before his tenancy comes to an end and loses his right to do so afterwards. However, where the tenant is allowed to remove fixtures under a provision of his tenancy agreement he is permitted to remove them within a reasonable time after his tenancy has come to an end.

ASSIGNING AND SUB-LETTING

'ASSIGNMENT' is the word used to describe the transaction when a tenant hands over, to someone other than the landlord, all his rights in the premises which are let to him. When a tenant *sub-lets* premises, however, he remains the tenant of the premises as far as his landlord is concerned: this is so whether he sub-lets only part of the premises or whether he moves out of occupation altogether and allows his sub-tenant to enjoy the whole of the premises.

Only in one case does the law treat a sub-letting as if it were an assignment. This is where a tenant has a lease for a term of years and he purports to sub-let the premises for as long as, or longer than, the remainder of the term of the lease. Here, he is trying to give his sub-tenant all the interest which he has in the premises or even more. The result is that the tenant is treated as having assigned the lease to the sub-tenant for the remainder of the term and the tenant himself ceases to have any rights in the premises. This means that he cannot distrain for unpaid rent, though he can, of course, sue his sub-tenant for the rent as a debt, and it also means that the landlord and sub-tenant become liable to one another on the covenants in the original lease to the tenant. This rule about a sub-letting taking effect as an assignment does not apply to a tenant from year to year who grants a sub-lease for, say, three years, for the tenancy from year to year may last longer than three years.

Covenants against assignment or sub-letting

Whatever kind of tenancy there may be, unless the agreement forbids the tenant to do so, he is free to assign the tenancy, or to sub-let the whole or part of the premises, without his landlord's permission. Obviously, however, the

117

landlord will frequently want to restrict this freedom as he may wish to have some voice in deciding who is to occupy his property. It is very common, therefore, to find a clause in a tenancy agreement which restricts the tenant's rights to assign and under-let. There is no reason why such a clause should not altogether forbid the tenant to do either of these things. But in practice an unqualified covenant by the tenant not to assign is unusual. This is because very few tenants would accept a long tenancy which obliged them to make this covenant unless there was such a shortage of houses or flats to be let that they had no option. If the tenant's circumstances changed—he might find himself unable to pay the rent or he might have to go and work in another town, for example—he would be prevented from finding another tenant to take over the tenancy. A landlord who insisted on this covenant might find few tenants for his property, except in a 'landlords' market', so to speak. For this reason, the covenant against assignment usually takes the form of a promise by the tenant not to assign *without the landlord's consent.*

When this form of promise is made, the law adds, *i.e.* implies, a proviso that the landlord's consent is not to be unreasonably withheld. In a case decided soon after the First World War, a landlord refused to consent to an assignment because he objected to the person to whom the tenant proposed to pass the tenancy. The ground of objection was that he was of German birth and only a naturalized British subject. It was decided that this was unreasonable. The landlord is only entitled to object to personal qualities in the intended new tenant which may make him an unsatisfactory tenant. Thus, it is reasonable to refuse where the intended new tenant is a married woman who has no means of her own. The objection may also be reasonable where the kind of use to which the property is to be put is different from the use which the original tenant makes of a property. A landlord may reasonably object if the new tenant intends to run a business in what has formerly been a dwelling-house, even though the tenancy agreement does not forbid the use of the premises for business purposes. If the tenant considers that the refusal is unreasonable he can assign the property without consent, but he would be better advised to apply to the High Court or the County Court for a declaration that he has a right to do so.

The landlord is not obliged to tell the tenant why he refuses his consent and it is up to the tenant to satisfy the Court that the refusal is unreasonable, but the Court may be more ready to decide that it is unreasonable if the landlord has not given any reason. Sometimes a landlord of business premises, for example, may be reluctant to allow an assignment when the lease is coming to an end because the new tenant will have the protection of the Landlord and Tenant Act of 1954. However, this is not in itself a sufficient reason for refusing consent. On the other hand, it was decided in one case that a landlord was not unreasonable when he refused to allow an assignment of a tenancy controlled by the Rent Acts only twelve days before the tenancy came to an end; but in this case it was clear that the only object of the assignment was to give the benefit of a statutory tenancy to the new tenant.

The landlord is allowed to lay down reasonable conditions as the price of his consent to a proposed assignment. He may demand that the original tenant should make good any breaches of his agreement to repair before he assigns, or that all the legal costs of the landlord in connection with the assignment should be paid by the tenant. What the landlord cannot do is to impose conditions which materially affect the terms of the original tenancy agreement—for example, by increasing the rent or by requiring the new tenant to pay the rates, for which the original tenant was not liable.

Whenever the agreement compels the tenant to ask the landlord's permission to assign, he must do so clearly (it would be wise to make a written request) and he must give the landlord a reasonable time in which to give his consent. He must also give the landlord full information about the transaction and about the intended new tenant. If the landlord unreasonably withholds consent the new tenant, despite the difficult position in which he may be, is still bound by his agreement to accept an assignment from the old tenant. In these circumstances he should try to ensure that the old tenant applies to the Court for a declaration that the landlord's refusal to consent is unreasonable.

An assignment must be made by deed in order to pass the legal estate to the new tenant. For most purposes, however, a written agreement to assign which sets out all the terms of the assignment will be equally effective. (See 'Leases and Agreements for Leases': the same principles apply to assignments.)

The obligations of the original tenant

Because the original tenancy agreement was made between the landlord and the original tenant, the latter remains liable to the landlord for breaches which may occur after he has assigned. For example, if a lease of a flat for seven years contains a covenant by the tenant not to carry on any business there and the original tenant assigns the lease after four years, he remains liable to be sued by the landlord for the three years which are left of the lease, if the new tenant starts to use the flat as business premises.

When an assignment is made, however, the law implies a covenant by the new tenant to indemnify the original tenant if he is sued by the landlord for the new tenant's wrongdoings. In other words, if damages are awarded against the original tenant, he can recover these from the new tenant. This provides a strong reason why a tenant who wants to assign should try to make sure that any prospective new tenant has reasonable means and, also, is someone who is likely to be a good tenant. It is wise to make the new tenant enter into an express covenant, in the agreement to assign, that he will indemnify the original tenant against liabilities under the tenancy. This is only one strong and obvious reason why a tenant who wants to assign his agreement or lease should have a solicitor to advise and act for him.

After the assignment has been made the new tenant, generally speaking, comes under an obligation to the landlord to observe all the terms of the tenancy which has passed to him. Conversely, the landlord's obligations under the tenancy agreement become enforceable by the new tenant. Not all the provisions of the original agreement bind the landlord and the new tenant. The provisions which are transferred are directly concerned with the land and premises which are the subject of the tenancy. On the other hand, an undertaking by the original tenant, for example, which is contained in the tenancy

F.L.—9

119

agreement, to acquire adjoining land would be regarded as a personal agreement unconnected with the tenancy and the new tenant would not be required to observe it.

We have seen that the original tenant remains under obligations to the landlord even after the assignment. If the new tenant himself subsequently re-assigns the premises to someone else, however, his obligations under the tenancy come to an end, unless he has expressly agreed that they shall not. The reason for this is that the new tenant was not a party to the original tenancy agreement and, therefore, his obligations to the landlord only last as long as he is tenant. The landlord will often, however, when he gives consent to an assignment, require that the new tenant should agree to be liable under the tenancy agreement for the remainder of the tenancy. This has the effect of making him liable under the agreement after he has made a re-assignment.

The original tenancy as a valuable asset

A tenancy of premises may be a valuable asset, particularly if it is a lease for a long period of years. It does not ordinarily come to an end on the death of the tenant but will pass to his personal representatives to be administered with the rest of his assets. Again, if a tenant becomes bankrupt, the benefit of the tenancy will pass to his trustee in bankruptcy to use for the benefit of the tenant's creditors. In both these cases an assignment occurs. As neither of these assignments is a voluntary act on the tenant's part there is no question of obtaining the landlord's permission, even if the tenancy agreement forbids assignment without consent.

Sometimes, however, the tenancy agreement or lease may contain a clause which demands the personal occupation of the premises by the tenant. If it does, death or bankruptcy may terminate the tenancy.

Again, many formal leases give the right to the landlord to re-enter and bring the lease to an end if the tenant becomes bankrupt or even if execution is levied on the tenant's goods on the premises. In this way the landlord may prevent an involuntary assignment of the lease.

An agreement by the tenant not to assign is not broken by a sub-letting of all or part of the premises. Therefore, if the landlord wishes to prevent sub-letting he must make sure that the agreement contains a further provision. It is not enough for the agreement to prohibit sub-letting simply, for it has been decided that this provision only prevents the tenant from sub-letting the whole premises and does not prevent a sub-letting of a part only. The only fully effective provision, therefore, is one by which the tenant agrees not to sub-let the premises or any part of them.

Lodgers

Even this provision will not prevent the tenant from taking in lodgers, as they acquire no interest in the premises as such but only have permission to live there. However, many formal leases contain an express covenant by the tenant that he will use the premises as a private dwelling-house. This covenant will be broken if he turns the house into a guest-house or even if he takes in friends as lodgers or paying guests, for the effect of his action is to use the house for business purposes—*i.e.* for the business of letting rooms.

Relationship of sub-tenant to original landlord

When a tenant creates a sub-tenancy he puts himself in the position of a landlord as far as the sub-tenant is concerned. Moreover, there is no contract between the sub-tenant and the tenant's own landlord. But the sub-tenant should always ask to see the main tenancy agreement (or 'head-lease') and he is presumed to have done so and to be aware of its terms. If he does something on the premises which is forbidden in the main agreement the head landlord can obtain an injunction to prevent him from doing it although he cannot sue the sub-tenant for damages, for he has not broken any agreement with the head landlord. In addition, the tenant himself may be liable to the landlord if he leads the sub-tenant to believe that he may do something which the main agreement forbids, or even if he stands by and takes no steps to prevent the sub-tenant from doing something which amounts to a breach of a covenant in the main agreement. Obviously therefore, a tenant should always be completely frank with a proposed sub-tenant, and let him see his own tenancy agreement or lease.

After a prospective sub-tenant has agreed to take a sub-tenancy he may nevertheless repudiate the agreement if he finds that there are unduly heavy burdens in the way of covenants in the main agreement. As we have seen, though he is usually not directly liable to the head landlord he may be indirectly controlled by the head landlord's seeking an injunction, and the sub-tenant may therefore put an end to his agreement with the tenant if he has not been told of unusual terms in the main agreement. There is one case, however, where the sub-tenant becomes directly liable to the landlord. This is where he agrees to take a sub-lease on the same terms as the head-lease. The head landlord may then enforce the terms of head-lease against him by suing for damages, for example, for a breach of covenant.

Sometimes the main agreement may contain a clause, similar to the one restricting assignment, requiring the tenant to get the landlord's consent before he *sub-lets*. In this case, no requirement is implied by law that consent must not be unreasonably withheld. If the sub-tenant finds that consent is required and that the tenant has not obtained it he may repudiate his agreement to take a sub-tenancy.

LONG LEASEHOLDS

INTRODUCTION

THE RENT ACTS have never applied to any house the rent of which was less than two-thirds of the rateable value.

This has created a considerable problem for tenants under a long lease. A long lease is usually granted—today, as it has been for many hundreds of years—in return for a substantial capital sum plus an agreement to pay a comparatively small ground rent.

For instance, in 1860 a house was built and offered for sale for a term of ninety-nine years at a price of £800 with an annual ground rent of £10. If the house had been for sale freehold, *i.e.* to pass to the purchaser and to his descendants or purchasers from him for ever, the price would, of course, have been substantially higher and there would have been no ground rent.

In effect the purchaser of a leasehold interest buys only the right to possession for the period of the lease. He is still primarily a tenant. He has, in effect, paid the bulk of his rent by one lump sum in advance. During the period of the lease he can sell what is left of it, and maybe make a profit. He gets that, not the ground landlord. But ultimately, many generations afterwards, perhaps, the house and land revert, *i.e.* pass back, to whoever is then the ground landlord.

And, as stated, because the ground rent was almost always small and less than two-thirds of the rateable value, the Rent Acts did not apply and the then tenant could be turned out unless the ground landlord was willing to grant a new tenancy at a full rent, or a new long lease for a premium and a low ground rent.

There was a tremendous expansion of house building in the mid-nineteenth century owing to the growth of industrialization and many houses were built on leasehold land. An owner of freehold land would grant a lease to a builder for ninety-nine years, say (which was the favourite period), at a low ground rent on condition that the builder would erect so many houses upon it which would conform to a particular plan and specification. The land would be divided into building plots and the builder would then sell his interest in the plot, together with the house which he had built, for what remained of the term granted to him by the owner.

The builder charged a lump sum in return for granting the long lease from which he would recover his building costs and make his profit. The tenant would be required to pay a small annual ground rent for his plot to the freehold owner. At the end of the term, the plot and the house would return to the freehold owner.

This created a severe problem after the war when many of these long leases were beginning to fall in at a time when there was a severe shortage of housing. Moreover, it was a condition of most of these leases that the tenant should keep the house in good repair both inside and out. The Landlord and Tenant Act, 1954, Part I (the rest of this Act deals with Business premises), was passed to deal with the problem.

THE 1954 ACT

The objects of the Act were to provide that—

    (a) When the long lease came to an end the tenant should have a chance of staying on, as tenant, provided that he could pay a new rent, a reasonable 'market' rent, or 'full' rent, to be fixed, in the absence of agreement, by a County Court Judge.

(b) Reasonable arrangements should be made about previous repairing obligations—again, to be fixed by the County Court Judge, in the absence of agreement.

(c) If the tenant wanted to stay on and could accept and afford a new agreement on the terms agreed or fixed under (a) and (b) above, he should not be evicted unless the landlord could establish one or other of the grounds which would enable a landlord of rent-controlled premises to get possession or on the further ground that the landlord genuinely intended to demolish or substantially develop the premises.

For the provisions of the 1954 Act to apply to a house the following conditions must be satisfied:

(a) The tenancy must originally have been granted for a term of more than twenty-one years whether or not it has subsequently been extended by agreement or by some enactment.

(b) The rateable value of the house in 1939 must have been not more than £100 in the London metropolitan area, and not more than £75 if it is anywhere else in England and Wales.

(c) The tenant must be living in the house when the lease comes to an end.

When the 1954 Act was passed it only applied to long leaseholds where the rent payable was less than two-thirds of the rateable value. The rent qualification has now been removed by the Rent Act, 1957, which has brought *all long leaseholds* into the scope of the 1954 Act provided they are within the 1939 rateable value limits.

The tenant of a long leasehold does not have to take any initiative when his contractual tenancy comes to an end. He simply stays where he is and continues to pay the rent due under the lease and to observe the conditions contained in it, which apply equally to the landlord. The effect of the Act is to continue his tenancy. If the tenant is only occupying a part of the premises comprised in the lease as a house and the rest is sub-let to someone else for business purposes, for example, his protection under the 1954 Act extends only to the part which he is occupying *as a home*, and the 1954 Act provides that he is entitled to remain as tenant of that part at an apportioned rent, which can be fixed by the Court on the application of either party in default of agreement.

ACTION TO BE TAKEN BY LANDLORD OR TENANT

At any time up to twelve months before a long leasehold comes to an end, the landlord has the right to apply to the Court for an order declaring that the tenancy is not protected by the 1954 Act. He could do this, for example, if the tenant was not living in the house at the time of the application. However, the Court would not make the order if the tenant were merely temporarily absent. Once an order has been made, a change of circumstances afterwards will not make the 1954 Act apply. The value of this provision from a landlord's point of view is that he can, by obtaining an order, prevent his tenant from moving into the house just before his long leasehold comes to an end simply for the purpose of qualifying for the protection of the Act when he has not been using it as his home perhaps for a very long time.

If the tenant does not wish his tenancy to continue after the end of his term he can bring it to an end by giving his landlord notice in writing at least one month before its termination date. If his tenancy has continued after the end of his term by the operation of the 1954 Act the tenant can bring it to an end at any time by giving his landlord not less than one month's notice in writing. He can also bring the tenancy to an end by such a notice even if the landlord has served on him a notice of the kinds referred to in the following paragraph.

A landlord who does not wish the tenancy to continue under the Act has two courses open to him. He may either offer the tenant a new tenancy on new terms, referred to in the Act as a statutory tenancy, or he may give the tenant notice that he wants possession. In either case, he must give notice to the tenant in a prescribed form not more than twelve months or less than six months before it is to take effect and the date on which it is to take effect cannot be earlier than the day on which the original tenancy would have come to an end but for the Act. This notice must specify the premises which the landlord believes to be, or to be likely to be, the premises which qualify for the protection of the Act. It must also contain the landlord's proposals for the terms of the statutory tenancy or, if he is seeking possession, notice that if the tenant is not willing to give up possession at the date of termination of the tenancy, the landlord proposes to apply to the Court for possession of the property comprised in the tenancy on one or more of the grounds which the 1954 Act allows.

This notice by the landlord must state the grounds for possession on which the landlord is seeking to rely and the landlord is not permitted in subsequent Court proceedings to put forward any ground for possession which he has not set out in his notice.

Finally, the landlord's notice must also invite the tenant to notify the landlord, in writing, within two months of the giving of the landlord's notice whether he is willing to give up possession of the relevant premises at the expiration of the landlord's notice.

If the tenant informs the landlord within two months of the giving to him of the landlord's notice that he is unwilling to give possession at the end of the two months' period after service of the landlord's notice, and if the tenancy fulfils the conditions necessary to qualify for the protection of the Act, the landlord may apply to the Court for possession on the grounds specified in the notice. However, if the tenant does not elect to retain possession in response to the landlord's notice and if his tenancy does not fulfil the qualifying conditions for protection at the end of the two months' period, the landlord has the right to an order for possession without having to establish that any of the special grounds mentioned in the Act exist. A tenant who elects to retain possession of his house but who is not occupying it as his home on the date when the landlord's notice expires will not be protected against an order for possession in favour of the landlord.

GROUNDS FOR POSSESSION

The grounds on which a landlord may seek an order for possession of the property comprised in a long leasehold are, with one addition, substantially the same as those for which an order for possession can be obtained under the provisions of the Rent Acts, and it is not proposed to set them all out in detail here, as they are described elsewhere. It should be noted, however, that whereas a landlord is entitled to seek possession under the Rent Acts if 'any rent lawfully due from the tenant has not been paid, or any other obligation of the tenancy . . . has been broken or not performed' the corresponding provision of the 1954 Act is more limited in scope and applies only where 'the tenant has failed to comply with any term of the tenancy as to payment of rent or rates or as to insuring or keeping insured the premises'.

The Court has to be satisfied, so far as those provisions of the 1954 Act which correspond with those in the Rent Acts for recovering possession are concerned, that the landlord has established his ground for possession and that it is reasonable that the landlord be granted possession. The *additional ground for possession* provided by the 1954 Act arises where the landlord is proposing to demolish or reconstruct the whole or a substantial part of the premises for the purposes of redevelopment.

The landlord has to satisfy the Court that he requires the premises for this purpose on the termination of the tenancy and that he has made such preparations for proceeding with the redevelopment as are reasonable in the circumstances. These preparations must include the obtaining of, or preparations for the obtaining of, for example, any necessary planning consent for the redevelopment. There must also be evidence that the landlord has very definitely made up his mind to do the new work and has the money necessary to enable him to do it. If the Court is not satisfied that the landlord requires the premises for redevelopment on the termination of the tenancy but is satisfied that they are so required on some date not more than a year later than the termination date, the Court must, if the landlord so requires, order that possession be given up on that later date. In the meantime, the tenant is entitled to remain in possession at the same rent and on the same terms as before the landlord's notice was given.

APPLICATIONS FOR POSSESSION

The landlord must make his application to the Court for possession not later than four months after the service of his notice terminating the tenancy or, if the tenant elects to retain possession, not later than two months after the tenant's election. If he fails to do so, his notice ceases to have effect and the tenancy continues under the old terms.

In a case where a landlord fails to establish his claim for possession the tenancy continues on the old terms, but the landlord then has the right to serve on the tenant a notice proposing a new tenancy which becomes effective in three months. In other words, the tenant then has a shorter time in which to decide whether to have a new tenancy or to give up possession.

125

NEW TENANCIES

If the landlord decides to offer *a new tenancy* (the statutory tenancy) to the tenant his notice must contain his proposals as to the terms of the tenancy. He must, for example, state the proposed rent, the instalments by which it is to be paid, and whether in advance or arrear. He must also state whether he is proposing that repairs should be carried out and, if so, whether by himself or by the tenant, or both. Finally, if he wishes to propose other terms for the tenancy, he must state them.

It is open to the landlord and the tenant to agree upon all these matters if they can. Their agreement must be in writing. If they cannot, the landlord can apply to the Court to determine any of the matters on which they have failed to agree and the County Court Judge can then decide—either all the terms of the new tenancy or those which are not agreed upon by the parties. He must do so during the currency of his notice, but not earlier than two months after giving it unless the tenant elects to retain possession, in which case the minimum time is one month. If the landlord and the tenant fail to agree on all the terms of the new tenancy and the landlord has failed to apply to the Court before his notice expires, the notice ceases to have any effect and the tenancy continues on the old terms.

The 1954 Act does not give the Court unrestricted power to regulate the terms of the new or statutory tenancy. It cannot order the tenant to execute repairs at the start of the new tenancy unless he consents. Furthermore, it cannot order the landlord to carry out any repairs not specified by the landlord in his application to the Court as repairs which he is willing to carry out. Again, unless the landlord and tenant both consent, the Court cannot require either to execute repairs at the start of the new tenancy in excess of what is necessary to bring the house into good structural and decorative repair, having regard to the age, character, and locality of the house. The Court can make provisions as to the keeping of the house in repair by the landlord or the tenant during the subsistence of the statutory tenancy, but must not require the house to be kept in a better state of repair than it will be in after any initial repairs have been carried out, or, if none are to be carried out, than the state of repair at the time of the Court's decision.

The effect of this provision may well be that the tenant's liability for repairs will be *less rigorous* under his new statutory tenancy than it was under the original lease. Indeed, all the tenant's liabilities under the old lease come to an end when a statutory tenancy begins. If the landlord establishes that repairs are necessary at the start of the statutory tenancy in consequence of the tenant's failure to fulfil his obligations under the original lease, he is entitled to payment by the tenant of the cost reasonably incurred by him in finding out what those repairs are and in carrying them out, but the Court can order that this cost be paid by instalments.

If the rateable value of the house on November 7th, 1956, exceeded £40 in London and £30 elsewhere in England and Wales the Court is free to fix the rent, irrespective of the personal circumstances of the parties, at a figure it considers to be a reasonable rent having regard (i) to the state of repair of the house after any initial repairs have been carried out and, if there are to be none, the state of repair at the time of its decision and (ii) to the other terms of the new tenancy.

However, if the rateable value of the house does not exceed the above-mentioned limits, the rent has to be fixed in accordance with the provisions of the Rent Act, 1957, which is considered elsewhere. In this event, it should be noted, the landlord and the tenant cannot themselves agree a rent which is in excess of the limit fixed by the Rent Act, 1957. The rent fixed by the Court or agreed is subject to reduction by order of the Court if the landlord fails within a reasonable time to carry out any initial repairs which he has agreed or been ordered to do. This order will be discharged when the landlord does in fact execute those repairs.

The new or statutory tenancy continues until the tenant relinquishes possession or until the landlord obtains an order for possession on substantially any of the grounds on which possession is claimed under the Rent Act, and no previous notice need be given. Hence the tenant receives a new and substantial degree of protection.

The Court in which proceedings are brought under any of the provisions of the Act is the local County Court.

CONCLUSION

A criticism which has been levelled at the Act is that although it helps the tenant who wants to stay in occupation, and can afford to do it does nothing to help the tenant who either wants to go, or *has* to go because he could not in any event afford to stay on even on the most favourable new terms that might be available to him, either offered by the landlord or fixed by the County Court Judge. As far as the Act is concerned it has been said that he is exposed to the full blast of the landlord's lawful demands under the repairing obligations of the old lease.

This is not altogether true because there is another Act of Parliament which may come to his rescue and relieve him of some of these liabilities, if not of all. This is the Landlord and Tenant Act of 1927, which applies to all tenancies, not only to long leases. The effect of the 1927 Act is that where a landlord complains of a tenant's failure to carry out all the repairs that he ought to have done and sues the tenant for damages for this failure, the Courts will apply quite different tests from those applied by the landlord or his surveyor. The surveyor will produce his list of dilapidations and say that this is the work which has to be done if the repairing covenants in the lease are to be fully carried out. The Court will say that this is not the point. They must ask how much the property which has now come back into the landlord's hands has been reduced in value simply by reason of the failure to do the repairs. You may well have a situation in which the property has suffered no loss of value. The state of the market may be such that the property in its unrepaired state may be just as valuable as it would be if all the repairs had been done. Even if this is not true the Court may find that it is only necessary to carry out some of the more essential repairs to ensure that the value of the property is not reduced. Obviously, the circumstances may vary a great deal, but, in practice, it has usually been found that the tenant's liability as decided by the Court is less than it would have been if the repair obligations had been strictly enforced.

Moreover, if there is any evidence that the premises were likely to have been pulled down or substantially reconstructed after the lease so that any repairs the tenant might have done would have been wasted anyway, then the damages awarded to the landlord for a breach of the obligation to repair would be nil.

RENT CONTROLLED HOUSES

INTRODUCTION

RENT CONTROL began in 1915 as a temporary emergency measure, but has survived for nearly half a century and will almost certainly celebrate many more anniversaries yet. The First World War brought building gradually to a halt and produced inflationary pressure on the economy. If a free market had been left to operate for rented accommodation, it would inevitably have meant that rents would have gone up and up. Many tenants would have been unable to match the pace of the rise and would have been evicted. Rent control was designed to prevent this. Since its inception it has had *two* main objects: first, to limit a landlord's right to raise his rent, and secondly, to confer security of tenure on the sitting tenant.

It was found in 1919 that the problems created by the war did not disappear with the armistice, and rent control was continued. However, between the two wars there was a substantial movement back to free market conditions for rented accommodation, as from time to time various classes of property were freed from control by successive Acts of Parliament. In 1939, on the eve of another war, the scope of rent control was enormously enlarged. It was then provided that rent control should apply to all dwelling-houses which in the metropolitan police district and the city of London had a rateable value not exceeding £100 on April 6th, 1939, in Scotland £90 on May 16th, 1939, and elsewhere in England and Wales £75 on April 1st, 1939. This meant that the vast majority of unfurnished rented accommodation became subject to rent control: probably about three-quarters of all available property became controlled.

The effect of the 1939 rent control was first to freeze the rents of the dwelling-houses to which it applied. It provided that the rent at which such dwelling-houses were actually let on September 1st, 1939, or the rent at which they were first let after that date, should become the *standard rent* which could only be increased thereafter for certain limited reasons and to a limited extent. Secondly, the 1939 legislation imposed restrictions on the landlord's right to recover possession of a dwelling-house let by him.

The structure and scope of rent control remained substantially unaltered after 1939 until the passing of the Rent Act, 1957. By then, striking anomalies had arisen since there could be and were, for example, enormous differences between the maximum rents recoverable for identical houses in the same road. This created hardship and unfairness for both landlords and tenants. The decline in the value in money in the post-war years meant that landlords who were receiving rents based on 1939 values often found that these were inadequate to meet even the bare cost of maintenance and repair. A tenant taking a house which had never been let, say, before 1955 found that he was being asked to pay an infinitely higher rent than his neighbour in identical accommodation. His neighbour had a lower standard rent for an identical house simply because it had been let years earlier. It was in this context that the Rent Act, 1957, was passed.

MEANING OF STATUTORY AND CONTRACTUAL TENANCIES

Because these terms occur so often in any discussion about the Rent Acts, it is desirable to explain them at the beginning.

A statutory tenancy is something created by the Rent Acts, although none of them actually used the words 'statutory tenancy'.

Originally every tenancy must be 'contractual'; *i.e.* it must begin as the result of an agreement, or *contract*, between landlord and tenant, that the one will let, and the other will take certain premises on certain terms.

If the premises are a dwelling-house to which the Rent Acts apply, then when the landlord gives his 'contractual' tenant notice to quit, the tenant need not go out, but is legally entitled to remain in occupation by virtue of the protection given to him by the Rent Acts, *i.e.* given by a Statute, or Act of Parliament. Hence he becomes a tenant protected by a Statute: hence the phrase 'statutory tenant'.

THE RENT ACT, 1957

The Rent Act, 1957, had two major effects. First, it released certain classes of property entirely from rent control. Secondly, it created a new formula for determining what rent a landlord was entitled to receive from premises which remained subject to rent control.

To deal first with the decontrol provisions:

(a) Any new letting of unfurnished premises to a new tenant starting after July 6th, 1957, is not subject to rent control—whatever its rateable value may be. This means that a landlord has been entitled to let premises to a new tenant since this date at whatever rent he can get the tenant to pay, and that the tenant has no right to remain in the premises when the contractual tenancy, *i.e.* the period of tenancy fixed in the agreement, comes to an end.

(b) The 1957 Act released from rent control all dwelling-houses which had on November 7th, 1956 in the metropolitan police district or city of London a rateable value exceeding £40, elsewhere in England and Wales £30, and in Scotland £40.

It is necessary to emphasize that the test is *rateable value* on that date: not the rates actually paid. That has nothing to do with the question. Neither rates paid nor rent paid matters for this purpose.

Note too that it is *rateable* value, not gross value. Every separately assessed property has two figures in the rate-book at the town hall; the Gross Value and the Rateable Value. The latter is arrived at by the Rating Valuer by making certain statutory deductions for the theoretical cost of repairs. Gross value is important in another context in this section.

It is also important to know that the metropolitan police district goes far into Essex, Kent, Surrey, Bucks, and Herts. Its boundaries are indicated on the back of the government sixpenny pamphlet called *The Rent Act and You*, published by H.M. Stationery Office.

However, tenants affected by this provision did not lose their right to remain in occupation of their houses straight away. Landlords were prohibited from seeking possession of their premises (unless they could do so on one of the grounds allowed by the former Rent Acts) before October 6th, 1958, at the earliest, and had to give at least six months' notice in writing to their tenants before doing so. The present position is that a tenant who already held a statutory tenancy of premises which were decontrolled by the 1957 Act at the time when the Act came into force, is not obliged to give up possession to his landlord until he has received from him at least six months' notice in writing requiring him to do so.

No such notice was required in the case of a tenant who at the time of decontrol held premises on a contractual tenancy which did not expire or could not have been brought to an end by the landlord before October 6th, 1958, because his tenancy was safe until after October, 1958. But a minimum of six months' notice must be given by the landlord to a contractual tenant whose contractual tenancy expired or could have been ended by a notice to quit before October 6th, 1958.

Power was given by the Rent Act, 1957, to the Minister of Housing and Local Government to extend the scope of decontrol to any class of property at any time by means of an order which has to be confirmed by a resolution of both Houses of Parliament. This means that the government of the day could in practice speedily bring rent control to an end without going through the elaborate process of parliamentary legislation, although it seems doubtful whether such a step is likely to be taken in the foreseeable future.

In 1958 there was passed the Landlord and Tenant (Temporary Provisions) Act which gave a temporary measure of additional protection from eviction to tenants whose premises had been decontrolled by the 1957 Act and to whom six months' notice as referred to above had been given. They had been unable to negotiate a new agreement with their landlords during the fifteen months' period between July, 1957, and October, 1958, and still had nowhere to go.

The 1958 Act prohibited landlords from requiring possession to be given without an order from the local County Court. The Court was given power, on the application of the tenant, to postpone the landlord's right to recover possession provided that the tenant had satisfied certain stringent conditions. The 1958 Act, however, expired on July 31st, 1961. It gave valuable extensions of time to these 'decontrolled' tenants who had done their best to find other accommodation but had failed. And the extensions lasted in some cases into 1962. But by now they have all come to an end.

COMPENSATION FOR IMPROVEMENTS

In cases where the landlord is obliged to give at least six months' notice in writing to his tenant before he can recover possession, and the tenant actually does give up possession at the expiration of his landlord's notice, the tenant is entitled to compensation from the landlord for any improvements which have been made to the premises since August 15th, 1945. To qualify for compensation, the tenant must make a claim on his landlord before giving up possession. It is not necessary that the tenant should have made the improvement himself. He is equally entitled to compensation if he became a tenant by assignment of a contractual tenancy to him by a previous tenant who made the improvement, or if he inherited a contractual tenancy on the death of a person who made the improvement, or again if he became entitled to succeed to a statutory tenancy, say, on the death of his father, who made the improvement.

What is an improvement which qualifies for compensation? The 1957 Act says that this includes structural alterations, extensions, or additions, and the provision of additional fixtures or fittings but does not include anything done by way of decoration or repair.

No compensation is payable if the improvement was made because the tenant was under an *obligation* in his tenancy agreement with the landlord to make it, or if it was made in *breach* of the terms of the tenancy, or if, before it was completed, the landlord notified the person who made it, in writing, that he objected to it. Compensation is also excluded if the tenant occupied the premises for business purposes and has become entitled to make a claim for improvements under the Landlord and Tenant Act, 1927. Finally, the tenant cannot claim compensation for a fixture which he is entitled to take away when he leaves the premises. (See chapter on Fixtures.)

To qualify for compensation, the tenant must show that the improvement adds to the value of the premises on the date when he gives up possession to his landlord. The amount of compensation is limited to the amount by which the improvement adds to the value of the premises as a whole after taking into account any payments or allowances the landlord may already have made in respect of the improvement. In calculating the value of an improvement regard also has to be paid to the use to which the premises are to be put after possession is given up. If, therefore, the premises are to be demolished immediately, the improvement obviously has no value. However, if demolition is not intended to take place immediately, the tenant would be entitled to some compensation, since the improvement would then obviously have some value during the interim period.

If the landlord and tenant cannot agree on the question of compensation, either party may apply to the local County Court to determine the question whether compensation is payable at all or the question of amount.

In general no tenant of a dwelling-house can get compensation from his landlord for improvements which he has made and which he has to leave behind him. This special provision in the 1957 Rent Act is an exception to the general rule.

RENT PAYABLE ON DECONTROL

Where premises became decontrolled under the 1957 Act, the maximum rent which the landlord could recover from the tenant was limited to the amount of rent legally recoverable immediately before the time of decontrol, subject only to the landlord's right to increase it to cover increases of rates payable by the landlord. This provision naturally gave landlords a strong incentive to serve on their tenants the notice of at least *six months*' duration requiring them to give up possession, which has been referred to above. But as stated above it had to be six months expiring on or after October 5th, 1958—not sooner. This was the fifteen months 'cushion' to protect the decontrolled from immediate shock. On the expiration of this notice the landlord could, of course, offer the tenant a new contractual tenancy at whatever rent he liked. The old control, by reference to a standard rent, had gone for all houses decontrolled by the Act because they were above the new rateable value figures. The only criterion now was what the premises were truly worth under ordinary conditions in the open market.

BUSINESS PREMISES

Finally, on the question of decontrol, it should be noted that it was not necessary for landlords to give the minimum period of six months' notice to tenants of decontrolled premises which qualified for protection under Part II of the Landlord and Tenant Act, 1954, which protects tenants occupying premises for the purpose of a trade or business. A tenant who, for example, held a tenancy of a shop with a flat above it before July 6th, 1957, when the Rent Act, 1957, came into force, enjoyed the protection of the Rent Acts if the rateable value of the whole premises was within the limits set by the 1939 Act. If the rateable value was outside the new and lower limits set by the 1957 Act for the continuation of coutrol, the Rent Acts' provisions ceased to apply on July 6th, 1957. And thereon, the tenant immediately qualified for the valuable protective provisions of the Landlord and Tenant Act, 1954.

THE PROVISIONS OF THE 1957 ACT RELATING TO RENT

As already stated, the 1957 Act established an entirely new formula for determining the rent recoverable by landlords for premises subject to rent control.

132

This formula was designed to ensure that rents could be fixed at a reasonable level for each house and each letting and not, like the old standard-rent formula, depend quite arbitrarily on the date of the first letting. It was also the policy of the Act to ensure that if tenants had to pay higher rents under the new formula, as they had to do in the great majority of cases, the increases would not become payable all at once. Provision was also made in the Act to prevent landlords from recovering increases to which the Act entitled them if and as long as

". . . an entirely new formula for determining the rent . . ."

133

their premises were out of repair. It is now necessary to consider these provisions in some detail.

The main factor in determining the maximum rent recoverable by the landlord in respect of a controlled tenancy is the responsibility for repairs. The first situation to be considered is where the tenant is not obliged by the terms of his tenancy to do any repairs to the premises. (For this purpose, the fact that he may be obliged to do internal decorative repairs is ignored.) In these circumstances, the annual rate of rent must not exceed a sum equal to *twice the gross value* for rating purposes of the premises as shown in the rating authority's valuation list on November 7th, 1956, with two possible additions.

First, if the landlord is responsible for paying the rates, there will be added to the figure represented by twice the gross annual value, the annual amount of the rates payable by the landlord on July 6th, 1957.

Secondly, if the landlord was providing services or furniture for the tenant on July 6th, 1957, there will be added an annual amount representing a reasonable charge for these services and the furniture. Services cover, for example, the provisions by a landlord of central heating or the provision of porterage in a block of flats. The annual amount to be charged for services and the use of furniture has to be agreed, in writing, between the landlord and the tenant. If they fail to agree, either may apply to the local County Court to fix the figure.

It often happens that the controlled premises occupied by the tenant are only part of a house and are not separately rated, so that no gross value for the premises is shown in the valuation list. Where this happens, the landlord and tenant must try to agree, in writing, what the gross value of the relevant premises is in relation to the value of the whole house before the recoverable rent can be determined. If they fail to agree, either can apply to the local County Court for the gross value to be determined for them.

The second situation is where the tenant is responsible under the terms of his tenancy for all repairs to the premises. (Repairs in this context again does not include internal decorative repairs.) In this event, the formula described above is again followed with the important difference that the gross value has to be multiplied by four thirds instead of two. In short, a tenant who is responsible for keeping his premises in repair is not expected to pay as high a rent as a tenant who is not.

The third situation is where the tenant is responsible for some but not all the repairs, again ignoring internal decorative repairs. Here, also, the above formula is followed, this time with the difference that the gross value has to be multiplied by a figure which must be less than two but greater than four thirds. It is left to the landlord and tenant to agree what this multiplier should be if they can, the obvious intention being that the rent should be fixed at a figure which fairly reflects the value to the landlord of the tenant's obligation to do repairs. Any agreement must be made in writing to have any legal effect, and if the landlord and tenant cannot agree, either can apply to the local County Court to fix the multiplier for them.

If the landlord is responsible under the terms of the tenancy for carrying out internal decorative repairs, the multiplier in the three situations considered above has to be altered. In the first situation, where the tenant is not responsible for any repairs, the multiplier becomes seven thirds instead of two. In the second situation, where the tenant is responsible for all repairs (except, of course, internal decorative repairs) the multiplier is fixed at five thirds instead of four thirds. Lastly, in the third situation, where the tenant has to do some but not all of the repairs, the multiplier has to be fixed at a figure which is less than seven thirds but greater than five thirds. This multiplier has to be agreed, in writing, between the landlord and the tenant or determined by the local County Court in default of agreement as already described.

Where, as often happens, the tenancy agreement is silent on t e question of internal decorative repairs so that neither the landlord nor the tenant is obliged to do them, the landlord can if he wishes elect to become responsible for doing internal decorative repairs, and after doing so, can take advantage of the higher multipliers described in the foregoing paragraphs and thus obtain a higher rent. If he makes this election, he must do so by serving a notice on the tenant in a form prescribed under the Rent Act, 1957. An informal notice not in the form prescribed will not do and will have no effect. However, the tenant can refuse to allow the landlord to take over responsibility for internal decorative repairs, provided he writes to his landlord saying that he is unwilling for him to do so within a month of receiving the notice from the landlord referred to above. If the tenant does this, he himself becomes obliged to keep his premises in a reasonable state of internal decorative repair, having regard to the age, character, and locality of the premises. If he fails to meet this obligation, the landlord will be entitled to seek an order for possession against him in the local County Court.

If the rent, calculated on whichever of the bases considered above was the relevant one, happened to be less than the rent legally recoverable by the landlord immediately before July 6th, 1957, it is the latter which became the rent limit for the premises.

As already indicated, the 1957 Act protected tenants from too sudden and sharp increases in their rent after the Act came into force on July 6th, 1957. First of all, rents cannot be raised unless the landlord gives three months' notice on a form prescribed by the Act. Failure to use the prescribed form could be fatal to the validity of the notice of increase.

Secondly, the increase is limited to a maximum of seven shillings and six-pence a week during the period of nine months immediately following the service of the notice of increase upon the tenant. However, this second limitation does not apply in the case of increases to which the landlord might have become entitled in respect of a rise in the amount of rates payable by him, a rise in the cost of services provided by him or improvements to the premises finished by him after July 6th, 1957.

It should be noted that where a tenant was a contractual tenant on July 6th, 1957, the landlord cannot take advantage of the 1957 Act to increase his rent until he can end the contractual tenancy. This is because the landlord and the tenant are bound by the terms of their agreement and, of course, this always fixes the rent payable until it comes to an end. Thus, for example, a tenant who was given a seven-year lease of controlled premises in January 1957 will continue to enjoy them until January 1964 at the rent fixed by the tenancy agreement. When a contractual tenancy could be ended by a notice to quit expiring on an earlier date than a notice of increase, assuming it to have been served on the same date as the notice of increase, the latter is given the effect of a notice to quit by the Act and converts the contractual tenancy into a statutory tenancy on the day on which it provides for the increase to become payable.

It has already been seen that some matters may have to be agreed between the landlord and the tenant or settled by the local County Court before the rent limit can be determined. When this happens, a landlord cannot serve a notice of increase before the relevant matters have been agreed or settled by the Court. The landlord's remedy is to make a speedy application to the Court when he finds that he cannot reach agreement with his tenant.

When notice of increase has no effect. In certain circumstances a notice of increase served by a landlord has no effect, except in respect of a rise in the rates payable by him or for an improvement finished after July 6th, 1957. This will be so if at the time any increase is to be payable the premises to which the increase relates are in an area which a local authority has designated to be cleared of houses or if a local authority has made a demolition order affecting the particular premises. This will again be so where the local authority has (as it may do in certain circumstances) ordered the landlord to do repairs which he has not carried out, and finally where it has made an order declaring the premises to be unfit for human habitation and not capable of being made so at reasonable expense.

How a new maximum rent may be fixed. Even when the rent of premises has been raised to the rent limit fixed by the 1957 Act it is not indefinitely frozen at that figure. The landlord is entitled to raise the rent above the rent limit in three circumstances.

(a) If he pays the rates and they go up, he can pass the increase on to the tenant immediately. He must give notice in writing and is entitled to back-date his claim for a period of up to six weeks before the date on which a notice is served.

(b) If the cost to the landlord of providing any furniture or services to the tenant goes up, he can recover the increased cost from the tenant. In this event, no notice of increase is necessary as the increase has to be agreed, in writing, between the landlord and the tenant or determined by the local County Court if they cannot agree. Any such increase can be back-dated to the time when the landlord began to incur the additional cost which he is seeking to pass on to the tenant.

(c) Finally, when the landlord has made an improvement (as already defined above) to the premises after the rent limit has been fixed, he can increase his tenant's rent by twelve and a half per cent. per annum of the cost of the improvement. To obtain this increase, he must serve a notice in writing, on the tenant, but the increase can be made payable from any date after the tenant receives the notice. The tenant has the right, so long as he does so within a month of receiving his landlord's notice, to ask the local County Court to make an order cancelling the notice provided that he can show either that the improvement was unnecessary or that more was spent on it than was reasonable. This right is, however, taken away if the landlord received an improvement grant for the particular improvement from the local authority, or if the tenant gave his consent in writing to the landlord for the making of the improvement and gave some acknowledgement to the landlord in doing so that he could increase the rent for the improvement.

RESTRICTIONS ON FOREIGN COMPANIES OWNING HOUSES IN THE UNITED KINGDOM

Some landlords adopted the device of transferring premises owned by them to companies formed for the purpose in Eire with the express object of making it difficult for their tenants to enforce their rights. To counter this, the 1957 Act prevented overseas' companies from issuing notices of increase after July 6th, 1957, in order to bring rents up to the new rent limit, unless they first obtained a certificate from the local authority in whose district the premises were situated stating that it was satisfied that the condition of the premises was such that no certificate of disrepair could be issued. A copy of the local authority's certificate has to be served by it on the tenant. After this has been done, any notice of increase served in the next twelve months is valid. If the overseas company gives a notice of increase which is valid and takes effect, it can afterwards serve further notices of increase on the tenant without seeking a further certificate of repair from the local authority.

This restriction on the right of foreign companies to serve notices of increase to bring the rent up to the rent limit does not apply if the tenant is himself responsible for all repairs under the terms of his tenancy.

CERTIFICATES OF DISREPAIR

It was part of the policy of the 1957 Act to prevent landlords from obtaining increases of rent, to which the Act might otherwise have entitled them, while the premises were not in a proper state of repair. The Act has created a rather complex machinery to achieve this object.

When a tenant considers that his premises are in a state of disrepair and have defects which ought reasonably to be remedied, having due regard to the age, character, and locality of the premises, he is entitled to serve upon his landlord a notice in writing in a form prescribed by the Act specifying the defects and requesting him to remedy them. Such defects can, for example, include a leaking roof or a worn staircase in a block of flats which affect the tenant of one of the flats, although the defects do not exist in the flat which he actually occupies. The notice cannot specify any defects in the state of internal decorative repair unless the landlord is responsible for internal decorative repairs under the terms of the tenancy or has elected to become responsible for these under the provision which has already been considered. The notice must then say that the landlord is liable for internal decorative repairs.

If within six weeks after receiving the tenant's notice the landlord fails to remedy the defects specified in the notice, or does not give an undertaking in writing to the tenant to remedy them or such of them as the tenant may agree in writing to accept as sufficient, the tenant can apply to the local authority for a certificate of disrepair.

The landlord is given six months in which to carry out his undertaking. If he fails to do so, the same consequences follow as if the local authority had issued a certificate of disrepair at the end of the six months' period.

On receiving the tenant's application for a certificate of disrepair, the local authority has to be satisfied that the defects contained in the tenant's notice to the landlord ought reasonably to be remedied having due regard to the age, character, and locality of the premises. The local authority is not concerned to inquire whether the landlord or the tenant is under an obligation to remedy any particular defect specified in the notice. However, if the local authority does issue a certificate of disrepair in respect of any defects which it was *the tenant's duty* under the terms of his tenancy to remedy, the landlord is entitled to apply to the local County Court to have the certificate of disrepair cancelled in respect of such defects. But the landlord cannot ask the County Court to cancel a certificate of disrepair on the grounds that he is not responsible under the terms of the tenancy for carrying out repairs. That is not relevant; if he wants the full rent allowed by the Act he must do the work needed to put the premises in repair, *i.e.* all except repairs for which the tenant is made responsible in the agreement. If he wishes to increase the rent to the rent limit, he must in fact remedy all the defects stated on the certificate which are not the liability of the tenant.

Both the landlord and the tenant have the right to apply to the local County Court for a certificate of disrepair which has been issued by the local authority to be amended, if he is tenant, he considers that the local authority's certificate has improperly omitted some of the defects specified in his notice or, he is a landlord, he considers that some of the defects which are contained in the certificate of disrepair are not defects which ought to be remedied by him if due regard be had to the age, character, and locality of the premises or, indeed, that they are not defects at all.

Once the local authority has decided which of the defects contained in the tenant's notice to the landlord ought to be remedied by the latter and that it will accordingly issue a certificate of disrepair in respect of those defects, it must send a notice to the landlord informing him that it is proposing to issue a certificate of disrepair and specifying the defects to which it will relate. The certificate of disrepair will not be issued if the landlord gives an undertaking, in writing, within three weeks of receiving this notice from the local authority undertaking to remedy the defects referred to in the notice.

However, the local authority is not obliged to accept this undertaking and may nevertheless issue a certificate of disrepair where, for instance, the landlord's record is a bad one with regard to repairs required to be done to his property by the local authority, and it is plain that his undertaking cannot be relied on. For example, the local authority can ignore the landlord's undertaking if on a previous occasion he has given a similar undertaking and failed to honour it within six months of giving it. If the local authority accepts an undertaking and the landlord fails to remedy the defects within six months, the certificate of disrepair is issued and takes effect from the end of that six months.

How long does a certificate of disrepair last? Once a certificate of disrepair has been issued, it remains in force until the defects to which it relates have been remedied. Even then it does not automatically lapse. A landlord who considers that he has remedied the defects must apply to the local authority for the certificate of disrepair to be cancelled. It is then the duty of the local authority to inform the tenant by a notice, in writing, that unless an objection

Both landlord and tenant have the right to apply to the local County Court for a certificate of disrepair to be amended.

is received from the tenant within three weeks, it proposes to cancel the certificate. If the local authority receives no objection from the tenant within three weeks or if it considers that a tenant's objection is not justified, it must cancel the certificate of disrepair. The landlord is entitled to apply to the local County Court for an order cancelling the certificate of disrepair if he considers that the

139

local authority has wrongly upheld an objection by a tenant and refused to cancel a certificate. Similarly, if a tenant thinks that the local authority has wrongly cancelled a certificate of disrepair in face of his objection that the defects to which a certificate relates have not been remedied by the landlord, he can apply to the local County Court for an order revoking the local authority's act in cancelling the certificate.

The rent position where a certificate of disrepair is in force

While the certificate of disrepair is in force, the rent recoverable by the landlord cannot, in any case, exceed the limit produced by multiplying the gross value of the relevant premises by four-thirds, with the possible additions for rates and improvements already considered. If the landlord raised the rent by a notice of increase served *more than six months* before the date of a tenant's application for the certificate of disrepair, this formula will in fact produce the rent actually payable during the life of the certificate of disrepair.

However, if the landlord has served a notice of increase *during the period of six months immediately before* the date of the tenant's application for a certificate of disrepair the rent recoverable by him while the certificate of disrepair is in force will be limited to the sum produced by multiplying the gross value by two-thirds, or to the rent actually recoverable before the notice of increase was served, whichever is the *less*, together with any increase to which he may be entitled for rates or improvements.

When a certificate of disrepair is issued by a local authority the Rent Act, 1957, *also back-dates the reduction in rent* to the date of the tenant's application. On every rent day after the certificate has been issued the tenant may withhold from his rent an amount equal to the sum by which his rent has been reduced until he has recovered from his landlord the difference between the rent actually paid by him between the period of his application for and the issuing of the certificate of disrepair, and the rent he would have paid if the certificate of disrepair had been issued on the date of his application for it. It is important to note that the only way in which a tenant can recover the rent overpaid (in consequence of the issue of a certificate of disrepair) by him between the date of his application for and the issuing of a certificate of disrepair is by making this deduction.

Finally, it should be noted that if a landlord serves a notice of increase while a certificate of disrepair is in force, it can never be of value to him as a basis for claiming an increase of rent unless it is specifically stated in the notice that it will not take effect while the certificate of disrepair is in force, except in so far as it is a notice claiming an increase in respect of rates or improvements.

MISCELLANEOUS PROVISIONS ON DECONTROL

It has been already stated that *new* tenancies of premises created after July 6th, 1957, to *new* tenants are not subject to rent control. It was also indicated that a tenant who was not 'new' might still be protected. In three cases, new tenancies will be controlled provided, of course, that the premises are within the control limits fixed by the 1957 Act. First, a new tenancy after July 6th, 1957, to a *sitting* tenant will remain subject to control if the tenant was a controlled tenant immediately before he acquired the new tenancy, and if the premises occupied under the new tenancy are the same as, or comprise a *part* of the premises occupied by him previously. One room common to both old an new is sufficient to protect the new if the rateable value of the new is within the 1957 Act limits.

Sitting tenant.

Secondly, when a landlord has obtained possession of premises on the grounds that they are overcrowded, the first letting afterwards is subject to control. Thirdly, the occupier of premises requisitioned by a local authority from the landlord enjoys a controlled tenancy if the landlord accepts him as a tenant when the premises are derequisitioned.

Tenants of controlled premises are usually, for obvious reasons, reluctant to give up, by moving, the advantages which they enjoy. In order to encourage mobility, it has been provided that a statutory tenant of controlled premises can, with the consent of his landlord, pass the benefit of his statutory tenancy to a new tenant, provided he does so in writing. The person giving up the tenancy is not allowed to charge any premium to the incoming tenant.

NOTICES TO QUIT

The 1957 Act has enacted that since July 6th, 1957, no notice to quit is valid unless it is given not less than four weeks before it is to take effect. So all notices to quit must now be at least four weeks, whatever the agreement says. This new rule applies both to furnished and to unfurnished lettings. Four weeks is now the minimum in every case for every tenancy. This provision does guarantee tenants of uncontrolled premises a little breathing space when their landlords determine their contractual tenancies. Before the 1957 Act came into force the great majority of tenancies were weekly, that is to say, that the tenants not only paid their rent weekly, but their contractual tenancies could be determined by a week's notice to quit. This did not particularly matter after 1939, since these tenancies were mostly controlled and the tenants could not be ejected after their contractual tenancies had been determined. The position would, of course, have been otherwise in the case of new tenants of premises after July 6th, 1957, and Parliament thought it was plainly unreasonable to leave landlords the power of turning tenants out at a week's notice in the present day when difficulties of finding accommodation are very great.

WHAT CONTROL MEANS

It has already been explained that, broadly, control has a two-fold object: it involves restricting a landlord's right to recover possession of his premises when the contractual tenancy comes to an end, and limiting his Common Law right to charge whatever rent he can persuade a tenant to pay. It has also been seen that control has been continued in force by the Rent Act, 1957, for certain classes of property, depending on their rateable values on a fixed date.

Now it is necessary to consider four further matters:

(a) what kind of lettings of premises falling within the rateable value limits set by the 1957 Act are in fact subject to control;

(b) what is meant by a statutory tenancy;

(c) the circumstances in which the benefit of a controlled tenancy can pass from one tenant to another; and

(d) the circumstances in which a landlord can recover possession of controlled premises from his tenant.

(a) *Premises subject to control.* The Rent Acts apply to 'a house or a part of a house let as a separate dwelling'. There must therefore first be a letting. If a person occupies premises under an arrangement which lacks the normal characteristics of a tenancy he may only be a licensee and his occupation is not protected by the Rent Acts.

Generally speaking, most people know straightaway whether they are 'tenants' to whom premises are 'let' or not. The agreement probably uses words which make the arrangement perfectly clear.

The issue of a rent book by the landlord implies a tenancy.

The borderline cases are people allowed to occupy premises or to use premises but who are not granted a tenancy.

A lodger, although he may occupy a room in the house, is not a tenant and he cannot, therefore, be a protected tenant. This situation is more fully discussed in the section dealing with lodgers, licences, service tenants, and occupiers.

Next, there must be a tenancy of a *house* or part of a *house*. This may sometimes give rise to difficulty. For example, can a caravan with its wheels removed properly be described as a house? It seems that it probably cannot be, at least so long as it remains in an easily portable state.

The letting of one room in a house can attract the protection of the Rent Acts, but the premises let must be a *separate dwelling*. This does not mean that the room or rooms must be 'self-contained', *i.e.* with their own front-door. That does not matter. 'Separate dwelling' means let to a tenant for his or her exclusive use.

This gave rise to difficulties of interpretation where a tenant had exclusive use of, say, two rooms but shared a third, a kitchen or other living-room, with another tenant. Did either have a separate dwelling? The problem was settled by an Act of Parliament which provided that a tenant who under the terms of his tenancy is obliged to share living-rooms with *another tenant* in the same house is to be in exactly the same position as if he enjoyed the use of a separate dwelling. But when a tenant shares living-rooms with *his landlord*, he does not enjoy the protection of the Rent Acts generally but only the limited measure of protection afforded to tenants of furnished premises under the Furnished Houses (Rent Control) Act, 1946, which is discussed in another section.

A number of other types of letting fall outside the Rent Acts' control. Premises let rent free, or at a rent which is less than two-thirds of the 1939 net rateable value are outside the Acts. This was one way of letting to a friend, relative, for a time, or to an employee, and avoiding the creation of a controlled tenancy where the tenant could, if he turned nasty, claim the protection of the Rent Acts.

A tenancy of a public house cannot enjoy the protection of the Acts.

Furnished lettings are outside the general system of control and are governed by the Furnished Houses (Rent Control) Act, 1946.

Premises owned by local authorities, the new town development corporations, the commission for the new towns, and, in certain circumstances, by housing associations and housing trusts, are not subject to control.

Land which is let with a dwelling subject to control can be equally protected with the dwelling if it all forms one unit. However, if *agricu tural* land exceeding two acres in extent is let with a dwelling, the dwelling will be protected by the Rent Acts, but the land will not. This means that the landlord would be entitled as of right to recover possession of the land on the determination of the contractual tenancy.

A tenant cannot enjoy the protection of the Acts when the Crown is his landlord.

A new exception was created by the Housing Repairs and Rents Act, 1954. A dwelling-house, maisonette, or flat which was made by converting a large house into self-contained flats, etc., was not to be controlled if the conversion was completed after August 30th, 1954. The same Act excluded from control *new* premises completed after the same date. These provisions of the 1954 Act were made to encourage the provision of dwellings for renting, of which there was, and still is, a great shortage.

". . . a special system of protection for farmer tenants . . ."

Rent control was not excluded, however, from dwellings which were converted or built with the assistance of grants from the local authority.

The Agricultural Holdings Act, 1948, established a special system of protection for farmer tenants, and a person farming agricultural land who lives in a house let with the land cannot claim the protection of the Rent Acts.

The Landlord and Tenant Act, 1954, as described in another section, conferred valuable rights on tenants enjoying long tenancies, that is, tenancies which were originally granted for more than twenty-one years. When it was passed, this Act only applied to long tenancies of premises the rent of which was less than two-thirds of the net rateable value as it stood in 1939.

The Rent Act, 1957, extended the provisions of the 1954 Act to *all long tenancies* (*i.e.* originally granted for more than twenty-one years) at whatever rent, and at the same time excluded long tenancies from Rent Acts' control.

A limited company, or any kind of corporate body, holding a tenancy of premises can never enjoy the security of tenure given by the Rent Acts after the contractual tenancy has come to an end. This is because the aim of the Rent Acts is to prevent a tenant from being deprived of his *home*, and a company or corporate body is obviously incapable of occupying a home. However, if a company or corporate body was given a tenancy of premises before July 6th, 1957, which has continued to be within the control limits set by the 1957 Act, it enjoys the protection of the Act so far as its rent provisions are concerned.

Where premises are let to a tenant partly for residential purposes and partly for business purposes, the Rent Acts apply to the letting provided it was made before July 6th, 1957, and the rateable value of the whole premises is within the limits fixed by the 1957 Act. However, the Rent Acts do not apply if the intention of the landlord and the tenant at the time of the letting was that the premises should be used exclusively for business purposes. In this event, the tenant will enjoy the protection provided by the Landlord and Tenant Act, 1954.

Finally, of course, all new lettings to new tenants since July 6th, 1957, are free of control. The word 'new' must be emphasized, because a letting to a former tenant, although made by an agreement dated after July 6th, 1957, may be controlled.

(b) *What is meant by a statutory tenancy.* A statutory tenancy is in short the right of continuing in occupation after notice to quit has been given, since the Rent Acts compel the landlord to go on accepting the former contractual tenant of his premises as a tenant, although an agreement between them no longer exists. When a statutory tenancy arises, the landlord can only recover possession of the premises by bringing proceedings in the County Court for the district in which the premises are situated and asking for an order for possession, unless, of course, the tenant voluntarily goes out of occupation. The grounds on which a landlord can bring proceedings for possession are limited and will be considered later.

When a tenant becomes a statutory tenant he is obliged to observe and is entitled to enjoy the benefit of all those terms of his former contractual tenancy which are consistent with the provisions of the Rent Acts. In other words, all the terms of the original contractual tenancy continue to apply during the life of the statutory tenancy except those which would obviously be repugnant to the scheme of the Acts. The most obvious example of a term of the original contractual tenancy which does not apply when a statutory tenancy arises is the term relating to the payment of rent. Once the contractual tenancy ends, the landlord's right to rent and the amount which he can charge is governed by the Rent Act, 1957. Another term which does not survive the contractual tenancy is the right to assign the benefit of the tenancy, since this would be alien to the Rent Acts' aim of giving security of tenure to a sitting tenant.

145

However, a covenant in a lease by a tenant to keep the premises in repair will continue in force while the statutory tenancy exists and it has been held that a landlord can sue his statutory tenant for damages for failing to observe such a covenant.

(c) *The transfer of the benefit of a controlled tenancy from one person to another*. A contractual tenancy can always be assigned by the tenant to another person unless there is a provision in the tenancy agreement forbidding him from doing so.

Sometimes the lease, agreement, or rent-book says in so many words 'no sub-letting and no assigning' (assigning means passing on to someone else the tenancy of the whole house, flat, etc.). That prohibits either.

Or it may say 'no sub-letting or assigning without landlord's consent'. In that case with consent, either is possible. Or it may say nothing, in which case the contractual tenant is free to do either.

But weekly, monthly, quarterly, and even yearly tenants are seldom interested in assigning their tenancies.

An assignment is usually only of value and interest when the tenant has a fixed definite period of years which he can pass on, indeed he will usually *sell* the remainder of his tenancy for money.

But what is vitally important for thousands of controlled tenants is what happens when the tenant dies.

And the cardinal point is that the tenancy does *not* automatically end with the tenant's death.

His right to the tenancy is part of his property, part of his estate which passes on his death.

Where a tenant of controlled premises dies leaving a widow who was residing with him at the time of his death, she is entitled to step into her husband's shoes as tenant. All that is required to satisfy the provision that the widow was residing with her husband at the time of his death is that the premises of which he was the tenant were then her home. The fact that she might have been away on holiday or in hospital when her husband died does not matter.

It makes no difference whether the husband was a contractual or a statutory tenant when he died. His widow will in either case be entitled to succeed to the tenancy.

It might happen that the husband, having quarrelled with his wife, left the benefit of his contractual tenancy by his will to someone other than his widow. In this event, the rights of the beneficiary are postponed to those of the widow. This means that the beneficiary might never enjoy any benefit from his bequest at all, since the contractual tenancy left to him might come to an end before the widow ceases to occupy the premises under her prior statutory right. A contractual tenancy can be left by will, because as stated above it forms part of the estate. This is equally true whether it is a tenancy by the week or a lease for, say, twenty-one years. But the House of Lords have decided that when the premises are controlled by the Rent Acts, the widow or the family have prior, overriding rights.

If the tenant of controlled premises who dies is a woman, or is a man who does not leave a widow, then any member of the tenant's family who was

146

residing with the tenant at the time of his death, and had been doing so for not less than six months previously, is entitled to take over the tenancy, whether it be a contractual or a statutory one, just as in the case of a widow. This provision obviously would enable a husband of a deceased tenant to stay in the matrimonial home after his wife's death. If there are several members of the deceased tenant's family who qualify to step into the tenant's shoes they can agree among themselves who the new tenant shall be, and the landlord has no say in the matter at all. If they fail to agree, they can apply to the local County Court to determine which of them ought to replace the deceased tenant.

Who qualifies as a member of the deceased tenant's family? Obviously a husband or child do so. So, indeed, would grandparents, grandchildren, brothers and sisters, nephews, nieces, aunts, and uncles of the deceased tenant. It is not necessary, however, that a blood relationship should exist between the deceased tenant and the person claiming to step into his shoes. Close relations by marriage have qualified by decisions of the Courts; so, too, have persons who had no relationship to the deceased tenant by blood or marriage where, for example, the deceased tenant stood *in loco parentis*, *i.e.* in the place of a parent, to the claimant. The more remote the relationship between the deceased tenant and the claimant, the less easy it becomes to say that the claimant is a member of the deceased's family in the ordinary sense of the word. Servants and lodgers do not qualify as members of the family.

The vital, indeed critical, feature of these provisions whereby a controlled tenancy can pass on to a member of the family—widow, widower, children, etc.—is that the succession to the tenancy is totally independent of the landlord's wishes and totally independent of the terms of the original agreement or rent book. The transfer of the tenancy within the family is the result of Act of Parliament and is independent of any private agreement.

If the tenancy is still a contractual tenancy at the tenant's death then the tenancy is transmitted according to his will, or according to the laws which govern an intestacy; if he left no valid will, subject only to a widow's overriding right, described above, if he cut her out.

And if a contractual tenancy is inherited by widow, widower, son, daughter, etc., it can pass on in exactly the same way on the next death.

But if the tenancy has been converted into a statutory tenancy because the tenant has been given notice to quit but has stayed on by virtue of his Rent Act protection, then the tenancy can be passed on after his death *once and once only*.

The statutory provisions entitling a widow or a member of a deceased tenant's family to succeed to a statutory tenancy can only operate *once* in relation to that tenancy. They are powerful, but they operate once and once only against the landlord's will. Thus, if a tenant dies leaving a widow and a daughter, the widow succeeds to his tenancy under the provisions applying to a statutory tenancy; if the widow were to die after succeeding to her late husband's statutory tenancy, the daughter would have no right to claim the tenancy in succession to her mother under these provisions. She could only take over the tenancy if the landlord were willing to accept her as a new tenant.

The last situation in which the benefit of a controlled tenancy can pass from one tenant to another has already been referred to in the discussion of the provisions of the Rent Act, 1957. This is where the statutory tenant of controlled premises can pass the benefit of his tenancy to a new tenant provided he does so in writing with the consent of his landlord. If the tenant who is transferring the benefit of his statutory tenancy has succeeded to his tenancy on the death of his predecessor as tenant under the provisions just considered, no further such transmission of the tenancy can take place on the death of the incoming tenant. However, the incoming tenant can be given the right to transmit his tenancy to his widow or a member of his family if his agreement, in writing, with the outgoing tenant for the transfer of the tenancy specifically so provides and the landlord consents to this provision.

(d) *Recovery of possession of controlled premises by the landlord.* A landlord is not entitled to eject a tenant of controlled premises from these premises without obtaining an order from the local County Court requiring the tenant to go, and he commits an offence if he does so. If a tenant of *uncontrolled* premises refuses to go at the end of his contractual tenancy, the landlord has an unconditional right to require the local County Court to order the tenant to go, and the Court would order him to give up possession not later than two months from the date of the judgment. However, in the case of *controlled* premises, even if the landlord has the right to bring proceedings for possession against the tenant, the Court is not bound to order the tenant to leave the premises. It will only do so if it considers that it is reasonable to make an order compelling the tenant to go.

So, a landlord asking the County Court for an order for possession against a tenant of rent-controlled premises must establish a case under two distinct and separate heads:

(i) that in all the circumstances of the case it is *reasonable* for the Judge to make an order for possession; *and*

(ii) that he can prove one or other of certain specific reasons why an order should be made.

He must, in practice, start by proving a specific reason under (ii) above. These are considered in detail below, but can briefly be summarized as follows:

(a) That the tenant is seriously in arrears with his payment of rent.

(b) That the tenant has broken some other condition of the tenancy.

(c) That the tenant or a member of his family or someone living with him has been guilty of nuisance or annoyance to adjoining occupiers, or has been convicted of using or allowing the premises to be used for an immoral or illegal purpose, or has allowed the premises to deteriorate by his neglect or default.

(d) That the tenant has himself served notice to quit, but afterwards changed his mind to the landlord's prejudice, *e.g.* if the landlord had contracted to sell the premises with vacant possession on the strength of the tenant's notice to quit, the tenant ought not to be allowed to change his mind.

(e) That the tenant, without the landlord's consent, has sub- et the whole of the premises, or assigned his tenancy of the whole, thus showing that he does not need the premises as his home. This is quite independent of conditions in the agreement against sub-letting, etc. It shows that he does not *need* the protection of the Rent Acts to protect his home.

(f) That the tenant has overcharged a sub-tenant, *i.e.* made a profit out of a sub-letting.

(g) That a tenancy of an off-licence is in jeopardy because the tenant has committed offences against the licensing laws.

(h) That the landlord needs the premises for a new employee and that the existing tenant occupied the premises as an employee whose employment has ceased.

(i) That the premises are required for occupation by the landlord himself or by certain members of his family.

(j) That suitable alternative accommodation is available for the tenant.

It is impossible to catalogue all the circumstances which the Court will have regard to in deciding whether it is *reasonable* to order a tenant to give up possession, after the landlord has established one of the grounds which entitles him to ask the Court to order the tenant out. Obviously, the conduct of the landlord and the tenant is a relevant consideration, as is the gravity of the tenant's breach of some obligation of the tenancy which has occasioned the landlord's action for possession.

The Court has a wide discretion to postpone the operation of an order for possession against a statutory tenant. It may, for example, order him to give up possession as long as six months or even more after the date of the Court's judgment. Again, it can make its order for possession a conditional one. To give an example, it might provide that the tenant is to give up possession if he has not fulfilled some obligations of his tenancy within, say, three months of the date of the Court's judgment.

It is now necessary to consider in a little more detail the grounds on which a landlord may seek an order for possession.

First, there are those grounds arising out of a tenant's failure to behave as a good tenant should (a) to (c) above. The landlord is entitled to seek an order for possession against the tenant when the latter has failed to pay his rent, or to carry out one of the other terms on which he holds his tenancy, for example, to keep the premises in good repair.

Next, a landlord can do so where his tenant or anyone living or lodging with him, or even a sub-tenant, has been guilty of conduct which is a nuisance or annoyance to people living in adjoining premises. The words nuisance or annoyance in this context have no technical legal meaning and are used in the popular sense. The act alleged to be a nuisance or annoyance must be such that it would be so regarded by a reasonably minded person. Thus, a landlord might be able to obtain an order for possession against the tenant of a flat whose wife persistently allowed large quantities of milk bottles to accumulate on a communal staircase or whose son persistently played a gramophone loudly in the early hours.

Again, if the tenant or any of the other persons mentioned above have been convicted of using the premises for some immoral or illegal purpose or if one of them has caused the condition of the premises to deteriorate by wilful acts of damage or gross neglect, an action for possession may be brought.

However, in all these cases, the tenant will not have an order for possession made against him if the matter complained of by the landlord was brought about by a lodger or sub-tenant, and he shows that he has taken such steps as

". . . wilful acts of damage or gross neglect . . ."

he reasonably ought to have done to eject the lodger or sub-tenant before the day of the hearing of the landlord's claim for possession.

Where the statutory tenancy includes premises having an off-licence (paragraph (g) above), the landlord can sue for possession if the tenant has not conducted the business to the satisfaction of the licensing justices or the police

150

authority, or has carried it on in a manner detrimental to the public interest, or the renewal of the licence has been refused.

A landlord can sue his tenant for possession when the tenant has charged a sub-tenant a rent in excess of the amount which the Rent Act, 1957, now permits him to charge (paragraph (f) above). Obviously, this provision only applies where the sub-tenancy is itself controlled.

Lastly, in this category, a statutory tenant who assigns or sub-lets all of the premises comprised in his tenancy without first obtaining his landlord's consent opens himself to an order for possession, even though there was no provision in the original contractual tenancy prohibiting such an assignment or sub-letting (paragraph (e) above). In any event, however, a statutory tenant who did this would probably be unable to resist an order for possession on another ground, namely, that he had ceased to occupy the premises since, as already indicated above, one aim of the Rent Acts is to give security of tenure to tenants using premises as their *home*. In the case of a tenant who ceases to occupy the premises comprised in the statutory tenancy, the landlord is entitled as of right to an order for possession and the Court cannot postpone the operation of the order for more than two months after the date of the judgment.

There is another category of circumstances in which the landlord may seek an order for possession which does not arise out of any misbehaviour on the part of a tenant.

First, a tenant who has given notice to quit to his landlord in consequence of which the landlord makes a contract to sell the premises with vacant possession or takes some other step which would seriously prejudice his position, opens himself to the possibility of having an order for possession made against him if he changes his mind and refuses to go (paragraph (d) above).

Secondly, a landlord may ask for an order for possession when the tenant was formerly in his employment and was given the tenancy only because he was an employee, and the landlord now wishes to accommodate a new employee in the premises (see the section on service tenants and occupiers, and paragraph (h) above).

Thirdly, provided that the landlord has not bought the premises after November 7th, 1956, subject to the statutory tenancy which he wishes to bring to an end, he may claim possession if he can show that he has a reasonable need for the premises as a house for *himself, or any son or daughter of his over eighteen years of age, or his father or mother* (paragraph (i) above).

The proviso in this case is designed to prevent people from buying houses with the express object of getting sitting controlled tenants out with a view to moving in themselves or to re-selling the premises, which would obviously appreciate in value if vacant possession could be offered to a prospective purchaser.

The tenant can defeat the landlord's claim if he shows that *greater hardship will be caused to him, if he is compelled to go, than to the landlord, if he is allowed to stay.* In deciding this question, the Court must take into account the question whether other accommodation is available both to the landlord and the tenant.

If the landlord does obtain an order for possession on this head by presenting a false case when he really intends to sell the premises, the dispossessed tenant can claim from him compensation for damage or loss which he may have sustained as a result of being compelled to move out.

Fourthly, a Court may make an order for possession against a tenant if it is satisfied that suitable alternative accommodation will be available to the tenant when the Court's order for possession would take effect (paragraph (j) above).

If a certificate is produced to the Court from the local authority by the landlord certifying that the local authority will provide suitable alternative accommodation by a date specified in the certificate, he discharges the burden of showing that suitable alternative accommodation is available. It is very difficult for a landlord if the local authority does not undertake to rehouse his tenant. In this event, he has to satisfy the Court that:

(a) there is alternative accommodation available to the tenant which is either protected by the Rent Acts or which will give the tenant security of tenure reasonably equivalent to that afforded by the Rent Acts;

(b) the accommodation is reasonably accessible to the places of work of the tenant and his family, and *either* that the rent and size of the accommodation is similar to that of dwellings provided in the neighbourhood by the local authority for persons who, in the opinion of the Court, have a similar requirement to the tenant as regards size of accommodation, *or* that it is otherwise reasonably suitable to the means of the tenant and to the needs of the tenant and his family as regards extent and character.

The requirement that the accommodation should be reasonably suited to the *needs* of the tenant and his family, as regards extent and character, open up a wide field of circumstances for the consideration of the Court.

Suppose the tenant has a garage and a car and the alternative accommodation offered has no garage, can the tenant say that it is not reasonably suited to his needs? The Courts have answered the question in this particular instance in the negative on the ground that what has to be considered is the *living* accommodation. However, if the tenant used his car for the purposes of his business or work, the Court would certainly give weight to the fact that alternative accommodation had no garage in deciding whether it was reasonable to make an order for possession. Again, the fact that the alternative accommodation is not big enough to accommodate the tenant's lodgers is not relevant in deciding its suitability, since all the Court is concerned with is to see that the tenant and his family will be suitably housed; but here, too, the absence of accommodation for lodgers will be a factor in determining the reasonableness of making an order for possession. The suitable alternative accommodation may consist of part of the premises already occupied by the tenant. A landlord might reasonably offer to a widow, whose family has grown up and left home, part of a large house occupied by her which now contains far more accommodation than she needs.

Since the coming into force of the Rent Act, 1957, which excludes new tenancies created after July 6th, 1957, from control, it will be difficult for landlords to offer alternative accommodation which is subject to control. They would be able to do so if the premises offered were part of the premises comprised in the tenancy they are seeking to end, or if they can find a tenant of another landlord who is willing to assign his statutory tenancy to an incoming tenant and has the consent of his own landlord to do so under the Rent Act, 1957, provision which has been mentioned above. If they cannot provide alternative rent-controlled accommodation, they must then offer the tenant a lease of the alternative accommodation for a fixed term of years to meet the requirement that the alternative accommodation must provide security of tenure reasonably equivalent to that enjoyed by controlled premises. Usually, the Courts will accept a five-year term for this purpose.

It should be stressed again, with regard to the grounds for possession in the category just considered, that even if one or other grounds is proved, no order for possession can be made unless the Court also thinks that it is *reasonable* to make an order, and reasonableness is a matter for the Judge's discretion.

SUB-TENANTS

To conclude this section on rent control, a word should be said on the position of sub-tenants. Broadly, their position is the same as that of tenants of the owners of premises. Provided that the tenant was lawfully entitled to sub-let part of his premises, the sub-tenant will enjoy the protection of a controlled tenancy if the rateable value of *his part* of the premises has remained within the limits set by the Rent Act, 1957. If the main tenancy comes to an end or the head landlord obtains an order for possession against the tenant, *the sub-tenant is entitled to remain in occupation of his part of the premises as a tenant of the head landlord.*

SCOTLAND

Finally, it should be noted that there are differences in the application of the Rent Acts in Scotland on the one hand and England and Wales on the other. The law dealt with in this section is that of England and Wales.

Note: for the Landlord and Tenant Act, 1962, see p. 859.

FURNISHED LETTINGS

FITNESS FOR HABITATION

WHERE FURNISHED PREMISES are let they must be reasonably fit for habitation at the beginning of the tenancy. A tenant who agrees to take furnished premises may withdraw from the agreement without incurring any liability if he discovers that the premises are unfit before he goes in. Even if he has gone into occupation he can rescind the agreement if he acts reasonably promptly.

153

Furnished premises must be reasonably fit for habitation at the beginning of the tenancy—

—but the landlord is under no obligation to remedy defects which develop later, unless the agreement provides for this.

The premises may be unfit for habitation if they have defective drains; if they are infested with vermin; if they have been occupied by someone suffering from infectious or contagious disease; if they are badly affected by damp or if they are in any way in a state to endanger the health of occupants. This liability on the landlord applies only to the beginning of the tenancy and he is under no obligation to remedy defects, however serious, which develop later, unless the tenancy agreement provides that he must. As far as the tenant is concerned, unless he has accepted special burdens of repair in the agreement he is obliged only to use the premises in a reasonable way and he need not do any repairs, but if he, or his family, or people whom he allows on the premises, damage them or the furniture he must make the damage good.

RENT TRIBUNALS

Under the Furnished Houses (Rent Control) Act, 1946, rent tribunals have been set up which have power to fix rents for certain premises in their areas. They may also be able to give security of tenure to tenants.

A tribunal only has power where the rateable value of the premises is £40 or less (in the Metropolitan Police District) or £30 or less elsewhere in England and Wales. In addition, there must be a letting at a rent which includes either payment for the use of furniture or payment for services provided by the landlord. The tribunal also has jurisdiction in one type of letting where no furniture or services are provided at all. This is where the tenancy agreement gives the right of exclusive occupation of accommodation to the tenant but also gives him the right to share other accommodation (*e.g.* a kitchen) with his landlord. This type of letting, where there is no payment for furniture or services, may also be controlled by the Rent Acts. If it is, the tribunal may not fix a rent below the rent limit under the Rent Act, 1957.

FURNITURE AND SERVICES

For the letting to be subject to control by a rent tribunal (and to be outside the Rent Acts) because furniture or services are provided by the landlord, the rent paid must include an appreciable amount for the tenant's enjoyment of furniture or services. To deal with furniture first, this must be sufficient in amount for the premises to be genuinely described as furnished. Also, it must be sufficient in value for the proportion of the rent attributable to the use of furniture to be substantial. Curtains and an electric clock, which was all the landlord provided in one case, are clearly not enough. There should probably be at least the basic furniture and floor covering appropriate to the use to which each room is to be put. It is not necessary for a landlord to provide linen or eating or cooking utensils. The value attributable to the furniture has sometimes been very roughly assessed in this way. Divide the total value of the hard furniture by ten and the total value of soft furnishings by five and add the two

155

figures. The answers give an approximate annual value for the furnishings (on the basis that ten and five years respectively represent the likely useful life of these items) and, when this is compared with the total annual rent, it will be seen whether the proportion of the rent attributable to furniture is substantial. This, of course, will be a matter of degree in each case. But if the rental value of the furniture worked out on this basis is about 20–25 per cent. of the whole rent the Court is likely to regard it as 'substantial'.

If an appreciable amount of services is provided by the landlord the agreement is treated as a furnished letting although he may provide no furniture. Basic requirements such as a cold water supply or sanitary facilities are not regarded as services, nor is the occasional work done by the caretaker of a block of flats, for example, who sometimes acts as a porter for the tenants. Permanently available attendance provided by the landlord's staff on the premises, on the other hand, is one kind of service which would be sufficient. The service must be personal to the tenant and not be shared in common with other tenants. Thus, provision of central heating to all the tenants of a block of flats is not considered as a service for these purposes, but if heating, hot water, or lighting is provided specially for one tenant, this might be a sufficient service. Again, the rent in respect of the services provided must be a substantial part of the total rent, and the percentage proportion is the same as that stated above for furniture.

There is one kind of service which takes a letting out of control both of the Rent Acts and of rent tribunals—this is the provision of board for the tenant, whether or not he occupies furnished rooms. Again, the value of this service must be appreciable in relation to the total rent. Thus, if the agreement provides that breakfast should be supplied to the tenant, this is probably enough. If the agreement gives the tenant the right to an evening meal as well, this will make the position certain. On the other hand, an early morning cup of tea would not be enough to be regarded as the provision of board.

The nature of the tenancy is determined at the beginning. If a genuine furnished tenancy is created it will not become an unfurnished one merely because the landlord later permits the tenant to replace the furniture originally provided with his own. In the same way if it is agreed that the tenant shall be supplied with meals, the fact that he ceases to have the meals will not alter the nature of the agreement. If some alteration of the terms of the tenancy occurs, however (*e.g.* if the landlord agrees to reduce the rent because the tenant has provided his own furniture or because he no longer wants meals), it is possible that a new tenancy agreement of a different nature may be deemed to have been made.

RATEABLE VALUE

If the rateable value of the part of a house which is the subject of a reference to a rent tribunal has not been separately assessed the tribunal may decide whether the rateable value of the part with which they are concerned would be within the limits of their jurisdiction if it had been separately assessed. At the hearing by the tribunal, however, the landlord may say that he requires an apportionment of the rateable value of the part concerned to be made by the County Court. If he takes proceedings to have this done within two weeks the tribunal cannot consider the reference until the County Court has made an apportionment.

PROCEEDINGS BEFORE THE RENT TRIBUNAL

The tenant or the landlord may apply to the tribunal to fix a reasonable rent. The application must be made in writing, either in an informal letter giving the parties' names and addresses, or on forms which can be obtained from the tribunal's offices or from the local authority (which may itself refer cases to the tribunal). When a reference has been made the tribunal can compel the landlord to give them all the information about the tenancy which it is reasonable for them to have. The date of the hearing is notified to the landlord and the tenant and both parties may send in written statements of their case beforehand, whether they intend to appear at the hearing or not. At the hearing both parties may personally present their arguments to the tribunal or they may have a lawyer or anyone else they please to represent or advise them. The members of the tribunal will often arrange to visit the premises to see for themselves the accommodation and furniture provided. When the tribunal are fixing what they consider to be the proper rent they will take into account the landlord's capital expenditure in buying the premises and furniture, for example, and the cost of management and of keeping the premises in repair. The landlord should therefore take care to produce as much documentary evidence as he can to support the expenditure which he claims to have incurred.

POWERS OF THE TRIBUNAL

First, the tribunal has power to fix a reasonable rent for the premises. If they do so the rent which they fix is recorded by the local authority in a register open to inspection by the public. After this has been done the landlord may not charge a higher rent for the premises, even to a new tenant, but if there is a change of circumstances either party may go back to the tribunal and ask them to reconsider the rent which has been fixed. This may occur, for example, where the amount of furniture on the premises is altered or where a service provided by the landlord becomes more expensive to maintain. If a landlord asks for or receives a higher rent than the one fixed by the tribunal he may be fined up to £100, as well as having to repay to the tenant the sums overpaid. Further, a similar penalty may be imposed on a landlord who demands from an existing or future tenant a premium as the price of a renewal or grant of a tenancy.

The tribunal have also a limited power to grant security of tenure to the tenant. If a landlord gives notice to quit after a tenant has applied to the

157

tribunal to fix the rent the notice is automatically prevented from taking effect until three months after the tribunal give their decision. In special circumstances (if the landlord has genuine and urgent personal need for the accommodation for his own use, for example) the tribunal may substitute a shorter period for the three months. Before the period of three months expires (but not if the tribunal have substituted a shorter period) the tenant may apply for a further period of security. The sort of case where this application may be granted will be where the tenant shows that he has genuinely been unable to find other accommodation. The maximum further period of security which the tribunal have power to give at one time is three months, but the tenant may apply again, and there is, in theory at least, no limit on the number of extensions which may be given. On the other hand, if the tenant does not apply to the tribunal to fix the rent until after he has received notice to quit, he cannot be given security of tenure and, though the tribunal may fix a rent for the premises, the notice will take effect on the date of its expiration. Where a tenancy agreement for furnished premises is made for a fixed term no notice to quit is needed to bring the tenancy to an end on the agreed date, and here again, though the tenant may ask the tribunal to fix a rent, they cannot give him security of tenure. By making successive agreements for a fixed length of time a landlord may therefore protect himself against the danger that his tenant may get an order for security of tenure, so long as there is no provision in the agreement for its continuance until it is determined.

There is ordinarily no appeal against a tribunal's decision. The High Court will only interfere where it is apparent that the tribunal have altogether erred in law in their decision.

NOTICE TO QUIT AND RENT BOOKS

The requirement of the Rent Act, 1957, that not less than four weeks' notice to quit must be given even in a weekly tenancy applies to furnished lettings. The landlord is also required by the Act to provide a rent book giving particulars of the rent and of the other terms and conditions of the tenancy.

DECONTROL

The rent tribunals continue to have jurisdiction to deal with furnished lettings within the limits of rateable value laid down by the Rent Act, 1957, even in the case of tenancy agreements made on or after July 6th, 1957. Furnished premises which have a rateable value in excess of the limits are no longer controlled by the tribunals. In a few cases, however, where the rent of decontrolled premises had been fixed by a tribunal before decontrol and where the tenant is still in occupation under an agreement made before the above date, the rent which the landlord can charge remains the same but such a tenant has no security of tenure.

LODGINGS

IT IS difficult to draw the dividing line between a tenant and a lodger with any degree of precision. Two men may occupy separate rooms in one house and each of them may have exclusive occupation of his own room, but one of them may be a lodger and the other a tenant.

The test that has to be applied is the landlord's right of control over the man occupying each room. For example, if the landlord has a right to come in and to eject visitors whom he does not wish to be on the premises, or if he has a right to interfere with the occupant's use of the room by preventing him from altering the arrangement of the furniture, then it could be said with certainty that the occupant is a lodger. Of course a prudent landlord who takes lodgers into his house will not often wish to exercise his rights or he will probably find that his lodgers will resent his interference and leave. The important point is that, in the case of lodgers, the landlord has this right of control which he can exercise if necessary, whereas he cannot do so as far as any part of premises occupied by tenants is concerned (unless they have expressly agreed to let him do so and this will be very unusual).

The reason for the difference is that the law regards a tenant as having a proprietary interest in the property let to him. A lodger, on the other hand, has a mere licence or permission to occupy a room or rooms at the landlord's pleasure. It is not necessary that the landlord should live on the premises for the occupants to be lodgers though, most commonly, he will do so. In the ordinary case it will be clear that the occupant of a bed-sitting-room in a house, who is probably allowed to use the bathroom and is perhaps also supplied with breakfast, is a lodger who has no proprietary interest in his room as a tenant has.

In much the same way as a tenant, however, the lodger will be entitled to notice to leave the room but there is no need for written notice (though it may be preferable to give written notice and keep a copy if any difficulty is expected in getting the lodger to vacate the room). The length of notice need not be a minimum of four weeks as in a tenancy but will, if nothing different has been agreed, be as long as the interval at which rent falls due. Most often, a lodger will pay rent weekly and he should be given at least a week's notice.

A lodger may have the right to go to a rent tribunal if his rent includes payment for furniture or services, but not if he is entitled to substantial board under his agreement.

Rates and rent

If the lodger's landlord is the person who ordinarily pays the rates for the premises and he falls in arrear with them the rating authority may serve notice of the amount of the arrears upon anyone (including lodgers) who pays rent to the landlord, and may require that future payments of rent should be made directly to them (if no notice has been served by a superior landlord requiring payment of rent direct to him—see Distress for Rent). If the rating authority gives such notice they may recover the rent from the lodger in the sa ne way as his landlord could have done. Payment made by the lodger operates as a discharge of his liability to pay rent to his landlord until the arrears are satisfied.

The lodger's landlord may not himself own the premises. If he does not, and if he falls behind with his rent, goods on the premises may be seized to cover the deficiency. The lodger can take steps to protect himself in this event (see Distress for Rent).

Covenants restricting use of premises

The tenant of a house who has agreed in his lease or tenancy agreement that he will not sub-let the premises, may take in lodgers. But if he has been

"... a few friends as paying guests ..."

required to go further and agree that he will use the premises as a private dwelling-house he will be in breach of his agreement by taking lodgers. His landlord may prevent him from using the house in this way or may even take steps to bring the lease to an end. The Courts have decided that this applies as much to a tenant who takes in a few friends as paying guests as to a tenant who turns the house into a guest-house with numerous lodgers.

Overcrowding: health: infectious diseases

Many provisions in Acts of Parliament and in by-laws of local authorities are aimed at ensuring that basic standards are observed when numerous people live in one house. It is only possible to describe some of the most important.

Under the Housing Act, 1957, a local authority may, by giving twenty-four hours' notice enter a house to measure the accommodation there. If the authority is satisfied that a house let in lodgings (or occupied, even as tenants, by more than one family) is overcrowded it may serve notice on the owner or occupier specifying how many people may use each room as sleeping accommodation, or it may declare any room to be unsuitable for such use. Any person who contravenes the notice may be fined in a Magistrates' Court up to £5 and up to £2 per day for every day on which the offence is continued. There is a right of appeal to the County Court against the notice within twenty-one days of its service.

Under the same Act a local authority which finds that a house let in lodgings has inadequate natural lighting, ventilation, water supply, drainage, sanitary conveniences, facilities for storage, preparation and cooking of food, or facilities for disposal of waste water may serve notice on the person who receives the rents. This notice must specify the work which the local authority consider necessary to remedy the defects and must give a time limit for the work to be done. It must go on to require the person who receives the rent to take steps to limit the number of people or households on the premises to the number stated in the notice, unless the work specified is done. Similar penalties and rights of appeal apply as in relation to overcrowding.

The Public Health Act, 1936, makes it an offence to let any part of a house which has been occupied by a person who has been suffering from certain serious infectious diseases (*e.g.* tuberculosis, poliomyelitis, diphtheria, measles, whooping cough) without having the house and any contents which may retain the infection disinfected to a doctor's satisfaction. An outgoing lodger (or occuper of any premises) who vacates a house where someone, to his knowledge, has been suffering from such a disease within the previous six weeks without having the house and contents disinfected, also commits an offence. In either case, there may be a fine of as much as £20. It is also an offence to give a wilfully false answer to a question on the subject and this carries a fine of up to £20 or imprisonment for up to a month.

Common lodging-houses

No one may keep a lodging-house for the night accommodation of the poor where the inmates (not being members of the same family) use a common room for sleeping or eating, unless he is registered by the local authority as keeper of a common lodging-house. The local authority must inspect the lodging-house before it is registered and may refuse registration if the premises are unfit or are likely to be a nuisance to neighbours. By-laws may be made by the local authorities to regulate the conduct of lodging-houses.

AGRICULTURAL HOLDINGS

WHAT IS AN AGRICULTURAL HOLDING?

THE LAW has been codified and is now contained in two important Acts of Parliament which govern the relationship of the landlord and tenant of an agricultural holding. They are the Agricultural Holdings Act, 1948, and the Agriculture Act, 1958.

As defined in the Acts an agricultural holding is a tenancy of land of any size provided that it is used for agriculture for the purpose of a trade or business. If you rent a paddock for grazing horses which you ride purely for pleasure, that would not be an agricultural holding. It has been held, however, that a woman who taught riding and rented a paddock for grazing her horses had an agricultural holding, because the grazing was in connection with a trade or business.

' "Agriculture" includes horticulture, fruit growing, seed growing, dairy farming, and livestock breeding and keeping, the use of land as grazing land, meadow land, osier land, market gardens, and nursery grounds, and the use of land for woodlands where that use is ancillary to the farming of land for other agricultural purposes, and "agricultural" shall be construed accordingly.'

This list is not necessarily exhaustive and the Courts could decide that some other activity came under the heading of agriculture if it had some similarity with the activities described.

Land which is let to a tenant because he is in a particular employment, *i.e.* what is commonly known as a 'tied holding', is not an agricultural holding within the Acts.

Land which is only used in part for agriculture may come within the Acts if the overall general character of the land is agricultural. This has the result that the Acts may apply to a building, in which case that building would lose any protection of the Rent Acts to which it might otherwise be entitled, even in respect of a sub-tenancy.

Some of the most important objects of the Acts are to provide a degree of protection for the agricultural tenant against eviction; to give him certain rights with regard to removal of fixtures and to compensation for improvements which he may have made during the course of his tenancy; and to provide for the fixing of new rents by arbitration.

THE TENANCY AGREEMENT

All tenancies which were *less than* a tenancy from year to year, *e.g.* a periodic tenancy from month to month, quarter to quarter, etc., in respect of agricultural land granted since February 1948 *take effect as a tenancy from year to year* unless prior approval to a shorter tenancy has been given by the County Agricultural Executive Committee.

An exception to this rule is that it is not to apply to an agreement or a licence where the land is used only for grazing or mowing during some specified period of the year, nor does it apply to allotment gardens.

Agricultural holding!

The former Agriculture Acts applied only to tenancies from year to year and longer, with the result that their provisions could be shut out simply by granting a tenancy for 364 days or less. This provision has now gone and such a tenancy would now take effect as a tenancy from year to year.

One further interesting exception is that if a tenancy to agricultural land is granted for a fixed definite period which is more than one year but less than two, then while it is an agricultural holding for the purposes of compensation for improvements, it does not become converted into a tenancy from year to year and it automatically terminates at the end of the fixed period.

Either party to an oral tenancy agreement may ask the other party to enter into a written agreement. If this is refused he can apply to an arbitrator to have the terms of the tenancy put into writing. (See heading *Arbitration* p. 167.) Similarly where, in the interests of more efficient farming, either party seeks to vary the terms of a tenancy relating to permanent pasture, provision is made for reference to arbitration. A tenant may also apply to arbitration for relief from contractual or customary obligations for the cropping and disposal of produce from arable land. He must show the arbitrator that he has taken suitable and adequate precautions against deterioration or injury to the land, for if he fails to do so, the landlord may obtain an injunction to prevent the new arrangements, or claim compensation from the tenant at the end of the tenancy.

FIXTURES

At Common Law anything attached to the land becomes the property of the owner of the land, except articles attached by the tenant for trade, ornamental,

". . . the old tenant's fixtures . . ."

or domestic reasons. Agricultural fixtures do not come within the definition of 'trade fixtures', but by statute, the tenant of an agricultural holding may remove any fixtures which he has attached to the land either during his tenancy or within two months of its termination. The tenant must, however, observe conditions. He must pay all rent which is due and satisfy all his obligations under the tenancy. He must give a minimum of one month's written notice of his intention to remove fixtures at least one month before the end of the tenancy; and, during the currency of this notice the landlord may serve a counter-notice offering to buy the fixtures and provided he pays a fair price he must be allowed to retain them. Finally, in removing the fixtures no avoidable damage must be caused and any actual damage must be made good at once. Provided the landlord gives his consent, an incoming tenant may, of course, purchase the old tenant's fixtures.

164

NOTICE TO QUIT

A tenant is guaranteed at least a year's security of tenure in that any notice to quit must be given at least twelve months before the date on which the landlord requires possession, and the notice must expire on the last day of the year of the tenancy. This rule does not apply where a receiving order has been made against a tenant, nor where repossession is sought for some non-agricultural use of the land authorized by the tenancy agreement, nor where notice is given by a tenant to a sub-tenant.

There is the further restriction on a landlord's right to regain possession in that if within one month of receiving a notice to quit the tenant gives the landlord a written counter-notice, then with seven exceptions the notice to quit is rendered ineffective unless the Agricultural Lands Tribunal consents to its taking effect. The seven exceptions where a tenant has no right to serve a counter-notice are:

(1) Where land is required for non-agricultural use and planning permission has been given, or is not required.
(2) Where the landlord has secured the consent of the Agricultural Lands Tribunal before serving the notice.
(3) Where the landlord has obtained a certificate of bad husbandry against the tenant.
(4) Where the tenant has failed to pay rent.
(5) Where the tenant is in breach of a condition in the tenancy agreement.
(6) Where the tenant has become bankrupt or compounded with his creditors.
(7) Where notice is given within three months of the death of the tenant.

Where the tenant exercises his right to serve a counter-notice there are five cases in which the Agricultural Lands Tribunal may declare the notice to quit to be effective, in spite of the counter-notice. These are where the termination of the tenancy is desirable in the interests of efficient farming or of efficient management, or for agricultural research, where some non-agricultural use is proposed, or where the landlord can show that he would suffer greater hardship if the notice to quit is refused than the tenant would suffer if the notice to quit is granted.

The position of sub-tenants is complicated, but the general effect is as follows. Where the tenant gives his sub-tenant notice to quit, they stand in the same relationship to each other as any other landlord and tenant under the Act, and the sub-tenant enjoys all the security of tenure and right to serve a counter-notice which any tenant possesses. Where the head landlord serves a notice on his tenant which is effective to put an end to the tenancy, then any sub-tenancy is automatically destroyed, whether or not the tenant has given his sub-tenant notice to quit. However, a notice to quit given by a tenant to his landlord will not by itself destroy the sub-tenancy, although a tenant may, of course, determine the sub-tenancy, by an effective notice to quit served on the sub-tenant. Similarly, a tenant cannot destroy a sub-tenancy by surrendering his own interest in the land to the landlord, for in this case the sub-tenant will move up' and hold his tenancy on the same terms as previously, from his

165

former head landlord. Finally, if a tenant forfeits his land, the sub-tenancy is destroyed unless the Court makes an order allowing the sub-tenant to retain his interest in the land.

A tenant may treat a notice to quit part of the holding as a notice to quit the whole, by serving a counter-notice to that effect usually within a month after the giving of the notice to quit.

COMPENSATION

An evicted tenant has a right to claim compensation for disturbance except in the five cases where the Agricultural Lands Tribunal has declared that a notice to quit is effective. The amount recoverable is the combined total of the loss suffered and expenses incurred as a direct result of the quitting, and while the tenant has a right to compensation equivalent to one year's rent, if he wishes to claim more than this he must prove his loss and expense up to a maximum permitted claim equivalent to two years' rent. Where the landlord has given notice to quit part of the holding and the tenant has served a counter-notice to quit the whole, compensation for disturbance can be claimed for the whole, except in a few special cases.

The landlord has a statutory right to recover compensation from the tenant on the termination of the tenancy in respect of particular instances of dilapidation, deterioration, or damage, and the amount recoverable is the cost of repair. If the landlord considers that compensation for specific damage is insufficient, he may, provided proper notice is given, claim compensation for general deterioration up to the amount by which value of the holding has been reduced. Any agreement as to compensation which is contrary to these statutory rights is invalid.

IMPROVEMENTS

Compensation for improvements which the tenant has made to the holding may be governed by the contract of tenancy or by custom. In all other cases statute prescribes the compensation which a tenant is to receive when he quits the holding. Generally speaking, where the improvements were begun before March 1948 the tenant has a right to compensation only if they were carried out with the landlord's consent, or in the case of drainage if he was first given notice. The amount of compensation is the value of the improvements to an incoming tenant.

Improvements begun since March 1948 fall into three categories. First there are long-term improvements for which an outgoing tenant will receive compensation provided that he first obtained the landlord's written consent, or in some cases the approval of the Minister or of the Agricultural Land Tribunal. Secondly, there are seven improvements of a short-term nature for which the landlord's consent is not a condition of compensation. These are: mole drainage; protection of fruit trees against animals; chalking of land; clay

166

burning; liming of land; application to land of purchased manure (not manure produced on the holding); consumption of corn or of purchased cake or other feeding-stuff by horses, cattle, sheep, pigs, or poultry folded on the land. The amount of compensation for long-term improvements is the increase in the value of the holding and for short-term improvements is the value of the improvement to the incoming tenant. Thirdly, the outgoing tenant is entitled to compensation for most 'tenant right' matters. This means the cost of labour and materials expended on such matters as growing crops, making hay, straw, or silage. The amount of compensation is the value of the improvement to an incoming tenant.

Subject to certain conditions and exceptions a tenant also has the right to claim compensation on quitting a holding at the end of a tenancy for the continuous use of a special system of farming, more beneficial than that required by the tenancy agreement or than that prevalent on similar holdings. The amount of the claim is the increase in the value of the holding.

Where a landlord has carried out improvements to a holding at the request or with the agreement of the tenant, he may increase the rent by an amount equal to the increase in rateable value, provided that he gave written notice of the intended increase within six months of completing the work.

Finally a tenant has a right to compensation for damage done by game if caused either by an unreasonable increase of game brought on to the land or where the right in game is solely vested in the landlord.

ARBITRATION

A most important and inexpensive method of settling disputes under the 1948 Act is by way of arbitration. This is a form of inquiry conducted by an arbitrator acting in the capacity of a Judge and not as a valuer. There is a special code of procedure, with conditions as to the qualifications and appointment of arbitrator. Certain matters, such as disputes between landlord and tenant, must be determined by arbitration. The arbitrator's award is final and binding on the parties, although he may be required to state in the form of a special case for the consideration of the County Court any question of law arising in the course of the arbitration. If he is requested to do so, before the award is made, an arbitrator appointed otherwise than by agreement between the parties must give his reasons for making the award.

In order that a fair rent may be assessed impartially, either party may demand, by written notice, that the rent payable for the holding shall be determined by reference to arbitration. The arbitrator then assesses what would be a reasonable rent in an open market. This procedure may only be invoked once in every three years.

Another important body for the settling of claims is the Agricultural Lands Tribunal. There are special rules as to the constitution of tribunals which consist of a chairman and deputy chairman and representatives from a panel of farmers and landowners. Tribunals are constituted separately for each hearing and give a written decision together with the reasons which led them to make it. There is a right of appeal to the High Court on questions of law.

MARKET GARDENS

The tenant of a market garden has all the rights of the tenant of an agricultural holding and has certain additional rights which are dealt with below.

There is no definition in the Acts of market garden but some of the cases are helpful. In one case the Judge said:

"Market gardening means the trade or business which produces the class of goods characteristic of a greengrocer's shop and which, in the ordinary course, reaches that shop via the early morning market where such goods are disposed of wholesale."

Market 'gardens'!

The two essential points are that the goods must be of this category and that the market gardener must run his garden as a business. The fact that the occupier of a country house regularly sells a good deal of the produce of the gardens or even a regular one half of the produce of the gardens does not make those gardens 'a market garden'.

The fact that the holding is wholly or mainly covered with glasshouses will not prevent it from being a market garden.

The Act of 1948 divides market gardens into two classes:

(1) Those where the original tenancy began on or after January 1st, 1896.

(2) Those which under a tenancy current on January 1st, 1896, were in use or cultivation as a market garden with the knowledge of the landlord.

In cases coming under category (1) above the tenant, in order to claim the special advantages given to market gardens by the Act, must have an agreement in writing from the landlord that his premises shall be let or treated as a market garden.

If a tenant who has land available wishes to use all or part of it as a market garden and the landlord refuses or fails within a reasonable period to give his consent in writing, the tenant may apply to the Agricultural Land Tribunal. The Tribunal may, if they are satisfied that the holding or part of it is suitable for market gardening, direct that the special privileges of the Act applicable to market gardens shall apply. In giving this direction they have power to impose certain conditions for the protection of the landlord.

Tenants falling within class (2) above have an advantage over the tenants in class (1). So long as they fulfil the conditions set out below there is no need to have the landlord's consent that the holding is let or shall be treated as a market garden and compensation will be payable for the improvements which are listed below.

The conditions are those already stated as applying to class (2) above and also that before January 1st, 1896, the tenant had, without having received a written notice of dissent from the landlord, carried out one of those improvements (other than one consisting of merely altering the building without actually enlarging it).

Special rights of market gardeners

The special rights of a tenant of a market garden, *i.e.* those in class (1) who have the landlord's permission or the approval of the Tribunal or those in class (2), as defined above, are as follows:

(a) On quitting the holding the tenant is entitled to compensation for the improvement set out below without having had to obtain leave of the landlord to carry them out or having had to give him notice of an intention to carry them out. These improvements are:

(1) Planting of standard or other fruit trees permanently set out.

(2) Planting of fruit bushes permanently set out.

(3) Planting of strawberry plants.

(4) Planting of asparagus, rhubarb, and other vegetable crops which continue productive for two or more years.

(5) Erection, alteration, or enlargement of buildings for the purpose of the trade or business of a market gardener.

(b) In addition to the right to remove fixtures as described above, with

169

reference to agricultural holdings generally, the tenant may, subject to the general rules about removing fixtures described above, remove any fixtures which he has affixed or erected for the purposes of his trade or business of a market gardener, whenever he may have done so. The limit of January 1st, 1884, does not apply to him as it does in the case of ordinary fixtures.

(c) The tenant may remove all fruit trees and fruit bushes not permanently set out that he has planted on the holding at any time during the tenancy. He must, however, do this before the end of the tenancy. He has no two months' extra period as he has with fixtures. If he does not, they become the property of the landlord, who need pay no compensation for them.

(d) The tenant may claim compensation for the whole or part of any improvement which he has purchased from a previous tenant even though the landlord gave no consent in writing for such purchase. This contrasts with the necessity for a tenant of an ordinary agricultural holding to obtain leave for the purchase of improvements.

SERVICE TENANTS AND OCCUPIERS

THIS SECTION is concerned with the position of persons who are provided with houses owned by their employers. They may be tenants or what is technically called licensees but, more usually, service occupiers. The distinction between the two can have important consequences, but it is sometimes difficult to determine whether an employee has the benefit of a tenancy from his employer or whether he is merely a service occupier.

THE SERVICE OCCUPIER

Where it is one of the terms of his contract of service that an employee *shall* live in a house owned and provided for him by his employer, and where it is necessary for him to do so in order that he can more conveniently perform his work, the employee will usually be only a service occupier. This will be so even if he is required to pay a small weekly sum for his use of the house or if his wages are reduced to take into account the value of the house to him. Often, of course, the service occupier will not pay anything at all. It makes no difference whether the contract of service is in writing or whether this is a mere verbal arrangement, as is very often the case. The service occupier is not a tenant at all. He has the mere right to use the house during the time he remains in the employment of the owner. Thus it is that, for example, a caretaker of a school who is required to live in a house in the school grounds as a condition of his employment or a farm labourer who has to live in a cottage on his employer's farm or the manager of a shop who is provided with and required to live in a flat above the shop will usually be service occupiers. This means that when their employment ceases for whatever reason, their right to remain in the house or flat, as the case may be, comes to an end too. The employer does not have to give a service occupier any notice to quit; the right to live in the house finishes with the employment. If the contract of service is in writing, as it would be more often than not in the case of school caretakers employed by local authorities or shop managers employed by large concerns, it will nearly always specifically say so. When the employment finishes the employer is entitled to obtain an order for possession against the former employee from the Court if the employee does not move out, and he will also be entitled to recover from the tenant a sum of money for his use and occupation of the house for the period after his right to occupy it ended. This sum will be equivalent to the notional rental value of the house over the period. In the case of a service occupier the Court cannot postpone the operation of its order for possession against the occupier for more than two months after the date of the hearing of the case.

THE SERVICE TENANT

A tenancy will usually be created between an employer and his employee if the employer charges him the market rent for the house and gives him a rent book, or if, in a written contract of service or in an agreement in writing made separately with regard to the house, use is made of expressions such as 'landlord', 'tenant', or 'notice to quit', which are, of course, words appropriate to the

". . . normal landlord and tenant relationship . . ."

normal landlord and tenant relationship. It is this kind of tenancy, where an employer lets a house to an employee, that is usually described as a service tenancy.

Service tenancies created *after* the coming into force of Section 11 of the Rent Act, 1957, on July 6th, 1957 (which is dealt with elsewhere), are not subject to any Rent Acts' control and the service tenant's rights are governed entirely by his agreement with his employer landlord. Normally, as has been said, the tenancy agreement will provide that the tenancy shall come to an end when the tenant ceases to work for his employer. When this happens the employee has to go and, if he does not, the employer can obtain an order for possession against him from the Court. Sometimes the agreement will provide that the employer shall be entitled to give the employee notice to quit. Since the Rent Act, 1957, this must be at least a four weeks' notice.

If, however, the house was let to an employee *before* July 6th, 1957, by his employer, the employee will still enjoy the full protection of the Rent Acts, provided that the rateable value is inside the control limits set by Section 11 of the Rent Act, 1957. This means that even if the tenant ceases to be in the employment of his landlord he can continue to occupy the house as a statutory tenant. His landlord can only evict him by securing an order for possession against him on one of the grounds allowed by the Rent Acts, which are considered elsewhere. However, an additional ground for an order for possession is given in these circumstances. Where the tenant has left his employment and is still occupying a house let to him as an employee, the Court can make an order for possession if it considers it reasonable to do so, and if the landlord proves that he requires the house as a home for some other person who is in his whole-time employment, or in the full-time employment of a tenant of his, or whom he has agreed to employ conditionally on his being able to provide him with housing accommodation. This provision is of obvious assistance to landlords who cannot, for example, find anyone to replace the former employee (who may have taken a job with someone else) without offering the newcomer the house which the former employee is still occupying.

The service tenant whose house was let to him before July 6th, 1957, but which became decontrolled as a result of the operation of Section 11 of the Rent Act, 1957, is in precisely the same position as any other tenant similarly situated when his right to occupy his house under his agreement with his landlord has come to an end.

MODE OF PAYMENT OF RENT

THE landlord and tenant will usually have agreed how and when the rent is to be paid and the day or days on which the rent falls due will be written into the rent book or be stated in the written lease or agreement. The periods at which rent is payable will often reflect the kind of tenancy which has been granted, so that a weekly tenant will pay his rent weekly and a quarterly tenant quarterly: a tenant from year to year, on the other hand, will commonly agree to pay rent monthly or quarterly without affecting the nature of his tenancy.

In advance or in arrear?

Unless there is express agreement rent is not due in advance and a yearly tenant may pay on the last day of the year, if he has not promised to pay by instalments. The parties should agree when the first and subsequent payments are to be made. When rent is to be paid quarterly, instead of specifying dates it may be agreed to pay on the 'usual quarter days'—that is, Lady Day (March 25th), Midsummer Day (June 24th), Michaelmas Day (September 29th), and Christmas Day (December 25th). A quarterly tenant who goes into possession between the dates for payment should see it is agreed that only part of a quarter's rent should be due for the incomplete quarter. Otherwise he will be liable for a full quarter's rent on the first date of payment.

Due dates

If there are no agreed dates for payment rent will fall due three months after the beginning of a quarterly tenancy. Thus, a tenant who enters on March 1st will pay the first quarter's rent on May 31st. In the same way a weekly tenant, paying rent in arrear, who enters on a Thursday will pay the rent on the following Wednesday and will continue to pay on that day. A tenant may pay his rent at any time on the date named for payment and it does not fall into arrear until midnight.

Alteration of amount

An agreement to raise or lower the rent fixed by a written tenancy agreement or lease should be evidenced in writing and some material benefit should be given in return for the change; for example, the landlord may agree to improve the premises or the tenant may agree to give up some right. A variation in the rent does not by itself put an end to the old agreement so as to create a new tenancy between the parties from the date of the change.

In money or in kind

Rent need not be paid in money. In the Middle Ages the peasants gave so many days' work to their lord by way of rent for their smallholdings and even now there is no reason why services should not, by agreement, take the place of a money rent. In a modern case an agreement between a man and the trustees of a synagogue that he should clean the synagogue in return for occupying a certain house was ruled to be a true tenancy agreement, his cleaning duties constituting rent. There are still many leaseholds in existence for which a nominal or 'peppercorn' rent is payable and such leases are occasionally created today, usually as an act of benevolence by the owner of land in favour of some charity. In these cases, though the rent is only nominal, payment of it maintains the relationship of landlord and tenant between the parties so that, at the end of the term of the lease, the property will revert to the landlord just as it does when an economic rent is paid. In addition there will probably be other covenants in the lease which impose material burdens designed to preserve the value of the property—duties to maintain the property in a good state of repair, for example.

Variable rents

Rent need not be fixed in amount, it may fluctuate according to the tenant's income or according to variations in the cost of living or the purchasing power of money. If it does fluctuate, however, there must be clear agreement on how the rent for any rental period is to be calculated.

Cash or cheque?

If the agreed rent is stated in terms of money the tenant is obliged, strictly speaking, to pay his rent in cash and payment by cheque does not fulfil the agreement. However, for practical purposes the increased use of banking accounts and of cheque books has caused this strict rule to be ignored. Payment by a post-dated cheque, however, is still no payment, and an agent for the landlord who is not authorized to take cheques may have to reimburse the landlord if he accepts from the tenant a cheque which is not met.

Collect or send?

Must the landlord call at the house to collect the rent, or must the tenant get the money to the landlord wherever he might be? If the agreement or rent book merely says that the amount of the rent is so and so, and does not include a specific promise to pay, then the landlord or his agent must call to collect the rent.

If, however, the agreement contains a specific promise, such as 'I promise to pay'—as most agreements do nowadays, then the tenant has an obligation to get the money to the landlord, and if it is lost on the way he would have to pay again.

Who pays?

The landlord is not obliged to accept rent from a third party, unless that person is authorized to pay it by the tenant. If a landlord wishes to obtain possession of premises because his tenant is in arrear with rent, he need not accept a payment which someone other than the tenant himself offers to preserve the tenant against eviction: the landlord's contract is with the tenant. In the same way, if a house is let under an agreement which provides that the tenant shall pay 'rent' to someone who is not the landlord, this is strictly not rent at all and, although the amount can be sued for if not paid, the important remedy of distress is not available to enforce it.

Who receives?

Rent should be paid to the landlord or to his authorized agent and the tenant should be wary of paying someone who does not ordinarily collect rent on behalf of his landlord, for if that person has no actual authority or if the landlord has not acted so as to make it appear that that person is his agent, the tenant will remain liable for the rent if it is misappropriated. If the landlord assigns his interest in the property, the tenant must, after he has had notice of the assignment, pay rent to the assignee. And if the landlord dies, payment should be made to his personal representatives until the landlord's interest passes, for example, to the person entitled under his will.

". . . be wary of paying someone who does not ordinarily collect the rent . . ."

When tenant pays Schedule A; and rates

In certain circumstances the tenant may be entitled to withhold all or part of the rent due to the landlord. For example, if Schedule A is assessed on the tenant occupier (usually it falls on the *owner* of the property) he may deduct the tax actually paid from future rent payments. But he must deduct it from the next rent due. If the tenant is a sub-lessee and his landlord's own landlord demands payment from the tenant of rent due under the head-lease, he may protect himself against paying twice over by withholding rent due to his own landlord. Ordinarily local authorities' rates are payable by the occupier and most leases will contain a provision imposing liability for rates on the tenant, but where premises are let for a term not exceeding three months, in the absence of contrary agreement, the tenant may deduct from his rent payments which he has made of the general rates. Apart from the general rates, the tenant is not liable for special charges imposed for local purposes (road improvement and drainage, for example) and he may deduct such payments from his rent. A covenant to pay rates does not impose liability for these charges. But the tenant is liable if he covenants to meet *all* outgoings in respect of the property— an exceptional, but possible covenant, and one the tenant should not accept if he can get his tenancy without it.

175

MARRIAGE

INTRODUCTION

BY ENGLISH LAW marriage is the 'voluntary union for life of one man with one woman to the exclusion of all others'. In order to be valid a marriage by our law must fulfil certain requirements, which are as follows;

(a) the parties must be 'capable', as regards age, etc., of marrying;
(b) they must not be prohibited from marrying by reasons of 'kindred or affinity', *i.e.* too close a relationship;
(c) they must not be validly married already;
(d) they must observe certain formalities;
(e) they must genuinely consent to marry.

The type of 'incapacity' for marriage most frequently met with is that one or other of the pair is too young. A marriage between people either of whom is *under sixteen* is void. Persons between the ages of sixteen and twenty-one may only marry with their parents' consent. If one parent is dead the consent of the surviving parent is enough, but if there is a guardian appointed he must consent too. If parents refuse their consent the couple may apply to the Court for its permission. Such an application can be made either to the Magistrates' Court, the County Court or the High Court, but the Magistrates' Court is usually chosen. The Court will be willing to disregard the parents' objections to the marriage if, for instance, the objection is shown to be based on mere prejudice or some other unreasonable ground, but parents' wishes are usually accorded considerable weight.

Persons of unsound mind who have been so certified cannot, while certified, contract a valid marriage. Persons of unsound mind who have *not* been certified can do so, unless it is established that they do not understand the nature of the contract of marriage and their responsibilities under it.

The consent of both persons must be freely given, and must be based on full knowledge of the fact that the contract is one of marriage. Marriages have been held not to be valid where one party believed the ceremony to be only one of betrothal, and also where the bride was threatened with physical violence unless she agreed to wed, or when as in one case the girl was drugged and did not know what was going on.

177

FAMILY LAWYER

'Kindred or affinity'

This is the law which forbids a man or a woman to marry anyone who stands in too close a relationship.

The full list of prohibited degrees of relationship is very long and some of it is only of theoretical interest. Few men are likely to want to marry their grandmother. The complete list is set out in the Marriage Act, 1949 and this can be seen in any public library. But the following summary of the logical basis of the list may be helpful.

(1) Ascendants and descendants may not intermarry. Hence a man may not marry his mother, mother's mother, father's mother, his grandfather's wife and so on up the scale from which he is descended.

So too, going down the scale, he may not marry his daughter, his son's daughter, his daughter's daughter. He may not marry his wife's daughter (*e.g.* his second wife's previously born daughter). Relationship of the half-blood is as great a bar as the whole-blood. And there need be no blood relationship at all. Kindred means blood relationship: affinity, relationship by marriage as it would be shown in the standard form of family tree.

(2) Persons related to each other within the *third* degree may not marry. Hence a man may not marry the daughter of a brother or sister of his. She is within the third degree: his father is related to him in the first degree; from his father to his brother or sister is the second degree; from there to their child is the third degree.

(3) Cousins may marry each other because they are one degree further away.

(4) Blood relations of the husband are not affinity (as defined above) of the wife. So two brothers may marry two sisters.

It is, however, legal by statutory exception to the rules for a man to marry his *deceased* wife's sister, deceased brother's wife, deceased wife's brother's daughter and deceased wife's sister's daughter, and also certain other relatives, further removed, of his deceased wife. Again, the full list is to be found in the Marriage Act, 1949. It is also legal for a woman to marry her deceased sister's husband, deceased husband's brother, as well as a list of less likely relatives also set out in the Act.

But the permission for a man to marry his deceased wife's sister, etc., and for a woman to marry her deceased husband's brother, did not, until 1960, extend to sister or brother of a *divorced* wife or husband. So if a man divorced his wife he could not marry her sister during the lifetime of his former wife, and vice versa.

This was changed in 1960 by the Marriage (Enabling) Act which allows a valid marriage to be entered into between a man and a woman who is the sister, aunt or niece of his former wife—whether living or not. It also allows such a marriage between a man and a woman who was previously the wife of his brother, uncle or nephew—whether they are living or not.

FORMALITIES OF MARRIAGE

(1) Church of England marriages

(a) *Marriage by Banns*. This is the commonest type of marriage in the Church of England. Banns must be read out in Church on three Sundays pre-

178

ceding the marriage ceremony. Where the proposed husband and wife live in different parishes the banns must be published in both. The parties must give to the clergyman at least seven days notice in writing of their intention to marry and their wish to have banns published, but he may not insist upon this if the people concerned are well known to him. Most clergymen will be ready to give a young couple all the information they need about the formalities of their marriage.

(b) *Marriage by common licence.* A licence removes the need for the calling of banns. In order to get a licence one of the parties must have lived for at least fifteen days before the marriage in the parish of the Church where the marriage is to be held, or the Church must be the usual place of worship of one of the parties. The marriage can take place as soon as the licence is issued, and the licence remains in force for three months. Licences can be obtained in London from The Faculty Office, 1 The Sanctuary, Westminster, S.W.1. Outside London they can be obtained from the offices of the Registrar for the Bishop of the Diocese.

(c) *Marriage by special licence.* A special licence can authorize a marriage *anywhere* (not necessarily in a parish church), and is therefore required where the ceremony is to be held, *e.g.* in a private house or chapel. It can only be granted by the Archbishop of Canterbury, and a fee of £25 is payable. Such licences are comparatively rare.

(d) *Marriage by Superintendent Registrar's certificate.* If the clergyman agrees, a marriage can be held in a Church on the authority of this type of certificate, without banns or licence. The certificate is obtained from the local Register Office.

(2) Other marriages

Those who intend to get married otherwise than according to the rites of the Church of England may do so in a Church of a different denomination (*e.g.* a Roman Catholic or Non-Conformist Church) or in a Register Office. First, notice of intention to marry must be given to the superintendent registrar for marriages. The form for this may be obtained from the local Register Office. A notice is then exhibited at the office for public inspection for twenty-one successive days. The registrar will then issue his certificate, and as soon as this is done the marriage may take place. It may be held in the Register Office or in the Church of the parties concerned (*e.g.* the Roman Catholic or Non-Conformist Church) so long as the Church is registered for such marriages.

It is possible, also, to apply to the Register Office for a certificate *with licence.* One of the parties must have lived in the district for at least fifteen days before the giving of the notice. The notice need not be exhibited for twenty-one days, and the certificate can be issued one clear day after the notice is given. The marriage can take place on any day within three months from the date of the entry of the notice at the office.

Where a marriage is held at a Church other than a Church of England Church either the registrar or else an authorised person under the Marriage Act, 1949 must be present. Clergy of the various denominations are usually so authorized, and their presence alone is therefore sufficient. The ceremony must take place between 8 a.m. and 6 p.m., and the Church doors must be open to the public. No special form of words need be used for the service, except that at some point the parties must declare that they know of no impediment to the marriage and state that each takes the other as husband or as wife.

HUSBAND AND WIFE—LEGAL DUTIES

Marriage alters the 'status' of husband and wife at law: in other words, their legal relationship with the rest of the community is changed. Each takes on new rights and duties.

The best known of such duties is the husband's duty to support his wife, which he is bound to do according to his means. The duty ceases if the wife unjustifiably leaves her husband or if she commits adultery, but if they part by

". . . the wife has power to 'pledge her husband's credit' and he can be compelled to pay for articles which are 'necessaries' to their way of living. For a well-to-do couple a fur coat *may* be a necessary."

mutual agreement the duty continues. The wife can enforce her right to be supported by obtaining a *maintenance order* (see below). What is more, the wife has power to 'pledge her husband's credit', *i.e.* she can order articles for their use, and the husband can be compelled to pay for them. He can only be made to pay, however, for articles which are 'necessaries' for their style of living. 'Necessaries' does not only mean such articles as food and drink: it covers all that goes with the couple's way of life. So for a well-to-do couple a fur coat or even a car *may* be a necessary. If the husband and wife are living together the husband must pay for such articles unless he can prove that his wife had been forbidden to pledge his credit or that at the time she was already provided with them sufficiently, or had an adequate allowance to buy them. A husband may, by inserting an advertisement in the newspaper, give notice to tradesmen that he will not be responsible for his wife's debts and this will help him to establish that he has forbidden his wife to 'pledge his credit'.

When the couple are living apart the right to pledge the husband's credit usually ceases, unless the wife's living away from her husband is due to his misconduct. If the couple enter into a separation agreement the wife may not pledge her husband's credit so long as he keeps to the terms of the agreement.

A second duty, which today is of less practical importance than formerly, is the wife's duty to live with her husband. Formerly a husband was entitled to compel his wife to carry out this duty, by force if required, and she could be sent to prison for failing to obey a Court order that she should return. Nowadays this does not apply, but if a wife leaves her husband she runs the risk of losing her right to financial support. She cannot, however, be *forced* to return to him.

Married women now have the same legal rights as other individuals, and their money and property do not pass automatically into their husband's ownership. Nor are marriage partners legally liable for each other's wrong-doings.

"... if a wife runs down a cyclist in the family car, it is the wife who must be sued. ..." (*Marriage partners are not legally liable for each other's wrong-doings.*)

Thus if a wife carelessly runs down a cyclist in the family car it is the wife who must be sued—the cyclist cannot obtain damages from the husband. A husband is not allowed to sue his wife for damages for 'torts' (*i.e.* civil wrongs, such as negligence) which she may commit, and a wife can only sue her husband in such a case when she is seeking to protect and secure her own property. Therefore, if Mr Smith is run over by Mrs Smith and injured he cannot obtain damages against her for negligence, nor could she sue him if the position was reversed. On the other hand, if Mr Smith collides with Mrs Smith and damages her bicycle she can sue him for such damage, since her property is affected. Husbands and wives may also make contracts with each other which are legally binding, and can sue one another for a failure to keep to such contracts. However, the Courts tend to be reluctant to hold that an arrangement between husband and wife is a legally binding contract, for most couples when arranging matters between themselves do not intend their agreement to have any legal force.

If a husband loses the company and help of his wife, which at law is called 'consortium', he may sue the person by whose act he loses them. Thus a husband may sue a motorist who by his negligence knocks over and kills or injures his

181

wife. Among the sums he can recover are the costs of medical treatment and convalescence. Equally, a husband can sue the person who entices his wife away from him. For example, in a well-known case a doctor who said to the wife of a shop assistant, "Come on, Gwen. We will go" was held to have 'enticed' her away and to be liable in damages to her husband. A wife in the same way can sue the person who entices away her husband. But it has been held that a wife cannot claim against someone who has so injured her husband that his sexual capacity is seriously impaired or destroyed, notwithstanding the consequent ill-affect on her health and happiness.

"If, however, the wife had treated her husband with neglect . . ."

A husband and a wife can make a will and leave their property in any way they choose. Nothing need be left to the surviving partner. However, if either dies domiciled in England (that is, having made this country his or her permanent home) the surviving partner can make application to the Court on the ground that the will does not make reasonable provision for his or her maintenance. The Court, if satisfied that this is so, has power to order that reasonable provision shall be made for the maintenance of the applicant, and to this extent can override and, in affect, amend the will. Generally the application has to be made within six months of the grant of probate of the will. No application is permitted by the husband or wife concerned where the testator (i.e. the maker of the will) left two-thirds of his net income to the survivor. The Court will usually only be prepared to override the provisions of a will where the husband or wife concerned has been treated with obvious unfairness, for instance where a husband at the end of his life was associating with a young girl and finally left all his money to her and nothing to his wife. In applications like this, the Court will expect to have evidence about the history of the married life. If the marriage was happy, a husband's last-minute aberrations will be overruled. If, however, the wife had for years treated her husband with indifference, neglect or cruelty, she may find her application turned down.

When a wife commits an offence against the Criminal Law the husband is not liable, unless he ordered her to commit it; nor is a wife liable, as such, for her husband's acts. But of course she may be a participant in the crime herself, and if so, she is liable. A wife may be able to prove, if accused of a crime, that she committed it in her husband's presence and under his coercion. If she can do so, she will be acquitted. Generally speaking, neither a wife nor a husband

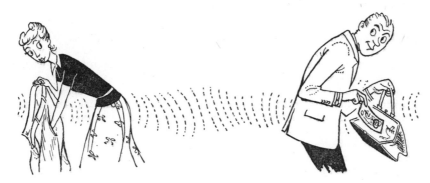

"When a husband and wife are living together it does not amount to stealing if one takes away the other's property."

can be *compelled* in a criminal case to give evidence against the other for the prosecution. Either can give evidence for the defence.

When a husband and wife are living together it does not amount to stealing if one takes away the other's property. On the other hand it *is* stealing, and the offender can be prosecuted, if the property is taken by a husband or wife about to leave or desert the other partner.

DIVORCE

There are five grounds for divorce by our law. They are·

(1) Adultery.
(2) Desertion.
(3) Cruelty.
(4) Incurable insanity.
(5) Commission by a husband of certain sexual offences.

We will consider these in turn.

(1) Adultery

Adultery means voluntary sexual intercourse between a married person and a person of the opposite sex. Only one act of adultery need be proved for a divorce to be granted. The difficulty usually met with, of course, is to *prove* the adultery, since parties are very seldom caught in the act. In order to prove adultery it is generally considered essential to have evidence of 'inclination and opportunity'; in other words it must be shown that the man and woman concerned were attracted to one another, and that they had an opportunity to commit adultery. The fact that the husband or wife has confessed to the adultery is not in itself enough, since such confessions are often made by parties who want to be free. A confession will therefore usually need to be corroborated by the evidence. Where a man and woman have been living together in a house 'as man and wife' for a considerable time, adultery will generally be implied. Where the only proof is evidence that the husband slept the night with a woman in a hotel the Courts are inclined to be hesitant about granting a decree of divorce, since the episode may be a mere sham. It will generally be necessary, therefore, to have some further evidence, for instance, to show that the man and woman concerned had been going about together for some time. In many cases the evidence of adultery is given by an inquiry agent (*i.e.* a private detective) who has taken a written statement from the person concerned, and can also say that on visiting the house concerned he found evidence to suggest that a man and woman were living there together.

The man with whom a wife is alleged to have committed adultery is known as the co-respondent. It is of course open to him to defend the case and deny the adultery—even if the wife does not choose to do so. Where a co-respondent is found guilty of adultery he may be ordered to pay damages to the husband. The object of these damages is to compensate the husband for what he has lost, and the Court has therefore to carry out the tricky job of estimating the financial value of a wife. A wife who in the past has been true and faithful and a good housekeeper is regarded as of more value than one who has been flighty and of little help in the house. A wife who has been of assistance in her husband's business is also regarded as of higher financial value. No attention is paid—in theory, at least—to the means of the co-respondent, unless he has made use of his money to attract the wife away from her husband. But whatever the husband may claim the Court is usually unwilling to order a co-respondent to pay a sum which he cannot possibly afford and thus expose him to bankruptcy or loss of home and furniture. Even if damages are not claimed against him the co-respondent usually has to pay the costs of the husband in obtaining his divorce.

(2) Desertion

Desertion means the leaving of a husband or wife by the other partner to the marriage, who intends to bring the married life permanently to an end. In order to be a ground for divorce the desertion must continue for at least three years immediately before the divorce proceedings are started. It is not every wife or husband who is left by the other partner who can claim to be deserted. The desertion must be 'without cause'. If a husband commits adultery, or treats his wife with cruelty, the wife has 'just cause' for departing, and does not commit desertion when she goes. Even if a husband or wife is not actually guilty of cruelty, he or she may give the other party 'just cause' for leaving. For a husband to carry on an association with another woman, even if it is not an adulterous one, gives his wife, in the law's eyes, good cause for leaving home. Prolonged nagging, to take another example, might also constitute good cause.

Once the desertion has started, it continues until it is brought to an end in one of the ways recognized by the law. One such way is an offer to return by the deserting husband or wife. It is not enough if the person concerned merely makes up his mind to come back. He must notify the other partner of his intention and offer to start again—and his offer must be genuine. If he has been guilty of behaving badly in the past it will usually be up to him to assure his partner that he will conduct himself better in future. If there is a real doubt about the genuineness of the offer to come back the deserted wife may refuse it. If it is a genuine offer, however, it puts an end to the desertion. What is more, the husband or wife who refuses it is then regarded as being a deserter. This can be illustrated by an example. Mr A. deserts his wife and lives away from her for two years. Then he writes and says he would like to return, and promises to give up the long but not adulterous flirtation he has been having with his secretary. This is a genuine offer, but Mrs A. refuses it. The result of this is that Mrs A. is now 'in desertion' herself, having declined a genuine offer by her husband to start married life again.

If the couple *are* re-united the desertion is brought to an end—but they must be properly re-united. If Mr B. merely comes to stay with his wife for a weekend in order to talk things over, married life (the law calls it 'cohabitation') has not been resumed. On the other hand, it can be resumed even though they do not live under the same roof, if, for instance, Mr and Mrs B. are reconciled and begin to spend regular visits together at a hotel, or a friend's house. If they have sexual intercourse the Court will be strongly inclined to regard cohabitation as having begun again. Before the desertion can be said to have been ended both Mr and Mrs B. must intend that the past is forgotten and that their marriage shall be re-established.

If a couple part by agreement it does not count as desertion. Thus if Mr and Mrs C. decide that they cannot make a go of things, and that it will be best to live apart, Mr C. will not be regarded as a deserter if he leaves home and remains away permanently.

On the other hand, if Mr. C. *does* desert his wife—if he leaves her without her consent—it does not make any difference that he continues to provide her with money for maintenance. He is just as much 'in desertion' although he is still supporting his deserted wife.

A husband or wife can still be deserted even if it is he or she who leaves home first. A wife, for example, may be driven out of the home by her husband's conduct. If so, after three years she can petition for a divorce on the ground of her husband's desertion. This type of case, where one partner is driven away by the other's misconduct, is known as 'constructive desertion'. Misconduct must, however, be extremely serious to justify a husband or wife in leaving. The ordinary wear and tear of married life is not enough, since couples take one another for better or worse. It is not necessary, however, for the conduct to amount to 'cruelty' in the legal sense so long as it is 'grave and weighty'. Unwarrantable indifference and prolonged unkindness may be enough, as may

185

prolonged drunkenness and niggardliness over money matters. No exhaustive list can be given of what may be regarded as conduct bad enough to drive away a husband or wife: all that can be said is that it must be serious, and usually must have continued for a long time.

A husband or wife may be in desertion even if he or she is living under the same roof as the deserted partner. For instance if Mrs E. cuts herself completely off from her husband and retires to live alone in a spare room, refusing to cook or sew for him, or to have any conversation or contact with him at all, she may be held to be a deserter even though they are still in the same house. She must, however, have cut herself off from virtually all contacts with her husband before this will be held to be the case. If she is merely neglectful of her household duties it will not be enough.

When the couple are parted involuntarily (for example because one of them is posted abroad) it does not count as desertion. In all desertion cases the *fact* of separation and the *intention* to desert must be proved: where the parting is involuntary there can be no such intention.

(3) Cruelty

Cruelty in the legal sense means conduct of such a character as to have caused danger to life, limb, or health, or as to give rise to a reasonable apprehension of such danger. Both husbands and wives can be guilty of cruelty. In most cruelty cases there is some element of physical violence, but this is not necessary. Nagging, if prolonged and serious, can constitute cruelty, as can a persistence in sexual practices which are known to be repellent to the other party. Theoretically one act of cruelty alone—such as one assault on a wife—could amount to cruelty, and so be ground for a divorce: but generally the Court requires evidence of a series of acts. Drunkenness by itself is not cruelty, but if a husband or wife persists in a course of heavy drinking which is known to be causing distress to the other party it may amount to cruelty. Husbands and wives can be cruel in the legal sense even when they do not intend to be so. For example, if Mr F. is boorish and taciturn toward his wife, and refuses to co-operate in running the house, and allows himself to become so dirty and unwashed that he becomes nauseating to her it may well be that she will after a time come near to a nervous breakdown. It cannot be said, however, that he has any intention to be cruel: he is merely indifferent to the effect his behaviour has upon his wife. Mr F. may well be held in such a case to be guilty of cruelty, whatever his intention may have been. Cases of involuntary cruelty, however tend to be rare: more usual are the cases where the husband or wife concerned is actuated by definite ill will toward the other partner.

Conduct which might be cruelty to one husband or wife is not necessarily cruelty to another. A sensitive wife will be more affected by abuse and indifference than an insensitive one. Words which would be unforgivable if spoken in one household may be commonplace in another. In deciding whether there has been cruelty the Court will pay attention to the social background and personality of the couple concerned. A long series of minor acts of unkindness which by themselves would not count as legal cruelty may do so if they are taken together. Criminal conduct by a husband or wife is not in itself cruelty, but if a partner indulges in a course of crime knowing that it is causing the other anxiety and distress it may amount to cruelty. In all cases it is essential to show that there has been some injury to life, limb, or health, or some real danger thereof. In many cases, of course, it is injury to mental and nervous health that can be established —for example, a husband's conduct may cause his wife to lose weight or to become depressed and 'jumpy'. In defended cases of cruelty a doctor's evidence is usually required to establish this. The refusal of sexual intercourse by either party, or the practice of 'coitus interruptus', can constitute cruelty, as may a series of inordinate sexual demands.

It is a defence to a charge of cruelty that the conduct in question was provoked by the victim. To amount to provocation, behaviour must be such as to deprive a reasonable person of his self-control. For example, if Mr G. sees his wife kissing Mr H. in public, after having promised never to see him again, it

"It cannot be said he has any intention to be cruel; he is merely indifferent. . . ."

would probably not count as cruelty if he thereupon slapped her face—since her conduct would be regarded as having provoked him. Acts done in self defence also do not count as cruelty. If, therefore, Mr J. slaps Mrs J. on the face when she attacks him with the carving knife his blow will not be regarded as being 'cruel'. The acts of an insane husband (or wife) are not regarded as being cruel if it is shown that he either did not know what he was doing, or if he did know, did not realize that it was wrong. For example, it is normally cruel to make groundless accusations of unfaithfulness against an innocent husband. But a wife suffering from delusional insanity may genuinely believe that her husband has been guilty of infidelity, and if so she would not be 'cruel' in the legal sense if she accused him of it—since she would not realize that her accusations were morally wrong.

(4) Incurable insanity

This is a ground for divorce if the husband or wife in question has been continuously under care and treatment for at least five years before the petition is brought. No divorce can be granted if the petitioner's own conduct helped to bring about the insanity. Until 1960 there was no possibility of a petition being brought on grounds of incurable insanity unless the insane husband or wife had been *certified*. This was quite out of line with modern ideas and practice which do everything possible to encourage voluntary treatment. The Divorce (Insanity and Desertion) Act of 1960, therefore, abolished the need for certification. The only essential point is five years' continuous treatment with, of course, convincing medical evidence that the mental disease appears to be incurable. The care and treatment must be continuous for five years, but it is not broken if the patient is allowed out 'on trial', for up to twenty-eight days.

(5) Sexual offences by a husband

Rape, sodomy, and bestiality by a husband are grounds for divorce on a wife's petition.

Bars to relief

A petitioner seeking a divorce may find himself faced with certain 'bars' to relief which can prevent his getting his divorce. These can be 'absolute' or 'discretionary'. If an absolute bar is proved no divorce can be granted: if, however, the bar is only discretionary the Judge may grant the divorce despite the existence of the bar, if he thinks fit.

The absolute bars are: Connivance; Collusion; Condonation.

The discretionary bars are: Delay; The petitioner's own adultery; The petitioner's own cruelty; The petitioner's own desertion; 'Conduct conducing'.

The absolute bars

(1) *Connivance.* This means turning a blind eye to the misconduct in question. Thus if a husband knows that his wife is having a love affair with another man, but takes no steps to stop it, or encourages it, he will be held to have connived at it, and therefore will not be entitled to a divorce in respect of it. Indifference, with knowledge, is enough. Encouragement is merely an aggravation. It is, however, not connivance to follow or 'shadow' a husband or wife—even one known to be committing adultery—if the object is simply to obtain evidence of his or her guilt. Nowadays pleas of connivance are comparatively rare.

(2) *Collusion.* Collusion means a bargain between husband and wife, making arrangements for a divorce case. An obvious case of collusion would be where a wife desired her freedom, and her husband in order to help her agreed to go to a hotel with another woman in order to provide her with evidence. If the agreement became known the wife would be unable to get her divorce. Another typical case of collusion is where a wife agrees to pay the costs of the case if her husband will give her her freedom. On the other hand, it is not collusion where Mrs K. writes to Mr K. saying that she knows he has committed adultery, and asking him to send her the necessary evidence of it, so that she can start a divorce case.

It is, however, often very difficult to draw the line between what is collusion and what is not. When a husband writes to his wife asking for the name of the man with whom she has committed adultery, and saying that if she gives it he will not claim any damages in the divorce suit there is a real danger of collusion being held to exist, since the Court frowns on any sort of bargain made by the parties in secret. The fact that both husband and wife want a divorce, however, does not make the case collusive, so long as they do not enter into any arrangements 'behind the Court's back'.

(3) *Condonation.* Condonation means the forgiveness of an erring husband or wife by the other partner, who intends to overlook what has been done. For instance, if Mr L. goes away for a weekend at Brighton with Miss M., and there commits adultery, his wife has grounds for divorce. But if she takes her husband back with full knowledge of what he has done and if their married life is resumed on its old footing, Mrs L. will be held to have condoned the adultery, and so to have no ground for divorce. There are two elements in condonation both of which have to be proved. One is the reinstatement of the offender, and the other is the intention to forgive in the mind of the wronged partner. If, in the example given, Mrs L. were to say to her husband "You can come back, but you must sleep in a separate room and I will give you a six months' trial to see if you can behave in future", there would be no real 'reinstatement', and hence no condonation. The resumption of sexual intercourse is conclusive proof of an intention to forgive on a husband's part, since the law does not permit him to have intercourse with an erring wife and yet continue to say that she is not forgiven. It is not conclusive, however, in a wife's case: since a wife may have difficulty in repelling her husband's sexual advances. Adultery is not regarded as condoned unless the party alleged to have forgiven it is shown to have known all about it: it is not sufficient that he or she had some suspicions.

Cruelty or adultery which has been condoned may be 'revived' if the forgiven parties go astray again. For example, if Mrs N. takes back her husband and decides to overlook and condone his adultery with Miss O. the condonation will only last for as long as Mr N. behaves himself. His past offences may be revived in the law's eyes, even if he does not actually commit adultery again. If he merely indulges in 'gross familiarities' with another woman, not amounting to actual adultery, his former misdeeds will be revived, and Mrs N. will have grounds for a divorce. It is just the same when the second offence is of a different sort from the first one. Thus, if Mr R. treats his wife with cruelty, which she condones, the cruelty would be revived if he were thereafter to commit adultery. Or, if Mrs P. were guilty of adultery and forgiven by her husband, her condoned adultery would be brought to life again, for legal purposes, if she started to treat him with cruelty.

The discretionary bars

(1) *Delay.* The Court will not assist a husband or wife 'who goes to sleep on his rights' and delays unduly in starting a case for divorce. So if Mrs Q. is deserted by Mr Q. she is expected, if she wants a divorce, to begin her case within a reasonable time. If she does not choose to seek her freedom for, say, twenty years, the Court will want an explanation of why she has delayed for so long. If all she can say is "I didn't bother about it" she may well be refused a divorce. On the other hand, there may be some reasonable excuse for the delay.

189

One such excuse would be that she had no money for legal proceedings, and had not heard of the Legal Aid Scheme which enables people of small means to obtain a divorce at reduced or at no cost. In desertion cases a wife may be able to explain the delay by showing that she continued for a long while to hope that her husband would return, and it has sometimes been held to be an excuse that a husband or wife wanted to wait until the family was grown up before ending the marriage. Nowadays very few divorce cases fail on the ground of delay, if there is any sort of excuse.

(2) *The petitioner's own adultery.* If the person bringing the divorce case, who is called the petitioner, has been guilty of adultery himself, he may not be granted his decree. It depends on whether the Court thinks fit to give it to him. He is bound to disclose his own adultery in a special statement to the Court, which he has to verify on oath, although it is not read out in public. We can illustrate this by a simple example: Mr R. committed adultery with Miss S. in 1955. He told his wife about it, and she decided to forgive him. Five years later Mrs R. goes off and lives in adultery with Mr T. Mr R. decides to divorce her. He will have to disclose his own offence with Miss S. to the Court, and it will be a matter for the Court's 'discretion' whether or not he is granted his decree. Probably he will get it, because it is Mrs R.'s adultery that has effectively brought his marriage to an end. Everything, however, will depend on the Court's view of the circumstances.

A more difficult case would be that of Mr U., who commits adultery with Miss V. Mrs U. starts a divorce case, but has to admit her own adultery with Mr W. This began *before* her husband's, and was one of the reasons why he left home and found consolation with Miss V. In this case the Court may be less willing to grant a divorce to Mrs U., because it was *her* conduct which really caused the marriage to fail. However, before making up his mind the Judge will have to consider a number of factors which have been laid down by the House of Lords as guides for the exercise of his discretion in cases of this kind. First of all he must think of the children and their interests: for their sake it *may* be desirable for the marriage to be brought to an end. Next he must think of Mr W.'s position. If he and Mrs U. are going to get married after the divorce, and live together respectably, it may be desirable to let this happen. Then he must decide if Mr and Mrs U. have any chance of being reconciled, since it would be unfortunate to put an end to the marriage if there were any hope of their coming together again. Then there is Mrs U.'s own position: if possible she should be allowed to re-marry and live a proper married life again. Lastly the interests of the whole community must be considered. On the one hand, it is little use to preserve a marriage which has utterly collapsed, and cannot be revived. On the other hand, the sanctity of marriage is of great importance, and marriages ought not to be dissolved too easily when the petitioner is at fault as well as the respondent. Weighing up all these considerations the Judge may give Mrs U. her decree—but it is by no means certain.

(3) *The petitioner's own cruelty and desertion.* These are also 'discretionary' bars, and the Court may, but is not bound to, grant a decree where the petitioner has been guilty of them.

(4) *Conduct Conducing.* If the Court finds that the petitioner has been guilty of such wilful neglect or misconduct as had 'conduced' to the other

partner's adultery or desertion, it may decline to grant a divorce. In Victorian days it used to be thought that a husband who abandoned his wife for long periods could be said to have 'conduced' to her adultery in that she would in such circumstances be likely to find another 'protector'. Nowadays 'conduct conducing' is comparatively seldom pleaded in the divorce court, but it is still part of the law. The conduct must be such that it can be said to have *caused* the adultery or desertion of the respondent: for example, a husband who habitually neglects and ill-treats his wife and who then permits her to go on holiday with another man may be held to have virtually caused her adultery. The refusal of sexual intercourse by either a husband or a wife may also be held to have conduced to misconduct by the other party.

The three-year period. A divorce decree cannot as a rule be granted unless three years have passed since the date of the marriage. The only exception to this rule is where the Court has given special leave for the case to be brought, on the ground that the petitioner has suffered 'exceptional hardship', or that the other partner has been guilty of 'exceptional depravity'. No hard and fast rules can be laid down as to what is 'exceptional hardship' or 'exceptional depravity', but examples can be given. It was held to be 'exceptional hardship' where a wife lost her job because she had got married, and was then promptly deserted by her husband two weeks after the ceremony. The husband then committed adultery. It was proved that if the wife were divorced she would be able to get her job back—and the Court therefore allowed her to start proceedings at once, without waiting for three years. It was held to be 'exceptional depravity' where a husband was convicted of a crime and sent to prison within three weeks of marriage. The mere fact that a husband or wife commits adultery very soon after marriage is not, however, generally to be regarded as 'exceptional depravity', unless the adultery is with a wife's sister or husband's brother, or a domestic servant of the household or is quite promiscuous and continuous.

Procedure in divorce cases

A divorce case is started by a petition, in which the petitioner sets out the basic history of the marriage and the grounds which he has for asking for a divorce.

Here is an example of a divorce petition:

IN THE HIGH COURT OF JUSTICE
PROBATE DIVORCE AND ADMIRALTY DIVISION (DIVORCE)
WESTCHESTER DISTRICT REGISTRY
TO THE HIGH COURT OF JUSTICE

The 1*st day of June* 1961

THE PETITION 0f GEORGE SMITH SHEWETH:

1. That on the 12th day of November 1954, the Petitioner was lawfully married to Mary Smith who was then Mary White, spinster (hereinafter called 'the Respondent'), at St. Anselm's Church, Barchester in the County of Barset.
2. That after the said marriage the Petitioner and the Respondent lived and cohabited principally at 12 High Street, Barchester in the said County and finally at 'White Oaks', Plumstead in the said County.

3. That there are two children of the family now living namely Alfred Smith who was born on the 1st day of April 1958, and Winifred Smith who was born on the 2nd day of March 1960.

4. That the said children are living with the Petitioner at 'White Oaks', Plumstead aforesaid and are to be educated at local schools and are being cared for by the Petitioner's mother and maintained out of the Petitioner's earnings. The Petitioner proposes that the said arrangements shall continue.

5. That the Petitioner, who is a Clerk, is now living at 'White Oaks', Plumstead: that the Respondent is now living at 74 Station Road, Puddleby in the County of Wessex; and that both the Petitioner and the Respondent are domiciled in England.

6. That there have been no previous proceedings in the High Court, or in any County Court, or Court of Summary Jurisdiction with reference to the said marriage or to any of the said children of the family.

7. That the Respondent has frequently committed adultery with James Black (hereinafter called 'the Co-Respondent').

8. That from about the 3rd day of January 1961 to the date hereof the Respondent has lived and cohabited and habitually committed adultery with the Co-Respondent at 74 Station Road, Puddleby aforesaid.

9. That the Petitioner has not in any way been accessory to or connived at or condoned the said adultery.

10. That this Petition is not presented or prosecuted in collusion with the Respondent or the Co-Respondent.

WHEREFORE THE PETITIONER PRAYS that the Court will decree:
(1) that his said marriage be dissolved;
(2) that he may be granted the custody of the said children of the family;
(3) that the Co-Respondent be condemned in the sum of £500 in respect of the adultery by him committed;
(4) that the Co-Respondent be condemned in the costs of these proceedings;
(5) that he may have such further and other relief as may be just.

The Petition is served on the respondent, as the other party is now called, and on any person named as having committed adultery—in the example given, on Mr Black. If the address of the respondent is unknown—if he has vanished—the Court may allow the Petition to be advertised in a newspaper, which is known as 'substituted' as opposed to personal service. With the Petition there is also served a document which gives the respondent instructions as to the action he must take. He may wish to defend the case, in which case there is a document called a 'Memorandum of Appearance' to be filled in, and in due course an Answer to the Petition to be filed. If the respondent does not wish to defend he may nevertheless wish to be heard on such questions as custody of the children, costs, and maintenance. If so, he must say so on the form served with the Petition.

If the respondent wishes to defend the case, he may also wish to file a 'Cross-Petition', i.e. to ask for a divorce on his own account. In the example above, for instance, Mrs Smith may wish to deny adultery, and claim that Mr Smith has treated her with cruelty, entitling her to a divorce. If so, she will say so in the Answer. Let us assume, however, that she does not wish to defend, or to be heard at all: she is simply willing for her husband's case to go through as quickly as possible. All she does, then, is to sign the 'Acknowledgement of Service' that comes with the Petition. In due course the case will come up for hearing as an undefended one. It may be dealt with in London or at one of the large towns in the country where divorce cases are heard. Mr Smith will be represented by a barrister (the services of a barrister are required in all divorce cases) and the case is likely to last only some ten minutes or so. It does not follow, however, that because it is undefended, Mr Smith is certain to succeed and to get his divorce. Even in an undefended case the Judge must be satisfied that one of the recognized grounds for a divorce exists, and Mrs Smith's adultery will have to be strictly and properly proved.

The Answer which will be filed if the case is to be defended is a document similar to a Petition, but setting out the respondent's allegations. The petitioner may counter this with a Reply—and finally the case will be fought out in Court.

If the facts warrant it, both parties may be granted decrees, but it is also possible that the Judge may not be satisfied that either has proved what is required, in which case there will be a stalemate, with neither side getting a divorce.

If the Judge does decide to grant a divorce, he pronounces what is called a 'decree nisi'. This is a provisional decree which says that the marriage is to be dissolved *unless* sufficient cause is shown why the decree should not be made absolute. ('Nisi' is the Latin word for unless.) The parties are not free to marry again until the decree is made absolute. The petitioner applies for this by her solicitor after three months. It is generally granted as a matter of form: no further court hearing is required.

Expediting decrees. In some cases the interval between decree nisi and decree absolute may be shortened, and the final decree 'expedited'. This is sometimes allowed where, for instance, a wife in whose favour discretion has been exercised is expecting a baby, and wishes to be free to marry again so that it may be born in wedlock.

Arrangements for children. In all Petitions, full particulars of the arrangements proposed for the children have to be stated (see Mr Smith's Petition above). Unless the Court is satisfied with the arrangements for the children, or that it is impracticable for the parties to make such arrangements, it may decline to grant a decree absolute.

'*Ancillary Relief.*' The most usual forms of 'ancillary relief' (orders, that is, which the Divorce Court can make in addition to the decree of divorce) are: (1) Alimony pending suit; (2) Permanent maintenance; (3) Custody of children.

(1) *Alimony pending suit.* Alimony pending suit is an allowance ordered to be paid by the husband to the wife between the petition and the hearing. Where there is a dispute the amount to be paid is usually decided by one of the Registrars of the Divorce Court, an official who supervises all the preliminary parts of the proceedings. The object of such alimony is to maintain the wife until the case is heard. The alimony continues to be payable until the date when the decree is made absolute. Such alimony is payable pending the hearing of suits for divorce, nullity, judicial separation, or the restitution of conjugal rights. In many divorce cases, of course, the wife is already in possession of an Order made

by the Magistrates' Court, and she cannot obtain alimony in the High Court while this is still in force. She can, however, apply to the Magistrates' Court to have the maintenance order discharged, so that she is free to seek alimony in the High Court.

There are various ways in which the Court can ascertain the means of the parties so as to decide how much alimony ought to be ordered. Usually the parties have to swear affidavits showing their financial position and sometimes one or both may be ordered to attend in person and be cross-examined as to their means. The registrar also has power to order books and documents to be produced, when he wishes to discover what the true position is. How much a wife will get depends on all the circumstances of the case, and there is no hard and fast rule. As a rough guide, the wife will usually be awarded enough to

". . . cross-examined as to their means . . ."

bring her income up to one-fifth of the joint incomes of the couple. For instance, if Mr Grey is earning £2,300 a year and his wife has a part-time job giving her an income of £200 a year the joint income is £2,500. One-fifth of this is £500, so Mrs Grey might be awarded £300 a year as alimony pending suit. She may also get an allowance for the children. The Court will usually take an average of Mr Grey's earnings when considering what he is to pay, so as to allow for fluctuations.

(2) *Maintenance*. Permanent maintenance may be awarded after a decree of divorce, nullity, or judicial separation has been pronounced. Here again, if the sum is not agreed between a husband and wife the Court will generally decide it after a hearing before a Registrar. Here, too, there is no fixed rule as to the amount which is granted, but, again, as a guide, the wife may be awarded a sum equal to one-third of the joint income, less the wife's income. So, for instance, if Mrs Black is earning £600 a year and her husband £3,000 a year the joint income is £3,600. One-third of this is £1,200. But from this must be deducted Mrs Black's own income of £600. She might therefore be awarded a sum of £600 as maintenance. In assessing what is to be ordered the Court has to consider the wife's income (if any), the ability of the husband to pay, and the conduct of the parties. A 'guilty wife' who has lost her case is allowed to apply for maintenance, but she is unlikely to be awarded anything very substantial—usually

all she will get is a small 'compassionate allowance'. On the other hand, there are cases where, although the wife is held guilty, her husband is not blameless either. He may, for instance, be asking the Court to exercise discretion in respect of his own adultery. In such a case the wife can expect to fare rather better in regard to maintenance.

The earning capacity of a wife is obviously an important factor. Mrs Brown who is an able business woman with a good income can expect to receive less by way of maintenance in her divorce proceedings than Mrs White, who is a housewife and mother, and has never developed any business ability. A wife who has never worked and who is getting on in years will seldom be required to take a job simply in order to reduce the maintenance which her husband could otherwise be ordered to pay.

"If Mr White has a fortunate win his wife can apply for an increased sum. . . ."

The taxation of maintenance often provides difficult problems. There are two sorts of order that can be made: those 'less tax' and those 'free of tax'. Where £40 a month less tax is ordered it means that £40 must be paid in full. Where £40 free of tax is ordered the meaning is that such a sum is to be paid as will, *after deduction of tax*, at the standard rate leave the sum named in the Order; in other words, more than £40.

Some of the complications in regard to tax have been removed by an Act which allows for small maintenance payments to be made in full without any deduction of tax. The husband pays the full amount. It is deducted from his income for tax purposes and the wife pays tax as a single woman.

Maintenance orders may be varied at any time on application by the parties. Before making a variation the Court will look into all the circumstances of the case including any increase or decrease in the parties' means. For instance, when Mr and Mrs White are divorced on the ground of Mrs White's adultery, Mr White if earning a good salary, may be ordered to pay his wife a sizeable sum as maintenance. If Mrs White finds a new husband to support her, Mr White's obligation to pay may be reduced or extinguished altogether. Mr White, of course, will have to apply to the Court for such a reduction if he wants

195

it to be made. In the same way if, for instance, Mr White has a fortunate win on the Pools and becomes much wealthier than before, his wife can apply for an increased sum by reason of this change of circumstance.

A maintenance order is not always an order to pay so much a week or so much a month. If the husband has property such as land, or houses, or stocks and shares the Court may order that some of that capital shall be settled, *i.e.* put in trust for the wife's benefit for her life. One great advantage is that whereas the other kind of order ceases on the husband's death, property settled in trust for the wife in this way brings her an income so long as she lives. However, such an order obviously cannot be made unless the husband has some fairly substantial means.

A wife who is rich in her own right may be ordered to make a settlement of this kind on her husband if she is the guilty party or if she has petitioned for divorce on the grounds of her husband's insanity.

Private maintenance agreements. The Courts have also a comparatively new power to review and revise *private* maintenance agreements made between husband and wife. The power was created in August 1957 by the Maintenance Agreements Act and it covers not only agreements made subsequently but also all those already in existence, whenever they were made.

Many of these agreements made some years ago are grossly unfair in the light of changed circumstances: the husband may have prospered greatly or he may have lost work and fallen on hard times. Yet the agreement could not be altered unless the parties agreed—and they were seldom likely to.

Since the Act, either husband or wife can apply to the Court and ask for a revision, and the Court will fix what is fair.

Sometimes these agreements contain a clause under which the parties agree that they will never apply to the Court for an order for Maintenance. The Act provides that any such clause is to be null and void.

(3) *Custody of children.* When a decree of divorce or judicial separation is pronounced, the Court has power to make an order for the custody of the children. Usually such orders are only made in respect of children under the age of sixteen: after that age the child is regarded as being able to care for himself. The paramount consideration in all such cases is the welfare of the child. It used to be the Court's view that if a wife was found guilty of adultery she would forfeit all right to the custody of or access to her children. But this harsh rule has now been abolished, and the Court does not use custody orders as a means of punishing the guilty party by taking away the children. Nevertheless the guilt or innocence of the parents has some effect on custody, because the wishes of an innocent parent will be given strong weight where the balance of advantage is equal from the child's point of view. Young children of either sex will, however, generally be allowed to stay with their mother even if the latter is the 'guilty' party.

Where a parent is awarded custody of a child it does not necessarily follow that the child resides with the parent. Custody may, for example, be awarded to the father while the mother is given 'care and control'. The father will then have a decisive voice in the upbringing of his son or daughter, but the child will live with the mother. Orders are also made as to the 'access' which parents are to have to their children. Such orders may provide for the parents concerned to visit the child at stated times, or for 'staying access' when the child goes to stay with the parent. Like maintenance orders, custody and access orders are by no means unchangeable. The Court will vary them where a change of circumstances seems to require it. Over-frequent changes are, however, frowned upon, since it is not considered that it is in a child's interest that he or she shall be 'bandied about' between the parents.

Orders for the children's maintenance can be and frequently are made in the same way as orders for the maintenance of a wife. The Court has power to make such orders for children up to the age of twenty-one, but orders in respect of those over sixteen are comparatively rare.

Persons other than the parents are allowed to apply to the Court for the custody of children. For instance, custody is sometimes granted to grandparents where neither the father nor the mother is in a position to provide a proper home for the child. It is unusual, however, to grant custody to a third party where either parent is available and is able and willing to have the custody.

The Queen's Proctor

It is the duty of this official to intervene in a divorce case if there is some reason why the decree should not be granted. For instance, a petitioner may have failed to disclose his own adultery to the Court. If the Queen's Proctor has reason to suspect this, he will step in, and the case will come before the Court again. (An anonymous letter often puts the Queen's Proctor on the alert.) If it is established that the adultery was not disclosed the decree nisi may be rescinded. The Court may also call in the assistance of the Queen's Proctor if any suspicious circumstances arise during the hearing which suggest, for instance, that the parties have been guilty of collusion.

Domicil

In the specimen divorce petition printed above it will be seen that both the parties are stated to be 'domiciled in England'. It is a rule that domicil must always be stated in such petitions, its importance being that the law will generally only grant a decree of divorce to those domiciled in this country (that is, in England and Wales) at the time when the proceedings are started.

What does a domicil mean? A person is said to be domiciled where he has his permanent home. Everyone has some domicil, but nobody can have more than one at any given time. The law regards each individual as having from birth a 'domicil of origin'. Thus a person born in Edinburgh has a Scottish domicil of origin and one born in London or in Cardiff has an English domicil of origin (England for this purpose includes Wales). This original domicil may be lost and a new domicil, called a 'domicil of choice', acquired if the person concerned resides in a different country with the intention of continuing to reside there for an indefinite time and with no intention of going back to live in the country of origin. When this happens, the old domicil of origin is lost and remains in abeyance until the individual in question abandons his new domicil. Then, unless he acquires a fresh domicil of choice, the domicil of origin comes into operation once again. Domicil, it should be noted, is different from nationality. A person of British nationality may well be domiciled in the U.S.A., France, and vice versa.

How the law of domicil works in practice can be best illustrated by an example. Mr North was born and lives in Bristol. He marries a Bristol girl. They both have an English domicil. Then Mr North is made sales manager for his firm in Scotland, and goes to live in Dundee. After a few years he decides that he will settle in Scotland permanently and live there when he retires. He sells his house in Bristol, buys one in Dundee, and lets it be widely known that he has decided to make a permanent home in Scotland. He now acquires a Scottish domicil of choice. Next, Mr North leaves his wife and commits adultery with Miss East. Mrs North cannot bring divorce proceedings in the English Courts, because neither she nor her husband are domiciled in England. A wife's domicil follows that of her husband, and so both the Norths are now domiciled in Scotland, and it is to the courts of that country that Mrs North must go for her divorce.

To take another example—Miss South marries M. Ouest, a Frenchman. Thus she loses her English domicil and acquires a French one. They go to live in France. Unless M. Ouest later chooses to come and live permanently in England, thereby taking an English domicil for his wife and himself, Mme Ouest would generally be precluded from suing for divorce in the English Courts. She would not be allowed, for instance, to complain in the English Courts of adultery committed by her husband—either in France or England.

There are, however, certain exceptions, in favour of a wife only, to the general rule that both parties must be domiciled in England before divorce proceedings can be brought. One is that a wife who lives in England, and has been 'ordinarily resident' there for a period of three years immediately before the commencement of the proceedings, can sue for a divorce so long as the husband is not domiciled in any other part of the United Kingdom or the Isle of Man. This exception would enable Mme Ouest in our second example to bring divorce proceedings if, for instance, she had left M. Ouest in France and come to live in England for three years before starting her case. Her domicil in such a case would still be France, since even if a woman with a foreign-domiciled husband is living in England and intends for her own part to do so permanently, she is still not regarded as being domiciled here. However, despite her foreign domicil, Mme Ouest would, under this special rule, be enabled to start a divorce case in England.

Another exception occurs where a husband has deserted his wife, or been deported from the United Kingdom, and was immediately before such desertion or deportation domiciled in England. We can illustrate this by the case of Mrs South. She is deserted by her husband, who leaves her and goes to Australia where he acquires a fresh domicil. Immediately before leaving her he had an English domicil: that is to say, he had been born and bred in England, and not lost this domicil of origin. Mrs South can sue for a divorce in England. She will not in this case have to show that she has been 'ordinarily resident' in England for the last three years. But this exception only applies when the husband has deserted his wife or been deported. It does not help a wife in a case when, for instance, her foreign-domiciled husband has been guilty of adultery.

The English Courts do not recognize as valid all divorces pronounced by the Courts of foreign countries. British subjects who obtain divorces abroad and subsequently re-marry have been convicted of bigamy when the foreign divorce has been one that our Courts do not recognize. The general rule is that our Courts do not regard a divorce abroad as valid unless the parties are both domiciled in the foreign country concerned at the time when proceedings are started, or unless the country of their domicil would recognize the divorce. A British husband who goes to Mexico *meaning to settle there for good* may thus obtain a Mexican divorce which will be valid in England. Our Courts would regard him as having acquired a Mexican domicil, and his wife (even though she

"A British husband who goes to Mexico . . ."

was resident in England) would also be so regarded, on the principle that a wife's domicil follows her husband's. But if a British husband obtains a Mexican divorce on a mere flying visit to that country—and thus while he still has his English domicil—the divorce will not be valid in England and according to our law he will still be married.

Recently, however, our Courts have begun to recognize some foreign divorces, even when they were granted when the parties were not both domiciled in the foreign country, *if the circumstances are such that in a similar case the English Court would grant a divorce.* For example, our Courts as we have seen will grant a wife a decree when she has been 'ordinarily resident' in England for the three years prior to the proceedings, even if she is not domiciled here. In the same way a wife who is 'ordinarily resident' in, say, Switzerland (even though not domiciled there) may be able to obtain a divorce in the Swiss Courts which would be recognized in England. The English Courts have only relaxed their strict rule in favour of wives, and they will still not recognize a foreign divorce which has been obtained by a husband in a country where he was not domiciled or which would not be recognized by the country of his domicil. The principle of this new extension is that our Courts consider that they should not refuse to recognize the power of foreign Courts to dissolve marriages when they claim a similar power for themselves.

Costs

When a wife wins a divorce case her husband usually has to pay the costs: that is to say, he is ordered to pay her legal expenses, as well as having to meet his own. A wife who loses is not usually ordered to pay her husband's costs, since generally speaking she has little means to do so—but costs *can* be ordered against her. When adultery is proved against a co-respondent the latter is usually ordered to pay the husband's costs, at any rate if it can be shown that he committed adultery with the wife knowing that she was a married woman. He may be able to escape an order for costs if he was under the impression that she was single at the time of the adultery.

A husband who is being sued for divorce may be ordered to give 'security' for his wife's costs. This means that he is ordered to put down a sum of money to help in meeting the costs of her suit. This rule is based on the old idea that a wife had no money of her own, and that if she was to bring legal proceedings she would have to obtain the money to do so from her husband. The law used to regard the provision of such money as one of a husband's legal duties, for unless he paid it the wife could not obtain justice. Nowadays orders for security are less common, one reason, for instance, being that wives with little money or none can now obtain Legal Aid.

Enforcing orders in the High Court

There are a number of ways in which the Court can make sure that its orders are obeyed. Parties in divorce cases who obtain orders for custody, maintenance, etc., should always seek advice as soon as possible when such orders are not complied with, as it is advisable to get the machinery of the law in motion with a minimum of delay. One common method is the Judgment Summons, whereby a debtor (for instance a husband who has failed to pay his wife the maintenance which has been ordered) can be brought before the Court, and examined as to his means. The final object of this procedure is to obtain an order committing him to prison for a period which is not to exceed six weeks. The operation of such an order is often suspended so long as the debtor pays the debt and costs by specified instalments. The Judgment Summons can be obtained in the Divorce Court or in the local County Court, and the latter is often a convenient place to issue it, since less travelling and expense is involved for the applicant.

High Court maintenance orders can now be registered in the Magistrates' Court and enforced by that Court: this procedure is dealt with later under the section dealing with magistrates' courts. The procedure for 'attaching' the earnings of a debtor, *i.e.* stopping the maintenance payments out of the husband's

THE FAMILY

pay, which is available in the High Court and the Magistrates' Court, is also dealt with in that section.

The Court has powers to restrain one party in a divorce case from molesting another pending the hearing. A wife, for example, who has been driven from home by her husband's cruelty may be pestered by him to return before the petition has come up for trial. If she were induced to go back her case might well be prejudiced. In such a case the Court will step in to prevent the husband's 'molestation' and if he persists in it thereafter he may be committed to prison for contempt of Court.

NULLITY OF MARRIAGE

A decree of divorce has the effect of dissolving a marriage—untying the knot binding the parties together. The effect of a decree of nullity is to pronounce that what seems to be a genuine marriage is in fact null and void.

Nullity suits may be brought in respect of two different sorts of marriage. One type of marriage is automatically void, and strictly speaking no legal proceedings are required to establish this. However, the parties concerned are often not agreed about the nullity of such a marriage, and a law case is then necessary to decide the point. An example of such an 'automatically void' marriage is one that is celebrated between parties under age. In England both parties must be sixteen at least. Another type of marriage which is automatically void is when one of the parties is mentally incapable of understanding the marriage contract. Another is when the marriage is bigamous; another, when the parties are within the prohibited degrees of relationship.

More frequently met with are 'voidable' marriages, i.e. those which are valid until their invalidity is pronounced by a competent Court. There are five grounds on which a marriage may be voidable. They are:

1. Impotence of the respondent.
2. Wilful refusal to consummate the marriage.
3. The fact that either party was at the time of marriage of unsound mind, or a mental defective, or subject to recurrent fits of insanity or epilepsy.
4. The fact that the respondent was at the time of the marriage suffering from communicable venereal disease.
5. The fact that the wife was at the time of the marriage pregnant by some person other than the petitioner.

These grounds need to be considered separately.

(1) *Impotence* means the inability by a man or woman to effect or permit the consummation of the marriage. The impotence may be due to physical or psychological causes. A man or woman who has a 'hysterical' or morbid repugnance to sexual intercourse is, legally speaking, impotent. Impotence may be general, or confined to a particular person. A husband, for instance, may be unable to have sexual intercourse with his wife although quite capable of having it with other women. He is 'impotent' in this sense. In the same way a wife may for various reasons be frigid toward her husband, although fully

201

capable of intercourse with other men. She, too, is legally 'impotent'. Sterility is not the same as impotence, and a husband who is incapable of begetting a child upon his wife will not be regarded as impotent so long as he is capable of having sexual intercourse with her. Medical evidence is, of course, usually required in cases where impotence is alleged.

(2) *Wilful refusal.* To establish this ground it must be shown that the marriage has not been consummated, and that this is due to the refusal of the party concerned. A husband or a wife is not regarded as having refused unless consummation has been proposed with reasonable 'tact, persuasion, or encouragement'. It may count as refusal if a wife or husband declines to seek medical advice where consummation has not been effected. Consummation does not necessarily mean an act of sexual intercourse from which the birth of a child may result. This was decided as a result of two well-known recent cases. In the first a young couple were living in Persia, and felt that they did not want a child to be born until they were home in England. They therefore used contraceptives. When they returned to England on leave the wife asked her husband to give up using contraceptives, so that she could have a child. He refused. When they then returned to Persia the wife considered that it would now be safe to have a child. Her husband still refused. Finally the wife returned to England and from there wrote to her husband asking him to have a 'normal married life'. He did nothing, nor did he accede to her requests when they were reunited in Persia. Finally she started nullity proceedings. It was held that she was entitled to a decree, as there had not been complete sexual intercourse between them by reason of her husband's wilful refusal to give up using contraceptives. This decision was, however, reversed a few years later by the House of Lords in another case where intercourse had been refused except with contraceptives. It was held that such intercourse, even though no children could result from it, counted as consummation of the marriage and that therefore it precluded the granting of a decree of nullity.

(3) *Unsoundness of mind.* We have seen that a marriage may be automatically void if one of the people concerned is mentally incapable of understanding the nature of the contract. But even where this cannot be established a marriage may be voidable if one of the parties was at the time of unsound mind, or a mental defective, or subject to fits of epilepsy or insanity. There is a qualification here, however. No decree will be granted on this ground unless the Court is satisfied

(a) that at the time of the marriage the husband or wife seeking a decree was ignorant of the insanity or epilepsy;
(b) that proceedings were started within a year of the marriage;
(c) that marital intercourse with the consent of the petitioner has not taken place since the discovery by the petitioner of grounds for a decree.

In other words, if a husband or wife knowingly takes a partner who is subject to this type of disability he or she cannot afterwards seek to have the marriage declared void. In the same way he or she must act to end the marriage within its first year. If the case is not begun within this period it will be too late. If the discovery of the disability is not made until after the year has passed no decree will be obtainable. The husband or wife who has marital intercourse after finding out about the other party's disability is regarded as having chosen to continue the marriage, and therefore not to be free to bring it to an end.

(4) *Venereal disease.* A marriage can also only be declared void on this ground where the conditions (a), (b), (c), above are satisfied.

(5) *Pregnancy by another person.* The same conditions apply here. It is sometimes very hard to decide just when a husband discovered the ground that he had for a decree. In one case a young serviceman's wife had a baby seven months after marriage. The husband believed it to be his, but he was then shown an anonymous letter which suggested that his wife was two months' pregnant at the time of her marriage. He consulted the doctor who had been in charge of the pre-natal clinic, to be told that the baby seemed to be a full-time one. The midwife confirmed this suggestion, but the husband had intercourse with his wife before tackling her upon the subject. Later she confessed that the baby was another man's, and he at once brought nullity proceedings. The Court held that although he had not been positively *convinced* of his wife's pre-marriage pregnancy at the time when they had intercourse he had nevertheless virtually 'discovered' it, and that therefore he was not entitled to a decree of nullity.

Nullity and children. When a decree of nullity is granted in respect of a 'voidable' marriage any child of the parties born during the marriage is deemed to be legitimate. Although, therefore, the effect of a decree of nullity is to 'wipe out' the marriage as if it had never taken place, it does not bastardize the children.

If, however, the so-called marriage was one of those which is automatically void from the beginning (as described above) any children are necessarily illegitimate.

PRESUMPTION OF DEATH

Any married person who believes that the other party to the marriage is dead, *e.g.* when he or she has disappeared for many years without word or trace, may petition the Court to have it 'presumed' that the death has occurred, and to dissolve the marriage. The Court then may make an order saying that the death is to be presumed and that the marriage is dissolved. The death of the husband or wife, of course, brings the marriage to an end, but the difficulty often is to prove that the death has taken place. Suppose that Mr and Mrs White part—by agreement—and Mrs White does not see Mr White for ten years. Then she wants to marry again. She does her best to make contact with her husband, writing to his last known address and to all his relatives. There is no result. Mrs White feels sure that Mr White is dead but she cannot prove it. What is she to do? The answer is that she can petition the Court to have the death presumed. The fact that Mr White has been absent for seven years and that nothing has happened to give Mrs White reason to believe that he is still alive will be a great help to her in her case, because it constitutes evidence of death unless the contrary is proved. Mrs White, however, will probably not get her decree unless she can prove to the Court that she has made all reasonable inquiries. These inquiries do not only mean writing to relatives and to the last known address: they mean putting advertisements in newspapers where it is reasonable to suppose that Mr White may see them. Of course, if Mr White does see them, and communicates with his wife, her hope of having him presumed dead will be gone. But unless efforts of this sort are made it will usually be very hard to persuade the Court to dissolve the marriage.

If a decree nisi is made on this ground and the respondent appears before decree absolute the decree will be rescinded. If he or she reappears only after decree absolute the decree stands, and the marriage is dissolved for good. A husband, however, may not be entirely finished with his wife after such a decree. If after she has been presumed dead she appears on the scene and asks for maintenance he may be compelled to maintain her. She is in one sense legally dead: but not so dead that she will not need a regular sum of money for her subsistence. After a very long absence by a wife, however, the Court would be

"... she can petition the Court to have death presumed ..."

slow to order any substantial sum to be paid by the husband. It should be noted that even when the husband or wife has been absent for seven years or more the Court is not *bound* to make a decree presuming death. This is another 'discretionary' ground: and the Court will only make the order if it sees fit to do so.

JUDICIAL SEPARATION

A decree of judicial separation can be made on the same grounds as a decree of divorce, *i.e.* Adultery; Cruelty; Desertion; Incurable insanity; (On a wife's Petition) Rape, sodomy, and bestiality.

The effect of a decree of judicial separation is that the parties are still married.

but do not any longer have to live together. Since they cannot nowadays be compelled to do so in any case, the decree is not of great practical use, and is seldom met with today. Mostly such decrees are obtained by people who feel a conscientious objection to divorce. A decree of judicial separation, unlike a decree of divorce, can be obtained within three years of the marriage. The arrangements for obtaining maintenance after such a decree are the same as those after a decree of divorce. Just as in a divorce case, the Judge will not

"If after she has been presumed dead she appears on the scene . . ."

pronounce a decree of judicial separation unless he is satisfied about the arrangements for the children under sixteen, or is ready to accept an undertaking from the parties that such arrangements will be brought before the Court within a specified time.

RESTITUTION OF CONJUGAL RIGHTS

Another type of order which the Divorce Court has power to make is that for the restitution of conjugal rights. This means an order by the Court that a husband or wife shall return home and 'render conjugal rights' to the other party. This decree, also, is seldom met with today, because even if it is not complied with there is little which the injured party can do. At one time a husband or wife who failed to obey such an order could be committed to prison, or seized by the other party and forcibly compelled to live at home. Today the only practical result of a failure to obey such an order is that the disobedient party is at law a deserter. But there is no need nowadays to obtain an order for restitution in order to establish desertion, and the procedure is therefore becoming obsolete.

DEEDS OF SEPARATION

It is nowadays possible for parties who do not wish to live together to enter into separation agreements, providing, for instance, that the husband will pay his wife a stipulated sum of money at regular intervals. In the past this was not so, and the Courts used to look on such agreements with a great deal of suspicion, since it was considered that it was against public policy for husbands and wives to agree to live apart. Today this attitude has disappeared and separation agreements can be enforced in the Courts just like any ordinary contract. Such agreements need not, strictly speaking, even be in writing but it is much better that they should be, as this prevents disputes about what the parties have actually agreed. The best course for a husband and wife who are contemplating

"Separation agreements provide for the parties to live apart."

making such an agreement is to consult a solicitor and have the document drawn up by him. Preferably each party should have his or her own solicitor although one can act for both. It is usual for the agreement to be drawn up as a deed, that is, a document under seal. There is a distinction which is not always clearly understood, between 'maintenance agreements' and 'separation agreements'. The former deal only with the financial support which the wife is to receive, while the latter provide for the parties to live apart.

Although separation agreements are now recognized by the Courts it is still not felt to be desirable that the parties should be able to 'oust' the jurisdiction of the Courts by agreeing not to apply to the Court for a sum beyond that laid down in the agreement. Suppose, for instance, Mr and Mrs Green decide to enter into a separation deed. Mr Green agrees to pay Mrs Green £8 a week. He would like that to be the maximum for which he can ever be liable, and he does not want Mrs Green to be able, once they have signed and sealed the deed, to go along to the Court and ask for more. So he inserts a clause in the deed saying that Mrs Green is not to take proceedings for maintenance beyond the provisions made in the deed. Under the Maintenance Agreements Act, 1957, such a provision is void and has no legal effect. Mrs Green can therefore apply to the Court for a larger allowance whenever she wishes, but the Court will not be very ready to make an order granting her, say, £10 a week when she has agreed to £8 only a short while before, unless for instance, her husband's income has substantially increased.

Where it is desired to alter a separation agreement an application can be made to the High Court or the Magistrates' Court for an order making the variation. Alternatively, of course, the parties can make the alterations for themselves, if they are agreed upon what is to be done. But all too often no such agreement can be reached, and it is then that an application has to be made. Let us take another of our imaginary couples—Mr and Mrs Gray, who have entered into a separation agreement by which they agree to live apart. Mr Gray undertakes to pay his wife £800 a year. This agreement is on the basis that Mr Gray is earning a salary of some £2,400 a year. But after three years Mr Gray's income greatly increases: he takes a new job with a new firm and is now making over £4,000 a year. Mrs Gray feels that she should now have more than her original £800, but Mr Gray declines to pay up. He says she must abide by the agreement. It is now open to Mrs Gray to apply to the Court. She will have to establish that there has been a change in the circumstances in the light of which the financial agreements were included in the separation agreement, and that as a result of the change the arrangements ought to be revoked. Her task should not be hard: Mr Gray's increase in salary is certainly a big change in the circumstances. So the Court will probably order her an increase in maintenance. Even if she were unable to show any change in circumstances she might be able to get the sum increased if she could satisfy the Court that the agreement did not contain proper financial arrangements for any child of the marriage. If, therefore, a couple omit in this agreement to provide for the children it is open to either of them to go to Court to have this rectified.

Which Court may they go to? This depends on the amount which is to be ordered. The Magistrates' Court cannot insert into an agreement any provision whereby the amount to be paid exceeds £7 10s a week for husband or wife or 50s for a child. Nor can the Magistrates' Court increase any provision beyond these limits. The High Court's powers are unlimited. It is therefore to the High Court that Mrs Gray would have to go in the example given above. When an order altering the financial arrangements in the deed has been made the deed takes effect with the alteration. Mr and Mrs Gray, therefore, will not have to make any further agreement: the old one will continue, with altered provisions about money. It will, however, not necessarily continue for ever, for either party is free to come to the Court again and ask for a further alteration if it appears that there are grounds for doing so. The Court, however, naturally discourages too frequent applications.

WILFUL NEGLECT TO MAINTAIN— HIGH COURT

The High Court now has power to order a husband to pay maintenance to his wife when he has been guilty of a wilful failure to do so. There is no need to prove that any 'matrimonial offence' has been committed: all that has to be shown is that the husband in question has not maintained his wife and children as he ought to have done.

A wife who wants to obtain such an order can apply on the same ground in the Magistrates' Court (see below), but there the maximum sum that can be ordered is £7 10s a week and 50s for a child. In the High Court the amount is unlimited. A wife who thinks that her husband can pay more than these sums is therefore free to apply to the High Court. Usually the solicitors acting for her will make inquiries beforehand to see what income and liabilities the husband actually has. If they fail to do this they may find that the application is made in vain, since the husband may be held to have no means of paying his wife maintenance at the rate desired. When an application fails on these grounds the wife may be ordered to pay the costs, since she could have started her case in the Magistrates' Court, and thus saved a great deal of expense.

It is a defence to such an application for wilful neglect to maintain that the wife has committed adultery, and a case of this kind sometimes results in a lengthy trial of the issue as to whether such adultery has occurred. Applications are heard in open court before a Judge, who may adjourn the case to enable a Registrar to inquire in detail into the means of the parties so that he may know what sum ought to be ordered. Where a Court makes a maintenance order under this procedure it may also make an order for the custody of the children.

DISPUTES OVER PROPERTY

When a marriage breaks down, or seems about to do so, there are very frequently disputes about property. When a husband and wife are living together happily they often do not give much attention to the question of 'whose is what'—they regard all their belongings as shared. But when they come to part, acute disagreements often arise about the furniture and the household equipment which they have accumulated. When a dispute of this kind arises between husband and wife a convenient means for settling it is provided by the Married Women's Property Act, 1882, which enables a Court in such cases to make any order as to the ownership or possession of any property which it thinks right. For instance, it can order that the husband is to keep the dining-room chairs and the wife is to have the curtains, and so on. By an Act passed in 1958 the Court now has power not only to deal with actual property, but with money that may have been raised by selling property. Thus if Mrs Smith sells the sideboard which the husband bought, Mr Smith may be able to get back from her the £50 which she has got for it, and which is now in her bank account. The Court may even make an order in respect of property which has been bought with the proceeds of such a sale. Suppose that Mr Smith sells the beds and bedding for £100, and with the money buys a carpet. If the Court thinks it proper to do so it may order him to hand the carpet over to his wife. The Court can also order that the property shall be sold and the proceeds of the sale divided as seems just. The Court has no power to transfer the ownership of property from one party to another. But it can say who is to have the *possession* of the article concerned, and it can also decide where the ownership lies.

Many articles, of course, are owned by the husband and wife in common. In such a case the Court's order may be that they are to be sold and the proceeds divided, or that one party or the other is to retain them for the time being. Goods bought by the husband out of his own earnings are regarded as his, while those bought by a wife out of her wages are hers. Articles bought by a wife out of money saved from her housekeeping allowance are regarded as the husband's. In one case, for example, money saved from the housekeeping was regularly spent by a husband and wife on the football pools. Eventually they had a sizeable win and decided to spend the money on buying furniture for the home. Later the marriage broke up and it was held that the furniture belonged to the husband. He had provided the stake money out of the housekeeping allowance which he gave to his wife, and the proceeds were therefore his.

". . . if Mrs Smith sells the sideboard Mr Smith may be able to get back the money she got for it . . ."

The ownership of the wedding presents is frequently a source of dispute. When friends and relatives give presents to the young couple they often think of them as going to both. Some presents of course are by their nature intended for one party or the other: a set of kitchen implements being (usually) for the wife and a set of tools being (usually) for a husband. In many other cases the giver's intention is hard to discover. In cases of doubt a gift from one of the wife's friends is presumed to be for the wife, and a gift from one of the husband's friends is regarded as the husband's. But even here the gift will be regarded as belonging to them jointly if the facts seem to warrant it.

Probably it is the ownership of the house where the couple have lived that gives rise to most difficulties. It is quite common for a husband to buy a house in his own name although his wife may find some of the money. Does this mean that the house will be regarded as entirely his? The law does not think so. The house was probably bought as a family asset intended as a continuous provision for both, and it therefore belongs to them jointly even though the money the wife contributed is only a very small part of the price. However, if a husband buys some chattel—a second-hand motor-car for instance—in the wife's name for her personal use the law will presume it to be a gift to the wife, and the car will be regarded as her property.

"In many cases the giver's intention is hard to discover . . ."

Although a husband owns the home in which the parties have been living it does not follow that he can turn his wife out of it when the marriage breaks down. A husband who is trying to sell the house where his wife and children are living without providing them with alternative accommodation may be stopped from doing so by a Court order. When a wife has been deserted by the husband she has a right (as against her husband) to stay on in the house: but if the house is held on mortgage (a Building Society, for instance) the mortgagee may be able to obtain possession against her if the instalments are not paid.

Proceedings under the Married Women's Property Act can be taken in the High Court or in a County Court and may be started at any time up to decree absolute. They are simple and comparatively inexpensive. In the High Court they are dealt with by a Registrar in his Chambers (or private room) and not by a Judge. If a husband or wife thinks that the other partner is likely to sell any property before the case comes to trial he or she may prevent this by obtaining an injunction. After the decree absolute has been obtained the Married

Women's Property Act procedure no longer applies, but it is still possible for a husband and wife to recover property which is in possession of the other. One means is by an application to the Court to alter a 'post-nuptial' or 'ante-nuptial' settlement. A settlement in this sense means an agreement between two parties giving property to one or the other in consideration of the marriage. It may well be unjust that such agreements shall continue in force when the marriage has come to an end by divorce. If so, they can be altered by the Court. For instance, Mr Smith may have made over a house to his wife in consideration of their marriage. Mrs Smith may then have gone off and committed adultery with another man. After obtaining his decree of divorce Mr Smith can apply to the Court to have the 'marriage settlement' changed and the house transferred to himself.

MATRIMONIAL PROCEEDINGS IN THE MAGISTRATES' COURT

By far the largest number of law cases between husbands and wives are dealt with in the Magistrates' Courts. These Courts have power to make a wide variety of orders which are sometimes loosely called 'separation orders' and sometimes 'maintenance orders'. The proper term now is 'matrimonial orders'. Generally it is the wife who applies for such an order, but as we shall see husbands may also now apply, since the law has now given them more or less equal rights with the wives.

Here are the grounds on which an application to the Court can be made by a husband or a wife:

(a) That the 'defendant' (*i.e.* the other party to the marriage) has deserted the complainant (*i.e.* the person applying to the Court).

(b) That the defendant has been guilty of persistent cruelty to the complainant, or to a child of the complainant, or to a child of his or her own who at the time of the cruelty was a 'child of the family'. A child of the family means any child of both parties, and any other child of either party who has been accepted as one of the family by the other party.

(c) (i) That the defendant has been found guilty at Quarter Sessions or Assizes of assaulting the complainant.

(ii) That the defendant has been found guilty in the Magistrates' Court of certain offences involving bodily injury against the complainant. (Where the offence is common assault it must have resulted in the imprisonment of the offender for a month or more.)

(iii) That the defendant has been found guilty of committing or attempting to commit, certain sexual offences against the children.

(d) That the defendant has committed adultery.

(e) That the defendant while knowingly suffering from venereal disease has insisted on, or without the complainant knowing of it, has permitted, sexual intercourse between them.

(f) That the defendant is an habitual drunkard or a drug addict.

(g) (This applies only to husbands)—That the defendant has wilfully neglected to provide reasonable maintenance for the wife or a dependant child.

(h) (This applies only to husbands)—That the defendant has compelled the wife to submit to prostitution, or been guilty of conduct likely to lead to that result which has resulted in the wife submitting to prostitution.

(i) (This applies only to wives)—That the defendant has wilfully neglected to provide, or to contribute properly towards, reasonable maintenance for her husband or a dependant child in a case where she might reasonably be expected to provide or contribute to such maintenance, having regard to the couple's resources and to the impairment of the husband's capacity to earn.

(a) *Desertion*. This is the same as desertion in the Divorce Court (see above). But in the Magistrates' Court an order can be obtained as soon as the desertion has occurred: there is no need to wait for three years before the application can be made. For example, if Mr Brown gets tired of married life and walks out of the home making no provision for his wife, Mrs Brown can apply to the Magistrates right away for an order. If the Court considers that Mr Brown has deserted her (*i.e.* left home without good cause) she will get her order. In three years' time, if they have not come together again, Mrs Brown will be able to sue for a divorce.

(b) *Cruelty*. Cruelty, too, means much the same in the Magistrates' Court as in the Divorce Court, except that it is necessary in the Magistrates' Court to show that it was 'persistent'. One single act of cruelty is not enough, but, for instance, a series of blows delivered over a period of a week will be regarded as 'persistent'. As will be seen, a husband or a wife can obtain an order where the cruelty has been directed not only against him or her, but also where it has been directed against a child. If Mr Gray, for instance, has ill-treated her small boy, Mrs Gray will be able to get a Court order. She can also get one when the child who is ill-treated is not in fact hers, but is a child of her husband's whom she has accepted as one of the family. An example of this would be the case where Mr Gray has a child by a former marriage who is being brought up by him and his new wife. If he is guilty of cruelty to such a child the new wife will have a ground for obtaining a Court order.

(c) *Offences against the other party or the children*. This ground largely explains itself. I t is to be noted that there must be a Court finding of guilt. An assault on a husband by a wife, or vice versa, may in itself be cruelty: where it leads to a Court case and to a conviction that conviction constitutes a separate ground for a Court order.

(d) *Adultery*. As in the Divorce Court an order in the Magistrates' Court cannot be made where there has been condonation, connivance, or conduct conducing to the adultery.

(e) *Venereal disease*. This again is self-explanatory. Insisting on intercourse does not involve physical compulsion, but it involves something more than a mere request.

(f) *Drunkenness and drug addiction*. A habitual drunkard means a person who is not mentally disordered but who by reason of habitual drinking is at times dangerous to himself or others, or incapable of managing himself or his affairs, or who behaves in such a way that it would not be reasonable to expect the other partner to the marriage to live with him.

A drug addict means a person (it can, of course, be a husband or a wife) who is not mentally disordered but who by reason of habitually taking drugs otherwise than on medical advice is at times dangerous to himself and others, or incapable of managing himself or his affairs, behaves in such a way that it would be unreasonable to expect a wife of ordinary susceptibilities to live with him.

(g) *Submitting to prostitution.* This is a ground which is rarely encountered nowadays.

(h) *Wilful neglect by a husband to maintain his wife or dependant children.* This is one of the commonest grounds, and it calls for some explanation. A husband is guilty of wilful neglect to maintain when he has means and fails to use them to carry out his duty of supporting his wife or children. If a husband is totally without means he cannot be said to be wilfully neglecting to maintain his family. A husband is also not bound to support a wife who has deserted him or who is guilty of adultery. A husband may be guilty of wilful neglect when he is providing some maintenance, but not enough: it is not necessary to prove a total failure. An order can be made not only in respect of a failure to maintain the wife, but also for a failure to maintain the children. This applies to all 'children of the family' (defined above). A husband can, therefore, be made liable for other children besides his own. For example, Mr and Mrs Green are the parents of George, a son born before the marriage. He is a 'child of the family'. Mrs Green is also the mother of Mary whose father is Mr White. Mr Green, however, has always accepted Mary as part of his household. She therefore also becomes a child of the family, and Mr Green can be made to support her. He is *not* allowed to say 'She is not my daughter and I decline to provide her with maintenance'.

(i) *Wilful neglect to maintain by a wife.* This is a totally new ground, and rather a revolutionary one. It was introduced in recognition of the fact that wives nowadays are often capable of earning, and *may* sometimes have means when their husbands have none. It is to be noted, however, that a wife can only be made liable to maintain her husband and children when:

(*i*) the husband's earning capacity is impaired by age, illness, or disability of mind or body—
and

(*ii*) it is reasonable to expect the wife to provide maintenance, having regard to the resources of the husband and wife which are or should properly be made available for the purpose. An example of a case where an order might be made on this ground is where the wife is a well-to-do business woman running a successful shop, and the husband is in hospital and unable to work at all. His earning capacity is 'impaired through illness' and since his wife has resources it would be reasonable to expect her to contribute to his maintenance. Cases where a husband will be entitled to financial support from his wife are fairly rare: but the Court is now enabled to entertain such applications.

The Court has power on a husband's or a wife's application to make a wide variety of orders, to provide for the future of the family. Here are the most important of the orders it can make:

(1) *A non-cohabitation clause.* This provides that the couple are no longer

bound to live together. Its effect is exactly the same as a decree of judicial separation in the High Court.

(2) *An order for maintenance for a wife.* The chief object of a wife in going to the Magistrates' Court is usually to obtain such an order. The *maximum* that can now be awarded is £7 10s a week. In deciding the amount to be ordered the Court has to consider carefully the means of the parties, and an order for the maximum amount is comparatively seldom made.

(3) An order for the maintenance of a husband, where the latter's earning capacity is impaired by age, illness, or disability of mind or body and it seems reasonable in all the circumstances for the Court to make such an order. Suppose Mr Black is under treatment for a nervous breakdown and unable to work. Mrs Black who has a sizeable income is then guilty of desertion, in that she leaves home without good cause. Mr Black is entitled to apply to the Court on that ground (see above) for an order, and if he can establish that his earning capacity is impaired he will be awarded maintenance. The sum awarded can be up to £7 10s a week. In such a case Mr Black might also be able to apply on the separate ground of wilful neglect to maintain by his wife (see above).

(4) *An order for the custody of any child of the family up to the age of 16 years.* The same principles apply to custody in the Magistrates' Court as in the Divorce Court. The chief consideration is the welfare of the child concerned.

The Court also has a number of other special powers with regard to children. It can, of course, make orders for their maintenance, the maximum amount being 50s for each child. It can also make an order that the child is to be committed to the care of the local Council where it is impracticable or undesirable that the parents should have charge of it. Where a custody order has been made the Court has the further power of ordering that the child shall be under the supervision either of the probation officer or of the Council. Orders of this kind are made when the Court has reason to think the person who is to have custody may prove unreliable, and that an independent supervision of the child is desirable.

Magistrates' Court orders are of course subject to variation at any time. A husband, for instance, who has been ordered to maintain his wife at the rate of £5 a week may fall out of work and find himself unable to pay. If he is wise he will at once apply for a variation. This will involve a Court hearing at which, if the Magistrates are satisfied that the former order is no longer within his means, they will reduce the sum to be paid, or even absolve the husband altogether.

The Court must revoke a matrimonial order if it is proved that the parties have resumed cohabitation (that is, taken up married life together again) or if it is proved that the complainant has committed adultery, but in such cases any order relating to children may remain in force. So if Mrs Brown gets an order on the ground of her husband's wilful neglect to maintain her, but later decides to have him back to live with her again, Mr Brown can go to Court and have the order revoked. In the same way Mr Brown can apply for a revocation if he discovers that his wife has committed adultery. The law does not make any provision for the exercise of 'discretion' in the Magistrates' Court, as it does in the case of the Petitioner's own adultery in divorce proceedings. If a husband or wife commits adultery, his or her right to the matrimonial order is forfeited.

Court orders automatically cease to have effect when the parties resume cohabitation, although where there is a dispute as to whether this has happened, either party can, as we have seen, apply to the Court and prove it. If an order is made while the parties are actually cohabiting, it is not effective until they cease to cohabit. If they continue to cohabit for a period of three months starting from the date of the order, it ceases to have effect at the end of the period, although certain provisions concerning the children remain in force.

There is a time limit in regard to complaint to the Court on the ground of adultery. The complaint must be made within six months of the date when the act became known to the complainant. Thus, if Mrs Smith discovers that her husband has committed adultery and wants to apply for a maintenance order she must act within six months from the date when she discovers his guilt. If she lets a longer period elapse, her right to an order will be gone. There are, however, certain exceptions to this rule which help a person who has been abroad during the period in question.

There is an appeal from the Magistrates to the Judges of the Divorce Court in London. These appeals are not 'rehearings' of the facts of the case: they are restricted to arguments based on the evidence given before the Magistrates.

An order in the Magistrates' Court on the ground of adultery, desertion, or cruelty often leads in due course to a divorce. The fact that the Magistrates' Court has found the husband or wife guilty of the offence concerned does not mean that a divorce will automatically be granted. But the High Court can, if it chooses, regard the granting of the Magistrates' order as sufficient proof of the offence concerned, although it will require to hear some evidence of the facts. The granting of a decree of divorce does not terminate a maintenance order granted by the Magistrates, so that it often happens that wives or husbands with small means do not trouble to ask for maintenance in divorce proceedings, being content with the order they have obtained in the Magistrates' Court.

The enforcement of Maintenance Orders in the Magistrates' Court

Maintenance payments are usually made through a court official called the 'collecting officer'. If they fall into arrear the party to whom they should be made can start proceedings to recover the arrears, or the collecting officer may be asked to do so. A summons is issued calling upon the debtor to attend Court and to explain why the arrears have occurred. He can be arrested if he does not attend. If he attends and gives a really good reason for his non-payment, such as that he has been unable to get work despite constant efforts, the arrears, or some of them, may be 'remitted'. A debtor who persistently and wilfully refuses to pay can be sent to prison for a maximum period of three months. This does not cancel the unpaid arrears, but if the husband loses his job as a result it may be of little practical help to the party to whom the money is owed.

However, the threat of prison may cause an obstinate husband to pay up, and sometimes the issue of the warrant committing the debtor to prison is suspended on condition that the arrears are paid off by specified instalments. This means that the threat of imprisonment is, as it were, kept hanging over the debtor's head, and it is often an effective way of getting the money paid. In deciding whether to remit arrears the Magistrates have to consider all the circumstances: one reason for allowing remission would be that the arrears occurred at a time when a husband did not realize that he was under a liability to pay, for instance, when he mistakenly thought that the order had been revoked. Another consideration that would influence the Court to allow a remission would be that it is not of much practical use to have so large a sum of arrears outstanding that a man would prefer to go to prison rather than pay it off.

Under the Maintenance Orders Act, 1958, two new aids for the enforcement of such orders were provided. One is that High Court maintenance orders may now be registered with the Magistrates' Court, and vice versa. Registration of a High Court order enables the quicker, simpler, and cheaper procedure of the lower Court to be used for enforcing it. An application for such registration can be made at the time when the maintenance order is granted, or at any time thereafter. Once an order has been registered in this way the debtor may, if he falls into arrear, be summoned before the Magistrates' Court for the area where he lives just as if that Court had made the order.

The second aid to enforcement given by the Act is the power to 'attach' the earnings of a husband. The Court will not make such an order unless at the time when it is applied for not less than four weekly payments are unpaid, or two instalments if they are due at longer intervals than a week. Nor will the Court make the order if it appears that the default was not due to 'wilful refusal or culpable neglect'.

But the order when made is very powerful. Its effect is to require the debtor's employer to deduct payments for the wife out of his earnings. If the Court decides to make the order it specifies two rates: the 'normal deduction rate' (which is the rate at which the Court thinks a deduction ought to be made from the debtor's pay) and the 'protected earnings rate', which is the amount below which the Court thinks the debtor's earnings should not be reduced by any deductions that are to be made under the order. Details of these rates are sent with an explanatory booklet to the employer concerned.

On the first pay day after the order comes into force the employer must begin to operate it and must deduct and send to the Court the proper amount. The employer is required to continue operating the order until he is notified that it has been discharged. If the Court wishes to know how much pay the husband is earning, it can inquire from his employer, who is bound to supply the information requested. The husband can apply to the Court at any time to have the attachment of earnings order varied. The normal deduction rate, of course, is usually higher than the rate of maintenance, because it is made with the object of clearing off arrears. As soon as the arrears are paid off the debtor is notified, and an 'appropriate variation' order is then usually made reducing the normal deduction rate to the rate of current maintenance. For example, Mr X. who has been ordered to pay his wife £3 a week may be in arrears to the amount of £30. The Court might then make an attachment of earnings order requiring Mr X.'s employer to deduct £8 a week from his pay. After six weeks the £30 arrears would be paid off, and the Court would then be ready to make an 'appropriate variation' order reducing the weekly deductions to £3, the rate of the current maintenance.

Orders made outside England

Maintenance orders made in Scotland and Northern Ireland may be registered for enforcement in England and Wales, and vice versa. The person to whom the payments are to be made applies to the Court which made the order, and the Court if satisfied that it would be convenient to register the order at the place named by the applicant sends a copy of the order to the Court of the place concerned. For instance, a wife who obtains a maintenance order in Perth may apply to have it registered in Birmingham if her husband is living there. It can then be enforced as if it had been made by the Birmingham Court. Maintenance orders made in the Commonwealth countries may also be extended to the United Kingdom for enforcement and vice versa. So if a wife obtains a maintenance order in England, and her husband then goes to Southern Rhodesia, she may apply to the Court to have the order registered in that country. It will then be sent to the Governor of the territory concerned, and it can be enforced there as if it had been made locally. Thus the arm of the law is theoretically long enough to reach over the sea, and compel a husband to pay up. It is nevertheless often a very long and difficult business to obtain maintenance from a husband who has gone overseas and is determined not to meet his obligations.

PARENTS AND CHILDREN

BIRTH

The general law

LEGISLATION has made it compulsory to do two things when a child is born—to *notify* the birth, and to *register* the birth. Both these things must be done even if the child is born dead, provided this happened after the twenty-eighth week of pregnancy.

The duty to *notify* can be described quite briefly. Written notice of the birth must be given within thirty-six hours to the medical officer of health of the local health authority for the area in which the birth takes place, which means, in the case of a county, the county council, and in the case of a county borough, the county borough council. This duty is imposed on the father of the child if at the time of the birth he is actually residing on the premises where the birth takes place and on any person in attendance upon the mother at the time of, or within six hours after, the birth. A person within these categories who fails to give this notice is liable to a fine not exceeding £1, unless he satisfies the Court that he believed on reasonable grounds that notice had duly been given by some other person. In most cases this notification is given by the midwife or doctor attending at the birth, and the father need not worry. But it is important that he should know of his legal duty so that he may ask if notification has been given.

217

The duty to *register* is quite distinct from the duty to notify. It is fulfilled by the giving of certain particulars by what is called a 'qualified informant' to the local Registrar of Births and Deaths, who records them in the register kept by him for this purpose, and by his or her signing the register in the presence of the Registrar, all within certain time limits.

If the child is legitimate the qualified informants who are under a duty to give the particulars are—the father or the mother, or if the father and mother are dead or unable to do so, the occupier of the house in which the birth occurred, if he knows about it, or one of the persons, if any, present at the birth, or the person having charge of the child. In the vast majority of cases, of course, this information is given by the father or the mother.

If the child is illegitimate the same persons are required to give the particulars except for the father. Indeed the Registrar is prohibited from entering him in the register as the father of the child except at the joint request of the mother and himself.

If the child is found new-born, alive and exposed, the person finding the child and any person in whose charge the child is placed are required to give such information of the prescribed particulars as they possess.

If the child is still-born, which, for the purposes of registration, means that the child issued forth from its mother after the twenty-eighth week of pregnancy and did not at any time after being completely expelled from its mother breathe or show any signs of life, unless there has been an inquest, the prescribed particulars must be given by the person who would, if the child had been born alive, be under the duty to give the particulars. If there has been an inquest, then on receipt of the Coroner's Certificate, the Registrar will register the birth from the particulars contained in the certificate.

Details to be given to Registrar

If the child is born alive, the prescribed particulars are (1) the date and place of birth; (2) the name, if any, and sex of the child; (3) the name and sur-name and occupation of the father unless the child is illegitimate, in which case this information will only be recorded at the joint request of the mother and father, who will both sign the register; (4) the name, surname, and maiden surname of the mother; (5) the signature, description (*i.e.* of the capacity in which the informant is qualified to give information), and residence of the informant; (6) the date of registration; and (7) the signature of the Registrar.

If the child is still-born, the prescribed particulars are the same, except that no provision is made for the name of the child and the nature of the evidence upon which the child is registered as still-born must be recorded. This evidence will normally be a certificate that the child was not born alive, signed by a registered medical practitioner or certified midwife who was either in attendance at the birth or who has examined the body of the child.

The Registrar will normally be the Registrar of Births and Deaths for the registration sub-district in which the birth occurred. For the purpose of registra-tion, for every county and county borough there are one or more registration districts (in England and Wales there are some five hundred registration dis-tricts) subdivided into one or more sub-districts. In the case of a living new-born child found exposed, if there is no information as to the place of birth, the Registrar will be the one for the sub-district where the child is found. However, on payment of a fee the birth can be registered before a Registrar other than the above.

Method of registration

Registration can be effected by attending at the register office, in which case it will be free of charge within three months of the birth or the finding of the living new-born child found exposed. It can also be done at home, if the Registrar is requested in writing to do so, but the informant must pay to the Registrar a fee of 1s 6d. However, in either case, this should be done before the expiration of forty-two days from the date of the birth or of the finding. If it is not, the Registrar is empowered to require any qualified informant to attend personally at his office to do so, and in the case of a parent failing to do so he or she is liable to a fine not exceeding 40s.

If the birth is not registered within three months, the informant must give the information and sign the register in the presence of both the Registrar and the Superintendent Registrar, and a fee of 3s 9d is payable to both of them. Registration after twelve months from the date of birth cannot be effected without the written authority of the Registrar-General, and a fee of 7s 6d is payable to both the Superintendent Registrar and the Registrar. Registration in contravention of these requirements is an offence punishable with a fine not exceeding £10.

Certificates

When the birth is registered, a birth certificate can be obtained from the Registrar on payment of a small fee, and if the informant wishes, this can be in a shortened form, from which all reference to parentage is omitted.

New or added names

If the child is registered without a name, the name can be registered subsequently, or indeed the registered name altered within twelve months of registration, provided a certificate of name given in baptism, or if the child is not baptized, a certificate of name given otherwise is delivered to the Registrar or Superintendent Registrar.

Legitimation

If an illegitimate child is legitimated by the subsequent marriage of the parents, the birth can and should be re-registered on the authority of the Registrar-General. If this is done within three months of the marriage, no fee is chargeable, otherwise a fee not exceeding 10s is payable.

False statements

It is an offence, broadly speaking, to make a false statement for the purposes of registration, punishable in certain cases with imprisonment.

Registers are public

Finally it may be worth remarking that registers of births are public documents, and any person is entitled to search for any entry and, on payment of a fee, to obtain a certified copy of any entry. This can be done, for instance, either at the local register office or at the General Register Office situated at Somerset House, Strand, London, W.C.2. At the General Register Office the Adopted Children Register is kept which contains particulars of adoptions, and from this certified copies of entries can be similarly obtained. But although records are kept for the purpose of tracing the connection between entries in the registers of births marked 'adopted' in pursuance to an adoption order, and the corresponding entries in the Adopted Children Register, these records are not open to inspection. Indeed the Registrar-General cannot furnish any person with information contained in these records without a Court order.

ADOPTION

Meaning and effect of adoption

To adopt is to acquire by law the rights, liabilities, and duties of a parent. This acquisition was not possible in this country until legislation passed in 1926 made it so. Until the Adoption of Children Act, 1926, the position broadly was that English Law regarded such rights and duties as not to be transferred by any act of the parents. One result of this was that if a parent agreed, however formally, to transfer such rights and duties to another and that other having cared for the child was subsequently presented with a demand for its return by the parent, the would-be adopter might well be unable to resist the demand. It is, therefore, essential for anyone who wishes to become a parent by adoption to make use of the procedure laid down by the successive Adoption Acts which enable him or her to acquire parental rights and duties by Court order.

It is this procedure and its consequences which will be discussed below, but it may be as well to mention here that if the preliminary problem arises of finding a child to adopt, it is possible to consult the children's department for the county or county borough, or in London, the London County Council's area Children's Officer. It is also possible to consult an adoption society. There are over fifty such societies in England and Wales, which are controlled by law. Some of these are non-denominational, while others require applicants to be of the same religious faith as that to which the society is affiliated. None may charge for their services. These bodies may accept donations. They may be paid, as may also local authorities, for expenses reasonably incurred in connection with the adoption, and the Court to which the application is made has power to authorize a payment or reward. It should be noted that it is not lawful for any body of persons, as opposed to an individual, to enter into any agreement or arrangement for the adoption of an infant, unless it is a registered adoption society or a local authority, and that even the individual is prohibited by law from advertising about proposed adoptions and, broadly speaking, from making any payment, save those mentioned above, to any person in connection with the adoption of an infant.

To adopt legally, then, you must apply to the Court, which can be either the High Court, or the local County Court or Juvenile Court for the district in which either the applicant or the infant resides.

220

Who may apply for an adoption order?

The question can best be answered by setting out who cannot, since the position in effect now is that subject to the restrictions set out below anyone now can. This is not, of course, to say that anyone will be granted an adoption order, since the making of such an order is in all cases discretionary. No one has an automatic or absolute right to an adoption order. However, before these restrictions are set out, it may be worth mentioning that adoption orders can be made authorizing the adoption of an illegitimate child by its natural father or by its unmarried mother.

The restrictions are these. More than one person may not be authorized to adopt except in the case of a husband and wife. The only possible joint applicants, therefore, are husband and wife. If the applicant, or one of the joint applicants, is the mother or father of the infant, there is no qualification as to age. Otherwise, joint applicants must both be at least twenty-one, and unless the infant is a relative of one of them, one of the applicants must be at least twenty-five. A sole applicant who is not the infant's mother or father must be at least twenty-five unless he or she is a relative, when twenty-one is the minimum age. If the infant is a female, an adoption order will not be made in favour of a sole male applicant unless the Court is satisfied that there are special circumstances justifying the making of the order as an exceptional measure.

Normally both the applicant and the infant will be resident in this country, but an applicant not ordinarily resident here may be granted an adoption order subject to certain special requirements, provided the applicant is domiciled here, as might happen, for instance, if though ordinarily resident abroad now the applicant had been born here and resided here, and still intends to return here permanently.

If the applicant is not domiciled here, *e.g.* if this country has never been his home, an application cannot be made for a full adoption order, but on certain conditions he or she can apply to the High Court or the County Court for a provisional adoption order, which will authorize the removal of the infant from this country so that he can be adopted by the applicant under the law of the country in which the applicant is domiciled.

Who may be adopted?

Any unmarried person under the age of twenty-one and resident here. The unmarried infant need not be a British subject, nor need he or she be domiciled here, but if the infant is a ward of Court, the leave of the Judge under whose control the ward is, is necessary.

Essential preliminaries

There are three matters vital to the making of an application to the Court. An applicant must normally have obtained the consent of certain persons to the adoption in question, and the infant normally must have been in the care and possession of the applicant for at least three consecutive months immediately preceding the date of the adoption order. Further, with two exceptions, the local authority has to be notified of the applicant's intention to adopt at least three months before this date. These matters will be discussed separately.

221

Consent of natural parents, etc.

Every parent or guardian of the infant must give consent, and if the application is being made by one spouse only, the consent of the other must be given to the adoption in question. There is a form for documentary consent, though consent may be given in person at the hearing. Consent may be given either unconditionally or subject to conditions as to the religious persuasion in which it is proposed to bring up the infant. Part of the policy behind the modern procedure is that generally the identity of the applicant shall not be known to the natural parent. It is, therefore, possible for an applicant who wishes his identity to remain confidential to obtain a serial number for his application, and for a parent or guardian to give consent without knowing who the applicant is—the form of consent in such a case identifying the applicant by the serial number only.

Consent can be withdrawn at any time up to the making of the order. If it is withdrawn, then unless the Court exercises a discretion which it has in certain cases to dispense with consent, an adoption order cannot be made. The discretion of the Court to override or ignore a change of mind and withdrawal of consent may be exercised if the Court is satisfied that the child's parent or guardian concerned has abandoned, neglected, or persistently ill-treated the infant or has persistently failed without reasonable cause to discharge the obligations of a parent or guardian, or cannot be found, or is incapable of giving consent, or is unreasonably withholding it; and it is specifically provided that if a person gives his consent to the making of an adoption order without knowing the applicant's identity and subsequently withdraws his consent only because of this lack of knowledge, his consent shall be deemed to have been unreasonably withheld. The Court has a discretion to dispense with the consent of the applicant's spouse, if it is satisfied that he or she cannot be found or is incapable of giving consent or that the spouses have separated and are living apart and that the separation is likely to be permanent. It should be noted finally that, so far as the giving of her consent is concerned, a mother is protected against herself, so to speak, in that she cannot effectively consent to her child's adoption until it is at least six weeks old.

The probationary period

The first six weeks of the infant's life are also excluded from the calculation of the period of three months, during which, for every adoption now, the infant has to have been continuously in the care and possession of the applicant. It should be noted that care and possession must be continuous for this period. To construe this requirement literally would lead to absurdities, e.g. an argument that since the infant had gone to hospital for a night during this period, the adoption order could not be made. But it should be appreciated that the voluntary transfer of both care and possession of the infant for even a short time during this three-month period may be fatal to a successful application. In a recent case the applicants had permitted the infant to return to his mother for a night and part of a day and this voluntary transfer of care and possession was regarded by the Court as fatal to the success of the application.

If an application is pending, a parent or guardian who has signified his or her consent to the making of the adoption order cannot remove the infant from the care and possession of the applicant except by leave of the Court. If such leave is requested, the Court will have regard to the infant's welfare in deciding whether to grant or refuse it. The parent or guardian may, of course, even if leave is refused, still revoke his consent to the adoption, but the Court can always dispense with his or her consent on the grounds that it is unreasonably withheld. If the application is for a provisional adoption order, *i.e.* by someone not domiciled here, the requisite period is six and not three months. The object of this three or six months' requirement is to ensure that for every intended adoption there shall be this 'trying out' or probationary period.

Informing the local authority

It is during this probationary period that the local authority exercises a protective supervision over the infant, *e.g.* by visits from its officers to satisfy themselves as to its well-being. For this reason an applicant has to notify in writing the local authority within whose area he is resident, *i.e.* the local county council or county borough council, of his intention to apply for the adoption order at least three months before the anticipated date of the making of the order, or six months in the case of a provisional order. The two exceptions to the requirement are that no such notice need be given if the applicant or one of two joint applicants is a parent of the infant or if the infant is above school age.

Methods of applying to the Court

The method of putting the application before the Court and the procedure at the hearing of the application differ, depending on whether the application is made to the High Court or the County Court or the Juvenile Court, but there are certain matters common to each type of application worth while mentioning.

For every application a guardian of the infant for the purposes of the application, known as a guardian *ad litem*, is appointed by the Court. His function is to safeguard the infant's interests. The usually appointed guardians are—in the High Court, the Official Solicitor; in the County Court, the children's officer of the local authority; and in the Juvenile Court, a probation officer. The guardian will investigate all the circumstances relevant to the proposed adoption. For instance, he will interview the applicant and ascertain particulars about his or her household, the accommodation in the home, the means and, broadly speaking, the health of the applicant, and whether the applicant understands the nature of an adoption order. The guardian will also, for instance, ascertain whether the infant is able to understand the nature of an adoption order and, if so, whether he or she wishes to be adopted by the applicant; and whether every consent to the order has been freely given with a full understanding of the nature and effect of an adoption order. When the guardian completes his investigation, he makes a confidential report in writing to the Court.

Court sits in private

The hearing of an application does not take place in open Court. In the High Court it is heard in Chancery Chambers, which are private, and also in private in the County or Juvenile Courts. Further, if the applicant, wishing to keep his identity confidential, has obtained a serial number for his application, the whole of the proceedings will be conducted with a view to securing that he or she is not seen by or made known to any party not already aware of his or her identity, except with the applicant's consent. For instance, if necessary, the applicant and any such party will attend before the Court separately.

Three essential conditions

Before the Court can make an adoption order, it must be satisfied of three things.

One—that every person whose consent is necessary and has not been dispensed with has consented to and understands the nature and effect of the adoption order, and in particular, that a parent understands that its effect will be permanently to deprive him of his parental rights.

Two—that the order will be for the welfare of the infant. When considering this point the Court will have regard, amongst other things, to the health of the applicant, and it should be noted that a doctor's certificate dealing with the applicant's health must be filed in support of every application, except when the applicant or one of them is the father or mother of the infant or the infant is above school age. The Court will also take into consideration the wishes of the infant, having regard to his age and understanding.

Three—that neither has the applicant received or agreed to receive any payment or reward in consideration of the adoption except such as the Court may sanction.

The Court has a discretionary power to impose such terms and conditions in the order as it thinks fit, and in particular it may require the adopter by bond or otherwise to make for the infant such provision, if any, as it thinks just and expedient. For instance, an undertaking to bring up the child in a particular religion is sometimes exacted.

The Register of Adopted Children

As stated in the section on birth, the Registrar-General maintains at Somerset House a special register for adopted children, and if the Court does make an adoption order, it will direct the Registrar-General to make a special entry in this Adopted Children Register, which will not reveal who the child's parents were, and if necessary, to mark the relevant entry in the Register of Births with the word 'adopted'. Although records are kept at the General Register Office for the purpose of tracing the connection between such entries in the Register of Births and the corresponding ones in the Adopted Children Register, these records are *not* open to inspection. Information contained in those records can only be obtained from the Registrar-General by means of a Court order. The Adopted Children Register itself is, of course, open to inspection and certified copies of entries in it can be obtained on payment of a fee. Such a certified copy is evidence of the adoption to which it relates.

Rights of appeal from the Court's decision

It is possible to appeal from either the making or the refusal to make an adoption order. From orders of the High Court or the County Court appeal lies to the Court of Appeal, and from the Juvenile Court either, in certain circumstances, to the Divisional Court of the Queen's Bench Division of the High Court or to a Judge of the Chancery Division of the High Court. If such an appeal is allowed, then the relevant marking on the Register of Births and the relevant entry in the Adopted Children Register will, in an appropriate case, be cancelled.

Summary

This section will be concluded with a reminder of what was stated at the outset. To adopt properly it is essential to make use of the procedure which has been discussed and so obtain an adoption order from the Court. The effect of such an order is permanently to deprive the natural parent of his or her parental rights and to transfer to the adopter all the rights, duties, and liabilities of the infant's parent or guardian in relation to the future custody of the infant, its maintenance and education, including all rights to appoint a guardian or to consent or to give notice of dissent from marriage. So far as custody, maintenance, and education are concerned the whole of the rights and obligations that flow from parenthood become the adopter's. It should be noted, however, that an order does not put the adopter and child into the position of natural parent and child for all purposes. For instance, it would appear that for the purpose of obtaining relief from income tax by way of child allowance, the adopter must prove, *inter alia*, that he has the custody of, and maintains the child at his own expense and does not merely through the making of the order become entitled to claim such relief as though it were a child of his own. On the other hand, for the purposes of the law relating to marriage the adopter and adopted are deemed to be within the prohibited degrees of consanguinity.

So far as the law of succession is concerned, the position now is that property passes on an intestacy, *i.e.* when there is no valid will, as though the adopted person were the child of the adopter and not the child of any other person, and if property is given by, for instance, a deed of gift whilst the parties are alive, or by will, the position is similar—a reference express or implied to the child or children of the adopter being construed as, or as including, the adopted person and a reference to the child or children of the natural parents being construed as excluding the adopted person—provided the deed or will was made after the date of the adoption order. It should be noted that unless a husband and wife make a joint application and so adopt jointly the infant, the adopter will, of course, be the spouse who makes the application, and what has been set out above would relate only to him or her. For instance, the infant adopted in these circumstances would not merely by virtue of his adoption acquire any right to share in the estate of the spouse of the sole adopter. Finally, it may be worth mentioning that a British subject will not necessarily lose his British nationality if adopted by someone who is not a British subject, and that the adoption of someone not a British subject will give the adopted person British nationality if the adopter or, in the case of a joint adoption, the male adopter, is a citizen of the United Kingdom and Colonies.

CUSTODY

The Common Law of England recognizes the right of the father, in priority to all other persons, to have custody of his child under the age of twenty-one. This right to custody will often prevail against the mother. The father can, if necessary, take *habeas corpus* proceedings against a third person, however well-intentioned, who has the child in his custody and who refuses or fails to return the child to the father.

What does the right to custody amount to? It gives the father the right to the services of a child living at home (and this right extends to children over twenty-one) so he can require the child to help with the washing-up, in the garden, or in general duties round the house. It also gives the right to exert discipline over the child by corporal punishment, if necessary, provided that the punishment given is reasonable. When a child goes to school this right

The Common Law recognizes the priority right of the father to have custody of his child.

may be delegated to a schoolmaster. An elder brother is not permitted to discipline younger children in this way unless, perhaps through the death of the parents, he is in the position of a parent toward them. If a mature child is not in the father's custody the Court will not always permit the father to reassert his right to custody if the child does not want to return to the father. On the other hand, if the Court considers that the welfare of the child demands it, the Court can, and quite often does, disregard the child's wishes.

EDUCATION

Closely associated with the right to custody are the father's rights to educate the child as he wishes and to bring the child up to follow the father's religious beliefs. The right to educate is qualified by a duty under the Education Act to

226

see that the child receives full-time education of a kind which is suitable to his abilities. Failure to make a child attend school regularly is an offence for which the father, or the mother if she has custody, is liable. Where religion is concerned the Court may interfere with the father's claim if the welfare of the child may be adversely affected: for example, if the father allows the child to be brought up in another religion, and later changes his mind, the Court may prevent the father from exercising his right. The poet Shelley was deprived of the upbringing of his children in favour of his deceased wife's parents, for the Court considered that the children would be injured by his irreligious opinions.

RIGHTS OF A MOTHER

Even under the Common Law the Court will sometimes reject the father's claims in favour of the mother's. It may do this where the welfare of the child— which is always the most important consideration where questions involving children come before the Court—is best served by doing so. This may happen where it is shown that the husband has treated the children with cruelty or where he has shown himself unsuitable to have control over the children in some other way.

In addition to these long-standing powers to heed the mother's wishes in preference to the father's, modern Acts of Parliament have gone far toward putting the mother on an equal footing with the father where a child is concerned. Thus, under the Guardianship of Infants Acts, the mother has a right to apply to the Court for the custody of a child. Again, under the Matrimonial Causes Act, custody of the children may be given to the mother when a divorce decree is granted. Indeed, nowadays, the mother will usually be given the custody of very young children after a divorce, whoever is the guilty party in the divorce proceedings. In other cases, the technical custody may be given to the father but the mother may be given actual care and control. In almost all cases the parent who has not control of the child will be given rights of access, unless there are very strong reasons for denying this right. If the father dies the mother has long been recognized as having the right to the custody of young children (though she must follow the deceased father's wishes on religious upbringing) and it would be very rare now for a surviving mother's claim to custody of older children, perhaps against paternal grandparents, for example, to be overridden by the Court. The father may, however, appoint a guardian to act with the mother after his death.

LOSS OF PARENTAL RIGHTS

Either or both of the parents may lose their parental rights. This may occur contrary to their wishes. If a father is found guilty of incest or attempted incest with a daughter who is under twenty-one, the Court may order that he shall be deprived of all authority over her. Again, there is power to deprive parents of control in favour of the local authority or some person the Court considers suitable where children under seventeen are found to be in need of care and protection. This order may be made in respect of girls where some member of the family has been found guilty of incest or attempted incest, or in respect of any children where other sexual offences have been committed against them or any of them. The order can also be made where the parents are not exercising proper care over a child or where they neglect or ill-treat a child or cause the child to be exposed to moral danger or fail to keep proper control over the child. All these orders may be appealed against. Also, they are not irrevocable and they may be revoked if circumstances change.

"Occasionally parents will themselves wish to divest themselves of parental powers."

Occasionally parents will themselves wish to divest themselves of parental powers. Thus, if they find it impossible to control an unruly child who is under seventeen, they may themselves go to the Court and the Court may order the child to be committed to the care of the local authority. All these powers are exercised by the Juvenile Court and it must be remembered that this Court can take other measures than depriving the parents of control: for example, they may put the child under the supervision of a probation officer while still living at home or order the parents to bind themselves to keep the child under control, with a penalty of forfeiture of recognizances—i.e. sums of money which they recognize may be payable to the Court—if they fail to observe the order. Lastly, parents may voluntarily divest themselves of power over a child by agreeing that other people should adopt the child.

228

MAINTENANCE OF CHILDREN

Both parents are liable to maintain their children and this duty is not necessarily altered by the fact that a child may have substantial means of his own—perhaps the result of a legacy from a grandparent—so that the Court may prevent a parent from trying to maintain a child out of his property so as to relieve the parent from doing so. Despite this, the trustees of settlements have wide powers, which the Court will sometimes extend, to use the income from a child's property for his support in proper cases. Where a larger sum of money is needed for purposes like paying for the training of a child for a profession or trade, or for setting a child up in business, the trustees may even resort to the child's capital for this purpose, though they will frequently have to get an order of the Chancery Division to be able to do this.

In most cases the child will not have substantial means and then the primary duty to maintain is on the father. If the parents separate, the father's duty continues, even though the children go with the mother who has committed adultery, or deserted the father, and the wife can obtain a maintenance order for the children in the High Court or in a Magistrates' Court. On the other hand, if the husband has no income because he is unable to work through old age or ill-health, a maintenance order may be made against the wife. Further, after a divorce, the High Court can order a guilty wife who has property of her own to settle part of it on the children, although the husband is able to maintain them himself. Where children under sixteen are concerned, continued neglect to maintain a child is an offence of which either or both parents may be convicted under the National Assistance Act. If a child is committed to the care of the local authority, or to a foster-parent, the natural parents still remain liable to maintain the child and will usually be required to make contributions for this purpose.

A CHILD'S PROPERTY

Under English Law there are certain legal disadvantages in being an infant. Some of these are dealt with elsewhere, *e.g.* the position of infants in contract and in tort and in making a will, and the special position under Scots Law is dealt with under the section describing some of the differences between English and Scots Law. What of the infant's position with regard to ownership of property? And first let us get clear when under English Law, a child ceases to be an infant? The answer is when he becomes twenty-one. But this prompts a further question—when precisely does he become twenty-one? Not, as is sometimes said, on his twenty-first birthday, but on the day before that birthday. There are cases in the Law Reports going back to 1699 from which it emerges very clearly that minority, or infancy, comes to an end on the day before the twenty-first birthday, and, because the law takes no account of fractions of a day, the infant is of full age from the first moment of the day before his twenty-first birthday. Hence on that day he can inherit a title, own a legal estate, vote at an election, sit on a jury, make a will, enter into a binding legal contract, and do all the other things that in law are the prerogative of full age.

If a child is born in a leap year on February 29th he may perhaps suffer over birthdays, only getting one in every fourth year, but he will not suffer the fate of the hero of the *Pirates of Penzance* who had to wait eighty-four years before he became twenty-one. If he was born on February 29th, 1960, for example, he will be twenty-one on February 28th, 1981.

An infant cannot own real property, *i.e.* he cannot be the legal owner of freehold land or the buildings on that land. So if, for instance, a freehold house

A child's property!

or land is sold to him or left to him by will, there must be trustees who will be the nominal owners of the legal estate to hold it for him until he is twenty-one.

He can, however, own personal property, *e.g.* money, furniture, books, clothes, a bicycle, a motor car, a horse, and so on. He can open a current account and deposit account at a bank. The opening of an account by anyone, infant or not, is of course subject to the right of a bank to refuse. But their refusal has nothing to do with the infant's legal rights. If they accept him as a customer he is legally empowered to own the money in his account, to draw cheques, etc. The bank may be particularly careful about an infant's overdraft. That again, however, is merely a matter of the bank's discretion.

Certain investments are available to an infant, *e.g.* the Post Office Savings Bank, the Trustee Savings Bank, National Savings Certificates, and Premium Bonds may be held by an infant. So may those Government Stocks which can be bought through a Post Office.

If, however, the Government Stock is one which is on the Bank of England Register they will not accept the infant alone. It is necessary for a trustee to be the nominal holder until the infant is twenty-one, either alone, or jointly with the infant. In the latter case they become joint owners.

As to the stocks and shares of public companies, their rules vary but, in general, they are unwilling to accept an infant shareholder alone. They want the shares to be held in the way described above for Government Stock on the Bank of England Register.

A problem may arise when a legacy of money is left by will to an infant. As stated above, an infant is legally entitled to own money. So one would expect that the legacy could be paid to him straight-away. The difficulty arises from the fact that an infant cannot give the executors of the will a valid binding legal receipt. For his own protection, the law is that an infant's signature to a contract or a receipt does not legally bind him, except for the special cases which are mentioned in the section on Infants and Contract. This is not one of the special cases so, as a general rule, an infant to whom money is left by will must wait to receive it until he is twenty-one—unless of course the testator has specified a higher age—and the trustees must hold the money in trust for him.

A few years ago there was an interesting case on this point which did disclose one exception to this rule. In his will a father left part of his estate on trust for his daughter's children. It was to be invested until the children became twenty-one, or married. There was in fact only one grandchild, a daughter who married when she was eighteen. Could she have her money then? The executors of the will asked the Court for guidance. The judge held that if a will says in clear words that a child is to receive a legacy at a specified age which is under twenty-one, or on the happening of some particular event like marriage, the executors can safely pay it and the receipt will be a good legal receipt, although the recipient may be under twenty-one when he or she signs it.

MARRIAGE OF CHILDREN

A child between sixteen and twenty-one who wishes to marry requires the consent of both parents if they are alive, or of the surviving parent, or of the guardian (if any) if both parents are dead. If any of these persons refuses to give consent, the child may apply to the Court for permission. Application is almost always made to the Magistrates' Court. There is no appeal against the Court's decision. If the child intends to marry under a common licence from the Registrar, the Registrar must ensure that the parents or guardian have consented expressly. If it is impossible to get the parents' consent—where they are untraceable, for example—the Registrar may dispense with consent or may require an application to the Court. If the marriage is to be after publication of banns, no consent is needed for publication. An objecting parent must make his objection known in church at the time when the banns are called. If a marriage is celebrated without the necessary consent being given, however, the marriage remains perfectly valid.

LEGAL PROCEEDINGS
BY OR AGAINST A CHILD

A child under twenty-one cannot bring civil proceedings on his own behalf. He requires a 'next friend' to act for him, who will be responsible for the costs if the action fails. Often a parent will be named as the 'next friend'. In a High Court action the 'next friend' must give written authority before he can be named to act. If a child is named as defendant to a civil action, he must be represented by someone called a 'guardian *ad litem*': again, this will often be the child's father but in this case he is not usually liable to pay the costs if the action succeeds against the child. An action which involves a child cannot be settled without the approval of the Court, which will require to be satisfied that the settlement is in the child's best interests.

When a child under seventeen is charged with a criminal offence the Court can compel the parent who has custody of the child to be present. It must do so where the parent lives reasonably near and where there are no special circumstances which would make the parent's attendance unreasonable. If a child under seventeen is found guilty of an offence, the parent may be required to pay any fine imposed, or any costs or compensation which is awarded. The parent can also be compelled to give security for the child's subsequent good behaviour.

Parents are not directly liable for their children's torts. They are only liable for injuries and damage which their children inflict on others if they were caused by the parent's own negligence in exercising their parental duties. For example, if a father allows a young child to drive his motor-car and the child knocks someone down, the father will be liable for his negligence in allowing the child to drive. Again, if a parent gives a potentially dangerous present to a child—an air-rifle, for example—and the child injures someone, the Court might find that the parent was liable in one of two ways. First, if the child was very young, it might be decided that the parent was negligent in giving the child an air-rifle at all. Secondly, even in the case of an older child, it might be decided that the parent was negligent in not properly supervising the child's use of the rifle, although the Court considered the child old enough to have an air-rifle under proper supervision.

NATIONALITY

Children generally acquire the nationality of the father at the time of their birth, except that a child born in the United Kingdom is almost always entitled to citizenship by birth. Children cannot become United Kingdom citizens by naturalization, for only persons of full age can become naturalized. However, if a parent is applying for naturalization he can apply to have his children registered as citizens. The Home Secretary then has a discretion, if he grants naturalization to the parent, to register the children, who then acquire citizenship. If no application is made, the children remain aliens, although the father (or both parents) has become naturalized. An alien child which is adopted by a male citizen acquires citizenship of the United Kingdom from the time of the adoption.

ILLEGITIMACY

An illegitimate child is one whose parents are not lawfully married when it is born. A subsequent marriage of its parents may in certain circumstances make that child legitimate—as will be described later. But originally, a child born *before* the marriage of its parents is born illegitimate.

Lawful marriage between the parents *before* the birth, even if it takes place after conception, makes a child legitimate from birth. A child may, therefore, be illegitimate either because the mother is not married at all, or because the child is begotten between the married woman and another than her lawful husband. However, the law presumes in favour of every child born of a married woman during the continuance of the marriage that it is legitimate. Even after the marriage has ceased, whether through death or divorce, this presumption still applies provided the child is born not more than the possible period after such an event—270 to 280 days are recognized as being the normal period of gestation, *i.e.* the normal interval between conception and birth, but in a number of cases quite different periods have been treated as possible, *e.g.* 174, and 307 days. This is not to say that such a child cannot be shown to be illegitimate. The presumption can be rebutted, *e.g.* by it being shown that the husband could not be the father because this would be physically impossible, for instance, through separation or impotency. But the law is reluctant to allow this presumption to be displaced. It places the burden of doing this on those who deny the legitimacy, and to take just one example, it would not be enough to show that the wife had committed adultery. The question in such a case is regarded not as being whether the husband or some other man is more likely to be the father, but whether it can be proved that the husband did not have sexual intercourse with his wife at the time when the child was conceived.

Effects of illegitimacy

The main reason behind this reluctance of law to declare a child illegitimate is that such a child suffers certain disabilities under the law. For example, so far as the law of succession to property is concerned, although the illegitimate person may succeed to the property of his mother should she die intestate, *i.e.* without leaving any valid will, he will only do so if the mother had no legitimate children, and he has no right at all to succeed to the estate of his father or any other of his relations on an intestacy. He can, of course, acquire property by gift or will, but acquisition in this way is less certain than if he were legitimate, since a gift by will of property to the 'children' of a particular person is regarded as designating only the legitimate children unless, for instance,

233

there were no legitimate children or it appears from the will when properly construed that 'children' was intended to include illegitimate children.

To take another example, the rights under the law of the illegitimate child to be maintained are restricted. Although his mother is bound to maintain him until the age of sixteen, he has no such right as against his father. It is true that legislation has made it possible for an order to be made by the Magistrates, called an 'affiliation' order, compelling the father to pay for the child's maintenance until that age, and these affiliation proceedings will be discussed later. Further, for the purposes of the National Assistance Act, 1948, a husband is liable to maintain his wife and children, including illegitimate children. It is also true that under various statutes an illegitimate child is entitled to receive benefits as a dependant of his parents. For instance, if the father is killed through the negligence of someone and a claim is brought under the Fatal Accidents Acts against that person on behalf of his dependants, who will normally be his wife and children, his children, for this purpose, can include an illegitimate child. But when all this is said, the fundamental disadvantage under the law remains that being illegitimate he can only look to his mother to maintain him unless an affiliation order is made.

How a child born illegitimate may be made legitimate

Such disabilities as those outlined above can largely be overcome if the illegitimate child is legitimated. Before the Legitimacy Act, 1926, children born out of lawful wedlock could only be made legitimate if a special Act of Parliament was passed to legitimate them. For instance, John of Gaunt's illegitimate children were made legitimate by an Act passed in the reign of Richard II.

But in this century legislation has made a considerable difference to children born illegitimate. It seems that the temper and spirit of the times are that if a child is born illegitimate because its parents are not married before its birth, yet if those parents subsequently do marry each other the child should be made legitimate.

This has been carried into effect by two Acts of Parliament, one in 1926 and one in 1959.

The object of the Act of 1926 was to make legitimate a child who was born illegitimate, if that child's parents subsequently married each other, *provided that*—and this was the awkward exception in many cases—neither parent was married to a third party at the time when that child was born.

For example, if Miss A. bore a child by Mr X. at a time when Mr X. was already married to Mrs X., then although he might subsequently have been divorced by her, and although he subsequently married Miss A., that child could not be made legitimate. The child of an adulterous union could never be legitimated under the 1926 Act. In many cases one or other of the parents was married to someone else. There was adultery, and the consequent birth of a child was followed by a divorce. But the subsequent marriage of the parents could not legitimate that child.

On the other hand, if at the time of the birth of the child, the father and the mother, though not married to each other, but not either of them married to anyone else, did subsequently marry each other, then that child, under the 1926 Act, was legitimated. In many cases, indeed, the 1926 Act did result in

234

the legitimation of children who were born illegitimate. But the Act did not legitimate children who were born of an adulterous union.

This situation was dramatically altered by the Act of 1959 which introduced an amendment to the 1926 Act. The effect of the 1959 Act in this respect was simply to repeal the proviso in the 1926 Act that neither parent should have been married to anyone else at the time when the child was born. So now it does not matter that either or both parents may have been married to someone else at the time of the birth of the child; the fact is that *when they do marry each other the child is legitimated from the date of the marriage* and a new birth certificate in the form appropriate to a legitimate birth can be obtained.

So to follow that example given earlier: if today Miss A. has a child by Mr X. at a time when he is still married to Mrs X. and subsequently there is a divorce and Mr X. marries Miss A., then the child is legitimated from the date of the marriage.

Moreover, the 1959 Act affects the past as well as the future. It makes legitimate many children who until that Act came into force on October 29th, 1959, were necessarily illegitimate because they were born as a result of an act of adultery. If it is established that their parents did subsequently marry, then from the date of the marriage those children were legitimated.

Is there anything else they need do, such as re-registering their birth? The position is that they are legitimated by the Act of Parliament; that is the effect of the law. But clearly they may want to prove it by getting a new certificate, and it is in any case the legal duty of the parents to re-register the birth of the child. As many of the people made legitimate by this new Act may have been born a good many years ago, the parents may be dead. Indeed, people legitimated by this new Act could themselves be getting on in years. The procedure is that if the parents are alive they should apply to the local Registrar or to the Registrar-General at Somerset House in London for a new certificate. If the parents are dead the children themselves can apply. The Registrar-General will send a form, a fairly simple one, which has to be sent to Somerset House with the birth and marriage certificates. The eventual result, if the application is right, will be a new birth certificate in the ordinary legitimate form.

The father's rights

Another interesting feature of the 1959 Act is that it gives the father of an illegitimate child a legal right to take an interest in him. Hitherto, the father had had no rights at all. He had only had an obligation, that is an obligation to pay if the mother obtained an affiliation order against him. The father of an illegitimate child can now apply to the Courts for an order giving him custody of that child, or an order giving him the right to see and visit the child.

This is something substantially new; it has of course no relevance to the situation where the actual parents of the child have married and so the child has become legitimate. But it is of value to the father where their marriage has not taken place, where the child remains illegitimate but the father feels a considerable responsibility toward him; a responsibility which is not satisfied by his making payments for the child's maintenance, either voluntary payments, or payments under an affiliation order made by the Courts.

Illustration of effects of 1959 Act

In order to illustrate the remarkable effect of the 1959 Act, a typical question and the answer to it may be of interest. The question is as follows:

"I was a married woman living apart from my husband when my son was born in 1939. He had to take my name. Some years later I got a divorce from my husband and married my son's father. After that my son was legally adopted by us and his name changed to his father's. Is my son still illegitimate or does the new Act of 1959 alter this?"

This is a perfect example of the kind of case which is affected by the new Act. This woman's son is now legitimate. His parents were able to marry a few years ago after the divorce and therefore he became legitimate on October 29th, 1959, automatically, as a result of the Act. The fact that his parents adopted him does not alter this and indeed as a result of the Adoption Act of 1960 they can apply to the Court to have the adoption order, which they no longer need, revoked. If they do this the adoption certificates will be cancelled and a new birth certificate showing him to be legitimate can be issued.

Adoption orders

This reference to adoption orders is interesting. Very often after the 1926 Act when the parents of an illegitimate child did marry, but the child was not automatically legitimated for the reasons explained above (that at the time of the birth of the child the parents were not free to marry each other), the parents were able legally to disguise the fact that the child was illegitimate by applying for an adoption order. It may on the face of it seem odd for the two natural parents of the child to adopt him. But this was very frequently done for the simple reason that once an adoption order had been obtained, a new certificate —the ordinary adoption certificate—was issued, and instead of the child then having a birth certificate which might indicate on the face of it that he must have been born illegitimate, he had an adopted child's certificate which completely concealed his origins and the fact that he was born illegitimate. So far as documentation was concerned, whenever it was necessary for him to produce a birth certificate it appeared merely that he was an adopted child, lawfully entitled to the surname of his adopting father. Moreover he could obtain the shortened form of birth certificate which merely indicates date and place of birth and contains no reference to parentage. This short birth certificate has for many years been normally accepted by insurance companies, pension funds, would-be employers, and so on, without question. It got over the difficulty and problem which so many illegitimate children faced that they had no legal entitlement to their father's surname.

The 1959 Act has done away with the necessity for all these innocent and justifiable subterfuges. The adoption orders obtained before that can be cancelled and the child is now legitimated.

Those children who remain illegitimate

The result of the 1926 Act as amended by the 1959 Act is, of course, that any child who was born illegitimate is automatically legitimated when its

THE FAMILY

parents marry each other. Nevertheless this will leave illegitimate those children of parents who never do actually marry each other. Even in this situation the father or the mother of such children may feel genuine moral obligations toward those children and may want to leave them legacies in their wills. The important point to note is that there is a risk in using general words like 'my child' or 'my children'. For the *mother* to use such words creates no difficulty because the illegitimate children are the children of her body and that is that. For the *father* to use such general words will almost certainly mean that any illegitimate children of his will not benefit. If, therefore, he particularly desires an illegitimate child to benefit, it is absolutely essential that in making his will he should mention that child *by name*.

Void marriages

Another remarkable provision of the 1959 Act concerns the children of marriages which are legally void. Before this Act if the marriage was void the children were automatically illegitimate. A marriage may be void for various reasons: for instance it may be bigamous—one or other of the parties may have a wife or husband still living—or one or other of the parties may be under sixteen years of age at the time of the marriage, or they may be within the prohibited degrees of relationship. Under the Act if the parents—or even only one of them—are genuinely unaware that the marriage is void, and if he or she or they both honestly and reasonably think that it is a valid marriage, then the child of that marriage can be legitimate. It is a condition that the father must be domiciled in England or Wales at the child's birth and also a condition that the innocent belief that the marriage is valid is still held when the child is conceived.

It is a difficult problem and this is a paraphrase of a complex section in the Act. The point is that the Act has gone a very long way to save a child from being legally illegitimate when, although the marriage of its parents was void, there was a genuine belief on the part of one or other of them that it was valid. The belief must not only be genuine but also reasonable. Clearly, if circumstances exist when this section of the Act might be applied, the child or the parents would need legal advice. The purpose of this paraphrase of this section of the Act is to draw attention to its existence and to indicate the circumstances in which it might apply and in which it might be possible to obtain from the Registrar-General a certificate of birth which indicates a legitimate birth.

The effect of legitimation is that from the date of the marriage, such a child is regarded, for most purposes, as though he had been born in lawful wedlock. He may, for instance, succeed to the property of his parents on their death intestate, and he has as against his father the normal right to be maintained.

Affiliation proceedings

As the name implies these are proceedings which, if successful, result in a finding by the Court that the child is in truth the child of the alleged or *putative* father and, as already stated, in an order that the father pay for the maintenance of the child.

A single woman who has an illegitimate child may apply for such an order

237

and so may a widow or married woman, but in the married woman's case she will be faced with the presumption of legitimacy, and, of course, no order will be made unless she can displace this presumption. Further no order can be made in her favour whilst she is living with her husband. This does not mean that no order can be made whilst she lives under the same roof as her husband, since a married couple may, although they share the same residence, live separate and apart from one another. Indeed, for the purposes of the law of divorce, one may desert the other and still share a residence in common.

The only other possible applicants for such an order are the National Assistance Board and a local authority, *i.e.* a county or county borough council. The National Assistance Board may apply, if, for instance, under the National Assistance Act, 1948, assistance has been given to the mother of an illegitimate child, or a local authority may, for example, apply where it has in the interests of the child's welfare received it into its care.

The application by the mother is made by complaint to any one Justice of the Peace, sitting in the mother's local Magistrates' Court. If the mother resides in Scotland or Northern Ireland, then application can be made to the father's local Magistrates' Court in England.

The application by the mother may be made before the birth, though no order can be made until the child is born, or at any time within twelve months from the birth. No application can be made after this period unless the putative father has within this twelve months' period paid money for the child's maintenance, or unless the mother proves that before the birth she married the putative father invalidly because either she or he was under age and that the putative father had access to her within the twelve months before the birth of the child.

After the complaint is made a summons will be issued requiring the putative father to attend at the Court, and the case will then be heard on the day appointed for the trial. The parties may, of course, be represented by counsel or solicitor, but whether or not the mother is the complainant, she must herself be present and give evidence. On the other hand, the actual presence in Court of the putative father is not essential. He is, of course, a competent witness on his own behalf. He is also a compellable witness on behalf of the mother, should she or her legal advisers consider it in the mother's interests to call him. The mother's evidence as to paternity must be corroborated by some independent evidence. Such corroborative evidence may be direct or circumstantial. For instance, it may consist of evidence independently confirming acts of familiarity, even though such proven acts took place before the child could have been begotten, or it may consist of an admission of paternity contained in a letter from the putative father. If being compelled to do so, the putative father gives evidence, corroboration may emerge from him in giving his evidence. Without corroboration of the mother's evidence as to paternity no order can be made.

The maximum contribution which the father will be ordered to make towards the child's maintenance is now £2 10s a week. The Court may also order him to pay the expenses incidental to the birth of the child and if the child has died before the making of the order, the child's funeral expenses. It will order payment to be made to the clerk of the Court unless on representation made by the applicant it is satisfied that it would be undesirable to do so. If the clerk is under the order to receive the payments on behalf of the mother, he can institute proceedings to enforce such payments, should they fall into arrear. The mother can, in any event, start her own proceedings with this end in view, which she will do again by complaint to the Magistrates' Court, and the Court may, for instance, commit the father to prison, but not in any case for longer than six weeks, if it is satisfied that his default was due to his wilful refusal or culpable neglect, or it may, in an appropriate case, make an order attaching his wages or salary or pension, *i.e.* compelling some of such money to be paid to the Court so that it may be paid over to the mother.

If the application for an affiliation order is made before birth, or within two months thereafter, the payments may be back-dated to the birth, but in other cases they are calculated from the date of the order. They will cease when the child attains the age of thirteen, unless the order contains a direction that they are to continue until the child is sixteen, when they will then cease. However, the Court does have power to make further orders continuing such payments thereafter if it is satisfied that the child is or will be engaged in a course of education or training after the age of sixteen and that it is expedient for payments to be made for that purpose. But such subsequent continuations cannot extend beyond the age of twenty-one. Payments must be made without deduction of income tax, but the father is entitled to deduct the amount of payments from the computation of his total income for income tax purposes.

The Magistrates' Court has power to revoke, revive, or vary the affiliation order on application to it by way of complaint. It might be asked, for instance, to vary the order because the mother's or father's means have materially altered since the making of the order, or the mother may wish to apply for a continuance of payments beyond the age of sixteen on the grounds set out above.

Finally, it is worth mentioning that the findings of the Magistrates' Courts in affiliation proceedings are subject to the review of the Appellate Courts, and an appeal lies either to Quarter Sessions or by way of case stated to the High Court.

GUARDIANSHIP

The legal meaning

A guardian is usually thought of as someone other than the parent who exercises parental rights over, and assumes parental duties for a child, but in its legal sense, the term 'guardian' includes a parent. The Common Law regards parents as the *natural* guardians of their children, and, by statute, after the death of one parent the surviving parent is the guardian of the children, either alone or jointly with any testamentary guardian appointed by the other, *i.e.* appointed by his or her will. Parental rights and duties have already been discussed. This section will deal, therefore, only with persons standing in the place of parents, *i.e. in loco parentis.* These are they who replace a parent and become legal guardians.

Unless some special customary right can be relied on—for instance, the City of London has a customary right to the guardianship of orphans of deceased freemen—this can only happen by appointment in one of a number of ways, *e.g.* by a Court order or under the will of a deceased parent. In other words, legal guardianship is different from actual care and control.

Suppose, for example, both parents die without appointing a testamentary guardian, *i.e.* a guardian appointed by a will, and some relation of the child

"The Common Law regards parents as the *natural* guardians of their children . . ."

assumes the care and takes over the control of the child. This act of guardianship gives rise to certain rights and duties. If there is no dispute as to the custody of the child, the actual custodians of the child will be entitled to continue to care for it and to exercise control over it. They must also, for instance, protect the child, and this duty may continue after the child comes of age if the child is unable to look after itself through some mental or physical disability. Further, by way of example, they must see that it receives full-time education. However, unless and until they take steps to have themselves appointed by the Court, they will not become the legal guardians of the child.

Appointment of guardians

Who may appoint a guardian? A parent can, the Court can, and an infant, supposing, for instance, there were no appointment by parent or Court, may appoint a guardian for himself. However, an infant's power to do this is ill-defined and rarely exercised and, in practice, guardians are normally the subject of either parental or Court appointment.

Both the father and mother have power to appoint a guardian or guardians either by deed or will to act after their respective deaths, if the child is then an infant. Persons so appointed need not, of course, accept the office, but if they

". . . an infant may appoint a guardian for himself . . ."

do so, they cannot thereafter resign at will. Such guardians are referred to as testamentary guardians even though the appointment is by deed, and testamentary guardians act jointly with the surviving parent unless the parent objects. If there is such an objection, or if the guardian considers the parent unfit to have the custody of the child, he may apply to the Court, and ask it to decide whether guardian or parent should act alone or whether they should act jointly. In all questions of guardianship, the child's welfare will be the Court's chief consideration, but if the Court, for instance, orders that the guardian should have the custody of the child, it would normally give the parent the right to have reasonable access to the child. If each parent appoints a guardian, they act as joint guardians after the death of both parents.

The jurisdiction of the Courts

The Courts which have jurisdiction in matters of guardianship are the High Court, or the local County Court or Magistrates' Court for the locality in which, for example, the infant in question resides. However, this jurisdiction of the Magistrates' Courts is more restricted than that of the two other Courts. For instance, the child must normally be under sixteen, and Magistrates' Courts cannot order more than 50s a week maintenance for the child. The High Court, through its Chancery Division, exercises the jurisdiction of the old Court of Chancery over infants, which will be discussed later when wards of Court are dealt with—but quite apart from this inherent jurisdiction, the High Court, together with the County Courts and Magistrates' Courts, have a statutory power to appoint a guardian in certain circumstances.

Suppose, for instance, an infant has no parent or guardian or other person exercising parental rights over him or the testamentary guardian refuses to act, the Court may appoint a guardian. In making the appointment, the Court will as always regard the welfare of the infant as the paramount consideration, but subject to this principle it will normally give preference to the nearest blood relations over strangers provided they are fit to act. Again the wishes of the deceased parent, if they are ascertainable, will be considered, even though he may not have appointed a testamentary guardian. The religion of the prospective guardian and the ward may be a relevant factor, since it would obviously be undesirable to risk a possible conflict between the two because of such a difference.

A guardian may have rights and duties either over the person or the property of the infant or both. A guardian of the *person* has no authority over the infant's *property*, and vice versa. Testamentary guardians are guardians both of the infant's property and his person. Guardians appointed by the Court are, unless otherwise expressly ordered, guardians only of the infant's person.

The guardian's rights and duties

What are a guardian's rights and duties over the person of the ward? They are similar to but not identical with those which a parent has over his children. He owes the ward a duty to provide physical and moral protection. His consent to the marriage of his infant ward is necessary and he must see that such a proposed marriage is suitable. Indeed he must endeavour to stop an unsuitable marriage.

He is under a duty to apply the income of the infant's property, in so far as he has control over it (a topic which will be dealt with below) for his proper maintenance, according to his position in life and expectations, and to take, when necessary, the advice of the Court on the question. He is not obliged to spend his own money on the maintenance of the ward.

If the guardian is acting jointly with the surviving parent, or the Court has ordered that he act to the exclusion of the parent, the Court may order the parent to pay such periodical sums to the guardian for the ward's maintenance as are reasonable having regard to the parent's means. The monetary limit of such a maintenance order in a Magistrates' Court has already been mentioned.

The guardian is entitled to the custody and control of the ward, and he can enforce this right by legal proceedings. But the Court can interfere with this right and commit the custody of the infant to another. Further, where a guardian is acting with a surviving parent, it will usually be the parent who will be entitled to custody to the exclusion of the guardian.

The guardian must also ensure that the ward receives full-time education, and he has the right to control the education of the ward. However, this right of control over education is subject to a duty to educate the ward according to the latter's position in life and the expectations and the wishes of his father and mother so far as these are known.

It is a crime to remove a ward under the age of fourteen and a female ward under the age of sixteen from the guardian's custody, and a crime to remove children of these age groups from the custody of their parents.

What are a guardian's rights and duties over the property of his ward? Subject to the rights and powers of others in whom the ward's property may be vested, he is, broadly speaking, entitled to receive income on behalf of the ward and has certain powers of management over his ward's property, which powers he must exercise for the benefit of the latter until the ward attains full age, or during any shorter period for which he is appointed guardian. However, as shown elsewhere, modern legislation has tended to ensure that a great deal of an infant's property is held by trustees. Thus, normally, a large part of the ward's property will be vested in others whose rights and powers override those of the guardian.

The importance of guardianship of property has in this way been reduced and the function of modern guardianship, therefore, concentrated more on the ward's person than on his estate. However, when the guardianship comes to an end, the guardian must account to the ward for all property that has come into his possession. Furthermore, so far as transactions between guardian and ward are concerned, the law protects the ward by presuming in the latter's favour, if a dispute arises between them, that, for instance, any financial advantage resulting to the guardian from the transaction was procured by undue influence on the part of the guardian. A Court will, therefore, regard the transaction, *e.g.* the contract or gift, as ineffective and if necessary set it aside, unless the guardian rebuts the presumption. He may be able to do this, for instance, by showing that the ward received independent advice before completing the contract or making the gift. The reason for this protection is that a guardian like a parent, for example, has peculiar opportunities for exercising influence over infants under his authority. It will be remembered that it was suggested when discussing this aspect of the relationship between parents and children that the safe course is to ensure that the child is given independent legal advice before completing a transaction that benefits the parent, and this is also the safest course for a guardian in similar circumstances.

When guardianship ceases

Guardianship ceases when the ward comes of age, or if the ward dies before then, or the appointment is for some lesser period, at the relevant earlier date.

The guardianship of a female is terminated by her marriage, but the guardianship of a son will not cease on his marriage unless it was made determinable on marriage. Moreover, the High Court has power to intervene whenever a guardian acts in a manner calculated to prejudice the infant, and if it is satisfied that the infant's welfare requires it, the Court may remove any testamentary guardian from office and, if necessary, appoint another in his place.

Wards of Court

The Chancery Division of the High Court inherited an old supervisory jurisdiction of the Court of Chancery over infants. This jurisdiction can be exercised irrespective of whether the infant has any property or not, or even of whether he is a foreign subject. Under it an infant can by application be made a ward of Court.

Once a child is made a ward of Court, in effect, the Court becomes its guardian. It is true that an actual guardian may be appointed to supervise the ward's activities, but it is the Court which controls. Thus, it may control the ward's education, maintenance, and custody. In particular, the Court will control the residence and marriage of its wards. Thus it will not allow one of its wards to be removed out of its jurisdiction, even by the father, unless it is satisfied that it will be for the benefit of the ward, and it will order a ward who has been removed without its leave to be brought back. Further, to effect such a removal without its leave will be treated as contempt of Court, which may, therefore, result in imprisonment.

A ward of Court may not marry without the consent of the Court even though all other necessary consents have been obtained, and marriage with one of its wards without leave is also contempt of Court punishable with imprisonment. Even the ward may be imprisoned for marrying without leave. Further, the Court will, if necessary, grant an injunction to restrain a contemplated marriage to which it has not given its consent, and may do so, even against the parent of the other intended party or a guardian who is consenting to the proposed marriage. It will also, if necessary, order that the other party refrain from communicating with the ward.

So the Chancery Division of the High Court through this procedure affords an effective method of protecting the welfare of infants, particularly, perhaps, of wayward infants. Many readers of this section will have become acquainted with the procedure through the reports in newspapers dealing with wealthy infants or ones with great expectations who have been made wards of Court to protect them from certain suitors. However, as stated earlier, any infant may be made a ward of Court irrespective of his of her wealth or poverty.

CHANGING YOUR NAME

ON THIS QUESTION the law varies according to whether the name which it is desired to change is a surname, a Christian name, or a forename. And let us get clear at the outset that the difference between a Christian name and the forename is that a Christian name is one given at baptism, and a forename is one which is not. In other words, it is a recognized first name, but not given at a christening or baptism.

SURNAMES

Dealing first with surnames, the basic principle is that any British subject is completely free to change his surname at will. The law is now, and always has been, that a surname is purely a matter of reputation, in other words, the name by which a man is known to his friends, relations, and business acquaintanceships, and so on. There is nothing sacred, legal, and binding about a surname; it is merely the name by which you happen to be known. Originally a surname denoted little more than the place from which you came. For instance, a man was called Peter of York, or John of Warwick. Over a period of time that slid insensibly into Peter York or John Warwick. Other surnames had nothing to do with geographical connotations, but indicated a family relationship. For example, David the son of Peter, hence David Peter or David Peters. A surname might also have indicated an occupation as so many of them did. For example, the blacksmith became Smith, the wheelwright became Wright; Baker, Butcher, and so on—it is perfectly obvious what those mean. The surname Little derived from a man who was below average height. The surname Biggs from one who was very tall. Although those surnames became attached to a man or to a family, it has been the law for many centuries that that man could change his surname simply by announcing the fact that he wished to do so, and so five hundred years ago, as today, Mr Peter Smith could overnight become Mr Peter Baker, simply by his deciding that he wished to make the change and telling all those concerned that he wished to do so.

We have all become so accustomed to laws and rules and regulations about what we can do and what we can't do, that it is surprising to most of us to meet such simplicity, to find that if, for example, our surname is Brown, we can, if we like, change it to White without asking anyone's permission, and even without any documentary formula of any kind.

The reason for this is that for hundreds of years the Common Law of this country has upheld the principle that a man's surname is not a right of property, and not surrounded by the solemnity and complication of the law of property, but as stated above, it is simply a matter of reputation: in other words, it is the name by which people know you.

A name which is a trade-mark is a different matter. Acts of Parliament give special rights of property in trade marks, and these are dealt with in another section. There may also be a legally enforceable right to the ownership of a pseudonym under which a man writes or broadcasts. But no one owns his personal surname in the same way as he may own his freehold house, or his books, or his clothes—another man may assume his surname and use it as his own, and no one could stop him unless there was some fraud or deception involved. That is the basic legal theory.

Why then do so many people change their names by what is called a Deed Poll? The fact is that there may be many practical reasons, not legal reasons, but practical ones, why a man's change of name may need more permanent

Anyone can adopt a new name—

but it is important to ensure—

that all concerned—

recognize that you are—

the same person under—

your new name!

evidence than it used to, years ago. Today it is not only the neighbours in the village who have to be told about a change of name. The Inspector of Taxes, the Collector of Rates, the Ministry of Pensions and National Insurance, the Electoral Registration Officer who keeps the Roll of Voters, to mention only a few, will all be concerned and want to know about the change of name.

None of them will challenge anyone's right to change his name; they would be grossly exceeding their powers and duties if they did. It has nothing to do with them. The legal right to change your name is as strong today as it ever was, but these people and others are entitled to be convinced that you, under your new name, are the same person as they already know under your old name on their records.

Then coming to more personal affairs, you may have a banking account, you may own a house, you may own stocks and shares, Savings Certificates, and so on. Clearly, if you own these in the name of John Brown, and you have decided that you want to change the name of Brown to White, it is a matter of urgent practical importance for you to ensure that the bank where you have your account, the Insurance Company who have insured your life, or your house, the companies in which you own shares, and all others who are concerned are left in no doubt about your change of name, and recognize that you are the same person under your new name. It may be very necessary that you should give them some good evidence on which they can rely, and which will convince them that you are not your impostor.

A DEED POLL

Indeed, to change your surname, although in law it is a matter of the utmost simplicity, a matter of free will and free choice, which in theory you can do overnight by simply announcing your change of name, yet in practice it may be very necessary to produce some good solid evidence of your honesty and good faith. The fact is that the more goods and possessions and property which you own, the more complicated your life is, so to speak, the stronger the evidence which may be needed. The best evidence of a change of name is a document called a Deed Poll. The word 'poll' simply means that the deed is signed and sealed only by one person—that is, of course, the one who is changing his name. Very briefly, the background to this, which may be interesting, is that Deeds of Sale of property from one person to another used to be written on parchment which was then cut into two pieces—not straight across but by a wavy or indented line. The seller kept one part and the buyer the other. It was a precaution against forgery in the days when many people could not read or write. If the two genuine parts were put together they fitted like the parts of a jigsaw puzzle, the *indented* lines matched and the documents were, as a result, called *Indentures*. But as a Deed Poll was signed only by one person there was no other part to the deed, and the top of the parchment was shaved clean with a straight edge. In other words, it was a Deed Poll and not an Indenture; 'poll' means a straight line. 'Indenture' implies an indented line.

The advantage of a Deed Poll today is that it will be universally accepted as proof of your change of name. And because it is a technical legal document it is obviously essential to consult a solicitor and ask him to draw it up for you. A very pertinent question at this point is, how much will it cost? The solicitor's fees, including the cost of advertisements, because it is desirable, even if not necessary, to advertise the change effected by a Deed Poll in one or two papers, will be something in the neighbourhood of ten guineas. That is only a rough guide; there is no fixed scale and the figure is given merely as a broad general indication of what the costs might be.

Another advantage of a Deed Poll is that it can be enrolled or registered in the Central Office at the Royal Courts of Justice. It need not be. But if it is so registered there is a permanent record of your change of name and official copies of the Deed can be supplied to those who have to satisfy themselves that you, under your new name, are indeed the same person as you were under your old name. There is no legal obligation, either to advertise, or to enrol the Deed. If you do neither, the figure of costs mentioned above will obviously be less, but there are advantages both in the advertisement and in the enrolment; both emphasize the genuineness of the change of name and both provide valuable evidence of your sincerity and ident'ty.

Moreover, enrolment of the Deed ensures that a permanent record is kept. There is also the advantage that after a Deed Poll has been registered, or enrolled in this way, the Passport Office will issue a new passport in your new name without even mentioning the old name on the passport. When the Deed has not been enrolled, the Passport Office usually writes both the old and the new name on the passport. But when it has been enrolled the old name disappears for good. It should be mentioned here that where a new name has been used for all purposes for at least the previous ten years, and there is evidence of this, the Passport Office may be willing to accept it and mention only the new name on the passport, but short of this kind of evidence, or apart, as stated above, from a Deed Poll, they write both names on the passport, both the old and the new, so the Deed Poll is the one certain way of ensuring that only your new present name appears on the passport.

A Deed Poll executed by a married man can, and usually will, include his wife's change of name to correspond with his. It will also include his children's names if they are under twenty-one. But a child who is over twenty-one will keep his former name regardless of his father's change, unless he wants to follow his father in changing his surname. In that case, he must also sign the Deed Poll.

In Scotland there is nothing exactly like a Deed Poll. The two established ways of proving a change of name in Scotland are either a petition to the Lord Lyon King of Arms, who may grant the petition and issue a certificate of change of name, or a declaration of change which can be registered in the books of Council and Session in Edinburgh or in the local Sheriff Court.

The Deed Poll, or the petition, or the declaration in Scotland are the strongest and perhaps most effective way of proving your change of name. It must be emphasized that it is not the documents themselves that effect the change. The documents are only evidence of your decision. But in this complicated world, and especially where the person changing his name may have property and possessions in his old name, which it is essential for him to ensure shall be his in his new name, it is useful that such evidence, effective evidence, is available to prove the change, and to prove his identity.

CHANGE WITHOUT A DEED POLL

But many thousands of people have in fact changed their names, who have never heard of Deeds Poll or petitions to the Lord Lyon King of Arms. They have simply at one time or another in their lives adopted another surname which is quite different from the names on their birth certificates; they may even have changed their names more than once. They are people who do not as a rule consult solicitors, people who may not have banking accounts, or insurance policies, or stocks and shares, and who do not own house property.

It is perfectly clear that they are legally free to change their names, and if they have done so, then what they have done is within their competence. But they may one day want to prove, for some reason or another, that they, under their new names, are the same persons as they were under the old names; in other words, that they haven't changed their identities, although they may have changed their names.

How are they to prove this? The answer is not a Deed Poll, but another document called a Statutory Declaration. A Deed Poll is intended to announce an *immediate* change of name, it deals with the present and the future, not with the past. But by a Statutory Declaration you may declare that for so many years past you have been known by your present name; it is meant to prove a change that you have made many years ago. A Statutory Declaration is rightly regarded as one which ought to be believed, because under the Act of Parliament which empowers the making of a Statutory Declaration it is provided that if the statements in it are false, the person who makes it is liable to face a criminal charge of perjury. It is for this reason that statements in the Statutory Declaration are accorded the greatest respect. Here again it is very desirable, in fact, for most people absolutely essential, that they should have a solicitor's advice and help in drawing up the Declaration. The cost is less than that of a Deed Poll, mainly because it is not customary to advertise a Statutory Declaration, but merely to have the document available to produce to those who may be concerned to prove that the change of name is a genuine one, involving the same person without change of identity, but only with change of name.

CHANGE OF NAME ON MARRIAGE

So far, we have been considering a voluntary change of name by a man or woman. But there is another way in which a woman, at any rate, most frequently changes her name, *viz.* when she marries. This is a matter of social convention, not of law. As a general rule, when a woman marries she takes her husband's surname, and the evidence of her change of name is her marriage certificate. However, it is not necessary for her to take her husband's surname; there is no legal obligation on her to do so. It may be inconvenient or possibly socially embarrassing, if she persists in being known by her maiden name after she is

249

married, but a good many professional people use their maiden names for acting, or writing, or for their practice as a doctor, or a lawyer, and their married name for social life.

Another question affecting married women is what name they should or may use after their marriage is ended by divorce. The answer is that a divorced woman is legally entitled to continue using her husband's surname by which she was known during her marriage. Equally she can, if she likes, revert to her maiden name. A divorced woman may even continue to use a title which she acquired by virtue of her marriage. There is a case, for example, where a woman who married the Earl of Cowley and therefore became known as Countess Cowley continued to call herself Countess Cowley after a divorce, although her husband had married again and there was another Countess Cowley. This caused a good deal of trouble and inconvenience and the matter had to be thrashed out in the Courts. The House of Lords upheld the first wife's right to continue to use the title of Countess and the surname of Cowley if she wished to do so.

CHRISTIAN NAMES

A change of surname, therefore, is a comparatively simple matter. A change of Christian name, i.e. a name given at baptism, is not quite so simple. There is one special difficulty about a change of Christian name. There is not a great deal of legal 'authority' (i.e. decided cases) on this point, but the Common Law appears to be that a Christian name given at baptism cannot be legally changed except at confirmation by the Bishop. This is occasionally done in the Anglican Church, and in the Roman Catholic Church it is indeed the general practice for the child who is being confirmed to take an additional Christian name, the name of a saint. There is no other certain way of effecting a legal change of Christian name. Even then the birth certificate which indicates the names originally given to the child cannot be altered, but as the new name given at confirmation is a legal change, the child or its parents can insist on the new name being used notwithstanding the difference from the birth certificate.

There is no such legal difficulty about changing a first name or forename which is not a Christian name, i.e. which was not given at baptism. Such a name can be changed at will as readily as a surname. The change may require evidence in the shape of a Deed Poll or Statutory Declaration, as described above in relation to surnames, but that is merely evidence of change.

But even though a Christian name may only lawfully be changed at confirmation, there is nothing to prevent anyone assuming and using and being known by a different first name. He may not be able to compel an official recognition of the change. It may be necessary for him to continue to use his original name in documents of title to land or property, in insurance policies or share certificates, and so on, but in ordinary everyday life there is no reason on earth why he should not use a different first name. Incidentally it is not uncommon for a Deed Poll to contain a change of Christian names as well as surnames, and the Central Office of the Royal Courts of Justice will not on that account refuse to enrol the Deed. They accept the Deed but send a formal note to the person who has signed it pointing out that the purported change of Christian name may not be recognized legally.

CHANGE OF NAME
WITHOUT LEGAL FORMALITIES

A good many people have been very concerned when they have discovered that important events in their lives have been carried out in names which differ from those on their birth certificate. There is a fear that a marriage or the purchase of a house, or some other important event in the person's life has been rendered invalid because those ceremonies or transactions have been carried out in other names and there has been no formal announcement of change of name by a Deed Poll or a Statutory Declaration.

These differences are very seldom of any importance if the ceremony or the transaction was entered into in the name by which they were known at the time. The facts of a case which was heard in the Courts illustrate this point very well.

The parents of a certain girl parted shortly before she was born and they never lived together again. When she was only three years old her mother went to live with a man, not her husband. She lived with him for some fourteen years. She could not marry him because her husband was still alive, but she took his surname and they had several children, all of whom, of course, were necessarily illegitimate.

The girl in this case was brought up by her mother to use this man's surname, to regard him as her father and to regard the other children as her lawful brothers and sisters. Her birth had been registered and she had been baptized. Her birth certificate would have shown the name of her real father, the surname which she would ordinarily have borne, but in fact she never saw it. She had no inkling of the truth until she was sixteen. Then her mother told her the whole story and begged her to go on using the surname she had always used until then. The girl agreed and, of course, it was obviously natural that she should.

Some years later she was going to be married and the question cropped up again. What name was she to give? Was she to give the name on her birth certificate which was the name of the father whom she had never seen, or should she give the surname which she had been brought up to use and indeed used for the greater part of her life?

She told her future husband and together they discussed the problem with the vicar who was going to marry them. He advised that she should stick to the name which she had always used and the banns were published in that name.

The Courts would never have been concerned with this story if the girl's marriage had been a success. But it failed, and the husband chose to petition the Court for a decree of nullity. He based his petition on the allegation that there had never been a lawful marriage, because the banns were not published in his wife's true name. In order to succeed in his petition he would have had to prove that both he and his wife wilfully and knowingly allowed a false name

251

to be published for the purpose of concealing the truth. It may seem strange, but he was prepared to assert and prove that if he possibly could.

But the truth was, of course, that the girl had used the name she had always used and did so on the vicar's advice for the very purpose of *avoiding* concealment. Indeed if she had given the name on her birth certificate, that might have been concealment, because no one hearing the name when the banns were published would have known who she was. The Court held that she was right to use the name which she had in fact given. The law is that banns and notices of marriages at Registrars' Offices are published in order to give publicity to the intending marriage. That purpose is destroyed if the banns are called or the notices given in names which have long since been abandoned.

The point it is desired to emphasize is that not merely is it a very simple matter to change a surname, or a first name, and even to use a name other than the Christian name which has been given at baptism, but that the use of names other than those on birth certificates for the purpose of transactions like buying or selling property, or stocks and shares, or vitally important ceremonies like marriages, does not necessarily invalidate those transactions or those ceremonies. There is nothing wrong about assuming other names unless it is part of a deliberate fraud. It may be very desirable, indeed it may even be essential, that a change of name shall be proved by formal documents like Deeds Poll or Statutory Declarations. But these documents are evidence of sincerity and genuineness, not the means of effecting the change. In fact this is one of the rare occasions on which the law, as it stands today, permits the greatest possible freedom of choice to an individual and he is not usually likely to be involved in difficulties unless, *e.g.* he is embarking on a course of fraud or endeavouring to avoid a criminal prosecution.

MENTAL ILLNESS

THE attitude of the law to those who are mentally ill has been substantially changed by the Mental Health Act, 1959. This Act of Parliament creates something of a revolution in the law about mental illness. As the figures show that one person out of every twenty goes into a mental hospital at least once in his lifetime, this Act is going to affect a large number of people. Moreover, it will affect not only those who need treatment but also their families and relatives.

The new attitude of the law is shown by the fact that the old names like lunatic, idiot, imbecile, feeble-minded person, and moral or mental defective disappear. The term in the new Act is 'mental disorder', and this covers every type of mental illness, whether it is due to arrested development, sub-normality, or disease of the mind.

No one would pretend that a mere change of name in itself would achieve very much. In fact however, this change which buries all those old words which have so many shameful implications and associations, is only one instance of the new legal and medical attitude to mental illness.

The voluntary patient

One of the principle objects of the Act is to make it simpler and easier than ever before for anyone suffering from mental illness or mental depression of which he is keenly aware, to get treatment or to go into hospital as a vo'untary patient. This ability to go voluntarily for treatment is not new in itself. What is new is that by repealing provisions in former Acts of Parliament, the new Act sweeps away many previous legal formalities which a voluntary patient had to go through. In particular, it abolishes the need for him to sign a form of consent.

Under the new Act it is as easy for him to get treatment for mental illness as it is to get treatment for any physical illness like bronchitis or a broken leg. He simply consults his own family doctor who can then send him to hospital for specialist examination. He may either be admitted to hospital there and then, or just asked to come to the out-patients' clinic for treatment.

Another advantage of sweeping away the previous formalities is that someone who is not actually unwilling to be treated, but is nevertheless incapable of taking the positive steps like going through the former formalities of signing forms of consent, can now be treated as a voluntary patient. Previously he probably had to be certified. Now he can be treated as a voluntary patient.

Reducing the need for certification

But even allowing for the tremendous increase in voluntary treatment over the last thirty years or so, and the considerable new facilities for voluntary treatment, there will still, of course, remain those for whom treatment must be compulsory. They will be a minority, perhaps only 10 per cent. of those who are treated, but whatever the proportion, the new Act is very important for them and their families.

It makes a considerable change by abolishing the former rules about certifying mental patients and requiring Magistrates' orders before such patients could be taken into a mental hospital.

One serious objection to the old arrangements for certification was that so many took it to mean that there was some permanent mental illness or instability. In truth, with modern methods of treatment, this need not be true at all.

So the old system of certifying is completely abolished. The new system is quite different. No Magistrate's order is necessary. All that is needed is for the nearest relative to apply to a hospital to admit the patient. The application must be backed up by recommendations from *two* doctors, one of whom must have had special psychiatric experience.

If the nearest relative does not want to take the initiative and the necessary action, this application can be made by an official of the local authority who is known as the Mental Welfare Officer.

This application made either by a relative or by the Mental Welfare Officer takes the place of the former Magistrate's order, an order which was commonly known as a reception order. This application is the authority to the hospital to detain the patient by compulsion if necessary. There are a lot of safeguards about this which will be described later on. The point which it is desired to make here is that the whole procedure is so much simpler than it used to be.

It may well be thought that this very simplicity could be dangerous, that a mere application by the nearest relative is highly dangerous for the patient and puts undue power in the relative's hands. So let us consider the safeguards.

Safeguards against wrongful detention

First is the two doctors' recommendations. This in itself is not new, but the need for one of the doctors to have certain special experience in mental illness *is* new. It is true that in an emergency a hospital can act on the recommendation of only one doctor. But a second recommendation must be produced within seventy-two hours if the patient is to be detained.

Next, if the request for admission is that it is to be for *observation* only, the patient is not as a rule to be detained for more than one month, or, to be precise, twenty-eight days.

If the application is for admission for *treatment* the patient may not be kept in hospital for more than a year unless the authority is renewed.

Moreover, the patient himself can apply to a new body set up under the Act called the Mental Health Review Tribunal at any time within six months of the day he went into hospital.

So during the first six months the patient has the right to apply to this tribunal and if he has not already been discharged, then after one year he must be allowed to go unless the authority for keeping him is renewed. How is the renewal of the authority achieved?

The Act says that within two months before the end of the year of the patient's detention, the responsible medical officer must examine him and report. If he reports to the managers of the hospital that the patient should be detained, either in the interests of his own health and safety, or for the protection of other people, then the authority to keep the patient there is automatically renewed: it is automatic on the doctor's recommendation, unless the managers refuse to accept it.

This, depending as it might on one man's opinion, may be too restrictive of the patient's liberty, so the managers are obliged to inform the patient of the decision, and he may then apply to the Mental Health Review Tribunal if he thinks that he is being unjustifiably detained.

After the first period of one year, if the authority to detain the patient is renewed as described, it lasts for one more year. If at the end of that second year it is renewed, it lasts for two years, and thereafter for two years at a time. So there must be the fullest consideration, a medical examination and recommendation to the managers, a managerial decision at the end of the first year, at the end of the second year, and then every two years thereafter, with, at each stage, a right of appeal by the patient to the Mental Health Review Tribunal.

The Mental Health Review Tribunal

What is this Mental Health Review Tribunal? It takes the place of the old Board of Control, which is abolished. There are fifteen tribunals, one for each regional hospital board area, and it is probably wise that there should be fifteen such tribunals, and not as formerly, just one in London. On every tribunal there must be lawyers, doctors, and people with experience of social work. In view of the fact that the liberty of the subject is involved, the Chairman at every meeting must be a lawyer. What is more, there is provision for appeal to the High Court on any question of law.

As a patient who is compulsorily detained has certain specific rights of appealing to this tribunal, the Act provides that a letter written by a patient to the tribunal at any time when he is entitled to appeal must be forwarded unopened.

The patient's letters

That is a clear right given by the Act to the patient. In other respects the Act does give certain powers to the responsible medical officer in the hospital to hold up letters sent by or sent to the patient. A letter to the patient can be held up if the doctor thinks it would interfere with treatment or cause unnecessary distress. But even in this case it is very important to note that the doctor must not just suppress a letter; he must return it to the writer, assuming, of course, that the name and address are clear.

As to letters written by the patient: if they are to someone who has given written notice to the hospital that he does not want to receive letters from the patient, the hospital will act on this instruction and detain the letters. If the letters seem to the medical officer to be unreasonably offensive to the person written to, or defamatory of anyone (except the hospital staff who have to endure this), or if they are likely to prejudice the patient's interests, they can be kept back from the Post Office.

These powers are rather wide and general. But these provisions about interfering with letters do not apply to any letter addressed to the Minister of Health, to any M.P., to any officer of the Court of Protection, which is a branch of the High Court dealing with the affairs of mental patients, or to the managers of the hospital.

So these provisions about letters are designed in the main to keep a fair balance; clearly some letters written by or to a patient are better never sent, but over and above the restrictive provisions there are the rights of the patient, to write at certain times to the tribunal, and to write to the Minister, the Member of Parliament, and the others mentioned above, when no restriction is allowed to apply.

The duties of the 'nearest relative'

It was stated earlier that the initiative for applying to a hospital to take a mental patient and to keep him there if necessary would usually, or at any rate very often, come from the nearest relative, and that this application, backed by the necessary medical recommendations, constituted the hospital's authority to receive and detain the patient.

This term 'nearest relative' is defined in the Act. It is not left to individual interpretation as to what might be 'nearest'. There is a specified order of precedence. The list is a long one, but the important ones, which come first, are husband or wife, secondly, if either of them is dead, son or daughter; failing either son or daughter, the father or mother, and then it goes on to other generations for which reference should be made to the Act itself. There are provisions for shutting out a husband or wife if there is permanent separation or desertion. It is interesting to note that for this purpose, as for many others, an adopted child is to be treated solely as the child of the adopting parents.

The situation may occur where the nearest relative refuses absolutely to do anything about a serious case, or even to allow anyone else to do anything. For example, say a wife is mentally ill, maybe seriously and even dangerously so, but the husband refuses to send her to hospital and objects to anyone else doing so. Can anyone else act when he, the nearest relative, will not act?

The Act deals with this situation by providing that a County Court Judge may direct that the functions of the nearest relative may be carried out by someone else. Another relative may apply to the Court for such an order, and so may the Mental Welfare Officer of the local authority. In response to such an application, the Judge may appoint either the relative who applies or some other relative, or someone with whom the patient is living, or the Mental Welfare Officer himself.

The application to the Judge may be made, not only because the nearest relative unreasonably objects to an application, but for a variety of other reasons, such as that no nearest relative can be traced, or that the relative himself is ill and incapable of acting. So this ultimate power of the County Court fills a gap which might otherwise wreck the scheme of the new Act.

The discharge of the patient from hospital

Next, what about the discharge of a patient from hospital? As stated earlier, the patient must automatically be discharged at the end of a year, unless the authority to keep him is renewed in the way which has been described. The same situation will arise at the end of the second year, and subsequently at the end of every two years. But quite apart from this rule in the Act, the nearest relative can *at any time* direct that the patient shall be discharged. The relative in fact can *order* it.

This order must be acted on, unless the medical officer of the hospital certifies that discharge would be dangerous either to other people or to the patient himself. If that is done, the relative cannot again request discharge for another six months, but if the relative disagrees with the medical officer's report, he is entitled to apply within twenty-eight days after he is told about it to the Mental Health Review Tribunal for their independent decision.

The hospitals

Another very important change made by the Act concerns the type of hospital which is considered competent to take in, and if necessary to detain, mental patients. Under the former Act no hospital could take more than one person suffering from mental illness unless it was a hospital specially designated, certified, or approved for taking these patients. That has all gone. Any general hospital can now take a patient suffering from any form of mental disorder. The hospital is not compelled to; obviously it is right that it should have some discretion, but the freedom to take such patients is valuable. So many of them are not dangerously mentally ill at all, in fact the majority are not, and it is particularly good for such patients that they should not be segregated in a mental hospital.

256

Moreover, with modern methods of treatment, a patient suffering from depression may be as curable as one suffering from appendicitis, and some general hospitals can deal expertly with both, to the mental patient's great advantage.

The Criminal Law

Another great change made by the new Act is one which many people interested in Criminal Law think is perhaps the most important feature. Briefly it is this. If someone is convicted of a crime and there is medical evidence that he is suffering from mental illness, psychopathic disorder, or subnormality of a degree requiring hospital treatment or guardianship, the Court instead of ordering imprisonment or some other punishment, can instead direct his admission to hospital, or direct that he be put under guardianship.

That is a simplified summary of these sections of the Act, but is enough to indicate their general purport. It means something entirely new in our criminal jurisdiction. It means that in certain cases hospital psychiatric treatment may be a better answer by society to a crime than punishment. How it will work out depends on the Judges, the Magistrates, the doctors, and the hospitals. The Act of Parliament can only provide a framework within which they can decide and act; but already since the passing of the Act, Courts have taken advantage of this provision to direct admission to hospital and treatment instead of punishment by imprisonment.

Summary

To sum up this new Act, it makes admission to hospital more informal and easier for voluntary patients. It also greatly simplifies the procedure for admitting patients who are incapable of going, or unwilling to go voluntarily for treatment. There are new and better safeguards against unnecessary, unjustifiable detention, better rights for the patient to appeal to the outside world and to get in touch with the outside world. The provisions with regard to appeals and letters do, so far as an Act of Parliament can, ensure that unjustifiable detention can in no circumstances be possible.

With all this, there are stricter safeguards against the release of someone who may be dangerous to himself or to others. The amount of compulsion has been reduced to what the framers of the Act considered necessary for public safety. On recent statistics this degree of compulsion will apply to something like 10 per cent., or even less, of mental patients admitted. The overwhelming majority of mental patients will be treated like any other sick person. The overriding purpose of the Act has been to do everything possible to destroy all the old stigmas attached to mental illness, so as to ensure as far as any legislative measure can ensure, that the mentally ill will seek the treatment which is available to them, and which under modern methods is greatly superior to anything which existed before, and provides a much better chance of alleviation or even cure.

IN BUSINESS ON YOUR OWN

A BUSINESS of your own is something you may build up from scratch, or something you may acquire from a previous owner.

If you are proposing to buy, let us say, a tobacco and confectionery shop, you will probably find that the transaction consists in:

(a) purchasing the freehold or taking an 'assignment' of the lease of the premises,
(b) buying the stock-in-trade at a valuation, and
(c) buying the goodwill of the business (and perhaps also the book-debts).

Goodwill has been described as 'the probability that the old customers will resort to the old place', and as 'the whole advantage . . . of the reputation and connection of the firm, which may have been built up by years of honest work or gained by lavish expenditure of money'. It may well be the most valuable asset of all.

A person who acquires the goodwill of a business is alone entitled to represent himself as continuing the business of the vendor. But unless the vendor gives an undertaking that he will not carry on a similar business in competition with the purchaser, there is nothing to prevent him from opening a similar business a few doors away. And—provided he does not *solicit* his old customers: for this the law does not allow him to do—he can deprive the purchaser of much of the value of the goodwill. It is, therefore, necessary for the purchaser to obtain an undertaking from the vendor that the vendor will not set up in competition. This is one of the first things a solicitor acting for the purchaser would see to.

The law looks with disfavour, however, on what is called 'restraint of trade', or rather, *unreasonable* restraint of trade; for it regards competition as being generally in the public interest. The purchaser of a business is not therefore entitled to impose upon the vendor any greater degree of restriction than is necessary to preserve for the purchaser the benefit of the goodwill he has bought. The restriction must be reasonable as regards both the vendor and the public.

In deciding what is reasonable, the law will have regard to all the circumstances, and in particular to the nature of the business. Thus, in the case of a

259

small local business, like a tobacco and confectionery shop, a restriction preventing the vendor from opening a similar business within a radius of ten miles
would obviously be unreasonable (for a shop only a couple of miles away
would hardly draw custom away from the business that has been sold). On the
other hand—to take an extreme case—it has been decided that an armament
manufacturer who sold his business to a company was bound by his undertaking not to manufacture armaments *in any part of the world* for twenty-five
years, the business being so international in character that competition from
any place at all could affect the goodwill that the company had bought.

". . . nothing to prevent him from opening a similar business a few doors away . . ."

At one time a person, or group of persons (*i.e.* a partnership firm), could
carry on a business under any name he or they liked. This freedom of choice,
however, gave rise to certain abuses and difficulties: and so a number of restrictions and regulations were imposed by the Registration of Business Names
Act, 1916.

The Act requires that every person or partnership with a place of business
in the United Kingdom that carries on business under a name which does not
consist only of the true surname or surnames of the individual or all the partners
(with or without Christian names or initials) shall be registered. Registration is
also required where a person has changed his name—though this does not
apply to a woman's change of name on marriage.

Registration is effected by sending to the Registrar of the district in which
the principal place of business is situated, within fourteen days of the commencement of business, a statement containing certain particulars. These must show:

AT WORK; BUSINESS; INDUSTRY; THE PROFESSIONS

(a) The business name,
(b) The general nature of the business,
(c) The principal place of business,
(d) The present Christian name and surname (and also any former names) of each partner,
(e) The nationality (and, where different, the nationality of origin) of each partner,
(f) The usual residence of each partner,
(g) Any other business occupation of each partner.

Any change that occurs in respect of any of these particulars must also be reported in writing within fourteen days.

To find the address of the appropriate Registrar, make inquiry of the Registrar of Business Names, whose London address is Lacon House, Theobalds Road, London, W.C.1.

Failure to comply with these requirements renders each offender liable to a fine not exceeding £5 for every day on which business is carried on in default, and also places the individual or firm under certain legal disabilities. For instance, the offender cannot enforce any contract entered into during the period of default, he cannot even sue for money due, unless the Judge grants relief from this provision: and such relief will only be granted if the Judge is satisfied that the default was accidental or on some other ground ought to be excused.

Upon registration, a certificate is issued, which must be displayed in a conspicuous position at the principal place of business. If this requirement is not complied with, each partner is liable to a fine not exceeding £20.

The Registration of Business Names Act also requires persons or firms carrying on business under a registered business name to set out similar particulars as to true names and nationalities on all trade catalogues, trade circulars, show cards, and business letters. An offence against this provision carries a penalty not exceeding £5.

The Act also contains a special provision to protect British firms from unfair competition. Where a business name contains the word 'British' or any other word suggesting that the business is under British control, when in fact it is not, the Registrar may refuse to register the name or may remove it from the register.

Where a person or firm registered under the Act ceases to carry on business, the person (or his executors or administrators if he is dead) or the partners must within three months send a written notice to the Registrar stating that the business has ceased to be carried on. Failure to do so renders the offender liable to a fine not exceeding £20.

Three other matters which affect the setting up of a business are:

(i) Tax;
(ii) Town Planning;
(iii) Security of Tenure for business premises under the Landlord and Tenant Act, 1954.

All these are dealt with under their separate headings.

261

PARTNERSHIP

FOR a variety of reasons a business man may prefer to work in association with others than on his own account, and so a great many businesses of every kind are partnership concerns or 'firms'.

Partnership is defined (in the Partnership Act, 1890) as 'the relation which subsists between persons carrying on a business in common with a view of profit'. It is by no means easy to say, in every case, whether a number of persons associated in a business enterprise are partners. The best evidence of partnership is the sharing of profits. But this is not a conclusive test. In many firms employees share in the profits. They are not, however, partners, because the business is not carried on for them, and in general they do not share in its control. The widow or child of a deceased partner who receives a share of the profits does not thereby become a partner. A creditor may receive payment of his debt by instalments varying in amount with the profits of the business; but this does not make him a partner. If a person lends money to the business at a rate of interest that varies with the profits, then, provided all the parties concerned sign the contract relating to the loan, the lender does not, merely by reason of such a loan, become a partner. Nor does the seller of a business who takes the purchase price in the form of an annual share of the profits. The joint ownership of property or the sharing of gross returns does not, of itself, create a partnership, though it may go some way to indicating that a partnership exists. A formal Partnership Agreement will, of course, be decisive evidence.

A partnership may not consist of more than twenty persons or, in the case of a banking firm, ten. A business association of greater numbers must generally be 'incorporated' as a limited company under the Companies Act, 1948.

There are many differences between a partnership firm and a limited company. Perhaps the most important is that a firm, unlike a company, is not regarded as a 'legal entity' in itself, as distinct from its members. In consequence, each member (partner) of a firm is *personally liable* for the firm's debts, while the members (shareholders) of a company are not personally liable because the company, having a 'legal personality' of its own, is itself liable for its debts. It is true that for certain limited purposes a partnership firm may be regarded as having a personality distinct from that of the partners: for example, a firm called 'Williams & Co.'—of which the partners are John Roberts and his sons Henry and Michael—may be sued in the firm's name. But this is really only a matter of formal or procedural convenience: in substance, if the case goes against the firm, it is John, Henry, and Michael Roberts who may lose every penny they possess. Had the defendant been 'Williams and Co. Ltd', an incorporated company, then although an adverse decision might cause the company to become insolvent and to be wound up, its shareholders would stand to lose no more than the value of their investment in the company.

This is why it is so important to distinguish between those persons who are partners in a firm and those who (like persons associated with it in one of the ways mentioned above) are not partners. For it is only to the partners that the creditors of the firm can look for payment of their debts.

When a partnership firm is created, a name must be chosen for it. In most cases the names of the partners, or of the chief partners, are used—perhaps abbreviated by the use of the term 'and Co.'—but a firm called 'Williams and Co.' may no longer have anyone by the name of Williams in it (the founders of the firm having perhaps died or retired), so that it may be necessary to inspect the Register of Business Names to see who the partners actually are.

Partners!

A partnership can be created without formalities of any kind. But it is not unusual for the partners to define their rights and duties toward each other in a legal document setting out the 'Articles of Partnership' in a formal Agreement: and this is certainly a sensible course to adopt, for the purpose of avoiding disputes between the partners in the future.

Anyone, including a married woman and an infant (*i.e.* a person under the age of twenty-one), can be a partner. But an infant does not render himself personally liable to the creditors of the firm; and he can always withdraw from the partnership before reaching full age or within a reasonable time of reaching it.

New partners may be admitted, but only, of course, with the consent of all the original partners.

The legal position of partners must be considered under two separate heads:

(a) their relation to persons dealing with the firm, and
(b) their relation to each other.

RELATION OF PARTNERS TO PERSONS DEALING WITH THE FIRM

Every partner is regarded in law as an agent of the firm. This means that every act he does in the ordinary course of business is binding not only upon himself *but also upon his partners*. Thus, unless the person he is dealing with knows that the partner has no authority to act in the particular matter, any partner can sell the firm's goods, purchase goods for the firm of the kind that it usually needs, receive payment of debts owed to the firm, and engage servants for the firm. The liability of the firm, *i.e.* of all the partners, extends even to *wrongful* acts done in furtherance of the business. Thus a firm has been held liable in damages for the act of a partner who bribed the clerk of a business competitor to disclose information about his employer's contracts. Partners are not, however, liable on a contract which is outside the usual scope of the firm's business, unless the partner who made it was specially authorized to do so.

The estate of a partner who has died is liable for the debts and obligations of the firm so far as they remain unsatisfied: but his own separate debts take priority.

When a partner dies and the business is continued under the same name, his estate will not be liable on that account for partnership debts contracted after his death (for example, for goods ordered in his lifetime but not delivered until after his death).

On the retirement of a partner, the other partners may agree that he shall be free of all liabilities already incurred. If the creditors are parties to this agreement, he is completely released: but if they are not, he is still indebted to them, though he may have a right of indemnity against his former partners.

A retiring partner is not, in general, liable for partnership debts incurred after his retirement, but he may be so liable if he has allowed himself to be represented as a partner, for example, by letting his name remain in the firm's name. To protect himself against such liability, therefore, a retiring partner should give notice of his retirement to all persons who have previously had dealings with the firm, and should advertise his retirement in the *London Gazette*.

A person who is admitted to partnership in an existing firm does not thereby become liable to the creditors of the firm for debts incurred before he became a partner. He may, however, become liable if there is an agreement (called in law a 'novation') between the creditors, the old firm and the new firm, by which the original liability of the old firm is discharged by the new firm's accepting liability in its place.

RELATION OF PARTNERS TO EACH OTHER

The property of a firm consists of all the property that was originally brought into the partnership stock and all that was later acquired for the firm. The partners may use such property for the purposes of the firm, and not for their individual purposes. Any property bought with partnership money belongs to the firm: so if one partner buys shares in his own name out of partnership funds, without the authority of the other partners, the shares are regarded in law as partnership property. If the firm occupies land or a building as tenant of one of the partners, then unless the lease is stated to be for a specific, limited period, the tenancy will continue until the partnership is dissolved.

Unless the articles of partnership otherwise provide, each partner has an equal share of the profits in the firm—even a partner who has made no contribution to the firm's capital. It is, therefore, usual for the articles to lay down the proportions in which the profits are to be divided, larger shares normally being given to partners who are of senior standing or who have brought in more capital. Losses must also be borne by the partners in equal shares, unless otherwise agreed. A partner who makes a payment, or incurs an obligation, on behalf of the firm in the ordinary course of business is entitled to be repaid or indemnified by the firm. The question of each partner's right to share in the capital of the firm on its dissolution is discussed below.

All partners are entitled to share in the management of the business (though there may be 'sleeping partners' who prefer not to do so); but unless otherwise agreed, no partner is entitled to remuneration for his services, i.e. pay beyond his share in the profits. Every partner may inspect the accounts, which must be kept at the firm's principal place of business.

When a dispute arises between the partners as regards ordinary business matters the opinion of the majority prevails: but if it is a question of changing the nature of the business, all the partners must consent to the change. Unless the articles provide for expulsion, no partner may be expelled by the others; and the consent of all partners is needed before a new partner can be introduced.

A partnership may normally be terminated by notice given by any partner at any time. Such notice—if it does not specify a date—will take effect as soon as it is received by the other partners. If the articles provide, however, that the partnership can be terminated 'by mutual arrangement only' then it cannot be terminated except with the consent of all the partners—or through the death of a partner. The retirement of a partner must cause the dissolution of the partnership; if the business continues to be carried on by the other partners they constitute a new firm.

If partners carry on the business beyond the time fixed in the articles for the duration of the partnership, the partnership will so far as possible continue on the terms contained in the articles.

Partners are bound to render true accounts and full information to each other, as well as to the executor or administrator of a deceased partner. A partner who derives a profit from his use of the partnership property or goodwill must bring it into the partnership account. And if, without his partners' consent, he carries on a business in competition with the partnership business, he must pay over any profits he makes to the partnership.

If the other partners consent, a partner can transfer his share of the partnership to another person. This amounts to the resignation of the old partner and the admission of a new one, with the consequence that the former firm is dissolved and a new firm brought into being. Even without his partners' consent, however, a partner can assign his financial interest in the partnership to another person (whether by way of sale or gift, or as security for a loan): but that other person does not then become a partner. He is not entitled to interfere in the management of the business or to inspect the books; his only right is to take the share of the profits to which the partner (the 'assignor') would have been entitled. Moreover, an assignment of this kind does not relieve the partner of his duties and liabilities.

DISSOLUTION OF PARTNERSHIP

A partnership may be dissolved through the expiration of any period for which it was agreed that it should continue, by the retirement, death, or bankruptcy of a partner, or on the happening of an event which makes it unlawful for the firm to carry on business (for example, if a partner becomes an alien enemy through the outbreak of war). A partnership may also be dissolved by a decree of the Court when a partner becomes permanently incapable of carrying out his partnership duties (through unsoundness of mind or otherwise), or is guilty of conduct which is damaging to the business, or so conducts himself that it is not reasonably practicable for the other partners to remain in partnership with him; and the Court may also decree dissolution if it is satisfied that the partnership can only be carried on at a loss, or that circumstances have arisen which make it 'just and equitable' that the partnership should be dissolved.

If, after the dissolution of a partnership, a new partnership continues with the old firm's name, the former customers are entitled to assume that they are dealing with the old firm (and so to hold its members liable) until they are notified of its dissolution.

Even after dissolution, one partner can still bind the others in all matters necessary for the winding up of the partnership affairs.

After the firm's liabilities have been discharged out of the partnership property, any surplus is divided among the partners in the same proportions as the profits were shared. But before such a distribution is made, each partner (where the partners contributed to the firm's capital in unequal shares) is entitled to repayment of the capital he subscribed.

When a partnership is dissolved, all its property must be sold, including the goodwill of the business. The buyer of the goodwill is entitled to use the firm's name (provided that old customers are not led to believe that the old partners are still members of the firm), and the old partners may not use it.

COMPANIES

A COMPANY (by which is meant, for our purposes, a limited company incorporated under the Companies Act, 1948, or one of the earlier Companies Acts) is a 'corporation', that is to say, a corporate body, which in the eyes of the law has its own personality, distinct from that of its members. This may fairly be described as the cardinal principle of company law. The company is an 'artificial legal person', capable of having rights and liabilities of its own. Its directors and shareholders are not liable to the creditors of the company, and in this respect, as we have seen, are in a radically different position from the partners in a firm.

When a company enters into a contract, the shareholders acquire no rights or liabilities under it. It is true that if it is a profitable contract, the shareholders will benefit, because the company's profits ultimately come to them: and for the same reason, if it involves the company in a loss, their pockets will ultimately suffer. But this does not alter the basic fact that it is the company's contract and not theirs, and that the company alone can sue and be sued on it. And if the company should be unable to pay its debts and be forced into liquidation, the shareholders will not be liable to its creditors for the amount of its debts. Their liability is *limited* (hence the name 'limited company') to the amount, if any, which they have not yet been required to pay on the shares they hold in the company: that is the full extent of their financial risk; *e.g.* if they buy £1 shares and for the time being are only asked to pay 10*s*, their liability is to pay the balance of 10*s* a share. Once they have paid the full £1, *i.e.* once the share is fully paid, they have no liability. Their shares may lose value, but they cannot be called on actually to pay out any more.

What, then, are the advantages and disadvantages of converting a business which has been carried on by an individual or a partnership into a limited company? The first advantage we have just considered—the limitation of liability. This enables a person who wishes to retire from the active running of a business to retain his financial interest in it without remaining liable for its debts. Another advantage of incorporation is that new money can be put into the business by shareholders who will not demand participation in the management, and employees can be enabled to acquire a financial interest without sharing in the control.

Then again, incorporation avoids the inconveniences which a partnership suffers on the death, retirement, or bankruptcy of a partner, the admission of a new partner, or the assignment of a partner's shares. A company's identity is not affected by any such changes: it remains the same person in the eyes of the law.

A company can hold property more conveniently than a partnership can. The death, retirement, or bankruptcy of a partner, or the admission of a new partner, generally involves some dealing, by conveyance or otherwise, with the firm's property, while a company's property remains unaffected by the coming and going of shareholders.

Difficulties which might well arise for his dependants when the proprietor of a business, or a partner in a firm, dies can also to a great extent be avoided, if the business is incorporated.

Among other advantages enjoyed by a company—for there is not space to mention them all—is the greater ease with which it can obtain the money it needs for the promotion of the business, whether by way of loans (through the issue of debentures or debenture stock) or by the raising of further capital by issuing shares on the Stock Exchange and inviting purchasers. Finally, mention may be made here of possible tax advantages on which expert advice is essential: the alleged advantages may be illusory.

There are, inevitably of course, certain disadvantages in converting a business into a company. Apart from the expense of floating (*i.e.* creating) the company, there may be a tax snag—for income received by a shareholder as dividends does not count as earned income. And a company (other than an 'exempt private company'—see below) is required by law to make public a considerable amount of information relating to its accounts and the carrying on of its business, and this might in some cases give an advantage to trade competitors. Moreover, by buying up shares on the Stock Exchange and then making an attractive offer to the remaining shareholders (a 'Take-over Bid') a stranger

'Floating' a company!

can sometimes acquire control. Ultimately, control rests with the majority of the ordinary shareholders, not with the directors.

Companies are of two kinds, private and public. A private company is one which restricts the right to transfer its shares, limits the number of its members to fifty (exclusive of employees), and prohibits any invitation to the public to subscribe for shares or debentures.

A private company is very often a family concern, resulting from the conversion of a business, and it is quite common to provide that only a member of the family may be a shareholder. Such companies are frequently created for the purpose of reducing the estate duty liability of individual members of the family, who will be liable only on the value of the shares each personally holds.

Any company which does not answer the above description is a public company, even if it does not invite the public to subscribe for its shares. In practice, however, nearly all public companies make a public issue of shares.

A private company may be formed by two persons: seven are needed for a public company.

A private company has certain privileges, *e.g.*:

(a) a member can appoint a proxy to speak on his behalf at a general meeting;

(b) directors need not file at the Companies' Registry a consent to act or a contract to take qualification shares and a list of directors need not be filed. The Register of Directors need not include the date of birth. A director is under no obligation to state his age or to retire on reaching seventy unless the company is a subsidiary of a public company;

(c) it need not issue a prospectus or file a statement in lieu of prospectus.

A private company may acquire further privileges and be known as 'an exempt private company' provided it satisfies three further conditions. The main additional privilege of an exempt private company is that the ordinary annual return to the Registrar of Companies need not include the balance sheet or the auditors' report. Thus an exempt private company can keep its financial affairs completely secret.

The additional conditions necessary to enable a private company to claim the privileges of an exempt private company are as follows:

(a) None of the shares or debentures is held by another company and no person other than the holder has any interest in any of its shares or debentures;

(b) Not more than fifty persons hold debentures (except a bank holding them as a security for a loan or when they are held by the trustees of a will or a family settlement);

(c) None of the directors is a company and its policy is not controlled by anybody except the directors, members, debenture holders, or trustees for debenture holders.

If these conditions are complied with, the company is an exempt private company and, as stated above, need not file its balance sheet or auditors' report with its annual return to the Registrar of Companies. It must, however, send with the annual return a certificate signed by a director or the secretary that, to the best of their knowledge and belief, these conditions have been satisfied.

FORMATION OF A COMPANY

A company is formed by delivering to the Registrar of Companies a document called the 'Memorandum of Association', which is signed by the persons proposing to create the company (each of them taking at least one share). The Registrar enters the company on a register and grants a certificate of incorporation. The register is open to public inspection, so that anyone who is interested to see what, for example, the objects of the company are, can do so.

The Memorandum of Association contains six essential clauses:

(1) The name of the company (which must end with the word 'Limited').
(2) The country of the registered office (England or Scotland).
(3) The objects of the company.
(4) The limitation of liability (this may be by 'guarantee' and not by shares: but we are concerned here only with companies limited by shares, which are by far the most numerous).
(5) The share capital (with the number and amount of the shares).
(6) The subscription clause (followed by the names of the subscribers and the number of shares each is taking).

The objects clause is of great importance, because a company—being an artificial creation of the law—does not have full legal capacity (like an adult person of sound mind), but only the capacity to do those things which are 'fairly incidental' to the carrying out of its stated objects. Thus whereas an individual ironmonger who is minded to do so can become a dairyman instead (and the same applies to a partnership firm of ironmongers), a company which is formed with the stated object of carrying on the business of ironmongers only, cannot lawfully transform its business into a dairy. If it sought to do so, its act would be *ultra vires* (beyond its powers) and of no legal effect, and the contracts of the dairy business would be void. This limitation is necessary for the protection of shareholders: for a person who sees fit to invest his money in one type of business may not want it to be used in another.

It is usual for an objects clause to be drawn in very wide terms, so as to give the company ample scope for its operations. Moreover, a company may by special resolution alter its memorandum so as to enable it.

(i)   to carry on its business more economically or efficiently,
(ii) to attain its main purpose by new or improved means,
(iii) to enlarge or change the local area of its operations,
(iv) to carry on some other business which may be conveniently combined with its own,
(v)   to restrict or abandon any of its objects,
(vi) to sell or dispose of the whole or part of its undertaking, or
(vii) to amalgamate with any other company or body of persons.

An alteration of the objects may require to be sanctioned by the Court if an application is made to the Court by a certain proportion of shareholders who are opposed to it.

The Memorandum of Association defines the powers of the company in what might be called its external relations.

The Articles of Association, which are lodged with the Registrar at the same time, control the internal management of the company, being concerned with such matters as voting rights and powers of the directors. Except in the case of a private company, it is not essential for Articles of Association to be registered, because the Companies Acts contain—in 'Table A'—a list of regulations which form every company's articles except in so far as they are excluded or modified by any special articles of the company.

A company may alter its articles by special resolution in any way which does not go outside the powers of the memorandum. An alteration must also not deal unfairly with minority shareholders; but such an alteration will be allowed if it is honestly made for the benefit of the company as a whole. Thus, in one case, an alteration of articles was permitted so as to enable a competing shareholder to be expelled by requiring him to transfer his shares—at their full value—to a person nominated by the directors.

As the powers of the directors are set out in the Articles of Association, directors who act in a manner unauthorized by the Articles will be acting *ultra vires*. There is, however, a fundamental difference in legal effect between an act which is *ultra vires* the company and one which is merely *ultra vires* the directors. To take the example mentioned earlier, if an ironmongery company, through its directors, made a contract for the carriage of milk, such a contract would be absolutely void so far as the company is concerned; any money paid out by the directors under the contract would have to come out of their own pockets, and no action could be brought against the company for any breach of such a contract. If, however, the contract is one which it is not beyond the powers of the company to make, but the contract is made on its behalf by a director acting in an unauthorized manner, the company may be bound if it ratifies the director's act (that is to say, approves it in a general meeting of the shareholders) or even without such ratification if the director has, to all appearances, authority to enter into the contract on the company's behalf (as, for example, if he is the managing director). A person entering into a contract with a company is not bound to inquire into its 'indoor management': so if the directors require the authority of a general meeting for the doing of a certain act on behalf of the company, an outsider (unless he is actually aware of an irregularity) is entitled to assume that they have duly obtained such authority.

If it is desired to raise money by the issue of shares to the public, a 'prospectus' is required. This term covers any form of notice or invitation offering to the public for subscription or purchase any shares or debentures. If a prospectus contains any untrue or misleading statement, an allotment of shares may be set aside on the ground of misrepresentation, while those responsible may be liable to pay damages and also to be prosecuted. For the protection of the investing public, the law requires a prospectus to set out a large number of particulars relating to the company's management and business.

A public company which has issued a prospectus cannot commence business or borrow money unless shares have been allotted to an amount not less than the minimum subscription (that is, the amount named in the prospectus as the minimum needed to make all necessary payments and to provide working capital) and unless every director has paid on shares for which he is liable to pay in cash the same proportion as is payable by the public. A public company which does not issue a prospectus must file a 'statement in lieu of prospectus' containing most of the information required in a prospectus.

On compliance with the above (and certain other) requirements the Registrar will certify that the company is entitled to commence business.

The 'capital' of a company may mean

(a) the *nominal* capital (*i.e.* the nominal value of the shares which the company is authorized to issue by its Memorandum of Association), or

271

(b) the *issued* capital (*i.e.* the nominal value of the shares actually issued), or
(c) the *paid-up* capital (*i.e.* the amount paid up or credited as paid up on the shares).

A company which needs more funds after the whole of its authorized capital has been issued may increase its capital, in general meeting, if power to do so is contained in the Articles. Where capital is increased, the Memorandum must be altered accordingly and notice given to the Registrar.

A company may also reduce its capital, if so authorized by the Articles; but as this may adversely affect creditors, it can only do so by special resolution confirmed by the Court. Capital is often reduced to enable a company to pay dividends safely when assets have been lost. The Court may require the company to publish the reasons for reduction.

The members of a company are the signatories of the Memorandum of Association and the other shareholders, that is to say, those to whom shares in the company are allotted or who acquire shares, on the open market (through the Stock Exchange) or otherwise, from their previous owners. The company must keep a register of members. Any person—including another company—can become a member (though a person under the age of twenty-one can repudiate his shares and cease to be a member).

Shares (which are discussed more fully below) entitle their holders to receive part of the company's profits when declared as dividends, and to participate in the share-out of the company's property on winding-up. They must generally be issued by the company at a price not less than their face (or 'nominal') value, and are usually issued for cash—though where the company is purchasing a business, the sellers may agree to take shares instead of money as the price of the business. Shares are sometimes not 'fully paid up': that is to say, the company is still owed part of the price of the shares. The owners of such shares are liable to be called upon to pay the balance, and in the event of the company's insolvency that balance (in addition to the amount they have already invested in the shares) will be the limit of their loss.

A transfer of shares from one shareholder to another is quite different from an allotment of shares by the company. Every shareholder in a public company is entitled to transfer his shares, in the manner prescribed in the company's Articles. A transfer is usually made in three stages. First, there is a contract for the sale and purchase. (If the shares are quoted on the Stock Exchange, this will be made—by a series of transactions which do not concern us here—through a stockbroker.) A transfer form is then signed by the seller and is delivered to the buyer with the share certificate—the document which a company issues to every shareholder, certifying the number of shares held by him. The buyer sends the transfer and certificate to the company, and the company is then bound to insert his name on the register as the holder of these shares and to send him a share certificate, made out in his name, within two months.

There may be various classes of shares, conferring different rights upon their holders. Thus the holders of preference shares are normally entitled under the Articles to be paid a fixed dividend before any dividend is paid on the ordinary shares (and they may also be entitled to prior repayment of capital).

272

Preference shares are sometimes 'cumulative', in which case a deficiency in any year's dividend is made up in subsequent years—so far as money is available.

Then come the ordinary shares, on which, generally speaking, the greater part of a company's net profits is paid as dividends. Sometimes 'A' ordinary shares are issued, the holders of which are not entitled to vote.

Deferred (or founders') shares are usually taken by the promoters of a company—sometimes being allotted to them as fully paid up in consideration of their work and expense in floating it. These shares usually entitle their holders to a proportion of the profits if the dividend on the ordinary shares exceeds a fixed amount; for example, the deferred shares may be entitled to half the profits after a dividend of 10 per cent. has been paid on the ordinary shares.

A company in general meeting may, if authorized by the Articles, convert fully paid shares into stock. Stock differs from shares in that it can be split up into any fractional amount for the purposes of transfer.

Debenture holders are not, like shareholders, members of the company; they are creditors who have advanced loans in return for the payment of interest, and who hold documents called 'Debentures' which certify the company's indebtedness. Their loans are usually secured by a mortgage or charge upon the company's property (known as a 'floating charge' if it is not attached to any specific asset), which entitles them to receive payment, if the company should become insolvent, in priority to other creditors.

The mode of paying dividends is determined by the Articles. They are usually declared by the directors with the sanction of a general meeting. It is a fundamental rule that dividends must not be paid out of capital. Any loss or depreciation of capital must be taken into account before the amount of profits can be ascertained and dividends paid. On the other hand, any increase in the value of the capital assets may be paid out as dividends, provided that the whole accounts for the year are taken into consideration.

An annual general meeting of members must be held once a year, and an extraordinary general meeting may be requisitioned any time by the holders of one-tenth of the paid-up capital carrying the right to vote. Three types of resolution may be passed at a general meeting. An ordinary resolution is passed by a majority of those present. An extraordinary resolution is one passed by a three-quarters majority of members entitled to vote and voting (in person or by proxy) at a meeting of which notice specifying the intention to propose the resolution as an extraordinary resolution has been duly given. A special resolution resembles an extraordinary resolution, except that it requires not less than twenty-one days' notice specifying the intention to propose the resolution as a special resolution.

A company's business is managed by its directors. A private company may have only one director, but a public company (if registered after October 31st, 1929) must have at least two. Every company must also have a secretary (who must not be the sole director).

Directors are, in the eyes of the law, both trustees and agents for the company. The first directors may be appointed by the Articles or by the subscribers to the Memorandum. The Articles normally provide for the appointment of directors from time to time, such appointments being made or confirmed by the company in general meeting. A director may at any time be removed from office by ordinary resolution. It is not lawful, in connection with the transfer of the whole or any part of the undertaking or property of a company, for any payment to be made to a director for loss of office or as consideration for his retirement unless particulars of the proposed payment have been disclosed to the members and the proposal approved by the company.

A director must disclose his interest in any contract to his co-directors. A person who has been convicted of any offence in connection with the promotion or management of a company, or who in a winding-up has been found to be guilty of fraudulent trading or any breach of duty to the company, may be prohibited from taking part in the management of a company for up to five years. A director responsible for fraudulent trading (*e.g.* carrying on business and incurring debts when there is no reasonable prospect of the creditors ever receiving payment) may be declared personally liable without any limitation for the debts of the company, and may also be sent to prison.

The subject of company winding-up is discussed elsewhere.

CONTRACTS GENERALLY

A FEW COMMENTS on the general fundamental law of contracts may be helpful.

A contract is an agreement which may be enforced by law. Not all agreements are legally binding. Some, like social engagements or domestic arrangements between husband and wife, are not intended to have legal effect. Others may be invalid in law because they lack some essential element.

To constitute a valid contract there must be:

(a) an offer by one party (the 'offeror') and acceptance of it by the other (the 'offeree'),
(b) 'consideration', or writing under seal,
(c) legality of object,
(d) legal capacity of the parties, and
(e) genuineness of consent.

These are explained below.

OFFER AND ACCEPTANCE

An offer may be express (as when one merchant offers to sell goods to another at a stated price), or it may be implied (like the offer of the Post Office to deliver letters posted in its boxes at the prescribed postage rates). It may be addressed to a single individual, or it may, like an advertisement, be made to the world at large. In one well-known case the manufacturers of a patent medicine advertised that they would pay £100 to any person who caught 'flu after using their medicament: the plaintiff used it but nevertheless caught 'flu, and it was held that, having accepted the offer contained in the advertisement by complying with the conditions, she was entitled to the £100.

An offer may be made subject to certain conditions; and provided reasonable steps are taken to bring them to the attention of the offeree, he will be bound by them even if he does not trouble to find out what they are. Thus a railway passenger who receives a ticket on which is printed 'Subject to the conditions contained in the current timetables' is bound by those conditions whether he has read them or not. And a person who puts his signature to an

"When an article is displayed in a shop window, it is not, in the strict legal sense, being 'offered' to the public."

order form or other such document cannot—unless he can prove actual fraud—be heard to say that he did not know the terms contained in it.

An offer must be distinguished from an 'invitation to treat', or an invitation to do business. When an article is displayed in a shop window, it is not, in the strict legal sense, being 'offered' to the public. If it were, the shopkeeper would be bound to sell it to anyone who tendered the price. But the shopkeeper is entitled to refuse: for in law it is the customer who offers to buy, and the shopkeeper is free to accept or reject the offer as he pleases.

Usually, of course, he is anxious to sell. But he may have reasons for wanting to keep some particular thing, which he may want for purposes of prestige or advertising or any other reason, and the fact that it is displayed in the window or on a counter does not oblige him to sell to a customer who offers the price.

On Monday *A*. posts a letter making an offer to *B*.

B. receives the offer on Tuesday morning—

and sends a letter of acceptance right away.

In the meantime *A*. writes on Tuesday revoking his previous offer.

On Wednesday *B*. receives the notice of withdrawal of the offer—

but as *B*. had accepted before *A*.'s offer was withdrawn—

there is a binding contract between them!

The same principle applies to a catalogue circulated to potential customers. The catalogue is an indication of the goods dealt in and an invitation to customers to ask, *i.e.* to offer to buy. It is not in itself an offer which can be at once converted into a contract by a customer's asking for an article and tendering the money.

The acceptance must be in the exact terms of the offer. If it introduces a variation it is a counter-offer, and amounts to a rejection of the offer. So if A. offers to sell his car to B. for £500 down and B. says he will pay £200 down and £300 in six months, he cannot (if that counter-offer is refused) claim to accept the offer at £500 down. A.'s offer, having been rejected by B.'s counter-offer, may no longer be available for acceptance. It is now B. who is making the offer to buy for £500 down—an offer which A., if he has now changed his mind, is entitled to reject.

To be effective, acceptance must be communicated to the offeror. Where a resolution appointing a headmaster was passed by a board of school managers, and was rescinded before it had been formally communicated to the applicant, it was held that his offer (in applying for the post) had not been accepted, and there was therefore no breach of contract. And the offeror is not entitled to say to the offeree, "I will assume you accept my offer unless I hear to the contrary".

An offer remains open until it is rejected, or revoked (before acceptance), or until the period for which it is stated to be open expires or (if no such period is stated) until a reasonable time has elapsed. What is a reasonable time depends on all the circumstances.

If the offer requires that acceptance be communicated in a particular way (*e.g.* by telegram), then it must be communicated in that way. If an offer is made by post, the law implies that it may be accepted by post. An offer (by whatever means it is communicated) only takes effect when it reaches the offeree. An acceptance by post, however, takes effect as soon as it is put into the letter-box. Thus if the letter of acceptance is delayed—or even lost—in the post, any resulting inconvenience must be borne by the offeror. For the contract is complete *as soon as the acceptance is posted.*

The revocation of an offer—like the offer itself—takes effect only when it reaches the offeree. If A. sends B. a letter on Monday offering to sell him certain goods at a stated price, and B., on receiving the letter on Tuesday, posts a letter of acceptance which reaches A. on Wednesday, there is a binding contract between them. And this is so even if A., having changed his mind, posts on Tuesday morning a letter revoking his offer, and B. does not post his letter of acceptance until Tuesday afternoon. For at the time when B. accepts he does not know that the offer has been revoked: and the contract would therefore have been completed before the revocation reached him.

CONSIDERATION

Except when it is made under seal (which is explained below), a gratuitous promise ('something for nothing') is not enforceable. Some *quid pro quo*— what the law calls 'consideration'—is essential.

The word 'consideration' in this sense sounds strange to our ears today, and indeed it is a very old use of the word. But we do use it in this sense, as, for instance, when we say: "In consideration of your paying me £50 I will allow you to drive over my private road for one year." So 'consideration' in this sense is what one party gains and the other party pays.

It may take the form either of a benefit received by the party who makes a promise or does an act, or a detriment suffered by the party who receives a promise. If A. promises to make B. *a present* of his watch, and then fails to keep the promise, B. cannot sue him: there is no contract between the parties, because there was no consideration for A.'s promise. If, however, A. had agreed to *sell* his watch to B., B. could sue him if he failed to do so: and it would be immaterial that the agreed price was far less than the real value, for the law does not concern itself with the adequacy of the consideration (leaving that for the parties to decide). In this example, the consideration would be both the benefit received by A. and the detriment suffered by B. (namely, the payment of money by B. to A.): but the consideration would be equally valid if A.'s promise had been to give B. the watch in return for B.'s doing something which was of no actual benefit to A. but occasioned some detriment or trouble to B., such as giving (or promising to give) money to a charity, or running a mile in under five minutes.

While consideration need not be adequate, it must be of *some* value. And it must relate to something done or paid at the time of the contract—the mutual promises which make a contract—or to a promise to do something in the future. Something *already done* cannot be a valid consideration in law.

ILLEGALITY

Contracts which are illegal are void. Among them are contracts tainted with immorality, contracts to commit crimes or civil wrongs, contracts for the sale of public offices or for the procurement of titles of honour, and contracts tending to impede the administration of justice.

Contracts in restraint of trade, if unreasonable in their terms, are regarded as against public policy, and are therefore void.

Gaming and wagering contracts are void by Statute: and any subsequent promise to pay a bet—even if supported by fresh consideration—is also void.

(As to contracts which contravene the Moneylenders Acts, 1900 to 1927, see the chapter on *Moneylending*.)

As the law refuses to countenance illegal contracts, any money paid or goods supplied under such a contract cannot generally be recovered. However, an exception to this rule may be made, where the parties are not both to blame, in favour of the innocent party; and where no part of the illegal purpose has been carried out, either party may recover money paid in respect of it. Moreover, if only part of a contract is illegal and the illegal part can be severed from the remainder, the contract may be enforceable as to the remainder.

CAPACITY

The most important form of incapacity today is infancy (see the chapter on *Parents and Children*). With a very few exceptions an infant is not legally bound by contracts into which he has entered.

A contract made with a person of unsound mind or in a state of drunkenness is valid, unless it was known, at the time of contracting, that he was mentally disordered or did not know what he was doing. Such a person—like an infant—is liable to pay a reasonable price (which might not be the agreed price) for necessaries.

GENUINENESS OF CONSENT

Where the parties were mistaken on so fundamental a matter that there was never a real (but only an apparent) agreement between them, the contract is void. But generally speaking, a contract is not 'avoided' by mistake.

If I buy a ring mistakenly thinking it to be gold, that is my fault and my misfortune. I cannot repudiate the contract because of my mistake.

It would be an entirely different matter, of course, if the seller had fraudulently or even innocently misrepresented the quality of the ring. But if he gave no representation, said nothing about its quality, I cannot get out of the contract or get damages.

Similarly where a young woman signed a contract for a series of dancing lessons: she thought she could stop the lessons at any time, only paying for those she had received. In fact, the terms of the contract which she had apparently not read, or at any rate not understood, obliged her to pay for the whole series whether she actually had the lessons or not.

But there are some occasions when a mistake can so affect the genuineness of the consent and mutual understanding between the parties that there is no contract in law. A detailed discussion of these occasions is too complicated for this work but as one general guide to this kind of mistake it can be said that it must be *mutual*, in other words that both parties are under serious misapprehension. For example:

(1) An auctioneer put up for sale lots of hemp and tow. The sale catalogue was misleading. The defendant intended to bid for hemp. A lot of tow was put up for which he bid, thinking it was hemp. The bid was accepted. The Court found that the auctioneer intended to sell tow while the defendant intended to bid for hemp and that the auctioneer thought the high bid offered was merely an overvaluation by the defendant. It was held that owing to mutual mistake there was no contract.

(2) The defendants contracted to buy a cargo of cotton to arrive 'ex *Peerless* from Bombay'. There were two ships of that name and both sailed from Bombay, but one arrived in October and the other in December. The two parties each intended to contract in respect of different vessels. The description of the cargo would have fitted either vessel but there was nothing to show clearly which cargo was the subject of the contract and therefore no binding contract.

An agreement which is induced by misrepresentation may be voidable; *i.e.* it may be enforceable by the person who has been deceived if he nevertheless for reasons which seem good to him wants to have the contract honoured and carried out; but it will not be enforceable against him. This question of the effect and results of misrepresentation is dealt with in the chapter on *Misrepresentation.*

WRITING AND 'UNDER SEAL'

Most contracts are just as legally valid and enforceable when they are made orally—by word of mouth—as when they are made in writing. It is not essential for most contracts to be in writing and duly signed. Obviously it is often an advantage, first because the existence of the contract is easier to establish if a written and signed document or letters exist, and secondly because if the terms are complicated a written record is safer than memory.

But there are two classes of contracts which are not enforceable in the Courts unless they are in writing or unless a written memorandum of the contract—signed by the party to be accused of failure to carry out the contract—is in existence. Notice that this memorandum in writing need not be signed by both parties. It will be accepted as evidence against the defaulting party if *he* has signed it.

The two classes of contracts are:

(i) contracts for the sale or other disposition of land or an interest in land. The words 'or other disposition' include a 'mortgage, charge, lease, assent, vesting declaration, vesting instrument, disclaimer, release, and every assurance of land or interest in land';

(ii) contracts of guarantee, *e.g.* where A. promises to stand guarantor for B. and to pay his debt to C. if he defaults.

For both these, writing is necessary. There used to be other classes of this kind. To mention only one, a contract for the sale of goods of the value of £10 and upwards had to be evidenced in writing. But this requirement (in the Sale of Goods Act, 1893) was abolished by statute in 1954.

The words 'under seal' mean that in addition to signing the document the parties press a wax seal, or imitation wax wafer as a token of their impressing a wax seal. The wax may be impressed by a seal or signet bearing a crest or initials or other emblem. Old deeds were always so sealed. But for some fifty years it has become a common practice only to have a red wafer imitation of the wax and for the signatories to touch the wafer opposite their signatures.

The point is that sealing or the imitation of sealing is regarded as giving greater solemnity to the document, which when sealed becomes known in law as a 'deed'. A man's seal was thought to be even more binding than his signature, especially in days when a nobleman might not be able to write but could impress wax with his family crest. Hence, as explained earlier, a contract under seal was binding even though no money or other consideration passed.

TERMINATION OF CONTRACT

A contract is normally brought to an end by performance, *i.e.* by both parties doing what they agreed to do. It may also be discharged by an agreement between the parties to rescind it, or in accordance with a provision in the contract that on the happening of a certain event (such as the outbreak of war) it shall cease to have effect.

Other modes of discharge are acceptance of breach, and impossibility.

280

A party to a contract may commit a breach of it

(a) by repudiating his obligations before the time for performance is due,
(b) by disabling himself from performance (*e.g.* by selling to B. the house which he had contracted to sell to C.), or
(c) by failing to carry out his obligations properly.

Any such breach entitles the other party to damages: but he cannot treat the breach as putting an end to the contract, and so releasing him from his own obligations under it, unless it is a breach of the entire contract or of some vital term that goes to the root of the contract.

A contract is not discharged by one party's repudiation of it, but only by the other party's acceptance of the repudiation. If the repudiation is not accepted (for the injured party is not bound to accept it as putting an end to the contract), the contract continues in force.

Generally speaking, a party who finds it impossible to perform his obligations through an event which occurs after the making of the contract is not thereby excused: for he could have provided against such a contingency by a term in the contract; *e.g.* a man who books a hotel room and cancels because he falls ill is liable for his breach of contract. (See section on Hotels.) However, there are a number of exceptions to this rule.

If performance becomes impossible through an alteration in the law, or through the act of a body with statutory authority (such as compulsory purchase by a public corporation), the contract is discharged.

It is also discharged if a specific object which is necessary for the performance of the contract is destroyed (*e.g.* the hall in which the concert is to take place, or the ship specified for the carriage of the goods sold), or if certain circumstances which form the basis of the contract fail to obtain (as when a room was hired for the purpose of viewing the coronation procession of Edward VII, which was then cancelled on account of his illness).

A contract may also be discharged when its commercial object can no longer be achieved. 'Frustration', as it is called, usually arises through a delay which is not due to the fault of either party (*e.g.* when a ship suffers accidental damage on the way to the port of loading, so as to be unable to perform the contract of carriage within a reasonable time).

At Common Law, frustration of contract often gave rise to injustice where one party had incurred expense in carrying out part of the contract, for which he could get no recompense. The Law Reform (Frustrated Contracts) Act, 1943, enables the Court to make orders for the payment of money or recovery of money paid so as to do justice between the parties.

REMEDIES FOR BREACH OF CONTRACT

The injured party may in all cases claim damages, and may sometimes sue for specific performance or an injunction, or refuse to perform his own obligations under the contract.

The amount of damages recoverable is such as will put the plaintiff in the same financial position as if the contract had not been broken. This rule is, however, subject to the limitation that a defendant will not be liable for damage which would not arise in the ordinary course of things and which he could not be reasonably expected to foresee.

Specific performance means the actual carrying out of the contract, and in a proper case the Court will order this. It is, however, a discretionary remedy, and will not be granted where damages would be an adequate remedy (as in the vast majority of contracts), where the contract is for personal services, where one of the parties is an infant, or where the contract is for the loan of money. Specific performance is usually obtained where the contract relates to houses, buildings, or land.

An injunction, which is also discretionary, may be granted to enforce a negative stipulation in a contract, such as an undertaking by the vendor of a business not to carry on a competing business within a certain radius for a certain length of time.

CONTRACTS FOR BUYING AND SELLING GOODS

THE LAW about the sale of goods has developed over the centuries and it was codified in a most important Act of Parliament called the Sale of Goods Act, 1893. This was out of the run of ordinary Acts of Parliament in that it did not make new law. What it set out to do was to put into one place a long series of Court decisions about the various rights of buyers and sellers of goods.

It is a long Act, and in places a complicated one. Therefore, it is proposed to deal first and in detail with those parts of the Act which make the greatest impact on the ordinary citizen. Those, of course, are primarily the conditions about the quality of goods, and the remedies available if the goods one has bought are defective in quality. After that will follow some account of the rest of the Act.

The word 'goods' covers pretty well everything except land and houses. The Act can apply equally to a merchant buying 10,000 tons of steel plate as to someone buying a cake, to someone buying a radio set or a vacuum cleaner or some other expensive piece of electrical apparatus as to a child buying a toy catapult.

All these things are goods, and the basic provisions of the Act about quality state that when someone buys goods from a dealer who regularly deals in that kind of goods, from one whose business it is to supply them, he is legally entitled to expect certain obligations to be fulfilled.

The seller must be someone whose business it is to deal in that class of goods. So if you buy a second-hand car or a sewing machine or a radio or a television set from a friend and it breaks down or is found to be generally defective soon afterwards, the Act does not help you. This is not because the goods are second-hand, but simply because your friend is not in that trade. The transaction was a purely private one, not a deal in the course of business which gives you legal rights under the Act.

The first basic provision is as follows:

> Where the buyer makes known to the seller the particular purpose for which the goods are required so as to show that he relies on the seller's skill or judgment and the goods are of a description wh'ch it is in the course of the seller's business to supply, the goods must be reasonably fit for such purpose.

This can be illustrated by a few examples which are taken from actual cases which have been fought in the Courts.

You buy a bun in a confectioner's shop. Unknown to you or to the shop-keeper it contains a stone on which you break a tooth. You are entitled to recover damages from the shop to compensate you for the pain you have suffered and for the cost of dental attention. The shopkeeper may say, "But this was a pure accident. With all my care I couldn't prevent it." That may well be true. But this principle has nothing to do with negligence. The shop-keeper's legal liability does not depend upon your proving that he or the bakers were negligent. It need not be his fault. You have not received goods of the quality you were legally entitled to expect and under the Act that's what matters. The bun was not fit for its intended purpose, which, of course, was to be eaten.

Then there was a case about a rubber hot-water bottle bought from the chemist, which burst a few days later and scalded the purchaser's wife. He sued the chemist and was awarded damages which included the expenses he incurred in the treatment of his wife's injury.

In the basic rule which is stated above, it is provided that the buyer has to make known to the seller the particular purpose for which the goods are required so as to show that he relies on the seller's skill or judgment. Now this does not mean that in every case when you buy articles in a shop that you must pompously say to the shopkeeper exactly how you are going to use the goods. It is quite enough if their purpose is obvious. If you buy a watch it is obvious that you want it to tell the time. A hot-water bottle is to keep you warm in bed, a bun is to be eaten. There is absolutely no reason for you to go out of your way to explain the purpose for which you want the articles; it is perfectly obvious and therefore they come within the condition.

On the other hand it sometimes happens that the purpose is not obvious. For instance, you may buy an electric motor which might be adaptable to a variety of uses. To bring yourself within the provisions of the Sale of Goods Act, you should make it quite clear to the shopkeeper what particular use or uses you have in mind. For instance, he would not be liable if you put an electric motor to heavy work and it broke down when it was really only suitable for much lighter work and you did not tell him how you were going to use it.

The second very important provision of the Sale of Goods Act is as follows:

> Where goods are bought by description from a seller who deals in goods of that description (whether he be the manufacturer or not) there is an implied condition that the goods shall be of merchantable quality.

283

Now this is needed to cover the situation where the purchase does not come under the first heading described above but you buy goods by some branded name or by a trade mark or some other precise description. If you ask for, let us say, the A.B.C. electric motor (which is an imaginary name, of course) the shopkeeper is not to be blamed if the motor he sells you is made

"... it sometimes happens that the purpose is not obvious ..."

exclusively for an A.C. supply whereas yours is D.C. That is a mistake whose consequences you would have to bear. When a customer buys something by some definite name or by some definite description the shopkeeper is not responsible for ensuring that it is fit for the purpose for which he intended it. Clearly, he cannot be made responsible for this, because he may not know the purpose for which it is intended. In any case the customer is not buying with the purpose made known or declared; he has only asked for a named article which he has described. Its fitness for its purpose is therefore entirely a matter for him. He must be presumed to know what he wanted.

284

To meet the situation and to continue to ensure that the shopkeeper is nevertheless responsible for its quality this second rule provides that 'the goods shall be of merchantable quality'. It is quite clear that these words are wide enough to mean that the goods are fit to be sold, or worthy of a good merchant.

If a man asked for and bought 'Slicko' hair cream (and that's an invented name, by the way) at a chemist and it made him bald, he could not sue the chemist on the intended purpose rule, because he had specified 'Slicko' and he got what he asked for. But he could rely on the rule about 'merchantable quality'. 'Slicko' obviously was not fit to be sold as a hair cream.

There is a third provision which is also of great importance:

Where there is a contract for the sale of goods by description there is an implied condition that the goods shall correspond with the description, and if the sale is by sample as well as by description it is not sufficient that the bulk of the goods corresponds with the sample if the goods do not also correspond with the description.

At first sight it may seem unnecessary for an Act of Parliament to say that the goods you have ordered must correspond to their description. The advantage of the provision is that if you do not get exactly what you have asked for you are not obliged to accept what is sold to you because it is just as good or because it is virtually the same. The quality may be just as high as what you wanted. The goods may be equally fit for your intended purpose, and under the previous provisions mentioned above you would not be able to reject them. Under this provision you are. For instance, if you buy rose trees by name and you find that when the buds appear in bloom the varieties are not exactly what you have ordered, arguments about quality are irrelevant. You would be entitled to damages. In one case which was heard in the Courts, the buyer ordered a new car of a certain make. The car had in fact done some very low mileage indeed and was virtually as good as new, but it was held that he was entitled to reject it because it was not in fact new.

If any of these conditions described above are broken what can the buyer do about it? What are his remedies? He may be entitled to reject the goods, *i.e.* to repudiate the contract and return them, or he may be entitled to damages. If he is going to reject the goods and return them he has to act very promptly before he has used them to any extent, before he can be said to have accepted them. If he has used them to such an extent that it may be said that he has accepted them and only discovered their defects rather late, then he is entitled to damages. He is entitled to damages from the trader or shopkeeper who sold to him.

It is very common for that shopkeeper to hide behind the manufacturer. He is apt to say that it is not his fault, that he had no responsibility. He merely sold what he had received. This is not the law. He is directly responsible to his customer. If he has to take the goods back or to pay damages, he may in his turn be able to sue the manufacturer from whom he bought them. But that is a matter between him and the manufacturer. The customer, the direct purchaser, can look for redress to the man who sold to him and leave the shopkeeper to pursue his remedies against the manufacturer; and no doubt the shopkeeper would be successful if he could show that he had not himself mis-handled the goods in any way and had sold them in the same condition as he had received them.

This was made quite clear by a famous case about some underwear which was sold to a doctor. He bought some underclothes from a reputable man's shop and contracted dermatitis. The medical evidence proved that the dermatitis was due to some chemical in the material which had not been completely removed during the process of manufacture. The Courts held that the shop-keeper was liable to pay damgaes to the customer. As the shopkeeper was personally blameless he could look in turn to the manufacturer to repay him.

Incidentally, the case also illustrates what was mentioned above, that conditions as to fitness for purpose and the condition about merchantable quality sometimes go hand in hand. Those underclothes had been bought from a shop which dealt in that kind of article, and it was obvious for what purpose the purchaser intended to use them. As they gave him dermatitis they were not fit for their intended purpose. In addition they were obviously not of merchantable quality. The advantage of the second one is that it would come into operation when the customer had not relied on the seller's skill and judgment to choose a particular article for him but had specifically asked for these garments by their trade name.

The attitude of the shopkeeper to the customer who comes along with unsuitable goods and says that they are defective very often varies not with the shopkeeper's knowledge of the law but with his concern for his own reputation. The first-class shop will usually not hesitate to do everything in its power to satisfy the customer and will readily take back defective goods without argument, and supply others which are up to standard. The less good shopkeeper will do everything in his power to avoid anything of the sort and, when driven into a corner and unable perhaps to produce other goods which are satisfactory, will offer the customer a credit note so that he can buy something else in the shop. The last thing he wants to do is to pay money back. No customer should ever be fobbed off by this kind of ruse, which is unworthy of any good shopkeeper and, of course, not in accordance with the Sale of Goods Act.

The three important conditions described above,

(1) fitness for purpose,
(2) merchantable quality,
(3) goods to correspond with description,

are conditions which are implied in the contract of sale of goods unless the terms of the contract specifically exclude them. This is extremely important, because it is quite lawful for the manufacturer or shopkeeper to invite the customer to enter into a contract, a written contract under which the conditions and warranties and provisions generally of the Sale of Goods Act are not to apply to that particular transaction. In return the customer is usually offered some other kind of promise. This arrangement is frequently made by what is commonly known as a guarantee.

Now guarantees often look very impressive. But although they certainly give the customer some advantages they may also deprive him of his rights under the Sale of Goods Act. A guarantee may be presented to the buyer for instance when he buys a piece of apparatus like a refrigerator, a vacuum cleaner, or a radio set and the apparatus is delivered to him accompanied by a document of guarantee. He is invited to return a part of the document, signed. If he does this he is given such rights as the manufacturer is willing to offer and gives up, as a rule, all his rights under Common Law or under the Sale of Goods Act which are described above.

Guarantees of this kind vary enormously. The period for which the guarantee is given may be six months or a year, although some manufacturers of some apparatus offer a much longer guarantee. They usually provide that if certain defects which are described appear within the period of the guarantee, the manufacturer will repair or replace what is defective.

However, this is often accompanied by a clause requiring the customer to pay all the labour charges involved in the repair and very often the cost of sending the goods to the manufacturer's premises. Costs of transport may not be high but labour costs very often form by far the highest proportion of the cost of doing the work. Indeed even if the manufacturer sends a service engineer to the customer's house to repair the defect he will very often under such a guarantee make what is called a service charge and this may be quite a considerable item.

If the buyer does not want to give up his Sale of Goods Act rights, he is free to decide whether or not to sign and return the guarantee and if he does not do so he will rely entirely on his Sale of Goods Act rights against the retailer. Whether he should do this or not is a question far beyond the scope of this work. Some people consider it valuable to have the manufacturer's promise to do the work of repair to what may be a complicated piece of apparatus.

One objection to signing the guarantee is that by agreeing to surrender all rights implied by Common Law or by statute the customer is prevented from suing the manufacturer for consequential loss or damage which might result from a defective machine. For instance, if an electric fire or some other electrical apparatus caused a serious fire to break out in the house or business premises and it was shown that the fire was due to faulty construction of the electric fire, there would in Common Law be a claim for damages against the manufacturer for negligence. But the acceptance of the guarantee excludes the possibility of making such a claim. This may not be financially serious if such catastrophes are covered by the buyer's own insurance policies. There are many factors to weigh up and each has to be considered on its merits, particularly because the terms of guarantees vary so widely.

One objectionable clause which occurs in some guarantees is the clause which makes the manufacturer the sole judge of his liability under the terms of the guarantee, particularly, for instance, the question whether the goods have been mishandled by the customer and whether the defect is really due to that mishandling or not. Occasionally buyers have struck out this clause and initialled the deletion and in returning the guarantee to the manufacturers have asked them to accept the deletion. Sometimes the manufacturers have done so.

To sign the guarantee offered by the manufacturer does not necessarily mean that the customer signs away his Sale of Goods Act rights against *the retailer.* In fact, it very seldom does. It could happen only if it is made an express condition of the sale, accepted by the customer, that he give up these rights—usually referred to as statutory conditions and warranties. If no such condition is accepted by the customer he still has his remedies against the retailer.

In view of the importance of the Sale of Goods Act there follows an account and brief interpretation of other parts of the Act. This will include a mention of the basic provisions as to quality which have been discussed above simply to show how they fit into the general scheme of the Act.

THE MEANING OF 'CONTRACT OF SALE OF GOODS'

The Act defines a contract of sale of goods as 'a contract whereby the seller transfers or agrees to transfer the property in goods to the buyer for a money consideration, called the price' (s. 1 (1)).

There is a distinction between a 'sale' and a mere 'agreement to sell'. Under a 'sale' the 'property in goods' (*i.e.* the ownership of them) is transferred from the seller to the buyer, while under 'an agreement to sell' the transfer of the

". . . may take the form of part exchange . . ."

property does not take place immediately but at a future time or subject to the fulfilment of conditions. An agreement to sell becomes a sale when the time elapses or the conditions are fulfilled subject to which the property in the goods is to be transferred. Both these transactions are covered by the expression 'contract of sale' (s. 1 (3)).

There must be money consideration for a sale: but it may take the form of 'part exchange', in which the consideration is partly in money and partly in goods.

The price may be fixed by the contract or determined by the course of dealing between the parties. If not so fixed or determined, the buyer must pay a reasonable price (s. 8). Thus there may be a perfectly valid contract of sale although no price has been agreed.

A contract of sale is to be distinguished from a contract for work and materials. The purpose of a contract of sale is the delivery of goods rather than the exercise of skill. It is not always easy to distinguish between them (which of the two, for example, is a contract by a dentist to make a set of false teeth, or a contract by an artist to paint a picture (a) for a private person, (b) for a picture dealer?). The relevance of the distinction is that the sale of goods is governed by the Act (with its implied conditions and warranties, etc.), while a contract for work and materials is not.

The seller is, of course, under a duty to supply the goods which he has contracted to sell. If these are 'specific goods', that is, an identified article, such as a particular second-hand car, and the goods have, without his knowledge, 'perished' (*i.e.* been destroyed or stolen) at the time when the contract was made, the contract is void (s. 6). But if the goods were not 'specific', if they were, for example, a new motor-car of a given make ('generic goods', or goods defined by description only), it is immaterial that the goods which the seller was intending to supply had perished at the time of the sale: he must fulfil his obligations by procuring other goods of the same description for the buyer.

CONDITIONS AND WARRANTIES

In order to give buyers of goods some measure of protection, certain conditions and warranties as to title (ownership of the goods), quality, and suitability are implied in every contract of sale. This means that the contract is deemed to include them unless they are excluded by express agreement, course of dealing between the parties, or custom of the trade.

A condition is a term which goes to the root of the contract; it is so vital that if it is broken the injured party can treat the contract as repudiated.

A warranty is a term of lesser importance: the breach of it gives rise to an action for damages, but does not entitle the injured party to reject the goods and treat the contract as repudiated (s. 62).

Whether a term is a condition or a warranty depends on the construction (*i.e.* the true interpretation) of the contract, and not on the particular word used.

Where a condition is broken by the seller, the buyer may, if he prefers, bring an action for damages only, instead of rejecting the goods: and generally speaking, once he has accepted the goods (or part of them) he is limited to an action for damages (s. 11 (1)).

The implied conditions and warranties are as follows:

(1) There is an implied condition on the part of the seller that he has (or will at the material time have) a right to sell the goods (s. 12 (1)).

If he is not entitled to sell the goods (because they are not his, and he does not have the owner's authority to sell), the buyer may recover the whole of the price paid—even though he may have enjoyed the use of the goods for a time: or he may, as happened in a case where the goods bore labels which infringed a registered trade mark, claim damages for any loss he may incur.

There are also implied warranties that he will not be disturbed in his possession of the goods, and that they are not subject to third-party rights.

(2) Where there is a sale of goods by description (or by sample and description), there is an implied condition that the goods shall correspond with the description (s. 13).

". . . there is an implied condition that the goods shall correspond with the description . . ."

Thus where the buyer has not seen the goods, but has bought them in reliance on a description (*e.g.* when he orders them from a catalogue), he can reject them if he finds that they do not correspond with the description.

(3) Where the buyer makes known to the seller the particular purpose for which the goods are required, so as to show that he relies on the seller's skill or judgment, and the goods are of a description which it is in the course of the seller's business to supply, the goods must be reasonably fit for such purpose (s. 14 (1)).

The purpose for which the goods are required need not be expressly stated, if that is clear from their description. Thus damages were recovered by a plaintiff who asked for a hot-water bottle, and was sold one which burst.

If an article is ordered under its patent or trade name, there is generally no implied condition as to its fitness for any particular purpose; but even in these circumstances, if the article is bought on the recommendation of the seller the condition as to fitness is implied. So a plaintiff who told the defendant motor-car dealers that he wanted a comfortable car suitable for touring purposes, and on their recommendation ordered a powerful sports-car, recovered damages when it proved uncomfortable and unsuitable.

(4) Where goods are bought by description from a seller who deals in goods of that description, they must be of 'merchantable quality' (s. 14 (2)). This probably means (for the matter is not beyond doubt) that they are in such condition that a reasonable man would accept them, after full examination, in performance of the contract.

Thus a consignment of coalite in which an explosive substance was contained was held to be unmerchantable, and the purchaser recovered damages.

This condition is not implied, however, if the buyer has examined the goods (or been given the opportunity of examining them), and the defects are such as the examination ought to have revealed.

It should be noted that the last two conditions are only implied where the goods are bought from a seller who regularly deals in such goods.

(5) Where the sale is by sample, there are implied conditions that the bulk shall correspond with the sample in quality, that the buyer shall have a reasonable opportunity of comparing the bulk with the sample (before accepting the goods), and that the goods shall be free from any defect rendering them unmerchantable which would not be apparent on reasonable examination of the sample (s. 15).

Apart from the above-mentioned conditions and warranties, there is no implied term as to the quality or fitness for any particular purpose of goods under a contract of sale. The maxim of the law is *caveat emptor* ('let the buyer take care'). Moreover, the conditions and warranties implied by the Act may be, and in written contracts frequently are, expressly excluded by agreement of the parties. If the seller is shrewd enough to exclude all conditions and warranties, express and implied, the buyer may have no remedy—unless the goods supplied are quite different from what he ordered, *e.g.* a second-hand instead of a new car.

TRANSFER OF THE PROPERTY

It is important to know when the property in the goods passes from the seller to the buyer, because generally speaking 'risk' and 'property' go together, and if the goods should accidentally be destroyed or damaged it is the owner at the time who must bear the loss. Moreover, in the case of bankruptcy of either party, it is necessary to know whether the goods can be claimed by his trustee in bankruptcy.

Where the goods are 'unascertained', the property does not pass until they are ascertained (s. 16). Unascertained goods are goods defined by general description only, *e.g.* '100 bags of sugar', as opposed to specific goods which are identified when the contract is made, *e.g.* 'the 100 bags of sugar now lying at X.'s wharf'. In the former case, the property in the goods cannot pass at the time when the contract is made, because at that time it is not known which 100 bags out of a larger number will be appropriated to the contract (*i.e.* picked out for delivery to the buyer): when appropriated, the goods are 'ascertained'.

Subject to this rule, the property in goods is transferred to the buyer at such time as the parties intend it to be transferred (s. 17): and the Act lays down rules for determining their intention where a different intention does not appear (s. 18).

The rules are:

(1) Where there is an unconditional contract for the sale of specific goods in a deliverable state (that is to say, when the contract is not made subject to the fulfilment of any condition and the goods are at the time ready for delivery), the property passes to the buyer when the contract is made: and it is immaterial whether the time of payment or delivery (or both) be postponed. So if a lady chooses a dress in a shop, and asks for it to be sent to her home and put down to her account, and the shopkeeper agrees to this, the dress becomes her property then and there, and if it is destroyed by fire she would nevertheless be liable to pay.

(2) Where there is a contract for the sale of specific goods and the seller has to do something to them to put them into a deliverable state, the property does not pass until that thing has been done and the buyer has notice of it.

(3) Where there is a contract for the sale of specific goods in a deliverable state, but the seller has to weigh, measure, or test them for the purpose of ascertaining the price, the property does not pass until he has done so and the buyer has notice of it.

(4) When goods are delivered to the buyer on approval or 'on sale or return' or similar terms, the property passes to the buyer

(a) when he signifies his approval or acceptance to the seller, or does any other act 'adopting the transaction' (*e.g.* selling or pledging the goods), or

(b) if he retains the goods, without giving notice of rejection, beyond the time fixed for returning them, or (if no time has been fixed) beyond a reasonable time.

(5) Where there is a contract for the sale of unascertained or future goods by description (future goods are goods to be manufactured or acquired by the seller after the making of the contract of sale), and goods of that description and in a deliverable state are unconditionally appropriated to the contract— by the seller with the assent (express or implied) of the buyer, or vice versa— the property in the goods thereupon passes to the buyer.

Such an unconditional appropriation is made when the seller delivers the goods to the buyer, or to a carrier for transmission to the buyer, without reserving the right of disposal (*i.e.* the right to recall the goods, or re-direct them to another person). Apart from express reservation, the seller is deemed to reserve the right of disposal where goods are shipped and by the bill of lading are deliverable to the seller or his agent, or where the seller sends, together with the bill of lading, a bill of exchange for the price of the goods—in which case the property in the goods does not pass to the buyer unless he accepts the bill of exchange (s. 19).

"... in a deliverable state ..."

Unless otherwise agreed, the goods are at the seller's risk until the property in them passes to the buyer, after which they are at the buyer's risk. This is so whether or not the goods themselves have been delivered. However, if delivery has been delayed through the fault of either party, the goods are at that party's risk, as regards any loss which might not have occurred but for such fault (s. 20). Thus, where apple juice which had been sold by the plaintiffs to the defendant deteriorated at the plaintiffs' premises because the defendant failed over a long

293

period to give delivery instructions, it was held that the loss fell on the defendant although (on the facts of the case) the property in the apple juice had not passed to him.

SALE BY PERSON NOT THE OWNER

As a rule, a sale of goods by a person who neither owns them nor has the owner's authority to sell gives no title to the buyer: and the true owner can claim them from the buyer without recompense. In order, however, to protect commercial transactions entered into in good faith, this rule is subject to the following exceptions.

(1) If the owner stands by and allows an innocent buyer to pay another person money for the goods, he is precluded (or 'estopped') from denying that person's right to sell them (s. 21 (1)).

(2) Under the Factors Act, 1889, a mercantile agent, who in the ordinary course of business has authority to sell goods in his possession which he does not own, can pass a good title to an innocent buyer even without the owner's authority for the transaction in question (s. 21 (2)).

(3) Where goods are sold in 'market overt' (that is, in a recognized market, or by a shopkeeper dealing in goods of that kind in the City of London), a person who buys them in good faith and without notice of any defect or want of title on the part of the seller gets a good title to them (s. 22). However, if the goods are stolen (and not merely obtained by fraud), and the thief is convicted, the property in them revests in the owner, notwithstanding a sale in market overt (s. 24).

(4) If the seller has a 'voidable' title to goods—if, for example, he obtained them by a fraudulent contract with the owner, which the owner can 'avoid' (rescind)—and his title has not been avoided at the time of the sale, he can pass a good title to a buyer who does not know of the seller's defect of title and buys in good faith (s. 23).

(5) A person who has sold goods and remains in possession of them can pass a good title to a person who buys them in good faith, without notice of the previous sale. And conversely, a person who has bought or agreed to buy goods, and has, with the seller's consent, obtained possession before paying for them, can pass a good title to a person who buys them in good faith and without notice of the seller's rights. The same rules apply to documents of title to goods, such as bills of lading (s. 25).

It may be briefly noted, also, that certain persons have a legal right to sell the goods of others, so as to be able to pass a good title. They include sheriffs, pawnbrokers, innkeepers, and repairers of goods (under the Disposal of Uncollected Goods Act, 1952).

PERFORMANCE OF THE CONTRACT

Unless otherwise agreed, the seller is entitled to payment on delivery of the goods, and if the buyer refuses to pay, the seller can refuse delivery (s. 28).

In the absence of express agreement as to delivery, the rules laid down by the Act are as follows.

The place of delivery is the seller's place of business, or if he has none, his residence. But if the contract is for the sale of specific goods which both parties know to be at another place, that place is the place of delivery (s. 29 (1)).

Where under the contract the seller is bound to send the goods to the buyer, but no time is fixed, he must send them within a reasonable time (s. 29 (2)).

If the goods are in the possession of a third party (such as a warehouseman), there is no delivery until the third party acknowledges to the buyer that he holds the goods on his behalf (s. 29 (3)).

Demand or tender of delivery must be made at a reasonable hour (s. 29 (4)).

Unless otherwise agreed, the expenses of putting the goods into a deliverable state must be borne by the seller (s. 29 (5)).

Delivery to a carrier for transmission to the buyer is as a rule deemed to be delivery to the buyer. But the seller must make a reasonable contract with the carrier, and where the carriage involves sea transit must give the buyer sufficient notice to enable him to insure (s. 32).

Where the seller agrees to deliver goods at a place other than that where they are when sold, the buyer must take the risk of deterioration in transit (s. 33).

Where the buyer fails to take delivery, at the seller's request, within a reasonable time, he is liable for any loss caused thereby, and must pay the seller a reasonable charge for custody of the goods (s. 37).

If the seller sends the buyer a larger or smaller quantity of goods than he ordered, the buyer may accept the whole, reject the whole, or accept the quantity he ordered and reject the rest (s. 30).

The buyer is deemed to have accepted the goods (and so to have lost any right of rejection) when he informs the seller that he has accepted them, when he does any act inconsistent with the seller's ownership (*e.g.* re-selling them), or when, after a reasonable lapse of time, he retains them without informing the seller that he has rejected them (s. 35).

A buyer who is entitled to reject goods is not, as a rule, bound to return them to the seller: he need only inform the seller that he refuses to accept them (s. 36).

RIGHTS OF THE UNPAID SELLER

A seller who has not been paid the whole of the price has the following rights *against the goods*, although the property in them has passed to the buyer (s. 39 (1)).

(1) A lien, *i.e.* a right to retain possession of the goods, if
   (a) there was no agreement for credit, or
   (b) the term of credit has expired, or
   (c) the buyer becomes insolvent (s. 41).

(2) A right of 'stoppage in transitu', *i.e.* while they are on the way. If the buyer becomes insolvent when the goods are in transit (*i.e.* in the custody of a carrier), the seller can take them back, and assume possession of them (s. 44).

(3) A right of resale
   (a) where the goods are perishable,
   (b) where the seller notifies the buyer of his intention to resell and the buyer does not tender the price within a reasonable time, or
   (c) where the seller expressly reserves a right of resale in the event of buyer's default (s. 48 (3), (4)).

If the property in the goods has not passed to the buyer, the unpaid seller has a right to withhold delivery similar to his rights of lien and stoppage in transit (s. 39 (2)).

ACTIONS FOR BREACH OF CONTRACT

In addition to his above-mentioned rights against the goods, the seller has two rights of action against the buyer.

When the property in the goods has passed to the buyer (or when the price is payable on a fixed day, irrespective of delivery or the passing of the property) the seller can sue for the price (s. 49).

If the buyer refuses to accept the goods, the seller can claim damages for non-acceptance. The measure of damages is the estimated loss directly and naturally resulting in the ordinary course of events from the buyer's breach of contract, and where there is an available market for the goods this will be the difference between the contract price and the market price (s. 50). Thus, if the seller finds another buyer at the same or a higher price, he will not as a rule be able to recover damages.

The buyer has corresponding rights of action against the seller.

If the seller fails to deliver the goods, the buyer can claim damages, the measure of damages corresponding to that which the seller can obtain in case of non-acceptance (above) (s. 51). If he has paid the price, he can recover the amount paid.

In the case of goods which are unique or of special value (such as a picture, rare book, or piece of jewellery) the Court may grant the buyer an order for specific performance: it will not do so where the goods are ordinary articles of commerce, for damages would then be an adequate remedy.

Where there is a breach of condition, the buyer can reject the goods. Instead of rejecting them, however, he can claim damages as for a breach of warranty. And once he has accepted the goods (or part of them if the contract is indivisible), or if the property in the goods has passed to him, he loses his right of rejection and can only claim damages (s. 11).

On breach of warranty, the buyer can claim damages or (what comes to the same thing) pay a reduced price. The measure of damages is the difference between the value of the goods delivered and the value they would have had if they had answered to the warranty (s. 53).

RIGHTS AGAINST THE MANUFACTURER

Though not really part of the law of contracts for the sale of goods, it is perhaps fitting to mention here that a buyer of goods who suffers injury through a defect in their manufacture (*e.g.* a skin disease caused by chemicals left in underwear) may be able to recover damages from the manufacturer.

While any damages he might be awarded against the seller would be for breach of contract, the liability of the manufacturer (with whom he has no contract) would be in tort for negligence.

Hence as mentioned earlier the 'Guarantee' which many manufacturers supply with their goods may be a trap for the unwary. For frequently, in exchange for the free replacement of defective components (a minor concession where the major part of the cost is for labour, for which the buyer has to pay), the buyer signs away the valuable rights which he enjoys at Common Law in respect of any negligence of the manufacturer that might cause him damage.

MISREPRESENTATION

GENERALLY

WHERE one of the parties to a contract breaks any of its terms, the other party can bring an action for damages (and can sometimes avail himself of other remedies too). The term infringed may be an express term, or it may be a term implied by law: but in either case it is a part of the contract itself.

It frequently happens that a person is induced to enter into a contract by a representation which he later finds to be false. If that representation was incorporated in the contract itself, there is no difficulty in enforcing it like any other term. But what if it never became part of the actual contract?

The short answer to this question is that if the misrepresentation was made in good faith, the party who was misled by it cannot claim damages, but may—if it has not become too late to do so—rescind or cancel the contract: if, on the other hand, it was made fraudulently, the injured party may both rescind or cancel the contract (subject to certain conditions) and may claim damages for the tort (civil wrong) of deceit.

We must first consider what constitutes a misrepresentation: for not every statement which proves to be false is regarded as a misrepresentation in law.

A misrepresentation is, in the first place, a false statement as to a material *fact*. A false statement as to the general law (as opposed to a question of private rights, to say, for example, that A. owes B. £1,000 is generally regarded as a matter of fact rather than of law) is not a misrepresentation—perhaps because for this purpose everyone is presumed to know the law.

As a general rule, too, a declaration of intention which is not carried into effect does not amount to a misrepresentation—though it has been said that 'the state of a man's mind is as much a fact as the state of his digestion', so that if it could be shown that the declared intention was never entertained at all, the declaration would constitute a misrepresentation.

A mere expression of opinion is not a misrepresentation, unless it is uttered in circumstances which imply that the person expressing it has reasonable grounds for his opinion, and there are in fact no such grounds.

It is, however, important—and not always easy—to distinguish a statement of opinion from a statement of fact. A statement that the spoons offered to a customer are 'equal to Elkington's A' (to quote an example from a decided case) is a statement of opinion. So, too, is a statement that they are the best in the market at the price. (Indeed even if this statement were demonstrably false, it

Misrepresentation!

would not be regarded in law as a misrepresentation, but merely as a 'puff': for tradesmen are expected to speak in exaggerated praise of their wares, and no reasonable person would claim to have been deceived by such exaggeration.) To say, on the other hand, that the spoons 'have as much silver in them as Elkington's A' is to make a statement of fact, and if untrue it is a misrepresentation.

A representation which is true when made, but which to the knowledge of the person making it becomes untrue before the contract is entered into, must be corrected: for to leave it uncorrected amounts to a misrepresentation. Thus in one case, the vendor of a medical practice, while negotiating a sale in January, stated (quite truly) that the takings were at the rate of £2,000 a year, but in May, when the contract was signed, they had fallen, owing to his illness, to £5 a week: it was held that the purchaser could rescind the contract by reason of the vendor's failure to disclose the fall in takings.

It may be convenient to mention at this point a special category of contracts in which non-disclosure in general (and not merely after a statement which has since become untrue) is tantamount to a misrepresentation entitling the injured party to rescind the contract.

It is not generally the duty of a contracting party to disclose to the other party material facts which might be expected to influence his decision. Thus in one case a man sold 'with all faults' pigs which he knew were suffering from swine-fever, and it was held that the sale was good. Exceptionally, however, there are certain types of contract in which there is a duty to make full disclosure: and for this reason these are called contracts *uberrimae fidei*

... as an advertising 'puff' ...

('of the most abundant good faith'). Among them are contracts for *insurance* (in which the assured must notify the insurer of every circumstance which might influence him in fixing the premium or agreeing to take the risk) (see section on Insurance), contracts arising out of invitations to the public to subscribe for a company's shares, contracts between members of a family for settlement of the family property, and—to some extent—contracts for the sale of land (in so far, only, as the vendor must disclose certain defects in his title).

FRAUDULENT MISREPRESENTATION

A fraudulent misrepresentation is commonly defined as a misrepresentation made by a person who knows that it is false or who makes it recklessly, not caring whether it be true or false. It could be described more shortly, and with equal accuracy, as a misrepresentation made without honest belief in its truth. For if a false statement is made honestly, it cannot amount to a fraudulent misrepresentation, even if there were no reasonable grounds for believing it to be true.

Thus if the vendor of a business 'cooks the books' in order to show a prospective purchaser a bigger weekly profit than he really enjoys, he is of course guilty of fraud. But if he is a muddle-headed person, incapable of keeping accurate books (or perhaps any books at all), and he mis-states the profit because he honestly believes that it is much bigger than it really is, then, careless though he may be, his misrepresentation is not fraudulent.

To establish a right to damages, a person who claims to have suffered loss through a fraudulent misrepresentation must show that it was intended to be acted upon by him. Thus where fraudulent statements were made in a company prospectus, and a claim for damages was brought, not by the original applicants for shares, to whom the prospectus had been addressed, but by persons who had become shareholders afterwards, the claim failed. It was held in a later case, however, that if a prospectus was issued to induce not merely applications for allotment of shares but also purchases of shares on the market, anyone who bought them on the faith of the prospectus would be entitled to claim damages.

The plaintiff must also prove that he was deceived by the misrepresentation. If a shopkeeper takes active steps to conceal a serious flaw in an article, as, for example, by plugging a hole in a gun, he is making (by conduct instead of words) a misrepresentation about it. But if the buyer does not examine it, his mind cannot be said to have been affected by the concealment, and he cannot therefore claim damages.

It is not necessary, however, for the injured party to prove that the mis-representation was solely responsible for his entering into the contract. It is enough if it was one inducing cause, making him less careful in his inquiries than he would otherwise have been. Moreover, he will not be deprived of his remedy because he had the means of discovering the falsity of the representation and did not avail himself of them. In one case the vendor of a business told the prospective purchaser that the takings were so much a year, and produced papers which, he said, bore out his statement. If the purchaser had examined these papers, he would have discovered that the takings were in fact sub-stantially less: but he bought the business without examining them. It was held, nevertheless, that he was entitled to rely on the vendor's statement with-out checking it, and that he therefore had the right to rescind the contract.

REMEDIES

As we have seen, damages can be recovered for fraudulent, but not for innocent, misrepresentation. Moreover, damages and rescission are not alternative remedies: a party injured by fraud can both claim damages and (subject to what is said below) rescind the contract, or, if he so prefers, he can claim damages and let the contract stand. The measure of damages is the amount of financial loss caused to him by the defendant's deceit: if he rescinds the contract, this will be the value (less the agreed price) of what he had contracted for, while if he lets the contract stand, it will be the difference in value between what he contracted for and what he actually got.

A contract induced by misrepresentation is voidable at the option of the party to whom the misrepresentation was made, but not of the party who made it (for a person cannot take advantage of his own wrong). The remedy of rescission must, however, be exercised before it is too late—and in this respect, again, there is a difference between innocent and fraudulent misrepresentation.

If the contract has been completed by conveyance, grant, or other disposition of property, it is doubtful whether it can be rescinded on the ground of innocent misrepresentation, while there is no doubt that it can be rescinded for fraud. Even in the case of fraud, however, it will be too late to rescind if third-party rights would be affected (as, for example, where a house which A. had been induced by B.'s fraud to sell to B. had been re-sold by B. to C. before A. attempted to rescind the contract), or where there has been such a lapse of time since the contract was entered into that it would be unduly oppressive even toward the wrongdoer to set it aside. The remedy of rescission, therefore, should always be invoked as soon as the representation is discovered to be false.

The third remedy which is available, in cases of innocent and fraudulent misrepresentation alike, is for the injured party to refuse to perform the contract, and to set up the misrepresentation as a defence in any action that may be brought against him for specific performance or damages.

HIRE PURCHASE AND CREDIT SALES

IT HAS become common practice nowadays for the consumer to enjoy the immediate possession of goods for which he pays on an instalment basis. This may be effected by either a hire-purchase or a credit sale agreement.

DIFFERENCE BETWEEN H.P. AND CREDIT SALE

A credit sale is simply an agreement for the sale of goods under which the price is payable by instalments. The important point is that the goods may straight away become the property of the buyer, and he can then do with them as he pleases: and even if they do not, he can pass a good title (*i.e.* ownership of the goods) to a person who buys them from him before he has finished paying for them.

Hire purchase is of quite a different nature. The goods hired by the Agreement are quite literally and strictly only 'hired'. There are two separate elements in this transaction: the hiring of the goods and their purchase. The hiring lasts for the period specified in the agreement (unless, of course, it is lawfully terminated before that hire) and then the hirer has an option to purchase the

301

goods. He usually exercises his option by paying a final nominal sum which may be as low as a shilling, but is commonly £1. Then the goods are his: not before.

It is true that the real object of a hire-purchase transaction is the purchase of the goods. This, however, does not affect the essential nature of the transaction. The vital feature is the choice given to the hirer to return or purchase the goods at the end of the hiring. Of course he will hardly want at that stage to return the goods, and lose the instalments he has paid. The point is he must have a choice: if he has an option to buy, equally he has free choice not to. This distinguishes hire purchase from the sort of agreement under which the goods automatically become the property of the hirer at the end of a certain period, and which is in effect a simple agreement to purchase.

The difference is of practical importance in this way. If a person who has goods on hire purchase sells them to someone else, the sale is of no effect in law, and the true owner can recover them from the buyer. The only exception to this rule is where the sale by the hirer takes place in market overt, that is to say in an open, public, and legally constituted market. On the other hand, the owner will lose his goods if they are sold by someone who holds them under a simple agreement to purchase. Moreover, a hire purchase, as opposed to a credit sale, gives the owner a right to recover possession of his goods if the hirer defaults in payment or commits some other breach of the agreement. Finally, a hirer who disposes of goods which are still subject to a hire-purchase agreement commits the crime of larceny (theft).

So—very important for all who are buying on the 'never never': do not sell the goods while the agreement lasts; do not sell before the goods have legally become yours as described above.

THE FINANCE COMPANY AND HIRE PURCHASE

When goods are bought on hire purchase, the usual practice is for the dealer to sell the goods to a finance company, which then hires them to the purchaser. The contract of hire purchase in these circumstances is thus made by the purchaser with the finance company, so that the rights and duties which arise under that contract are enforceable by and against the finance company, and not the dealer. This is so, even though, as usually happens, the purchaser pays the initial deposit to the dealer, who keeps it and sets it off against the amount owed him by the finance company. The finance company may require the purchaser to provide a guarantor. It will normally have an arrangement with the dealer (known as a 'recourse agreement'), under which the dealer agrees to indemnify it against any default by the purchaser.

STATUTORY RULES FOR CERTAIN GOODS

The dealer and finance company are usually more capable of looking after their interests than the customer is, and in consequence the terms of a hire-purchase agreement may sometimes be oppressive. Moreover, persons who buy goods on a hire-purchase or credit sale basis do not always read or fully understand every clause in the agreement which they sign. Parliament has therefore thought fit to give some protection to the purchaser of less expensive goods by certain provisions in the Hire Purchase Acts of 1938 and 1954. These Acts apply to hire-purchase and credit sale transactions in which the total price involved does not exceed £300, or, in the case of livestock, £1,000, but only apply to credit sales when the price is payable by at least five instalments.

HOW THE ACTS PROTECT THE HIRER

The first way in which the above Acts protect the purchaser is by ensuring that he is made aware of the terms of the agreement. This they do by requiring the owner to furnish the hirer, within seven days of the making of the agreement,

Hidden defects!

with a copy of a Note or Memorandum of the agreement in which the following must be set out: the hire-purchase price and cash price, the amount of each instalment and the time when each becomes due, and a list of the goods to which the agreement relates.

This Note or Memorandum must be signed by the hirer and by or on behalf of all other parties to the agreement. The Acts also require that *before* the agreement is made, and independently of the Note or Memorandum, the cash price of the goods must be stated *in writing* to the hirer. The penalty for non-compliance with these requirements is that the owner is not entitled to enforce the agreement or recover the goods. If, however, the fault of the owner consists merely in not setting out in the Note or Memorandum the whole of the required information, the Court may, if it thinks it fair, in the circumstances, allow the owner to enforce the agreement nonetheless.

These Acts also help to safeguard the hirer by providing that certain terms are to be *implied* in every agreement. These implied terms consist of a number of warranties, *i.e.* in non-technical language, promises, which the owner is deemed to give to the hirer.

First, he is deemed to warrant that he will have the power to transfer the title in the goods to the hirer at the time when this is called for by the agreement (normally, of course, at the end of the hiring); secondly, that the goods are of 'merchantable quality', *i.e.* fit to be sold; and thirdly, that they are reasonably fit for the purpose for which they are required.

Even in those agreements which are outside the scope of the statutes there are a certain number of implied terms of the same type. Thus, there is in every hire-purchase agreement, whether covered by the Acts or not, an implied warranty by the owner that the goods are his at the time of the hiring. Those hirers who are protected by the statutes will have the benefit of those implied terms as well. Apart from the statutes, the only warranty to be implied as to the condition of the goods is that they are as reasonably fit as reasonable care and skill can make them for the purpose for which they are required. Thus, the owner will not be liable for hidden defects in the goods unless the transaction is one to which the Hire Purchase Acts apply.

The Acts also forbid the owner from seizing the goods when one-third of the price has been paid, unless he gets an order from the County Court, and also permit the hirer to cancel the agreement on payment of one-half of the H.P. price. Both these points are dealt with in more detail below.

WHAT RIGHTS HAS THE HIRER IF THE GOODS PROVE UNSATISFACTORY?

The difficulty often is that any representations as to quality were made by the dealer, who is not a party to the hire-purchase contract, rather than by the finance company which is. In most cases the dealer does not act as the agent of the finance company in relation to the transaction. Generally speaking, therefore, it is no answer, in a claim by the finance company for arrears of payment or damages, to argue that the goods were defective. It has been decided, however, that should representations made by the dealer prove false, he may be liable to pay damages to the hirer, provided that the hirer was induced to enter into the agreement on the strength of them. Moreover, the dealer may also be liable for negligence to anyone who is injured as a result of the defective condition of the goods which he supplies.

Most hire-purchase agreements contain clauses in very wide terms which purport to exclude all liability of the owner (*i.e.* generally the finance company) in respect of warranties, representations, etc. Such an exemption clause will be construed strictly against the owner, so that any ambiguity will be resolved in favour of the hirer. In any case, it will not be effective when the fault is so serious as to amount to *a fundamental breach of the contract*. There was such a fundamental breach, for instance, in the case of the hire purchase of a car, which on delivery was in such a totally different condition from when the agreement was made that it could not be considered the same car, if, in fact, it deserved to be called a car at all.

So far as the terms to be implied by statute are concerned: (a) the condition as to title cannot be excluded by agreement of the parties; (b) the one about merchantable quality can be excluded only if the goods are second-hand, and are stated to be such in the memorandum; and (c) the one as to reasonable fitness can be excluded *only* if the hirer is expressly notified of the exclusion, and of its effect.

The Hire Purchase Acts not only provide that certain terms shall be implied, but also render void certain provisions that may be expressly included in both hire-purchase and credit sale agreements. In particular, a term which relieves the owner or seller from liability for the acts or defaults of anyone acting on his behalf in connection with the formation of the agreement is void.

DUTY OF HIRER TO CARE FOR THE GOODS

During the currency of the hiring the hirer is under a duty to take reasonable care of the goods, but if they should be damaged or destroyed otherwise than by failure to take such care, *e.g.* damage by lightning or catastrophes like floods or severe storms, he is under no liability either to repair them or to pay damages to the owner. He is also required by the statutes to inform the owner, on demand, of the whereabouts of the goods.

HIRER'S RIGHT TO TERMINATE THE AGREEMENT

We have seen that in all true hire-purchase transactions the hirer is not compelled to buy the goods; but in practice his right to return them at any time is usually limited. A definite period may be fixed for the hiring, in which case the hirer, if he terminates the agreement before the end of that period, will nevertheless be liable to pay for the whole period. Alternatively, there may be a provision in the agreement requiring the hirer to pay an additional sum if he terminates the hiring before a certain amount is paid. Generally, if he terminates the hiring, he will be liable for that amount, as the price of his power to give notice to terminate.

But when the transactions come within the scope of the Hire Purchase Acts, the position of the hirer is more favourable. These Acts provide that his right to end the agreement and return the goods is not to be ousted or modified by any provision in the agreement. If he ends the agreement, as he is entitled to do *at any time,* by giving notice to the person entitled to receive the moneys payable, he is liable to pay what has already become due, plus the amount,

The hirer is under duty—

to take reasonable care—

of the goods—

but should they be damaged—

by a catastrophe—

he is only required to inform the owner—

of the whereabouts of the goods!

if any, by which half of the hire-purchase price exceeds the total of the sums paid and the sums already due. (In other words, his total payments will amount to one-half of the price.) *This right to cancel by paying half* is a valuable protection, because although the hirer loses the goods, he is enabled to escape what would otherwise be his legal liability to pay the whole H.P. price.

Generally the hirer will be allowed to buy the goods outright at any time during the period of hire. A purchaser under a credit sale has always the right of paying off the full amount of the balance at any time.

OWNER'S RIGHT TO TAKE THE GOODS BACK

Invariably, in the agreement, the right is reserved to the owner to determine the hiring and/or the whole agreement and to retake possession of the goods on default of payment by the hirer or breach by him of any term of the agreement. The owner has no right, however, to enter on the hirer's land for the purpose of retaking the goods unless the agreement expressly gives him a licence to do so. He is never permitted to use force for the purpose of entering and seizing the goods, nor can he ever enter as of right on a third person's premises for the purpose of so doing.

The agreement, besides giving the owner a right to recover possession upon failure to pay a due instalment or breach of some other term, may purport to make the hirer liable in such event to pay some penalty or to make up what he has already paid to a certain sum. Whether or not such a clause is enforceable depends on whether the amount stipulated for represents a genuine pre-estimate of the damage suffered by the owner as a result of depreciation, or is in the nature of a penalty held over the head of the hirer to deter him from defaulting in any way. If it is a penalty, the owner will be unable to recover it. The question of whether a clause falls into one category or the other will depend on the reasonableness, in all the circumstances, of the amount which the hirer is called upon to pay.

The right of the owner to recover possession of his goods is restricted, however, by the Act of 1938 for those agreements which fall within its scope. If *one-third* of the hire-purchase price has been paid, the owner cannot recover possession *except by bringing an action in the County Court*. If the owner flouts this requirement, the agreement is automatically terminated, the hirer is released from all liability under the agreement and, what is more, may recover from the owner everything paid by him under the agreement.

When an action is brought to recover possession in those cases where one-third of the purchase price has been paid, the Court has power to do one of the following things: (i) order delivery of all the goods to the owner, (ii) order delivery to the owner of part of the goods and transfer of his title to the remainder to the hirer, or (iii) make what is called a postponed order for delivery of the goods. In the last case, the operation of the order for delivery is suspended on condition that the hirer pays the unpaid balance of the purchase price on terms fixed by the Court. If the hirer then pays off the unpaid balance in accordance with these terms the goods will become his. If, however, he fails to pay the instalments fixed by the Court the owner may proceed to retake the goods himself without the need of applying to the Court again.

If the hirer defaults in payment or commits some other breach of the agreement, the owner is not, of course, bound to terminate the agreement but may, if he chooses, merely sue for the arrears or for damages. This course may well be the better one if the value of the goods has fallen appreciably. When an action is brought against a hirer who is wrongfully keeping the goods, after the agreement has been terminated, he will normally be given the choice of either paying their value or returning them. When the agreements are within the scope of the Acts, the owner must, before bringing an action to recover them, make a written request for the surrender of the goods.

THE HIRER'S LANDLORD AND H.P. GOODS

In certain circumstances the interest of the owner in goods held on hire purchase may be overridden by a right in some third party. Thus, a landlord may distrain for rent upon goods that are held by his tenant under a hire-purchase agreement. Goods on the premises held on hire purchase by someone other than the tenant may also be subject to distress if they are within the 'reputed ownership' of the tenant. (This occurs when the goods are in the possession, or under the control of, the tenant with the consent of the true owner in such circumstances that the tenant is reputed to be the owner of them.)

LIEN ON H.P. GOODS BY REPAIRER, ETC.

A repairer of the goods who has done work on them at the request of the hirer may have a lien on them for his charges (*i.e.* a right to retain them until he is paid), provided the hirer has the implied authority of the owner to effect repairs. Likewise, a common carrier or an inn-keeper may have a lien on the goods as against both hirer and owner for charges incurred by the hirer.

SOME POINTS SPECIAL TO CREDIT SALES

Credit sales, as has been pointed out, are a type of transaction essentially different from hire purchase, and are governed by the Sale of Goods Act, 1893. In addition, however, the Hire Purchase Acts have a limited application to those credit sales which fall within their scope. In particular, the requirement of a Note or Memorandum of the Agreement in the prescribed terms is applicable to a credit sale if the total purchase price exceeds £5. Also, the sections which render null and void certain types of clauses apply as in the case of hire purchase. Moreover, it appears that the purchaser under a credit sale will have the advantage of those terms implied by the Hire Purchase Acts as well as the similar but somewhat wider terms to be implied under the Sale of Goods Act. The seller generally cannot retake the goods upon the default of the buyer unless the agreement expressly provides for this, or unless he has the buyer's consent. The normal remedy of the seller under a credit sale is to sue on the contract for the unpaid balance of the price.

SOME SPECIAL CONTROLS

In recent years there have been a series of regulations made by the Government under powers conferred by the Defence (General) Regulations, 1939, which impose a degree of control on hire-purchase and credit sale transactions. The effect of these regulations is to require in the case of any hire-purchase or credit sale agreement: (a) that the agreement should be in writing, (b) that it should state the cash price of the goods and the amount payable for the installation or maintenance, (c) that before the agreement is made, payment should be made of not less than a certain percentage of the cash price and installation charges, (d) that the agreement should provide for payment of the balance by approximately equal instalments at equal intervals spread over not more than a specific period or, in the case of hire purchase, by one payment within three months. The percentage which is required to be paid by way of a deposit, and the period over which instalments may be paid, are varied from time to time, and from one type of goods to another. Credit sales are exempt when the whole of the price is to be paid within nine months in equal instalments, or by one payment within three months. It is made an offence punishable by fine for anyone to be party to or connected with a transaction which contravenes these regulations. There are also provisions to prevent circumvention of these requirements: *e.g.* the money for the deposit must not be borrowed from the owner or dealer, and the deposit must not be repaid unless and until the goods are returned.

Another form of control was instituted by the Advertisements (Hire Purchase) Act, 1957, which makes detailed provisions controlling advertisements of goods offered for sale on an instalment basis. The general tenor of the Act is to require that when an advertisement gives some particulars of the terms offered, it must give with equal prominence all of the relevant terms, such as the amount of the deposit, number of instalments, etc.—so that the words one used to see: 'Yours for only 10*s*' in large type, are not to be larger than the words stating how many instalments of how much.

PATENTS

THE PURPOSE of the law relating to patents, which is now set out in the Patents Act, 1949, is to enable an inventor (or a person to whom he has assigned his rights) to enjoy the fruits of his invention by exploiting it for his own profit exclusively over a period of years, and at the same time to protect the public at large against the unfair use of that monopoly.

'Letters patent' (as they were called in the Statute of Monopolies of 1623, and are called to this day) may be applied for by any person claiming to be the true and first inventor, by his assignee (*i.e.* the person to whom the inventor has transferred or assigned his rights), or by his (or his assignee's) personal representative. The application must be made, to the Comptroller General of Patents at the Patent Office, in the form prescribed, and must contain either a complete specification (*i.e.* technical description) of the invention or a provisional specification, to be followed by a complete specification within twelve months. The claim generally obtains a priority date as from the first application.

The specification is referred to an examiner, who has to investigate whether the invention has previously been published or whether any prior claim has been made. The applicant may be ordered to refer explicitly, in the complete specification, to an earlier patent which the use of the invention would infringe.

The application may be refused if it appears to the comptroller (to whom the examiner reports) to be frivolous or to be illegal in its use or on other grounds laid down in the Act (Section 10).

If the specification is accepted, the applicant has the same privileges and rights as if the patent had been sealed on the date of acceptance; but he cannot institute proceedings for infringement until the patent is sealed.

After acceptance of the specification, any person may oppose the grant of letters patent within three months from the date of publication of a complete specification on any of the following grounds:

(a) that the applicant obtained the invention from him;
(b) that it has been previously published in the United Kingdom;
(c) that it has been claimed in a complete specification deposited pursuant to an application of an earlier priority date;
(d) that it was used in the United Kingdom before the priority date of the claim;
(e) that it is obvious and clearly does not involve any inventive step;
(f) that it is not an invention within the meaning of the Act;
(g) that the complete specification is insufficient;
(h) that (in the case of a 'convention application') the application was not made within twelve months from the date of first application in a country which has a patent treaty or convention with the United Kingdom.

Duration of a patent

A patent, when sealed, is granted for sixteen years. But the term may be extended on the application of the patentee, or of a person to whom he has granted an exclusive licence, for a further period of five years, or in exceptional cases ten, on the grounds of inadequate remuneration or loss through war.

A patentee may apply for a patent for an *improvement* in his invention as a 'patent of addition' which lasts as long as the original patent; and in certain circumstances he may make amendments of his patent.

At any time after the expiration of three years from the sealing of a patent, any person interested may complain to the comptroller that there has been an abuse of the monopoly rights under it. The purpose of granting patents is not only to reward and so encourage invention but also to promote the working of new inventions on a commercial scale in the United Kingdom without undue delay. It is an abuse of monopoly rights, therefore, if the patentee is not working his patent on a commercial scale as fully as is reasonably practicable, or is not meeting the demand for the article in the United Kingdom to an adequate extent and on reasonable terms, or if he is hindering the working of the invention on a commercial scale by importing the patented article from abroad, or prejudicing the export trade or home industry by refusing to grant a licence or insisting on unreasonable terms.

If satisfied that there is such an abuse of rights, the comptroller may grant the complainant a licence on such terms as he may think expedient, or may order the patent to be indorsed 'licences of right' (which means that any person is entitled to a licence upon terms to be agreed between the parties or, in default of agreement, settled by the comptroller).

Revocation of a patent

There are various grounds on which the revocation of a patent may be obtained on petition to the Court. The most important of these are:

(a) that the patent is not for an invention within the meaning of the Patents Act;
(b) that the invention was not new;
(c) that it was obvious;
(d) that it is useless;
(e) that the claims of the complete specification are ambiguous;
(f) that the complete specification is insufficiently explicit; and
(g) that the application for the patent was not in order.

(Some of these grounds, as we have already seen, are also grounds for refusing the grant of a patent in the first place.)

Nature of a patentable invention

An invention is a new and original method of making a known article or a method of making an article previously unknown. It does not include the discovery of a new principle or theory in itself, but only a mechanical application of it. Generally speaking, in order to be patentable, an invention must be something applied to a 'vendible (*i.e.* saleable) commodity'. So a method of fumigating buildings by spraying them with an already-known substance would not qualify for a patent.

An invention is *not new* if it was known or used in the United Kingdom before the claim was made. It is *obvious* if it did not involve any 'inventive step' in the light of what was already known and used. It is *not useful* if it does not serve the purpose for which the specification shows it to have been intended. A machine which is claimed by its inventor to peel potatoes may be held by the Court to be useless if it only washes them.

A claim must not be *ambiguous*; that is to say, it should be expressed with such precision as to enable one to say what particular acts would infringe it. However, a claim would not normally be held invalid because it could have been more precisely expressed.

The specification must sufficiently and fairly describe the invention and the method by which it is to be performed, and must disclose the best method of performing it which was known to the applicant for the patent. It must contain adequate instructions to enable the kind of person for whom the instructions are intended to carry out the invention without having to add anything new on his own part, and must not be misleading or withhold useful information.

A patent is invalid if it is granted on the application of a preson who is not in fact entitled to apply, or is obtained at the expense, or in violation, of the rights of another person (for example, where the application is made without the authority of the inventor or his successors in title, *i.e.* those who have lawfully acquired his right to the invention).

A petition for revocation may also be presented by a Government department on the ground that the patentee has failed to comply with a request to use the invention upon reasonable terms for the services of the Crown.

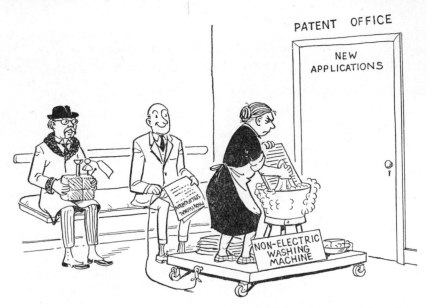

"An invention is a new and original method of making a known article . . ."

The comptroller also has power, subject to an appeal to the Court, to revoke a patent in circumstances which would have justified him in refusing to grant it, if a person who would have been entitled to oppose the grant applies within twelve months from the date of sealing the patent for an order revoking it. Alternatively, the comptroller may order the specification to be amended by qualification, correction, or explanation of the claim.

Subject to the prohibition of certain restrictions, a patentee may impose restrictive conditions on the sale of a patented article so as to bind all persons acquiring it with notice of the restrictions.

A person who is threatened with an action for infringement may himself institute proceedings for a declaration that the threat is unjustifiable, for an injunction restraining any repetition of the threat, and for damages (if he has

312

sustained any). If the threats were in fact justified, the defendant patentee can then counter-claim in the 'threats action' for infringement of his patent.

It is a criminal offence (punishable on summary conviction by a fine not exceeding £5) to represent falsely that an article is patented.

REGISTERED DESIGNS

Under the Registered Designs Act, 1949, copyright protection for five years from the date of registration can be obtained for a new or original design which is 'applied to any article by any industrial process or means'. The proprietor can also get two extensions of five years each. The registered number of the design must be marked on the article.

A design is the shape, form, or ornamentation of the finished article (not the process by which it is produced, which might be the subject-matter of a patent), and is quite different from a trade mark, which is usually an unimportant part of the article, placed upon it for the sole purpose of indicating its origin.

TRADE MARKS

INTRODUCTION

ANYONE who seeks to 'pass off' his goods as goods manufactured or supplied by another person (so as to derive an improper benefit from that other person's reputation) may be sued at Common Law. One obvious method of 'passing off' is to adopt or imitate the distinguishing marks which other persons apply to their goods for the purpose of identification. As such identification is in the interest of the public and the trader alike, these so-called 'trade marks' have been protected by legislation, which is now to be found in the Trade Marks Act, 1938. Thus, while other forms of 'passing off' may only be prevented by an action at Common Law, the infringement of trade marks may give rise both to a 'passing off' action and to proceedings under the Act.

'A trade mark', it has been said, 'means the mark under which a particular individual trades, and which indicates the goods to be his goods—either goods manufactured by him, or goods selected by him, or goods which, in some way or other, pass through his hands in the course of trade.'

REGISTRATION

To obtain the protection of the Act, a trade mark must be registered in the Registry kept by the Trade Mark Registrar at the Patent Office. The registration of a person as the proprietor of a trade mark gives him the exclusive right to

313

use it in connection with the goods for which it is registered. If another person adopts or imitates it in connection with similar goods, the registered proprietor has a right of action for infringement: and in an action for 'passing off' (with which an infringement action is usually combined) the defendant's use of a registered trade mark is conclusive evidence against him.

A trade mark can only be registered in respect of particular *goods* or classes of goods. Thus, it has been held that it cannot be registered in connection with a *process* for the repair of stockings.

The register of trade marks is divided into Part A and Part B, of which the former gives fuller protection.

In order to be registrable in Part A, the trade mark must contain, or consist of, *at least one* of the following:

(a) The name of an actual company, individual, or firm, represented in some special manner. The name alone, in ordinary letters, would not suffice; for registration might cause hardship to other persons of the same name.

(b) The signature of the applicant (or of a predecessor in his business).

(c) An invented word or words. Words which are descriptive of the goods concerned, such as 'quick-firing' or 'perfect', cannot be registered, because it would be unfair for one trader to have a monopoly of them. An invented word which is merely a phonetic spelling of an ordinary word is not sufficient for this purpose.

(d) A word or words having no direct reference to the character or quality of the goods (and not being a geographical name or a surname). Thus, there could be no objection to the word 'Sunset' in connection with, say, a perfume; for it could not affect the rights of any other trader.

(e) Any other distinctive mark. This covers pictorial marks, and may also include colours.

Registration in Part A gives the proprietor an *exclusive* right to use the trade mark.

To be registrable under Part B, it is sufficient if the mark is merely distinctive, *i.e.* capable of distinguishing the proprietor's goods from the goods of other persons.

The protection afforded by a class B registration is limited. In an action for infringement no relief will be granted if the infringer satisfies the Court that his use of the mark is not likely to deceive or cause confusion.

A person who is not the proprietor of a trade mark may—on the joint application of himself and the proprietor—be registered as a 'registered user' of it in relation to goods with which he is connected.

The proprietor may 'disclaim' part of his trade mark, and limit his rights to the remainder. By so doing he may avoid being opposed on the ground that his trade mark lacks the essential features. Or again, the Registrar may require the applicant, as a condition of registration, to disclaim part. Thus, in order to register 'motorine' and 'absorbine', applicants have been obliged to disclaim the exclusive right to the use of the words 'motor' and 'absorb'.

Where a trade mark consisting of an invented word or words is registered in respect of any goods, and is so well-known that other persons might be tempted to use it in relation to *other goods*, a 'defensive' trade mark may be registered (although it is not intended to use it) to prevent such use in relation to other goods.

Application for the registration of a trade mark must be made in writing to the Registrar. A trade mark which is likely to cause confusion by reason of its similarity to another mark, or which is 'scandalous' (that is, objectionable or ridiculous), or contrary to morality or law, cannot be registered. If the Registrar refuses the application on one of these grounds, the applicant can appeal either to the Board of Trade or to the Court.

If the Registrar accepts the application, he causes it to be advertised. Any person who desires to object may do so within one month by giving notice of opposition, setting out his reasons. The matter is then decided by the Registrar, subject to an appeal to the Court.

The registration of a trade mark lasts for seven years; it may from time to time be renewed for further periods of fourteen years.

If the proprietor does not use his trade mark for five years, any aggrieved person may apply to the Court to have it removed from the register.

In the event of infringement, the proprietor of a registered trade mark can apply for an injunction restraining further use of the mark, and for an order that all infringing marks be destroyed, and that the infringer hand over all stamps, dies, etc., employed to make them. He will not get damages, however, unless he can prove fraud, or at least knowledge, on the part of the defendant, and he can only get an account of profits for the time when the defendant continued to use the mark after he became aware of the plaintiff's rights or knew that the trade mark was not his own.

Several defences are open to the 'infringer'. He can deny that his mark is similar to the plaintiff's; he can show that the goods in respect of which he used the mark were not of the kind in respect of which the trade mark was registered; and he can counter-claim for the removal of the plaintiff's mark from the register.

TRADE NAMES AND PASSING OFF

As we have seen, there is, quite apart from the registration of trade marks, a Common Law action to prevent other persons from knowingly using a name or mark which has become associated with the goods or business of the plaintiff. Generally speaking, a man is entitled to trade under his own name even if it is the same as that of a well-known trader in the same business; but he may be restrained from doing so in such a manner as to represent that his business is that of the well-known trader. Thus, it was held that the makers of 'Wright's Coal Tar Soap' could not only prevent a Mr W. F. Wright from selling toilet preparations under such names as 'Wright's Baby Powder', but could get an injunction restraining him from carrying on business under any name of which 'Wright' or 'Wright's' formed part without clearly distinguishing it from the business of the plaintiffs.

An injunction was granted, at the suit of a representative group of wine-producers from the French district of Champagne, restraining the defendants from using the description 'Spanish Champagne' to describe their wine, on the ground that a substantial part of the public were likely to be misled by the description into thinking that they were getting the produce of Champagne, and that the description was intended to attract to the Spanish product the goodwill connected with Champagne, and was dishonest trading.

Passing off!

COPYRIGHT

INTRODUCTION

THE AUTHOR of a book, the painter of a picture, or the composer of a song might get little profit from their labours if other persons were at liberty to copy or reproduce their work without permission or payment. It is the law of copyright that protects their interests.

'Copyright' means what the word suggests—the right to copy or reproduce. The Copyright Act, 1956, which now governs the law on the subject (introducing many changes from the previous law), defines copyright as the exclusive right to do, and to authorize other persons to do, certain acts in relation to the work in question. These acts are all forms of copying or reproduction, their exact nature depending, as we shall see, upon the nature of the work.

Copyright is not to be confused with ownership: a person who owns an original work frequently does not enjoy the copyright in it. For example, if an artist sells a picture to a person who did not commission it, the copyright belongs to the artist, although the picture itself becomes the property of the buyer.

Copyright differs from patents and the registration of industrial designs in that it arises automatically by operation of law: in other words, no formalities need be complied with, generally speaking, in order to secure copyright.

"*Copyright* means the right to copy or reproduce."

WORKS IN WHICH COPYRIGHT EXISTS

Copyright exists (subject to certain conditions which will be considered later) in every '*original literary, dramatic, or musical work*'. The expression 'literary work' includes any written table or compilation: so it has been held that copyright exists in a list of football fixtures and that the Pools should not copy the League's fixture list without permission. 'Dramatic work' includes a choreographic work (*i.e.* ballet), but not a film: films are also the subject of copyright, but under a separate provision of the Act. A dramatic work, for

317

copyright purposes, is something which is capable of being printed and published. So it has been held that there was no infringement of copyright where what was copied was not the text of a play but only the scenic effects, stage directions, and other aspects of its production. 'Musical work' means music and nothing else. In a vocal composition, therefore, the words constitute a literary or dramatic work: so there are two copyrights, one in the music and the other in the words (*e.g.* Gilbert and Sullivan each had his own separate copyright).

Copyright also exists in every '*original artistic work*'. An artistic work means a work of any of the following descriptions:

(a) paintings, sculptures, drawings, engravings, and photographs—all irrespective of artistic quality;
(b) works of architecture—either buildings or models for buildings;
(c) other words of artistic craftsmanship.

A drawing includes any diagram, map, chart, or plan: an engraving includes any etching, lithograph, woodcut, print, or similar work.

The works of artistic craftsmanship are those of silversmiths, potters, woodworkers, hand-embroiderers, and so forth. (The Copyright Act is not concerned with articles manufactured under conditions of ordinary industrial production: these can be protected under the Registered Designs Act, 1949.) An outline drawing of the heel of a shoe made for the purpose of illustrating a tradesman's catalogue has been held to be an original artistic work and therefore the subject of copyright. A dress design or pattern would certainly be, though a Judge has expressed doubts as to whether a dress itself could be the subject of copyright as a work of artistic craftsmanship, on the ground that the article to be protected must by itself gratify the aesthetic emotions!

The word 'original' means simply that the work must not have been copied from another work: it does not mean that it must express an original thought or be produced in an original form. Thus although the work is based upon, or consists of, existing material and has involved no literary skill or judgment whatsoever, it may well be original if it is arranged in some new form: on this basis, directories and railway guides are the subject of copyright. As we have seen, it has been held that a list of football fixtures, the compilation of which required much work, skill, and ingenuity, constituted an original literary work, although it was pointed out by the Court that there can be no copyright in information as such. On the other hand, it has been held that a school textbook, which was produced by cutting down the text of another work and joining the retained portions together into a continuous narrative, was not original. Whether or not an abridged version of a literary work will qualify as 'original' depends on the nature of the abridgment. If it takes the form simply of eliminating certain portions of the text, then it is not original: but if it also involves some alteration of the text and the exercise of skill and ingenuity, then it may well be original for the purposes of copyright.

Subject to certain conditions, copyright exists in every sound recording—defined in the Act as 'the aggregate of the sounds embodied in, and capable of being reproduced by means of, a record of every description, other than a sound-track associated with a cinematograph film'. A record includes any 'disc, tape, perforated roll, or other device in which sounds are embodied'. Copyright also exists in every 'cinematograph film', this expression including the sound-track.

Finally, there is copyright in every television and sound broadcast made by the British Broadcasting Corporation or Independent Television Authority from any place in the United Kingdom or in certain other countries.

CONDITIONS FOR THE
EXISTENCE OF COPYRIGHT

The work in question must have been written, composed, or made by a 'qualified person' if it is to be the subject of copyright. A qualified person is, in the case of an individual, a British subject, a British protected person, a citizen of the Republic of Ireland, or a person domiciled or resident in the United Kingdom or in another country to which the relevant provision extends. In the case of corporate bodies, it is a body incorporated under the laws of any part of the United Kingdom (or such other country). The Act contains provisions for its extension to the Isle of Man, the Channel Islands, colonies and dependencies, and for its application to countries which by a Convention agree to afford similar treatment to works protected in this country.

In the case of literary, dramatic, musical, and artistic works which are *unpublished*, copyright will only exist if the author 'was a qualified person at the time when the work was made, or, if the making of the work extended over a period, was a qualified person for a substantial part of that period'. In the case of *published* works, copyright will exist only if one of the following conditions is satisfied:

(a) the first publication took place in the United Kingdom (or other country as above), or

(b) the author was a qualified person at the time when the work was first published, or

(c) the author had died before that time, but was a qualified person immediately before his death.

'Publication' here means that a reproduction of the work has been issued to the public: it does not mean the mere performance of a literary, dramatic, or musical work, the issue of records of such works, the exhibition of an artistic work, the construction of a work of architecture, and the issue of photographs or engravings of a work of architecture or of sculpture.

In the case of sound recordings, copyright will exist if the maker of the recording was a qualified person when the recording was made, or, in the case of a published recording, if the first publication took place in the United Kingdom (or other country as above). 'Publication' in regard to sound recordings means simply the issue of the recording to the public. In the case of films, copyright will exist where the maker was a qualified person for the whole or a substantial part of the period during which the film was made, or, if the film has been published, the first publication of the film took place in the United

Kingdom (etc.). Here, 'publication' means 'the sale, letting on hire, or offer for sale or hire, of copies of the film to the public'.

OWNERSHIP OF COPYRIGHT

Ownership of copyright may be acquired automatically, that is, simply because the Act says that in the given circumstances copyright exists and the author or maker of the work is entitled to it. The general rule is that in the case of a literary, dramatic, musical, or artistic work 'the author . . . shall be entitled to any copyright subsisting in the work'.

Sometimes the 'author' is obvious. Occasionally the meaning is not so obvious. Thus it has been held that a person who conceived the idea of a particular drawing for commercial use, but being himself unable to draw, employed an artist to execute it in accordance with his directions, was not the author of the drawing. It has also been held that when a journalist contributed an article to his newspaper, which was then drastically altered by a sub-editor, the author of the final version was the sub-editor and not the journalist. And it has been held that a person who merely provided the material for a biographical work written by another was not a joint author with the writer. Broadly speaking, therefore, the author of a work is the person responsible for clothing the idea, information, or material in the form in which it ultimately appears; not necessarily the writer of the first draft.

To this general rule as to the ownership of copyright in literary, dramatic musical, and artistic works there are certain important exceptions:

(i) Where a literary, dramatic, or artistic work is made by the author *in the course of his employment* by the proprietor of a newspaper, magazine, or similar periodical under a contract of service or apprenticeship, and is made for the purpose of publication in that newspaper or magazine, the proprietor is entitled to any copyright in the work so far as relates to any publication in the newspaper or magazine, or to the reproduction of the work for the purpose of such publication. Thus—unless the parties have otherwise agreed—there is a division of copyright in a work contributed by a journalist or artist in the course of his employment on the staff of a newspaper or magazine. So far as publication in the newspaper or magazine is concerned, the copyright is owned by the employer: as regards publication in any other context, the copyright, following the normal rule, is owned by the author. The words 'in the course of his employment' mean in the course of the work which the author is employed to do.

(ii) When someone *commissions* the taking of a photograph, the painting or drawing of a portrait, or the making of an engraving, and pays or agrees to pay for it in money or money's worth, the copyright, in the absence of agreement to the contrary, belongs to him, not to the photographer, the painter, or the draughtsman.

(iii) As to sound recordings, the maker is generally entitled to any copyright: but there is a similar exception here, the person who commissions it, and pays, is entitled to the copyright.

320

The copyright in a cinematograph film is owned by the maker, who is 'the person by whom the arrangements necessary for the making of the film are undertaken': in most cases, of course, this will be the film company responsible for financing and organizing the shooting of the film. In sound and television broadcasts, ownership of the copyright vests in the B.B.C. or I.T.A., although they may, and usually do, agree that the artist shall retain the copyright provided that they have the right—on payment—to broadcast and to repeat the broadcast, paying an agreed fee for each repeat.

The ownership of copyright may be transferred to another person by a valid 'assignment'. This must be distinguished from a 'licence', which is a mere permission to copy or reproduce, *e.g.* the right to repeat a broadcast or to reprint an article. An assignment is the grant of a specific interest in the copyright, the assignee taking the place of the assignor, and becoming entitled to sue in respect of any infringement of the right assigned. A licence, on the other hand, transfers no interest: it merely enables the licensee to do what would otherwise constitute an infringement.

HOW LONG DOES COPYRIGHT LAST?

Generally speaking, copyright lasts for the life of the author and for fifty years after his death. But the time at which the fifty-year period begins varies according to the circumstances. For literary, dramatic, and musical works, it begins at the end of the year in which the author dies, if the work was published before his death.

If the work has not been so published, performed in public, offered for sale in the form of records or broadcast, then the period begins from the end of the year in which one of these acts is first done to the work or to an adaptation of it.

For artistic works, the period begins at the end of the year in which the artist died.

For a photograph or an engraving not published before the author's death, the period begins at the end of the year of first publication.

For sound recordings, films, and broadcasts, the fifty years runs from the end of the year when the recording or film is first published or the broadcast first made.

INFRINGEMENTS OF COPYRIGHT

The acts restricted by the copyright in a literary, dramatic, or musical work are:

(a) reproducing the work in any material form;
(b) publishing the work;
(c) performing the work in public;
(d) broadcasting the work;
(e) causing the work to be transmitted to subscribers to a diffusion service;

321

(f) making an adaptation of the work; and

(g) doing in relation to an adaptation any of the acts (a) to (e) above.

The acts restricted in the case of artistic works are:

(a) and (b) above, and

(c) including the work in a television broadcast;

(d) causing a television programme which includes the work to be transmitted to subscribers on a rediffusion service.

For sound recordings, films, and broadcasts, the restrictions are as follows:

(1) As regards sound recordings, it is an infringement to make a record embodying the recording, to cause the recording to be heard in public, or to broadcast the recording. It is not an infringement, however, to cause the recording to be heard in residential hotels (unless a special charge is made for admission to the part where the recording is to be heard) or in certain non-profit-making clubs (unless the proceeds of any charge made are applied otherwise than to the purposes of the club).

(2) As to films, the acts restricted are the making of a copy, causing it to be seen or heard in public, broadcasting it or causing it to be transmitted to subscribers to a diffusion service.

(3) For television and sound broadcasts, the acts restricted are the making (*otherwise than for private purposes*) of a film, copy of a film, or a recording, causing them to be seen or heard in public by a paying audience, or broadcasting them.

The law recognizes that it is sometimes in the public interest to permit acts restricted by copyright. Thus 'fair dealing' with a literary, dramatic, or musical work is permitted for the purposes of research or private study, criticism or review, or in the reporting of current events in a newspaper or periodical (accompanied by a suitable acknowledgement), or by means of broadcasting or in a film. So, too, recitation by one person in public of a literary or dramatic work, with suitable acknowledgement, is not an infringement. Nor (if certain conditions are fulfilled) is the inclusion of a short passage in a collection for school use. Where, by virtue of an assignment or licence, there is a right to broadcast a copyright work, a record or film of it may be made for the purpose of the broadcast (though such reproduction must be destroyed within twenty-eight days of being used.

Similar exemptions apply in relation to artistic works also. It is not an infringement to paint, draw, photograph, etc., a sculpture which is permanently situated in a public place or a work of architecture. An artist who does not own the copyright in a work of his may reproduce parts of it as long as he does not repeat or imitate the main design. The reconstruction of a building is not an infringement of copyright. Certain libraries are entitled to make copies of literary, dramatic, and musical works. Where records of a musical work have been made or imported for retail sale, any manufacturer can make copies on giving notice to the owner of the copyright and paying a royalty fixed under the Act.

REMEDIES FOR INFRINGEMENT

The owner of copyright may sue for damages (or alternatively for an account of profits made by the infringer) and for an injunction to restrain infringement. He may treat infringing copies as his own property, and claim delivery up of those in the infringer's possession. He cannot, however, get damages from an innocent infringer, that is, a person who was not aware and had no reasonable grounds for suspecting that the work was the subject of copyright. On the other hand, exemplary damages may be awarded where there is a flagrant infringement and ordinary damages would in the opinion of the Court be inadequate.

Deliberate infringements of copyright are punishable as criminal offences in Magistrates' Courts. And by the Dramatic and Musical Performers Protection Act, 1958, it is an offence to make a record, film. or broadcast of a dramatic or musical performance without the written consent of the performers.

PERFORMING RIGHT TRIBUNAL

To assist composers, music publishers, and makers of records to collect royalties from places of entertainment, a number of societies have been formed (the best known being the Performing Right Society) to keep an eye on performances, conduct negotiations, collect royalties, and distribute them.

The Copyright Act, 1956, established the Performing Right Tribunal to determine disputes between these licensing societies and persons requiring such licences.

CONTRACTS OF EMPLOYMENT

WRITTEN AND ORAL CONTRACTS

IN law there is no reason why a contract of employment should not be made simply by word of mouth. An oral contract of employment is legally valid. Certain contracts, as we have seen in other sections of this work, are not legally enforceable unless they are evidenced by writing, e.g. a contract for the sale or other disposition of land or an interest in land. That must be evidenced in writing if it is to be enforceable. But a contract under which A. engages B. to work for him can be just as valid if it is made by word of mouth alone, as if it is made in writing.

Thousands of such contracts are, of course, made orally. Take, for example, the contract whereby a building worker is engaged on a site to work for the builder who is putting up a building. In that trade the practice is to engage many workers by the hour or by the day. They are told what to do by their foreman. Their pay is calculated at so much per hour, they can be sacked at an hour's

323

or a day's notice. Much the same applies in many other trades. But it can also apply in a job where both employer and employee anticipate that the employee will be paid, not so much an hour or so much a day, or paid on piece-work rates, but rather will be paid a fixed rate per week which will be quite independent of the amount of work he does, and that he will be engaged in a job which may last for not merely days or weeks or months, but years and years. There are many such jobs where the employee is engaged simply on a verbal contract.

Such a contract is perfectly legal. But it may be very disadvantageous if disputes subsequently arise about the precise terms of the engagement. For example, matters which ought to be settled and made perfectly clear between employer and employee may be overlooked, *e.g.*:

(a) the amount of holiday to which the employee is entitled;
(b) whether that holiday is to be with pay or not;
(c) after what period of service he may be entitled to have a holiday with pay;
(d) what is his position if he falls sick. Is he entitled to be paid his ordinary salary or wages while he is away ill, and, if so, for what period;
(e) if the employer wishes to terminate his employment, or if the employee wishes to go, what notice ought to be given on either side;
(f) the precise nature of the duties which he can be reasonably asked to perform.

Many of these matters are settled with perfect amity between employer and employee, even though they have not been set down in the contract. But over and over again one finds cases which occasionally find their way into the Law Courts and much more often lead to explosive disputes and considerable distress, simply because nothing has been clearly settled about them at the time the contract was entered into.

PAY DURING SICKNESS

An outstanding example of this particular kind of disagreement is the question of what wages or salary are to be paid during absence through sickness and for how long. Let us take the situation where the contract of employment, whether it is written or oral, says nothing about this problem at all. Therefore, when it happens, when the employee is away ill, the rights and wrongs must either be settled by friendly agreement, or, if not, must be determined according to the Common Law. What is the law about payment during absence through sickness?

Let us first look at a number of actual cases which have been heard in the Courts. First, the case of a man working at a weekly wage as a fruit salesman. He was away ill for three months. Was he or was he not entitled to wages during that three months' absence? His employers refused to pay anything; he claimed full pay and the dispute came to Court. The Court held that there was nothing in his contract of employment to cut down or to abolish what they considered to be his Common Law right to wages during illness. It was held, therefore, that he was entitled to be paid in full for his three months' illness.

In the next case a man was employed as a smoker of smoked salmon, and of herrings, at a weekly wage. His contract, such as it was, said nothing at all about pay during absence through illness, but, some time before he was taken on, a notice had been put up in the place where he worked. The terms of the notice are important. The notice read thus:

'During sickness half pay allowed up to a total of twenty-one days a year. This allowance is purely an act of grace on the Company's part and cannot be claimed as a right.'

Now it was proved that he never personally actually saw this notice. On the other hand, it was also proved that his fellow-workmen knew about the practice of half pay for twenty-one days and no pay for absence after twenty-one days. It was also proved that they had told him about this custom of the firm. Moreover, when he fell sick and was away for a week or so he accepted his half pay. This was at a time when the twenty-one day period was never in question. He had only been away for a week or two. Some years later he had a more serious illness, and on this occasion he was away for several months, and this time, after taking advice, he sued the company for full wages for the whole time of his absence.

He, unlike the man in the first case mentioned above, lost his case. He lost it for this reason: the Court held that the arrangement about half pay for twenty-one days as an act of grace had become so much a part of the *general custom of employment* in that company that it had become a term of his particular contract. They held on the evidence that the man himself must have known about it, that he had recognized it previously when he had been ill for short periods. Therefore, although it was not, in so many words, contained in his particular contract with the Company, it had, in fact, become part of his contract; it was an implied term of the contract, and the Court so held as a matter of law.

It follows from this case that when there is a long- and well-established custom in a particular employment about wages or salary during illness, then that custom may become part of the contract of service. It is because of the difficulty which obviously frequently arises, of proving that there is such a custom, that many employers prefer to make their sick leave arrangements clear in writing, and to get it into the contract.

The judgments in these two cases, both of which were heard in the early 1950's, indicated that if the contract of service says nothing one way or the other about pay while sick, and if there is no established custom in a particular employment which fixes this sick pay, then the man is entitled to full pay while he is away ill, and it does not matter how long his illness goes on. As long as he is in the employment of his firm, company, or other employer, he is entitled to sick pay. If, however, there is some custom such as the one described, which is quite independent of the term of the contract, but which is so well established and well recognized that the Courts will hold that the man must know it, and that it therefore must be regarded as an implied contract of the term of service, the Courts will uphold that clause.

In the years following these cases it was frequently doubted whether it really was the law that in the absence of specific arrangements in the contract of service an employee was entitled to indefinite sick pay during absence through illness.

An authoritative answer was given in a very important High Court case decided in 1960. The facts of this case were these: a firm advertised for a production manager experienced in the design and manufacture of women's skirts. They offered the post to an applicant who refused their original terms of £30 a week and eventually accepted a salary of £30 a week with an addition of 2*d* a skirt bonus for all skirts made at the factory. So it was perfectly clear that the bonus of 2*d* a skirt, whatever that amounted to, made a substantial difference to his earnings. There was nothing in the contract of service to say what was to happen if the new manager fell ill.

Pay during sickness

He started work in January 1955. In November 1956 he suffered from a coronary thrombosis. He recovered from this in January 1957, but when he was then ready to return to work he found that someone else had been appointed production manager, and that he would be required to work on somewhat different terms.

He was not prepared to agree to this. But the facts of that quarrel are irrelevant for this present purpose. The point of the case which is relevant here is what pay, if any, was he legally entitled to receive during the nine months when he was away ill. There was nothing in his contract about this; it merely provided for a weekly rate of pay, and said nothing at all about pay during absence through sickness.

The Judge considered the cases which I have described above, and other cases dealing with this problem. And he quite clearly came down on the side of this general principle: where the written terms of the contract say nothing either way about the employee's right to be paid while he is absent from work during sickness, *i.e.* where the contract is silent on the point, the employer must pay the employee's full salary or wages. The only possible exception is that there might be some implied term which provides otherwise, but obviously an implied term is very difficult to establish.

Applying this general principle the Court decided in this case that the manager was entitled to his full salary of £30 a week for the whole period of his illness, and also the 2*d* per skirt bonus for skirts produced while he was away ill, although he could have had no personal responsibility for them. The point was that this weekly pay plus this bonus was his contractual pay. That was the only point that mattered, and that was the pay to which he was entitled while he was away sick. The Court was not asked to apply itself to the question whether the company, the employer, was entitled to give notice to terminate the employment; that was an entirely different matter. The only question was what pay the employee was entitled to receive while he was away sick, and the answer was perfectly clear: full pay plus the bonus, because the bonus was part of his contractual pay.

HOW MUCH NOTICE SHOULD BE GIVEN TO TERMINATE A CONTRACT WHERE THE CONTRACT DOES NOT FIX A PERIOD OF NOTICE?

The situation may arise where either a written contract does not specify in express terms what length of notice should be given by either side to terminate the contract, or there is no written contract at all, and whatever may have been agreed orally between the parties has long since been forgotten or is subject to contradictory recollections.

When it is neither clearly expressed nor unanimously agreed between the parties what length of notice should be given, then by Common Law, which the Courts will apply if they are asked to do so, the rule is that the notice should be reasonable.

The first and most important point to note about this is that a reasonable notice does not necessarily depend upon the periods at which salary or wages are paid. For example, it is quite commonly assumed that if the employee is paid weekly, then in the absence of agreement as to the length of notice needed to terminate the contract, it is reasonable, by the Common Law standard, to give him a week's notice. That is not always so. It is also very generally assumed that the man who is paid monthly can have his contract terminated by a month's notice. This, too, is not an accurate statement of the law.

These ideas probably derive from the weekly and monthly tenancies, where it is a much more strongly accepted custom that the amount of notice required shall depend very largely upon the intervals of time at which rent is paid. This is considerably less true today than it was, very largely because, since the 1957 Rent Act, any tenancy requires a four-weeks' notice, even though it is a tenancy on which the rent is paid weekly, but even allowing for that distinction, it was and is probably true that in the absence of express agreement in the tenancy agreement or lease, the notice required had some dependence on the periods at which rent was paid.

This has never been such a strong general rule in contracts of employment. In the cases in which they have been asked to decide this question, the Courts have tended to disregard the periods of payment, and have considered instead the degree of responsibility for the work. Broadly speaking, the higher the responsibility, the longer the notice they have decided ought to be given.

The more valuable the employee is, the higher and the more responsible his job, the longer notice he ought to give if he wants to go, and the longer notice he ought to be given if his employers want to get rid of him. This really is a matter of pure common sense. A junior clerk doing comparatively routine clerical work might reasonably be dismissed at a week's notice. From the employer's point of view he can be replaced comparatively easily; from his point of view he can find a comparable job comparatively easily. To go to the other extreme, the editor of a national newspaper might reasonably expect something like six or even twelve months' notice. It might be a very long time before he can find another comparable job.

In considering the question of what is reasonable notice, the Courts try to be fair to both sides, and must pay particular regard to the position of the employee who is thrown out of a job. It may seem odd that a person occupying such an important job as editor of a national newspaper should have no agreement which lays down in terms the amount of notice to which he is entitled if his employers want to get rid of him, but it is a fact that there are many such important posts where these terms are not properly explored beforehand. It may be that both sides prefer to take a chance.

The following few examples are taken from actual cases decided by the Courts where the Judges had to say what was a reasonable notice in each case in the absence of any express term in the contract of employment:

A milk roundsman—one week.
A foreign correspondent of *The Times* who was paid monthly—six months.
A manager of a medium-sized shop who was paid weekly—one month.
A commercial traveller with a fairly wide territory—three months.
An engineering salesman—three months.

All these cases depended on their particular facts, but they do provide a sort of rough guide.

It may help an understanding of this general topic to consider two comparatively recent cases concerned with the same type of employment. The first one concerned a sales representative whose territory covered a great part of the Midlands and Wales. He was given two weeks' notice. He claimed damages for loss of salary and commission on the grounds that two weeks was far too short a notice, and that he had therefore been wrongfully dismissed. He maintained that he was entitled to three months' notice, *i.e.* that three months' notice was reasonable for a man in his position. His contract did not specify any particular period of notice.

His former employers argued on the other hand that the two weeks' notice he had been given was fair enough, or if the Court did not agree with them that two weeks was fair, then a month was the most he should have been given. The

Judge heard an account of the work which this sales representative had to do, and the responsibilities which he had to accept. He was impressed by the very wide extent of the territory which the man covered. It was a great part of the Midlands and Wales. The Judge ultimately decided that it was wholly unreasonable to give only two weeks' notice and that the three months the plaintiff had claimed was the right period. Therefore he awarded damages accordingly, *i.e.* salary and estimated commission for three months.

The next case concerned a clerk who was employed at a wage of £10 a week. He was an unqualified book-keeper accountant. He had no professional accountancy qualifications, but he had some twelve junior office employees under him. He was given one week's notice, and when he sued his employers for wrongful dismissal because they had given him too short a notice, he claimed that he ought to be given three months' notice. The Judge decided that his position and responsibilities did not merit the three months' notice which he claimed, but that certainly one week was too short. It was decided that in this case one month was the right period. Here again, of course, there was nothing in the contract of service to specify what notice should be given on either side to end the contract.

One more case about notice, although there was no argument here as to the length of the notice. This was a rather novel point which was taken up by the manager of a shop. His employers owned a number of shops and he ran one of them. On the very eve of going off on his summer holiday he was given notice. It was the right length of notice according to the written agreement. There was no dispute about that, no problem about what was right and reasonable, because, as previously explained, arguments about what is right and reasonable can only arise if there is no clear agreement about the length of notice before the employment starts. In this case there was no dispute about the length of notice. But the manager took the point before the Court that it was illegal for any employer to give notice to one of his staff when he was about to go on holiday if that notice was going to expire during the holiday period. He argued—and this was a very interesting argument—that the purpose of a period of notice was to give the employee a chance to get another job. If he was on holiday he would not have that chance. Therefore, for an employer to give him notice on the eve of his holiday was virtually to deprive him of that vital chance to obtain other employment. He asked for an additional week's salary to compensate him.

This novel claim aroused a great deal of interest, but the Judge refused to accept it and said that there was no Common Law principle that a notice was not to be given so as to expire during a holiday. It might be hard on the man concerned, indeed he thought that in this case it was very hard indeed, but it was not illegal, provided that the notice was in accordance with the written contract of employment.

IS THE EMPLOYER RESPONSIBLE FOR THE SAFETY OF HIS EMPLOYEES' PROPERTY?

An employee will naturally take to his place of work a hat, a coat or a macintosh, or an umbrella, a handbag, a briefcase, and so on, all the ordinary paraphernalia which most of us at one time or another carry on our way to work, and we expect to be able to leave it at our place of work in safety. Has the employer any legal responsibility if, during the day, one or other of those articles is stolen or a handbag is opened and money taken?

Curiously enough, although both the Common Law and successive Acts of Parliament have compelled employers to shoulder immensely heavy responsibilities for the personal safety of their employees, to ensure that the place where they work is safe, that tools and machines are safe, that the system of work is one which will give every possible protection to the workpeople and so on, yet there is no such legal duty on the employer to ensure the safety of his employees' personal property. Many employers do, of course, provide lock-up cupboards where their staff can put their personal belongings, but that is what might be called part of good industrial relations, a common-sense management of the factory or office. It is not based on any legal duty on the employer.

This principle that the employer has no legal responsibility for the safety of his employees' belongings was firmly established by a Court of Appeal decision in 1946 where all the previous law on the matter was reviewed.

There was an interesting development in a case heard in 1957, where the facts were such as to suggest that in certain circumstances the employer might be liable. In this case a doctor was employed as a resident house physician at a hospital, and it was one of the terms of his employment that he had to live in a hostel which was near the hospital. It is clear that this introduces a different consideration. He was not just the daily office or factory worker, but was actually required to live in the hostel. Therefore he would naturally have many personal belongings in his bed-sitting-room. Moreover, he could not even lock the door and take the key away. He was required to leave the key in the lock, no doubt so that the room could be cleaned.

A number of things were stolen from his room, and his employers, the hospital management committee, refused to accept any responsibility for the loss. He felt acutely about this, and the point was a novel one in view of the fact that he was required to live in the hostel. He took legal proceedings against the hospital management committee. The Court, however, held that they were legally entitled to refuse to accept responsibility. As in the previous cases, it was held that they were not responsible for the safety of his personal property just because they were his employers, and the fact that they ran a hostel in connection with the hospital where he had to live did not turn them into hotel-keepers who do have special responsibility for the safety of their guests' property.

What, then, can be done by the employee, at least to mitigate or minimize his loss? Anyone in the position of that doctor should surely take out an insurance policy on his personal property in the furnished room or rooms where he is required to live. There would not be much difficulty about getting such a policy, although it is possible that the premium might be a little higher than it would be for someone living in a private house or self-contained flat. With regard to office workers and factory workers in general, there has recently been a change in the insurance cover provided by comprehensive insurance policies on one's goods and chattels at home. It is now possible, if you have a comprehensive policy on your furniture and goods in your own home, to have that policy extended to cover certain personal belongings which you normally and usually take to your place of work.

DUTY OF EMPLOYEE
TO KEEP HIS EMPLOYER'S SECRETS

Every employee has a duty by law to keep his employer's trade and business secrets, and to keep them not merely while his employment lasts, but also after it has ended and he has gone to another job.

One very common temptation is to steal a list of customers. For example, in one case which came before the Courts it was described how a young man was taught how to run a business which was mainly concerned with the manufacture of a particular kind of cloth of very high quality. It was high-grade quality and inevitably very expensive. It followed, of course, that the market for such cloth was small, and a list of the customers who were accustomed to buy it was very valuable.

In this case it appeared that the employee surreptitiously copied out a complete list of customers from his employer's order book. Few people had access to this book, which was kept as secret as possible, but he did have access to the book in the ordinary course of his employment. Later on he gave up this job and set up on his own and invited those customers to order the cloth through him.

This was such a serious matter that his former employer felt obliged to bring legal proceedings to stop him. The Court upheld the employer's claim and not only awarded him damages for loss of trade, but also made an injunction ordering the ex-employee to cease canvassing the former customers of his former master and to hand over the list which he had made, and all copies.

It is interesting to note that in this case the Court was not enforcing a clause in the contract of employment. There was nothing whatever in the contract of employment dealing with the employee's duty to preserve his master's secrets. The Court was, in fact, applying a basic general principle of the Common Law that all employees owe this duty toward their employer. It is very often written into the contract of employment. Many such contracts do contain such a clause so that it may be brought clearly home to the attention of the employee. There is, however, no legal necessity for the clause to be there. It is binding in law whether it is there or not.

CAN AN EMPLOYEE BE PROHIBITED FROM
TAKING EMPLOYMENT WITH A COMPETITOR?

Every employer who entrusts trade secrets to an employee knows that he runs the risk that at some time or another the employee may leave him and set up on his own, or go to a competitor, and that those trade secrets will be secrets no longer. The problem applies to all sorts of confidential information.

Another aspect of the problem is the employee's association with clients and customers. It is inevitable that a responsible employee will build up some sort

331

of personal connection; indeed, the more valuable the employee the more likely he is to have influence with clients and customers and to be in possession of confidential information and secrets.

The case already described where an employer successfully enforced, with the help of the Courts, his right to have his list of special customers kept secret shows that the Courts will intervene to assist the employer in this respect. Very often, however, the former employee's use of secret or confidential information is never so clearly shown as it was in that case where he blatantly stole his former employer's customers from him. The fact is that the secret information is in his hands. It may, for example, concern a process of manufacture and it may be virtually impossible to prove that he is using it in unfair competition with his former employer.

So, for many years, employers have cast around for other methods of doing all that they legally can to ensure that those whom they have taught, and those whom they trust, will not, later on, either set up on their own on the strength of all that they have been taught and learnt, or help competitors.

The usual method by which the employer hopes to achieve this is to put a clause in the original contract of service under which the employee agrees that within so many years after leaving that employment, he will not set up in a competing business of his own, or go to a competitor within a certain radius. A tailor in the West End of London may put in the clause that if his head cutter leaves him he will not join another firm within a radius of five miles of the present establishment, and this will be stated to last either for ever, or for a limited period of time, say two to three years. The owner of a butcher's shop in a country market-town may require the manager of his shop to undertake not to work for a competitor in the town for at least one year after leaving his employment. A partnership agreement between a number of doctors setting up in practice together will almost certainly contain a clause providing that if one doctor wants to leave the partnership he will not set up in practice on his own within a certain radius and within a certain period of time. All such provisions are intended either to protect trade or business secrets, or to prevent competition and canvassing of customers and clients.

It is important to realize that the fact that a clause is in a contract voluntarily entered into between the two parties, the employer and the employee, does not mean that it will necessarily be upheld by the Courts. This general principle, of course, must be stated with extreme caution. By and large the Courts will uphold the written terms of a contract apparently freely and voluntarily entered into by two adults, even though the contract turns out to be extremely harsh, and perhaps even was not properly understood by one of the parties. Nevertheless there are a few, a very limited number of cases where the Courts will, on the grounds of public policy, be prepared *not* to uphold a particular clause of the contract.

These clauses of the type we are now discussing are examined by the Courts with the greatest suspicion. There have been a number of cases where the employee has broken the contract by setting up in business within the prohibited radius or within the prohibited time, or both, and his former employer has gone to the Courts to ask for an injunction to stop him, and possibly to ask for damages as well.

The general attitude of the Courts is that the employer has to justify the individual clause in the circumstances to which he wishes it to be applied. The clause is to be null and void *unless the employer can justify it*, and the tests for justification are as follows:

(1) That the restriction was reasonably necessary for the protection of his business or profession, and that it was imposed only for that reason.
(2) That it is not unduly harsh and oppressive on the employee.
(3) That it is not an unreasonable interference with the public interest.
   (The public interest and the employee's interest can often be the same because the Courts say that, in general, it is against the public interest that a man with knowledge and skill should be prevented from exercising it.)

With those general principles in mind, it is interesting to consider some actual cases.

The first one concerns a man who was employed by an engineering firm to do work on thin-wall bearings. This work was connected with a new type of racing car, and the thin-wall bearings involved a knowledge of secret processes. This was a matter of enormous importance to the man who was financing the whole of this new conception of racing car design. The employee entered into an agreement whereby he undertook not to work for any competitor for two years after his employment should have ended.

He did join the service of a competitor within that time, and his employers applied to the Court for an injunction to stop him. The Judge held that the clause in the agreement was too wide to be enforceable. It was too wide because there was no limitation on the area to be covered by the agreement. In fact, it appeared to mean that he could not work for any competitor anywhere in England, Wales, Scotland, or Ireland, that any such competitor could be prohibited from employing him by an injunction, and if employment had begun could be compelled to dismiss him.

It is highly probable that if the limitation on future employment had also contained a limitation of distance as well as of time, the Court would probably have been prepared to hold it reasonable. But one very important feature of all these cases is that if the Court finds that an agreement is unenforceable because it is against public policy to put undue restrictions on employees, the Court will not re-write the agreement; they will not substitute what would have been reasonable in the first place. The contract either stands or falls, and will not be revived in a new form by the Judge. In this case the problem was so important for the employers that they appealed, but the Court of Appeal agreed with the Judge's view that the covenant was too wide in area. They also added an objection of their own, which was that the clause would never have had a chance of succeeding unless it had been limited *to the particular secret processes in which the man was engaged*. It was quite wrong to exclude him from any other competitor of the employers in any other branch of their business. It meant that he could not work for any motor manufacturer or any garage at all, and that restriction they thought was very much too wide.

As a contrast, consider the case concerning the manager of one of a group of butchers' shops. He entered into an agreement with the owner of the shops that he would not engage, either directly or indirectly, in the business of a retail butcher for twelve months after the ending of his employment within a radius of one mile from the shop where he was employed. However, when he left that employment he immediately found a job with another butcher within one mile of that shop. The Court held that as his work had brought him into personal

Secret Processes!

contact with the owner's customers, so as to gain some influence with them, and as the clause was reasonable and moderate, only covering a mile radius, and only lasting for twelve months, it ought to be enforced.

In another case a clerk in an estate office in Portsmouth had a contract which barred him from going to another estate agent in the town for one year after leaving his present post. The Courts considered that that was not reasonable, being too wide in area, covering as it did the whole of a large town.

On the other hand, a solicitor's clerk had been employed by a firm of solicitors since he was fifteen. They taught him his job. They even went so far as to train him to become a solicitor. When he was twenty-seven he had passed all his examinations and qualified as a solicitor. They agreed to take him on in his new capacity, and he signed an agreement that he would not at any time after it ended be engaged in work as a solicitor within seven miles of the town. Some time later he broke the agreement. He pleaded that it was unreasonably wide because it prevented him from so practising 'at any time after the agreement ended'. But the Courts considered that this was a reasonable restriction and upheld it. The distance was only seven miles and there was no reason why he should compete within that radius.

And lastly, a rather exceptional and difficult case, about a man who had a very responsible job as supervising agent in West Africa for a firm in England which had a large export business to West Africa. His contract of service debarred him from taking a similar post, for five years after his present one ended, within the radius of fifty miles of *any* West African port. In effect, a clause like this shut him out of that kind of job in West Africa altogether. Nevertheless, the Courts did not think it was too wide; when it was challenged they upheld it and decided that it was reasonable.

It is clear that one important point which the Courts take very carefully into consideration is the status of the employee in the concern. Either he is near the top of the concern in the kind of post where he knows everything about it, and therefore is a very important person in that concern, one with special knowledge, or he has a post which actually brings him into direct personal touch with the clients or the customers. It may be that the kind of job he has comes into both categories. The estate agent's clerk in the example given above certainly met clients, but they were always new clients. He did not have a close, long-standing, personal relationship with any of them, and that was a point which influenced the Court to hold that the restrictive clause was too wide. The solicitor's clerk, on the other hand, who afterwards became a qualified solicitor himself, knew a great deal about some of the clients' personal affairs. They were permanent clients, constantly coming about their legal troubles. He did not merely know them as persons; he knew their histories, knew a great deal about their family affairs, and because of his knowledge was all the better able to give them good advice.

Even that tailor's cutter had in the opinion of the Court a far more personal knowledge of the permanent regular customers, a knowledge which the customers relied on, than say an assistant in a very different kind of shop, an ordinary retail shop, or the estate agent's clerk in Portsmouth. The man who was in charge of the West African side of his company's business had immense influence and local knowledge. If he in West Africa was free to work for another export firm it is quite possible that his former employers would have lost a great deal of their business.

So, where an employee does fill a post where his personal relationship with the clients or customers of the firm is vitally important, it will be reasonable and lawful to stop him from competing for a time, and within an area, after he leaves. How long a time and how wide an area is bound to vary with every case. It is fair to say that the Courts will try to cut down both the time and the area to the minimum which they think is consistent with the three principles specified above. It must never be forgotten that it is for the employer to justify the restrictions. The general principle is that all such restrictions are apparently against the public interest. It is for the employer to justify them in the particular circumstances of his particular case, and if he can do so, they will be upheld and enforced by the Courts.

WHO OWNS INVENTIONS MADE BY THE EMPLOYEE IN THE COURSE OF HIS EMPLOYMENT?

This is a very difficult question. Certain inventions and discoveries made by employees in a certain class quite clearly belong by law to the employer, and it is the employee's duty to give to his employer all the necessary information about his invention or discovery, *i.e.* to impart what is necessary to enable it to be put into practice, or if it is patentable, to enable it to be patented (see the chapter on *Patents*). On the other hand, there are inventions and discoveries outside this class to which the employee can claim complete legal right of ownership.

Much depends upon the status of the employee. For example, if a man who is purely a manual worker has a bright idea which leads him to some original invention, then in the vast majority of cases that invention would certainly belong to him. For example, a certain man was employed to drive a fork-lift truck, and that was the beginning and end of his duty to his employer. He noticed that the truck tended to be overloaded, and that there was no means of warning the loaders or the driver when a dangerous state of overloading was likely to occur. He devised a valve which had the effect of preventing overloading by giving automatic warning. This was so far outside the usual functions of a driver of this kind of truck that he was entitled to claim ownership of the invention.

Then there was the case of a night-shift foreman in a producer gas plant. He was promoted to a higher grade of superintendent, but even though in that position he did superintend the gas plant, his status was comparatively lowly. Over him were a manager, an assistant manager, and a number of engineers. He invented a process, an apparatus for extracting sulphate of ammonia from producer gas, which was superior to that previously used by his employers. He patented the process and the apparatus, and when his employers claimed that they were entitled to the patent—and they had some evidence in support, such as his post as a superintendent—the Court held that the invention was so far outside the ordinary scope of this particular superintendent's duties that he was entitled to retain the invention for himself.

A relevant factor is the amount of wage or salary that the person is paid. This foreman, at the time the case was heard, which was in 1926, was earning between £7 and £8 a week. It is difficult accurately to say what he would be earning in a comparable position today. Perhaps between £15 and £20 a week. The driver of the truck in the first example given was also earning something round about the same figure.

It is quite clear from the cases that when you move higher up the scale, higher up the ranks to persons who have wider and more general responsibility, and therefore a higher duty to their employers, and a higher skill which they are expected to exercise on their employer's behalf, if they light upon some discovery or invention, then the likelihood that the Courts would hold that they

". . . inventions made by the employee in the course of his employment"

must communicate that to their employers is considerable. For example, an American company employed a man as their agent and manager in England. His job was to endeavour to get exported to England a certain type of pump which was manufactured in America. Although the basic design of the pump was American it was frequently necessary to make alterations to meet the requirements of English customers. When modifications were made, it was as a result of discussion and negotiation between this agent and the English customers. In the course of these discussions, which went on over the years, he elaborated several new designs and secretly patented them in his own name. The Courts held that in his responsible position he had a duty to disclose the nature of his inventions to his employers and to hand over the patents to them.

To take the matter one stage further, where a man is employed as, for example, a research chemist or physicist, or as an engineering draughtsman or designer, and in the course of doing the work which he is paid to do, he lights on some new and improved method of doing old work, or some completely new formula, it is quite clear from the Court's decisions that he must communicate his invention to his employers at once.

In one very famous case concerning a research chemist, the Judge said: "Any invention or discovery made in the course of the employment of the employee in doing that which he is engaged and instructed to do during working hours, and using the materials of his employer, is the property of the employer, and not that of the employee. Having made such a discovery or invention, the employee becomes a *trustee* for the employer of that invention or discovery. He is therefore, as a trustee, bound to give the benefit of any such discovery or invention to his employer."

The situation described in the above cases rests on the Common Law. This has nothing whatever to do with particular clauses in contracts of employment. It is a general basis of the Common Law that responsible employees occupying a high position in a company, or even if their position is not so high, yet if they are carrying out work which they are specifically employed to do—and this applies particularly to research workers and technical workers—then the inventions they may make in the course of their employment must be given to their employer. He has provided the opportunity for the work to be done, he has provided the tools, the raw material, the laboratories, the experience, and so on. While engaged in this work they have a moral and legal duty to communicate all that they learn to their employer.

That is the Common Law. But this can so often give rise to difficulties and disputes that it is the general practice in those employments where people regularly make inventions—one can think of the great chemical and engineering firms for example—that it is the general practice for the employer to include in the contract of service a clause which specifically obliges the employee to communicate to the employer inventions made in the course of his employment. One such clause reads as follows:

'You agree that any invention, improvement, process or design, wholly or in part invented or made by you during the continuance of your employment with the Company, and intended for use or capable of being used in connection with any of the operations of the Company, and which arises directly or indirectly out of, or in consequence of, work in which you have been at any time engaged during the course of your employment with the Company, shall be communicated to the Company and to no other person.'

The clause goes on to say that the employee will join the Company in applying for letters patent if necessary, either in the United Kingdom or abroad, and in general do all things possible to enable the company to have the full use of that invention.

It will be noticed that the clause refers to inventions, etc., made during the continuance of the employment with the company. Now it is perfectly clear that a man may be engaged in a particular branch of work for Company A. for many years and subsequently move to Company B., and after he has been with Company B. for, say, a few months, engaged on work very similar to that he was doing for Company A., he suddenly sees a great light and realizes that he is on the point of making a considerable new discovery. That discovery probably emanates more from the work he did for Company A. than for Company B. It is therefore quite common for that clause to cover inventions and discoveries made not merely during continuance of employment, but for a period afterwards, and a period of one year after the employment by Company A. comes to an end would probably be accepted by the Courts as reasonable.

Finally, on this difficult subject of ownership of inventions, it should be added that most large concerns who hope and expect their employees to make inventions, do have some scheme for rewarding exceptional skill. Much depends on how far the invention arose ordinarily and naturally out of work the man was directed and employed to do. It may very well be the result of an inspired direction given by his chief. But if it is not—if it is something which was his own inspiration and really goes outside the precise field of the work he is employed to do—he would probably qualify for some sort of reward under the reward scheme which many companies now operate. The amount of the reward is usually proportionate—so far as can be foreseen—to the commercial value of the invention to the employer.

NOTICE TO TERMINATE EMPLOYMENT

We have dealt earlier with the situation which arises where there is nothing in the contract of service either oral or written, to specify how long a notice is necessary on either side to terminate the contract. The notice in that case has to be what the Common Law Courts describe as a reasonable notice and, as described above, this depends upon the status and importance of the job. The more important it is the longer the notice which the Courts would consider to be reasonable.

However, even when a period of notice is specified, the contract sometimes neglects to say on what day it should be given, or neglects to say, as some contracts do, that it can be given on *any* day, a very convenient and sensible arrangement. And the same difficulty may arise when employer and employee agree together that although no fixed period of notice is stated in the agreement, that in that particular case the right notice, let us say, shall be a month, but they cannot agree on what day it shall be given: the employee perhaps contending for the first day of the following month, the employer saying that he can give it tomorrow provided it runs for a month.

There is no rule of law to fix the day, but it has been clearly decided in a number of cases that a week's notice must be seven days, and that a month's notice must be a calendar month. For example, if a girl is employed on a contract which provides for a week's notice on either side, it would be wrong for the employer to give her notice on Monday morning to expire on the following

Saturday. Equally it would be wrong for her to give such a notice to her employer. Monday to Saturday is, in fact, her working week, but it is not a week's notice in law. The notice in such a case should be given on Saturday to expire on the following Saturday. That is the absolute minimum. In considering these matters, it is important to note that the day on which wages or salary happen to be paid, or the day on which work happened to begin, is irrelevant.

If the notice is to be a month, or is to be three months, or longer, and no day of the month has been specified in the contract, it may be given on any day, and the notice will run until the corresponding day one calendar month, or three calendar months later, and so on.

WRONGFUL DISMISSAL

From time to time there are cases in the Courts where a servant complains that he has been wrongfully dismissed and asks for damages for unlawful or wrongful dismissal. There is a fairly common assumption that what the particular employee is complaining about is that the employer's reasons for dismissing him were totally unjustified; either they were not true at all, or, if they were true, they were not sufficiently serious to justify the extreme measure of dismissal.

This is such a general and serious misunderstanding that it is most important to get it perfectly clear that provided an employer gives the notice prescribed in the contract of service, he is not obliged to justify or explain his reason. For example, a foreign correspondent is engaged by a newspaper on a contract which is to be terminable by three months' notice on either side. He goes abroad, he does his work, sends back his despatches, many of which are printed, and everything appears to be going well. After some twelve months in such employment, his employer gives him three months' notice. He complains bitterly, and asks what he has done wrong, and gets no answer. He is told to go at the end of the three months' notice period, and he goes. But, brooding over what he considers to be gross injustice, he takes proceedings for damages for wrongful dismissal. Those proceedings are bound to fail. There can be no question of wrongful dismissal where the employer has exercised the legal rights under the contract of giving the notice prescribed by the contract. Exactly the same rules apply to every such situation. It makes no difference at all whether the notice to be given is a week, a month, six months, or a year, or whatever it might be. Provided the proper notice is given on either side, there is no need for any reason to be given.

As a matter of good staff relations an employer may prefer not to exercise the right of terminating the contract unless, indeed, he has a reason which he is prepared to disclose. One reason may be cutting down of staff owing to falling off in work. Other reasons may be falling below a certain standard of skill and competence. Other reasons may depend on personal behaviour. But whatever the reasons may be, it is entirely up to the employer whether he discloses them or not. He is not obliged to give any reason whatever when he is exercising the right of terminating the contract by the notice prescribed by that contract.

Occasionally, however, an action for damages for wrongful dismissal succeeds, and when it does it is based either on the fact that the notice given was not lawful, *i.e.* it was either not in accordance with the contract, or not in accordance with what the Common Law would find to be reasonable notice, or that some other special provision of the contract has not been observed.

The latter situation obtained in a case which was decided in 1960. The plaintiff in this case was the manager of an insurance company's branch office. His contract provided that for a certain period of years he was not to be given notice to terminate his employment, unless he was guilty of negligence or misconduct in his work. This, of course, is an extremely unusual contract. You do from time to time see contracts where an employer agrees to employ someone for a fixed definite period of time, agrees to employ him for ten years, fifteen years, or whatever the period might be. Obviously this is exceptional. It only arises where the prospective employee is a person of such outstanding distinction that the employers are anxious to secure his services for as long as reasonably possible, are prepared to pay for them, and are prepared also to guarantee that his employment will not be terminated for a period.

The particular contract in this case was not quite as firm as that, but they did guarantee his employment for a definite period of years, leaving to themselves only the loophole that if he was guilty of negligence or misconduct, they could give notice.

His behaviour over a period of time caused considerable concern to his employers. It is not necessary to go too closely into detail, but in general they complained bitterly that he was very seldom in his office, that he was spending too much on entertaining customers of the firm, and that he gave the general impression of enjoying himself and not giving proper attention to the affairs of his employers.

He challenged this in the Courts. He issued a writ claiming damages for wrongful dismissal, and thereby he alleged that he had not been guilty of any such negligence or misconduct as would justify his employers' action. The case was fought, and therefore it was necessary to go into considerable detail about all his activities in the office. The employers elaborated their complaints, which have been briefly outlined above, the plaintiff explained exactly what he was doing and why he was doing it, and established to the satisfaction of the Court that so far from neglecting his employers' interests, he had in fact furthered them considerably, and that when he was out of his office he was probably doing far better work from their point of view, or at least as good work from their point of view, as when he was in his office. The Courts found in his favour; they decided that the employers had dismissed him wrongly because they could not prove either negligence or misconduct. In the result he was awarded a sum of damages amounting to more than £15,000, plus, of course, his costs.

SUMMARY DISMISSAL

Summary dismissal means the termination of the contract without giving any notice at all. It means in effect giving the sack on the spot, or at any rate within a matter of hours.

The first point to note about summary dismissal is that it is, on the face of it, a breach of contract. A contract of employment, like any other contract, must be observed on both sides, and one of the clauses of every such contract is that it is only to be ended by the period of notice stated in the contract or if, as often happens, no such period is stated, then by reasonable notice.

Nevertheless, there are certain circumstances in which an employer can justify his apparent breaking of the contract by ordering his employee to go at once, *i.e.* by giving him the sack summarily. Summary dismissal is justified when the employee has been guilty of such a gross piece of misconduct that he has done something which strikes at the root of his contract, *i.e.* strikes at the fundamental relationship between master and man. It indicates either deliberate disobedience, or deliberate defiance, or reckless disregard of his ordinary

Summary dismissal!

obligations. An outstanding example, of course, is the engine driver who comes on duty drunk, and takes a train with many coaches and hundreds of passengers on a perilous journey. The same principle would apply to anyone in such a responsible position where the safety of people and property are imperilled by his deliberate disregard of his normal obligations.

Another example is a deliberate disobedience to a lawful order given by the employer or by a superior officer. Another is a course of conduct where the employee's personal interests and those of his firm come into conflict. For example, there is a very famous case of a trusted clerk in a firm of stockbrokers. His duty was to give expert advice to the firm's clients, but he himself went in for gambling transactions in secret on the stock exchange.

When his firm discovered this they sacked him at once, although he happened to be one of those unusual employees who was entitled to a very long period of notice indeed. In fact, he had a fixed contract for ten years, and the contract was only terminable after that period had expired. However, all that is by the way. It matters not how long the period of notice to which you are entitled may be; the point is, have you substantially committed a grave breach of your basic contract of employment which entitles the employer to terminate it? The Court held in this case that the employers were entitled to sack him on the spot, because he could not give expert and impartial advice to clients when he himself was gambling to the extent of hundreds and thousands of pounds per annum. It was far too dangerous. He was tempted quite obviously to advise the firm's clients to buy and sell stocks and shares, not because of their likely worth and future prospects, but because they would help him to make money on his own transactions.

On the whole it is wiser for the employer to use the weapon of summary dismissal with considerable discretion. It does indeed need a gross dereliction of duty to justify the sack on the spot. In the case of the trusted confidential clerk mentioned above, any dismissal within the period of ten years was bound to be 'wrong' unless they could justify it, so there was no point in not giving immediate summary dismissal. In general, however, acts of slackness, incompetence, general unsatisfactoriness, are best dealt with by giving the ordinary normal notice, whatever it might be.

It is sometimes said that the employer tells a man to go at once, but gives him wages or salary 'in lieu of notice'. This is not an accurate way of describing the situation. It is not possible to give pay in lieu of notice. There is nothing in lieu of notice which is legally permissible. Either notice must be given or summary dismissal resorted to, which has to be justified, or nothing. There is no alternative. But this shorthand phrase disguises a means which often appeals to both the employer and employee. Let us suppose the employee's contract is terminable by a month's notice, the employer says to him that he proposes to give him a month's notice starting tomorrow. He hands the written notice to him, and he further says, "I do not want you to work out your period of notice. You can go now, but you will be paid up to the end of the month".

That is a simple and sensible device to get the unwanted employee out of the premises, out of the place, with proper notice, but he gets a month's pay for doing no work, an arrangement which may still be very convenient for the employer.

GIVING OF REFERENCES

In very many cases the employer has no difficulty at all in writing an appropriate reference for an ex-employee who is seeking employment somewhere else. But if that employee left under a cloud, if he was given notice for incompetence or disobedience or untrustworthiness, still worse if he was sacked summarily for a really gross dereliction of duty of the kind described above, the employer's task is a very difficult one.

The first point to note is that there is no legal obligation on an employer to give a reference at all. If he says that he will not do so, or if he simply ignores the request for a reference, there is no power on earth which can make him give one.

On the other hand, to give no reference at all may in some cases be unkinder to the ex-employee than even to give a rather tepid one. Moreover, the employer has certainly a social if not a legal duty to other prospective employers to give a fair and honest account of the ex-employee who is seeking new employment.

The fair and honest account may involve writing things which reflect upon the man's ability, trustworthiness, or otherwise upon his character. Does the

The reference is sent privately and confidentially to the future employer—and it must tell the truth!

employer, if he writes such a reference, run any risk of proceedings for libel? Alternatively, if instead of writing the reference, he talks to the prospective future employer on the telephone, and says damaging things, does he run a risk of an action for slander if what he has said is subsequently reported?

The principles which must guide the employer in writing his reference are a scrupulous determination to be absolutely fair and absolutely honest. If he sticks to those two principles there is no doubt at all that if, by any chance, he is sued for damages for libel, he would have a defence, the defence of honest comment on a privileged occasion. The reference is entitled to what the law calls privilege. This is discussed in detail on the section on libel and slander. Here it is only necessary to say that the privilege lasts so long as the employer

(a) is scrupulously fair and honest in all that he writes;
(b) is not actuated by any ulterior, improper, or unworthy motive, in fact actuated by no other motive than a desire to give an honest reference; and
(c) the reference is sent privately and confidentially to the future employer who has asked for it, and it is not broadcast abroad for other people, either in the employer's office, or in the office of the future employer, to read.

Provided these conditions are satisfied, the occasion on which the reference is given is a privileged occasion, and therefore the reference will be privileged and that will be a defence to an action for libel.

It should be noted that if the employee was given notice because the employer long suspected that he had been fiddling with the petty cash, but had never succeeded in proving it, it would be a great mistake for him to state that in his reference. There he is stating a suspicion which, however well founded, may not be accurate. He can say in general terms that he had some doubts about the man's general suitability for his work, but he must be very careful not to state facts which are not capable of being proved. On the other hand, if it is a clear fact, for example, that the man was regularly late for four days out of five over and over and over again, that is a fact which could and should be stated. If it was a fact that he was not capable of carrying out certain of the more difficult tasks entrusted to him, that is a fact which should be stated. That fact may be indistinguishable from an opinion. In this case it is opinion that matters; the employer's opinion is that the man was not up to his particular job, intellectually or physically. That is a matter which it is fair to state. Whether a man is a thief or not is not a matter about which you can have an opinion, because this is nothing to do with competence, it is a matter of fact.

CONTRACTS FOR WORK TO BE DONE

THE type of contracts to be dealt with under this section covers a very wide field. The element common to them all is that one party agrees in return for payment to do some job or perform some service for another: but the job or service may vary from something as vast as the building of a block of offices to something as comparatively trifling as the repair of a watch.

The price for the work

Usually a price for the work will be agreed in advance, and if it is, the workman is entitled to the agreed amount. If no price is agreed, however, the workman is still entitled to be paid something. He will be entitled to be paid on the basis of what is a reasonable remuneration for the amount of time, labour, and skill which he has expended on the job, and also for the materials used by him in its performance. In some cases, however, the workman may do work for which the hirer is not bound to pay. This is the case where the work done was never requested, or agreed to, by the hirer. For example, if the workman does extra work without the approval of the hirer, then even though this extra work is essential to the proper performance of the contract, the hirer is not bound to pay any more than the sum originally agreed between the parties. Again, where a person is brought in to do a job which he holds himself out as able to do, and then does it so badly that the work, when completed, is of no use to the hirer, such a person cannot claim to be paid. If, for example, an architect is employed to design a house, and when it is built to his design it proves to be a dangerous structure in which no one could safely live, he is not entitled to any payment.

It may also happen, in some cases, that a workman who has not completed a job will be unable to recover any payment, though, in general, failure to complete will only mean a reduction in the price. One must look carefully both at the terms of the agreement and at the reason for non-completion. Generally, a person who undertakes to do a specific job for an agreed sum, payable on completion of that job, and who fails substantially to complete the job, is not entitled to recover the agreed sum *or any part of it*. One exception to this rule is where it is the employer himself who has prevented the work being completed. In this case the workman may sue for damages for breach of contract, or may treat the contract as at an end and sue for reasonable remuneration. Another exception is where, through no fault of the workman, it becomes impossible for him to perform his contract in full, or where the contract has been frustrated.

The employer, however, cannot refuse payment on the ground that in some trifling respect the work is incomplete, though he can deduct the cost of making good the defect or omission.

In some cases the workman is employed to do work on the basis that he shall be paid for what he actually does. In such a case his right to payment does not depend on his completing the job. On the contrary, he may abandon it at any time and claim to be paid for what he has done. It is a question of the proper construction of the contract and the degree to which the workman has departed from its terms.

Quality of the work

So far as the standard of the work is concerned, the workman must exercise the degree of skill and ability that one would normally expect from a person who holds himself out as qualified to do the job in question. If he falls below that standard, he will forfeit, in whole or in part, his right to payment. Moreover, if the result of his lack of skill or ability results in the creation of a dangerous state of affairs, he may be liable to compensate the hirer, or even a third party, who is injured or whose property is damaged as a result. If, for instance, the repairer of a car fails to replace one of the wheels securely, he may be liable to any member of the public as well as to the owner of the car who is injured as a result of the wheel coming off on the road.

When the workman is required to supply his own materials, and the employer makes known the purpose for which these materials are intended and that he relies on the workman's skill and judgment, then there is an implied absolute warranty by the workman that the materials are fit for the purpose for which

". . . a person who holds himself out as qualified to do the job . . ."

they are required. The effect of this is that the workman again is liable for any damage or injury which results from the unfitness of the materials; and it is no excuse for him to show that the materials were in fact supplied by some third party.

Care of the article on which work is to be done

Where the workman receives from the employer some article on which he has to do work, he must take ordinary care of that article whilst it is in his possession, and must return it when the work is complete. If the employer's chattel is lost, owing to some unauthorized act of the workman or his servant, then (providing the servant was acting within the scope of his employment)

347

the workman is liable for its loss. For example, an employee of a garage was ordered to take a customer's car back to him. Instead of proceeding by a direct route, the employee made a detour for his own convenience and while doing so was involved in an accident. The garage proprietor was held liable for the damage to the car.

The workman's duty to return his employer's chattel is subject to his proper charges being paid, but if he keeps it in exercise of his lien (see chapter on *Liens*) he cannot claim extra payment for warehousing or storage.

Delegation of work

The question often arises whether a workman is bound to do the job himself, or whether he can delegate performance, either in whole or in part, to someone else. The answer is that, in general, no complaint can be made that the work has been done by someone to whom he has delegated the job, provided it is done up to the agreed standard. In fact, some contracts, especially building contracts, are entered into on the express understanding that most of the work will be sub-contracted out. But there are cases where delegation is not permissible. These are where the work involves individual skill, judgment, or taste of one sort or another. The creation of anything artistic would fall into this category. In any case, if there is something in the contract itself to indicate that the contractor is promising personal performance, then he is bound to give this.

Time limits

It is common to stipulate for a time-limit within which work is to be done. Generally, failure by the workman to comply with a time-limit will not entitle his employer to withdraw from the contract altogether, and to refuse the work done. But there are some cases in which the contract specifically provides that time is to be 'of the essence', *i.e.* all-important, or the circumstances or nature of the contract may make this clear. In these cases, belated performance is not good enough, and the hirer is entitled to refuse it. Whenever the time appointed for completion is past, the hirer is entitled to call upon the workman to complete the job within a reasonable time thereafter. If the workman fails to comply with that request, he will forfeit his right to payment in every case.

Penalties and damages

Sometimes hirers attempt to reinforce stipulations as to time for completion by inserting in the contract a clause requiring the workman to pay a certain sum if he does not complete on time. If, having regard to all the circumstances, and in particular to the size of the sum and the circumstances in which it is to become payable, the proper inference is that the clause constitutes a sort of threat to deter the workman from delay, then the sum is a penalty, and as such is not recoverable. If the clause represents a genuine attempt to estimate the loss which the hirer will suffer as a result of the job not being completed on time, then the sum fixed, and no other, will be recoverable as damages for late completion, no matter what the loss actually incurred turns out to be.

When a building contractor makes a tender in respect of the erection or repair of a building, he may be expected to calculate his margin of profit with an eye to the nature of the work required and the length of time it will take. Should he be required to do work which is widely different in nature or extent, he may be unwilling to be bound by the terms of his tender. The original contract usually envisages a certain number of variations, but the variations may increase out of all proportion as the work progresses. If the variations have been so numerous as to change the whole nature of the job, and if the builder has at some stage made known to the other party that he considers the work being done to be no longer covered by the contract, it may be held that the original contract has been abrogated, and in such a case the builder will be entitled to reasonable remuneration for the work he has done.

Reasonable remuneration

We have noted a number of cases where the workman is entitled to 'reasonable remuneration'. A claim to such remuneration is known as a *quantum meruit* ('as much as he has earned'), and is available generally wherever the contract is silent on the question of price, or where the work done is in some way different from that contracted for, or where the contract is for some reason no longer operative.

Court order for specific performance

In other types of contract a party who is unwilling to perform his obligation may sometimes be forced to do so by a decree of specific performance granted by a Court, *i.e.* an order to do the work. This remedy is appropriate when damages would not adequately compensate the aggrieved party. Specific performance, however, is never available when the contract to be enforced involves the doing of some personal service by one party for the other. The law will not compel a man to work for another against his will, as this would be to countenance a form of personal servitude, and is not likely to conduce to good service. The only remedy against an unwilling workman, therefore, is damages for breach of contract.

THE TENANT OF BUSINESS AND PROFESSIONAL PREMISES

THE PURPOSE of this chapter is to describe the protection which is offered to the tenants of business and professional premises by the Landlord and Tenant Act of 1954. This Act of Parliament falls into two parts. The first deals with the tenant of dwelling-houses let under long leases, and this is dealt with in the chapter on *Long Leaseholds*. The present chapter deals with Part II of this Act which deals with the tenant of business or professional premises. Many tenants of shops and offices during the nineteen-fifties will remember how very unfavourably they were placed in comparison with tenants of dwelling-houses. The vast majority of tenants of dwelling-houses were protected by the Rent Acts—a protection which meant that the rent could not be increased beyond certain limits, and that the tenants could not be evicted, save by an order of the County Court, an order which it was difficult to obtain. Tenants of business premises had no such protection and during the nineteen-fifties this became a very serious problem, because as such tenancies and leases ran out the rents asked for a renewal were such that many tenants could not afford them. The object of the new Act is to give some protection to such tenants.

What premises are protected?

First of all let us consider what kind of premises are covered by this general description of 'business and professional' premises. The definition in the Act of the word 'business' is so wide that the list of premises can include shops, garages, offices, factories, warehouses, laboratories, schools, hotels, cinemas, clubs, and premises occupied by a charity or by a trade union. It will include a doctor's surgery, a dentist's consulting-room, a solicitor's offices, a barrister's chambers, and so on. It is clear that the Act will cover any premises used for pretty well any activity which one could mention, any trade, any business, any profession, and also activities like social clubs, trade union clubs, charitable clubs, and so on.

Under the Rent Acts the test is rateable value. Under this Act rateable value does not come into the picture at all. It does not matter what the rateable value of the premises is. All that matters is that they should be used for some kind of business, trade, or profession.

It is also important to note that the Act may apply to a dwelling-house, although only a part of it is used for a trade, business, or profession. For example, a shopkeeper may have a shop on the ground floor and live above it; or a doctor may use the ground-floor rooms as a surgery and a waiting-room and live above it. Nevertheless, the whole of that house can be covered by this Act. Some such premises may also be covered by the Rent Acts, and when that is so the tenant must rely on the Rent Acts. But when any premises like these are taken outside the scope of the Rent Acts, as a good many were by the Rent Act of 1957, it is valuable for the tenant to know that, although he may have lost his Rent Act protection, he may still be able to fall back on the protection of the 1954 Act for the whole house.

In considering this wide general list of premises which is covered by the Act, it is important to mention the few which are expressly excluded. The Act excludes an agricultural holding, a mining lease, a public house, service tenancies, and a short tenancy—that is, a tenancy which has been granted for a term of not more than three months.

Agricultural holdings are excluded, because they are covered by the Agricultural Holdings Act of 1948. (See the chapter on *Agricultural Holdings*.) Service tenancies are excluded, because they are so closely related to and so closely dependant on the tenant's job. The whole point of service tenancies is that they are meant to last only so long as the tenant is in particular employment, and the tenant is required to live in those particular premises, and the Act does not interfere with that kind of arrangement.

Public houses are not covered, because they have rather a special relation-ship to the owners, the brewers, who may own and run them. But an hotel or a restaurant is covered by the Act.

Short lettings up to three months are excluded simply to avoid bringing the whole weight of this legislation to bear upon seasonal lettings for limited periods; for example, the letting of a little shop on the promenade of a seaside town during the season. A landlord who lets premises for a trade or business for a short term of not more than three months will be able to recover possession at the end of the term, so long as he does not include in the agreement a pro-vision for renewing it or extending it beyond the three months, and so long as the same tenant has not been in occupation for a period which, together with any period during which any predecessor in the carrying on of the business carried on by the tenant was in occupation, exceeds six months. With those few exceptions all premises let for trade, or a business, or a profession, may benefit from the Act.

What protection does the Act offer?

First, when the period fixed by the letting comes to an end the tenant is not obliged to go. He can stay on in the premises, go on offering to pay the rent fixed by his original agreement, and if that rent is accepted he remains there as a protected tenant under the Act.

The landlord may be perfectly happy to let this state of affairs continue, at least for a time. If, on the other hand, he does not want to retain that tenant, or if he has other plans for the premises, or if he wants to obtain a higher rent, which he thinks he can under the market conditions prevailing at the time, what can he do?

His first step is to give the tenant notice: not just the notice which the tenancy agreement or lease may prescribe, but a notice in the special form laid down by the Act. This notice must be at least a six months' notice. Even a weekly tenant is entitled to at least six months, and in particular circumstances the notice may have to be as much as twelve months.

The notice must also include two very important statements:

(I) It must invite the tenant to reply *within two months* stating whether he is willing to accept the notice and to go, or whether he wants to stay.

(ii) It must state whether the landlord will oppose any application for a new tenancy, and if so, for what reasons.

Here then is the first basic provision of the Act: that the tenant need not go when the lease or tenancy agreement expires, and that if the landlord wants him to go he must serve a notice which is quite independent of the terms of the agreement; it must be a notice which complies with the Act, *i.e.* at least a six months' notice.

If the landlord lets things slide and gives no such notice, as is required by the Act to the tenant, the tenant may be perfectly happy to go on living and working in the premises until the landlord brings matters to a head. On the other hand, the tenant may feel that this kind of situation is unsatisfactory. He may feel uncertain, because he is running perhaps an expensive business, and his tenancy depends upon this Act of Parliament continuing in existence unchanged. The tenant may feel that this is not very satisfactory and that he would prefer to have the security of a long definite term ahead of him. So the Act provides that if his original tenancy was granted for a period of more than one year, or granted for some fixed period of years and then from year to year, he can take the initiative and apply to the landlord for the grant of a new lease.

Another point which the tenant must take into consideration is that the protection given by the Act is personal to him. It lasts as long as he is personally in occupation. If he dies, the special protection of the Act comes to an end. Looking ahead to the future of his trade, or business, or profession. he may think this a very tenuous protection, and he may prefer to feel that his living and the living which he may want to bequeath to his heirs, is dependent on something more substantial.

So for any one of these reasons the tenant may expressly apply to the landlord for a new tenancy or lease. Just as the landlord's notice prescribed by the Act must follow a special form, so must the tenant's application. He must say how long he wants the new tenancy to last, what amount of rent he proposes, and what other terms he considers ought to be in the new agreement. In fact, he must draft the basic terms of a new agreement, and this is very much a matter on which the individual business or professional tenant may need expert professional advice. This is exactly the moment when he ought to consult a solicitor and get him to draft the terms of the notice, including the terms of the new agreement which he would like to have.

At this stage you have the situation where either the landlord has taken the initiative and given the tenant notice to go, a notice which complies with the terms of the Act, or the tenant has given the landlord notice that he wants to stay, and this too, a notice complying with the terms of the Act.

Here you have the conflict of two interests—the tenant who wants to stay, the landlord who wants him to go, and both, let us assume under expert legal advice, have given the proper forms of notice—forms which, as explained above, have nothing to do with the provisions of the agreement which may have been entered into a very long time ago, but which comply with the provisions laid down in the new Act.

Here then is the situation which the Act quite explicitly envisages: that the landlord wants to get the tenant out, but cannot do so as he used to be able to do, because the Act gives a tenant protection, and that the tenant is anxious to stay and to get a new lease. What is the next step?

A new tenancy

First, both parties should get together and negotiate. The Act envisages that at this stage, when both parties know that ultimately, in accordance with the provisions of the Act, a Judge of the County Court or the High Court may be asked to act as a kind of arbitrator between them, they should get together and discuss the terms of a new tenancy or lease. Very often they will do so. If they cannot reach agreement, what is the next stage?

If the tenant wants to stay on in the premises, and the landlord is not willing to let him do so on the only terms that the tenant is willing to offer, the tenant should apply to the Court and ask for an order that a new tenancy should be granted to him on such terms and conditions as the Judge thinks fit. It is vital for the tenant to know that there is a time limit within which this application can be made. If he is going to apply to the Court, he must apply *within four months* after the landlord has served the notice requiring him to give up possession. If he lets this period of four months go by without initiating an application to the Court, *he has lost all his rights under the Act.*

It is most important that a tenant should realize this, because there is no provision in the Act for a Court exercising discretion and extending the time. If four months go by after the landlord has served his notice, and within this

". . . both parties should get together . . ."

time the tenant has not come to terms with him, and has not applied to the Court, there is nothing whatever he can do. It is important, therefore, that within the four months, even if negotiations are still going on, he should get his application to the Court set on foot. Most tenants will probably be represented by solicitors who will be very well aware of this time limit. But some may not be so represented. They may not know of this time limit, and it is important that they should, because there is no scope for extending it. If the time goes by and the tenant has not made his application, there is nothing the Court can do, however great the hardship to the tenant may be.

Which Court is the appropriate Court for hearing these applications? The answer is that if the rateable value of the premises is £500 or under, the Court is the County Court, and if the premises are of a rateable value of more than £500, the appropriate Court is the High Court.

The powers of the Court

When hearing an application for a new tenancy, the Court, whether a County Court or High Court, has power to grant a new tenancy or lease for any period up to fourteen years. The Court may not necessarily fix fourteen years. In many cases which have come before them they have fixed shorter periods, such as three, five, or seven years, but they have power to fix up to fourteen years. The period they fix depends very much upon their view of the nature of the tenant's work, how important it is that there should be continuity in the same premises for the same work, and how difficult it might be for the tenant to find other equally suitable premises.

The period of time for which a new tenancy fixed by the Court is to last is, of course, only one aspect of the matter. Another very important point is how much rent the tenant is to pay. There is no question of a renewal on exactly the same rent as the tenant was paying before. Under the Rent Acts applying to dwelling-houses, the rent is fixed by the Acts, which lay down a precise formula. Under this Act for business premises, there is no such precise arithmetical formula. The rent is to be a fair and reasonable rent according to present-day market conditions. And that rent is to be fixed by the Judge. The question is what rent would the premises command in a free market? In other words, a rent governed by the law of supply and demand, subject only to the Judge's view of what is fair and reasonable. This is the kind of question on which there could be a great deal of argument. And the cases in the Courts which have been brought since this Act came into force have revealed considerable differences of opinion as you might imagine. As a rule, both landlord and tenant have called expert witnesses to give evidence of what the fair market rent ought to be. The ultimate decision, however, rests with the Judge. It is in his power to order the grant of a new tenancy to the tenant for as long as fourteen years, or for such lesser period as he may think fair, considering the nature of the tenant's work, and the nature of the landlord's objection, and what the landlord wants the premises for, and at the same time to fix a fair rent, having regard to the free market conditions.

An important point is that in assessing the new rent the Judge is directed by the Act to pay regard to the question how far the higher rent assessed by witnesses is due to the tenant's own exertions in improving the property. He must pay regard to the tenant's past exertions and consider how far they may have contributed to an increase in rental value. He must take them into account and deduct them from his calculation of what the new market rental ought to be on the evidence he has heard.

The Judge must also consider other terms of the tenancy, because they may be equally important. For example, he must decide who should be responsible for repairs, both to the inside and to the outside. And his decision on this point will naturally affect the rent which he fixes. For example, if he decides that the tenant is to be responsible for interior repairs and the landlord for exterior repairs, he will fix a lower rent than if he decided that the landlord should be responsible for all repairs, both exterior and interior. Or if he decided that the tenant should be responsible for all repairs, both interior and exterior, the rent would be lower still. If he was disposed to grant a fourteen-year lease he would probably decide, in accordance with standard practice, that the tenant was to be responsible for all repairs, outside and inside. And in that case the rent he fixes would take account of those responsibilities. If, on the other hand, he decided that a very small extension was all that was necessary, say two to three years, he would probably decide that at least during that time the exterior repairs should be the responsibility of the landlord, and in that case, he would fix a higher rent to be paid by the tenant.

It may be thought that once a tenancy has come to an end, and has been renewed, by an order of the Court under the 1954 Act, then, when the new agreement comes to an end, the landlord is automatically entitled to possession. This is not so. The Act is available to both landlord and tenant whenever any agreement or extension of agreement comes to an end, whether that extension is based on a freely negotiated arrangement or based on an order of the Court. It is possible that a tenant may be granted a continuous succession of new tenancies.

It is perfectly clear that the Act was designed, and deliberately designed, to give a substantial measure of protection to the business and professional tenant. Not as remarkable a protection as is given to the tenant of a dwelling-house which is protected by the Rent Acts, but nevertheless a considerable degree of protection and continuity.

Grounds on which the landlord must be given possession

Nevertheless there are certain circumstances under which, however badly the tenant may need a renewal of his tenancy, in order to preserve his business, his trade, or his practice, the Court must pay heed to the landlord's plea that the tenancy should be ended. There are certain grounds specified in the Act on which—if they are proved—the Court must give the landlord possession.

If the landlord tells the tenant when he gives him notice that he will oppose any application for a new tenancy, he must state precisely why. And 'why' must be phrased in terms permitted by the Act. The Act specifies certain reasons for which a landlord may oppose a new tenancy. They are laid down in detail in Section 30 of the Act.

The first three of the reasons for which a landlord may oppose a grant of a new tenancy are concerned with the behaviour of the tenant:

(1) That the tenant has failed to carry out his repairing obligations under the agreement and that as a result the premises are in a bad state of repair.

(2) That the tenant is constantly in arrears with his rent.

(3) That there are other serious breaches by the tenant of the terms of his agreement, or that for other reasons connected with his use or management of the premises it is reasonable for the landlord to be given possession.

These first three reasons give the landlord an opportunity of getting rid of a bad tenant if he can prove any one or more of these points to the Judge's satisfaction.

(4) The fourth reason for which a landlord may be granted possession is that the landlord has offered alternative accommodation to the tenant: accommodation which is reasonable, considering the terms of the previous tenancy, and which is suitable for the tenant's needs considering the kind of business he carries on.

355

The fifth and sixth reasons are concerned with the landlord's future plans for the premises:

(5) The tenancy was created by the sub-letting of only a part of the property. If the landlord is the owner of the whole property he might be able to prove to the Court that the tenant should not be granted a new tenancy of only a part, when he, the landlord, might reasonably expect to obtain a higher rent by letting the whole property as one, instead of in a number of separate parts. If the landlord can show that his intention to let or sell the whole property as one is genuine, he might successfully substantiate an objection to the Court's renewing a tenancy of a separate part.

(6) The landlord may establish to the Court's satisfaction that he intends to pull down or to reconstruct the premises, or to carry out such substantial work of reconstruction, that he could not do so without obtaining vacant possession of the whole.

Looking back over the litigation which has resulted from this Act, it is quite clear that in the majority of cases the landlord who has desired to obtain possession of business premises has applied to the Court not so often on the grounds of his tenant's bad behaviour, his tenant's failure to pay rent, or to observe the covenants, or because he wants to deal with the whole property which is sub-let to a series of tenants, but because he wants to demolish or reconstruct the building of which the tenancy forms a part.

There has, of course, been the odd case where the landlord has obtained possession because his tenant is utterly worthless and has not paid his rent and has not observed his obligations. These are easy cases and have not led to much litigation, or if they have, the decision of the Court has not been hard to reach. The most difficult cases have occurred where the landlord wants possession so that he can reconstruct the premises. The obligation under the Act is that the landlord should *prove* that he intends to demolish or reconstruct the premises. Proof of intention is not very easy. His intention itself may be quite sincere. But the Courts have made it very clear that they are not going to accept as evidence of intention a mere pious hope. They have to be satisfied that the landlord not merely hopes to carry out work of demolition or reconstruction, but that there is real evidence that he will do so. The landlord will have to prove that he has made positive plans; that the money to carry out those plans is available; that the architect's drawings are prepared; that the builder's estimates have been given, and that in every possible way, short of actually doing the work, he can establish to the Court's satisfaction that this is what he is going to do, as soon as he is given vacant possession of the property. It is not easy to be precise about this. The point which must be emphasized is that it is not enough for the landlord even to put plans before the Court. He must be able to convince them by solid evidence that as soon as he is given vacant possession he has the *capacity* to put those plans into operation; the *will* to do so, and the *fixed definite intention* that this will be done as soon as possible.

(7) Finally, the Court may accede to a landlord's opposition to a tenant's request, because the landlord proves that he wants to occupy the premises himself; that he will occupy them for the purpose of a business, or trade, or profession, which he will carry on, or, partly for such a business, trade, or pro-

fession, and partly as a home in which he will live. (There is a proviso to this, namely, that the landlord shall have been owner of the premises for more than five years.)

If the Judge is not convinced by the landlord's opposition on any of the grounds mentioned above, he will order the grant of a new tenancy on terms which he will decide: terms which will fix the rent, the length of the tenancy, and the other conditions such as repairing obligations.

If an order for possession is made

If the Judge, on the other hand, accepts that the landlord's opposition is reasonable and comes under the headings laid down by the Act which are described above, he will make an order for possession.

To avoid immediate hardship it is provided that this order for possession shall not take effect for three months. In other words, the tenant is given three months in which to move.

Moreover, in certain circumstances, the tenant may be entitled to compensation. If the Judge makes the order for possession, not because the tenant was a bad tenant, that is, not for the first three reasons mentioned above, but because the landlord wanted the premises for his own purposes, that is, for one of the last three reasons mentioned above, then the tenant is entitled to recover from the landlord a sum of money by way of compensation.

How much will the compensation be? The compensation will usually be an amount equal to the rateable value of the premises. But if the tenant can show that during the whole of the fourteen years before the expiration of the tenancy, the premises have been occupied by him for the purposes of his business, or that he was the immediate successor to someone who occupied the premises for his business, he may receive twice the rateable value. That is a broad general description of Section 37 of this Act, a section which can lead to some difficulties in interpretation. Anyone who is concerned should certainly get legal advice on the facts of his particular case in relation to Section 37 of the Act. He may be entitled either to a sum equal to the rateable value of the premises, or to a sum equal to twice that value, and to decide exactly which is his entitlement is a very nice matter of construction of the section as applied to the facts of his particular case.

The Act also contains provisions for giving a tenant compensation for improvements if he is not granted a new tenancy: and here, too, it is essential for the tenant to get legal advice.

Summary

Any Act which overrides the basic principles of contract between landlord and tenant, or any other two contracting parties, is necessarily complicated, particularly as when in the case of this Act, it strives to preserve a fair balance. This Act was something of a new venture. For the first time it gives tenants of trade, business, and professional premises, of hotels, theatres, clubs, and so on, something akin to the Rent Act protection of the tenants of dwelling-houses. It goes nothing like as far, of course, because it provides that a renewal of such a tenancy is to be based on a market rent, fixed if necessary by an independent tribunal, namely, a Judge of the County Court or the High Court. It also gives a landlord extended powers of recovering possession; powers which go beyond his powers under the Rent Acts. Nevertheless, by and large it gives the tenants of these business premises a considerable degree of protection against unfair or extortionate rents for renewal of their tenancies.

The preceding account describes the basic principles of the Act, but it is absolutely vital that any landlord or tenant who is particularly concerned should get legal advice on his particular case.

PENSION SCHEMES

(A) GENERAL

(1) The nature of a pension scheme

A PENSION SCHEME is usually an arrangement, consisting of a Trust Deed and Rules, which is brought into existence by an employer for the principal purpose of providing pensions for his employees when they retire. The essential idea behind any such scheme is that the pensions and any other benefits which will eventually become due should be paid out of a fund, which will gradually be built up as the years go past, from the regular contributions which the employer, and in most cases the employees as well, are obliged to pay under the rules of the scheme.

It goes without saying that from the employee's point of view, whether he has to contribute or not, it is very important that such a scheme should create a set of legally enforceable rights and obligations; that in return for long service with his employer and compliance with the rules of the scheme he should obtain a legal right to a pension which he can, if need be, enforce in the Courts against his employer or the trustees of the scheme. An employee who is offered terms of service which include a pension payable at the discretion of his employer or the payment of which is made dependent in some way upon the continued prosperity of the employer's business should regard this as a very important factor when making up his mind whether or not to accept the job, especially in these days when the chances of reaching a ripe old age improve each year. Furthermore, benefits vary considerably from scheme to scheme. All too often the details are not made available to the employee until after he has taken the job, but a prospective employer will think none the worse of an applicant who prudently asks to see the terms of the scheme before he makes up his mind.

Where there is a properly constituted Trust Deed, the legal position is usually satisfactory. Such a deed is normally made between the employer and the trustees. The latter will be a bank or other corporate body, or named individuals some of whom will be nominated by the employer and some, if the employees have to make contributions, by the employees themselves. What the deed does basically is to establish the pension scheme as a legal entity which has an existence separate from that of the employer. The employer binds himself to pay over the contributions—both his own and those he will collect from the employees—to the trustees, and the trustees in turn bind themselves to set up the fund out of which the benefits are to be paid and to manage the scheme in accordance with the rules which are usually appended to the Trust Deed in the form of a schedule. It will be the duty of the trustees to invest the fund to the best advantage and in many cases this takes the form of paying it out by way of premiums for group life policies in a named insurance company. Such a scheme is known as a life office scheme, and the details of it will probably

" Ripe old age "

have been worked out by the insurance company themselves to suit the particular employer's requirements. There is, however, no obligation upon the employer to set up an insured scheme in this way; he is free to decide whether it would be more advantageous for the fund to be invested in interest-bearing securities; and to resolve any doubts which he may have he would normally consult an actuary to advise him what benefits the scheme should provide, how much the contributions should be and how the fund should be dealt with so as to produce the best results in his particular circumstances.

If the scheme provides substantial benefits (two-thirds of salary at normal retiring age will usually be the maximum pension which it is possible to earn) the contributions will normally be based on a percentage of salary, and if the employee has to contribute, the percentage which he has to pay will often be only half that which his employer pays. If, however, the scheme is intended to provide smaller flat rate benefits to supplement the State Retirement Pension for employees whose level of wages make this a more suitable form of provision, then the contributions will also be on a flat rate basis—so much per week regardless of the amount earned during the week.

The primary benefit to be provided is, of course, the pension payable from retirement until death. Other benefits commonly found are an ill-health pension payable where an early retirement is due to physical or mental ill-health; death benefit payable to the employee's family where the employee dies before reaching retirement age; and pensions for widows and orphans.

Schemes of this basic type are very flexible: they can be established for the benefit of a mere handful of employees—sometimes for one employee only—but they are equally suitable for firms which employ many thousands of people.

(2) Other types of pension scheme

It has been estimated that in 1961 probably some 5,000,000 men and women were members of private pension schemes of the type just described. But in addition to these, about another 4,000,000 men and women were covered by the schemes of the civil service, the armed forces, local government authorities, the nationalized industries, public utility undertakings, and other public authorities of many kinds. The legal basis of these other schemes seldom takes the form of a Trust Deed: they are usually set up by a public or private Act of Parliament, or by a Statutory Instrument made under a public Act. Such schemes provide legally enforceable rights for those who participate in them, in the same way as Trust Deeds, and in general their rules and provisions are far more extensive and complex than those of private schemes. This is undoubtedly due to the fact that the statutory schemes tend to have very large numbers of members, and for this reason it is necessary for them to cater in greater detail for the wider variety of situations and difficulties which is likely to arise in the course of their administration.

Most pensionable employees are covered by one or other of these two major categories of pension scheme, but a not inconsiderable minority belong to yet other types of scheme, which have often been specially designed to fit unusual sets of circumstances. From the legal point of view, there is no reason why such schemes should not be just as satisfactory as the more normal types, although to achieve this result very often the legal arrangements will be more complicated. An example of such a scheme would be one which is set up by an organization of employees of a particular sort, e.g. merchant navy officers or the printing trade, to which members of the organization may or must subscribe, regardless of who may employ them.

(3) Annuities under the Finance Act, 1956

For some people there may be no opportunity to join a pension scheme, perhaps because their employer does not run one, or, more commonly because they themselves are self-employed. Since the Finance Act, 1956, it has become attractive financially for such persons to enter into individual contracts with an insurance company for the provision of an annuity (i.e. an annual payment for life), to commence at a specified age not earlier than sixty nor later than seventy. The premiums for such a contract need not be at a fixed annual rate, which is useful for those whose incomes fluctuate from year to year, and within certain limits they qualify in full for income tax relief. This was the great change made by the 1956 Finance Act, that now for the first time a person who was not employed but worked on a fee-paying basis—doctor, solicitor, craftsman—anyone who worked on his own, could contribute toward his personal pension and have all his contributions allowed in full for tax relief. The annuity, when received, is regarded as earned income so that earned income relief can then be obtained.

Another much-used method of providing an individual pension is to effect an endowment policy. Such a policy provides a fixed sum of money at a fixed age or upon earlier death. The money can be used to purchase an annuity

"Self-employed"

either for the insurer or perhaps for his widow, if he should have died before reaching the fixed age. Here again, the Finance Act, 1956, has helped, this time by treating as exempt from tax that part of the annuity which represents repayment of capital. An endowment policy has some advantages over an annuity contract, notably that it can be used as security for a temporary loan or, in the last resort, surrendered in return for its value at the date of surrender. On the other hand, tax relief is only granted on two-fifths of the policy premiums if, as is the general case, the premiums are more than £25 p.a. Thus, the choice between an annuity contract and an endowment policy may for some people be a difficult one to make.

(4) National Insurance

National Insurance incorporates within its tremendous scope the scheme from which are paid Retirement Pensions, Sickness Benefit, Death Grants, and

361

various benefits for widows and orphans. These benefits correspond to the normal benefits provided by private pension schemes, but in addition National Insurance provides important Maternity Benefits, Unemployment Benefit, and benefits for those who are injured at work or who suffer from certain diseases which arise out of their work, *e.g.* pneumoconiosis.

The legal basis for National Insurance is to be found in the National Insurance Acts, 1946–63, the National Insurance (Industrial Injuries) Acts, 1946–63, and the great mass of statutory instruments which have been, and continue to be, made under these Acts. Under this legislation, insured persons, as they are called, acquire legally enforceable rights to the benefits to which they are entitled, but if there is any doubt whether an insured person is entitled to any particular benefit, this has to be decided first of all by an independently appointed Insurance Officer or, in appropriate cases, a Medical Board, with a right for the insured person to appeal to the local National Insurance tribunal or a medical appeal tribunal, as the case may be. From these tribunals, there is a further right of appeal in some cases to a Commissioner specially appointed for that purpose by the Crown. Questions about contributions (*e.g.* whether enough have been paid to earn a particular benefit) and classification (*i.e.* whether a person is to be regarded as employed, self-employed, or non-employed) are decided by the Minister of Pensions and National Insurance, with a right for the insured person to appeal to the High Court in England or the Court of Session in Scotland, if a point of law is involved.

In the field of pensions, National Insurance is in many respects unique: in one way or another it provides benefits for practically every man, woman, and child in this country: it has no fund, the contributions having been calculated on the basis that they will be roughly sufficient to pay the current benefits: and many people (those who earn between £9 and £18 per week and who have not been 'contracted-out' of the graduated scheme which started in April 1961) pay both flat-rate and percentage contributions.

Tax relief is granted in full in respect of an employer's contributions to National Insurance: but the contributions of employed, self-employed, and non-employed persons are given relief only in part, according to a table (see Finance Acts, 1960 and 1961). Thus the relief for an employed person over eighteen years of age is granted on £22.

When the benefits are received under National Insurance, they are taxable as though they were earned income, but this does not apply to unemployment, sickness, or maternity benefits, nor, of course, to death grants, all of which are exempt from tax.

It would be outside the scope of this work to go into National Insurance in any further detail. Anybody who has a National Insurance problem should apply in the first instance to his local National Insurance Office, who are always ready to give such help as they can and who will supply him with such of the very clear leaflets published by the Minister as relate to his case. If he is still not satisfied, he would do well to consult a solicitor, since it is virtually impossible for even the most intelligent layman to find his way unaided around the very great number of Acts and Regulations which determine his legal rights.

AT WORK; BUSINESS; INDUSTRY; THE PROFESSIONS

(B) PENSION SCHEMES AND THE LAW

(1) General

The primary task of the lawyer in relation to a pension scheme is to establish it as a separate legal entity against which the members will, by virtue of their membership, acquire legally enforceable rights, and towards which the employer and the members will undertake legally enforceable obligations. Several common ways in which this can be done have already been mentioned.

The lawyer's secondary but equally important task is to draft the rules of the scheme in such a way that the scheme will be valid in law and workable in practice, while at the same time there will be the maximum possible saving of income tax and estate duty. This calls for experience, skilled draftsmanship, and a clear understanding of the pitfalls which await the unwary. To take a simple example, in a scheme for manual workers provision might be made for the member's contributions to be deducted from his wages each week. This may sound reasonable and harmless enough: but in fact, unless and until the Truck Acts, 1831–1940, are amended or repealed, such a deduction may be illegal. In such a case, it is necessary to provide that the employee's contributions shall be paid over by the employer to a third party; it must not be possible for the employer to derive any possible benefit from the contributions; and evidence must be available that the member's consent to the deductions was freely given. Then the deductions will be valid.

Another example concerns the technical rule of law known as the Perpetuity Rule. In effect, this rule provides that a trust (and a pension scheme is usually a trust for this purpose) is void if it can possibly last for a longer period than a life or lives in being at the date when the trust is established, plus a further period of twenty-one years. Any life or lives can be chosen for the purpose of imposing the necessary limit, and it is quite common at the present time to ensure a long period of existence for the scheme by limiting its duration to twenty-one years after the death of the last survivor of all the lineal descendants of King George V who may be living at the date when the scheme begins. Another solution, not often used because the conditions attaching to it are onerous, is to register the scheme under the Superannuation and other Trust Funds (Validation) Act, 1927, which has the effect of exempting the scheme from the Perpetuity Rule.

For our third example, we might take the case of the member of a scheme who dies before reaching retirement age. His widow is entitled to be paid a substantial death benefit, which she desperately needs because there are young children to be brought up. To her disappointment she finds that estate duty has to be paid on the value of the death benefit. Had the rules of this scheme been drafted so as to give the trustees of the scheme a discretion as to whom the death benefit should be paid, they would, of course, have exercised their discretion in the widow's favour, but no estate duty would have been payable. This is one of the exceptional cases where it may benefit the member, or in this instance his family, not to have a legally enforceable right to payment.

Some other points which require careful consideration in the rules are as follows: if the employer's intention is to contract some or all of his employees out of the graduated part of the National Insurance Scheme, the rules must be drafted so that they comply with the requirements of the National Insurance Acts, 1959 and 1963, as to contracting-out: if the fund is to be invested (as opposed to being used to pay life policy premiums) the trustees of the scheme must be given investment powers which are wide enough to enable them to make the best possible use of the money at their disposal: provision should be made for those employees who come from other pensionable employment to bring with them in suitable cases their accumulated pensionable service in return for a money payment from the other scheme (known as a transfer value payment): and vice versa: finally, provision must be made for alterations to the rules to be carried through without undue difficulty, subject, of course, to adequate safeguards for the accrued rights of existing members.

(2) Taxation

If you belong to a private pension scheme you may have heard the secretary or some other officer of it say, "We wanted to make such and such a provision in the rules, but the Inland Revenue would not allow it" or "We had to put such and such a provision in the rules to satisfy the Inland Revenue". Why is it that the Commissioners of Inland Revenue take such an interest in pension schemes, and why are those who manage the schemes so anxious to secure their approval?

Naturally, there is a very good reason. A pension scheme which has been 'approved' by the Inland Revenue under the provisions of s. 379, Income Tax Act, 1952, enjoys four extremely valuable income tax advantages:

First, the employer, in computing his profits, is allowed to deduct his ordinary annual contributions to the pension scheme as a business expense. Secondly, the employer's contributions in respect of any particular member are not regarded for income tax purposes as being an addition to that member's income. It is not generally realized that, except where the employer is an individual or a partnership, the employer's contributions would be so regarded but for Inland Revenue approval of the scheme. Thirdly, each member is allowed to deduct his own ordinary annual contributions from his income for income tax purposes. Fourthly, the income of the pension fund, arising from its investment, is not subject to tax.

These special advantages are given to approved pension schemes because it is the national policy to encourage the making of provision for old age. But to obtain them, the scheme must satisfy the detailed and intricate requirements of the Inland Revenue who are very much concerned to see that what they are being asked to approve is in fact a pension scheme and not something else masquerading under that name; that the rules of the scheme are not so drafted that the privileges set out above are capable of being abused; and that the rules are not drafted in such a way as to deprive them of the tax (at one-quarter of the standard rate) which they levy upon the trustees when contributions are repaid to a member who leaves the scheme, or when small pensions are commuted into a lump sum payment. If the scheme does not quite fulfil all their requirements, the Inland Revenue are sometimes able to give partial approval to it, e.g. 75 per cent., and in that case the privileges will be reduced accordingly.

Approval under s. 379, Income Tax Act, 1952, is not the only way of obtaining taxation privileges for a pension scheme. For instance, statutory schemes, *i.e.* those set up under a public general Act of Parliament, are dealt with under s. 378; and a scheme which is not fully approvable under s. 379, *e.g.* because it provides that up to 25 per cent. of the pension may be taken in the form of a lump sum, or one which is not approvable at all under s. 379, *e.g.* because no fund has been set up from which to pay the benefits, may nevertheless be approvable under yet another section of the Income Tax Act, 1952, namely s. 388. The tax concessions here are not so extensive as those under s. 379, but they are still well worth having, particularly in these days of high personal taxation.

". . . provision for old age"

It is not, of course, essential or in any way obligatory for a pension scheme to be approved by the Inland Revenue: however, the cost of providing pensions under an unapproved scheme is obviously far greater than it would be under an approved scheme, and there can be few cases indeed where individual circumstances are such that the disadvantage of having to comply with the Inland Revenue requirements outweighs the advantage of reduced taxation.

A person who is receiving a pension from an 'approved' scheme must pay income tax on it, but the pension is regarded as earned income, with the result that earned income relief can be obtained; and, of course, any other relevant allowances can be claimed.

365

ARBITRATION

INTRODUCTION

A GREAT many disputes—especially among merchants in particular trades, and between insurance companies and insured persons—are determined not in a Court of Law but by arbitration.

Arbitration affords some advantages over Court proceedings. In the first place, it is not attended by any publicity, because the proceedings are not—like a Court hearing—open to the Press and public: and this may be of great importance to business men who want to preserve their trade secrets, or to insurance companies who might hesitate to repudiate claims—even though they would be justified in doing so—for fear of the damage which the publicity of Court proceedings might cause to their reputation.

Another advantage of arbitration is that a technical expert can be appointed to decide a technical issue within his expert knowledge. If there is a dispute as to the quality of goods, involving such questions as the right to reject them or the amount to be deducted from the agreed price on account of their defective condition, Court proceedings may be both protracted and unsatisfactory. The Judge will have to hear expert witnesses (that is to say, persons with long experience in the particular trade) for both sides, weigh up their evidence (which may be of an extremely technical nature), and arrive at a conclusion on a matter in which he has no first-hand, practical experience. On the other hand, an arbitrator could be appointed who is an expert in the trade, and who could come to a speedy and reliable conclusion based largely on his own knowledge.

So it is very useful when the *only* questions in dispute are purely technical ones. It is not so useful when questions of interpretation of documents and of law are involved, as will appear further on in this section.

Arbitration may be more expeditious and convenient than legal proceedings. The arbitrator can usually agree with the parties on the time and place of the hearing, at a date as early as they wish, and they do not have to await their turn in the Court list. This advantage is not so marked as it used to be, owing to the growing practice of the Commercial Court and other Courts giving fixed dates for hearing. A 'fixed date' in a Court list may, however, be upset by the previous cases overrunning their estimated time: and, of course, it may be necessary to wait some time for a date to be fixed.

It is commonly supposed that arbitration is less expensive than litigation: but this depends very much on the nature of the dispute. If it is merely as to quality, and the parties agree to abide by the decision of a single arbitrator who is an expert in the trade and is willing to act for a reasonable fee, then certainly the cost will be considerably less than that of a trial (with solicitors, barristers, the drafting of pleadings, and so forth). But if other questions arise, which necessarily give rise to legal argument if justice is to be done, then arbitration can be more expensive than litigation. In the first place, there are the fees of the arbitrator (perhaps of two arbitrators and an umpire) to be paid, whereas a Judge is paid out of public funds, and not by the parties to the dispute. Secondly, where the dispute is complicated and it is necessary to have the facts presented with clarity and force, many people find it essential to engage solicitors or both solicitors and barristers just as they would in a Court case.

Arbitration!

Thirdly, as we shall see, an arbitration—particularly where points of law are involved—is not always the end of the dispute: for either party can invoke the jurisdiction of the Court, with the result that in the end the expenses of litigation as well as of arbitration may be incurred.

The law relating to arbitration is to be found in the Arbitration Act, 1950, which consolidates earlier enactments and contains provisions that are mainly designed to ensure the effectiveness of any arbitration to which the parties have agreed (in writing) to submit their dispute.

367

ARBITRATION AGREEMENTS AND LEGAL PROCEEDINGS

Arbitration arises by agreement of the parties (save for arbitrations by order of the Court or under certain statutes with which we are not here concerned). There may be an agreement to submit to arbitration either an existing dispute or any dispute that may arise in the future. The former is often called a 'submission', the latter an 'agreement to refer': both are included in the term 'arbitration agreement'. An arbitration agreement may be made by word of mouth, but in that case it will not be governed by the Arbitration Act, which only applies to written agreements.

If the parties have agreed to submit their differences to arbitration, then for either of them to start legal proceedings is a breach of that agreement. The Court is reluctant to permit such a breach, and will normally, therefore, on the application of the other party, '*stay*' (that is, put a stop to) the action. It will not do so, however, unless it is satisfied:

(a) that the party applying for a stay has not taken any step in the action (other than the formal step of 'entering an appearance'),

(b) that he is ready and willing to do all things necessary for the proper conduct of the arbitration,

(c) that the matter in issue is within the scope of the arbitration agreement,

(d) that there is no sufficient reason why it should not be referred to arbitration.

Thus, the Court has a discretion to grant or refuse a 'stay'. In particular, it may refuse a 'stay' if in the circumstances the arbitrator may not be impartial, or if the dispute involves an allegation of fraud. It will also usually refuse a 'stay' if the only point in issue is one of law, as such a point is better decided by a Court.

If the Court has refused to stay an action (or if no application for a stay has been made), it has sole jurisdiction, and will not permit arbitration proceedings with regard to the matter in dispute while the action is pending.

In order to ensure, so far as possible, that any disputes arising out of their contract are referred to arbitration and not brought before the Court, parties sometimes provide in the contract that no right of action shall accrue until an arbitration award has been made. Thus in the case of *Scott* v. *Avery* (1856), a policy of insurance on a ship provided that the amount of any loss should be referred, in case of dispute, to arbitration, and that the award of the arbitrators was to be a condition precedent to the maintaining of an action: and it was held that until an award was made no action was maintainable.

Thus, where the agreement contains a '*Scott* v. *Avery* clause', as it is called, failure to refer the dispute to arbitration will normally afford a defence to the action. However, it is provided by the Arbitration Act that if the Court orders that the arbitration agreement shall cease to have effect as regards any particular dispute, it may also order that a provision in the agreement making an award a condition precedent to the bringing of an action shall also cease to have effect as regards that dispute. So although the existence of a *Scott* v. *Avery* clause makes it more likely that the parties will adhere to their agreement and refer their disputes to arbitration, the Court may—if the circumstances warrant it—nullify the clause and accept jurisdiction over the matter in question.

This provision is in line with the policy of English Law, which looks with disfavour on any agreement to oust completely the jurisdiction of the Court. As was said in one case, "There must be no Alsatia in England where the King's writ does not run". In this respect the English Law of arbitration differs from that of other countries (including Scotland), where the parties may effectively agree that the Court shall have no jurisdiction and that the award of the arbitrator shall be conclusive. In English Law, the jurisdiction of the Court *cannot* be entirely ousted and, as we shall see, there are various grounds on which an arbitration award may be brought under the control or correction of the Court.

A question sometimes arises as to whether the particular dispute is covered by the arbitration agreement: for if it is not, the parties are not bound to have it determined by arbitration. It has been held that words which refer to disputes arising 'under' or 'in respect of' a contract are to be widely construed, and include disputes as to whether the contract has been repudiated or frustrated. A party who admits the existence of a contract but denies liability under it can set up an arbitration clause in it as a defence to the action: but he cannot do so if he denies the existence or validity of the contract, for the arbitration clause is part of the contract, and if there is no valid contract the arbitration clause is itself null and void.

An arbitration must be distinguished from a valuation (to which the Arbitration Act does not apply). A third party who is appointed not to decide a disputed question by a judicial process, but to use his own skill and knowledge for a purpose such as fixing the value of property, is not an arbitrator, and the parties are contractually bound by his decision, which can only be set aside if made fraudulently or on an evidently wrong basis.

REVOCATION OF AUTHORITY OR REMOVAL OF ARBITRATOR

The authority of an arbitrator or umpire appointed by virtue of an arbitration agreement cannot be revoked—unless a contrary intention is expressed in the agreement—except by leave of the Court. In certain circumstances the Court will remove or give leave to revoke the authority of a particular arbitrator, or order that the arbitration agreement shall cease to have effect. It can remove an arbitrator who has 'misconducted himself or the proceedings', or who 'fails to use all reasonable despatch' in hearing the case and making an award, *i.e.* giving a decision. It may also give leave to revoke the authority of an arbitrator for other good cause, such as lack of impartiality. Where the Court has given leave to revoke the authority of the arbitrator or has removed him, it may appoint a person to act as sole arbitrator in his place, or may order that the arbitration agreement shall cease to have effect with respect to the particular dispute.

Where there is an agreement to refer future disputes to arbitration, and a

369

dispute arises which involves a charge of fraud against a party to the agreement, the Court may order that the agreement shall cease to have effect and give leave to revoke the authority of the arbitrator, in order that the question of fraud may be determined by the Court.

ARBITRATORS AND UMPIRE

An arbitration agreement may name the arbitrator or arbitrators, or may provide for the appointment to be made by a third person, such as the President of a professional body (like the Law Society or the Royal Institute of British Architects), or of a Trade Association or Chamber of Commerce.

Unless otherwise agreed, the reference is to a single arbitrator. If the parties do not concur in appointing one, or if the appointed arbitrator refuses, or is unable to act, or dies, and the parties do not appoint another person in his place, any party may serve the others with notice to concur in an appointment, and if no appointment is made after seven days the Court may make the appointment. (Thus, even where the parties to a contract make no further provision in it for arbitration than the bald statement, 'All disputes hereunder shall be determined by arbitration', this is sufficient to bring into operation all the machinery of the Arbitration Act.)

Where the agreement provides that the reference shall be to two arbitrators, one to be appointed by each party, and one party fails to appoint an arbitrator (or a substitute for one who refuses, or is unable to act, or dies), the other party may serve notice on him to make an appointment within seven days. If the notice is not complied with, the party who served it may appoint his arbitrator to act as sole arbitrator.

Where arbitrators have been removed or their authority revoked by leave of the Court, the Court may appoint a person or persons to act in their place.

Where the reference is to two arbitrators, then—unless a contrary intention is expressed—they must appoint an umpire immediately after they are themselves appointed. The Court has similar powers to appoint an umpire as in the case of a sole arbitrator. An umpire's duties commence only when he is called upon to act, and this is when the arbitrators give written notice that they cannot agree: he may, however, on the application of any party to the reference, be ordered by the Court to take and hear the proceedings in lieu of the arbitrators as if he were a sole arbitrator.

If the agreement provides for the appointment of an arbitrator by each party, and for the appointment by arbitrators of a third arbitrator, it takes effect as if it provided for the appointment of an umpire: but if it provides simply for the appointment of three arbitrators, the award of any two of them is binding.

When the umpire takes over the arbitration, the arbitrators cease to act in a judicial capacity. Indeed it is quite customary, in a commercial arbitration, for each of the arbitrators to act as an advocate for the party who appointed him—and even (where the arbitrator has, for example, examined perishable goods before they were disposed of) to give evidence on his behalf.

AT WORK; BUSINESS; INDUSTRY; THE PROFESSIONS

CONDUCT OF THE PROCEEDINGS

Arbitrations vary greatly in the matters of evidence and procedure: for parties who have agreed to set up their own tribunal can also agree to waive any of the rules of evidence and procedure which would be applied in a Court of Law.

Contracts which are entered into on the standard printed forms of the various trade associations normally provide that the reference to arbitration shall be in accordance with the association's rules: these rules govern the form of arbitration, and sometimes provide for an appeal from the original arbitrator to an appellate committee.

Unless they are expressly excluded, an arbitrator has most of the powers of a Court, such as the power to order pleadings (*i.e.* the written formulation by each party of the points of claim and defence) and the disclosure of relevant documents, and the proceedings resemble those in an action in the Courts.

The arbitrator notifies the parties of the time and place of the hearing, and if he has given clear notice of his intention to do so, can then proceed even though one of them fails to attend.

A lay arbitrator is generally allowed to have the assistance of a legal adviser during the hearing, and may always employ legal assistance in drawing up his award. He may also, as a rule, take the advice of experts, though he should not do so without the consent of the parties.

Unless expressly agreed to the contrary, the rules of evidence must be observed. The arbitrator must hear both sides, must examine the parties on oath, and—if he thinks fit—administer the oath to their witnesses, and the evidence must be given in the presence of both parties. An arbitrator cannot call a witness himself without the consent of the parties.

It is a peculiar characteristic of the English law of arbitration that, notwithstanding their agreement to refer disputes to arbitration, either of the parties can *insist* on obtaining the decision of the Court on a point of law. This is done by asking the arbitrator to 'state a special case', and, if he refuses, applying to the Court to make him do so. A special case may take one of two forms. It may be a question of law submitted to the Court by the arbitrator, at the request of either or both of the parties before he makes his award. This is called a 'consultative case', the arbitrator then making his award in the light of the Court's ruling on the legal question. The other method is for the arbitrator to make his award in the form of a special case. In this so-called 'award case', the arbitrator declares his findings of fact, and makes his award in alternative forms, so that the final outcome depends on the Court's ruling on the question of law stated by the arbitrator. He can, however, state his award in the form of a special case with a limited time for setting it down for hearing, and with an alternative final award which is to become operative if the case is not set down within that time.

An arbitrator must, if the question of his jurisdiction is raised, consider the point. But if he wrongly decides that he has jurisdiction, his award is not made good by his decision on that point.

He should decide all matters submitted to him, but should not go beyond them: otherwise his award will be void (unless the bad part can be separated from the good).

An arbitrator may award costs, which are taxable (*i.e.* assessable by a 'Taxing Master') in the High Court.

REMISSION AND SETTING ASIDE OF AWARDS

There are several grounds on which the Court may remit an award to the arbitrator for reconsideration or may set it aside.

The grounds for remission are:

(1) Inadvertent omission (as, for example, where the arbitrator has stated a case but has not declared his findings on all the facts relevant to the decision in law).

(2) The discovery of new material evidence after the making of the award.

(3) A mistake admitted by the arbitrator, who asks for the matter to be remitted to him.

(4) A mistake in law apparent on the face of the award.

(5) Where the arbitrator has misconducted himself or the proceedings, or the award has been improperly procured (without any improper motive on the part of the arbitrator).

(6) Where the award is uncertain or not final. An award which is uncertain (such as that A. *or* B. shall do something), or which is not final (as, for example, where it provides that a third party shall certify the loss arising from a breach of contract), cannot be enforced.

The remission of an award enables the arbitrator to correct it, and so to do justice between the parties, without the inconvenience and expense of starting the proceedings all over again. If possible, therefore, the Court would rather take this course than set an award aside.

The Court can, however, set an award aside for any of the three last-mentioned reasons, and it will set it aside and not remit, where the arbitrator behaved corruptly or in defiance of the law, so as to forfeit the confidence of the Court. It will also set aside an award based on an illegal contract.

It should be noted that the Court will not remit or set aside an award for mistake, unless the award is, on the face of it (or on the face of a document forming part of the award), bad in law. The general principle is that the parties, having chosen their own tribunal, must accept its decision. Indeed, even an evident mistake in law would not be a ground for remitting or setting aside an award if the point of law (such as the proper construction of a term in a contract) was the very question referred to arbitration, but only if it was a point arising incidentally in the course of the reference. If the arbitrator does not give reasons for his decision, his award will, of course, not be open to challenge on this ground.

ENFORCEMENT OF AWARDS

There are two methods of enforcing an award if the losing party fails to comply with it. One is to bring an action on the award (for if A. undertakes to pay B.

any sum awarded to B. by the arbitrator, and the arbitrator awards B. £1,000, that is tantamount to an enforceable promise by A. to pay B. £1,000): and this is the only method available in the case of an *oral* submission. The other method is to obtain leave of the Court to enforce the award in the same manner as a judgment of a Court of Law.

ENFORCEMENT OF PAYMENT OF DEBTS

THE FIRST step toward the recovery of a debt by process of law is the bringing of an action and the obtaining of judgment against the debtor. If the 'judgment debtor', as he is then called, still fails to pay, the creditor can proceed to 'execution' of the judgment, that is, can set in motion the legal machinery for exacting payment. This can be done in a number of ways.

In the first place, the judgment creditor can have the debtor's 'goods and chattels' seized and sold to satisfy the debt. This is effected by a writ of *fieri facias* (known for short as 'fi. fa.', pronounced 'fie fay'). It is obtained, usually by the creditor's solicitor, from the Central Office of the Supreme Court, or from a local District Registry, and is directed to the sheriff of the county in which the goods are situated. The sheriff is responsible for the seizure and sale of the debtor's goods: and he acts through the bailiff or other sheriff's officer. The writ being directed to goods, chattels, furniture, etc., does not authorize the seizure of freehold land or fixtures to such land. The bedding and wearing apparel of the debtor and his family are exempt from seizure, and so are the tools of his trade, up to a total value of £20. The goods are normally sold by public auction (though where the circumstances warrant it, the Court may authorize a sale 'by private treaty'). The proceeds of the sale are applied, after discharge of the costs of execution, in payment of the judgment debt (including any award of costs), and any excess is returned to the debtor.

It is sometimes necessary for the judgment creditor to ascertain the nature and extent of the debtor's assets, his salary, and so forth (if only to avoid incurring useless or disproportionate costs in seeking to execute the judgment). He may do this in either of two ways. He may apply to a Master of the High Court to obtain an order for the examination of the debtor as to his means: or, more simply, he may issue a judgment summons out of the County Court of the district in which the debtor resides. The debtor must attend for cross-examination in the County Court (if the latter course is adopted), where the Judge will order him to pay the debt by such instalments as he can afford—having regard to his income and outgoings, and may order that he be committed to prison if he defaults. Thus, although imprisonment for debt was abolished by the Debtors Act, 1869, a recalcitrant debtor may still find himself in prison today—not, however, for the failure to pay but for contempt of

Court in refusing to pay, the Court having been convinced that he has means to do so, that he *can* pay. Application may be made to the County Court, by either the creditor or the debtor, for variation of an instalment order on account of a change in the financial position of the debtor.

Another weapon in the judgment creditor's armoury is the 'garnishee order' or 'attachment of debts'. This enables him to get hold of money due to the debtor while it is still in the hands of a third person, who is the garnishee. The garnishee might well be a bank in which there is money standing to the debtor's credit in his account. The procedure is that the creditor first applies to a Master for a 'garnishee order *nisi*', supporting his application with an affidavit setting out the material facts. A 'garnishee order *nisi*' is then made, and served on the garnishee: and the money is then 'frozen' in the hands of the garnishee. *Unless* (and this is the meaning of the Latin word '*nisi*') the garnishee can show cause why he should not pay to the judgment creditor the debt alleged to be due from him to the debtor, the order will be made absolute, and the garnishee must pay the creditor direct. In order to be 'attached' in this way, a debt must already be an existing debt, and not one that will fall due in future. Salary can be attached once it has been earned, and is therefore owed by the employer, but not in advance. Moreover, certain debts are protected by statute from attachment. These include the wages of seamen and labourers, and police and service pensions. Generally speaking, any debt that cannot be assigned (such as maintenance due from a husband to his wife) cannot be garnished.

If the judgment debtor owns land, whether freehold or leasehold, a 'charging order' may be obtained over his land. The effect of such an order (which is first made *nisi*, and then, unless cause is shown to the contrary, made *absolute*) is to charge the land with the payment of the debt, so that the creditor may then apply to the Court to have the land sold or to have a receiver appointed, who will discharge the judgment debt from the rents received.

A charging order may also be obtained over stocks and shares owned by the judgment debtor. Notice of such an order is given to the company concerned, and has the effect of preventing any transfer of the stock or shares charged. The debtor can also be prevented from receiving dividends on them. After waiting six months, the creditor can bring an action to have the stock or shares sold.

A debtor's interest in partnership property and profits may be charged, under the Partnership Act, 1890, with the amount of a judgment given against him for a private debt. Such an order is usually accompanied by the appointment of a receiver.

The appointment of a receiver is supplementary to the usual modes of execution in some cases, and a substitute for them in others. In the case of land and partnership property, a receiver may be appointed to receive on behalf of the creditor, and—in so far as there is any excess—on behalf of the debtor as well, the rents and profits accruing from it, and the proceeds of sale. Where the debtor is possessed of an equitable interest in property under a settlement or trust, the only method of reaching it is by means of a receiver, into whose hands the income from the property will be diverted. A receiver can be appointed only with the consent of a Master of the High Court, who will take into account the amount of the debt, the amount likely to be recovered by a receiver, and the probable cost of his appointment.

Finally, it may be noted that the service of a bankruptcy notice—though it is not a form of execution—may often be the cheapest, quickest, and most effective method of extracting payment from a judgment debtor who is not willing to pay up.

ENFORCEMENT OF CLAIMS

LIMITATIONS ON THE RIGHT OF BRINGING LEGAL PROCEEDINGS

THE section on *Receipts* refers to the limitation of power to enforce payment of debts after six years. This section explains the general principles which apply in all cases.

The law does not allow a person to 'sleep on his rights', and to bring an action after so many years that the defendant may have forgotten the true facts. He may no longer be in possession of evidence to rebut the claim. He may have acted in such a way (for example, by spending the money which the plaintiff now claims), under the impression that there was no claim against him or that any such claim had been abandoned, that it would now be oppressive to allow such a claim to be put forward.

Accordingly there are a number of statutory provisions, some contained in general Statutes of Limitation, others in enactments concerned with particular topics, which lay down a 'limitation period', that is, a length of time within which an action must be commenced. After that period has expired, the claim is 'statute-barred'.

An action founded on a contract under seal (defined in section on 'Contracts Generally') or on a judgment debt (*i.e.* a Court order) cannot be brought after the expiration of *twelve* years from the date on which the cause of action accrued, while actions on ordinary written or oral contracts must be brought within *six* years: *e.g.* the ordinary debt for work done or goods supplied.

If, however, a debt is secured by a mortgage or charge on property, the right to recover the money due is not barred until twelve years from the date when the right to receive it accrued: and even if the right to sue for the money is barred, the right to enforce the mortgage or charge by foreclosure is not barred until the debtor has remained in possession of the property without paying interest for twelve years.

The right of action in contract accrues at the time when the contract is broken or payment becomes due. In general, if the parties do not agree on a future time for repayment, money lent is due for repayment immediately, so that the limitation period runs from the time of the loan. But where money is payable on demand (as between banker and customer), time only runs from the date of the demand.

A right of action which is barred by lapse of time may be revived by acknowledgement of the debt or part payment. The right of action is deemed to have accrued on the date of the acknowledgement or last payment. The payment of interest revives the right of action in respect of the principal, but not in respect of statute-barred instalments of interest.

Acknowledgement must be in writing, signed by or on behalf of the debtor and made to the creditor or his agent. If there is a clear admission that the debt is owing, it is immaterial that there is no promise to pay, *or even that the acknowledgement is coupled with a refusal to pay*. The letter recognizes that there is a debt, or a claim for a debt, and that is enough to preserve the creditor's right to have his claim decided by the Court.

In tort, the general limitation period is six years. But where damages are claimed for *personal injuries* (whether in tort or in contract), the action must be brought within *three years*.

The limitation period does not run against persons under certain disabilities. Thus if, when the right of action accrued, a plaintiff was under twenty-one or of unsound mind, he may bring an action at any time before the expiration of six years from the date when his disability ceased. In the case of personal injuries, however, there is no extension of the three-year period of limitation if the person under disability was, at the time when the right of action accrued, in the custody of a parent.

If the action is based on fraud, or the right of action has been concealed by fraud, or the action is for relief from the consequences of a mistake, time does not run until the plaintiff has discovered the fraud or mistake, or could with reasonable diligence have discovered it. Thus a plaintiff who bought plum trees which the defendant fraudulently warranted to be of a particular variety was able to pursue his claim for damages when he discovered that they were of a different variety seven years later.

An action to recover land or rent must be brought within twelve years.

Shorter periods of limitation are laid down in various statutes: an action must be brought within one year, for example, by a moneylender or the holder of a bill of lading.

Until recent years, claims against the Crown, public authorities, and public corporations (such as the National Coal Board) had to be brought within shorter periods than against other defendants; but this special privilege has now been abolished.

BANKRUPTCY

THE LAW of bankruptcy serves two purposes:

    (a) it enables a person who is hopelessly burdened with debts to rid himself of his liabilities so as to be able to make a fresh start, and

    (b) it ensures the fair distribution of his property among his creditors.

A person may be made bankrupt on the petition of a creditor or on his own petition.

WHO MAY BE MADE BANKRUPT

Under the earlier Bankruptcy Acts, which go back to the reign of Henry VIII, only traders could be made bankrupt. But under the modern law (which is enacted in the Bankruptcy Act, 1914) all persons can be made bankrupt, subject to the following exceptions:

An *infant* (*i.e.* a person under the age of twenty-one) can only be made bankrupt in respect of debts which are legally binding on him.

An *alien* cannot be made bankrupt unless he is domiciled in England, or has had a residence or place of business, or carried on business personally, or through a partner, or agent, in England.

A *limited company* cannot be made bankrupt, but may be wound up under the Companies Act, 1948.

ACTS OF BANKRUPTCY

Before bankruptcy proceedings can be taken, the debtor must have committed an act of bankruptcy, so as to make his insolvency manifest. An act of bankruptcy is committed in any of the following ways:

(1) If the debtor makes a conveyance or assignment of his property to a trustee or trustees for the benefit of his creditors *generally* (*i.e.* not to particular creditors, or for the benefit of trade creditors only).

(2) If the debtor makes a fraudulent conveyance, gift, delivery or transfer of his property, or of any part of it.

The term 'fraudulent' is here used both in a narrower and in a wider sense. In the narrower sense it means that there is an actual intention to defraud creditors; and if this is proved, then such a conveyance can be set aside, *i.e.* cancelled, at any time, except as against an innocent purchaser of the property, who gave value for it, without knowledge of such an intention on the part of the vendor. In the wider sense (as the term 'fraudulent' is generally used in bankruptcy law) it means an intention to prevent the distribution of the debtor's property in accordance with the bankruptcy rules. And if the transaction is fraudulent in this sense, then even a person who takes the property in good faith and for value will get no title to it if a bankruptcy petition is presented within three months of the transfer of the property to him.

If an assignment has the effect of defeating or delaying creditors, it will, in this wider sense, be fraudulent even though the debtor makes it in good faith. Thus, where an insolvent debtor assigned his business to a company which was formed to take it over, it was held that this must delay the creditors, and therefore constituted an act of bankruptcy.

Where an insolvent debtor assigns his property in payment of a past debt, this, whatever his motives may be, is an act of bankruptcy. But if the consideration for the transfer is partly a past debt and partly a further advance, and the further advance is genuinely intended to enable the debtor to continue his business, it may be held that the transfer is not an act of bankruptcy.

"... an actual intention to defraud ...

(3) If the debtor makes any conveyance or transfer of his property or any part of it, or creates any charge on it, which would be void as a fraudulent preference if he were adjudged bankrupt. (The meaning of fraudulent preference is discussed later.

(4) If, with intent to defeat or delay his creditors, the debtor departs out of

England, or remains out of England or departs from his dwelling-house, or otherwise absents himself, or begins to 'keep house' (*i.e.* remain indoors). For such conduct to constitute an act of bankruptcy there must be an intent to defeat or delay creditors: but this intent will readily be inferred if a debtor avoids his creditors (*e.g.* by leaving his place of business without informing them of his new address).

(5) If execution has been levied against the debtor by seizure of his goods, and the goods have either been sold by the sheriff or held by him for twenty-one days.

(6) If the debtor files in the Court a declaration of his inability to pay his debts, or presents a bankruptcy petition against himself.

(7) If a bankruptcy notice is served on the debtor by a creditor who has obtained a final judgment or order against him, and the debtor does not, within seven days after service of the notice (if it is effected in England—a longer time may be granted in the case of a notice served abroad), either comply with the requirements of the notice or satisfy the Court that he has a counter-claim or set-off which equals or exceeds the amount of the judgment debt and which he could not set up in the action in which the judgment was obtained.

A bankruptcy notice calls upon the debtor to pay the judgment debt or to secure or compound for it to the creditor's satisfaction. It must be accurate in its terms, and must state the consequences of non-compliance: otherwise it will be void.

If a bankruptcy notice is not complied with, *any* creditor can found a petition upon it. Failure to comply with a bankruptcy notice is, in practice, the most common act of bankruptcy.

(8) If the debtor gives notice to any of his creditors that he has suspended, or is about to suspend, payment of his debts.

It is not necessary for such notice to be in writing, so long as it is deliberate. A letter summoning a meeting of creditors may or may not constitute such a notice: the test is whether a reasonable person would infer from its terms that the debtor intended to suspend payment. Thus, where a debtor wrote to his creditors, 'Being unable to meet my engagements as they fall due, I invite your attendance at .... when I will submit a statement of my position for your consideration and decision', this was held to be an act of bankruptcy.

THE PETITION

A debtor's petition declares that he is unable to pay his debts, and its presentation constitutes an act of bankruptcy.

A creditor (or a number of creditors) may petition, *within three months* after the occurrence of an act of bankruptcy, provided that the debt owing to him (or to the petitioning creditors in the aggregate) is at least £50, and that it is liquidated (*i.e.* a definite sum) and is payable immediately or at a certain future time.

A creditor's petition, in setting out the amount of the debt, must also disclose any security which the creditor holds for it.

The petition must be presented in the County Court of the district in which the debtor has carried on business or resided during the greater part of the preceding six months, or in the High Court if during the greater part of that period he has carried on business or resided within the London bankruptcy district, or if he is not resident in England, or his residence is unknown.

A *receiving order* is made by the Court immediately upon the presentation of a debtor's petition. A creditor's petition is heard not less than eight days after the service of the petition, and the Court, if satisfied as to the continuance of the debt, the service of the petition and the act of bankruptcy, will then make a receiving order, unless there is good reason to the contrary (as, for example, where the debtor's only asset is a life interest which will be forfeited on bankruptcy).

The effect of a receiving order is to make the Official Receiver (an officer of the Board of Trade who is appointed for a particular district) the receiver of all the debtor's property, and to take away from the creditors—with certain exceptions—all remedies against the property or person of the debtor. No legal action can then be started against the debtor without leave of the Court. Where the debtor's business is such as to require it, the Official Receiver may, on the application of a creditor, appoint a special manager to run it. The property does not, by virtue of a receiving order, cease to belong to the debtor, but it is put into the charge and control of the Official Receiver, so that the debtor cannot deal with it and the creditors cannot seize it by legal process.

A receiving order must be advertised in the *London Gazette* and in a local paper, and should be registered at the Land Registry if the debtor owns land.

In certain circumstances (as when a composition or scheme of arrangement is sanctioned by the Court, or when it appears that the debts will be paid in full) a receiving order may be rescinded. The debtor can then resume control of his property, and the bankruptcy proceedings are at an end.

PROCEEDINGS AFTER RECEIVING ORDER

The debtor attends a private interview with the Official Receiver, where he is instructed as to the preparation of his *Statement of Affairs*. If he cannot prepare it himself, he may be allowed assistance. It must contain a list of his assets and liabilities, his creditors and the securities (if any) which they hold. The Statement of Affairs must be verified by affidavit (*i.e.* a document to whose truth the debtor swears) and submitted to the Official Receiver within three days of the receiving order in the case of a debtor's petition or within seven days in the case of a creditor's petition. It is open to inspection by anyone who states in writing that he is a creditor. Failure to submit it may result in the debtor's being adjudged bankrupt on the application of the Official Receiver or a creditor.

Not more than fourteen days after the receiving order is made, the Official Receiver must call a meeting of creditors, by giving six days' notice in the *London Gazette* and a local paper, and by notice to the creditors named in the Statement of Affairs. The notice to the creditors should be accompanied by a summary of the debtor's statement, and observations on the causes of his failure. The first meeting of creditors is presided over by the Official Receiver, and its main business is to decide whether a composition or scheme of arrangement is to be accepted (*e.g.* an offer by the debtor to pay 8*s* in the pound), or whether the debtor is to be made bankrupt.

If the debtor puts forward a scheme which is accepted by a majority in number and three-fourths in value of the creditors, and if (after completion of the debtor's public examination) the scheme is approved by the Court—which will have regard to the public interest as well as to the wishes of the creditors—the receiving order will be discharged.

As soon as is convenient, the debtor must undergo a *public exa·nination* in Court as to his conduct, dealings, and property. The examination is taken before the Registrar; the debtor is examined on oath, and his answers are taken down in writing and signed by him.

The public examination is designed not only to obtain in the interests of creditors a full disclosure of the debtor's assets and the facts relating to his insolvency, but also to protect the public: the debtor cannot, therefore, refuse to answer questions on the ground that they may incriminate him. If a debtor refuses to answer questions, he may be reported to the Judge, who may commit him for contempt of Court: and if he fails to attend his public examination, a warrant may be issued for his arrest.

The public examination may be adjourned from time to time, to enable the debtor's answers to be checked (*e.g.* his explanation of apparent gifts of property, or payments to friends and relations that appear in his bank pass-book): it must not be concluded until after the first meeting of creditors.

ADJUDICATION

Unless the creditors adopt a scheme or accept a composition which is satisfactory to the Court and is carried into effect, the debtor is adjudicated bankrupt. On adjudication, the property of the bankrupt passes to his *trustee in bankruptcy*, and becomes divisible among his creditors. This is explained in more detail below.

The trustee is a person appointed by the creditors, or by the Board of Trade (if the creditors do not appoint a trustee within four weeks of adjudication), and his appointment is not complete until it has been certified by the Board of Trade, which may refuse to certify an unsuitable appointment.

The creditors may appoint a *committee of inspection* to superintend (and sometimes to appoint) the trustee. The committee of inspection consists of three to five persons who are creditors or hold creditors' proxies. The trustee requires the consent of the committee (or—if there is no committee—of the Board of Trade) for certain purposes.

An adjudication may be annulled if a scheme is accepted after it, or when it is shown that the debtor ought not to have been adjudicated bankrupt, or when his debts are paid in full (and his conduct had not been such that the Court will refuse to exercise its discretion in his favour).

Notices of the adjudication, of the appointment of a trustee, and of any annulment of adjudication, must be published in the *London Gazette* and a local paper.

Adjudication subjects the bankrupt to certain disqualifications. Any property he acquires after bankruptcy (a legacy, for example) may be claimed by the trustee. He must not obtain credit for £10 or more without disclosing that he is bankrupt, or engage in business under another name without disclosing his name when he was made bankrupt. He cannot be a company director without leave of the Court.

DISCHARGE

A bankrupt may at any time apply for an order of discharge releasing him from the status of bankruptcy. The application is heard in open court, and may be opposed by the trustee, the creditors, and the Official Receiver. If the Court grants a discharge, it may be unconditional, or conditional (*e.g.* requiring the bankrupt to set aside so much from his earnings per month for the benefit of his creditors), or suspensive (*e.g.* staying the operation of the order for a certain time, or until a certain dividend is paid), or both conditional and suspensive.

The Court *cannot* grant an unconditional discharge:

(a) when the bankrupt's assets are worth less than 10*s* in the pound on his unsecured liabilities (unless he was not to blame for this), or

(b) when he has not kept proper books of account for the three years preceding his bankruptcy, or

(c) has continued to trade knowing himself to be insolvent, or

(d) has contracted any debt without reasonable expectation of being able to pay it, or

(e) fails to account satisfactorily for any loss or deficiency of assets, or

(f) has brought on his bankruptcy by rash speculations, extravagance, gambling, or neglect of his business, or

(g) has put any of his creditors to expense or incurred expense by pointless litigation, or

(h) has given an undue preference to any creditor within three months of the receiving order (when unable to pay his debts as they became due), or

(i) incurred liabilities within that period with a view of making his assets equal to 10*s* in the pound, or

(j) has been previously adjudged bankrupt or made a composition or arrangement with his creditors, or

(k) has been guilty of any fraud or fraudulent breach of trust, or

(l) committed any indictable offence in connection with the bankruptcy.

The Court will take into account the manner in which the bankrupt has carried out his duty to assist the trustee in collecting his property for the benefit of his creditors.

An order of discharge releases the bankrupt from all debts provable in the bankruptcy, except for certain debts due to the Crown or incurred through fraud or under a Court order in affiliation or similar proceedings. It will not protect him from criminal proceedings.

The order also removes the disqualifications mentioned above, but certain statutory disqualifications prevent a bankrupt from taking part in public affairs for five years from the date of his discharge, unless the Court certifies that his bankruptcy was caused by misfortune without any misconduct on his part (as, for example, where he was let down by a fraudulent partner).

A bankrupt's discharge is quite unconnected with the realization of his property by the trustee: it may take place long before the distribution to creditors is completed, or long after—or it may never take place at all.

PROPERTY DIVISIBLE AMONGST CREDITORS

Not all the property of a bankrupt becomes divisible amongst his creditors: and, on the other hand, certain property which is not his may be divisible amongst them. The property so divisible is as follows:

Property belonging to the bankrupt at the commencement of the bankruptcy

This includes some, but not all, his rights of action, *i.e.* rights of legal action to enforce claims which he might have; and also his contracts (other than those involving his personal skill), though the trustee may disclaim them.

The bankruptcy commences with the earliest act of bankruptcy on which the petition could have been founded. However, certain transactions which take place after the commencement of the bankruptcy but before the date of the receiving order are *protected, i.e.* valid as against the trustee, if they are made in good faith and for valuable consideration, *i.e.* usually money. Examples are payments made by the bankrupt to any of his creditors, assignments by him for valuable consideration, and payment of money or delivery of property to him.

Property acquired by the bankrupt before his discharge

Property which belongs to the bankrupt at the commencement of the bankruptcy or which he acquires before adjudication passes *automatically* to the trustee (excepting property which the bankrupt holds in trust for others, and the tools of his trade, clothing, and bedding of himself and his family to a total value of £20): but property acquired after adjudication must be *claimed* by the trustee. He cannot claim such part of the bankrupt's personal earnings as are necessary for the maintenance of himself and his family, and his claim is subject to certain other restrictions.

Goods in the bankrupt's reputed ownership

This means all goods in the possession of the bankrupt in his trade or business, with the consent of the owner, under such circumstances that the bankrupt is the reputed owner of them. 'Reputed owner' means that he reasonably appears to own the goods and can justifiably be assumed to do so by the world at large. Where it is the established custom in any trade for the trader to have the goods of other persons in his possession, reputed ownership does not arise: for example, it is well known that hotel-keepers often hire, instead of buying, their furniture, and that antique furniture dealers hold articles belonging to other dealers 'on sale or return'. Goods on hire purchase may be within the reputed ownership of the bankrupt: but once notice has been given determining the hiring, they are no longer in his possession with the owner's consent.

Property comprised in certain voluntary settlements

All settlements made within two years of the beginning of the bankruptcy are void, with the exception of settlements made before and in consideration of marriage, or in good faith and for value, or for the wife or children of the bankrupt in respect of property acquired through his wife. If the bankruptcy occurs after two but within ten years, a settlement is void unless it can be proved that the settlor, at the time of the settlement, was able to pay his debts without the aid of the property settled, and that he retained no interest in it.

A settlement in this connection implies an intention on the part of the settlor that the property shall be retained and not immediately sold so that the proceeds cannot be traced. Thus a gift of jewellery by a husband to his wife was held to be a settlement, whereas a gift of money to a son to enable him to commence business was held not to be. The jewellery was retained intact and meant to be: the money was meant to be expended.

Covenants in marriage settlements to settle after-acquired property are in some circumstances void against the trustee in bankruptcy.

A general assignment of book debts by a trader is void against the trustee as to debts not paid at the commencement of the bankruptcy, unless registered under the Bills of Sale Act, 1878. This rule does not apply, however, to debts due from specific debtors or growing due under specified contracts (though in these cases notice of the assignment should be given to the debtors): nor does it apply to book debts included in a transfer of a business made in good faith and for value, or to debts included in any assignment of assets for the benefit of creditors generally.

Property so used as to give a fraudulent preference

If a person unable to pay his debts as they fall due transfers property to a creditor, or pays him, within six months before the presentation of the bankruptcy petition, with a view to giving that creditor a preference over other creditors, the transfer or payment is void, and the creditor must hand over the property or money to the trustee in bankruptcy. There is no 'fraudulent preference', however, if the transfer or payment was not made voluntarily but was due to pressure by the creditor, or was for the purpose of averting criminal proceedings or enabling the debtor to carry on business.

REALIZATION OF THE DEBTOR'S PROPERTY

There are extensive means of obtaining 'discovery', *i.e.* finding out all about the debtor's property. Not only must the debtor disclose all his assets in his statement of affairs and answer questions on oath at his public examination, but he must, if required, attend meetings of his creditors and make a full disclosure of his property to them, and not only the debtor but also his wife and any person believed to have any of the debtor's property in his possession or to be able to give information as to the debtor's affairs may be ordered by the

Court to give evidence on oath at a private examination. Further, the Court has power to order that for a period of up to three months letters and telegrams addressed to the debtor be directed to the Official Receiver oʳ trustee.

It is the trustee's duty to take possession of the bankrupt's property as soon as possible. Subject to certain rules, he may disclaim land burdened with onerous covenants (though in the case of leases the leave of the Court may be required), shares or stock in companies which might involve a liability, unprofitable contracts, or property that is not readily saleable. A person injured by the disclaimer of any property may prove for the damage he has suffered as a debt under the bankruptcy, and may apply to the Court for an order vesting in him any disclaimed property in which he has an interest.

The trustee can sell the bankrupt's property by public auction or private contract and claim any debt due to the bankrupt: and with the specific permission of the committee of inspection he has considerably wider powers, including the carrying on of the bankrupt's business so far as is necessary for beneficial winding up.

PROOF OF DEBTS AND DIVIDENDS

A creditor must 'prove' his debt before he is entitled to any share in the bankrupt's property. Provable debts are 'all debts and liabilities, present or future, certain or contingent, to which the debtor is subject at the date of the receiving order, or to which he may become subject before his discharge by reason of any obligations incurred before the date of the receiving order'.

In the case of a contingent debt (such as a claim for non-performance of a covenant to leave premises in good repair, when the lease has not yet expired), the trustee must estimate the value of the liability, subject to the creditor's right to appeal to the Court. If, in the opinion of the Court, the liability cannot be fairly estimated, the debt will not be provable in the bankruptcy.

Unliquidated claims, *i.e.* claims which have not been or cannot yet be put into terms of an exact sum of money, cannot be proved in bankruptcy unless they arise out of a contract or breach of trust. Nor can debts contracted after the creditor has notice of an act of bankruptcy, or after the receiving order has been made. Nor can alimony ordered to be paid periodically to the debtor's wife, or arrears of alimony or of maintenance.

A creditor who is himself indebted to the bankrupt is entitled to set off the amount he owes against the amount owed him by the bankrupt, and to claim the balance: for otherwise he would have to pay what he owes in full, while receiving only a dividend in respect of what he is owed. But a creditor cannot claim the benefit of such a set-off if, at the time when he gave credit to the debtor, he had notice of an act of bankruptcy.

A creditor should prove his debt, as soon as possible after the receiving order, by an affidavit verifying the debt, specifying any supporting vouchers, and stating whether he is a secured creditor. (Failure to state that he is secured may result in his having to surrender the security for the general benefit of the creditors.) A secured creditor is one who holds some security for his debt, such as a mortgage or bill of sale. He has the choice of (a) realizing his security and proving for the balance, (b) surrendering his security to the trustee and proving for the whole debt, or (c) valuing his security and proving for the balance. If he values his security, the trustee may, if he wishes, redeem it at that value or require it to be sold.

Certain debts are 'preferential', because the debtor's estate (after the discharge of all costs of the bankruptcy proceedings, including the petitioning creditor's costs and the trustee's remuneration) must be applied in payment of them in priority to other debts. The *preferential debts* (which rank equally among themselves) are:

(1) Rates and purchase tax due within the preceding year, and other taxes assessed up to the preceding April 5th, and not exceeding one year's assessment.

(2) Wages or salary of a clerk or servant, labourer or workman, not exceeding £200, for services rendered during four months before the receiving order, and accrued holiday remuneration.

(3) Amounts due in respect of contributions payable during the preceding year for industrial injuries insurance or national insurance.

The debtor's landlord, if he has levied distress for rent, is also to a certain extent a preferential creditor.

Certain other debts are '*deferred*', being payable only after all other debts proved in the bankruptcy have been paid in full. These include:

(1) Interest exceeding 5 per cent. under a moneylending contract.

(2) A loan to a person engaged in business at a rate of interest varying with the profits, or an amount due to the vendor of a business under a contract whereby he is to receive from the purchaser a share of the profits.

(3) Loans between husband and wife for business purposes.

The trustee must distribute dividends with all convenient speed, and must distribute all money in hand after making provision for disputed claims, expenses, and the claims of creditors residing at such distance that they may not have had time to tender their proofs.

The first dividend must be distributed within four months of the first meeting of creditors (unless the committee of inspection think there is good reason for postponing it), and subsequent dividends at intervals of not more than six months. Before declaring a dividend, the trustee must give notice of his intention to the Board of Trade and to all creditors mentioned in the bankrupt's statement who have not proved their debts, and the notice must be published in the *London Gazette*.

The final dividend is declared when all the bankrupt's property has been realized. Before declaring it, the trustee must notify all creditors whose proofs he has rejected that if they do not establish their claims to the satisfaction of the Court within a stated time he will proceed to make a final dividend without regard to their claims.

Any surplus which may remain after payment of all the creditors in full with interest, and of the cost of the bankruptcy, belongs to the bankrupt.

The trustee, whose conduct is under the supervision of the Board of Trade, may apply to the Board of Trade for release after declaring the final dividend: and if his accounts are found to be satisfactory, and no objection is raised by any creditor, his release may be granted.

THE LIQUIDATION OF A COMPANY

A COMPANY'S EXISTENCE comes to an end when it is 'wound up' or 'liquidated'. There are various reasons for liquidation. One obvious one is insolvency: if the company cannot pay its debts, the creditors are entitled to have its assets distributed among themselves, just as in the case of an individual who is made bankrupt. But there are, as we shall see, other reasons for the dissolution of a company.

A company may be dissolved in three ways:

(a) compulsory winding up,
(b) voluntary winding up, and
(c) winding up under the supervision of the Court.

Whichever the method, a liquidator is appointed to administer the company's property and distribute the assets, first among the creditors and then (where the company is solvent) among the shareholders.

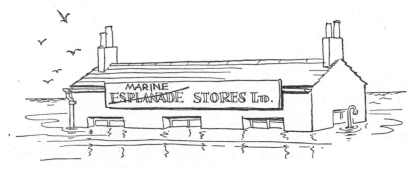

Liquidation!

COMPULSORY LIQUIDATION

The grounds on which a company may be wound up compulsorily, *i.e.* by order of the Court, are:

(1) That the company is unable to pay its debts. A company is deemed to be insolvent if a creditor for over £50 has formally demanded payment and not received satisfaction within three weeks, or if execution on a judgment is not

387

wholly satisfied, or if it is proved to the Court, taking into account contingent and prospective liabilities, that the company cannot pay its debts.

(2) That the number of members has fallen below the statutory minimum (two in a private and seven in a public company).

(3) That the company has not commenced business within a year of its incorporation or has suspended business for a year.

(4) That the 'statutory report' has not been delivered to the Registrar or the 'statutory meeting' has not been held.

(5) That the company has passed a special resolution to that effect.

(6) That it is 'just and equitable' that the company be wound up—a residual reason giving the Court wide discretionary powers on hearing an application.

If, for example, the main object of a company was to work a particular mine, and the mine is now worked out; or if it is carrying on business at a loss, with no prospect of improvement; or if it is impossible to carry on business because of internal disputes in the company; or if the misconduct of directors can only be properly investigated in a winding up: in such circumstances the Court may decide that it is just and equitable that the company be wound up.

A petition for a compulsory winding-up order may be presented by either the company itself, or a creditor, or a shareholder.

If an order is made (and it may, of course, be refused if the petition is opposed), the winding up commences at the date of the petition, and the Official Receiver becomes provisional liquidator until a liquidator is appointed. He must then summon separate meetings of creditors and shareholders, to decide whether application should be made to the Court to appoint another person as liquidator and to appoint a committee of inspection (consisting of creditors, shareholders, and persons holding their power of attorney). If both meetings pass the same resolutions, the Court makes the appointments: if there is a difference, the Court decides.

If a person other than the Official Receiver is appointed liquidator, he must notify his appointment to the Registrar of Companies and give security, and he must give the Official Receiver all such information and access to the company's books as may be required.

Except where the Court so directs, the company's property does not vest in the liquidator in the way that a bankrupt's property vests in his trustee.

When a winding-up order has been made, the Official Receiver may call upon certain persons (including past and present directors and employees of the company) to submit a statement of affairs giving particulars of the company's assets, liabilities, creditors, and the securities held by them.

The Official Receiver then makes his report on the state of the company's finances and the cause of its failure, and states whether further inquiry is desirable. He may make a further report stating that in his opinion fraud has been committed by a promoter or officer of the company, and the Court may order such officer to be publicly examined.

A special manager of the company's business may be appointed by the Court on the application of the Official Receiver.

If all the issued shares are fully paid up, the shareholders cannot be called upon to make any contribution to the discharge of the company's debts, etc., their liability being limited to the amount of their shares (for which they have already paid in full). In the case of shares which are not fully paid up, they may be called upon to pay up to the limit of the unpaid balance. Moreover, if existing shareholders (who are called 'A' contributories) leave any call unpaid, former shareholders who held the corresponding shares within a year of the commencement of winding up (the 'B' contributories) may be called upon.

The liquidator requires the sanction of the committee of inspection or of the Court for bringing and defending actions in the name of the company, for carrying on the company's business, and for certain other purposes: but for most purposes (including sale of the company's property) no sanction is required.

Creditors must prove their debts by affidavit, specifying vouchers, and stating whether the debts are secured.

Creditors whose proofs are rejected can apply to the Court within twenty-one days of the rejection, and the Court may admit the proof of debt.

Before declaring a dividend, the liquidator must give two months' notice to the Board of Trade (to be published in the *London Gazette*), and to any creditors mentioned in the statement of affairs who have not proved.

The liquidator may (and on sufficient demand, must) hold meetings of creditors and shareholders from time to time, to ascertain their views.

If a winding up is not concluded within one year, the liquidator must send the Registrar a statement of receipts and payments and particulars regarding the liquidation, and must continue to report in the same way at half-yearly intervals.

The preferential debts in a company winding up are the same as in bankruptcy. And the bankruptcy rules (as to proofs of debt, secured creditors, fraudulent preferences, and so forth) apply generally in the winding up of an insolvent company.

VOLUNTARY LIQUIDATION

A company may be wound up voluntarily:

(a) when the period fixed by the articles for its duration expires, or on the occurrence of an event on which the articles provide for its dissolution, or

(b) if the company passes a special or extraordinary resolution to that effect (as it may—among other reasons—for the purposes of amalgamation or reconstruction).

The winding up may be either 'a members' voluntary winding up' or 'a creditors' voluntary winding up'.

A members' winding up can only take place when the company is solvent. The directors (or a majority of them) must within the five weeks preceding the resolution deliver to the Registrar a statutory declaration setting out the company's assets and liabilities and stating that in their opinion the company will be able to pay its debts in full within twelve months.

The liquidator is appointed by the company in general meeting. When its affairs are fully wound up, the liquidator must lay his account before a final general meeting (of which at least one month's notice must be given in the *London Gazette*) and then send it to the Registrar: and three months after, the company is deemed to be dissolved.

If it turns out that the company is insolvent, the liquidator must call a meeting of creditors, and subsequent meetings are held as in a creditor's winding up.

There must be a creditors' winding up if a declaration of solvency is not made. A meeting of creditors (advertised in the *London Gazette* and two local papers) must be convened for the day of, or day after, the meeting at which it is proposed to pass the resolution for voluntary winding up, and a full statement of the company's affairs must be laid before the creditors' meeting.

Each of the meetings (the company's and the creditors') may nominate a liquidator, but if different persons are nominated the creditors' nominee will be appointed, unless the Court otherwise orders.

The creditors may also appoint a committee of inspection consisting of not more than five persons. The company may appoint not more than five persons to act with them, but the creditors may object to all or any of them (the Court having power to appoint others in their place).

If the winding up lasts more than a year, the liquidator must call annual meetings of the creditors and of the company, and lay his accounts before each meeting.

When the company's affairs are fully wound up, the liquidator must call final meetings of the company and its creditors, and submit his accounts to each meeting and to the Registrar; and as in a members' winding up, the company is deemed to be dissolved three months later.

In both a members' and a creditors' winding up the liquidator, after discharging the expenses properly incurred in the winding up (including his own remuneration), must pay first the preferential and then the ordinary debts, and finally distribute any surplus assets among the members according to their rights. The liquidator or a creditor or contributory may apply to the Court to determine any question in the winding up.

LIQUIDATION UNDER SUPERVISION

When a company has resolved to wind up voluntarily, the Court may order that the winding up shall continue under its supervision. Any disposition of property made after the commencement of the winding up is then void, unless the Court otherwise orders: so, too, is any distress for rent or execution. The liquidator has the same powers as in a voluntary winding up, subject to any restrictions imposed by the Court.

It is not often that an order for winding up under supervision is made, because in cases where it is not desired to make a compulsory order the Court can generally exercise sufficient control, without a supervision order, over a voluntary winding up.

390

EMPLOYERS' LIABILITY

THE BACKGROUND

EMPLOYERS' LIABILITY means the liability of an employer to pay damages to his servants for personal injuries which they have sustained in the course of their work. This is the employer's personal liability. But there is also what is called his *vicarious* liability, which is *his responsibility for the acts of his servants* to each other and to outsiders, so long as those acts occur in the course of their employment. The employer's liability may arise under Common Law, *i.e.* usually for negligence as described above. But in this field, Acts of Parliament like the Factories Acts have imposed some very strict obligations on employers, and these obligations are independent of negligence. In other words the injured man need only prove failure to observe the obligations, not why the failure happened, nor negligence.

There are no recorded cases of servants suing their employer in English Law before 1837. The general mood prevailing at and after that time was that every workman should look after himself, and if he entered a dangerous employment he accepted its risks. Gradually it came to be recognized that workmen needed special protection against dangerous conditions of work, and this more humane attitude was reflected in the courts. As time has gone on since then, employers have been made subject to statutes and regulations in the most minute detail, and the workman's rights have been more and more extended, partly by Acts of Parliament and partly by a series of decisions in the courts.

The very existence of vicarious liability crept in only gradually, but the courts ultimately laid down in terms the general principle: "I am liable for what is done for me and under my orders by the men I employ, for the reason that by employing them I set the whole thing in motion." The basis of the doctrine of vicarious liability is that in the eyes of an outsider, master and servant are one.

In 1837, a butcher's van owned by a certain Mr Fowler was overloaded. While being driven by his employee, one Priestley, it collapsed. Priestley made legal history by suing Fowler, for the fact was that the overloading of the van was the fault of a fellow servant, and not of the employer, Fowler himself. The action failed, it being held that a master was not liable to his servant for an injury caused by the negligence of a fellow-servant with whom he was engaged in *a common employment.* This principle was at first even further extended, and indeed it was not finally abolished until 1948. Enlightened courts and Parliaments, however, had by 1948 made very considerable breaches in a doctrine which came to be recognized as indefensible.

The first major breach was in 1880, with the passing of the first Employers' Liability Act. Under this Act, if a workman could prove that his accident arose from a defect in the plant or machinery, or from defective superintendence by a superior, then he could recover for the negligence of a fellow-servant. As if to counterbalance this concession, however, he could not recover more in amount than three years' wages.

The Act of 1880 proved in due course to be inadequate, and in 1897 a new principle was brought in with the passing of the first Workmen's Compensation Act. Under this Act an injured workman did not have to prove negligence. Whenever a workman had an accident arising out of and in the course of his employment, which incapacitated him from work, he received weekly compensation. But the compensation was much smaller than would have been his Common Law damages for negligence, and though the original Act was extended, the Common Law rules and rights were not affected. The difficulty facing a workman was that he had to make a choice—either to claim compensation for the fact of the accident, or to sue for damages for negligence. He could not do both.

Meanwhile, a new field of Common Law liability had been born in the courts—liability of the employer for breach of statutory duty. The basis of it was this: if a statute gave rights but did not impose a specific remedy, a person injured by someone else's breach of the statute could sue at Common Law. But most of the Acts regulating factories and such premises had criminal penalties attaching to them. It was at one time thought that persons injured by these breaches had no Common Law action for damages. But the courts began to hold that if an Act was passed for the benefit or protection of a class of person, a member of that class could recover damages for a breach of the statute even where there was a criminal penalty for the breach. To such actions, common employment was held to be no defence. And in actions where it did still apply, the Courts were getting more and more ingenious in finding ways to avoid obstructing the workman by this defence. Finally, in 1948, the Employers' Liability Act of 1880 and the set of Workmen's Compensation Acts were repealed and the doctrine of common employment was killed at the same time.

THE EMPLOYER'S COMMON LAW DUTY OF CARE TODAY

The general duty of an employer, whether personally or acting through his other servants or agents, is to take reasonable care for the safety of his men during the course of their employment. This applies particularly to:

(a) the place of work;
(b) the plant and machinery; and
(c) the method of working.

It exists, furthermore, whether the employment is inherently dangerous or not. The law is sometimes stated as that the employer must not expose his employees to unnecessary or unreasonable risk. If there is a risk, and the employer cannot eliminate it, he must at least take steps to reduce it as far as possible. If all due care has been exercised, and the inherent risk brings injury to a workman, he can only sue his employer successfully if he can prove negligence against him.

It might be thought that the principal duties of an employer to his workman arose from contract, rather than tort, but such is by no means the case. And once you enter the field of tort, the Common Law rule applies—you must prove negligence. This section is concerned with the Common Law duty of care; specific statutory duties are dealt with later.

It may well be asked—to whom is this duty of care owed? When is a man a servant of a particular master? The answer seems to be that the relationship of master and servant exists when the master has the right to tell the servant not merely *what* to do, but *how* to do it. If a man is paid to do certain work but can decide for himself how he is going to do it, then that man is not a servant, but what is known in law as an independent contractor.

"The general duty of an employer . . . is to take reasonable care for the safety of his men . . ."

As may be imagined, difficulties can arise when a workman is temporarily lent by one employer to another. In such cases, a clear distinction must be made between lending a workman, passing the control (*and the liability* for his safety) to another master, and merely 'making available the workman's services', when control *and liability* remain with the original employer. Then there is the problem of the man who volunteers to do work without pay under the orders of another. Here the law is that provided that the master knows and consents, the man ranks in law as a workman. And it must be remembered that the employer's duty of care is owed to each workman as an individual, so that account must be taken of any special peculiarity of the workman in question— his having only one eye, for example (*Paris* v. *Stepney Borough Council*, 1951 described in the section on *Negligence*).

An employer under our present law is liable for the negligence of his servants toward the world at large. This extends to their negligence toward one another. In both instances, it must be established that the negligence took place in the course of the man's employment.

When is an act 'in the course of employment'? There are many cases, all of which have to be studied in detail, to establish the answer to this question, and the result is far too complicated to be put into a concise statement. Certain factors may, however, act as pointers. Consider, for example, the case of the workman who strays away from his place of work to another part of the factory

". . . unaware of something wrong . . ."

where he meets a danger. It has been held that provided he is doing his employer's work, he is still 'in the course of his employment', even though he may be doing it in a place forbidden to him by rule, or even by statute.

The general duty of the employer may be said to divide itself into three main branches—plant, place of work, method of work. But it always remains one general duty, and such factors as the selection and supervision of fellow-servants may be of importance, too.

What acts have to be established against an employer to show him to have been negligent? Firstly, the employer may have done nothing at all to fulfil his statutory obligations; secondly, he may have been informed of a defect but have done nothing to remedy it; thirdly, being aware of a risk, he may have taken inadequate steps to eliminate that risk or at least to reduce it; and, fourthly, he may be found to have been unaware of something wrong about which he ought to have known.

AT WORK; BUSINESS; INDUSTRY; THE PROFESSIONS

BREACH OF STATUTORY DUTY

We now turn directly to the nature and the general principles applicable in instances of breach of statutory duty. In general, as it has been already mentioned, where an Act of Parliament imposes a duty on anyone and that duty is broken, then someone injured by that breach can bring an action for damages against him—not always, but whenever the statute in question is clearly intended for the protection and safety of the workmen engaged in a particular operation.

At least, however, it can be said that any workman injured as a result of his employer's breach of the safety provisions in the Factories or Coal Mines Acts can sue for personal damages, despite the penalties imposed criminally.

The exact nature of an action for breach of statutory duty is analogous to, but not quite identical with, an ordinary Common Law action for negligence. The plaintiff in the action for damages arising from the employer's failure to observe his statutory duty must prove:

(a) that the statute imposes on the employer a duty *which is intended to protect the plaintiff workman* against harm of some kind;

(b) that the employer has failed in this duty; and

(c) that the breach has directly resulted in harm being done to the plaintiff of the kind contemplated by the statute.

Of these, perhaps the most difficult may be the third point—a complete chain of causation must be established.

It used to be the law that where a breach of the duty was followed by injuries of the type the statute was there to prevent, there was a presumption that the injuries were caused by the breach. The recent case of *Bonnington Castings Ltd.* v. *Wardlaw*, which went to the House of Lords, completely overruled this presumption, and said that the chain of causation has to be strictly proved, *i.e.* that if it is shown to have been broken the claim will fail.

Is this duty an absolute one? It is, in the sense that the employer cannot, delegate his duty of care, and blame a subordinate if he has fallen down on his job.

If a statute imposes a duty on a person and he delegates that duty to a superintendent, foreman, or workman, or contractor, he remains liable if the duty is not carried out. Moreover, liability in this respect does not depend on negligence. In most cases, the defendent cannot even escape by proving that it was impracticable to comply fully with the statute.

Let us turn now to examine briefly the possible defences open to the defendant in an action for breach of statutory duty. He may deny that he was subject to the duty, he may say the duty was not as wide or as absolute as the plaintiff alleges, or again he may claim that the plaintiff is not one of those entitled to benefit from the particular statute, or deny that the accident was the type which the statute was designed to prevent. For all these points are essential ingredients in the plaintiff's case. But there are also certain partial defences.

He can claim that the plaintiff's contributory negligence was the total or partial cause of the accident, or he may be able to take advantage of the particular wording of the statute.

In this last connection, the Factories Acts limit some of the duties they impose by using the words 'practicable' and sometimes 'reasonably practicable'. To do what is practicable involves more than just taking reasonable care, for 'practicable' really means 'feasible'—something which can be done. But in considering whether the defendant has done all that was practicable, account must be taken of the available knowledge at the time of the accident. It is no good the plaintiff complaining in, say, 1957, at the trial of his action, that the defendant had not taken at the time of the accident in, say, 1955, precautions that were not invented until 1956.

If, instead of demanding 'all practicable measures', the statute limits the defendant's obligation under it to doing 'what is reasonably practicable', though the duty is less than before, it still imputes a standard higher than 'reasonable care' to the defendant.

THE FACTORIES ACT, 1937

This important Act replaced the Factories Act of 1901. At the moment there is a new Factories Bill before Parliament which may modify it in its turn, if passed. But taking the 1937 Act as it is applied today, the first rule of importance it makes is that, with a few exceptions, it is the occupier of the factory who, in the event of a breach of duty, is normally liable for this type of civil action as well as for any criminal penalties imposed.

It also created for the first time a new, long, and complicated definition of a factory. This begins with the general definition that it includes 'every place where manual labour is used in the manufacture of goods or analogous processes for trade or profit'. This definition alone has been the subject of scores of cases, any or all of which may be vital to a plaintiff. One point established is that it need not include a building—it may be carried on entirely in the open air. But it seems that it is a place with definite boundaries, and the Act applies only within those boundaries. On the other hand, if there is a clearly demarcated area within the factory which has a distinct and separate non-factory purpose, this area may be excluded. Examples of this are a dwelling-house adjoining the factory, or offices within it.

As to processes which make up a factory, the manufacture of part of an article, the altering, repairing, finishing, cleaning, or breaking-up and demolition of any article, or adapting it for sale, including work like packing chocolates in boxes, have all at different times been held to be processes which constitute a factory. The section also specifically includes Crown premises or premises owned by a public authority if they are places which would be factories under the general definition if they were carried on for profit.

As to when newly constructed premises first become a factory, one case held that even though no production proper had started, and there was no electricity yet laid on, nevertheless, as a lorry was being painted when a workman fell into an inspection pit beside it, that was enough to bring the premises within the Act.

In addition to the Factories Act itself, there are powers under it for regulations to be made and have the force of law when made. In very many cases, special regulations have been made to cover the special hazards of a number of dangerous trades.

Many of the statutory provisions apply to the fencing of machinery in the factory. The Act itself divides machinery into three classes: (a) prime movers, *i.e.* engines and sources of power; (b) transmission machinery; and (c) other dangerous parts. There have been very many cases on the subject of just what is secure fencing as demanded by statute. A recent case established certain conclusions which over-ride all those made before it. This case held that the duty to fence machinery is a strict and absolute one, that it is no longer a defence to claim that fencing is impracticable, or to claim that the machine, if fenced, will become unusable, and that fencing itself cannot be secure unless it provides complete protection against every danger contemplated by the statute.

Once it has been established that there is a right of action by the plaintiff, there is no distinction at all between a physical injury and a disease—he can sue in respect of either equally well. This forms a great field on its own within this section of the law, and it is here only possible to say that almost every kind of disease that can arise from factory work has been the subject of a set of regulations, as have the conditions which can give rise to them. Obvious ones are dermatitis and similar skin troubles caused by contact with harmful substances, but the subjects covered by regulations specially made include ventilation, humidity, dust, fumes, infectious materials, inflammable substances, the special protection of the eyes, and even the lifting of excessive weights.

ESTABLISHMENTS SUBJECT TO SPECIAL REGULATIONS

These cover industries and trades over a truly enormous field. There are regulations which cover the special circumstances applicable in iron and steel foundries. Others are made to concern shipbuilding yards and dry docks. Building and engineering operations have extensive regulations of their own, as do electrical stations.

Mines and quarries have now a complete Act to themselves—the Mines and Quarries Act, 1954, which covers control and management, roofs, shafts, entrances, ventilation, lighting, and so forth. It also contains most detailed provisions on the subject of explosive substances and how they are to be controlled and used. These include duties imposed sometimes direct upon the workman, such as the shot-firer in a coal-mine.

Railways are subject to a set of regulations called the Prevention of Accidents Rules, which have been built up and added to between 1902 and 1931. Merchant shipping, as is well known, is subject to the very stringent terms of the Merchant Shipping Acts, 1894 and 1949. Even agriculture has special statutory provisions to regulate it and protect its workers, in the form of the Agriculture (Safety, Health, and Welfare Provisions) Act, 1956, and this covers operations much wider than mere farms. Altogether, it will be seen that there are few fields indeed where danger may be met with during employment, which are not the subject of statutory provisions of one sort or another. And it should finally be stressed that unless expressly stated otherwise, nothing in such provisions is to lessen the duties of the employer at Common Law—in particular the duty to provide the man with a safe system of working.

THE WORKMAN AT FAULT

In all we have said so far in this section, it has been assumed that the negligence or breach of statutory duty was the sole cause of the injuries to the plaintiff. However, an accident may be due to two or more defendants being at fault (in which case there are provisions to allow them to claim contribution from each other) and the accident may have been caused wholly or partly by the plaintiff's

Contributory Negligence

failure to take reasonable care for his own safety. There falls upon him an over-riding obligation so to do. The main significance of the Contributory Negligence Act, 1945, was that whereas before that, the courts set out to select, perhaps from several causes, what they regarded as *the* cause for the accident, now they have regard to all the causes and apportion the damages accordingly.

When contributory negligence by the plaintiff is brought up as a defence to an action for breach of statutory duty, it has the same effect generally as if the action was one for Common Law negligence. But, as was emphasized in one very important case, the degree of care demanded of a plaintiff for his own safety varies according to the circumstances, and allowance must be made for the conditions under which work is carried on.

A man may be obliged to give his attention to more than one thing. Then again, just as a defendant is entitled to balance the disadvantage of alternative safety measures against the risk involved, so too a plaintiff may expose himself to some degree of risk rather than submit to his activities being curtailed. All these factors must be considered in deciding whether or not the plaintiff was acting reasonably or whether he was guilty of some contributory negligence. It is not incumbent on the workman to run himself blindly into danger by following his employers' instructions to the letter. Nor need he devise a safer method if he finds the present one dangerous—he may simply refuse to follow what he has been told. Looking at it from another point of view, a workman may choose to take a deliberate risk for the benefit of his employer and not be condemned if an accident results. There have been many cases where inadvertence has been excused. It has been held by the House of Lords that direct disobedience to orders might be evidence of some negligence on the workman's part, but it can sometimes be satisfactorily explained. On the other hand, if a workman totally ignores obvious dangers he is himself guilty of negligence. There is a border-line, on one side of which any lapse is excusable, but beyond which it is inexcusable, and there are many cases all of which bear upon this very indefinite line.

A further point of view may arise where a statute imposes duties on a workman as well as on an employer, and the workman breaks his part of the regulations. This breach, if it causes the accident, may be total or partial contributory negligence. And as a matter of general principle, it has been held that if he finds that his employer has failed to carry out a statutory duty, the workman's proper act should be to report it—not try and put it right!

CONCLUSION

The law of tort is such a vast subject that it should perhaps be emphasized in conclusion that there has been room here for a statement purely of some of the general principles applying in that realm. There may be—indeed there are—further principles for which there has been no room here, and it may be that your personal problem is governed by one of those principles.

Further, do remember that each case is decided on its own particular facts. If you should happen to find that one of the illustrations given in the text seems to be exactly 'on all fours' with your own problem do not imagine that you have an immediate cause of action certain of success. One tiny factor which you may not think even significant at all may make all the difference between success and failure. There is only one thing to do about it—consult your solicitor. Put your problem to him, and ask him to advise you generally. His knowledge of the whole field of the law of tort will enable him to advise you whether or not you have a good cause of action. So do not be misled by a basic principle simply stated here, nor yet by an example of a past decision. In any event, there may be a case being heard at the moment you are reading this, the effect of which may be to reverse a long-established principle and render a whole section of this book out of date, for the law changes fractionally almost day by day, as each case heard adds its weight to that of the many many thousands decided before it.

TRADE UNIONS

TRADE UNIONS began as combinations of workers for the improvement of wages and conditions. Parliament and the Courts for a long time regarded them with hostility as conspiracies in restraint of trade. In 1800, the Combination Act was passed, making all such combinations to regulate working conditions illegal. This statutory ban was lifted in 1824, but even after that the Trade Unions, though tolerated, were not given any assistance by the law in enforcing their contracts or protecting their funds. They were no longer against the law, but were still outside it. The Trade Union Act, 1871, the so-called 'Charter' of the Trade Unions, partially legalized them and introduced a system of voluntary registration. The intention of the legislature in this Act and in others passed about this time was to some extent defeated by the narrow way in which the Courts interpreted them. So Parliament was forced to intervene from time to time to reverse the decisions of the Courts in Trade Union cases. This it did, for instance, in the Trade Disputes Act, 1906 (see below), which gave certain immunities from liability for civil wrongs, and again in the Trade Union Act, 1913, which empowered Trade Unions to collect money for political purposes.

A Trade Union at the present day is any combination of persons, whether temporary or permanent, which has as its principal objects the regulation of the relations between workmen and masters, or between workmen, or between masters, or the imposing of restrictive conditions on the conduct of any trade, business, or profession. (Employed persons of every kind are covered by the term 'workmen'.) A Trade Union may have as an additional object, but not as its sole object, the provision of benefits (*e.g.* sick pay, pensions, etc.) to its members. All these form what are known as the 'Statutory Objects' of Trade Unions.

It should be noted that the term 'Trade Union' covers not only unions of workmen, but also employers' associations, which are formed for the purpose of regulating relations between masters.

As a general rule, English Law disapproves of what are called 'restraints of trade'. Thus, any agreement which interferes with the individual's freedom of action in carrying on his trade or business is void and unenforceable, unless it can be shown that, in all the circumstances, a certain degree of interference is reasonable in the interests of the parties, and that it is not contrary to the public good. It is obvious that most Trade Unions come into headlong collision with this principle, because of the limits they impose on the freedom of their own members in the conduct of their trade or business. The position in this regard was regulated by the 1871 Act, which provided that 'the purposes of any Trade Union shall not, by reason merely that they are in restraint of trade, be unlawful so as to render void or voidable any agreement or trust'. The practical effect of the doctrine of restraint of trade on Unions has for most purposes, therefore, been nullified; but we shall see that it may still be important to distinguish between Unions which are 'legal' and 'illegal' at Common Law, according to the extent to which their objects are in restraint of trade.

The 1871 Act provided a system by which a Trade Union may be registered, if it so chooses. There are certain advantages in being registered, and also certain duties. The principal effect of registration is to give the Union a legal personality of its own, separate from that of its members. In this respect registration is akin to incorporation under the Companies Acts. A registered Trade Union is recognized by the law as a separate entity. It can sue and be sued in its registered name, it can own property, buy and sell land. An unregistered Trade Union, on the other hand, is in the eyes of the law merely the sum total of its members, and its separate existence is not recognized. Among other advantages enjoyed by a registered Trade Union are special methods of protecting its funds, certain exemptions from tax, and the right of any member to nominate a person to receive, on the death of the member, any sums payable by the Union up to £200. Besides, registration is conclusive proof that a body is a Trade Union. An unregistered Trade Union may apply to the Registrar for a certificate that it is a Trade Union, and this certificate has the same conclusive effect.

Application for registration must be made to the Chief Registrar of Friendly Societies. An application must be signed by seven members, and must be accompanied by printed copies of the rules of the Union. The Registrar will only register the Union if he is satisfied (a) that its principal objects are 'Statutory Objects' (as defined above), (b) that none of its purposes is illegal, and (c) that none of its rules is contrary to the provisions of the Trade Union Acts. If he refuses registration, there is a right of appeal to the High Court. Registration may be subsequently withdrawn or cancelled by the Chief Registrar, either at the request of the Trade Union, or on his own initiative if it is proved that registration was obtained by fraud, or has become void in circumstances laid down by statute, or that the Union has wilfully, and after notice, violated any of the provisions of the Trade Union Acts. Immediately registration is withdrawn or cancelled, the Union ceases to enjoy the privileges of a registered Trade Union, though none of its liabilities are affected.

A registered Trade Union, being a recognized 'person' in law, can make contracts which are enforceable both by and against the Union. If it breaks its contract, damages are payable out of the Union's funds. If an unregistered Union, on the other hand, purports to make a contract, those members who were directly responsible for making the contract, or who authorized the making of it, will be personally liable—but not the Union as such.

The 1871 Act, which, as we have seen, provided that the contracts and trusts of Trade Unions were no longer to be void merely because the purposes of the Unions were in restraint of trade, did not make enforceable certain agreements of a domestic nature. The exact wording of the Act is important, and it is this: 'Nothing in this Act shall enable a Court to entertain any legal proceeding instituted with the object of directly enforcing or recovering damages for the breach of' any of a certain number of specified agreements. The agreements in question are as follows:

(1) any agreement between members of a Trade Union about the conditions on which any member shall sell goods, transact business, employ or be employed;

(2) any agreement for the payment of a subscription or penalty to a Trade Union;

(3) any agreement for the application of the funds of a Trade Union
    (a) to provide benefits to members,
    (b) to furnish contributions to non-members for acting in accordance with the Trade Union's rules or resolutions, or
    (c) to discharge any fine imposed upon any person by a Court of Justice;

(4) any agreement between one Trade Union and another;

(5) any bond to secure the performance of any of the above agreements.

Some of these agreements are obviously of a type which it would be undesirable to require the Courts to enforce. It would be strange, for example, if a Court were to compel a man to strike. There are two points, however, which must be made about agreements of the specified types. The first is that they may be enforceable if they are made by a Union which does not have objects that are illegal for restraint of trade. For such agreements would then be valid independently of the 1871 Act. The second point is that the Act does not prevent such agreements being enforced indirectly by means of a declaration or injunction, which are two other remedies, besides damages, that may be sought from a Court of Law.

A Court will usually be prepared to consider, on some particular issue, what is the true meaning and effect of any rule of a Trade Union, and to express its decision in the form of a declaration, which is not a method of direct enforcement and so falls outside the Act. Once their rights have been determined in this way, parties can generally be relied on to act in accordance with the declaration. Thus in this way a member might be able to obtain a benefit which he claims to be due to him.

It is quite common for Trade Unions and Employers' Associations to negotiate general agreements as to the terms of employment in a particular trade. These 'collective agreements' do not bind the parties to them, but may be incorporated expressly or by necessary implication in the contract of employment of the individual workman. Moreover, under the Terms and Conditions of Employment Act, 1959, a claim may be made to the Minister of Labour and National Service, if an employer fails to observe a collective agreement applicable to his trade and area, provided the agreement was negotiated by bodies representing substantial proportions of the employers and workers which it concerns. The Minister may refer the claim to the Industrial Court, which may require the employer to observe the terms of the agreement, if the claim is well founded.

The objects of Trade Unions, and the means they use to achieve them, must involve some degree of interference with people in the conduct of their trade or business. This interference often results in damage of one sort or another. The question how far a Trade Union or its members may be held liable for such damage is therefore of great importance. To answer it we must consider to what extent the rules generally applicable to certain torts (civil wrongs) are modified in the case of Trade Unions.

A tort is a civil wrong for which a person may be made to pay damages. Familiar examples are libel, trespass, negligence, and malicious prosecution. Three types of tort which are of special interest to trade unionists are intimidation, inducement of breach of contract, and conspiracy.

Intimidation means compelling a person by means of an illegal threat to act, against his will, in a way which is in itself perfectly legal, but which causes damage to a third person. An illegal threat means a threat to do something illegal, *e.g.* to use violence, etc. The person injured in such circumstances can recover damages from the one who issued the threat. There will be no liability, however, for a warning, as opposed to a threat, or if the threat was merely to do something lawful.

It is also a civil wrong (save in exceptional circumstances which might justify such action) to persuade another to break his existing contract with a third person, or to make it impossible for him to perform such a contract by doing something illegal, *e.g.* hiding his tools. In such a case, not only is the contract-breaker liable to the third person, but also the one who induced the breach.

Where there is an agreement between two or more persons to do an act which is either illegal in itself or done for an unlawful purpose, then all the parties to the agreement are liable to any person who suffers damage as a result. This is the tort of conspiracy. Normally, in the case of an individual, the law is not concerned with motive. But the motive with which a combination of two or more act is important. An act done by an individual with the intention of injuring another does not become illegal if in itself lawful: the same act done by two or more for a like purpose may render them liable for conspiracy. If the predominant motive is the infliction of injury on another, rather than the protection of their own interests, two or more persons may thus be liable for an act which one person alone could do with impunity.

The Trade Disputes Act, 1906, exempted Trade Unions, and their members to a certain extent, from these general rules of liability. Trade Unions themselves were given a complete exemption from liability in tort. The individual member was given a limited protection when acting 'in contemplation or furtherance of a trade dispute'. The Act provides, in the first place, that an act done in contemplation or furtherance of a trade dispute is not actionable on

403

the ground only that it induces some other person to break a contract of employment. Secondly, it provides that an act done in pursuance of an agreement or combination by two or more persons shall, if done in contemplation or furtherance of a trade dispute, not be actionable unless the act, if done without any such agreement or combination, would be actionable. The latter provision is obviously meant to cover those cases where a malicious motive would make actionable an act, otherwise innocent, done by a combination. It can be argued, however, that any act done for a malicious motive cannot be said to have been done 'in contemplation or furtherance of a trade dispute', and therefore is not protected by the statute. This interpretation would really deprive this part of the statute of any meaning.

In any case, these provisions do not protect meddlers or trouble-makers or those who act out of sheer vindictiveness. Acts in contemplation of a trade dispute are acts done in preparation for, and with reference to, a dispute which is imminent—not acts done in the hope of creating such a dispute. Acts in furtherance of a trade dispute are acts done to advance the interests of one side to a genuine, existing dispute.

The rules of civil liability, as amended by statute, leave a great deal of room for legitimate interference with another in the defence of trade interests. If one is acting 'within one's rights', the enormity of the damage that may be caused to a rival is totally irrelevant. Thus the attainment of a 'closed shop', i.e. the monopoly of all jobs in a particular business or factory by the members of a certain Union, is a legitimate form of self-advancement, and therefore a combination for this purpose will not be actionable. And a strike is not illegal unless the strikers act in breach of their contract of employment, commit some other illegal act, or act for an illegal motive, e.g. the overthrow of the Government.

The acts of Trade Union members may involve them not only in civil liability, but in certain circumstances in criminal liability also. Thus, the same facts which give rise to liability for civil conspiracy will also constitute the offence of criminal conspiracy. In fact, a criminal conspiracy is more easily proved, since it is not necessary to show that anyone has suffered damage as a result of it.

Certain acts of intimidation are also made punishable by statute as criminal offences, for which there is a maximum penalty of £20 or three months' imprisonment. These consist of:

(a) using violence to, or intimidating, another or his wife or children, or injuring his property;
(b) persistently following another about from place to place;
(c) hiding, or depriving another of, any tools, clothes, or other property owned or used by him;
(d) watching or besetting the house or other place where he resides, or works, or carries on business, or happens to be; or
(e) following another with two or more persons in a disorderly manner in any street or road,

provided that any of these things is done with the intention of compelling the other to act in a way in which he is not bound by law to act.

404

Peaceful picketing is generally not an offence. One Act specifically provides that persons acting in contemplation or furtherance of a trade dispute may attend at or near a house or place where a person resides or carries on business, if they do so for the purpose of peacefully obtaining or communicating information, or of peacefully persuading any person to work or to refrain from working. It is not legitimate, however, for pickets to try to boycott premises by persuading customers to go away. Pickets must also be careful to behave in a manner which is strictly within the law, and must not, for example, cause an obstruction, use violence or intimidation, or remain on private premises without the owner's consent.

"Peaceful picketing is generally not an offence."

What a Trade Union may and may not do is controlled, not only by the general law, but also by its own rules. It cannot, for instance, use its funds for any object that is not provided for in its constitution. If it attempts to do so, any member may apply to the Court for a declaration that it is acting beyond its powers, and for an injunction to restrain it from so acting. In addition to its Statutory Objects, a Trade Union is allowed to have any number of other objects, so long as they are lawful. It is only allowed to have 'political objects', however, if these are approved by a resolution passed by a majority of the members voting. 'Political objects' refer particularly to paying the expenses of any candidate for Parliament or any local government body, the holding of political meetings or the distribution of political literature, and the maintenance of a Member of Parliament or holder of certain public offices. Every member may claim exemption from contributing to the political fund, which must be kept separate from the other funds of the Union. Each member must be given notice of this right to 'contract out', and no one who does not contribute can be made to suffer any penalty or disadvantage on that account. If these rules are not observed, a member may complain to the Registrar, who has power, after hearing both sides, to make such order as he thinks just.

The rules of a Trade Union constitute a contract between the Union and each member. One of the most important parts of that contract from the member's point of view is the power of the Union to expel him, since expulsion so often means deprivation also of livelihood. There is no power of expulsion unless it is expressly provided for by the rules. In every case, it must be exercised in strict accordance with the rules. The slightest departure from the procedure laid down in the rules will make the expulsion invalid. Moreover, there are certain basic principles of natural justice to which a committee (or whoever has the power to expel) must conform, in deciding whether a member is to be expelled or not. The member in question must be told what the charge against him is, and be given a chance of answering it. The committee must reach the decision honestly, and without malice or bias. If there is any departure from the rules or from these principles of natural justice, a member can sue for a declaration and/or an injunction, and may even recover damages from the Union for breach of contract (at least if it is a registered Trade Union). These remedies are available for breach of any of the Union's rules, except that it is not possible to enforce directly any of those domestic agreements specified in the 1871 Act (above) or to recover damages for breach of them.

A registered Trade Union must comply with certain statutory requirements. Its rules must provide for certain things, including the appointment and removal of a committee of management, trustees, and officers, and the inspection of its books by anyone with an interest in its funds. Also, every alteration of its rules must be registered, and approved by the Registrar. Every registered Trade Union must have a registered office. No Trade Union is allowed to be registered in a name which is the same, or nearly the same, as that of another registered Trade Union. A Union may, with the approval in writing of the Chief Registrar of Friendly Societies, and the consent of at least two-thirds of its members, change its name. The Chief Registrar will not give his approval lightly, and there must be shown to be some good cause for the change. Every registered Trade Union must send to the Registrar by June 1st of every year a general statement of its receipts, funds, assets, and expenses. This must be accompanied by a copy of all alterations of rules and new rules, and changes of officers during the preceding year. A registered Trade Union is required to have a trustee (or trustees) and treasurer, besides the committee of management. A secretary is also an essential officer in practice.

All the property of any Trade Union is held in the names of the trustees. They control the Union's funds and look after its litigation. A trustee of a registered Trade Union is not liable for deficiencies generally in the Union's fund, but only has to account for the moneys which he has actually received on behalf of the Union. The treasurer and other officers have to account to the trustees, and hand over money, papers, etc., in their possession at the request of the trustees. There is a special statutory provision which allows a prosecution to be brought in a Magistrates' Court against any person who obtains by false pretences, or wilfully withholds or fraudulently misapplies, funds, books, or other property belonging to a Trade Union. The offender may be ordered to deliver up the property or repay the money, and in addition, if the Court thinks fit, to pay a fine of up to £20.

Trade Unions may amalgamate, provided the following conditions are fulfilled:

(1) a ballot must be taken by each of the Unions at which at least 50 per cent. of the members in each Union cast a vote;

(2) at least 60 per cent. of those voting in each Union must vote for amalgamation;

(3) the notice of amalgamation must be sent to the Registrar, signed by seven members and the secretary of each Union.

There is nothing to prevent a registered Trade Union amalgamating with an unregistered one.

The rules of every registered Trade Union must provide for the manner in which the Union may be dissolved. They must not be such as to make dissolution virtually impossible. On dissolution, the funds that are left, after all the Union's liabilities have been met, are divided between all the existing members, in the proportions to which they have contributed.

Action by or against a registered Trade Union may be brought in the name of its trustees, if such action concerns the property, or a right or claim to the property, of the Union. When the action is in contract, a registered Union may be sued in its registered name, and it may sue, in contract or in tort, in its registered name. When an action is brought by or against an unregistered Trade Union, the procedure is the same as in the case of any large body of persons who have the same interest in certain proceedings brought by or against themselves. A few are chosen to represent the whole, and the action is brought in their names or against them. The Court must authorize the choice of representatives. In the case of a Union, they are usually the trustees and the members of the committee.

FRIENDLY SOCIETIES

A FRIENDLY SOCIETY is a voluntary association formed for the purpose of raising funds by members' subscriptions to enable advances to be made to them in times of need and for similar objects. Statutes dealing with Friendly Societies go back as far as 1793. Those which are operative today are known as the Friendly Societies Acts, 1896 to 1958. The general purpose of these statutes has been to encourage the promotion of thrift by providing for the better management of Friendly Societies and the protection of their funds. The benefit of these statutes generally is reserved to those Societies which are registered.

In order to be eligible for registration under these Acts as a Friendly Society, a society must be formed for the purpose of providing, by means of voluntary subscriptions of members, for one or more of the following purposes:

(1) Relief of members and their families during sickness, or in old age or widowhood;
(2) Insuring money to be paid on the birth of a member's child, or on the death of a member or of the husband or wife, parent or grandparent, of a member;
(3) Relief of members when out of work or in distressed circumstances;
(4) Endowment of members or their nominees at any age or on marriage;
(5) Insuring money to be paid to a member if the member or the husband or wife of the member is alive at a certain specified date in the future;
(6) Insuring members' tools against fire;
(7) Guaranteeing that the Society's officers and servants will perform their duties.

A Trade Union cannot be registered as a Friendly Society, nor do the Friendly Societies Acts apply to Trade Unions, whether they are registered or not.

Generally, registration is voluntary: but a registered Society enjoys certain privileges. It can sue and be sued, and can own land in the names of its trustees. It can carry on life assurance business without being subject to the Assurance Companies Acts of 1909 and 1946. It has priority over the other creditors of its deceased and bankrupt officers, and is exempt from certain stamp duties. Some of the other advantages appear from what follows.

Registered Societies are subject to the supervision of the Chief Registrar of Friendly Societies and his Assistant Registrars. A Society which wishes to be registered must make application to the Central Office, and registration is only effective when the Registrar, being satisfied that the various statutory provisions have been complied with, issues to the Society an 'acknowledgement of registry'.

A Society may have one or more branches, which may be registered independently of the Society. To constitute such a branch, there must be a number of members of a registered Society who are under the control of the central body, have a separate fund administered by themselves, and are also bound to contribute to a fund under the control of the central body.

A registered Society or Branch must have the following officers: a secretary, a treasurer, trustees, a committee of management, and auditors. There may be others. The property of the Society is vested in the trustees, and they are usually the proper persons to sue or be sued on behalf of the Society. The trustees with the consent of the Committee of Management, or of a majority of the members, must invest the Society's funds in such securities as are either expressly directed by the rules, or approved by statute, or within the categories of normal trustee investments.

A member of a registered Society or Branch is guaranteed certain rights. He may inspect the books of the Society, and may nominate a person to whom money payable on his death, up to £200, is to be paid.

An important right enjoyed by the members collectively is that one-fifth of them can apply to the Chief Registrar to appoint an inspector to investigate the affairs of the Society, or to call a special general meeting, or to investigate the Society himself with a view to dissolving it. The Chief Registrar, therefore, has greater powers of control over a registered Friendly Society than he has over a registered Trade Union.

A member of a registered Society or Branch cannot be sued for arrears or current subscriptions, as all payments are voluntary; but fines imposed by the rules for non-payment may be recovered, provided they are reasonable, in a Magistrates' Court. If the rules so provide, a member may be expelled if in arrears for a stated period, or for some other breach of the rules. If, however, a member is wrongly expelled or suffers some other wrong due to the violation of the rules by an officer, it appears that he can sue the Society for damages. There are statutory provisions, which apply to unregistered Societies as well, which relieve members from the effects of failure to pay sums that have fallen due, when such failure is caused by military service.

The rules of a registered Society must provide a method of holding general meetings. Certain transactions can only be carried out by means of a 'special resolution', *e.g.* changing the name, amalgamating with another Society, etc. Such a resolution must be passed initially by a majority of three-quarters of the members present and entitled to vote at a general meeting, and then must be confirmed by a simple majority at a general meeting held between fourteen days and a month later.

The rules must also provide for the manner in which disputes between the member and the Society or the Branch and the Society are to be decided. The method usually provided for is reference to arbitrators or to justices. Once a decision is given in accordance with these rules, there is no appeal. The parties to a dispute may, however, by consent, refer the dispute to the Chief Registrar.

There is also a system of supervision, introduced by Statute, over the finances of a registered Society. Such a Society is required, every five years, to have its assets and liabilities valued and to submit this valuation to the Central Office. Also accounts must be kept and audited at least once a year, and the audited return of receipts and expenditure sent to the registry.

A registered Society may go out of existence in various ways. It may amalgamate with, or transfer its engagements to, another registered Society or to a Company; it may dissolve itself, or the Chief Registrar may, as a result of application by one-fifth of the members, dissolve it. He may also on his own initiative cancel or suspend the registry of the Society in appropriate circumstances.

The 1896 Act imposes penalties for default by a registered Society or its officers in fulfilling their various obligations under the Act. Such penalties are recoverable in the Magistrates' Courts. More important, perhaps, provision is made for the recovery of property or money belonging to a registered Society which has been wrongly obtained, withheld, or misapplied by any person. If such a person has acted with fraudulent intent, he is liable to a fine in addition to being ordered to re-deliver the property or repay the money. This provides the Society with a cheap, quick way of protecting its property, for these proceedings may be brought in a Magistrates' Court.

CARRIAGE OF GOODS

INTRODUCTION

AT COMMON LAW there are two classes of carrier, *viz.* common carriers and private carriers. A common carrier is one who holds himself out as being ready to carry goods (or passengers) as a regular business, *e.g.* the railways: a private carrier undertakes such carriage only as a casual occupation. The

"Common carriers!"

common carrier is bound to carry all goods offered to him by persons willing to pay his reasonable hire, unless (a) he has no room in his vehicles, (b) the goods are not of the kind he professes to carry, (c) the goods are of such a nature as to subject him to extraordinary risk, or (d) the destination is not one to which he usually travels. If he wrongfully refuses to carry any goods he may be prosecuted or sued for damages.

A common carrier—unlike a private carrier, who is only bound to carry with due care—is 'in the nature of an insurer' of the goods he carries. He must make good any loss or damage, whether caused by his negligence or not, unless it be due to:

(a) act of God (*i.e.* a violent natural force, such as a hurricane),
(b) enemy action,
(c) inherent defect in the goods, or
(d) bad packing.

Even at common law a common carrier could limit his liability by expressly contracting with his customer to that effect, and might do so by posting a notice in a conspicuous position or issuing a ticket in such terms.

We shall see, however, that the liability of a common carrier is now generally excluded, in respect of all forms of transport, by various statutes and special contracts, and therefore the distinction between a common carrier and a private carrier is less important than it used to be.

CARRIAGE BY LAND

By the Carriers Act, 1830, it is enacted that no common carrier by land shall be liable for loss or injury to certain articles when the value exceeds £10, unless the value is declared and an increased charge paid. The articles include gold and silver, jewellery, watches, bank-notes, title deeds, paintings, china, and furs.

When a parcel containing any of these articles is delivered to a carrier and its contents declared, the carrier may demand an increased charge, provided that he affixes in a conspicuous part of his office a legible notice stating the increased rate.

Except as provided by the Act, a common carrier cannot limit his liability by public notice. He can still, however, make a special contract with his customer varying his common law liability. If a special contract is made, it will not deprive the carrier of the protection of the Act unless its terms are inconsistent with his having received the goods as a common carrier.

Nothing in the Act protects a common carrier from liability for loss or damage arising from the felonious act (*e.g.* stealing) of any servant or subcontractor of his, or from his own neglect or misconduct. Nor does it exempt him from liability for damage caused by *delay*.

Road

The carriage of goods by road is subject to the licensing of vehicles by the 'Licensing Authority' under the Road Traffic Act, 1960.

A licence is generally necessary for the carriage of goods for hire or reward, or for, or in connection with, a trade or business. (No licence is required, however, for the ordinary delivery by a tradesman of goods sold by him, and there are certain other exceptions.)

There are three classes of licence—'A', 'B', and 'C'.

The 'A' licence, or Public Carriers' Licence, entitles the holder to use authorized vehicles in connection with the general business of a carrier.

The 'B' licence, or Limited Carriers' Licence, entitles the holder to use authorized vehicles for the carriage of goods in connection with any business carried on by him or, subject to any conditions of the licence, for the carriage of other goods for payment. (See below.)

"Nothing in the Act protects a common carrier from liability . . . for damage caused by delay."

The 'C' licence, or Private Carriers' Licence, entitles the holder to use authorized vehicles for the carriage of goods in connection with a business carried on by him, but not other goods for payment.

Thus while 'A' and 'B' licences authorize the carriage of another's goods for payment, a 'C' licence only permits the carriage of goods in connection with the holder's own business. The 'B' licence is intended for the owners of vehicles who use them in the main in their own business, but find they are not fully loaded (particularly on return journeys), and wish to use them partly to carry goods for others, in return for payment.

The Licensing Authority has a wide discretion as to whether to grant 'A' and 'B' licences, and is under a duty to consider first the interests of those requiring transport facilities and then the interests of those providing them. Applications for such licences have to be published by the Licensing Authority, and objections may be made by other carriers, on the ground that the transport services they are already providing are sufficient to meet the demand (or on certain other grounds).

For the purpose of avoiding uneconomic competition, a 'B' licence may be limited as regards the places between which the vehicles may operate, the classes of goods which may be carried, the persons for whom they may be carried, and otherwise. No condition can be imposed, however, as to rates or charges.

An applicant for a licence who is aggrieved by the refusal of the Authority to grant it or by conditions attached to a 'B' licence has a right of appeal to the Transport Tribunal. An objector has a similar right of appeal.

An applicant for a 'C' licence is usually entitled to it as of right.

Rail

Before the Transport Act, 1947, the railway companies had to prepare schedules of charges for the approval of the Railway Rates Tribunal, and were not allowed to give any undue or unreasonable preference to any particular person or type of traffic. The Railway Rates Tribunal also settled the conditions of carriage.

The rates differed according to whether the goods were carried at the company's or at the owner's risk. Company's risk applied unless the owner requested in writing that they should be carried, at a lower rate, at his own risk.

Subject to certain modifications, the Carriers Act, 1830, applied to railway companies.

By the Transport Act, 1947 (as modified by the Transport Act, 1953), a new public corporation, the British Transport Commission, took over the railway companies. It is the duty of the Commission to submit to the Transport Tribunal 'charges schemes' setting out both charges and other terms and conditions (including those relating to liability for loss or damage). The former rules with regard to equality of charges and undue preference do not apply to the Commission, but anyone who wishes to send goods by rail which cannot reasonably be carried by other forms of transport and considers that the charges are unfair may complain to the Transport Tribunal.

Thus the terms on which goods are today carried by rail depend on the 'charges schemes', which supersede both the common law and earlier statutory provisions (such as those contained in the Carriers Act, 1830).

CARRIAGE BY SEA

A carrier by sea could be a common carrier; but it is much more usual for his legal rights and obligations to depend on a special contract relating to the goods he carries. This is called a 'contract of affreightment' ('freight' being the price of the carriage), and may take the form of either (a) a charter-party, or (b) a bill of lading.

A charter-party provides for the hiring of the ship itself; a bill of lading, for the conveyance of goods in it. These two contracts have much in common, and may exist at the same time, as where the charterer wants to be able to sell the goods while they are still in course of carriage, or is himself using the ship as a 'general ship', carrying the goods of third parties under bills of lading.

As between the shipowners and the charterer himself, the terms of the contract of carriage will usually be found in the charter-party, and the main purpose of any bill of lading will be to serve as a receipt for the goods shipped on board. But for an assignee (that is, a person to whom a bill of lading is transferred, such as a purchaser of the goods), the bill of lading will contain the terms of the contract of carriage made with the shipowners, and an assignee is not affected by the charter-party except to the extent that its terms are incorporated in the bill of lading (by such words as 'freight and all other conditions as per charter-party') and are not inconsistent with it.

Charter-parties

A charter-party may be either a voyage charter or a time charter. In the former, the ship is chartered for a specified voyage or voyages, and both the port of loading and the port of discharge are specified (though the charterer may be given the right to order the ship to any port within the limits named in the charter-party). In the latter, the ship may be placed at the charterer's disposal for a specified time from a particular date or from the day on which the ship arrives at a named port, to use for what voyages he chooses for the time the ship is at his disposal.

Charter-parties, while varying from one trade or area to another, to suit the particular conditions, tend to follow a certain form of words and contain expressions to which the Courts, in the course of centuries, have assigned a definite meaning and legal significance. Among these expressions and meanings are the following:

'*Now at*' (*name of port*). If the charterer knows where the ship is at the date of the charter-party, he can work out approximately when it will be at his disposal at the agreed place. Accordingly the statement as to the position of the ship is generally construed as a *condition* (*i.e.* a fundamental term of the contract), and if it proves to be untrue the charterer can rescind the contract in addition to suing for damages.

'*Proceed to* (*Liverpool*) *and there load.*' The owner must bring his ship to the agreed or usual place of loading at the port where the voyage is to commence (unless the charter provides otherwise). The charterer, on receiving notice that the ship is ready to load, must deliver the cargo alongside the ship, and may be liable in damages for delay in producing it. The shipowner is generally responsible for proper stowage.

'*A full and complete cargo.*' As the shipowner is normally paid at the rate of so much per ton carried, he will not want any of his space to be wasted. If the charter specifies the amount to be loaded, a cargo to approximately that amount (say 3 per cent. more if the ship can take it) will suffice, and it is not necessary for the charterer to fill the whole ship; but if he undertakes to load a full and complete cargo within specified limits, he must fill the ship within those limits. Breach of his obligation to load a complete cargo renders a charterer liable for 'dead freight', *i.e.* damages for the unoccupied space, payable at the same rate as if the space had been occupied by cargo.

The charterer is entitled to the full benefit of the ship, so the owner cannot take up space by loading bunker coal intended for a future voyage.

'*Demurrage.*' The proper meaning of this word is the agreed extra payment (usually per day) for the permitted detention of the ship, while loading or unloading, beyond the period specified in the charter-party (or if no period is specified, beyond a reasonable time): but it is also used to describe the damages to which the shipowner is entitled if the ship is detained beyond the period for which a demurrage rate was agreed, or where there was no agreement for demurrage.

The period allowed for loading and unloading is called 'the lay days', and begins to run when the ship arrives at the agreed place and the charterer has notice that she is ready to load or unload. The lay days may be expressly stated, *e.g.* 'thirty running days (Sundays and holidays excepted)', or may be left to be calculated according to the agreed rate of loading, *e.g.* 'at the rate of 100 tons per day'.

If the charterer has agreed to load or unload within a fixed time, he is absolutely obliged to do so, and in the absence of express agreement to the contrary he will not be excused if delay is caused by the crowded state of the docks, dock strikes, bad weather, or other factors beyond his control.

The counterpart of demurrage is '*despatch money*', which the charterer may claim from the shipowner if the loading or unloading is completed early.

'*Always excepted.*' A charter-party always contains a clause setting out 'the excepted perils', *i.e.* those risks for which the shipowner is not to be held liable. These—couched in somewhat archaic terms which have been hallowed by usage—include 'restraints of princes and rulers', 'the Queen's enemies', 'act of God', and 'perils of the sea'.

A blockade or embargo is a 'restraint of princes': and this phrase was held to cover an order of the Argentine government prohibiting the landing of diseased cattle, and the diversion of a ship from Hamburg to a British port, at the suggestion of the Admiralty, on the outbreak of war with Germany.

The term 'Queen's enemies' applies only to foreign enemies in time of war, and not to traitors, pirates, or robbers.

'Perils of the sea' means something beyond the ordinary action of wind and waves; it covers storms, sunken rocks or icebergs, collisions due to the negligence of other ships, entry of water into the ship through a hole made by rats (but not direct damage to cargo by rats), and other maritime accidents of an unexpected nature.

Other matters which are frequently contained in the excepted perils clause are 'barratry of the master and mariners' ('barratry' is any wrongful act wilfully committed by the master or crew to the prejudice of the shipowner or charterer, such as scuttling the ship, smuggling, or mutiny), 'negligence of the master and mariners', 'pirates, robbers, or thieves', and 'jettison'.

An unjustified deviation in the course of the voyage may render the contract

415

of affreightment void; in that case the terms of the charter-party will no longer apply (irrespective of when or where the deviation takes place), and the shipowner will lose the protection of the excepted perils clause. Deviation is, however, justified if it is necessary for the safety of the ship or crew (even though

"An unjustified deviation in the course of a voyage. . . ."

necessitated by unseaworthiness caused by the master). And a ship need not proceed by the shortest route if it is usual and commercially reasonable to use another route, *e.g.* for the purpose of calling at certain ports for bunkering.

Bills of lading

A bill of lading is a document acknowledging the shipment of goods and setting out the terms and conditions of carriage. Where the ship is chartered, and the charterer provides the cargo himself, the bill of lading may be a mere receipt for the goods given by the master: if the charterer takes the goods of others, it contains the contract he makes with them.

In addition to being
(a) a receipt for the goods shipped, and
(b) evidence of the contract for the carriage of the goods, a bill of lading is also
(c) a document of title to the goods specified in it, enabling them to be sold or pledged while still in transit.

It is usual for a less formal document, called a '*mate's receipt*', to be given at the time when the goods are shipped, and for this to be exchanged later for a bill of lading signed by the master. The master normally signs as agent of the shipowners; but where a ship is chartered and then put up as a 'general ship' (*i.e.* for the carriage of the goods of shippers generally, and not merely of the charterer), the master may—in some cases—be the agent of the charterer.

The master can bind the shipowners by any terms which he has express or implied authority to make. But if the ship is chartered, he may not sign bills of lading varying the terms of the charter unless the charter so permits or he obtains express instructions to do so.

A bill of lading which states that the goods are 'in good order and condition' is called a '*clean*' *bill of lading*. The words refer only to the apparent or external condition. If they are untrue, the shipowner will be liable in damages to an assignee of the bill of lading who suffers loss by acting on the faith of the representation.

The person to whom the bill of lading is made out may in most cases assign his rights under it, thus transferring the property in the goods to which it relates, by indorsing—*i.e.* signing—the bill (if it is drawn to 'order') and delivering it to the assignee.

The bill may pass through any number of hands (like a cheque or other negotiable instrument), the ultimate holder being entitled to demand delivery of the goods and to sue on the contract of carriage in case of damage, loss, or delay.

Limitations of liability

The Merchant Shipping Act, 1894 (as amended), gives protection to ship-owners and charterers when goods are lost or damaged *without actual fault on their part* by enabling them to limit their total liability to a sum of so much a ton on the tonnage of the ship calculated on a formula too complicated to be set out here. They have, incidentally, a similar right to limit their total liability in cases of personal injury or loss of life. They are not liable for loss or damage caused by fire. They are not liable for the theft of precious articles, unless there was a written declaration of their true nature and value at the time of shipment. For other loss or damage to goods their liability is limited according to the ship's tonnage.

The Carriage of Goods by Sea Act, 1924, sets out rules determining the responsibilities, liabilities, rights, and immunities attaching to carriers under *bills of lading* in ships carrying goods *from* any port in Great Britain or Northern Ireland.

Under these rules, the undertaking to provide a seaworthy ship is not absolute: but the carrier must exercise due diligence to make the ship sea-worthy and fit for the carriage of goods, and must properly and carefully load, keep, and discharge the goods. He is not responsible (a) for any act, neglect, or default of the master or the carrier's servants in the navigation or management of the *ship* (as opposed to the cargo), (b) for a number of other mishaps set out in the rules (including such events as strikes and lock-outs, which would not exempt him at common law), or (c) for 'any other cause arising without the actual fault or privity of the carrier' or his agents or servants. The rules

417

expressly permit 'any reasonable deviation', and in particular deviation for the purpose of saving life or property.

The rules require that a bill of lading issued by the carrier shall contain certain particulars, and an express statement that it is subject to the rules. Written notice of loss or damage should be given at the time when the goods are discharged, or within three days: and liability comes to an end if an action is not brought within one year after the delivery date.

The carrier's liability is limited to £100 per package unless the bill of lading states the nature and value of the goods (or the parties agree to a higher maximum).

General average

Where a sacrifice is made at sea (*e.g.* by jettisoning cargo in a storm, to save both the ship and the remaining cargo), the loss is borne proportionately by the interests involved—the shipowner in respect of his ship and freight, the charterer (if any) in respect of freight payable to him under the bills of lading, and the cargo owners in respect of their cargo. The contribution made by those who have benefited from such a 'general average act' is called 'general average contribution'. The amount due is settled by 'average adjusters' according to the law of the country where the adjustment is made.

CARRIAGE BY AIR

The carriage of goods (and passengers) by air will henceforth be regulated by Orders in Council made under the Carriage by Air Act, 1961. This statute has replaced the Carriage by Air Act, 1932, which gave effect in English law to the Warsaw Convention of 1929 for the unification of the rules relating to international carriage by air. The Convention was amended at The Hague, and 'the Warsaw Convention as amended at The Hague, 1955' is incorporated in the Act of 1961.

An 'air waybill' is made out in respect of each consignment, giving full particulars of the goods, the place of departure and destination, and so forth, and this constitutes the air carriage equivalent of the bill of lading in carriage by sea.

Subject to his obligations under the contract of carriage, and until such time as the consignee becomes entitled to delivery, the consignor retains all rights of disposal of the goods, as by withdrawing them at the place of departure or destination, stopping them in transit, calling for them to be delivered to a person other than the named consignee, or requiring them to be returned. Unless the consignor has stopped the goods, the consignee is entitled to delivery of them on payment of the charges due and on complying with any conditions set out in the air waybill.

The carrier must notify the consignee as soon as the goods arrive. If he admits having lost them, or if they have not arrived seven days after the due date, the consignee may sue him.

Subject to the exemptions mentioned below, the carrier is liable for any loss of—or damage to—goods which occurs during the carriage by air (*i.e.* while they are in his charge at an aerodrome or in the air). His liability is limited (at present to about £6 per kilogramme), unless the consignor has at the time of handing over the package to the carrier made a special declaration of value and paid any additional charge, or unless it is proved that the damage resulted from an act (or omission) of the carrier or his agent or servant acting within the scope of his employment, done with intent to cause damage, or recklessly and with knowledge that damage would probably result. The carrier is also liable for delay in the carriage of goods.

"In the case of damage to cargo, a written complaint must be made. . . ."

The carrier is exempt from liability if he and his agents or servants took all necessary measures to avoid the damage, or if such measures were impossible.

Any provision in the contract of carriage which tends to relieve the carrier of liability or fixes a lower limit of liability is null and void.

In the case of damage to cargo, a written complaint must be made to the carrier within fourteen days of receipt, and in the case of delay within twenty-one days. Otherwise the carrier, unless guilty of fraud, cannot be sued.

The right to recover damages is lost if an action is not commenced within two years.

BILLS OF EXCHANGE, CHEQUES, AND PROMISSORY NOTES

INTRODUCTION

THE LAW relating to bills of exchange, cheques, and promissory notes, which may be described collectively as 'negotiable instruments', is mainly to be found in the Bills of Exchange Act, 1882. They are all substitutes for money, invented by the commercial world, recognized by the old 'law merchant', and finally incorporated into the ordinary law of the land.

They are substitutes for money in that they can eventually be converted into the amounts of money which they represent. Their usefulness lies principally in their negotiability. This means that like money (and unlike other forms of property, such as leases, mortgages, or stocks and shares) they can be transferred from one holder to another by mere delivery, or signature (endorsement) and delivery, with the effect of transferring the property in them, that is, the right to the money they represent. Moreover, anyone who gives value for a negotiable instrument (*i.e.* does not receive it as a gift), and who takes it in good faith, will not be affected by any defect in the title of the person from whom he gets it, *i.e.* it will not matter if that person had no right to it, *e.g.* had stolen it.

This is an exception to the usual rule of law that no one can give to another a better title than he himself possesses. If a person sells to a jeweller a watch which he has found in the street, the watch does not become the property of the jeweller, but can be claimed from him by the rightful owner: and if the jeweller has sold it, he can be sued for its value. On the other hand, if a person is dishonest enough to buy groceries with a cheque made payable to bearer which he has found in the street, the grocer will not be liable, after he has received payment on the cheque, to refund the money to the rightful owner of the cheque or to the person on whose account it was drawn. In this respect, as in others, the cheque resembles actual money.

Bills of exchange

A bill of exchange, which is a form of payment especially useful and common in international trade, is an order in writing, requiring the person to whom it is addressed to pay a certain sum of money to a specified person (or his order, *i.e.* as he may direct) or to bearer. There are three parties involved—the *drawer* who makes the order, the *drawee* to whom it is addressed, and the *payee* in whose favour it is made.

The order may be to pay on demand, or at a fixed future date, or so many weeks or months after 'presentation' to the person liable on it. It must not have any conditions attached to it (such as 'pay if the goods are in sound

420

condition'): for this would obviously make it less readily transferable. The fact that a bill of exchange may be—and generally is—payable at some future time makes it especially useful as a means of obtaining credit for goods for which the buyer may not be able to pay until he has himself, perhaps after processing them in some way, re-sold them. The seller, while giving the buyer the necessary time to pay, is able to obtain payment himself without waiting for the bill to 'mature', by 'discounting' it, *i.e.* selling it (in effect) to a bank or 'discount house', which pays him the amount of the bill less a discount (in the nature of interest) for the advance payment. The discount house then presents the bill to the buyer at the time when payment of it is due.

The drawee of a bill of exchange is only liable on it if he 'accepts' it, *i.e.* indicates his intention to pay it by writing 'Accepted', together with his signature, across the face of the bill. The drawee thereby becomes the '*acceptor*', and is the person primarily liable on the bill. If he does not pay, the drawer is bound to pay. The bill may be 'negotiated' by the payee, and so pass through the hands of a number of subsequent holders. Anyone who 'endorses' the bill (*i.e.* puts his signature on the back) in the course of negotiating it—or otherwise (for example, to 'accommodate' a party to the bill, by guaranteeing its payment)—thereby undertakes the same obligation as the drawer, that is, to pay it if the drawee does not.

Thus, if A. sells goods to B., B. may draw a bill of exchange on C. (who perhaps owes B. money, or has undertaken to finance him), in favour of A., for the price of the goods. If C. accepts the bill, he becomes primarily liable to A. or to whoever subsequently holds it. A. then, let us suppose, endorses the bill over to X. (that is, signs it on the back and hands it to X., perhaps in payment for goods supplied by X. to A., or because X. is discounting the bill for him), X. endorses it over to Y., and Y. to Z. If payment is refused when the bill is presented by the ultimate holder Z. to the acceptor C., Z. can demand payment from—and if necessary sue—not only C. but also B. as drawer, and X. and Y. as endorsers.

Cheques

A cheque is a special type of bill of exchange. It is always *drawn on a banker* and *payable on demand*. The banker never 'accepts' a cheque, and so never assumes any obligation toward the payee or holder. But a bank is under a duty to its customer to pay the cheques which he draws, provided his account is in credit or arrangements have been made for an overdraft. If a bank wrongly refuses to pay a customer's cheque, it will be liable to pay damages for the injury done to his credit, and in the case of a trader these damages will be substantial. A customer may countermand payment, *i.e.* 'stop' a cheque, in which case the bank must refuse payment (the cheque being 'Referred to drawer'). The bank's duty and authority to pay cheques are also ended when it gets notice of the customer's death or bankruptcy.

Promissory notes

A promissory note is a promise in writing, signed by the maker, to pay a certain sum of money to a specified person (or his order) or to bearer. Whereas a bill is an order to someone else to pay, a note is a promise to pay oneself.

Initially, therefore, there are only two, and not three, parties to it, though as in the case of a bill or cheque a number of persons may become liable on it through endorsement.

RULES RELATING TO
NEGOTIABLE INSTRUMENTS GENERALLY

We must now consider the rules which are common to all these types of negotiable instrument, before turning to more detailed consideration of each one in turn.

"A person must know the nature of the document he (or she) is signing. . . ."

No one can be held liable on a bill, cheque, or note unless his signature appears on it. Moreover, a person must know the *nature* of the document he is signing. If he is deceived into believing that he is signing as witness to a share transfer when in fact he is signing a promissory note, his signature will not bind him: but he will be bound to pay a holder in due course (see below) the full amount of, say, £10,000 which is stated on the note, if he knew he was signing a note, even though he did not have his glasses with him at the time and was deceived into thinking that the note was only for £1,000! In other words, he is responsible for his own folly in signing a negotiable instrument when he could not read clearly.

A person who signs a negotiable instrument is bound, even though he chooses to sign in a fictitious name. An agent may bind his principal by signing the principal's name, provided he has authority to do so. A company, of course, can only sign through the medium of its agents. An agent may add his own name as well, but if he does so he should be careful to add 'per pro.' or some other words to show that he is acting as an agent only. Otherwise, he may find himself personally liable on the instrument. A member of a trading partnership has power to bind his partners by signing the firm's name without express authority to do so.

Negotiable instruments require to be stamped with a 2d stamp. A fine of £10 may be imposed for issuing or negotiating a bill or note that is not stamped, and such a bill or note cannot be sued on or put in evidence.

Payment of a negotiable instrument cannot be enforced unless at some stage consideration was given for it (though for this purpose it may be 'past consideration' such as payment for goods already delivered or discharge of an existing debt). This means that some holder of the instrument must have given value for it. It is not necessary for the person who sues to have given value himself. Thus an engaged couple who are given a cheque as a wedding present cannot sue the drawer if it is dishonoured, no consideration having been given for it. If, however, they endorse it over to a shopkeeper in payment for some article, the shopkeeper can sue on the cheque if it is dishonoured; and so also can anyone to whom the shopkeeper may give the cheque as a present, because at one stage in its history (namely, when the shopkeeper supplied goods in exchange for it) consideration was given for it.

The consideration must not be illegal. A holder who gives illegal consideration for an instrument cannot enforce it; nor can any subsequent holder who takes it with knowledge of the prior illegality. An instrument which is given to pay a gambling debt, for instance, is deemed to be given for an illegal consideration. A bookmaker, therefore, has no legal rights on a cheque received from a client if it is dishonoured.

Any defect in title of any parties to the instrument, and any personal defence available to prior parties as between themselves, will not defeat the claim of a 'holder in due course'. A 'holder in due course' is defined as a holder of the cheque or bill of exchange, etc., who takes it when it is complete and regular on the face of it, in good faith and for value, before it is overdue, and without notice either of its previous dishonour or of any defect in the title of the person who negotiated it to him. (As an instrument is not 'negotiated' to the original payee, he cannot be a holder in due course.) Thus it is immaterial, so far as a holder in due course is concerned, that at some stage—whether at the time it was issued or in the course of negotiation—there was an element of fraud or illegality in the history of the instrument: the holder in due course is entitled to be paid.

A bill or note is 'issued' when delivered complete in form by the drawer or maker to the payee. If it is made payable to bearer, it can be negotiated without endorsement. If it is made payable to a specified person (or his order), it must be endorsed—save that the Cheques Act, 1957, provides that a person who pays into his own bank account a cheque made payable to himself need not endorse it. The holder of an instrument may endorse in blank or specially. To endorse in blank, he merely signs his name on the back: and the instrument then becomes payable to bearer. To endorse specially, he must also indicate the name of the person who is to be paid: and that person must himself endorse in order to receive payment or negotiate the instrument further. Every holder can choose whether to endorse specially or in blank.

Instruments made payable to a specified person are safer than those payable to bearer. If an endorsement is forged on a bill, cheque, or note, not only does the forger himself not get a good title, but no other person into whose hands it subsequently comes can claim against the drawer or maker, or against anyone who was a party to the document before the forgery was committed. A holder who has received payment in good faith, but whose title is derived through a forged endorsement, may be compelled to return the money paid. And a person who pays out on a forged bill or cheque remains liable to the true owner, and cannot debit the drawer with the amount (save that a banker has statutory protection with regard to forged endorsements: see below).

An endorsement should correspond with the description of the payee on the bill or note. If the payee is wrongly described or his name is misspelt, he may endorse the bill as he is described, adding his proper signature if he wishes to.

We now turn to the individual types of negotiable instrument.

Bills of exchange

Here is an example of a bill of exchange:

London, January 1st, 1962

£500   Three months after date pay X.Y. or order the
(Stamp)   sum of five hundred pounds sterling for value
(2*d*)   received.

                            (Signed) A. B.

To O. P.
London

As we have seen, the drawee of a bill (O. P. in the above example) only becomes liable when he accepts it. The holder of a bill must formally present it to the drawee for acceptance if the bill is made payable a certain time after sight (the time when it is so presented being the time when it is 'seen'), or if the bill expressly requires presentment, or if it is made payable elsewhere than at the residence or place of business of the drawee. In other cases, the bill need not be presented to the drawee until the time comes for payment. Presentment must be made at a reasonable hour on a business day before the bill is overdue. Presentment is excused if the drawee is dead or bankrupt (or is a fictitious person), and also if it cannot be effected despite diligent efforts by the holder. The drawee has twenty-four hours from presentment within which to accept. If he does not accept, the bill is dishonoured, and the holder may proceed straightaway against the drawer or (if the bill has been negotiated) against any endorsers.

The drawee may give a general or a qualified acceptance. He may qualify his acceptance by, for example, making payment conditional on the happening of some event, such as the arrival of a cargo or receipt of a bill of lading, or by agreeing to pay only part of the amount for which the bill is drawn: or he may introduce a stipulation as to the time or place of payment (writing across it, for instance, 'Accepted payable at Lloyd's Bank, Law Courts Branch, only').

The holder is always entitled to refuse a qualified acceptance, and if he is prepared to take it must do so with the consent of the drawer and endorsers: otherwise, their liability on the bill will cease.

The acceptor is under the duty to pay the bill, according to the terms of his acceptance, to the payee or to any holder to whom it has been validly negotiated. (It may be noted, in passing, that bills of exchange are sometimes called 'acceptances'.)

The drawer and endorsers, whose undertaking is to pay if the drawee does not, become liable only if the bill has been presented to the drawee for payment and has not been paid. A drawer is liable even without presentment if the drawee is under no duty, as between himself and the drawer, to accept or pay the bill, and the drawer has no reason to suppose that the bill would be paid if presented.

When a bill has been dishonoured, either by non-acceptance or by non-payment, the holder may immediately claim, in the former case against the drawer and endorsers, and in the latter case against the acceptor, drawer, and endorsers. But the drawer and endorsers have a right to be given notice of dishonour, as a rule, and those who do not receive the requisite notice are freed from liability. The reason why notice is required is to enable the person to whom notice is given to take steps promptly to protect his own interests. If, for example, he has endorsed a bill, due for payment on April 1st, and does not hear of its non-acceptance or non-payment until the end of the month, he may by that time have lost the opportunity of enforcing his remedies against the drawer or earlier endorsers. Notice must be given within a reasonable time (which means within a day or two). The prudent holder will give immediate notice to all those against whom he may wish to proceed.

Cheques

A cheque, as we have seen, is a bill of exchange which is drawn on a banker and payable on demand. Many of the rules which apply to other types of bills of exchange have no relevance to cheques: and conversely, cheques are subject to many special rules relating to the obligations of bankers and the protection afforded them by statute.

It is a common practice to write 'Cash' (or 'Wages' or 'Office') after the word 'Pay' on a cheque form. Strictly speaking, in such cases there is no payee, and the document is not a cheque at all: but it is obviously a direction to pay bearer, and the bank will treat it as such.

'Blank cheques' can be very dangerous. If the recipient of a blank cheque (*i.e.* one on which the amount is not filled in) inserts a greater amount than he should, a person who subsequently takes the cheque for value without knowing of the fraud will be entitled to payment of the full amount.

The amount of a cheque should be denoted both in words and in figures; but in case of a discrepancy, preference is given to the words.

A cheque may be '*open*' or '*crossed*'. A cheque is crossed when two parallel lines are drawn diagonally across it, with or without the words '& Co.' written between them. A crossed cheque can only be paid to a banker. This means that it can only be properly cashed by being paid into an account at a bank, which then collects payment of it on behalf of its customer. The crossing of a cheque is thus a safeguard against theft and forgery. For this reason banks encourage their customers to cross their cheques, and commonly supply cheque-books with a crossing already printed on them. A customer who wants to get cash at his bank for one of these has only to strike out the crossing and write 'Pay cash' on the cheque and add his signature to this direction: for the drawer (but nobody else) is entitled to 'open' a crossed cheque.

A cheque may be *crossed* '*specially*' by writing the name of a bank between the diagonal lines. The effect of this is that the cheque can be safely paid to that bank only. Every holder of a cheque is entitled to cross it generally or specially: and it is a wise precaution to take if there is any risk of the cheque going astray.

A banker who pays a crossed cheque to someone other than another banker (or, in the case of a special crossing, the named banker) is liable to the true owner of the cheque for any loss he may sustain: but the banker will be excused if the crossing was not apparent or was obliterated.

A crossed cheque may be marked 'Not negotiable'. Such a cheque may still be transferred from one holder to another, but (contrary to the general rule of negotiability) no holder can get a better title than his predecessor had. Thus in one case a partnership agreement provided that all partnership money should be paid to partner A. Partner B. received a cheque payable to the firm and marked 'Not negotiable'. X. in good faith cashed it for him. It was held that X. must pay the amount of the cheque to A.

The words '*Account payee*' on a cheque do not make the cheque non-transferable, but put upon the bank which collects payment on behalf of any person other than the original payee the duty of proper inquiry as to that person's authority to receive it, and if they are negligent they may be liable to the true owner for the amount of the cheque. The only effective way of preventing the transfer of a cheque (or other negotiable instrument) is to write the word '*only*' after the name of the payee: the mere omission of the words 'or order' does not make the cheque non-transferable.

A bank runs the risk of having to bear losses caused by fraudulent dealings with cheques. It is bound to know its own customer's signature, and if it pays a cheque on which the drawer's signature is forged it cannot normally debit its customer with the amount. (In one case a customer who knew that his wife was forging his signature on cheques did not inform his bank until after her death: in those exceptional circumstances it was held that the bank was not liable to him.) Furthermore, if the amount of a genuine cheque is fraudulently increased, the bank must bear the loss of the excess, unless the drawer has by his own negligence facilitated the alteration, *e.g.* by writing the amount in a way which makes it easy to insert extra words and figures.

A bank may also have to pay out to a true owner who has suffered loss through the bank's dealing with his cheque. Banks have, however, been granted some measure of exemption from the usual consequences of conversion. A banker is protected if in good faith, and in the ordinary course of business, he pays a cheque which is not endorsed, or is improperly endorsed, or bears a forged endorsement. He is protected both in the sense that he does not incur liability to the true owner of the cheque and in the sense that he is entitled to debit the drawer with the amount.

So far as the collecting bank is concerned (that is, the bank which collects payment of a cheque for its customer), this statutory protection originally applied only to crossed cheques: but it has been extended, by the Cheques Act, 1957, to cheques of every kind, as well as to other instruments in the nature of cheques. Where a banker, in good faith and without negligence, receives payment for a customer of a cheque (or similar instrument), and the customer has no title or a defective title, the banker incurs no liability to the true owner. The banker must, however, show that he was not negligent. Thus he would be expected to make inquiries if a cheque payable to a customer's employers were paid into the customer's own account. A banker must also satisfy himself so far as is possible as to the honesty of a new customer, and if he fails to do so he may lose his statutory protection in respect of cheques collected on the customer's behalf.

The Act of 1957 specifically provides that failure by a bank to detect an irregularity in—or absence of—endorsement shall not amount to negligence. This has to a large extent relieved banks of the onerous duty of scrutinizing endorsements, whether they are collecting or paying cheques.

The question whether a bank can recover money which it has paid in error is a difficult one. The general rule is that money paid under a mistake of law cannot be recovered, but money paid under a mistake of fact can be. The mistake of fact must, however, be as between the payer of the money and the recipient. Thus money paid on a cheque in the mistaken belief that the drawer's account is in credit cannot be reclaimed once payment is complete (which is when the money is placed on the counter, and touched by the recipient), for the mistake here is as between the bank and the drawer. Money paid out on a negotiable instrument must be reclaimed immediately if it is to be recovered at all.

There are, however, two exceptions to this rule. First, money can always be recovered from one who receives it knowing that he is not entitled to it; and secondly, money paid on a cheque (or bill) on which the signature of the drawer (or acceptor) is forged is always recoverable. Money paid to an agent, for example, to a bank collecting on behalf of a customer, may be recovered before the agent transfers the money to his principal or otherwise prejudices his position: and in this connection a bank which merely credits a customer's account with the amount received is not deemed to have transferred it as yet.

A customer cannot demand to have his cheques cashed at any branch of the bank, but only at the one where he keeps his account. Different branches of the same bank are treated as separate for some purposes, but not for all. Thus, if a customer has an account at two branches, the balance at one may be used to reduce his overdraft at the other, unless there is in force an agreement to the contrary. (See pp. 453–456 on cheques and receipts.)

Promissory notes (and I.O.U.s)

A typical example of a promissory note would be:

London, January 1*st*, 1962

£100   Three months after date I promise to pay X. Y.

(Stamp)   or order one hundred pounds.

(2*d*)   (Signed) A. B.

A promissory note, unlike a bill of exchange, may be made by two or more persons, whose liability may be either joint or joint and several. If the note states, 'We promise to pay . . .', it is joint: if 'I promise . . .', it is joint and several. In the former case, all the makers must be sued together: in the latter, the holder can sue one without suing the others.

Presentment is not usually necessary in the case of a promissory note (unless it is payable in a specified place only) to render the maker of the note liable: but it is always necessary to render an indorser liable.

"An I.O.U. is merely evidence of the state of accounts between the parties to it."

Unlike a cheque or bill, a promissory note is a continuing security, and will not be overdue as against the maker merely because it has not been presented for payment within a reasonable time of its being issued or becoming payable. In cases where presentment for payment is necessary, the limitation period will not commence to run until that has taken place. The Stamp duty on a promissory note used to vary according to the amount of the money promised, but since the Finance Act, 1961, the stamp on bills of exchange and promissory notes is a fixed stamp of 2*d*. An adhesive stamp may be used. It must be cancelled by the person by whom it is signed before he delivers the note.

A promissory note is not to be confused with an I.O.U. A promissory note (as the name implies) is a *promise* to pay money, and not merely—like an I.O.U.—an acknowledgement that it is owing. A promissory note is negotiable, that is (as we have seen) transferable by delivery—or endorsement and delivery—from one person to another, so as to entitle the ultimate holder to claim the money promised in it from the maker (or, if he dishonours it, from previous endorsers): an I.O.U., on the other hand, is not negotiable. An I.O.U. is merely evidence of the state of accounts between the parties to it. The creditor cannot sue *on* the I.O.U. (as the holder of a promissory note sues on the note): he can only sue for the debt in respect of which the I.O.U. was given, using the I.O.U. as evidence, and not as the cause of action.

No stamp is needed on an I.O.U.—unless it incorporates the terms of an agreement or contains an express promise to pay, in which case it should be stamped as an agreement or as a promissory note.

CONTRACTS OF GUARANTEE (SURETYSHIP)

A CONTRACT OF GUARANTEE is an undertaking by one person to be answerable for the 'debt, default or miscarriage' of another, and is usually one whereby a third person, who is called the *guarantor* or *surety*, undertakes to discharge a debtor's liability to his creditor if the debtor himself fails to do so. (Guarantee in this sense is, of course, entirely different from the 'guarantee' given by the manufacturer or seller of goods, which is a warranty as to their quality.)

A familiar example is the guarantee which a bank may require before allowing a customer to overdraw. If Mr Jones is known to be a substantial business man, while it is doubtful whether Mrs Jones has means of her own, the bank may be willing to grant her overdraft facilities provided that her husband signs a guarantee, but not otherwise. Or again, goods may be supplied to a limited company of doubtful financial status on the terms that its directors personally guarantee payment for the goods, so that if the company is insolvent, or for any reason fails to pay, a claim for the amount due may be made against the directors themselves.

A contract of guarantee must be evidenced in writing: if there is no memorandum of its terms, signed by the guarantor or his agent, it is unenforceable against him. In this respect a contract of guarantee must be distinguished from a contract of indemnity, which does not require to be evidenced in writing. In a contract of indemnity there are only two parties, the creditor and the person giving the indemnity: and the person giving the indemnity has some interest in the transaction apart from the indemnity (for example, a *del credere* agent).

The guarantor's liability is secondary, in the sense that it only arises if the principal debtor, who is primarily liable, makes default.

LIABILITY OF THE SURETY OR GUARANTOR

A surety or guarantor—the words mean the same thing—can avoid liability under the guarantee if he can show that he was not informed of facts which in

429

the circumstances ought to have been disclosed to him by the person to whom the guarantee is given, such as the previous dishonesty of a servant whose fidelity he guarantees.

The surety is only liable if the terms of his obligation are strictly observed. If, for example, he agrees to be only one of several co-sureties, he will not be under any liability unless the others execute the guarantee: and any other conditions on which his liability depends must be fulfilled before the creditor can have recourse against him. However, unless the contract of guarantee expressly provides to the contrary, the surety can be sued without being given notice of the debtor's default and without any prior claim being made or proceedings taken by the creditor against the debtor.

A guarantee may be intended to cover a single transaction only (such as payment for goods to be supplied on a particular occasion), or it may be a continuing guarantee (as for goods to be supplied from time to time up to a specified total). If it is continuing, it remains in being until it is revoked, and is not exhausted by the first advance up to the limit of the amount guaranteed. For instance, suppose Mr Jones guarantees his wife's overdraft up to £500. If she overdraws up to that limit, but then reduces the overdraft by payments in, her husband's guarantee will continue to cover future drawings up to the limit of £500, and will not be terminated by reason of her previous overdrawing to the full amount of the guarantee.

SURETY'S RIGHTS AGAINST CREDITOR

The surety may, at any time after the guaranteed debt has become due, and even before he has been called upon to pay it, require the creditor to claim it from the debtor. The reason for this is, of course, that the surety stands to lose if there is delay in the collection of payment, for the debtor may in the meantime abscond or become insolvent; and the surety is entitled to protect himself against that risk. He must, however, undertake to indemnify the creditor for any expense incurred in claiming from the debtor, and he cannot compel the creditor to *sue* the debtor before he is himself sued on the guarantee.

If the surety is sued, he may rely on any set-off or counter-claim on which the debtor could have relied against the creditor.

On payment of the amount due under the guarantee, the surety steps into the shoes of the creditor (in legal parlance he is 'subrogated' to the rights of the creditor) so far as the guaranteed debt is concerned, and can claim it from the debtor; and he is entitled to have assigned to him every judgment or security held by the creditor in respect of the debt.

SURETY'S RIGHTS AGAINST DEBTOR

The surety has a legal right to call on the debtor to pay off the debt as soon as it is ascertained and due.

If any payment has been made by the surety, he is entitled to be indemnified by the debtor. This right of indemnity may be expressly contained in the contract of guarantee, or it may be implied whenever the guarantee has been undertaken at the request, express or implied, of the debtor. It arises as soon as a payment has been made under the guarantee, the surety becoming a creditor of the debtor for the amount he has paid and interest. He cannot, however, recover the costs of an action brought against him on the guarantee, unless he was authorised by the debtor to defend the action and there were reasonable grounds of defence.

If the surety is sued, he can claim an indemnity against the debtor in the same action.

RIGHTS OF CO-SURETIES

One of several sureties who has paid more than his share under the guarantee is entitled to contribution from his co-sureties, whether they are bound by the same or different instruments, and whether he knew of the existence of co-sureties or not at the time when he agreed to be bound.

If his sureties have not guaranteed equal amounts, he can claim contribution from each of them in proportion to the amount guaranteed.

Before recovering contribution, however, he must bring into account any securities which he may have received from the creditor in respect of the debt. Thus if A. and B. guarantee C.'s account at the bank, and A. then pays off C.'s overdraft and receives from the bank the securities which C. had deposited against the overdraft, A. can only recover contribution from B. if he brings into account the value of those securities. And the same rule applies when a surety who claims contribution has received security from the debtor himself.

DISCHARGE OF SURETY

A surety is discharged from his obligation if without his consent the contract between creditor and debtor is varied. For except in those cases where the variation is clearly immaterial to the surety (or necessarily beneficial to him), he is entitled to be consulted.

The surety is discharged if the creditor makes a binding contract to give time to the debtor, though not if he merely omits to press him for payment or delays suing him. If, however, the creditor, when giving time to the debtor, expressly reserves his rights against the surety, the surety is not discharged. In this case, the creditor can press the surety for payment, and the surety can press the debtor: so the agreement to give time to the debtor may be of little value.

The surety is also discharged if the creditor omits to do anything which he is bound to do for the surety's protection, as, for example, if he fails (where necessary) to register a deed giving security, so as to lose the benefit of the security. So, too, if the creditor relinquishes any security he holds in respect of the guaranteed debt. For the surety, on payment of the debt, is, as we have seen, entitled to have handed over to him all the securities held by the creditor in respect of the debt.

If the creditor discharges the debtor, whether expressly or impliedly, the surety will also be discharged. Thus in one case, where goods were let on hire-purchase by X. to Y., Z. guaranteeing the payment of the instalments, it was held that Z. could not be sued on the guarantee after X. had seized the goods (the instalments being in arrear), because under that particular hire-purchase agreement the seizure of the goods released the debtor from liability. In the same way, if a lease is determined before the expiration of the term, the guarantor of rent payable under it is discharged from liability. However, a surety is not discharged if the debtor goes bankrupt and is then discharged from bankruptcy.

A surety is discharged if the creditor discharges a co-surety or in any way prejudices the surety's right of contribution from his co-sureties.

A guarantee cannot be revoked (save by mutual consent) if the consideration for it was given once for all. If, for example, a fidelity bond (a guarantee as to the honesty of a servant or agent) is given to a prospective employer, and in consequence the servant or agent is employed by him, the surety cannot revoke the guarantee, and even after his death his estate will be liable on it. A continuing guarantee can, however, be revoked in respect of future transactions, and the surety is thenceforth discharged.

MONEYLENDING

THE PURPOSE of the Moneylenders Acts, 1900 and 1927, is to regulate the business of moneylending, so as to protect borrowers from extortionate rates of interest and other forms of oppression.

A moneylender is defined as a person who carries on the *business* of money-lending. This definition excludes one who may from time to time lend money to his friends (even at interest): and expressly excluded are friendly societies, banks, insurance companies, and persons carrying on, in good faith, any business in the course of which money is lent, but which does not have as its primary object the lending of money.

A moneylender must take out an annual licence in respect of every address at which he carries on his business. To qualify for this, he must first obtain a certificate from the Magistrates' Court of the district. The certificate must show his true name, and the name under which, and address at which, he is authorized to carry on business. A certificate can only authorize a moneylender to carry on business at one address: so a separate certificate must be taken out in respect of each licence.

The necessity to apply for a certificate imposes a form of control over moneylenders: for a certificate may be refused if the application is opposed on sufficient grounds, *e.g.* that the moneylender is not of good character. If a certificate is suspended or forfeited, the licence becomes suspended or void.

A moneylender who carries on business without a valid licence is liable to heavy penalties (including imprisonment), and any moneylending contract into which he enters is void.

All business must be carried on under the authorized name and at the authorized address, and all agreements must be made and securities taken in that name. All documents issued by a moneylender must bear his authorized name, and must not suggest that his business is banking.

A moneylender may not send out circulars inviting people to borrow or employ agents or canvassers.

Before any money is given or security taken by a moneylender, a memorandum or note setting out the date of the loan, the amount lent and the rate of interest, and all other terms of the contract, must be signed by the borrower; *and a copy must be sent to him within seven days*. Neither principal nor interest can be recovered, nor can the security be enforced, if this is not done.

A moneylender may not make any charge for the expenses of the contract. An agreement to pay any sum in this regard is void, and any sum so paid can be recovered by the borrower or set off against the loan. It is not permitted to charge compound interest. If there is default in the payment of any sum due, no increased rate of interest can be charged, but only simple interest at the ordinary rate on the sum in default. Any agreement to the contrary is void, and any sum so paid can be recovered or set off by the borrower.

It is illegal for a moneylender to make any charge for negotiating or granting a loan, and any sum so charged may be set off or recovered by the borrower or intending borrower.

After the loan is made, a moneylender must, on written request and on payment of one shilling, supply the borrower with a statement showing (i) the date, amount, and rate of interest of the loan, (ii) the date and amount of all payments by the borrower, (iii) the amount of all sums due but unpaid, with the dates when they became due and the amount of interest which is due and unpaid on them, and (iv) the amount and date of all future payments due from the borrower.

The moneylender must also, on written request and on payment of a reasonable sum for expenses, supply the borrower with copies of all documents.

If he fails to comply with any such request within a month, he cannot sue for any sum due or charge interest until he has done so.

A moneylender's right to take proceedings either to recover money lent and interest, or to enforce a security is barred within twelve months from the date on which the cause of action accrued, *i.e.* when repayment becomes due. However, where payments become due from time to time in one transaction, the limitation period does not begin to run until the last instalment is due. If during the twelve months the debtor acknowledges in writing the amount due and undertakes in writing to pay it, the moneylender has twelve months from then in which to sue. This short limitation period prevents a moneylender from allowing heavy interest charges to mount up.

The Court has power to reopen moneylending transactions when (a) the interest charged is excessive or the amounts charged for bonuses or commission are excessive, and (b) the transaction is harsh and unconscionable, or 'is otherwise such that a court of equity would grant relief'. The Court may then either cancel the whole transaction, or vary any of its terms and order an account to be taken on the basis of the new terms (*e.g.* a lower rate of interest), and will order the borrower to pay any sum which may be found due on that basis.

This relief may be obtainable by the borrower when he is sued: or he can himself apply at any time to have the transaction reopened.

A moneylending transaction may be held to be harsh and unconscionable solely on account of the excessive rate of interest or because of other circumstances as well.

If the rate of interest *exceeds* 48 *per cent. per annum, there is a presumption that it is harsh and unconscionable.* The onus would then be on the moneylender to justify it, as he might by showing, for example, that no security was given, or that the borrower had no financial prospects, or that the loan was for a very short period.

On the other hand, the Court may well be satisfied that interest at a smaller rate than 48 per cent. is excessive, if, for example, the moneylender made misstatements during the negotiations, or the borrower was too stupid to understand the terms of the transaction, and the moneylender appeared to have taken advantage of the borrower's obvious ignorance.

BAILMENTS

A BAILMENT (the word comes from the old French *bailler*, 'to deliver') occurs whenever the owner of an article puts it in the hands of another for a limited period for a particular purpose. In other words, a bailment may be defined as a temporary transfer of possession for a special purpose.

Bailments may be classified according to the purpose for which the transfer is made. It may be intended that the recipient should merely keep the article safe for the owner, or he may be given it to use or to work on. Another division, and one of greater significance from the legal point of view, is into bailments which are gratuitous, *i.e.* made on a friendly basis without payment on either side, and bailments of a commercial type for which one of the parties receives payment. As we shall see, this distinction is very relevant to the question of how much care the recipient or bailee is required to take of the article.

DEPOSIT

Possibly the most common type of bailment is the deposit of an article with another for safe-keeping. The liability of the bailee in respect of the article deposited with him varies according to whether he is receiving payment for his trouble or not. If he is not being paid, he is only required to conform to that

434

standard of care which a reasonably prudent man would exercise in respect of his own property. It would seem, indeed, that if the owner is content to leave his property with someone who is notoriously careless, he cannot complain if the bailee shows no greater diligence in safeguarding the other's property than he would show in safeguarding his own. In any case, the depositee who receives no reward is only liable for such loss or injury as results from his gross negligence or fraud, or from not following the owner's instructions. Even though he is unpaid, he is not entitled to use the article left with him, and if he does so without the owner's express consent, he is liable for any loss or damage resulting from his unauthorized use. He is bound to return the article on the owner's demand.

"The most common type of bailment is the deposit of an article with another for safe keeping."

A person may be an involuntary bailee, if goods are delivered to his premises without any request by him. This situation may arise when goods are delivered by mistake, or in the hope that the recipient will agree to buy them. In such a case, he should not use the goods, but is not liable for their safe custody. If someone arrives claiming to be the owner, he can safely hand them over to him.

Persons who receive goods for safe-keeping in return for payment are required to conform to a higher standard. Warehousemen, railway left-luggage officers, and those who store furs or furniture fall into this category. They must use such care as a vigilant man would take of his own property of a similar kind. The question of liability will most often arise when the goods have been

435

stolen while in the bailee's possession. In these circumstances, it is necessary to examine the precautions which were taken to guard against theft. Obviously these precautions must be greater in the case of more valuable articles such as jewellery, which in the ordinary way should be kept only in a safe or some form of strongbox. The mere fact that a thief has succeeded in his venture does not necessarily imply negligence on the part of the custodian. One must consider whether the precautions taken by way of locking, supervision, etc., could be expected to have proved adequate normally.

The custodian is liable for the negligence, fraud, and other wrongful acts of his employees, servants, and agents, unless they are acts committed outside the scope of their employment. In any case, if he has negligently employed a servant of bad character, he will be liable for any loss caused by him. A person who undertakes to keep goods is not entitled without authority to pass them on to another for storage. If he does so, he is liable for all resulting loss.

These general principles governing the duties of the warehouseman (and others who perform the same function) may be varied by special agreement between the parties. The terms of the contract may limit his liability to a certain amount, or may absolve him from liability for loss arising in certain ways. But the Courts will do their best to limit the effect of such clauses, which are only effective if brought to the notice of the other party. In any event, the burden always falls on the warehouseman to prove that the loss occurred without his fault, or that it falls within the terms of some exempting clause.

Innkeepers (an expression which includes the proprietors of hotels) enjoy special statutory protection, provided they display the notice required under the Innkeepers Acts.

Generally a person who keeps goods for reward has no lien on them, *i.e.* no right to retain them until his charges are paid. But the railway has a lien on all goods deposited with it for safe custody for the amount of its storage charges. Wharfingers, packers, and possibly warehousemen have a similar lien. If a bailee does have a lien over goods, he cannot charge for keeping them during the period when the goods were being retained against the owner's wishes.

LOAN FOR USE AND HIRE

There is a different type of bailment when an article is transferred temporarily, not merely for the purpose of safe-keeping, but to be used by the recipient for his own convenience. The bailee may get the use of it either on free loan, or in return for payment under a contract of hire. In the former case the whole transaction is for the benefit of the borrower alone, and he therefore assumes a correspondingly high degree of responsibility in respect of the article. He is liable even for slight negligence, and must exercise the greatest amount of care while it is in his possession. On the other hand, it is meant for him to use, and so he is not liable for loss or injury caused by third persons whose wrongful acts could not be reasonably foreseen or prevented. He must bear the ordinary running expenses involved in the use of the particular article, *e.g.*

If the article is on free
loan—

—the borrower assumes a high
degree of responsibility—

—and must exercise the greatest care
while it is in his possession.

He must bear the ordinary
running expenses involved—

—and must not use it for any
unauthorised purpose—

—or lend it to a third person.

If he does, any loss or injury which occurs falls
on his shoulders.

the price of fodder for a horse, or petrol for a car. He must not use the article for an unauthorized purpose, nor lend it to a third person without the owner's consent. If he does, any loss or injury which occurs, even without his fault, falls on his shoulders. The owner owes practically no duties to the borrower. All he is required to do is to warn the borrower of any hidden defects in the article of which he himself knows. He would be expected, for instance, to let him know if he had not used the thing himself for some time.

The owner or bailor is in quite a different position when he lets his property out on hire. Here the advantages, and consequently the duties, are more evenly divided between both parties. The owner guarantees impliedly, even if he does not do so expressly, that the thing hired is reasonably fit for the purpose which the hirer has in mind. He is liable for damage or loss caused to the hirer by defects of which the owner *ought* to have known, as well as by those of which he actually did know. The hirer's first duty, of course, is the payment of the agreed rent (usually there will be an agreement for repossession by the owner if the hirer defaults). So far as the care of the article is concerned, the hirer will be liable for any loss which occurs as a result of his negligence or the negligence of his servants. He is not bound to do repairs, and should not do them without consulting the owner, or he may find himself unable to recover the cost of them.

MANDATE AND HIRE OF WORK AND LABOUR

The third possibility is that the bailee, *i.e.* the person with whom the goods are deposited, may be required to do something to, or with, the thing bailed. If he undertakes to perform such a service gratuitously the transaction is one of 'mandate'; if for reward, it is a hiring of his work and labour. The rules applicable to a person undertaking to do work on a chattel in return for payment are dealt with elsewhere (see *Contracts for Work to be Done*). The mandatory bailee is not bound to such a high standard as the professional bailee. In performing the task entrusted to him it is sufficient if he acts with reasonable care and diligence, and with such skill as he possesses or holds himself out as possessing. On completion of his task, the mandatory bailee must return the chattel to its owner, but is entitled to claim from the latter such necessary expenses as he has incurred.

There is one rule which is applicable to bailments of every kind, whether gratuitous or for reward. It is that the bailee cannot refuse to return the article entrusted to him on the ground that some other person has a better right or title to it than the bailor, unless he does so on behalf, and with the express authority, of that third person. Thus if A. borrows or hires a car from B., he cannot refuse to return it to B. on the ground that he has now learned that it really belongs to C.—unless his refusal is made on behalf, or at the express request, of C.

The bailor may sue the bailee for the return of the article or for its value if the bailee wrongfully refuses to comply with his demand for its return, or if he deals with it in a manner inconsistent with the bailor's right, *e.g.* by selling it.

If a third party damages or destroys the property, the bailee may sue him even though he himself is not liable to the bailor for its loss or damage. If he receives by way of damages more than his own interest in the chattel is worth, he must account to the bailor for the excess. The bailor ordinarily can sue a third person for damage to the article only if the article is permanently damaged or totally destroyed. So far as the world at large is concerned, the person who enjoys the rights and owes the duties in respect of an article is the one who has possession of it, that is, the bailee.

STATUTORY POWERS OF SALE

At Common Law a bailee had no right to sell articles bailed to him, as they remain the property of the bailor. However, various statutes give a power of sale, in certain circumstances, to innkeepers, warehousemen and wharfingers, and persons with whom goods have been left for repair (if the bailor fails to pay and take delivery).

One of the most interesting of the statutory powers of sale arises under an Act of Parliament of 1952 which deals with the problem where goods are left for repair, the repairs are done, but the owner never turns up to collect them.

Before this Act there was nothing that the repairer could do—with legal safety. If he got rid of the goods or sold them, he was always under a possible liability for years that the owner would call for them. If he could not produce them he was liable for damages.

The Act, the Disposal of Uncollected Goods Act, was designed to give the repairer the right to sell the goods after a certain time and on certain conditions. The conditions are as follows:

(a) The repairer must display conspicuously on his premises a notice stating that he avails himself of the provisions of the Act and that the Act gives him power to sell the goods after twelve months from the time when they are ready to be handed back to their owner.

(b) He must give the owner notice that the goods (describing them) are ready, state his charges, and state also that after twelve months he has a legal right to sell them unless they are claimed or directions given as to delivery.

(c) After the twelve months he must give a further notice, again describing the goods and stating his charges, and stating that the goods may be sold if the owner does not take delivery or give directions for delivery and pay the charges due.

If in the final notice he states the lowest price he is prepared to accept for the goods he is not obliged—as he otherwise is—to sell the goods by public auction, provided of course that he sells at not less than that price.

The notice of the repairer's intention to sell the goods is to be sent by registered letter to the address which the repairer was given by the owner.

The repairer who has sold goods under the powers conferred by this Act must within seven days from the date of the sale prepare a record stating:

(a) the goods sold (describing them), the method, date, and place of sale;
(b) the name and address of the auctioneer if the goods were sold by auction, or if not by auction and the sale price was £1 or more, the name and address of the buyer;
(c) the gross proceeds of sale, and a statement of the repairer's charges.

He must keep this record, together with a copy of his notice of intention to sell, for six years.

It all seems very complicated. But the provisions of the Act are very useful where, for instance, something of real value is left for treatment or repair, *e.g.* a valuable clock, antique furniture, valuable jewellery, etc. Before the Act, the repairer had no legal right to do anything except keep the goods until the owner collected them and paid his charges. Under the Act, he can dispose of them by sale under conditions which protect the owner and also protect the repairer or 'bailee' as he is, to use the technical term described above.

The complications derive, of course, from a desire to be fair to both sides.

The account given here is necessarily compressed. Any bailee desiring to avail himself of these powers should study the Act itself—it is quite short—and preferably also get legal advice.

CONDITIONS OF COVENANT
EXEMPTING THE BAILEE FROM LIABILITY

It is not uncommon for a bailee accepting goods for safe custody, or for repair or treatment, to put forward a contract under which he exempts himself from liability for loss by fire or theft, or even by his own negligence or that of his servants.

There is nothing unlawful about this, and the exempting conditions may be upheld by a Court, provided that he can prove that the contractual conditions were clearly brought to the notice of his customer (the bailor) and that the customer accepted them. If the goods are sufficiently valuable the customer can and probably will insure them. Insurance will not affect the bailee's liability. It will affect the bailor's peace of mind, because he will recover the amount of the loss from his insurers. But his insurers then stand in his place (by subrogation—see Insurance) and can take against the bailee any legal proceedings for damages for loss or damage which would have been available to the bailor.

But in everyday transactions like sending clothes to the laundry or drycleaners the conditions may be unduly onerous. Sometimes their onerousness is mitigated by the bailee accepting liability up to some specified amount—but it may be less than the value of the articles deposited.

Nevertheless, the conditions may be legally valid if the customer has read them and accepted them and the bailee can prove this.

In one famous case relating to dry-cleaning, the dress was ruined. The customer sued for damages. The dry-cleaner produced his conditions of contract which were printed on the back of the receipt and which apparently exonerated him.

But in the evidence given to the Court the Judge accepted the plaintiff's word that she regarded that slip of paper as nothing more than a *receipt* acknowledging the deposit of the dress for cleaning and which she would produce when claiming the dress. She said she had no idea there were contractual conditions on the back which she was accepting by the mere act of leaving her dress for cleaning.

The Judge believed her, and emphasized that as far as he could see from all the evidence given, the dry-cleaners took no steps to draw their customers' attention specifically to these conditions. There was nothing unlawful about them, but they had not been brought to the customer's attention. So he held that they were not binding on the customer and awarded her damages.

In another case the customer left a valuable mink coat at a furrier's. She was given a receipt which declared that furs were left at 'owner's risk'. The point of special interest here is that the customer knew of this clause and accepted it. It had been explicitly drawn to her attention by the bailee.

When she asked for her coat back it could not be found. As the bailee was not prepared to pay up, she consulted her solicitor and, on his advice, sued for damages.

The bailee, of course, relied on the contract: deposit 'at owner's risk'.

You might think that that would be the end of the matter.

But the Judge who heard the case decided otherwise. He was very concerned about the fact that the defendants, *i.e.* the bailees, could give no account at all of how the coat had disappeared, nor could they offer any credible explanation of how it *might* have disappeared.

If they could have shown and admitted that they or one of their staff had been negligent, and, say, delivered the coat wrongly to someone else, then the owner's risk condition might have protected them. It was there partly to protect them from carelessness on the part of their staff.

But there was nothing to establish that any member of the staff had been negligent.

It was possible on the evidence that the coat had been put into someone else's cold store by the bailee—*i.e.* handed over to a sub-contractor for safekeeping. If that had been done it was against the contract, which was that the bailee himself should look after the coat.

The Judge held that there was an unexplained and fundamental breach of contract, and that therefore the contract was brought to an end and its conditions could not apply. He awarded the plaintiff £600 damages, the value of the coat.

These cases are described only to show that exempting conditions must no be accepted by the customer at their face value. If the loss is serious, he woulc be well-advised to get legal advice to see whether they will stand up to attack or whether a compromise can be negotiated, or whether he must accept the loss. The essential point for all parties, bailors and bailees, is that a Court will always scrutinize very carefully any contract conditions which purport to relieve the bailee of his basic common law liability to take reasonable and proper care of goods entrusted to his care.

LIENS

LIENS are certain types of right which one person has over the property of another.

The most common kind of lien is the *possessory* lien. This is the right of a creditor *to retain possession of another person's property* until his claim is satisfied.

A possessory lien may be (a) particular or (b) general.

A particular lien is a right to retain goods until all charges incurred in respect of those goods have been paid. It may arise by express agreement between the parties, but much more usually it arises by implication of law, *i.e.* as a general legal right. Thus carriers have a lien in respect of the freight on goods carried, and hotel-keepers have a lien on luggage and other property brought to the hotel if the guest does not pay his bill. A repairer of goods has a lien on them until the cost of repairs has been paid: but there is generally no lien on goods unless they have been *improved*, so that a garage proprietor, who would have a lien for repairs done to a car, has no lien for merely garaging it or supplying petrol.

A general lien is a right to retain possession of goods not only for a debt incurred in respect of those goods but for debts generally due from their owner to the person exercising the lien.

In most cases a possessory lien is particular and not general. Thus if a man sends a suit to be cleaned, the cleaner may refuse to hand it back until the amount due for cleaning it has been paid: but he cannot hold on to the suit until amounts owed for the cleaning of other articles have been paid, for his lien relates only to the particular debt incurred in respect of the suit. If he had a general lien, he could hold on to the suit until the customer had paid all that he owed generally.

A general lien may arise by contract, but more frequently arises by the custom of certain trades or professions. It is well established that a general lien can be exercised by factors, bankers, stockbrokers, solicitors, and—in some cases—insurance brokers. Thus a solicitor can retain all papers belonging to a client until the client has paid all his fees, whether incurred in respect of the papers detained or in other matters.

A possessory lien is lost if possession of the goods is given up to the debtor (unless it be given up for a specific and limited purpose only). Thus if a garage proprietor allows a customer who owes him money for repairs to his car to take the car out and use it as he pleases, the lien is lost, and cannot be exercised if the customer brings the car back to the garage.

A possessory lien is also extinguished on payment or tender of the amount due, or if security for the debt is taken in such circumstances as to show that the security was taken in substitution for the lien.

Save for certain statutory powers of sale (see under *Bailments*), a possessory lien can only be enforced by detention of the goods, and no claim can be made for storage or any other expenses of exercising the lien.

It remains to note briefly two other forms of lien, the maritime and the equitable.

A maritime lien is one which attaches to a ship or a ship's tackle, cargo and freight, for payment of a claim founded on maritime law. It does not depend on possession, but travels (so to speak) with the ship, etc., into whosoever's hands it may come—even if the ship be sold to a purchaser who does not know of the existence of the lien. It is exercised by arrest and by sale (unless security is given) through the Admiralty Court.

A maritime lien can be exercised by salvors on the property salvaged, by seamen for their wages, by a ship's master for wages and disbursements, and by claimants in respect of damage through collision caused by the ship's negligence.

A maritime lien may come into conflict with a possessory lien. The possessory lien of a shipwright for the cost of repairs is subject to maritime liens attaching to the ship before it was brought into his shipyard, but it takes precedence over all later maritime liens.

An equitable lien is a charge on property conferred by law until certain claims have been satisfied. It is independent of possession. It binds all persons who acquire the property subject to the lien with knowledge of its existence.

An unpaid vendor of land has an equitable lien on it for the balance of the purchase money, and the purchaser has a lien on it for the amount of the deposit he has paid.

When a partnership is dissolved, retiring partners have an equitable lien on the partnership assets existing at the date of dissolution for payment of all the partnership debts then owing.

An equitable lien is enforced by sale after a declaration by the Court that the lien exists.

AGENCY

INTRODUCTION

IN LAW, an agent is a person who acts on behalf of another person, who is called the principal. In ordinary language the term 'agent' is sometimes used more loosely: for example, a motor dealer may be described as the 'sole agent' for a particular make of car. But in law such a person is a principal in any contract he makes with a customer: for he sells cars on his own account, and not on behalf of the manufacturer.

The distinction is of fundamental importance. When an agent enters into a contract, it is, as a rule, not he, but his principal who is bound by it and able to enforce it against the other contracting party.

The bus conductor, the telephone operator, the waitress are all the agents (as well as the servants) of their employers. So, too, the solicitor, the estate agent, the auctioneer are the agents (though not the servants) of those who engage them. Agency, in fact, is one of the most common legal relationships.

An agent may have authority to do one specific act, *e.g.* to buy a particular article (he is then called a 'special agent'): or he may be authorized to do anything which comes within the scope of management of a business (he is then a 'general agent'): or he may—though this is less common—have unlimited authority to do anything at all on behalf of his principal.

"A wife has the implied authority of her husband to purchase on his account . . . necessaries suitable to their style of living."

No formality is generally required for the appointment of an agent, and in fact most agencies are created by word of mouth or by conduct. An agency may also arise out of the relationship between the parties: thus a wife has the implied authority of her husband to purchase on his account (to 'pledge his credit for') necessaries suitable to their style of living.

The principal can at any time revoke the agent's authority (though he may remain liable on any contract which the agent may make before it is known to the other party that his authority has been revoked). However, if the agent is a salaried servant of the principal he has an implied right to reasonable notice, and cannot be summarily dismissed except for misconduct.

Agency may be terminated by 'operation of law', *e.g.* where the principal dies or becomes bankrupt, or insane, or becomes an enemy alien (through the outbreak of war). It may also come to an end if the time agreed upon for its continuance has expired, or when its subject-matter is destroyed (*e.g.* a house which the agent is employed to let).

RIGHTS AND DUTIES BETWEEN AGENT AND PRINCIPAL

An agent must be diligent in the performance of his duties. If he is employed to sell, he must obtain the best price reasonably obtainable, and must disclose to his principal anything likely to influence him in the making of the contract. Thus, in one case an agent was employed to sell the lease of the principal's premises, and after getting the superior landlords' consent to the use of the premises for certain business purposes, he allowed his principal to remain under the impression that such consent would be refused, with the result that the principal was induced to sell for a lower figure than he would have been able to obtain. It was held that the agent was not entitled to his commission.

An agent must not become a principal as against his employer: for example, a stockbroker who is employed to buy shares must not, while pretending to buy shares on the market, sell his own shares to his principal.

He must render an account when required, and must not make any profit beyond the commission or remuneration paid by his principal. If an agent takes a bribe or secret profit from the party with whom he contracts on behalf of his principal, the principal may refuse to pay the agent and may even recover the amount of the secret profit from him. Furthermore, he may sue both the agent and the third party for damages for any loss that he may have sustained through entering into the contract: and he may also repudiate the contract.

The relationship of agency is one which so readily lends itself to improper inducements that it has been made a criminal offence (under the Prevention of Corruption Act, 1906) both for a person to offer an agent a bribe and for the agent to accept it.

An agent cannot recover a commission from two principals whose interests are inconsistent without making full disclosure of his own position and getting the consent of both of them.

An agent must not delegate his authority by getting someone else to do the work, except in the ordinary way of business (as by employing clerks or assistants).

He must not disclose confidential information or documents entrusted to him by his principal: he is under a strict obligation of secrecy.

The principal must pay the agent the agreed commission or remuneration in accordance with the contract between them. It is often difficult (especially in estate agency contracts) to determine whether in the events which have arisen the agent is entitled to his commission. If the terms are that he shall be paid a commission on completion of a sale, then he is not entitled to commission if no sale takes place, even though he introduced a person ready, able, and willing to purchase, and the principal then refused to sell. If, however, the contract clearly stipulates that the agent is entitled to commission on the introduction of a person ready, able, and willing to purchase at a certain price, and the sale goes off through the fault of the principal, the agent will be entitled to the

445

agreed commission for effecting the introduction. (See further on this the chapter on 'Selling a House'.)

If an agent is appointed as 'sole agent' to sell a house, no other agent can be employed: but the owner may still sell it himself, without paying commission.

Where an agency has been created for a fixed time, and the agent's authority is revoked before that time has expired, he may be entitled to damages for being prevented from earning his commission. Questions frequently arise as to whether an agent is entitled to commission in respect only of the first transaction effected through his introduction, or whether he can claim it on all subsequent orders; or again, whether he is entitled to commission on transactions which are only completed after his agency is terminated. It is impossible to lay down general rules: for the answer must depend on the express terms of the agency agreement and on the terms which are in all the circumstances reasonably to be implied in it. Commission may even be payable to the agents' executors on orders received after his death, if the agreement provides for the payment of commission as long as the principal does business with the customers introduced by the agent.

The principal must indemnify the agent for acts lawfully done and liabilities incurred in the execution of his authority. If, for example, the agent is—by the custom of the particular trade or market—personally liable on a contract which he makes for a principal, he can recover from the principal any loss he incurs on such a contract.

EFFECT OF CONTRACTS MADE BY AGENTS

It is necessary to distinguish between three cases:

(a) where the agent discloses the name of his principal,
(b) where he discloses the existence, but not the name, of his principal, *i.e.* discloses the fact that he is an agent but not for whom, and
(c) where he discloses neither the name nor the existence of his principal, *i.e.* where he appears to be the principal himself.

In the first case, the agent himself, as a general rule, incurs neither personal rights nor personal liabilities under the contract. The only exceptions to this rule are where the custom of the particular trade makes the agent liable, or where he in reality has no principal, or where he executes a deed or signs a bill of exchange in his own name.

An agent who expressly contracts as agent, though without disclosing the name of his principal, will not be personally liable. But if he does not, on the face of the contract, show that he is only an agent (and the mere addition of some such word as 'broker' or 'manager' after his signature is not sufficient for this purpose), the other party to the contract can sue either the agent or the principal, when he discovers who he is, at his option.

Where neither the name nor the existence of the principal is disclosed, the other party—on learning that the agent was acting on behalf of an undisclosed principal—can sue either the agent or the principal at his option, and conversely can be sued by either of them. But he must make up his mind. If he clearly indicates that he regards the agent as liable on the contract, he cannot afterwards sue the principal: and vice versa. The principal cannot sue if he allowed his agent to contract in terms inconsistent with agency (*e.g.* where an agent described himself, in a charter-party, as the 'shipowner'), and he can be met with any defence that the other party could have raised against the agent before he discovered the existence of the principal.

AUTHORITY OF AN AGENT

An agent who is employed to conduct a particular trade or business has implied authority to do whatever is incidental to it. His acts are binding on the principal if they are within the scope of his apparent authority, *i.e.* the authority he appears to the outside world to possess, and a restriction on his apparent authority will not be effective as against the other party to the contract unless known to that other party.

If, for example, the proprietors of a public house forbid their manager to purchase cigarettes on credit for use in the public house, they will nevertheless be liable for the price of any cigarettes he orders, such orders being within the apparent authority of a public house manager, unless the suppliers actually know that he has no authority to order cigarettes.

Moreover, a person who has 'held out' another as his agent, *i.e.* indicated by various means that he is his agent, for example, by regularly paying for goods ordered by him, may be prevented in law from denying that that other person was his agent in any similar transaction. He must do all he can to publicize the end of the agency. (This is what underlies the unfortunate notices that appear from time to time in the newspapers, to the effect that Mr X. will no longer be responsible for debts contracted by his wife.)

A person who professes to act as agent but has no authority from his alleged principal, or who exceeds his authority, is liable to an action for 'breach of warranty of authority' at the suit of the party with whom he purported to contract. The action is based on the implied warranty, *i.e.* implied legally binding promise, by the agent that he had authority to make the contract.

Liability of this kind may be incurred without any fraudulent intent. In one case solicitors were instructed by a client to defend certain proceedings. Before the proceedings started, the client, without the solicitors' knowledge, became insane, and in consequence the solicitors' authority was automatically terminated by operation of law, *i.e.* a rule of the law of agency). The solicitors were held personally liable to the plaintiff for certain costs in the action against their client, because in acting for him they had impliedly warranted that they had authority to do so, and it was immaterial that they had done so in all good faith.

RATIFICATION

Where a person purports to make a contract on behalf of a principal when he has no authority to do so, the principal may, if he so wishes, confirm and adopt the contract. This is known as ratification, and its effect is to make the contract as binding on the principal as if the agent had been properly authorized to make it on his behalf.

Ratification is only possible where the agent contracted expressly as agent, and at the time named as his principal the person ratifying the contract. The principal can ratify even though the agent never intended that he should, but wanted to keep the benefit of the contract for himself.

Ratification may be either expressed or implied by the conduct of the principal (as, for example, where he pays for goods ordered without his authority).

CLASSES OF AGENT

Certain classes of agent are recognized by law as having particular kinds of authority, rights, and obligations.

Factors are mercantile agents (sometimes called consignees or commission agents) who are in possession of their principals' goods and can sell them in their own name. They are authorized to give a warranty if it is usual in the course of business. They can bind the owners of the goods by any sale, pledge, or disposition of them. They have a lien on goods and on the proceeds of sale for the balance of account between themselves and their principals.

Brokers are agents employed to buy or sell on behalf of others. They differ from factors in not having possession of their principals' goods (and so not having any lien), and in not contracting in their own name so as to be able to sue on the contracts they make.

Del credere agents are agents, employed to sell goods, who undertake that the purchasers they procure will pay for the goods they take. In other words, they guarantee the credit of the customers they introduce: and in consideration of the responsibility they assume, they are, of course, paid a higher rate of commission.

POWERS OF ATTORNEY

AS WE HAVE SEEN in the preceding section of this book, it is very common, especially in the business world, for one person (the 'principal') to ask another (the 'agent') to perform some act on his behalf. In general, the law does not require the principal to instruct his agent in any particular form, or in any precise detail—thus, an agent may receive his authority either orally or in writing, and indeed in some cases his authority may be implied from the surrounding circumstances.

There are, however, some exceptions to this general rule. A very important one occurs when the principal wishes his agent to enter into a deed, *i.e.* a

448

document under seal, not merely on the principal's behalf but also *in his name*. In this case, the authority to the agent must itself be contained in a deed, and by long-established practice such a document is called a Power of Attorney. 'Attorney', here, is used in its original sense meaning an 'agent', and not in its later restricted sense of a lawyer appearing as an advocate in Court. If you want to appoint an attorney to execute a deed on your behalf, it is not necessary for you to appoint your solicitor, although very often this can be the most convenient course.

Although a power of attorney is essential in the circumstances mentioned above, this is by no means its only function. Agents can be appointed in this way to prosecute a lawsuit, to manage a business, to obtain a grant of Letters of Administration of the estate of a deceased person (where the principal is unable to carry out the administration of the estate himself), to perform the principal's duties as trustee of a will or settlement (*N.B.* this is only permissible if the principal is going abroad for a period of not less than one month), and generally in any case where it is important that there should be clear evidence of the agent's appointment.

The power of attorney itself is usually a very straightforward document. It first of all states who the agent is to be, and then goes on to describe the purpose for which he is being appointed and the powers which he is to have. Nevertheless, it is often a difficult document to draft because the precise extent of the agent's authority must not be left in any doubt. If it is, the person with whom the agent is dealing on behalf of his principal may question the agent's power to bind his principal, and important business transactions may thus be delayed or even permanently frustrated.

Another hazard which attends all agency dealings but which is of particular importance in the case of powers of attorney is the possibility that the agent's authority may have come to an end by reason of his principal's supervening death, insanity, or bankruptcy. If his principal is abroad, the agent himself may not hear for several days, or even weeks, of the happening of such an event which in law has the effect of automatically revoking his authority to act on behalf of his principal. In the case of the person who is dealing with the agent, there is also the added hazard that the principal may have expressly revoked his agent's authority, a fact which the agent may be concealing fraudulently.

To deal with difficulties of this sort, the Law of Property Act, 1925, provides that if a power of attorney is expressed to be irrevocable for a fixed time, not exceeding one year from the date of the power, persons dealing with the agent during that period shall be protected, as is also the agent himself, whatever the principal may do or suffer. However, it is not always possible or desirable to include a clause of this sort in a power of attorney and, where it is not present, the agent may have to make a statutory declaration to satisfy the person with whom he is dealing that he has not received any notice of the revocation of his authority. If a declaration of this sort is made within three months of the dealing in question, another section in the Law of Property Act, 1925, provides that it shall be conclusive evidence that the power of attorney has not in fact been revoked.

It follows from what has been said above about supervening insanity that it is a most unsatisfactory, if not dangerous, course for an agent to obtain a power of attorney from a principal whose mental powers are clearly failing. It is often difficult in this type of case to determine the exact moment of time when the principal crosses the borderline from sanity to insanity, so that the agent will never be quite certain whether his authority to act has been revoked. This is an important matter for him, because if he has dealings with anybody under the power of attorney after his authority has been revoked, he runs the risk of being sued by that person for breach of warranty of his authority. The proper course in such a case is to apply to the Court of Protection, which is a branch of the High Court, for the appointment of a Receiver to manage the principal's affairs.

In these days of telephone and airmail post, foreign travel does not necessarily cause delays in communication, and this has to some extent removed what used to be a very common reason for the granting of a power of attorney, particularly in relation to the carrying through of dealings with land.

If land is involved, and a power has been granted, there are certain statutory requirements for the filing of the power at the Central Office of the High Court, or, in the case of registered land, at H.M. Land Registry, unless the power is only to be used for one transaction and is to be handed over to the buyer or seller of the land, as the case may be, on completion of that transaction.

A power of attorney may also give the agent (or attorney) power to operate a bank account in the name of the grantor of the power (or authority). But if this is all that is needed, it is simpler to sign an authority to the bank on one of its own forms.

MONEY

LEGAL TENDER

IT IS the duty of a debtor to seek out his creditor (and not vice versa), and to offer him payment, at a reasonable time and place, by way of 'legal tender'.

Legal tender is the offer of *money* made in accordance with the Coinage Acts and certain other legal provisions. A creditor is not bound to accept payment by cheque (or other such instrument), and if he does so for the convenience of the debtor the payment is only conditional, in the sense that if the cheque is dishonoured the debt is revived.

At the present day Bank of England notes are legal tender up to any amount. (So too are gold coins issued by the Mint: but as their intrinsic value, since Britain went off the gold standard, is so much more than their face value, they are nowadays regarded as a commodity rather than as currency.) Silver or cupro-nickel coins are legal tender up to an amount not exceeding 40s, twelve-sided threepenny pieces up to 2s, and coppers (*i.e.* pennies and halfpennies—

for farthings are no longer legal tender) up to 1s. Legal tender must be accepted in discharge of a debt: money in any other form can be refused.

Thus you can pay the travel agent the £100 due for the family holiday with the 4,000 sixpences saved up during the year for that purpose—if he will accept payment in that form: but he is not obliged to do so!

It may be mentioned, in passing, that in Scotland and Northern Ireland the only Bank of England notes which are legal tender are £1 and 10s notes. (The circulation of Scottish or Irish notes for sums under £5 in England is actually prohibited.)

"To constitute legal tender, the exact amount due must be offered. . . ."

To constitute legal tender, the exact amount due must be offered, and offered unconditionally. The debtor can offer a larger sum than is due in satisfaction of his debt, but he cannot demand change as of right. A passenger on a bus has no legal right to require change of a £1 note (or even of a sixpenny piece) for a 3d fare, though if the conductor has change he will naturally give it, and not insist on the passenger's either forgoing his change or getting off the bus!

The significance of legal tender lies in this: that if a debtor is sued after making legal tender (which for some reason the creditor has refused), he can pay the money into Court—for the debt is not extinguished—and the creditor will have to pay all the costs of the action: while if the debtor never made legal tender before the action was commenced, the creditor will be entitled to any costs incurred before legal tender is made or the money paid into Court.

451

It is the debtor's duty to ensure that payment reaches the creditor, but he is entitled to rely on any method of transmission which is indicated as acceptable by the creditor. If, therefore, the creditor asks for remittance by post, the debt will be discharged if the money due is posted, even though it should be lost in the post—provided it is posted in a reasonable way. It would not be reasonable to post money in an unregistered envelope, or even in a registered envelope if the amount is very large. (The Post Office is not liable for the loss of an unregistered letter: and the amount recoverable when a registered letter is lost is limited under the Post Office Regulations.)

APPROPRIATION

Where a debtor owes money to his creditor on more than one account, *e.g.* where he has bought various articles from him at different times, he is entitled, at the time of payment, to 'appropriate' the money paid to a particular account, that is, to state in respect of which debt it is paid. If the debtor does not do so at that time, then the creditor is entitled to make the appropriation at any time. The right of appropriation may be important when a debt is statute-barred: for if the debtor does not appropriate his payment to an enforceable debt, the creditor will be able to appropriate it to one which has, through lapse of time, become unenforceable.

There are, however, certain legal presumptions which apply when no appropriation is expressly made. Thus, if A. owes B. £7 9s 11d for repairs to his radiogram and £65 for a television set, and hands him (or sends him a cheque for) £7 9s 11d, without stating on what account it is paid, the law presumes that the payment is made in discharge of the debt of that exact amount, and not as part-payment of the other debt. And if there is a current account between debtor and creditor (*i.e.* where a balance is carried forward, payments made being deducted from the balance and further debts added to it), the presumption is that payments are appropriated to the debts in order of date, so that the earliest are discharged first.

RECEIPTS

(1) GENERAL

A RECEIPT is an acknowledgement in writing, usually signed, that money has been paid (or goods received).

A person paying a sum of under £2 cannot insist on being given a receipt. For payments of £2 or more, however, a receipt can be demanded as of right: for the Stamp Act, 1891, renders a creditor liable to a penalty of £10 if he refuses to give a stamped receipt (*i.e.* a receipt bearing a 2*d* stamp) on payment of £2 or more.

A receipt for £2 or more which is not duly stamped cannot be put before a Court as evidence that money was paid or for any other purpose. However, it was enacted by the Cheques Act, 1957, that a cheque is good evidence of payment: so although a receipt for a payment of £2 or more can still be demanded, it is now frequently regarded as unnecessary when payment is made by cheque, and it has become customary (though it may be doubted if this consequence was intended by the Act) for stamped receipts not to be given, unless specifically asked for, when payment is made by cheque. (This is dealt with in detail below.)

It is the duty of the person giving a stamped receipt to cancel the stamp—usually by writing the date and his name or initials across it—before the receipt leaves his hands. Failure to stamp a receipt which requires stamping may be redeemed within fourteen days on payment of a penalty of £5, and within a month on payment of £10. If affixed at the right time, the stamp may be of the adhesive type (an ordinary postage stamp), but if put on later it must be an impressed stamp.

Some receipts are exempt from stamp duty: the most important exemptions are where money is deposited with a banker or in a Post Office Savings Bank, where it is paid by way of wages or pension, and where paid in satisfaction of a parliamentary tax or duty.

(II) THE CHEQUES ACT, 1957

What was the true effect of the Cheques Act of 1957? One of the main objects of the Act was to do away with the need for endorsement. It says in effect that if A. writes out a cheque payable to B. and B. pays it straight into his account at his bank he need not endorse it; *i.e.* need not write his name on the back of the cheque, as was the usual practice before this Act came into force.

That was the fundamental purpose of the Act. It was designed to save time and work and it has achieved this purpose, because bank cashiers need not turn over every cheque and examine every endorsement. An endorsement is still necessary if the cheque carries a large capital letter R on the face of it, because that indicates that an endorsement is necessary in order to act as a receipt. But the number of cheques which carry this large capital letter R and require an endorsement is very small. The vast majority of cheques do not: provided the payee in whose favour they are drawn pays it into his own bank account, he need not endorse it, and the bank cashiers need not turn the cheque over to find out whether it has been endorsed or not. In itself that single operation does not amount to very much; multiplied by thousands or hundreds of thousands it amounts to a great deal, and the Act has done away with much unnecessary work. The practical working of the Act since it came into force in October, 1957, has proved that it was unnecessary to have all these endorsements.

The Act, however, has had some unexpected results. Business concerns of many kinds from the vast nationalized electrical and gas industries down to quite small shops have told their customers that if bills are paid by cheque they will not send a receipt unless one is specially requested. Some businesses have even gone so far as to say that because of the Cheques Act they need not send a receipt, and will not do so. In fact, some refuse point-blank to give a receipt when payment is made by cheque, explaining that because of the Cheques Act they are relieved of any legal obligation to give a receipt.

This is not true; but to explain exactly what the true position is since the Cheques Act, it is necessary to begin by examining the situation which obtained before the Cheques Act.

Suppose you bought goods to the value of, let us say, £10 6s 8d from Messrs A. B. & Co., for which they sent you a bill which you later paid by cheque. They would pay this cheque into their bank, and in time it would come back to you from your bank. As a general rule it would be included with your usual bank statement, which would include all cheques you had drawn during a certain period. The practice of different banks varies slightly, but either they would send it back to you, or would keep it for you. On the back of the cheque you would see the payee's endorsement which at that time was necessary, the endorsement A. B. & Co.

Probably the company also sent you a receipt, stamped with a 2d stamp, and you probably kept it as evidence that you had paid the bill, in case by mistake they later on sent in another demand for payment.

But—and this is the important point—even if they did not return the account receipted, that cheque of yours which was endorsed by them was good evidence that you had paid. The rubber stamp which banks put on these cheques would show that it had been paid and apparently credited to the account of A. B. & Co.

If the bill they sent you was dated, say, March 1st, 1957, and your cheque was dated March 10th and was for the exact amount of the bill, it would hardly need a High Court Judge to say that the odds were very heavily in favour of your having paid that bill. It is not very likely that you would give A. B. & Co. a cheque for £10 6s 8d unless you were paying their bill for the same amount. In fact a High Court Judge did decide some 160 years ago that an endorsed cheque would be such strong evidence of payment that it could be accepted in a Court of Law as equivalent to a signed receipt.

There could be difficulties, of course. If you gave a cheque for a round sum of, say, £20 to a tradesman to pay a bill, or part of a bill, he might, if he was dishonest, say that he had cashed the cheque for you as a favour and given you the amount of the cheque. But even a signed and stamped receipt might be forged, so there could be difficulties in that case also. The Courts have never accepted the principle that a signed receipt is necessarily genuine if there is evidence that it might not be. A signed receipt is what the lawyers call *prima facie* evidence, *i.e.* apparently sound, but it can be contradicted and overthrown by evidence to the contrary.

The signed and stamped receipt is good enough for most of us, good enough for most business transactions, but it is not a sacred document which can never be questioned, never be destroyed by strong evidence to the contrary. The endorsed cheque was probably just about as good as a signed and stamped receipt. The only advantage of the receipt over the cheque was that the receipt on the actual bill identified the goods for which the money had been paid.

So that was the position before the Cheques Act. An *endorsed* cheque was accepted by the Court as good evidence that the amount demanded had been paid and was virtually as good as a signed, stamped receipt. All that the Cheques Act has done is to say in effect that an *unendorsed* cheque may be received as evidence of payment in just the same way that an endorsed cheque used to be.

As explained earlier, the Cheques Act said that cheques paid directly into the account of the person in whose favour they were drawn need not be endorsed. It would have been a great pity if the old principle that an endorsed cheque was evidence of payment had been lost simply because so many cheques would no longer be endorsed. Hence the Act contains a short section to say, in effect, that if the cheque appears to have been paid by the bank on which it is drawn it is to be evidence that the person to whom it was payable has received the money. In other words, going back to the example given earlier, if you give A. B. & Co. a cheque today for £10 6s 8d and they pay it into their bank, they need not endorse it. When it comes back to you through your bank you will see from the marks on it that it has passed through your bank and passed through A. B. & Co.'s bank, and although their name is not endorsed on the back of the cheque, the Act provides in effect that it is to be prima facie evidence that you have paid the money and that they have received it.

There is no new principle here, as so many people and so many business houses have seemed to assume. The only difference is that the statement of the law about unendorsed cheques is in an Act of Parliament, whereas the old principle, which we have described, depended upon a decision of the courts a long time ago, and it looks very much as if the world of business in general knew nothing about it.

It is very important to know that in spite of this section of the Cheques Act providing that an unendorsed cheque is to be evidence of payment, just as the old endorsed cheque used to be, this does not mean that anyone who pays a bill is not to be entitled to a proper receipt. Anyone who pays a bill, whether by cheque or by cash, is just as much legally entitled to a proper receipt as he always was. The Cheques Act does not in any way diminish his rights in this respect.

The law is, as stated in the first part of this section, that if anyone pays a bill for £2 or over, and wants a receipt, he can ask for it and is entitled to receive it. One way of asking for it, if he pays by cheque and sends it off by post, is to write the words 'please send receipt' on the bill itself.

The Stamp Act of 1891, which deals with payments of £2 or over, provides that if anyone gives a receipt which is not stamped, that is with a 2d stamp, or refuses to give a receipt when one is legally due, he shall incur a fine of £10.

This incurring of the fine of £10 is not a penalty which the private individual can enforce; it is not in his power to do so; it is for the Inland Revenue authorities to do so. And anyone who has either been refused a receipt or given a receipt which is not signed over a 2d stamp, when he has paid a bill for £2 or over (and it matters not whether he has paid by cheque or by cash), can report the matter to the Inland Revenue and let them deal with the tradesman or the other creditor who has refused to give a proper receipt.

On the other hand, if you are willing to accept your cheque which comes back to you from your bank as good evidence of payment, then there is no reason why you should not fall in with the tradesman's wishes. Some businesses, including, for instance, some local authorities who collect rates, some of the Electricity and Gas Boards, and many of the large shops, have adopted a system whereby you keep the main part of the bill and only send to them with your cheque a counterfoil which is detachable, because it can be torn off along a perforated edge. You send them that counterfoil with your cheque. The counterfoil usually shows just your name, address, and the amount due and some reference number. You keep the main bill, which you can file away and mark on it that you have paid by cheque, and you need only send to the creditor the counterfoil with your cheque.

If you keep your bills carefully you will file away the main bill with a note on it that you paid by cheque numbered so and so on such and such a date, and then you can forget about it. If you are extra careful you will perhaps file with the bill the cancelled cheque when it comes back to you from the bank. You will get no further letter enclosing a receipt from the company concerned, and obviously this method saves the creditor a great deal of time and money and it is hoped that this saving in time and money may possibly lead to some reduction in the overheads of that business, and a possible benefit to the customer.

The point which must be strongly emphasized is that the person who pays is free to choose whether he will have his bill receipted and stamped, or whether he will rely on his paid cheque. If he wants a receipt he is just as much entitled to it as he was before the Cheques Act was passed, and anyone who refuses to give a duly stamped receipt is, as stated above, liable to incur a fine at the instance of the Inland Revenue.

Incidentally, some businesses think that they can get round all this trouble by returning the bill or the invoice with only the word 'paid' written on it, and no 2d stamp. This is just as much a receipt as if the word 'received' had been written. There is no technical let-out here; any words which indicate that the money has been paid are as much a receipt as specific words indicating receipt.

Another vexed and difficult question concerns purchases for cash in a shop. In many of the large shops it is quite a common practice for the assistant to give the customer a bill in duplicate or triplicate, even if he is going to pay cash. The customer will take the bill to a cashier at the cash desk, pay the money, and then be given back one or two copies of the bill which the cashier has stamped with a rubber stamp or perforated with some symbolic marking. The customer takes them back to the counter and the assistant gives him his goods. He may be given one copy to keep, but that copy is not usually intended to be and is not usually a receipt in the legal sense of the word. It is as a rule only a device for bookkeeping and accountancy in the shop. For most customers that may be all that they will want. They have paid their money and they have got the goods. Many people have had such tickets or counterfoils and so on given to them and they lie in their pockets for weeks until they are eventually thrown away. They are not receipts; they are merely an indication to the assistant at the counter that the customer has paid his money at the cashier's desk and they are an authority to the assistant to hand over the goods. There is no record of the transaction under the customer's name and the customer as a rule wants neither a bill nor a receipt.

But if the customer genuinely needs a proper receipt, perhaps for tax purposes, or perhaps for evidence to his employer that money has been paid for particular goods, he is still entitled to demand a stamped receipt, that is, a receipt signed over a 2d stamp, for any purchase of the value of £2 and over, even if he has paid cash. Paying cash makes no difference to his right to a receipt. If the amount of the bill is less than £2 there is no law requiring a proper stamped receipt to be given.

How long should receipts be kept?

A common question is, "How long should I keep receipts?" And if many people fall in with the present stream of requests since the Cheques Act not to ask for receipts when we pay by cheque, but to be content with the cancelled cheque as evidence of payment, the question is how long to keep such cheques? The answer is six years, because after six years a simple debt for money due for goods supplied or work done becomes what is known as 'Statute barred', or to put it in plain language—dead.

This calls for a little more explanation. For some hundreds of years it has been a general principle of our law that a time shall come when stale or dormant claims shall be finally dead and buried—dead in the sense that the machinery of the law is not available to enforce them. The claim may be still 'alive' in the sense that the money has not been paid. But if a creditor has not bothered to pursue it for so long as six years he must pay the penalty for his neglect. In short, although the claim may theoretically be a good one the Courts will not help him to enforce it.

To take a simple example, if Mr A., a watchmaker, repairs your watch and sends a bill which you do not pay and you persist in not paying it for six years after he has delivered the bill, he cannot thereafter compel you to pay. If he sues you, that is, if he issues a summons in the County Court, your first defence is that the debt is more than six years old. If that is established that is an end of the case. You may, in fact, never have paid; alternatively, you may have paid but have no receipt or cancelled cheque to prove that you have. But none of this need be established. Whatever the reason, the six years' interval is a complete defence in itself. The watchmaker's claim is barred by what are known as the Statutes of Limitation—'limitation' because they put a limit of time to claims for debts of this kind.

The point to watch, for both creditors and debtors, is that the period of time may not be a simple six years from the date when the debt became due. For instance, if the debtor pays something on account, or if he writes a letter promising that he will pay soon, the six-year period runs not from the date when the debt originally became due but from the date when something was paid on account, or when a promise was made to meet the bill.

The six-year period of limitation is revived, so to speak, whenever the customer acknowledges his indebtedness, by whatever means he does it—a promise, or a payment on account.

This is, of course, just as much a warning to a creditor as advice to a debtor. No creditor should ever let a six-year period go by without issuing a writ or a summons to enforce payment. In Scotland there is no such fixed definite period of six years, but in England and Wales the period is definite.

457

FAMILY LAWYER

Sunday

A question which is often asked: is is it illegal either to write a cheque or to give a receipt on a Sunday? It is difficult to guess at the origin of this idea, but whatever its origin there is not now any authority for it. Both are as legal if given on a Sunday as on any other day.

It is difficult to guess at the origin of the idea that it is illegal to write a cheque or give a receipt on a Sunday.

Payments marked on a rent book

There is a much-disputed question whether, on a rent book, where the rents are collected weekly and the collector initials the weekly payment, the payment should be signed for over a 2d stamp when the amount is £2 or over.

Ordinarily, any payment for £2 or over must be acknowledged by a receipt signed over a 2d stamp if the payer demands it. But the question of a receipt on a rent book is subject to some rather special considerations. The answer to the question depends upon whether the rent book belongs to the tenant or to the landlord. As a general rule, a rent book supplied by the landlord for the use of the tenant under a rent controlled tenancy, remains the landlord's property. He hands it to the tenant to keep while he is the tenant; it remains a record of the rent paid but the book belongs to the landlord and is merely kept by the tenant as a record of the conditions of the tenancy and the payments of rent. The landlord does not give it to the tenant for ever. In the ordinary way it does not become the tenant's property. That being so, a weekly payment of rent of £2 or more, initialled or acknowledged in the book itself, need not be receipted over a 2*d* stamp.

It is a curious piece of law. But that is what has been decided in a High Court case which concerned not a rent book but a card supplied by an Electricity Board which hung over the tenant's meter. On that card it was the custom of the collector to mark the units consumed and to initial the amount paid. It was held that that did not mean that he was giving a receipt to the consumer. A receipt for money paid for £2 or more need only be stamped when it is a piece of paper or other signed document handed to the payer for him to keep. When the document remains the property of the creditor, whether he be a landlord or an Electricity Board, or anyone else, it is not, under the terms of the Stamp Act, a receipt and therefore it need not be signed over a 2*d* stamp.

In the overwhelming majority of cases a rent book supplied by a landlord on a controlled tenancy remains his property and is merely left in the custody of the tenant as a record of payments made and a record of conditions on which the tenancy is granted or held by the tenant. Therefore no 2*d* stamp is needed.

However, if the tenant is not content to rely on the entry in the rent book, and if he demands a properly stamped receipt which he can keep for each weekly payment of £2 or more, the landlord is bound to give him one.

BILLS OF SALE

THE PURPOSES OF BILLS OF SALE

WHERE goods remain in their original owner's possession but are assigned or mortgaged to another person, the transaction is effected, or evidenced, by a document called a 'bill of sale'. (The name is somewhat misleading, for bills of sale may effect not only a sale, but also transfers by way of gift, and they mostly arise out of mortgage transactions, in which the borrower assigns certain goods to the lender as security for a loan.)

A bill of sale serves two main purposes. In addition to effecting, or evidencing, the transfer of the property in the goods, so as to enable the grantee to claim them from the grantor, it can—if made available to public inspection—notify anyone concerned as to their ownership that *the person in possession of the goods is not the owner*, because he has sold or given them to someone else, *or is not the absolute owner*, because he has mortgaged them to another person as security for a loan.

As the ownership of chattels commonly passes by delivery, *i.e.* handing over the goods themselves, it tends to be assumed that one who is in *possession* of chattels also *owns* them. Such an assumption may enable a person to obtain

459

credit on the strength of his apparent prosperity when he is in fact in the gravest financial difficulty, and has had to raise a loan on the security of his trade machinery or drawing-room furniture.

The law relating to bills of sale is contained in two statutes, the Bills of Sale Acts, 1878 and 1882. In addition to promoting the two purposes mentioned above, it also has as its object the protection of impecunious borrowers, who might suffer at the hands of moneylenders through executing documents of an oppressive nature whose real purport they do not understand. Thus, the former Act (which originally applied to all bills of sale) makes void as against a person's creditors any secret disposition, by bill of sale, of goods of which he retains possession, while the latter invalidates bills of sale given by way of security for money if they are not made in the prescribed form.

Secrecy is avoided by the requirement that bills of sale shall be *registered* if they are not to be void as against creditors of the grantor. This applies equally to *absolute bills of sale* (which relate to out-and-out assignments) and to *conditional bills of sale* (which relate to mortgages, and are subject to the condition that when the loan is repaid, with interest, the property in the goods shall revert to the borrower).

WHAT CONSTITUTES A BILL OF SALE

The term 'bill of sale' is so defined in the Acts as to include not only bills of sale strictly so called (*i.e.* assignments of personal chattels of which the assignor retains possession) but also transfers, declarations of trust, inventories of goods with receipt thereto attached or receipts for purchase moneys of goods, powers of attorney, authorities or licences to take possession of goods as security for any debt, agreements by which a right in equity to any goods or to any charge or security on them is conferred, and certain other written agreements of similar effect.

The assignments which require to be registered as bills of sale are those of personal chattels, *i.e.* goods, furniture, trade machinery, and articles capable of complete transfer by delivery, and also fixtures and growing crops when assigned or charged separately, *i.e.* apart from the land.

To be a bill of sale within the meaning of the Acts, a document must be one on which the title of the transferee of the chattels depends, either as the actual transfer (or agreement to transfer) or as a document of title taken at the time as a record of the transaction. Thus, while a mortgage of land and buildings in course of erection, which gave the mortgagee power, on default of the mortgagor, to seize and sell materials, was held to be a bill of sale, an agreement in an ordinary building contract, that all materials brought by the builder upon the land should become the property of the landowner, was held not to be a bill of sale.

A hire-purchase agreement, under which the property in the goods does not pass until final payment and the seller has a right to retake possession on default in payment, is not a bill of sale. But where—for the purpose of raising a loan—the owner of goods purports to sell or assign them to another, and then enters into a hire-purchase agreement under which the goods are again to become his property on payment of the agreed amount, the court will inquire into the real nature of the transaction and may decide that the document is a bill of sale.

Assignments of stocks or shares, of contracts or of book debts, are not governed by the law relating to bills of sale: but certain assignments of book debts must be registered 'as if they were bills of sale', if they are not to be void against the assignor's trustee in bankruptcy, and there is a special register for assignments of book debts.

ABSOLUTE BILLS OF SALE

In the case of an absolute bill of sale, *i.e.* where ownership is transferred, the law is concerned only to protect persons who do business with the grantor of the bill, and not to protect the grantor himself (as in the case of a conditional bill of sale—see below). For this purpose the law merely requires publicity by means of registration, without prescribing the particular form in which the transaction is to be carried out.

The bill must be registered within seven days after execution, it must be attested (*i.e.* witnessed and signed) by a solicitor, and the attestation clause must state that the effect of the bill has been duly explained by the solicitor to the grantor.

REGISTRATION OF BILLS OF SALE

Registration is effected by taking to the Bills of Sale Department in the Royal Courts of Justice the original bill with every schedule or inventory attached to it, a true copy of the bill and schedules, and an affidavit which verifies the execution and attestation, and states the time of execution and names, addresses, and occupations of the grantor and of every attesting witness.

The bill must state the consideration for which it is granted, and the statement must be substantially true. Thus, if the consideration is the payment of money, and part of the money is not to be paid until some time after the bill is signed, the bill should not state that the money is 'now paid'. If it is made subject to any defeasance (*i.e.* agreement enabling it to be avoided), or to any condition or declaration of trust, it must contain a statement to that effect.

Where the affidavit describes the residence of the grantor as outside the London Bankruptcy District, or where the goods are stated to be outside that district, a copy of the bill is sent to the local County Court of the district where the grantor resides or the goods are situated.

Anyone is entitled, without giving any reason, to examine the register on payment of a small fee, and notice of registrations is regularly given in the publications of Trade Protection Societies, to keep their subscribers informed as to the financial status of their customers or prospective customers.

Registration lasts for five years, and may be renewed by filing with the registrar an affidavit stating the last registration of the bill. A bill which is not renewed in proper time becomes void, as though it had never been registered.

461

CONDITIONAL BILLS OF SALE

Here the object of the law is two-fold, to protect both the public and the borrower himself.

The former object is achieved by the requirement of registration, and the rules are the same as those applying to absolute bills of sale, except that attestation need not be by a solicitor, but can be by any 'credible witness' who is not a party to the bill.

For the protection of the borrower, a very detailed form is prescribed, which must be exactly complied with. It sets out the date of the bill, the names and addresses of the grantor and grantee, the consideration for which the bill is granted (which must be not less than £30), the transfer of the property as security for payment of the money lent and interest, and the promise by the grantor to pay the principal sum and the agreed interest at definite times, and to do all acts necessary for the maintenance of the security (such as keeping the goods insured).

The goods must be set out in an inventory scheduled to the bill of sale. The bill will be void, except as against the grantor, in respect of any goods which are not specifically described. Thus, if the schedule includes 'the Sheraton table and other furniture in the drawing-room', the grantee will not be able to claim the other pieces of furniture against any person such as the trustee in bankruptcy or an execution creditor of the grantor, though he could claim them against the grantor himself. The reason for this rule is, of course, that unless goods are specifically described in the bill of sale, it is only too easy for other goods to be substituted for them, or to be added (by being brought in, for example, from another room) in fraud of the grantor's creditors.

The goods in the schedule must belong to the grantor at the time when the bill is executed. A bill of sale cannot be granted over stock which a tradesman has not yet acquired: it cannot have the effect of a 'floating charge' created by a debenture on the property of a limited company.

The object of a conditional bill of sale (or '*bill of sale in security*') is to enable the lender (the grantee) to seize the goods if he thinks that the borrower (the grantor) cannot repay the loan. But the law will only permit such seizure in certain events. These are:

(1) If the grantor fails to pay any money secured by the bill at a stipulated time, or fails to perform any other obligation he has undertaken, such as to insure the goods.

(2) If the grantor becomes bankrupt or allows any of the goods to be distrained for rent, rates, or taxes.

(3) If the grantor fraudulently, *i.e.* with intent to prevent the grantee seizing the goods, removes them or allows them to be removed from his premises.

(4) If the grantor fails, without reasonable excuse, to produce to the grantee his last receipt for rent, rates, and taxes, after being required by the grantee in writing to do so.

(5) If execution has been levied against *any* goods of the grantor (even goods not included in the bill of sale) under any judgment.

After seizing the goods, the grantee must not remove them from the place of seizure for five days; for within that period the grantor may apply to a High

Court Judge, and the Judge, if satisfied that the cause of seizure no longer exists (*e.g.* if the money due has been paid), may restrain the removal or sale of the goods, or make such other order as may seem just.

THE EFFECTS OF INVALIDITY

An *absolute* bill of sale which is unregistered is void only as against creditors of the grantor: for it is for their protection alone that registration is required.

If the bill of sale is void for want of registration, *all* goods in the 'apparent possession' of the grantor may be taken by his trustee in bankruptcy, by any person to whom his goods have been assigned for the benefit of his creditors, or by anyone seizing them in execution of a judgment. Goods are in a person's 'apparent possession' so long as they are on any premises—private or business—occupied by him, or are used and enjoyed by him on the premises of another.

Although unregistered, an absolute bill of sale is valid as between grantor and grantee, so that the grantee can claim the goods from the grantor under it.

If the bill is registered, the goods comprised in it are not within the 'order and disposition' of the grantor for the purposes of bankruptcy.

As the rules relating to *conditional* bills of sale are designed to protect both the public and the borrower, the effect when such a bill is invalid depends on the nature of the defect.

If the bill is not in the proper form, or the consideration for it is less than £30, it is void for all purposes. The grantee's only right will be to claim repayment of his loan, with interest at the rate of 5 per cent. per annum.

If the bill is not registered or not properly attested, or if the consideration is not clearly stated, it is again void as a *security* both as between the parties and as against third parties, but the grantee may claim principal and interest at the rate specified in the bill.

If the schedule to the bill does not specifically describe the goods comprised in it, or if the grantor was not the true owner of the goods when the bill was executed, the bill is void as against third parties, so far as those goods are concerned, but it may be enforced against the grantor.

BASIC PRINCIPLES OF TORT

WHAT IS A TORT?

LET us start with a practical example. Mrs Brown is on her way to do her weekly shopping in the High Street. Round the corner and along the pavement she comes, past the post office and across the front of the 'Dog and Duck'. Mrs Brown disapproves of intoxicating liquor in any form, and she is entitled to her opinion. She even averts her eyes as she passes, looking steadfastly across to the other side of the road. At this moment there is a splintering crash, and to the startled eyes of three small boys playing hopscotch further along the pavement Mrs Brown suddenly and totally disappears—if not actually into the bowels of the earth, then at least into the cellar of the 'Dog and Duck'—a factor which increases her shame as she lies, in some pain, with her right leg fractured just above the knee.

Passing over the six weeks Mrs Brown spent in hospital, the pain, the suffering, and the inconvenience of it all—not to mention the agony of reflecting that she of all people was observed by a curious crowd being carried semi-conscious out of a public house on a stretcher—we turn to the morning when Mrs Brown sits, now completely recovered, at least physically, in the office of her solicitor. All she can see clearly is that she was doing nothing wrong, and she has been injured. She wants damages. And in this particular case she is likely to recover them. For there has been committed against her what the lawyers call a 'Tort'.

This is an old Norman-French word, literally meaning simple 'wrong'. But there is more to it than that, and the word means little to Mrs Brown. "What is a tort?", she may well ask her solicitor. And she may be surprised at her solicitor's hesitation in answering what to her is a simple and straightforward question. In fact, however, the solicitor is doubtless reflecting that literally volumes have been written on the subject of what is an exact all-embracing definition of a tort.

From the vast number of definitions attempted, let us take one which may not be absolutely complete, but which is at least comprehensive and straight-forward. 'A tort is a wrong, done to the property or person of another, for which the appropriate remedy is a Common Law action for damages', or in colloquial terms, compensation. It is not the same thing as a breach of contract, nor is it a crime.

It is true that the same act may be both a tort and a breach of contract, *e.g.*

465

negligence in carrying out a contract as where a doctor performs an operation negligently. But the tort, or wrong, of negligence exists as a separate issue, a separate right of *action* which means a right and power to bring legal proceedings in the courts.

A tort may also be a crime, *e.g.* to assault someone may be the *crime* of assault and also the *tort* of trespass to the person. For the latter, the assaulted

"Mrs Brown is on her way . . ."

person has a right of action for damages quite apart from any prosecution for assault which may ensue.

When someone has suffered injury to his person or property through the act of another one very important question is: has that person committed a tort or wrong which the law recognizes as a wrong in law for which the courts would award damages?

Another way of answering the question is to give a list of the wrongs for which a man may sue another, *e.g.*:

Trespass on or over his property.
Trespass to the person (*e.g.* assault or false imprisonment).
Nuisance (*e.g.* excessive noise, bad smells, etc.).
Liability to visitors injured on dangerous premises.
Libel and slander.
Negligence.
Taking another person's goods in circumstances when there is no question of the crime of stealing but the taker thinks he owns them or has a right to take them, *e.g.* Innkeeper's Lien.
Deceit (*e.g.* false representations), etc.

Trespass is invasion of, an interference with the owner's or occupier's right to his land or his house. Even if no physical damage is done, it is a wrong for which damages may be awarded even if they are only nominal. More important, usually, the court may issue an order called an injunction forbidding the trespasser to repeat his wrongful act on pain of imprisonment for contempt of court.

Nuisance is some act which interferes with a man's reasonable peaceful enjoyment of the peace and comfort of his own home. It includes, *e.g.*, the making of excessive noise which interferes with neighbours' reasonable peace.

Libel and slander are a wrong done to someone's good name and reputation.

Taking and asserting a right of ownership to another's goods or refusing to return them is the tort of 'conversion', *i.e.* converting another's property to your own use.

Motive, *i.e.* the reason why you do these things, is seldom of any importance. What matters is that a wrong has been done which falls within the classification of torts.

Negligence is the careless disregard of the legal duty to take care which everyone owes to his 'neighbour'. Who his neighbour may be is discussed below.

Happily, in Mrs Brown's case, the matter is one without any real difficulty. Unhappily, in this quality, her case is rare. One of the main reasons for this is that whereas the principles of tort have been laid down and written about exhaustively, they are no more than principles. Each single case depends completely on its own merits when it comes to applying those principles. And the principles themselves are repeatedly being modified as they are reported in this case and that case and applied with justice to each one. The law of tort is largely judge-made law. Each case that comes before the court is measured against the other leading cases which have been fully reported in the various Law Reports. Facts are compared, and a decision is made which is in accordance with the basic principles of tort as applied to the facts of the case in point.

This is why the law of tort has been described as a collection of more or less independent topics, governed each by its own peculiar history. One can say dogmatically only that it is impossible to be dogmatic about the law of tort. This is not, as has unfairly been suggested at times, merely a device formulated by lawyers to provide lucrative business for themselves! It is because strict rules make for occasional hard cases, and the only completely fair system for deciding disputes between parties is to have very fluid principles and apply them, with the guidance of existing cases, to each individual problem before the court.

467

FAMILY LAWYER

WHO IS MY NEIGHBOUR?

In essence, the most basic principle of all on the subject of tort is that which forms one of the primary roots of Christian teaching. 'Love thy neighbour', says the Commandment. Now this principle becomes, in law, 'You must not injure your neighbour'. Immediately comes the lawyer's question—'And who is my neighbour?', and already we are in the realm of argument. The answer seems to be that put so well by Lord Atkin in the course of his judgment in a leading case in 1932: My neighbours are 'persons who are so closely and directly affected by my acts, that I ought to have them reasonably in my contemplation when I am directing my mind to the acts or omissions which are called in question'.

Applying this basic principle directly to the facts of Mrs Brown's case, the solution is clear. The wood forming the cellar flap outside the 'Dog and Duck' was rotten. Any proper examination would have revealed this. It was patently in a dangerous state. To omit to keep it in a proper state, or to repair it if it deteriorated was the clear liability of the brewers as owners of the pub in question. This is the more so as the cellar flap, when closed, forms part of the public highway. Mrs Brown has had a grievous wrong done to her—a wrong independent of contract—and her appropriate remedy is a Common Law action. For the good lady, much though she would hate to admit it socially, is in the eyes of the law 'the neighbour' of the brewery company. She is a person so closely and directly affected by the acts (and in this case the omissions) of the company that they ought reasonably to have had her in contemplation, as indeed anyone else who walked over that pavement, when it came to keeping their cellar flap in a proper state of repair.

HAS ANYONE INFRINGED
MY LAWFUL RIGHTS?

Another definition of a tort—the reverse side of the same coin, as it were—is 'a breach of a right'. Mrs Brown's absolute right of free and safe passage along the public highway has been infringed by the brewers. She is entitled to recover damages.

Sometimes, however, a plaintiff finds it difficult, if not impossible, to establish the exact right which has been broken by the defendant. Consider the imaginary case of Mr Smith, a long-distance lorry driver of skill and experience. Suppose that he is driving his heavily loaded lorry up a steep hill. He goes to change down into bottom gear, and for some reason—it can happen to anyone—he misses a gear. The lorry starts to run backwards. Glancing in his mirror, Mr Smith sees that there is quite a stream of traffic coming up the hill behind him. His brakes are insufficient to hold the weight of the lorry and the load on so steep a hill. There is little he can do. In a desperate endeavour to save the lives of those behind him, at the risk of his own, Mr Smith takes a hasty and courageous decision. Swinging the wheel over, he turns the lorry sharply into the bank. The load is high, and despite all his good intentions and efforts, the lorry overturns. Happily, it does so in such a way that the following traffic can avoid it.

Mr Smith is dragged out from beneath the wreckage with a broken arm. He wants damages.

But he is bound to fail because he has no right of action, *i.e.* there is no one against whom he can bring legal proceedings with any prospect of success. True, he has been injured, and he was not to blame—indeed he deserves credit for his unselfish action in saving the following traffic. But it is found that there was nothing mechanically wrong with the lorry. No one has infringed his rights as an individual. No one has done him any wrong. He cannot recover. He can, of course, claim National Insurance Benefits—that is exactly the reason for the National Insurance Scheme—but he has no claim in tort.

"Has anyone infringed my lawful rights?"

There are many kinds of 'right' which, if infringed by others, may give grounds for an action in tort. There are rights which attach to status—the status of a husband, for example, who may sue anyone who entices his wife away from him, so infringing his right of 'consortium', as the law calls it. Parents have rights over their children—masters have rights over their servants —and servants over their masters, too. These are rights conferred by status.

More complicated, but no less effective, are the right of personal safety and the right not to be deceived by misrepresentation. On the other hand, there are duties imposed by the law, and if these are not fulfilled, then the rights of others may be infringed—the duties attaching to owners of certain types of animals, for example.

Then there are rights attaching to property. Infringements of these rights involve the torts of trespass and nuisance already mentioned. Infringement of the right to a good reputation is in law the tort 'defamation', *i.e.* libel and slander.

469

WHAT SHOULD I ANTICIPATE?

At a time of festival and rejoicing in the year 1773, there was a fair taking place in a country town, packed with stalls and thronged with people. As might be expected, there were also a few rowdies present, one of whom did a most stupid and dangerous thing. Lighting the blue paper of a firework squib, he tossed it on to the stall nearest him, and stood back to see the fun. The stall-holder happened to see it land, grabbed it quickly before it exploded, and hurled it away from him. It chanced to land upon another stall, whose owner just had time to do exactly the same thing. Finally it exploded, seriously injuring an innocent bystander who was totally unconnected with the original author of the misadventure. And yet it was the squib-thrower who was justly held liable for the injury, because all the people between him and the plaintiff had acted only in the agony of the moment, and could not be held to blame, whereas the defendant should have realized that his action might be expected to cause serious injury to someone or other in the crowded fair.

The case is an old one, but the principle it established remains good law today, and it has been applied repeatedly since. The guiding rule may be put in the form of a simple question—ought the defendant to have *anticipated* the final result? If the answer to this is 'Yes', then he will be held liable to the plaintiff in damages.

But though the principle is clear, the application of it may be fraught with difficulty. Again and again the courts have to deal with cases where the claim arises from an act admittedly negligent and wrongful, but where the defendant pleads that the harm done to the plaintiff was 'too remote' from the act or omission of which he was guilty, in other words it was so far away that he could not reasonably have anticipated it. And the court has to apply the principle afresh to each new set of facts.

For example, in 1925 a lorry, wrongfully left unattended by the defendants at the top of a hill, ran away out of control. In its headlong course, it injured a small child. The mother of the child was in her front garden. She saw the lorry rushing down the hill with no one in it, and she knew that somewhere further down the hill, round a bend out of her sight, her child was playing with others. When, after a few minutes, someone told her that a child answering the description of her child (it was indeed her child, as it turned out) had been injured, she suffered a nervous shock from which she actually died. The negligent lorry-owners were held liable for her death, on the application of this same old principle, because they should have anticipated this as a reasonable consequence of their negligence.

HOW DOES 'MALICE' AFFECT TORTS?

There are some special torts where certain special elements have to be established —malice, for example. Take the imaginary case of a theatrical agent, more keen than scrupulous—who finds exactly the dancer he is looking for to play the lead in a big London production. He finds her, let us say, at a sea-side concert party, at the start of the summer season. He goes back-stage to see her, and puts to

470

her his proposition. She is crestfallen as she realizes that she has signed a contract for the whole of the summer season with the concert party promoter. The agent, dangling the bait of the London show before her, assures her that on the salary she will be getting she will be able comfortably to settle the claim for damages for breach of contract which the promoter is likely to make. And, so assured, the lady leaves for London. But it is the agent who receives the greatest shock, when the promoter brings an action not against the girl but against *him*, for 'inducing her to break her contract'. When the agent hears that in this class of tort, malice is an essential ingredient, he is confident, for he has never even met the plaintiff and so could hardly be found guilty of spite or hatred toward him, the accepted meaning of 'malice'. But he does not know that 'malice' in tort has a special meaning—it means that a man has acted 'with improper motives'. Obviously, it is basically improper ever to induce someone to break their contract with someone else. So the agent in our imaginary example will be found liable in damages to the concert party promoter.

Another, more obvious, example of a case where 'malice' is an essential ingredient is an action for 'malicious prosecution', where it is proved that the defendant laid information before the police, from improper motives, as a result of which, criminal proceedings were taken unsuccessfully against the plaintiff.

But here again, the same coin has another side to it. In 1885, a certain Mr Pickles, who owned some land on the outskirts of Bradford, chose to dig a deep well on that land. He knew that one effect of this act would be to deplete the water supplies of the Bradford Corporation, but he insisted on exercising what he considered were his rights. In the action which ensued, it was established that the water abstracted by Mr Pickles as it flowed underground was not in any channel, or through a defined area—it just percolated haphazardly through the soil. This might have been expected to give him victory, but the Corporation were by no means dismayed. They alleged—and indeed they proved—that when he dug his well, Mr Pickles was fully aware that he would be depleting the water supplies of the Corporation. 'Malice!' they claimed. 'The motives of Mr Pickles were essentially improper!' But the court upheld Mr Pickles, establishing another very important principle in tort—that motive, however wrong, can never turn the exercise of an absolute right into a tort. He had an absolute right to the water percolating through his soil. He could therefore take it, and never mind why he did so.

DAMAGE

Another element which must not be ignored in tort is damage. This will be dealt with in some detail later on. At this stage, two points only may be made. Firstly, the damage claimed by the plaintiff must not be too remote. And secondly, there are some special torts where, unless damage is proved, or can legally be presumed, there is no tort at all, despite an admittedly wrong action on the part of the defendant. On the other hand, there are certain special torts which are held not to require proof of damage at all (see below).

DEFENCES TO ACTIONS IN TORT

What types of defence are available?

Perhaps the defence most often raised in actions of tort is that the plaintiff has not proved that he has been wronged by the defendant. But the question of the burden of proof is to be dealt with in more detail a little later on.

There are other cases where the law permits certain special defences. For example, a statement which is admittedly defamatory may have been made on an occasion which was 'privileged' in law, *e.g.* in Parliament. (See chapter on 'Libel and Slander'.)

Thirdly, there are instances where a defence arises from the status or position of the defendant, *vis-à-vis* the plaintiff. For example, the Queen has complete personal immunity in tort. Another instance, which affects far more people, is the position regarding husbands and wives.

The general rule is that while they are living together as a married couple, no husband or wife may sue the other in tort, except in one instance—and that applies only to a wife suing a husband for a tort to 'her property'. The husband has no such corresponding right against his wife. He cannot sue her at all for a wrong she does him. The position alters after divorce or judicial separation.

There is a summary method of settling disputes between them, under Section 17 of the Married Women's Property Act, 1882, but this is not an action in tort.

This bar to actions in tort between husband and wife can sometimes have surprising effects upon other people. Supposing a wife is travelling as a passenger in her husband's car and there is an accident and it is held that the husband was 50 per cent. to blame and the driver of the other car involved also 50 per cent. to blame. The wife, unable to sue her husband, has brought an action against the other driver only. But he has been found to have been guilty of some negligence—not all the negligence which caused the accident, but some. Oddly enough, he will have to pay the wife the whole 100 per cent. of her damages. Should he claim 'contribution' from the husband amounting to half the damages, he will fail, because this would be but a method of making a husband pay damages to his wife, in tort, and he is not liable in law for that.

More serious is the situation where the only negligence is on the part of the husband who is driving. His wife is hurt. Anyone but his wife would have a claim against him for the tort of negligence and through him against his insurance company. But because she cannot sue him, she cannot claim under the policy. Some comprehensive policies have a special section giving a wife or husband the right to certain payments in these circumstances. But they are limited in amount and may not cover the wife's or husband's just claim.

(The wise course is for husband and wife each to have an accident policy when money is payable on specified injuries occurring regardless of the cause.)

The defence that 'It was an accident'

The above categories apart, however, there are some specific groups of defence to actions in tort which come under the general heading of 'Accident'. They fall conveniently into three distinct sections.

Take, for instance, the position which arises when a man fires a gun at a rabbit—legally and innocently. He misses the rabbit (a bad shot, but not a wrongful act in itself, especially from the point of view of the rabbit!), but the bullet, before it is spent, ricochets off a nearby tree and is deflected into the eye of the plaintiff, who is innocently standing by. This would be a complete accident and the man with the gun would not be condemned in damages to the plaintiff.

Then there is the example of something in the nature of a quite phenomenal rainfall which, let us say, renders the drainage facilities of a mountain village completely inadequate, so that many innocent householders suffer seriously from flooding. If they take action against the local authority, they will fail if it is proved that the rainfall on this particular occasion was so completely abnormal that it could not have been within the anticipation of the local authority. But it is as well to remember that if the mountain village was, for instance, in the Welsh valleys, it would take a lot more rain to make the event 'an Act of God' (which this defence is called) than would be the case if the village were, for instance, in the Sahara, where any sizeable rainfall might well be quite phenomenal.

The third section in this group of defences is that which might arise if a man awoke one night, convinced that he heard a burglar. Creeping quietly downstairs and picking up a poker, he waits anxiously behind a door as the footsteps come nearer and nearer. The door softly opens, and a dim shape is seen. Down comes the poker, the intruder slumps to the floor unconscious, on go the lights, and the harassed householder finds that he has hit not a burglar but his mother-in-law, staying for the weekend, who has been unable to sleep and has come down to get herself a hot drink. In such a case—assuming the court accepted the facts and did not regard them as a false but ingenious excuse—the defendant would not have to pay damages, for the event was in law 'an accident arising from a genuine and innocent mistake of fact'.

There is another defence which is often allied to the last section, and this is based upon the proposition that a man cannot recover damages from someone else for an injury which was basically his own fault. For example, a man who lets his cattle stray on to the land of his neighbour through his own negligence cannot get damages if his valuable beasts are poisoned through eating his neighbour's yew trees.

On the other hand, this rule must not be carried too far. A man may acquire a dangerous dog for the protection of his property and may warn people about this by means of a written notice, but he will still be liable to a man lawfully coming there on business who cannot read.

Did I accept the risk?

The next great class of defence to actions in tort is one which can be pleaded if you voluntarily, of your own free will, accepted the risk of injury. If you undertake a risk quite voluntarily, with your eyes open, as it were, and you get hurt, you cannot claim damages from the person originally at fault.

For example, if I lend you my double-barrelled shot-gun at your request, and I tell you at the time that one of the barrels is defective, but you still elect to take the gun—then if you fire that barrel and injure yourself, you cannot recover damages from me, for I will plead the defence that you voluntarily accepted the risk.

But this principle, too, cannot be carried too far. In 1935, a policeman looking out of the window of his police station saw that there was a runaway horse in the crowded street outside. Hardly thinking about it, he dashed out and hurled himself at the head of the terrified animal and brought it under control, but not without sustaining serious injuries. When he sued the horse-owner, that man pleaded the policeman's voluntary acceptance of risk. But the defence failed, and the courageous officer recovered damages. The court held that the emergency was such that he could not be said to have acted deliberately in the face of a risk which he chose to accept. He acted spontaneously. The emergency, in other words, rendered his action quite involuntary, especially in view of the office he held.

How far may this principle be carried? An interesting question which has often intrigued lawyers arises when a man accepts a lift in a car from a driver who he can see is drunk. If the car crashes, can the driver, on being sued, plead that the passenger voluntarily accepted the risk? The consensus of opinion seems to be that only in the most extreme circumstances would the driver thus be able to escape liability for injury to his passenger.

The defence of 'Contributory Negligence'?

The next major category of defence to actions in tort is more often a partial, rather than a total, defence. It is that of 'Contributory Negligence'. Let us consider an example from a real case which arose out of a nasty accident during a journey in a long-distance coach. The plaintiff was a Mr Jones, one of a number of passengers who had the appalling experience of realizing that the coach in which they were travelling down a long, steep hill, was out of control. Whatever the feelings of the other passengers were, those of Mr Jones became widely known. He felt sure that his only hope of escaping a terrible death was to jump to the door, fling it open, and leap for his life. Leap he duly did, and sustained a serious injury in the process. When he sued the coach firm, they proved that in fact the driver, by an almost superhuman effort, had actually managed to regain control of the coach farther down the hill, so that if only Mr Jones had stayed where he was and swallowed his fear, he would not have been injured at all. They claimed that Mr Jones was guilty of 'contributory negligence'—that he had *contributed* to his own injury by his *negligent* act in leaping wildly and unnecessarily from the moving coach. In the event, they failed, the court holding that if A.'s negligence puts B. in a dilemma, B. is not guilty of contributory negligence if he takes a wrong decision in the agony of the moment.

But in order to explain exactly what amounts to 'contributory negligence', it is necessary to give a brief historical account of its development as a legal doctrine. The key date is the year 1945. Before then, the law was that if you wanted to secure damages from anyone else, you had to prove that you yourself acted faultlessly. If you were found to have contributed at all—even by the merest fraction—to your own misfortune, then technically you lost your action. This was seen to be manifestly unjust, but the original principle had been laid down by a court so high that its ruling bound all those judges regularly meeting this point. Here was a principle that was, alas, too inflexible, and which was causing injustice. What the courts did was to busy themselves finding ingenious ways round this unjust principle. Finally, Parliament was prevailed upon to act, so that the principle itself could be amended by Statute which would bind all courts.

Consequently, the Law Reform (Contributory Negligence) Act, 1945, was passed, which made compulsory the principle which the recent practice of the courts had proved was so desirable. Ever since that Act came into force, anyone found to have been, say, 50 per cent. to blame for his own misfortune has had his damages assessed and then reduced by that percentage. This was a doctrine which for years had proved itself to be effective in the specialized jurisdiction of Admiralty. Thenceforward it was applied to the whole law of tort.

Contributory Negligence.

In assessing the contributory negligence of any plaintiff the court has to take into account his or her physical and mental condition. A motor-car, let us say, may be driven negligently, but a young and active person may be found to have contributed in part to his own injury if he made no attempt at all to jump clear when he could and should have done so. Under identical circumstances, an elderly or handicapped person would be found not to have contributed at all. Once more you see how a principle, provided it is flexible, may be adapted and applied with justice to the facts of each and every case before the courts.

Other defences

Before leaving the subject of defences to actions in tort, there are one or two others worthy of mention. For example, the defendant may escape liability by proving successfully that the wrong done to the plaintiff was in fact the fault of someone else. Personal immunity created by statute—*e.g.* Diplomatic Immunity —is another special defence. Further, if a person establishes that he was expressly authorized by statute to do what he did, he will escape liability, though he has to satisfy the court that the statute really did authorize the act in question, and did not merely 'permit' it to be done.

NEGLIGENCE

WHAT IS THE 'DUTY OF CARE'?

FROM all that has been said so far, it will be very clear that 'negligence' plays a vital part in most torts. Indeed, for many of them, negligence goes to the root of the action. However, 'negligence' may be an actual tort in its own right. We have treated it, up to now, as being more or less 'failure in the performance of a legal duty'. It must now be looked at from the point of view of *the absence of that amount of care which the law demands at all times of the 'reasonable man'*. This applies whenever (a) there is a duty of care in law, and (b) damage results from the lack of that care. In this sense of the word, there are no 'degrees of negligence' at all. Either it is present, in which case there is a valid cause of action, or it is not, in which case the action must fail.

Let us look at some examples of the tort of negligence. One obvious example is the motorist driving faster than he reasonably should. In every situation there is a speed which reasonable people considering the matter impartially would consider safe. It is always a matter of judgment in the light of particular conditions: the amount of traffic, the state of the weather, and so on. The motorist drives at 60 m.p.h. when reasonable people would have said that anything over 40 m.p.h. was risky. He has to brake to take a corner safely, but because the road is wet he skids and knocks down a woman on the pavement. This is a clear case where he is liable for damages for his negligence.

A surveyor is instructed on behalf of a potential buyer of a house to do a thorough structural survey. He fails to spot an outbreak of dry rot. The client buys the house and subsequently has to spend hundreds of pounds on eliminating the dry rot. The surveyor is liable for damages for his negligence.

A doctor diagnoses that a patient has influenza and tells him to go to bed and take aspirin, when he is actually in the early stages of poliomyelitis. If the patient suffers as a result of this faulty diagnosis, and if the medical evidence of other doctors convinces the court that the doctor could and should have known better he would be found negligent.

A workman superintending the operations of a crane and giving signals to the crane driver high up in his cabin who cannot see what is happening on the ground is negligent if he signals a load to be lowered when men below are still moving an earlier load and they are struck by the descending new load.

These are examples of lack of proper, reasonable skill and care: failure to observe the legal duty of care. And the persons affected are in an obvious direct and immediate relationship to the negligent person.

But you may get difficult cases when the person injured is not very close to the negligent person. He is not the doctor's patient, the surveyor's client, the workman's mate, the pedestrian or other person on the road whom the motorist knocks down. How far does the duty of care extend?

When we consider this vital question 'was there a duty of care owed in this case?' we are really back again to the question we previously discussed—'who is my neighbour?' And there is a very good example of this, in the facts of a case which fell to be decided first in 1943.

Mr Young was a motor-cyclist, who had a serious accident when he collided with a car in the main shopping street of a large and busy town. Just at that moment, a certain Mrs Bourhill was being assisted off a tram-car at least fifty feet away from the accident. On her back she was carrying a heavy basket. She did not see the accident, but she heard it. Still, she was never in any personal danger—nor, in all fairness to her, did she imagine that she was. But she did suffer a serious shock, and soon afterwards gave birth to a still-born child. In due course, she sued Mr Young for damages (it having been agreed that he was to blame for his collision with the car), and the question the court had to decide was—'did Mr Young's duty of care extend as far as Mrs Bourhill?' Should he, do you think, have had her in mind when he drove negligently? The final decision of the House of Lords was 'No'. In other words she was too far away from the scene of the accident. So, the plaintiff failed.

It is important to note that she did not fail because her shock was only nervous, and not physical. In our very first example, Mrs Brown, who fell into the cellar of the 'Dog and Duck', will be able to recover damages for nervous shock as well as for her fractured leg. But Mrs Bourhill failed because the court held that the duty of care of Mr Young did not extend as far as her.

On the other hand, the same principle was applied with an opposite effect in another case, which was decided in 1939. There, a Liverpool Corporation tram-car collided with, of all unfortunate things, a hearse on its way to a funeral. One may imagine the effect upon the principal mourners in the car behind, though they were not injured. And they secured damages for this mental shock, for the judge held that the duty of care certainly did extend to them on the facts of this case.

You will appreciate the difficulty of deciding in advance what view the court may take of the fresh facts in each case—for no two cases are ever identically the same. A widespread national disaster provided a particularly difficult legal problem of this nature, in 1946, when a 'test action' was brought (one of several similar actions which was tried while the other similarly placed plaintiffs awaited the decision and agreed to be bound by it) arising out of the tragic loss of the submarine *Thetis*.

The case in question was brought by the relatives of one of the seamen who lost their lives in that disaster. Evidence was given by technical experts that the sea had entered the *Thetis* through a torpedo tube and by way of a door, which the deceased, Seaman Woods, had opened. But it was further shown that Woods had opened that door only after examining a test cock, which showed no sign of

477

water in that tube. Now the test cock was proved to have been faulty, because it was in fact blocked with paint, through the negligence of the builders and painters of the submarine.

On those facts, the question before the court was—could the painters be held liable for the loss of life of Woods, and for that matter of many others as well? After long argument and much hesitation, the court decided that they were not so liable. No theoretical reasonable painter could have foreseen the ultimate result in this tragic case. There was actually some difference of opinion among the various judges as to whether the duty of care extended so far, and some thought that it did. But they all agreed that whether or not the duty did extend, the negligence of the painters was not connected directly enough with the accident, and so the damage suffered was 'too remote'.

From these several examples, can a conclusion be drawn? It has been stated that a duty to take care exists when a person does, or fails to do, an act which may have as its reasonable and probable result injury to others. This duty is general, although it does not become 'actionable' until damage has been caused. And the damage must be directly connected with the act or omission, and not therefore too remote.

One final point on negligence. Supposing you are walking along the bank of a river or canal and you see someone push someone else in. Can you be sued for negligence if you refrain from jumping in and attempting a rescue—particularly if you cannot swim? The answer is definitely 'No', as the example comes directly within the principle that a man is under no duty to prevent someone else from suffering damage as a result of the negligence of a third person.

THE BURDEN OF PROOF

On whom does it lie?

Suppose that there are two cars travelling in opposite directions along the same stretch of country road and they collide. The driver of one is killed, the driver of the other is concussed and suffers a state which is well known to both doctors and lawyers, known as 'retrograde amnesia'—which is to say he can recall nothing of the accident, nor of anything for some time before it. The relatives of the deceased man start an action against the survivor, the driver of the other car. There are no eye-witnesses to the accident. Under these circumstances, who has to prove what? On whom, to use the legal terms, rests the onus (the burden) of proof?

Basically and primarily this rests upon the plaintiff in any action. He (or in our example above, his relatives) alleges that the surviving driver drove negligently. He has to prove that this is the case—or most probably was so—from the evidence available, to the extent that if the defendant made no answer and called no evidence at all, the court would have to decide in the plaintiff's favour.

But certain general principles must be stated. Firstly, the mere fact that an accident has happened and someone has been hurt is not in itself evidence that anyone has been at fault. Secondly, in such a case as the one suggested, where

478

there are no eye-witnesses, it is not going to be enough for the plaintiff to produce a theory showing how the accident *might* have happened. On the other hand, he does not have to prove that the defendant must have been negligent 'beyond all reasonable doubt'. That is a maxim which applies to the Criminal Law alone. He must show that '*on the balance of probabilities*' the defendant was negligent.

He can, of course, do this by means of circumstantial evidence. Marks on the road, damage to vehicles, injuries to bodies, and the positions in which they were found—all these things can be combined to discharge fully the plaintiff's burden of proof, *provided* that the proper inference to be drawn from those facts makes it reasonably probable, on balance, that the defendant was negligent. Many cases come before the courts each week in which the questions to be resolved are the same, namely, 'what is the reasonable and proper inference to be drawn from this set of facts?'

What is '*Res Ipsa Loquitur*'?

So much for the general rule. But to it, as to almost all rules, there is an exception—or what appears to be an exception, for in fact it is not quite so, in this case. It has for many years been described by lawyers in a convenient brief Latin expression: *Res ipsa loquitur*—which means 'the thing speaks for itself'. This doctrine comes into operation in those cases in which the mere happening of an accident itself constitutes some primary evidence of negligence—enough, indeed, to discharge the plaintiff's primary burden of proof. When this happens, the burden shifts to the defendant, who must set about proving that on the balance of probabilities he was not negligent, though it might *appear* so.

A few simple examples will illustrate this doctrine quite clearly. Take, for instance, a claim by a railway passenger who is injured when two trains going in opposite directions collide. Whatever the actual reason for the collision, the railway authorities are bound to have been to some extent at fault unless they can prove that the incident arose through the fault of someone or something outside their control. Without fault on somebody's part, trains going in opposite directions cannot collide—*the thing speaks for itself.*

Again, as actually arose in one case, where a man went into hospital with two stiff fingers and emerged later with four stiff fingers, there was a presumption that someone had blundered—the thing spoke for itself! Not that the hospital authorities were unable to prove that there was no negligence, in fact, but in default of such proof the evidence of the facts alone was sufficient to discharge the plaintiff's primary burden.

Take a motoring example—it has been held that while a skid is not in itself evidence of negligence (it may be so caused, but it can happen without any negligence at all), nevertheless, if a vehicle skids for a long way and then mounts the pavement and hits down a pedestrian from behind, there is enough evidence of negligence from the mere facts of the case to throw the burden of proof on to the car driver, who must then establish that on the balance of probabilities he was innocent. The importance of this doctrine is that unless the defendant can prove positively that he is innocent, he must be found liable.

"Res ipsa loquitur."

What if there is more than one cause?

There is now one topic bearing on the question of the burden of proof which must be examined with some care. This is the distinction between two types of 'cause' of an accident. A preliminary example, taken from a real case, may help. It was decided in 1877, long before railways were nationalized, and the defendants were an ordinary public company.

Contrary to proper practice, the railway company had allowed far too many people to crowd into one of the carriages when the train stopped at a station. This, it was established, was negligence on their part. One of the people jammed like sardines inside the carriage was the plaintiff in this action, a Mr Jackson.

Trying to make more room for himself and those around him, he rose from his corner seat and put his hand on the jamb of the door. At that very moment, a desperate porter on the platform outside forced away the crowd of people who were still trying to press into the overcrowded carriage, and slammed the door— hard! The results to the plaintiff may well be imagined.

The court ultimately held that the porter was not negligent. He was acting with the best of intentions and had no opportunity to see Mr Jackson's hand in its unfortunate position. If he had been negligent, as a servant of the company, that would have been the end of the matter, and Jackson would have secured damages. But, in fact, Jackson failed, despite the fact that he had successfully proved the company were negligent in allowing too many people to jam into the carriage in the first place. And he failed because this was found by the court to have been only an indirect cause. The direct cause was the innocent but unfortunate action of the porter, which you will remember the court had decided was not negligent at all. The negligence of the railway company in allowing too many people into the carriage was not directly enough connected with the accident to Mr Jackson to make them pay damages to him.

From this case we learn that there may be two causes to an accident, and the plaintiff's burden is to prove not merely that he suffered damage, and not merely that the defendant was negligent, but that the proved negligence was the actual and direct cause of the accident.

This having been established, there must also be remembered a very important qualification. Although the defendant's negligence must be the direct cause of the accident, it need not by any means necessarily be the *immediate* cause. Take the case of a man negligently leaving a horse unattended on a highway, and the horse being whipped up by a mischievous lad so that it bolted and injured someone. In such a case, the court would hold the horse-owner to blame, because this was an accident which his mind should have contemplated, and he should not therefore have left the horse unattended.

THE STANDARD OF CARE

How high is the standard?

We have spoken of the 'duty of care' which is owed by ordinary people to one another, and how far this may be made to extend. But one question remains unanswered—'How high a standard of care must the person owing a duty of care exercise?' And also such subsidiary questions as, for example, 'Is the standard invariable, or does it vary from time to time under different circumstances?'

The principle is a particularly flexible one, varying in every case according to its individual circumstances. The whole proposition is based upon a general rule which has one key word of the greatest importance. That word is 'foreseeability'—a long word and not an attractive one, but one which has been found to be the only satisfactory basis for the general rule.

In 1951 a very famous leading case was heard which, after prolonged argument in the High Court and the Court of Appeal, finally went before the House of Lords.

The case arose through the employment by the Stepney Borough Council in one of their transport garages of a Mr Paris. Paris had, some time before he took this job, sustained a serious accident elsewhere and had lost an eye. He did not conceal this from the Council when he applied for the job. They set him to work doing mechanical welding, and after some time he had the terrible misfortune to have another accident which caused him to lose the sight of the remaining eye. He was thus totally blind. When he sued the Council, the whole action revolved around the question of how much the Council should have foreseen—in particular whether their duty was to exercise a higher standard of care toward a man they knew was one-eyed than they should have exercised to a man who had two eyes.

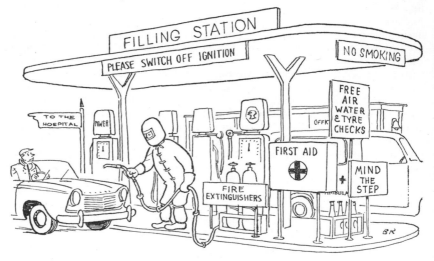

Foreseeability!

The Council asked, with logic—if their standard of care was high enough to protect them against a claim by Tom or Dick, who had two eyes apiece, why should that same standard not be enough to protect them from the claim of Harry, it not being their fault that Harry had only one eye? For Paris it was argued that the case would have been different if the Council had been ignorant of his condition when they took him on, but in this case they engaged a one-eyed man knowingly. That made it *foreseeable* that an accident to his remaining eye would render him totally blind. Therefore they should have provided him with protective goggles, although goggles were not usually provided for this kind of work. And this argument prevailed, and Paris won his action.

Immediately, lawyers started asking about the application of the converse—in other words, if the solution rests upon 'foreseeability', and a risk is foreseen but it also discovered that to eliminate it would be impossible from a financial point of view—perhaps even rendering the whole operation incapable of performance without the risk—do the cost and practicability of overcoming that risk affect the standard of care required? And in the year following the Paris case it was decided that such indeed is the rule.

We can thus summarize the law regarding the standard of care as follows. The basic standard required is that not of the brilliant but of the 'reasonable' man—the mythical 'man in the street'. And what standard of care is the reasonable man supposed to have? Answer: he must guard against those dangers which are reasonably probable, or foreseeable. He does not have to guard against those dangers which might conceivably be possible. The rule cannot afford to lose its value by being carried too far. If too high a standard were demanded, the reasonable man might be too frightened to do almost anything.

Further, this standard of care which the law demands of him (and in default of which it will award damages against him) varies not merely according to the general circumstances, but with the degree of the risk and (in the light of the principle in the Paris case) with the potential seriousness of the consequences.

Another statement of the general rule adds that if 'the usual practice' has led to a reasonable belief that accidents seldom or never occur when it is being carried out, then such usual practice is the standard required. Therefore, whether or not it should be raised depends upon the experience of the past.

There is, however, one particular section of this rule which contains a special modification. This comes in cases which involve work demanding 'special skills'. It is based upon the proposition that the 'reasonable man' is not likely to undertake the work at all unless he has acquired that special skill. Thus, the standard required is that normally found among men with this special skill.

To illustrate the principle, consider the case of a lady who, conscious of the fashion of the moment, decided she would like to wear that type of ear-ring which demands the ear being pierced and a tiny ring inserted. She went to a jeweller and asked him to do the necessary minor operation. The jeweller pointed out that she could have it done by a doctor—that doctors were generally the people to do it. The lady, however, having evident faith in this jeweller, wished him to pierce her ears for her. He consented, and used all the care which might be expected from him. Naturally, his skill was not equal to that of a surgeon, nor did he know what doctors know about sterilization, the dangers of infection, and so forth. And when the operation went awry, and the lady suffered from an infected ear, her action against the jeweller was unsuccessful. The standard of care demanded of him was not the same as would have been demanded of a surgeon. For it would be wrong to impose upon a person of whom a task is requested a standard of care and knowledge which can only be expected from a man in whose professional field this lies. It would have been very different if the jeweller had held himself out to the lady as having all the special skill required, so that she relied upon his self-advertised standard and suffered as a result.

SPECIAL CATEGORIES OF PEOPLE

Carriers of passengers

Apart from the modification regarding work involving special skills, there are several specific exceptions to the general rule, involving special categories of people. And by 'carriers of passengers' is meant essentially people who do carry people for hire or reward.

If I agree to drive you, my friend and neighbour, to the station in my car in the morning—a free lift—and I am not aware of any danger present in my car, then you must take things as you find them. You cannot afterwards claim that I should have warned you about dangers which I myself did not know were there. But if, for example, you catch a bus to the same station, over the same route, your position in law is very different, for the bus-owner by taking your fare as his reward thereby creates for himself a duty to be sure that the vehicle in which he carries you is safe. And if it turns out not to be so, even if the owner knew nothing about the defect, and you are injured in consequence, you can secure damages from him. And this duty affects not merely the condition of the vehicle, but also the way in which the journey is carried out. In other words, the owner of the bus, whether he be a private person or a great organization like London Transport, in return for your fare, makes you what is in effect a guarantee that his vehicle is safe and his driver competent and careful.

The law goes even further regarding passenger-carriers. Suppose you get on a train and by fraud avoid paying your fare. If that train is involved in an accident and you are injured, will your claim now be barred if it comes out that you were a fraud? No, you will succeed, because the railway organization accepted you as a passenger and that makes them liable to you under the general rule. The rule does not, however, apply to the stupid fellow who is at the time of the accident sitting, let us say, on some part of the undercarriage, as people have been known to do, before now. He has not been accepted as a passenger. He is a trespasser. In one sense, you are a trespasser, too, but the railway has taken you at your face value as you sit in your compartment.

Applying this to road transport again, and to the type of occurrence which one has been led to believe is all too common, it is general knowledge that very many big firms who run great fleets of lorries make strict regulations forbidding their drivers to pick up anyone, upon pain of losing their jobs. Now, supposing a lonely long-distance night driver falls for the temptation of a pair of pretty legs standing on the roadside and the appeal of a daintily pointed thumb—suppose he gives the girl a lift, and while she is travelling with him he has a crash, for which he is responsible. Will the girl succeed in a claim against the lorry-owners? Emphatically not. She may sue the driver personally, and if he is worth 'powder and shot' she may recover damages from him, but she has no claim against his employers.

Dangerous premises

Supposing you have a pot-hole in your drive—something that may affect many people. And supposing someone comes to visit you after dark, at your invitation, catches his heel in it, falls and injures himself. What is your position? To answer this, some history is essential.

Until fairly recently, legal liability arising from 'dangerous premises' was particularly complicated. All depended upon whether the plaintiff was what the law called 'an invitee', 'a licensee', or 'a trespasser'. It proved difficult clearly to define these terms, and action after action involved sustained legal argument as to exactly what category the plaintiff was in at the time of the accident.

The law was changed by the Occupiers' Liability Act, passed in 1957. This alters the duty, laying it down in a new form, a clear form, and a thoroughly desirable form. Since that Act became law, there has been no more argument about whether the plaintiff was 'an invitee' or 'a licensee' because it no longer matters. There may be some argument as to whether the defendant is 'the occupier', but the plaintiff is easily identified as either a 'visitor' or a 'trespasser'.

If he is a 'visitor' (and provided he is not a trespasser, he can be nothing else) then the Act lays down in terms that the occupier of the premises must 'take such care as is reasonable in all the circumstances of the case to see that the visitor will be reasonably safe in using the premises for the purpose for which he is invited or permitted by the occupier to be there'.

The Act goes even further than this. It gives specific guidance as to how the words 'in all the circumstances of the case' shall be interpreted. For instance, it allows the occupier to raise the defence of *volenti non fit injuria*, *i.e.* that the injured person voluntarily accepted the risk, if it applies. On the other hand, it says that if a visitor is on the premises as the result of a contract with the occupier, then the occupier cannot by that contract restrict or exclude the duty of care laid down by the Act.

These are but a few of many points made by this Act. But the mention of 'contracting out' of liability brings up the general question of when, if ever, this may be done. The answer is very rarely, and only when expressly permitted by an Act of Parliament. The Merchant Shipping Act, 1894, enables ship-owners to limit the amount payable by them to anyone injured or killed while travelling on a ship. The Carriage by Air Act, 1932, makes similar provisions regarding aircraft passengers. On the other hand, many statutes do not merely refrain from expressly authorizing 'contracting out'—they expressly forbid it. The Road Traffic Act, 1930, for example, specifically stopped carriers of passengers from imposing upon their passengers an agreement that the carrier would not be liable to them, or liable only within certain limits.

Manufacturers, distributors, repairers, and contractors

From dangerous vehicles and dangerous premises, let us turn for a moment to another category whose members are subject to a rather special liability— beyond the general Common Law rule. These include manufacturers, distributors, and repairers. The rule applicable to them was, if not actually founded, then at least very clearly defined in the celebrated leading case of *Donoghue* v. *Stevenson*, which reached the House of Lords in 1932.

The action arose when a lady purchased a bottle of ginger beer. It is not merely picturesque detail to emphasize that this bottle was of the opaque type common in the sale of ginger beer—indeed it is a point of absolutely vital importance in the decision. This lady bought this bottle which she could see neither through nor into. She poured some and drank it. Then she refilled her glass with the remaining contents of the bottle. To her horror, there emerged, she said, from the neck of the bottle a brown sludgy mess which, upon later examination, turned out to be a decomposed snail. The effect of this discovery upon the lady was not merely emotional, it was physical as well. The question now arose—who was liable in damages to her? This is why the opaque quality of the bottle became important. The retailer, from whom she bought it, had

485

received it, sealed and opaque, from the wholesaler, and had neither any idea nor any possibility of examining the horror that lay within. Surely the retailer could not be condemned? And exactly the same consideration applied to the wholesaler. Mrs Donoghue accordingly chose to sue the manufacturer. And it was held on a preliminary point of law that if it was true that the snail was actually there she should get damages. As was stated in terms in the House of Lords, "A manufacturer of products which he sells in such a form as to show that he intends them to reach the ultimate consumer in the form in which they left him, with no reasonable possibility of intermediate examination, and with knowledge that the absence of reasonable care in the preparation or putting-up of the products will result in injury to the consumer's life or property, owes a duty to the consumer to take reasonable care".

"The presence of a 'foreign body' . . ."

This rule stands as firmly today as when it was made, and its application extends, of course, far beyond bottles of ginger beer! The same rule applies to repairers. In one case a garage repairer had so negligently replaced the wheel of a lorry which he had been repairing that it came off, without warning, and hit a man walking along the road. The court felt that it could not impose upon the lorry driver a duty of removing all four hub-caps and checking the tightness of the wheel nuts, and justly made the repairer liable. On the other hand, if a car emerges from a repairer with a hugely excessive and entirely obvious play in the steering wheel, the driver cannot make the same claim with the same chance of success. He should have spotted the defect at once.

What about distributors? Supposing a hair-dye is distributed without any preliminary test being made of it at all, and the distributors advertise it as safe when they ought to have known or could have known if they had been careful that it was nothing of the kind—are they liable to any customer injured by using the dye? Indeed they are, provided only that the court is satisfied that the goods were distributed in such a way as to exclude examination of them by the customer before use.

It is as well to emphasize, however, that in all such cases as this, the burden remains squarely on the plaintiff to prove some negligence on the part of the defendant. But proof of the presence of an article such as that notorious snail is in itself evidence of negligence except where the defendant can give a satisfactory explanation. And from the plaintiff's point of view, it must be remembered that the presence of a 'foreign body' in a manufactured article is only evidence of negligence against the manufacturer *if* it is able to be proved that the article, when used, was in the same condition as it was when it left the hands of the manufacturer.

This has been put rather neatly in the phrase 'responsibility ceases when control ceases'. In other words—if intermediate examination of a product is both practical and expected, then liability may shift from the manufacturer to the person who should have made that examination.

Finally, consider contractors. Are they a special category? Yes, in that a person who does work under a contract and does it negligently so that some outside party gets hurt, may not be liable to that person in damages. But this must not be taken too far. If by his negligence he has created a dangerous state of things, he will be liable to anyone whom he should reasonably have contemplated as being likely to be injured by it *unless* (and here comes the same principle again) he had grounds for believing that his work would be tested or examined before it was used. And once it has been examined and passed, the contractor is free of all liability from that moment on, whatever may happen.

DAMAGES

How much will I get?

It has already been stated that in any action based on negligence, it is the general rule that you must prove that you have suffered damage. Without that proof, the action will fail. And we have already seen that damage may be found to have been too remote from the negligence, even where there has been a breach of the duty to take care.

What is the measure of damages recoverable? Supposing I have a rather dilapidated old wall at the bottom of my garden which has for years almost been tumbling down. While it is still up—just!—however, a passing motorist swerves through negligent driving, hits the wall a glancing blow, and there is my wall—a heap of rubble on the ground. Let us concede the motorist to be liable, here. What sum can I recover from him? Strictly speaking, I can only recover such a sum as will enable that wall to be restored to its pre-accident condition, and not a better condition. I might also get some amount of money which will represent the loss of 'the amenity' before it is restored. You can see at once what a fearfully difficult problem this may be.

However, it is a simple matter compared with some of the problems which arise when trying to assess damages for personal injuries. Even as a general proposition it must be recognized that it is impossible to convert pain and suffering into pounds, shillings, and pence. If you have been only slightly injured in a road accident, for example, you might truthfully say that you would not voluntarily go through that experience again for fifty thousand pounds, but that would hardly make your damage claim worth that sum.

Apart from this initial impossibility, though, an example will illustrate the basic difficulty of this problem. Let us say you have sustained a broken finger through someone's negligence. You go to your solicitor and ask him how much you are likely to recover by way of damages, assuming you win your action. And his hesitation in replying is only to be expected. For, how much is a broken finger worth? You will surely agree that a 'tariff'—so much for a broken finger, so much for a broken leg, and so on—would mean grave injustice. Suppose you are a business executive. A broken finger may mean little more than pain and inconvenience. Suppose, on the other hand, that you are a labourer, normally wielding a pick. Your grip may be affected, and you may have to go on to light (and less well paid) work, until it mends. But now suppose that you are a concert pianist. Until that finger mends, you will be totally deprived of earning your fees, even of practice. It may mean thousands of pounds lost before you have recovered your former ability, and your former prestige. And if the finger never totally recovers, remaining always slightly stiff, you might manage, even if you were a labourer—but your career as a pianist might well be ruined.

From this you will see that every single case has to be assessed on its own merits; other cases will not necessarily help, and even full knowledge and great experience can often lead only to an intelligent guess. And there are many other variants, which it is impossible to plan for or against—things such as future suffering, estimated future loss of wages, or amenities, perhaps even loss of expectation of life.

In the claim of almost every plaintiff in an action for damages there are certain items which can be worked out mathematically—loss of wages, for example, certain allowable expenses, and so forth. These give little trouble, generally, and they are known as 'Special Damages', in contrast to any damages for pain and suffering, which are referred to always as 'General Damages'.

There are one or two factors which happily present no problem at all, for statutes have laid down what is to be done to assess the rights and duties of those concerned. For example, a plaintiff at the time of the trial may have received sums of money by way of National Insurance Benefits, and is scheduled to receive certain further benefits in the future. In this case, it has been laid down that the benefits, which can be accurately calculated, will be halved, notionally, and the figure representing half the benefits receivable within five years of the accident will be deducted from the final 'Special Damages' awarded.

The plaintiff's duty

There is one further point which should be mentioned on the subject of damages, for it affects every single case. Again, let us take a simple example. My little Austin Seven car, parked at the side of a road, is smashed into by a negligent driver. It is going to take at least two months to complete the repairs. A car is desirable and pleasant for me, but not essential to my work. I can claim reasonable 'loss of use' by way of Special Damages. If, however, a car is necessary to me in my work, I can hire one and claim the hire charges. But I cannot hire a Rolls-Royce limousine and claim the cost of that.

The example is perhaps a little exaggerated, but the principle is a sound one. It is that upon every plaintiff lies an absolute duty to minimize, so far as is reasonably possible, the amount of his claim, and if he does not, the court will.

No one can be permitted, having sustained damage and having a good claim in law, to capitalize on his own misfortune at the expense of the wrong-doer, to sulk, and refuse to co-operate, so that the ultimate claim is higher than it might otherwise be.

But these are just a few of the enormous number of problems which arise out of the consideration of damages. We have only illustrated a few of the principles involved. But even these may lead to an appreciation of your solicitor's difficulties in giving you a fair and definite answer to your natural question: "How much am I likely to recover in pounds, shillings, and pence?"

FATAL ACCIDENTS

WE COME NOW to the situation where through someone's wrong-doing, someone's tort, another person is killed. Death may be immediate or may follow months later. What can be done, by way of bringing an action for the negligence which caused the accident and the death, if the injured person dies before he can initiate and complete legal proceedings?

THE OLD RULE

The old Common Law rule was that all actions of tort, whether for negligence or anything else, automatically ceased if either the plaintiff or the defendant died before the action was heard and determined. It made no difference whether the person who died was the plaintiff, *i.e.* the one who had been injured, or whether it was the defendant, *i.e.* the one alleged to be guilty of the tort. The result was precisely the same; the whole action was wiped out.

If it was the injured man who had died the cessation of the action could have no effect on him, but it could mean severe loss to his estate and therefore to those entitled to his property on his death. The cessation of the action was a great benefit to the negligent person because he escaped the consequences of his negligence.

The same rule applied to breaches of contract. To illustrate the operation of the rule, take the example of Mr A. entering into a contract with a builder to construct an addition to his house. The work is done, but done so badly that in a storm the roof of the added part is stripped off. Damage is, as a result, caused to the original house and the new addition is rendered useless.

Mr A. gets advice from his solicitor and his surveyor. He is advised that he has a good cause of action for damages and he decides to ask his solicitor to issue a writ against the builder, and this is done. The action might be based on contract, *i.e.* breach of the contract to do a workmanlike job; or on tort, *i.e.* the tort of negligence. This is a perfect example of the way in which contract and tort can overlap.

But then Mr A. suddenly dies of a stroke. Under the old rule that was an end of the legal proceedings and an end of the claim. Although Mr A.'s estate, *i.e.* his property, was seriously diminished in value as a result of the builder's wrong-doing, Mr A.'s heirs could not sue him.

The same result would follow if it was the builder who died unless he was in a partnership—in which case his partners would be liable—or was a company which, of course, continues in existence (see the chapters on *Partnership* and *Companies*).

Take another example: A., a pedestrian, is knocked down and severely injured by B. driving a car. A. starts proceedings for damages. B. dies—nothing to do with this accident—he dies after an illness. A. could get nothing, not even from B.'s insurance company. The cause of action ceased on B.'s death.

In the same situation if A. had died when he was knocked down, certain of his near dependants could claim compensation against B. for the financial loss they had suffered. This special right was created by the Fatal Accidents Act of 1846, and this Act is discussed in detail below. It is of the greatest importance.

But A.'s *estate, i.e.* his representatives (executors or administrators) acting on A.'s behalf, could not sue B. The right of action ceased on A.'s death.

And the right of certain near relatives to claim compensation depended on their proving some degree of financial dependence on A. Only a widow, widower, child, or parent could apply. So if A. was a man with no near relatives B. would pay nothing. No one could sue him.

THE NEW RULE

This unjust situation was substantially altered by an Act of Parliament in 1934. It was called the Law Reform (Miscellaneous Provisions) Act and it lays down the general rule that on the death of any person, any cause of action which he had at the time of his death, that is to say if he was in the position of being able to issue a writ for damages for negligence, or any other tort or breach of contract, or any other cause of action at the time of his death, then that right should not die with him, but should survive for the benefit of his estate. In other words, the right would pass to his legal personal representatives, *i.e.* either his executors, if he has made a will, or his administrators.

The Act also lays down the rule that if it is the alleged wrong-doer who dies and a writ has, or could have been issued against him before the date of his death, then the right to continue with the action survives against his estate. The injured person can continue proceedings against the alleged wrong-doer's personal representatives.

There are four exceptions to this new rule and they are:

(1) Actions for defamation.
(2) Actions for seduction.

(3) Actions for inducing one's spouse to leave or remain apart from another, *i.e.* the tort of enticement.
(4) Claims for damages for adultery.

In these four cases the cause of action still dies with either the wrong-doer or the injured person. It is difficult to understand why (1) above is excluded. The other three are not of great importance. The fact that a claim for damages for adultery ceases on the death of a co-respondent would not, of course, have any effect upon the divorce proceedings, or, at least, would not necessarily have any effect, unless the co-respondent was an essential witness.

Certain time limits apply when either the plaintiff or the defendant in such cases has died before an action is brought to an end by a decision of the Courts. If the action is brought *on behalf* of the estate of a deceased person, then the ordinary rules of limitation apply and time runs from the date when the cause of action arose. In the case of death caused by the tort of negligence the period of time at present is three years.

When the action is *against* the estates of deceased persons a special rule applies. The rule is that either proceedings must have been pending against him at the date of his death or that proceedings are taken out and begun not later than six months after his personal representatives take out a Grant of Representation, that is not later than six months after his executors or administrators get a Grant of Probate or a Grant of Letters of Administration.

This six months after the obtaining of the grant has the effect that the periods of limitation mentioned above may be exceeded if by chance the personal representatives do not obtain a grant for say four years after the death of the deceased person. They still may be faced with an action within six months after they get the grant. It is useless therefore for personal representatives to delay obtaining a grant in the hope that the course of action against the estate will die. It will not.

When the cause of action survives for the benefit of a deceased person's estate the damages will usually be the same as those which would have been recoverable by him if he had survived.

DAMAGES FOR LOSS OF EXPECTATION OF LIFE

A serious injury may not kill a man, but it may shorten his life. The Common Law courts over a period of years developed the doctrine that a man had a claim for diminution of his life, a claim, as it was called, for 'loss of expectation of life'. Thus, for example, a pedestrian knocked down by a motor-car and seriously injured would have a claim for damages, first for the pain and suffering caused by his injuries, secondly for loss of earnings, thirdly for any other special damage which he suffered as a result of the accident, and lastly, a separate item for loss of expectation of life if he could prove that his injuries were so severe that his reasonable expectation of life had been substantially cut down.

In one well-known case a Mr Flint brought an action against a Mr and Mrs Lovell to recover damages for personal injuries caused by Mrs Lovell's negligence in driving a motor-car so as to cause it to collide with the plaintiff's car. The collision was obviously a very serious one because he suffered very grave injuries indeed. In giving his judgment, the judge said: "In this case a gentleman of seventy years of age who, according to the evidence, was a man in good health and good condition for a man of his years, who was living an exceptionally active and energetic life and was able to do so without the slightest inconvenience, met with this terrible accident as a result of which his life will be very materially shortened. He is now, unhappily, according to the unanimous testimony of the doctors whom I have heard in this case, not expected to live very long. Probably something under a year.

"It is a most difficult thing to estimate damages in those circumstances. There is no doubt that Mr Flint suffered terribly as a result of this accident; there is no doubt that he will go on suffering from the effects—although, of course, the acute pain is now over—until the time arrives when he dies as a result of the accident. There is no doubt that he has lost the prospect of an enjoyable, vigorous, and happy old age which I am satisfied on the medical testimony might have gone on for a number of years if this unhappy accident had not occurred."

It appeared from the evidence that the old gentleman's life had probably been shortened by eight or nine years allowing, of course, for all the chances and perils of this mortal life.

The judge awarded £4,000 damages and it was clear that he was taking into account both the actual pain and suffering and the loss of expectation of what he called a happy and vigorous old age.

The judge's right to take loss of expectation of life into account was challenged in the Court of Appeal. But the Court of Appeal upheld the principle. Mr Flint was likely to die within two years of the accident instead of, as he might reasonably have expected, within ten years or even more.

Now, as the injured man in this case had not died as the result of the accident, *i.e.* as the immediate result of the accident, the Law Reform (Miscellaneous Provisions) Act of 1934 had no application to that case. But the case did clearly establish a legal right to claim damages for loss of expectation of life. The next interesting development was its application when the injured person died at once or very soon after the injury. The first case in which the 1934 Act was applied was one heard in 1936 where the injured man was knocked down by a motor-car, rendered unconscious, and died two days later without having recovered consciousness.

The judge held that as the dead man had been unconscious and incapable of pain, he had no cause of action to survive for the benefit of his estate and consequently refused to award damages for the shortening of his life. What influenced the judge was his view that damages for shortening of life were really given for the pain and distress which a person would feel when he realizes that his life had been shortened, when he realizes that he is likely to die within a calculable period of time, or at any rate an estimated period of time according to medical evidence when in the ordinary way he might have lived much longer.

It is an intelligible view. It is the kind of problem which shows how difficult these problems can be. The decision was quite reasonably accepted by the parties to that case. But the basis of the decision was subsequently over-ruled by an important case in 1937 where a young woman of twenty-three sustained severe injuries through the negligence of the defendant and as a result her leg was amputated and she died four days after the accident, having been unconscious practically the whole of that time.

The plaintiff in the case was her administrator, who claimed under the 1934 Act for damages for the pain and suffering of the deceased girl, for the loss of her leg and for the diminution of her expectation of life.

Both the trial judge and the Court of Appeal followed the decision mentioned above and refused to give damages for loss of expectation of life in view of the girl's unconsciousness for four days before her death. But the House of Lords reversed this decision and took the view that 'the object of the Law Reform Act is to put a person who by his negligence causes damage to someone, who subsequently dies, in precisely the same position in regard to liability (with certain qualifications which do not apply in this case) as he would have been in if the injured person had not died then, but had sued and recovered damages'. It followed, therefore, that the cause of action survived the death, and that damages for loss of expectation of life should be awarded to this girl, or rather to her estate, although she personally was possibly, or indeed very probably, quite unaware of the fact that her life had been shortened and that she was dying.

What is the basis for the assessment of damages for loss of expectation of life? This, of course, is an appallingly difficult question. In a case in 1941 which came to the House of Lords, an infant two and a half years old was fatally injured in a motor-car collision. She actually survived the collision but died the same day after having been unconscious all the time. Now, at the trial, damages for loss of expectation of life were assessed at £1,200. The Court of Appeal who were asked to reduce the figure, refused to do so by two judges to one, the dissenting judge thinking that the figure ought to be £350. So the House of Lords were asked to decide. The House of Lords decided that the way to look at this matter was to call it not loss of expectation of life but loss of expectation of happiness. As they pointed out, to live for twenty years in conditions of acute misery, acute poverty, and so on, may not be a very happy existence, and twenty years of such a life is not worth as much in terms of money as fewer years of a happy life.

Therefore, said the judges, one must try to find out not merely how long the injured person might have been reasonably expected to live and by how much that period has been shortened, but what kind of life could he or she have reasonably been expected to live. The various considerations to be taken into account can be summarized as follows:

(a) The courts must be satisfied that the circumstances of the life of the person who was killed were likely on balance to lead to a positive measure of future happiness. It is for the loss of prospective happiness measured objectively by the courts that damages are awarded.

(b) No regard must be paid to financial losses or gain during the period of life of which the victim had been deprived. Thus no consideration for loss of future earnings under this head of damage. This particular head of damage is in respect of loss of life alone, not of loss of future earnings or inheritance, etc.

(c) The damages should be reduced in the case of a very young child as there is necessarily so much uncertainty about the child's future that no confident estimate of prospective happiness can be named.

(d) Wealth and social status should not in themselves result in increased damages because happiness does not depend on them.

(e) Finally, the Lord Chancellor emphasized that damages which would be proper for a *disabling injury* may be much greater than the damages for loss of life altogether, and that for damages for loss of expectation of life by itself, only very moderate figures should be chosen.

With all those considerations in mind, the House of Lords reduced the damages under this particular heading in this case from £1,200 to £200. It must be remembered that the victim was a child of two and a half. She was living in modest but quite favourable circumstances in a village where her father had been in continuous employment for fifteen years.

As a result of this leading decision which, of course, binds all the other courts in the land, damages for loss of expectation of life in subsequent cases have generally tended to follow this pattern and are nowadays in the neighbourhood of £500 where the deceased person is in the prime of life and otherwise conforms to, or the facts of his case comply with, the conditions laid down by the House of Lords. Where a very young child is concerned the figure is usually less, nearer to the £200 awarded in this particular case.

Damages for loss of earnings suffered by the deceased must be limited to the period during which he survived the injury. His personal representative suing on behalf of his estate cannot claim the loss of earnings which he would not have made if he had not died.

The same considerations apply to damages for pain and suffering or the loss of a leg or arm or other limb. Here again the damages must be limited to the period for which the deceased person lived after receiving the injuries.

DAMAGES WHEN DEATH IS INSTANTANEOUS

When death is instantaneous the only damages which could be awarded under the Law Reform Act described above are damages for the loss of expectation of life, and those are necessarily small compared with what the damages would be for pain and suffering or loss of earnings if the deceased survived for a period of time. Damages for loss of expectation of life are not likely to exceed £500. The loss to any dependants of the deceased could, however, be substantial. But as briefly mentioned at the beginning of this section, dependants were given a special personal right to compensation for *their* financial loss by the Fatal Accidents Act, 1846, generally known among lawyers as Lord Campbell's Act because he was the person mainly responsible for having it introduced into Parliament and getting it passed into law.

The basis of the Fatal Accidents Act is that it shall give compensation to the dependants of the deceased. The Law Reform action described above is one brought or contested entirely on behalf of the deceased himself or the estate of

494

the deceased. The Fatal Accidents Act action is one brought by the deceased's personal representative on behalf of *the dependants* of the deceased. So if there are no certain specified dependants as defined below, no action can be brought.

Although the right of action under the Act exists for the benefit of the dependants of the deceased it must be brought by and in the name of the personal representative, *i.e.* the executors or the administrators.

If, however, the executor or the administrator is slack about this and does not start proceedings within six months after the death, or where no executor or administrator has been appointed (for example, there may be no estate at all except this possible claim for damages), then one or any of the dependants may themselves bring the action.

Who are the dependants on whose behalf the action may be brought? Under the original Act of 1846, the action might be brought for the benefit of the wife, husband, parent, and child, but no other. In other words, a fairly limited class of dependants, although they are the most important ones and the nearest in blood or marriage relationship to the deceased person. However, the classes of dependants have been extended by the Fatal Accidents Act of 1959 so as to include the brother, sister, uncle, or aunt of the deceased, or the issue of any of these. It is further provided that in working out any relationship for the purpose of the Act,

(i) an adopted person is to be treated as the child of the person by whom he is adopted;

(ii) a relationship by affinity should be treated as a relationship by consanguinity;

(iii) a relationship of half blood is to be treated as a relationship of whole blood;

(iv) the step-child of the person is to be treated as that person's child;

(v) an illegitimate child should be treated as the legitimate child of his mother and reputed father.

(The terms consanguinity and affinity are explained in the chapter on *Marriage*. Briefly, consanguinity means a relationship by blood while affinity means a relationship as a result of a marriage.)

The executors or administrators of the estate may very well be among the dependants described above. That makes no difference. They still sue in their representative capacity, *i.e.* as personal representative, not as whatever relation they may happen to be.

There is a time limit within which the action must be brought. It must be started within three years after the death of the deceased person. If the claim for the loss of life arises out of an action involving ships, the action should be brought within two years of the death of the deceased, as such an action may have to be brought in the Admiralty Court where, in this particular class of case, a two-year period of limitation applies.

How are damages payable under the Fatal Accidents Acts assessed? There is no question under these Acts of trying to turn into money the pain and suffering which is a standard item in claims of damages where the injured person is hurt but does not die. Similarly there is no difficulty about estimating the value of a shortened life. The basis is loss to dependants. What loss have they suffered as a result of the deceased's death? They cannot be awarded damages to console them for his loss. If they prove their case, *i.e.* prove that it was, for instance, the negligence of the defendant which caused the deceased's death, they must then go on to prove financial loss and if they cannot prove financial loss the defendant in effect wins his case.

It is not necessary that the plaintiffs should prove that they were actually getting financial benefit from the deceased at the time of his death. It is possible to assess *prospective* loss provided there is a reasonable expectation of financial advantage and not a mere speculative possibility. But in most cases, of course, there is actual immediate loss.

Assuming that the plaintiffs will have incurred funeral expenses, these will be awarded, but they must be reasonable. When the judge is deciding what is reasonable he will not necessarily allow the full cost of some very elaborate and expensive funeral or grave stone.

The amount of damages under these Fatal Accidents Acts is therefore purely a matter of applying a series of mathematical rules, or as one judge said: "A hard matter of pounds, shillings, and pence, subject to the element of reasonable future probabilities."

Now this may make the working out of the damages appear extremely simple: hard mathematical rules; a matter of pounds, shillings, and pence. On the contrary it is a difficult problem.

The reason why it's difficult can be seen at once when one applies oneself to working out a particular problem. For example, a man who earns £20 a week and is aged forty has a wife and three children to support and is killed in an accident which is due to someone else's negligence. There is a clear claim against the wrong-doer which is duly brought by the personal representatives of the injured man and they have to put forward a statement of what they think ought to be paid to the dependants, that is the widow and the three children.

The dead man was earning £20 a week. First of all there must be deducted from that £20 a week what he needed for personal expenditure. That may not be very difficult: the amount he spent on himself in the way of clothes, food away from home, travelling, and so on, is probably readily ascertainable within a reasonable degree of approximation. These figures, together with the income tax he pays and any other personal expenditure, have to be deducted from his gross wage of £20 a week to discover what is then left for the maintenance of his wife and family. Let us assume that one arrives at a figure of, say, £16 a week. This is merely guesswork and not meant to indicate what might apply in any particular case.

How is one to capitalize, that is represent by one lump sum, the value of £16 a week to his dependants? And for how many weeks, months, and years is one to assume that this £16 a week would have continued to be earned? He might in the future earn substantially more. By the time he is fifty he might be earning £40 a week. On the other hand there might be periods of shortage of work, short time, complete unemployment which would mean that his earnings would be very substantially reduced and might come down to figures like £3–4 a week.

One must also take into account that if he had not been injured and killed in this accident he might later on, owing to the chances of our mortal life, suffer another accident and either be seriously incapacitated or killed, when there might be no claim for negligence because it was pure accident.

How is anyone to make an intelligent guess under these circumstances? To add to the difficulty he might suffer from illness—serious illnesses like bronchitis, a long bout of pneumonia, tuberculosis, cancer, other things that may seriously affect his earnings. Then again one has the situation where his habits of life may change. He may become a drunkard instead of a sober and industrious person.

Clearly the future is not something which can be worked out with mathematical exactitude. Nevertheless it is the duty of the judge to award to the dependants a sum which represents what in his opinion is the fair immediate capital value of the deceased man's future net earnings. For example, if the man is aged forty, he might very well be reasonably entitled to say that, allowing for all the mischances of this life, he would have had, say, ten to fifteen years working life before him at a wage of £20 a week gross. The kind of work must also be taken into account. If the man was aged fifty at his death he would take a figure of less than ten. It is perfectly true that all being well a man of forty might work for twenty-five years and a man of fifty might work for fifteen years. Possibly both might work for more. But the judge has to put into the scale all the imponderables which no one can know about. And, taking all the factors into account, he has to work on some sort of rough measure of justice of this kind.

Another matter which the judge has got to take into account is the possibility of the widow marrying again. For example, if the man leaves a young and attractive woman, he may realize and feel obliged to take into account the possibility that she may marry again.

He must also take into account the ages of the children, the possibility of their earning, and when they are likely to earn.

The point is that he must be fair *not only to the dependants* of the man who has been killed, *but also to the man who has to pay* the damages. It is not a question of awarding some penal sum to punish the man who has committed this wrong-doing. After all, the wrong-doing is a tort, not a deliberate crime. It is a fault of carelessness rather than a deliberate act such as the commission of a crime. So there is no question of punishing the man who has committed the act of negligence, it is only a question of finding a fair and reasonable figure of compensation. Probably no sum of money is going to be fair, adequate, and right in every case, to compensate for the death of a person who has family responsibilities. It is no use hoping that the law will work magic. The law, working through the judges, can only do its best to be fair and reasonable to both sides.

As the basis of the action is the monetary loss suffered by the dependants it would follow that all monetary advantages must be taken into account in assessing the damages. This principle, of course, would mean that if the death of the injured person meant that an insurance policy on his life became payable, the amount of that policy would have to be deducted from the amount of the damages. It is obviously right in general that any incidental monetary advantages which might follow after the death should be taken into account. But it was thought to be rather hard that if the deceased had, for instance, an insurance policy or a right to benefit under a Pension Scheme, these sums should be set against the amount of compensation which the wrong-doer would otherwise have to pay. It is therefore provided in the Fatal Accidents Act of 1959 that in assessing damages under this heading there shall not be taken into account any insurance money, any benefit under the National Insurance Acts, or payments by a Friendly Society or Trade Union, or any pension or any gratuity which has been or will be paid as a result of the death. All these sums will go to the people who are entitled to them—widows, other dependants, and so on, or according to the will—and they will not affect the amount of the damages assessed by the court to be paid by the wrong-doing defendant.

In most cases, actions under the Law Reform Act of 1934 mentioned above where you may have a claim for loss of expectation of life, and actions under the Fatal Accidents Acts are tried at the same time. Very often the persons entitled to the deceased's estate are the same as the persons entitled to damages under the Fatal Accidents Acts. Quite obviously, where the persons entitled to the estate are a widow or children they are exactly the same people as those entitled to damages as dependants by virtue of the Fatal Accidents Acts. In such cases the question arises whether the damages given under one Act should affect the damages given under the other. Now it is provided in the 1934 Act that the rights conferred by that Act for the benefit of the estates of deceased persons shall be *in addition to* and shall not take away from any rights conferred on the dependants of the deceased by the Fatal Accidents Acts.

On the other hand, in assessing damages under the Fatal Accidents Act the court must pay regard to damages recoverable under the earlier Act. For example, the court decides that under the Law Reform Act £500 is to be paid for loss of expectation of life, but under the Fatal Accidents Act £5,000 is to be paid to the widow as compensation. If the widow is also entitled to the £500 by virtue of the fact that her husband had left all his property to her in his will, then the judge can take that £500 into account and he may knock the £5,000 down to £4,500.

WHEN TORT AND CONTRACT OVERLAP

OUTSIDE the realm of torts, damages can, as has been said, be recovered in the courts in actions brought by parties to a contract. The basic difference between contract and tort is that in the case of a contract the parties to the contract have fixed their duties to each other between themselves. If one party breaks the contract, the other can successfully sue him for damages which it can be proved resulted to him as a consequence of that breach.

For instance, if A. contracts with B. to repair B.'s motor-car by a certain date and he knows that it is essential to B.'s business that the car should be

498

available by that date, then if A. fails to keep his promise he may be liable to B. for loss which B. suffers as a result. That is a straight example of money damages being payable to compensate for actual provable loss. There is not necessarily any tort here (*e.g.* negligence). There *may* be negligence, but in essence the action is one for breach of contract, failure to honour a term of the contract.

On the other hand, if A. does the work on time, but does it so badly (*i.e.* negligently) that the car soon breaks down, B. can sue him for that negligence in performing the contract. A. is, in fact, in breach of contract in failing to observe a term implied in any such contract to do the work skilfully, but also guilty of negligence. But only one set of damages will be awarded.

There are a number of instances where the rights and duties existing between two people may arise either out of contract or out of tort, or sometimes from both.

When an action arises strictly out of contract, it is a governing principle that only parties to that contract can sue on it, either to enforce it, or to claim damages for the breach of it. A duty arising from a contract between A. and B. cannot normally be expected to bind C. who is not a party to the contract.

On the other hand, in some cases, a breach of contract signed between A. and B. may result in a tort being committed against C. For example, if a man employs a surgeon to perform an operation on his (the man's) son and the surgeon is guilty of negligence, the son can sue the surgeon in tort, although his link with the surgeon arose purely by reason of the contract between the surgeon and his father.

Another instance where tort overlaps contract is where one party is induced by the efforts of an outsider to break the valid contract he has made. In such a case, the man who has held to his part of the contract may sue the outsider in tort, for inducing the breach.

Again, professional men owe a duty to their patients or clients in tort as well as in contract. The duty owed by a solicitor to his client is to do his work with proper skill. He is liable to his client for professional negligence, he is not liable to other people. That is primarily a breach of contract. But medical men, as we have already seen from the example given above, owe a duty in tort to their patients, whether or not there has been any contract between them. Dentists, and also nurses, are vulnerable in exactly the same way.

Considering the position of hospitals, it provides us with a good example of how a principle can be changed by the Courts. It used to be accepted as the law that in the case of a voluntary hospital, the duty owed by the governors or management committee of the hospital toward a patient in the hospital was limited to the exercise by them of reasonable care and skill in their selection of medical staff. Gradually it came to be realized that this principle, once fair, was now creating an anomalous position. Finally, a case was decided which called for a restatement of the principle, and this was used to modify the original principle. From that case onward, a hospital is recognized as being liable for any negligence of its servants, just as any other employer is, as a basic rule. And today, the patient injured by the negligence of hospital staff has but to show that the act which caused his injury was committed under the general control of the hospital—that those who caused his injury were in the employment of the hospital. But he must bear in mind that consultants are not on the staff of hospitals, though they treat people there, so that if it is a mistake by a consultant which caused the injury or damage, then the consultant must be sued personally, and an action against the hospital alone will fail if all the hospital staff were innocent of fault.

LIABILITY OF AND FOR INFANTS

IN ORDINARY SPEECH, 'infancy' may mean a number of different things. In law, it has a definite meaning. It means an individual, male or female, who has not yet attained the age of twenty-one. It is with the position of the infant

In law 'infant' means an individual, male or female, under the age of 21.

in law that we are here going to deal—that is, the infant in relation to the Civil Law, for his position in relation to the Criminal Law is governed by quite different considerations. We must consider the liability of the infant and the liability to him and for him, under two separate heads, namely, contract and tort. The meaning of 'contract' is clear enough; the meaning of 'tort' will be explained when we come to it.

THE POSITION OF THE INFANT IN CONTRACT

The position of the person under twenty-one in the field of the law of contract is one which has been established over very many years, mainly by the Common Law, and to a lesser extent by statute, particularly the important Infants Relief Act of 1874. Generally speaking, an infant cannot enter into a legally binding contract.

Most contracts entered into by infants are either null and void, or are voidable, *i.e.* can be cancelled by the infant. They may be binding on the other party to the contract if he is an adult, but may be voidable by the infant. In other words, he could cancel them either during his infancy or within a reasonable time after he becomes twenty-one.

The Infants Relief Act of 1874 declared three classes of contracts by an infant to be absolutely void. They are:

(a) a contract for the repayment of money lent to the infant or to be lent to him;

(b) a contract for goods supplied or to be supplied to the infant (except necessaries), and

(c) admissions by the infant that he owes money, *e.g.* this would cover such items as promissory notes, post-dated cheques, and so on.

However, this law, which is designed, of course, for the protection of young people under twenty-one and to enable them to get out of the consequences of having rashly entered into an unwise contract, is subject to two very important exceptions.

Two kinds of contracts entered into by an infant are legally binding on him. They are:

(a) contracts for the supply to him of necessaries;

(b) contracts which are wholly or partly for his benefit.

The term 'necessaries' has a special meaning in law. It covers items which are held by the courts to be suitable to the infant's social position (usually dependent on his parents' position in life), *provided they are also genuinely needed* by him at the time of the contract.

There is a very good illustration of this in a case decided in 1908, the principle of which is still good law today. Inman was a Cambridge undergraduate, the son of a well-to-do architect. He went to a Cambridge tailor called Nash, and ordered a number of clothes, including no less than eleven fancy waistcoats. When he would not pay, Nash issued a writ. Inman said that he was an infant. Nash said that eleven fancy waistcoats were quite suitable as a wardrobe for a wealthy young undergraduate. But Inman called his father, who said in evidence that his son was already amply supplied with clothes. Nash lost his case. He had not proved that they were actually required by the infant at the time of the contract. So the fancy waistcoats were not in law 'necessaries', and the tailor's bill was never paid, for the contract was not one of those binding on the infant. The tailor was, of course, taking a chance. If, on the other hand, the contract had been for *one* suit or even perhaps for *one* fancy waistcoat, the court would probably have held the articles to be necessaries and therefore that the contract was legally binding.

The other type of contract binding on the infant is one which is for his benefit. This type covers contracts of apprenticeship and also of service. One of the leading cases on this point concerns a young man who later became a very famous professional boxer—Jack Doyle. In 1935, Doyle, who was still under twenty-one, held a licence to box professionally from the British Boxing Board of Control. One of the terms of that licence (which was the result of a contract between Doyle and the Board), said that if Doyle was disqualified, the Board could order his purse to be forfeited. Doyle fought at the White City and was disqualified. Forfeiture of his purse was ordered. Doyle sued the White City for his purse, saying that as he was an infant, he could not be bound by the clause which permitted forfeiture of his purse. But the court held that the contract under which he held his licence was the means whereby he could earn his living, even though he was an infant. It was thus for his benefit, and he was bound by it in law. And so he lost his purse for that fight.

Next there is the class of contract which is voidable by him, provided he repudiates it during his infancy or within a reasonable time of his reaching twenty-one. This class includes contracts of tenancy, and also marriage settlements. But the infant who exercises his rights cannot have it quite all his own way. Because if the infant has derived some benefit from the contract—he cannot recover from the other party what he has already paid under the contract, whether in money or otherwise. For example, an infant rented a house and agreed to pay the landlord £100 for the furniture. He paid £60 and gave a promissory note for the balance. After some months' use of the house and furniture he came of age, and then took proceedings to get the contract and the promissory note set aside, and to recover the money which he had paid. He obtained relief from *future liabilities on the contract, and the promissory note*. But he could not recover the money paid for furniture of which he had enjoyed the benefit. "No doubt", said Lord Coleridge, C.J., "the words of the Infants Relief Act, 1874, are strong and general; but a reasonable construction ought to be put upon them. . . . When an infant has paid for something and has *consumed* or *used* it, it is contrary to natural justice that he should recover back the money *which he has paid*." Then, as another example, an infant who in 1929 exchanged his motor-cycle combination for a motor-car, was unable to recover his motor-cycle combination when the car broke down after some time, because he had already derived some benefit from the car.

What is the position of an infant who, while entering into a contract, does so by fraudulently misrepresenting his age as being over twenty-one. When the other party then seeks to enforce it, can the infant say to him, "Whatever I said at the time, I was in fact an infant, and you therefore cannot sue me"? The answer to this question is not by any means simple. Certain plaintiffs in the past, finding themselves facing this situation, tried ingeniously to sue the infant not under the contract, but in tort, where infancy is no defence, claiming damages for fraud equivalent to the amount due under the contract, the fraud being the false representation that the infant was actually twenty-one. But the courts would not have this. They considered it was merely an ingenious method of enforcing a contract. The example shows how far the law goes to protect an infant from actions for damages for breach of contract. It is evident why people are reluctant to enter into any kind of contract with infants. Even though infants are liable on contracts for 'necessaries', or contracts for their benefit as defined above, it may be necessary to prove the point in a court. Many a business man will take a chance when he knows with whom he is dealing and the family background. But when he does not, he rightly insists on cash down before delivery of the goods he is asked to supply.

If an infant who has misrepresented his age to be over twenty-one has secured possession of goods which are still in his possession at the time of the hearing, he can be made by the court to return them to the seller. If, however, he has parted with those goods, the seller cannot recover the goods from whomever has bought them from the infant, nor can he recover from the infant the money obtained by the infant for them. This is because to enforce the sale would entail suing the infant in contract, to which the infant has a complete defence, whereas the restoration of the goods, if the infant still has them, is an equitable obligation.

THE POSITION OF THE INFANT IN TORT

The general rule is that an infant is liable personally to anyone whom he has wronged. He may be too young to be able to foresee the consequences of, for example, an act of trespass or the publishing of a slander or a libel, on his part, but if he intended to do the act which involved the trespass or the slander or libel, he is liable for the consequences of it, even though he was unable to foresee those consequences—he knew perfectly well he was doing wrong from the start. But if the tort is one which depends upon either malice or negligence, it is an arguable question of fact which the court must decide—was the infant of sufficient age to foresee the consequences of his act, or was he old enough to form a malicious intention?

A parent is not normally responsible in law for the wrongful act of his child. But if the infant was acting as an employee of the parent at the time, then the parent can be liable in his capacity of employer, provided that the tort was committed by the infant in the course of his service. The parent may also be liable in certain cases for his own personal negligence in allowing the infant to have the opportunity to commit the tort.

PARENTAL RIGHT OF CONTROL
OVER A CHILD

The general rule is that the father of an infant (or in the case of an illegitimate child, the mother) has custody and control of him up to the age of twenty-one, unless those rights of custody and control have been removed by the court. In addition, the father has the right to the infant's services. His exercise of authority over his child must never be unreasonable, but provided it is not that, a parent can prevent any child under twenty-one from leaving his roof against the parent's will. In all cases, the welfare of the child is the very first consideration of any court. It is suggested by the legal authorities, though not directly stated, that no action for false imprisonment will lie against a father who forcibly stops a daughter of sixteen from eloping to Gretna Green, for example. And a father may regain possession of his child by reasonable force if the child has been removed from him—something that he certainly cannot do in respect of his wife.

Within the bounds of reason, a father may beat or even imprison a child in his legal custody, either to punish the child, or to prevent any threatened misconduct, *but* the force used must always be reasonable, and the father must act in good faith. This is because the parent's authority exists only for the benefit of the child and the maintenance of domestic discipline. There must be no arbitrary punishment. And, for example, if a father orders his son to commit a crime, and beats him when the son refuses, that is most clearly an assault.

This same general authority applies also to guardians appointed by the court or by the father through his will or by deed. And during those periods when it exists, the authority of a schoolmaster and the right to chastise the child is exactly the same as that of a parent, as is also the authority of a master of his legally bound apprentice, demanding only the exercise of judgment and prudence.

DUTY OF CARE TOWARD CHILDREN

The duties of a schoolmaster have been the subject of a large number of cases. Basically, the teacher's duty is to exercise such care toward a child in his charge as would be exercised by a reasonably careful parent. Where a master sent a thirteen-year-old girl to poke the fire and adjust a damper with which she was not in any way familiar, and she was injured doing this, he was held to have been negligent. On the other hand, where a boy of twelve was told to carry a long-spouted oil-can from one classroom to another, and another boy came suddenly round a corner and caught his eye on the spout, the teacher was found not to have been negligent. A teacher cannot be expected to go too far in law in his efforts to prevent injury arising between children playing together when in his care. He must, for example, supervise young children at play, though this can hardly be continuous or complete supervision. And the older they are the less supervision they are presumed to need. It is a matter of common-sense precaution in the light of particular circumstances. A fairly recent case which contained so much law of public importance that it went for final decision to the House of Lords, may serve as an excellent example. This arose out of a very tragic accident where a little boy of four, who was at a nursery school, was dressed up ready to go for a walk. During the short period when the teacher left the classroom to attend to some other child who had cut himself, he wandered out of the classroom, down the drive, through the gates, and toddled into the main road outside. At that very moment, a lorry was passing, the driver of which, in the agony of the moment, swerved desperately to avoid him. The lorry never touched the child, but it crashed into a telegraph pole, and the driver was killed. His relatives brought an action against the Education Authority (the employer of the teacher), claiming that the accident was due solely to their servant, the teacher, having failed in her duty to take care. It was argued by the defendants first that their duty did not extend so far—that they owed no duty to the passing lorry driver. And they further claimed that it would have taken 'almost superhuman vision' to foresee such an accident as this. The final decision of the House of Lords was to the effect that people in charge of tiny tots in premises adjoining a busy road do owe a duty to users of that road to see that children who are too young to have acquired any road sense cannot possibly escape unattended in this way from the premises, because they should foresee that an accident involving users of the road, as well as to the children, might well result from such an escape. So the Education Authority were held liable.

There is one more point regarding schools. The school premises must be kept in a properly safe condition. School authorities have been found liable to children who have suffered in accidents arising from such things as the defective condition of the school playground or even from unswept snow on the steps of the school chapel. Moreover, if the school takes it upon itself to provide a bus to and from school for the pupils, it has to see that such vehicle is reasonably safe.

A parent who gives a child a gun, or air-gun, without proper instruction, may be liable if anyone is hurt owing to that child's negligence.

CHILDREN AND DANGEROUS PREMISES, ETC.

As stated above, the general liability both by and toward infants in tort is the same as that concerning adults. There is, however, one particular field of tort where there are specially stringent precautions which have to be observed for the protection of those of tender years—in other words, where the basic duty owed is the same as to adults, but where the scope of those duties is wider. This is in respect of dangerous premises, dangerous property, and dangerous things.

In another section we have dealt with the special duties owed to the main categories of persons coming on to such premises. The duty of care toward children is the same, basically, as that owed to adults—to take reasonable care that the visitor will be reasonably safe in using the premises for his lawful purposes. But the occupier must expect children to be less careful than adults. Warnings, adequate for adults, might be quite insufficient in respect of children.

A special duty toward children may still, therefore, be said to come into operation whenever there is something on the premises which is first an *allurement* or attraction to children, the sort of thing that children would be tempted to play about with, or near, or on—and secondly, which is *dangerous* or porentially dangerous. The leading cases on this point contain an abundance of examples: a turntable on a railway company's premises which was known to be frequented by children; a bank where children were allowed to play at the foot of which were tins and broken glass; the poisonous berries of attractive appearance in a public park. In all these cases the owners or occupiers of the land were held to be liable in damages to the children who were hurt or poisoned, because they knew the children played there and did not do enough to stop or

505

protect them. Further, where a company moved a truck by means of a long wire rope without first taking steps to warn off any children who might be playing in the area, they were held liable to a child injured by their action, it being held that they had acted 'in reckless disregard of the child's presence'.

If there is a clear and rigidly enforced rule that children may not come on to the land unless accompanied by adults, then there is no special duty owed to children higher than that owed to the adults. When a child is trespassing, also, the duty is no higher to the child than it is to an adult trespasser, with one exception—if children are *known* to be present on the land, you must not do anything which will injure the child unless the child is specifically warned first. In general, the landowner must assume that the public may include little children. But his duty rarely extends beyond not creating or sustaining concealed dangers and giving proper and sufficient warning. "Parents can hardly shift the burden of looking after their children on to the shoulders of those who happen to have accessible bits of land," as a judge said in one case, "but different considerations may well apply to public parks or recognized playgrounds where parents allow their children to go unaccompanied in the reasonable belief that they are safe." Even so, if the danger in such places is obvious and unconcealed, even to a child of tender years, the playground authority may not be liable.

Elsewhere, we have examined the position of the plaintiff in an action who has been guilty of some contributory negligence. Do the same rules apply to children? It is certainly true that what may be contributory negligence in an adult is not necessarily negligence in a child. Negligence means 'want of ordinary care' and 'ordinary care' means such care as may reasonably be expected from the plaintiff in the particular case. So, although there is no definite age below which a child may be said in law to be incapable of contributory negligence (as, for example, in the Criminal Law where a child under the age of eight is deemed totally incapable of forming a criminal intention), nevertheless a tiny tot who cannot appreciate very much at all can clearly not be capable of bearing any duty of care at all, and so cannot be guilty of contributory negligence.

There is one very old case on this point which established a principle which has remained good law ever since. This arose when a Mr Nurdin left a horse and cart unattended in the street. When a little boy named Lynch climbed on to the back of the cart, and another boy whacked the horse, which moved sharply forward, throwing little Lynch to the ground and injuring him, it was Mr Nurdin who was held liable to him.

The general rule may thus be stated to be that in considering whether a child has taken reasonable care for its own safety, you must have regard to the age of the child, the whole circumstances of the case, as well as the knowledge which the particular child may be expected to have had of the dangers to which the negligence of an adult may have exposed him.

A final point—a child can only sue someone 'through his next friend', who is usually his father. The father becomes, therefore, the plaintiff in the action to this extent. Supposing a child has been injured partly by the negligence of his father, and partly by the negligence of another, the contributory negligence of the father will not mean that the damages to the child will be in any way reduced.

506

SOME POINTS OF GENERAL LAW ABOUT CHILDREN

It has already been stated that an infant in law is one who is not yet twenty-one years of age. When does he become twenty-one? By English Law, at the beginning of the day immediately *before* his twenty-first birthday. By Scots Law, at the beginning of the day of his twenty-first birthday.

So if a child is born in a leap year on February 29th, he does not have to suffer the fate erroneously imagined by W. S. Gilbert in *The Pirates of Penzance*. He will not have to wait for eighty-four years until he is legally twenty-one! If, for instance, he was born on February 29th, 1956, he will be twenty-one in English Law from the beginning of February 28th, 1977. Under Scots Law he will be twenty-one immediately after midnight on February 28th, 1977.

MOTOR ACCIDENTS

THE FACTORS that must be considered under this heading fall into two categories—criminal liability and civil liability. As the former may sometimes have some effect upon the latter, and as criminal developments invariably precede civil in point of time, some mention may be made of that aspect first, but only very briefly as Road Traffic Law, from a criminal standpoint, is so large and important a subject that a complete Section of this book has been framed to deal with it.

In general terms, it may here be said only that the current and most recent statute concerning users of the highway (not merely motorists but motor-cyclists, pedal-cyclists and pedestrians too) is the Road Traffic Act, 1960. Under its authority exist also numerous Regulations, such as the Construction and Use Regulations, Traffic Sign Regulations and so forth. But the Act of 1960 serves to codify and to consolidate most of the criminal law to which the ordinary road-user is subject.

Turning from the criminal to the civil aspect of motor accidents, the first vital difference between civil and criminal liability is that in a criminal court there is not such a thing as 'contributory negligence'. A man may be only 1 per cent. to blame for an accident, and yet if the other party, who may perhaps not even be summoned, is found during the hearing to have been 99 per cent. to blame, it matters not—any man driving with a slight degree of carelessness can correctly be convicted under the Road Traffic Act. In Civil Law, however, the exact proportions of blame attaching to each party concerned is of the most vital importance, and will materially affect the award of damages. This is why a conviction for, say, careless driving against one party to a civil motoring action may have but little relevance to, and effect on, that action, though it arises out of the same accident.

In Civil Law, for example, the rule of the road is necessarily not absolutely inflexible. Being on the 'wrong side of the road' is in itself but slight evidence of negligence—it may be reasonably explained—at times it may be almost obligatory, for there are occasions when a collision can only be avoided by means of a sudden move to the 'wrong side'. Regarding speed, the general guiding rule is that all drivers must proceed at such a speed that they can pull up to a stop within the limits of their vision, should any emergency arise. Failure to do this, will almost inevitably involve at least partial responsibility for any accident.

Another distinction between criminal and civil cases is that whereas in the former, negligence of the defendant must be proved 'beyond a reasonable doubt', the rule applicable to civil cases is that the plaintiff must show that 'the balance of probability' is in his favour. And this applies not only to motorists but to all road users. It may be little realized that in a civil court, a pedestrian who steps into the road when a car is so near that its driver has no reasonable chance of stopping, may be liable in damages to the motorist. It has been held to be some evidence of civil negligence against a driver if a tyre bursts, if a vehicle overturns, or if the vehicle is so loaded that it hits a bridge under which it is passing.

Further, in Civil Law, a reasonable man must anticipate a certain degree of negligence by others and take steps to avoid it, if the particular form of negligence is frequently acknowledged as a hazard. A driver faced with a green traffic light may proceed across, ignoring the possibility that a driver coming from his right or left may cross in face of the red light which faces him. On the other hand, a driver approaching a zebra crossing must guard against the possibility that behind a vehicle blocking his view of the pavement ahead may be a pedestrian waiting to move out on to the crossing.

Regarding vehicle insurance, though this has been fully dealt with elsewhere, it should be stressed that the breach of the duty to insure will not merely make the offender guilty of a criminal offence. It will also render him personally liable in damages for breach of statutory duty at the suit of any person thereby deprived of an effective remedy through that breach.

As has been fully dealt with in the section of this book dealing with torts, there are cases where the circumstances of the accident may in themselves be sufficient to discharge the plaintiff's civil onus of primary proof—these are the cases which come within the principle of *res ipsa loquitur*.

The procedure in a civil action

Lastly, a word regarding the civil procedure with which the lawyer attending any party to a civil motoring action will be concerned. The plaintiff commences the action by issuing and serving upon the defendant a writ—of which the defendant's solicitor may accept service on his behalf. The defendant, within a short and strictly defined period, files a document at the court called an 'Appearance', indicating that he intends to contest the matter. The plaintiff now delivers a 'Statement of Claim', setting out the facts he alleges, and his detailed allegations of negligence. Subject to certain procedural exceptions, he is thereafter restricted to those allegations which he makes in that document and cannot shift his ground at the trial. The defendant for his part delivers to the plaintiff a 'Defence', answering fully all those allegations and facts which he contests. He may also contend that the plaintiff has done some wrong and damaged him. In this case, associated with the defence, he may make a 'Counter-Claim'. The plaintiff, if this is the case, files a 'Reply' (to the Defence) 'and Defence to Counter-Claim'. Further pleadings are more rarely seen, though either side may request the Court to order that 'Further and Better Particulars' of the opponent's case should be delivered. At this stage, the pleadings are said to be closed, and the plaintiff issues a 'Summons for Directions', at the hearing of which all points of procedure and evidence likely to be relevant at the trial of the action are discussed between the parties' representatives and the court makes the appropriate order. Incidentally, all summonses of this nature are dealt with by a Master (or District Registrar, in the provinces), who is a court official, part of whose duty is to deal with this type of dispute or discussion in his private chambers.

Once the Order for Directions has been made, both sides make final preparations for trial and wait, patiently or otherwise, for the action to appear in the court list for hearing. When the case has been heard and judgment given, the successful party enters and files the judgment itself and a copy is served upon the unsuccessful party. Subject to any possible questions of an appeal, the only remaining steps are for the costs of the action to be scrutinized (or 'taxed', as the lawyers call it) and allowed at a figure decided upon by one of the Taxing Masters, and when this has been completed, the successful party can take steps to enforce the terms of the judgment, should the loser not comply with the terms of it. These steps may be many and various and are known collectively as the 'execution' of the judgment.

THE LEGAL AID AND ADVICE SCHEME

INTRODUCTORY

IF ANYONE urgently needs the services of a lawyer to bring or to defend a case, or to give advice, it is very hard that he should be deprived of this and perhaps deprived of justice if he simply has not got the money to pay the fees.

It was the realization of this basic point that governed the minds of those responsible for the introduction of the Legal Aid and Advice Act, 1949. It had taken a long time to put this principle into statutory form, because of the difficulties of working out a practical method, and the history of Legal Aid as we know it in England today is a long, as well as an interesting one—too long to be set out here, where the reader's principal concern is much more with the important questions "What aid can I get?" and "How can I get it?". But it is fair to say that this great benefit to society was entirely conceived by lawyers, formulated by lawyers, and is today administered by lawyers.

In such fields as divorce, for example, there had long been in existence what was known as the 'Poor Persons' Divorce Department, and also certain provisions for men and women in the Forces. Furthermore, it had long been a principle of English Law that anyone in the dock for a criminal offence could always be sure of representation, at least if the charge against him was of any real consequence. Even today, it is commonly reported in the Press that 'Mr So-and-so, charged with housebreaking, applied to the court for legal aid,

Legal Aid!

his application was granted, and the case was adjourned for fourteen days' or words to that effect. But legal aid in criminal matters is something that has always been available through the ordinary courts. Most solicitors who deal with crime have agreed to provide their services for a very nominal fee paid by the court, and many barristers have done the same. Criminal legal aid does not form part of the Legal Aid and Advice Scheme, and we exclude it from consideration here, for that reason.

After many years of careful discussion and argument, the Legal Aid and Advice Act, 1949, became Law. At first, legal aid was available only for certain types of case, but it has gradually been extended as more and more parts of the Act have been brought into operation, until today there is very little by way of legal trouble where the ordinary citizen cannot get first of all advice, and later, should it be required, financial aid to enable him to acquire the services of both solicitor and counsel, without paying for this one penny more than he can genuinely afford.

The one golden principle underlying the Scheme is that, under it, the lawyers provide the legal help and assistance which a reasonable man would obtain for himself if he had the money to do so. Once a man has been granted legal aid, he has the absolute right to choose any solicitor or barrister who is in the Scheme and, with very few restrictions, deal with the matter exactly as if he was paying the lawyer's bill, himself. Legal aid is not some special type of assistance which can only be obtained through some official department. It is fundamentally just another method whereby the services of a lawyer can be made available to a wider public.

One other general point should perhaps be made about the Scheme as a whole before going into details about it. Over the years since 1949, the Scheme has undergone a great number of small additions and improvements. Further, the financial levels under which you must come to be entitled to aid in one form or another have been steadily raised as the general cost of living has risen. But, these financial limits apart, there are very few points now remaining to be amended or further implemented.

Nevertheless, further alterations here and there may still have to be made to keep the Scheme completely up to date. There are pamphlets available to everyone at all Legal Aid Offices and many other places, apart from which any solicitor will be able to answer most of your queries. There are organizations such as the Citizens' Advice Bureaux to perform the same general function in this respect. Subject to your means you can be pretty well guaranteed whatever financial assistance is necessary for you to obtain legal aid and advice in almost every kind of legal difficulty.

WHEN IS LEGAL AID AVAILABLE

Legal Aid is available for so nearly every form of legal trouble that it is easier and quicker to set out here those few sets of circumstances where it is *not* available. In general terms, whenever you need advice or assistance in any problem which has a legal aspect, whenever you have a cause of action against someone, or whenever anyone has taken action, or is threatening to take action, against you which you have grounds for defending—then legal aid in one form or another is available to you, subject to means.

When is legal aid *not* available, then? Basically, not unless there is a problem or dispute of some kind. It is to help people in trouble. If you can raise the money to buy a house, you cannot get legal aid to pay the legal charges involved in the purchase, for instance, but if any dispute arises out of the purchase, you probably can.

In matters of dispute, legal aid is available to all who come within the financial limits of the Scheme and who need it, *except* for the following few instances:

    (a) Defamation. (Libel and slander.)
    (b) Breach of Promise of Marriage.

(c) Seduction. (Claim for loss of wife's services after she has been seduced.)
(d) Enticement. (Damages for enticing a wife or child away.)
(e) Election Petitions.
(f) Proceedings arising out of Judgment Summonses for debts.
(g) Relator Actions. (Not affecting ordinary persons and very rare.)
(h) Instances where private organizations can take proceedings for penalties under certain Acts, *e.g.* Lord's Day Observance Society.

The list looks long, but in fact only (a) and (b) are of any importance to most people.

With these few exceptions, and with the additional exception of securing representation at a Coroner's Inquest, there are virtually no disputes in law for which you cannot obtain total or partial assistance, depending only on your means.

Assistance when granted is, of course, not always total. If you are earning enough to be able to afford a certain amount, you may be offered legal aid provided you agree to pay a contribution which is assessed by the local Legal Aid Committee based on the findings made to them by the National Assistance Board who have examined your resources. The Committee also fix the method of payment—the initial payment and the amount of any instalments. If later you win your action with costs, you may sometimes wind up with the return of some of your original contribution. Regarding that contribution, should your financial circumstances change completely during the course of your action, its total, and the instalments, may be varied in the discretion of the Committee.

It is important to say here that the fact that the National Assistance Board come into the picture does *not* mean that legal aid is a form of national assistance. The National Assistance Board officers are available to help the local Legal Aid Committee solely because of their experience in assessing people's means. They advise on finance and nothing else.

Where does all the money come from, to work this Scheme? In the first place, since the Legal Aid authorities finance you, then if you win your case and are awarded costs against the other party, it is the Fund, and not you, who gets these costs back. In the second place, the lawyers who are in the Scheme (and very few are not) have agreed to take a reduced fee from the Fund for the work they do on your behalf. The Fund itself is non-profit-making. It has a certain income from the contributions, and it does not at present have to meet any costs awarded in favour of successful opponents. We say 'at present' there, because there is a body of opinion which thinks that hardship may sometimes be suffered by someone just too well-off to be granted legal aid, who is sued by an assisted person, and who successfully defends the action at his own expense. In such a case, it can be said to have been established by the court that he had done nothing wrong, and yet he has had to pay all his own costs, whereas the State has financed the action brought against him and in that sense put him to all the trouble and expense of fighting and winning. That is something which may or may not be the subject of a future alteration in the Scheme.

Whatever amount the Legal Aid Fund is 'in the red' at the end of each year, is covered by Government funds—in other words by the taxpayer. So no one has any grounds for being 'too proud' to apply for legal aid. It is not charity and you will be assisted exactly as much as your means make it necessary for you to secure justice.

Finally it should be mentioned that you can secure financial aid not merely to take a dispute to court. You can also under the Scheme get ordinary legal advice, as well as action short of actual litigation.

The four main departments of the Scheme, with which we will now deal separately, are as follows:

(1) Legal Aid for High Court and County Court Actions.
(2) Legal Aid for Proceedings before Magistrates.
(3) Legal Aid for Action other than in the Courts.
(4) Legal Advice not requiring any action by the lawyer.

(1) Legal Aid for High Court and County Court Actions

First, the financial limits at the time of writing. You must not have a 'disposable income' of more than £700 per year. Also, if you have a 'disposable capital' of more than £500 you may be barred from obtaining legal aid, but the Committee have a discretion.

That word 'disposable' is vital. It may be very different indeed from your normal income and capital. It has been authoritatively stated that a man with three children may have an actual income as high as £1,600 per year and yet be within these limits. It is not possible to work out conclusively in advance whether or not you come within those limits, for there are many variants covered by the regulations now current and there is always the opportunity for discretion to be exercised by the Committee, or by the Assistance Board who work out the figures and present them to the Committee. But it is possible to give you some idea of the allowances which will be deducted in order to convert your actual income and capital into your 'disposable' income and capital.

First of all the question of your income. The estimated amount of Income Tax you will pay is deducted. Next, there may be deducted up to a total of 30s per week any of the following—the first 15s of sick pay being received from a Trade Union or Friendly Society, the first 15s of any private pension, any maternity or attendance allowance under the National Insurance Acts, and any disablement pension or similar State payment.

Your 'net rent' (which means rent plus rates, repairs allowance and mortgage payments but less rent gained by sub-letting part of your home) will further be deducted, and if you are not a householder, a reasonable living allowance. Further deductions may be made in respect of the support you provide for your wife or husband and any dependent relatives.

Regarding your capital and savings, you may first take it that the value of your furniture and effects, personal clothing and tools of your trade will be deducted. The Board will also deduct one half of whatever your house would realize over £3,000. You will not have to regard as capital the first £125 of any life or endowment policy you may own. If you have a debt which must be paid during the coming twelve months, this will be deducted. Regarding dependent relatives, including children, and also your wife or husband, there is

513

an allowance of £75 for the first person dependent, £50 for the second, and £25 for each other person.

But you do not have to work these details out. You only have to fill in a short and simple form which you can get from any Legal Aid Office, or direct from your solicitor, who will also help you fill it in. Not every solicitor in the country is available to you, but from the Law List in your Public Library or at the Legal Aid Office you can get a list of those in the Scheme in your area. Any Citizen's Advice Bureau will help you with the form and also to find a solicitor.

The solicitor you choose has a primary right to decline to act for you—for example, he may already have been instructed by the other party to the dispute. But assuming he agrees to act for you, then with his help you will complete the form with brief details of your claim as well as your financial position.

When completed, your form goes to the Legal Aid authorities, where it comes before what is called a Certifying Committee. This committee is made up of practising solicitors and barristers. Each case is considered on its merits. To get legal aid, you do not have to show that you have a 'stone wall certainty' of a case. You have only to show that you have apparently got a reasonable cause of action. The committee will grant (or refuse) your Certificate on the basis of the details of the case on your form. They will not hear the other side's point of view. Later, a different committee may possibly consider a similar form submitted by the man you are suing, and it may be that both of you will be granted Certificates.

Your Certificate, once granted, lasts until it is discharged. If during the period before the actual trial something new turns up which renders your action absolutely certain to fail, then your solicitor is in duty bound to report this to the Legal Aid authorities, who may reconsider the case and discharge your Certificate from that date onwards. And if, for example, the man you are suing makes a reasonable offer which your legal advisers say should be accepted by you and you refuse, insisting on carrying on to try and get more, again the authorities can discharge your Certificate at that point, for to proceed may mean risking an award of costs against you.

But assuming your case has apparent merit and the Committee grant you a Certificate, then the papers pass through a special (and confidential) department of the National Assistance Board. Their representative interviews you, and a report is made to the committee, who assess your contribution and the way you can afford to pay it. You are then offered the Certificate, provided you accept liability for the contribution and agree to pay the instalments demanded. If you should default in those instalments, then your Certificate can be discharged for that, too, of course.

As to what your contributions may be, you may take it that if your disposable capital is under £125 and your disposable income under £250, your contribution will be nothing. If you have more than this, your contribution may be for all your disposable capital over £125, plus one-third of such part of your disposable income as is over £250. Your assets, incidentally, are coupled with those of your spouse, unless he or she is the opposing party in your action.

Once you have accepted the terms offered you, and keep your part of the arrangement, you can forget about lawyers' bills in connection with that matter altogether, with one exception. That is that if your action comes to trial, and if you lose, and if the judge, bearing in mind not only the merits of your case but your general conduct, decides in effect that you have been 'pulling a fast one' over the Legal Aid authorities and over your lawyers—then the judge can make an order condemning you personally in whatever costs he thinks fit. But if both your case and your conduct are reasonable, and you just happen to lose, then the judge will generally not make any order for costs against you, a legally assisted person.

If you lose the trial of the action, you may yet, if your case is strong enough, sometimes get legal aid to undertake an appeal to the Court of Appeal against the decision. It is even possible, now, to have your legal aid extended to cover an appeal to the House of Lords, although the Lords can only be appealed to where there is a point of law of public importance at issue in the case.

A final point. The law imposes certain time limits in various matters, and you may find yourself in an emergency. Going through the normal full process of getting a Certificate and having your contribution assessed may be too long to prevent your claim from being barred. In that event, your solicitor will guide you how to secure the immediate issue of an Emergency Certificate.

(2) Legal Aid for Proceedings before Magistrates

First of all—what type of case does this part of the Scheme cover? Five types, in fact. First, cases relating to orders under the Matrimonial Proceedings (Magistrates' Courts) Act, 1960. Do not confuse this with divorce, which is a High Court matter, and so comes under the part of the Scheme we have just dealt with. This is a question of separation orders, and the like, where the parties remain married but live apart, the guilty party paying a weekly sum to the other, the court both assessing the sum and collecting it.

Secondly, this part of the Scheme covers orders made under the Guardianship of Infants Acts, where neither husband nor wife may have committed an actual matrimonial offence, but where they may agree to live apart, and the Court has to consider the financial upkeep of the children, as well as custody, access, and their general welfare.

Thirdly, this part of the Scheme covers those matters where an illegitimate child is born, and the mother summons the man she claims to be the father, asking the magistrates for an order that he shall make regular payments toward the child's upkeep. As in matrimonial cases, either or both parties may be granted legal aid.

Fourthly, if either party to a bastardy summons (or affiliation summons, as it is also known) has reasonable grounds for an appeal from the magistrates to Quarter Sessions, this, too, can be the subject of a Legal Aid Certificate.

The fifth and final type of case is so rare as to be almost non-existent, today. It covers proceedings for possession under the Small Tenements Recovery Act, 1838. Normally, possession cases are heard in the County Court and thus come under the part of the Scheme already dealt with. But very occasionally a dwelling bears so small an annual sum by way of rent and rates that the magistrates can deal with the case. All property has risen so much in value since 1838 that today there must be very few places which still remain within the scope of this Act. Should it arise, however, legal aid is available to either party, or both.

The procedure for obtaining legal aid and also the financial limits are exactly the same as those for High Court and County Court actions.

Cases before the magistrates sometimes involve rather more urgency than, for example, High Court actions, and so the Local Secretary has power to grant the Certificate without waiting for the Certifying Committee to consider it.

(3) Legal Aid for Action other than in the Courts

This part of the Scheme, which is authorized by the Act of 1949, was only brought into operation in 1960, but has already proved of great value. It concerns problems which demand action of some sort by a solicitor, but which fall short of an actual High Court or County Court case.

For example, supposing you have a dispute with your neighbour which will call for a solicitor's letter to put matters right. Or supposing you have reasonable grounds for thinking that your husband or wife has been committing adultery but you have no proof, and you need an inquiry agent to do some work for you. Or again, supposing you have been knocked down on a zebra crossing but were knocked unconscious and have little recollection and no witnesses—you want investigations made, a Police Report acquired (and paid for), statements taken from witnesses and so forth. You may not be able to afford the normal charges and disbursements involved.

All you have to do is to put your problem to any solicitor who is in the Scheme. He will guide you on how to fill in the appropriate form, which you can get either from him or from the Legal Aid Office. The Certificate for which you apply here is called a 'Claims Certificate'. Legal aid can be obtained to cover all his services in connection with your problem, short of litigation.

In the case of our supposed accident, for example, the solicitor may pursue the matter until he has obtained some admission of liability, or at any rate a reasonable offer, from the other party. If the claim is settled without any need for litigation, the solicitor's work for you will be fully covered by this type of Certificate. On the other hand, if the motorist proves stubborn so that proceedings have to be started, your Claims Certificate can be converted into a full Litigation Certificate.

The financial limits for this type of legal aid are firstly that your 'disposable capital' must not be more than £125, and your 'disposable income' must not be more than would attract a contribution of more than £25. This last is because £25 is the maximum contribution you will be asked to pay for this type of legal aid.

(4) Legal Advice

The first point about getting Legal Advice, as opposed to Legal Aid, is that there are two complete sections to this part of the Scheme. There is the Statutory Scheme, founded by the 1949 Act, and brought into operation in 1960. But also there is the Voluntary Scheme, introduced also in 1960, but which is quite outside the 1949 Act, being purely a conception of the Law Society, which is the governing body of the solicitors' profession.

To deal with the Voluntary Scheme first, this applies to anyone, whatever their income, whatever their capital. Quite irrespective of their means, anyone in England and Wales is entitled to walk into the office of any solicitor in the Scheme, pay exactly £1, and consult him about any kind of problem at all, involving up to half an hour of the solicitor's time. What you can get is his verbal advice. He may agree to confirm this in a written note if you ask him. That is the Voluntary Scheme.

Under the Statutory Scheme you will pay only 2s 6d or even nothing, if you have not more than £125 capital, ignoring the value of your house, your furniture, and the tools of your trade, and you have not earned more than £7 10s during the seven days immediately before your call on the solicitor. In assessing this £7 10s, from your actual income you may deduct all Income Tax and National Insurance contributions, and also £2 5s in respect of each adult dependant, including your spouse, and £1 7s in respect of each child.

If these conditions apply to you, you may take advantage of the Statutory Scheme. Your solicitor will assist you to complete a form, and then for up to an hour and a half you can discuss your problem with him and receive the benefit of his advice. For this privilege you will have to pay him exactly half a crown. If you are on National Assistance you get the same privilege for nothing at all.

Legal advice supplied under the Statutory Scheme is based purely on your statements on the form. The correctness of those statements may afterwards be checked, and naturally any false statements will land you in very serious trouble.

If you and your spouse both have assets and income, they must be added together as before, unless of course it is your spouse who is the other party to the problem.

There are so many occasions in life today when people could have avoided serious trouble if only they had made it their business to find out right at the start what their legal position was, quite independent of any action that needed to be taken. The true work of a solicitor is not merely getting people out of trouble as far as possible, but stopping them from getting into trouble in the first place. And he cannot do this at all if he is not consulted until trouble has already arisen. This part of the Legal Aid and Advice Scheme can serve to help you avoid much trouble and expense.

NEIGHBOURS

OVERHANGING TREES

MANY PEOPLE are concerned about trees which, though they stand in their neighbours' gardens, have spreading branches which overhang their gardens. Their concern and objection is not as a rule based on the mere fact that the branches overhang. They are concerned because those branches, when

If the overhanging branches of your neighbour's tree offend—

—you are entitled to remove them.

If the roots obtrude—

—you may dig them up.

But you have no right to the fruit—

—or to the use of the cut branches.

These belong—

—to the owner of the tree!

in full leaf, prevent rain falling on a flower-bed or give so much shade that nothing will grow in their gardens below it. Furthermore, in the autumn the leaves from these branches may cause them a considerable amount of additional work when they fall into their own gardens. Is there anything that can be done, if the owner of those trees is not willing to lop or trim back the overhanging branches?

The law is that you are entitled, that you have the *right* to cut back the branches which overhang your garden or land and also to trim hedges which hang over your property. If the overhanging branches or tops of the hedges are doing actual damage, it may be possible by a court order to compel their owner to trim and lop them. When they overhang, without doing actual measurable damage—and this, of course, is the usual case—your legal remedy, if their owner is not willing to cut them back, is to carry out the work yourself.

You should strictly limit yourself to cutting them at the boundary line; at the point where they cross the boundary between your garden and your neighbour's. To go beyond would be trespassing. Moreover, what you cut off does not belong to you. It remains your neighbour's property and the best thing to do is to deposit it gently on his land. It would be a great mistake to spoil the legality of what you have done in actually cutting off the branches by assuming ownership of them. In a famous case which came to the courts a man cut off the branches of an apple tree which overhung his land. He behaved with strict legal correctitude by cutting them off at the point where they crossed the boundary line, but he stepped beyond the bounds of legal correctitude when he assumed ownership over the branches, and the fruit which they bore, and actually sold the fruit. When his neighbour sued him for damages, the courts upheld his right to cut the branches at the point where they crossed his land but equally upheld his neighbour's right to ownership of the branches and the fruit, and he had to pay damages. The damages were the amount of money which he had received by the sale of the apples which those branches bore.

ENCROACHING ROOTS

The same principles apply to the roots of the neighbour's trees which encroach under your land. As these are usually invisible, you may not worry about them unless you suddenly find that they are causing damage. Whether they do cause damage or not is utterly irrelevant to your right to cut them; just as it is irrelevant whether the overhanging branches cause damage or not. As a matter of practical common sense you may worry about neither the overhanging branches nor the encroaching roots unless, in fact, they are doing some damage like interfering with the growth of your own plants, or sucking moisture from your own ground. Nevertheless the same principle applies to roots or to branches —you need not prove damage, you have the right to cut the roots at the point where they encroach on your land, just as you have the right to cut the branches at the point where they overhang your land.

There have been a number of cases in the courts where the encroaching roots, which have grown invisibly and stealthily under the ground of a neighbour have ultimately done damage to his house. The roots of the beautiful Lombardy poplar, for instance, travel horizontally for a considerable distance. Owing to their immense power of sucking moisture from the soil, they can, when they get near to the foundations of a house, cause considerable damage. They can cause the soil to dry and contract, the house to settle, and the foundations to crack. There have been cases where the damage has been so great that a considerable amount of money has been necessary to underpin the building. In such cases the courts have awarded damages to the owner of the house against the owner of the trees.

When such dramatic damage has been caused, an argument which is sometimes put forward by the owner of the trees, if they were there before the house was built, is that he is not legally liable for the damage to the house. The argument runs something like this:

> "My trees were here before you came along and built your house; therefore I am not responsible. You should never have built your house where you did."

This is no answer in law. It does not matter in the least whether the trees were there first or not. It sounds an ingenious argument but it is fundamentally unsound in law. Nothing alters the fact that the owner of the neighbouring land is legally entitled to be protected from this kind of nuisance in law and if he suffers actual loss or harm he can claim damages. As stated above, if he suffers no loss or harm or only suffers loss or damage to some minor extent he still has his remedy of cutting off the encroaching roots at the point where they cross his boundary. If additionally he suffers actual provable loss or damage he has a claim for damages to compensate him. Underpinning foundations has of course led to heavy claims for damages and they have been successful in a number of reported cases.

A further argument which has also been advanced in cases over the last thirty years is that if the trees were self-sown, *i.e.* natural-grown trees which no human had planted, then the owner of the land on which those trees grow is not responsible to his neighbour for any damage which they may cause. This interesting new argument has been heard in the courts and decisively settled in favour of the owner of the damaged property. It concerned elms whose roots damaged the foundations of a neighbouring house. The courts held clearly that it was irrelevant whether the trees were self-sown or actually planted by the owner of the adjoining land or by his predecessor in title. All that mattered was that their roots had caused damage. That entitled the householder to claim compensation for the harm done to his property.

BOUNDARY FENCES, WALLS, AND HEDGES

There is no general legal obligation on anyone to build a fence or wall or to plant a hedge to mark the boundaries of his garden or his land. He may very well think it desirable in his own interests to mark out the limits of his property and put something up on the boundary to show clearly to the world where his territory begins and ends and what property he claims. But as a matter of ordinary general law he is not obliged to do so; *i.e.* apart from a special private agreement he is not, in general, obliged to erect boundary fences, hedges, or walls. Neither is his neighbour.

It follows from this basic principle that if you do put up a fence or wall purely to please yourself you are under no debt or obligation to anyone else to keep it in good repair. As you need never have put it up in the first place you are not legally bound to anyone if you let it fall into disrepair. That may be unneighbourly behaviour but no one can compel you to repair it. It must be emphasized that that is the general legal position under the Common Law where there is no private agreement or private obligation under the deeds of the property, or no public nuisance as when your wall is a danger to users of the highway.

You may, however, find that when you buy a house you are obliged to accept an obligation to put up one or more fences or to keep them in repair if they are already erected. It is not unusual today when large areas of land are being divided up into building plots that the Deed of Conveyance or the Deed of Transfer of *each* property contains a covenant, that is to say an obligation on each owner to erect one or more of the fences or walls around his property, or if they are already erected, to continue to maintain them.

Nevertheless, many owners of houses have no such obligation in their title deeds. It is also very often extremely difficult to find out who owns the fences, the walls, or the hedges which are already there.

If you feel grieved at the sight of a decayed wall or decrepit fence along the side of your garden and would like to have it repaired, or restored, the first question obviously is to decide who owns it. If that boundary fence, hedge, or wall is your property then the repairs must be a matter for you. If they belong to your neighbour you must rely on friendly persuasion, unless you happen to know of a covenant in his title deeds obliging him to repair that particular boundary wall, fence, or hedge. You might know, because there could well be a reference to that covenant in your own deeds.

How is ownership to be decided if the title deeds do not make it clear? The first point is that if the fence stands on your land it is your fence, whoever erected it. Even if it was erected by your immediate neighbour, if he built it on your land, it becomes your property. The same principle applies to a wall and to a hedge. That gives the answer to the question of ownership so long as the extent of your land is clear. If the title deeds contain accurate measurements and plans the matter can be settled with precision.

But suppose the measurements are not exact. So often they are not. To deal with this kind of problem the law applies certain presumptions which have grown up by long custom and are now legally recognized. One of these is that a fence belongs to the person who owns the land on the same side as the supporting upright posts. It is assumed that whoever built the fence placed the supports on his own ground and the fence itself on the precise limits of his land.

This presumption is not of great help in deciding the ownership of a hedge which has a habit of spreading not merely upwards but also horizontally.

There are other presumptions here which may sometimes help. First, if a boundary line is marked on the Ordnance Survey maps, the courts will, in the absence of other evidence, accept that line as marking the boundary, even if it goes slap through the middle of the hedge. Secondly, if there is a ditch beyond the hedge it is presumed that whoever planted the hedge threw up earth from the ditch to make a foundation in which the hedge could be planted and that when he dug the ditch he dug it *on his own land*. In other words that he did not trespass but that when he dug the ditch he was operating on his own property. It is assumed that the ditch is his and that, therefore, so also is the hedge on his side of the ditch.

The ownership of a wall can often be settled by the same test as that mentioned above for the ownership of a fence. If the measurements of the land are clear and the wall is entirely within the boundary line, then the whole of it belongs to the owner of the land on that side of the boundary. If the wall is half-way across the boundary, it probably belongs half to each of the neighbours. If the boundary measurements are not clear, then one can usually fall back on the presumption that it belongs to the owner of the land on the side of the supporting buttresses.

These are general legal presumptions which the court will apply in the absence of more precise evidence about ownership. If there is precise evidence about ownership, then, of course, that will override these general presumptions.

When it is possible to decide the ownership of a wall, a fence, or a hedge in one or other of these ways, there is some hope of putting an end to disputes between neighbours about who should maintain and repair the boundary walls, fences, and hedges. For instance, if your neighbour asks you to repair a boundary fence which is falling into ruin and you can show that the fence must belong to him, that should be the end of pressure upon you. If, on the other hand, he can show that it belongs to you, can he compel you to repair it?

The answer is that he cannot do so unless there is some specific obligation in your title deeds which he can invoke against you. His own deeds will usually provide a clue to the existence of such an obligation. It is the kind of point a solicitor is alert to discover when he is acting for a proposed purchaser of a house.

THE LAW OF NUISANCE

Noise

The question when one neighbour may legitimately and with the force of law behind him complain about the amount of noise his neighbour makes and, more important, invoke the powers of the courts to stop that noise, is a matter of very considerable importance in any urban community. It can be important in a rural community too, as some of the cases show, but in the main it is a problem for those who live in towns and cities.

The question comes under the general heading of the law of nuisance. Nuisance is a tort. Before trying to give a general definition and description of nuisance, it may be helpful to describe a number of particular cases where the courts have exercised their powers to stop certain noises which they have deemed to be a nuisance in law.

Some actual Court cases

For example, a certain Miss T. was a keen pianist, who practised and played her piano a great deal and also taught singing. Her neighbour, Mr M., was so incensed by this continuous playing and singing that he retaliated by fixing up a buzzer which made the maximum amount of noise in her house and practically none in his. It would probably be anti-social to describe the mechanics of this device, but that was its effect.

Miss T. ultimately took proceedings in the local County Court, asking for an injunction to stop Mr M.'s buzzer. The County Court Judge decided that the noise of the buzzer was a nuisance in law; that Mr M. was to blame, and he awarded a sum of damages against him which he assessed at £48. How he arrived at this particular figure is not a matter of general importance. The important point is that in addition to awarding a small sum of damages he also granted an injunction forbidding the buzzer to be used again.

He did, on the other hand, also find that Miss T.'s activities were excessive and he ordered her to pay a small sum of damages to Mr M., the sum amounting to £7 10s, and to stop her playing by 8 p.m. on each day.

She appealed against this order to stop at 8 p.m., but the Court of Appeal thought that that time was late enough in that particular neighbourhood and upheld the judge's order. They were influenced partly by the fact that much of her playing was merely piano exercises or tunes for children's singing, which they felt was not 'an inspiring thing for any listener'.

That case follows the decision in the leading case decided as long ago as 1893 where a Mr Christie sued a Mr Davey. It is so famous and has governed so much of the courts' thinking on this problem ever since that a short account must be given. Mr Christie was a teacher of music and dancing. His next-door neighbour, Mr Davey, was extremely irritated and he wrote a very cross letter to Mr Christie which Mr Christie did not answer, because he thought it was rude. As a result Mr Davey began to make a series of offensive noises in his own house. He beat on tin trays, he whistled and shrieked, and it became so intolerable that Mr Christie had to take legal proceedings, asking the court for an injunction to stop Mr Davey from making these offensive noises.

The court held that there was nothing wrong in Mr Christie giving music lessons and playing the piano in his own house, and that the volume and extent of the noise was not unreasonable. On the other hand, they thought that Mr Davey's activities, banging on trays, shouting, whistling, and making other noises, were not a reasonable and legitimate use of his own property, and they ordered him to stop. It is interesting to note that they did consider that the successful plaintiff, Mr Christie, should in fact see to it that musical instruments should not be played in his house after 11 p.m. This is a later hour than the court fixed in that case which has just been described above. It may be that today where music lessons are being given, a court would incline to the earlier hour rather than to the later. But the overriding test which both courts applied was whether the activities were reasonable. A point which counted against both defendants in these cases is that their retaliatory noises were malicious. They were made out of a desire to revenge themselves for the noise which they thought they had suffered, and to cause acute embarrassment to their neighbours. Malice is not an essential element in proving nuisance in law. A great deal of noise can be a nuisance whether it is maliciously made or not. Nevertheless, if malice can be established, as it obviously could be by inference iᴅ both these cases, it is a point which counts against the malicious noise-maker.

Both the people whose activities were challenged in these cases were professionally engaged in teaching music. But it must not be thought that allegations of nuisance are limited to that kind of activity. One of the most frequent sources of complaint is against those who play their wireless sets, television sets, record players, and so on, continuously at a high volume. There is no doubt at all that if the volume is consistently so high that it becomes burdensome to the neighbours, they have a right of action for nuisance in the courts. There must be a certain degree of 'live and let live', but as everyone will know, people frequently can bear in their own room an amount of volume from wireless or television set or record player which is far louder than may be necessary for their own enjoyment, and can be an intolerable nuisance to their neighbours. If this goes on day after day, there is no doubt at all that their neighbours have a right of action against them. Such proceedings can be brought in the County Court, where litigation is not expensive, and of course legal aid may be available. (See section on Legal Aid.)

Another kind of disturbance is sometimes caused by a man who runs a coffee bar or a restaurant or, as in one recent case, a fish and chip shop. The case concerned a man who had opened a fish and chip shop in what had previously been a reasonably quiet residential road. It was primarily residential, although it did have one or two shops in it. Nevertheless, those shops caused no disturbance and closed at a reasonable time at night. The fish and chip shop, on the other hand, stayed open very late. The worst trouble was caused, not so much by noise from the fish and chip shop itself, but from the noise caused by those who came from far and wide to visit it, and after it had closed, hung about outside, indulging in noisy conversation, making considerable noises with their motor-bikes, and generally causing great disturbances until the small hours of the morning.

A number of residents got together and took legal proceedings. The owner of the fish and chip shop pointed out, with some justice, that the noise of which they mainly complained came not from his premises but was caused by customers who stayed outside in the road till a late hour talking and laughing and making considerable noises with their cars and motor-bikes. The court decided, however, that although he was not to blame for the behaviour of his customers, yet they would not be there staying to late hours unless the fish and chip shop was open to a late hour, and they made an order that it should close down not later than 11 p.m., although that meant the loss of business to him, and although he was not responsible for the activities of his noisy customers in the road.

In another case, some people who lived in a generally quiet residential road complained bitterly about a club which had late nights at least once a week. The members were there until about two o'clock in the morning, and when they left in a very merry state they talked loudly to each other, slammed car doors, 'revved' up their engines, sounded their horns, and sleep was almost impossible in that road until the last club member had gone, which was usually about three o'clock. When the residents complained to the manager, he made the point that the club had actually been in existence long before the other houses were built, and said that while he was very sorry about the disturbance the members caused, there was little he could do to control them once they had left the club, and in any case the club had been there first.

The fact that he could not control them after they had left the club was, of course, no answer in the light of the case described immediately above. What of his other point, that the club had been there first? This, it has been decisively held, is no answer at all. The real question is whether a nuisance has been caused. If the answer is 'Yes', then it does not matter in the least that those who suffer from the nuisance came on to the scene after the nuisance had been going on for many years. (The same principle is applied to overhanging trees, etc., see above.)

In another case, a certain well-known film actor gave frequent late-night parties in his flat in a quiet street in the West End of London. The parties were somewhat noisy, and the guests were apparently extremely noisy when they left. The neighbours joined together and took legal proceedings, and the court found the noise went beyond all reason, and granted an injunction, ordering the noise and the late-night parties to stop.

It is quite clear from all these cases that if that kind of noise is only occasional, the courts would probably not interfere. As has already been stated, there must be a degree of 'live and let live'. When, however, the noise is beyond all reason, and frequent, the courts will interfere and grant an injunction to stop it.

Another type of nuisance by noise arises from building operations. Such work can be extremely trying in these days when power-drills, power-operated hammers, and pile-drivers can make a most fearful and appalling noise. The difficulty here is that the rebuilding operations are in themselves perfectly legitimate and it is very difficult to carry them out without noise. The question is, how great is the noise, and how far must it be endured? In one case the plaintiffs were a firm of solicitors with offices on the first floor of a building in London. Those who owned the ground floor decided to remove their existing windows and replace them with much larger windows. This involved using electric drills and power-driven hammers on the walls. The noise was unendurable, and the evidence was that it not merely made work difficult in the solicitor's offices, but absolutely impossible, every day. On this evidence, the court decided to act and to grant an injunction to stop the work during ordinary business hours. This was bitterly contested, because if the contractors had to do all this work out of ordinary hours they would have to pay heavy overtime rates to their workmen, and the cost of the work would be greatly increased. However, the court decided that the interference with ordinary life and work was so intolerable that the order should be granted. They forbade any noise by drills or power-driven hammers, between the hours of 10 a.m. and 5 p.m., from Monday to Friday. Clearly such an order would not be made for all building operations. It is always a matter of evidence and of degree, and when work of new building or rebuilding is going on, neighbours must suffer some inconvenience. The noise and inconvenience here was so great that it made the life and work of those in the solicitor's offices absolutely intolerable, and the courts decided therefore that they must intervene and stop it.

To come to a rural case, the neighbours complained of the noise of cockerels.

They described that between 2 a.m. and 7 a.m. every morning their sleep was utterly destroyed by the crowing of something like 750 cockerels kept by their farmer neighbour. He kept the cockerels as part of his farm, as a business. But this made no difference. The court thought that to have 750 cockerels in a pen *near* an adjoining house was unjustifiable, and they granted an injunction. In effect, they gave the farmer the alternative of either altering the layout of his farm, so that the cockerels were removed to a considerable distance from the neighbours' houses, or getting rid of them altogether.

The basic legal principle

The basic legal principle underlying all these decisions is that anyone has a right to be protected from excessive noise which seriously interferes with his comfort and convenience, whether in his home or his office, or his shop, wherever he may live and work. The test always is whether it unreasonably deprives him of a reasonable degree of pleasure and comfort. The basic legal rule is that he has a right to the reasonable enjoyment of the premises in which he lives or works, free from interference by noise from his neighbour.

The difficulty, of course, is to decide what is unreasonable interference. One point to note is that he cannot expect the same degree of peace and quiet if he lives in the middle of an industrial city as he might expect if he lives in the heart of the country. There is no standard test which applies all over the country. The court must look at all the circumstances and all the surroundings. As one Judge said in a famous case, which has often been quoted: "What would be a nuisance in Belgrave Square would not necessarily be so in Bermondsey." That is not a piece of needless class distinction. It is a simple statement of fact in this context of the Common Law about nuisance.

It is clear from all these cases that noise, to be actionable in law, must be a substantial interference with one's peace and happiness. Secondly, it is not necessary to prove any actual financial loss, nor to prove any injury to health in order to succeed in a court action. Loud and constant noise, whether it be from a wireless or from a mechanical hammer, may in itself be wrong in law because of the inconvenience and discomfort it causes.

Thirdly, it is no defence for the man who operates the noisy wireless or the noisy factory, or who owns the noisy cockerels, to say that he did all this before you came to live as a neighbour, and that as he was there first, you must put up with it. It is a favourite reply of factory owners to complaints about the nuisance caused by their factory, but in law it is no answer.

INTERFERENCE WITH WIRELESS RECEPTION

Electrical apparatus which is not fitted with suppressors can cause serious interference with television or wireless reception. If anyone who offends in this way is unwilling to fit suppressors, it is worth knowing that the Post Office have certain legal powers under which they can compel suppressors to be fitted. Complaints of such interference should be made to the Post Office.

Smoke and smells

The principles described as applying to excessive noise, of course, also apply to excessive smoke and excessive smells. All of these are nuisances which

"To offend against the law, the noise, the smoke or the smell must be excessive and unreasonable."

do not cause actual damage to property, but which cause an intolerable inconvenience to ordinary life. So there are always two things to be considered. The right of the plaintiff who complains about the noise, the smoke, or the smell,

527

and the right of the defendant who has, after all, a right to use his own property legitimately. As has been said in one case: the affairs of life cannot be carried on without the mutual sacrifices of comfort and 'the law must regard the principle of mutual adjustment'.

To hear more than you would like to hear of your neighbour does not necessarily make his behaviour actionable at law; nor does it follow, if you are ill or exceptionally sensitive, that you can bring an action or get an objection. To offend against the law, the noise, the smoke, or the smell must be excessive and unreasonable.

That is why, as explained above, the law must consider the locality, and must also consider the standard of reasonable comfort of the ordinary reasonable man.

Other nuisances

There is another class of case where *actual damage* is caused to neighbouring property. Examples of this kind of injury are:

(a) damage to the plaintiff's trees or shrubs or fruit through fumes from the works of a copper smelting company;

(b) damage caused by a stove which was used for heating water in the defendant's house, but which happened to be on a wall adjoining a cellar in the house of the neighbour, who kept a hotel. He kept wine in that cellar and by reason of the heat from the boiler covering the wall the wine was rendered undrinkable;

(c) injury to a well by the escape of sewage from the defendant's land.

Those are examples of nuisance coming from one territory on to another and causing actual damage. These are easier cases to prove than the nuisance by noise, smoke, and smell, which are mainly matters destroying the peace of mind, injuring the health, destroying the comfort and convenience of occupiers.

A point which is sometimes argued by those against whom a complaint of noise is made, is that they have received permission under the Town and Country Planning Acts from the local authority for the work they are about to do. It is most important to realize that the granting of permission under these Acts, or the granting of permission under the local building by-laws, is totally irrelevant to this question of nuisance. Sanction under Town and Country Planning, sanction under the local building by-laws, does not legitimate what is otherwise a nuisance.

COURT PROCEEDINGS FOR NUISANCE

In discussing the rights under the law of those who are deeply aggrieved by nuisances created by their neighbours, reference has frequently been made to legal proceedings leading to an injunction. These proceedings may be brought either in the County Court or in the High Court, or in Scotland in the Sheriff Court or in the Court of Session. Wherever they may be brought, legal aid is available for those who are within the limits of income and capital described in the section dealing with legal aid in this work. The case, of course, must be very carefully prepared, evidence must be collected over a period of time, and it must be evidence which will convince the court that an unreasonable nuisance, *i.e.* a nuisance in law, has been created. Once the judge is convinced, he will award some sum of damages if he is satisfied that some damage has been caused which needs to be compensated by a money award.

That, however, is probably the least of the plaintiff's concerns; what he usually wants more, is an order of the court to prohibit the nuisance being repeated or continued. This order is known as an Injunction in England and Wales, and an Interdict in Scotland. It is a powerful weapon, because the penalty for its breach is imprisonment of the defendant for contempt of court.

There are, however, two possibilities which do not involve legal proceedings in the civil courts.

The Noise Abatement Act

One alternative is that offered by the Noise Abatement Act of 1960. This Act provides, in effect, that if noise would be a nuisance under the general Common Law principles which have been described, then it is also to be a statutory nuisance under the Public Health Acts. This means that the local authority can take proceedings. It means that instead of the private citizen consulting his solicitor and starting legal proceedings, at his own expense and risk if he cannot get legal aid, he can ask the local authority to prosecute under the Noise Abatement Act. If the local authority are willing to do so, they will first give a warning to the offender, requiring him to abate the nuisance, *i.e.* to cut down or stop the noise. If he does not do so, they can prosecute him.

Furthermore, quite apart from action by the local authority, any three private citizens who occupy land or premises and as such occupiers suffer from the noise, can themselves initiate a prosecution just as the local authority can.

By-laws

It is sometimes possible to take other proceedings against noise from loud-speakers and record players. This can be done when the local authority has made a by-law to deal with the nuisance of noise from such instruments. If they have made such a by-law, and you wish to take advantage of it, you will need the help and collaboration of two other neighbours who suffer as you do. The three of you must prepare a form of notice, a form which you can usually obtain from the local authority, and it only remains for you to complete the blank parts of the form. Then you have to serve this formal notice on the offender. Under the standard form of by-law, he has a fortnight in which to abate the nuisance. If he does not do so within this time, you can initiate a prosecution, and he may be fined up to £5. How effective proceedings under these by-laws are it is very difficult to say, because there are no national records to show how many people have taken advantage of the by-laws, and what the results of their actions have been. Nevertheless, when there is nuisance from wireless, television, or record-playing instruments, it is well worth investigating the possibility of proceedings under the by-law if you can find at least two other neighbours to join with you.

NUISANCE NOT A CRIMINAL OFFENCE

So often one hears of cases where the suffering neighbour calls the police to deal with a serious outbreak of noise or other nuisance from adjoining premises. In general the answer of the police must be: "This is not a criminal offence; we have no power to enter private premises unless a criminal offence has been committed, and there is nothing we can do to stop this. We would only come into this matter if a breach of the peace has been occasioned."

In fact, of course, no such criminal offence has been committed or breach of the peace has been occasioned, and the answer for the suffering neighbour is to invoke the Civil Law of nuisance. It may work slowly, but if he can prove the seriousness of the nuisance he will get the most effective remedy, *i.e.* an injunction plus damages.

Aeroplane noise

On the question of noise from aeroplanes, it must be said that the protection ordinarily given under the Common Law by the courts is lacking. The Civil Aviation Act of 1949 contains a section which provides that no private citizen, nor anyone else, shall be able to bring an action in the courts, to stop the nuisance of noise and vibration of aircraft on certain aerodromes, so long as certain rules laid down for the reduction of this noise and vibration are complied with. In other words, an Act of Parliament, as of course it can, has taken away the general Common Law rights in this respect.

Parliament has in effect decided that one must bow to the inevitable, and that if aeroplanes are necessary for transport and defence, then so also is the noise that they make.

The Minister of Civil Aviation has made rules for the conduct of these aerodromes, with a view to reducing noise and vibration, and if the rules are broken any private citizen can take legal action. Apart from that, however, he cannot do so. The rules are published, and are to be found in the Air Navigation (General) Regulations of 1954. The Act originally applied only to aerodromes owned and licensed by the government, and those licensed for civil aviation, but it has since been extended to cover aerodromes operated by manufacturers of aircraft.

Garden bonfires

A frequent cause of complaint is the smoke from garden bonfires. In most cases everyone puts up with a certain amount of smoke from a bonfire; most people with gardens have to light bonfires from time to time to burn garden rubbish which they cannot usefully put on a compost heap. The question of nuisance usually only arises where the burning of rubbish on neighbouring land is so constant that it becomes an intolerable nuisance. If, of course, it is so constant that it makes the reasonable comfort and enjoyment of your own home impossible, it comes within the general Common Law definition of nuisance set out above. If it is not so constant and continuous, then it clearly does not. The Clean Air Act (1956) forbids the emission of dark smoke beyond certain narrow limits from factory chimneys and the funnels of ships and steam trains, and it also gives local authorities the right to make smoke control orders under which it will be an offence to allow any smoke to come from the chimneys of houses, or indeed of any other building. The Act, however, does not touch the ordinary garden bonfire.

There is a possibility that if the smoke is a constant and considerable nuisance, the local authority may be willing to take action against the offender, on the grounds that the bonfire is a statutory nuisance under the Public Health Acts. This is additional to the possible right of the private individual to take a civil action at Common Law.

Furthermore, there is the possibility that if the bonfire does damage to the neighbour's fruit trees or his fence, then he has a right of action for damages for the actual harm which has been caused. This goes beyond the question of nuisance interfering with comfort and convenience, and comes under the heading also described above, of a nuisance which causes actual damage to property, whether it be growing trees, plants or shrubs, or a boundary fence or whatever it might be.

THE LAW OF TRESPASS

Trespass is the tort or wrong that is committed by unlawfully entering upon someone else's land or placing any material object upon it.

The commonest form of trespass, of course, consists in wrongful entry on someone else's land, e.g., by walking, riding, or driving over it without permission. It follows that to remain upon that land, having once wrongfully entered it, is also a trespass. Trespass is a continuing offence so that the owner or lawful occupier of the land could, if he were so minded, take legal proceedings against the trespasser, not merely for the first wrongful entry, but for every subsequent day during which the trespasser remains there.

An important distinction between trespass and nuisance—which, as we have seen, also involves an invasion of someone else's rights of property—is that legal proceedings can be brought in respect of a trespass even though no actual damage of any kind has been caused. There is no need to bring any evidence of damage. It is enough to establish the fact of the trespass. To succeed in an action for nuisance, however, it is necessary to prove that some damage has been caused to the occupier's beneficial enjoyment of his own property.

If legal proceedings for trespass are taken and no damage has been caused, an award of damages by the court would obviously be nominal and would merely mark the fact that a wrong had been committed. If, however, there is also actual damage, the money award would take account of that. The value to the lawful occupier of the land of this right of action without proving damages is that he can get an injunction against the trespasser forbidding him to repeat his trespass, even though no physical harm has been done to the property.

Notice boards on property frequently contain the legend 'Trespassers will be prosecuted'. This is sometimes described as a 'wooden lie', because the word 'prosecution' implies a crime. Trespass is not a crime—save rarely, under wartime legislation, or possibly special legislation relating to government-owned territory used by the Armed Forces. Apart from these rare exceptions, trespass is a tort or civil wrong for which the appropriate remedy is proceedings in the Civil Courts.

The ordinary casual trespass does not usually lead to such serious action. It is invaluable, however, for the occupier of the land to know that, in the case of repeated trespasses, powerful remedies are available to him to prevent their repetition.

It is said that the lawful occupier of the property is entitled not merely to request a trespasser to go, but to exercise reasonable force to eject him if he refuses to go. 'Reasonable' in this sense means that it must not be greater than is strictly necessary for the purpose, and anyone seeking to exercise this remedy of self-help must be extremely careful about the degree of force he exercises in case he exposes himself to a summons for assault to which he would have no defence unless the degree of force he used was thought by the court to be reasonable. A forcible removal, after the trespasser has been given a reasonable time and polite requests to go, may well be justified. But even then 'reasonable' could never include beating, wounding, or other physical injury, unless the trespasser himself makes such a vicious physical attack, that the occupier has to defend himself.

Apart from actually entering another person's land, it is a trespass to cause any physical object to cross the boundary, or even to come into contact with the land, even though there is no actual crossing of the boundary. For instance, it is a trespass to throw stones into your neighbour's garden, to drive nails into his wall, to let a creeper grow up it, to pile rubbish against his fence or wall, or even to lean a ladder against it. Many a neighbour will give permission for some of these things to be done if his consent is sought first. If it is not and he objects, he has a right to demand the removal of the offending object and his right can be enforced by County Court Order if such an extreme measure becomes necessary.

PRIVACY AND THE LAW

A RIGHT of privacy is something which many people value very highly. They might reasonably expect that it is a legal right which can be enforced and protected by law. In spite of complaints that some parts of the law are in some people's eyes very silly indeed, for instance some of the laws about licensing, about betting and gaming, about Sunday observance, and so on, nevertheless most people recognize that it is the law as a whole which ensures their reasonable liberty to live, to read, to think, and to worship as they choose. That is the broad meaning of the 'rule of law' in our civilization. In totalitarian countries the law is apt to be the servant of the dictatorial government. There, the law is what the executive government wants it to be, and the courts of those countries apply the law which the dictator ordains.

In those parts of the world which are subject to what is conveniently and generally known as the 'rule of law', the executive cannot override the law. The courts are independent of the executive, and can give decisions in favour of the citizen against the government. It might therefore be expected that in this civilization which values privacy and personal liberty so very highly, there would be some special legal right to protect privacy just as there undoubtedly is legal power to assert the right of personal liberty.

It is therefore rather odd to find that there is no specific law protecting privacy. There is not, for instance, anything similar to the law protecting a man's right to his good name and reputation. If this is wrongly attacked he can bring an action for libel or slander, because his right to his good name, if it is a justified right, is a legal right. If someone walks across your property you have a legal right to stop him because he is trespassing, and trespass is a wrong in itself. Not only have you a legal right to stop him, but you have power to sue him in the courts for damages. Trespass to your good name, trespass to your property, are rights which can be enforced by due process of law.

But there is no legal right to protection of privacy *in itself*. You have to hang your claim to privacy on to something else, to some other legal right.

Light and air

Let us have a few practical examples. Sometimes people are worried about new building which is going on around them. A house is being built nearby which will have windows overlooking their garden, or windows from which it will be possible to see into their house. Or to take another example, new houses are being built so near that they are going to take away light from the house. What can be done, if anything? There is certainly a loss of privacy, there is a loss of light, and perhaps a loss of the free flow of air.

Apart from voluntary agreement, nothing can be done to preserve that enviable seclusion and privacy of the garden. That garden may not have been overlooked before, it may have been completely secluded, but there is no such thing as a legal right to ensure that nothing can ever be built which will overlook it, if the only result of that overlooking is to interfere with the garden's seclusion and privacy.

But something might be done to stop a loss of light to the house. Under English Law, if a house or any other building has enjoyed uninterrupted light for twenty years, no new building is to be put up which will take it away. That is the legal basis for the expression 'ancient lights'. After twenty years without interruption, a legal right is established, and that means a right which the courts will enforce by ordering the offending building to be pulled down or reduced in height. Before twenty years have passed, no such right exists, except, of course, by voluntary agreement.

But even then, when the right exists, there must be some measure of tolerance and common sense. Even if one house-owner has acquired this right to light, whether after twenty years' enjoyment of uninterrupted light, or by voluntary agreement, the law will not prevent the erection of any adjoining building which may take away *some* of the light. The test is, not how much light has been

533

taken away, but how much is left. Is the house-owner left with a reasonable amount? If rooms which used to be light are substantially darkened he can legitimately complain and, what is more, the courts will take notice of his complaint and enforce such alterations in the adjoining building as will preserve a reasonable amount of light to himself. This matter is dealt with in more detail in 'Easements, Natural Rights and Licences' in the chapter on Problems of Land Ownership. It is mentioned here as an instance of the fact that while there is no inherent legal right to privacy, the fact that there may be a legal right to light which may result in the courts enforcing alterations in adjoining buildings, may give the house-owner privacy as an incidental result to his legal right to a certain amount of light.

Boundary fences and hedges

Another question between neighbours affecting privacy is the dividing fence or hedge. One question which occurs from time to time springs up as a result of the owner of one property cutting down a dividing hedge which has hitherto provided a splendid barrier between the two properties, and provided some seclusion and privacy for both. Nevertheless, if the owner of one house dislikes the hedge so much—perhaps it is straggling and untidy—that he cuts it down, can the neighbour on the other side of the hedge do anything about it in the way, say, of having the neighbour erect something in its place? The answer, apart again from voluntary agreement or some obligation in the deeds of the house, is 'No'. If the offended neighbour has to rely on a claim to privacy and seclusion, he has no legal ground for his claim, and his only answer is to build a new hedge, fence, or wall on his own property.

The tenant's privacy

An example of a right to privacy being gained incidentally to another right is to be found in the tenant's right to shut his front door on everyone, including his landlord. There is a good deal of misunderstanding about this, particularly when the tenant is the occupier of one or two rooms in a house, which is let out to a large number of tenants. So often the landlord of that kind of house assumes that he has some basic right to enter any of his tenant's rooms at any time. This is not the law. A tenant, whether he is a tenant of a house or a flat or merely rooms in a house, has the absolute right to refuse admission to anyone, including his landlord. So long as he pays his rent and observes the conditions of the tenancy, he is, so long as that tenancy lasts, a king in his own castle. There is no such thing as an automatic right by a landlord to enter a tenant's property, so long as the tenancy lasts.

If a landlord wants to have this right, he must reserve it expressly in the tenancy agreement. It is quite common in a well-drawn tenancy agreement to find a clause which gives the landlord the right, after giving due notice and making a proper appointment, to enter on the premises at certain intervals, perhaps two or three times a year, for the specific purpose of viewing the state of repair of the property. He may require this right because the tenant has certain express obligations about repair, and the landlord wants to see if they're carried out; or the landlord may have accepted express obligations about repair and he may

534

need the right of access either for himself or for his workmen in order to carry out those repairs. Whatever the reason, he has no right to enter unless it is by agreement with the tenant, and, of course, the best way of ensuring that agreement is to have an express clause in the tenancy agreement which the tenant

The tenant's privacy.

has signed. That is something the tenant can never revoke, and it means that on giving proper notice the landlord can insist on a right of entry.

If such a clause is not there, the tenant has the same right to exclude his landlord as to exclude any other visitor. It is not fundamentally based on any legal right of privacy—it is a right of property, and the right of privacy follows incidentally as a consequence, not as an original right.

In another section dealing with the difference between lodgers and tenants, it is explained that a lodger has no such right to exclude his landlord. In fact, one of the main differences between a lodger and a tenant is that the tenant has the right to exclude the landlord and the lodger hasn't.

Wills

Another aspect of privacy which attracts a good deal of attention from time to time is the publication of wills. Many people bitterly resent the fact that their wills may be published or quoted after their death, or at any rate that anyone, whether he has any genuine interest or not, can go and read their wills at Somerset House. Some years ago, indeed, a Bill was introduced in Parliament with the object of preventing newspapers from saying how much money anyone had left and to whom he had left it. This Bill did not become law, but it is not the only one of its kind, and it was followed by another attempt by a private member to introduce a Bill to stop the publication of wills or summaries of wills, if not indeed to stop the right of people to go and read them at Somerset House. Nevertheless, the law as it stands at the moment is that once a will has been proved, or as in Scotland, the executors confirmed in their appointment, the will is a public document. The Press can publish its substance, or as much of it as they like to quote, and anyone can go and read it, and indeed anyone can have a copy on paying a small copying charge.

Secret trusts

This being so, it may be worth mentioning how the substance of a will can nevertheless be kept secret, even under the law as it now stands. Under English Law this can be done by the simple expedient of making a secret trust.

The secret trust will not stop the total amount of the will being stated in the probate and subsequently published, but it can stop the identity of the beneficiaries being disclosed.

One kind of secret trust is to leave a sum of money in the will to the executors and to say in the will that they are to deal with it according to instructions which have been privately given to them.

The other kind of trust is even more secret, because in the will the money or property is left to the executors, apparently as an out and out gift, without even mentioning the fact that they are to deal with it according to private directions which the testator, *i.e.* the maker of the will, has given to them.

The first method discloses that there is, in fact, some secret trust, but does not say what it is; the second hides even the fact that there may be a secret trust. Both methods, of course, involve a high degree of confidence in the chosen executors, and the time when the testator tells them the terms of the secret trust depends upon which method he has chosen.

This question of communicating the terms of the secret trust to the executors is vitally important, and the time, as stated, depends upon the method which the testator chooses. It is undesirable in this work to give further detailed explanations of the method because it is absolutely essential that anyone who wishes to take advantage of this method of securing absolute privacy for the terms of his will to get legal advice. It is absolutely essential that he should consult a solicitor and not dabble in secret trusts for himself. The only point to be emphasized here is that by one or other of these methods, which are well known to the law, complete secrecy can be achieved

536

LIBEL AND SLANDER

INTRODUCTION

LIBEL AND SLANDER are an attack on a person's good name, on his reputation. Libel is written, slander is spoken. To put it in another way, libel is set down in some permanent form; slander is the transitory, passing spoken word.

Libel.

So although writing is one permanent form in which the offensive words may be recorded, there are others. For instance, the words spoken on a 'talking film' are libel, so are words spoken on to a recording apparatus. Equally libel are words carved or painted on stone. Essentially the difference is that to be a libel the words must have some degree of permanence and be capable of being read or heard again and again, whereas to be a slander, the words need only be spoken once, and not recorded.

The practical significance of the distinction is this: a person who is libelled can bring legal proceedings without having to prove that he has actually suffered any loss or damage as a result of the libel.

537

It may be that no one believed it. Never mind: if the offensive words were in some permanent form—and therefore a libel—he need not prove that he had actually suffered any loss.

On the other hand, if the offensive words are only spoken, then as a general rule the person of whom they are spoken cannot sue for damages unless he can show that he has actually suffered loss or damage. There are a few exceptions to this rule, exceptions which are set out below. But the general rule is that libel is actionable without proof of actual damage, whereas slander is not unless actual damage can be proved.

There is a common-sense justification for this rule. If the damaging and offensive statements can be read over and over again and read by many people, or if they can be repeatedly heard as when they are recorded, it is reasonable to suppose that they *must* do damage, and that actual damage need not therefore be proved.

When the words are merely spoken, and therefore impermanent, it may be reasonable to suppose that they will not necessarily cause lasting damage.

Actually the true basis for the distinction is an accident of history and legal procedure in the seventeenth century. The law today does, however, recognize that certain slanders may be so inherently serious that they must be treated like libels and that no actual damage need be proved. These are dealt with below under the heading 'Slanders actionable without proof of special damage'.

DEFINITION

The legal expression which covers both libel and slander is DEFAMATION. Many attempts have been made to define defamation. One definition is that it is:

> The publication of a statement which tends to lower a person in the estimation of right-thinking members of society generally, or which tends to make them shun or avoid him.

Another is that it is:

> The publication of a statement which tends to bring a person into hatred, ridicule, or contempt.

No definition can be completely satisfactory. In the first place, if the statement is true it may be desirable that the person 'defamed' should be lowered in the public estimation. In the second place, whether the statement is true or false, who is the 'right-thinking member of society' whose 'hatred, ridicule, or contempt' is involved—the 'reasonable' man's (whoever he may be) or that of the narrow-minded man who is glad to lower his estimation of other people and finds it only too easy to hate?

These definitions are helpful in that they indicate that the statement must have been '*damaging*'; but they do not cover the real difficulties about an action for defamation. For example, they do not indicate that in order to get damages the statement must be *untrue* or, in the case of comment, 'unfair'; nor do they take into account the circumstances where motive is important, or those where neither motive nor truth have any relevance.

CRIMINAL LIBEL

Libel can be a crime, but it very seldom is. In the Middle Ages it was regarded as a crime because it tended to provoke a breach of the peace, in that it might result in a duel, or the like. Nowadays it may be said that, generally, defamation is a 'civil' matter—that is to say, one where the injured person himself has to bring proceedings for damages. It is a 'criminal' matter, in the sense that the offender can be prosecuted and punished, only if the statement provokes, or is likely to provoke, a breach of the peace.

One important distinction between criminal and civil libel is that a defamatory statement can be criminal even though it is not published to anybody except the person defamed; but no action can be taken on a civil libel unless it is published to someone else than the person defamed. The reason for the distinction is that a breach of the peace is just as much to be feared—perhaps even more to be feared—if you insult a man to his face, whereas loss of reputation, which is the reason for a civil action for damages, depends on what has been said to other people and not on what is said to you.

Another important distinction between criminal and civil libel is that *truth* is a complete defence to a civil action for libel, but that in a criminal prosecution the defendant must prove that his statements were not only true but also that it was in the public interest that he should publish them.

There is a common saying that, "The greater the truth, the greater the libel". This applies *only* when the libelled person has brought criminal proceedings. Its logic is obvious. If the libellous imputation is true, how much greater is the risk of a breach of the peace. The truth strikes home. The nearer the libel is to the truth, the more damning it is.

So where the injured person takes criminal proceedings the defendant does not escape by proving truth: he must also prove that the public interest required or justified the publication of the libel.

Criminal proceedings for libel are rare because the injured person usually wants damages. In a prosecution, even if the defendant is found guilty, the plaintiff gets no money damages and very little, if anything, toward his costs. The punishment is usually an order directing the defendant not to repeat his libel on pain of imprisonment; perhaps a fine; and very rarely, imprisonment. A plaintiff who wants to recover damages and his costs will naturally take civil proceedings. And to these, as explained in detail below, truth or justification is a complete defence—if it can be proved.

Probably the only value of the right to prosecute for libel is, as stated above, that the prosecution can be brought, and an order to prohibit repetition of the libel obtained, even when it has not been published to any third person.

SPECIAL DAMAGE

Another distinction between libel and slander, apart from the distinction of the degree of permanence, is that you can bring an action for libel without proof of special damage, whereas with a few exceptions (as to which see below) in the case of slander SPECIAL DAMAGE must be proved.

What is meant by special damage is some material loss which can be measured in money, such as the loss of a job. It has been held to cover such a loss as that of a wife and even of the hospitality of friends. But it must be measurable in money, and the damage must be the natural and probable result of the publication of the words complained of.

SLANDER ACTIONABLE
WITHOUT PROOF OF DAMAGE SUFFERED

There are four cases where slander is actionable in itself and without the need to prove special damage.

Slander.

(1) Imputations of unfitness for job, etc.

If you make a statement which imputes that a man is unfit for some office which he holds or for a profession, calling, trade, or business which he carries on then he can bring an action against you without having to prove that he has suffered any actual damage as a result of it. Thus to accuse a tradesman of dishonesty or insolvency would be actionable in itself. In other words he could sue you for damages for what you said and would not have to prove that he had lost any trade because of your slander because either of those things would impute unfitness for his occupation. On the other hand, to accuse an actor of having committed adultery might not be, because it is possible to commit adultery and still be an excellent actor. It would be different if the actor could show that he had lost a job because, say, some unusually strait-laced producer had refused to engage him as a result. Here he would be able to show special damage, and, as we have seen, any slander is actionable in those circumstances.

However, to accuse a clergyman of having committed adultery would clearly be another matter.

It must be borne in mind that the words must be spoken 'in the way of' the plaintiff's office, profession, etc. Consequently he must hold that office or carry on the profession or whatever it may be. If, therefore, an accusation of adultery were made of a *retired* clergyman it could not be made 'in the way of' his calling.

At one time not only did the words have to be said in the way of the calling, they had to be said of him in connection with his calling. This led to some curious results. In one case the courts felt obliged, on this principle, to decide that an accusation that a schoolmaster had committed adultery with the school cleaner had not been made of him in his capacity as a schoolmaster and was therefore not actionable without proof that actual damage had been caused. This rather absurd position has been remedied by the Defamation Act, 1952, s. 2, which lays down:

> In an action for slander in respect of words *calculated to disparage the plaintiff* in any office, profession, calling, trade, or business held or carried on by him at the time of the publication, it shall not be necessary to allege or prove special damage, whether or not the words are spoken of the plaintiff in the way of his office, profession, calling, trade, or business.

(2) Imputations of disease

It may be a slander to say that someone is suffering from an infectious or contagious disease. It is uncertain what diseases are included, but there are decisions of the courts going back at least to the beginning of the seventeenth century. The idea is that a person suffering from such a disease may be 'shunned' or 'avoided': consequently, although diseases which reflect adversely upon the person suffering from them (for example, a venereal disease) are certainly included, other diseases which are due solely to misfortune (for example, leprosy and even scarlet fever) are to be found in the list.

(3) Accusation of crime

It is a slander actionable without proof of actual loss or damage to accuse a person of having committed a crime for which he could be punished bodily —for example by execution or imprisonment. Of course the words used must have been understood to mean an actual accusation: if you say to someone, for example, "This is sheer robbery," nobody would understand you to mean that the person had in fact committed that crime.

If the crime is not punishable bodily—for example, where the penalty is a fine—then an accusation of having committed it is not slanderous; and this is so even though, in the event of non-payment of the fine, the person could be sent to prison.

(4) Imputations of unchastity in females

All the preceding examples of slanders actionable without proof of actual loss or damage come from the Common Law; this one is the creation of an

541

Act of Parliament. By the Slander of Women Act, 1891 (which does not apply to Scotland), words 'which impute unchastity or adultery to any woman or girl shall not require special damage to render them actionable'.

PUBLICATION

From the point of view of a civil action—that is, where the purpose is to get damages—there is no libel or slander unless the defamatory matter (written, spoken, or whatever it may be) has been '*published*'—that is, communicated to somebody else.

The reason is that the plaintiff's real cause for complaint is that his *reputation* has suffered in the eyes of other people, and no such harm has been done if you or he are the only ones to read or hear the statement.

As we have seen, in the case of criminal libel, publication to the plaintiff is enough because here the question is the possibility of a breach of the peace, and the plaintiff himself may be provoked by reading the libel. There is no such thing as 'criminal slander', so merely speaking words to the plaintiff would not be publication: on the other hand, to do so might involve some other offence such as 'insulting words and behaviour'.

Husband and wife

A true exception to the above rule about publication does exist, however, in the case of communications between husband and wife. The law regards it as impossible, and indeed undesirable, to attempt to limit freedom of communication between spouses. Consequently, things written or said by one to the other are not 'published' in a legal sense. However, two points must be borne in mind.

First, the exception extends only to communications made in private. If Mr Jones writes to Mrs Jones that Mr Smith is a thief, there is nothing Mr Smith can do about it provided—and provided only—that the letter does not get into somebody else's hands, as by Mrs Jones showing it to somebody else or its being written on a postcard so that anybody could read it. There is also the possibility that the letter may be opened by the wrong person: this is dealt with in the next sub-section below. Equally, if Mr Jones says by word of mouth to Mrs Jones that Mr Smith is a thief, and somebody overhears him, it will be no defence for Mr Jones to say that he was only talking to his wife.

Secondly, although Mr Jones may write and speak freely to his own wife about Mr Smith, he cannot write or speak freely to Mrs *Smith* either about Mrs Jones or about Mr Smith. Husbands and wives may be free to pull other people's reputations to pieces, in private, in talking or writing to each other, but they have the right to preserve their own reputations in each other's eyes and in the eyes of the outside world.

What is publication?

It is common sense that if you deliberately write or say something to somebody you are intending to publish it to him, and it will be a publication provided he reads it or hears it and also understands it. But it is also possible to publish unintentionally, by the communication being read or the statement being overheard by someone for whom it was not intended. For example, what is the position if a letter is opened by somebody else—a postman, a clerk in the addressee's office, a servant at his house, his wife, or somebody who happens to be inquisitive? Here a third party is involved without your intention.

The general rule is that if a defamatory statement is not deliberately published to a third party, the author will not be liable unless he knew, or ought to have known or anticipated the possibility, that it might come to the eyes or ears of that third party. So, in the case of a written communication, if it were sent by postcard or telegram, the chances of its being read by someone other than the person to whom it is addressed would be very high. If, however, it is enclosed in an envelope, the courts have decided that there is no presumption that the postman will read the contents; but there remains the risk that it may be opened and read, say, by a secretary at the office to which it is addressed, and if you ought to have anticipated this possibility you may be liable. For that reason the question of whether you put such words as 'Private and Confidential' on the envelope may be relevant.

Husbands and wives

The question of the possibility of a letter being opened by the husband or wife of the person to whom it is addressed is less certain. In a case which came before the Court of Appeal at the end of 1961 a man (call him Mr Jones) wrote a libellous letter about a lady (call her Mrs Smith). The letter was addressed to Mrs Smith and was very securely fastened. Mrs Smith was out when the letter arrived but her husband was at home, and he opened it. There is, of course, no doubt that if the letter had been addressed to *Mr* Smith his wife could have claimed damages against Mr Jones; nor is there any doubt that if it had been opened by Mrs Smith she would have had no claim at all. The point was, should Mr Jones have foreseen the possibility that Mr Smith would open his wife's letter? The jury thought he should. Mr Jones appealed on the ground that the verdict was 'perverse' in that it rested on the false assumption that people open other people's letters. One judge agreed; but the other two judges were of the opinion that the possibility existed and that therefore it was properly left to the jury to decide whether Mr Jones ought to have foreseen it in this particular case. This decision does not mean that it must now be presumed that husbands and wives open each other's letters, but that it is a possibility for the jury to consider.

General rule

The test, therefore, is what you should reasonably anticipate. For that reason you will not be liable if your letter is read by a thief: it is, of course, a possibility, but it is too unlikely to require serious consideration.

Equally, you will not usually be liable if the person to whom you say or write the defamatory statement repeats it or passes it on to another. If you defame Mr Jones to his face or by letter addressed to and opened by him, and Mr Jones repeats it to his wife or hands the letter to a friend, there has, of course, been a publication, but it is Mr Jones's publication, and not yours.

543

Distributors and others

There is another possibility—particularly in the case of libel—and that is for a person to be responsible for a statement which he has not written and indeed of which he is unaware. This often happens in the case of books, magazines, and (particularly) newspapers. Here many people may be liable: the actual writer, the owner of the publication, the editor, the printer, the distributor or retailer of the publication or the librarian who lends it.

Here the general rule is that 'innocent dissemination' does not amount to publication. In other words, you have not 'published' simply because the libellous material has passed through your hands; but the point is that you must have been 'innocent'—that is, unaware and not to be expected reasonably to be aware that what you were handling contained a libel. It is not an easy thing to prove: you must show that you did not know and that your lack of knowledge was not due to negligence.

A postman, for example, cannot be expected to know what is in the letters he delivers. At the other end of the scale, the actual writer must know what he has written; and persons such as publishers and editors and printers are equally held to be necessarily aware of what they have published or set up in type.

The doubtful cases are those, such as distributors or librarians, who play an active part in 'publishing'. They should have less responsibility than the actual writer or publisher, because the original 'publication' was not by the distributors; but at the same time they ought to have more responsibility than the postman, because they should be more concerned with the contents of what they distribute.

Here again the rule of 'innocent dissemination' is applied: did the distributor know, or was he negligent in not knowing, that the publication in question contained a libel? Obviously big distributors, newsagents, booksellers, and librarians cannot read all the thousands of publications which pass through their hands. At the same time they must show reasonable alertness: if the libel is contained in a glaring front-page article or displayed on a poster, or if the libel has been pointed out to them, they cannot claim to have exercised reasonable care and so to be 'innocent disseminators'. Two examples can be taken from cases. In one, a poster (for which the defendants were responsible) was not justifiable by the facts of the story which it advertised; in the other a lending library continued to circulate a book although it had been warned by the publishers to withdraw it. In both instances there was lack of reasonable care.

UNINTENTIONAL DEFAMATION

Introduction

Under the heading of 'publication' we have considered cases where one person can defame another without intending to do so—because, for example, his statement is overheard or read by someone for whom it was not intended, or a publisher or distributor allowed something to go out which he had failed to see was libellous.

By 'unintentional defamation' lawyers usually mean something a little different from this. They are thinking of cases which most people would call 'bad luck', because there is an unexpected coincidence which ordinary care would not have foreseen. This kind of difficulty arises over the choice of a name in a story, so that readers think a real person of that name is meant. It can arise even in a true story, because there are two people of the same name and the defamatory thing said of one of them (and truly said about him) is understood by readers to refer to the other. A few examples may help to illustrate this.

Examples

One of the most famous cases concerns a 'gossip column' written over fifty years ago. Then, as now, gossip-writers invented their characters and stories, and this one was about a character called 'Artemus Jones' (comic name), who was represented as a Peckham churchwarden (respectable neighbourhood and occupation) enjoying himself at a motor rally at Dieppe (France, a 'naughty' country) with a lady who was not his wife. This was a typical gossip-writer's set-up; but unfortunately there was a real man called Artemus Jones. He was a barrister (and a respectable one); he did not live in Peckham; he was not a churchwarden; nor had he visited Dieppe. A number of persons, however, gave evidence that they had taken the article to refer to him—after all, it is a most distinctive and unusual name—and he was awarded damages. The writer had not intended to refer to the real Artemus Jones; but in fact Artemus Jones had been employed by the paper—a very curious coincidence— so there was some evidence of negligence. On the other hand, the decision has been described by a distinguished barrister, Sir Valentine Holmes, Q.C., as 'repugnant to common sense'.

In another case a newspaper published a photograph of a Mr C. and a Miss X. with a caption saying that they were engaged. This information had been supplied by Mr C. himself; but in fact Mr C. was married already. Mrs C. brought, and won, an action against the newspaper on the ground that the announcement suggested that she was not married to Mr C. but was living in sin with him. This case is an example of 'innuendo' (which is dealt with below) as well as of unintentional defamation.

In a third case a newspaper published that 'Harold Newstead, thirty-year-old Camberwell man', had been convicted of bigamy. This was true of a Harold Newstead who was aged thirty and was a barman in Camberwell. Unfortunately there was another Harold Newstead, also aged about thirty, who also worked in Camberwell, but as a hairdresser. This second Harold Newstead brought a successful action for damages.

Offer of amends

The hardship of this situation has to some extent been relieved by the Defamation Act, 1952, s. 4, which allows a person who has 'innocently' published words which are defamatory of another person to make what is called 'an offer of amends'.

This section contains a lot of technicalities: anybody using the 'offer of amends' procedure should do so only under professional advice.

In brief, the 'publisher' has to make the offer and accompany it by an affidavit showing the facts which he says display his 'innocence'. To establish 'innocence' he must show: *either*

(a) that he did not intend the words to refer to the other person and did not know any circumstances which might make them understood to refer to him; *or*

(b) that the words were not defamatory on the face of them and, equally, he did not know any circumstances which might make them so understood; *and*

(c) that in either case he 'exercised all reasonable care in relation to the publication'.

The 'offer of amends' must always include an offer to publish a 'suitable correction' and a 'sufficient apology', and, where appropriate, an offer to 'take such steps as are reasonably practicable' to notify persons to whom the words have been distributed.

If the offer is accepted by the 'other party' and 'performed' by the 'publisher', the other party cannot take or continue an action for libel or slander. If it is not accepted, it is a defence for the publisher to prove that he published innocently, made the offer in good time, and has not withdrawn it. A major difficulty here (and one which applies particularly to publishers of newspapers, books, and the like) is that if the 'publisher' was not the actual author he must prove in addition that the actual author wrote 'without malice'.

INNUENDO

Introduction

Before coming to the defences to an action for libel or slander there is another circumstance to consider in which a statement may be defamatory.

As we have seen, a statement of fact about a particular person—for example, "Mr Jones stole the petty cash"—may, if untrue, be a good cause of action. As we have also seen, an imaginary statement of fact about an imaginary Mr Jones may be actionable if there is a real Mr Jones to whom people reasonably suppose the statement refers. A third possibility, however, is that what you say does not refer to Mr Jones by name, but people realize that he is meant; alternatively, that although you mention Mr Jones's name what you say about him is not defamatory on the face of it but is understood to be so by people who are aware of the special circumstances in which you said or wrote what you did.

Examples will be helpful. If you say, "A cashier in this town stole the petty cash", you have not referred to Mr Jones by name; but, if Mr Jones is the cashier to whom people suppose you to be referring, it is no good your saying you 'mentioned no names'. Similarly, suppose you mention Mr Jones by name —for example, by saying, "The firm had no trouble about petty cash before last August; Mr Jones is now the cashier"—on the face of it this looks like two statements of fact; but these two statements might look sinister to anybody who knew that Mr Jones had become cashier in that August.

In a case which came before the courts a magazine produced a picture of the plaintiff who appeared to be operating a camera and to have a placard which read, 'Your photo finished in one minute', and alongside were shown two respectable ladies who appeared to be looking at his photographs. On the facing page was a picture of a naked lady; and, running across both pages, were the words, 'Of course for another shilling, madam, you can have something like this'. You may think there is nothing defamatory in those words by themselves; but the jury decided that in those particular circumstances there was a hidden meaning—there was the suggestion that the plaintiff dealt in indecent pictures.

Innuendo.

Definition

When the alleged libel or slander is not clear on the face of it but will be understood to be defamatory by somebody who has reasonably deduced a 'secondary meaning' this secondary meaning is known as the INNUENDO. The word comes from Latin and means 'nodding at'. Dean Swift, the author of *Gulliver's Travels*, puts it this way (in another work): 'Convey a libel in a frown, and wink a reputation down.' In short, even though what you say is not itself defamatory, the way in which you say it (the frown or wink or nod which accompanies it, for example) may be the deciding factor. So also will be the secondary meaning (whether you intended it or not, and whether or not there was a frown or wink) which a reasonable person understood in such cases as those of Mr Jones or the photographer mentioned above.

Burden of proof

Although in most cases of defamation it is assumed that the words (or whatever it may be) ought not to have been used, and therefore it is for the

547

defendant (the one who is being sued) to show he had some right to use them, in the case of innuendo the 'burden of proof', as it is called, shifts from the defendant to the plaintiff. The reason is that in what might be called the 'straight-forward' libel the meaning is clear, but when you are alleging a secondary or concealed meaning it is right that you should have the responsibility of saying what that secondary meaning is and also of proving that the words were so understood by the person who read or heard them. In the example given above about Mr Jones and the petty cash, if you say, "A cashier in this town stole the petty cash," to someone who has never heard of Mr Jones it will not occur to him that it was defamatory of Mr Jones.

PRIVILEGE

One of the defences to an action for defamation is that, although the statement may have been defamatory, it was written or said on a 'privileged' occasion. The two major points here are (1) what is meant by privilege, and (2) how far does the privilege go?

What is privilege?

In effect, privilege is a protection given by the law to defamatory statements made in certain circumstances. If these circumstances exist, then the defendant (that is, the person who made the statement) is protected from liability— sometimes completely, sometimes only partly. It is for the judge to decide as a matter of law whether the circumstances amount to a privileged occasion.

Extent of privilege

The extent of the privilege or protection allowed by law varies according to what is necessary or desirable in the circumstances. If complete protection is considered necessary, the defendant has what is known as ABSOLUTE PRIVILEGE; but usually something less than complete protection is insufficient, and this is known as QUALIFIED PRIVILEGE.

(1) Absolute privilege

Where the occasion provides absolute privilege, then anything written or said is protected, however false it may be, however much damage it may cause, and however malicious, improper, or negligent the motives or conduct of the publisher may have been.

Naturally the occasions enjoying such wide protection are very few; they are as follows:

(1) *Judicial proceedings.* Judges, Counsel, Juries, parties in a case, and witnesses enjoy complete protection as regards any words spoken in relation to proceedings in a Court of Law or similar tribunal. This, of course, does not mean that someone who made improper observations might not find himself in some other form of trouble—for example, punishment for contempt of court—but he could not be sued for defamation. The same protection extends to documents used in such proceedings and to preliminary statements made in

connection with them—for example, communications between solicitor and client.

(2) *Parliamentary proceedings*. Members of the House of Lords and of the House of Commons enjoy absolute privilege in respect of anything said by them in the course of a parliamentary debate or proceeding. This absolute privilege would not extend to the same thing said in another part of the Houses of Parliament (say, in a bar or smoking-room) or, of course, outside. For this reason, when someone is defamed in Parliament, he often asks for the remark to be 'repeated outside', so that he can bring an action. The invitation is seldom accepted.

(3) *Affairs of state*. It is not quite clear how far this absolute privilege goes; but ministers of the Crown in giving advice to the Sovereign, officers of state in making communications to each other on state affairs, and military, naval, and R.A.F. officers in making reports or otherwise acting in the course of duty, are all given absolute privilege.

Absolute privilege is given in the above cases because it is considered that in the public interest it is better to have complete freedom of expression, even though the risk of malice, inaccuracy, or damage to reputation may be increased. In all other cases the privilege is only 'qualified'.

(2) Qualified privilege

It is difficult to describe precisely all the circumstances which enjoy qualified privilege, but some are reasonably clear. In general, the circumstances must be such that the person who makes the statement must have some kind of recognizable legal, social, or moral duty or interest to make it to the other person who must have a similar duty or interest to read or hear the statement.

This rules out idle gossip or things which are said out of spite, but recognizes that it is sometimes right that you should be allowed to speak freely and without fear that what you say is not completely accurate, provided that you do so honestly and that the person you speak to ought to be told about it.

An obvious example would be that of an employee's reference. If you are proposing to employ somebody, you have a legitimate interest in how he behaved with his previous employer. His previous employer is not bound to give a reference, but if he does so he has the duty to give you his honest impression. It is 'for the common convenience and welfare of society' that such occasions should be privileged; but at the same time it is impossible to draw up an exact list of what those occasions are.

Some things are certain, however. Firstly, the occasion ceases to be privileged if the defendant was 'malicious'; secondly, the statement must not go beyond what is necessary for the occasion; thirdly, publication must be confined to those who have the duty or interest to receive it.

Malice

This means ill-will or spite, but also includes any improper motive in the mind of the defendant. In the case of an employee's reference, if you say something defamatory about him because you dislike him, you are being malicious out of ill-will; but even if you say it simply out of a desire to gossip, that is

549

still 'malicious' in a legal sense, because you had an improper motive in saying it.

Mere carelessness is not malice: you may be the sort of person who believes anything. On the other hand, if you know you have received unreliable information and yet recklessly use it, that may well be evidence of malice.

Over-wide statement

Because the qualified privilege applies only to the occasion, the privilege may be lost if what is said (or written) is unconnected with the occasion. To take again the example of the employee's reference, if in addition to commenting about his work you also write something which 'brings him into hatred, ridicule, or contempt' and which has nothing to do with his work—for instance, that he is cruel to his wife—this might destroy the privilege. It might also be evidence of malice.

Over-wide publication

The same principle applies to publication to persons unconnected with the occasion. It is right that you should give a candid reference to the new employer, but it would be wrong that you should send it by postcard so that it could be read by everybody or that you should give it in the presence of other people who had no proper interest in the question.

On the other hand, your publication to your stenographer by dictating a letter to her, or to the plaintiff's secretary by her opening the letter, may be covered by the privilege.

When qualified privilege arises

As has already been said, it is not possible to make a complete list of the occasions which provide qualified privilege; but the following are some of the circumstances in which a statement may be so covered.

(1) *Legal, moral, or social duty.* Here a question of duty is involved. For example, it is your legal duty to give information to the police about suspected crime, your moral duty to warn your daughter about her boy-friend's bad reputation, your social duty to give a reference (if you give one at all) which is honest. They are the sorts of duty which would be 'recognized by English people of ordinary intelligence and moral principles'; but difficulties may arise if a person exceeds that duty—for example, by talking to others than the police, the daughter, or the employer, as the case may be.

(2) *Common interest.* Here *all* the parties concerned must have a genuine and proper interest, both the one who makes the statement and the one who receives it. For example, husbands and wives may be properly interested to hear that their married partners have been unfaithful, but this does not mean that any meddlesome busybody has a genuine 'interest' in telling them about it.

(3) *Self-interest.* It has been said that privilege attaches to any statement 'fairly made by a person in the conduct of his own affairs, in matters where his own interest is concerned'. For example, you have a right to protect your reputation, and consequently defamatory statements you make about your

attacker, provided they are not unnecessarily violent or over-widely published, enjoy a qualified privilege. If you are attacked in a newspaper it may be reasonable to reply through a newspaper; but this would be excessive if the defamatory statement was made to only one or two people.

Reports

So far we have been considering the privilege (if any) enjoyed by the author of a defamatory statement. The next point is the privilege enjoyed by a person who reports such a statement. Obviously a person who reports a privileged statement does not necessarily enjoy the same privilege—it may be right that you should be privileged in giving a reference, but there is no reason why the new employer should be privileged if he chooses to 'report' the reference to somebody else. There must, consequently, be some public good served by the report being made.

(1) *Judicial proceedings.* It is in the common interest that fair and accurate reports of judicial proceedings should be published, whether by newspapers or anyone else and whether contemporaneously or later, and therefore such reports which are published without malice enjoy at Common Law a qualified privilege, provided they are neither blasphemous, seditious nor obscene, and their publication has not been forbidden by law (as in the case of certain details of divorce cases or where children are involved) or by order of the Judge.

In the case of newspapers and broadcasts, rather more protection (possibly amounting to absolute privilege) is given by the Defamation Act, 1952, ss. 8 and 9, if the report is (a) of the proceedings of a court exercising judicial authority within the United Kingdom, and (b) contemporaneous. It follows that if the report is of proceedings in, say, a foreign court or is not a contemporaneous report, the privilege is only 'qualified'; and in no case other than a newspaper or broadcast can there be more than qualified privilege.

By 'fair and accurate' is meant that the report must be impartial, not inspired by 'malice'; but it need not be a verbatim report. It follows that it must not distort the picture—as, for example, by picking out only the damaging things said about a man, or failing to report any answer he may have had. In particular, the protection extends only to the factual side of the report, and not to comment.

(2) *Parliamentary proceedings.* There is a similar protection for reports of parliamentary proceedings.

By the Parliamentary Papers Act, 1840, all reports, papers, votes, and proceedings published under the authority of the House of Lords or House of Commons are absolutely privileged. This applies only to such reports, etc. All other reports are subject to the rules explained above in connection with reports of judicial proceedings.

(3) *Other proceedings.* The Defamation Act, 1952, s. 7, provides a schedule which gives a list of 'newspaper statements having qualified privilege'. The same privilege extends to broadcast statements.

The list is divided into two parts. Those in Part I enjoy the privilege without the publisher being required to make any explanation or contradiction if the plaintiff (that is, the person who thinks he has been defamed by the statement) complains that it is inaccurate. Those in Part II enjoy the privilege only if the defendant, on request by the plaintiff, has published 'a reasonable letter or statement by way of explanation or contradiction'.

The lists are too long for inclusion here. Part I covers fair and accurate reports of proceedings in the Parliaments or Courts of the rest of the British Dominions, of certain international organisations and of any International Court. Part II covers fair and accurate reports of the decisions of certain associations 'formed in the United Kingdom for the purpose of promoting or encouraging' such miscellaneous activities as art, science, religion, learning, trade, business, industry, profession, game, sport, or pastime. It also covers fair and accurate reports of public meetings lawfully held in connection with a matter of public concern, as well as such meetings as those of local authorities and public (but not private) companies.

JUSTIFICATION

Definition

It is a complete defence to a civil action for libel or slander that the statement complained of was true. This is called the defence of JUSTIFICATION. In so far as the statement consists of the expression of opinions or the drawing of inferences, those opinions or inferences must also be true. This does not mean true simply in the sense that the defendant truly held the opinion, but that the opinion or inference itself was true in the light of the facts. For example, if a cashier had failed on one occasion to balance his books and I expressed the opinion that he was an unreliable cashier, I might truly think this was the proper inference to draw; but the test would be whether this was a true inference to draw from a single failure.

Distinction from 'fair comment'

There is another defence, dealt with below, which is called 'FAIR COMMENT ON A MATTER OF PUBLIC INTEREST'. It must not be confused with the defence of justification because there are some important differences.

(1) In justification the question of malice is not important: if the statement is true it does not matter that you made it out of spite or other improper motive, but in the case of fair comment it does.

(2) In the case of justification any opinion, inference, or comment must, as we have seen above, be 'true', but in fair comment it does not have to be true in any absolute sense: if it is made without malice, it is enough if it is a comment that might fairly be made. In fact a better description might be '*honest* comment', *i.e.*, expressing an opinion which *could* be honestly held by a reasonable person even if most other people would disagree with it.

(3) The defence of fair comment applies only to comments on matters of public interest: the defence of justification applies to a comment on anything.

Difficulties

Although justification is a complete defence, it is not an easy one for a number of reasons.

(1) The law presumes to start with that the statement was false. In other

words, if I say the cashier failed to balance the accounts, I have to prove the truth of my words.

(2) If I fail to prove the truth of what I said, I may well make the damages I have to pay that much more severe: the jury may well feel that it was bad enough to have made the statement in the first place, and that I have made things worse by continuing to maintain that it was true in open court.

(3) It does not matter how good the defendant's grounds may be for believing the statement to be true: I may have got the statement from a source on which I had every reasonable right to rely, but it makes no difference if the story in fact is not true.

Nor can the defendant protect himself by qualifying the statement with such words as, "I believe", or, "There is a rumour". It is equally not enough to add that one does not believe the story or that it has yet to be proved. It may be entirely true that the defendant believed the story or that there is a rumour, but that is not the point: what has to be proved is not what the defendant truly believed but that what he believed was true.

(4) It is not what you meant to say which necessarily counts, it is what you have said. Conversely, it may not be what you have said which counts, but what you meant to say. An example of the former would be where you meant to say, "He is not a dishonest man", but unfortunately you omitted the word 'not'. An example of the latter would be where, although you had said, "He is not a dishonest man", you intended to mean that he was pretty near it, or had been dishonest on that occasion, or needed watching, or something of that kind. This is what you meant to say; and usually what is involved here is an 'innuendo', a subject which is dealt with elsewhere.

(5) It is not enough to prove that most of what you said was true: you must prove that all the material statements were true. At Common Law it was 'sufficient if the substance of the libellous statement be proved. . . . As much must be justified as meets the sting of the charge, and if anything be contained in a charge which does not add to it, that need not be justified.' By statute the position has been expressed in a different way. The Defamation Act, 1952, s. 5, says:

> In an action for libel or slander in respect of words containing two or more distinct charges against the plaintiff, a defence of justification shall not fail by reason only that the truth of every charge is not proved if the words not proved to be true do not materially injure the plaintiff's reputation having regard to the truth of the remaining charges.

FAIR COMMENT

Introduction

As we have seen, you may defame somebody by making a simple statement of fact, as by saying that he is a thief; and here, if it has been 'published', the only possible defences will be that it was true or that it was written or said on a privileged occasion.

Or you may defame a person, not by the statement of fact at its face value, but by some hidden meaning (or 'innuendo') which it has—as by saying, "We had no trouble with the petty cash till last August": this in itself damages no one; but, if a new cashier arrived last August, it may conceal an accusation that he was responsible for the trouble.

Lastly, you may defame a person, not by the statement of fact (which may be true) but by what you say about it—the opinion you express or the inference you draw. As we have just seen, you can plead justification and succeed if you can prove that the opinion or inference was 'true'.

Fair Comment (?)

Now we have to consider another line of defence involving opinion, inference, or comment, but where the comment does not have to be 'true' in the same sense that it has to be in a plea of justification. It is known shortly as FAIR COMMENT.

Definition

This defence is rather more complex than a simple plea that the comment was fair. A better idea of what is involved can be got from looking at the way in which this defence is usually expressed.

In so far as the words complained of consist of allegations of fact they are true in substance and in fact, and in so far as they consist of expressions of opinion they are fair comment made in good faith and without malice upon a matter of public interest.

554

There are a number of points to notice about this formula:—

(1) *Fact and opinion.* With the defence of fair comment you are concerned not only with the comment but also with the fact or facts on which it is based, and it is important to keep them separate.

(a) For the defence of fair comment to succeed it is necessary to show that the facts on which the comment was made are true: if the facts are untrue the comment on them can hardly be fair.

(b) If the facts and the comment are so mixed up that one cannot tell which is which, there is a risk that something which was intended as comment may be taken as a statement of fact. If so, it will have to be 'justified' (that is, proved true), whereas, if it is clear that it is comment, all that has to be done is to show that it is 'fair'—not necessarily 'true'. This subtle distinction is explained below.

The 'rolled-up' plea. The form of pleading given above is known as the 'rolled-up' plea, because it tries to cover and combine both the factual and the commenting aspects of this defence and to suggest a defence of justification. However, the courts have not allowed it to be used in this way. It is not an alternative defence of justification and/or fair comment: it is simply a defence of fair comment, and the defendant must make it clear which of the words are statements of fact and how he proposes to show that they are true. If he fails to prove the truth of the statements of fact he will fail on the fair comment issue as well.

(2) *'True.'* What the pleading says is 'true in substance and in fact'. What is meant by 'true' in connection with facts has been explained above in connection with the defence of justification, and the Defamation Act, 1952, has made a similar provision about failure to prove the truth of every fact where the defence is one of fair comment. By Section 6 it is provided that:

a defence of fair comment shall not fail by reason only that the truth of every allegation of fact is not proved if the expression of opinion is fair comment having regard to such of the facts alleged or referred to in the words complained of as are proved.

(3) *'Fair.'* If there is a jury, it is for them and not for the judge to decide whether the comment is 'fair'. This, of course, is a very difficult task. Everybody has a legal right to his own opinions and a legal right to express them. Therefore there may be a great variety of opinions legally expressed; and the 'fair' opinion is not necessarily the one with which you happen to agree. It follows that the 'fair' opinion in a particular case is not the one which that jury holds—even if they have an agreed opinion. An alternative would be to imagine what the opinion of a 'reasonable man' might be: this would equally create difficulties because reasonable men can hold different opinions.

In a famous case, which concerned a criticism of a play, the judge said the question was:

"Would any fair man, however prejudiced he may be, however exaggerated or obstinate his views, have said that which this criticism has said . . .?"

This may at first sight appear to be strange guidance, because one does not expect a fair man to be prejudiced or exaggerated and obstinate in his views.

Nevertheless, it is good guidance, because it stresses the most important aspect of 'fairness', which is that the commentator believed in his comment, *i.e.* that he was honest even if wrongheaded, and was not actuated by spite or any other improper motive.

(4) *Malice.* The words 'without malice' are intended to reinforce what has just been said about 'fairness', but they go a bit further. A person may hold and express strong, unpopular, and even wrongheaded views but still be regarded as making a 'fair comment'. On the other hand, a person may hold views with which a large proportion of people are prepared to agree, but if he does not express those views *honestly, because (for example) his primary purpose is to wound*, it is right that the jury should take that into account in deciding whether his comment was 'fair'. Similarly, if he goes beyond comment on (again, for example) something a man has done and without justification attacks the man who did it or his motives in doing it, again he may have gone beyond the bounds of fair comment and displayed malice.

(5) *'Public interest.'* Even though you have shown that the facts were true, that the comment was fair and that it was made in good faith and without malice, you have still got to show that the matter on which you commented was one of 'public interest'.

Although it is for the jury to decide whether facts are true, comment is fair, and malice is absent, it is for the judge to decide as a question of law whether the matter is one of public interest.

It is impossible to say precisely what is of public interest. There is no doubt that public affairs such as the administration of the law, Parliament, the Churches, the Armed Services, and the like are of public interest. As for other matters, it has been suggested that the test is whether the person or activity commented on exposes himself or itself to the public gaze and is therefore a legitimate object of public criticism. This criterion brings in such persons as politicians and priests, authors and actors, professional sportsmen, and others whose occupations are designed to attract public attention or whose living depends on it. It also brings in their activities—the political speeches they make, the books they write, the pictures they paint or film, or the sports they practise. Furthermore, it includes such persons as company directors who, though they may not seek publicity, must expect comment on what they do.

'INJURIOUS FALSEHOOD'

There is another type of action, very like an action for defamation, which is sometimes called INJURIOUS FALSEHOOD and in other connections is known as SLANDER OF TITLE or SLANDER OF GOODS. The major distinction is that in the case of injurious falsehood the statement, though damaging, need not necessarily be defamatory; but it must, of course, be untrue.

Examples

In one case the defendant told people that a certain firm had ceased to exist. There is nothing necessarily defamatory about such a statement, but the result of this untrue statement was that the firm lost business.

556

In another case the defendant told the man to whom the plaintiff was engaged that she was already married. Again there is nothing necessarily defamatory in this, but the result was that the man broke off the engagement.

Property rights

There is a similar right of action where the 'injurious falsehood' concerns not a person or business but a right of property. For example, I might throw doubt on your title to some land, so that you could not sell it; or on your right to some patent or trade mark so that people would refuse to deal with your goods. Similarly, I might slander your goods themselves by suggesting that they were of poor quality.

What must be proved

In all such cases the injured party may bring an action provided he can show the following things:

(1) That the statement was 'published' by the defendant and to someone else than the plaintiff (the injured party).

(2) That the statement was false.

(3) That it was published 'maliciously'—that is, with the intention of injuring the plaintiff. Mere carelessness is not enough; but, on the other hand, a person who recklessly makes a statement which he knows is likely to injure may have shown malice from his recklessness.

(4) That the plaintiff has suffered damage as a result. Under the Defamation Act, 1952, s. 3, he is not bound to show this if either:

(a) the words are published in some permanent form (which includes broadcasting); or

(b) the words are 'calculated to cause pecuniary damage to the plaintiff in respect of any office, profession, calling, trade, or business held or carried on by him at the time of the publication'.

Slander of goods

In the case of slander of goods it must be shown that the statement was made 'of and concerning' the goods in question. A mere 'puffing' of one's own goods, implying that other people's goods are inferior to one's own, is not enough. There must be some more precise statement—for example, that the goods contain some harmful substance or do not contain some ingredient which they are said to contain—so that there is a particular slander of those goods or a particular imputation that the person who deals in them is dishonest or incompetent.

JURIES

Libel and slander are two of the few remaining civil actions in which a jury can be demanded by either party. The others of this miscellaneous collection are malicious prosecution, false imprisonment, seduction, and breach of promise of marriage.

One reason for defamation being a jury case is that in earlier days libel was primarily a criminal matter. It used to be tried by the Star Chamber, where there was no jury, and the judges were judges of both law and fact. After the abolition of the Star Chamber the judges were reluctant to leave it to a jury to decide whether the matter complained of was defamatory: their task was confined to deciding whether the words were published by the defendant and whether they referred to the plaintiff, and it was for the judges to decide whether the words amounted to a libel. The question was finally settled by Fox's Libel Act, 1792; and the position now is that it is for the judge to decide whether the words are *capable* of being defamatory: if he decides that they are not, then he must withdraw the case from the jury; if he decides that they are capable, then he must leave it to the jury to decide whether in fact they *are* defamatory.

There are other aspects of a defamation action where the judge and jury have separate functions. Where the defence is put up that the words were spoken or written on a 'privileged' occasion, the jury only come into it if there is a dispute about the facts: it is for the judge to decide as a matter of law whether the facts amounted to a privileged occasion. Where the defence is 'fair comment on a matter of public interest', it is for the jury to decide whether the comment is fair but, perhaps rather curiously, it is for the judge to say whether the matter is of public interest.

The basic rule is that questions of fact are for the jury and questions of law for the judge.

Example

The partnership between judge and jury is not always an easy one. In a famous case the following telegram was sent:

> 'Edith has resumed her service with us today. Please send her possessions and the money you borrowed, also her wages.'

The judge decided as a matter of law that these words were capable of being defamatory; the jury decided as a matter of fact that they were. The case went to the Court of Appeal where two judges agreed they could be defamatory but one said they could not. In the House of Lords the division went the other way: three judges agreed that the words were not capable of being defamatory but the other two said they were. Altogether, therefore, there were four judges who thought the words could not be defamatory, five judges who thought they could, and a jury who thought that in fact they were. Nevertheless, the minority opinion which thought they could not be prevailed, because that was the view taken by the House of Lords.

This, of course, is not a typical case. It is rare that there is such a conflict of judicial opinion. What is more unpredictable is the view which a jury may take on any particular case—and, still more, the view they may take on the right amount of damages to award. For these reasons, and also because fashion and even the meanings of words change from generation to generation, decisions reached in previous cases are not such reliable guides in the field of defamation as they are in most branches of the law.

CRIMINAL LAW

WHAT IS CRIMINAL LAW?

CRIMINAL LAW is the subject of this part of the FAMILY LAWYER. It will tell you what you must have done to make you guilty of a large variety of crimes, some of the defences you may have against being found guilty, what courts decide whether you are guilty or not, and what can be done if you are found guilty.

These are most important aspects of the Criminal Law from a practical point of view; but knowing about them does not tell you what a 'crime' is by nature or how 'criminal' law differs from other aspects of the law.

In short, what is a 'crime' and why is Criminal Law a separate branch of the law?

What is a crime?

In other parts of this book you will find the law dealt with under many headings, such as CONTRACT, TORT, HUSBAND & WIFE, RENT RESTRICTION, and each of these headings is subdivided into particular headings according to the type of 'contract' (*e.g.* CONTRACT OF EMPLOYMENT) or 'tort' (*e.g.* TRESPASS) or 'husband and wife' problems (*e.g.* MAINTENANCE) or whatever it may be.

All these divisions are logical and convenient, although they may overlap in some cases. The one thing they have in common is that on the whole they concern only the people involved. Generally speaking, if I enter into a contract with you, you can make me carry it out, but if you don't think it worth while to do so nobody is going to do it for you; if I trespass on your property and legal action is to be taken to stop me it must be taken by you. Things of this sort, though they cause harm and are legal wrongs, are almost entirely a matter for the civilian concerned—and they are therefore left to be dealt with in what are called CIVIL COURTS.

Why, then, the CRIMINAL COURTS and a special legal liability for CRIME?

(A) Definition

There is no generally agreed or complete definition of crime. However, a crime has at least two distinguishing marks.

(a) *Community interest.* As explained above, only the people concerned are usually interested in enforcing a contract or dealing with trespassers. (That is one of the reasons why the notice, 'Trespassers Will Be Prosecuted' is usually a lie: trespass is seldom a crime, and so you cannot be prosecuted for it.)

One of the distinguishing marks of a crime is that the public *as a whole* are interested in what has been done, as well as the particular people concerned. If I make a brutal attack on an old lady, she can sue me in the 'civil' court and get compensation for the damage I have done her; but that is not enough.

559

The public as a whole—the community—are concerned (a) that I don't do it again, and (b) that other people don't follow my example. Therefore, in addition to any steps the old lady may take, the community must also take action against me. The importance of this will be even more obvious if we suppose that I start to make the attack, but you stop me before I can carry it out: as I have not injured the old lady she would have no claim against me, and I would go scot-free if it were not for the Criminal Law.

(b) *Punishment.* Another distinguishing mark of a crime is that it carries a penalty. In 'civil' disputes there is usually no question of punishment or retribution. If I break my contract with you or damage your property, I must pay

"Trespass is seldom a crime, and so you cannot be prosecuted for it . . ."

what you have lost through my failure to carry out my side of the bargain or the cost of putting the damage right, but there is no question of my paying something extra by way of punishment for having done wrong.

In the case of crime one of the important features is the punishment of the criminal—partly for his own good, in the hope that he may reform or at least perceive that crime does not pay; partly for the benefit of the community, in the hope that fear of a like punishment will deter him or others from similar wrong-doing.

(B) Origins

Once a particular act (or omission) has become classified as a crime it is recognized as something forbidden and something which carries a penalty of fine, imprisonment, or even death. But how does it reach that classification?

It is almost impossible to understand the meaning of 'crime' without knowing something about the history of the idea and how it has been (and still is) influenced by moral and political considerations.

In a primitive community there is really no distinction between crime and anything else you happen to dislike. The strongest man prevails: he takes his weapon and deals personally with the wrong-doer—whether the 'wrong' was murder or merely making a face at him. With better organization the strong man takes companions to help him; but it is still a trial of strength, without much regard to the justice of his cause or the importance of the dispute.

At a later stage of development the strong men begin to see that SELF-HELP —untidy and unregulated—is dangerous and inconvenient. They therefore set up a kind of tariff for various wrongs. Over 1,000 years ago, in the reigns of King Alfred and his elder brothers Ethelbert and Ethelred, there was an elaborate

"In a primitive community there is really no distinction between crime and anything else you happen to dislike . . ."

tariff which included such rates of compensation as 3–12 times the value for damage to property (according to whose property it was) and 5s–20s for damage to toes (according to which toe). However, the difficulty still remained that if the wrong-doer refused to pay the tariff price the old system of 'self-help' was employed, and a BLOOD FEUD or OUTLAWRY probably followed. And there was still no distinction between wrongs to the community and merely private wrongs.

The next stages are therefore concerned with the KING'S PEACE and KEEPING THE PEACE. This involves three major problems:

(a) Defining 'crimes' and separating them from 'civil disputes';
(b) Enforcing the law as consistently as possible;
(c) Preventing crime.

To begin with, these problems were dealt with on a local basis. In the days when it was a good deal more difficult to go from London to Newcastle than it is now to go from London to Australia, and when people lived in isolated communities, the local chieftains administered their own laws; but over 900 years ago, in the reign of King Canute, there was the beginning of a distinction between criminal offences and private disputes.

One of the great merits of William the Conqueror was that he left English laws more or less as they were: he and his successors for the next hundred years concentrated more on making the system efficient. Within that hundred years, in the reign of his grandson Henry II (a keen amateur lawyer and administrator), we had a JURY system and Royal Judges travelling the length and breadth of the country on CIRCUIT to try crime.

It was in this way that a COMMON LAW was established. The judges on their return to London would compare notes on how they had dealt with cases at

"What was good enough for William the Conqueror . . ."

their ASSIZES, and so there began to be uniformity in their decisions. Over 600 years ago LAW REPORTS began to be published, so that what had been decided could be seen and followed in subsequent cases. As a result we now have a record of what are 'Common Law' crimes and a system of what is called JUDICIAL PRECEDENT, which means (roughly) that judges are bound by preceding judgments to follow the existing definitions of crimes and to deal with them as they were dealt with by their predecessors. This makes the law as 'certain' as can be, and largely removes the possibility of personal prejudice.

The major disadvantage of this system is that, although it gives you 'certainty', it also gives you 'inflexibility'. It is a good thing that judges should be bound by the existing law; but, on the other hand, what was good enough for William the Conqueror may not be good enough for us today. How, then, to alter the law? To what extent is the law concerned with changes in moral or religious views?

The courts are not directly concerned with morals or religion: they are concerned only with *legal* rights and wrongs. People's moral or religious conduct and opinion vary enormously in a free society. To take obvious examples: many people disapprove of adultery, betting, drinking alcoholic beverages, and working on the Sabbath; many people do one or more of them. But none of them are 'crimes', however offensive they may be to a particular person's religious or moral code, and therefore no judge (whatever his own veiws) can treat them as such.

On the other hand, if the community feel that the courts should concern themselves with any of these problems they can change the law. Supreme over the courts is PARLIAMENT. By an ACT OF PARLIAMENT (or STATUTE, as it is also called) centuries' old law can be changed in as many weeks, and the new law takes the place of the old. Thus betting, drinking alcohol, and working on Sunday have become crimes in certain circumstances; and adultery, though still not a crime, can lead to legal consequences—*e.g.* in connection with divorce.

Thus our Criminal Law today is found partly in Common Law decisions of judges, partly in Acts of Parliament or Statutes. The more obvious evils, such as murder and stealing, were naturally enough early inventions of the Common Law; less obvious evils or those which appear only with a more enlightened social consciousness (such as indiscriminate selling of drugs or cruelty to animals) are usually the creation of Statute. Many old Common Law crimes (including murder and stealing) have been re-defined, revised, or brought up to date by more modern Statutes.

That, then, is a very brief account of how the Criminal Law developed and still develops. Wherever the definition of a crime is to be found, it is the judge's duty to interpret the law as he finds it; he must follow the established practice as to the way in which the guilt of the accused person is proved; and if the accused is found guilty he must pass the appropriate sentence, exercising such discretion as the law allows him.

METHODS OF CLASSIFICATION

There are two obvious ways of classifying crimes—first, according to the purpose of the crime; second, according to the seriousness of the crime. Neither of them is very satisfactory because there is a good deal of overlapping.

(A) Purpose

One distinction that can be made is between:

(a) offences which are primarily against the State or community; and
(b) offences which are primarily against the individual; and these can be
   further subdivided according to whether they are:
   (*i*) against their persons, or
   (*ii*) against their property.

563

How crime is classified

(a) Offences against the State
such as—

TREASON.

SMUGGLING.

MUTINY.

INCOME TAX
DODGING.

(b) Offences against the Individual, his person and his property,
such as—

MURDER.

ASSAULT.

MALICIOUS DAMAGE.

BURGLARY.

The offences under (a) include such crimes as TREASON, MUTINY, and RIOT—crimes which may affect individuals, but whose importance is rather that they affect the community as a whole. These are crimes which most of us do not have much temptation to commit; but there are others, such as INCOME-TAX DODGING and SMUGGLING through the customs, which are fairly widespread and certainly affect the community because the rest of us have to pay higher taxes to make up for those which have been dodged. However, it is only the second type of crime that is dealt with in this work.

The offences under (b) include everything from MURDER to simple ASSAULT as far as offences against the person are concerned, and such things as BURGLARY and HOUSEBREAKING in connection with property.

In a sense all crimes are offences against the community because a civilized State is concerned to see that its members are not victims of crime. Furthermore, it is the State which has the responsibility of preventing, detecting, trying, and punishing crime.

(B) Seriousness

Another distinction that can be made is between:

(a) Indictable Offences:
    (*i*) Felonies (including TREASON);
    (*ii*) Misdemeanours; and
(b) Petty Offences.

Indictable and petty offences. Indictable offences are crimes which are usually tried by a judge and jury; petty offences are those which are usually tried summarily before magistrates without juries. However, some indictable offences can be tried summarily, and some petty offences can be tried on indictment. Broadly speaking, indictable offences are the more serious ones' but in the case of the more serious petty offences the accused person may prefer trial by jury' and, conversely, in the case of a less serious indictable offence it may be preferable to 'get it over before the magistrates'.

Felonies and misdemeanours. The distinction between these two types of indictable offence is largely historical and has practically no importance today.

On the whole felonies are the graver crimes; but there are a lot of exceptions. It is a felony to do more than £1's worth of damage to a tree in a park; it is only a misdemeanour to ill-treat a child 'in a manner likely to cause him unnecessary suffering or injury to health'—which includes 'injury to or loss of sight, hearing or limb, or organ of the body and any mental derangement'. Moreover, both offences—whether to the tree or the child, are punishable with a term of imprisonment not exceeding five years.

The distinction used to be important because until the nineteenth century they involved the DEATH PENALTY and FORFEITURE of the felon's land and goods. Today the only felonies punishable with death are TREASON, SETTING FIRE TO HER MAJESTY'S SHIPS AND DOCKYARDS, PIRACY involving danger to life, and MURDER in certain circumstances. Forfeiture was abolished in 1870. Another disadvantage enjoyed by the person accused of felony was that he could not call witnesses in his defence or have a barrister to defend him except on questions of law; but these disadvantages no longer exist.

(C) Powers of arrest

The most important distinction which exists today concerns the power of arrest. The police naturally have wider powers than the private citizen.

On the whole, there cannot be an arrest for a misdemeanour without a WARRANT: but in the case of a felony committed in his presence even a private citizen may have power to arrest without warrant. Indeed, in some cases he has a duty to do so.

TYPES OF CRIMINAL

(A) Principal in the first degree

This usually means the person who actually does the deed—fires the shot, coshes the cashier, blows the safe, burgles the house, or whatever it may be. There may, of course, be more than one principal in the first degree—as where several people shoot or cosh. But the person who does the deed without which the crime would not have been committed may not be a criminal at all. If I hand you a poisoned drink to pass to my wife and you know nothing about the poison, *you* are guilty of no crime at all but *I* am the principal in the first degree.

(B) Principal in the second degree

This means a person who 'AIDS AND ABETS' the principal in the first degree. To aid and abet you have got to be present at the commission of the crime and actually assisting the principal in the first degree, even if only by encouraging him. Your presence might consist only in keeping watch—possibly at some distance from the actual scene of the crime; your encouragement would have to be a little more active than just happening to be present so that your friend felt braver when he attacked the old lady. In the imaginary case given above, where my wife is poisoned, if we had both agreed to poison her you would be the principal in the first degree; I would be the principal in the second degree.

(C) Accessory before the fact

An ACCESSORY BEFORE THE FACT is rather like a principal in the second degree, except that he is not present at the actual commission of the felony. He is someone who gives help or encouragement beforehand—as, for example, by providing implements which he knows are to be used for housebreaking.

(D) Accessory after the fact

This means, obviously, a person who starts to help only after the felony has been committed. He may, after the crime, help the criminal to escape justice.

Equally obviously, not everybody who helps a criminal to escape is an accessory after the fact: the porter who takes him down in the lift from the flat he has burgled, the taxi-driver who drives him to his 'fence', are all helping him. To be found guilty of being an accessory after the fact you must know of the felony *and* you must give some active help in connection with it.

In this connection there is an interesting example of sex discrimination. A wife is not an accessory after the fact by hiding her felonious husband—but this is not so in the reverse situation.

Types of criminal

Principal in the first degree—generally the person who actually does the deed.
Principal in the second degree—one who aids and abets at the time.

Accessory before the Fact—helps *before* the crime.

Accessory after the Fact—one who . . .

. . . helps .

. . . after the crime!

REQUISITES FOR CRIME

(1) 'Actus non facet reum nisi mens sit rea'

This Latin maxim means that, to commit a crime, you have not only got to do *something forbidden by law*, you have also got to have a particular *wrongful intention* at the time when you did it.

These two requirements have been described by Lord Goddard as 'a cardinal doctrine of the Criminal Law'.

(a) *The guilty act.* It is important to remember that not all evil conduct is a crime, and not every crime is really evil. 'Envy, hatred, malice, and all uncharitableness' is no crime—but parking without lights is.

Although a large part of what most people think ought to be criminal is included in the list of crimes, nevertheless to be found guilty you must be shown to have done some 'guilty act' which is established as a crime either by Common Law or by Statute. 'Common Law' crimes are on the whole the more obvious ones which were recognized as 'anti-social' in our early history; 'statutory' crimes are either new ones created by Parliament or old ones which have been newly defined or brought up to date by particular Statutes or Acts of Parliament. Nowadays it is true enough to say that the vast majority of crimes have been included in some Act of Parliament which defines *what* 'guilty act' must be performed to make it a crime.

Consequently, you cannot be found guilty unless you have done that particular act. For 'murder' you must have killed somebody (if you poison someone, but before it takes effect he falls downstairs and breaks his neck you are not guilty of murder); for 'burglary' you must have done it 'by night'; for 'stealing' you must have 'taken and carried away' (if you just touch you haven't stolen); for 'embezzlement' you must have done it as a 'clerk or servant'; and so on.

The 'guilty act' can, of course, consist of an *omission* to do something which you had a legal duty to do. If I have charge of a baby or some helpless old person and I deliberately cause their death by omitting to feed them, it is the same as if I had done a positive act.

The 'guilty act' need not be actually performed by the guilty person. If I send you a box of poisoned chocolates it makes no difference that you would not have eaten them if the postman had not delivered them or your wife had not pressed you to do so. I am still your murderer, and the postman or your wife are innocent because they have no 'guilty mind'.

(b) *The guilty mind.* So, in addition to doing a guilty deed the accused person must have a 'guilty mind'.

This means something more than a general evil intention or moral culpability. It usually involves having an intention of some kind, though in some cases the accused is presumed to have the intention of a 'reasonable man', even though in fact he did not have that intention, and in other cases the lack of intention amounts to 'criminal negligence'—that is, a degree of recklessness which is as bad as having a positive intention to perform the 'guilty act'. This will become clearer when we discuss such crimes as murder and manslaughter.

In the majority of crimes there must be not only an evil intention but a *particular* evil intention. For example, in the case of burglary the statutory definition says that the breaking in to the house must have been 'with intent to commit any felony therein , so if the intent was to get a night's shelter it could not be burglary, whatever other offence it might have been.

It is the intention that counts, whatever the consequences. If I shoot with the intention of killing you but instead I kill your brother, it is still murder; but if I shoot with the intention of killing a rabbit but instead I kill your brother, it is not.

(2) 'Intention'

However, you cannot form an intention unless you are able to do so and have freedom of choice. For that reason infancy or lunacy, for example, may be a defence because they mean you haven't got the capacity to form the intention; and if you are forced to do something at pistol-point, for example, it may be a defence because it prevented you from having freedom of choice. These things are dealt with below.

DEFENCES

Because the law requires a criminal to have a 'guilty mind' there are certain types of individuals who cannot commit crimes, and certain circumstances in which what is done is either not a crime at all or, if it is, is considered to be less blameworthy.

(1) 'Infancy'

An INFANT in English Law means someone under the age of twenty-one. Obviously a person can have a 'guilty mind' at a very early age, though it is difficult to believe that a baby in arms can do so. The trouble is to know at what age a person ought to be assumed to be 'responsible'. English Law (perhaps inevitably) fixes arbitrary dividing lines.

(a) *'Under eight.'* Under the age of eight a child cannot be guilty of any offence: he may in fact have killed somebody, but nevertheless the presumption that he cannot commit murder or manslaughter is IRREBUTTABLE. By 'irrebuttable' is meant that, whatever the evidence to the contrary, our courts will not admit the possibility that the child *could* (let alone *did*) have the necessary 'intention'.

(b) *'Over fourteen.'* From the age of fourteen a child is considered fully capable of committing a crime. But the way in which he is 'tried' for the crime, and the penalty if he is found guilty, takes into account the fact that he is still an 'infant'.

(c) *'Eight to fourteen.'* A child who is eight but under fourteen is in a kind of half-way house. It is presumed that he is incapable of committing a crime but (unlike the case of children under eight) this presumption, except on a charge of rape, is REBUTTABLE. This means that you start with the same presumption that the child could not have the intention to commit a crime, but you can bring evidence to 'rebut' that presumption—*i.e.* to show that the child did in fact have the capacity to realize that what he did was gravely wrong.

(d) *In general.* These distinctions about age, trial, and treatment are artificial and unsatisfactory. At the end of October 1960 a Committee on Children and

569

Young Persons, having spent four years looking into the matter, recommended the raising of the age for 'criminal responsibility' to twelve or even fourteen; but at the same time they suggested a 'new look' at the criminal side and more attention to 'protection or discipline' and the responsibility of parents.

"Under the age of eight a child cannot be guilty of any offence . . ."

". . . from the age of fourteen a child is considered fully capable of committing a crime."

(2) Insanity

It is difficult to define INSANITY, or to say how 'insane' a person must be before he ought to be regarded as incapable of a 'guilty mind'. Even lawyers (without taking into account the valuable discoveries of psychologists) have long realized that 'insanity' is only a comparative term, ranging from complete mental inability to slight mental instability. From a practical point of view there are two problems: (1) how to define insanity so that a jury (who are no more experts in this matter than you or I) can decide whether the *particular* accused person falls on this side or the other of the agreed line; and (2) what to do with the accused person if he is found to be insane. This second difficulty can often be got over in a rough way because the judge, in sentencing him, can take into account (among other things) his ability to resist temptation.

A further problem is, even if you can agree on a definition of insanity, can you get Parliament to make the necessary change in the law? Don't forget that judges cannot change this sort of law: for 'capital murder', for example, they must pronounce sentence of death, and their own feelings do not come into it. This may be a pity; but on the whole it is better that the Law should be 'certain'.

'*M'Naghten Rules*.' Apart from an Act of Parliament passed as recently as

1957 (the Homicide Act) and concerned only with murder, the only guidance comes from what are known as the M'NAGHTEN RULES, which are neither 'judgments' by judges nor an Act of Parliament, but 'advice' given by judges in connection with a mentally deranged man who had a fancied grievance which led him to shoot at a prominent statesman of the time—well over 100 years ago.

Although these 'rules' started with neither Common Law nor statutory uthority, they are applied in all cases where 'insanity' is pleaded as a defence. The M'Naghten Rules were laid down in 1843; and they can be summarized as follows:

(a) Everyone is presumed sane. It is up to him to prove that he is not.

(b) If he proves he was insane, his insanity is a defence only if at the time when he committed the crime the accused 'was labouring under such a defect of reason, from disease of the mind, as not to know the nature and quality of what he was doing or, if he did know, that he did not know he was doing wrong'.

(c) If the insanity takes the form of a delusion about *facts* the accused must be treated as though those facts were actually true.

These 'rules' have been much criticized on the grounds that they are out of date, vague, and unscientific. Rule (a), that you must be presumed sane unless you can show the contrary, is sound enough. Rule (c), that if you have delusions about facts you must be treated as a sane man would be if those facts were true, is also sound. For example, if I kill somebody (assuming, because of my insanity, that he is a rabbit) it should be a good defence because shooting a rabbit is not murder. But if I kill somebody (assuming, because of my insanity, that he has swindled me) it should not be a good defence because, even if it were *true* that he had swindled me, I should not have been justified in shooting him.

Rule (b) is the one most criticized. What is meant by 'defect of reason' or 'disease of the mind' and what is 'wrong'? On the other hand it is little use discarding this definition of insanity unless you can think of a better one—*i.e* one suitable for an unscientific jury. It is said that juries do not get confused by the M'Naghten Rules: they ask themselves the simple question, 'Is he mad?' and give the simple answer, 'Yes' or 'No', according to their common-sense instinct.

'*Less than insanity.*' Lesser degrees of mental instability do not usually provide a defence—*e.g.* 'irresistible impulse', which, of course, may be only an impulse which was not resisted, *e.g.* because of drunkenness. There is a curious exception created by Act of Parliament (Infanticide Act, 1938) to take care of mothers who kill their babies in certain circumstances (see below). And there is the Scottish conception of 'diminished responsibility' which has been introduced into English Law only since 1957 and which is dealt with in the 'Homicide' section below.

(3) 'Intoxication'

INTOXICATION of course is not the same thing as being 'drunk' in a popular sense; and it can arise from alcohol, drugs, or anything else which introduces 'toxic' elements, the effect of which is to influence the 'intention' (from the 'guilty mind' point of view) of the person who has taken them.

571

It is the effect that counts. So you may have what the 'ordinary man' might call the 'unfair' result that a drunk person might have a good defence even though it was his own fault he was drunk, while another would have no defence even though his intoxication was caused by somebody else.

The cause of the intoxication does not matter from the point of view of guilt (though it would probably affect the sentence): what matters is the effect the intoxication has on the ability of the accused person to form an intention. If a man is so drunk (whether from his own fault or not) as to be incapable of forming any intention at all, it may be impossible for him to be guilty of the crime in

Intoxication has a wider meaning   —It can come from anything
than being drunk—   toxic—

the effect of which is—   —to influence the 'intention'!

question. If, however, though drunk (again, whether from his own fault or not), he can form *some* intention, the question is whether his intention is enough for that particular crime.

A few examples may help. To commit murder I must have the intention either to kill or to cause grievous bodily harm or to do an act likely to kill or cause grievous bodily harm. If, though drunk, I have the intention to give my wife a slight slap but because of my drunkenness I hit her harder than I meant to and kill her. it is not murder because I have not got the 'intention' required for murder. If, however, though drunk, I have the intention to cause her grievous bodily harm but because of my drunkenness I overdo it and kill her, it is murder because I had one of the necessary 'intentions'—the intention to do grievous bodily harm. It is obviously difficult to discover the 'intention' of an intoxicated person; but, if it can be discovered, it is the intention which counts and not the cause of the intoxication.

It is no defence to say that because of drink or drugs you were more open to temptation. Nor, of course, is drunkenness a defence when it is in fact the crime itself—*e.g.* being drunk in charge of a car under the Road Traffic Acts, 1930 and 1960.

(4) Provocation

This defence is mostly relevant to a charge of homicide, and so is dealt with under that heading.

(5) Compulsion

It is still uncertain how far compulsion is a defence. Although the law does not expect outstanding heroism it probably does expect reasonable fortitude—and some relationship between the threat and the crime. If I threaten to burn down your house unless you kill my wife the law will expect you to run the risk of my burning your house; but if I threaten to kill your wife unless you burn down your house, although that might be the crime of arson you might be excused for selecting what is presumably the less serious alternative.

Certainly the threat must be one of death or grievous bodily harm to yourself or your family. A threat to property is not enough; and it must be a threat which is likely to be carried out immediately. However serious the threat it will not justify murder.

It used to be presumed that if a wife committed a felony (other than homicide) in her husband's presence she did it under his compulsion. This rather absurd presumption was abolished in 1925; but it is still a defence (except in treason or murder) if the wife can show that in fact she did commit the offence in the presence and under the coercion of her husband.

(6) Necessity

There is still no certain answer to the question whether 'necessity' (whatever it may mean) can justify a crime. A doctor is still guilty of unlawful parking even though he felt that life would be endangered by his continuing to search for a parking meter. So-called 'necessity' may limit the penalty; it does not destroy the guilt. The famous 'sea-lawyer's' dilemma about the two mountaineers on a rope only strong enough to support one is still not solved. Is it murder for one to push the other off and thus save himself? If he does not, both die. The only case bearing on the subject concerned two shipwrecked men who ate the cabin-boy, believing that he would die in any event and that they would also die if they did not eat him. In fact, they had misjudged the situation, for they were picked up a few days later. They were found guilty of murder because they had caused the death of the cabin-boy before he would have died naturally, and their 'necessity' was no defence.

(7) Self-defence

SELF-DEFENCE is, of course, a form of 'Necessity'; but it has an obvious difference in that when you are defending yourself or your property your conflict' is between you and the person who is attacking you—and no innocent third person is involved. In the case of 'Necessity', however, such as the ship-wrecked men or the two men on a rope, the 'conflict' is between you and some-body who has done you no harm at all.

Self-defence is therefore recognized as a good defence for a person accused of a crime of violence—and even of homicide—if he can show that what he did was necessary to protect himself, his property, or someone else, against the actual attacker.

But for the defence to succeed he must be able to convince a reasonable jury on two major matters:

(1) That what he did was 'reasonable' in the circumstances—*i.e.* reasonably proportionate to the danger with which he was faced. If an unarmed man

Self-Defence.

attacks me it would not normally be 'reasonable' or 'proportionate' to my danger of injury for me to shoot him. On the other hand, if I am attacked by several unarmed men, or if I am a woman attacked by even only one unarmed man, what is 'reasonable' or 'proportionate' must obviously be different.

(2) That the 'violence' on his part was the only 'reasonable' alternative—say, to calling a policeman. Unheroic though it may be, you are usually expected to run away (if you can) rather than do violence. It has been said that this does not apply to the protection of your property (particularly your house), because by running away you would in fact be ceasing to protect it; but it is by no means safe to suppose that you are legally entitled to blaze away at every trespasser on your property. You would, however, probably be held legally entitled to shoot an armed raider who was attacking your house or your family.

'OFFENCES AGAINST THE PERSON'

INTRODUCTION

'Fatal' and 'Non-fatal'

THERE is nothing particularly logical about dividing crimes between those 'against the person' or those 'against property', or those which are 'against the community' and those which are 'against the individual', or those 'against the person' which turn out to be 'fatal' or 'non-fatal'. All crimes affect the 'community'; many crimes 'against the person' affect his 'property' as well (and vice versa); some crimes turn out to be 'fatal' or 'non-fatal' simply as a matter of luck.

However, they are convenient divisions. In the next section we shall be dealing with 'fatal' crimes—*i.e.* as a result somebody dies. This is called HOMICIDE. But, as you will see, homicide in some circumstances may not be a crime at all or, if it is a crime, will be punished according to what type of homicide it is in law.

1: 'FATAL'

Homicide

Definition: Homicide simply means the killing of a human being. The killing, however, may be LAWFUL or UNLAWFUL.

Types of homicide

(1) *Lawful.* Obviously in some circumstances 'killing of a human being' is lawful—as in case of war. But there are circumstances when it is lawful in times of peace; and these can be summarized as follows:

(a) *Advancement of public justice.* Carrying out an arrest might be an example. The person accused of homicide would naturally have to show that he used no more force than was needed to carry out the arrest. That would mean that he would have to show it was better to arrest at the risk of death than let the man escape. That in turn would mean that the crime for which he was being arrested was a serious one—or at least that serious results would be likely to follow if he was not arrested. You cannot legally kill just because you are arresting for a felony.

(b) *Execution of a lawful sentence.* The public hangman is thus protected. But the sentence must have been lawful, and the execution must be carried out in a lawful way. If the sentence was not lawful, or an

573

unauthorized person carried it out, or it was carried out in an unlawful way (*e.g.* by poisoning), the homicide might be murder.

(c) *Prevention of crime.*
(d) *Self-defence* (see above).
(e) *Protection of property.*

Apart from carrying out the requirements of justice there are circumstances where homicide may be better in the eyes of the law than the alternatives open to the person accused of the homicide. If you see your father about to kill your mother it is better to restrain him, even at the risk of his death, than to stand by and let the deed be done. If you see someone about to kill you it is better, even at the risk of your assailant's life, to kill him before he kills you.

But in all these cases you will have to show that the crime in question was one which justified such drastic treatment: in other words, the crime must usually have been one which was serious and involved violence (*e.g.* murder or rape), and, moreover, one which at the moment when you retaliated violently did involve serious risk of death or serious bodily injury to you or the person you were protecting. Most important of all, you will have to show that there was no reasonable alternative open to you—*e.g.* you could not have retreated rather than killed; you could not have got help from a bystander or from the police.

Obviously it is far more difficult to justify homicide in protection of your property than in protection of your (or somebody else's) life. It used to be believed that you were justified, or at least excused, if you shot at a trespasser by night; but it would be unsafe to rely on that belief today.

(f) *Misadventure.* This is a different sort of case. The person who causes the death may not have intended any sort of violence at all. The hangman, the person who arrests, the person who protects himself or someone else, each knows that violence is or may be involved. The person who causes death by MISADVENTURE causes it by bad luck.

Bad luck can arise in so many ways that it will be simplest to take two examples:

(1) A surgeon operates, but the patient dies.
(2) A boxer hits his opponent, and his opponent dies.

Most of us would feel that neither the surgeon nor the boxer was to blame; and in general that would be true.

The surgeon or the boxer, however, might be charged with murder or manslaughter; and they might be convicted if they could not at least show the following two things:

(*a*) The operation (or the boxing) was 'legal'. If the operation was (for example) a criminal abortion or the boxing was a 'prize fight', then a death resulting from it might be murder or manslaughter.
(*b*) The operation (or the boxing), though legal, was carried out in a proper way. If the surgeon used the operation deliberately to kill his patient or was criminally negligent in carrying out the

operation, he would be guilty of murder or manslaughter. If the boxer deliberately hit to kill or flagrantly disregarded the rules of the game, he too might be guilty of murder or manslaughter.

(2) *Unlawful.* Unlawful killing goes by different names according to the circumstances in which it is done, the person who does it, and the person to whom it is done. As you will see later, the survivor of a suicide pact is guilty of manslaughter, not murder; the person who kills a child is guilty of abortion, child-destruction, or murder, according to the circumstances.

Murder

Definition. MURDER is, of course, one of the most serious crimes, and can be punished by death. The only other crimes still punishable by death are TREASON, PIRACY, and SETTING FIRE TO THE QUEEN'S SHIPS.

Murder is not fully defined in any Statute. In *Halsbury's Laws of England* there is a Common Law definition which goes back to the sixteenth century at least:

> It is murder for a person of sound memory and discretion unlawfully to kill any human creature in being and under the Queen's peace, with malice aforethought . . . provided the person dies of the injury inflicted within a year and a day after the same.

All the expressions in this definition are important; but in particular:

(a) 'A person of sound memory and discretion.' This refers to capacity to commit a crime. This 'capacity', of course, can be reduced or eliminated altogether by such things as infancy or insanity (see above).

(b) 'Unlawfully.' This word is, of course, to distinguish murder from 'lawful homicide'.

(c) 'Human creature in being.' The word 'human' excludes animals. The words 'in being' made it necessary to create new offences to include the killing of unborn or partly born children (see ABORTION and CHILD DESTRUCTION).

(d) 'With malice aforethought.' This is the most difficult part of the whole definition, and the most important. As you will have seen above to be guilty of a crime you have almost always got to have a 'guilty mind'—an 'intention'. In murder the 'intention' is called 'malice aforethought'. What is 'malice' and what is 'aforethought'?

Malice aforethought. In the simplest case the 'murderer' has thought about it beforehand, and that covers the 'aforethought'. But this does not necessarily mean long premeditation or planning of the murder: a sudden killing may be murder even though the 'intention' was 'aforethought' only a moment before the blow was struck.

The 'malice' means an intention either to kill or to do grievous bodily harm or to do an act which the 'murderer' knows (or, as a reasonable man, must be assumed to anticipate) is likely to kill or cause grievous bodily harm. The 'act' may take the form of failure to act where there is a duty to act—*e.g.* to leave your baby without food with the intention that he shall die of starvation.

It is simple enough when the 'murderer' definitely intends to kill or do grievous bodily harm. It is more difficult when the death results without the accused person having intended it.

Constructive malice. Until 1957 if you killed in the course of committing a violent felony or in the course of resisting arrest you were guilty of murder whether or not you intended to kill or cause grievous bodily harm. This was called 'CONSTRUCTIVE' MALICE, and it was considered so unsatisfactory that in 1957 an attempt was made to abolish it by Act of Parliament. It is not quite certain how far the attempt has been successful because of a decision by the House of Lords in 1960. In that case a man was trying to shake a policeman from his car, having no intention to hurt him but only to avoid being arrested by him. The policeman fell and was killed by another car. The House of Lords said it was murder, despite the lack of intention.

Capital murder. Before 1957 the penalty for all murders was death by hanging and no other sentence could be passed unless the accused was under eighteen or pregnant or unless he was found GUILTY BUT INSANE, in which case he was (as he would be now) sentenced to be kept in custody as a 'Broadmoor patient'.

Since the Homicide Act of 1957 the death penalty has been abolished for all murders except the following:

(a) murder done in course of theft;
(b) murder by shooting or explosion;
(c) murder done in course of preventing lawful arrest or effecting or assisting escape from legal custody;
(d) murder of a police officer (or anyone helping him) while in the execution of his duty;
(e) murder by a prisoner of a prison officer (or anyone helping him) while in the execution of his duty;
(f) a second murder—provided both murders were done in Great Britain.

The punishment for all other murders, apart from persons found 'guilty but insane' or found to be suffering from 'diminished responsibility', is now imprisonment for life.

Manslaughter

This is another type of unlawful homicide. Its main difference from murder is over the question of 'malice aforethought'; and the following circumstances (though they can never make the killing lawful) may reduce the homicide from murder to manslaughter.

1. '*Involuntary manslaughter.*' Homicide is INVOLUNTARY MANSLAUGHTER where it does not amount to murder but the killing was the result either of (a) CRIMINAL NEGLIGENCE in the course of doing a lawful act, or (b) doing an unlawful act of a dangerous nature.

Criminal negligence means recklessness as to whether or not one's conduct will cause bodily harm to another. Again one's conduct may consist in failure to act where there is a duty to do so, as in the case of one's babies or other helpless people in one's care: if the failure is intended to result in death and does, it will be murder; if it is without intention and results from criminal negligence, it will be manslaughter.

In the case of fatal motor accidents it is often difficult to determine whether the negligence is 'criminal', and various statutory offences connected with driving have therefore been invented—*e.g.* DANGEROUS DRIVING, DRIVING WITHOUT DUE CARE, CAUSING DEATH BY DANGEROUS DRIVING, DRIVING UNDER THE INFLUENCE OF DRINK OR DRUGS, CAUSING BODILY HARM BY THE WANTON DRIVING OF A VEHICLE, DRIVING RECKLESSLY, DRIVING WITHOUT REASONABLE CONSIDERATION. All these offences involve negligence and if death results the question is whether it is sufficiently gross to justify a charge of manslaughter.

'Unlawful acts of a dangerous character' include such things as the examples given above, of an illegal operation or a prize-fight: if death results it will be manslaughter. If the operation or the boxing match are legal and there is no negligence it will be a case of lawful homicide (by misadventure); but if there is criminal negligence it will again be manslaughter; and if there is an intent to kill or do grievous bodily harm it will be murder.

2. '*Diminished responsibility.*' Although long known in Scottish Law, DIMINISHED RESPONSIBILITY appeared in English Law only in 1957. 'Diminished responsibility' is different from 'insanity' under the *M'Naghten Rules.*

If the accused person succeeds in establishing insanity under the *M'Naghten Rules* he is truly not guilty because he could not form the necessary intention. It is said that Queen Victoria, who had been attacked by several mad people, could not bear the idea of their being found not guilty even though they were mad, and insisted on the illogical definition 'guilty but insane' when it should have been 'not guilty because insane'.

In the case of 'diminished responsibility' the accused person has *some* responsibility for what he has done, but ought to receive a different punishment for his crime because his responsibility is *diminished* by the state of his mind.

The law therefore now provides, by the Homicide Act of 1957, that if the accused can show 'such abnormality of mind . . . as substantially impaired his mental responsibility' he is to be found guilty of manslaughter where otherwise he would have been guilty of murder.

3. '*Provocation.*' Even the law recognizes that people have human weaknesses, and therefore it has long been allowed that a person may be so provoked or goaded that he cannot help retaliating, and if the retaliation results in death it ought to be manslaughter rather than murder.

However, the mere fact that you have been provoked is not enough. If your retaliation results in the death of the person who provoked you, to get the homicide reduced from murder to manslaughter you will have to show:

(a) The provocation was so gross as to deprive a reasonable man of his self-control. You may be unusually quick-tempered, but that is not the standard: the standard is that of the reasonable man.

(b) The provocation must in fact have deprived you of your self-control. You cannot take advantage of a provocation which has not deprived you of your self-control to work off an old score.

(c) Your retaliation must be in the heat of the moment. You cannot go

579

away and cool down and then retaliate in a way that might have been understandable if you had done it at once.

(d) Your retaliation must be proportionate to the provocation. If, for example, someone keeps ruffling your hair, it would be disproportionate retaliation to give him a blow which kills him.

It used to be thought that words without deeds would not constitute provocation—you should meet words with words. Since 1957 it has become clear that words or deeds or a combination of the two will do.

Killing in self-defence may be lawful (see above); killing through provocation is never lawful. The most that provocation, however gross, can do is to reduce what would otherwise have been murder to manslaughter.

Suicide

The law used to be that suicide was a crime, *viz.*, the crime of self-murder. If the crime succeeded, the criminal, of course, was beyond the reach of human justice. If he did not succeed, he could be convicted of the attempt to commit the crime.

It has been said that in the years 1959 and 1960 the police were aware of 5,000 cases of attempted suicide, but that prosecutions were taken against only about 500 people.

The Suicide Act of 1961 has abolished the old rule of law whereby it was a crime for a person to commit suicide. Suicide has ceased to be a crime, and English Law is brought into line with Scottish Law on this point.

Furthermore, there are now no legal restrictions on the burial or burial services of suicides.

In a suicide pact all the persons concerned have agreed to end their lives, but one or more may nevertheless survive. The survivor of such a pact was at one time prosecuted for murder, after 1957 for manslaughter, but under the new Act there is an offence which is neither murder nor manslaughter. The Act creates a new offence, namely, that of complicity in another person's suicide. The person who gives some active incitement or encouragement or advice, or even assent or approval, may be guilty of this offence which is defined as follows:

> "A person who aids, abets, counsels or procures the suicide of another, or an attempt by another to commit suicide, shall be liable on conviction on indictment to imprisonment for a term not exceeding 14 years."

Infanticide

This is the killing of a child of under twelve months by its mother in circumstances which would otherwise be murder, but where the balance of her mind is disturbed by the effects of giving birth to the child. The offence was created by Act of Parliament (Infanticide Acts of 1922 and 1938), and one of its obvious advantages was that the death sentence need not be pronounced when a reprieve is almost certain: it is a felony carrying a maximum penalty of life imprisonment, but that leaves the judge discretion to pass a suitable sentence—which may even mean immediate release.

580

Abortion

Definition. As a crime, it is unlawfully procuring or attempting to procure a miscarriage. It can be committed by the pregnant woman herself, but she will be guilty only if she was in fact pregnant. If it is committed by anyone else, he will be guilty whether she was pregnant or not.

Procuring a miscarriage may, however, be lawful. A qualified doctor, for example, is entitled to do so, but only provided that it is for the purpose of preserving the mother's life—which includes the preservation of her sanity (Rex *v.* Bourne, 1939).

2: 'NON-FATAL'

Introduction

The law protects you not only against death or grievous bodily harm at some-one else's hands but also against almost any interference with your person to which you have not consented.

'Consent'

Obviously, if you consent to run the risk of injury you cannot usually complain if it happens to you, and the person who injures you will not be guilty of a crime nor can you sue him for damages. For example, if you agree to box or play football there is no crime, and you cannot complain if you suffer the sort of injuries that are likely to result from such sports even when they are played legitimately. Equally, if you agree to a legitimate surgical operation you cannot complain of the inevitable discomfort or the loss of the limb (or whatever it may be) which must follow.

But if what you have consented to is not legitimate, then consent is no defence and the person who injures you may still be guilty of a crime—and you may be also. If the assault involves a breach of the peace, as in the case of a prize-fight or the risk of causing 'actual bodily harm' for which there is no legal justification, or in the case of certain sexual offences against persons under sixteen, the consent of the victim is irrelevant.

Other defences

(1) *Furtherance of public authority.* Such things as lawful arrest or the carrying out of lawful sentences must obviously sometimes involve force which in other circumstances might be criminal assault. Force which is reasonable in the circumstances may be used.

(2) *Correction of children.* Parents or persons having the authority of parents, or persons (like schoolmasters) to whom they have delegated authority, may punish children—again obviously using only such force as is reasonable.

(3) *Defence of self or property.* You can obviously defend yourself from force by using reasonable force. You can also defend your property against trespassers; but you should not use force until persuasion has failed.

(4) *Mistake.* This covers such things as accidental jostling in the street; but nevertheless the law requires you to take reasonable care.

'ASSAULT AND BATTERY'

Technically an ASSAULT is only the *display* of force in such a way that the other person anticipates it is going to be used on him; and BATTERY is the *actual use* of the force. You can have 'battery' without 'assault'—if I come up and hit

Technically *Assault* is the display of force.

Battery is the actual use of force.

But if you are attacked without seeing your assailant—it is *Battery* without *Assault*.

In practice, however, the word *Assault* is often used to cover both assault and battery.

you from behind it is a 'battery', but there has been no 'assault', because you did not 'anticipate' it. However, the word 'assault' is often used to cover both assault and battery.

Types of assault

Most assaults, and the punishments for them, are now covered by Act of Parliament. Some examples are given below, with the maximum sentences in brackets.

(1) *Common assault.* This is a misdemeanour which may be tried on indictment (one year) but is usually tried summarily (two months). The difference between 'trial on indictment' and 'summary trial' is explained below.

(2) *Aggravated assault.* This is a common assault committed on a child under fourteen or on any female, but of 'such an aggravated nature' that magistrates may award higher punishments (six months or £20, followed by 'binding over' for six months thereafter).

(3) *'With intent to commit felony'*, etc. An assault 'with intent to commit felony' or in connection with the police (or people helping the police) in their duty is a misdemeanour (two years).

(4) '*Occasioning actual bodily harm.*' 'Actual bodily harm' means any harm which interferes with the health or comfort of the victim, even temporarily. An assault which occasions actual bodily harm is a misdemeanour (five years).

(5) '*Wounding or inflicting any grievous bodily harm.*' 'Wounding' means breaking the skin—not a mere bruise or scratch. 'Grievous bodily harm' means a more serious interference with health or comfort than 'actual bodily harm'. Wounding is a misdemeanour (five years); but if it is done with intent to do grievous bodily harm or to prevent an arrest it is a felony (life imprisonment).

(6) '*Administering poison or other noxious thing.*' If this is done 'with intent to injure, aggrieve, or annoy' it is a misdemeanour (three years); but if it is done so as to endanger life or inflict grievous bodily harm it is a felony (ten years).

(7) '*Explosions.*' Causing explosions which injure or are intended to injure is a felony punishable with various sentences according to the circumstances (fourteen years to life imprisonment).

(8) '*Attempt to choke, suffocate, or strangle.*' An attempt to choke, suffocate, or strangle with intent to commit any indictable offence is a felony (life imprisonment).

The same applies to using chloroform or other 'stupefying drugs'.

Firearms

Many of the above assaults, including even common assault, may involve an additional penalty of up to seven years' imprisonment if the offender was carrying a firearm *or* imitation firearm at the time of the assault *or* at the time when he was arrested.

3: 'SEXUAL'

Introduction

Although there may be no very good logical reason for dividing crimes between those which are 'against the person' or 'against property', or 'against the community' or 'against the individual', or 'fatal' or 'non-fatal', there are rather better reasons than convenience for dividing 'offences against the person' into 'sexual' and 'non-sexual'.

Both types of offence are invasions of the 'privacy of person' to which we are usually entitled unless we agree to share that privacy with another, and as such are really only different examples of assault. In the case of 'sexual' offences, however, there are certain sociological factors—not always corresponding with religious views—which make it necessary to forbid certain sexual activities even though the persons concerned have consented.

Fornication (sexual intercourse between unmarried persons) and adultery (sexual intercourse between persons, one or both of whom is married to a third person) are sins according to many religious beliefs, but they are not crimes in English Law. Prostitution is sinful, but has criminal consequences only in certain circumstances, *e.g.* under the Street Offences Act, 1959. Sexual intercourse with girls below the age of sixteen is no sin according to some religions, but it *is* a crime in English Law. Some 'unnatural offences' are crimes in English Law, but not all.

For the protection of women and children and in the interests of public morality (or decency) a large number of sexual activities, generally agreed to be undesirable, have been made criminal. The following are some examples.

RAPE

Definition

This felony, punishable by imprisonment for life, is committed by a man who has sexual intercourse with a woman against her will. It need not be carried out by violence: anything which deprives the woman of real consent is enough. Thus it is rape if the intercourse is achieved by intimidation, by a trick (as by pretending to be her husband), by stupefying her, or by taking advantage of her unconsciousness or of her being too mentally retarded to be able to assent or dissent.

Exceptions

A husband cannot be guilty of raping his wife unless they are separated by court order or by agreement, though of course (apart from the decency of the matter) he may be guilty of causing her 'bodily harm'.

A boy under fourteen cannot commit rape because there is an 'irrebuttable legal presumption' (see above), whatever the facts, that he is incapable of doing so; but he can be found guilty of helping another person to commit rape.

Defence

The only defence is true consent. This, of course, is difficult to prove. The accused person is therefore allowed to bring rather wider evidence than would usually be permitted. He can, for example, show the likelihood of consent by producing evidence that the woman in question was unchaste.

UNLAWFUL SEXUAL INTERCOURSE

(1) Mentally afflicted

For the protection of the mentally afflicted it has been made a felony for a man to have unlawful sexual intercourse with a woman, knowing her to be an idiot or imbecile. That she may have appeared to consent is immaterial.

(2) Young girls

To have sexual intercourse with a girl of under thirteen is a felony punishable with life imprisonment, and her consent is no defence. If she is over thirteen but under sixteen it is a misdemeanour punishable with two years' imprisonment.

It is a defence that the accused man reasonably believed the girl to be sixteen—*provided* (a) he himself is under twenty-four, *and* (b) he has not been previously charged with such an offence. It is also a defence that the accused man reasonably believed the girl to be his wife.

(3) Incest

INCEST means sexual intercourse with near blood relations, such as your mother, daughter, or sister in the case of a man (and similar relationships in the case of a woman), knowing of the blood relationship. It is incest whether the relationship is 'legitimate' (*i.e.* arising out of lawful wedlock) or not. The exact relationships are laid down in the Sexual Offences Act, 1956 (they range from grandparents to grandchildren) which makes incest a misdemeanour punishable with seven years' imprisonment.

(4) Miscellaneous

There are a great many other provisions against such things as ABDUCTING women or girls for immoral purposes, causing prostitution or unlawful intercourse, and the like.

INDECENT ASSAULT

As the name implies, INDECENT ASSAULT consists not only of indecency but also of assault. It is punishable with anything up to ten years' imprisonment according to the purpose of the assault and whether the person assaulted is a man or a woman.

UNNATURAL OFFENCES

These are offences which are variously described as BUGGERY, SODOMY, and BESTIALITY. They have long been Common Law offences (see above). They can take place between men and men, men and women, or between men or women and animals. 'Unnatural offences' between women are not covered by the Sexual Offences Act, and are not crimes in English Law

'OFFENCES AGAINST PROPERTY'

INTRODUCTION

YOU will see in the 'OFFENCES AGAINST THE PERSON' section of this work that the offences were divided into 'fatal' and 'non-fatal' and then further subdivided—a reasonably logical and convenient arrangement.

As for 'OFFENCES AGAINST PROPERTY', the pattern chosen here is as follows:

(i) Offences consisting mainly of damage *to* property.
(ii) Offences consisting mainly of being *on* property.
(iii) Offences consisting mainly of *stealing* property.

Obviously the three can overlap: a burglar (for example) may damage the property getting in, commit a further crime by being on the property with intent to steal, and complete the pattern by actually stealing.

MALICIOUS DAMAGE

If I damage your property, even by mistake, I must usually pay for it; and if I don't you can force me to do so by a 'civil action'. Here we are concerned with damage which makes me liable also from a 'criminal' point of view.

Definition

This sort of damage is called 'unlawful and malicious destruction of or injury to property'; and it is a felony or misdemeanour punishable by anything from a fine to imprisonment for life according to the seriousness of the offence.

Types of property included are buildings, machinery, crops, animals, goods, mines, ships, and works of art. Types of injury include ARSON (*i.e.* setting fire to a building or things in it) and the use of explosives.

Defences

Apart from the usual defences to a criminal charge (see above), your major defence will be to show that what you did was not 'unlawful'. To be 'lawful', what you did must be something you had a legal right to do. It may be enough for you to have an honest belief that you had the legal right; but unfortunately 'ignorance of the law' is no excuse. You are presumed to know the whole of the general law of the country, but not necessarily to know individual rights. For example, if you dig up a bush on my land, honestly believing it is on your land, the 'law' concerned here isn't 'general' or 'public' law: it depends on 'private' rights ('legal' rights none the less)—rights which have been established by the personal agreements you and I made about our land when we bought it or leased it. But, if you dig up a bush in Hyde Park, honestly believing you have the right to take bushes from public parks, the 'law' concerned here is 'public' or 'general' law: you are expected to know the statutory or other regulations about public bushes.

Restitution

Usually the fact that a criminal has been found guilty does not mean that the person he has injured will get 'restitution' or 'reparation'. But there is a useful provision for the summary trial and punishment of persons who have done damage not exceeding £20 *and* for them to pay compensation to the injured party.

BURGLARY

Definition

BURGLARY is one of the offences in connection with property that need not involve any stealing or any damage to the property in question, but simply consists in having got on to the property (or out of the property) in a particular

586

criminal way for a particular criminal reason. It is defined by statute (Larceny Act, 1916) as follows:

Every person who in the night
  (1) breaks and enters the dwelling-house of another with intent to commit any felony therein; or
  (2) breaks out of the dwelling-house of another, having
      (a) entered with intent to commit any felony therein; or
      (b) committed any felony in the said dwelling-house
shall be guilty of felony called burglary.

Most of these words need some explanation.

(a) '*In the night.*' This means between 9 p.m. and 6 a.m., Greenwich Mean Time or Summer Time as the case may be.

(b) '*Breaks* . . .' Nothing need in fact be 'broken'; it is sufficient merely to open a closed door or window. If the door or window is already open, it probably does not amount to 'breaking' to open it wider—unless it is latched in some way and you have to break or undo the latch. On the other hand, it *is* 'breaking' to use a naturally open aperture, like a chimney, which cannot be closed. It also counts as 'breaking' if you get in by deceit or the threat of violence—*e.g.* by pretending to be a friend of someone in the house or ringing the bell and frightening the person who answers the door or, as in one case, claiming to be authorized by the B.B.C. to inspect the wireless set.

(c) '. . . *and enters.*' This means that, apart from the 'breaking', some part of the body of the burglar must go into the house. Consequently, if the 'breaking' consists of breaking a window with the hand and the hand goes through the window you have 'breaking and entering'; but if it is done with some instrument and only the instrument goes through the window there is a 'breaking' but no 'entry'. However, if the instrument is to be used not only for the 'breaking' but also to carry out the subsequent felony (*e.g.* to fish out the loot) there is a 'breaking and entering' even though no part of the burglar's body goes into the house.

(d) '*Dwelling-house of another.*' Dwelling-house means some permanent structure where that other person usually sleeps and which he regards as his permanent home, even though he may be temporarily absent. So a tent or a movable caravan is probably not sufficiently 'permanent' to constitute a dwelling-house. On the other hand, a flat or even a single room may be a dwelling-house even though there are other flats and rooms in the same house. The room of a mere lodger or a guest at a hotel is, however, not his dwelling-house; it is part of the dwelling-house of the landlady or hotel-keeper: so the landlady or hotel-keeper cannot burgle his room, but he can burgle their rooms —including the rooms of fellow lodgers or guests.

Once the premises are established as a dwelling-house then any part can be burgled, even though it is used as a shop or office, provided there is internal communication between the dwelling and the business part. Outbuildings are also included, provided they are permanent structures occupied together with the dwelling-house and provided there is communication between the house and the outbuilding (such as a garage) either directly or by a covered and enclosed passage.

587

Burglary

A person is guilty of burglary who—

(a) In the night—(9 p.m.–6 a.m.)

(b) breaks—(nothing need in fact be broken).

(c) and enters—(if only an arm enters it constitutes 'entering')

(d) the dwelling-house of another —(a single room may be a 'dwelling-house')

(e) with intent to commit any felony therein

(f) or breaks out having intended or actually committed a feony

(e) '*With intent to commit any felony therein.*' This part of the definition means that in the case of 'breaking and entering' the accused person can be guilty of burglary only if he already had the 'intent to commit any felony therein'. If he 'broke and entered' without intending to commit a felony it would not be burglary. (But it might be 'housebreaking', on which, see below.)

(f) '*Breaks out . . .*', *etc.* 'Breaking out' is much the same thing as 'breaking in'; but this part of the definition shows that in the case of 'breaking out' it is a burglary *either* if the entry was done 'with intent to commit any felony' *or* if (even without previous intent) the robber has actually committed a felony in the house.

A 'technical' crime

You may well feel that some of the above distinctions are over-subtle and absurd. But here you have an example of a serious crime which has got a precise technical definition laid down by Parliament (not by lawyers)—and it is the duty of the courts to administer the law as they find it, not as they would like it to be. There are other such crimes, *e.g.* larceny. These distinctions may be most important from the point of view of the accused person, and they *are* most important if the law is to be certain.

There are at least two considerations which justify the courts in 'splitting hairs' over such crimes as burglary.

(1) As recently as 1837 burglary was still a 'capital' offence, and therefore defence counsel (even prosecuting counsel), judges, and juries were anxious to give proper weight to any distinction that could be made. Even now burglary is punishable with anything from a fine to life imprisonment.

(2) Irrespective of the penalty involved, it is a principle of our law that an Act of Parliament (which, after all, goes through many processes before it is passed) contains what Parliament meant to say—no more and no less. Therefore, although a 'reasonable man' might think it makes little difference whether the burglar enters at nine in the evening or a second earlier, that cannot be the right way to look at it, because Parliament has said quite clearly that it must be by night and 'night' means between 9 p.m. and 6 a.m. Similarly the 'reasonable man' may think it makes little difference whether the robber formed the 'intent to commit any felony' before or just after he 'broke and entered'; but if Parliament thought so, it did not say so. It is for Parliament, not the courts, to alter the law.

HOUSEBREAKING

This is another felony created by Act of Parliament (Larceny Act, 1916). The definition is very like that for burglary, but, as the following major differences will show, you may be guilty of housebreaking (with a smaller maximum penalty) when you could not be guilty of burglary.

(1) Housebreaking can be committed by day *or* by night.

(2) The building, in addition to a dwelling-house, can be a 'schoolhouse, shop, warehouse, counting-house, office, store, garage, pavilion, factory, or workshop, or any building belonging to Her Majesty, or to any government department, or to any municipal or other public authority'.

(3) In the case of 'breaking in' and committing a felony, it does not matter that there was no previous intent.

(4) In the case of 'breaking out' without having committed a felony, it is not housebreaking, even though there *was* a previous intent.

(5) The maximum punishments are fourteen or seven years' imprisonment, according to whether or not a felony has actually been committed.

'BEING FOUND BY NIGHT . . .'

In addition to burglary and housebreaking, there are a large number of other offences, of which the following are examples.

It is a misdemeanour to be found by night in possession of housebreaking implements without lawful excuse—and you have to prove the 'lawful excuse'.

It is also a misdemeanour to be found by night, and having the intent to commit a felony:

(a) in any building, or
(b) armed with an offensive instrument,
(c) with your face blackened or disguised.

All these misdemeanours are punishable with five years' imprisonment—or ten years' if you have been previously convicted for one of them or for any felony.

LARCENY

LARCENY is just another word for THEFT or STEALING. It is a very ancient Common Law offence, which was later defined by Act of Parliament.

It is also a very technical offence; and consequently many offences which might look like stealing to the ordinary man are not stealing in law. The main reason for these technicalities, some of which may seem artificial and even absurd, is that at one time if the thing stolen was worth more than twelve pence the crime was GRAND LARCENY, punishable with death: consequently judges, juries, and counsel were anxious to find any loophole which they could.

The statutory definition referred to above runs as follows:

> . . . a person steals who, without the consent of the owner, fraudulently and without claim of right made in good faith, takes and carries away anything capable of being stolen with intent, at the time of such taking, permanently to deprive the owner thereof . . .
>
> (Larceny Act, 1916)

This language may sound legalistic; but in fact almost all the words or expressions used are important, and may make all the difference between a 'GUILTY' or 'NOT GUILTY' verdict. They are therefore worth looking at.

(a) '*Consent*.' The consent must obviously be a real consent. If I persuade you to 'consent' by frightening you or by misleading you, there is no true consent on your part. Stealing effected in these ways is known by such names as LARCENY BY THREATS, LARCENY BY A TRICK, LARCENY BY MISTAKE, and so on.

But in the case of 'mistake' I must have been aware of the mistake at the

Larceny

LARCENY means "taking without the owner's consent"—("Consent obtained by a trick is no justification").

"Fraudulently without claim of right"—(However, to take property by mistake is not larceny.)

"taking and . . ." (Handling is not taking.)

". . . carrying away . . ."

". . . anything capable of being stolen . . ."

". . . with intent permanently to deprive the owner thereof." (Borrowing is not larceny.)

time I am said to have stolen. If I ask you to lend me two shillings, which I put in my pocket and later find to be half a crown, I have not 'stolen' the sixpence so far; but if I then decide to keep the sixpence, that is the moment when I steal it.

(b) '*Owner.*' This means anybody who has a better right to the property than the 'stealer'. If I trespass on a golf course and take away the 'lost' balls, I have no right to them: even if the original owners cannot be found, the golf club has a better right to them than I have. 'Findings are keepings' is *not* a rule of English Law.

(c) '*Fraudulently and without claim of right.*' This means that if I had no intention to deceive you but honestly (even though incorrectly) thought I had the right to take the thing, I could not be guilty of larceny. If I take your overcoat, believing it to be mine, I do it under a 'claim of right made in good faith'; if I take it when I am too drunk to realize whose overcoat it is, then I am incapable of acting 'fraudulently'.

(d) '*Takes and carries away.*' This means what it says: there must be a 'taking' *and* a 'carrying away'.

'*Taking.*' This means laying hands on a thing so as to get it into one's possession. If, for example, I finger goods in a shop or pick up a book in your house to look at it, I am not 'taking' these things because there is no question of my trying to get them into my 'possession'.

'*Carrying away.*' This means that the thing must not only be 'taken' but also moved from where it was. The slightest movement will usually do even though the thing is, for example, not completely removed from the victim's pocket or catches on something.

(e) '*Anything capable of being stolen.*' Most things can be stolen; but there are some exceptions. Land cannot because it cannot be taken away; but things which grow or are found on land can be. A debt or the plot of a play cannot be stolen because there is nothing tangible to pick up. Things belonging to nobody cannot be stolen: as explained above, lost property may still belong to someone; but if I throw away, say, an old pencil stump I have abandoned my ownership and it is yours if you pick it up. There are special rules about animals, according to whether they are tame or wild, and so on.

(f) '*With intent . . .*' This is another case where 'intent' is very important. There must have been an intent *at the time of the taking*, and that intent must have been *permanently to deprive the owner*. As we saw in the case of 'mistake', it is not easy to be sure when the intent was formed or whether the intent was not permanently to deprive but only to 'borrow'. Borrowing is not larceny, because there is an intention to return the thing in question; but it has been made an offence by Act of Parliament to borrow a motor vehicle even though you do intend to return it.

AGGRAVATED LARCENY

Definitions

The statutory definition of larceny has already been given; but obviously some larcenies are graver than others and so demand greater punishment.

It is therefore provided by the Larceny Act that for SIMPLE LARCENY—*i.e.* stealing for which no other punishment is provided—the maximum punishment shall be five years' imprisonment.

Other larceny is known as AGGRAVATED LARCENY, *i.e.* larceny which is aggravated (made more serious) by such things as the method used (*e.g.* violence), the nature of the thing taken (*e.g.* somebody's Will), the position of the thief (*e.g.* a policeman), and/or the place where the theft took place (*e.g.* somebody's 'dwelling-house').

Here are some examples.

Larceny from the person

This means stealing from someone's actual person, but without using force. Stealing by a pickpocket is an obvious example. It is punishable with fourteen years' imprisonment.

Robbery

This also means stealing from someone's actual person (or at least in his immediate presence)—but here the thief uses some force, even though it is only by frightening his victim in some way. It is punishable by anything from a fine to life imprisonment, according to the circumstances.

Here a lot depends on whether the thief had a weapon (ARMED ROBBERY), whether force or fear were used, and whether the thief was alone.

If actual force is used the maximum penalty can be imposed. Even if no force is used the maximum penalty can still be imposed if the thief was either (a) 'armed with any offensive weapon or instrument' or (b) accompanied by a confederate.

Even if the robbery is unsuccessful the maximum penalty can be imposed if the assault with intent to rob was made either by (a) one armed person or (b) two or more persons, whether armed or not. If it is done by a single unarmed person the maximum penalty is limited to five years.

Where 'fear' is used, it need not be fear of personal violence: it can be fear of violence to a member of the victim's family or of serious injury to his property, or even (in some circumstances) to his job or reputation.

Burglary, etc.

Burglary, housebreaking, and similar offences committed in houses and other 'enclosed premises' have already been dealt with (see above). They are, of course, aggravated larcenies, mainly because of the place where they are done.

Other 'aggravated larcenies'

Here are a few examples of other larcenies which are 'aggravated' by the importance of the thing stolen, the position of the thief or the place where the theft takes place.

(1) *Wills*, '*postal packets*', *etc.* Because of their importance the theft of such things carries a maximum penalty of life imprisonment.

(2) *Policemen and servants.* Because persons in positions of trust owe a

special duty the maximum penalty for thefts by them is fourteen years' imprisonment, when in the case of others it might be a 'simple larceny' punishable with a maximum of five years.

(3) *Ships, docks, etc.* Because of the special opportunities offered by such places as ships and docks (and many other premises), thefts from them also carry a maximum penalty of fourteen years' imprisonment.

LARCENY BY A SERVANT AND EMBEZZLEMENT

Technical difficulty

LARCENY (or STEALING) means, among other things, not having 'the consent of the owner' and 'taking and carrying away' the object stolen (see above). Therefore, technically, a servant cannot 'steal' goods entrusted to him by his master because he already has them with his master's 'consent'. Equally, if goods are given to a servant to deliver to his master and the servant misappropriates them, he has not 'stolen' them from his master, because they have never been in his master's possession. And in neither case is there any 'taking and carrying away' from the 'owner'.

To get over the first difficulty the courts a long time ago invented a theory that when a master entrusted goods to his servant he only gave him 'custody' of them, and not 'possession': consequently, as the master still had 'possession', the servant could steal from him. This ingenious device would not, however, cover the second difficulty (where somebody else had entrusted the goods to the servant), because here the master had never had 'possession' of the goods at all.

Statutory definition

However, both these situations are now covered by Act of Parliament (Larceny Act, 1916), which says that anyone employed as a 'clerk or servant' who

> 'steals any chattel, money, or valuable security belonging to . . . his master . . . or fraudulently embezzles . . . any chattel, money, or valuable security . . . taken into possession by him for . . . his master'

is guilty of felony punishable with fourteen years' imprisonment—as compared with five years' imprisonment for simple larceny. 'Embezzlement' means stealing goods, etc., entrusted to the servant *for* his master but not *by* his master, and thus covers the second difficulty described above.

Further difficulties

The statutory definition mentions a 'clerk or servant'. It follows that if the accused person doesn't fall into that category—for example, he is your trustee or your solicitor—you cannot successfully prosecute him under this section of the Act. There is a further 'statutory offence' called FRAUDULENT CONVERSION to cover this. Another difficulty arises if the criminal, 'clerk or servant' or not, gets hold of the goods, etc., by some other method than 'stealing' or

594

'embezzling'—the two methods mentioned in the section. The statutory offence of OBTAINING BY FALSE PRETENCES may cover this. These two offences are dealt with below.

FRAUDULENT CONVERSION

Definition

This misdemeanour, punishable by seven years' imprisonment as opposed to fourteen years' for LARCENY BY A SERVANT or EMBEZZLEMENT, covers people who, though neither 'clerks' nor 'servants', have behaved dishonestly. It includes such people as the following:

(1) Someone with a power of attorney (*i.e.* someone with possibly very wide powers over somebody else's property).
(2) A director, member, or officer of a company.
(3) Trustees and others to whom property has been entrusted.

Such people commit FRAUDULENT CONVERSION if they deal with the 'property' (which includes money) entrusted to them otherwise than for the purpose for which it was 'entrusted'. It is often difficult to decide whether the property or money has been 'entrusted' or 'given' out and out, or whether the accused person has been 'fraudulent' or merely careless.

Examples

If you employ me to paint your house and I say I shall need £5 to buy the paint, have I been 'fraudulent' if I later use the money for the ladders and scaffolding? If you give me £5 to pay to Mr X. and I lose it on the way, or Mr Y. tells me (and I honestly, if foolishly, believe him) that Mr X. has authorized him to take it, have I been 'fraudulent' if I pay it to Mr Y.?

Hire-purchase agreements. If I dispose of property which I am buying on hire purchase and for which I have not paid all the instalments due, I shall almost certainly be guilty of fraudulent conversion. I may be a fool, and I may be mistaken, but that does not excuse me from knowing the law—which in this case is quite simple: it is not my property.

FALSE PRETENCES

Introduction

This is another 'technical' offence. Just as fraudulent conversion had to be invented to cover people who were neither 'clerks' nor 'servants' (and so could not be guilty of larceny by a servant or embezzlement) so FALSE PRETENCES had to be made a crime to cover dishonest persons who did not merely 'steal' but persuaded the other person to hand over not only the 'possession' of his goods but the 'ownership' as well.

Examples. Two simple examples may help to make this clearer. They are examples of what is known to lawyers as the 'ring-dropping' trick. There are many forms of it, and people are constantly being deceived by it. In the following examples you assume 'I' am a rogue and 'you' are deceived by my trick.

(1) *Larceny by 'Ring Trick'.* I come up to you and show you a ring which you think is valuable but which I know is not. I offer to share the proceeds if you will sell it for me. You agree and take the ring, but I ask you to leave me your watch as security for my share. You agree to do so because on what I have told you about the ring your watch is worth less than your share, and anyhow you will get your watch back when you turn up with the proceeds of sale. Then, of course, you discover that the ring is worthless; you turn up at our agreed meeting-place; I am not there. The result is that you have a worthless ring, but I have your watch. My crime is larceny by a trick, because you only parted with the *possession* of your watch—not the *ownership*: you kept that all the time—and you expected to recover the possession when we divided the proceeds of the sale of the ring.

(2) *False pretences by 'Ring Trick'.* Here I tell you exactly the same untrue story about the ring; but instead of the arrangement for you to sell it and for us to divide the proceeds you agree to take the ring in exchange for your watch. I hand you the ring; you hand me your watch. This is not a contract for the SALE OF GOODS, but it *is* a contract which involves you in passing to me not only the *possession* but also the *ownership* of your watch. My crime is therefore not larceny (just getting possession): it is obtaining by false pretences.

Definition

The statutory definition is that anyone who 'by any false pretence' *and* 'with intent to defraud' *either* (a) obtains or procures for himself or someone else 'any chattel, money, or valuable security' *or* (b) 'fraudulently causes . . . any other person' to do certain things in connection with a 'valuable security' (*e.g.* signing it, sealing it, destroying it) is guilty of a misdemeanour punishable with five years' imprisonment.

Explanation. As this is another crime which is defined in technical terms by Act of Parliament the precise wording is important.

(a) '*False pretence.*' This means writing, saying, or doing something (or even doing nothing) which is likely to deceive, is meant to deceive and does deceive. However, the 'something' must relate to a present or past *fact* and not to an *opinion* or something to take place in the *future*, such as a promise. Therefore exaggerations by advertisers, though untrue, are not false pretences if they keep to vague statements of opinion ('Brand X is the Best') and do not contain an untrue statement of fact, *e.g.* that the product contains some ingredient which it does not contain. If I go into your restaurant and order a meal for which I cannot pay, I am not guilty of 'false pretences', because I have not made any 'pretence' at all. On the other hand, if you had asked me whether I had the necessary money on me, I might be guilty of 'false pretences' if I had replied, "Of course", or even if I had said nothing but by means of a haughty gesture had given you the impression that I had. However, if I go into your restaurant, unable to pay and not intending to pay, although I may not be guilty of 'obtaining by false pretences', I am probably guilty of another offence called 'obtaining credit by fraud'.

You might think that a 'promise' to do something was a statement of the *fact* that one had the present intention to do it. However, it is not necessarily so. On the other hand, if I give you a cheque, it has been decided that I am impliedly making the following statements of fact: (1) I have an account at that bank, (2) I have authority to draw on it, and (3) the present facts are that the cheque will be met on presentation. But I am *not* implying that the money is necessarily in the account now.

(b) '*With intent* . . .' The 'false pretence' must have been 'with intent to defraud' (or 'defraud *or* injure', as the case may be), so if you had neither of those intents you will not be guilty of this crime. For example, if you make a 'false pretence' to get money out of somebody who already owes you it, there is no intention to defraud.

(c) '*Chattel* . . .', *etc.* The 'false pretence' must have been in connection with a 'chattel' (which is roughly some physical object you can touch), 'money' or 'valuable security' (something like a cheque). So, if you get something which is none of these three—for example, a night's lodging at a hotel—then, whatever crime you may have committed, it is not the crime of 'false pretences'.

OTHER FRAUDS AND CHEATS

Introduction

In a sense almost any crime (larceny or rape, for example), if not done by violence, may be done by fraud or cheating.

There are, however, a great many crimes which depend for their success primarily on deceiving people; and both Common Law and Statute Law contain a great many provisions to protect people from their simplicity. Two of them, fraudulent conversion and false pretences, have already been discussed. Only a further two or three examples can be given here.

(1) Obtaining credit by fraud

As already explained, there were difficulties about making a 'servant' guilty of 'stealing' and so larceny by a servant and embezzlement were created; because someone like a 'trustee' was not a 'servant', fraudulent conversion had to be invented; because you cannot steal when you have got not only possession but also ownership, false pretences had to be invented.

OBTAINING CREDIT BY FRAUD had to be invented because false pretences covered only a 'chattel, money, or valuable security' and not such matters as a meal or a night's lodging, which are none of these things. Fraudulently getting credit for services of this kind is the statutory misdemeanour of obtaining credit by fraud, and is punishable by one year's imprisonment.

(2) 'Cheating'

This is an old Common Law offence which has been applied by statute to particular forms of CHEATING.

In particular, winning money by cheating at any game or sport counts as

Examples of frauds

1. FALSE PRETENCES.

Example: Exchanging a valueless ring for a valuable watch—"The Ring Trick".

(Exaggerations by advertisers are not 'false pretences' if they keep to a statement of opinion.)

2. FRAUDULENT CONVERSION.

3. OBTAINING CREDIT BY FRAUD.

Example: Disposing of hired property.

Example: Paying for a meal with a bad cheque.

4. CHEATING.

5. SHORT WEIGHT, ETC.

Example: Winning money by cheating at games or sports.

Example: To give short measure of foods sold by weight or numbers.

6. STOCKS AND SHARES.

Example: Misleading statements to induce share purchase.

obtaining by false pretences, and so does cheating over the betting in connection with them.

(3) 'Short weight', etc.

There are many statutory provisions about giving short weight or adulterated goods. For example, it is a summary offence to sell food by weight, number, etc., and deliver short quantity. Even on summary conviction it is punishable by a fine of £5 for the first, £20 for the second, and £50 for any subsequent offence.

(4) Moneylenders

It is a misdemeanour, punishable with two years' imprisonment, for a moneylender (and others) fraudulently to induce or attempt to induce anyone to borrow or agree to borrow money by false representation or promise.

(5) Stocks and shares

To protect the public from the activities of 'sharepushers' and the like, it has been made an offence, punishable with seven years' imprisonment, to make misleading statements to induce people to buy shares—or indeed to deal in shares at all unless legally authorized (Prevention of Fraud (Investments) Act, 1958).

RECEIVING

This offence is often called 'Receiving Stolen Property'; and, for the sake of simplicity, we shall assume in what follows that the property has been stolen. But in fact for the offence of RECEIVING to be committed the property need not necessarily have been *stolen*.

Definition

This is another offence which has been defined by Act of Parliament (Larceny Act, 1916):

> Every person who receives any property knowing the same to have been stolen or obtained in any way whatsoever under circumstances which amount to felony or misdemeanour, shall be guilty of an offence of the like degree . . .

Punishment

The maximum punishments are fourteen years if the circumstances amount to a felony, seven years in the case of a misdemeanour, and whatever the appropriate penalty may be in the case of petty offences triable summarily in a magistrates' court.

What must be proved

Therefore if property has been obtained in any way amounting to a felony or misdemeanour—for example, by obtaining credit under false pretences—

F.L.—39   599 the person receiving it will be guilty provided the following things are also proved:

(1) At the time of the receiving the goods had been stolen. If, for example, I take my wife's diamond ring and pass it to you to dispose of, you may not be guilty of receiving because a husband cannot steal from his wife unless he has left or deserted her or is about to do so. Even if the property has originally been stolen there is no 'receiving' if it was not still stolen at the time of the receipt. Suppose I steal something and wrap it up to send it to you, and then the true owner finds the parcel but nevertheless lets it go on to you so as to

". . . the possession of stolen property raises a presumption of either stealing or receiving . . ."

trap us, you will not be guilty of receiving, because the owner had got the parcel back into his possession and so the property had ceased to be stolen.

(2) The property must be 'received'. This means that the property must come into the receiver's possession—either actually or into the hands of someone on his behalf, such as his wife or servant. If he knows the property is stolen it does not matter that his wife or servant is unaware of it. If he does not know, but when he finds out he then takes possession of the property, he becomes a receiver. But he must have accepted the goods in order to receive them: if he is arrested while he is still examining the goods but before he has made up his mind to accept them, he has not yet 'received' them.

(3) The accused must know the property to have been stolen. That is to say, he must know it was stolen or acquired in circumstances amounting to a felony or misdemeanour: it is not enough for him merely to know that they

600

have been acquired by dishonest means. Also he must know it at the time he receives the property—not find out later, for example.

(4) The accused must have intended to deal dishonestly with the goods at the time he accepted them. Consequently, if you accept goods believing them to be your own or intending to hand them over to the police, you cannot be guilty of receiving, because your intention at the time was innocent; and this is true even though you later change your mind and misappropriate them.

Methods of proof

In the case of receiving it is, of course, particularly difficult to prove the necessary 'knowledge' on the part of the receiver, and therefore rather wider evidence is admissible than normally.

Circumstantial evidence is always admissible. If I take goods at an absurdly low price or surreptitiously down some dark alley, I ought to suspect there may be something fishy about them and I shall find it hard to convince a jury that I did not deliberately shut my eyes.

But in addition to circumstantial evidence, the mere fact that I am in possession of recently stolen property is *by itself* enough to raise a presumption that I either stole it myself or received it with the knowledge that it had been stolen. Normally it would be for the prosecution to prove I *did*, not for me to prove I *didn't*. However, it is only a *presumption*. This means that the jury *may* convict me if I offer no explanation, but they do not *have* to. And if I *do* offer an explanation the jury must *not* convict me *unless* they are satisfied I did in fact have the guilty knowledge.

Lastly, evidence is admissible that I have been in possession of other stolen property within the last twelve months and that I have been convicted within the last five years of any offence involving fraud or dishonesty.

'BLACKMAIL'

DEFINITIONS

(1) Popular

BLACKMAIL is a popular name for getting, or trying to get, something out of somebody by threatening him. It is not a technical term in law; and in fact many things which ordinary people might regard as blackmail are not legal offences at all.

The first thing to bear in mind is that threatening somebody is not necessarily either a moral wrong or a legal offence. If I have owed you money for a long time and at last you tell me that if I do not repay it by the end of the month you will bring proceedings against me, this is a threat but it is not blackmail—nor is there anything morally wrong about it. In this example you have a right to your money and you have the right to sue me if I do not pay. So you are threatening only to do something you have a right to do, and trying to get something you have a right to have. The point about blackmail is that either the *threat itself* must be illegal, or the *purpose* for which it is used must be illegal—or both.

(2) Legal

Offences which amount in law to blackmail are usually described as 'demanding with menaces and without any reasonable or probable cause'. There are, of course, a number of offences which involve 'menaces' but which are just on the other side of the thin dividing line.

'Near-Blackmail' (*i.e.* making threats, but not *demanding* anything)

Under two Acts of Parliament of 1861 criminal offences (in this case felonies) are committed by anyone who shall

'send, deliver, or utter, or directly or indirectly cause to be received, knowing the contents thereof, any letter or writing'

which threatens to do various things. These include threats

(a) 'to kill or murder any person', or
(b) 'to burn or destroy'
    (i) 'any house, barn or other building', or
    (ii) 'any rick or stack of grain, hay, straw, or other agricultural produce in or under any building, or any ship or vessel', or
(c) 'to kill, maim, or wound any cattle'.

You will notice that these threats have to be in writing, and that if you knowingly have anything to do with such a threatening message coming into another person's hands you have committed a felony even though you did not write it yourself and even though the motive is not to get something out of that person.

Under a recent Act

'It is an offence by threats or intimidation to procure or attempt to procure any woman or girl to have any unlawful sexual intercourse in any part of the world.'

This is nearer to blackmail as generally understood; although the person making the threats may himself get nothing out of the person threatened; but here again the point is that it is an offence in itself to make such threats, and this is so even though the intention is not achieved.

'True Blackmail'

The 'true' blackmail offences, *i.e.* demanding with menaces, are contained in an Act of 1916.

The Act makes it a felony punishable by life imprisonment for any person:

(i) to utter, knowing the contents thereof, any letter or writing demanding of any person, with menaces, and without any reasonable or probable cause, any property or valuable thing;

(ii) to utter, knowing the contents thereof, any letter or writing accusing or threatening to accuse any other person (living or dead) of any crime to which the Act applies (the crimes in question will be described later) with the intent to extort or gain any property, or valuable thing from any person;

(iii) to accuse or threaten to accuse any person (living or dead) of any such crime with the intention of extorting any property or valuable thing.

Now let's consider these definitions in a little more detail. It is necessary to explain the meaning of some of the words. First, what is the meaning of the word '*utter*'.

It really means very much the same thing as sending or delivering so it can be done by anyone who takes a conscious part in getting the writing to the threatened person.

Menaces. This means rather more than threats of violence; it covers threats of violence, of course, but it also covers the threat of any action which may be unpleasant to the person threatened, *e.g.* to threaten to tell a wife of her husband's infidelity.

Without any reasonable or probable cause. These words refer to the threats or *menaces*, and not to the demand. At the beginning of this section on blackmail there was the example of someone owing you money and your threatening him with legal proceedings if he did not pay. You have *a reasonable cause* to demand this money, and you also have a right to threaten him with proceedings. That is why it is not blackmail to threaten to issue a writ unless the money is paid as demanded, or unless your neighbour stops trespassing or making unreasonable noise, etc. Everyone has a right to apply to the courts for legal remedies. Hence the words 'reasonable or probable cause' protect your seeking to invoke the law. But, of course, there is no right to threaten to beat someone up, because for this there can be no 'reasonable or probable cause', not in law, at any rate.

Accusing of any crime. On the face of it these words are very clear and it is only necessary to add that the person who is going to be accused of the crime need not be the one to whom the letter was written; it can be any other person, whether living or dead. It will naturally be someone very close to him, otherwise there is no powerful threat which would have the effect of extorting any money or other property out of him. For instance, if the letter threatens to reveal the fact that the recipient's father was a murderer, that would be a sufficient threat. Incidentally, the property demanded need not belong to him. It may belong to someone over whom he has influence.

The crimes which are specified in the Act are all the serious crimes. They need not be set out in detail but are all those which are punishable with death or imprisonment for not less than seven years, or certain serious sexual crimes. This description covers virtually all the serious crimes, because the punishment of seven years' imprisonment is, of course, the maximum laid down by law, not necessarily the punishment which may more generally be awarded.

This covers paragraphs (i) and (ii) in the definition of blackmail given above: the letter which demands with menaces or threatens to make an accusation of crime.

Paragraph (iii) covers the offence of accusing or threatening to accuse of a crime with intention to extort property where the accusation is *not* contained in a letter or any other writing. It may be in writing, but it need not be for this act to be an offence. This is designed to cover the threat by word of mouth, because many a blackmailer would be far too cunning or too afraid to put his threats in writing.

It is also blackmail if the threats are used not to extort money or property but in order to secure an appointment for yourself or another to a much-coveted job. Threats to publish (*i.e.* write or speak) a libel upon any other person, whether living or dead, if made with the object of procuring a job, are an offence. For instance, if you said to the chairman of a public company that unless he made your son managing director you would let it be known that the chairman's wife had been convicted of shoplifting some long time ago (a fact not known locally), you would be guilty of this offence. And it would not matter whether what you said about the chairman's wife was true or not. If he sued you for libel, as will be seen in another part of this encyclopaedia, you would have a defence to the libel if you proved its truth, but that is no justification for blackmail.

Finally, a person who with intent 'to extort any valuable thing from any person'

'publishes or threatens to publish any libel upon any other person (whether living or dead)

is guilty of a misdemeanour, punishable with up to two years' imprisonment.

Of course, if the libel were an accusation of one of the crimes mentioned above it would be a felony punishable with life imprisonment.

A person commits a similar offence who, with the same intent,

'directly or indirectly threaten to print or publish, or directly or indirectly proposes to abstain from or offers to prevent the printing or publishing of any matter or thing touching any other person (whether living or dead)'.

This is quite a useful provision if you are faced with vague threats that somebody will say something about you ('publishing' includes saying things by word of mouth), but the threat must be accompanied by an intent to extort some 'valuable thing'.

FORGERY

THE verb 'to forge' originally meant simply 'to make' and had no suggestion of falsity or fraud. It is still used in that sense, as when a blacksmith forges a shoe. But for some hundreds of years it has also been used in its criminal sense.

The crime of forgery is defined by the Forgery Act of 1913 as follows:

'Forgery is making a false document in order that it may be used as genuine' —a delightfully simple definition, although when you examine it you will see that it does need some explanation. The Act also makes it a forgery to counterfeit certain seals and dies.

What is 'a false document' in this sense? It is false:

(i) if it pretends to be made by someone who did not make it, or did not authorize its making;

(ii) if the time when it was made or the place where it is made (if either of those is important) are falsely stated;

(iii) if material alterations have been made.

A document is not a forgery when it merely contains statements which are false. That definition just quoted goes far beyond the statements in the document itself; to be a forgery the document must pretend to be something which it is not. A letter containing a number of false statements is not necessarily a forgery. But it would become a forgery if it purported, for instance, to be signed by A. when in fact A. knew nothing about it, but B. had written A.'s signature. The point has been well summed up by this definition:

'a forgery is a document which not merely tells a lie, but tells a lie about itself.'

An example of a forgery resulting from the mis-statement of the time or the place where the document was made is the false ante-dating of a cheque. So too, if a telegraph clerk immediately on hearing the result of a race sends the bookmaker a telegram backing the winning horse and indicates by his stamp that the telegram was handed in at the Post Office before the race was run, he commits a forgery of that telegram.

The word 'document' in the definition quoted above covers *any writing*. A picture, not being written, has been held not to be a document; therefore it was not a forgery to sign the picture with the name of a painter who had nothing to do with its painting. However, this is not to be taken as invitation to cheat by putting false signatures on paintings, because another offence is committed. The offence is the very old one known as 'a Common Law cheat'.

As with all other crimes, it is essential to prove that the accused was acting with some wrongful intent, not merely by accident or mistake.

At Common Law, before the 1913 Statute, it was necessary that the forger should intend not merely to deceive (*i.e.* to persuade someone to believe a thing to be true when it is actually false), but also to defraud.

But the Act specifies many kinds of writing which it makes it criminal to forge, even for the purpose of merely deceiving without any intention of defrauding. These are important public documents of various kinds, *e.g.*

(i) Any document to which is affixed the stamp or impression of the Great Seal or the United Kingdom or Her Majesty's Privy Seal.

(ii) Any register or record or certificate of births, baptisms, namings, dedications, marriages, deaths, burials, or cremations.

(iii) The documents and registers of any Court of Justice.

The full list is set out in Section 3 of the Act, but these examples show the kind of document which it is a crime to forge, even if you want only to tell a lie about your age (*i.e.* to deceive) and have no intention of defrauding.

The penalties vary at their maximum from life imprisonment to seven years, according to the importance of the document.

But generally it is necessary to prove intent to defraud; *i.e.* an intent to persuade some other person to act, or refrain from acting, to his own disadvantage. To deceive is to induce a state of mind; to defraud is to injure by causing another to behave to his prejudice.

Examples of documents which it is a crime to forge with intent to defraud are:

(i) Any will or codicil either of a dead or living person, any probate or letters of administration.

(ii) Any deed or bond.

(iii) Any valuable security (*e.g.* cheque or bill of exchange).

(iv) Any document of title to land or goods.

(v) Any power of attorney.

(vi) Any insurance policy.

(The penalties vary from life imprisonment to imprisonment for fourteen years.)

The full list is in Section 2 of the Act.

It is important to note that it does not matter whether any person was *actually* defrauded or deceived. What matters is the intention in the mind of the forger, and intentions can be and are inferred by the court from the acts of the accused.

Then, in case the Act by specifying certain documents, a few of which have been mentioned above, should have left out others, there is a rounding-up section to cover any other document, not already mentioned. The reason why some are particularly mentioned is partly to make it a crime to forge some of them with intent only to deceive and partly to lay down the sentences which can be awarded. The more serious and more important the document which has been forged, the heavier the sentence. The sentence can run even to life imprisonment. The rounding up section dealing with other documents not particularly mentioned which are forged with intent to defraud or to deceive lays down a sentence which, compared with the much heavier sentences prescribed for the particular documents named in the Act, is comparatively light, because it is a term not exceeding two years.

The Act deals also with seals and dies as well as with documents. It is, of course, vitally important that there should be public confidence in the many official seals and dies which are used to indicate that a document is authentic. For instance the seal of any of the Courts of Justice, the seal of the Office of the Registrar-General of Births, Deaths, and Marriages. Any die or stamp used by the Commissioners of Inland Revenue or the Commissioners of Customs and Excise, and so on.

The offence of forgery consists in making the document or counterfeiting the seal or die, but it is also an offence to 'utter' the document and utter in this sense means in effect to cause the document to go into circulation or to be received by the person whom it is intended to defraud or to deceive. Anyone who utters any forged document, seal, or die is guilty of an offence as serious as the person who actually made the forgery, and if he is convicted is liable to the same punishment as if he himself had forged the document, seal, or die. He must, of course, know that the document is forged or the seal has been counterfeited, and he must have the intent to defraud or deceive which is necessary to make the document itself a forgery and the forger guilty of an offence.

CONTEMPT OF COURT

INTRODUCTION

THIS offence is perhaps not very happily named. On the one hand, it sounds rather pompous, and so has become a popular 'joke-phrase': that does not much matter, because the law can stand jokes against itself, and indeed enjoys them. On the other hand, from a more serious standpoint, lawyers and judges themselves feel uneasy about CONTEMPT OF COURT, because (1) the phrase gives the impression that it is tied up with the personal vanity of the judge, and (2) a judge can COMMIT somebody to prison for contempt of court without trial and, until recently, without right of appeal. In fact, judges are very reluctant to commit people to prison for 'contempt'.

The true reason why contempt of court is punished is not that judges are particularly sensitive about their personal dignity but that it is important in the public interest that nothing should be done to interfere with the proper administration of justice. To ensure that it is essential that

(1) the trial is carried out in a decent way, and
(2) any order made by the court is obeyed.

Therefore to fling an egg at a judge in court would be a contempt, though to do so elsewhere would not necessarily be so—the reason being that the protection of the judge's dignity in court is one of the necessities for the due administration of justice.

'Contempt', however, covers a much wider variety of activities than are implied in the word in its simplest sense. It covers almost any conduct that may impede the course of justice, from things done before a case has even started (e.g. bringing pressure on somebody not to start the action or not to give evidence), to things which happen after the case is over (e.g. failure to carry out a court order or improper comment while there is still time for appeal).

TYPES OF CONTEMPT

It is impossible to give a full list of 'contempts'. In what follows a reasonably comprehensive description of the types of contempt will be given, together with examples.

Contempt of court can be roughly divided into two classes: (1) Words or deeds which obstruct or may obstruct the course of justice, and (2) disobedience to an order of the court made as a result of the trial. The first type of contempt covers things said or done during the course of the trial (or in connection with it), and is often called CRIMINAL CONTEMPT; the second covers words or deeds after the trial, and is often called CONTEMPT IN PROCEDURE. Though the types are obviously distinct, the technical descriptions are not very helpful. A more practical distinction might be between those contempts which allow the judge to imprison you at once because you are present in his court, and those where you have to be found and arrested, for example, when you have run away to another country with a young woman who is a 'ward of court'.

(1) 'Criminal Contempt'

'Criminal Contempt' can be divided into those done in front of the judge himself and 'others'.

(A) '*Contempt in the face of the Court.*' This means conduct, whether by word or deed, in the presence of the court or when the court is actually sitting, such as to disturb or obstruct the due administration of justice. The conduct need not be deliberately aimed at the judge—it can be aimed at counsel or solicitors, or the jury, or the parties or their witnesses; and counsel, solicitors, etc., in their turn can *commit* contempt, as will be seen later. Presumably a judge himself cannot commit contempt in the face of his own court—though it is conceivable that in a court of two or more judges (as Sessions or Assizes or Appeal Courts) one judge might be in contempt of the rest of the bench; but it is so improbable that a judge would act in such a way that the idea is more entertaining to imagine than practical to discuss.

The following are some of the ways in which contempt can be committed by words or deeds by or to persons in the presence of the court.

(a) *Judges.* The position of judges has already been discussed. Obviously any sort of physical attack would be a contempt. Almost certainly any insult to a judge would be contempt; but there is a dividing line between insult and discourtesy. It is not a question of whether a judge's vanity is hurt (some people are hurt more easily than others), but whether the conduct is likely to destroy that dignity which any court must have if justice is to be done.

(b) *Counsel and solicitors.* Insults to them, though undesirable and imprudent, are not in themselves contempt unless likely to lead to disorder or unless persisted in after warning by the judge. Physical attacks on them would probably be contempt if committed in the presence of the judge; but an attack within the precincts of the court, though not in his presence, would probably only amount to contempt if it interfered with the discharge of their duties.

Solicitors and barristers can, of course, themselves commit contempt. Solicitors are particularly vulnerable because they are officers of the court.

Barristers, though not officers of the court, have a duty toward it and may be guilty of contempt for such malpractice as wilfully deceiving the court.

(c) *Juries and witnesses.* Offences *toward* juries and witnesses are dealt with below. The kinds of contempts they can commit in the face of the court are, in the case of jurors, wrongfully refusing to return a verdict, or in the case of witnesses, refusing to be sworn or to answer questions put to them. A witness is, however, allowed by law to refuse to answer a question if the court is satisfied that the answer might incriminate him.

(B) *Other criminal contempts.* The following are examples of contempts which, though not done in the face of the court, are nevertheless criminal.

(a) *Embracery.* EMBRACERY means attempting 'to corrupt, influence, or instruct a juror or to incline him to favour one side more than the other, whether by money, promises, letters, threats or persuasion, or by any other means than by evidence and arguments in open court at the trial'. This is not only a contempt but also a Common Law misdemeanour punishable by fine and imprisonment.

(b) *Interfering with a witness.* This may take almost any form—*e.g.* intimidating him, bribing him, trying to influence him, keeping him hidden. It is contempt to dismiss a servant for giving evidence for the other side.

(c) *Interfering with a party.* The same principles apply to attempts to influence or obstruct the plaintiff or defendant in an action.

(d) *Speeches or writings tending to defeat the ends of justice.* Any speeches or writings, public or private, may be a contempt if they tend to defeat the ends of justice—and the tendency need not be very strong. Merely to write to a judge to influence his decision may be enough, even though the writing is not accompanied by a bribe or a threat, and even though it is improbable that it will in fact influence him. To make scandalous attacks on a judge is contempt, because it is in the public interest to maintain respect for the courts. To comment on a trial while it is in progress may be a contempt, because, for example, the comment may affect the minds of the jury.

On the other hand, criticism and comment in good faith is permissible after a case is over. The difficulties arise in connection with cases which are pending or which are not yet over. When does a case begin to be 'pending'? When is it 'over'? It has been held that a criminal prosecution may be 'pending' even though the accused has not been committed for trial; and as regards when a case is 'over', one must always remember that although the trial is finished there is the possibility of an appeal.

It used to make no difference whether or not you were aware that proceedings were pending, and if it was your trade to distribute the publication in which the contempt was printed (*e.g.* as newsagent or bookseller) you would be liable even though you did not know it was there.

Since October 27th, 1960, however, the law has been changed; and a new Act of Parliament (The Administration of Justice Act, 1960) puts it very simply (as statutes go) as follows:

A person shall not be guilty of contempt of court on the ground that he has published any matter calculated to interfere with the course of justice in connection with any proceedings pending or imminent at the time of publication if at that time (having taken all reasonable care) he did not know and had no reason to suspect that the proceedings were pending, or that such proceedings were imminent, as the case may be.

The Act also protects the distributor who, having taken all reasonable care, at the time of distributing the publication 'did not know that it contained any such matter as aforesaid and had no reason to suspect that it was likely to do so'.

Finally, the Act provides that the publication of information relating to proceedings before a court sitting in private shall not in itself be contempt, with a few exceptions. These are fairly obvious ones such as certain proceedings in connection with guardianship, etc., of infants and under the Mental Health Act, 1959, or where national security or secret processes are involved, or where publication has been expressly forbidden by the court.

(2) 'Contempt in Procedure'

These are contempts which do not tend to obstruct the administration of justice but which represent disobedience to the orders of the court and probably involve injury to somebody.

The most obvious example is failure to pay a sum of money which has been ordered to be paid. There is no longer in most cases imprisonment for debt as such—*i.e.* merely because you are unable to pay—but if you are able to pay and refuse to do so, then it may amount to contempt.

But there are other court orders than orders to pay money, and failure to carry them out is equally contempt. For example, the court may have granted an INJUNCTION (*i.e.* ordered you not to do something, such as continuing to trespass on someone's property): disobedience would be contempt. In a divorce case the court may have awarded CUSTODY of the children to the mother; if the father refuses to hand them over he will be guilty of contempt. Another well-known example is interference with a WARD OF COURT (*i.e.* a person under the age of twenty-one who has come under the care of the court), such as by taking him or her out of the country or marrying the ward without the permission of the court.

PUNISHMENT

In the most serious cases of contempt in the face of the court the judge can summarily commit the offender to prison, and he is immediately taken there by the TIPSTAFF. The judge need not specify the length of the sentence, and the offender will have to apply for his discharge. If the judge then decides he has sufficiently PURGED his contempt (*e.g.* by apology and, if necessary, making amends) he may then release him; but he is not bound to do so and may decide that the offender should remain longer in prison and make another application later.

Where the contempt is less serious the judge may impose only a fine, or merely require the offender to be of good behaviour.

Persons committed to prison for contempt are not treated as convicted criminals. For example, they need not wear prison clothes.

APPEAL

Until very recently there was no appeal from a committal order for contempt; but it is now provided in the Administration of Justice Act, 1960, that an appeal can be brought (much in the same way as any other appeal) to the High Court, the Court of Appeal, or the House of Lords, as the case may be.

THE CRIMINAL COURTS

INTRODUCTION

Courts for all purposes

YOU will have seen from the earlier part of the CRIMINAL LAW section of this work that there is every sort of crime from TREASON to PARKING. Each of them has to be *tried*; and the citizen who feels he has been wrongly convicted or sentenced ought to have some right of *appeal*.

At the same time it would be ridiculous to spend as much time or ability on an offence carrying a maximum penalty of a £2 fine as you would spend on one involving fourteen years' imprisonment or a capital sentence.

Consequently there are many hundreds of courts throughout the country, of various degrees of dignity and importance, which provide for the suitable trial of all types of criminal offence and for appeal against their decisions.

A simple diagram

The diagram shows in simplified form the COURTS which deal with crime, the JUDGES who preside over those courts, and the way in which APPEALS go from one court to another.

MAGISTRATES' COURTS

General Purpose Courts

Although MAGISTRATES' COURTS appear at the bottom of the diagram they are by far the most numerous of criminal courts. One way or another practically all prosecutions for crime pass through these courts.

The Magistrates

(1) *In general.* Most magistrates' courts are presided over by JUSTICES OF THE PEACE. These are men and women who give their services without payment and who usually have no legal training. They do, however, often have considerable experience of life; and, as far as the law is concerned, they have the advantage of the advice and guidance of the CLERK TO THE JUSTICES—a solicitor with considerable knowledge both of the law and of the practice of the magistrates' courts. He usually has considerable experience of life as well[1].

611

(2) *In large towns.* In London and some other large towns, instead of 'lay' and unpaid magistrates, there are professional paid magistrates called STIPENDIARY MAGISTRATES. They must be barristers or solicitors of seven years' standing; but they have usually been in practice longer than that. Because of his legal qualification a stipendiary has, generally speaking, the powers of two 'lay' magistrates.

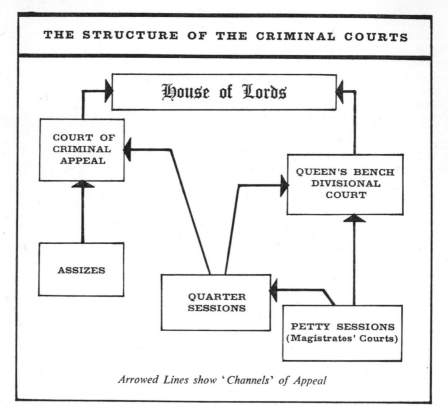

THE STRUCTURE OF THE CRIMINAL COURTS

𝕳𝖔𝖚𝖘𝖊 𝖔𝖋 𝕷𝖔𝖗𝖉𝖘

COURT OF CRIMINAL APPEAL

QUEEN'S BENCH DIVISIONAL COURT

ASSIZES

QUARTER SESSIONS

PETTY SESSIONS (Magistrates' Courts)

Arrowed Lines show 'Channels' of Appeal

(3) *In the City of London.* The City of London, as in so many other matters, has its own rules: there the Lord Mayor or any Alderman (legally qualified or not) may sit as sole magistrate and still have the powers of two lay magistrates elsewhere. Lord Mayors and Aldermen of other cities do not have these powers.

The Courts

Two functions. Magistrates' courts have two most important but quite separate jobs to do. *First,* they may actually try the offender and deal with him if he is found guilty. This is their major work: most crimes are the simple work of simple men, involving very little question of law but requiring proof that the accused person committed the crime of which he is charged. *Secondly,*

612

in the case of more serious crimes where the penalty may also be more serious so that the accused ought to have the benefit of a more expert judge and a jury, they may not have the power to try the accused; but at the same time there is no point in sending him for trial unless at least there is some case for him to answer: so in these cases the magistrates act as 'examining justices' to decide whether there appears to be evidence of a case that ought to be tried by some superior court.

(1) *Summary jurisdiction.* The first function described above is what is known as the magistrates' 'SUMMARY JURISDICTION'—*i.e.* the case is tried summarily or quickly, without a jury and without many of the complications that are necessary or desirable in more serious cases.

However, there must be not less than two magistrates present if it is a 'lay bench'. The decision is taken by a majority: the chairman does not have a casting vote, so it is obviously desirable to have an uneven number on the lay bench.

Summary offences. The sorts of offences which magistrates may try are in general laid down by Act of Parliament.

They show an extraordinary variety—from keeping a dog without a licence to smuggling ten thousand watches; from drinking in a pub after closing time to thrashing a child with merciless cruelty.

They have power to levy fines of up to £50 or sometimes £100, and in a few instances (*e.g.* pollution of the sea by oil) very much heavier fines. They also have power to sentence to imprisonment of up to six months, and in a few special cases, up to a year or even two years.

If, however, the offence is one which if proved could carry a sentence of more than three months' imprisonment, the accused has the right to ask for trial by jury at a superior court—usually Quarter Sessions. For instance, a charge of careless driving must be dealt with by the magistrates summarily. The maximum sentence is three months' imprisonment or a fine of up to £20 or £50, depending upon whether the conviction is the first or not.

But if, however, the charge is dangerous driving the accused can insist on trial by jury, because the possible sentence is more than three months' imprisonment without the option of a fine.

Starting proceedings. Anybody can start most criminal proceedings—*e.g.* a private individual, the police, or some other authority. To start, you 'LAY AN INFORMATION' or 'MAKE A COMPLAINT' against the person concerned, and this must almost always be within six months of the offence. The 'Information' is usually in writing, but it need not be on oath unless the informant wants a warrant to be issued for the arrest of the person concerned.

Arrest. In many cases the person charged is not arrested. If the offence is not serious, or there is a reasonable chance that he will turn up, it is enough to issue a SUMMONS: this describes the offence alleged and orders him to appear before the magistrates at a certain place and time. Sometimes, of course, the offender has been arrested before the information has been laid. He may be arrested on a warrant issued by the magistrates, or if he has committed a serious felony he may have been arrested without warrant.

Trial. The next thing is the trial. To save time and trouble where the accused person does not wish to deny the accusation, it is now provided that if the offence is not triable on indictment or punishable with more than three months' imprisonment (*i.e.* it is a fairly unimportant offence, like parking in the wrong place) and the accused wishes to plead guilty, he can do so by post, and the court can deal with the case in his absence. If, of course, he wishes to plead not guilty he must turn up to argue his case either by himself or through a solicitor or barrister.

If the accused pleads not guilty the trial starts by the prosecutor 'opening his case': that is to say, he (or his counsel or solicitor) outlines the case against the accused and the evidence that will be brought to prove it. He then calls his witnesses into the box to give their evidence, which they do in reply to questions by him. This is called EXAMINATION-IN-CHIEF. After each witness has been so examined the accused (or his counsel or solicitor) has the opportunity of CROSS-EXAMINATION—that is to say, of asking questions of the witness to show that his evidence is untrue, unreliable, or capable of a different interpretation.

When all the prosecution witnesses have been dealt with in this way the accused can submit that he has no case to answer—for example, on the grounds that the prosecution's evidence does not show that he committed the crime he is charged with. The court will very seldom allow the prosecution to try again by producing further evidence: it either accepts the submission, in which case the summons is dismissed and the accused goes free, or they reject it and the accused has to tell his side of the story.

This he does in much the same way. He can make a speech and call his witnesses, who are examined and cross-examined like the prosecution witnesses. He is also allowed to make a speech after his witnesses have given evidence; but if he has already made a speech he can only make the second one with the leave of the court, and the prosecutor is also given a second speech. After the evidence for the defence has been heard the prosecutor also has the right to call evidence to REBUT it—*i.e.* to show that it is not to be relied on.

Decision. As there is no jury at a court of summary jurisdiction, the magistrates themselves have to decide whether the accused is guilty or not guilty. If they wish to, they may retire to their room to consider their decision. They can also ask the clerk to join them to advise them about the law, but he should not accompany them as a matter of course when there is no point of law involved, because it is for the magistrates themselves, and not the clerk, to decide.

If the magistrates decide that the case has not been proved then they DISMISS THE INFORMATION and discharge the defendant.

Sentence. If, on the other hand, they find him guilty they must decide what is the appropriate sentence. Before doing this they are informed of any previous convictions against the accused. During the course of the trial these will not have been revealed, because they are usually irrelevant to his guilt in the present case and might create prejudice; but as regards sentence they are obviously relevant, because a person who has committed previous crimes merits different treatment from a first offender. They can also hear evidence about the accused's character. Furthermore, the defence can make a PLEA IN MITIGATION—*i.e.* point out to the court any factors which favour merciful treatment.

Sentences can vary from an ABSOLUTE DISCHARGE to IMPRISONMENT—usually for a maximum of six months, though in some cases if the court thinks the offender deserves a more serious punishment than it has power to inflict it may send him to Quarter Sessions (see below) for sentence. The court has also, of course, the power to fine.

Absolute discharge means that in effect the guilty person is convicted of the offence but not punished; but the court can order him to pay costs and also damages or compensation up to £100.

There can, however, be CONDITIONAL DISCHARGE—*i.e.* subject to the condition that he commits no further offence for a period not exceeding twelve months and that if he does he will be sentenced for the original offence. Alternatively, for offences where the sentence is not fixed by law (and thus the magistrates can use their discretion) the court can order the offender (if he consents to the order) to be under the supervision of a PROBATION OFFICER for not less than one or more than three years. In this way the offender has a chance to reform his life under the care of a sympathetic and devoted officer of the probation service without the 'sentence' being regarded otherwise as a 'conviction'. If the offender disobeys the probation order or commits another offence the court may summon him—or even issue a warrant for his arrest—and award the appropriate punishment.

Children and young persons. Summary trials of CHILDREN (*i.e.* those under fourteen) and YOUNG PERSONS (*i.e.* those of fourteen but under seventeen) are held at special JUVENILE COURTS, usually before three magistrates, of whom one must be a man and one a woman, drawn from a special panel. In order that young people who 'get into trouble' shall have the best possible chance, not only are the magistrates selected from people who are likely to be understanding (*e.g.* people with children of their own, and people who are not too old) but also the law provides that the young people shall be kept free from adult offenders and from undesirable publicity. The court must sit in a different building (or at least at a different time) from the ordinary magistrates' court. Only people who have business there are allowed to be present. But in order to avoid any suggestion of secrecy the press are allowed to attend; nevertheless, without permission, they must not publish names, addresses, or any other particulars (such as pictures) which may identify the parties or witnesses under seventeen years of age.

(2) *Preliminary examination.* (i) *Explanation.* What has been described above is the 'summary jurisdiction' of magistrates' courts, where the magistrates actually try the case and sentence the accused person if he is found guilty. What is now going to be described is the PRELIMINARY EXAMINATION which magistrates carry out in the case of offences which are serious enough to go to a higher court, but ought not to go there unless the prosecution can show at least a reasonable case (see above).

When magistrates are carrying out a 'preliminary examination' they are known as EXAMINING JUSTICES. A single magistrate is enough for a preliminary examination, as opposed to the two which are generally required for the exercise of summary jurisdiction.

As the purpose of the preliminary examination is not to try the accused but to discover whether there is a case to go for trial, the accused does not start by pleading guilty or not guilty.

(ii) *Depositions.* The prosecutor opens the case in much the same way as in a summary trial, and examines his witnesses. After that the hearing may go rather differently.

First, the accused person (or his counsel or solicitor) may decide not to cross-examine (see above), because he knows that these same witnesses will probably appear again at the 'real' trial in the superior court, if there is one, and he may not want to alert them as to the sort of questions he is going to ask.

Secondly, the hearing is bound to go rather differently, because the law requires that all the answers of the witnesses must be written down in their own words by the clerk to the justices and then read over to them and signed by them and by the presiding magistrate. The purpose of this is that these statements, called DEPOSITIONS, shall be available if necessary for the superior court. But it all takes a great deal of time.

Thirdly, counsel or solicitor for the accused may decide to call no witnesses, particularly if he sees that his client is likely to be sent for trial. He may feel that, as in the case of cross-examining the prosecution witnesses, it is better not to reveal his own case at this early stage.

Although any evidence which is given (and any statement made by the accused in court) is taken down in the 'depositions', the witnesses themselves may nevertheless have to attend the trial in person. For this purpose they are BOUND OVER—*i.e.* they enter into a 'recognisance' or promise to pay a fine if they do not turn up. If their evidence is unlikely to be needed at the trial they may be bound over 'conditionally'—*i.e.* they need not turn up unless they receive a notice to do so.

(3) *Committal.* As a result of this preliminary hearing the court may decide that the case put forward by the prosecution is not strong enough to justify their committing the accused for trial. If so, he is released.

If not, then the justices must decide to *which* court to commit him for trial. As will be seen later, there are two choices—Quarter Sessions or Assizes (which include the Central Criminal Court, popularly known as the Old Bailey, and the Crown Courts at Liverpool and Manchester, which are the Quarter Sessions and Assizes for the areas concerned). In general, the choice depends on the gravity of the charge—the most serious offences go to Assizes.

Appeals

Obviously no appeal is needed from the magistrates when they are sitting as 'examining justices': either they discharge you there and then or you have the opportunity to put your case at the actual trial.

But from a court of summary jurisdiction there are two ways of appealing.

The first is to the Queen's Bench Division, if a point of *law* only is involved. The second is to Quarter Sessions, if the appeal is against *conviction* or *sentence* or both.

These two methods of appeal are described below under the headings of the two courts concerned.

QUARTER SESSIONS

Dual function

As just explained, one function of Quarter Sessions is to act as an appeal court from the magistrates; but they also act as 'courts of first instance'—

616

that is to say, courts where a case is *tried for the first time*. They try cases which are rather too important for the magistrates but not important enough for the Assizes. Consequently they have a jury, and usually more experienced persons sit on the bench.

They have power to try all criminal offences with certain specified exceptions—the most important of which are treason, murder, manslaughter, bigamy, and certain perjuries, forgeries, and unlawful conspiracies, and also certain felonies which are punishable by imprisonment for life.

All these offences must go for trial at an Assize Court presided over by a High Court Judge.

There are two kinds of Quarter Sessions: County Sessions and Borough Sessions. County Sessions are composed of unpaid lay justices (like the magistrates' courts), but they usually have a legally qualified Chairman. Borough Sessions are to be found in cities and large boroughs and they are presided over by one man, called a Recorder, who is paid and who is a qualified lawyer.

As Court of First Instance

As explained above, a person who is going to be tried at Quarter Sessions will already have appeared before the 'examining justices', who will have 'committed him for trial'. Between then and the trial he will have been REMANDED IN CUSTODY or released on BAIL, according to the seriousness of the offence and the likelihood that he will turn up for trial.

Indictment. At Quarter Sessions proceedings are started by INDICTMENT, instead of 'information' as at Petty Sessions. The indictment gives the name and place of the court; a statement of the offence, with reference to the relevant statute if necessary (*e.g.* 'Arson contrary to section 3 of the Malicious Damage Act, 1861'); and finally particulars of the offence, such as the time and place.

Trial. At the actual trial the accused person appears at the bar of the court and is ARRAIGNED—*i.e.* the indictment is read to him and he has to plead to it, guilty or not guilty, as the case may be.

The trial itself follows much the same pattern as at Petty Sessions, except that, as there is a jury, it is for them and not for the magistrates or the Recorder to decide whether the accused person is guilty or not. Consequently, after the prosecution and the defence have completed their cases, the Chairman or the Recorder sums up to the jury. The SUMMING UP is intended to instruct the jury about the *law* they must apply to the matter; it can also deal with the *facts*, but it is always for the jury to make up their own minds about them and to return a VERDICT accordingly.

Appeals. A verdict at Quarter Sessions is not necessarily final. The convicted man has a right of appeal. If the only ground of appeal is whether the court has correctly interpreted or applied the law, he will usually appeal to the Queen's Bench Division of the High Court, which is described below.

If the appeal is based on wider grounds, for instance, that he denied the truth and accuracy of the so-called facts given in evidence, or that the magistrates or the Recorder gave an unbalanced or inaccurate summing up, he will appeal to the Court of Criminal Appeal.

The functions and powers of both these courts are described under separate headings.

As Appeal Court

Quarter Sessions also act as a Court of Appeal from Petty Sessions. A convicted person can appeal against his conviction or against his sentence or against both— unless, of course, he has pleaded guilty, in which case he obviously cannot appeal against conviction (apart from very exceptional circumstances). He may, however, still appeal against the severity of his sentence.

The interesting feature of an appeal from the magistrates' court to Quarter Sessions is that the appeal is a new hearing of the whole case. In other words, Quarter Sessions do not take the evidence given in the court below 'as read', but require that it shall all be given again. The witnesses have to appear and are examined and cross-examined just as if it was a new trial—which indeed it is.

If the true answer turns upon the credibility and reliability of the witnesses, this is a valuable right to the accused.

If, however, the facts given in evidence to the magistrates are admitted to be true, and the only question is whether, in law, those facts show that an offence has been committed, it is quicker and cheaper to appeal to the Queen's Bench Division to have the point of law determined. This method of appeal is described next under the heading 'Queen's Bench Division'.

QUEEN'S BENCH DIVISION

Description

This Court is a division of the Supreme Court of Judicature, and the Judges are Her Majesty's Justices of the High Court, who have the title of the 'Honourable Mr Justice X.', are invariably given a knighthood on appointment (if not already knighted), and are addressed in court as 'My Lord'.

As Appeal Court

Appeals on a point of law can be made from the magistrates' court or Quarter Sessions, and the appeal is heard by at least two Queen's Bench Judges.

Case Stated. The method is by CASE STATED. This means that the person who wants to appeal asks the magistrates (or the Chairman or Recorder) to 'state a case'. The 'case stated' for the opinion of the Divisional Court has to include a brief account of the facts involved, any submissions (legal arguments about the facts) made by the prosecution or the defence, and the conclusions on the point of law which the bench made. As a result, the Queen's Bench Division Judges have a neat summary of the situation and of the legal point in question: no time need be wasted on the agreed facts, and the argument can be confined to discovering the answer to the legal question.

Either the prosecution *or* the defence may ask the magistrates to 'state a case'. Furthermore, if the magistrates refuse to state a case, they may be compelled to do so by the High Court.

ASSIZES

Highest Court of First Instance

The Assize Courts are simply the courts presided over by the High Court Judges travelling round the country 'on circuit' as they have done since the reign of King Henry II. When he established the system in 1166 the means and methods of travel were so primitive and hazardous that it would have been a virtual denial of justice to compel every serious criminal trial to be heard in London. So instead of the accused having to come to London, the judges had in effect to go to him.

That is a simplified but basically true account of the origins of the system whereby judges since the twelfth century have travelled on circuit and heard cases in all the larger towns in the whole country.

The Central Criminal Court in the Old Bailey is a virtually permanent Assize Court.

The account already given of the powers of Courts of Quarter Session has shown that certain of the gravest crimes can only be tried by the High Court at Assizes, e.g. murder, manslaughter, certain perjuries and forgeries and conspiracies, bigamy, and certain other offences punishable with life imprisonment.

Quite apart from this division of powers, the examining justices who have to decide whether there is a case to answer have some discretion whether to commit the accused for trial at Quarter Sessions or at the Central Criminal Court or Assizes. If the case is very serious, e.g. fraud or burglary with violence, then notwithstanding the fact that Quarter Sessions may technically have power to deal with it, they may commit the accused to the next Assizes, or to the Central Criminal Court.

They may also be influenced by the fact that a speedier trial may sometimes be achieved by so doing, because it is a cardinal principle of the British administration of justice that a man shall not be kept waiting a long time for his trial. A wait of more than, say, six weeks can in itself amount to a denial of justice.

England and Wales are divided into seven CIRCUITS, and at a number of important cities or towns within those circuits there are Assize Courts which are visited by COMMISSIONERS OF ASSIZE in the winter, summer and autumn of every year. The visits may last several days, and there may be several judges, according to the amount of business that needs to be done.

The Judges are called 'Commissioners', because, although they may be (and usually are) in fact Judges of the High Court, their right to be Judges at Assizes comes from a Royal Commission (with such ancient names as OYER ET TERMINER and GAOL DELIVERY) issued to them by LETTERS PATENT. For the most part the Commissioners are Judges of the Queen's Bench; but eminent barristers (usually Queen's Counsel) are often appointed as Commissioners.

The Central Criminal Court. The CENTRAL CRIMINAL COURT (popularly known as the OLD BAILEY) is the Assize Court for London and a large part of the home counties.

The general work of the Court (which is partly Assize work and partly Quarter Sessions work) is done by full-time professional judges—the RECORDER, the COMMON SERJEANT, and one or two JUDGES OF THE MAYOR'S AND CITY OF LONDON COURT.

The most important work—the trial of grave crimes such as murder—is done by Queen's Bench Judges (sometimes by the Lord Chief Justice himself), one or more of whom are specially assigned to sit at the Old Bailey as may be required.

Crown Courts. These were established in 1956 in Liverpool and Manchester.

619

They perform much the same functions as Assize and Quarter Sessions Courts for the areas concerned as does the Central Criminal Court in London.

Procedure and appeal

The procedure at the trial of criminal cases in these Courts is much the same as at Quarter Sessions. Unlike Quarter Sessions, however, the Assizes, though a higher Court of *first instance* than Quarter Sessions, is not an *appeal* Court from Quarter Sessions or indeed any other Court.

Appeals *from* Assizes go to the Court of Criminal Appeal.

COURT OF CRIMINAL APPEAL

Description

The present system of criminal appeals was created by the Criminal Appeal Act, 1907.

Before that Act it was possible for a Judge of Assize to reserve any difficult point of Law to enable him to consult the other Judges of the Common Law Courts. But that was quite a different matter from a right of appeal against conviction, or sentence, or both.

This Act established a new Court, the Court of Criminal Appeal.

The Court consists of the Lord Chief Justice of England and all the other Queen's Bench Judges. At least three of them must sit to form a Court, and they must be an odd number. Normally only three sit; but in cases of exceptional difficulty the Lord Chief Justice may convene a Court of five or even more: on one occasion thirteen judges sat.

There is no jury; and only on very rare occasions are there any witnesses: they are not necessary, because the judges are in effect reviewing what happened in the Court below (and there will be a *verbatim* transcript of all the evidence and legal arguments), and, *on the basis of what happened there* (not what ought to have happened) they decide whether the conviction or sentence ought to be allowed to stand.

The Right of Appeal

There is no automatic right of appeal in all circumstances.

In the first place, the prosecution has no right of appeal at all: if the accused person is acquitted, that is the end of the matter; if he is found guilty, the prosecution cannot appeal against the sentence on the ground that it was too lenient.

In the second place, a convicted person has a right of appeal without leave if (1) he is appealing only against conviction, and (2) the ground of appeal is on a question of law only. The usual questions of law are either that the judge misdirected the jury or that evidence was improperly admitted.

In all other cases—for example, if the appeal is against sentence, or the grounds of appeal are a question of fact or of law and fact mixed—the accused must have the leave either of the judge who tried his case or of the court of Criminal Appeal. The trial judge will obviously give leave unless he thinks the appeal is so hopeless or frivolous that it ought not to be brought. If the trial judge refuses leave the accused can ask for it from the Court of Criminal Appeal. If they grant it they usually treat the application for leave as the actual hearing of the appeal, and hear it then and there, thus saving both time and money.

Decision

If, on an appeal against conviction, the court comes to the conclusion that the verdict of the jury was unreasonable or the judgment was wrong in law or that there was a miscarriage of justice, they will quash the conviction unless they consider that in fact there was no substantial miscarriage of justice. Obviously it would be absurd for a guilty person to be discharged because of a single and wholly unimportant error, and the court is expressly given the power to ignore matters which may be technically wrong but which did not in their view result in a substantial miscarriage of justice. Even so, they will often allow appeals which the ordinary man—whoever he may be—would have rejected, if they feel that there is a chance that a properly instructed Jury might have acquitted him. A serious doubt is resolved in favour of the accused.

On an appeal against sentence, the court has the power to vary it. Rash appeals against sentence are discouraged by the fact that the court may vary sentences *upwards* as well as downwards.

HOUSE OF LORDS

Introduction

The HOUSE OF LORDS is the highest and final Court of Appeal for the whole of Great Britain. This includes Scotland, whose law in many respects is different from that of the rest of Great Britain.

Composition

The name 'House of Lords' is rather misleading. As a Court of Appeal the House of Lords does not mean anybody with a title which gives him a seat in that House but only certain peers who have judicial qualifications—and very high qualifications.

These peers include the LORD CHANCELLOR, past Lord Chancellors, others who hold or have held high judicial appointments and are also peers, and nine specially appointed life-peers called LORDS OF APPEAL IN ORDINARY, who have usually had long experience in the High Court or the Court of Appeal or both. Whereas the Court of Criminal Appeal usually consists of three judges, the House of Lords sitting as a judicial tribunal usually consists of five, but it may be more.

Appeal regulations

The same Act of Parliament which created the Court of Criminal Appeal regulated appeals from that court to the House of Lords; but the rules differed

621

in two important ways from those which regulated appeals from lower courts to the Court of Criminal Appeal:

(1) The *prosecution* as well as the convicted person could appeal (whereas only the *convicted person* could appeal to the Court of Criminal Appeal).

(2) Leave to appeal was not in the hands of the courts but depended on a 'certificate' by the ATTORNEY-GENERAL (called his 'FIAT'—Latin for 'Let it be done'). This had to certify that the appeal ought to be taken to the House of Lords because the decision of the Court of Criminal Appeal involved a point of law of exceptional public importance *and* that it was desirable in the public interest that a further appeal should be brought.

The second rule has long been a subject of adverse criticism. It was felt to be wrong in principle that such an important decision should rest on one man, not a judge but someone appointed by the political party in power, and from whose decision no appeal could be brought. In practice the system worked well enough, and nobody has seriously doubted that successive Attorney-Generals of all parties took every possible step to reach a wise decision and were wholly unswayed by any improper considerations, political or other.

However, the rules about leave to appeal have been changed with effect from October 27th, 1960. It is now provided by the Administration of Justice Act, 1960, that appeals can be taken to the House of Lords from a Divisional Court of Queen's Bench in a 'criminal cause or matter' or from the Court of Criminal Appeal with the leave *either* of the lower Court in question *or* of the House of Lords, *but* that such leave shall not be granted:

unless it is certified by the court below that a point of law of general public importance is involved in the decision and it appears to that court or to the House of Lords, as the case may be, that the point is one which ought to be considered by that House.

The major differences from the old method are that the decision is taken from the Attorney-General and given to the courts (with a right of appeal), and that for a 'favourable' decision you do not have to have 'exceptional public importance' ('*general* public importance' is enough) or 'public interest' (it is enough if the point '*ought* to be considered').

Application for leave to appeal has to be made within fourteen days of the decision from which you are appealing. If leave is refused you have another fourteen days to apply to the House of Lords; but, of course, you will not be successful unless the 'court below' certified that a point of law of general public importance was involved.

Many people, whether they approve of the death penalty or not, find it difficult to understand why a person convicted of capital murder should not have better rights of appeal than other criminals, or why, although his conviction may not involve 'a point of law of general public importance', it should not be a point 'which ought to be considered' by the House of Lords. The short answer is that there may be no 'point of law' involved which any further consideration could alter. If he is undoubtedly guilty, the ludge has no choice but to pass sentence of death, and the question of whether he shall be executed or not is no longer a legal matter. It is a problem which can be settled only by one of the methods explained below.

PARDON AND PARLIAMENT

Final Judgment

The decision of the House of Lords, being final, represents the law as it stands at that moment. There are, however, two further possibilities, neither of which has much to do with the 'rightness' of the sentence or the 'rightness' of the law, neither of which are on the whole under the control of the courts or within the discretion of the judges who preside over those courts.

The proper 'legal' sentence can be altered by the Queen (or King, as the case may be); the 'law' under which the accused person was found guilty may be altered—though usually too late to help the particular guilty man. These two 'alterations' are done in the following ways.

Royal Prerogative

If there are special circumstances—where, for example, a person is undoubtedly guilty and quite properly convicted, but nevertheless there are reasons of sympathy or humanity why the sentence should not be carried out— there remains what is called the ROYAL PREROGATIVE OF MERCY. The Queen, of course, does not in these days of a 'constitutional monarchy' exercise this prerogative according to her personal feelings: she accepts the advice of the Home Secretary who, in his turn, has been advised by experts—including, as a rule, the judge who tried the case and would have shown 'mercy' himself, had he had the legal power to do so.

Changing the Law

But 'hard cases make bad laws'. It is unsatisfactory that sentences which do not command public approval should be regularly set aside by the use of the 'Royal prerogative' or that juries should shrink from reaching the right verdict because they fear the consequences which follow. The 'Royal prerogative' should be available for exceptional cases which even the most perfect system of law cannot cover—but for those only. Juries should feel generally that their verdict suits their social conscience and that the sentence is likely to appear just to them. If the law is such that the 'Royal prerogative' has to be over-employed or juries are tempted to shirk their duty, it is better that the law should be changed.

Changes in the law can be effected only by Parliament—the elected representatives of the people as a whole. This is not the place to describe the procedure by which it is done. It is long and laborious. But if public opinion feels sufficiently strongly, for example, that all capital punishment is wrong, or that certain murders ought not to be punished by death, or that the 'diminished responsibility' of certain murderers ought to be taken into account, then eventually the wishes of the public prevail and an Act of Parliament such as the Homicide Act, 1957, is passed which gets near to the 'public opinion' of the time and becomes the law of the land.

It is surprising that, with so many people with so many different views, our Criminal Law keeps reasonably up to date, provides a fair trial and right of appeal, seldom makes mistakes, and is still the admiration of the civilized world.

RIGHTS OF A FINDER

You are walking along a street and see something shining in the gutter. You pick it up and find that it appears to be a diamond ring. You may be mistaken and it may only be a piece of cut glass. But suppose it is valuable. Is it yours because you found it?

The answer, certainly, is that it is not. You should take it to a police-station, describe how you found it and leave it there. The police then do what they can to find the owner. If the ring is really valuable the loss will probably have been reported to them and the ring will be restored to its owner. Any reward for your honesty is a matter for his good-will. But let us be quite clear that if you had kept it, or sold it, you would have committed a crime—the crime known as 'larceny by finding'. The owner could also sue you in the civil courts for damages or for the return of the ring.

So in this case, quite clearly, findings are not keepings.

If the loss has not been reported, and if the police enquiries do not lead to the owner being found, it is their usual practice to return the lost property to the finder after a time. Then he can keep it or dispose or it without fear of a prosecution for stealing. But if the true owner ever turns up and proves his ownership he will have to return it or pay its value.

But the finder has a better right to the ring than anyone else, except the true owner. That is why the police give it back to him if the owner cannot be found. To that extent, findings *are* keepings.

In one case, it was reported that a man found a wad of bank-notes lying on the floor in the public part of a shop. He handed them to the shopkeeper so that they could be returned to their owner if they were claimed. As they were not claimed, he demanded them back. The shopkeeper refused. The customer took legal proceedings and the court held that the shopkeeper must hand them back because the finder had a better right to them than the shopkeeper.

These bank-notes were found on the floor in the public part of the shop. If something is found on property to which the public had no right of access, *e.g.* in a private garden, or under the floorboards in a house, the general rule is that the *owner or occupier of the premises*—the garden, or house, etc. has a better right to keep it than the finder.

It is true that in a case during the last war a soldier who found a brooch in a requisitioned house where he was billeted was held to have a better right to it than the owner of the house. But it appeared that the owner had never occupied the house before it was requisitioned and the judge felt able to decide that the soldier who had honestly declared his 'find' had a better right to it than the man who then owned the house but had never lived there.

If you find something while travelling on a train or bus your legal duty may be governed by bye-laws. For instance, under the Railway Bye-laws you are legally obliged to hand over any such lost property to the British Transport Commission.

Treasure trove

Treasure Trove means gold, silver, plate, bullion, or coins, found in the earth or in a building. The finder should declare his find to the police. Then the local coroner will hold an inquest. Inquest means 'enquiry', and the purpose of this particular inquest is to establish on the evidence whether the original inquest is to establish on the evidence whether the original owner deliberately hid, buried, or concealed his treasure, or whether he merely abandoned it. Carefully buried treasure was obviously deliberately hidden. Scattered coins may merely have been abandoned. The law is that deliberately hidden treasure belongs to the Crown, whereas abandoned treasure belongs to the finder. But the finder is rewarded either way, because if the coroner finds that the treasure belongs to the Crown it is the invariable custom for the Crown—through the Treasury—to pay the finder the present-day market value of his find.

INVESTMENT

WHAT is meant by investment?

Simply putting one's money out to work—in other words, to earn its keep. It is wise to remember that money's wages, like those of human beings, are often higher when there is more risk involved.

There are three ways in which money can earn its keep: by interest, by dividends, and by capital appreciation.

It follows from this that money in a current account at the bank is not invested, because it is not earning anything for its owner. Therefore there is no point in keeping one's savings there. All that it is necessary to keep is enough for current needs, paying the rent, household bills, insurance premiums, and so on.

After making provision for running expenses, a man—or woman—should consider how much money is necessary to meet a sudden crisis. The next step is to put that amount—perhaps one hundred pounds or more, according to one's personal liabilities—into some form of savings scheme where the capital is secure, earns interest, and is readily available.

NATIONAL SAVINGS

The question to be asked here is: "Can I be sure of getting back £1 for every pound I have put in if I need the money in a hurry?"

First on the list comes some form of National Savings.

The *Post Office Savings Bank* pays $2\frac{1}{2}$ per cent. on all deposits. The interest on the first £600, giving an income of £15 a year, is tax free, *i.e.* free of income tax, but it must be included in a surtax return. Up to £10 can be withdrawn on demand: larger amounts take a few days. Individual deposits in the Post Office Savings Bank must not exceed £5,000.

The same facilities are available from *Trustee Savings Banks*, which form part of the National Savings Movement, and, as they are under Government supervision, give an equally high degree of security.

National Savings Certificates offer a higher rate of interest, which is not subject to income tax or surtax. But to gain the full benefit, they should be held for six years. Units, which are in denominations of 20s become worth

627

25s at the end of that period. This accumulated interest represents a yearly increase of £6 3s 8d per cent. for people who pay tax at the standard rate of 7s 9d in the £. The maximum holding in the present issue, the Eleventh, is limited to 300 units. If money invested in Savings Certificates is needed urgently, only a few days are necessary to get repayment.

Defence Bonds, also part of the National Savings Scheme, give an annual return of £4 10s per cent., which is subject to tax. They are sold in multiples of £5, and are designed for people wishing to leave their money invested for a seven-year term. At the end of seven years, investors in this form of saving receive an

". . . the chance of winning a prize . . ."

additional capital payment of £2 10s per cent., which is tax free. Six months' notice is required if the money is withdrawn before the end of the seven-year period. If it is taken out without this notice, each £100 of bonds is subject to £2 10s deduction.

The maximum holding of Defence Bonds (4½ per cent. Second Issue) is limited to £5,000 for each person.

Final category in the National Savings Scheme is the *Premium Bond*. Here money does not earn any interest, but holders of bonds stand the chance of winning a prize. The amount of prize money available is geared to the number of Premium Bonds in issue, and prizes ranging from £25 to £5,000 are awarded monthly. Each Premium Bond costs £1, and individual holdings are limited to £800.

Although ordinary deposits in *Trustee Savings Banks* earn the same rate of interest—2½ per cent.—as money deposited in the Post Office Savings Bank, Trustee Savings Banks offer facilities not available through the Post Office for higher rates of interest. But at these higher rates, the money is not so easily available. Three and a half per cent. is paid on deposits which are subject to one month's notice. For deposits which can be withdrawn only at three months' notice, the interest rate rises to 5 per cent. But before being able to take advantage of these higher interest rates, a depositor must have at least £50 in an ordinary savings account. There is a top aggregate limit of £3,000 in these three sections.

In all these forms of saving, with the exception of Premium Bonds, which do not earn any interest, the rate is fixed and does not fluctuate. But there are other forms of savings where the capital is just as secure and the depositor can be certain of getting £1 back for every £1 he has put in. The rate of interest is not fixed, however, and varies with Bank Rate. *Note: the figures quoted for interest, etc., are correct at June* 1963.

BANK RATE

Bank Rate is fixed by the Bank of England, and in effect it controls the rate of interest which the Government pays on its short-term borrowings, and it governs the general rate of interest which banks and other financial institutions pay.

For the ordinary man, its effect is most obvious if he has money in a deposit account at his bank. The rate the clearing banks pay on money deposited with them is 2 per cent. below Bank Rate. There is no limit on the amount of money that can be held. It can be withdrawn at seven days' notice, and the interest on it is subject to income tax and surtax.

Bank Rate also influences the interest which building societies pay. Shares and deposits with building societies are yet another form of saving in which the investor can be certain his capital will remain intact and he will be able to withdraw his money at short notice in case of need. Amounts up to £100 can usually be withdrawn immediately. Larger amounts take a few days.

BUILDING SOCIETIES

There are two different classes of investment in building societies. Money can either be placed on deposit or can be used to buy shares. The interest paid to depositors is slightly lower than the rate paid to shareholders. The reason for this? Money on deposit is a loan to the society, and depositors rank as creditors. As such, they come before shareholders in having a prior claim to the society's assets.

Investment in building societies is limited to £5,000 per person; husbands and wives are treated as one person and are limited to £5,000 jointly.

A point to remember about money invested with a building society is that income tax is paid by the society at the standard rate, and the income payment the investor receives is net of tax. This tax cannot be reclaimed from the Inland

Revenue, even if the investor is paying tax at less than the standard rate, or even no tax at all.

Here is an example to illustrate this point: if a building society is paying 3¼ per cent. on deposits, that represents all the return a man who does not pay any tax would receive. If his rate of tax were 5s in the £, the return for him would be the equivalent of 4½ per cent. If his rate were the standard one of 7s 9d in the £, it would be equal to his money earning a gross rate of nearly 5⅓ per cent.

Investing money in a building society is therefore more profitable to a man who pays a high rate of tax than a man who is in a lower tax bracket. Income received from a building society is subject to surtax.

Building societies use the money that is deposited with them to finance other people's home-buying. It can be taken for granted that money put into the hands of a reputable building society is as 'safe as houses'.

For absolute security, the investor should choose a society that is a member of the Building Societies Association, which lays down strict rules of conduct for its members.

Rates of interest paid by building societies are to some extent geared to Bank Rate, but they do not vary immediately, as do clearing bank deposit rates, with Bank Rate changes.

LOCAL AUTHORITIES

Local authorities will pay good rates of interest to people who are prepared to lend money on mortgage loans for a set period, usually terms of two years and upwards. The rate offered is higher than that obtainable from building societies, and although the interest obtainable at any time varies with changes in Bank Rate, the terms on which individual loans are accepted are adhered to throughout the period of the loan.

Big corporations usually offer a slightly lower rate of interest than the smaller ones. But all represent a safe form of investment and a good return on capital.

A point that has to be remembered is that income tax at the standard rate is deducted at source from the interest payments.

HIRE PURCHASE FINANCE HOUSES

With the growth of hire purchase in this country, finance houses are eager for funds to carry on their operations. The big ones—members of the Finance Houses Association—deal only in very large sums. But the not-so-large ones welcome deposits. The minimum amount is usually £50. Rates of interest that can be obtained on loans to these companies are higher if the money is deposited for a period of six months or more. A conservative company will probably offer 1 per cent. above Bank Rate for short-term loans, and an extra 1½ per cent. for a longer term.

But caution is needed. Much money has been lost by hire purchase companies which have not been run on sound business principles. If an investor is attracted by the higher return on his money which he can obtain by placing it with a finance house, he would be well advised to choose one which is a member of the Industrial Bankers Association. As a general rule, he should be wary of any concern offering more than 1 or 1½ per cent. more than Bank Rate. A higher return usually involves some degree of risk.

These are the principal channels for investment where capital is not subject to fluctuation, and the investor knows the terms on which he can get repayment should he need the money.

LIFE ASSURANCE

Life assurance offers a wide range of facilities for saving, and has the advantage that it can be paid for out of income. But one disadvantage that must be borne in mind is that if a policy has to be surrendered, some loss of capital is involved, particularly in the early years.

Life assurance falls into two main categories:

(1) Life assurance, where the sum assured is payable on the death of the policy-holder.
(2) Endowment assurance, where the sum assured is payable at the end of a certain number of years, or on the death of the policy-holder if he should die before the end of that period.

For a higher yearly premium, both life and endowment assurances 'with profits' can be taken out. This means that policy-holders will share in the profits of the insurance company with which they are insured. Part of the huge sums of money that are received in premiums each year is invested by the insurance companies. Their investment managers have the reputation of being just about the wisest there are. Of course, the amount of profit on investments that individual companies make can vary, and so therefore does the amount of 'profit' they add to their policies. A with-profits policy provides a means of investing, to some extent, in stocks and shares, through experts, and without worry.

Saving through life assurance obviously has more attractions for a man with dependants than for one without them. But the payment of regular premiums provides a disciplined form of saving and also gives the policy-holder certain tax reliefs.

The Government encourages saving through life assurance, and for the past 160 years has put its encouragement into the practical form of allowing tax relief on part of the premiums. At present, rebate at the standard rate can be obtained on two-fifths of the annual premium. There are two conditions to this. The yearly premium must not exceed 7 per cent. of the sum insured, nor may a policy-holder claim rebate on premiums that amount to more than a sixth of his income.

Once an endowment policy has matured, its owner is faced with the problem of what to do with the lump sum which he receives. Usually, when he receives it, he has reached retirement age, when income is all-important.

ANNUITIES

It is at this time of life that annuities become attractive. For the payment of a lump sum, life assurance companies will undertake to pay a guaranteed income for the rest of the annuitant's life. Or a married man can purchase an annuity that will be paid throughout his life and that of his wife if she should outlive him.

The scheme has many attractions for those who do not have to provide for dependants after death. They can be sure of receiving a fixed income for the remainder of their lives—with no worry involved. And, an important point in these days of high taxation, part of the income from an annuity is treated as return of capital—and no income tax has to be paid on that portion.

British insurance companies are considered the world's best. Their foundation is rock solid; but they also move with the times. If a person has a particular problem which is not provided for in one of their standard schemes, they are always willing to try and work one out to meet his special needs.

THE STOCK EXCHANGE

So far all the investments and forms of savings dealt with have been 'safe'—that is to say, the initial capital is secure and the return on it predictable within certain limits.

All have the advantage that no expenses are involved.

But safety of capital has one big drawback. In an inflationary period such as we have been going through since the end of the war, the value of money has declined rapidly. According to official estimates £1 in 1938 was worth only 6s 11d in 1961, when reckoned in terms of what it would buy.

It is the desire to keep up with inflation which has largely led to the tremendous increase in the number of people investing through the Stock Exchange in the post-war years. The number is now put at over three million.

What has the Stock Exchange to offer that the 'safe' schemes have not? The answer is the prospect of beating inflation by increasing one's capital.

To understand how this comes about, it is necessary to know a little about the stock market and how the Stock Exchange works.

When the directors of a company seek a Stock Exchange quotation for the company, they are obliged to make a proportion of the shares in the company available to the public. In this way, they are in effect giving the public the opportunity of becoming part-owners of the concern. If the company prospers, the people who have bought the shares—the shareholders—will have a part in that prosperity. If it should do badly, they will see the value of their shareholding go down.

However, if a shareholder does not wish to keep shares he has bought, he can sell them. There is no time limit. The same shares can be bought and sold again within the hour.

The Stock Exchange provides the means of doing this. Think of it as a vast market place, where stocks and shares take the place of fruit and vegetables, fish and meat; a market place where the law of supply and demand operates, and the price of things in demand goes up and the things nobody much wants can be bought cheaply.

Business on the Stock Exchange can be done only through members. These members are divided into two categories: stockbrokers and stockjobbers.

Jobbers are the wholesalers of the stock market. In the House—as the vast room in Throgmorton Street where business is done is called—they have their 'pitches'. They stand at these pitches all day, waiting for customers, much as a man at a market stall might stand.

Their customers are the stockbrokers, who act on behalf of clients who wish to buy or sell shares. But there is one big difference between a jobber and a market stallholder: the jobber does not know whether his customer wants to buy or sell. If a customer in a market asks "How much are the oranges?" the salesman knows he is interested only in buying.

In the stock market it is different. The broker goes up to a jobber who specializes in the type of share he wants to deal in, and asks for the price of the shares of the company he is interested in. But he does not say whether he is wanting to buy or sell. And the jobber in his turn quotes two prices. One— the lower—at which he is prepared to buy. And a higher one at which he will sell.

This difference in price is called the 'jobber's turn', and represents his profit. If the price is acceptable to the broker, he will say whether he wants to buy or sell, how many shares are involved. Then, simply by word of mouth, the bargain is clinched. It is on this way of doing business that the Stock Exchange's motto, *Dictum meum pactum*, is based: MY WORD IS MY BOND.

The transaction is confirmed the following morning, when jobbers' and brokers' clerks get together in the Settling Room under the Stock Exchange.

Only members of the Stock Exchange and their authorized clerks—all men—are allowed on the 'floor' of the House. A few years ago a public gallery was built, from which outsiders can now watch the Stock Exchange in action. But only watch: the gallery is firmly glassed in and the activities of the members, like those of good children, can be seen but not heard.

The Stock Exchange year is divided into 'Accounts', most of them running for two-week periods; a few are of three weeks' duration. The normal Account runs from Monday to the Friday of the following week, a period of ten working days.

Business is transacted within the framework of these Accounts. In practice, this means that a buyer of shares will not have to pay for them immediately. Nor will a seller receive payment. In both cases, payment is due on Account Day, which is the Tuesday ten days after the last Friday in each Account.

An exception is when gilt-edged stocks are bought or sold. Then, 'settlement is for cash', which means payment has to be made immediately.

Altogether, more than 9,000 securities are quoted on the London Stock Exchange. Many are household words with which shoppers on the High Street, readers of newspapers, and watchers of television advertisements are familiar. Others are small, obscure companies—tea and rubber plantations, and so on— that most people have never heard of.

DIFFERENT KINDS OF STOCKS AND SHARES

The capital of a company is divided into shares or stock units, which have a nominal, or par, value. (The word 'par' is simply Latin for 'equal'.) Most usual nominal values are 20s, 5s, and 1s. These nominal values rarely correspond to the prices at which the shares are bought and sold.

Within this framework there can be several different types of shares, which offer the investor different things.

First on the list are *Debenture Stocks*. Debentures are loans, and they are secured on the company's assets. The rate of interest payable on Debenture Stocks is fixed, but if, for any reason, it is not paid, holders have the right to demand that the company's assets should be sold to make good their loss.

Next come *Preference shares*. Here again the rate of interest is fixed, but at a higher rate than on Debenture Stocks, because the security is not so great. Preference shareholders, as the name implies, get preferential treatment: their dividends must be paid before those of Ordinary shareholders. And, if they hold Cumulative Preference shares, they are entitled to the payment of arrears if, when profits fall, payment of their dividend is passed in any year or years. These arrears, too, take precedence over the payment of dividends on Ordinary shares.

As the rates of interest or dividend on Debenture and Preference Stocks are fixed, the price of the shares fluctuates as Bank Rate and the general level of interest rates vary. So it must be remembered that a holder of either of these types of stocks cannot be sure how much he would get at any time if he wished to sell.

Next we come to *Ordinary shares*, which account for more than half the market value of the securities quoted on the London Stock Exchange. In 1961, that value was £30,000,000,000.

Ordinary—or equity shares as they are sometimes called—do not carry a fixed dividend rate. But they have the right to all the company's profits after the prior claims of Debenture and Preference Stocks have been met.

A well-run company does not pay out all its profits in dividends. It ploughs some of them back, either to reserve or to finance future expansion. Even though shareholders do not receive these ploughed back profits in the form of dividends, they still benefit. The assets of the company, of which they are, in effect, part-owners, are increased.

If a company does badly, profits will naturally fall. It may even trade at a loss. Usually, then, Ordinary shareholders will get no dividend at all. But if the company has followed a conservative dividend policy in previous years and has put money into its reserves, it may decide to pay a dividend out of these reserves.

It is for this reason that an investor should, when considering investing his money in a company, find out how many times the dividend is covered by earnings. Earnings are the net amount a company has available after all charges, including taxation, have been paid. And this is the amount that could, in theory, be paid out as dividend to Ordinary shareholders. The number of times the dividend that is actually paid divides into the sum earned, represents the 'times covered'. High dividend cover gives a measure of safety; the reverse when cover is low.

Although a few British companies announce their dividend payments in shillings and pence, it is more usual for them to be expressed in percentage terms. To those with no knowledge of how the Stock Exchange works, these percentage rates often seem much too high. The important point to remember here is that they relate to the nominal value of the shares, and not to the current market price.

Except in certain circumstances, which are subject to shareholders' agreement, the nominal value of a share does not change; it is fixed when the company is formed. The market price, however, is subject to the law of supply and demand and may fluctuate daily.

There are three main factors which affect the market price of a share:

(1) The company's record as a profit-earner.
(2) Its future prospects.
(3) The value of its reserves.

If all these are good, the price of the share will be high; it can be ten, twelve, or even more times greater than the nominal value.

Shareholders must, however, relate dividend rates to the market price of the share. For example, a company may announce a 20 per cent. dividend. Its shares have a nominal value of 5s: 20 per cent. of 5s is 1s. The investor is therefore, getting a return of 1s on every 5s share he holds. But the market, value of the share may be, say, 25s, so, in fact, the investor is getting only 1s on every 25s he has invested: equal to a return of 4 per cent. This return on the actual money invested is termed 'yield', as opposed to the 'rate', which applies to the par value of a share.

There is a simple formula for working out a yield:

$$\frac{\text{Dividend rate per cent.} \times \text{Nominal value of share}}{\text{Price of share}} = \text{Yield per cent.}$$

The yield on Ordinary shares varies enormously. On some speculative shares, it is as high as 25 per cent. On others, it is little more than 1 per cent.

When a share is on a low yield basis, it usually means that its 'growth' prospects are high. Experienced investors look ahead, and many are willing to sacrifice current income to hopes of steadily growing profits in the years to come. If their judgment is right, they can expect to get bigger dividends in the future, and also see the value of their capital increase.

Ordinary shareholders are the owners of a public company. They are entitled to go to the company's Annual General Meeting and ask the directors questions if they are not satisfied with the way it is being run. Normally, each share they hold entitles them to one vote, which they can use when decisions involving the conduct of the company's affairs arise.

In recent years, however, many companies have issued non-voting shares—they usually have the label 'A' shares. Non-voting shares receive the same dividends and other benefits as voting shares, but their holders have no say in the conduct of the company. Because their holders have no votes, 'A' shares are usually cheaper than voting shares. In general, the voteless do not suffer; but there is one circumstance in particular where they could. If their company were to be taken over by another, they could not protest effectively if they felt they were not getting fair treatment.

There is no royal road to fortune through the Stock Exchange. Money can be lost there more easily than it can be made.

Yet investment in equity shares does offer the opportunity to take part in the industrial growth of the country and so offset the effects of inflation.

UNIT TRUSTS

Probably the best means for a person inexperienced in money matters to invest in Ordinary shares is through a unit trust. The unit trust movement has grown with the increasing interest in investing that has been a feature of post-war Britain. By buying units in a unit trust, the investor is able to purchase a holding in a wide spread of investments that would be impossible for a person of average means.

Unit trust funds are administered by firms of managers, under strict rules laid down by the Board of Trade. The managers charge for their services. This service charge, also subject to Board of Trade rules, is incorporated in the price at which units are offered for sale or re-purchase.

Unit trusts are framed to meet investment needs of all kinds. In some the accent is on income; in others on capital appreciation. Amounts invested through a unit trust can be small; one accepts a minimum of around £3. And most trusts run a savings plan, by which regular monthly payments can be invested. The investor can choose whether his dividends shall be paid to him or retained by the trust to buy further units. The advantage here is that small amounts can be invested, much smaller than it would be practicable to invest through normal Stock Exchange channels.

Some unit trusts have introduced plans whereby endowment assurance can be linked to investment in stocks and shares. There are two main advantages to these schemes. The first is that the usual tax relief is granted on the premiums. Secondly, the value of the sum assured, based as it is on a holding of units representing equity shares, should grow as the years to the maturity date of the policy pass.

GILT-EDGED SECURITIES

Interest in equity shares has overshadowed, in recent years, the other great section of the investment market: gilt-edged securities.

Gilt-edged stocks are those issued by the Government, corporations, Dominions, and so on. The name gilt-edged comes from the fact that gilt-edged was the best quality paper, and once upon a time Government stocks enjoyed the reputation of being the best possible investments.

They have fallen from favour because the rate of interest on them is fixed. And as interest rates generally have risen, so the capital value of gilt-edged stocks has fallen.

Apart from interest rates, another force is at work in the gilt-edged market: the date on which the issuing body undertakes to repay—or redeem—the loan at par; that is, for every £100 nominal value of stock held it undertakes to repay £100.

According to the date on which the issuing body is pledged to redeem them, gilt-edged stocks fall into four categories: short, medium, long, and undated.

(1) Short—when the redemption date falls within five years.

(2) Medium—when repayment is due between five and fifteen years.

(3) Long—when repayment will not be in less than fifteen years.

(4) Undated—when the Government, or other body, says it will repay the loan on a certain date 'or after'. 'After' may never come, because it is unlikely that it will be possible to raise loans on such favourable terms in the future.

The most famous—or notorious—undated gilt-edged stock is $3\frac{1}{2}$ per cent. War Loan, which has dwindled to almost half its nominal value since it was issued in the First World War. There have been many campaigns to urge the Government to fix a date on which it will repay War Loan. It is a particular case, because so many of those who hold it are people of small means who bought it for patriotic reasons.

So far successive Governments have shown no signs of yielding. Their view is that if the terms on which a stock is issued can be altered in one case, they can be altered in others—and not necessarily to the benefit of the stockholders.

This underlines the great advantage gilt-edged stocks have over others: the rate of interest payable on each £100 nominal value of stock has the full weight of Government guarantee behind it.

The undertaking to redeem at par is also guaranteed by the Government or other body whose loans fall within the gilt-edged section. Therefore, if an investor buys a dated gilt-edged stock at less than par, he can be sure that on a certain future date he will receive £100 for each £100 nominal value of stock he holds. Thus, he can be sure of a definite amount of capital appreciation within a given number of years. And, as the law stands at present, capital gains are subject to tax only if profits are taken within six months of the purchase date. This capital appreciation aspect of gilt-edged investment is particularly attractive to people who pay a high rate of tax.

COST OF INVESTING

When considering the best means of putting one's money to work, the cost involved in the various forms of investment must be taken into account.

With the exception of some Government stocks, all securities quoted on the Stock Exchange must be bought and sold through a stockbroker. He charges commission for his services. This commission is reckoned on the 'consideration'—that is, the money actually paid, not the nominal value of the stock. For gilt-edged stocks the rate of commission is ⅜ per cent.; for the rest 1¼ per cent.

There is another charge. The Government levies a Stamp Duty of £1 per cent. on the cost of buying stocks; no Stamp Duty is incurred when stocks are sold. Nor does it have to be paid if the same shares are bought and sold again in the same Account.

Gilt-edged stocks are not subject to Stamp Duty. And on some of them it is possible to cut commission costs by buying and selling through the Post Office or through a Trustee Savings Bank. The stocks which can be bought and sold in this way are contained in the Post Office Register. There are over thirty of them, and they comprise all the British Government stocks, with the exception of the 'nationalization' issues—Gas, Electricity, and Transport.

The Post Office and Trustee Savings Banks charge a small commission for carrying out the transactions, but it is considerably smaller than that charged by brokers.

There are limits, however. Not more than £1,000 may be dealt with in any one transaction. It takes longer than through a broker, and the investor is not able to stipulate the price at which he will buy or sell.

TAX ON INVESTMENT INCOME

Another point about investment that has to be remembered is that in most cases where interest or dividends are paid, the law demands that income tax at the standard rate must be deducted before the payments are made. People who pay tax at less than the standard rate must reclaim from the Inland Revenue the excess of tax that has been deducted.

Again there are exceptions. Tax is not deducted at source from the interest on War Loan. Nor from Government stocks that are purchased through the Post Office or Trustee Savings Banks. But if they are bought through a stockbroker, then income tax is deducted before payment is made.

Interest on deposits in Post Office and Trustee Savings Banks is paid without deduction of tax. So is that paid on deposits by clearing banks and some industrial bankers.

On the other hand, tax is deducted from interest and dividend payments on building society shares and deposits and on local authority mortgage loans. It is important to remember that an investor cannot reclaim tax on building society payments if he is in a lower-than-standard tax bracket.

Many people who would like to invest on the Stock Exchange do not know how to go about it. If they do not know a stockbroker, or cannot obtain the name of one from friends, the London Stock Exchange will provide a list of brokers who are willing to take on clients. Otherwise, bank managers can arrange for securities to be bought and sold. They have to put the business through a stockbroker, but this does not lead to extra expense for the investor. Stockbroker and bank share the usual commission on a 75:25 per cent. basis.

CONCLUSION

It must be emphasized that there is no watertight security of capital when money is invested through the Stock Exchange. Nor, except on gilt-edged stocks, is a fixed income absolutely certain.

Because of this, everybody's first investment should be a 'safe' one. And these are the points to be considered in deciding which form it should take: what income the investment gives, how quickly cash is available in case of need, and how individual tax rates affect the income that is offered by different schemes.

Until a really secure 'nest egg' has been provided, nobody should think about buying stocks and shares.

After that, unit trusts offer a wide spread of investments under the constant supervision of experienced managers. For the beginner, this is a means of investment with the minimum of worry.

Another way of investing a little money without too much worry—and with a certain amount of social enjoyment—is to join an investment club.

These have become quite fashionable over the past five years, and are usually formed of people who work together, live in the same neighbourhood, or have some other common interest. Any number of people, from half a dozen upwards, contribute a regular sum. They meet at intervals to discuss how the money should be invested, and share the gains or losses.

A club provides a pleasant introduction to investment for the beginner, as well as the opportunity of learning more about it from the club's discussions.

There are two investment club associations in Britain, both willing to give advice on the practical steps involved in setting up and running a club. They are:

National Association of Investment Clubs,
40/41 St. Andrew's Hill,
London, E.C.4.

Association of Investment Clubs Ltd.,
31 Dale Street,
Liverpool, 2.

What about the man who prefers to back his own judgment?

If he is wise, he will choose the shares of a company he knows about. Or he will try to find out all about it before he buys. He will listen to advice and will ignore 'red-hot tips'.

If he chooses a large, well-run company, which supplies goods or services which will continue to be in good demand in the future, he should be able to watch his capital and his income increase as the years go by.

But he will also remember that share prices can fall as well as rise. If there were infallible rules for making money on the Stock Exchange, all stockbrokers would be millionaires! In spite of occasional allegations that they are, they are not.

INSURANCE

GENERAL

WHAT, in essence, is insurance? It is the system by which a man may shift the bearing of a burden, a worry as to what is to happen if something unfortunate happens to him, from himself to an insurance company. He pays a premium, or more often a series of regular premiums, and if the unhappy event against which he is insuring never happens, then these sums will be wasted, except that they may be regarded as having been the 'rent' for the storage of his worry. But he knows that if the blow does fall, his loss will be met, wholly or partially, by the insurance company. From the company's angle, if they can receive sufficient premiums from a sufficiently large number of people, they will be likely only to have to pay out losses of a fraction of those subscribers, and the rest of the premiums collected, after deduction of overheads, should leave them with a profit.

But surely, it may be asked, is this not very like gambling? It must be conceded that once, a couple of centuries ago, it was used very often for purposes akin to gambling. At one time, for example, anyone could insure the life of anyone else in the world. You could 'have a bit' on the King of Siam or the Chancellor of the Exchequer, if you liked! But this was stopped, firstly by the Life Assurance Act of 1774, which said that all life insurances should be null and void unless the person insuring had '*an insurable interest*' in the life he was insuring. Later, this general principle was extended, for instance, by the effect of the Gaming Act, 1845, so that in due course it came to be applied to every class of insurance.

Today, it is recognized, for example, that everyone has an 'interest' in his own life, and indeed his own health, for he may pay premiums to a company against the possibility that accident or illness may deprive him of the ability to work for his living. But if it is someone else's life or health that he wishes to insure, in what circumstances can he have that essential 'insurable interest'?

A creditor may insure against the death or incapacity of a man who owes him money. He has insurable interest in the debtor's life. There is also a recognized 'insurable interest' in the life of your husband or wife. Sometimes two people or more may have an 'insurable interest' in someone or something—for example, a mortgagor and a mortgagee both have an 'insurable interest' in the house with which they are concerned. And in the case of a manufactured food, for example, the manufacturer, the wholesaler, and the retailer all have an 'insurable interest' against it going bad and becoming harmful. Without some such insurable interest the insurance is void, or voidable.

It may well be asked—at what moment of time must this 'insurable interest' exist? At the time the policy is taken out? At the time of the loss? It depends on whether the interest depends purely on the contract between the customer and the insurance company, or whether it derives originally from statute.

For example, the Life Assurance Act, 1774, says that an insurable interest is an essential and it has been established that this interest must exist at the time the policy is entered into. In the case of an ordinary policy not directly under the control of a statute, the important moment is the time of the loss which gives rise to the claim under the policy. Unless the claimant can prove he had an insurable interest at that time, he cannot recover.

The amount of the premiums is fixed by the insurance companies. They are worked out on what is known as an 'actuarial' basis, a method of forecasting the law of average and how it will be likely to work. But competition between the various companies has its influence, too.

"Proposal Form."

You sometimes read of 'assurance' and sometimes of 'insurance'. What is the difference? In general terms, 'assurance' is the way in which a sum is fixed as payable upon the happening of something which is quite inevitable—such as death. 'Insurance' is strictly the method of arranging for a sum to be paid should something happen which may, in fact, never happen at all—a fire, for example. But in practice, both terms are often used quite indiscriminately, without misunderstanding, though the word 'assurance' is commonly reserved to apply to life policies, and 'insurance' is used for the other types of policy. Throughout this section, for convenience, only the word 'insurance' will be used, as including 'assurance' as well.

The normal contract of insurance is entered into by means of a proposal form being completed by the person taking out the insurance. The company, of course, supplies the form. In this he discloses all the relevant details from which the insurance company can assess the risk. They then, in effect, make the customer an offer—"We will insure you against this risk if you will pay us a premium of so-and-so." This offer may be accepted by the customer by his paying the first premium. As a matter of practice, the policy, which is the document containing the full terms of the contract of insurance, is drawn up later and sent to the customer, but the general rule is that the risk is covered from the payment of the first premium.

However, the customer may want immediate protection against the risk well before the company have completed their inquiries and agreed to issue a policy. And the company may be prepared to give this protection provided that they may withdraw from the risk if they wish to, when full inquiries have been made. In such event, a 'cover note' is given to the customer—a document evidencing a temporary and provisional cover for a specific limited period of time. At the end of that time, if the 'cover note' is not renewed, or the policy issued, the temporary insurance expires.

But, before he ever gets his policy, there are certain legal obligations on the customer which arise when he is completing his proposal form. As you may be aware, the general commercial principle is expressed in the old Latin term *caveat emptor*—'let the buyer beware'. Provided the seller acts in good faith and does not deceive the buyer, it is the buyer's own responsibility to see he has got all he thinks he is paying for. No more than this ordinary good faith is necessary from the seller. But in contracts of insurance, a different principle applies. The insurance contract is one described by the Latin phrase *uberrimae fidei*, which means literally 'of the utmost good faith'. And if either party to the insurance contract departs from this utmost good faith, the whole contract is voidable, *i.e.* can be cancelled by the party aggrieved. This is because the full extent of any risk must be known to anyone who is covering that risk. Any other principle would be manifestly unfair. The proposal form is the basis of the contract between the insured and the insurers, and it is a basic principle of the Common Law relating to insurance that this contract must be based on the utmost good faith and that every relevant and material fact should be disclosed.

Most insurance companies take care to ask a sufficient number of extremely pertinent questions to ensure that every relevant fact is disclosed to them, and as a rule wind up with some general question asking whether there is any other matter which has not been covered by particular questions and which would, if they knew it, affect their consideration of the insurance. It is most important that full and truthful answers should be given to all these questions. In a case which came to the courts in 1956 a man sued his insurance company for some £800 which he said was the loss and damage he had suffered as the result of a burglary at his house, and he claimed that he was entitled to be repaid this sum under the terms of his policy. The insurance company had refused to pay and the grounds of their refusal were that in filling in his proposal form he had not disclosed the fact that he had suffered a loss by burglary or housebreaking at a house at which he had previously lived when he made a claim against another insurance company who paid his claim. The printed statement on the proposal form was this:

'I have never sustained a loss in respect of any of the contingencies specified in this proposal except..........................'

The proposer left this declaration as it was, the blank not filled in. There was a good deal of argument about the possibility of some ambiguity about his simply leaving this statement blank. He had not said in so many words, "I have never suffered a burglary before," or words to that effect. He had not told a direct lie. But it was held that in view of this failure to give a complete and unambiguous answer the insurance company were entitled to treat the policy as void. The background to the case is, of course, the fact that if a man has previously suffered a burglary, that is a fact relevant for the insurance company

"Any particular hazards of your occupation must be frankly revealed."

to take into account. Clearly the insurers are entitled to know the proposer's insurance record. Some people and some properties are more likely to be burgled than others and they are entitled to know that the proposer may fall into this category.

The same considerations obviously apply to a proposal for life assurance. Any illnesses you have suffered or any particular hazards of your occupation must be frankly revealed. If they are suppressed there is a risk that you may pay premiums for years on a policy which may fail of its purpose.

Assuming the proposal form to have been filled in with the utmost good faith, the contract between the company and the customer is, as we have said, evidenced by the issue of the policy. Insurance policies are often extremely worrying, even frightening, to the layman, because they are worded sometimes in most complicated terms—often with whole sections in tiny print, and some-times with typed or printed slips known as 'endorsements' stuck on the back of them, which may appear to contradict the wording inside in some respects.

Let us therefore at least give the worried customer some crumb of comfort. If the policy is found by a court to have been ambiguous, the court will always place on the ambiguous wording the interpretation most favourable to the customer. In general, however, the appalling complication of some policy wording will readily be translated for the customer by the company or broker concerned, and the real reason for the apparent incomprehensible verbosity of some policies is that except where statutes have laid down specific rulings, insurance law is entirely judge-made law. And the wording of the policy is often governed by the wording of the judgments in the test cases of the past. Any departure from that wording 'lifted' bodily from those judgments might set up a whole series of further test cases, with consequent trouble and expense to all concerned, including the policy-holder. So bear with the abstruse wording on your policy—it may even be there for your protection. As has been said— it is always better to be long-winded now than to risk omitting some provision which alone could solve a future problem.

Most policies are worded to include a preamble (the names of the parties and the fact that they have agreed to enter into the contract of insurance), an operative clause (setting out the risks and events insured against), and several conditions. Among these conditions, there is likely to be one saying that a claim must be notified by the customer within a specified or reasonable time for the company to investigate it. There will probably be a condition setting out the terms upon which either party may cancel the contract, and there will often be found an arbitration clause, which says that in the event of any disputes, particularly as to the amount of the claim, the matter shall be decided not by the courts but by an arbitrator or arbitrators. In practice, this clause is very rarely insisted upon, but it is almost always there in the policy.

Regarding endorsements—where their wording differs from that of the printed policy, they override the original terms, for they are meant to be the special terms applicable to the particular policy to which they are attached.

In respect of most policies of insurance, the general principle of *indemnity* applies and must be briefly explained. First of all, it may be described as the provision which stops anyone from making a financial profit out of his own misfortune. You have a car, worth, say, £500. You insure it for £1,000. It is wrecked. You cannot recover more than its true value at the time of its destruction—£500. That is the general principle of indemnity, although sometimes the policy specifies that this principle is not to apply. For example, some policies have an 'agreed value' clause, wherein the value of an article insured is agreed upon and whatever its value at time of loss the agreed value will be paid. Again, there is sometimes a provision for 'reinstatement' where the company agree to replace the article specified completely, whatever the cost to them. Subject to exceptions of this nature, however, the general principle is that of indemnity as above stated

Two further doctrines need brief explanation, also, as they play an important prat in insurance law. The first of these is 'Contribution'. The principle of indemnity itself indicates that where a man has insured the same risk with two companies, payment in full by one will discharge the other. But this principle of contribution allows a company which has paid, to make the other company pay part of the sum received by the customer. This does not apply to personal accident and illness insurance policies—a man can take out as many of those as he likes and receive payments under them all. But it does apply to fire, burglary, and similar insurances.

The other principle that must be borne in mind is that of 'Subrogation'.

One meaning of this word 'subrogation' is that the insurance company which has paid the insured person's claim can take legal proceedings in his name. For instance, A. insures a consignment of carpets against risks of fire and theft. The carpets are destroyed by a fire in the warehouse where they are stored. The company pays him their insured value. But there is evidence that the fire was caused by the negligence of one of the warehousekeeper's servants and therefore that the warehousekeeper is liable for the tort of negligence.

The insured person may be quite happy, because he has been paid in full by the insurance company. But in such a case they can sue, *i.e.* take legal proceedings against the warehousekeeper for damages for negligence. They can sue in the name of the insured who must lend his name for this purpose. He is under no risk. If the case is lost the insurance company pays. He is merely the nominal plaintiff. The proceedings are actually begun and carried through by the company, who 'stand in his shoes'. That phrase picturesquely describes one meaning of subrogation.

Many people are apt to think that if through their negligence or other wrong-doing they have caused loss or damage to some other person they need not worry if that person is insured. "The insurance company will pay up," they say. So they will. But the company then has the power and the right to take legal proceedings in the name of the insured against them, the persons who caused the loss or damage. And if they win, the damages awarded belong to them. So in every such case if there is a right of action, *i.e.* if there is evidence of a breach of legal obligation, the insurance company will naturally and rightly take action.

Supposing a man has a motor accident, through the negligent driving of Mr X. He sues Mr X., who cannot stand up in court and say, "They cannot make *me* pay you any damages because you have already received, or will receive, a payment of damages from an insurance company." So, where a man has at any time certain rights both against his insurers and also against an independent individual, he may succeed in getting a cash award totalling more than he has lost. This is another case where the principle of subrogation applies. If, after being paid by insurers, the plaintiff gets further compensation out of someone else, then the plaintiff must hold those 'profits' in trust for his insurance company, to whom he must pay them later.

It will at once be seen that subrogation is but an extension or an application of the principle of indemnity. A recent case, adopting this principle, by means of it established that if a firm is insured against damages payable by it arising from any negligence by the firm's servants, and an accident happens through the negligence of a servant and the insurers pay the damages to the person hurt, they, the insurers, are entitled to bring an action against the servant personally for the amount thus paid by them. It would be rarely that the servant would be worth suing, under such circumstances, of course, but the right has been established.

But when considering subrogation, one factor is essential. No right of subrogation accrues to the insurance company until after it has paid over to its customer under its policy. And, of course, the customer must himself have had the legal right to sue, for the very meaning of subrogation is 'stepping into the shoes' of the customer.

There remains one other very important term which, as it affects the ordinary insured person directly and frequently, must be considered and explained. Indeed, it is little understood, and often leaves customers bewildered and angry after their claims have not been met in full. This is the term 'average'.

The normal policy which covers fire, theft, and so forth, usually does not contain an 'average clause'. If it does not, or if 'average' is specifically excepted under the policy, then it is simple. But if it does—what then? An example may help. You are insured for loss by theft, let us say, in respect of a valuable antique of which you are justly proud. You value it at £1,000, but you find that to insure it for that sum will demand a premium larger than you can afford. So you pay a smaller premium and insure it for £500. Then one night, a perspicacious burglar with an eye for antiques, makes away with it. You put in a claim for £500 under the policy, rather annoyed with yourself now that you did not insure it for its full value. Discussing the point with the insurance claims man, you tell him how lucky he is only to have a £500 claim and not a £1,000 claim. And you fail to understand why, once the insurance company know this, they are prepared to pay you only £250. They point out the 'average' clause. You only insured it for *half* its true value. You named its value at £500 instead of £1,000. Then half the value you put on it is all you are going to recover. And, try as you may, you will not recover more than £250. If you had insured it for £750, three-quarters of its true value, and the insurers found out, they would pay you only three-quarters of £750. Thus, if the policy is going to contain an 'average' clause (and not every policy does) be very sure that you are insuring up to the full value of the articles involved, or you may pay dearly for your thrift!

There are other general principles which affect the very large field of insurance law, but while there is no room here in which to discuss them all, one point should perhaps be mentioned. It is that which arises when the loss, and the consequent claim under the policy, arise out of an act which was criminal. The basic principle applied here is that which is a fundamental seen in many aspects of the law of torts, and it is discussed in full in that section. In general terms, it states that you may not make a profit or recover monies lost through your *own fault*. If you take out a policy on your own life and then murder someone and are hanged for it, it is hardly to be expected that the insurance company should pay your relatives in full! That is why ordinary life policies invariably contain a reference to suicide. Often, however, the policy directs that only suicide within a specified period, say a year, shall invalidate the policy. Taking advantage of this clause, as he thought, a very brave man by the name of Beresford, who had insured his life with the Royal Insurance Company Ltd, in 1925, found in 1934 that his family finances were in a serious state. Anxious to provide for his widow and children, he quite dispassionately and deliberately shot himself so that his family could receive the benefit under that life policy. The usual 'suicide within one year' clause was there, but this was nine years after the policy was taken out. The widow made the planned claim, but the insurers refused to pay. After much argument, the court held them not liable to pay, on the grounds that suicide was at that time a crime in law, and a man cannot obtain monies for himself or for others by means of a crime. It is important to note that all such cases depend on the exact wording of each policy. It may be, for example, that 'suicide while the balance of mind is disturbed', thus rendering the suicide not a crime, might have saved the Beresford family. But in that case there was absolutely no doubt that Beresford was both sane and courageous, and did what he did, deliberately and with full knowledge, and his family lost their claim. (Suicide is no longer a crime. See p. 646.)

This principle, however, cannot be carried too far, and it seems to have been established that it does not apply to instances of death by criminal negligence. A man with an ordinary third party motor policy may drive so recklessly that he kills another. He may later be convicted of manslaughter—obviously a serious crime. But the insurers will still be held liable to pay the relatives of the innocent deceased under the policy, because the criminal act was accidental in one sense. It may well be asked—if a man insures his own life, and he is killed by the negligence of the very person claiming the benefit under that policy, will the insurance company then be made to pay out in full? While not definite in the form of a decided case, the answer would seem to be 'no'.

As a final thought—can you take out a policy of insurance to cover any fines imposed by a Criminal Court? Most definitely not—because such a policy would be subject to the over-riding principle that no contract can be enforced which is contrary to public policy, and this it clearly is for it would defeat the whole purpose of punishment, as you will doubtless agree.

LIFE INSURANCE

Life insurance has been defined in several ways, one of the most clear definitions being simply 'insurance under which the insurers' liability is dependent on human life, or on the happening of some contingency which is itself dependent on human life'.

There are three basic types of life insurance—'term', 'whole-life', and 'endowment' insurances. The early life policies were 'term' insurances, for the company agreed to pay a fixed sum if the customer died within the term specified in the policy—five, ten, fifteen years, or whatever it might be. If he survived beyond that term, nothing was payable.

Under the 'whole-life' insurance, the company agree to pay a specific sum to the customer's estate upon his death whenever that happens. The only question, therefore, is not 'if' they will have to pay, but 'when'.

Under the third type, endowment insurance, the company agree to pay an agreed sum at the end of a fixed term of years, or earlier if the person insured dies before the expiry of that term. For instance, a man of thirty takes out an endowment policy to be paid when he reaches the age of sixty or on his death if he dies before that age. If he dies at, say, fifty, the whole of the policy money is payable to his estate. If he survives to sixty he himself collects the money. Thus it has been for him a form of compulsory saving.

This type of insurance is itself sub-divided. There is the pure endowment policy, which is really a form of investment. If the insured person dies within a fixed period, his estate will have to keep up the premiums until the end of the fixed period, in order to receive the ultimate payment.

On the other hand, the policy may be an 'annuity policy', which is in one sense the exact converse of ordinary life insurance. Here, in consideration of an advance sum paid by the customer, the company agree to pay him a regular income for so long as he survives, but nothing upon his death. This is really in order that a man with capital, with no dependents to provide for, surrenders that capital to the company in return for the guarantee of a fixed income during his lifetime, or for an agreed period.

Annuity policies themselves may be of more than one kind. The simplest is that where all payments stop upon the death of the person insured. Then there is the 'deferred annuity', used mainly for the provision of retirement benefits—the regular payments start only on the insured person reaching a certain agreed age. Further, there are what is known as 'contingent annuity' policies, where the income starts being paid by the company only if something specific happens—for example, to a wife is she should survive her husband. This type of policy is very valuable where the husband is living on a retirement pension which dies with him, and he might therefore leave his widow badly off.

It is now necessary to consider the risk in life insurance. The normal policy covers death from any cause—disease, natural causes, accident, and so on. But the provisions of the policy must be carefully studied when death occurs through the wilful misconduct of the insured person himself. It may, however, be stated that as far as a murdered person is concerned, being murdered by other people is one of the risks covered by the ordinary life policy. In that sense, murder may be an 'accident' as far as the victim is concerned! The suicide question has been already dealt with in the introductory part of this section. The vital question in all cases is 'what is the exact wording of the policy?' For example, policies occasionally say that in the event of suicide during temporary insanity, the policy shall be treated as surrendered at that point, and only its 'surrender value' (every policy of insurance has a 'surrender value' calculable to any moment of time) paid to the estate of the dead person.

With regard to 'insurable interest' in life policies, which we have already stated is absolutely necessary, it should be said that insurance policies can be assigned—i.e. transferred for a consideration, usually a money payment—to anyone else. And there is nothing against Mr X. insuring his own life, in which as we have seen he has an insurable interest, even though it is his intention immediately to assign the policy to someone without an insurable interest in his life. On the other hand, where the customer is not really the customer at all, but merely lends his name to a stranger in order to create a fraudulent insurable interest, the whole policy may be illegal under the Act of 1774.

When a life policy is proposed, the company who are going to shoulder the risk naturally have a number of inquiries to make to ascertain the full extent of that risk. This is where that principle of 'the utmost good faith' applies most strongly. However, in general, it may be stated with authority that the customer risks the subsequent total avoidance of liability by the company only if he *knowingly* misrepresents his state of health at the time of taking out the policy.

However, to counteract this, insurance companies frequently make the answers of the customer in this respect specific 'warranties' on his part. If they are then wrong, there may be no liability on the company, no matter how innocently the wrong answers may be given. The customer, for his part, may protect himself by qualifying his answer as being 'to his own knowledge' or some similar phrase.

Questions regarding past illnesses—medical history of the customer—these are facts, pure and simple, and must be accurate and cannot be qualified. Questions are sometimes inserted regarding the customer's 'temperate habits'. The answers to such questions must, of course, be taken on their own merits in each case. There is no judicial definition of 'intemperance'. Another question to which the accuracy of the answer is vital and unqualified is that of the exact age of the customer—it is obvious how material an effect this may have upon the risk to be undertaken by the company concerned.

At this point in this very complicated subject it may be helpful to sum up the points about the three commonest kinds of life policies: Whole-Life, Endowment, and Fixed Term (or Term Life as it is sometimes called).

A whole-life assurance policy is one which is not paid until death, the death of the life assured. If a young married man with a family seeks the cheapest way of providing a capital sum or an income, or both, for his dependants in the event of his death at any time, a whole-life policy is the answer. But he himself will never receive the money and he may feel that he would like to receive the capital sum when, say, he is sixty-five, or later. In that case he should take out an endowment policy, under which the sum assured is paid when he reaches a certain age—whatever age is agreed upon when the policy is taken out—or if he dies before he reaches that age, then of course the whole sum is payable on his death.

The premiums on an endowment policy are usually higher than the premiums on a whole-life policy. It is certain that the sum assured will have to be paid at a certain date at the latest, whereas if the money is not payable until death the assurance company may have the benefit of the premiums for much longer. Hence they are lower on a whole-life policy. The advantage to the policy-holder of an endowment policy is that he is not only providing for dependants after his death, but if he survives he is also saving for his own old age.

The idea behind the Term Life policy is to give insurance cover against death during a certain fixed period, usually a comparatively short one. Take, for instance, the man who is just about to start on his own in some business or profession. He puts all the capital, all the savings he can lay his hands on, into his new business. Maybe he also borrows. If his business or his practice flourishes he may at the end of, say, five years have something really substantial to show for his labours. If he died then, there would be perhaps a valuable asset for his widow or other dependants to carry on or to sell. But if he died before he had got his new business on its feet he would leave them not merely penniless, but also saddled with heavy liabilities.

So it is worth knowing that for a comparatively low premium, usually substantially lower than a premium on the other two kinds of policy mentioned, he can insure against his death within a short definite period, three, five, ten years or whatever he thinks it ought to be. If he survives beyond that period he gets nothing. The policy has exhausted itself. It is not an endowment policy. He will have paid his premiums and still get no money in return. The point, however, is that during the critical years he will have given his family the protection of the policy and because that protection is only to last for some short and definite time he can, as we said, provide for a large sum to be paid to them in return for quite a reasonable premium.

It is sometimes said in criticism of life assurance policies that even on an endowment policy when a capital sum is paid to the man who has survived for the period of the policy, he will not get much more than he has paid in. This is not really a valid criticism. He *will* get something more than he has paid in and if he takes into account the income tax relief which is allowed on premiums, most, if not all, of these policies will show quite a reasonable profit. But the real argument against the criticism is, of course, that even if he does not make a substantial profit, he has committed himself to what is virtually compulsory saving, a saving which he might not otherwise achieve if it was left to haphazard efforts and, more important, he has provided protection for his family against his untimely death. The fundamental purpose of the policy is protection of his dependants against his untimely death.

Suppose the insured person has a long illness, suffers a heavy loss of earnings and cannot find the money to pay the next premium on his life policy. Should he surrender the policy and take what money the insurance company would give him. In general it is usually unwise to surrender a policy. A surrender is likely to involve loss. The man who surrenders a policy will usually receive less than he has actually paid in by way of premiums. This is not to be taken as a certain, unalterable rule, because different insurers may vary and much may depend on how many premiums have been paid. But the man who surrenders may receive less than he has paid in. Moreover, he has said goodbye to the policy for ever, and if in the future he wanted to reinsure his life he would have to pay higher premiums because he is older, and he may not then be such a 'good' life from the insurers' point of view. In short, rather than surrender it s better to make every effort to find the amount of the premium and it is worth knowing that the insurance company may be willing to lend the premium. They may lend the amount of the following year's premium too. No company wants to see the policy fail, even though it may only make a very small profit for them. It is not good for their reputation for policies to be surrendered in this way and it is not at all uncommon for them to be willing to lend a premium or two against the security of the policy.

One interesting variation of the Term Life policy is the Decreasing Temporary Assurance. For instance, a man of forty-six could take out a policy for £1,800 for eighteen years, decreasing by £100 a year, for a yearly premium of only £10. (As rates may vary in the future, it must be stated that this was a particular policy offered in 1957.) The idea behind this policy is very similar to the Term Life policy, as it provides the maximum protection for the first year but decreases and ultimately vanishes to nothing, because as the years go by the assured person has reason to believe that his other assets will increase and money will be available from other sources in the event of his death during the period. It is usually cheaper than Term Life, because it provides for a decreasing capital sum.

WITH PROFITS AND WITHOUT PROFITS

Life policies may be 'with profits' or 'without profits'. The former entitle the policy-holder to a share in the profits made by the company; the latter do not.

"In a period of inflation it is better to have a 'with-profits' policy."

Thus, on a 'with-profits' policy, the company will every so often add a bonus to the policy. The bonus will be an additional capital sum. A policy with profits for £1000 may be increased by bonuses to, say, £1,500 over its full term. The bonuses will vary according to the prosperity of the company and also according to the economic climate. In a period of inflation it is better to have a 'with-profits' policy. In a period of economic difficulties, a policy 'without-profits' is safer. The insured person is at least reasonably certain of the actual amount promised at the end of the term.

The premium for a 'with-profits' policy is always higher than for a policy 'without-profits'. The choice is a matter for expert advice in the light of the company's future financial prosperity and the general economic situation.

ASSIGNMENT OR SALE OF LIFE POLICIES

The fact that life policies can be 'assigned' was mentioned above, and now needs some discussion and enlargement. Firstly, such assignment may be either 'legal' or 'equitable'. 'Legal' here is not used to contrast with 'illegal', let it be stated, but means a full and complete assignment in every way, as opposed to the 'equitable' assignment which transfers rights which are enforceable by law on fundamental moral grounds.

Whichever method is adopted, an assignment is a means of getting an immediate sum of money.

'Legal' assignments of policies may be made under either of two statutes. Firstly, there is the Policies of Assurance Act, 1867, which applies only to life policies, and which, though nearly a century old already, is still good law. Under this Act, the assignment of a policy can be legally effected by means of a written endorsement on the back of the policy, or by a separate document in the proper form set out in the Act and properly stamped. To sue the company on the policy, the person to whom it is assigned must give them notice of the assignment. The date on which this notice is given is important, because there may be more than one assignment of any policy, and priority ranks by the date on which notice was received by the company, in each case.

'Legal' assignment of a life policy may alternatively be effected under the Law of Property Act, 1925, Section 136, provided the assignment is to be an absolute one, and not merely something like a mortgage or other security. This Act demands that the assignment must be in writing and under the hand of the assignor, *and* that express notice in writing must be given to the company, though it may under this Act be given at any time, even after the death of the original customer. This type of 'legal' assignment, if properly carried out, gives the assignee the right to sue the company, and also allows the company to obtain a final discharge of their liability by paying the assignee. But the assignment must be in proper form and must be stamped.

With regard to 'equitable' assignments of policies, no special form is required—it may even be effected verbally. It may be done by transferring the physical possession of the policy, if this is done in circumstances from which the intention of the assignor can be reasonably inferred. Bare physical possession without some evidence of intention will not be enough for the assignee to found a claim against the company, as a general rule. A promise to assign, accompanied by valuable consideration (money or the like) will be a valid equitable assignment of a life policy. But a bare voluntary promise is not enough except in the case of it being made by a person literally on the point of death. In that case,

652

and provided the intention was clear, and physical possession of the policy is handed over by the dying man, the company will have to pay over the money due under the policy to the estate of the deceased, but his executors will be deemed to hold that money on trust for the holder of the policy. There is no need for any notice to be given to the company to complete an equitable assignment of a life policy. So, in fact, a legal assignment which fails only through lack of this notice being given may yet be enforceable in equity.

The next question to be considered is the priority between assignees of a policy if there are more than one. In the case of a legal assignment, the date of receipt of the notice is the vital factor, as has been stated. But in 1828, the case of *Dearle* v. *Hall* laid down the rule that by giving notice to the company, any assignee in good faith who has given value for the policy may gain priority over earlier assignees who have not given value. But their good faith, as well as their having given value, must be strictly proved, to upset the general rule that the date on which assignments were made governs the priority. It follows from the rule in *Dearle* v. *Hall*, that anyone intending to lend money on the security of a life policy should not do so before checking with the company that they have had no notice of any previous dealings with other assignees.

What is the effect of an assignment, whether legal or equitable? Any assignment other than to a person acting in good faith, who gave good consideration for the transfer and had no knowledge of any fraud, is bad in law if the effect is to defraud honest creditors of the original policy-holder. Assignments may also be void as against a Trustee in Bankruptcy under certain circumstances.

It is a further general rule, alterable only by express provisions in the policy, that the assignee of a policy can acquire no greater rights than the person who assigned it to him. So if the original policy-holder had, for example, failed to disclose a material fact so that the policy was voidable by the company, it is voidable by them against the assignee even though he knew nothing of the error. And if the original holder's fraud is not discovered, and the company pay the assignee under the policy in full, they can recover the money so paid from him if and when they discover the fraud.

If the original holder, after the assignment, obtains an extension of the policy, the assignee will have the advantage of this extension.

Then again, apart from his rights against the company, a man holding a policy transferred to him by way of security for a loan which has not been repaid, may exercise a power of sale or a foreclosure directly against the original policy-holder. By means of the latter, the original policy-holder may lose his right to have the policy re-transferred to him upon his paying the loan concerned. But it is important to note that the mere assignment of a policy does not of itself oblige the original holder to keep up the premiums, and it is usual to find such a term in a separate instrument or endorsement assigning the policy.

Upon the death of any policy-holder, the company who have to pay out may be in some difficulty as to whom they are legally bound to pay. The rule is that, provided they have had no notice of assignment, they may safely pay whomsoever produces the policy to them, irrespective of that person's obligations of trust, if any.

As has been noted, if the assignment is a 'legal' one, one of the consequences is that in law the assignee can give a complete discharge to the company,

653

irrespective of what the original holder may think, or say, or do. If the assignment is an equitable one, the consent of the original holder is necessary before a discharge can be validly obtained by the company from any assignee.

Under the Life Assurance Companies Act, 1896, companies who cannot be sure from whom they may obtain a final legal discharge may pay the sum due under the policy into court and let the rival claimants fight it out between themselves as to who gets the ultimate benefit. The same provision applies, for example, where the original policy has been lost, stolen or strayed.

It should also be stated that some policies contain provisions expressly making them non-assignable. It is therefore vital to check the exact wording of the policy in the fullest detail before any assignment is entered into.

Life policies may be disposed of sometimes by methods other than assignment. Nomination, for example. The policy-holder may nominate a beneficiary at the time of taking out the policy, but the nominee will have no legal rights unless the nomination was made under certain Acts of Parliament or it amounted to a declaration of trust. The company will pay directly to the policy-holder's estate. Of course, it may be made the subject of a specific legacy in that person's will. One Act, the Married Women's Property Act, 1882, has laid it down in terms that a policy taken out by a man or woman on their own life and expressly stated to be for the benefit of spouse or children will be enforced in those terms.

What if a policy-holder goes bankrupt? The answer is that the policy passes with all his other effects to his Trustee in Bankruptcy, even though, through his having failed to keep up the premiums, it may in fact be a liability rather than an asset. That is a matter for the creditors to sort out among themselves.

Finally, on the subject of life policies, the question of Estate Duty may emerge as one of immense importance. The general position here is that the holder of a policy on his own life can escape Estate Duty altogether on its benefits, provided that he assigns it at least five years before his death to someone else by way of an absolute gift, or if he assigns it at least five years before his death expressly to trustees giving certain named persons of his choice an immediate interest in the whole of the policy. Anyone who has suffered from the depradations of the Estate Duty Office will immediately recognize the vital importance of these alternative provisions.

HOUSE INSURANCE

One of the principal rules is that, unless expressed in terms to be so, property insurance generally is *not* subject to 'average' (which was discussed in the first part of this section).

Regarding fire insurance in particular, first, for the company to be liable, there must be actual 'ignition' and the loss must be caused directly (the actual term is 'proximately') by such ignition. But so long as there is loss through fire, it does not matter that the fire remains only in the grate. For example, where a lady hid her insured jewellery in her fireplace, forgot it, and lit a fire there and lost her jewels, her fire policy covered her loss. The origin of the fire is immaterial, whether it is by accident or by design. In one case where a ship was set on fire expressly to avoid capture, the owners recovered from the company concerned. But it is as well to note that subject to the express wording or the policy, explosion is not the same as fire, nor is spontaneous combustiou, although if by either of these means fire develops and loss is sustained to independent substances, recovery may be possible. Also recoverable is loss sustained from efforts made in good faith to quench a fire—the spoiling of goods by water from hoses is a common example of this.

Disclosure of material facts may very well be vital in fire policies. The risk may be materially increased by the nature of the structure itself or of the state of adjoining premises. Failure to disclose such points may result in the policy being avoidable, later, by the company concerned. On the other hand, except where the use of premises, for example, is made the subject of a warranty that it will not be changed in the future, a subsequent alteration and increase of the risk will not as a rule invalidate a fire policy. Often, however, there is to be found in fire policies an express condition that later alterations in the fire risk will be disclosed to the company and their consent obtained. Questions have been raised in several cases as to whether leaving of a house unoccupied for a time is 'an increase in the fire risk', but generally each case must depend upon its own facts. In passing, 'continuous occupation' is frequently found as a condition in burglary policies, though it is rarely found in a fire policy, in Britain.

Apart from provisions exclusively relating to fire policies, however, most private dwellings in this country are insured under normal comprehensive policies. There is an important distinction to be drawn between the insurance of the building and the insurance of the contents, although the two kinds of policy may sometimes be found combined in one.

The normal building policy taken out by a house-owner has a standard premium of 2s 3d per £100 of the value of the building. It covers loss or damage caused by a series of standard perils, including fire, explosion, riot, civil commotion, aircraft, storm, tempest (flood is customarily specifically excluded), burglary, bursting water tanks or pipes, earthquake, vehicle impact, larceny of fittings and fixtures, loss of rent (if the house is made uninhabitable through an insured peril), and also indemnity to the owner in respect of accidents to members of the public resulting from defects in the premises.

FURNITURE INSURANCE

The standard policy covering the furniture of a house—the contents generally, in fact—which is usually taken out by the occupier of a house if someone other than the owner has a standard premium of 5s for each £100 of value. It covers most of the perils listed in the house-owner's policy described above, and it also covers such factors as hotel expenses, should the house be rendered uninhabitable by an insured peril. It covers damage to the goods of servants, if any, sometimes of guests as well. It also commonly covers damages payable by the occupier after personal injury to servants, guests, members of the public generally, and even the insured himself if fatally injured. Further it frequently covers loss or damage to property normally in the house but removed temporarily by the occupier—for example, taken with him on holiday.

The occupier is required and obliged to insure up to full value in respect of the contents of his residence. He must usually specify any items worth, in themselves, more than 5 per cent. of the total sum insured. Moreover, the standard 'contents' policy will usually not cover loss or damage to his car, even if it is in the garage attached to the house.

Also with regard to dwelling-houses one does sometimes find special burglary policies taken out in order to cover items of special value which may consist of furniture. These are really more likely to be found covering business premises than dwelling-houses. A notable feature about such policies is that the company usually insists on a high standard of protection before they will accept a separate risk. This, of course, plays its own important part in the general prevention of crime.

As has already been mentioned, the standard comprehensive policy on the contents of a house does of itself provide some cover, but the householder must be careful to distinguish 'burglary and housebreaking' from 'larceny'. It is as well to ensure that larceny is one of the perils insured against, for this is the only way to recover any of the contents of the house 'snitched' by a lodger, a servant, or a visitor to the premises, as 'burglary and housebreaking' necessarily entail actual wrongful entry and the occupier will need protection from theft not necessarily accompanied by breaking in, nor, for that matter, breaking out.

A proposal for a comprehensive policy on a house or on furniture must state the full value of the property to be insured. In this respect it differs from a fire policy. If you insure your house against fire and the other risks which are included in the expression 'fire policy', you are not obliged to insure for the full value of the house. It may have a market value at that date of, say, £3,000, but you are at liberty to choose to insure it for only £2,000. It follows, of course, that if the house is totally destroyed, you can never get more than that £2,000. On a comprehensive policy, however, you are not free to insure for less than the true value. Suppose the furniture and personal possessions in your house would, on a fair valuation, amount to £3,000. If you merely insure them for £1,000 and someone breaks in and steals, say some rings and silver, and you make a claim, you then receive a visit from an inspector of the insurance company, who would probably see at a glance that you had not insured the contents of your house for their full value. In other words, you were in breach of the contract on the form of proposal which contains a clear declaration that you have insured for the full value. Such a breach of contract on your part would entitle the company to treat the policy as null and void. We do not say that they would do so. Many companies would be willing to pay your claim, or possibly part of your claim, if you undertake in future to reinsure for the full proper value of the whole of the contents. The point to be emphasized, however, is that they would be entitled to treat the policy as void and that is a risk which it is hardly worth running.

With this point in mind, how should you value the contents of your house? The answer is that insurance companies will not worry overmuch about the average householder getting precise and expert valuations. Most of us would have a rough idea about the present-day value of our belongings. This does not mean replacement value. The policy does not cover replacement value, it covers

656

the *present* value of whatever is lost or damaged in its present state. This means, broadly speaking, the price as between a willing buyer and a willing seller, not the price on a forced sale. The insurance companies will accept an honest valuation of the contents of the average home. If, however, you have things of special value, antique furniture, valuable silver, paintings, a library of first editions, and so on, then you would be well advised to get an expert valuation from someone qualified in that particular field. If you don't know who to go to, ask the insurance company, who will advise you about an independent expert, and his list and valuation can then be filed with your policy.

Incidentally, it is important to note that the comprehensive policy does not cover the full value of many things which are not furniture. The usual clause in the policy says that any article, other than a piece of furniture, a piano or an organ, is only insured to 5 per cent. of the full value for which you have insured all the contents, unless these items are specially mentioned in the policy. So this applies to silver, paintings, jewellery, furs, etc. Clearly, therefore, there is yet another argument in favour of at least a special list of these items, if not of an expert valuation.

The type of insurance worth considering, especially for small and valuable things, like jewellery and furs, is the All-Risks policy. A comprehensive policy, even if the articles are specially mentioned, does not cover the risk of losing something outside the house. The risks covered are only those specifically mentioned in the policy. Insurance against loss outside the home can be achieved by the All-Risks policy. If you take off your ring to wash your hands and leave it in a cloakroom, or your fur is stolen while you are attending a party, the All-Risks policy will cover the loss there as it would if you were at home. It is considerably more expensive in premiums, but may be worth considering for articles of special value, especially those which you may wear or carry.

One of the greatest advantages of a comprehensive policy, whether on the building or on the furniture, is that, apart from covering the serious risks we have already mentioned, it gives insurance against a possible liability to pay damages for injury to people who may visit you, either on a friendly call or on business, or to do work in your house. It must not be thought that you are automatically legally liable if your daily help falls and breaks her leg, or if an electrician who has come to work for you electrocutes himself, or if a friend paying a call trips over a defective step and hurts himself. The question of your legal liability depends on whether you were negligent: whether, for instance, the defective step was a danger which you knew or should have known and against which you should have warned or protected your visitor; whether the accident to the daily help was because you provided her with a piece of defective equipment to work with. The point is, of course, that you may not *necessarily* be liable for an accident to someone else on your property simply because it happens on your property. You must be proved to have failed in your reasonable duty of care.

But suppose the injured person or the dependants of somebody who is killed succeed in proving your negligence. In that event you will have a heavy claim for damages to meet, especially if the injury is serious or death follows. The advantage of a comprehensive policy is that the insurers will take over the defence of the claim and, if you are found liable, they will pay the amount of the damages up to the maximum amount stated on the policy. In recent years this maximum on most of the insurance companies' comprehensive policies has been increased to £25,000 for any one accident. Moreover, even if they are ultimately found to be free from blame, most people would be glad to be relieved of the worry and trouble of dealing with the claim and possibly fighting a legal action. The insurers will deal with all this and, of course, will pay the costs. Incidentally, it is vital that if such an accident occurs and you have such a policy, the insurers must be told at once. If you fail to tell them without the least possible delay there is the risk that you may lose the benefits of the policy.

As was stated earlier, the term 'comprehensive' is a misnomer, in that you are only covered against the risks which are stated in the policy. It is a common complaint that when an accident happens, people look at their policy for the first time and then find perhaps that that particular accident is not covered, that there is some condition which shuts out that claim. The answer to such a charge is to read the policy and, if a risk which you want covered seems to be excluded, to ask the insurance company whether it can be included. This is probably a counsel of perfection; most people do not read their policies, and even if they do, some policies are badly drafted and not at all easy to understand.

Expert advice on the merits of the various insurance companies or of a policy at Lloyds may be given by insurance brokers. An insurance agent is usually an agent for one particular company or perhaps more than one. It is hardly his function to give impartial advice about the merits of other companies or about a Lloyds policy. The broker, on the other hand, is not an agent for any particular company and it is his function to give impartial advice over the whole field of insurance.

INSURANCE OF JEWELLERY, FURS, ETC.

There are one or two factors to be borne in mind relative to the insurance of jewellery as opposed to other 'contents' of a dwelling-house or business premises. In the normal comprehensive cover for contents, there is usually a provision, as has been stated above, that any particular articles worth more than 5 per cent. of the total value covered by the policy must be separately listed and valued. This provision will certainly exclude expensive jewellery and furs.

But by far the most popular and satisfactory form of cover for jewellery or other valuables, the use of which is still further increasing all the time, is again the 'all-risks' insurance policy. This covers loss or damage of almost every possible kind, including accidental loss, theft, burglary, fire, and so on. The only normal exceptions are wear and tear and normal depreciation, neither of which are really applicable to jewellery.

The premiums are not unduly high, but strict inquiries as to the absolute integrity of the customer are insisted upon most properly by the company. More than integrity—the company needs to be satisfied that the customer is one normally careful with his property and possessions. Once obtained, the cover may be extended to include travel with such items to foreign countries.

In this type of policy, all the principal items are set out and a value specified for each item. This may not be the true value when loss or damage is sustained, but it ranks as the customer's estimate. Often it is advisable to have an expert certify the value for the purpose of the policy.

Regarding business premises dealing in jewellery, these are invariably made subject to the most detailed and stringent security measures—otherwise no company would accept the risk. Not only that, but there is a far greater temptation for criminals to steal such things as jewellery than, say, grand pianos—and indeed, when stolen, there is a far more ready market for jewels than most things. Further, business premises are usually unoccupied at night, when

"It is advisable to have an expert certify the value . . ."

thieves are more inclined to operate. Thus, the premiums and conditions are often high and strict for this type of insurance. They are, for example, frequently subject to inspection by the company's experts.

EDUCATION INSURANCE

Today there are infinitely wider opportunities for all for school and university education than ever before. Even so, to send a child to certain fee-paying schools (whether day or boarding schools) is a heavy drain on the parents' income, and even a grant for university education may fall far short of the child's needs. If the father dies young, the fees or the extra amounts needed may be beyond the widow's means.

There is a means of securing against this risk by way of education insurance. There are several types available to the parent. One is in fact a branch of

659

life assurance, called in this case a 'Children's Deferred Insurance'. The parent insures his own life until the child is twenty-one. It is agreed in advance that when the child reaches this age, any one of several courses is open for him to take. The child can elect to take a cash sum, or an assurance on his own life, or a future endowment, gaining the advantage of the premiums already paid by the parent, and thus obtaining far more favourable rates.

But though this method is frequently used in order to obtain capital for the child's technical education or trade apprenticeship, during which time capital must be available until earnings derive from the work after qualification, there are a few types of policy which have been developed more strictly for use by the parent in order that actual school and/or university fees may be paid.

The parent may, for example, take out a straightforward endowment policy, payable upon the child reaching a given age. If the child dies before reaching that age, the premiums are usually returned, sometimes with interest. In this type of policy, however, the parent cannot claim income tax allowance in respect of the premiums. A variation of the same type of policy ensures the payment of the endowment at the agreed age of the child, even though the father may die and the premiums in that case cease to be payable further.

Another type of policy is in the form of a straightforward endowment policy, payable on the death of the parent irrespective of the age of the child. Income tax rebate being available in respect of these premiums, the cost of cover may thus be considerably reduced. Again, this type of policy may be varied so as to ensure a series of endowments on the life of the parent—premiums continuing to be payable in some cases even while endowments are being paid out on others.

Then there is the straightforward 'School Fees' policy, where the premiums gain an assurance that the company will see that the child's education fees are continued to completion should the parent die while the child is still at school, making sure that his education will not only be completed but uninterrupted.

MOTOR INSURANCE

As the traffic on our roads increased steadily throughout the 1920's, many accidents brought to light the essential need for some form of motor insurance to be made compulsory, as many motorists condemned in negligence were found to be 'not worth powder and shot', with consequent serious suffering on the part of those innocently injured.

The Road Traffic Act, 1930, therefore, made it an offence for anyone to use a motor vehicle on a road without being insured in respect of his legal liability to third parties for bodily injury, and having evidence of that insurance in the form of a cover note or insurance certificate.

Once insurance was made compulsory, however, few motorists were content with this limited cover. Even the normal 'third party only' policy includes cover for the damage to the property of third parties. And many motorists adopted a 'comprehensive' cover, which included damage to their own vehicle and sundry other benefits of a minor nature as well.

It is important to note that the 1930 Act did not make insurance in respect of passengers compulsory except where they were being carried for hire or reward, or as employees. But passengers are covered by the normal motor-car 'third party' policy, all the same.

The scales of premiums took into consideration the occupation, as well as the motoring record, of motorists insuring, and to some extent even the district in which they drove. The condition of the car also had to be considered. On the other hand, consistently good driving free of accidents resulted in the introduction of the 'no claim bonus' system, whereby the premiums were materially reduced after certain agreed periods of time. The types of policy and scales of premiums relating to commercial vehicles were even more extensive and complicated. Again, there were now motor-cycles, which have always attracted a very much narrower market for obvious reasons—many companies even today will not touch this type of business at all. When granted, motor-cycle cover involves higher premiums, and many limitations such as not being comprehensive, nor covering passengers, nor more than the one named driver, even when increased premiums were demanded.

When claims arise, litigation being both long and expensive, insurance companies will often try and settle, whenever possible. And many companies have working agreements between themselves, which are known as 'Knock for Knock' agreements. These sometimes cause confusion to motorists and must be briefly explained for that reason. In the course of a year, let us say, many cars insured by one company will collide with many cars insured by another, and if every claim were fully investigated and some fought out in the courts, there would probably be little balance, in the long run, in favour of either company's recoveries and payments out. So the two companies may agree to let the loss lie where it falls, in every case involving them. No investigations into liability are made, no arguments as to rights and wrongs take place, and each company simply pays the losses (depending on the exact nature of the cover) of its own insured. The question which often arises from this system is that a man, quite innocent of any fault, may thus have a 'claim' registered on his policy and lose his 'no claim bonus' in consequence. It must be emphasized, of course, that it is a 'no claim bonus' and not a 'no blame bonus'. Still, where there is substance in an aggrieved customer's complaint, the discount is usually allowed provided that it is reasonable to conclude that but for the 'Knock for Knock' agreement his company would have been able without doubt to recover in full from the other company.

The provisions of the 1930 Act, in time proved inadequate. There were cases, for example, where a motorist used false pretences to obtain cover, or where he used his vehicle in breach of some condition in the policy. In all these cases, where the insurance company repudiated liability, as they were entitled to do, the third party was unable to recover, except if he was lucky, from the motorist personally. Clearly some further remedy was necessary. The 1934 Road Traffic Act, therefore, compelled insurance companies to satisfy the claims of injured third parties notwithstanding that they might be able legally to repudiate liability under the policy in question, save when the company could secure a declaration from the court that they would be unjustly served if they had to pay. Even this was by no means sufficient to prevent a number of injustices from occurring, however, and in 1946 the motor insurance companies and the

Ministry of Transport together came to an agreement, whereby a fund was set up from which would be paid all third parties injured in road accidents who should have had the benefit of the motorist's compulsory insurance, but who were unable to recover owing to that insurance being absent or ineffective. This is called the 'Motor Insurers' Bureau', and the only type of case it does

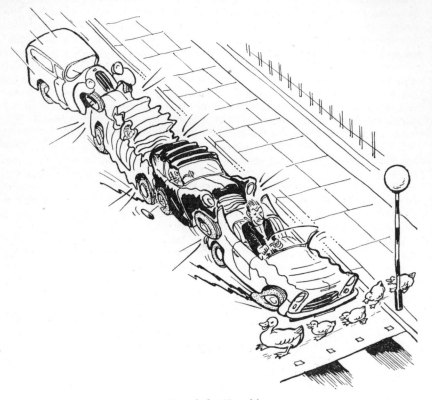

Knock for Knock!

not cover is that of the man injured by a motorist whose identity is never discovered. Even in those cases, sympathetic payments are frequently made by the Bureau.

The vast majority of motor policies are on an annual basis, and have to be renewed every year. As a matter of custom, there is usually included with the reminder note sent by the company to the car-owner a free fifteen-day cover-note. But motor insurances need not be annual, and anyone can take out a short-term policy to cover a summer season's use of their car, or perhaps a touring holiday. Premiums are usually proportionately higher than the annual ones, as driving is likely to be more concentrated into such short terms.

In 1960, the Road Traffic Acts up to that date, including the 1930 and 1934 Acts, were consolidated. Useful definitions appeared, to clear up problems which had arisen in the past. 'Motor vehicle', we now know for certain, does not extend to a diesel dumper employed solely on building roads, but it does include a motor-assisted pedal cycle—even when the engine is turned off!

Civil liability for breach of statutory duty is discussed elsewhere in this book, but it should here be emphasized that as the law now stands, a breach of the duty to insure will not merely make the owner liable to criminal penalties, but will also make him liable in damages for breach of statutory duty brought by an injured person.

The 1960 Act does not apply to police vehicles, local authority vehicles, Crown vehicles, nor to items like invalid carriages, but otherwise it applies to everyone 'using' or anyone 'causing or permitting anyone else to use' the vehicle in question. To be in this last-named position, one must be in a position to forbid the driver to use the car—one must be a person responsible for the car's care, management, or control. Assistance, such as lending purchase money for a car, or helping to pay for its insurance, are not sufficient acts to make someone responsible for seeing that a car is insured.

The insurance demanded by the 1960 Act must be with an 'authorized insurer'. It still need not extend to cover passengers, unless carried for reward, or as employees, or under a contract. It must be evidenced by a Certificate of Insurance, which is necessary to obtain a licence for the car at all. There is one way around the Act altogether, but as will be imagined, its use is infinitesimally small. One can drive without being insured provided one has previously deposited the sum of £15,000 with the Accountant General of the Supreme Court! Anyone who could do that could obviously afford a hired or chauffeured limousine, anyway!

The ordinary policy, going quite some way beyond the statutory demands of the Act, will indemnify the insured personally when he is driving other cars than his own, and also other persons when driving his, the insured's, car. This last provision can have occasional curious side-effects, as a leading case of 1943 served to show. It involved the noted film actress Miss Merle Oberon. Her chauffeur, a man named Digby, drove negligently, with Miss Oberon in the back, and she was injured. She sued Digby, who was found to be negligent, and secured judgment against him. Whereupon the interesting question arose— could Miss Oberon's insurers be made to cover the chauffeur's negligence and thus Miss Oberon's own claim? The company protested that this would make Miss Oberon a 'third party' in respect of her own policy. But the court held that this was indeed so. Her policy covered claims for injuries sustained by anyone, including herself, as long as they arose out of the negligent driving of Mr Digby, who was a named authorized driver in the policy. Actually, the insurers appealed successfully against this decision, but Miss Oberon countered further by appealing to the House of Lords, so important was the point, and they restored the original decision in her favour.

Complete change of ownership of a vehicle will put an end automatically to any policy in respect of it, however far that policy may extend to the owner driving other people's cars.

There are further provisions in the 1960 Act to cover the rights of hospitals and doctors up to specified limits, in respect of treatment given to persons injured in any motor accident.

Supposing, as is often the case, that the policy demands that the vehicle should be in a 'roadworthy condition'—is this condition effective at the start of the journey or the moment of the accident? It has been established that where the unroadworthiness occurs at the moment of the accident (a foot-brake failing, for example) then the policy is effective. If it is something like a failure of lights occurring some time before the accident, the policy is not effective. Knowledge of the insured is irrelevant on this point.

Some policies restrict the use of the vehicle to certain limited specified purposes only. A car allowed to be used for 'business and professional purposes' may not be covered for use by someone else authorized by the assured as a driver, but on their business and not his. Some policies exclude cover whenever the vehicle is used for a particular trade or business.

Other points of law established by past cases make it clear that 'the insured's household' means the household of which he is the head, and does not cover a man's liability for injury to his sister. A car insured for 'social, domestic, and pleasure purposes' does not cover a journey, however pleasant, that involves a business contact at the end of it. A policy which excludes use 'for hire or reward' has been held to cover instances where the passengers contribute to petrol and running costs, but not to cases where they pay the driver the equivalent of a train fare. And driving one's fellow employees to work for a regular weekly payment has been held to be using your car 'for hire or reward'. But a clause excluding cover where too great a load was being carried applies only to goods lorries or vans, and not to a tremendous crush of extra passengers.

ACCIDENT AND ILLNESS INSURANCE

There are three main forms of insurance under this heading which are customarily available to individuals, being graded in expense as regards their premiums, naturally. The cover may be against 'accident', purely and simply. It may be against 'accidents and specified diseases', or thirdly—the widest and most expensive cover—it may be against 'accidents and all sickness'.

A detailed proposal form has, of course, to be completed by the customer, in which his occupation and also his physical condition and medical history may be of particular relevance and importance. The normal accident policies are renewable annually, and as age increases, insurers are found to be increasingly reluctant to effect renewals, as not only does liability to illness and accident increase, but recovery time is apt to be materially longer.

A person in the light of his claims record may be found to be 'accident prone', and consequently an abnormally heavy insurance risk, and unless he has one of those rare types of policy under which the company binds itself to renew the insurance each year until the insured reaches a specific age, he may find renewal difficult to effect.

In this field of insurance, one facet is known as 'ticket insurance'. For example, when you buy a railway ticket, you can at any station booking office buy at the same time a short-term insurance for a low premium covering the journey in question. Similarly, many airports have slot machines in their waiting-rooms from which ticket insurance may be obtained to cover the flight you may be about to take.

Apart from the embracing policy covering accident and all sickness, however, those who are not content to rely upon the National Health Service can at any time take out a special policy to cover hospital expenses, so that they may enter a nursing home if ill or injured and know that the fees will be covered.

From the legal point of view, the first very important thing to be noted about accident insurance is that it is *not*, primarily, a contract of indemnity. It can be made so, or partially so, of course, as was done in a case decided in 1854. The policy in that case had two distinct contracts in it—firstly to pay £1,000 if the insured person was killed and secondly to compensate him up to £1,000 for expenses, pain, and loss arising out of an accident. The second was a contract of indemnity, the first was not.

The importance of this point has already been demonstrated above. It means that in a non-indemnity contract, the benefits named are payable regardless of the financial loss sustained. And there are further consequences, as you will remember—any number of non-indemnity insurances can be taken out, and there is not provision for contributions between companies. Further, companies who have paid out their customer cannot recover anything from any person at fault who caused the accident which gave rise to the claim under the policy.

But irrespective of indemnity, the Life Assurance Act, 1774, applies to all accident policies, and it follows that the customer must have an insurable interest in the life or health of the person insured.

The questions arising from the risk involved in these policies are many and complicated. It may first be asked—"What is an accident?" It does not of itself include disease, and implies that it had a cause dictated by chance. The condition of the person insured is, as has been said, important, as it has, for example, been held that where a person with a weak heart injures it while running to catch a train, there is no 'accident'. On the other hand, if a man stumbles while walking and sprains his ankle, that is an accident, for though he intends to walk he does not intend to stumble.

The cover obtained in accident and illness insurance may be limited. The policy may expressly say that the cover is limited to special kinds of accident only (railway accidents, for example). On the other hand, the policy may cover all accidents with certain express exceptions.

An interesting exception is that where the company excludes accident cover in all cases where the insured is injured due to his own fault. If the policy merely covers 'accident', then normally the negligence of the insured person himself does not bar a claim. But the policy may expressly except claims arising from accidents involving 'voluntary exposure to obvious risk' by the insured. Many cases have been reported on this point, and each must be taken on its own merits, but the legal arguments that can arise are extensive.

Another exception in a policy which may give rise to some argument is that covering 'injuries when the person insured is under the influence of liquor'. If this is the wording, it matters not that the drunkenness did not cause the accident—if the company show that the insured person was drunk at the time he was injured, they have been held entitled not to pay the claim.

PERSONAL LIABILITY INSURANCE

This field of insurance exists to provide indemnity against liability at law to pay damages for accidental injury or damage to property resulting from the activity of the person insured as defined in the policy—as a builder, a golfer, a cyclist, even as a private householder.

The protection available to the householder, whether owner or occupier, has already been touched upon in the part of this section dealing with house occupation and comprehensive policies. Probably the widest range of policies in this field are those issued to traders of various kinds. The limits of the cover are usually specified (for example, up to £100,000 per accident, or perhaps per year), and all legal costs and expenses in connection with investigating and contesting any claims are also normally included. The premium is naturally governed largely by the nature of the business in these cases. And a mere statement of occupation is frequently not enough, in itself. For example, the term 'builder' may cover anything from interior decoration to demolition of houses. There is ordinarily a provision demanding that the insured shall notify all accidents immediately, whether or not claims may arise, as investigation on the spot and at the time may be of vital importance should a claim later arise. The limits of indemnity should be high, because it is the rare but serious accident against which the greatest protection is needed.

There are many forms of personal liability insurance framed to cover various sections of the community. These policies normally exclude the type of cover found as a matter of practice in Motor policies, or Employers' Liability policies. But several of the types available are worthy of brief mention here.

There is what is known as 'Products Liability insurance', which protects all manufacturers, wholesalers, and retailers against harm done through a product being purchased or used by an ordinary member of the public. A hair-dye may cause a form of skin disease, for example, and food or drink may seriously poison a consumer through some unrealized defect.

Another class of insurance is that taken out by professional men, to cover any negligence by themselves or their servants in the course of giving the services they provide. These policies frequently contain an arbitration clause, for the reason that professional men will often be reluctant to defend, even where they should win, for fear of adverse publicity. Often found in this type of policy is a 'Q.C.' clause, under which all claims will be settled unless a Queen's Counsel advises that a win is sufficiently likely to warrant an action in any case.

There is a further small but lively market for insurers in the form of libel insurance, though these often demand that the insured bears a named fraction of any claim settled, for libels may be committed quite inadvertently by all authors, even when they intend their work to be nothing but pure fiction, if in fact someone alive is taken by others to be the model for an unpleasant character.

Another widely used form of personal liability insurance is that known as 'contract guarantee'. In many types of construction work, a contractor has to give an undertaking that the work will be completed on a specified date. All sorts of events may occur to prevent him from doing this, with the best will in the world, and contractors frequently insure with a company of their choice against the damages which will become payable should they fail to complete within the time demanded.

". . . certain family tendencies . . ."

Insurance regarding the weather is also useful to many people, and is certainly no joke. Thousands of pounds may be lost in agricultural projects, not to mention lesser losses to organizers of sporting and social events, should weather conditions prevent plans going through, and many individuals and organizations have been saved from heavy loss by means of a well-placed weather insurance.

It is even possible to insure against the possible birth of twins, which obviously causes a far greater expense to any household than one baby. Such insurance must naturally be effected in the earliest period of the pregnancy, and

667

premiums may depend upon certain family tendencies which are as yet unexplained by medical science but which make the risk materially greater than the normal statistical likelihood.

Finally there is what is known generally as 'Contingency Insurance', where the event insured against is unlikely but theoretically possible and which, should it happen, will cause an individual or firm a serious financial loss. One aspect of this type of insurance sometimes arises when a document of title to property, for example, is missing. Insurance companies, for a premium, will indemnify the document owner against any subsequent claim by anyone who may appear, holding the documents. From time to time, very serious potential trouble can be averted in this way, and with a satisfactory policy in existence, a sale of house or land can sometimes be effected when, without the indemnity, no one would buy.

THE RIGHTS OF THIRD PARTIES

Before 1930, injustices sometimes arose when an injured person who was covered against lawful claims by third parties, went bankrupt (or into liquidation, in the case of a company). The claim might be made, the person insured might receive the money in full from his insurers, but if he went bankrupt at the wrong moment, all the injured third party could do was to claim as a creditor against the general assets available for general distribution in the bankruptcy.

To afford a remedy for this, the Third Parties (Rights Against Insurers) Act, 1930, was passed, the primary purpose of which was to transfer the rights of the insured person against his insurers directly over to the third party, to whom the insurers would become directly liable.

It can, of course, only operate when two things have happened: first, the third party must have a valid right against a person or company who is insured against just such a risk (not a mere claim, but an established right); and, secondly, the insured person or company must have become insolvent.

The rights of the third party in such cases cannot, of course, be any greater than the rights of the original insured person. If the policy has a fault in it—if it had perhaps been actually repudiated by the insured person before the event—then the third party will have no relief from the insurers. The insurers can raise and use any defence against the third party which they could have raised and used against the original insured person, procedurally as well as otherwise—they can enforce an arbitration clause against the third party, for example.

It is, however, necessary to point out that the Road Traffic Acts also give third parties certain rights against insurers quite different from the 1930 Act. For example, Section 207 (1) of the Road Traffic Act, 1960, says that in a, motoring claim, where a third party gains judgment against an insured motorist, that third party may exercise that right directly against the motor insurers concerned. This right does not depend at all on the insolvency of the insured person. Provided the motorist had a certificate of insurance, judgment has been obtained against him, and the liability is covered by the policy, the third party may recover from the insurers the amount of the judgment, plus the costs of the action.

Further, if the policy restricts the liability of the motorist to a part only of the damages, the third party may recover the whole sum from the insurers, leaving them to pursue the motorist themselves, for the 'excess'. Moreover, the insurers cannot raise as a defence to a claim by a third party under the Road Traffic Acts, the fact that they may have cancelled the policy, or may have been entitled to cancel or avoid liability under the policy, although in such events, having paid out the third party in full, they may try to recover directly from the erring motorist. Thus it will be seen that in the case of compulsory motoring insurance, the rights of third parties extend even beyond those granted to them under the Third Parties (Rights Against Insurers) Act, 1930.

WILLS

MAKING A WILL

BEFORE ANYONE can make a valid legal will by English Law there are a few essential preliminary conditions to be satisfied. They are simple but important:

(a) You must have what is known to the law as 'testamentary capacity'. This means that you must be over twenty-one, and of sound mind. Under certain special circumstances someone under twenty-one can make a valid will. The exceptions will be described later in detail. But briefly they permit a valid will to be made by a soldier or airman on actual military service, or a mariner at sea, although they may be under age. These young people, under twenty-one, enjoy special privileges, and the nature of those privileges and the manner in which they should be exercised will be described later. Apart from those exceptions, no one can make a valid will until he has attained the age of twenty-one. Once he is over twenty-one he can make a valid will, unless he is of unsound mind.

(b) Secondly, it is an essential condition that you should *intend* to make a will. This may seem so obvious as not to be worth saying, but the point is that this condition is designed to cover the case where someone makes a will under duress, as a result of force or threats, or fraud. This heading, too, will be explained later when we deal with the question of the grounds on which a will may be set aside.

(c) Thirdly, the will must be made in writing. Here, too, there is an exception in favour of soldiers, airmen, or mariners in circumstances which will be described hereafter. But apart from the special privileges for them, the will must be made in writing. Writing, of course, does not merely mean handwriting; the will can be typed or printed.

Those are the three essential preliminary conditions. Capacity, intention and writing.

In addition to those preliminary conditions there are certain definite rules:

(a) The will must be signed by the testator, or alternatively it must be signed by someone on his behalf or at his direction. We will deal later with the manner in which a signature by someone else on behalf of the testator and

671

at his request will be effective. The general rule for all wills is that it must be signed by the testator.

(b) The signature must be at the foot or end of the will. In a sense this sounds almost too obvious to be mentioned and yet it is very remarkable how many people making wills put their signature anywhere except at the end of the will. There has been quite a spate of litigation arising out of the eccentric methods of testators who put their signatures all over the place. There is no point here in going into the varieties of these eccentricities; the rule is perfectly clear, the signature must come at the end of the will.

(c) The witnessing. This perhaps is one of the most important points of all. The testator must either sign his will in the presence of two witnesses or acknowledge his signature in the presence of two witnesses. This provision about acknowledgement covers the case where the testator has already signed his will and then suddenly realiz s the need for two witnesses, calls them in, points to his signature, and says: "This is my signature, I have signed this will and now will you please witness it."

(d) The witnesses, of whom there must be two, must each sign in the presence of the testator after he has signed the will, or acknowledged his signature in their joint presence, and they should append their signatures in the presence of each other and of the testator.

This rule about witnesses is probably the most important of all in the sense that more wills have failed through its breach than through the failure to observe any other rule. The simplest way of describing the manner in which

672

the rules about witnesses can be best complied with is to picture the testator sitting at a table and the two witnesses on either side of him. The testator should sign the will while the two witnesses watch him and then each of them in turn should sign his name while all three of them are still together. During this ceremony none of them should leave the room.

The vital importance of all three staying together during the signing and witnessing is shown by the following case. The father of two sons made a will leaving the greater part of his considerable estate to one son and only a token gift to the other. This was a deliberate choice and he knew exactly what he was doing. The will was signed at his home and was witnessed by a friend and the testator's housekeeper. It so happened that the testator signed the will in the presence of a friend who was his guest at dinner, and the friend then added his signature. Later on, after this friend had gone, the testator asked the housekeeper to add her signature.

Now clearly that was not in compliance with the rules, but on the face of it the will had been signed in the presence of both the friend and the housekeeper. However, after the testator's death the housekeeper told what had happened, told the son who had been left only a very small gift under the will, and he challenged it. As a result the will was declared invalid. Therefore the testator was deemed to have died intestate, *i.e.* without making a valid will, to the great advantage of this son, because then his estate was divided into two equal parts among the two brothers.

A will is probably the only document which by law needs the signature of two witnesses. The reason for this strict rule is that a will only comes into operation, is only legally effective, after the man who has made it is dead. Questions about various other documents may very well arise during the lifetime of the person who made them. True, they *may* only arise after he is dead, but the distinction between a will and any other document is that a will can *never* be operative until the person who made it is dead. That is why the law has long insisted that the signature of the maker of the will shall be witnessed by two people who were there together to watch the maker of the will—the testator—sign it and then that they should both sign while they are together in the testator's presence. It is a precaution against fraud and forgery; it is an absolutely strict rule, and as it is incorporated in an Act of Parliament, the courts must interpret it with the utmost strictness.

Now it is also important, though not essential in law, that after the testator's signature and alongside the signatures of the two witnesses there should be written what the lawyers call the 'attestation clause'. The attestation clause is simply a way of saying that the formalities about the signing and witnessing have been complied with. It says in terms that the witnesses were there together, that they watched the testator sign, and that they signed in the presence of each other and of the testator. It is not easy to state facts in words which mean no more and no less than is absolutely necessary. There are more ways than one of doing it but one quite common formula will be found in the model of a simple will which appears at the end of this section.

The reason why it is desirable to say on the face of the will that the rule has been complied with is this: if such a form of words is not there, if there are only the three signatures, the authorities at the Probate Registry or the Probate

Court will usually want one of the witnesses to swear that he was in fact there when the testator signed, that the other witness was also there, and that all three were together when the will was signed and witnessed.

If both the witnesses are dead or cannot be found, the absence of the attestation clause may cause some trouble. It is possible that someone else who knew the facts could swear. For example, a solicitor who had drawn up the will and who was present, but did not act as a witness. But there may not be such a person with the necessary knowledge.

It is also important that the two witnesses should be adults, that is, over twenty-one, and, of course, of sound mind. It is not legally necessary that they should add their addresses under their signatures, but it is useful in case questions arise later and the Probate authorities want to get in touch with them.

Another point to watch is that the witnesses should not be beneficiaries under the will. The law is that if a witness benefits under the will he loses that benefit. The will is not invalid; he is not treated as someone who has not witnessed the will, but he cannot legally insist on receiving any legacy or any benefit which may have been left to him under the will.

There is no reason why an executor named in the will should not be a witness; there is no conflict between being an executor and being a witness. The conflict only arises where the witness is left something under the will. He remains a valid witness but he loses his legal right to his legacy. The rule also extends to cover the wife or husband of a witness. For example, if Mr Jones witnesses a will and there is a gift to Mrs Jones in the will, the gift to her is void, and vice versa. The only exception to this rule is that if they were not married at the time when the will was made then the gift is not invalidated. Their marriage *after* the date of the will does not invalidate a legacy to either of them in the will.

Basically the making of a will is a very simple matter indeed; provided the few simple rules mentioned above are complied with, a will can be legally valid. Even the most obvious trap—that a witness cannot receive a benefit under the will nor the husband or wife of a witness if they were married at the time the will was made—can be avoided by the simple expedient of inviting two friends as witnesses who are in no way concerned with the benefits under the will. Yet it is quite surprising how many wills made privately—'home-made wills' as they are commonly known—are not admitted to Probate because of some defect. The trouble is that so many testators cannot resist the temptation to become rather complicated, particularly when they want to create trusts or life interests, *e.g.* when a man wants to leave something to his widow for life and thereafter to his children. So many such wills say, for example: 'I leave my house and all my property to my wife and thereafter to my children.' What does that mean? Does it mean that the wife only has a life interest, or does it mean that the property is left to her to deal with as she thinks fit? In fact the two gifts are contradictory. It is impossible to give something to one person and then to give it to another. What rights has the wife over the property during her lifetime?

To take another example. A man, by his will, left the house in which he was living with his family to his wife. He thought he ought to describe it and so in the will he put its exact address. Some years later he sold that house and bought another. If he had thought about it he would probably have changed his will, but he died leaving it unchanged. So no house whatever was left to his wife. When he died, the house he had mentioned in the will had already been sold. The house he was then living in wasn't mentioned at all.

Wills can appear to be simple and yet as soon as the will-maker—the testator—departs from the very simple business of leaving all he possesses to one person, or let us say a few legacies of particular sums of money or particular items like a gold watch, or a picture or a motor-car, and following it with a general round-up clause saying that he leaves everything absolutely to a particular person, so soon as he departs from that simple process infinite complications set in. (See section on 'Home-made Wills'.)

REVOKING A WILL

The rules are strict, and rightly so, because if it is alleged after the testator's death that a will has been revoked or cancelled, when he is not there to give evidence on his own behalf, it is very necessary that certain strict formalities should have been followed. For instance, it is not enough to write the word 'cancelled' in bold letters across the face of a will. It might have been written by anyone else. And so the rule is that any written revocation or cancellation of a will must comply with the same formalities as the making of a will. The testator must sign a written statement of his intention to revoke the previous will and his signature must be witnessed in precisely the same way and with the same strictness as if he was making a new will.

This is well illustrated by a case in the courts where a man wrote across his will 'THIS WILL IS CANCELLED' and threw the document into a wastepaper basket. A housemaid picked it out of the basket and kept it, and after the man's death that very will was admitted to Probate.

What's more, the tearing up or burning of a will does not necessarily by itself revoke it, because it may have been destroyed by mistake or by some third person with deliberate intent to get rid of a will which was unfavourable to him. There may be practical difficulties in the way of proving the contents of a will which has been destroyed, and a maliciously disposed person may achieve his object even though, if he is found out, he runs the risk of being prosecuted for this very serious criminal offence of destruction of a will. But very often he will fail in his purpose, because drafts or complete copies of the final will may be in existence, and in these circumstances, if the court can be convinced that the will was destroyed either accidentally or maliciously and that the testator had never actually intended to revoke it, they will consider and perhaps accept the next best evidence of the contents of the will. There are cases on record where they have admitted to Probate a copy of a will which has been destroyed.

The burning or tearing or otherwise destroying a will will only be accepted as evidence of revocation if there is independent evidence that the testator intended his will to be revoked, that he knew precisely what he was doing and meant to do it. There must be evidence either that he destroyed it himself, or

675

that if someone else did so, that he was actually present; that the will was destroyed in his presence, and at his request.

The best way of revoking a will is to make a written statement signed and witnessed just like a will. In the ordinary way this is done when you make a new will. The first clause in that will should be a statement that you revoke all previous wills, even if you are certain that the old wills have been destroyed, or even if you have never actually made a will before so far as you know. It is safe and certain, and certainly can do no harm, to begin a will by revoking any previous will or testamentary disposition. It is not at all far-fetched to suggest that you may have made a previous testamentary disposition or even possibly that one has been made in your name of which you are unaware.

There have been cases of wills being made and forgotten and coming to light many years later. Moreover, as has been said earlier, a soldier or sailor or airman has in special circumstances the privilege of making a will which may not even be in writing and he may well forget about it. It is important that when he sets out to make a will many years later, there should be no doubt about the revocation of any previous wills. The safe and certain way is to state in writing in a document which is signed and witnessed as a will, that all previous wills are revoked.

However, there is one way under English Law in which a will may be automatically revoked, possibly without the testator realizing it. The law is that marriage automatically revokes any previous will made either by the husband or the wife, unless that will was expressly made, in contemplation of that particular marriage. If John Smith is going to marry Mary Jones, and before his marriage he makes a will in which he says that it is made in contemplation of his forthcoming marriage to Mary Jones, the will remains valid after the marriage. But unless there is some such express reference to the marriage which

676

is about to be solemnized, and that marriage actually is solemnized, then any will made before the marriage is automatically revoked. The reason behind this provision is probably sound. It assumes that the will made before the marriage was contemplated would pay no regard to a wife or husband or children, and in that case it might be fairer for the family if there is no will at all and the estate is distributed according to the rules which operate on an intestacy. In Scotland, incidentally, the rule is different. There, a will is not revoked by marriage, but it is revoked automatically by the birth of a child of the marriage.

ALTERATIONS TO A WILL

Minor alterations to a will can be effected without signing a new will but simply by adding a postscript which has the technical name of a codicil. Major alterations to a will are best made by revoking the previous will and starting again, making a new will. But minor alterations can conveniently be made by a codicil.

As an example of a minor alteration, you have, say, left £50 to a friend and later on, because you are better off, or because you think that the original £50 was rather mean, you want to make it £500. You must not do that by altering the figure in the original will. It is a rule of law that the will as originally drawn will be admitted to Probate unless it can be proved that the alteration was made before the will was signed and witnessed. If it appears that the alteration was made afterwards, it is ignored, and the will as originally drawn is admitted to Probate. The broad and general rule is that once the will is made it cannot be altered. The only legal way to make the alteration is to add a codicil.

A codicil has to be made with precisely the same formalities as the will. The testator must sign it in the presence of two witnesses, both present at the same time to watch him sign, and who then add their signatures while all three are together. The witnesses to the codicil need not be the same people as the witnesses to the will, but there must be two witnesses who must follow the rules which are described above for the making of a will. Very often the codicil is written on the same paper as the original will. It appears exactly like a postscript to a letter. It need not be so; it can be on a completely separate piece of paper, but clearly it is desirable that the codicil and the will should be kept together.

HOME-MADE WILLS

There is no law which says that a will must be made by a solicitor or other legally qualified person. Although it is a legal document of immense importance, and although it is a document which doesn't come into effect until after the testator is dead, and is not there to explain it or alter it if necessary, yet there is nothing in law to prevent you from attempting to make your will yourself. Indeed, provided that you comply with the statutory rules which have been described in this chapter, there is no reason why you should not make an effective valid will which the Probate authorities will accept and on which they will grant Probate.

It is, however, necessary to give some very important words of warning on this point. First of all a will by itself is not an effective legal document; it does not become effective until it has been proved. Under English Law a will is proved by lodging it with the Probate Office either at Somerset House, or in one of the District Probate Registries which are established at most of the larger towns throughout England and Wales. In these District Probate Registries or at the Principal Probate Registry in Somerset House, the will is examined and if it appears to conform to the statutory rules for will-making it will be admitted to Probate. In other words a separate document which will be issued which will be the legal authority giving complete power to the executors to carry out the terms of the will. More will be said about this in a later chapter dealing with the effect

of Probate. The point which we now wish to make is simply that a will has to pass the statutory elementary tests before it can be admitted to Probate, and it is a sad fact that every year something like thirty to forty out of every hundred wills which are presented for Probate are not accepted because they fail to pass these tests. Those which fail are usually home-made wills.

If the Probate Registry throw out a will because of its failure to pass these tests, it is sometimes possible to get the Probate Court, that is a Judge of the High Court, to overrule the Probate Registry's decision and to accept a will. For instance, in one recent case a will was signed with the words 'Your loving mother'. The will was perfectly clear; it was obviously a will by a mother leaving all her property to her son and it was witnessed by two witnesses who said that they were present with the testatrix at the time when she signed the will. But, bless her heart, instead of signing her name she had signed the words 'your loving mother', just as if she was ending up a letter to her son. The Judge accepted it, and admitted the will to Probate. But that was a very exceptional case, and not a risk which we would recommend anyone to take.

Another kind of problem which will not prevent the will being admitted to

Probate, provided it is made in accordance with the rules, but which may lead to the purpose of the will being defeated, is where the testator making his will at home tries to be too ambitious. For instance, he wants to leave property to one person, *e.g.* to his wife, for life, and subsequently to arrange that the property shall go to a child or to children. It is terribly common for this to be done in such a way that the intention of the testator is completely frustrated. The will may be admitted to Probate because it apparently complies with the rules. But when it comes to carrying it out and trying to put the testator's intentions into effect the terms of the will make it impossible. Take, for example, a will made by a widow who had a married daughter, with a son who was about three or four years old. She was mainly concerned with ensuring that her property ultimately went to her grandson. But what she did was to make a will leaving everything to her daughter, and then to say that on her daughter's death everything was to go to the grandson. But these two provisions are completely incompatible. As she left everything to her daughter, it was an absolute gift and the daughter could do what she liked with it. The will was effective up to a point in that at least it could be proved. So the property could go to the daughter. But what the testator really wanted, which was that the daughter should only have a life interest, and that the capital—the value of the estate—should go to the grandson on the daughter's death, was completely frustrated.

The really sad thing about these problems is that so many of the people who make these home-made wills are completely unaware of the fact that it has long been a tradition in the solicitors' profession that wills shall be made for very low fees indeed. This does not mean that if a solicitor's client, who has been his client for years and is very well off, wants to make his will, the solicitor will not charge him a proper fee, *i.e.* a fee which will take into account the solicitor's skill and knowledge, will include a proper figure for the cost of the actual work done, plus overheads, plus a reasonable percentage for profit. What it does mean is that for others—people who are less well off, or people who are not established clients whom the solicitor knows well, it is the long established custom and tradition that the solicitor will be willing to make a will for a very small fee indeed. For example, for making a simple will, by which we mean a will which includes a few specific legacies and a gift of the bulk of the estate to one other person and perhaps a gift over to someone else in the event of that person dying, the average sort of fee is not likely to exceed three to five guineas. This is a figure which will certainly not cover the actual office costs involved in making the will, the solicitor's time in taking notes of what the client wants, the cost of the paper, the typist, the correspondence, and so on. Yet that is the standard custom and the vast majority of solicitors will honour it. If you want to make a will, go into a solicitor's office, tell him roughly what you want, and ask him what his fee will be before you incur any expense at all. In certain parts of the country it is known that solicitors will make wills—simple wills—for even less than the figure mentioned. In the bigger cities, where overheads are so much higher, they may ask a little more, but in any case it will be an extremely modest fee. It seems, therefore, there is very little excuse for anyone running the risk of making a home-made will.

Still, many people do, and many people buy will-forms from stationers and write out their wills on these forms.

Now there is nothing whatever wrong with these forms. The notes which they contain are comprehensive, and, in general, they are accurate. The complaint we have to make against them is that they do tempt people to be rather more elaborate than they would otherwise be, and it is elaboration which leads to trouble, *i.e.* lead to wills which either cannot be proved at all, or if they can be proved, cannot be carried into effect so as to observe the testator's real intentions. His intentions may be frustrated, simply because the terms of the will by law must be interpreted in another way. This is not to say that the law is obstinate or difficult; what it does mean is that if the legal interpretation gives A. substantial advantage, then although many people may know that the real intention was to give B. that advantage, yet A., if he is determined and maliciously minded, whatever he may know of the testator's intention, can insist on the interpretation which favours him being carried into effect. It is no use supposing that where benefits are concerned everyone who might be entitled under a will is going to be benevolent and kind and to say, "Well, it is quite clear that Uncle John intended this, and never mind what he has actually said. I will forego what he appears to have given me in favour of B. whom he really meant to benefit, but he didn't say it very well." It's not the law which is difficult on these occasions; it is those persons who, instead of being willing to allow what is generally known to be the testator's intentions to be carried into effect, will insist on the literal meaning of his words being carried into effect, because it is to their advantage. In fact, when people talk of the law being harsh and unkind in this situation, it is usually quite untrue and unjust; the real truth is that *they* are harsh and unkind.

In spite of all this adjuration that it is far, far better to get a solicitor to draw up a will, however straightforward your intentions may be, I feel it may be interesting and possibly helpful to conclude with an example of a simple will just to illustrate the form which a will should take. Here, then, is an example of such a simple will:

```
THIS IS THE LAST WILL AND TESTAMENT of me
DAVID BROWN of No. 1 Acacia Avenue, Any Town
in the County of Loamshire which I make this
First day of January One thousand nine hundred
and sixty-two
1. I HEREBY REVOKE all other Wills and testamentary
   dispositions of any kind heretofore made by me
2. I APPOINT my wife MARY and my friend ABEL BROWN
   to be Executors of my Will
3. I BEQUEATH the sum of Twenty Pounds to my friend
   JAMES EDWARDS of 50 Acacia Avenue, Any Town;
   my gold watch to my nephew JAMES, and a desk
   which stands in my study to my nephew GEORGE
   and my fishing rods to my nephew EDWARD
4. I DEVISE AND BEQUEATH the whole of my real estate
   and all the residue of my personal estate to my
   said wife absolutely
   IN WITNESS whereof I have set my hand the day
   and year first above written
```

SIGNED by the above-named DAVID BROWN
as his last Will in the presence of
us present at the same time, who in
his presence, at his request, and in
the presence of each other, have
hereunto subscribed our names as
witnesses

Signed: *David Brown*

Signed: *William White*
20 Acacia Avenue
Any Town
Grocer

Signed: *John Green*
30 Acacia Avenue
Any Town
Butcher

If any of the items which David Brown has mentioned in that will, and which he has given specifically as legacies to named persons, no longer exist at his death, then the legacies fail. There is no particular legal difficulty about this and if you leave your collection of paintings by Roger Fry—if you're so lucky as to have any—to a named person in a will which you make say twenty years before your death and at your death the paintings are no longer there, the legacy fails; that is perfectly simple. That is the only kind of difficulty which could occur with this sort of will and it is not really a legal difficulty at all, it is a practical one; the legacy cannot be carried out because the gift is not available and that's that. If the specific articles named are still in the testator's possession, the executors are under a duty to hand them over; if they are not, there is nothing they can do about it; that does not affect the validity of the will. The important part of the will, of course, is the clause which gives the real and personal estate to one person, namely, in this case, his widow, after certain specific gifts have been made. Real estate means his freehold land or houses, if he has any; his personal estate means everything else from a leasehold property down to the money which may be in the pockets of his suit. This is a simple will which disposes of what he has to leave once and for all.

WILLS OF SOLDIERS, SAILORS, AND AIRMEN

As was mentioned earlier, members of the armed forces of the Crown and mariners at sea have certain privileges with regard to making wills. The privileges are three:

(1) The will can be made orally, by word of mouth. It need not be in writing.
(2) The will need not be witnessed. Clearly, as it need not be written, it follows that there will be no witnesses in the ordinary way—that is two people who affix their signatures in the presence of the testator and of each other. But the privilege goes further. If the will is made purely by word of mouth its contents can be communicated to one person only and not necessarily to two.

681

(3) The person making the will need not be twenty-one. A legal will can be made by someone under that age provided that he falls within the privileged class.

Who belongs to this privileged class? It comprises a soldier, sailor, or airman who is on 'actual military service', and also a sailor who is at sea when he makes his will, and for him, the sailor at sea, the privilege applies whether he is on actual military (*i.e.* war) service or not. A soldier or airman whose domicil (*i.e.* permanent home) is in England or Wales can make a valid informal will purely by word of mouth and not witnessed, even though he is under twenty-one, so long as he is on 'actual military service'. A sailor has the same privileges on land, if he is also on 'actual military service'. (He may not call it 'military' service but the word 'military' has a technical significance in this context which

will be explained.) If he is *at sea* then it does not matter if he is on such service or not; the only test is that he is at sea. This privilege is not limited to sailors in the Royal Navy, but covers the Merchant Navy as well. It also covers administrative or clerical staff on a ship and includes women as well as men, *e.g.* a woman secretary to the purser.

The meaning of these words 'on actual military service' has been the subject of a good deal of discussion and consideration in the Courts. When is a soldier or sailor or airman on actual military service? One thing which is quite clear is that if he has been mobilized for the purpose of a war or some warlike operation, he is deemed to be on actual military service although he may not be engaged in actual warlike operations. For instance, it was decided in one case that a battery commander of the Territorial Army who had been called out on August 25th, 1939, which was before the embodiment of the Territorial Army, was on actual military service. So also was a member of the WAAF who was in charge of a balloon depot who at that time had never seen a shot fired in anger.

There have also been cases concerned with those who after the end of the Second World War were serving in the forces and were part of a garrison in an occupied country; for instance, in the British Army of the Rhine. The words are also wide enough to cover such military operations as those which were carried out against the Mau Mau in Kenya or against Communist bandits in Malaya. Neither of these operations was a war in the ordinary sense of the word. But the men concerned were in the forces; they were serving, and they were engaged in warlike operations. Members of the forces in Cyprus during the troubled period when terrorists belonging to the EOKA movement were doing such harm to property and to life would certainly have come under this rule.

We have referred to the fact that one of the privileges is that the soldier, sailor, or airman who comes within the classes described above can make a valid will although he is under twenty-one.

This relaxation of the basic rules applying to wills—rules which are ordinarily very strictly applied—has been made to cover the case of someone who, while on military service or at sea, is anxious to make a will in an emergency. It has an obvious application to someone who has been very seriously wounded and may not recover and who is anxious to express his wishes about his property. It is a wise and generous relaxation of the law that in those circumstances the man or woman concerned can make a will—a valid, legal will—simply by telling someone what he or she wants to be done with his or her property. As it can be done by word of mouth, there need be no document attested by two witnesses, and it doesn't matter whether the testator is twenty-one or not.

Nevertheless, there are obvious risks about wills made in such circumstances. The first is that the spoken wishes may be misinterpreted or inaccurately reported. The second is that if the testator has died the person to whom he has communicated his last wishes may have died too. So, although the privilege is valuable, and in quite a number of cases has been exercised, and the oral, unwitnessed will has been admitted to Probate, yet if the person concerned survives it is very strongly recommended that when he comes safely back to dry land he should make a written will with all the usual legal formalities as described above so that his wishes may be put on record. As we said, a good many wills made by soldiers and sailors and airmen on service, or by sailors on service or at sea, have been accepted for Probate on the strength of their communication to a friend or to their commanding officer who heard and made a note of the dying man's wishes. But although this relaxation in the law seems generous and wise, it obviously offers opportunities for mistake or even, possibly, in extreme cases, fraud. So, if possible, it is better to make a will which complies with the ordinary rules which, after all, are designed for no other purpose than to prevent mistake or fraud.

A further point which should be mentioned is that if a will is made orally under these circumstances and is therefore a valid will, it can be revoked orally with just the same informality. There may be the difficult situation where one friend will turn up to testify that John Jones made this will by word of mouth shortly before he died, but someone else will turn up to say that subsequently he changed his mind and revoked it. And, as you can imagine, such a conflict of evidence may lead to many complications.

It was mentioned above that any will can, under English Law, be revoked by a subsequent marriage or by Scots Law by the birth of a child of a marriage. The same rule applies to one of the oral wills made under the privilege extended to soldiers, sailors, and airmen.

Although some emphasis has been laid on the fact that the wills of people in these privileged classes can be made by word of mouth alone, such a will may also be made in writing, and signed without witnesses. There are many examples of members of the forces who wrote their wills in their pay-books and signed them but did not get them witnessed. If they were on actual military service at the time, and as we have seen, these words have a very wide and generous interpretation, those wills are valid. There have been cases where they have remained in existence for twenty or thirty years after the soldier in question returned from the wars and settled down again at home but had never thought of making another will. Perhaps he thought that with the end of the war that will which he had made had ceased to be valid. That is not so, the will remains valid because it was valid at the time it was made. And it may be very important for the man in question not only to know this but to consider whether in the light of circumstances many years later he would still wish that will to remain in force. If he thought about it he would very often wish to revoke it and make another.

THE DUTIES OF AN EXECUTOR

A will is the document in which the deceased sets down exactly how he wants his property to be divided up on his death. But by itself the will is not an effective legal document for this purpose. There is one more stage. The will must be *proved* so that a further legal document may be obtained which gives the executor or executors named in the will complete legal authority over all the estate of the deceased.

The Probate

In England and Wales, proving a will means that executors go through certain operations, which will be described, so that they may obtain from the Principal Probate Registry at Somerset House, London, or from a District Registry (and there are a good many District Registries in the principal towns of England and Wales), the document which is known as a Grant of Probate. This is very short. It usually is all comprised on one foolscap page. It states the fact of the death of the testator, the value of the estate as then known, the amount of death duties which have already been paid, and the fact that the executor or executors are duly appointed.

This document, which is familiarly and usually called the Probate, gives the executors legal recognition. The fact that the executor is named in the will is not enough in itself to enable him to deal with the estate. For example, the bank where the deceased had an account, the insurance company who insured his life, the Post Office where he had a savings account, and all the companies in which he held stocks or shares, are not prepared to read the will and accept that as authority to transfer the money or the shares into the name of the executor or to follow his directions. They want to know that the will complies with the statutory rules which have been described and that the executors named in the will are legally and validly appointed. Once the Probate Registry issues a Grant of Probate they know they are absolutely safe in acting upon it and paying to the executors therein named all the money and all the other property to which the deceased was entitled. In many cases, of course, the executors will not ask that the money should be paid to them, but that it should be paid direct to persons who may be entitled to it under the will. But the banks, insurance companies, the other companies, and so on, are not concerned about that. Once Probate has been granted they will implicitly follow the executor's directions. It is his responsibility from then on. He has the legal power and the legal responsibility.

It should be mentioned here that when the estate is very small indeed some of these concerns may not insist on Probate being obtained before they will distribute such assets of the deceased as they have. For example, the Post Office, when presented with a will in which a deceased man has left his widow all he has in the Post Office Savings Bank, will very often be willing to pay it to her provided the amount is not more than £100 or thereabouts. Some insurance companies may be willing to act on the will alone in such circumstances where the amount of money is very small. So will some employers where they have to administer a pension scheme and some grant is due to the deceased person under the scheme. They do this when it is quite clear that the estate is very small indeed and only small sums of money are involved. In other words they are willing to take a risk of doing the wrong thing, and they will not put the widow in such a case to the trouble of proving the will. This, however, is exceptional and it is only mentioned simply to tell those who may be concerned with very small estates that it may not always be absolutely necessary to prove the will. In the vast majority of cases, however, it is necessary.

The testator's estate

Obtaining a Grant of Probate may sound a strange and formidable operation. In fact, the actual mechanics of getting a Grant are not in the least difficult. What may make it difficult is to find out enough about the affairs of the deceased person. This is the point at which to urge everyone who makes a will to put with his will a list of the property which he owns at that time, and to try to keep it up to date. The Solicitors' Law Stationery Society, a well-known firm which supplies solicitors and barristers with many of the materials which they need for their work, publish a useful little book which bears the title *My Estate*. The particular merit of this little book is that it contains headings under which items may be entered, and so it serves as a reminder to people of the kind of things they ought to put down. It is not *necessary* to have such a little book. You can make your own list on your own pieces of paper. The book is just a helpful guide. The point is that you ought to prepare a separate list on which you put down the freehold property you may have, any leasehold property (and these two headings will cover houses and land), then a separate heading for stocks and shares, a separate heading for insurance policies, another for investments like National Savings Certificates or money in the Trustee Savings Bank, or the Post Office Savings Bank, and so on. It's not really very difficult for the testator to prepare this list and to keep it up to date, and it is of enormous help to those who, after he is dead, when he is no longer there to speak for himself, have to try to prepare a statement of what he owned.

In order to prove the will the executor's first duty is to prepare such a list of all that the testator owned. Everything must go down on it. All the assets already mentioned, and in addition, furniture, ornaments, clothes, personal possessions like motor-cars, books, pictures, and so on.

The Inland Revenue Affidavit

These items have to be entered on a form which is called the Inland Revenue Affidavit. It must be on the right form, and there are a good many different forms, varying according to the kind of estate which the testator left, *e.g.* whether he owned land or houses or shares, etc. But whichever particular form is appropriate, the basis is that it is a complete list of all the testator owned at the date of his death, together with the value of each item. The purpose, of course, is to enable the Inland Revenue to work out the amount of death duties which are payable out of the deceased's estate. It must be filled in and filed with the Inland Revenue, even though no duties are payable, owing, for instance, to the smallness of the estate. The rates of duty are set out later. The essential point is that, whatever the value, the Inland Revenue Affidavit must be filled in and must be testified to on oath in every case. That is why it is called an affidavit. It is not simply a form to be filled in. It is sworn to as a true statement and, if it is false, the executor may face an accusation of perjury.

One of the worst headaches for the executor may be to decide how he is going to value the property. Some items, of course, are easy; cash in the bank on current account or deposit account is simply the amount of that cash. Money in National Savings Certificates or in the Trustee Savings Bank or the Post Office Savings Bank, will be valued by the Post Office or the bank and an accurate figure given. Stocks and shares which are quoted on the Stock Exchange are to be valued in accordance with an established formula. For example, if the testator, let us say, had 100 shares of nominal £1 value in a particular company, and on the date of his death they were quoted on the Stock Exchange at 34*s* to 36*s*, that is to say the selling price was 34*s* and the buying price 36*s*, the value for the purposes of the Inland Revenue Affidavit is 34*s* 6*d*. The formula is to take the difference between the two prices, *i.e.* 2*s*, to divide it by a quarter and to add a quarter to the lower price. A quarter of 2*s* is 6*d* and so the value for the purposes of the affidavit is 34*s* 6*d*.

The value of land or houses may be more difficult to ascertain. If the house had recently been bought it might be reasonable to insert the purchase price of the house, but if it had been bought some time ago values may have changed, the character of the neighbourhood may have changed, the value may have gone up or down. An executor with considerable local knowledge may be able to put a value on the property himself. If not, it may be essential for him to get a valuation from a local estate agent and surveyor. Then furniture, clothes, and so on, may present a problem. If there is nothing of particular value the Inland Revenue authorities are not likely to worry and will accept some reasonable round figure. How far it is necessary for the executor to obtain expert professional assistance may depend very much upon the attitude of the Inland Revenue authorities. They have considerable discretion and they will decide in every particular case, looking at the value of the estate as a whole, whether they would accept the executor's figures or whether they will want them to be backed up by expert professional valuation. Much will depend upon the total value of the estate.

If there is money available to pay for expert help it is important for every executor to know that he is legally entitled to consult a solicitor, a surveyor and valuer, a stockbroker, and to obtain any other assistance he may reasonably need, and pay their fees out of the estate. He is not expected to bear these costs out of his own pocket. He himself is not entitled to charge any fee for his work unless the will provides for it, but he is allowed to pay for necessary expert advice, and recover the cost from the estate.

The Inland Revenue Affidavit must also contain a list of the debts which the deceased owed at the date of his death. These may vary from housekeeping expenses to substantial bills for things which he had bought before his death. Every debt which he owed ought to go into the affidavit because it is deductible from his total estate, and thus has an important bearing upon the amount of duty for which the estate is liable. An essential expense, of course, will always be the funeral expenses. They are a first charge on the estate. The executor will usually pay them, but he will, of course, recoup himself out of the assets of the estate as he gets them in and under his control.

Any executor who consults a solicitor will have complete advice and guidance on every step which he takes. What is more, the solicitor will be able to arrange for him to get an advance of money either from the bank where the deceased kept an account or from other sources, so that the executor can have at call a supply of ready cash with which to meet and deal with the debts before he gets under his control the property which the deceased left.

Estate Duty

The object of the Inland Revenue Affidavit is primarily to enable the Inland Revenue authorities to assess the amount of estate duty which is payable. Rates

687

of estate duty may vary from year to year as they are fixed in each year's budget which, of course, is always followed by the Finance Act which gives statutory sanction to the budget. The rates applicable on a death occurring in the financial year 1962–63 are set out at the end of this section.

Duty is payable on all property which passes or is deemed to pass on the death, and one of the effects of those words 'deemed to pass' means that the property passing on death can include among other things gifts made by the deceased within five years of his death (or indeed at any time if he actually retained some personal financial interest in the subject matter of his gift). For example, if Jones dies in 1961 and two years before that had given to his son shares to the value of £5,000, and left an estate worth, say, £15,000 to his wife by his will, the son would have to pay a substantial sum by way of estate duty on the gift to him made two years ago. This might come as rather a blow to the recipient of such a gift who was unaware of this law, especially as the rate of duty would be the rate appropriate to the *whole* estate, not just to the £5,000. It is therefore worth knowing that if anyone receives a gift of this kind he can cover the risk of having to meet substantial estate duty by taking out a policy of insurance against the possibility of the death of the giver within five years.

This five-year rule is, of course, designed to prevent the avoidance of duty by the simple device of a man's transferring his property to the persons whom he intends to leave it to on his death and coming to a private arrangement with them that they will in fact let him have the use of the property for the rest of his life.

So, on all gifts made within five years of the donor's death, estate duty was payable in full with certain exceptions.

These exceptions are as follows:

(a) If the gift is made to charity it will escape duty if it is made more than one year before the death of the donor.

(b) A gift made in consideration of marriage is exempt. Therefore if the gift of £5,000 mentioned above had been given to the son on the occasion of getting married, he could accept it knowing that even if his father were to die the next day it would not form part of the father's estate for death duty purposes and there would be no duty to pay.

(c) The gifts may also be exempted if they form part of the giver's normal expenditure. This, however, is a comparatively rare matter.

The severe impact of the five-year rule was mitigated a little by the Finance Act of 1960. The relevant section (Section 64) provides for a graduation of the scale of duty. If the giver dies in the first or second year after the gift, duty is payable in full. If, however, he dies in the third, fourth, or last year of the five-year period the principal value of the property is to be reduced for estate duty purposes as follows:

(a) By 15 per cent. of the principal value if the death takes place in the third year.

(b) By 30 per cent. if the death takes place in the fourth year.

(c) By 60 per cent. if the death takes place in the fifth year.

Thus, in effect, duty is reduced because the value of the property is deemed to be reduced for the purposes of estate duty.

Debts

One of the executor's problems is to know what debts may be outstanding. He will know, of course, about the bills which the creditors have sent in and which are among the deceased's papers. How can he be certain that there are not other debts? When can he safely distribute the estate among the beneficiaries feeling confident that he has paid all the debts and is not likely to receive a claim after he has wound up the estate? To protect himself against this risk, that is, if he thinks there is a risk, he should issue advertisements requiring any person concerned to send particulars of his claim to him, say, within two months after the date specified in the advertisement. The advertisement ought to appear in the *London Gazette*, and although there is no rule about it, it would be very desirable that it should also appear in some other newspaper or newspapers which the executor can select at his discretion. He would be wise to choose also a national newspaper, *e.g. The Times*, the *Daily Telegraph*, and the *Guardian*. If the testator owned land or houses the advertisement should appear also in a local newspaper circulating in the district where that property lies. If the deceased person had business interests in other parts of the country, he should see to it that advertisements appear in newspapers circulating in that part of the country.

At the end of the time specified in the advertisement for sending in claims, the executor is free to divide up the estate after paying all the debts or claims of which he has notice.

If he actually knows of a debt, but the creditor has not replied to the advertisement he must, of course, pay it. He must also pay late claims if there is still money in his hands with which to do so.

The advertisement protects him against personal liability for claims of which he had no knowledge and which have not been sent to him within the time stated in the advertisement. There is no rule of law that he *must* advertise, but he is wise to do so if he thinks there may be creditors he doesn't know about, because the fact of the advertisement will be a substantial protection to him against later claims.

From this account of the executor's duties certain clear points emerge. He must prove the will, he must pay the debts, he must distribute the estate among the beneficiaries according to the will. In a sense these are the most important, but there is one primary duty which has not yet been mentioned. It may be obvious, but it is not generally realized that it is the executor's duty, the first of all his duties, to arrange for the burial or the cremation of the testator whose estate is now in his charge.

A question which often is asked is whether a direction expressed in the will that the testator's body should be cremated is legally binding on the executor. The answer is that it is not, however imperatively it may be expressed. The executor is legally entitled, if he so wishes, to disregard that direction. If, for example, the surviving members of the family have strong views against cremation, the executor may lawfully pay regard to them and arrange for burial instead. It is, however, stated on good authority that if the will contains a direction *against* cremation, that direction is legally effective and the executor must obey it. He will, of course, be responsible for paying the expenses of the funeral or cremation he arranged, but those expenses are the first charge on the estate and he will naturally recoup himself out of the money of the estate as soon as he gets Probate and therefore legal control over the assets.

Summary of executors' duties

So at this stage it is possible to set down in plain and simple order the duties of the executor. They are as follows:

(a) To arrange for the burial or cremation.
(b) To prove the will.
(c) To pay the estate duty and all the debts, to collect the money due to the estate of the testator and to do everything else necessary to secure control over the assets of the deceased.
(d) To distribute those assets in accordance with the directions in the will.

Executors often get into trouble with the beneficiaries because they are, or appear to be, very slow about distributing the assets. There is an old rule of law that the executor is not bound to divide the estate among the beneficiaries before the end of one year from the date of the death. He may divide it sooner but he is not bound to. It is called the Executor's Year. This year is a period of grace and time during which he can carry out the work which, as is perfectly obvious from what has been said above, may be very onerous, of getting the assets under his control, paying the debts, paying the duty, and discovering how much he really has to distribute. In Scotland the executor under the same rule is given only six months.

Reasons for delay in distribution of estate

It is, of course, true that there may be good reasons why even after six months or the year is over the executor may be unable to distribute the estate. There may have been difficulties about getting the property into his hands, or in tracing the beneficiaries. There may be discussions with the Inland Revenue about the amount of death duties. Sometimes these discussions with the Revenue may be very prolonged indeed, because they involve considerable arguments as to the valuation of certain assets. For example, the testator may have had shares in a private company of which he was perhaps the principal proprietor. Those shares are not quoted on the Stock Exchange. What is the true market value to be placed on them? All kinds of considerations come into a decision on this question. The first, of course, is that the shares are not readily marketable. There may be restrictions in the Articles of Association of the company against the disposal of shares; they are not freely for sale as are the shares of public companies which are quoted on the Stock Exchange. The question of assessing their true value may be a matter for considerable argument. Other assets which may be very difficult to value are timber, or land which has not yet been developed and may have no immediate market value but which may have some potential value which is, so to speak, inherent in the land at the date of death and which the Revenue wish to take into account. There may be other rights such as rights of fishing, rights of shooting, on which it is not at all easy to place an exact figure. This is the kind of thing which may lead to very long discussions with the Revenue, where the executors are fighting for the lowest figure and the Revenue are fighting perhaps for some higher figure which they think is the true market value at the date of death.

Then there can be enormous difficulties about tracing beneficiaries, *e.g.* where property has to be divided among the children of X. and X. has died, and it is not certain how many of his children or their descendants are still living. Let us say two of them are readily traceable, but it is known that there were two others who have gone abroad and have lost touch with their families. Are they still alive? Where are they? And maybe it is necessary to find out

". . . difficulties about tracing beneficiaries . ."

whether those children themselves left children. The difficulty in this sort of situation, of course, is that it is not known for certain into how many shares the asset is to be divided.

It is worth mentioning here that where the inquiries are likely to be very prolonged it is sometimes possible by arrangement with an insurance company for the executors to get an indemnity policy under which they may be permitted to divide according to the facts they then know with the certainty that if the facts turn out to be different because a long-lost beneficiary turns up and claims a share which the executor no longer has in his hands, the insurance company will meet the claim.

Sometimes it is even necessary for the executor to make an application to the High Court for permission to distribute according to the facts which he has ascertained, and he can get protection against personal liability in that way.

The essential point for the executor to remember is that he must, under, we trust, advice from his solicitor, make quite certain that he is not exposing himself to personal liability in the future for doing the work according to the best information which he has in his hands. The fact that he can get directions from the court or can insure against the risk is a great protection to him. The point for him to remember is that he must, whenever there is any doubt at all, make sure that he gets this protection, otherwise he may expose himself to considerable personal liability, and as he is probably doing all this work for nothing or next to nothing, unless the testator has left him a substantial personal legacy, it would be very hard indeed if he subsequently found that he had to suffer out of his own pocket.

Telling the beneficiaries

Many beneficiaries are only too anxious to get their hands on what has been left to them and do not appreciate the problems of the executor. All executors should tell the beneficiaries fully and frankly what is happening. If there are serious difficulties which hold up distribution of the estate, the executor ought to explain what they are. There may be nothing to prevent an executor from dealing with specific legacies. A gift of £50 to John or £100 to Emily, probably presents no problems. The problems really arise when the residuary estate, that is the residue which is left after certain specific legacies have been given, has to be divided in accordance with the testator's wishes and the division depends upon the number of beneficiaries who are alive within a certain class, children, grandchildren, nephews, and so on. It is not at all unreasonable then for executors to delay until they are absolutely certain, but it *is* unreasonable for them not to tell those beneficiaries exactly what the problems are and why the delay exists.

Moreover, executors should realize that beneficiaries in general are legally entitled to see the accounts of the estate and to be told how the work of distribution is getting on. If they are not satisfied they may consult solicitors of their own and there is nothing to prevent them from applying to the court for an Order for an inquiry into the distribution of the estate. A beneficiary who merely has one specific legacy perhaps is not entitled to see the accounts, but a beneficiary who is entitled to more, in the sense that he has a share in an estate, a share which is not an exact figure, but depends upon the value of the estate after paying debts and duty and also upon the number of shares into which it is to be divided, certainly has a legal right to see the executor's accounts.

When the testator controlled a business

An executor of a testator who ran a business is often faced with the problem whether to continue running that business, and if so for how long. Clearly it may be to the advantage of the estate and therefore to the beneficiaries if the business can be run at least until it can be sold at a good price. If it stops dead on the death of the testator it will probably be sold at a forced price for less than it might have been worth.

Nevertheless, the executor in this position must be very careful. Unless there is a positive request in the will that he shall carry on, his duty is to sell it as a going concern as quickly as he can, or to wind it up. His difficulty is that if he runs it and then sells it at a very much higher figure than he might have done if he had sold it immediately on the death, he gets no reward and probably no thanks; but if he and the business run into heavy loss, or indeed any loss at all, he may be liable to the beneficiaries for that loss if he is carrying it on without the testator's authority. This, of course, makes it so important for any testator who is running a business not to indulge in the grave risks of making the will himself or with the aid of a friend who says he knows how to make wills. It makes it so vital that he should get a solicitor to draw his will up for him. However, that is a comment in parenthesis; at the moment it is just very desirable to warn executors, and to add that an executor can charge to the estate the cost of any legal advice he has reasonably sought from a solicitor.

The executor is personally liable for the debts of the business while he continues to run it. But, if the will authorizes him to carry it on, he can reimburse himself out of the estate for the debts he incurs. Unless he has the authority of the will expressly directing him to carry on the business, the only safe course is for him to get the consent of all the beneficiaries to his doing so, even if only for a short time while he can wind it up gradually and find a buyer at the best price. All the beneficiaries have to consent, and if one of them happens to be an infant, that is someone under twenty-one, that infant cannot give a legally binding consent. One way out of the difficulty is for the executor to apply to the court for directions as to the carrying on and the disposal of the business, and this may cause further expense to the estate. Obviously it is most important for testators who run a business to give considerable thought to this matter, and under the advice of the solicitor who draws up their will, to give some positive directions to their executors. If they do not, the executor can hardly be blamed for saying that he won't touch it and to sell the business at once.

How executors are appointed

Executors are as a rule named in the will. It is certain that the first clause of a will drawn up on legal advice will be 'I appoint .... and .... to be the Executors of this my Will'. Indeed, there may be more than two, and sometimes it is very desirable, particularly when there is going to be trust for a sale of land, that there should be four executors. But whatever the number it is quite certain that a will drawn up by a solicitor will contain an express appointment of certain named persons to be an executor or executors, or, if a woman or women, an executrix or executrices, and it is equally certain that there will be at least two, and on occasions there may be four. The reason for having at least two, of course, is to cover the possibility that one may die before the testator. It is very common for one of them to be a professional person, perhaps the solicitor himself or a partner in the firm of solicitors which draws up the will.

The executor, of course, need not be a person in the ordinary sense of the word. The executor can be a corporation like the Trustee Department of a bank, or the Public Trustee. It is impossible to generalize about the advantages of having the Public Trustee or a bank to act for you. Both have the obvious advantage of absolute security and continuity. A corporation of this kind never dies. But such a corporation may be less considerate or less 'human' in the administration of the estate than a solicitor who was a friend of the testator and knows the family and is a 'family friend' so to speak. Generalizations are really impossible on this subject, and it is a matter for each testator to consider in the light of the kind of estate he is likely to leave and the kind of persons whom he wishes to benefit, and how long any trusts he makes are likely to continue. It is a subject which he could profitably discuss with a solicitor, and one particular matter which he ought to take into account is what fees would be charged by the Public Trustee or by a bank.

The executor who is not expressly appointed

It often happens that in a home-made will the testator forgets to make an express appointment of an executor. Nevertheless, it is sometimes possible for someone to be accepted as an executor by the Probate Registry although he is not named in the will. This can come about if one of the people mentioned in the will is asked to undertake the duty of seeing to the funeral, paying the debts and generally dividing up the estate. Where one finds words of this kind the testator has, in effect, although not in so many words, asked some particular person to take on the job of an executor, without actually making the express appointment. Where this has happened that person will be allowed to prove the will as an executor. He is known to the law as an 'executor according to the tenor', because the 'tenor' or purport of those words is in fact to make him an executor, and this is recognized by the Probate Registry.

If, however, the will does not ask anyone to see to these duties, but simply makes a number of gifts, then it is rather more difficult. No one then can actually be appointed executor, but one or other of the main beneficiaries will have to apply to the Probate Registry for what is called a Grant of Letters of Administration. This is the authorizing document which is usually associated with an intestacy—that is when no will has been made. The difference in this case is that it will be called a 'Grant of Letters of Administration with the Will Annexed', because those to whom the authority of administration is given must carry out the terms of the will. It is a little more troublesome to get such a grant, and that is why it is always an advantage if an executor or executors are expressly named in the will.

There is a third type of executor, an *executor de son tort*. That means an executor through his own wrong. This is one who, although not appointed executor, unjustifiably meddles in some way with the deceased's estate, for example, by going to the house soon after his death, taking possession of some of his property, handing some over to others, and generally dealing with the estate as if he really was an executor appointed by the will.

It should be emphasized that an executor appointed by the will has authority to act from the date of the deceased's death. It is perfectly true that, as explained above, he may not be able to assert his legal authority until he has actually obtained the Grant of Probate. As explained, the bank, the insurance companies, the companies in which the deceased had stocks and shares, are not obliged to recognize anything except the Grant of Probate. Nevertheless, an executor can do anything in connection with the estate provided that he was appointed by the will, and then when he gets the Grant of Probate, it legalizes, back to the date of the death, all that he has done, provided, of course, he has acted properly. But one not appointed by the will has no authority at all. If he sets about dealing with the estate as if he were an executor he may find himself put into the position of being an *executor de son tort*, and it is not at all an advantageous position to be in, because he is liable to be sued by the deceased's creditors, is liable to be sued by those who may subsequently obtain a grant of representation to the estate, and, indeed, by the persons who are entitled to the estate. Probably few people do put themselves into this position, but it has happened; it has been known that a violent, headstrong, and domineering son has assumed powers and responsibilities which were not his at all, and has found himself in a position of legal liability in which he never expected to find himself. This is a warning. Unless you are appointed by the will do not attempt to act as an executor until a legal grant such as Probate, allowing you to be an executor according to the tenor, or a 'Grant of Letters of Administration with the Will Annexed', is given to you.

Executors: fees and miscellaneous points

It is apparent from what has been said that the work of an executor may be extremely onerous. It is true that, provided there is money enough in the estate, a great deal of that work can be put on to the shoulders of a solicitor. A solicitor will deal with all the documents, he will get all the expert advice that may be needed from valuers, stockbrokers, and others, he will deal with the Estate Duty Office and all the main burdens of the executor can be taken on to the solicitor's shoulders. Even so, a good deal remains for the executor to do, because unless the solicitor has acted for the testator for many years he cannot possibly know all the circumstances, cannot know what the deceased owned or what he owed, and it is for the executor to do his best with the papers at his disposal to give the solicitor that information. In other cases, where the estate is small and an executor tries to do the whole thing himself, it is a very heavy burden indeed. And so the moral is for all testators—don't ask people to become your executors, don't appoint them in your will without at least approaching them beforehand and asking them if they might be willing to undertake the work.

If someone is appointed executor without his previous knowledge, it is open to him to renounce that appointment if he does not wish to undertake the work. The fact that he is appointed executor by will does not impose a legal obligation upon him to accept the appointment. He can renounce it by making a written statement of formal renunciation and sending it to the Principal Probate Registry at Somerset House in London or to the District Probate Registry. The only point for him to watch is that, if he is going to renounce his appointment, he ought to do it before he has done any act which may mark him out as an executor, *e.g.* by paying the funeral expenses or in some way assuming authority over the estate of the deceased.

A lay executor is not entitled to charge any fees for his work, neither indeed is a professional executor such as a solicitor unless there is a clause in the will entitling him to charge. But a lay executor cannot charge any fees under any circumstances, and so again, as a pointer for testators, it is kind to provide that at least a legacy of an appropriate amount should be left to the person who is going to do this great deal of work in connection with your estate.

SCALES OF ESTATE DUTY WHERE DECEASED DIED ON OR AFTER APRIL 10th, 1962

PRINCIPAL VALUE			RATE PER CENT.
£		£	£
Does not exceed		5,000	Nil
Exceeds	5,000 but not	6,000	1
,,	6,000 ,, ,,	7,000	2
,,	7,000 ,, ,,	8,000	3
,,	8,000 ,, ,,	10,000	4
,,	10,000 ,, ,,	12,500	6
,,	12,500 ,, ,,	15,000	8
,,	15,000 ,, ,,	17,500	10
,,	17,500 ,, ,,	20,000	12
,,	20,000 ,, ,,	25,000	15
,,	25,000 ,, ,,	30,000	18
,,	30,000 ,, ,,	35,000	21
,,	35,000 ,, ,,	40,000	24
,,	40,000 ,, ,,	45,000	28
,,	45,000 ,, ,,	50,000	31
,,	50,000 ,, ,,	60,000	35
,,	60,000 ,, ,,	75,000	40
,,	75,000 ,, ,,	100,000	45
,,	100,000 ,, ,,	150,000	50
,,	150,000 ,, ,,	200,000	55
,,	200,000 ,, ,,	300,000	60
,,	300,000 ,, ,,	500,000	65
,,	500,000 ,, ,,	750,000	70
,,	750,000 ,, ,,	1,000,000	75
,,	1,000,000		80

RULES FOR THE DISTRIBUTION OF AN ESTATE WHEN THERE IS NO WILL

IN THE CHAPTER referring to the duties of an executor, we described how one of the first duties of an executor was to prove the will, *i.e.* to obtain what is known as a Grant of Probate, a document which is the executor's legal authority to deal with the estate.

LETTERS OF ADMINISTRATION

When there is no will, or no valid will, there can be no question of obtaining a Grant of Probate. When no will has been made, or when a will which has been made is not admitted to Probate, someone else with legal authority has to be found with legal powers to get the estate into his hands, to get it into his control and to distribute it, not in this case according to the wishes of the deceased person, but according to the rules which are laid down by law for the distribution of an estate on an intestacy. The word 'intestacy' means simply the situation which arises when either no will has been made or no will has been or can be proved.

In order to have legal authority to distribute an estate in these circumstances someone has to apply to the Probate Registry, either the Principal Probate Registry or a District Probate Registry, or if necessary (*i.e.* if the Registry are not prepared to accept the will without higher authority) to the court, for what is called a Grant of Letters of Administration. (Application can in certain cases be made to a local office of Customs and Excise: see below.)

This is a document issued by the Probate Registry, the purpose of which is to give one person, or it may be more than one person, similar powers to those conferred on an executor. The Grant may be given to one person, if there is no life interest or if no infant, *i.e.* someone under twenty-one, may be entitled legally to a share in the estate. But if anyone under twenty-one is entitled to some interest in the estate, or if anyone has a life interest, there must be at least two administrators, or else the Grant must be made to, for example, the Public Trustee, or some other corporation which comes within the legal category of a Trust Corporation.

If, for instance, a man dies leaving no will and the only person legally entitled to a share in his estate under the rules applying to the distribution of an intestate's estate is his widow, she might well be able to obtain a Grant of Letters of Administration in her name alone. If, however, there are children under twenty-one who might be entitled, she cannot do so, and there must either be another administrator to share with her, or as stated above, the Grant must be made to a Trust Corporation. Incidentally, a private person can be appointed jointly with a Trust Corporation.

One of the advantages of making a will and making it properly according to law is that those who are interested in the deceased's estate are saved a good deal of the extra trouble and extra expense associated with obtaining a Grant of Letters of Administration.

The method of obtaining such a Grant is very similar to that of obtaining a Grant of Probate. The same kind of documents, namely, a statement of the nature of the estate and its value, *i.e.* an Inland Revenue Affidavit, and the other documents described in the chapter on the duties of an executor must be prepared. The Inland Revenue authorities have precisely the same interests as regards estate duty, the Probate authorities have the same interests to ensure that those who apply for a Grant of Letters of Administration are legally entitled to do so. An additional document which may be necessary when an individual, or individuals, are applying for a Grant of Letters of Administration, is a bond entered into with an insurance company guaranteeing that those to whom the Grant may be made will carry out their duties according to law, and that if they do not do so, money will be available to make good their default. The taking out of this bond, which is a kind of insurance policy, requires the payment of a premium, and this is yet another reason why the obtaining of a Grant of Letters of Administration is more expensive than obtaining a Grant of Probate.

While it is possible to obtain a Grant of Letters of Administration by personal application to the Probate Registry, just as it is possible to obtain a Grant of Probate of a will by personal application, it is obviously very desirable, unless the value of the estate is small, to obtain the help and advice of a solicitor who can deal with the whole matter and all the complications on behalf of the proposed administrator or administrators. And just as a solicitor's costs are a proper charge on an estate where an executor is concerned, so they are also on an estate where an administrator is concerned. It is worth knowing that a local office of H.M. Customs and Excise can handle personal applications when the net value of the estate is not more than £1,000 and the gross value is not more than £3,000.

THE INTESTATES' ESTATES ACT, 1952

When a deceased person has left no will, or no will which can be proved, the whole of his property must be distributed according to rules laid down by Act of Parliament. The Act which is now operative is the Intestates' Estates Act, 1952, which came into force on January 1st, 1953. It applies to England and Wales but not to Scotland, where the laws of inheritance are markedly different from those which apply in England and Wales.

This Act of Parliament affects the estates of all who died after midnight on December 31st, 1952, and it made some considerable changes in the law of intestate succession which had obtained before that date.

The rules which operated before that date provided that a surviving wife or husband was to be entitled to the first £1,000 of the estate absolutely, to all the personal chattels, and to a life interest in the remainder of the estate, either the whole of the remainder or the half of the remainder, depending on whether there were children. There were other provisions for children and other relatives. But it is not necessary to go into details, because the rules have been so substantially changed by the 1952 Act

THE NEW RULES IN OPERATION

One of the most important changes introduced by this Act was the substantial increase in the amount to which the surviving widow or widower was to be entitled. It was increased from the old figure of £1,000 to £5,000, if there are children, and to a very much higher figure when there are no children.

The rules are somewhat complicated. They are set out in detail at the end of this chapter, but in order to illustrate some of their more important effects it is proposed here to explain how the Act might operate in the case of a family consisting of a husband and wife and, let us say, two children. It does not matter for the sake of the example who dies first, whether it be husband or wife, because exactly the same rules apply to the surviving spouse, whichever it may be. In order, however, to avoid the necessity of constantly writing 'his' or 'her', let us assume for the purpose of this illustration that the husband dies leaving a widow and two children, and that he leaves no will (or at any rate no will which can be proved). In this situation how will his money and his other assets be divided according to the law as laid down in the Intestates' Estates Act, 1952?

First, the widow has an absolute right to all his personal chattels. The expression 'personal chattels' means a great variety of things. First of all, let us get clear what it does not include, simply because the items excluded are comparatively few and can be explained in a very few words. First, it does not include land or an interest in land, or the buildings on land, or the trees or crops which grow on the land.

Secondly, it does not include share certificates, national savings certificates, and similar securities.

Thirdly, it does not include chattels used for the purpose of the deceased's business, or money, or any other securities for money.

It does, however, include such things as books, furniture, clothes, china, silver, jewellery, linen, watches, clocks, ornaments, pictures, motor-cars, horses, and other domestic animals. These things and others like them are the *personal chattels*, and there is obvious distinction between all these items and assets like land, or buildings, or securities for money. They are what we would colloquially describe as 'goods and chattels'.

Some of these personal chattels may be exceptionally valuable, but value is not the test. It does not matter in the least whether by chance the deceased person owned a painting worth, say, £50,000, or a stamp collection, or articles of silver or china which happen to have a considerable value. Value is totally irrelevant for this purpose. In our example the widow is entitled to receive all the personal chattels which come under the definition, whatever their value might be. The motor-car may be a Rolls-Royce or it may be a very unimportant small motor-car of some popular make which may be worth only £50. None of this makes any difference—the only test is whether it is a personal chattel. If it is, then the widow is entitled to receive it.

Secondly, the widow is entitled to receive up to £5,000 free of death duties, plus interest at 4 per cent. per annum from the date of death to the date of payment.

The position so far, therefore, is that the widow is entitled to:

(a) all the personal chattels, whatever their value might be;
(b) £5,000, free of death duties, plus interest at 4 per cent. per annum from the date of death to the date of payment, or so much up to £5,000 as the estate is worth.

If the estate is worth more than £5,000 after paying death duties, allowing for the interest payable to the surviving widow or widower, and excluding the personal chattels which are in any event payable to the surviving spouse, then the children may have an interest. The rules provide that in these circumstances the balance over the net figure of £5,000 is to be divided into two parts. The administrators must retain and invest one-half and hold it on trust for the widow, *i.e.* the income from this half will be paid to the widow for the rest of her life, and on her death the capital goes to the children.

The other half is held on trust for the two children in equal shares. Each of the children must be paid his share as soon as he or she reaches the age of twenty-one. If one child is already twenty-one he will be paid his immediate share in the estate at once. If any child is under twenty-one the trustees will keep his share in their hands. They may use the income for his general education and upbringing, but any income not used for that purpose is invested and so added to the capital to be paid over at twenty-one. If a child marries under twenty-one he or she then becomes entitled to be paid the income, but the capital must be retained until he or she is twenty-one.

Until a child becomes twenty-one, or until he marries under that age, his share is described as being contingent, *i.e.* it is contingent upon the happening of one or other of those events. If he dies under twenty-one and without marrying, his share is lost both to him and to his estate, *i.e.* to his successors in inheritance.

So when there are two children, both under twenty-one when the father dies, and one of those children dies under twenty-one, never having married, his share goes to the other child who does survive until twenty-one, or marries under that age.

When a child becomes twenty-one or marries under that age his share ceases to be contingent and becomes vested. This is a vitally important distinction. The child who marries under twenty-one is not entitled actually to have his share paid to him until he is twenty-one, but nevertheless he is, as stated above, entitled to receive the income, because his share has become vested in him. The importance of this is that if he marries at twenty, so that his share then becomes vested, and dies in an accident or for any reason, at, say, twenty years and six months, his share will form part of his estate and will be dealt with according to his will if he made one, or under the rules relating to intestacy if he did not.

Exactly the same rules apply to the other half which is held in trust for the widow during her life so that she receives the income on it. When she dies that half is divided among the children who attained *vested* interests in the manner described above. Even if all her children died before she did, yet if they had attained vested interests, their shares would form part of their estate.

There are special provisions affecting grandchildren. Suppose, when the father dies, two children survive him and attain a vested interest in the manner described, but that a third child had died before his father, leaving a son who is still a baby, the baby may still have a right to share in the estate. That grandchild, if he attains twenty-one or marries under twenty-one, has a right to exactly the same share as his father would have had if he had not died. If there is more than one such grandchild they all divide their own father's share between them.

Let us have a practical example to illustrate all this.

Mr Smith dies leaving an estate as follows:

Money in the bank	.	.	.	£200
Stocks and shares valued at	.	.	.	£3,000
Insurance policies on his life	.	.	.	£8,000
House valued at	.	.	.	£5,000
Personal chattels valued at	.	.	.	£700

Total . £16,900

He leaves a widow, two children over twenty-one, one child of fifteen, and two grandchildren, the offspring of a deceased daughter.

Let us assume his debts outstanding and funeral expenses add up to £500. His estate is therefore worth £16,400. Estate duty will be a little under £1,000, leaving a sum of £15,400 to be divided.

Mrs Smith receives at once the personal chattels, and £5,000 plus some interest from date of death until payment. Payment in such a case need not take long. It is an easily manageable and realizable estate. So for the purposes of this example let us ignore it altogether.

So after paying duty, and £5,000 and the personal chattels to Mrs Smith, there is left over a sum of £9,700.

Half is held in trust for Mrs Smith for life and thereafter for the children or children's children who attain vested interests. The other half is held in trust for the children who attain vested interests.

The two children over twenty-one may be paid their shares at once. The potential division is into four parts; and there is nothing to prevent their each getting one-quarter of one-half at once.

Another quarter of one-half is held in trust for the child of fifteen. The last quarter of one-half is held in trust for the two grandchildren.

When the child of fifteen attains twenty-one or marries he attains a vested interest in his share. If he dies before that, his share goes to swell the general pool.

When the two grandchildren attain twenty-one or marry their shares become vested: they divide their parent's share and so each have one-eighth of one-half.

When Mrs Smith dies, her half is divided in exactly the same way as the other half.

Although this chapter is primarily concerned with the rules for the distribution of an estate when no valid will is left, it may be appropriate to interpolate here some remarks to indicate why it may be better to make a valid will than to leave the distribution of an estate to be decided according to these rules which operate on an intestacy. Keeping to our example, where it is the husband who dies and leaves a widow and children, he might, if he had thought of it, have preferred to leave as specific legacies certain particular chattels to one or other of his children, or to friends; for example, if he had pictures or silver or books in which he had a particular interest, he might have wished to leave some of them to named persons. Under the intestacy rules, of course, his widow is entitled to them all.

Secondly, unless the value of his estate, excluding the personal chattels, exceeds £5,000 net, none of his children can be entitled to any share at all. He might, had he thought of it, have wished to leave a specific legacy to one child. There may be perfectly valid reasons for this. For example, one child may be

701

physically handicapped and might therefore have a greater claim on the benefits to be received from his father. Another child may be a daughter to whom he wants to leave a fairly substantial sum, according to his means, in order to give her a good start when she gets married. There may be a variety of reasons for distinguishing between his children, and indeed for distinguishing between his children and his widow. The Intestates' Estates Act obviously cannot possibly enter into fine distinctions of this kind. The most it can do is to give a fixed sum to the widow and thereafter to divide the balance equally between the children. No division by Act of Parliament can possibly do more.

POSITION WHERE THERE IS A SURVIVING SPOUSE BUT NO CHILDREN

So far we have considered the position where both a widow and children survive. Let us now consider the position where there is a surviving widow but no children. The same rules apply where the survivor is a widower with no children, but as explained above we are taking the situation where the husband dies first simply for the sake of grammatical convenience.

In this situation the surviving widow is very remarkably better off than ever before, provided, of course, there is enough money in the estate.

The surviving spouse is entitled to:

(a) the personal chattels;
(b) £20,000 (or up to £20,000), with interest at 4 per cent. from the date of death until payment, free of death duties.

The fate of the balance over £20,000 net depends upon what other relatives of certain degrees survive. Suppose the estate of Mr Smith in our example above was worth £30,000 net, exclusive of personal chattels which go to Mrs Smith anyway. She is entitled to half the balance over £20,000 absolutely—*i.e.* £5,000. The other half is payable to the surviving parent or parents of the deceased. If there are no parents it goes to surving brothers or sisters in equal shares. And the share of a deceased brother or sister is divided among their descendants if any, who attain twenty-one or marry under twenty-one.

WIDOW, BUT NO ISSUE, PARENTS, BROTHERS OR SISTERS, NEPHEWS OR NIECES

If the deceased husband leaves neither issue nor parents, nor brothers or sisters, nor issue of such brothers and sisters, then his surviving widow is absolutely entitled to the entire estate, the whole of it, however much it may be worth. More distant relatives are completely excluded where the deceased leaves a widow. And precisely the same rules apply where a woman dies leaving a widowed husband.

NO WIDOW, BUT CHILDREN OR OTHER ISSUE

It is now necessary to consider the position where the deceased husband leaves children or other issue but no surviving spouse. In this case his issue are

702

absolutely entitled to the estate on attaining twenty-one or marrying under that age. If more than one child survives and attains twenty-one the estate is divisible equally between those children. The shares which any child who dies unmarried and under twenty-one would have taken had he or she reached the age of twenty-one or married under that age, will be added to the shares of the other children.

NEITHER WIDOW NOR ISSUE

The next situation to consider is where there is no surviving spouse and no issue. If there is no surviving spouse and no issue who become twenty-one or marry under that age, the estate is divisible among the classes of relations in the order mentioned, set out in the summary at the end of this chapter.

OTHER CHANGES IN THE LAW

The Intestates' Estates Act of 1952 made two other substantial changes in the law.

The first of these is that it gave the surviving spouse a legal right to buy the matrimonial home. This is very important indeed. To illustrate its importance, consider the case where a husband dies leaving not very much in cash, but leaving a freehold house which at the date of his death was his absolutely. He might have owned it absolutely for some time or he might by the time he had died have paid off every penny owing under a mortgage. Whatever the circumstances, at the date of his death he owned it absolutely. Under the law as it stood before the 1952 Act, his widow had no legal right to the house at all. Her legal rights were limited to £1,000, free of duties, plus interest, and the personal chattels. But if there was money available in the estate to meet her cash claims, she had no claim to the house, and this could be very harsh if that house had been—as it most likely was—their married home for many years. If she had to get out of that home, the other benefits she might have got under the law of intestacy as it then existed would go nowhere to compensate her for the loss of her home.

The new Act increased her cash entitlement from £1,000 to £5,000; even that, however, by itself, might not have been enough to remedy this particular injustice which sometimes caused considerable hardship. The Act therefore goes further and provides that the surviving wife or husband has the right to insist that the actual house which was the family home shall be transferred to her or to him. It is true that the value of the house has to be set against the money to which she or he is entitled out of the estate; but as the entitlement is now £5,000 as opposed to the old £1,000, it is a considerable advantage and may cover a large number of houses. You may very well, therefore, have the situation where the surviving widow, to continue our example of the situation where is is the husband who dies—may be content to take £1,000 in cash and to allow the balance of £4,000, to which she is entitled, or any other money of her own, to be set against the value of the matrimonial home which was entirely in her husband's name and which he neglected to deal with because he neglected to make a will. Indeed, it may be worth far more to her to have the right to insist on having the deeds of this house transferred to her than to have a cash sum of money.

It is not only when the deceased person *owned* the house that the new law operates. It also operates if he had a lease or a long tenancy which cannot be brought to an end within two years from his death. The surviving spouse can require such a lease or a tenancy to be passed on to her or to him.

The next important change brought about by the new Act is the right of the surviving husband or wife to insist on being paid the capital value of a life interest, instead of being content with receiving only the income for life.

As explained above, a life interest occurs when, for instance, a husband dies leaving a widow and children, and leaves substantially more than £5,000. After the £5,000, free of death duties and plus interest, has been paid to the wife, the balance, as has been explained, has to be divided, half being invested and the income paid to the widow for her life, and half being paid to or kept for the children when they come of age or marry under age. The Act gives the surviving spouse the right to insist that his or her life interest in the half shall be redeemed, and that a capital sum representing the value of the income, should be paid over at once.

This can be very advantageous not only to the surviving spouse but also to the administrators of the estate, because they can distribute the whole estate at once. They can distribute it free of the life interest, and the distribution can be completed earlier probably than would otherwise be the case. It is an advantage to the surviving spouse, because he or she may prefer to have a capital sum rather than what might be a small yearly income.

That is a general description of the broad effects of the new law of intestacy, as laid down in the Intestates' Estates Act of 1952. Here now are set out in full the rules for distribution of the estate of an intestate.

SUMMARY OF THE RULES OF SUCCESSION ON INTESTACY

(1) When there is a surviving husband or wife.

    (a) If the deceased leaves no issue and no parent, brother or sister of the whole blood, or issue of such brother or sister, the surviving husband or wife is absolutely entitled to the whole estate.

    (b) If the deceased leaves issue, the surviving husband or wife is entitled to the personal chattels, and to £5,000 free of duty, with interest at the rate of 4 per cent. from the date of death until payment. The surviving husband or wife is also entitled to the income of half of the balance of the estate over that £5,000, the rest being divisible among the issue who attain twenty-one or marry under that age, absolutely, *per stirpes* (explained below).

    (c) If the deceased leaves no issue but is survived by a parent, or brother or sister of the whole blood, or issue of such brother or sister, the surviving husband or wife is entitled to the personal chattels, together with £20,000 free of duty, with interest at the rate of 4 per cent. from the date of death until the date of payment. The surviving husband or wife is also entitled to half the balance of the estate absolutely, the rest passing to the parents, if any, and if there are no parents, to the surviving brothers and sisters *per stirpes*.

(2) When there is issue, but no surviving husband or wife: the issue are absolutely entitled to the estate in equal shares, *per stirpes*, on attaining twenty-one or marrying under that age.

(3) When there is no surviving husband or wife or issue who become entitled to the estate, other relations are entitled to the estate in the following order:

(a) a parent, and if more than one, equally;

(b) if no parent, brothers and sisters of the whole blood; if more than one, equally, *per stirpes*;

(c) if no brothers and sisters of the whole blood, those of half blood, equally, *per stirpes*;

(d) if no parents or brothers and sisters, then grandparents, and if more than one, equally;

(e) if no grandparents, then uncles and aunts of the whole blood, equally, *per stirpes*;

(f) if no uncles and aunts of the whole blood, then those of half blood, equally, *per stirpes*.

(4) If no surviving husband or wife, or no surviving relations under paragraph (3), then the whole estate passes to the Crown, or the Duchy of Lancaster or the Duke of Cornwall. In practice they try to find any more distant relatives and share the estate between them, and only keep the money if no relatives can be found.

Note: The expression mentioned above, '*per stirpes*' means 'by stock' by 'by family'. Thus, in paragraph (1) (c) above, it means that if there were four children who attained twenty-one or married under that age, but three of them die before the intestate leaving children of theirs surviving, the division will still be into four equal parts. Any surviving child of the testator takes his full quarter share, but any children of a deceased child divide the share their parent would have taken. In other words, if one of the intestate's children had died leaving four children, his three brothers or sisters would each take a quarter share, while his children who attain twenty-one or marry under that age would divide among themselves *his* quarter share, *i.e.* each of them would take a sixteenth each. The division is not made by counting heads, but by counting stocks, and the division into stocks is decided by the number of children who, at the date of the death of the intestate, are either twenty-one or have married under that age. That division is final and decisive, and any one of those who dies after that time can bequeath to his children only the right to divide his share among them. They cannot claim a share of the proportions given to their uncles or aunts.

DISINHERITANCE AND HOW A WILL MAY BE CHALLENGED

TO CUT OFF a wife, a son, or a daughter with the conventional shilling has long been the right of every Englishman or Welshman, but not of a Scotsman. English Law has long accepted the principle that everyone should have complete freedom to dispose of his property by will, to bequeath it exactly as he likes, even to the extent of disregarding all family or any other moral obligations.

". . . the principle that everyone should have complete freedom to dispose of his property . . . exactly as he likes. . . ."

Many other systems of law in other parts of the world, particularly those which are founded on Roman Law, have prevented this by laying down that a widow and children must receive certain definite shares of the estate. Scots Law has followed this principle of Roman Law. Under Scots Law a wife who survives her husband, a husband who survives his wife, or a child who survives a parent has a right to a definite share in the estate of the deceased. The amount of the share is fixed by law and this right cannot be defeated by anything which is contained in the will.

For example, suppose a man, domiciled in Scotland, dies, leaving a wife and child, and that he had fallen out with his family and been living apart from them for years before his death. He might as a last act of spite make a will under which all his property was to go to relatives of his own, and nothing to his wife or child. His intention to cut out wife and child would, in part, be frustrated. His widow could claim one-third of his moveable estate, *i.e.* any money, stocks and shares, furniture, etc., and also a life interest in one-third of the value of any house or other heritable property which he left. (Broadly speaking, heritable property under Scots Law is similar to real property under English Law; land and buildings, etc.) The child would be entitled to a one-third share of the moveable estate. Nothing contained in a will could prevent a widow and child receiving those shares and the will would have effect only over that part of the dead man's property which remains after those shares have been paid. That freely disposable part of his estate is called the 'dead's part'. The widow and child would also have these rights and some additional rights as well if the husband and father had died without making a will.

THE ACT OF 1938

Under English Law, however, there was nothing until the Inheritance (Family Provision) Act of 1938 to authorize any interference along these lines with a will, however harsh the will might be. And even that Act did not go to the lengths of laying down that a widow or a widower or a child should have certain fixed and definite shares. It only provided that if a will did not make reasonable provision for certain dependants, they could apply to the Court for an order that some allowance or capital sum should be paid to them out of the estate. How much it is to be, if anything, depends entirely upon the Court's discretion —what the Judge thinks.

Who may apply under this Act for some such allowance to be made? A very limited class:

(i) The wife or husband.
(ii) A daughter who has not been married, or who is, by reason of some mental or physical disability, incapable of maintaining herself.
(iii) An infant son.
(iv) A son who, though over twenty-one, is by reason of some mental or physical disability, incapable of maintaining himself.

When this Act was passed it only affected wills. It was extended to intestacies by the Intestates Estates Act of 1952, which made it apply where the rules of distribution on an intestacy had the effect of leaving one of these dependants so badly off that it would be reasonable for the Court to order that some provision should be made out of the deceased's estate.

It is very important to be aware of the need to apply to the Court. The Act does not allocate fixed shares to any of the dependants. They must apply to the Court and it is entirely in the Court's discretion to decide how much, if anything, ought to be given to them.

Another important point is that there is a time limit within which this application must be made. The time limit is six months from the date on which a grant of representation to the deceased's estate is first taken out; in other words, the date when the will is proved and Probate granted, or the date when Letters of Administration are granted. The imposition of this time limit may be a hardship. It may operate particularly harshly when, say, a husband and wife have been separated, the husband has died, and his will has been proved without his widow even being aware of the fact of his death. On the other hand, there must be some time limit, because if there were not, executors or administrators would never know when they could safely complete the distribution of the estate, either in accordance with the will, or in accordance with the rules of distribution after intestacy. A period of six months was chosen as a compromise between the desire to give dependants a reasonable chance of making their application, and prolonging the winding up of the estate. There is no need, of course, for the application to be actually heard by the Courts within that time, it is only necessary for the application to be set on foot by issuing the appropriate summons in the High Court. It is absolutely essential to get legal advice.

The Court has power to extend the six months' time limit, but only on certain very limited grounds; for instance, that there was some doubt as to the true interpretation of the will and that an application under this Inheritance Act was waiting upon a decision on the meaning and effect of the will. But, the fact that the dependant might have been ignorant of the death of the person concerned, or had delayed through ignorance of his or her rights, or because of difficulty of communication, perhaps because the dependant was abroad, would not enable an extension of time to be granted.

THE COURT'S JURISDICTION

What principles guide the Court in deciding whether or not to interfere with a will? To a very large extent the Judge must exercise a kind of moral jurisdiction. He has to try to put himself in the position of the deceased and consider what he ought to have done by moral, reasonable standards. The burden is on the dependant to prove that he or she has been treated unreasonably, treated with a disregard for natural and moral obligations. And in considering the validity of the claim it is obviously necessary for the Judge to look at the reasons which may have influenced the making of that particular will.

Suppose that it is a widow who applies because she has been left nothing or very little under her husband's will. The Judge will want to know, first, what other resources she has, what she has got to live on; secondly, whether her husband expressed any reasons either in the will or elsewhere for cutting her out, and, thirdly, if no such reasons were given, whether they can be inferred from the history of their married life. For instance, in one case where a widow applied to the Court for additional provision to be made for her out of her late husband's estate, the question arose whether it was permissible to put in evidence a statement by one of the testator's sons based on hearsay. In this statement the son said that his father had told him that his mother was drinking too much, that he had found bottles of whisky and gin hidden in her wardrobe, and that this secret drinking had caused him much distress. His father had also told him that there had been constant nagging and quarrelling, that she was frequently the worse for drink, and that on one occasion she had seriously assaulted him. He said that whenever his father visited him he complained to him most bitterly of his mother's conduct and that his father spent weekends as often as possible away from his home, either with this son, or with sisters, in order to get away from his wife. In fact things had reached such a pitch that a year before his death his father had entered into a Deed of Separation.

It was argued that this kind of evidence should not be received, and that although the Act contemplated that the Court would pay attention to any statements signed by the testator, it did not contemplate hearsay evidence of this kind. The Judge decided that this evidence was admissible, and that it gave him essential information from which he could infer the reasons which had influenced the testator to leave his widow less than he otherwise might have. In the result the widow's application failed. This is particularly significant because, in other kinds of legal proceedings, a Court will not receive evidence of what a dead man is supposed to have told someone else, save in certain very special circumstances which are precisely defined, mostly in relation to sudden death and the cause of that death. But in applications under this Inheritance Act it is clear that the Court will receive any *credible* evidence which might help them to understand why the testator made the kind of will in question.

A short account of some other actual cases may help to show what kind of orders the Court may make. In one case, the widow who applied to the Court had become the testator's housekeeper in 1946, and married him in 1948. He died in 1951, leaving her an annuity of £2 a week out of an estate of £15,000. She asked the Court to order that more should be allowed to her. The brothers and sisters of the testator opposed her application, alleging that she had forced her way into the house, and more or less planted herself on the testator. The Judge held that £2 a week was not a reasonable provision out of an estate of this size and that whatever were the circumstances under which the marriage had taken place, nevertheless the fact remained that the testator had made her his wife, and had therefore made himself morally and legally responsible for her. Even if his family were right in saying that she had bullied him into it, this made no difference to the fact that she had a position which gave her not only moral rights but also legal rights under the Act against her former husband. He ordered that her annuity should be increased to £4 a week.

Another case which is interesting on the question of amount concerned a much smaller estate. The testator left the whole of his property, which amounted to over £5,000, to various charities. His widow applied for an order for an allowance to be made to her. It appeared that she had married the testator in 1947 when he was seventy-four and she was seventy. Both had been married previously. Her income, independent of her husband, was £1 7s 9d a week. She also owned a bungalow which was valued at £750 and had a small sum in the Post Office Savings Bank. The Judge directed that the whole income of the estate should be paid to her during her widowhood.

A comparatively wealthy woman died in childbirth, but the life of her baby son was saved. She had made a will under which she left the bulk of her property to the child of a former marriage, and a legacy to her second husband.

709

No doubt, if she had lived, she would have altered the will to bring in the child of her second marriage. Her second husband earned only a small salary, and had no private means, and so he applied to the Court asking that the will should be altered in order to give something to the baby son. This application was unusual because the Act was apparently designed only to help members of a family who had been deliberately left out of a will or left an unreasonably small amount. In this case the Court were being asked to do something for a child who was not even born before the will was made. Nevertheless they decided that they could vary the will so as to give a fair share to the child of the second marriage. The case is particularly interesting, because here the Court were doing what the deceased woman would probably have wanted to do if she had lived. In most other cases where the application succeeds they are doing what they think the deceased person ought to have and could have done, but did not, either through deliberate malice or through indifference.

A question much argued in another case was whether a widow applying for maintenance under this Act was to be treated as entitled only to a bare subsistence or to a fair share, whatever that might amount to. The facts were that a husband left his wife in 1925 at a time when he only had a very small income and had indeed landed himself in bankruptcy. He did, however, make her a weekly allowance of £2, which he later on increased to £3. But during the years of their separation he amassed considerable wealth. Indeed the increase from £2 to £3 a week was miserably inadequate considering the money that he was making at that time. By his will, which he made in 1939, he left his wife an annuity of £250 and included in it a dishonest statement of the circumstances of their separation. He also settled a legacy of £1,000 on his daughter. It was only after his death in 1946 that his wife discovered that his net residuary estate, after paying death duties, amounted to £130,000. Both she and her daughter applied for a reasonable provision to be made for them and were faced with the argument that as the wife had managed to live for twenty years on £3 a week and never complained, and that as her husband had left her more than he gave her during his lifetime, she was not entitled to receive any more. The Judge declined to accept this argument and awarded her £1,000 a year and the daughter £100 a year, out of the estate.

OTHER MEANS OF CHALLENGING A WILL

Applications under this Act of Parliament are not the only way to alter or upset the terms of a will. A will may be challenged in the Courts if it can be proved that at the time when the testator made his will he was under some *undue influence* or *under duress*. That is why people who are in a special position of trust or influence, like doctors, solicitors, priests or clergy, must be very careful indeed. They may be in close contact with a dying man or woman; they may have great influence. If a will is made which is greatly in their favour and ignores, or provides inadequately for, members of the family who ought to have been remembered, it is natural to suspect that they may have used their influence to their own advantage. A solicitor is in a specially vulnerable position because he may have drawn up the will, and it is the almost invariable practice, when a solicitor is told that anything more than a small legacy is to be left to him personally, for him to refuse to draw up the will, and to advise the testator or testatrix to get independent legal advice.

Another example of undue influence is the pressure and persuasion of a second wife who may induce her husband to leave all his property to her, although it would have been right and proper for him to have left something, at least, to the children of his first wife.

It is not enough only to suspect undue influence. It is not easy to upset a will which on the face of it is validly made and complies with all the rules. The disappointed family have to prove that there are solid grounds for their suspicion and prove further that the one to whom the bulk of the estate has been left has not merely unduly influenced the testator, but exercised a degree of influence amounting virtually to compulsion; a compelling influence where the testator's mind was actually controlled by another person.

Another ground on which a will may be upset is proof that the testator was so ill, or so mentally feeble, that he did not know what he was doing. Here, too, doubts and suspicions are not enough. There must be cogent evidence from which the testator's weakness or senility can be inferred with reasonable certainty. It must also be remembered that, in all these cases, there is someone who is vitally interested in upholding the validity of the will as it was drawn.

You may also have the situation where the testator has signed the document in complete ignorance that he was signing a will. He may be of perfectly sound mind, there may be no evidence of undue influence amounting to coercion, no evidence of duress. It is, however, extraordinary how many cases there are of people signing contracts, signing deeds transferring property, transfers of stocks and shares, and even wills without having the least idea what they were doing. As a signature to a will must be attested by two witnesses (unless it is a Scots will written out entirely in the testator's own handwriting) the act of deceiving someone into signing a will believing it to be something else usually involves the co-operation of two other people. Even so, it has been possible to obtain this, and even where it has not been possible the signatures of witnesses may be forged in the hope that no question will ever arise.

The Scots lawyers have a picturesque phrase to describe wills made under undue influence, or by trickery of the kinds I have described. They call them 'wills made by fraud, facility, and circumvention'. If a will is held by the Court to be invalid for any of these grounds, it is of course not admitted to Probate and the estate will be divided as if no will had ever been made.

TRAVELLING

TRAVEL GENERALLY, AND TICKETS IN PARTICULAR

SOONER OR LATER, almost everybody has to travel over some distance from place to place, whether it be by train, by bus, by ship, or by plane. In the section of this book which deals with the law of tort, the rights and duties of the 'common carrier' have been explored in some detail. But in general it will be remembered that a 'common carrier' has a special meaning in law. It describes a person carrying persons or goods for hire or reward as a business, and not by way of a casual encounter or occasion.

The common carrier may, of course, make a special contract with any member of the public. But apart from any question of special contracts, travel by public transport, whether on land, sea, or by air, is a matter of contract—a contract implied by the mere fact of the passenger travelling in return for a fare. And of this contract, the ticket is generally the written evidence.

You step on a bus, the conductor comes round and you pay your fare. He gives you your ticket, and you either hold it in your hand or you put it in your pocket, or your handbag, or the band of your hat. When you come to your stop, you probably screw it up and pop it in the little slot on the bus platform placed there for that purpose. If you are less thoughtful, you probably drop it in the gutter on the way home (and render yourself technically liable to a £10 fine for creating litter in a public place!). But how often have you thought to read it? How often have you even paused to read the tiny print on the train ticket that you place more carefully in your handbag or your wallet? And yet in most cases that ticket is the evidence of your contract with the bus company or the railway organization, and it either contains the terms and conditions by which you and they are bound, or it refers you to the place where you can see those conditions.

But, you say, you never even realized that you were travelling subject to conditions—they were not brought to your attention, so surely you cannot be bound by them! But, in fact, a traveller is bound in law by any reasonable conditions imposed, even if he has not taken the trouble to find them out, read them, and study them. You have paid your fare, you accept your ticket, the ticket refers you to the conditions, and it makes no difference at all that you have not bothered to read them. It is on those conditions and those conditions alone that you are offered transport. You accept the ride, you also accept the conditions. That is the basic law on the subject. Because travel is primarily a matter of contract.

Apart from any special conditions which may or may not be imposed—what is the general legal duty of a common carrier? It is to carry anyone who offers himself for carriage, who is ready to pay the fare, and who is in a fit state to travel—so long as there is sufficient accommodation. The carrier is bound to exercise due care so as to carry you safely—at least so far as reasonable care and foresight can attain that end.

Further than this—the carrier is responsible for the negligent actions and omissions of all his servants and all those directly connected with him in running the carriage service. That demands a very high degree of care, although it must be said that this does *not* extend to dangers outside the control of the carrier.

What is the degree of care required? All that can be said is that it depends entirely on the individual circumstances of each case. But this general duty, it should be made quite clear, is not any part of the contract between the carrier and you, the passenger. This is a *general* duty, independent of the conditions of contract, a breach of which is a tort. And if it is broken, the injured passenger has a right of action in tort against the carrier. In general, to succeed, he must prove negligence, though sometimes the doctrine of *res ipsa loquitur* (which is explained in the section on torts) may apply, lessening this burden of proof—a railway collision, in general terms, can hardly happen without negligence of some kind by railway servants or agents.

But let us for the moment take that duty generally imposed by the law as read, and return to the question of your ticket.

The ticket is the evidence of the contract you have made (whether you realized it or not) with the carrier, under the terms of which he is obliged to carry you to a named destination in a reasonable time and without negligence. So much is common to all such contracts. But the carrier and you may agree between you upon a number of special conditions—special terms, limiting, perhaps even eliminating, some of the general duties which you may in all innocence be taking for granted. And as you took your ticket and made no objection to the conditions which the carrier insisted on imposing, you are taken in law to have agreed to those conditions, even if you have not chosen to read them—provided only that the carrier had those conditions in writing clearly set out in detail, somewhere where you could have access to them, had you desired.

These conditions are usually to be found in the official timetables and so forth which are published by the railways. They are very lengthy, very dull, and very complicated. But you can find from them that the companies (now, of course, the British Transport Commission) do not promise that their trains will run to time, or even that they will run at all. You will find that they are not prepared to carry, free of charge, any amount or any kind of luggage you care to bring: you are entitled to take so many pounds of luggage—150 lb. with a First Class ticket, 100 lb. with a Second—but for more than that you must pay. And there are limitations on the size and kind of thing you may carry by rail. Obviously it would be out of the question if people were allowed to take dangerous or offensive articles—and in fact there are innumerable (and detailed) regulations concerning the carriage and the charges for every variety of thing. All these regulations you have agreed to by *buying your ticket—provided* the ticket really warns you of their existence.

In selling you a ticket the carrier is under contract to carry you to a named destination, in a reasonable time, and without negligence.

But, you say, you may be illiterate, and thus unable to read any conditions. You may be blind. Or to take a more probable and common example—you want to catch your train, and you really have not the time to seek out from whatever quarter is necessary a copy of the conditions—even if you had, you

715

would not have time to study them in detail, and you might feel that you needed a lawyer to explain the significance of some of them to you. All these objections matter not one bit. The conditions are there, available for you to read and study, and if you choose not to take the trouble to find them out, and understand the meaning of each and every one of them, then that is your own responsibility, and you will be taken to have accepted them. That is the general law, and it is very little realized.

The carrier is not likely to be using the law to impose unjust and demanding conditions upon you. Most of them you would expect to find anyway, you can take them for granted—all of them will be found to be reasonable, in general terms. But strictly speaking, you are bound by them, whatever they say—with the proviso that the Courts will refuse to apply any that are wholly unreasonable or improper. For example—in bus travel—the Road Traffic Act, 1930, contained a section specifically forbidding bus companies to restrict the general legal liability with regard to negligence, and if any public service vehicle owner tried to impose such a condition, it would not be enforced by the Courts against you.

These conditions are not 'secret'. They are public, if you only take the time and trouble to seek them out—they must be, or you will not be bound by them. And while the conditions applicable to ordinary traffic may contain little or nothing that would surprise you, that may very well not be the case when you take an excursion by train, let us say, although you are paying a greatly reduced fare and might expect to have some of the ordinary rights and duties altered in the circumstances.

There are a number of 'ticket cases' which have been decided by the Courts, over the years, and a selection of these will be referred to in detail a little later. But if your ticket says in tiny print 'For Conditions see the Company's Time-tables'—you cannot complain that you had not bought a timetable and read them, if at any time on that journey you find the company wishing to apply one of those conditions against you. For by those conditions you are bound, provided they were available to be studied by you, even if you chose not to bother.

Before going into some of the questions raised particularly by the most common forms of travel, it is worth while pausing a moment to examine the effect of this general point, as it has been brought up and discussed by various Courts—for any Court that tries your case may find itself bound by these decisions.

From the point of view of the carrier, who sets out the detailed terms and conditions on which he is prepared to carry you, the condition he would most like to impose upon you would be one under which you agree to relieve him of all liability for any damage arising to you out of the negligence of his servants or agents—or for that matter for any breaches of the contract itself committed by his servants or agents. If he could do that, you could not sue him for any negligence, whatever he or his servants did, in face of such a condition.

Now, as we mentioned, the Courts would refuse to enforce any condition that was wholly unreasonable. But it would have to enforce any condition that was reasonable, however strict, and however seriously it reacted upon an innocent and unwary passenger. And so in case after case ordinary passengers have been endeavouring to escape from any limiting conditions by which they have been caught, and in general the Courts have been supporting them as far as the law can be stretched to allow this.

In one such leading case in 1955 a man took a sea voyage, and did not notice that the ticket claimed complete exemption from liability arising out of the negligence of any of the shipping company's servants. This is an exemption which a private shipping line can seek by contract, but which British Railways cannot. There was an accident, and the passenger was hurt. It was beyond doubt that the actual employees responsible were the captain and bo'sun of the ship in question. The company stood by the contract and insisted on the condition. Seeing himself apparently bound by it and unable to escape, the passenger, on his solicitor's advice, said: "Very well, I will not sue the company at all. I will sue the captain and the bo'sun personally, in tort!" And, of course, he knew that no reputable company would fail to stand behind its employees and pay any damages awarded against them, and the plaintiff got his damages. The company tried to claim that the contract also barred personal actions against their employees, but the Court of Appeal decided that it did not.

Let us consider this principle when applied to another form of ticket which no doubt millions of people buy, every year, but which very very few ever really look at, at all—the simple railway platform ticket. This little slip of cardboard will probably do no more than refer the inquisitive to the 'British Railways Book of Regulations', and to Regulation 8, therein. But that regulation specifically frees the British Transport Commission from liability for the negligent acts of its servants and agents, and says in terms that it is a condition of the platform ticket that there shall be no liability at all falling upon the Commission. In fact, this even goes so far as to free them from liability for false imprisonment!

Now this is a condition which the Court has held to be wholly unreasonable and void, when it is put into a contract for train carriage. So a passenger on a train journey does not, cannot, lawfully exempt the railway from liability for negligence for personal injuries. But this is not a train ticket, it is a platform ticket. And this is not all. In the second paragraph of that same regulation, it lays down as a further condition that the acceptance of the platform ticket shall be regarded as conclusive evidence that the holder agrees that, should any of the Commission's servants be negligent, he will not hold any of them personally liable, either.

This is an important addition to the contract. For in the case above-mentioned, the reason why the passenger won his preliminary point and was able to sue the employees personally was that they, the employees, were not strictly parties to the contract between the company and the passenger. Behind this lies another very important principle—which is tested law—and this is that the only people who can sue on a contract or take advantage of any conditions in that contract are parties to that contract. And servants are not normally parties to any contracts made between outsiders and their employers. But this condition may well be an agreement between the passenger (who is a party to the contract) and the railway (the other party) that the passenger will recognize himself as being barred from taking a certain course (suing the employees personally) at all. And such a clause the Courts might have to

717

enforce. Because the passenger cannot later turn round and deny that he contracted not to sue the servants personally—the acceptance of the ticket without
objection amounts in law to that agreement.

Now the interesting thing about this example is that it has never yet been
tested in the Courts, so that one can only speculate within certain limits, as to
what might happen if it were so tested.

The important part about this condition is that it makes any servant of the
railway who is sued a party to the original contract, and it makes the ticket-
holder specifically agree to this. And lawyers who deal repeatedly with this
sort of problem are even now searching for loop-holes through which you, the
innocent passenger, may squeeze should you ever be landed in this position.

One of these loop-holes in which there is a little hope is that a contract is
only a true and enforceable contract if both parties to it give some 'consideration'—some service, or some value for a service. You for your part have given
your penny or twopence. The railway have given the use of their private property—the platform. But what about the servants who are said to be also
parties to the contract—are they truly parties?

There are a few cases which may or may not be held to have decided principles which are relevant to this compelling issue, but for the complete answer
we shall have to wait until a claim of this nature actually comes before a Court.
And attached to this main problem, there are a number of side issues—subsidiary problems—such as whether, if the servants were in law held responsible
for negligence, despite the condition, the railway would be strictly bound to
pay any damages awarded to you against them.

From this actual example you may glean some idea of the unexpected
importance that may lie in that little piece of cardboard which you may thrust
unthinkingly into your pocket. Let us use these facts to remind you that on it,
and on the conditions to which it leads, may rest the success or failure of a
claim, perhaps for thousands of pounds, which you might one day be in a
position to make, arising out of your decision to travel—or to be present at
a place where travel is the main concern of those with whom you deal.

And, of course, you must buy a ticket. It is no good saying, "Oh, I'll pay
at the other end". If a passenger has not bought a ticket he may legally be
removed from the train, even though he is willing to pay the fare. On the other
hand, if a passenger *has* bought a ticket but has mislaid it, then he cannot be
removed—even though he refuses to pay again. Much simpler to have a ticket
and be able to produce it.

You must produce your ticket if you are asked to do so by a servant of the
railway. If you have lost it, you must either pay the fare again (from the place
where you started) or you can give your name and address. If you refuse to do
one of these three things—show your ticket, pay again, or give your name and
address—you may be legally detained until you can be brought before a
Magistrate.

Not to produce a ticket is evidence of a fraudulent intention. This means
simply that if you can't produce it you will be presumed to be travelling with
intent to defraud the railway—and it will be up to you to convince the Court
that you are innocent. Of course, you may be able to do this quite easily by
afterwards finding the ticket; or the Court may believe you when you say

quite simply that you lost it. Where people who intend to defraud the railway get caught is when they lose their tickets too often; or say they were in a hurry and didn't buy one, but they got on the Tube at Piccadilly. Sooner or later they will find that they have been watched, and that it has been discovered that they never bought a ticket or that it wasn't Piccadilly but some far more distant station that they have come from.

Another thing you must not do is to use other people's tickets. Of course this does not mean that you cannot buy a ticket for a friend—in that case you

"Not to produce a ticket is evidence of a fraudulent intention."

are only acting as his agent. The sort of thing you must not do is to use other people's season tickets or the return half of other people's return tickets—and that seems to be true even if you don't gain anything by it. It is certainly true if you do. In one case a man wanted to go on to Manchester. There happened to be a day excursion from London to Manchester and back which was much cheaper than the ordinary single fare—so he bought the excursion ticket, as he was fully entitled to do; he wasn't obliged to use the other half, if he didn't want to. When he got to Manchester, however, he happened to meet a friend who wished to go to London, and he gave him the return half—which the friend used. The friend was clearly guilty of fraud, because he had got a cheap journey he was not entitled to—and the other man was guilty of aiding and abetting him.

FAMILY LAWYER

TRAVEL ON THE RAILWAYS

Apart entirely from the questions of contract which we have been discussing, however, there are certain *inalienable* rights existing at Common Law—not only rights but duties. A railway station, for example, is a place to which the public have right of access, either as intending travellers with a ticket, or as holders of a platform ticket, or without any ticket at all as when they can walk on to the platform to meet a friend, and the law demands that in respect of every such place there is an absolute duty not to allow any danger to exist if it is possible with reasonable care to avoid it, and in cases where it cannot be avoided, to bring the attention of the ordinary public to the danger, by warning, fencing, protection, or notice, so that no one may injure themselves in such a place. Breach of this duty will give anyone injured a right of action in tort, at Common Law—subject, of course, to contributory negligence on his part, for a full discussion of which see the section dealing with the law of tort.

It was back in 1888, when the railway was not the commonplace it is today, but still something a little unusual and rather special to many people, that a Mr Osborne, a season-ticket holder on the London and North Eastern Railway, was coming down the station steps, which were caked with snow from a recent fall, and patently slippery and dangerous. Mr Osborne slipped, crashed down the steps, and injured himself. He sued the railway company. In court he freely admitted that it was obvious that the steps were dangerous. But that made no difference—he was still entitled to recover, for he knew the danger, though not the extent of it. But even had he realized its extent, he would still have won his action for damages, for though they were dangerous, there was nothing about the station steps that would have made any attempt at descent by Mr Osborne 'unreasonable'—so he would in law have been entitled to descend and look to the railway company for the consequences of any injury incurred in doing so, because nothing could take away from the defendants their absolute Common Law duty not to allow a danger on their public premises to exist, or if it could not be remedied, to warn Mr Osborne.

But Mr Osborne was a season-ticket holder. What would have been the position had he been merely the holder of a platform ticket—and we shall for this purpose disregard the contractual problems arising there. Happily, we know, and the answer is that he would have succeeded, for there is a case right on the point, which happened as recently as 1949. A certain Dr Stowell was seeing someone arrive at, or someone leaving, a station, and he held a platform ticket and was on the platform when he slipped and went flying over a patch of oil or similar slippery substance—it may have been a piece of orange peel, as far as the legal point goes. He sued the Railway Executive (the Executive was later dissolved and the present standing defendant in such actions is now the British Transport Commission*), who replied, in effect, "What are you to us? You are not a traveller—you are a mere station user—we have no duty toward you!" But they were wrong, and Dr Stowell was successful in his action, the Court holding that a station is a place to which the general public has access, and whether the plaintiff is a train user or a mere platform user, in law the duty toward him is exactly the same.

* *Changes arising from the Transport Act, 1962, are described on p. 859.*

So much for slippery traps—but what about a factor which may also have its dangers, and which, at least in London, is so usual as to be almost invariable at certain hours of the day—what about overcrowding? Have the railways a duty in this respect? To some extent, they have. They have a duty not to let the platforms become so overcrowded that passengers are pushed on to the line and thereby injured or killed.

But this duty cannot be carried too far. There is no liability on the railways if, in the stress and strain of the 'rush hour' a fight develops and a passenger is assaulted by another. He can sue his attacker, but not the railways in that respect.

What about overcrowding actually on the trains themselves? Supposing a small child is caught in the tremendous surge from a packed carriage when a train pulls into a station, and is swept off his feet and injured. The duty not to allow overcrowded carriages remains, but the child in such a case would fail, as the passengers were leaving the carriage at the time and if there was negligence it was by one or more of them, and not by the railways.

On the subject of children, it might be as well to observe that all carriers of passengers are required to make provision for the safety of small children— but only on the basis that they will be accompanied on their journey by some adult person who is capable of looking after them.

On this 'escape clause', if one may so describe it informally, which the railways have used successfully, when they blame other passengers and thus escape liability—take an incident which one would imagine is more suited to an adventure novel than to real life—suppose that someone brings a bomb into a compartment of a train and it goes off, accidentally or intentionally, in the middle of the journey, injuring and killing innocent passengers. Is this a good ground for an action by an injured passenger against the railway? Strange as it may seem, this is not so imaginary an incident as you might suppose; it actually happened, in India, in 1918—and the passenger failed. It seems, therefore, that one may be quite dogmatic about it—there is no liability falling on the railways in respect of any injury to any passenger from his fellow-passengers.

What about the question of doors? There is a primary liability on the railways to take reasonable care to see that they are shut before the train starts. If the train starts to move, and as it slides away down the platform a compartment door swings open and strikes a person standing lawfully on the platform, the railways are primarily liable. But during the course of the journey, the doors of an actual compartment are obviously not continuously under the control of the railways and the Courts have so held. Supposing that while the train is going full speed ahead a door comes open and a brave, if foolhardy, passenger goes to shut it and falls out—whether the railways would be liable for his injury would depend on the degree of contributory negligence held against the plaintiff by the Court—it might be one hundred per cent. if the Court found that there was no real justification for his voluntary action.

Take another example which actually happened, fortunately without any injury in this case, so that there was no action. A non-smoking compartment, and a slightly befuddled passenger absent-mindedly lighting a cigarette is courteously reminded of where he is by a fellow-passenger. Apologising, and in some confusion, he goes to open the window to throw the cigarette out, but opens the door by mistake. Had anyone been injured as a result, would any claim for damages have lain against the railways? It may safely be said, "No".

There are very many possible problems which can arise concerned with doors of trains—the variations are almost infinite. But the general principles are the same in each case.

Let us turn to another not infrequent problem arising out of train travel. It is night. A slow suburban train plods along, stopping at every station. After some little time of running along, it pulls up. A man gets up, takes his hat and his umbrella, knowing that this is his stop. He opens the door and steps out—some six feet on to the side of the line, for the train has not in fact arrived at his station, or any station, but has pulled up at a signal. Would there be any liability on the railways in such a case? One may say definitely not with some certainty. Why not? Because the passenger never received any 'invitation to alight'. He made a wrong assumption which he had no right at all to make.

But now let us imagine the same set of circumstances, except that before he opens the door there is audible to everyone in the compartment the cry of a station official calling out the name of the station, and it is in response to this 'invitation' that the passenger opens the door and steps out, whereas in fact his particular end of the train has not yet reached the end of the platform, but is some yards short of it.

The position is simply this. If a passenger is genuinely led by the actions of the railway or its servants to believe that the train has arrived at its destination, and the passenger has acted on that invitation and is hurt in consequence, then he may recover damages. But whether the circumstances actually amount to such an invitation will depend on the facts in each individual case.

It is not in itself negligence for a train to over-shoot or stop short of the platform, though there are circumstances in which it could be negligence, and this might assist the passenger. Of course, the extent of his contributory negligence, if any, would be materially affected by the conditions of light and/or weather—in daylight he would have less excuse for stepping out than at night, or in thick fog, for example.

It has been held that the mere calling out of the name of a station by the railway staff may not of itself be an invitation, but if the station name is called out, and there is an interval, and no warning is similarly shouted out, then that will probably be considered an invitation to alight. In one case, the porter on the station, after calling out the station name, saw that part of the train was not against the platform and shouted, "Keep your seats!" but this was not heard by the man who fell out on to the line and was injured, and it was held that he could recover.

It may be added that if the passenger looks out, can see and does see the position, and the danger, and then nevertheless decides to jump down regardless, he will not be able to recover damages, for obvious reasons.

Turning next to the subject of platforms generally, it has been established that there is a legal duty on the railways to make sure that their platforms are reasonably safe. If there is a projection over which a passenger, particularly one in a crowd, may trip, then any passenger who does trip and is injured may recover. Previous examples already quoted here show that the presence of ice, snow, oil, or even fruit peel on a platform, will be held normally to constitute a 'trap', from which liability will fall on to the railway organization.

But if the railway can prove by evidence that they had noticed the danger, that they had done everything in their power to remove it, and that they had also taken proper and sufficient steps to warn passengers, then they will be cleared of liability. There is also the invariable question of contributory negligence by the passenger. If the danger is an obvious one, but the passenger takes no steps to avoid it, though he could see it in front of him, then any damages which he may recover will be reduced to the extent of his own negligence.

At night, the railways have a duty to light their platforms sufficiently and properly to make them safe. And they are also responsible for taking such precautions as may be necessary in fog. But it has been held that a passenger who slipped and fell without any contributory negligence on his part could recover damages fully, it being no valid answer on the part of the railways that the passenger could have selected a different, and safer, route.

These general rules apply not only to personal injuries—they also apply to the property of passengers. If through the negligence of the railway organization a passenger's luggage suffers damage, then he may sue for this damage, just as he could if he were personally injured. And it was held in one case that the owner of luggage had a perfectly good claim even though he, the owner, was not personally in charge of it, as it was being transported by a servant of his.

What is the position of trespassers—those strictly trespassers in law, for in the section of this book dealing with torts it was pointed out that a person accepted by the railways as a passenger, even if he was in some measure a fraud, is not in law a trespasser? The answer is that the railways have no general duty to trespassers, save that they must not deliberately set traps to injure them.

Take, for instance, the example of a level crossing. There is a large notice instructing all passengers to use a footbridge over the line—informing them that walking across the line itself is trespass. If a person walks across the line and gets hit by a train, one would think that he could have no claim at all. That may be the case, but if in fact it was proved in Court by evidence of several people that despite the notice, it had become almost traditional, certainly customary for people to walk across the line, ignoring the bridge, *to the knowledge of the railway servants* (the importance of that phrase cannot be exaggerated) then this knowledge and lack of action combined might be construed by the Court as an invitation to cross the line despite the notice, and in that event the pedestrian might recover damages.

Thinking of warnings, it is not perhaps generally known that the communication cord on an ordinary train is there not by caution as much as by statute. In fact, under the Regulation of Railways Act, 1868, any train travelling more than twenty miles from its start must provide some means of communication between the passengers on the train and those in control of it. And if the cord is not provided, or if it does not work, when pulled, and if it is later proved that an accident to a passenger might have been avoided if it had been in proper working order, then that may be regarded as evidence of some negligence against the railway organization.

There is one final point which has been demonstrated in Court and which

723

may come to the mind of the reader—and that is the drunk passenger. This selfish individual is almost inevitably going to cause acute embarrassment and distress to his fellow-passengers. What, if anything, can they do about it? Can they claim that it is negligent of a railway to allow a passenger on a train who is patently unfit to travel through gross intoxication? If annoyed, or even

"It is not in law negligence on the part of the railway to allow a drunken passenger to board a train."

injured, granted they can sue the drunk—but can they sue the railway? The answer is that they cannot. It has been established that it is not in law negligence on the part of the railway to allow a drunken passenger to board a train, and they will escape liability unless it can be shown that the condition and activities of the drunk were brought to the attention of the railway servants (ticket-collector, possibly, or even the guard) but nothing was done about it to restrain him.

724

On the other hand, if the drunk completes his journey and falls and injures himself after he has got off the train, the railway is not responsible, for they are in no way subject to a duty to care for, and look after, the drunk once he has reached his destination. Once there, their liability ceases, and if the drunk leaves the station and falls under a bus, he cannot blame the railway for having carried him to the place where he met with his accident.

If you buy a ticket for travel in a Second Class compartment, but cannot find a seat, are you therefore entitled to sit in a First Class compartment without paying the difference between the First and Second Class fares? The answer is that you are not.

LUGGAGE IN RAILWAY 'LEFT LUGGAGE' OFFICES OR ON THE TRAIN

If you leave your luggage in a railway 'left luggage' office, the general rule is that they are responsible for its safe-keeping. If it is lost, handed out to someone else or destroyed, the railway are primarily responsible.

But, as might be expected, they do protect themselves by contract from responsibility for exceptional risks.

The ordinary basic charge per parcel or per case is small. Why should they accept responsibility for all goods whatever their value? By contract, *i.e.* by the conditions on the cloakroom ticket, they make their position perfectly clear.

If the value of the luggage deposited is more than £5 the depositor has no right to compensation for its loss unless he has declared its value at the time when he deposited it and paid whatever small additional sum is appropriate on the railway's conditions of contract. The additional sum is comparatively small. The point is that unless it is paid, the railway are not liable for loss of the goods deposited. Or, to be precise, *probably* not liable. In general, the contract conditions on the cloakroom ticket are upheld by the Courts. But there have been instances where the total and inexplicable loss of the goods from the cloakroom has led the Courts to hold the railway liable, even though the goods were worth over £5 and should have been declared. But it is unwise to rely on such chances of litigation when you know full well that the luggage you are depositing contains clothes, furs, jewellery, books, etc., which are worth far more. In such a case it is wiser to declare an approximate value and pay the appropriate extra charge rather than the standard charge.

What of the safety of your luggage on the train while you are travelling?

If it has been put into the luggage-van, then the primary responsibility for its safety rests with the railway. They can escape this responsibility only if they can prove that its loss, or damage caused to it, is not their fault. The burden of proving this is on them, and it is not an easy burden to discharge, because the luggage is in their safe-keeping.

But this responsibility is also subject to a rule about value. If your luggage contains articles which put the total value over £25, the railway are not responsible unless you have declared the value and paid whatever additional sum may be required under their published list of rates.

725

If you take your luggage into your compartment with you, then *you* are responsible for its safe custody.

TRAVEL BY AIR

Apart from the special provisions of the Statute Law which apply to travelling by air, as set out by the Carriage by Air Act, 1961, and the Civil Aviation Act, 1949, the same general principles apply to common carriers by air as apply to all other common carriers. At Common Law, the liability of the owner of the plane (under certain circumstances the hirer, in his place) and his servants, notably the pilot and navigator, are exactly the same as if they were controlling any land-based vehicle.

This applies to the extent that should a plane crash while in course of take-off, or at all before reaching the normal height at which the journey is planned to be accomplished, this will be regarded as *prima facie* evidence of negligence—in other words, from the plaintiff's point of view he may plead *res ipsa loquitur*.

And the liability does not commence only when the plane moves off down the runway—nor does it apply only to passengers. One case arose where a man, seeing his wife and children off on a plane trip, was allowed or invited by the aircraft company to stand near the plane in such a position that when the engines started the poor fellow was hit by the end of the propellor and killed. The action against the company succeeded there.

What about a passenger in an aircraft who is not a fare-paying ticket-holder at all, but the guest of a munificent gentleman who has hired or chartered the plane? Suppose that he is injured in the course of the flight, through the negligence of the company. Can he sue them? He can. And will they be able to say, "But you were not a fare-payer—you were only a guest—we have no liability towards you"? No, they will not.

May there be express contract conditions imposed on the air traveller, as on the train traveller? Only to a limited extent, for the law has made it illegal for an aircraft company or organization to 'contract out' of its liability to fare-paying passengers.

Should the accident be a fatal one (and, of course, in aircraft crashes it very often is) then the relatives of the deceased have certain rights against the company. Under deaths caused by negligence other than in the air, the relatives pursue their claim under the Fatal Accidents Acts, 1846 and the Law Reform Acts. (See section of this book dealing with those rights in detail.) The normal period within which such claims must be started is three years.

By the provisions of the Carriage by Air Act, 1961, however, if a passenger in an aircraft 'on international carriage' (and there has been a mass of legal argument about the exact meaning of those vital words) is killed, his relatives bring their action under the terms of *this* Act—but they must remember that the statutory limit is reduced from three years to two years. And from when does this limitation run? It runs from the date when the aircraft was scheduled to arrive at its destination, or the date on which the carriage stopped. Moreover, it has been laid down that the method of calculating the 'period of limitation' as it is known—the two-year period—is to be decided by the law of the

726

country in which the action comes to be tried. Because one of the worst complications about travel to other countries is this difficult question about the country in which the action shall be heard, and the differences and similarities of the laws of that country and any other country with which the contract may

At one time lawyers described an aircraft as a 'dangerous thing',

but as flying progressed, this was—

—considered no longer true!

have been concerned. This is one of the most difficult and complicated subjects in the whole of the legal world—it is known as 'Private International Law', and is usually dealt with only by those who specialize in such problems.

It was mentioned above that no aircraft organization is allowed to make an express contract with its passengers whereby all liability for the negligence of its servants is agreed to be denied. But to a limited extent a company *may*, under other provisions of the Carriage by Air Act, 1961, provided the contract is one of 'international carriage', limit its liability to each passenger to a certain sum of money. Unfortunately, the values of different currencies in the economic conditions of today are so changeable and unstable that the sum provided for as the top limit of contractual liability in these cases is in terms of a notional currency against which all other currencies can be judged—the limit is 250,000 gold francs. The value of this changes almost from day to day, in pounds, but you may take it that it represents a very substantial sum. As a postscript to this, there are, though rarely, circumstances in which this limit can be topped—as established by one recent case, which held that really wilful misconduct on the part of the company, or possibly express agreement prior to the flight, will enable a higher figure to be obtained.

Referring back to general terms, it was at one time thought by some lawyers that an aircraft could be described as a 'dangerous thing' within the rule in *Rylands* v. *Fletcher*, which is discussed and explained at length in the section of this book which deals with torts. But as flying progressed, the success of this argument became less likely to succeed, and it has now been held in terms that an aircraft is definitely not, in itself, a 'dangerous thing' within the meaning of that rule.

Nevertheless, in cases of an aircraft in flight which crashes, it may be so difficult as to be almost impossible for the relatives of a passenger who is killed to prove that the crash was caused by the negligence of those concerned. And since the law was ultimately compelled to cover this provision, Parliament passed the Civil Aviation Act, 1949, under Section 40 of which if damage, death, or injury is caused in any way to any property or person arising out of an aircraft being in motion (these are not the words of the Act) then damages may be recovered by or on behalf of any person affected *without proof of negligence*. In other words, since 1949, liability for death or injury or loss or damage to person or property is 'absolute' upon the aircraft concern, and their only counter is to prove contributory negligence on the part of the plaintiff.

We say 'aircraft concern' there, as most travel by the public is through the medium of the big air-lines. But it is possible to fly by private plane, of course. In that event, it is the plane-owner who would normally suffer this 'absolute liability' created by the 1949 Act. The Act does, however, go on to provide that if the owner has hired the plane for fourteen days or more to someone else, who flies it himself or provides his own crew, then it is this hirer who has to bear this absolute liability, and not the owner.

TRAVEL BY SHIP

The first thing to remember about ships, as they affect the general traveller, is that in general terms, wherever it may go in the world, each and every British ship is a tiny piece of Britain—and similarly in respect of ships belonging to all other nationalities. This may not appear to the layman to have a great deal of significance, but its effect is far-reaching, because it means that on every British ship, wherever it may be, in port or on the high seas, British law applies on it, and to it, and to those travelling with it, or even temporarily on board it.

For example, if you have a fatal accident on board a British ship, your relatives may use the Fatal Accidents Act to sue those responsible, even though the ship may have been travelling between Singapore and Honolulu at the time.

Apart from this general consideration, however, it may be stated briefly that as between shipping companies and fare-paying passengers, their respective legal rights and liabilities, apart from special contract terms which are agreed between the parties to the contract (of which the ticket is evidence, as in the case of railways), the same Common Law rights and duties apply as if the carriage was over land.

Thus, apart from any special contractual exemptions which may be operative, the shipping company must take reasonable care, for example, to provide the passenger with proper access to a sleeping berth engaged by him, to make his cabin safe, in general terms, and to warn the passenger about the condition of the deck of the ship, should this contain any dangers.

Nevertheless, it must be stated as a general rule that the liability of the shipping company to the passenger is usually regulated by the terms of the contract between them. The shipping ticket is generally a much larger and more formal document than the train or the bus ticket, however, and the average passenger does not catch a ship with the same speed of action that he catches a train, so that he has usually far more time to study and to digest the very detailed conditions which are usually in tiny print on the ticket itself.

Statutes regulate the terms of contract for carriage by sea to some extent, and the principal Act with which the passenger may be concerned, whether he realizes it or not, is the Merchant Shipping Act of 1894. That Act lays down that shipowners *can* expressly limit their liability to passengers by express contract for loss of life or personal injury. But, whether they do so or not, Section 503 (1) (a) of that Act, since amended by later Acts, states that in the case of loss of life or personal injury to a passenger whilst aboard which occurs without negligence by the owners, the owners shall not be liable for a larger sum than is set out in the latest Act, at present the 1958 Act. Here again, like the 'gold franc' top limit in the Carriage by Air Act referred to above, the tonnage of most passenger ships is sufficiently large to make this an extremely high ceiling.

DAMAGES ARISING OUT OF TRAVEL

The problem of damages is a vast one, and it is impossible to do more than state a few general principles and quote a few examples. But the questions of damages arising out of negligence or breach of contract while travelling do raise some rather special problems, particularly in the case of trains. Before running through a few of them, however, it must be stated that it is in every case the overriding duty of the plaintiff in the action to do what he can to minimize his own loss or damage.

The basic rule is that damages may be recovered so as to effect compensation to the wronged plaintiff for all loss or damage *directly suffered*, whether or not that damage was reasonably foreseeable at the time. For example, damages for personal injury will cover not merely fractures, lacerations, and such-like, but will include shock, pain and suffering, loss of expectation of life,

729

and actual or even prospective disablement, as well as any actual expenses incurred as a result of the wrong.

Are damages recoverable when only shock has been sustained—or is that by itself too indefinite an item to be claimed? The answer is that such damages can be recovered, at least as regards the person injured by the wrong. It only becomes more complicated when one comes across the case of a pregnant woman, for example, who suffers shock as a result of negligence by a carrier, and finds that when her child is born, later, it is physically damaged by the shock sustained by the mother. This can, of course, happen, medically, although no actual case of this nature is recorded as having appeared before the Courts. It is therefore a point strictly debatable, but the general opinion seems to be that not only the woman but also the child could recover damages against the carrier. Sooner or later such a tragic instance may come for decision by the Courts and a definite ruling will then be made, converting an academic argument into a hard fact.

In the section of this book which deals with torts, you may recall the principle laid down by the case where a man, fearing for his life when the coach in which he was travelling got out of control down a steep hill, leaped for his life and suffered serious injuries. Although the coach later was controlled again so that had he not leaped out he would have been unhurt, nevertheless he recovered damages, as his action in the 'agony of the moment' was not held against him.

It is also perhaps a point worthy of mention that whether or not the defendants were insured against such risks as arise in claims against them is totally irrelevant to the question of damages. Damages are compensation to the injured, and not a punishment for the guilty—and if through careful insurance the defendants do not in fact have to pay out one penny of their own money (except, of course, for the policy premiums), the damages recoverable against them will be the same in any event.

But these, you may say, are very general points. They are, but there are a few extensions to or branches of the law relating to damages which particularly apply to travel. One of these arises out of the ordinary right, outside any express contract, of the passenger on, say, a train to be delivered safely to his destination *within a reasonable time*. You may well imagine that there have been very many arguments in Court as to the exact meaning of that term—when is the time, though delayed, still 'reasonable' and at what moment in time does it become 'unreasonable'. But assume for this purpose that it has been held or agreed to have been unreasonable, and the railways have to pay their passenger damages.

Let us now imagine a passenger who by reason of a delay caused through negligence has been prevented from reaching London by, say, 6 p.m. He was going to a dinner at 7.30—a dinner, moreover, for which he had bought in advance a £5 ticket. The train does not get him to London until 9.30. Will the £5 he has thus, in effect, lost be recoverable? Certainly.

Now let us take it a stage further. Suppose that, instead of a dinner, he planned to get to London by 6 p.m. in order that he could catch (from that station or another) the 7.15 evening train to his home out in the distant country—a place so small that the 7.15 is the last train to it at all until the following morning. He cannot now get a train until the next day, and this was the fault of the railways. He must spend the night in London, you say. And if he does, passing an angry, and probably a sleepless, night in a small hotel near the station, can he recover the cost of that night? Yes, he can, under normal circumstances—people before him have done so.

What if he simply *had* to reach his home that night—in order to be on time for a vitally important business appointment the following morning—and what if he hired a car, or took a taxi? This, too, he could probably recover, subject to one overriding test which the court would apply—a test formulated many years ago in a case on the point.

The test is simply this—supposing that the delay in question was not the fault of the railway but of himself. Under those circumstances, would he have incurred the same expense? If the court accepts that he would have, then he may recover the expenses from the railway if it was their fault. And, of course, he must not be unreasonable, extravagant or oppressive. That is but an application of the plaintiff's duty to minimize his own loss. Not that he is obliged to find a room in a doss-house for the night—not that he would be made to sit about in the waiting-room till morning. But he would not be able to drive to the most expensive hotel in London—somewhere he would normally never dream of staying—and acquire their best room at a huge price and expect to recover that.

Indeed, on one very celebrated occasion, many years ago now, in 1870, one gentleman, finding himself cut off from his destination through the fault of the railway company, actually went to the trouble and expense of hiring a special train to take him to where he wanted to go. On this subject the Court said that under the particular (and rare!) circumstances of his case, he could recover this expense, so you will see that even that *could* be held to be 'reasonable', though with the modern alternative methods of transport available it would be most unlikely, today!

Of course, when a train, through the fault of the railways, is seriously late, the passengers so delayed suffer not merely financial loss here and there, but almost invariably vexation and disappointment. Can damages be recovered under this head? No, that is going too far. But if any real and measureable inconvenience has been suffered, capable of being specifically stated, this is in principle recoverable by way of damages.

What about the man whose train is late so that he misses a business appointment and consequently suffers a financial loss of several thousand pounds, which he would have gained, had he been there on time—can he claim for the resulting loss of business, however much it is? The answer to that one is no—*unless* the railways were given specific notice at the time of the contract or ticket of the object of this special journey. Then they might be liable, but not otherwise.

Certainly there is authority for saying that a workman who loses a day's wages by reason of the railway's negligence, and there not being any special contractual protection for them, can recover a day's wages by way of damages.

ROADS, STREETS, AND PATHS

Lawyers usually think of 'roads, streets, and paths'—as being summarized in the single word 'highways'. And this word conjures up a whole field of the law, which it is our task now to deal with, pointing out the essential principles.

The initial basis on which this subject needs tackling has already been laid in earlier sections of this book. They are the general principles of negligence and of nuisance. They apply as much to highways as to anything else. Indeed, they are perhaps applied even more to highways than to anything else. Leaving aside the aspects already covered, such as the Road Traffic laws, and motor claims cases, it is necessary to examine the rights and the liabilities which affect ordinary members of the public as they pass along the highway.

As an example of how the general principles apply, take the doctrine of 'foreseeability' and *novus actus interveniens* (see section on torts). When a Water Board was responsible for a manhole with a flap cover in the highway which it was well known that children invariably played with, it was held to be foreseeable by them when someone tripped over the flap cover when the children had left it sticking up, and the injured plaintiff recovered damages.

Trees with branches projecting over a public highway have been held to be a 'nuisance' and gave rise to damages in another case. The principle of recoverable damages being the 'natural and probable cause of the act of the defendants' also applies. In an older case, the defendants by their negligence allowed a set of circumstances the effect of which was that water spouted up in the middle of a public road. Some horses travelling along near the spot took fright, swerved, fell into a nearby cutting, and were hurt. They would not have reached the cutting and the consequent drop, had this not been fenced carelessly by those constructing it. Despite this, their owner recovered damages against the company that caused the original danger.

Highway users—their duty to each other

The principles which apply here can best be illustrated by the famous case of *Bourhill* v. *Young*, which was dealt with in the section of this book dealing with torts. There the Courts examined in detail not merely the facts of the case but also the principles involved. They examined how far the duty of each highway user to each other extended. The case is worthy of detailed study in connection with this fundamental principle.

Many of the principles which still apply today in modern form were based originally on the ancient action of 'trespass', and if that was established on the part of the defendant, then the plaintiff recovered damages irrespective of whether actual negligence could be proved by him. But this does *not* apply to accidents on the highway, in general. If a pedestrian on the highway is run over, he has no valid claim for damages unless he can prove some degree of negligence against the defendant.

But in reported cases, old and new, we may find many examples of what may be found to be negligence. A horse and cart is left unattended on the highway—that has been held to be evidence of negligence in itself. If a vehicle is on the road, moving or stationary, without proper and sufficient 'tackle' (in other words, in proper working order) this is negligence in itself, also. But that was a principle decided at the beginning of the last century. Now bring it up to date and apply it to motor-cars. The basic difference between a horse and cart and a motor-car is that the former involves a horse or horses, which, if they take fright, may suddenly bolt, causing damage to innocent passers-by. But a car is not likely to start off on its own accord, and cannot 'bolt'. And so the modern development of this old principle shows us first that it is not evidence of negligence in itself to leave a motor-car unattended in a road *except* when it is left in such a position and in such a manner that it could move of its own accord—for example, on a steep slope if the brakes failed—or if it was open and could be started by a child.

Now let us apply this to a vehicle, such as a lorry, left unlit on the side of a road at night. There were two cases decided in 1944, and at first sight it seemed difficult indeed to reconcile the two decisions. If a lorry is left unlit on a highway at night, can this be a case of creating a 'nuisance' in law? Because if it can, then the injured plaintiff need not trouble himself about proving negligence at all—he has but to prove the nuisance and his damage resulting from it, and he will succeed. In the first of these two cases it was held that under certain circumstances an unlit lorry on the highway at night could indeed be a 'nuisance', and the plaintiff recovered in that case without proof of negligence. But in the second case the court really modified this by saying that while the principle in the first case was a correct one, the circumstances under which it could be exercised were very rare indeed, and that in all normal cases the plaintiff must prove negligence, to some extent, in order to entitle him to recover damages. It is this second case which is in general taken as the guiding one today.

On the other hand, there can be literal 'obstructions in the highway' that can only be described as 'public nuisances'. In a 1916 case it was held that the person or authority who created that obstruction would be liable in damages to anyone injured by it (or should one say 'against it'?) *unless* it was erected there by statutory authority *and* all proper and reasonable steps were taken to prevent it becoming a danger to the public, such as lighting it at night. To this principle, there is an exception, however, which must be remembered. The Act of Parliament which gave rise to its erection may have conferred upon the erecting body absolute immunity—that has been known. In general, and apart from that exception, however, the rule is that if a public body erect an obstruction and leave it unlighted at night, they will be liable, unless they can prove that the lack of illumination was not through their negligence but through unforeseeable circumstances.

Occupiers of premises adjoining a highway—their liability

Such people have certain very strict legal obligations and responsibilities over and above the ordinary householder. They must not in any circumstances create a potential public nuisance which, accidentally encroaching on to the public highway, causes injury or damage to a highway user. The leadin g case on this point concerned a hanging ornamental lamp which fell one day on to the head of an innocent passer-by. But the principle does not stop there. It has been extended to cover the case of a butcher, whose shop was on the roadside, outside whose shop there lay a lump of meat fat. Now the butcher had not put it there—but as there was nowhere else around whence it could have come, it was found as a question of fact that it must have been carried there on the sole or heel of a customer leaving the shop. Nevertheless, the butcher was liable in damages to the injured person who slipped on the piece of fat and seriously injured herself, because the butcher, by dealing in meat fat, among other things, had thereby, albeit unknowingly, been the cause of a danger on the public highway.

You may think that this could be particularly harsh on an occupier. Recognizing this, the courts have held that if the danger was something like a roof-slate falling on to the pavement, and if this was the responsibility of the owner, rather than the occupier, as the owner was liable for keeping the premises in good structural repair, then the liability for damages may pass to the owner, as opposed to the occupier. But this is only if the owner had a right to 'enter and do repairs' and an obligation to do them. If the owner's obligation were simply to effect any repairs reported to him by the occupier and no more, the position would be different and the occupier would remain liable.

What is the position of a landowner whose land adjoins a highway—suppose he has horses which graze on this land and a horse escapes from his land and gets on to the highway, where it inflicts damage upon a motor-car which comes into unexpected contact with it at night? Curiously enough, there will be no liability on the landowner for this *unless* the plaintiff can prove that the landowner was negligent in some specific way. This is because there is in law no duty on the part of a landowner in such a position to prevent the escape of anything from his land on to the highway—unless that something happens to be an intrinsically dangerous thing, when he becomes liable under the rule in *Rylands* v. *Fletcher*. But a horse is clearly not a thing essentially dangerous in itself.

We have been speaking of the duties attaching to owners or occupiers of premises 'adjoining the highway'. How near is 'adjoining', is a question which may well be asked. In answer it can only be said that no specific distance has been named as a dividing line, but there is a guide in a case decided in 1944. This arose out of a nasty accident when the plaintiff, on a dark foggy night, went headlong into a dock, quite inadvertently, the dock being forty-seven feet from the edge of the highway. He claimed, justifiably, that had the dock been fenced off, he would not have fallen in. This was true, but the duty so to fence would have applied if the dock had been 'adjoining the highway'. Did it apply when the property was forty-seven feet away, or was that too far from the highway to be strictly 'adjoining' it, in law? It was held to be too far, and the plaintiff failed on that count.

Premises adjoining the highway may, of course, take the form of sports grounds, golf clubs, and so forth. And it is happily rare, though not entirely unknown, for people travelling lawfully along the highway to be struck by golf balls, cricket balls, etc. What is the legal position in such cases? The answer is that it varies according to the circumstances—how regularly, or how unexpectedly, does such an event take place? In the case of one golf club, where a highway crossed part of the course and it was a fairly regular thing for balls to land on it, or shoot over it at a low trajectory and high velocity, a person who was hit and injured successfully sued the club, as the event had happened too often for it to be described by the defendants as 'unforeseeable'. On the other hand, a person lawfully proceeding along the highway outside a cricket ground and who was injured by a ball, ultimately failed in his claim, although the matter went as far as the House of Lords. The claim failed simply because the

"Trees . . . adjoining the highway . . ."

Court accepted that such a tremendous hit as the height of the boundary fence demanded was almost phenomenal, not to be reasonably expected, and therefore not reasonably foreseeable by the cricket club.

Next we turn to the subject of trees. These, rooted and flourishing on private land adjoining the highway, can sometimes be nothing less than a public nuisance if they are allowed to grow until they overhang the highway itself, endangering such passing innocents as those on the upper decks of buses. Again, branches of trees have been known to fall, sometimes entirely without warning, and they can injure or even kill, if this happens. What is the legal position here?

In general terms, the answer depends upon what is only really another aspect of that important word 'foreseeability'. The owner of the land on which the tree is planted will be liable to anyone in the highway who is hurt, provided that he knew of the potential danger, or if he *ought* to have known it, had he taken proper interest and proper precautions.

In one case, the tree owner was found not to have been liable for the fall of a tree, or part of it, on to the highway, because there was absolutely no reason to suppose that the tree was anything but stout and strong, although in fact it turned out to have had a 'latent defect' in the form of an arboreal disease which showed no outside symptoms. This could never have been discovered until the tree suddenly fell, unless at regular and short intervals the tree had been examined by an expert. To arrange such repeated and expensive examinations was held to be too high a duty to impose upon the owner of the tree, and the claim failed.

On the other hand, some years later, when a tree fell on to the highway and injured a passer-by, the claim succeeded. But in this case the tree was one which had been seen by all and sundry to have been dying, and a potential danger, for years. It did not need an expert to tell that. And consequently, this was a danger which its owner either knew, or ought to have known, and he was found liable.

Let us now take this matter of trees a stage further. Suppose that a tree falls without any negligence on the part of the owner. It was not a foreseeable danger. But the owner is made aware of its having fallen. Now—night is falling fast, and the tree lies right across part of a country road, where there is no street lighting. Has the tree owner here a duty to light the tree or to warn coming people or traffic of its presence? A decided case says that he has *not* such a duty.

But if a tree falls, and, for example, its falling can be deduced as being directly attributable to recent road-widening operations by a local authority, who went too near its roots so that the tree became unsafe, in such a case the person hurt by its fall can successfully sue the local authority as it was their negligence which was the direct cause of the accident and such an event should have been foreseen by them.

Before leaving the question of premises adjoining the highway, let us look for a moment at the position of owners and occupiers of such things as warehouses, where goods have sometimes to be hauled up to upper floors by means of pulleys and ropes. If this involves goods being raised or lowered over the heads of people lawfully and peaceably proceeding along the highway, then those performing such an operation have a very strong duty to take all reasonable care, and this applies whether there are any people actually on the highway at the time or not—again we see the effect of the 'foreseeability' rule, for whatever the actual position at the time, the operation must be done on the basis that there might be people coming along at any moment.

NUISANCE AND NEGLIGENCE EXAMINED TOGETHER

The first general rule on this important topic is that if a person *creates* a nuisance, or is responsible for it being created, or if he allowed it to continue as a nuisance after he became aware of it, he is liable for damage done as a result of that nuisance. But he is not going to be liable for a nuisance unless he either created it or allowed it to continue after becoming aware of it.

There was a startling incident in the East Anglian town of Lowestoft which provides a good illustration of this point. One day, without previous warning, there was an ominous rumbling in the main road and a whole section of it subsided and disappeared. The collapse was both sudden and dangerous, and a member of the public who suffered damage sued the local authority. The reasons for the collapse were gone into by experts, and it was revealed that, oddly enough, the damage had been caused by rats, which had eaten away the sewer joints, until finally the sewer caved in, with the results that we have seen. It was not due to any faulty construction of the sewer by the Lowestoft Corporation, nor indeed was there any means by which they could have been warned of the impending collapse, for it was not really discoverable at all until it actually happened. And the claim against them failed, in consequence.

On the other hand, this point of view cannot be carried too far. An important leading case was heard in 1940, which established that in the case of actual buildings which adjoined the highway, all property, wherever it is, does need checking and repairing from time to time, and there is accordingly a duty on such property owners to keep a constant eye on it at reasonable intervals. If they do not, and there is a collapse or similar disaster which they did not anticipate, they may be found liable to anybody hurt.

Having then assimilated the general rule about nuisance, it will be appreciated that one very significant thing about it is that if nuisance exists, and the other circumstances are right, then liability will be incurred *quite irrespective of negligence*. If there is nuisance, there does not have to be any negligence at all proved by a plaintiff wishing to succeed.

But that is not all. What is done may be done deliberately, in good faith, and under circumstances where the doer's general belief is quite justified. If it is a nuisance in law, then he will be condemned in damages if others are harmed by what he has done.

Let us now see some of the applications of these principles to the subject of highways. First of all, an obstruction in a highway at night and unlit is in law a nuisance. What about a moving vehicle travelling along the road with no lights? The lights may be out by reason of the driver's negligence—it is not inevitable but it is highly probable, let us say. And the driver can be sued for any negligence, if negligence can be proved (not just stated but *proved*) against

737

him. But what if it cannot be proved? Could the driver be sued for nuisance? The answer is an emphatic 'no'—because apart from anything else, nothing can be an 'obstruction' whilst it is continuing to move.

But now let us imagine that someone has drawn the driver's attention to the fact that his lights are out—it is, let us suppose, a case of only his rear lights. As soon as he becomes aware of the event, the driver pulls in to the side of the road and stops. Now if someone hits the lorry, can he be sued for creating a nuisance, even without any negligence on his part? No, unless or until he is proved negligent, there is no nuisance created by him—yet. If he stands by the vehicle in the darkness, if he waves a torch when other vehicles approach, if he continues to do his best to warn the public of the danger on the road formed by his unlit vehicle—whether he succeeds or fails, he is doing no wrong, unless he can be proved to have been negligent in some respect. But let him move away from that unlit vehicle, leaving it unlit—even in order to go and get help, or to borrow some proper lamps—and there is in law an 'abandonment' on his part. At that moment, the unlit vehicle becomes a nuisance in law. The most temporary abandonment will suffice. But provided he does not commit any act of negligence, then as long as he sticks by his vehicle to warn other traffic, or he leaves it properly lit—then any action will fail, because there is no nuisance in law.

On the other hand, if the action is based not on the defendant merely 'causing a nuisance' but on his 'causing *and continuing* a nuisance', then negligence does have to be proved in any event for the plaintiff to succeed, for he must prove that the defendant 'neglected to remedy' the nuisance.

A war-time case provides a good example of this. The blast of a bomb which fell near a house loosened some of the roof slates. It was found that under the circumstances the occupiers, who had not caused the nuisance, were not negligent in 'failing to remedy' it when later the slates fell into the highway and injured someone, for it could not be said that with reasonable care and skill they should have known about the continuing nuisance.

By contrast, an illustration of the 'other side of the coin', as it were, is provided by another case, decided in the same year, 1941. There, snow had fallen and it had been allowed to collect nearer and nearer the guttering of a roof which overhung the highway, with nobody having done a thing about it. One day, it fell with hurtful results to an innocent passer-by, without actual warning. The occupiers were held liable, because, in contrast to the previously mentioned case, here was an instance of a danger of which they clearly should have been aware, without the services of any expert being called in.

OBSTRUCTION OF THE HIGHWAY ITSELF

The basic principle that must first be stated is that it is in law a 'public nuisance' to obstruct or hinder the free passage of the ordinary public along any highway. And if it is satisfactorily proved, the person creating the nuisance is liable without proof of negligence. A private individual has a right of action if he sustains particular damage as a result of any such obstruction, but he must show that his suffering was for some reason greater than that suffered by the average member of the public, in order to make his damage recoverable. He is also subject to the principle that his damage must be substantial, and not too remote, but directly caused by the defendant.

An occupier of property either on, or immediately alongside, the highway can bring this type of action, also, and by 'immediately alongside' is meant 'sufficiently near the highway that he is affected by the nuisance'. For example, an old case held that where a plaintiff had been obstructed by the action of the defendant from carrying his corn from his field to his farm, so that the corn was damaged by rain, he had a good right of action.

"Frontagers"

People whose property actually is in contact with the highway—'frontagers' as they are sometimes known—have an interest over and above that of the ordinary public, in that they can sue for damage done to a road which affects them as frontagers. But mere personal inconvenience is not enough on which to base a claim—they must show that they have sustained actual financial loss. And although every man suffering from a nuisance has a right in law to take steps to abate that nuisance, a man cannot sue under this head for money which he spent in exercising his legal right to abate the nuisance of which he complains.

Examples which are taken from decided cases show that a shop-owner can sue another arising out of large vans continually being left right outside his front door, obstructing his light, offending his customers with offensive smells, and generally losing him business. It is also possible to make oneself liable to

739

action by a frontager by making one's own premises nearby so diverting and attractive that crowds are drawn to the place in such volume as to block the door of the plaintiff. If I have a shop which sells ice-cream, but instead of inviting people into my shop to buy it, I cut out a section of my front shop-window and sell it through there so that the highway is blocked and my neighbour suffers, he can sue me, but on the other hand, if my goods prove so popular that a queue collects outside my door and along the pavement, without my doing anything to create that queue outside of ordinary business, then you will not succeed in a claim against me, even if your shop, next door, is interfered with by the crowd wanting to buy my goods.

Suppose that I obstruct the highway in such a way that *prospective* customers are diverted from your shop, and you lose business—will you succeed in recovering damages against me? The answer must be that each case of this type is one of degree—one can point to examples indicating success, and others presaging failure.

One general principle affecting all frontagers: any one of them may use the highway for the purpose of loading or unloading his goods, and generally for securing access to his premises, even if thereby he effects a temporary inconvenience to the public—provided no serious or lasting obstruction is caused.

DANGERS IN THE HIGHWAY

In general terms, whether you dig a trench, or place a pile of stones in the highway, even when you are not negligent, you will be liable to anyone injuring themselves in consequence. It is no good being like the man who erected a little cairn of stones in the middle of a road out of the top of which emerged a wooden rod, attached to the end of which was a red light. When asked what the stones were for, this apocryphal being replied that they were to hold the light firmly, and when questioned about the reason for the light, he replied that it was to keep people and vehicles away from the stones!

If a highway authority has authorized and instructed an independent contractor to do work in the highway for them, they are liable if he, by negligence, fails to warn or protect the public from any danger to them thus created.

Nor need a thing actually impede the progress of the public along the highway to be a nuisance. For example, a small pile of slates placed in the gutter for collection was held to be a nuisance, and a pedestrian who tripped over it recovered damages under this heading. (Even so, it must be remembered by plaintiffs that it might be held to be contributory negligence by them not to see such an obstruction.) The piece of fat carried on to the pavement from the butcher's shop, a case mentioned earlier, was a nuisance, you will remember. And a company which built and used coke ovens beside the highway, so that clouds of smoke and steam constantly poured out across the highway, obstructing the view of drivers of vehicles on the highway, had to pay damages to a plaintiff injured as a result. This is a danger which many people have encountered, no doubt, when garden bonfires create such an 'obstruction', but happily it does not often result in an accident.

PROTECTION FOR THE INDIVIDUAL

If someone, either by his own act or by the act of independent contractors authorized and instructed by him, does place an obstruction in the highway—even when that is legal and authorized, as under certain circumstances it may be—he is still under a duty to protect the public by lighting the obstruction by night and warning them of it by day. A local authority frequently erects an obstruction in the highway under the authority of an Act of Parliament. And if the statute which authorizes them so to act does not mention any duty to light that structure at night, are they liable to someone injured? To this extent, certainly—that if the authority, having erected the obstruction, generally lights it at night, and then slips up so that one night it remains unlit, then the authority is liable to an injured plaintiff. This is because there are two factors involved which throw liability in any event on to a defendant—in the first place, negligence, and in the second, the creation of a nuisance.

In order to succeed in an action brought for nuisance, as opposed to an action for negligence, the plaintiff must show (a) that there was an obstruction placed in the highway by the defendant and (b) that there was a consequent danger to the public. Once having thus proved that there was a nuisance, in order to make it 'actionable', the plaintiff must establish that it was either unlighted or concealed by reason of the defendant's own fault or that the defendant allowed it to be unlit or concealed.

Street lighting may in fact be such as to disclose the obstruction, even without special individual lights attached to it, and if it is thus rendered perfectly clear—effectively lit—then the duty to light at night may be thus eliminated completely. But one local authority which built an air-raid shelter in a highway, or extending on to it, was liable when it was found unlit, even though the street lighting was all that the law allowed it to be at that time, and it had to pay damages to a motorist who hit it.

Again remember that 'nuisance' is a term which can embrace something more than a physical obstruction. The emission of sparks from a locomotive has been found to be a nuisance on a highway, and indeed the doctrine has been used to penalize those who place unmanageable vehicles on the road, or who use them in a way that brings hurt to others—for example, by organizing a motor-cycle race on the open highway. It must also be stressed that it is no answer to a claim that you have created a nuisance on the highway to say, "Ah, but though you personally may have been inconvenienced, it is a great convenience to the vast majority of the public". A tramway track may serve the public, but if it is laid without statutory authority it may well be a nuisance to other vehicles.

Under this heading, we once again encounter difficulties when dealing with a 'forecourt'. At least theoretically, there *can* be privately owned parts of property which have become, even if only by common use over many years, effectively part of the highway. But one recent case in which a woman actually left the highway and tripped and hurt herself over a stop-cock in a forecourt, the plaintiff's action failed, the Court holding that in that case the stop-cock in the forecourt could not properly be described, on the facts, as a 'nuisance to users of the *highway*'. It was not on the highway.

An excavation may be a nuisance. An unfenced 'area' immediately adjoining the highway into which a member of the public fell was a nuisance because it was unfenced. But this only applies when the dangerous place or thing is *immediately adjacent* to the highway—you remember the case where someone fell into a dock which was forty-seven feet from the highway—there was no liability there, even in thick fog.

On the other hand, there is no duty at all lying on a frontager to fence against a danger created by someone else on the highway, so that in one case where an organization had raised the level of the highway substantially at the edge of the defendants' property, leaving a drop to that property, the defendants were not liable when somebody fell from the newly raised portion of the highway over the drop on to the defendants' property.

One defence which can be raised in this sort of case, and which will cause the plaintiff to fail if it is proved, is to show that the highway as it was at the time of the accident is exactly the same as it was when the highway was 'dedicated to the public'—when it became a highway in law, in other words. In one case, where a cellar-flap had projected slightly above pavement level for as long as anybody could remember, the owner of the premises to which the cellar was attached was held to be not liable to a person who tripped over the projection in the dark—even where the plaintiff was a stranger. But it must be remembered that because a set of circumstances has existed for as long as anyone can remember, this raises only a presumption and, like all presumptions, it can occasionally be disproved.

Short of such successful presumptions of this nature, however, the occupier of premises which receive light or air by means of a grating in the highway is liable to anyone injured as a result of such grating becoming out of repair and thereby dangerous.

THE SPECIAL POSITION OF HIGHWAY AUTHORITIES

Highway authorities are at present in a very special and privileged position, with regard to claims arising for dangerous obstructions and so forth occurring in the highways. This privileged status is due to end on August 3rd 1964, but the present rule is that they are not liable for non-feasance, but only for misfeasance. This needs some explanation, and some people feel that it is almost without justification—but that matters not for the purpose of this book, because it is the duty of the lawyer to explain and to implement the law as it stands, and not the law as he would like it to be.

The first thing to be done is to explain these two terms. The most simple definition is as follows: 'Misfeasance' is actually creating a danger in the highway. 'Non-feasance' means failing to remedy a danger in the highway, of which they may or may not be aware, but which they did not create.

In addition to this explanation, it must be remembered that a local authority may be a number of things all bound up into one organization—they may be a sanitary authority, a tramway authority, a highway authority, and a whole host of other authorities. In their capacity as, for example, tramway authority,

Misfeasance !

Non-feasance!

they may be liable for non-feasance. It is only in their capacity of *highway* authority that they enjoy this peculiar protection.

The reason for the protection is historical. At Common Law, the general duty of keeping the highway repaired fell generally upon the whole of the parish. And as no one member of the parish could sue the parish generally (for this would have involved suing himself, among others), it followed that an accident arising out of failure to repair a highway could not be maintained by a member of the parish against the parish as a whole—*nor* (for it follows) against the parish surveyor, who was the parish representative in this field. Now when, later on in history, the powers of the parish surveyor were taken over by the local authority, they, then in their capacity as highway authority (but only then), enjoyed the same immunity as the old surveyor enjoyed.

This immunity brings with it some curious problems, and some decisions on the point have an effect which may seem both strange and even unreasonable, at first sight. Take, for example, a case which was decided in 1894. A local authority in its capacity as sanitary authority erected a sewer cover, in the highway. In time, the highway around the sewer cover became worn. It was not repaired, as it should have been, and this went on until one day the sewer cover actually projected above the level of the highway. At this point, a Mr Thompson tripped over it one day and hurt himself. He sued the corporation, and he lost, because the corporation insisted that there was nothing wrong with the erection of the sewer cover, and that was done in their capacity as sanitary authority. Where they had slipped up was in failing to repair the highway around it—but this failure was in their capacity of highway authority, and as a highway authority they could not be made liable for non-feasance, which this was. And Mr Thompson failed.

This cannot be carried too far, of course—though Mr Thompson would have thought it had already been carried much too far! For if that sewer cover had been negligently placed in the highway, and that is what had caused that subsidence round it, then he would have succeeded.

Moreover, if the accident happened not because the structure was slightly projecting (even though it may have been so) but because it was in itself defective, then the plaintiff will recover, provided only that the structure was placed there by the local authority in some capacity other than as highway authority (or by some other person or persons altogether).

It is also important to remember that this doctrine has no application at all to cases where the highway authority have made up or altered a highway and have omitted to take some precaution to render their work safe, so that it becomes dangerous, and someone gets hurt. In the case cited where a highway authority built up part of the road so that there was a drop on to the premises of a private company, over which the plaintiff fell, his claim against the company failed, but ultimately he succeeded against the highway authority. Again, where one highway authority built a road on a hillside but failed to make proper provision for the drainage of the water which now collected on that road, they were liable to a neighbouring landowner whose land was consequently flooded. On the other hand, where a highway authority took over a highway and carried out certain drainage works, which were properly carried out and improved the road, but the road still remained damp in one particular area, they were not liable to the driver of a car which skidded on ice formed on the road where it was damp. They had usually warned against the occasional flooding which still went on in very heavy rain, but they had put out no warnings, here. Still, the ice was not due to flood but to the damp patch becoming frozen, and this continuing dampness was a result of non-feasance, not misfeasance.

Again, where a highway authority placed a traffic stud in the highway negligently so that it was a danger to passing traffic and when a car went over it it flew up and injured a following cyclist, this was held to be misfeasance and they were liable.

And in another case, where there had been a road accident on a highway in 1937 and the highway authority had cleared the debris but had not replaced some railings after it, they were found liable to a pedestrian who fell through the gap in the railings in 1942 because they had 'made up the highway but had omitted a precaution necessary for the safety of the public', and this rendered their action misfeasance as opposed to non-feasance. But in contrast to this, where through non-feasance a hole has appeared in the highway and a poor temporary repair is done but wears away again so that the hole reappears and someone is injured through this, the highway authority escaped on the grounds that this was only non-feasance.

It will be appreciated that some of these cases are very difficult to reconcile, one with another, which makes it sometimes difficult for a lawyer to advise a claimant unless the facts of his case happen to be almost identical with those of a decided case.

As mentioned above, this privileged position of highway authorities is due to end in respect of damage occurring on or after August 3rd 1964. This is because of The Highways (Miscellaneous Provisions) Act 1961 which, however, also provides that after that date it shall be a defence for the authority to prove that they have taken all reasonable care to make the highway safe for traffic.

THE DEFENCE OF 'STATUTORY AUTHORIZATION'

If a public nuisance has been created, and an action based on it occurs, it may occasionally be a defence to such an action for the defendant to prove that he did what he did as a direct result of the authority of an Act of Parliament, provided every precaution has been taken to prevent it becoming a nuisance. But it must be emphasized that apart from the case of an express provision, or a necessary implication, a statute will never be taken to authorize the specific creation of a nuisance. And if the statute does not require the defendants to do something, but merely permits them to do it, and they do it in such a way as to cause a public nuisance, then they will still be liable, without negligence having to be proved against them.

A good example of the position of a local authority in these circumstances is to be found in a case decided in 1943. There the authority took over an abandoned tram-track, and gave public notice that they were going to remove it. The plaintiff was a cyclist who was injured through the disrepair of the tram-track before it was removed but after the authority had taken it over.

The local authority were liable to him because they took the track over from the former owners with a specific continuing liability for its disrepair, and although this was in a sense 'non-feasance', they were acting as tramway authority in this case, and not as highway authority, and they were liable despite any statutory authority they had to remove the tram-track.

It must also be remembered that even where a highway authority does something in pursuance of express statutory authority—they may still be liable at any time if negligence can be proved against them—if they can be proved to have made a slip in anything that they were actually doing. For instance, in one case, an authority were expressly authorized by a statute to make up a road, but they (or their contractors) used their tar-spray so negligently that an adjoining landowner who grew water-cress suffered material damage. He sued the authority, and won despite their attempt to say they were only doing what the statute had allowed, because he proved that they did that permitted act in a negligent manner.

Further, it must never be forgotten that if the cause of action is the escape of something intrinsically dangerous from the authority's land on to that of someone else, causing damage, that someone may call to his aid the rule in *Rylands* v. *Fletcher* (see section on torts), which applies as much to a local authority as to a private individual.

Finally, on this point we have seen that if a local authority does something in pursuance of powers given it by statute and does that thing negligently, it is going to be liable to anyone hurt. But what if the statute gives the local authority a specific power, and they fail to exercise that power—can they then be liable if damage results thereby to some individual? Basically, they cannot, because 'failure to exercise a power given by statute' is not of itself actionable. But if the exercise of that power is necessary if damage is to be prevented through their own previous acts, then in that case they will be liable for failing to exercise that power. And if a local authority commits a nuisance by, say, discharging sewage into a river, it cannot, in defence to claims arising therefrom, say "Oh, but we had powers to enlarge our sewage system—it is only that we failed to exercise them". They will still be liable to those damaged by that failure.

HOLIDAYS AT HOME AND ABROAD

HOTEL BOOKINGS

A HOLIDAY on which nothing goes wrong seldom involves any questions of law. The law is invoked when something goes wrong. So let us consider first the unfortunate situation which arises when someone has booked rooms at a hotel or boarding-house for his holiday and then something happens which makes it imperative that he should cancel his booking. What is the legal position? Suppose, for instance, that you have booked rooms for yourself and your family and something entirely beyond your control happens to prevent your travelling; for example, a national strike of all transport, not only railways but long-distance coaches. You have no car and you are not able to hire one. Another kind of situation may be due to something affecting only you

Holidays abroad!

and your family personally. For example, you fall seriously ill, or one of your children is taken ill with some serious and infectious disease.

These examples can be multiplied indefinitely. The common factor between them all is that the occurrence which prevents your going on your holiday is something beyond your control.

So many people in this situation take it for granted that they can just telephone or write to the hotel and say that they wish to cancel their booking, and that that is an end of the matter. Sometimes they may have paid a deposit at the time when they booked their rooms. They may recognize that they must forfeit that deposit, usually a comparatively small sum—comparative, that is to

747

say, with the amount which the bill would have been if they had taken up the booking and stayed at the hotel. It is quite commonly believed that they can cancel their booking either by sacrificing the deposit or, if they have not paid a deposit at all, then without any further monetary obligation on their part.

This is not the law. The law is quite simply that once a booking is made and accepted by the hotel proprietor, there is a legal contract, and so long as the hotel proprietor is ready and willing to receive you, that contract remains binding, and you are legally liable for damages for breaking the contract.

The fact that the reasons leading you to break their contract are good, so good indeed that from your point of view they are insuperable, does not mean that the breach of contract is something which the law would condone. From the point of view of the hotel-keeper who has reserved the rooms, the validity of the reasons leading to the breach is quite irrelevant. All that he knows is that rooms which he has kept available are no longer wanted, and he suffers loss.

There have been a good many cases of this kind which have come before the Courts, and the broad general rule which emerges is that in these circumstances the hotel proprietor is entitled to sue for damages for the loss which he has suffered. In the ordinary case where the person who has booked the rooms has booked them on full board or 'en pension' terms, the principle is that he is liable to pay the full cost for the accommodation which he has booked, less something for the food which he and his family did not eat. The general rule applied by the Courts is that the hotel is entitled to be paid about two-thirds of the full 'en pension' charge which includes all meals. In other words, a third is knocked off for the food which the prospective holidaymakers did not eat.

On the other hand, the hotel which demands compensation for a cancelled booking must be able to prove that it did everything possible to re-let the rooms. The law about this kind of contract is perfectly clear. The hotel manager must do everything he reasonably can to re-let the rooms which are no longer needed. If he has been given a reasonable period of notice, he must write to all those he may have previously refused and tell them that he now has a cancellation. Quite apart from this, if someone turns up at the last minute to whom he can offer the rooms, or some of them, then those who have cancelled must be given the benefit—it must be put to their credit in any claim he may have against them.

So to sum up, if you book rooms for your holiday and for reasons of illness or business, or any other reasons at all which affect you, and which are perfectly valid from your point of view, you are compelled to write to the hotel and say that you cannot take up the rooms, you must be prepared to face the fact that you may be required to pay a reasonable sum in compensation. At its highest, as we have explained, the figure would be something like two-thirds of the full 'en pension' charge for the period for which you had booked. But the hotel proprietors must do everything they possibly can to re-let the rooms which you have cancelled. The longer the notice you give them of your cancellation, the heavier is the burden on them to show that they have done all they reasonably can to re-let the rooms. If, for instance, your holiday was booked for a period in August at a popular seaside town, it would be rather surprising if the hotel proprietor was not able to re-let your rooms and relieve you of legal liability to compensate him, particularly if you had given him reasonable notice. If the period for which you had booked was at the time of year when he was not ordinarily full, it might be much more difficult for you to escape legal liability to compensate him.

Some hotels, particularly the larger ones, accept these cancellations with good grace. They probably consider that it is good for their reputation that they should do so. It must not be forgotten, however, that in so doing they are giving up their legal right to damages for a breach of contract and that many smaller hotels or boarding-houses which have set aside rooms for you for a definite period may suffer a real loss which they cannot afford, and that in these circumstances they are financially obliged to press for payment of proper compensation. If they take their case to Court the standard which the Court adopts is the one stated above, broadly speaking, two-thirds of the full board terms for the period for which you had booked, provided always that the hotel proprietor can show that he has done everything possible to re-let the rooms to someone else. If he is put to proof of this he would have to produce his letter files to show exactly what efforts he had made to re-let the rooms. It is important to know that he cannot just sit back and do nothing and assume that he is going to get full damages. He must do his best to do what the law calls 'mitigate' the damage which he has suffered by your cancellation.

There is, of course, another side to this problem. Sometimes the hotel accepts a booking and when you and your family arrive for your holiday you find that there has been some kind of muddle and that the rooms which you had booked are not available for you. In such a case, of course, you can claim damages for the hotel proprietor's breach of contract. The amount of damages may be rather harder to fix, but a Court would certainly award something to compensate you and your family, not merely for the actual financial loss incurred in travelling expenses, or the loss incurred by having to go to a more expensive hotel, but also some money compensation for general inconvenience and dis-appointment.

Moreover, if the hotel proprietor has promised that he will book for you certain specified rooms, *e.g.* rooms with a sea view, and when you get to the hotel you find that the sea view is non-existent, you have a claim for damages against him for breach of contract. In one such case which came to the Courts, the family found that the rooms were quite different from those described and booked, and although they accepted the less favourable rooms under protest, they were so incensed that they claimed a sum of damages, and when it was refused took the case to Court. The Court awarded them a sum of money as damages. True, it was not very large—something between £60 and £70, but it marked the Court's upholding of the law that a clear and definite contract must be honoured, and that it is not beyond the Court's power to fix in terms of money a sum by way of damages for a breach of contract of this nature.

THE HOTEL'S RESPONSIBILITY FOR THE SAFETY OF A GUEST'S PROPERTY

Hotels have varying degrees of responsibility according to whether they fall into one or other of two main classifications. The first classification is whether

749

the hotel is an inn in the old English Common Law sense of the word, or whether it is what is commonly known as a private hotel, or a boarding-house.

An inn in the old English Common Law sense of the word is not just what is known colloquially today as an inn or a public house. It is any hotel from the Ritz or the Dorchester downwards which offers food, drink, and a bed to any traveller who calls, who seems to be able and willing to pay, and who is in a fit state to be received. The essence of the definition is that any casual caller can walk in and ask for all these things, or any of them, and he must be received and given that for which he has asked, unless there is some very good reason

"... not in a fit state to be received ..."

for refusing him. For instance, that there is no room available, or no table at which he can be served, or, of course, that he is not in a fit state to be received because he is drunk or very dirty.

Hotels which are private hotels or boarding-houses usually so describe themselves, and they do not hold themselves out as willing to receive any casual caller. The way in which they do their business is to expect people to make written arrangements with them beforehand. The distinction may appear to be fine, but there is a genuine borderline. On one side of the borderline is the private hotel shielding itself behind its curtains which, as a rule, will not accept the traveller or the casual caller. On the other side of the line is the hotel ranging from the most magnificent and expensive down to the simple village inn which will take in the casual caller, provided that it has room available and the caller appears able and willing to pay and is in a fit state to be received.

The vast majority of hotels, of course, fall into the latter category and are quite happy to do so, although the grander they are the more likely it is that their business will be arranged by bookings beforehand. Nevertheless, they run their business on the basis that they are open to the world, or shall we say to all of the world who can pay the charges required, whether they are very expensive or very cheap.

The latter type of hotel is much the most common. What are its legal responsibilities for the safety of their guests' goods?

In principle the responsibilities are very heavy. The basic Common Law rule for some hundreds of years was that the hotel proprietor was liable to recompense the guest for any loss of his goods, although it could not be established that either he or any of his staff was in any way to blame. The proprietor was still liable for the loss, even though it was inexplicable or even though maybe some outside thief may have broken in and stolen the guest's property.

For instance, there was a case where a woman's diamond ring was found to be missing from her bedroom. She swore that she had left it there when she went out to a dance. She had left it in her jewellery case, and when she returned next morning her ring was missing. There was absolutely nothing to show who had taken it, nothing to show whether the thief was a member of the hotel staff or some complete outsider. There was no evidence of negligence on the part of the hotel proprietor or his staff. Nevertheless, under the law the hotel proprietor was liable.

Now this is something which runs counter to all the principles of the law relating to negligence described in another section of this work. That law depends on proof of negligence, proof of a breach of some legal duty. This liability on the hotel proprietor is an exception to the general rule, because it is not necessary to prove negligence of any kind whatsoever.

It may be interesting to state briefly the reasons for the apparent harshness of this rule. It derives from the days when many keepers of inns and hotels were in league with local thieves and highwaymen. It was all too easy for the proprietor of the inn to tip off a local thief that a wealthy guest was staying in his inn for the night and to tell him where the money or the valuables could be found, so that while the hotel proprietor was apparently innocently asleep in his bed the thief could break in and steal. The rule imposing this absolute liability on the proprietor was designed, of course, to act as a deterrent to him to becoming an accessory before the fact to theft by thieves and highwaymen.

Although that old justification for the rule has no doubt entirely disappeared, yet Parliament has been reluctant to remove it altogether. The most that has been achieved has been to modify it. It was modified by the well-known Innkeepers' Act of 1863, whose provisions must have often been seen at or near the entrances to hotels. The provisions of that Act have now been modified by the Hotel Proprietors' Act of 1956.

The broad general principles of this Act are that while they do not remove the hotel proprietor's liability for the loss of his guest's property, they do fix a maximum limit to the hotel proprietor's liability. The liability under the old Act

751

of 1863 was a maximum of £30. The new Act alters this maximum to £50 *for any one article or* £100 *in all*. If the articles stolen amount to more than £100, £100 is the most the guest can recover. If they are worth altogether less than that, the guest can only recover the actual value.

A fact which undoubtedly influenced Parliament in refusing to relieve the hotel proprietor of his absolute liability up to a certain amount, was their knowledge that it is not too difficult for hotels to insure against their maximum liability under the Act. Moreover, if any one hotel suffers a series of such losses, it is certain that the insurance company would increase their premium and thus do something to ensure that the hotel proprietor took better precautions, either in engaging his staff or in looking after the safety of his premises and of his guests' goods.

The hotel proprietor's right to limit the amount of his liability for loss in these cases depends upon his displaying a notice in a conspicuous place near the reception desk or in the front hall of his hotel. The present notice is headed Hotel Proprietors' Act, 1956, and the notice quotes certain sections of the Act which set out the limits of his liability as described above.

The right to the hotel proprietor to limit his liability to £50 for any one article, or £100 in total, depends of course upon there being no evidence of actual negligence or misconduct on the part of the hotel staff. These limits of liability are only fixed to meet the case where there is no evidence of negligence, where his liability depends on this old Common Law rule that he has got to take the risk whether he is negligent or not. The limits were merely fixed to relieve him of overpowering losses. He is liable as soon as the loss of the guest's goods is proved, and he would be liable for the full value were it not for the limited liability fixed by the Act. If, on the other hand, the loss can be proved to be due to carelessness or misconduct on the part of the proprietor himself or any member of his staff, then the limit of liability does not apply. The ordinary rules of negligence apply. If negligence can be proved, there is no statutory limitation, and the hotel proprietor must pay the full amount of the loss, whatever it might be.

There is one small compensatory factor to make up for this quite heavy liability on the proprietor of the hotel which, under Common Law, is a common inn. This is that if a guest leaves without paying his bill, the proprietor is entitled to keep his luggage, and if necessary to sell it to recover the amount the guest owed him on leaving. This is known as the Innkeeper's Lien. It's a special right given by law to the keepers of hotels which come within this definition, to detain and sell any property belonging to a defaulting guest.

The proprietor of the private hotel or boarding-house which is not a common inn within the Common Law definition, has no such heavy liability for the safety of the guest's goods. At such a place the guest would not be able to recover damages unless he could prove negligence or some such misconduct on the part of the proprietor or his staff. In fact, it is the ordinary relationship depending on negligence. And the proprietor of such an establishment has no right of lien, no right to detain and sell the goods of a guest who defaults in paying his bill.

The 1956 Hotel Proprietors' Act also deals with the situation as applied to the common inn, where goods have been deposited with the proprietor for safe keeping. The law under that Act is that if goods deposited with him are lost, the proprietor is absolutely liable. He is also liable if the guest has attempted to leave property with him but is unable to do so because the proprietor will not take it, or because he or his staff have no adequate arrangements for receiving valuables which a guest wants to entrust to them.

The Act, however, makes one change in the law which is in favour of the hotel proprietor. Before the Act there had been a number of claims against hotel proprietors for the loss of guests' motor-cars, stolen from hotel car parks or garages, and also for the theft of goods from those motor-cars. Under the old cases, before this new Act, the hotel-keeper was always held to be liable, because these things came under the category of guests' belongings, for which, as stated above, he had a very heavy responsibility indeed. The new Act of 1956 has changed this rule. The hotel proprietor is no longer absolutely responsible for the safety of his guests' motor-cars, or for anything left in them. Nor is he responsible for the safety of any other vehicle, whether it's a motor-bike, or scooter, or an ordinary bicycle, nor is he responsible for a horse, or its harness, or for any other animal. He is not responsible for any of these things which may be left on the hotel premises, in stable, barn, shed, garage, or car park. Previously he was, *now* he is not to be responsible, unless negligence can be proved against him or his staff. In other words, in this kind of case the ordinary principles of negligence apply. The principles of absolute liability, subject to the statutory maximum, apply only to the guests' belongings brought into the actual building of the hotel itself.

HOLIDAYS ABROAD

The first points to be dealt with if you are planning a holiday abroad are passports, visas, compulsory vaccinations or inoculations, and currency restrictions. All these matters are very apt to vary from country to country and from time to time. For example, at the moment of writing, currency restrictions on travellers from the U.K. have been virtually abolished for most countries of the world. But throughout the period from the end of the Second World War up to the middle of 1960, there were very severe currency restrictions on British people travelling abroad, and it may be that a change in the economic climate could lead to a resumption of restrictions on the amount of foreign currency which British people travelling abroad could carry. It is therefore unwise to be too specific in a work of this kind, particularly when immediate up-to-date information about currency problems can always be obtained very readily from a bank or travel agency.

The same considerations apply to passports and visas. The Passport Office or any travel agency is always able to give immediate up-to-date information on the present position relating to travel to any country in the world. There is no legal principle involved here; it is usually a matter of immediate political considerations, applied either by this country or by the country to which it is proposed to travel. Other countries' rules about inoculations or vaccinations are also apt to vary and here again the Passport Office or the travel agency can give the most recent information. The only point in mentioning these matters here is to indicate that they are matters which have to be considered and on which information is necessary, and to indicate the source from which that information may be obtained at any time.

A matter, however, of general and continuing interest, on which information is not so generally readily obtainable, is the question of insurance against illness or accident while on holiday abroad. This is important, because, although a few countries reciprocate our National Health Service, many of them do not.

Illness while on holiday!

Moreover, the charges made for medical attention in many foreign countries are very substantially higher than equivalent charges for medical attention in this country before the introduction of the National Health Service. In the United States of America, for example, charges for medical attention are very high indeed. They are also high in some countries in the continent of Europe. It is therefore well worth the prospective holidaymaker considering taking out an insurance policy against medical expenses before he sets out on a holiday abroad. The cost of such a policy will vary between different insurance companies, but a fair average is that a premium of £1 per person per fortnight will entitle the insured person to compensation of up to £100. For a higher premium, of course, higher compensation will be paid for any accident, or illness, or its consequences.

It is worth knowing that the money payable under the policy is not limited to paying the actual fees of the doctor in the foreign country. For example, suppose you are in Rome and you suffer some accident or some illness for which it is quite clear that prolonged medical attention is needed, and the last thing you want to do is to go to an Italian doctor or stay in an Italian hospital. You want immediately to get back home. The amount payable under the policy will enable you to take a special plane back home, or to cover any other expenses involved in travelling back home so that you can see your own doctor or go to a hospital at home. The point is that the money payable under the policy can be used as you think fit, either for medical attention where you are, or for the costs of returning to your own country.

The usual policy is one covering both accident and sickness, and relying on the terms of the policy you are entitled to take such steps as you think fit, and put in your claim for the money due.

Baggage insurance is extremely cheap. For example, some sample premiums for £100 worth of luggage for a fortnight are, in the United Kingdom, 4s; in the continent of Europe, 5s 6d; in the rest of the world, 7s 6d. It is probably advisable to take out the 'all risks baggage insurance' for the full period of the holiday and not merely for the actual time spent in travelling, in aeroplane, motor-car, or train. If the insurance is taken out for the full period of the holiday, the luggage is covered wherever you are, including the hotel at which you are staying. It is a condition of the policy that the amount for which the insurance is taken out should be the full value of the baggage, in other words, the replacement value of all the things you take away with you.

Taking a car abroad

If you take your car abroad there are some special points to watch about insurance. Even if you have a comprehensive policy, you must still give written notice to your insurance company of your intention to take your car abroad. If you do not, the policy may be void.

Moreover, some European countries have laid down special rules about insurance policies, and these can be very troublesome to the traveller who is going to cross a number of frontiers. If you give your insurance company a list of the countries whose frontiers you may cross, the company will give you a green card which is the equivalent of the insurance certificate in the United Kingdom. If you do not have a green card, you have to take out a local third-party insurance at very high rates in each country you visit. The green card applies only in Europe, so that if you take your car further afield, you will probably need a special policy.

Here again, as mentioned above on questions like passports and currency, the company which has insured your car, the motoring organization to which you belong, will obviously have up-to-date information and it is very desirable to consult them. In fact, so far as insurance is concerned, it is absolutely essential. The points herein mentioned are only indications of the kind of matters which have to be considered.

ROAD TRAFFIC LAW

THE STATUTORY BACKGROUND

THE ROAD TRAFFIC ACTS, which were wholly in keeping with contemporary public opinion, started with the law that no motor-car should progress in public at all except with a man walking in front of it with a red flag. But that rule, if it was intended to impede the progress of the internal combustion engine, was a signal failure—it was like trying to stop up a hole in a dyke with a finger.

Few commercial inventions can ever have made such progress, in what is relatively so short a time, as has the motor vehicle. It has made our ancient road system, founded by the Romans, totally inadequate. And it has also given rise to a whole host of Acts of Parliament, Rules, Orders and Regulations, as the law tries constantly to keep abreast of the vast flow of cars and lorries from the factories on to our roads.

The first major consolidating Act regarding road traffic was the Road Traffic Act of 1930. Year after year since then has seen further statutory provisions of many kinds. Recently, the Road Traffic Act, 1960, has again consolidated the position. Already it is the 'parent' of a small host of Statutory Rules and Orders, but it is now the principal Act on this huge and ever-growing subject.

Its scope is probably a great deal wider than is generally realized. It deals not merely with cars and drivers, but with Goods Traffic, and the complicated business of licensing it. It deals with public service vehicles, with traffic signs, with odd items like weighbridges, and with a whole range of subjects all involved in this vast problem of control, which is so often a problem of public safety. The Act of 1960 alone runs to 236 pages, in its official printed form. Books on Road Traffic Law run into literally millions of words. The Act itself has 271 Sections and 20 Schedules.

From this you will understand that this field of law, perhaps more than any other, is subject to constant change. Even taking the law as it is at the time of writing, it is not going to be possible to do more than summarize a few of the principal provisions which affect the ordinary motorist.

DRIVING AND DRIVING OFFENCES

The first three sections of the Act of 1960 are so important that they must be dealt with in some detail. They are as follows:

    (a) Causing death by reckless or dangerous driving.
    (b) Reckless and dangerous driving generally.
    (c) Careless and inconsiderate driving.

Causing death by dangerous driving

In a sense this is a new offence. Before 1956, if someone was killed on the roads as the result of the dangerous driving of a motor-car or other motor vehicle, the only charge which could be brought against the driver for the death of that person was manslaughter. This, of course, is a very serious offence, with a maximum penalty of life imprisonment. Over many years it became apparent that juries were reluctant to convict of manslaughter where death was caused by dangerous or reckless driving. Moreover, there was a decision of the House of Lords that the offence of reckless or dangerous driving could be committed, although the negligence was not of such a high degree as to amount to manslaughter if death ensued, so the reluctance of juries to convict of manslaughter had some solid legal basis.

As a result, therefore, Parliament decided to create this new and distinct offence of causing death by reckless or dangerous driving.

The essence of the offence is described in the Act in a form which can be paraphrased as follows:

Anyone who causes the death of another person by driving a motor vehicle recklessly or at a speed or in a manner which is dangerous to the public, having regard to all the circumstances of the case, including the nature, condition, and use of the road and the amount of traffic on the road, shall be liable to imprisonment for a term not exceeding five years.

The offence, being such a serious one, is not to be tried by Magistrates or Quarter Sessions but must be tried in the High Court, that is, at Assizes or at the Central Criminal Court.

If the person injured is not killed immediately or does not die within a year and a day, the prosecution cannot succeed under this section, the essence of which is causing death. This provision that the death must occur within a year and a day is not expressly stated in the Act. It is a fundamental rule of the Criminal Law.

Reckless and dangerous driving generally

The essence of this offence can be described as follows:

Driving a motor vehicle on a road recklessly or at a speed or in a manner which is dangerous to the public, having regard to all the circumstances of the case, including the nature, condition, and use of the road and the amount of traffic.

It will be seen, therefore, that it is the same as the preceding section, with the vital difference that death has not resulted from the dangerous driving.

The accused person has a right to demand a trial by Jury either at Quarter Sessions or at Assizes. However, the charge may, with his consent and the consent of the prosecution, be dealt with summarily, *i.e.* by a Magistrates' Court.

The penalty on conviction on indictment (*i.e.* when trial is at Sessions or Assizes) is a fine or imprisonment for a term not exceeding two years, or both a fine and imprisonment.

The penalty on conviction summarily (*i.e.* before the Magistrates) is a fine not exceeding £100, or imprisonment for a term not exceeding four months, or both fine and imprisonment, or in the case of a second or subsequent

757

conviction, a fine not exceeding £100, or of imprisonment for a term not exceeding six months, or both fine and imprisonment.

It is important to note that if someone is tried for the offence of causing death by dangerous driving and the jury are not satisfied that his driving was actually the cause of death, but are nevertheless quite satisfied that he was driving recklessly or dangerously, etc., then they can convict him of an offence under this section, *i.e.* of reckless and dangerous driving, although he had not been charged with it as such.

A man can be convicted under this section although charged under Section 1, and although no notice of intended prosecution was given to him. The charge under Section 1 of causing death does not require such a notice. A charge

A man can be convicted of reckless and dangerous driving although he did not touch or even seriously inconvenience any other road user.

under Section 2 of reckless driving does require such a notice and the failure to give it would normally result in the prosecution's being bound to lose their case. This does not apply, however, where, on the man being charged under Section 1, he is convicted of dangerous driving under Section 2 (notice of intended prosecution is dealt with in some detail below).

A study of the description of the offence as set out above shows that a motorist cannot escape by saying, "I was not involved in any accident. The road was perfectly clear." The charge is not one of being involved in an accident at all. The charge is reckless and dangerous driving and a man can so drive and be convicted, although there was no accident and although he did not touch or even seriously inconvenience any other road user.

If a police officer sees what he believes to be dangerous driving, he has the power to arrest the driver without a warrant. As a rule, however, the charge is laid by way of a summons.

Incidentally, one of the many novel features of the Act is that pedal cyclists can also be charged with driving in a manner dangerous to the public.

Of course, this section is very closely allied with Section 3, which deals with careless driving, and the problem immediately arises—when is driving to be held to be 'in a manner dangerous' and when is it only careless? The only answer that can possibly be given is that each case depends completely on its own facts. It is not a question of law at all. The law only comes into it if the decision of the Magistrates, or of the jury, is so completely against all the evidence as to be 'perverse'. In such cases only will the High Court, as a matter of law, alter the decision of the lower Court. There is one judicial statement which has been found to be a useful guide to the answer to this very tricky question, however. One High Court Judge has put it that the driving is dangerous, as opposed to being merely careless, if it was, "A deliberate choice of a course of driving whereby danger arose".

If a man is brought before a Court charged with dangerous driving under Section 2, the Court can find him not guilty of that charge but guilty of careless driving, although he was not formally charged with carelessness at all.

In the detailed wording of the charge, set out above, you will have noticed the reference to 'speed'. It is beyond any doubt that speed is in itself one of the elements of danger. Indeed, a man may sometimes be charged simply with 'driving at a speed dangerous . . .'

The charge is one frequently found allied to that of driving under the influence of drink or drugs, though by no means always. But, while there is no specific authority on the point, the view is generally held that if there is no drink charge, and simply one of dangerous driving, then it should not be mentioned in evidence that the driver concerned had been drinking, because such evidence is apt merely to create prejudice against him. If he was not so much under the influence as to be incapable of proper control of his vehicle, then this aspect of the matter should, as a matter of fair practice, be omitted in evidence.

What is perhaps less known about this charge is that a passenger can be convicted of it—even in cases where the driver is not summoned at all. In a case where the car owner was sitting in front, alongside the driver, and could control the course and speed of the car, and did so, he was rightly convicted of dangerous driving. A passenger may, of course, also be convicted of this offence jointly with the driver, on the well-established principle that two persons 'pursuing a common purpose' may be equally guilty, although only one of them actually did the driving.

As may be imagined, the Law Reports are packed with cases, some of which may be taken as a useful guide to any other case. But mostly, reported cases are no more than illustrations of how established principles have been applied in a given set of circumstances, and unless a principle itself is involved, a Court may not choose to make a similar decision in any case before it. However, here and there we find a principle clearly stated. For example, it has been held that if the only act alleged against the defendant is that he did something dangerous 'in the agony of the collision', then he should be acquitted. Other cases sometimes form useful guides—for example, the case of a driver who was found guilty of dangerous driving in that he overtook another vehicle in dangerous circumstances, under the mistaken belief that he was on a dual-carriageway, where such overtaking would have been perfectly safe.

On the subject of penalties, these may be very heavy indeed, and include imprisonment, even for a first offence. Whatever the penalty, the licence of the driver *must* be endorsed, and he *may* be disqualified from driving for a period on his first offence. If this is his second conviction for dangerous driving, he *must* be disqualified if within three years of his former offence. Naturally, the High Court has power to impose higher penalties than the Magistrates' Court, although the conviction is for the same offence.

Careless driving

First, let us examine the actual wording of the section. It makes it an offence to drive a motor vehicle on a road 'without due care and attention, or without reasonable consideration for other persons using the road'. And the reader may well ask—"How much care is due care?" and likewise, "What consideration is reasonable?" It must be stated firmly but regretfully that no direct answer to these understandable questions can be given in terms. It is a matter of fact for the Justices trying each particular case. It is not a question of law at all.

It is an offence which cannot normally be dealt with by a higher Court than a Magistrates' Court, although it has to be remembered that a person may be tried by a higher Court for dangerous driving and, although not specifically charged with careless driving, he may be convicted of that by a jury. Notice of intended prosecution (see below) is again necessary.

It was at one time thought that if a motorist made a 'mere error of judgment', he could not be convicted of this charge, but this has now been held not to be the case. It depends on how great was the error of judgment—and whether, in fact, it amounted to carelessness or not. And in looking for guidance among reported cases, it has also to be borne in mind that the Road Traffic Act cases are criminal ones—at least insofar as they are required to be proved 'beyond a reasonable doubt'—whereas civil actions, though they may concern motoring negligence, are decided always on 'the balance of probabilities'.

There are, however, a number of cases in which principles have been established which will hold good on the trial of any careless driving charge. Take, for example, the case of a man who comes up to a traffic light showing green in his favour. May he just sail across, regardless of anything coming from his right or left? No, he may not. While he may assume that the lights are in order and not showing green in all directions, and while he may also assume that other drivers will behave properly, he will be found to have been careless if he fails to take avoiding action in the face of someone else's mistake.

For in the case of offences under the Road Traffic Act, it must always be remembered that the charge is one of carelessness on the part of the 'man in the dock'. It does not matter if the facts establish that another man (who may or may not be summoned also) was 99 per cent. to blame for an accident. If the defendant was in any material degree at fault, he can be correctly found guilty. What 'the other fellow' did matters not one scrap, in this respect. Conversely, it is of the greatest importance in civil actions for damages (see section on Negligence).

What about the case of learner-drivers? Sometimes their inexperience will lead to their being involved in accidents which a driver of greater experience might avoid. This is true, but it has been established—and justly—that though a lesser standard of *skill* may be applied to them, the same high standard of *care* must be applied to them as to the most skilful driver.

How often it has been heard in a Court trying a careless driving case—"Yes, I turned right, but I signalled my intention of doing so first, and clearly, too". It is another established principle that a driver's duty is not confined to making signals. He must take care to see that those signals have been seen and understood, and if he makes his signal and drives on regardless, he may be found guilty of carelessness.

Another question that is often asked is the position in law of that useful and important little book *The Highway Code*. The answer is that it does not have the direct force of law, but observance of its provisions, or a breach of them, will tend to negative, or to establish, guilt in a careless driving case.

One example of a lack of consideration for other road users seen all too frequently in practice is the practice of some people never to dip their headlights, but to tear along, blinding many of those coming toward them. It is true that even when they cause accidents by this conduct, the offenders are rarely caught. But if they are caught, then this has been held to be an example of 'lack of reasonable consideration' in law as well as in fact, and they should be convicted.

On the subject of being blinded by headlights, the principles on this point are happily very clear. If you are driving along and you are blinded through no fault of your own, then your duty is to stop at once. If you meet with an accident in the few seconds it takes you to stop, then you will not be held to have been careless. But if you choose not to stop but to carry on as best you can until you can see again, and you meet with an accident during that time, then you will be found to have been careless—*not* for failing to keep a good look-out for people or traffic in front of you, *but* for proceeding instead of stopping when you were so discourteously blinded.

Theoretically a driver should always watch the road in front of him, but he has also to take momentary glances at his dashboard instruments, for example, and if he makes a mistake through such a momentary inattention, then he will usually not be found careless. But generally, inattention can rarely be excused, and of course its importance may be directly related to the speed you are travelling at. A half a second to glance away at fifteen miles an hour, and you will have gone forward a little less than four yards. The same momentary inattention at sixty miles an hour, and you will have travelled fifteen yards.

How about the driver who literally falls asleep at the wheel—even momentarily? He will inevitably be found to have driven carelessly, provided only that there is some evidence that the driving during his temporary lapse was at all improper. He will be found guilty not for falling asleep, however, but for continuing to drive when he was so tired that sleep was likely, or even probable. The same case established, however, that a sudden disability without warning—for example, a heart attack, or being hit by a flying stone—if proved, will excuse him of carelessness.

If you are found guilty of careless driving, then your licence *must* be endorsed with the conviction, unless there are 'special reasons' why it should not be. Those two words—sometimes they are found as 'special circumstances', but the meaning is the same—have a definite legal interpretation, which is important.

761

They must be reasons special to the *offence* as opposed to the offender. It does not matter who the guilty defendant is, nor what his job is in life, nor any other factor connected with him personally. But if the circumstances of the offence are in fact special—if, for example, he was driving someone to a hospital in an emergency—then these might be 'special reasons' in law.

Driving 'Under the Influence'

The first cardinal point to be made in connection with this serious and complicated series of offences is the wording of the Section (Section 6 of the Act). 'A person who, when driving, *or attempting to drive* a motor vehicle on a road or other public place, is unfit to drive through drink or drugs shall be liable . . .' Frequently this offence is spoken of as 'drunken driving' and defendants have so often been heard to complain most bitterly, "But I was not drunk", that it must be made abundantly clear that you do not have to be 'drunk' to be found guilty. Indeed, Section 6 (6) of the Act goes on to say, 'Unfit to drive through drink or drugs means under the influence of drink or a drug to such an extent as to be incapable of having proper control of a motor vehicle'. That may be a very long way short of being 'drunk' in the ordinary sense.

It may be as well to point out here that a later, but analogous, section (Section 11) of the Act places the same responsibilities upon pedal cyclists, though of course the charge is less serious in their case, as are the penalties—one cannot, for example, disqualify a cyclist, who does not hold a licence to drive. In the case of cyclists, therefore, there is no right of election, and they can only be tried summarily.

The motorist charged with this serious offence can elect, if he wishes, to be tried by a jury at Quarter Sessions or Assizes. There are prospects of evidence in future cases involving the use of the 'breathalyser'—a machine for measuring and analysing to some extent the contents of the defendant's breath. This is certainly going to be admissible evidence, though only time will tell how accurate and infallible it may or may not prove to be.

The words 'road or other public place' will not have escaped the attention of the vigilant reader. Road, yes—but what else may be held to be a 'public place'? There are several cases on this point to guide us. The car park attached to an inn, though off the road, has been held in terms to be a 'public place' for the purposes of this section. So was a private field to which the public were temporarily invited to watch racing, even though it was able to be closed to the public at any time. And it has also been held that a bombed site, strictly speaking private property, over which motorists were accustomed to take a 'short cut', was a 'public place' within the meaning of the section.

The offence is more frequently found in connection with drink than with drugs, but this does not make a person under the influence of drugs any the less seriously in trouble if he drives. 'Drug' is defined as 'medicament or medicine, something given to cure, alleviate, or assist an ailing body'. It has been held that a diabetic who took a wrong dose of insulin and thus rendered himself incapable was 'under the influence of a drug' to such an extent as to be incapable of proper control of his car. One waits with some interest for the first time that someone 'under the influence' of a 'tranquillizer' suggests that

that curious modern danger is not a drug within the meaning of the section, because it is given to alleviate an ailing mind in a body that may be perfectly healthy!

Two final points worthy of note in passing are firstly that the inhalation of fumes from a vat has been held to be 'taking drink' in this connection, and a man steering a towed vehicle is not 'driving', and so presumably cannot be convicted under this section if found to be under the influence of a drink or drug.

Drunk 'In Charge'

Section 6 of the Act has a number of sub-sections, and that which has probably given rise to more legal arguments than almost any point in this whole vast Act is Sub-section (2), which says first of all that 'a person who, when in charge of a motor vehicle which is on a road or other public place (but not driving the vehicle) is unfit to drive through drink or drugs, shall be liable. . . .'

The same sub-section later goes on with this unusual and noteworthy wording, which must here be quoted in full:

'A person shall be *deemed* for the purposes of this Sub-section *not* to have been in charge of a motor vehicle if he proves—

(i) that at the material time the circumstances were such that there was no likelihood of his driving the vehicle so long as he remained unfit to drive through drink or drugs; and

(ii) that between his becoming unfit to drive as aforesaid and the material time, he had not driven the vehicle on a road or other public place.'

Now, bearing those words carefully in mind, let us consider a few examples of the decisions arising from them.

A learner-driver, stone cold sober and trying very hard, was driving under the supervision of a 'competent driver' who was materially under the influence of drink. The 'competent driver' was held to be 'in charge' of the vehicle, and was found guilty.

A mechanic, 'under the influence', repairing a car at the side of the road, but with no ignition key and no authority to drive, was found *not* 'in charge' and not guilty.

A motor-cyclist left his machine in a public place and later got drunk. Friends, expressly intending that he should not ride in that state, took him to the parking place, soaked him with water, and tried to arrange for someone else to ride the machine. Some time later, the defendant was found, still under the influence of drink, some feet away from his cycle, saying that if he wanted to ride it no one was going to stop him. It was held that until he had given it into someone else's charge, he remained in charge. He was found guilty.

A man who owned a car got so drunk that his friends put him in a stupor in the back seat, in a car park, immobilized the car, and left him. When the police found him, some time later, he was still so much in a stupor he did not even know he was in the car. It was held that he had reached the car whilst insensible and was not a free agent. He was therefore *not* in charge.

763

A man borrowed his son's car. He got drunk and was found sitting in the driving seat, though no intention to drive was shown, and the car was mechanically incapable of being started. He was found to have been 'in charge' of it.

From these five conflicting and contrasting examples, can any single simple principle be extracted—something that can be used as an immediate and infallible guide for future cases? Alas, no. The only answer lies in a sixth example which, independent of its facts, said that whether or not a person was 'in charge' was a question of fact in each case, and possession of an ignition key was only one of several possible factors involved in making a decision.

Certainly it is correct, however paradoxical it may appear, that a defendant may be found to have been so drunk as to be incapable of forming any criminal intention at all—too drunk to know what he was doing, or to know that what he was doing was wrong. In these circumstances, whether in a motoring or any other criminal case, he will be entitled to an acquittal.

The reader may well ask—what about a man who parks his car, gets fairly drunk, and leaves it for the night and goes to bed? Is he possibly 'in charge'? The answer is clearly 'No', because of the wording of the sub-section quoted above—under such circumstances, there is no likelihood of his driving whilst unfit.

Under the second part of the sub-section as quoted, the defendant must show (and the burden of proof is on him) that he was unlikely to drive—if you like, that he had no intention of driving. If he can do this, he will escape. And he may do it in any one of a number of ways. For example, if he takes a bus to a friend's house and gives the friend his only ignition key, the friend agreeing to drive the car home for him, this would dispel any likelihood of his driving whilst under the influence. But the fact that a car is immobilized is not in itself a sufficient defence, for it is possible for a man to be 'driving' in law without the engine being started.

A defendant may call his friends to prove that they would have stopped him, if necessary by force, from driving. Whether he could plead that the police themselves would have prevented him from trying to drive, so drunk was he, and they being present, is a more moot point! One fact should be emphasized— when a burden of proof falls in a criminal case upon a defendant, he does not have to prove whatever it is 'beyond any reasonable doubt' but only 'on the balance of probability'—just as if he were in a Civil Court.

A word is now necessary on the subject of the man who is driving along after taking drink, and who realizes that he is either becoming, or actually already, unfit to drive. It is his duty to stop immediately—so much is beyond question—and he will naturally be given a matter of a few seconds in which to do this, and still bring himself under the protection of the second part of the sub-section quoted above. The question of fact for the Court to decide will then be whether he was under the influence of drink to such an extent that he must have been unfit to drive in fact, before he realized it. Really to escape, the defendant must satisfy the Court that between first becoming unfit to drive and his own realization that he was unfit to drive, he did not in fact drive that vehicle. And if it is a question of drugs, as opposed to drink, it must be realized that some drugs do take a considerable time before they start to act upon the human body.

SIGNS AND SIGNALS

Traffic signs are the subject of special regulations, made under the authority of the Act. Apart from those regulations, however, there is Section 14 of the Act itself, which makes road users liable to penalties which are, in fact, much heavier than those under the regulations, for failing to conform to properly erected traffic signs or to signals given by a policeman controlling traffic. To such charges, it is no defence at all for the motorist to say, "I did not see the sign". It is his duty to see it, and if he does not, and so disobeys, he is guilty of the offence.

As to the signs themselves, there is in the Act a presumption that they are properly erected, and of the prescribed size, shape, colour, etc. This is, however, only a presumption, to save the prosecution having to prove it in each case, and as with all presumptions, it can be rebutted by specific evidence given to the contrary.

It is as well to emphasize that temporary traffic lights and the 'Stop' and 'Go' signs worked by hand which are sometimes encountered near road works, have the force of law, and ignoring them means an offence against Section 14.

It is perhaps not as widely known as it might be that pedestrians, too, are subject to fines for not playing their part in the use of the roads. Section 15 lays down that if any pedestrian disobeys a signal given by a constable in uniform engaged in the direction of traffic he can be fined up to £10 for a first offence and up to £25 for further offences.

But whether it is a motorist or a pedestrian who is summoned for failing to obey a signal given by a constable on duty, the defence may well be raised— "I'm sorry—I never saw the signal". This is not a point on which there is any very clear authority. Certainly it is no defence that a driver failed to see a traffic *sign*, for they are always placed where they can always be seen, and the same might not apply to the signal of an officer at a crowded cross-roads, for example. Probably it would be held that unless it was under the circumstances negligent of the defendant to have failed to see the signal (which is a question of fact in each case), then he would not be found guilty for not obeying such a signal.

With regard to 'Halt' signs, it is clear that the vehicle affected must be actually brought to a standstill, even though only momentarily. It is not a defence to say, "I reached the sign and as I could see the road was absolutely clear, I went forward". Regarding 'Slow' signs, on the other hand, it is a question of more than a token reduction of speed. The vehicle must be slowed to a stage where the driver can pull up, should something appear from the roads other than that on which he is moving.

On the subject of white lines in the road, whereas a single line does not impose any statutory obligation—it is merely a warning, when it runs along the centre of the road—the position is different where there are double white lines, which are the subject of special regulations passed originally in 1959. And where there is a double white line, it is an offence to stop at all on the roadside except for the purpose of loading or unloading passengers or goods, or unless there is some kind of breakdown so that the stopping is unavoidable.

Another important section which deals with stationary vehicles is Section 16, under which penalties can be imposed on anyone who leaves a vehicle at rest in

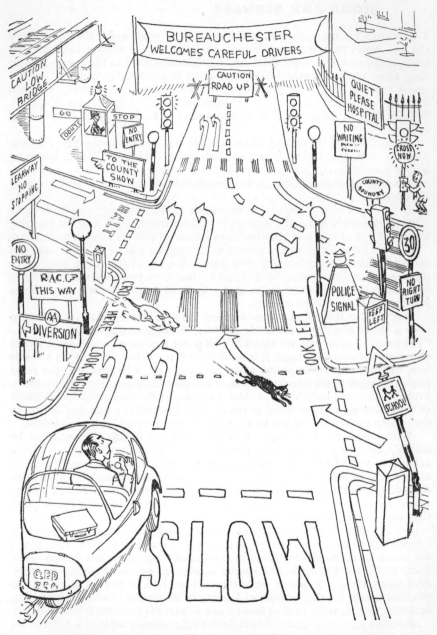

Disobedience of a lawful traffic sign is covered by a set of regulations.

such a position that danger is likely to be caused to other persons using the road. The point particularly to be noted here is that this applies not merely in cases where, for example, a vehicle is parked on the road-side just round a blind bend, but in any position where, though it is safe where it is, it would become dangerous if it moved forwards or backwards—which is sometimes the case if the brake is not set before the vehicle is left.

ACCIDENT PROCEDURE

Anyone who has the misfortune to be involved in an accident while in control of a vehicle is subject to a number of rules and regulations, which are a little complicated in that they are not all in the same, or even in adjacent sections of the Act. The position may therefore be summarized as follows.

If you are driving your car and you become involved in an accident whereby

(a) some person other than you is hurt, or
(b) some vehicle other than your car or any trailer you may be drawing suffers damage, or
(c) an animal (except a cat) other than an animal in your car or any trailer you happen to have, is hurt,

then you must stop. That is the first and absolute requirement, that you must stop.

The next requirement is that if you are required by any person who has reasonable grounds for making the request to give your name and address and also the name and address of the owner of the car if it is not your own, and also the identification marks of the vehicle, then you must do so. Clearly any person who has a reasonable ground for making the request must satisfy you that he has such a ground. You need not give these particulars to anyone who happens to be passing by.

If for some reason you do not give your name and address to a person with reasonable grounds for asking for them, then you must report the accident at a police station or to a police constable as soon as reasonably practicable and, in any case, within twenty-four hours.

It is obvious that situations may arise where there is no one to whom the particulars can be given. For example, you hit a car parked at the roadside and slightly dent its wing. You run over a stray dog. You knock down an unattended bicycle parked at the kerb. In all these cases you must stop, but as there is no one to whom you can give the particulars, then you must report the accident within twenty-four hours at the outside at a police station or to any police constable.

It is clear from the wording of the section and it has been so held in the Courts that where the full particulars as prescribed are given, then it is not necessary for an accident to be reported to the police.

In the description of the section given above it was assumed for the sake of example that you were driving a motor-car. To be precise, the section covers the situation which arises where the accident occurs 'owing to the presence of a motor vehicle on a road'. A motor vehicle, therefore, need not necessarily be moving, but the accident arises from the mere presence of the vehicle on the road.

Another part of the Act places a further obligation where the accident involves personal injury, a special obligation relating to personal injury cases. If, owing to the presence on a road of a motor vehicle, an accident occurs involving personal injury to some other person, then the driver of that vehicle must either

(a) at the time produce to a police constable, or to some person having good reason for asking, a certificate saying that he is insured, or

(b) report the accident as soon as possible and, in any case, within twenty-four hours, at a police station or to a police constable, and thereupon produce the certificate of insurance.

To incur these obligations, the motor vehicle must have been involved in some accident which can be said to be 'owing to the presence of that motor vehicle on the road'. This has nothing to do with blame—the driver's total innocence has nothing to do with it. But it has been held that there must be some direct connection between the vehicle in question and the accident—if, for example, a pedestrian steps backwards sharply to avoid a car and injures another pedestrian, the car driver is not obliged to stop.

On the other hand, it must be remembered that 'shock' is as much 'an injury' as, for example, a broken leg, in this connection. The only escape a driver who has been involved in an accident may have is that established by the leading case of *Harding* v. *Price*, 1948. There it was laid down that if the driver was genuinely and understandably ignorant of the accident in which he had been involved, then he was entitled to be acquitted of the charges of not stopping and not reporting it. But this escape does not apply if the driver is held to have been ignorant of it through his own fault—in other words, if he *ought* to have known about it, even if he did not, then he can be found guilty of an offence under Section 77.

From this it can be seen that if there is, for example, a collision between two cars, both of which are damaged, but where no one at all is in the least injured, then the two drivers concerned may simply exchange names and addresses and not report the matter to the police. But the slightest personal injury to anyone at all connected with the incident immediately draws the police into it.

LICENCES, AND THE LACK OF THEM

The basic position

This is that everyone driving a motor vehicle (and that includes that modern curiosity the 'motor-assisted pedal cycle' which ranks as a motor-cycle, even if it is only being pedalled at the time) must be in possession of a current driving licence. Anyone who lacks this commits an offence. But not only this. Any employer who sends a man out on the road in a motor vehicle when that driver is unlicensed commits an offence against Section 98 of the Act, *even* if he, the employer, was ignorant of the fact that the employee was unlicensed, for the liability is 'absolute' and does not require a 'guilty mind' to ensure a conviction.

The provisional licence holder must, as is generally known, carry 'L' plates of proper size, shape, etc., back and front, and if he is driving a motor-car, must be accompanied by a competent licensed driver in a position where he can exercise effective control of the vehicle. It is not good enough to have a licensed driver sleeping quietly in the back seat while the learner plods along, in effect alone. The law on this point is so worded that if a learner-driver has neither a current provisional licence, nor 'L' plates up, nor any competent driver, he should be charged only with the single and simple offence of driving without a licence.

Under the present law, the 'learner' who is satisfied always to drive with a competent driver alongside him, and who either repeatedly fails his driving test or never applies for one, cannot simply continue to obtain provisional licence after provisional licence. The local authority from whom he gets his licence now have power to refuse to grant a further provisional licence altogether.

It is not good enough to have as a 'competent driver' a qualified motor-cyclist. The competent driver must be licensed to drive that particular class of vehicle with which he is concerned at the time.

If a current licence holder contracts a disease which would render him unsafe on the road, his licence may be revoked by the local authority on their discovering this fact, and further licences refused. Sorry though we may be for epileptics, for example, it is really more than we can afford to have them at the wheel.

When a licence is applied for, the time of the application is noted as well as the date. Thus, if you are stopped because your licence has expired and you call immediately and take a fresh one out from that same day, you will still be guilty of the offence of driving without a licence. And it must always be remembered that driving without a current licence may well involve you in something a great deal more serious—driving without insurance—a topic which is to be dealt with in detail, below.

A foreigner, licensed in his own country, may drive without a British driving licence for twelve months from first coming here, or until his current international permit expires, whichever is the sooner.

DISQUALIFICATION FROM DRIVING

A Court *must* order a defendant to be disqualified from holding a driving licence for use on the highway on the occasion of his first conviction for driving under the influence of drink or drugs, on his second conviction for being drunk in charge of a motor vehicle, or at any time if he should be found guilty of taking part in the race or motor trial on the public highway. The period for all these is 'at least twelve months'. Further there is a compulsory disqualification for at least nine months on the occasion of a driver being convicted for the second time in three years of driving in a manner dangerous to the public, or for aiding and abetting a driver in this respect if the aiding and abetting was active in the sense that the defendant was actually present.

The disqualification must generally be for a specific period, except that it may be for life. But apart from this, it must not be for an unnamed and indefinite period.

There used to be a power exercisable by the Court to limit the disqualification to a certain class of vehicles—thus allowing a man to be, say, disqualified from driving a heavy lorry but not from riding a motor-cycle. That power has now been specifically abolished, and any disqualification must be for all classes of motor vehicles.

When it comes to assessing the period, it is laid down that the day on which disqualification is imposed is to rank as the first day of the period named. Of course, the defendant may appeal, whether against conviction and sentence, or even against sentence alone. If he does, the lower Court may, in its discretion, suspend the disqualification, which will then not start to run until or unless the appeal is unsuccessful. But this is an absolute discretion, and there is no appeal against a Court's decision not to suspend the disqualification pending an appeal.

Removal of disqualification

If the disqualification is for six months or less, it cannot be restored within that period. If it is for between six and twelve months, then it can be made the subject of an application to restore after six months. If the period imposed is from one to six years, then application can be made once half the period has expired. If the period is longer than six years, then application can be made at any time after three years have gone by.

The application takes the form of a summons against the police officer responsible for the original prosecution. The Court hearing such an application cannot vary the period—they can grant it or refuse it, and that is all—save that they can sometimes indicate that if the application is repeated in so many months, it will probably receive a favourable hearing. The disqualified person himself must go into the witness box and give evidence of his hardship, etc., on oath, and he can be cross-examined about the seriousness of the original offence by the prosecutor. The application to restore must be made to the same Court as that which imposed the original disqualification—not necessarily the same Judges or Magistrates, but the same Court. If it was an Assize Court which disqualified the defendant, he can apply only to an Assize Court for its restoration. If there is no application for early restoration and the sentence imposed expires, there is no need for any application at all—the new licence becomes available from the end of the period, automatically.

Driving while disqualified

We now turn to what is, with the exception of causing death by dangerous driving, probably the most serious offence dealt with in the Road Traffic Act. And quite rightly one of the most serious, for if a Court has found itself bound to pronounce a driver so unfit to control a vehicle on the road as to impose on him the penalty of disqualification, it would be hard to imagine an offence more serious than the open defiance of that sentence.

It is no doubt for this reason that in default of 'special circumstances' anyone found guilty of this offence must be sent to prison. Those whose lives bring them into contact with the law learn that there is hardly a single crime about which one can safely say, "There can be no possible excuse for this".

Even wilful killing can occasionally be justified in law. And there are instances reported where even this most serious driving offence can be said to be committed 'under special circumstances'—for example, a disqualified man out of reach of a doctor and with no telephone, rushing his child, injured in an accident, to hospital in order to save her life. But outside of such rare cases, this is an offence which is deserving of little, if any, sympathy. And the law is prepared to punish with nearly equal vigour anyone who knowingly aids and abets anyone to defy the Court in this way, making them liable also to imprisonment, though not inevitably so. It is not an offence which needs much information beyond the bare facts stated, for it can hardly be committed except deliberately, and there is accordingly no fear of those ignorant of the law from falling foul of this section, which is Section 110. Before leaving the topic, however, it is as well to mention that Section 244 of the Act does impose upon the prosecution certain time-limits within which they must bring their proceedings.

Disqualified until a driving test is passed

Under Section 104 of the Act, the Court may impose upon a driver whom it finds guilty of driving in a manner dangerous, driving without due care, or driving under the influence of drink or drugs, a condition that he shall not acquire a full licence to drive alone until such time as he has passed the standard Ministry of Transport Driving Test. If this is part of his punishment, a question often asked is—"Can the defendant, pending his test, drive a car provided he puts up 'L' plates and has a 'competent driver' to accompany him?" The answer to this is, "Yes, he can", as he is entitled to hold a provisional licence, this being only a partial disqualification, and one often used in cases involving careless driving by people who are elderly and whose faculties are getting less capable of dealing with the conditions of the roads today.

Driving tests generally

There are very few people indeed who, having failed the driving test, do not feel, and say, that they have been unjustly treated. This is natural. And it must be stated clearly that the Act does not allow any question of an appeal against the result of a driving test. The only thing to do is to take it again. Occasionally, however, it appears that there may be some definite irregularity about the test —not about the result, but about the way it has been conducted by the examiner. Section 99 of the Act allows the aggrieved person then to summon the examiner and to have the Court examine whether in fact the test has been carried out in accordance with the very stringent regulations which govern the conduct of driving tests.

MOTOR INSURANCE, AND THE LACK OF IT

The demands of the law

As motor vehicles in their early years stopped being rarities and curiosities, and became more and more generally used, so, inevitably, accidents increased, and innocent people were killed and injured by negligent driving. Some wise and careful drivers took out their own insurance against the risks involved in driving,

771

but there were many cases where the injured pedestrian, though he might secure from a Civil Court an award of heavy damages for his injuries, found the motorist 'not worth powder and shot'. In order to prevent this recurring, the law made it compulsory for all motorists to insure against what are known as 'third party risks'—that is to say to take out such an insurance policy that whatever claim they had would be met by the funds at the disposal of the insurance companies. Moreover, to ensure that this was obeyed, the law made it a criminal offence to drive whilst uninsured.

It must be pointed out that in recent years the offence has actually lessened in seriousness to some extent, because there has lately been established what is known as the Motor Insurers' Bureau (see Insurance), so that even if for any reason there is no effective insurance, the injured innocents will still be fully compensated. Nevertheless, it is still an extremely serious offence.

Section 201 of the Act is that which demands that every motorist shall be insured against third party risks. This provision extends to every kind of motor vehicle—including motor-assisted pedal cycles. By Section 203, the Act provides that this insurance shall cover risks arising from death or injury on the roads of all except passengers, and also that it shall cover any emergency medical treatment they may need. Passengers do not *have* to be covered, because a passenger is always in a position of a volunteer, and the law is really aimed at protecting the innocent bystander. Nor, in fact, does the policy have to cover employees when travelling in the course of their employment.

When a passenger is being carried for 'hire or reward', however, that puts him in quite a different position, and if a driver is going to carry passengers at all regularly for reward, then he must insure against death or injury to them. Not that every single journey where a generous passenger insists on making some contribution to the cost of the petrol, for example, makes the journey one which falls into this class—but if the practice is regularly indulged in, then it is as well for the driver to be sure his policy covers him, or he may find himself in serious trouble.

The provision about passengers carried for hire or reward, as a matter of more topical interest, is not confined to buses and to taxis plying for hire. A 'minicab' which cannot by law ply for hire, but which takes telephone bookings and picks up as directed, still takes its passengers 'for hire or reward' and must be covered for them.

Regarding employees, many people with staffs who may be required to drive have their vehicle covered for those occasions when the employee drives them. But if an employee finishes his business, and then takes the car off on what the law rather picturesquely describes as 'a frolic of his own', then the car during such frolic is uninsured. In such a case, the employer might well be summoned, as well as the employee, because the offence covers not only those who drive whilst uninsured but those who 'cause or permit' the vehicle to be driven under those conditions. Nevertheless, and though the liability seems to be absolute—one where knowledge and mental guilt do not have to be proved— it has been suggested that a genuinely ignorant car owner might have a defence if morally quite innocent. In such a case, however, he might well not be summoned at all, and if summoned and found guilty, he might be given a very nominal penalty or even an 'absolute discharge'.

How strict is this? In one case, an employee appears to have driven solely on his employer's business, and was thus fully covered—except for a detour of a couple of miles, during which he took a young lady home. It was held that his chivalry over so short a time and distance did not render the vehicle uninsured —the 'frolic' was too small to make it so serious! On the other hand, there have been cases where a morally innocent servant has been found not guilty, as he was misled, about the terms of a policy he had never seen, by his employer, while the employer has been found guilty and severely punished.

Section 202 of the Act lays down a number of specific exceptions to the normal demands of the law. Because of various reasons (usually because there is always enough money to cover all normal claims in any event), vehicles owned by the Crown (army vehicles and the like, for example) do not have to be insured as do private cars—nor do vehicles owned by local authorities, police vehicles, salvage vehicles, and nor do trams or trolley-buses. For different reasons, nor do invalid carriages have to be covered by insurance. Indeed, though it is little known and almost never used, an ordinary private motorist can drive without any insurance company gaining any premiums from him— but only upon terms that he first lodges the sum of £15,000 in the Supreme Court!

Worthy of mention also is Section 206, which details some special conditions which, if insurance companies demand they shall go in their policies, shall be null and void. It further prevents insurance companies, who have given a driver a good policy, from avoiding that policy after an accident by means of some technical breach by the driver or owner.

Naturally, there are many cases in which insurance policies have been the subject of vigorous arguments in Courts, against and on behalf of defendants charged with driving whilst uninsured. And the general rule which the Court will always follow first of all is, 'it depends on the wording of the actual policy'. If there is no cover provided by the terms of the actual policy, then there is an offence. If there is such cover, then the defendant is acquitted.

Not that it is by any means always as simple as that! For example, what if a policy is so wide as to cover the driver when in control of 'any motor-car', and the driver concerned steals a car and drives that? There have been instances where a thief has escaped liability under this section on such grounds, though few policies are so widely worded. Most of them say 'any motor-car being driven with the authority of the owner'. But even then, problems can arise. Suppose that a policy says just that and by means of a ruse the driver secures the authority of the owner. The policy itself might turn out to be avoidable, but still the fraud might enable the driver to be acquitted under this section of the Act, unless at the time of the prosecution the insurance company have already taken steps to avoid the policy.

Again, there are policies which cover a motor-car, when in the hands of any properly licensed driver. In that case, the driver might not have a policy of his own and still be fully covered. But, as was mentioned earlier on, an offence for driving without a licence may very well, if the policy is so worded, mean that the car is being driven whilst uninsured as well.

A final aspect on motor insurance as dealt with by the Road Traffic Act— one which is happily not seen very often in the Courts. Section 233 deals with the very serious offence of forging a certificate of insurance, or using, or even lending one to someone else, with intent to deceive the authorities. The wording of the section speaks of an act by the defendant 'calculated to deceive'—and it has been held that there need not be any active 'calculation' on the part of the defendant—the phrase means no more than 'likely to deceive'. And to this charge it is no defence at all for the defendant to say, "But I never gained any-thing out of it", for that is not the point.

MISCELLANEOUS

In an Act so vast as the Road Traffic Act, there are naturally a number of topics which may affect the ordinary motorist, and which it might be helpful to him to touch upon lightly, here. An attempt will be made to touch mainly or those aspects of the subjects which are unusual, little known, or not clear in some way.

Speeding

The law relating to exceeding the speed limits which are imposed on various stretches of road is in general extremely simple and needs little comment. But it might be pointed out that although fire engines, ambulances, and police cars are under no circumstances allowed to drive without all due care and except with full safety—nor may they 'jump' traffic lights without risking prosecution—nevertheless, Section 25 of the Act does specify that any of these three types of vehicle *when in the course of emergency duty* (and then only) may exceed the speed limit if necessity demands it. Thus, when a police car stops you and says, "I have been following you in this built-up area for a mile, and you have been doing between fifty and sixty miles an hour all the way", you have no right to suggest that he, too, is guilty of speeding, because he is not. On the other hand, you may not attempt revenge, for if you 'tail' a police car, or any other car for that matter, in order to check his speed and report him, then you will find yourself in trouble if in taking this course of action you yourself break a speed limit.

Hours at the wheel

For obvious reasons, some control must be exercised to prevent unscrupulous employers working their drivers so hard that their control suffers and the safety of innocent people is imperilled in consequence. Indeed, so carefully has this been borne in mind that many people complain that the precautions are unneces-sarily strict, but if this is so, it is certainly a fault on the right side, you may agree.

Section 73 of the Act, bearing in mind that all goods drivers have to keep full records, says that such drivers (and also bus and coach drivers) must first of all not drive for more than five and a half hours at a stretch. Secondly, they must not drive for more than a total of eleven hours in any period of twenty-four hours starting at 2 a.m. Thirdly, they must have at least ten hours' con-tinuous rest at some time in every twenty-four hours—except that if this is no more than nine consecutive hours' rest no offence will be committed if during the next period of twenty-four hours they have twelve full hours' consecutive rest. And in order to make driving not 'continuous', breaks must be for periods of not less than thirty minutes.

On the other hand, a proviso exists whereby if these rules are slightly broken in the course of the completion of a journey which has been delayed by unforeseeable circumstances, no offence will be deemed to have been committed. And there is a provision also which protects employers to the extent that their schedules must allow for such rest periods, but they are not responsible for

"Goods drivers must have at least ten hours' continuous rest in every twenty-four hours."

actually seeing that the drivers actually rest—that would be too great a burden upon them, of course. A final point not without interest is that a special rule of evidence in these cases allows the driver's records to be used in evidence against the employer, if he is prosecuted.

Taking and driving away

There is a very good reason for this charge. Originally, when anyone took a car that was not theirs, they were, when caught, charged with stealing the car.

But then one man, in the course of his defence, pointed out the undeniable fact that stealing, in law, demands as one of its ingredients, proof of 'an intention permanently to deprive the owner'. And he was acquitted, and in his small way made legal history. This was a serious blow in favour of the criminal, for it meant that they could all place their hands on their heart and say, "I never intended to keep the car for ever—only for the time I needed it". In fact, a very celebrated Lord Chief Justice thought up an answer equally strong to meet this ingenious defence, by recommending that such men be charged with stealing petrol—for if you take and drive away a car, even if you later bring it back or leave it somewhere, you must be taken to have incurred the theft of the petrol which was actually in the car at the time, in that this can never be replaced—not the petrol originally there, for it has gone up, literally, in smoke!

But while this charge of stealing petrol became common for a short time, and is even today sometimes, if rarely, seen, the law was added to, and a new crime came into the calendar—'taking and driving away a motor vehicle without lawful authority'.

It is, however, the law that if the defendant, though he took the car without authority, genuinely believed that if he had formally asked the owner he would have been certainly granted the necessary permission, then he is entitled to be acquitted. But the onus of proving such a belief, and its accurate foundation, is on him. It is not up to the prosecution to disprove it. And the section (Section 217) applies irrespective of where the car was at the time that it was taken—on the road, in a garage—anywhere.

Naturally, there have been cases testing every angle of this section. In one case three men came upon a parked lorry. Two pushed, the third steered, as they tried to get the engine going. They were caught before it started. It was held that 'driving away' meant moving the vehicle, whether on the engine or not, from the place where it was left, and they were all rightly convicted. Then, in another case, two men were found to have taken a car. Only one, of course, was driving, but as their purpose was common to both, they both were convicted. But it has since been established that while it does not matter which of two men so placed took the car if they had a common purpose, still, in order to convict a man found in the capacity of a passenger only, there must be some evidence given to show that he was a party to the taking. Even so, a recent case showed that a man who was not present at the taking, but who later secured a lift, heard all about the theft, ratified it for his part and joined the common enterprise, could be found guilty of this offence, too. A man found pedalling a 'moped' was found guilty though he had not at any time used its engine.

A van driver, lawfully in possession of his employer's van, who takes it on after work to use it for his own purposes, a use to which he is not supposed to put it, although his possession of it is allowed, is not guilty of this offence of taking and driving away. But if he returns it to his employer's garage, as instructed, and later comes back and removes it in order to take a ride, he is then committing this offence.

Supposing a man is caught in the act—about to take and drive away a vehicle, but not yet having done anything to move it. He cannot be charged with the main offence. Let us say he has not even done enough when caught to be charged with an attempt to take and drive away the vehicle. But if he has

776

already tampered with the brake, or perhaps even the lock on the door, then, provided the vehicle is on a road or parking place *provided by the local authority*, he can be convicted of an offence under Section 218 of the Act—tampering with the vehicle without lawful authority or reasonable cause. The penalties are serious—for a second offence he can even be imprisoned—but it must be remembered that there are many places which do not come within the description of the words italicized above.

Obstruction. (Parking)

The Act is the basic authority under which regulations have been made and are continuing to be made, concerning parking meters and traffic wardens, and so forth. But, apart from those special regulations, the Act itself not only recognizes that a vehicle can be an obstruction on the highway but, under Section 43, gives the police power to remove such vehicles and charge for the removal and storage until collected. There has been power to prosecute for general obstruction ever since the Town Police Clauses Act of 1847—long before the invention of the motor-car. And while there is clearly an offence if there is a material blocking of the road and interference with people or traffic, in fact it is an offence under the 1847 Act to use the highway in such a way as is likely ('calculated') to obstruct, and cases have been decided which emphasize that there is no need for any actual obstruction of anyone to be proved. Each case, of course, will depend on its own facts, but one which is useful to remember is that which held that a man whose car was in the middle of a line of other cars, all illegally parked, was still committing an obstruction, even though the cars behind him and in front of him were as wide as his.

We have all met the annoying little car who stays firmly in the middle of the road so that all those overtaking him have to go well over to their off-side. He, however, does not commit the offence of obstruction. But on the other hand, a lorry which drove slowly along the middle of the road specifically frustrating all attempts of other vehicles to overtake him was found guilty, on the particular facts, of causing an obstruction.

To dispose of another popular fallacy, it is no defence to an obstruction charge to claim that one left someone 'in charge' of the vehicle available to move it if any obstruction was caused.

If a vehicle breaks down and an obstruction is thereby caused, it has been held that there is no 'wilful' obstruction, provided the driver does his best to shift it in a reasonable time. Indeed, that word 'reasonable' is the most vital test in all these obstruction cases. If, in the light of all the facts, the use of the road by the vehicle in question was not unreasonable, there will generally be held not to be any obstruction. But it should be made clear that very many local authorities make their own by-laws which are applicable in their own areas, over and above any general Road Traffic Act provisions.

Interrupting free passage of highway

Motorists and their passengers occasionally find themselves in trouble through opening a door of a car which has drawn in to a kerb and hitting a passing cyclist, or even a pedestrian. This is a matter covered not by the Road Traffic Act, but by the Highways Act, 1835, in which Section 78 is the material section, and is frequently used today. It has two limbs, and the prosecution must be careful to go under the right one, or they will lose their case.

The first part deals with drivers on the highway causing hurt by negligence. It has been held that this part of the section deals with acts of driving alone, and not with anything done after the car has stopped.

This hurdle having been covered, it must be remembered that a driver who has opened his door only after taking a good look through available windows, etc., cannot be found guilty of causing 'wilful' obstruction to passers-by, though he still may be found guilty of 'interrupting by negligence' the free passage of anyone who bumps into the open door.

Such an accident, incidentally, is one 'arising out of the presence of a motor vehicle on a road', and as such has to be reported to the police (see Accidents, above), because that section does not demand that the vehicle in question should be moving at all. And a careless passenger can be found guilty if charged, even though the driver may not be prosecuted at all.

PROCEEDINGS

Notice of intended prosecution

"Now then—what's all this here?" Who does not recognize this as one of the formalities which are likely to follow some slight accident on the highway? It is traditionally delivered in a deep, rich, booming but kindly voice, the owner of which is encased in a uniform of navy blue in the pockets of which he feels for a stub of a pencil.

Traditionally there is a pause in the conversation (if one can call violent mutual recrimination between two angry drivers by such a refined word) before both sides give their version of what happened. Diligently, accurately, the 'man in blue' takes it all down, smooths out ruffled feelings, directs the blocked-up traffic, and generally straightens matters out. And then, before the drivers leave the scene, each is treated to a speech which runs always in the same way, which, subject to certain local variations, runs as follows: "I must inform you that the facts of this matter will be reported to my superior officers for the consideration of proceedings being taken against you arising out of this matter. You are not obliged to say anything now unless you wish to do so, but I must warn you that anything you say will be taken down in writing and may be given in evidence." (*Not* 'evidence *against you*', as one so often hears in plays and films, but that is another point.)

In due course, and perhaps weeks later, when he is congratulating himself that all is forgotten and forgiven, the motorist who was at fault (or it may be both motorists) will find himself served with a summons to appear in the local police court to answer a charge of, say, careless driving.

Now those who are responsible for taking proceedings under the Act are in certain respects subject to very strict regulations, when it comes to the actual issue of a summons. And if these have not been strictly complied with, the defendant may take full advantage of the prosecution's slip. And the particular restriction with which we now propose to deal is that which says that when proceedings are to be taken, the defendant must either be served with his summons within fourteen days of the incident in question, or he must within that time be served in proper form with a notice of intended prosecution, UNLESS he was warned at the time that the matter would be reported with a view to proceedings being taken. And that 'unless' is the reason for the first part of the constabulary formula quoted above.

To what types of offence is this rule applied? First of all, to all cases of dangerous or careless driving, to speeding cases, to cycling dangerously or carelessly, to any offence against a traffic sign, for disobeying a police signal, for leaving a vehicle in a dangerous position, or for aiding and abetting any of those offences.

There are many incidents where the defendant cannot be warned at the time of the incident. Perhaps it was a 'hit-and-run' case, perhaps the defendant himself was removed, unconscious, to hospital—there might be any one of a number of reasons precluding his being warned at the time. Occasionally the officer himself forgets the formula in the activity of the moment, a fact which an alert defendant has raised successfully on many occasions in the courts.

This is why, in almost every case, the police take the precaution, even if verbal notice was given at the time, of sending the notice of intended prosecution, usually by registered post, within fourteen days of the alleged offence. Warning does not have to be proved in court—unless the defendant raises the point and gives evidence about it, the court will assume it was done.

The formal notice may warn the defendant that proceedings may be taken against him for, say, alleged dangerous driving. Subsequently, he may be convicted of the lesser offence of careless driving, but though he was not warned of this, he cannot escape in that way. He may be charged with causing death by dangerous driving, which needs no such notice at all, and ultimately be convicted for dangerous driving. The lack of a notice here, too, will not allow him to escape.

In cases where the defendant was drunk—very drunk indeed—he may not even hear the warning through his stupor. If no notice was served he can, more than fourteen days later, be summoned for driving under the influence of drink (because that requires no notice), but not for dangerous driving (which does require notice).

The notice, if it must be served, must be in writing, and it must be served either personally or by registered post or by the recorded delivery service. It may be served upon the registered owner of the car, if the driver's identity is not established. It must be sent to the recipient's 'place of abode', though it is good service if it is received either by one of his family or even a servant, as then it is certain, for all practical purposes, that it will reach him. Even if it then does not, proof of such service will be enough to block up this loophole for the defendant. In one case, service of the notice upon a porter in a block of service flats was held, on the particular facts, to be sufficient.

On the other hand, the police cannot send a notice to the defendant's home if they know perfectly well that he is not there—because he is, for example, in hospital. The real point, however, is that the despatch, and not the receipt, of the notice is the vital point.

The day on which the offence took place is not to be counted as part of the necessary fourteen days. When the notice was sent to the wrong address, but still it was forwarded on and reached the defendant within the necessary time, it was held to be good service. And it should be emphasized that the police will not be condemned if neither the driver nor the registered owner could possibly have been found out by them in time to send the notice, despite all reasonable diligence on their part. And if the slip-up over the notice is held to have been due to the driver's own conduct, then he will not be allowed this technical escape.

Is the notice irrevocable? No, it is not. Many times a notice is duly sent and a summons is never ultimately taken out at all. It is used more as a precaution than anything else. One case further established that where a notice was duly served, and later a letter was written to the defendant telling him that it had been decided not to prosecute him, and later still, fresh evidence having come to light, that decision was reversed and he was prosecuted, the notice was effective and was not taken to have been withdrawn by the letter.

A notice giving warning of a careless driving charge has been held to be valid even for the laying of a dangerous driving charge, but the printed form of notice usually warns of both offences, as a matter of precaution.

Small typographical errors do not invalidate a notice otherwise in due form. The test to be applied in such disputes is—was the defendant prejudiced? If he was not, then the notice will be held to have been good.

Evidence at Court

One provision of importance is that contained in Section 242 of the Act, which allows a certificate to be given in evidence by a police constable stating purely formal evidence about (a) the identity of the driver at the time, (b) the fact that the car belonged to the registered owner's firm, or (c) to a company of which he was a director. Even so, and while this may save the trouble and expense of a witness being drawn to Court from far away, a copy of such a certificate must be delivered to the defendant seven days before the trial, and if he wishes to have the witness there, he must say so within four days, and the witness, however formal, will be brought to Court personally.

Limitation of time

Section 244 of the Act does set out certain provisions relative to the time within which proceedings must be brought, but it should be remembered that once a summons has been issued, it matters not how long after that it is served, or how long a time elapses before the case is actually heard in Court.

The general provisions about limitations of time are really contained in Section 104 of the Magistrates' Courts Act, 1952, which requires that in all cases to be tried summarily, the proceedings must be issued within six months of the offence in general cases. If it is a question of an indictable case—that is one which can only be dealt with by a higher Court, then there is no official time limit at all, unless expressly ordered by a particular Statute.

Section 244, however, does make certain express provisions. Under it, for example, if the charge is one of driving whilst disqualified, the summons must be issued within six months of the offence, *or* within three months of the offence becoming known, *or* within twelve months of the actual offence having taken place. The same provisions apply to cases of driving without insurance. The charges alleging forgery or fraud, previously mentioned, and charges dealing with the falsification of records and the like, are also subject to similar express provisions in Section 244 of the Act.

THE LAW RELATING TO CLUBS

Introduction

THE WORD 'club' has never been finally defined by lawyers. But it is usually taken to mean a society of persons who associate together to promote some object such as social intercourse, art, science, literature, sport, or politics. Generally, the provision of social intercourse for its members is one of a club's main objects. Various special laws apply to various special kinds of club. For instance, members of flying clubs are allowed to give instruction to other members without holding a public transport aircraft licence. Members of rifle clubs are exempted in some cases from holding a firearms certificate. But, in general, clubs are not exempt from ordinary legal rules, and must carry on their activities in accordance with the law of the land.

It is generally agreed that there are two main types of club. One is the proprietary club and the other is the members' club. In a proprietary club the property and money of the club belong to the proprietor. The members have to pay subscriptions to the proprietor and in return for that are allowed to make use of the club buildings and property. There may be a committee which is nominated by the proprietor, or perhaps partly elected by the members, but it is the proprietor who owns the club and all its fittings. A members' club, on the other hand, is one where all the property belongs to the members. Very often it is vested in trustees, who hold it on behalf of the members, but there is no 'proprietor'. The members all have a share in the ownership of the club's property. In such a club, the management of the club and its property is in the hands of the members, and is regulated by the club rules. When members join the club they undertake expressly or by implication to abide by such rules. Some clubs are 'incorporated' under Acts of Parliament. For example, the club may be a company under the Companies Acts. Usually, when a members' club is incorporated, it is registered as a company limited by guarantee. The club which is incorporated in this way may be allowed to drop the word 'limited' from its title, which it would have to use if it was an ordinary company. There are some advantages to incorporating a club in this way, but it is by no means essential. Many working-men's clubs are incorporated as Friendly Societies under the Friendly Societies Acts or the Industrial and Provident Societies Acts. This gives them certain advantages such as exemption from stamp duty upon receipts and certain other documents—but, again, there is no necessity for such registration.

781

Club rules

The rules of a club usually specify the purpose for which it was instituted and regulate the admission of members, the payment of subscriptions, the expulsion or suspension of members, the holding of meetings, the admission of guests, and so on. Members are deemed to be bound by the rules so long as they have reasonable access to them. Disputes sometimes arise because of an alteration in the rules, which some members may object to. All well-drafted club rules make provision for alterations, and if the alteration has been made in accordance with the rules, members have no right to object to it. The alteration, however, must be one that is made in good faith. The rules also usually provide for the expulsion of members in certain cases. So long as the expulsion is carried out strictly in accordance with the rules the member concerned will have no right of redress. Where a rule provides that a member may be expelled if in the committee's opinion, after inquiry, his conduct is injurious to the welfare and interests of the club, there must be a fair inquiry by the committee into the allegations against the member concerned, and he must be given an opportunity of stating his case to the committee. Here again, the power of expulsion must be exercised in good faith. If a club committee tried to expel a member, for instance, merely because he had exposed irregularities in the accounts, the Courts could intervene to prevent his expulsion.

Management of the club

The management of a club is usually, under the rules, in the hands of a committee, and the powers of the committee depend upon the rules. The committee is generally given power to employ and to dismiss club servants, to close the club premises when thought necessary, and so on. From a practical point of view it is impossible to over-emphasize the importance of every club having a good and clear set of rules. Such rules prevent disputes arising and allow all members to see exactly what their rights and duties are. It is usually sensible, when starting a club, to have the rules drafted, or at any rate supervised, by a lawyer.

Legal actions by and against clubs

An unincorporated members' club cannot sue or be sued in the Courts in the club's name. This is because such a club is not the legal 'entity', as is a limited company. However, in certain cases, one member will be allowed to bring what is called a 'representative action' on behalf of all the other members, and in the same way a person who wishes to sue the club may be allowed to sue one or more of its members as representing the others. If a club is a limited company (see above) it can sue or be sued in its own name. The proprietor of an unincorporated proprietary club can bring legal action in his own name or in the name of the club, and he can also be sued in his own name or the club name.

Dissolving a club

Very often the club rules provide for what is to happen on dissolution of the club. Even if there is no such provision the club can be dissolved if all or most of the members desire it. The property and assets of the club are then sold and after the club's debts have been paid the balance is to be divided equally amongst the members, except the honorary members—unless, of course, the rules provide for some different arrangement. The assistance of the Court can be called for if it is thought that the assets are not being properly distributed. The proprietor of a proprietary club can dissolve it by declining to accept any more subscriptions. Generally speaking, if the members of a proprietary club which is being dissolved have paid subscriptions for a period beyond the date of a dissolution, they can claim the proportion of the subscription from the proprietor.

Liquor in clubs

Where a club's stock of liquor belongs to the members (as it does in a genuine members' club) it is not necessary to get a licence in order to supply it to the members. The reason for this is that liquor licences are only needed to authorize *sales* of liquor: and the law does not consider that any sale takes place when a member is served with drink which is already, in a sense, his own property. Genuine members' clubs, therefore, do not require to be licensed. In recent years this rule that a club does not need to have a licence has caused a good deal of dissatisfaction among the licensees of ordinary hotels and public houses. They complained that in order to get their licences they had to apply to the Magistrates and undergo considerable expense and trouble. Moreover, even if they succeeded in obtaining licences, they were subject to rigorous control and inspection. Clubs, on the other hand, could serve drinks without a licence, and all that was necessary was that they should be registered with the local Clerk to the Magistrates. This registration was largely a matter of form involving only the payment of a small fee. Encouraged by this simple procedure, a large number of bogus clubs sprang up, and there was very little control of their activities. The Licensing Act of 1961 has drastically altered this position. Clubs in which intoxicating liquor is supplied now either have to obtain an ordinary licence from the Magistrates or a certificate of registration. The certificate of registration is not to be had merely for the asking—a club has to qualify in order to obtain one. Stated below are the five principle qualifications for registration.

(1) Members must not be admitted without at least two days' interval between nomination and admission. This is intended to put a stop to the practice which often existed in the old days, whereby a person entering a club could be made a member straight away, and could then buy drinks. By devices of this kind a club could turn itself, for practical purposes, almost into a public house, and any member of the public could get immediate service. Now the club rules must provide that there should be a two-day interval.

(2) The club must be conducted in good faith as a club, and have at least twenty-five members. There are many reasons why a club may not be regarded as being conducted 'in good faith'. Among the matters which the Court may consider before it decides to grant a registration certificate are any arrangements which the club may have restricting its freedom of purchase of liquor (in other words, any 'tie' it may have with a brewery), and any arrangements which exist for giving members information about the finances of the club. Bogus clubs, which are not really clubs at all but exist to enable an individual to sell liquor without a licence, may find this requirement about good faith a difficult

hurdle to surmount, since many Magistrates' Courts will probe deeply into any club which seems to be more a façade than a reality.

(3) Liquor must not be supplied to members except by the club. The club is therefore not qualified if it has some arrangement whereby liquor is supplied, for example, by an independent caterer.

(4) The control of liquor must be by the club or by an elected committee of the club. This does not prevent the club allowing its steward or bar manager to purchase liquor in its name. But the employee concerned must be under the control and supervision of the club or one of its elected committees.

(5) No person may receive a commission on purchases of liquor, or (generally speaking) a monetary benefit from its supply to members.

Where there is no objection to the issue or renewal of a certificate and the club's rules conform to the Act's requirements, the Court is bound to make certain assumptions in the club's favour. For example, it must then assume that it is conducted in good faith, and it is up to objectors to prove the contrary.

Applying for a registration certificate

A club which desires to have a certificate has to apply by lodging with the local Magistrate's Clerk certain particulars signed by the chairman or secretary. Where the club is a new one, notice of the application must be given to the public by displaying a notice on or near the premises, where the public can read it, for seven days before the application is made, or by advertising it in a local newspaper. The rules about the application are fairly strict, and a club applying for a certificate for the first time would be well advised to take the advice of a solicitor about how the application is to be made. For example, the club rules must be attached to the application, and the names and addresses of the committee members must also be given.

Inspection of club premises before registration

When a club applies for a certificate, the local council, the police, and the fire authority (this means the county council or other body which is responsible for fire brigade activities in the area) have the right to inspect the premises beforehand. There have, in recent years, been a number of serious fires in club premises, some of which gave rise to loss of life. Parliament has therefore thought it desirable that club premises should be inspected to see that there are suitable exits and appliances, and that the premises in other ways do not present special fire risks to those who use them.

Hearing the application

Applications by clubs for registration certificates are dealt with in open Court. A certificate may be granted without the club being represented at the Court, but before the application is refused the club must be given the opportunity of being heard. The club may be represented by a barrister or solicitor, or by its chairman or secretary, or some other member who has been authorized to appear for the club.

The police, the local council (including the fire authority), or any person who is affected by reason of the fact that he occupies or has an interest in other

784

premises, may come to Court and object to the grant of a certificate. A person, for example, who occupies a neighbouring house and who thinks that the existence of a club will disturb his peace is thus entitled to try preventing the Court from granting the certificate. The following are the grounds on which an objection can be made either to the grant of new certificate, or the renewal of an existing one:

(a) That the application does not give the information required by the Licensing Act, or that the information given is incomplete or inaccurate, or that the application in some other way fails to conform with the Act.

(b) That the premises are not suitable and convenient for the purpose of a registered club in view of their character and condition and of the size and nature of the club. It might therefore be objected that the proposed club premises were too old or tumbledown, or too small in view of the club membership.

(c) That the club does not comply with the requirements for qualification for registration (see above), or that the applicant is not a fit person, or that the premises are disqualified for use as a registered club.

(d) That the club is conducted in a disorderly manner or for an unlawful purpose, or that the rules of the club are habitually disregarded as respects the admission of persons to membership or any other material respect.

(e) That the club premises are habitually used for an unlawful purpose, or for indecent displays, or as a resort of criminals or prostitutes, or that there is frequent drunkenness in them, or that there have within the preceding twelve months been illegal sales of intoxicating liquor, or that persons not qualified to be supplied with intoxicating liquor in the premises are habitually admitted for the purpose of obtaining it.

Even when a club has been granted a certificate an application may be made to the Court for the certificate to be cancelled. Such an application can be made on any of the last three grounds shown above. A certificate normally lasts for a year and after that must be renewed. A renewal can be objected to on the same grounds as an original grant, and if it is refused the premises may be disqualified for use as a registered club for a fixed period.

The Courts, therefore, now have very wide powers to control registered clubs. They may refuse registration to clubs which they consider not to be qualified for it, and even when they have granted registration they may withdraw it if objection is made.

The sale of liquor in clubs

In ordinary cases, where drinks from the club's stock of liquor are served to members, no sale is regarded by the law as taking place. As we have already seen, this is because the drink already belongs to the member concerned, and he cannot be said to buy something which is his already. Thus members' clubs do not need to be licensed. But clubs from time to time do want to 'sell' drinks. They may, for example, wish to admit members of other clubs for a short period, when those other clubs are closed for a holiday period or undergoing repairs, or they may wish to provide that members of affiliated clubs shall be

785

allowed to use the club premises and to buy drinks at the bar. They can now do this, so long as there is a provision in their rules allowing for the admission of the people to whom it is desired to sell drinks. Since the supply of a drink in this way is at law a 'sale', a licence would normally be required to cover it. However, the Licensing Act, 1961, by a special exception, says that so long as the club rules permit the practice, persons other than members *can* be allowed to buy drinks in a club. Of course, this concession could give rise to serious abuse, because a club's rules might be framed so as to allow any member of the public to enter the premises and to buy a drink. In this way the club might be turned, for practical purposes, into a public house. But the law prevents this happening by giving the Magistrates power to impose conditions restricting

"... allowed in as members of another club ..."

sales to non-members in this way. The Magistrates, however, are not allowed to impose conditions so as to prevent the sale of drinks to a person who is admitted to the premises as being a member of another club if (1) the other club is a local one and is temporarily closed; or (2) both clubs exist for a learned, educational, or political object of a similar kind (for example, if both clubs were Conservative or Labour clubs); (3) each of the clubs is primarily one for ex-service men or women; (4) each of the clubs is a working-men's club registered under one of the Acts applicable to such clubs.

In short, the Courts have power to restrict the sales of drink in a club to people who are not members of it but who are allowed in under the rules. But their power to impose such restrictions is a limited one where the people concerned are allowed in as members of *another* club.

Licensed clubs

Clubs which want to serve drinks and which, for one reason or another, are unable to qualify to obtain a registration certificate, can apply for a licence, in just the same way as can a hotel or public house.

Hours for drinking in registered clubs

Registered clubs have a limited power to fix their own drinking hours. The limits depend on what are the general licensing hours for ordinary licensed premises, such as hotels, in the district. The hours which the club fixes for itself must not be longer than the ordinary general licensing hours for the district, and there must be a break of at least two hours in the afternoon. On Sundays, Christmas Day, and Good Friday, the hours must include the hours from three to five and there must be not more than three and a half hours after five.

Clubs must fix their permitted hours in the manner prescribed by their rules. If they omit to do this there will be no permitted hours.

General

In many other ways the rules about drinking in clubs are the same as those which apply in ordinary licensed premises. For example, there is a ten-minute 'drinking-up' time after the end of the ordinary permitted hours, during which drinks which have been bought before the hours came to an end can be finished up. 'Special orders of exemption' can be obtained for special occasions in clubs. Residents in clubs may have drinks at any time and are not bound by the ordinary permitted hours. A club which holds a registration certificate is permitted, under it, to supply its members with drinks in some place other than the ordinary club premises on a special occasion. For example, a club may supply drinks in a 'club tent' at a local cricket match, or at a village hall on the occasion of some special club festivity held there. The service of drinks on such special occasions must, of course, be confined to club members and their guests, and the place concerned must be open only to such members and guests. Clubs are permitted to make 'off-sales' to their members, but drinks supplied in this way must only be supplied to a member in person and may not be handed to a messenger. The penalties for supplying liquor to a member or guest on club premises if the club is not registered or licensed are severe. The offender may be sent to prison for a term not exceeding six months or may be fined up to £200, or both.

THE LICENSING SYSTEM

Introduction

THE RIGHT of the Englishman to drink has been controlled by the state for very many years. As long ago as 1828 an Alehouse Act was passed by Parliament, providing that licences to keep taverns should be granted by the Magistrates for each district once a year. But even before that date there had been numerous statutes, applying to different parts of the country, which contained similar restrictions. As the nineteenth century continued there was a whole spate of licensing legislation, most of which aimed at controlling the 'evils of drink', as they were known to the Victorians. Finally in 1910 a great Consolidation Act was passed, containing the whole code of licensing law. This code remained largely unchanged until 1953, when a further Consolidation Act was passed. During the 1950's there was much discussion of the reform of the licensing law, with a view to introducing more freedom into the system,

"The right of the Englishman to drink has been controlled by the state for very many years"

and getting rid of out-of-date restrictions. This finally gave rise to the Licensing Act, 1961, which introduced a measure of change, but disappointed many reformers by the timidity of its provisions. The drinking laws of the country still remain complicated, difficult to understand, and sometimes illogical.

The basic rule of licensing law is that intoxicating liquor may not be sold without the authority of two licences. These are the excise licence and the Justices' licence. The first to be obtained, and the more important, is the Justices' licence, which constitutes an authority to hold an excise licence. Once the would-be licensee has succeeded in obtaining his Justices' licence, he can go to the excise authorities and obtain his excise licence, on payment, more or less as a matter of course. The difficult hurdle which he has to surmount is obtaining the Justices' licence.

Excise licences are of many kinds. Probably the most familiar is the so-called 'publican's licence', which is properly called a 'spirits on-licence'. This authorizes the sale by retail of spirits, beer, cider, wine, and what are called 'sweets'. 'Sweets' is the legal name for liquors which are made from fruit and sugar which has been fermented. The term includes, for example, alcoholic cordials and mead. Other types of excise licence are the beer on-licence, which authorizes the sale by retail of beer and cider for consumption on or off the premises, the wine on-licence, the beer off-licence, and so on. Before any of these can be obtained, the necessary Justices' licence must be applied for from the 'licensing Justices'. The licensing Justices are merely a committee of ordinary J.P.'s who have the special task of dealing with the grant of licences for their area. They have an annual meeting once a year, which is often popularly referred to as 'Brewster Sessions' and a number of intervening 'Transfer Sessions'. The generic name for all their meetings is 'Licensing Sessions'.

Applying for a licence

How does an intending licensee set about getting a licence? Let us take the imaginary case of Mr Pott, who owns the Railway Hotel and who wishes to convert it from an unlicensed to a licensed house. We will assume that the licence which he wishes to obtain is the 'publican's licence', referred to above, which will enable him to sell all kinds of drink for on or off consumption. The first thing he must do is get a Justices' licence, and in order to do this he must make a formal application to the licensing Justices. Probably he will enlist the services of a solicitor, though there is nothing to prevent him tackling the job by himself, if he wishes to do so. He will have to give certain statutory notices to the police, to the local council, to the Magistrates' Clerk, and to the fire authority. He will also have to put up a notice of his application in his premises, where the public can see it, and to advertise it in a local newspaper, so that the world will know what he is intending to do. Then on the day of the licensing sessions he will go along to the Magistrates' Court and present his case. Until the day of the hearing he will not know what opposition there is going to be to his application. Anyone may oppose it, on any ground. Generally, opposition comes from rivals in the licensing trade who feel that they can supply all the requirements of the neighbourhood and that no new licensed premises are required. However, any member of the public is free to oppose, and, for example, advocates of the temperance movement may seek to have the application rejected. Evidence will be given on both sides, and then the Magistrates will deliver their decision. They have a complete discretion in cases such as Mr Pott's, to refuse the application or to grant it. Generally speaking, they will require to be satisfied that a 'need' for the new facilities exists, although the Licensing Act does not anywhere lay this down. If they grant the application, the licence will come into force right away and continue for a year. After the end of the year, it will have to be renewed. There may be opposition to the renewal, but generally speaking if a licence has been once granted, renewals are permitted as a matter of course, so long as the premises are well conducted. If Mr Pott's application is refused he will have a right of appeal to Quarter

Sessions, when the whole case will be heard again. This gives him, as it were, a 'second chance' of getting his licence. If his appeal fails, or if he decides not to appeal against a refusal, it is open to him to apply again at a later sessions; but if the Magistrates have recently refused his application they are scarcely likely to grant it again in a month or two's time—unless the circumstances have very much changed by then.

Mr Pott's application, of course, was for the ordinary 'publican's' licence, or, to be strictly accurate, for a Justices' licence authorizing him to hold a publican's licence. As we saw, in such applications the Magistrates have a complete discretion to grant the licence or to refuse it. The new Licensing Act, however, has set up three special kinds of Justices' licence, and in the case of these 'special' licences the Justices do not have such a wide discretion, and can only refuse the grant on certain fixed grounds. These special licences are called the restaurant licence, the residential licence and the restaurant and residential licence.

The *restaurant* licence covers the sale of liquor with meals and it is a licence which is granted to premises adapted and used for providing main meals at midday or in the evening, or both. A condition is attached to it that liquor is not to be sold or supplied except to persons taking meals on the premises for consumption at the meal or as a preliminary or a sequel to it.

The *residential* licence covers the sale of liquor to residents in boarding houses and residential hotels. It is a licence which is granted for premises which are used for providing board; lodging and breakfast and at least one other main meal. It is subject to the special condition that liquor is not to be sold or supplied on the premises except to persons residing there, or their private friends genuinely entertained by them. Moreover, the liquor must be for consumption by such a person or his friend either on the premises or with a meal which is supplied at but to be consumed off the premises. (For example, a picnic meal.)

A *residential and restaurant* licence is intended for residential hotels that have a public restaurant. It is a licence which is granted for such premises, and it is subject to the condition that liquor must not be supplied except in accordance with the conditions referred to above for a restaurant licence or a residential licence.

If our imaginary applicant Mr Pott had been applying not for an ordinary licence but for, say, a restaurant licence, he would have had the advantage that the Magistrates could only have refused his application on one of the fixed grounds. On the other hand, he would have had to put up with the disadvantage that he would only be able to serve drinks to people who were having main meals at his establishment. He would not have been able to serve casual pints to casual customers.

The grounds on which the grant of one of these special types of licence can be refused are too long to give here. Speaking generally, they may be said to be grounds connected with the character of the applicant, the suitability of the premises, the conduct of the premises in the past, or with the type of customer. For example, one ground for refusal is that, in the case either of a residential licence or of a residential and restaurant licence, a large proportion of the people staying at the premises is made up of young people unaccompanied (that is, persons under eighteen not accompanied and paid for by a parent or person of full age), or in the case either of a restaurant licence or a restaurant and residential licence that a large proportion of persons coming to the premises is habitually made up of young persons unaccompanied. Another ground for refusal is that the service of liquor is intended to be by self-service methods, that is to say any method allowing a customer to help himself on payment or before payment.

The introduction of these special licences has made it a good deal easier for hotels and restaurants to get licences of a limited type. But it is still as difficult as ever it was for any premises to get an ordinary licence, allowing drinks to be served to all comers, as in a public house.

The permitted hours

It is necessary, in all licensed premises, to comply with the permitted hours. Outside these hours liquor must not be sold, *or supplied, or consumed*. Mr Pott, our imaginary licensee, is not free to get round the licensing laws by saying, for instance, that a customer may have a drink free on him out of hours, instead of buying it. This would constitute the 'supply' of liquor, which is just as illegal out of hours as the sale of liquor. Moreover, the drinking of his drink by such a guest would count as a *consumption* out of hours, which is itself illegal on licensed premises. We shall see in a moment that there are exceptional cases when the sale or consumption of liquor *is* allowed outside the permitted hours: but first we must see exactly what *are* the permitted hours. They are laid down by the Licensing Act, 1961, and are as follows:

(a) on weekdays (not Christmas Day or Good Friday), the hours from eleven in the morning to half past ten in the evening, with a break of two and a half hours beginning at three in the afternoon; and

(b) on Sundays, Christmas Day and Good Friday, the hours from noon to half past ten in the evening, with a break of five hours beginning at two in the afternoon.

In London, and in certain districts outside London where a later end of permitted hours in the evening has been adopted, the terminal hour is eleven instead of half past ten. It is open to the licensing Justices anywhere outside London to adopt this later hour if they think that the requirements of the district make it desirable. Unless they make a special order to this effect, the end of evening hours stays at half past ten. There is another rule in the Licensing Act permitting the Justices to modify the hours for their district if they think it desirable, but the total number of hours of any day must not be more than nine (or nine and a half where the later evening closing is adopted) and the hours must not begin earlier than ten in the morning. Furthermore, there must be a single break of not less than two hours in each afternoon. These are the permitted hours for *on-licensed* premises.

For premises which only have an off-licence (for example, wine merchant's premises) the permitted hours on weekdays (except Christmas Day and Good Friday) begin at half past eight in the morning, and there is no afternoon break. In Wales there are no permitted hours on Sundays unless the particular district concerned has opted for such hours by a local vote. Speaking generally, the more rural parts of Wales are still 'dry' on Sundays, while the urban areas have mostly opted for Sunday opening.

'Drinking-up time'

One of the most noticeable changes brought about by the new Licensing Act is the relaxation of permitted hours to allow drinking for ten minutes after the end of the permitted hours in the afternoon and evening. This is the so-called 'drinking-up time'. It enables patrons of a bar to finish up drinks which they have bought during the permitted hours. They cannot buy any further drinks; but they *are* allowed to finish up such drinks as they already have. Formerly, the law was that you were allowed to buy a drink up to ten o'clock (if that was the end of hours in your district), but you could not drink any of it after the clock had struck. Now you may buy a drink up to ten o'clock and you have until ten-ten in which to finish it up.

Exceptions

There are, of course, certain exceptions to the rule that no purchase, supply, or consumption of drink may take place outside the permitted hours. Of these, one of the most important is that those who reside on licensed premises may buy a drink and consume it at any hour. Thus a guest at an hotel may have a drink at three a.m. if he wishes to do so, and if he can persuade the hotel staff to supply it to him. Of course, this does not mean that the hotel is *bound* to supply drinks after hours. If the management choose to close the bar at a certain time and to supply no drinks afterwards they are free to do so. But it is legal for a resident to have a drink at any hour. Moreover, under the new Act a resident at an hotel may stand a drink to his friend at any hour of the day, and the friend is at liberty to consume the drink which is so served to him. This again is a relaxation of the law, because the old rule was that while a resident at a hotel might have a drink at any time his guest could only consume one during the permitted hours. Another exception to the permitted hours' rules is that in respect of 'staff drinks'. A licensee is entitled to supply drinks to his staff after hours if he wishes to do so, and the staff do not break the law by consuming such drinks.

Staying open

A point about the permitted hours which is often not understood is that licensed premises do not have to be open for the whole permitted period. There is no rule that a public house *must* keep open for the whole of the hours, and a licensee may close his doors when it seems fit to him to do so. The only risk he runs by so doing is that it *may* constitute proof that his premises are not required for the accommodation of the public, and so could conceivably lead to the loss of his licence.

Extensions

Permitted hours can be extended by a special order of the 'local authority'. These orders, which are made on the application of the licensee concerned, are called 'special orders of exemption'. They enable the licensee to sell drinks at hours other than the ordinary ones on special occasions—for example, where an office party is being held at the licensed premises, or when the local carnival is in progress. The authority has a complete discretion as to whether it shall grant such extensions, and there is no appeal. It can also make 'general' orders of exemption, which allow drinks to be served outside the ordinary hours, on a more or less permanent basis, where some special need exists—for example, where the premises are situated near an all-night market such as Covent Garden. The authority which grants these exemption orders consists in London of the police and of the Magistrates elsewhere.

Not to be confused with orders of this kind is the 'occasional licence', which authorizes the sale of liquor not at a different *time* from the ordinary one but at a different *place*. For example, the licensee of a public house may wish to serve drinks at a dance being held in the local village hall, which is unlicensed. He will then apply for an occasional licence to sell his liquor not at his usual licensed premises but at the hall in question. If the Magistrates see fit, they can grant him permission to do so, naming the hours at which he will be free to sell.

Young customers

The licence-holder is bound by numerous legal rules which are designed to ensure good behaviour on his premises. Of these the most important are the rules concerning service to young persons. A licence-holder or his employee must not 'knowingly' sell liquor to a person under eighteen, or 'knowingly' allow a person under eighteen to consume liquor in a bar. A bar is interpreted in the Licensing Act as including any place 'mainly or exclusively used for the sale and consumption of liquor'. Moreover, a licence-holder must not 'knowingly' allow any person to sell liquor to a boy or girl under eighteen. Further, it is an offence for such a boy or girl to buy or to attempt to buy liquor on licensed premises, or to consume it in a bar. What is not always realized is that it is also an offence for any customer to buy or to attempt to buy liquor for consumption in a bar on licensed premises by a boy or girl under eighteen.

As to 'off-sales', the rule is that a licensee or his employee must not 'knowingly' hand to a boy or girl under eighteen any liquor sold in licensed premises for consumption off the premises. The exception to this is where a delivery is made at the residence or working place of the purchaser. Moreover, no one may 'knowingly' send a person under eighteen to obtain liquor from licensed premises for off-consumption. The word 'knowingly' in all the above cases means with knowledge of the age of the youngster concerned.

In addition to these rules for under-eighteens, the law also restricts those under fourteen as to their use of licensed premises. Such children are not allowed to be in bars on licensed premises at all during the permitted hours. Thus a father may not take his thirteen-year-old son into the saloon bar, even if he only proposes to let him have a glass of ginger beer. But a child of fourteen or over may be on licensed premises, although he may only have 'soft' drinks. A boy or girl of sixteen or over may buy beer, porter, cider, or perry for consumption at a meal in some part of licensed premises, such as a dining-room, which is usually set apart for the service of meals.

Refusing service

Contrary to popular belief, the licensee of a public house is *not* obliged to serve any and every member of the public. Some licensed premises count in law as 'inns', which in legal language means a place which is 'held out by its proprietor as offering food, drink, and, if required, sleeping accommodation to any traveller who presents himself and who is able and willing to pay a reasonable sum for the facilities provided, and is in a fit state to be received'. All ordinary residential hotels are therefore in the legal sense 'inns', and the rule is that all travellers who wish to make use of the inn must be allowed to do so, and none can be denied admittance. An ordinary public house, however, is not an 'inn', because it has no sleeping accommodation. The licence holder is therefore perfectly free to refuse to serve anyone he wishes. Nor need he give any reason for such a refusal. He can require any customer whose presence he no longer desires to leave the house, and if the customer refuses to go he can put him outside with such force as may be necessary. The licensee is at liberty to exercise this right even though the customer concerned is behaving at the time in a perfectly proper manner. Should the customer's behaviour deteriorate, the licensee is not only at liberty but actually under a duty to remove him, since the law forbids him to allow any 'drunken, violent, quarrelsome, or disorderly' conduct on the premises. He must also be careful not to allow his premises to become the resort of thieves or prostitutes, and he must admit the police whenever the latter wish to make a routine visit. He must not, however, serve any policeman on duty with liquor except with the authority of the policeman's superior officer. Nor must he allow a policeman on duty to remain on the premises unnecessarily.

Standard measures: credit

A further legal requirement which the licensee must observe concerns the sale of liquor in proper measures. No drink must be sold in quantities of half a pint or more unless it is in a measure marked according to the imperial standards. In other words, it must be marked 'one pint', 'half-pint', or whatever the quantity may be. The sale of liquor in a glass or tankard not properly marked is an offence. A customer, however, may be allowed to *consume* his liquor in an unmarked tankard so long as it is sold to him in one that is properly marked. After the sale it may be poured into an unmarked vessel (for example, an antique pewter mug), as long as this is done at the customer's request and in his presence. A further rule about the sale of liquor concerns credit sales. When liquor is sold for consumption on the premises it must be paid for before or at the time when it is sold or supplied. You cannot order a pint of bitter in the public bar and then lawfully ask the licensee to 'put it on the slate'. However, liquor that is served with a meal may be paid for at the time when the meal is paid for, which may be later on. Again, if liquor is sold or supplied for the consumption of a resident at a hotel, or his guests, it may be paid for when the hotel accommodation is paid for, in other words it may be put on the resident's bill. In all other cases the rule is payment by cash down.

Music, dancing, and gambling

Generally speaking, if a licensee wishes to provide public music and dancing at his premises he must get a special licence to cover it. Such a licence, however, is not required where the 'music' merely consists, for instance, of the occasional use of a bar-room piano, or where the performers are not more than two in number, or where the performance is of recorded music and singing only. The licensing Justices may, and sometimes do, insert a condition in a licence that no musical performances of any kind are to take place, for example, on Sundays, and where such a condition is imposed the licensee must, of course, comply with it. He is also free to make his own rules on the subject, and if he chooses to ban singing, or to allow it on certain special occasions only, he is at liberty to do so. As to gambling, here again the law lays down strict rules. No games of chance (that is to say, any games where an element of chance is involved) may be played in the public rooms of licensed premises for stakes of any kind, whether consisting of money, drinks, or anything else. The only exception to this rule is in respect of the games of dominoes and cribbage. Both of these are games of chance within the legal definition, but the law makes a special exception and allows them to be played in public houses for stakes (even monetary ones), because they do not normally give rise to obvious gambling. Games of pure skill such as skittles and darts may be played for stakes in the public rooms of on-licensed premises, but card games (all of which involve some element of chance) may not.

GAMING AND WAGERING

INTRODUCTION

'GAMING AND WAGERING' is the title used in most legal textbooks to describe what most people call gambling and betting; but it is far from clear what the difference is between them, and in some cases the same operation can be both.

Definitions
(a) *Gaming.* The only one defined in the latest statute on the subject (Betting and Gaming Act, 1960) is 'gaming'. This is said to mean 'the playing of a game of chance for winnings in money or money's worth'.
(b) *Game of chance.* The Act says that game of chance 'includes a game of chance and skill combined . . . but does not include any athletic game or sport'.
(c) *Wagering.* 'Wagering' has been described as 'an agreement between two persons whereby one will win and the other lose a stake on the outcome of an event in which they have otherwise no interest'.

Insurance, etc.
People sometimes feel that agreements such as insurance contracts and Stock Exchange transactions are a form of gambling—and so they may be. If, for example, you took out a policy on the life of a film star who was a stranger to you, it would be a disguised wager on how long he would live, because otherwise you had no financial interest in his life. The insurance policy would

be void or voidable, because you had no insurable interest. Similarly, if you entered into a Stock Exchange speculation on (say) 'options' or 'differences' where there was no intention that either party should take or deliver the securities in question but simply that one side would pay the other the difference involved, that again would be a disguised wager.

On the other hand, if you insure (say) your house, you have an 'insurable interest': you are not betting that your house will burn down, you are covering yourself against the risk that it may. Similarly, if you make a genuine purchase of some shares, although you naturally hope that they will increase in value it is not a wager, because you must do something with your savings and the risks of investment are something from which you cannot escape.

The simple distinction is that in genuine insurance or Stock Exchange transactions you are dealing with a risk which already exists, whereas in gaming or wagering you are dealing in a risk which did not exist until you created it.

Void contracts

Another important distinction between the two is that contracts such as those for insurance or dealings on the Stock Exchange (if genuine) give rise to legal obligations which can be enforced at law, whereas gaming and wagering contracts are 'void'. This does not necessarily mean that they are illegal—in fact, most of them are now legal. What it does mean is that if someone fails to pay you on a gambling debt the Courts will not help you to enforce your claim. This is sometimes referred to as 'pleading the Gaming Acts' and, though dishonourable, is a complete answer in law.

The fact that such contracts are void may affect other people than those involved in the actual gaming or wagering—for example, stakeholders, persons who have lent money for gambling or to pay gambling debts, or persons who hold cheques which were originally given in respect of a wager. In some cases the money or the amount of the cheque may not be recoverable. To go into all the considerable detail involved in considering which of these 'third-party' claims (so to speak) may be enforceable and which not is not possible here. It is only possible to sound a warning; a solicitor should be consulted.

Unlawful games

Apart from 'gaming' (that is, playing for money), a game itself may be illegal. At Common Law, it is said, all games were lawful except perhaps cockfighting; but any doubt about that was removed by the Cockfighting Act, 1952, making it clearly illegal. Bear-baiting and similar sports are illegal under the Metropolitan Police Act, 1839. Until the Betting and Gaming Act, 1960, certain other games with the old-fashioned names of 'pharoah', 'basset', 'hazard', and 'passage' were illegal, as were any dice-games other than backgammon.

MODERN LAW

Legislation concerning games and gaming and similar pastimes goes back many hundreds of years. Much of it has been repealed by the 1960 Act—the oldest being the Unlawful Games Act, 1541, and a 1621 Act of the Parliament of Scotland 'Anent Playing at Cardes and Dyce and Horse Races'.

Nevertheless a lot of old and not so old Acts of Parliament still apply to the many varieties of gaming and wagering; but they are not of great practical importance today and only the three major statutes (Betting and Lotteries Act, 1934, Small Lotteries and Gaming Act, 1956, and Betting and Gaming Act, 1960) will be dealt with in detail.

The law concerning the different forms of permitted betting and gambling, as well as the legal requirements in connection with such activities as lotteries, charity entertainments, small gaming parties, club gaming, 'bingo', and 'fruit machines' are dealt with under the relevant Acts and can be easily spotted by reference to the sub-headings.

BETTING AND LOTTERIES ACT, 1934

Racing

Part I of this Act provides for the restriction of betting on horse and dog race-courses and provides for the licensing of tracks and bookmakers, totalizators, and pool betting. For the latest legislation concerning bookmakers and betting shops reference should be made to the Betting and Gaming Act, 1960 (below).

Lotteries, e.g. raffles

Part II of the Act deals with lotteries, *e.g.* raffles. After dealing with unlawful lotteries it provides for two forms of lawful lottery called 'Lotteries at Entertainments' and 'Private Lotteries'. A third form of lawful lottery called 'Small Lotteries' is provided by the Small Lotteries and Gaming Act, 1956.

Unlawful lotteries. Section 22 of the Act lays down that, except as otherwise provided, all lotteries are unlawful and that anyone is guilty of an offence who in connection with an unlawful lottery does any of the following things:

(a) prints lottery tickets;
(b) distributes, offers for distribution, or has in his possession for the purpose of distribution, such tickets;
(c) prints, publishes, or distributes or has in his possession for such purpose any advertisement, list of prizewinners, ticket, or any other matter likely to induce persons to participate;
(d) brings or invites a person to send to Great Britain any ticket or advertisement for sale or distribution;
(e) sends or attempts to send out of Great Britain any money or valuable thing received in respect of the sale or distribution of a ticket;
(f) knowingly allows any premises to be used in connection with a lottery; or
(g) procures or causes to procure any person to do any of the above things.

Lotteries at entertainments and when they are lawful. By Section 23 a lottery 'promoted as an incident of an entertainment' is *not* an unlawful lottery, provided it is carried out subject to the following conditions:

(a) The whole proceeds (including the proceeds of the lottery) must be devoted to purposes other than private gain, after deducting the expenses of:
    (i) the entertainment (excluding the expenses of the lottery);

797

      (ii) printing the lottery tickets; and

      (iii) providing prizes in the lottery (not exceeding £10).

(b) There must be no money prizes.

(c) The tickets must be sold or issued and the result must be declared on the premises where the entertainment takes place and while it is in progress.

(d) The facilities for participating in a lottery must not be the only substantial inducement to attend the entertainment.

The 'entertainments' at which these lotteries may be promoted are defined by the Act, and they have been added to by the Betting and Gaming Act, 1960. The full list is now 'bazaars, sales of work, fêtes, dinners, dances, sporting or athletic events, and other entertainments of a similar nature'.

Private lotteries and when they are lawful. A private lottery is a lottery in Great Britain which is confined to the following people:

(a) members of a society (for example, a club or a trade union or trade union branch) which is not established for gaming, wagering, or lotteries; or

(b) persons all working on the same premises (for example, the staff of a factory); or

(c) persons all residing on the same premises (for example, guests in a hotel or the tenants of a block of flats).

The lottery must be promoted by and for such members or persons and the sale of tickets must be confined to them.

Such a lottery will *not* be an unlawful lottery provided the following conditions are observed:

(a) the whole proceeds, after deducting the expenses of printing and stationery, must be devoted to prizes or (in the case of a society) either to prizes or to the purposes of the society or both;

(b) there must be no advertisement of the lottery except on the premises or on the tickets;

(c) the price of every ticket must be the same and be stated on the ticket;

(d) every ticket must show the names and addresses of the promoters, the persons to whom tickets may be sold, and a statement that no prizes shall be paid to any person other than the one to whom the promoters sold the ticket (and no prize shall be paid to any other person);

(e) the full price must be paid on the sale of the ticket, and no money must be returnable;

(f) no tickets must be sent through the post.

Offences under this part of the Act committed when the conditions are not observed are punishable with fines of up to £500 for the first conviction and imprisonment for one year or a fine of £750 or both for subsequent convictions.

SMALL LOTTERIES AND GAMING ACT, 1956

Small lotteries

This Act creates yet a third type of lottery which in certain circumstances will *not* be unlawful. It also deals with what are called 'Small Gaming Parties' (see below).

The kind of lottery here dealt with is one promoted in Great Britain on behalf of a registered society 'established and conducted wholly or mainly' to raise money for charitable purposes or participation in or support of athletic or cultural activities or other purposes, *not being 'purposes of private gain or purposes of any commercial undertaking'*.

The society must first register. Registration is obtained on application to the local authority, specifying the purpose of the society, and on payment of an annual fee of £1. The registration can be refused—or, after having been granted, can be revoked—if it appears to the authority:

(a) that any person has been convicted of certain offences connected with lotteries promoted or projected by the society in question; or
(b) that the society is not a society which qualifies under the Act.

In case of refusal or revocation the society has a right to a hearing, and there is also a right of appeal. A society may itself apply for the registration to be cancelled.

If the society is registered then this type of lottery will *not* be unlawful if it conforms to the following conditions:

(a) The promoter must be a member of the society and have written authority from its governing body.
(b) No remuneration must be payable to him or to anyone employed by him who is engaged in the business of betting.
(c) No prize must have a value of more than £100, and no ticket must cost more than 1s.
(d) The whole proceeds, apart from the amounts of the expenses and the prizes, must be applied to the purposes of the society.
(e) The amount appropriated to expenses must not exceed the actual amount of the expenses or 10 per cent. of the proceeds, whichever is the *less*; and the amount appropriated to prizes must not exceed 50 per cent. of the proceeds.
(f) The price of every ticket must be the same.
(g) The total value of tickets sold must not exceed £750 —and if any other lottery is being conducted for the society on the same day the total value of all tickets sold must not exceed £750.
(h) The only written advertisements permitted are those exhibited on the society's premises or published exclusively to the members and such advertisement as there may be on the tickets.
(i) Every ticket and notice must give the name of the society, the name and address of the promoter, and the date of the draw.
(j) No ticket may be sent by post except to members.
(k) No person must participate in the lottery unless he has paid the full price of his ticket, and no money must be returnable.
(l) Only the proceeds of the lottery may be used for expenses or prizes.
(m) No tickets may be sold to a person under sixteen.

If any of these conditions is broken the promoter and any other person who was a party to it is guilty of an offence unless he can prove it took place without his knowledge. If, however, the offence comes under (e) or (l) above—

that is, it consists of having appropriated too much to expenses or prizes or of having used other money than the proceeds of the lottery for these purposes— it is also a defence to show that the proceeds fell short of what was reasonably estimated, that the appropriation was for expenses actually incurred or for prizes unconditionally promised on the sale of the tickets, and that the appropriation was not more than could legally have been made if the 'reasonable estimate' had been reached.

An example will make this clearer. Suppose you had estimated that your lottery would bring in £500 and had promised prizes of £100, £75, £50, and £25, and you had spent another £25 on expenses, that would make a total obligation of £275. Suppose further that your lottery actually brings in only £250: that will mean that you are £25 short and will have to find it from other money— in contravention of condition (1) which says, 'Only the proceeds of the lottery may be used for expenses or prizes'. However, if £500 was a 'reasonable estimate' you will have a good defence, because the total of the prizes (£250) would not have exceeded 50 per cent. of the estimated proceeds and the amount of the expenses (£25) would have been less than 10 per cent. of them.

There is one further obligation, and that is that within three months after the month when the draw is held the promoter must send a certified return to the local authority showing:

(a) the proceeds of the lottery;
(b) the appropriations for expenses and prizes respectively;
(c) the purpose (or purposes) to which the proceeds were applied and the amount (or amounts) so applied; and
(d) the dates between which the tickets were sold.

The maximum penalty for failure to do this, or for making a false or misleading statement, is £20.

Small gaming parties

As will shortly be seen (under 'Betting and Gaming Act, 1960'), the law has recently been changed, and any 'gaming' (that is, 'the playing of a game of chance for winnings in money or money's worth') may now be lawful, and premises are no longer regarded as 'a common gaming-house' (the keeping of which was a criminal offence) simply because of 'the carrying on of gaming thereon'.

Even before 1960, however, what were called 'Small Gaming Parties' had been legalized by the Small Lotteries and Gaming Act, 1956, and the Act is *still* useful for those who want to organize games of chance for charity, etc., and do not want to conform to all the requirements of the 1960 Act or find it inconvenient to do so.

Small Gaming Parties are entertainments promoted in Great Britain to raise money for purposes other than private gain at which games of chance or of chance and skill combined are played subject to the following conditions:

(a) Only one payment (not exceeding 5s) must be made by each player in respect of all the games.
(b) Only one distribution of prizes (not exceeding £20 in value) must be

made in respect of all the games; but at the final of a series in which the participants have played in the preceding games the maximum can be £100.

(c) The whole proceeds, apart from expenses and prizes, must be applied for purposes other than private gain.

(d) The amount appropriated to expenses must not exceed the reasonable cost of the facilities provided.

When two or more entertainments are promoted by the same person on the same premises on the same day they count as one for the above purposes.

BETTING AND GAMING ACT, 1960

Part I of this Act covers betting, bookmakers, and betting offices, and is dealt with below. Part II covers 'gaming', and makes considerable changes in the law.

Lawful gaming

The Act repeals much of the previous law on gaming, and declares that 'premises shall not be a common gaming-house by reason of the carrying on of gaming thereon'. 'Any gaming shall be lawful if, but only if, it is conducted in accordance with the following conditions':

(a) either the chances are equally favourable to all the players or the gaming is so conducted that they are; and

(b) all the money put down for stakes or payment of losses is paid to the winners; and

(c) no other payment is required for a person to take part in the gaming.

As will be seen later, the Act provides that in certain circumstances one or all of the above conditions need not be satisfied.

If proceedings are taken under this section and evidence is given *either*

(a) that the game was of a kind where the chances are not equally favourable and also that ten or more persons were present, *or*

(b) that an entrance fee was charged (if the exception for 'clubs', explained below, does not apply),

then it is for the accused to prove that the gaming *was* conducted in accordance with the three conditions given above and, if he fails to prove it, 'it shall be held that the gaming was unlawful'.

Persons under eighteen. Apart from observance of the above conditions the Act requires that a person under the age of eighteen must not be among the players unless:

(a) the gaming is at a private dwelling-house or in the presence of his parent or guardian, *and*

(b) he takes part with the permission of his parent or guardian.

It is, however, a defence for the accused person to prove that he had no reasonable cause to suspect that any of the players was under eighteen.

Penalties. Any person who organizes or manages gaming which is unlawful because of a breach of any of the conditions given above, or because persons under eighteen were allowed to play, is guilty of an offence; so is any person who knows or has reasonable cause to suspect that one of these offences will be committed on any premises and allows those premises to be used for gaming or makes them available to a person who commits such an offence.

There is a maximum fine of £500 for the first offence and of one year's imprisonment or £750 or both for subsequent offences. There is also a maximum fine of £50 for persons who take part in such unlawful gaming.

Gaming in clubs

Clubs are exempt from condition (c) for lawful gaming given above (that there must be no other payment than the stake money) if the following things are proved:

(a) that the gaming was carried on as a 'club activity';
(b) that the only other payment (apart from any annual subscription) was a fixed sum determined before the game began;
(c) that the only persons who took part were either members who had applied or been nominated more than twenty-four hours before or bona fide guests of such members; *and*
(d) that the club was not 'of a merely temporary character'.

This, of course, explains how the popular bingo clubs can be lawfully run.

Gaming machines

None of the above provisions of the Act about 'lawful gaming', including those about 'clubs', applies to what are called 'gaming machines'.

A gaming machine is defined by the Act as 'a machine for playing a game of chance, being a game which requires no action by any player other than the actuation or manipulation of the machine'. This definition, of course, covers what are popularly known as 'fruit machines' as well as any other gaming machines of a similar coin-in-the-slot nature; and this will be so even if the machine has some stopping or other controlling device, because, whether or no such device has any effect on the chances, it is only a 'manipulation of the machine' and the question of skill (if any) is irrelevant.

There are two sets of provisions for gaming machines:

(1) Any person who allows such gaming on premises to which the public have access or which are used mainly by persons under the age of eighteen (*e.g.* so-called fun fairs), and any person who, having cause to suspect that the premises will be so used, allows such a machine to be placed on them or makes the premises available, is guilty of an offence.

(2) As regards other premises gaming machines may be installed subject to the following conditions:

(a) there must be not more than two machines;
(b) the stake must be not more than 6*d* a time;
(c) all the stakes must go to the winners or for purposes other than private gain. It has been decided that the club funds are not a purpose other than private gain because the members derive a gain.

It is notorious that such machines can be so set as to provide heavy odds against an individual's winning.

Gaming in public places

Any person who takes part in gaming in any street or other place to which the public have access is liable to a maximum fine of £50; and a constable may arrest without warrant any person he finds in such a place and has reasonable cause to suspect of committing this offence.

". . . heavy odds against winning . . ."

Public houses. The playing of dominoes or cribbage, however, is permitted on 'on-licensed' premises. The licensing authority may impose requirements or restrictions to secure that the games are not played in such circumstances as to induce people to resort to the premises 'primarily for the purpose of taking part in gaming at those games', and also to secure that the gaming does not take place for high stakes.

Entertainments not held for private gain. 'Where gaming is carried on at an entertainment promoted for raising money to be applied for purposes other than private gain' the prohibition against Gaming in Public Places (above) does not apply (except as regards streets) and an entrance fee can be charged. The provisions of the Small Lotteries and Gaming Act, 1956, about Small Gaming Parties are applicable (see above).

Amusements with prizes

(1) *Non-commercial entertainments.* 'Lotteries at entertainments' are allowed subject to certain conditions by the Betting and Lotteries Act, 1934 (see above). By the 1960 Act at such entertainments there may also be 'amusements with prizes'.

In connection with such amusements the provisions of the 1960 Act about equal chances, all stakes having to go to the winners, and no other payment being required do not apply as they do in the case of ordinary gaming (see above); nor do the provisions of the same Act about non-participation by persons under eighteen or those which affect 'clubs' or 'gaming machines'.

However, this is so only if the following conditions are observed:

(a) the whole proceeds of the entertainment (including those of the 'amusements') must go to purposes other than private gain, apart from the deduction of expenses similar to those allowed in the case of 'lotteries at entertainments', *and*

(b) the opportunity to win prizes, participate in a lottery, or take part in gaming must not be the only substantial inducement to attend the entertainment.

(2) *Commercial entertainments.* Similar amusements may be provided on premises which have been granted a permit by the local authority and at certain 'pleasure fairs' provided by travelling showmen. But here the conditions are more severe, and they are as follows:

(a) The amount paid for a chance must not exceed 1*s.*

(b) The amount taken on one sale of chances must not exceed 50*s.*

(c) The sale of chances and the declaration of the result must take place on the same day and on the same premises.

(d) No money prize must exceed 1*s.*

(e) The winning of a prize or the purchase of a chance must not entitle a person to a further chance to win from any other amusement, gaming, or lottery—except that in the case of slot machines a further free chance may be offered if not more than another 1*s* can be won from it.

Enforcement and penalties

A Justice of the Peace (or his equivalent in Scotland) who is satisfied that there is reasonable ground to suspect that an offence 'is being, has been, or is about to be committed on any premises', can issue a warrant authorizing a constable to enter, if necessary by force, at any time within fourteen days and search them. The constable may seize anything which he reasonably believes may be used as evidence and may arrest and search any person he finds there whom he reasonably believes 'to be committing or to have committed any such offence'.

There are penalties ranging, according to the offence and according to whether the conviction is summary or on indictment, up to a maximum of £500 for the first offence and one year's imprisonment or £750 or both for subsequent offences.

This Act covers England, Wales, and Scotland, but not Northern Ireland.

Betting and bookmakers

Part I of the Betting and Gaming Act, 1960, deals with betting. It provides for the granting of 'bookmaker's permits' and 'betting agency permits' for persons who act as bookmakers or 'negotiate bets as servant or agent to another bookmaker', and establishes 'licensed betting offices' where such bets may be received.

It provides, further, that premises other than licensed betting offices must not be used for betting unless the persons concerned either reside or work on those premises, or are holders of bookmaker's permits, or are acting on behalf of such holders.

The maximum penalty for resorting to prohibited premises for betting is £50. The maximum penalties for 'street betting' are £100 for the first offence, £200 for the second, and three months' imprisonment or £200 or both for subsequent offences.

It is an offence to have a betting transaction with a person under eighteen.

Bookmakers. A bookmaker on his own account must hold a 'bookmaker's permit'. The way in which these permits are obtained and the grounds on which they may be refused are given below.

Furthermore, no person may negotiate or receive bets as agent to a bookmaker unless:

(a) he is twenty-one;
(b) he is authorized in writing by that bookmaker; *and*
(c) that bookmaker holds a bookmaker's permit or a betting agency permit.

A register must be kept of such authorized persons and must be produced to a constable on request.

Betting offices. The Act says that where there is a 'betting office licence' in force the premises licensed may be used for betting transactions with the holder of the licence and any servant or agent of his. The way in which such offices must be conducted, the method by which such licences are obtained, and the grounds on which they may be refused are given below.

Under the Act the only persons who may hold a betting office licence are:

(a) the holder of, or applicant for, a betting office licence;
(b) the Racecourse Betting Control Board (since renamed the Horserace Totalisator Board); or
(c) a person, not being one of the above, who is both
    (i) accredited by a bookmaker holding a bookmaker's permit or by the Board, *and*
    (ii) the holder of, or applicant for, a betting agency permit.

Conduct of betting offices. A licensed betting office must be managed according to rules contained in the Second Schedule to the Act.

(1) The premises must be closed throughout Good Friday, Christmas Day, and Sundays, and any other time prescribed.
(2) The premises must not be used for other purposes than betting.
(3) Persons under eighteen must not be admitted.
(4) The licensee must display on the premises his licence and any other

805

prescribed notice; and he must comply with any prescribed restrictions as to the exhibition of notices.

(5) Neither the licensee nor his servants or agents must encourage persons on the premises to bet.

(6) There must be no facilities for seeing television or listening to the radio or to anything broadcast other than information relating to the subject matter of the betting. (This is a reference to what is popularly known as 'the blower'.)

(7) There must be no music, dancing, or other entertainment, and no refreshment of any kind must be served.

(8) There must be no direct public access from the licensed premises to other premises used for non-betting transactions.

Enforcement and penalties. There is a maximum fine of £100 for contravention of any of the above rules. Furthermore, a constable may enter in order to find out if they are being complied with, and anyone who obstructs him is liable to a fine of £10.

Licensees or their servants may refuse to admit, or may expel 'any person who is drunken, violent, quarrelsome, or disorderly', or whose presence might subject the licensee to a penalty in connection with the above rules. If such a person refuses to go he may be fined up to £5; and a constable may help to expel such a person.

Granting of licences

The licensing authorities for England and Scotland for the granting or renewal of bookmakers' permits, betting agency permits, and betting office licences are a committee of the local Justices of the Peace. There must be at least four quarterly meetings of such authorities.

Application may be made at any time to the Clerk. Within seven days thereafter the applicant must send a copy to the police. There is a maximum penalty of £50 for false statements in either the application or the copy.

Within fourteen days of the application he must advertise in a 'newspaper circulating in the authority's area' that he has made the application, and that within a specified time any objectors must send two copies of their grounds for objection to the Clerk. In the case of a betting office licence this advertisement must also be posted on the entrance (or proposed entrance) to the premises concerned.

Within seven days of the newspaper publication the applicant must send a copy of it to the Clerk; and within a further specified period the Clerk must notify the applicant, the police, and any objector of the date of the meeting where the application will be considered.

Permits and licences can be granted without the applicant having to appear; but if there are objections there has to be a hearing.

Refusal of licences

Permits *must* be refused on a number of grounds, such as that the applicant is under twenty-one, and *may* be refused if he is not a fit and proper person, or has been convicted of any of a number of specified offences, including any offence involving fraud or dishonesty.

Betting office licences *must* be refused if the authority is not satisfied that the applicant will be the holder of a permit at the relevant time, or that the premises will be enclosed or that there will not be satisfactory means of access between the premises and the street. Licences *may* be refused on such grounds as that the premises are unsuitable or that there are enough such premises in the locality already; and an application for renewal may be refused on the ground that the premises have not been properly conducted under the licence.

There is a right of appeal.

Fees

The following fees are laid down for the grant or renewal of permits and licences:

			Grant	Renewal
Bookmaker's permit	.	.	.	£100	£1
Betting agency permit	.	.	.	£5	£1
Betting office licence	.	.	.	£1	£1

THE LAW RELATING TO FISHING

THE RIGHT TO FISH is such an extremely valuable legal right that it is jealously guarded. The right to fish in some of the carefully preserved and well-stocked private waters, particularly in the south of England, may cost the owner of a rod a surprisingly high amount of money.

The high seas

Let us therefore start by mentioning some stretches of water where anyone may fish without leave, licence, or permission from any other person. The first of such areas is the high seas. The high seas, by a general and accepted principle of International Law, are an area where anyone may fish. What the high seas means varies according to the laws of the neighbouring country. So far as the United Kingdom is concerned, the area is today what it has been for many hundreds of years, *viz.*, more than three nautical miles from the low-water mark of ordinary tides. Once outside this territorial limit of three nautical miles you are on the high seas, and so far as English Law is concerned free to fish for all that you can catch. Within recent years certain other countries have made other laws. One of the best-known is the new territorial limit created for Iceland, with a view to preserving certain of the fish around her coasts for her fishermen, and shutting out the English and Scottish trawlers.

However, a discussion of international territorial limits is quite outside the scope of this work, and indeed the law is far from being settled.

Territorial waters

Nearer inshore to the United Kingdom are the territorial waters of this realm, *i.e.* the waters lying *within* the distance of three nautical miles of the low-water mark of ordinary tides. It is said that the three-mile limit originates from the days when a particular type of gun could fire a shell that distance, but whatever its origin, three miles is still the limit.

"The high seas . . . are an area where anyone may fish . . ."

Within this three-mile limit, fishing is free to all the subjects of the United Kingdom of Great Britain and Northern Ireland; not to anyone else, except with permission from the Crown, but free to all subjects of the Kingdom, with the single exception of fishing for salmon and sea trout off the coast of Scotland. Fishing for salmon and sea trout off the coast of Scotland within territorial limits is strictly controlled.

The origin of this right for the subjects of the Kingdom to fish within territorial waters is said in the ancient law books to be that the bed of the sea within the three-mile limit belongs to the Crown, and that we as the subjects of the Crown can enjoy the right to fish in the waters which cover it.

Tidal rivers

The next area of water to consider is the tidal river, that is, the rivers in which the tide ebbs and flows, e.g. the Thames, the Ouse, the Tees, the Mersey, and so on. The general rule in England and Wales is that the public have the right to fish in tidal waters just as they have in the waters of the sea within the three-mile limit. The right extends as far as the tide goes, and this may be a considerable distance. This right is the right of the public in general becaus it is a right of the Crown, and the public derive their legal right from the Crown, so that it is paramount over any other right of the subject.

There are a few exceptions, because there are some stretches of tidal waters where a private individual has an ancient exclusive right to fish, probably as a result of a grant by the reigning monarch to a private subject, a grant which usually was made many hundreds of years ago. For example, there are such private rights of fishing in tidal waters in parts of the River Wye and the River Severn, both of which have tidal estuaries. There are similar rights in the Eden, the Coquet, the Yorkshire Ouse, the River Conway, and the River Loone, and possibly one or two others. All these, however, are exceptions to the *general rule* of freedom for all to fish in waters where the tide ebbs and flows.

In Scotland this freedom to fish in tidal waters is subject to a number of rather special exceptions, mainly because of the fact that the Scottish salmon fishery is of such tremendous value and importance. It is impossible here to go into all the details of these particular regulations, and anyone particularly concerned is advised to obtain from the Scottish Tourist Board a pamphlet which they publish at the price of two shillings, which is entitled *Guide to Fishing*.

Inland rivers

Coming next to rivers which are not tidal—the inland river which flows as a tributary into a main river making for the sea, or the upper reaches of a main river where the sea does not penetrate. Here the picture is quite different. There is no general public right to fish in fresh-water rivers above the flow of the tide.

It is very likely that many readers will know of fresh-water streams where they can go to fish without asking anyone's permission. Certainly there are such places. Not many today in the south of England, but there certainly are such places in parts of Wales, in the north of England, and in Ireland. They do not need to ask anyone's permission apparently, but that does not mean that there is a public *right* to fish those rivers. It only means that the owner of the fishing rights does not mind their fishing there and that he does not trouble to enforce his legal rights, or to treat the fishermen as trespassers. He is either good-natured and likes them to enjoy themselves, or else he is indifferent and does not care.

An odd legal point about rights of fishery is that the owner of the fishery and his successors in title never lose their rights of ownership simply by letting the public come to fish as often as they like. This may go on for generations. But even so the public never acquire a legal right. This is quite different from a right of way. For example, many public footpaths, many rights of way, have been made and created simply by people walking that way year after year without being stopped or without being given permission by the owner of the land. In time, usually after twenty years, a legal right of way is made, and the owner of the land or later owner of the land can never take it away.

"The right to walk on a public towpath does not mean that you can fish . . ."

But a permanent public right to fish can never be set up in this way. Even if public fishing has gone on from time immemorial, the owner of the fishing rights can stop it at any time. Indeed one Judge in a famous case went out of his way to tell the owners of the land on either side of a certain river that they need not worry about losing their rights by letting people fish. "Let people come and fish them," he said, "if you don't mind them doing it. You needn't fear that they have established a legal right." So anyone who owns the land through which a fishing river flows need not worry on that score about people who come to fish without his leave.

It is sometimes said that fishing is freely allowed, legally allowed, wherever you can sail a vessel. But this is not so. It is true that there are public rights to sail boats in many a fresh-water river, that is, a public right of navigation. But the man in the boat has no more right to trail lines or to anchor and fish with a rod and line than a motorist on the road has any right to shoot a pheasant flying overhead. (Incidentally, this public right to row or sail in fresh-water rivers *can* be acquired by long custom. It is something like the right of way over land which we mentioned earlier.) In Scotland you don't even need to show long custom. You may sail in any river which is navigable. But the right to navigate does not carry with it the right to fish. Equally, of course, the right to walk on a public towpath does not mean that you can fish the water.

The rights to fish in a fresh-water river always belong to someone. They may belong to the members of a fishing club. They may belong to the farmer through whose land the river flows, or to some large land-owning corporation like the National Trust. As a rule the owner of land abutting on a river is also the owner of half of the bed of the river, that is up to the half-way mark, the mid-stream, and also is the owner of the fishing rights in his half. If he owns the land on both sides, he usually owns the fishing rights over the whole width of the river which flows through his land.

Generally, in England and Wales, the right of fishing or fishery goes with the land, and is in the ownership of the adjoining, or riparian owner, as he is generally known. The word 'riparian', of course, refers to the bank of the river—the riparian owner is the person who owns the land on the bank adjoining the river.

Now, although, under English Law, the fishery will usually belong to the adjoining riparian owner, it may belong to someone who does not own the land. If, however, his right is challenged by the landowner, he would have to prove a good paper 'title'—that is to say deeds and documents proving his ownership of the fishery. As stated earlier, long custom or use, long practice of fishing in that particular river does not prove anything in this case. There is no such thing as free public fishing in fresh-water rivers, and no such thing as the acquiring of a right to do so by free public use over a period of years, as there is in the case of a right of way. So the person claiming a right of fishery against the owner of the land would have to prove that some way back a previous owner had, by the appropriate legal documents, granted the right to fish.

The fact is that when people say casually that fishing in such and such a stream or canal or lake is free, it only means, in law, that the owner allows anglers to fish in it without interference, and does not bother to make a charge.

Unfortunately for keen fishermen, such so-called free fishing is far from common and is becoming harder and harder to find. A good deal of the Thames is free—in this sense; up to the City Stone at Staines no permission is needed; above that point there are still free stretches of water, and the best way to find them is to ask the lock-keepers. You still need a permit from the Thames Conservancy Board which will cost about £1 a year, but it is granted for the asking. You can also get permission without charge, or for a small charge, to fish in the reservoirs which belong to the Metropolitan Water Board, or to a local authority.

But where the owner of the fishery is interested in the care of the river, and preserves the fish, you will not get leave to fish just for the asking. He must limit the number of rods. Too many would denude the river of fish and spoil everyone's sport. It is a fact that all the best fishing rivers are carefully preserved, and it is not at all easy for a new angler to be let in. When he is, there may well be a substantial fee to pay.

It would be a piece of valuable practical information if we could here and now give a list of good rivers in which any angler may be allowed to fish, either near his own home or in some distant spot where he might like to spend a fishing holiday. Unfortunately that is an ambitious task which no work of this kind could possibly undertake, simply because circumstances change from year to year. There is, however, a useful book which is published from time to time and is called *Where to Fish*. This work does not tell you how to fish, nor does it in any way advertise or praise one river over another. It is practical and factual. It states who owns or manages the fisheries, what licences or permissions are needed. It is published by the magazine called *The Field* and devoted to field sports in general, which will be familiar to everyone interested in hunting, shooting, or fishing.

Licences from the River Boards

Coming now to a point of practical importance to every angler: quite apart from any permission you may need from the legal owner of the fishing rights, you must also, in England and Wales, get *a licence from the local River Board*. It is always necessary to get a licence for salmon and trout fishing, and in certain areas it is also necessary to get a licence for coarse fishing.

You need a licence to wield a rod and net, just as you need a licence to carry a gun.

The licence is usually known as a rod licence. It is simply a licence to allow you to use a rod, and it is quite independent of the legal right of fishery. For example, even the owner of the fishery needs a rod licence from the local River Board before he can lawfully fish his own water. The law is that you must not fish for salmon or trout without a licence, nor for coarse fish without a licence if the River Board have made a local order applying to coarse fish.

However, the River Board must not refuse a licence unless the applicant has been convicted more than once of some offence against the fishery laws. He will pay a licence fee which varies in different districts, and may vary according to the fish which he intends or hopes to catch. The details about where to apply, and the amount of their fee, will be found in the book mentioned above, entitled *Where to Fish*, or they can be obtained on application to the Clerk of the local River Board.

The reason for these licences is not simply to place restrictions on fishermen for the sake of having restrictions. They are only one of the ways in which the River Boards carry out the duties they must perform under an Act of Parliament of 1923, called the Salmon and Fresh Water Fisheries Act. The Act is concerned very largely with laying down what are the lawful and unlawful ways of catching fish, the dates of the close seasons, and the granting of licences is a way in which the River Board can exercise some control over fishermen, and give them information about these points of the law which they otherwise might not know.

ANIMALS

INTRODUCTION

IN CONSIDERING the law about animals there is one very important distinction to be made between animals which are tame by nature and animals which are wild by nature. This distinction is important in considering the responsibilities of the owners of animals, and the rights of those who may come into conflict with those animals because they have caused either damage to property or injury to other animals or to people. The nature of these responsibilities and rights depends basically upon whether the animals are wild by nature or tame by nature.

THE WILD AND THE TAME

The domestic or tame animals are those which have lived with man for so long that their natures, generally speaking, have forgotten the old savage instincts. These are dogs, cattle, sheep, horses, asses, mules, goats, pigs, cats, and poultry. The word 'cattle' includes a bull. A bull may be thought of generally as a somewhat wild animal. In law the bull is not in that classification, and this is important as we shall see later. In law a bull comes under the category of a domestic or tame animal.

This description of a domestic animal is taken from the Protection of Animals Act of 1911, and the species actually named in the above definition are themselves inclusive of many other animals since, for example, the word 'bull' includes any cow, bullock, heifer, calf, steer, or ox, and the word 'fowl' or 'poultry' includes any cock, hen, chicken, capon, turkey, goose, gander, duck drake, guinea-fowl, peacock, pea-hen, etc.

Into the category of animals wild by nature come not only lions and tigers, which have a savage nature however benevolently they may appear to look at the visitor behind the bars in the zoo, but also monkeys, parrots, deer, foxes, all game, hares, rabbits, rooks, pigeons, and so on. The category also includes elephants, although an elephant may, in fact, attain a remarkable degree of domesticity, and as is well known they have been used in the East for generations as the servants of man, just as horses and cattle have been used in the West.

813

Nevertheless, by English Law, they are regarded fundamentally as wild by nature, and the distinction is exclusively a question of law.

The importance of the legal distinction is this: if you keep a wild animal, or, to be precise, an animal which belongs to this legal category of animals wild by nature, and that animal escapes and does damage or injury, you are absolutely liable for that damage or injury, although you or your agents, or staff, or any one for whom you may be responsible, may be in no way to blame. For example—a woman keeps a pet monkey which is usually a very obedient creature. One, day it flies at a boy and bites his face. Now the evidence in this case was that this particular monkey was as tame as any monkey ever has been. It had been born and bred in captivity and was devoted and obedient to its mistress. But on this

"In law a bull comes under the category of a domestic or tame animal"

one occasion it did harm for the first time in its life. The fact that it had never done harm before was no defence and its owner was absolutely and completely liable for the harm which it did. Anyone who keeps an animal of these species is absolutely responsible for any injury or damage the animal causes, even if it is not his fault, even though it may be someone else's fault, or even though it may be due to some catastrophe which the owner could not control, like a thunderstorm setting loose a frightened animal.

This class of animal, regarded in law as wild by nature, includes not only lions and tigers and leopards, which are never completely tamed, but also, as mentioned above, the obedient and peaceable Indian elephant, and also pet marmosets and monkeys.

The basis of the distinction appears to be that if an animal exists in a wild state anywhere in any part of the world, it is to be treated as an animal wild by nature. That clearly is why even a tame elephant still falls into that category.

It has long been accepted that a camel does not exist anywhere in a wild state and therefore in a case where a camel caused injury at a zoo, it was accepted that the camel's owner was not immediately and automatically absolutely liable.

As a matter of fact it has recently been found that camels do, though very rarely, exist in a wild state. But as the Courts have held that a camel is not to be treated as an animal wild by nature, that is the law.

Few people, perhaps, are likely to keep a lion or an elephant, but a good many people have pet marmosets. Moreover, if you are hurt by a lion, tiger, buffalo, etc., which has escaped from a circus or a zoo, it is well to know that in law the owner is absolutely responsible and liable to pay full compensation, and that you have no need to prove that he had been negligent.

A few years ago there was a case in the Courts in which two midgets, a husband and wife, sued the owners of the circus in which they performed. The facts were that some tame and well-mannered Burmese elephants were frightened

"If you are hurt by a lion . . . it is well to know that in law the owner is absolutely responsible"

by a dog which yapped at their heels, and one of the midgets was trampled on and hurt by an elephant and the other one was severely shocked.

It certainly was not the elephant's fault; it was the fault of the dog, and of the dog's owner. But the Judge felt bound to hold that the elephant's owner was legally liable simply because the elephant, however innocent and tame, belonged to the class of animals treated in law as wild by nature.

Some years ago a committee was appointed by the Lord Chancellor to consider this branch of the law, and that committee recommended that this old rule of absolute liability on the owner of an animal wild by nature, for any damage or injury which that animal occasioned, should be abolished and that liability should depend on the owner's negligence. So far, however, the old rule has not been changed and it still is that the owner is absolutely liable, so that there is no need to prove that he has been negligent in any respect. Anyone, whether a private individual or the proprietor of a circus or a zoo, is absolutely liable for any damage which one of these animals, which falls into the category of wild by nature, may cause at any time and in any circumstances.

The liability of the owner of domestic animals is entirely different. The responsibilities vary according to the animal and so we will treat them in turn.

815

CATS

Cats come into a very special category. What the reason for this is no one professes to know, but the facts are that cats are treated with a special leniency by the law. The owner of a cat is not legally liable if the cat trespasses on a neighbour's land and causes damage in following its natural instincts. A cat can attack anyone's poultry, devour his pigeons, dig up his seeds and plants, and yet the person aggrieved has no legal remedy against its owner. He can drive the cat away by any means in his power, short of such cruelty as would expose him to prosecution, but there is nothing else he can do. For instance, all bird-lovers regret that one of the cat's natural instincts is to kill birds, and in 1926 an owner of some hens and pigeons which had been mauled or killed by a cat belonging to his neighbour, decided to test the law on the point. He claimed damages for the destruction of his hens and pigeons; but he lost. The Court of Appeal decided that the law was that the owner of a cat was not liable if the cat trespassed and killed birds belonging to a neighbour, or indeed to anyone else. That is the law as it stands at the moment and nothing short of an Act of Parliament can alter it.

DOGS

From cats to dogs: dogs used to be in rather a similar favourable position, but this is no longer true of all a dog's activities. The position now is that if a dog trespasses on to another person's property, digs up the flowers, or interferes with crops, his owner is not legally liable. So far the dog shares the cat's immunity. If, however, the dog attacks other *animals*, his owner may be liable. Two Acts of Parliament, the Dogs Act in 1906 and the Dogs (Amendment) Act in 1928, have provided that the dog's owner will be liable for damage caused by his trespassing dog to cattle and to poultry. The word 'cattle' in the statutes includes horses, mules, asses, sheep, goats, and swine. There is an old tag about a dog being allowed a first bite. So far as a dog's attack on other animals is concerned, ignore this old tag—it has no relevance at all. The owner of the dog is absolutely liable if the trespassing dog attacks another person's animals which come within the definition above.

A cat can attack poultry or pigeons, and there is no legal remedy, but if the dog does the same thing its owner is absolutely liable, and therefore can be made to pay damages.

There remains, however, the privilege which a dog shares with a cat. If the dog which trespasses digs up crops, ravages a garden, and makes holes in the fences, the owner is not liable to pay damages. If any other animal, except only a cat and a dog, trespasses and does damage like this, the owner would usually have to pay, but neither cats nor dogs make him liable if they trespass and cause damage to growing plants and crops.

Although the Dogs Act of 1906 and the Dogs (Amendment) Act of 1928 provided that dog owners were liable for damages caused by their dogs worrying cattle—and as we have explained, cattle includes a variety of animals, including horses, mules, asses, sheep, goats, and swine—it was later thought that it was also desirable to make the dog owners criminally liable for such mischief by their dogs if it took place on agricultural land. The two Acts mentioned enable the owners of the injured animals to claim damages from the owner of the dog. But the Dogs (Protection of Livestock) Act, which was passed in 1953, was designed to provide the sanctions of the Criminal Law against the owners of such dogs. It came about as a result of long and bitter complaints by farmers over many years, against dogs which worried sheep and cattle and often caused them serious harm. Briefly the Act provides that if a dog worries *livestock* on any *agricultural land*, the owner of the dog and also the person in charge of the dog at the time, who may very well not be the dog's owner, is to be guilty of an offence under the Act.

If a dog or cat ravages a garden, the owner is not liable to pay damages

'Livestock' means cattle, sheep, goats, swine, horses, or poultry, and for the purposes of this definition 'cattle' includes bulls, cows, oxen, heifers, or calves, 'horses' includes asses and mules, and 'poultry' means domestic fowls, turkeys, geese, or ducks. 'Agricultural land' means land used as arable, meadow, or grazing land, or for the purpose of poultry farming, pig farming, market gardens, allotments, nursery grounds, or orchards.

Worrying livestock means either attacking or chasing the animals in such a way as may be expected to cause injury or suffering, or 'in the case of females abortions or loss or diminution in their produce'. For example, the loss of milk in a cow.

So the Act introduced another weapon against trespassing dogs for the benefit of farmers. On conviction the owner of the dog or the person in charge of the dog may be fined, and although the maximum fine is £10 for the first

817

offence, it may rise to a maximum of £50 for subsequent convictions in respect of the same dog.

So you will see that although a dog which digs up flowers or vegetables may escape scot-free, or let us rather say his owner may escape scot-free, the owner of a dog who attacks other domestic animals may either be liable in Civil Law for damages or, if the provisions of the Dogs (Protection of Livestock) Act apply by reason of the dog attacking cattle, sheep, etc., on agricultural land as defined, he also may be guilty of a criminal offence and liable to be fined in accordance with the Act.

Another question which often arises about dogs is whether the owner of animals which the dog is attacking is ever justified in taking the law into his own hands and shooting the dog. There have been a number of cases before the Courts during the last fifteen years about this problem. In one leading case it was described how a farmer shot a dog which was worrying his sheep because he could see no other way of saving his ewes. It was the middle of the night and very dark because there was no moon. Two dogs had penned the ewes into a corner and were barking violently at them. The farmer was unable to drive the dogs away. He said that their blood was up; they seemed so fierce and savage that he did not think it safe to try and catch them with his hands. Many of the ewes were heavy in lamb; the dogs had been at them for over an hour and eventually the farmer shot at them and killed one.

The owner of the dogs sued the farmer for damages. The Court of Appeal decided that an owner of animals was justified in shooting a dog only in certain special exceptional circumstances and they laid down two general principles. These are the tests on which these principles were based:

(a) Was the dog actually attacking the animals, or was it likely to renew his attack so that the animals were in real and imminent danger?
(b) Was it a fact that the farmer could do nothing else to save his animals except to shoot, or that he behaved reasonably in thinking that shooting was necessary to protect his animals?

In the judgments delivered in this case some of the remarks of one of the Judges are of great general importance. He said:

"To shoot a dog is hateful to anyone who is fond of animals. On the other hand those who keep dogs in the country, or take them there, are under a real and serious obligation not to allow their dogs to chase sheep or cattle. Even if the sheep or cattle are not physically attacked, serious injury may be done to them if they are frightened and chased, particularly when, as in the present case, the ewes are in lamb or the cattle in calf."

In this case many of the ewes did subsequently fail to carry their lambs. It must be emphasized that this decision of the Court of Appeal does not mean that the owner of animals is entitled to shoot with recklessness and with impunity any dog who happens to be worrying his sheep or his cattle. If he resorts to such extreme measures and he is sued for damages, the burden will be on him to prove that he was right in acting as he did in accordance with the basic principles described above.

The next question we must consider about dogs is what is the liability of their owner if they attack and bite or savage a human being. It is not a criminal offence for a dog to attack a human being, and therefore there is no question of the owner being liable to prosecution. But it is a civil wrong for which the injured person may claim damages, if and only if he can establish that the owner had reason to know that the dog *might* attack human beings.

If a dog attacks other domestic animals the owner may be immediately liable; he may be liable for damages; he may be liable to be fined under the Dogs (Protection of Livestock) Act; he may even risk his dog being shot and justifiably shot by the farmer who owns the animals attacked. But if a dog attacks and seriously harms a human being, he has no legal redress unless he can establish that the owner of the dog knew, or should have known, of the dog's vicious propensities.

This derives from the fact that in general dogs are friendly to human beings. It is said that a dog is allowed his first bite. That is not true. But like so many proverbial sayings it has some basis of truth. The law is this: a dog's owner is not liable if a dog bites or savages another person unless he had reason to know that his dog might behave in this savage way, and such knowledge might be imputed to him if it is proved that:

(a) the dog had previously bitten or savaged another person, or
(b) the dog had given *other evidence* of savage propensities.

The fact that the dog has actually bitten someone before is conclusive evidence of knowledge of its savage disposition by his owner. But other evidence of the dog's savage disposition might serve to establish the fact that the owner ought to have known of the risk.

Once the owner has been given evidence from which he should realize his dog's nature—evidence which would convince any reasonable person—then he is legally responsible and liable to pay damages if his dog attacks and injures any human being, even though it may be for the first time, and may be the first bite.

This leads to the question which is often asked, whether the owner of a dog may save himself from this liability if he puts up a notice saying, 'Beware of the dog'. The owner who puts up this kind of notice usually lives in a rather lonely part of the world and he usually keeps dogs which may be rather fierce with strangers. There is no reason in law why he should not keep a fierce watchdog, yet he does so at some risk. If the dog does bite or savage a lawful caller, whether it be a friend paying a social call or a tradesman delivering goods, or even a stranger who nevertheless has an honest reason for his visit, the owner is likely to be legally responsible for the harm the dog may do. The truth is, I am afraid, that notices like the 'Beware of the dog' are not a defence in law. In fact they really indicate the owner's knowledge that the dog may be rather savage and fierce.

Nevertheless from a purely practical point of view he is probably wise to put up the notices. They do act as a warning to those people who assume that they can approach any dog and expect that dog to make friends with them. Some people get bitten because they approach strange dogs in a rather bossy manner on the assumption that any dog is very pleased to welcome their attentions. Such a notice ought to do something to prevent that kind of rash behaviour.

819

Moreover, if the dog only bites because someone has come to him in that way, the notice may be a very good defence in law. In other words, the notice is not an absolute defence if the dog makes a wanton attack, but it may be a defence to a claim if the visitor himself, by his own behaviour, provokes a dog. The notice is really a warning to the visitor to take no notice of the dog and to go on as if the dog was not there. If the visitor chooses to behave in another manner it may very well be the visitor's own fault. In other words, the notice is not necessarily a complete defence in all circumstances, but it may be a defence in the circumstances described.

". . . the assumption that any dog is very pleased to welcome their attentions . . ."

Other domestic animals

The rules about the liability of the owner of dogs which attack human beings, apply to other domestic animals which attack human beings. For instance, take a bull, an animal of somewhat uncertain disposition. If a bull attacks a human being its owner is not legally liable unless—as with the dog—the owner knew that this bull had some savage inclinations, or that the bull had previously attacked human beings. It has been held in a number of cases that it is not the ordinary nature of bulls, or rams, or horses, or cats with kittens, to injure human beings. So the farmer or the owner of these domestic animals is not obliged to take extraordinary precautions to keep you and his bull, or the other animals, at a safe distance unless he has a reason to know that these animals are dangerous.

If he has any reason to believe that they might be dangerous he should never let these animals graze in a field through which a right of way or a public footpath runs.

Damage to property

This rule about it being necessary for a plaintiff to prove the defendant's knowledge of savage disposition, whether proved by a previous attack or by other evidence of fierceness, does not apply to damage which is done to another person's *property*. For example, if cattle or poultry invade your garden from a neighbouring field, eat the vegetables, and churn up the ground, their owner is liable to you for the trespass and for the damage. The privilege in this respect with regard to cats and dogs does not apply to any other domestic animal. If cattle, horses, pigs, or any other animal invade your land, whether it's your domestic garden or your agricultural land, and do damage, the owner of the animals is liable to you for the damage they have caused.

It is no answer for the owner of the animals in this sort of case to say that your fence or your hedge was defective. It is not your duty to keep them *out*, it is his duty to keep them *in*.

The same rule applies if his animals trespass and injure your animals: for example, if his horse trespasses on to your land and kicks your horse, or his cattle gore your dog. If his animals are trespassing he is responsible. In this kind of case you are under no obligation to prove that he had been careless or that he knew of their propensity to wander or to attack other animals; the mere fact of the damage and the injury is enough to make him liable.

Exception for animals being driven along the highway

There is, however, a curious exception which has an old historical basis and can be justified on no other basis. It concerns animals which are being driven along a highway. Let us suppose, for example, that your house borders on a road along which cattle are being driven on their way to market. If your garden gates are open and some of the cows wander in and trample over your lawn or your flower-beds, you would not be able successfully to sue their owner for damages simply because they had broken into your garden.

You *would* have this right if they had broken in from neighbouring land. But if they are being driven along the highway on their lawful occasions, because they are being driven to market or being driven to other land, you will not have this right unless you can prove that the cattle drover had been negligent. Now this is not very easy if he was driving them along in the normal slow and peaceful way. It would be said that you should have kept your gates shut. The law is that cattle and all the other domestic farm animals are fully entitled to travel along the highway just as we are, and if you live by a road along which they walk it is up to you to keep the gates shut.

The old adage of the bull in the china shop finds a parallel in the law reports, in the case of the ox who while being driven with his fellows along the street broke into an ironmonger's shop, where he stayed for some forty-five minutes, rampaging around among the pots and pans and the china, before he was persuaded to come out. You can imagine what damage he did. The unlucky ironmonger did not succeed in his claim for damages, because he could not prove that the herdsman had been negligent.

So the position is that if animals—always excepting cats and dogs—if animals other than these break into your land from your neighbour's land and cause damage, you can recover compensation without proving any negligence on the part of their owner. It is their owner's duty to keep them in and keep them safe. The fact of the trespass and the damage is enough. But if the animals are being lawfully driven on the highway and they break into your property, you have, in addition to proving the damage, to prove that whoever was in charge of them was negligent.

Animals on land adjoining a highway

There is another unusual point concerning animals on the highway, when they come from land which adjoins the highway. The law is that anyone who owns land adjoining the highway is not bound to keep a good fence or a good hedge between his land and the public road. A few years ago there was a case in the High Court in which the facts were that a motor-cyclist who was riding along the road in Cornwall had a terrible shock when a mare leapt over the hedge and landed on him. He was hurt and brought an action for damages against the owner of the mare. It was perfectly obvious that the hedge was not adequate to keep the mare in. The Court's decision went against him, because of this old rule that the owner of the land adjoining the highway is not obliged to take care to keep his animals off the highway. If he has reason to think that any one of his animals is exceptionally wild or savage by nature he must take special precautions. But in the absence of such knowledge he is not obliged to take special precautions to keep his animals off the highway.

The reason for this special favour showed to the owners of land adjoining the highway goes so far back that it is impossible nowadays to say what its origin is. Many lawyers think it is unjust and out of date, but it needs a new Act of Parliament to alter it.

A Judge in the Court of Appeal in a case heard in 1943 said:

"The rule appears to be ill-adapted to modern conditions. A farmer who allows his cow to stray through a gap in his hedge on to his neighbour's land, where it consumes a few cauliflowers, is liable in damages to his neighbour. But if, through a similar gap in the hedge, it strays on to the road and causes the overturning of a motor-omnibus with death or injury to thirty or forty people, he is under no liability at all. I scarcely think that this is a satisfactory state of affairs in the twentieth century."

Many people driving in cars in remote parts of the United Kingdom are well aware of the risks of meeting sheep or cattle wandering all over the road. It is as well that they should know that, so far as the law is concerned, if they hit one of these animals it is likely to be held that they are responsible and not the owner of the animal.

None of these exceptional considerations which apply to domestic animals apply to animals which are wild by nature. The basic rule for all animals wild by nature is, as already stated, that whoever keeps them, does so at his peril. If they escape and do harm to property or person, then notwithstanding any of these exceptions for domestic animals, the owner of the wild animal is absolutely liable without proof of negligence, without proof of previous knowledge of savage propensities. He is liable automatically for any harm they may cause.

In view of the fact that the owner of a dog may be liable if it attacks other animals, and also if it attacks human beings provided the owner has knowledge of its savage disposition, it is useful that the law requires a dog to carry some badge of identification. The law is that every dog—save for the few exceptions mentioned below—must wear a collar bearing the name and address of its owner whenever it is out in public, so to speak, whenever it is out in the roads or in the fields, and so on. The inscription may be on the collar itself, or on one of those little appendages which one often sees attached to the collar. A pack of hounds is excused from complying with this formality, so are sporting dogs while being used for sporting purposes, so are dogs being used for destroying vermin, or for driving or tending sheep or cattle. A dog not in one of these categories, if it is without a collar, may be seized and treated as a stray and its owner fined up to £50.

BEES

Many people keep bees and the law about them has some curious points of interest. So long as they are in their free wild state they are, of course, ownerless. If they are reclaimed and hived then they become the property of the owner of the hive. If they then leave the hive they are still his property so long as he can see and follow them. If the swarm happens to settle on a tree in neighbouring property the bee-keeper has no right to trespass on to his neighbour's property to get them, and if the owner of the land refuses his permission, or he does not risk getting their permission, he will have lost his property in the bees; they will become wild again until someone else reclaims them by catching the swarm and hiving it.

Questions arise from time to time about whether a neighbour's keeping of bees amounts to a nuisance or not. One can very easily imagine the situation in a suburban garden where an enthusiastic bee-keeper may keep so many bees that they frighten or disturb the people who live in adjoining houses, which in suburbia may be very close indeed, and they may not share his enthusiasm for bees.

The basic legal rule is that to keep a reasonable number of bees is no nuisance in the technical legal sense; a sense which is described in the section on neighbours. What is reasonable depends on the circumstances. There may be some 50,000 bees in the hive and obviously seven or eight hives may be too many for a small suburban garden with houses all round. But twenty or even thirty hives may not be too many in the open country. This is always a question of degree and of fairness of consideration for others, as in all these questions concerning nuisance between neighbours. Broadly speaking, the bee-keeper in a small suburban garden should be content with a very few hives, and the further he gets out into the country the more hives he can keep.

There have been a few cases in the Courts where the bees have been more than a nuisance but a positive danger. For instance, where bees have attacked other animals. In two of these cases they attacked horses and stung so viciously that the horses died. In another case a horse was attacked and threw and dragged its rider, who was severely injured. In all these cases the owner of the bees was liable in damages.

Bees are treated in law as wild animals and therefore belonging to no one until they are reclaimed from their wild state. So if a swarm settles on a tree in your garden the bees don't belong to you, but if you hive them they become your property. If they leave your hive they are still your property so long as you can see and follow them.

". . . to keep a reasonable number of bees is no nuisance in the technical legal sense . . ."

BIRDS

The law about birds was substantially changed by the Protection of Birds Act which became law in December, 1954, and applies to England, Wales, and Scotland. The great merit of this Act is that it makes the law protecting birds simpler and more severe. The earlier Acts did not give protection all over the country, all the year round, but now under the new Act it is a criminal offence to kill any wild bird at *any time*, *anywhere*, with very few exceptions. Among the exceptions are the destructive birds like the magpie, the hooded or the carrion-crow, the jay, the wood-pigeon, the jackdaw, the rook, the starling, the house sparrow, and certain gulls.

Another group which is not protected by this Act comprises the birds which are bred for the table and are already covered by the Game Acts—grouse, pheasant, partridge, black game, or ptarmigan. Nor does the Act protect certain birds which are usually shot and used for food like certain wild duck, wild geese, snipe, woodcock, plover, and one or two others. These birds are, of course, subject to a close season when shooting is forbidden.

But broadly speaking, apart from game birds, birds shot for food, and the destructive birds, it is now a criminal offence to take or kill any wild bird at any time. It is also an offence to destroy their nests while they are in use.

What about their eggs? What about the schoolboy's collection? This presented rather a problem. The answer is a compromise between the views of those who would stop anyone ever taking eggs from a nest, and those who think there is no harm in taking eggs from some birds' nests. The Act empowers the Home Secretary and the Secretary of State for Scotland to make orders containing a list of the birds from whose nests some eggs may be taken without fear of prosecution.

The Act necessarily goes into more detail than is possible here. What has been stated above gives a broad general picture of the scope and purpose of the Act. Anyone concerned to have precise details and full lists of the birds in the categories described can get full information from the Royal Society for the Protection of Birds, at 25 Eccleston Square, London, S.W.1.

RIGHTS OF OWNERSHIP OF ANIMALS

The rights of ownership in animals depends mainly upon the classification into which those animals fall.

(1) *Domestic animals:* an animal which falls into this category, which has already been described, is just as capable of being owned as any inanimate article. The owner of a domestic animal has the same right of ownership over that animal as he has over his house or his furniture. He can, for instance, bring an action for damages for injuries caused to his animals, and to compel someone who has stolen one of the animals to return it. (The theft would also, of course, expose the thief to risk of prosecution.)

(2) *Animals wild by nature:* such animals are not owned by anyone unless they have been taken into captivity. They may or may not have become tame as a result of captivity, but the point is that their movements are controlled. Thus, animals in a zoo, deer in a park, or bees in a hive are capable in law of being owned by someone.

If the wild animals are still in their natural state they are not owned by anyone. Thus, a man who owns land does not own the wild animals that may be on the land. He may have the exclusive right to hunt and shoot or otherwise kill them, simply because they are on his land, but that is a very different matter from owning animals themselves. When the animals are killed, or die, however, then the owner of the land on which they lie owns them. Thus if the animals are killed by a poacher, they remain the landowner's property.

An owner of land may let out shooting rights for all animals found on his land, or for certain animals, and in that event he temporarily deprives himself of his exclusive right to hunt those animals and the tenant of the shooting rights has the right of ownership of the animals which he kills.

(3) *Ownership of swans:* there is a point of special interest here, which will be familiar to many who have read of the ceremony of swan-upping on the River Thames. By very ancient law, the Crown has the exclusive right to the ownership of certain wild animals, in certain circumstances, *viz.*, swans, and those fish included in the term 'Fish Royal'.

White swans in open rivers belong to the Crown. Any person may own swans that are unmarked if they are in his own private waters. For example, the swans at Abbotsbury in Dorsetshire are in private ownership. Once, however, the swans fly away and become at liberty, they belong to the Crown and may be seized on behalf of the Crown. The swans on the River Thames belong either to the Crown, or to two of the City Companies; the Dyers' Company and the Vintners' Company. Every year, young swans on the Thames are marked to show whether they belong to the Crown or to one or other of the Companies. This is the ceremony known as swan-upping.

The Fish Royal are whales and sturgeon. If they are caught in territorial waters, or if they are stranded on the foreshore, they belong to the Crown. If the fish is caught outside territorial waters, then it belongs to whoever caught it.

(4) *Bees:* the ownership of bees has already been considered.

Some special provisions relating to dogs

(a) *Licences.* Everyone who keeps a dog must, unless it falls within one of the exceptions mentioned below, have a licence for it as soon as it attains the age of six months. The licence costs 7s 6d. It is obtainable from a post office, and it lasts for twelve months beginning with the first day of the month in which it is taken out.

Exceptions:

(i) No licence is necessary for a dog kept and used solely by a blind person for his guidance.

(ii) A hound under the age of twelve months which has never been entered in or used with a pack of hounds need not be licensed so long as the owner or master has taken out proper licences for all the hounds entered in or used with any pack kept by him.

(iii) It is possible to get exemption in respect of a dog kept and used solely for the purpose of tending sheep or cattle on a farm, or by a shepherd in the exercise of his calling, if the owner of the dog obtains a certificate of exemption from duty. It will be necessary to obtain the consent of the local Magistrates' Court, and details of the procedure will be obtained on application to the Court.

(b) *Stray dogs.* If an officer of the police has reason to think that a dog found wandering abroad is a stray dog, he may seize it and keep it until it is claimed and the expenses of its detention are paid. If the dog is wearing a collar with the owner's name and address inscribed on it, or attached to it as described above, the police will, of course, inform the owner that they have it. It is their practice also to inform the owner that unless the dog is claimed within seven days it is liable to be sold or painlessly destroyed. The police must keep a register of all dogs seized and detained by them, and this register is open to inspection by any member of the public at all reasonable times on payment of some small fee.

(d) *Dogs which are dangerous or out of control.* On complaint being made to the Magistrates' Court that a dog is dangerous and not kept under control, the magistrates may make an order, either for the dog to be kept under proper control, or for it to be destroyed. It should be noted that it is not an offence merely to keep a dangerous dog. Many people do keep dogs which have been trained to guard property and to be fierce with strangers. The offence consists, not just in keeping the dangerous dog, but in also failing to keep it under proper control.

THE LAW OF SCOTLAND
COMPARED WITH THE
LAW OF ENGLAND

INTRODUCTION

ALTHOUGH Scotland and England were united in 1707, this did not mean that one code of law was adopted for the whole of the United Kingdom. On the contrary, each of the two countries kept her own legal system. So far as Scotland was concerned, the existence and independence of her courts and her law were guaranteed by the Treaty which led to the union of the two countries, Article XVIII of which provided that, except for certain laws concerning trade—

> 'all other laws in use within the kingdom of Scotland do after the union and notwithstanding thereof remain in the same force as before (except such as are contrary to or inconsistent with this Treaty) but alterable by the Parliament of Great Britain with this difference betwixt the laws concerning publick right policy and civil government and those which concern private right that the laws which concern publick right policy and civil government may be made the same throughout the whole United Kingdom *but that no alteration be made in laws which concern private right except for evident utility of the subjects within Scotland*'.

Article XIX went on to safeguard the Scottish courts of law, including the Court of Session and the High Court of Justiciary, and provided that Scottish legal cases should not fall within the jurisdiction of the English High Court.

These articles in the Treaty of Union form, as it were, the 'fundamental law' which, during more than two and a half centuries, has preserved for the Scots their own highly individual legal code. That the Treaty has lost none of its force was shown as recently as 1953 in an unusual case which came before the Court of Session in Edinburgh. In this case the Court was asked to declare that the use of the numeral 'II' in the title of Her Majesty the Queen 'involved a contravention of Article I of the Treaty of Union'. The Court held that it did

829

not, but although the case failed the Judges nevertheless put on record their agreement with the petitioners that certain provisions of the Treaty (including those articles which related to the preservation of Scots Law) constituted a 'fundamental law', which held greater force than an ordinary Act of Parliament and which could not be altered or repealed by Parliament.

At the present time, therefore, Scotland has her own courts and judges, her own law officers and prosecutors, and her own legal profession. Such English dignitaries as the Lord Chief Justice and the Attorney-General have no powers north of the border, where their places are taken by the Lord Justice-General and the Lord Advocate respectively. Most important of all, Scotland has her own law, a system which traces its origins back to the earliest Scottish customs, which owes a great debt to both Roman Law and the law of the Church, and which through the centuries has developed, with the aid of many jurists of international eminence, into a unique and progressive modern code. Scots Law has, of course—especially in more recent times—been influenced by the law of England, but it has never succumbed to its more famous neighbour; and today, though similar in many fields, the two systems reveal wide differences of the greatest practical importance. It will be the purpose of this article to give some general impression of the Scottish legal system and, in particular, to point out some of the differences between it and English Law which are most likely to affect people in their everyday lives.

THE COURTS IN SCOTLAND

Turning first to the general framework of the law in Scotland, it may be of interest to say a word about the Scottish courts of law. The supreme court in civil matters (*i.e.*, where crimes are not involved), corresponding to the English High Court of Justice, is the Court of Session. This court is composed of sixteen judges and is presided over by the Lord President of the Court of Session. Certain of the judges sit alone in order to hear cases at first instance, and a judge sitting alone for this purpose is known as a 'Lord Ordinary'. (All the judges of the Court of Session bear the judicial title of 'Lord'.) Appeals from the judgment of a Lord Ordinary are heard by a Division of the Court composed generally of four of its members. The Court sits only in Edinburgh and does not go on circuit. The same judges who form the Court of Session also form the High Court of Justiciary, which is the supreme court of criminal justice in Scotland. The High Court has jurisdiction to try any crime committed in Scotland, except where its jurisdiction is ousted by statute, but in practice only the more serious offences are dealt with by it. The Lord President of the Court of Session heads this court also and, in this capacity, he is known as the Lord Justice-General. The other members of the court (who are, as has been said, the remaining judges of the Court of Session) are known as Lords Commissioners of Justiciary and, in this capacity, they go on circuit, trying criminal cases in the various circuit towns of Scotland. The High Court of Justiciary also acts as a court of criminal appeal, and when sitting as such is normally composed of three judges. An appeal lies to the House of Lords from the Court of Session in civil cases, but there is no appeal from the High Court of Justiciary to the House of Lords in criminal cases—a difference from the English system, which permits an appeal to the House of Lords in criminal cases where a point of law of general public importance is involved if leave to appeal is first obtained from either the court below or the House of Lords itself.

After the Court of Session and the High Court of Justiciary the next most important court in Scotland is the Sheriff Court. Scotland is divided into twelve sheriffdoms and for each of these sheriffdoms there is appointed a Sheriff

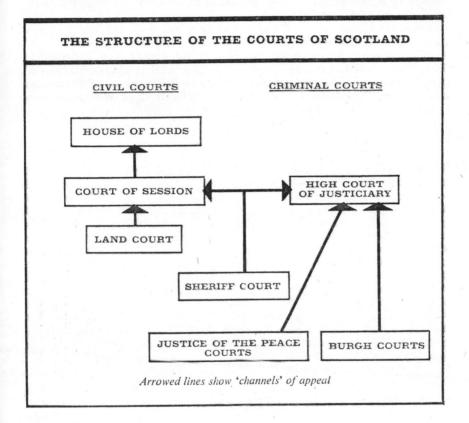

THE STRUCTURE OF THE COURTS OF SCOTLAND

CIVIL COURTS   CRIMINAL COURTS

HOUSE OF LORDS

COURT OF SESSION   HIGH COURT OF JUSTICIARY

LAND COURT

SHERIFF COURT

JUSTICE OF THE PEACE COURTS   BURGH COURTS

Arrowed lines show 'channels' of appeal

Principal and several Sheriffs Substitute. The latter hear both civil and criminal cases in the principal towns of the sheriffdom, while the principal duty of the former is to hear appeals in civil cases from the judgments of the sheriffs substitute in his sheriffdom. A sheriff principal is always a senior member of the Scottish Bar; a sheriff substitute must be either a member of the Bar or a solicitor, and in either case must be of at least five years' standing in his profession. Although the Sheriff Court is often—and understandably—compared with the English County Court, the sheriff's jurisdiction is in fact much wider than that of a County Court judge. Thus a County Court judge has no power to try criminal cases, whereas a sheriff substitute can and frequently does try all but the very gravest offences, such as murder and rape. Even in civil matters, a sheriff substitute has much greater powers than a judge of the County Court, for there is no upper limit to the value of the cases which he can hear, whereas a County Court judge cannot, except with the consent of the parties, decide cases of which the value exceeds £400. Indeed, in some parts of Scotland litigants tend to bring very important cases indeed before the sheriff, rather than go to the additional trouble and expense of raising an action in the Court of Session in Edinburgh.

Other Scottish courts which may be noticed are the Land Court, which deals with a host of problems relating to agricultural land, and the Court of the Lord Lyon King of Arms, which possesses a somewhat anachronistic jurisdiction in matters of heraldry. There are also in the counties the Justice of the Peace Courts, and in the burghs the Burgh Courts composed of Magistrates of the burgh. These last-named courts deal chiefly with minor criminal offences.

THE LAW OFFICERS

Just as England has two law officers of the Crown—the Attorney-General and the Solicitor-General—so also there are two Scottish law officers, the Lord Advocate and the Solicitor-General for Scotland. More is said below about the functions of these two officers in relation to the administration of criminal justice in Scotland. Apart from having these functions the Lord Advocate is the chief adviser to Her Majesty and the Government on matters involving the law of Scotland. His is an office of some antiquity, dating back to the fifteenth century, and at one time, after the Jacobite rebellions of 1715 and 1745, the Lord Advocate was the virtual ruler of Scotland. Though not quite so exalted today, the office is nonetheless one of very great importance. The holder is always a senior member of the Scottish Bar; he is one of the Ministers of the Crown (and by invariable practice is created a Privy Councillor); and so that he may play a full part in the work of the administration, he is almost always a Member of Parliament. He is, amongst other things, responsible for the drafting of Scottish legislation.

THE LEGAL PROFESSION

The legal profession in Scotland is divided, like its English counterpart, into two branches, namely, members of the Bar and solicitors. Members of the Scottish Bar are not known as barristers but as advocates, and they all belong to the Faculty of Advocates, a professional body dating from the sixteenth century. Its membership in 1961 was slightly less than three hundred, of whom, however, less than half were in active practice in the Court of Session in Edinburgh. Only a member of the Faculty of Advocates is entitled to plead on behalf of a client before that court or the High Court of Justiciary. At the head of the Faculty is the Dean of Faculty, elected by his fellow advocates, and under him the Faculty exercises a strict control over the professional conduct of its members.

The governing body of the solicitors' branch of the legal profession in Scotland is the Law Society of Scotland, which was created by Act of Parliament in 1949. Before he can practise, a solicitor must obtain a practising certificate from the Law Society, and a committee of the Society, known as the Discipline Committee, keeps watch over the conduct of solicitors in professional matters and investigates complaints made against any member of the profession. Some solicitors in Scotland are also members of one or other of certain private corporations or societies of solicitors, of which the oldest and most widely known is perhaps the Society of Writers to H.M. Signet. (Members of this society append the letters 'W.S.' to their name.) Membership of one of these bodies does not confer on a solicitor any particular rights or privileges in the practice of his profession, though it may, of course, lend some prestige to him or his firm.

SCOTS AND ENGLISH LAW

Mention has been made above of the many differences which exist between Scots Law and the law of England. This is not just an academic point, of interest only to students of law; the differences between the two systems are of very considerable practical importance and can easily affect the ordinary citizen in the conduct of his business and family affairs.

Inheritance

If we turn first to the law of succession, which lays down the rules governing the making of wills, the distribution of the property of deceased persons, and similar matters, several fundamental differences between Scots and English Law at once reveal themselves. One vital difference is that by the law of Scotland the immediate family of a deceased person are recognized as possessing certain 'legal rights' in his estate. What this means is that the widow and children of a Scotsman who dies are each entitled to claim a share of the property left by him, whether or not he left a will disposing of that property. Even if he left a valid will disposing of his whole estate, this could not defeat the legal rights of his widow and children.

Suppose, for instance, that a man dies domiciled in Scotland leaving a widow and children, and that it is found after his death that he has made a valid will under which his whole estate is to go to a stranger. The law will not give effect to this will if the dead man's widow and children choose to claim their legal rights out of his estate. If they claim these rights, then the widow will be entitled to a life interest in one-third of any land or houses which her deceased husband owned—a right which is known in Scots Law by the old name of 'terce'. She will also be entitled to '*jus relictae*'—that is, to a one-third share of any other property, such as money in the bank, stocks and shares, furniture, etc., which belonged to the deceased. The children, for their part, can claim 'legitim' (or 'bairn's part'), which is a one-third share of their father's estate (other than land and houses) and which is divided equally amongst the children. Only what remains of the estate after all these claims have been met (known picturesquely as 'dead's part') will be allowed by the law to go to the stranger in accordance with the terms of the will. A surviving husband has similar legal rights in the estate of his deceased wife. Instead of 'terce' he has 'courtesy', which is a life interest in the whole of any land or houses which his deceased wife owned, and his one-third share in her other property is known as '*jus relicti*'. (Incidentally, where there are no children the *us relictae* or *jus relicti* of a surviving spouse is increased to one half of the moveable estate of the deceased.)

It is in this way that the system of legal rights has always operated to protect the family of a deceased person in Scotland against the possibility of an unfair or spiteful will and to make futile any threat on the part of a Scottish father to cut off his son 'with a shilling'. In England, on the other hand, the widow and children of a deceased person do not possess any rights in his estate comparable with the legal rights recognized by Scots Law. If he has died without leaving a will, then his widow and children can, of course, each claim a share of his property, but if he has made a will leaving everything to a stranger, then neither his widow nor his children can claim anything out of his estate as of right. This rather harsh position has, however, been softened by the passing of the Inheritance (Family Provision) Act, 1938, which allows certain close relatives of a deceased person, such as his widow or unmarried daughter, to ask the court to order that some reasonable provision be made for their maintenance out of the deceased's estate, a request to which the court may accede if it is satisfied that the deceased's will does not make reasonable provision for them. (For a more detailed description see the chapter on Disinheritance.)

Scots and English Law differ also when it comes to the rules which govern the distribution of the estate of a person who has died intestate—that is to say, without having made a will. It is impossible within the compass of this article to deal fully with the rules of division in Scotland, but an example may be taken of a domiciled Scotsman who dies without leaving a will and whose property consists of, say, the family dwelling-house and the furniture in it, a small balance on current account at his bank and a rather larger one on deposit account, some National Savings certificates and premium bonds, and the family car. The solicitors who are winding up his estate have the house and furniture valued and also place a value on the car, and when all the various items are added up and the dead man's funeral expenses and debts deducted, and estate duty (if any) paid, the value of his estate is found to be in the region of £4,000. There are living the deceased's widow, his three sons and two of his daughters, his third and youngest daughter having died some years before her father; there are also two grandchildren, who are the children of the deceased's youngest daughter. How is the estate to be divided?

If the case had happened in England, there would have been no problem: the deceased's property would have gone in its entirety to his widow, and his children and grandchildren would have got nothing. This is the effect of the Intestates' Estates Act, 1952, which provides, in effect, that the estate of a man dying intestate and leaving a widow and children must, if its value is less than £5,000, go wholly to the widow. But in Scotland the rules are different and rather more complicated. In the first place, Scots Law regards the estate as falling into two separate categories, known as the 'heritable' estate and the 'moveable' estate. By heritable estate is meant in this case simply the deceased's house; the remainder of his estate is moveable. The distinction is important because what happens to the heritable estate is quite different from what happens to the moveable. The heritable property passes wholly and directly to the deceased's eldest son subject, however, to the widow's legal right of terce: that is to say, the eldest son gets his father's house, but his mother is entitled, if she claims it, to a life interest in one-third of the house. (The value of this life interest and how it is to be paid is normally settled by amicable agreement, but if there is any dispute the house may have to be sold and one-third of the proceeds invested for the benefit of the widow during her lifetime and for the eldest son on her death.)

How, then, is the deceased's moveable property divided up? His eldest son, having accepted his father's heritable estate, cannot claim any part of the moveables. The widow can, however, claim her legal right of *jus relictae* and thus obtains a one-third share of her husband's moveable property. The surviving children of the deceased (always excepting his eldest son) can also claim their legal right of legitim, and therefore another one-third share of the moveables is set aside and divided equally amongst these four children, so that each child receives one-twelfth of the total moveable estate. The remaining third, or residue, of the estate is also divided equally amongst the deceased's children (other than the eldest son) with, however, this difference, that in dividing up the residue the deceased's youngest daughter, who died before him, is taken into account for the first time. Her two children are entitled to take the share in the residue of their grandfather's estate to which their mother would have been entitled had she lived. In other words, the remaining third of the deceased's estate is divided into five parts; each of the deceased's four surviving children receives one part, and the last part (to which his youngest daughter would have been entitled had she survived him) is divided equally between her two children.

It can be seen from this example that the division of the estate of a person who has died intestate will be very different according to whether it is governed by Scots or English Law. But this is merely one example, and it illustrates only a few of the many differences which exist between the law of Scotland and that of England in this most important sphere of wills and succession. Obviously, it is essential to know which law is going to govern the winding up of your affairs after your death. What decides this vital question?

English or Scottish domicil?

The answer depends on what lawyers call your 'domicil'. If you are of English domicil, English Law will govern the winding up and distribution of your estate, so that, for example, if you die without leaving a will, your widow will normally be in a better position than if Scots Law applied. If you are of Scottish domicil, the law of Scotland will govern the winding up and distribution of your estate, and therefore it is no use trying to cut a disobedient son out of your will because, in spite of what you do, he will be able to claim his legal right of legitim out of your estate.

How, then, is one to know whether one is of English or Scottish domicil? Questions of domicil are sometimes easy but often extremely difficult: the answer may depend on where the person concerned was born and what domicil his father held, or it may depend on where he resides and whether he intends to stay there permanently. The answer is obvious in the case of a person who was born in England of English parents, who has lived and worked there all his life, whose home and possessions are there and whose family and friends are also there: he is evidently of English domicil. And the same is true of the Scotsman who does not move from his native country. But the matter may be much more difficult. A Scotsman, for example, may live in England for much of his life and yet keep his Scottish domicil. His business may have brought him south: he may have been sent by his employers to their London office and been compelled to buy a house and set up home in Surrey; but he may, nevertheless, regard himself as Scottish, may go back to Scotland for his holidays and may have the firm intention of returning permanently to that country as soon as his employers can find him a suitable post there, or at all events when he retires. Such a man remains of Scottish domicil, even during the years when he is living in England, and the law which will govern the winding up of his affairs on his death will be Scots Law.

It should be repeated that questions of domicil are frequently very difficult, and legal advice should always be obtained if there is the slightest doubt about the matter and the question looks like becoming important. Domicil is always important in the field of succession, as the example given above shows. Other examples abound. Suppose, for example, you wish to make your will—as you should, if you are a responsible person—here again, if you are of Scottish domicil, the rules of Scots Law regarding wills will apply to you; if you are of English domicil, English Law will apply; and the two are very different. If you are domiciled in Scotland and you make a will according to English Law, or vice versa, you run a great number of risks, including the risk that your will may not be valid at all and that, even if it is, it will not have the effects which you intended. Once again, it has to be repeated that in this field it is vital to take legal advice.

The law about making a will

How in fact do the two laws differ in the matter of wills? First of all, they differ in their opinion of the age which a young person ought to have reached before he (or she) can properly make a will. Under English Law an 'infant' (that is, a person under twenty-one) cannot make a valid will—a rule to which there is only one exception, mentioned below. In Scotland, however, a valid will can be made by a boy as soon as he reaches the age of fourteen or by a girl as soon as she reaches the age of twelve, the only qualification being that until they reach the age of twenty-one young persons are not allowed to put a clause in their will altering the succession to any heritable property which they may possess. Subject to this limitation, however, the power to make a valid will of a Scottish 'minor' (the correct Scottish legal term to describe a boy of between fourteen and twenty-one or a girl of between twelve and twenty-one) is unfettered.

The exception mentioned above to the rule of English Law that an infant cannot make a valid will occurs in the case of soldiers or airmen who are on actual military service, in the case of mariners or seamen (including merchant

THE LAW OF SCOTLAND

seamen) who are at sea, and in the case of members of the navy or marines who, though not at sea, are so circumstanced that if they were soldiers they would be on actual military service. These are enabled by a series of Acts of Parliament to make a valid will even although they have not reached twenty-one; and in the case of wills made by soldiers, sailors, or airmen in such circumstances the law of England dispenses with certain of the formalities which must normally be observed in making a will—even to the extent of recognizing as valid a will made by such a person by word of mouth in the presence of a witness. Such is the effect of these Acts in their application to a soldier (to use the military as an example) who is of English domicil. A soldier who is of Scottish domicil should, however, be very careful not to be misled by this if he wants to make a will while on active service, because the Acts do not apply to him in the same way. Indeed, so far as they relax the formalities necessary for making a valid will, they do not apply to him at all: in the case of a Scottish soldier the ordinary law of Scotland governs the making of his will whether he is on active service or not. Nor do the provisions allowing a soldier under twenty-one to make a will affect him, because being a domiciled Scotsman he can already do this. The only specialty which the Acts have introduced, as regards the making of a will by a Scottish soldier on active service who is under twenty-one, is that the soldier can validly dispose of his heritable property in his will—a thing which, as mentioned above, he could not otherwise do.

The legal formalities of a Scottish will

Certain formalities must be observed in making a will under Scots Law and it is unwise in the extreme for a person without legal training to attempt to make a will for himself. The formalities are, briefly, that the testator (that is, the person who is making the will) must sign each separate sheet of paper which forms part of the will and must subscribe the will—that is, sign it at the very end, after the last clause which it contains. His signature must be witnessed by two witnesses, who should also sign the will at the end and add their designations. (These witnesses, incidentally, do not need to be told that it is a will which they are witnessing, still less what the will contains.) This is the normal way of executing a will in Scotland, and it resembles closely, though by no means exactly, the method laid down in English Law. There are, however, two exceptional methods which can be used in Scotland and which are unknown to English Law. The first is really a way of leaving a legacy, rather than of making a complete will. In Scotland a man may bequeath a legacy not exceeding £100 Scots (which is equivalent to £8 6s 8d sterling) by word of mouth and without the necessity of any writing; such a legacy is known as a 'nuncupative' legacy.

The second method, which is much more common, is the 'holograph' will. A holograph will make take one of two forms. Either it is written out entirely by the testator *in his own handwriting* and signed by him, or else it is written (or typed) by another person and the testator writes at the end of it, in his own handwriting, the words '*adopted as holograph*' and signs it. In neither case are witnesses necessary and in both cases the will is a perfectly valid one.

In 1930 a case was taken on appeal from the Court of Session to the House of Lords which involved a holograph will and which, by reason of its unusual facts, emphasizes the rule mentioned earlier in this article, that the law governing the making of a will is the law of the country where the testator was domiciled at the time of his death, and also illustrates how difficult it sometimes is to decide what a person's domicil is. The case concerned a certain George Bowie, who was born in Glasgow in 1845 and who worked as a commercial traveller in that city until 1882, when he gave up work permanently, choosing to live for the remainder of his life on the bounty of his relatives. Around 1890 he left Glasgow and went to live in Liverpool—not, apparently, because he wished to abandon Scotland and greatly desired to settle in England, but because a brother and sister of his for whom he had some considerable affection (and who gave him an allowance) had already gone there. During the next thirty-seven years, until his death in 1927, George Bowie never returned to Scotland and, indeed, left Liverpool only twice for short periods. He died in Liverpool and was buried there. While Bowie had been living in Liverpool his brother and sister had died, leaving him a considerable amount of property, and when he died it was discovered that he had made a holograph will leaving the residue of his estate to be divided equally amongst four hospitals.

The question at once arose—where was Bowie domiciled at the time of his death? If his true domicil was Scottish the holograph will was, of course, valid, but if he had acquired an English domicil as a result of his long stay in Liverpool then the will was invalid, because a domiciled Englishman must make his will according to the forms of the law of England, which does not recognize a holograph will as valid. If his will were invalid the four hospitals could not, naturally, claim their bequests; instead, his whole estate would go to his niece, Mrs Ramsay, who was his sole next-of-kin.

In the event, the House of Lords decided that Bowie had retained his Scottish domicil and had not acquired an English domicil at the time of his death; that his holograph will was, therefore, valid; and that accordingly the residue of his estate must, after all, be divided up amongst the four hospitals in terms of his will. Their Lordships held that Bowie's domicil was originally Scottish, and that his long residence in England had not by itself changed his Scottish domicil into an English one. For such a change, they said, much more than mere residence in England would have been required; it would have been necessary to prove a clear intention on Bowie's part to abandon his domicil of origin and acquire a domicil in England. There was no evidence of such an intention: on the contrary, it seemed to be the case that he had gone to Liverpool only to be with his family and that he had always looked upon himself, with some pride, as a Glasgow man. (Another item of evidence lending support to this view was that Bowie ordered and read a Glasgow weekly newspaper every week.)

Although in this case the validity of the will was upheld and the testator's wishes regarding the distribution of his estate given effect to, the decision was rather a narrow one, and it underlines the importance of being quite certain about one's domicil before one even thinks of making a will. The case also emphasizes one of the most important principles of the law of domicil, namely, that it requires strong evidence to show that a person has voluntarily abandoned the domicil which he had at birth (that is, his domicil of origin) and adopted a new domicil.

Revocation of a Scottish will on the birth of a child

One final distinction between the law of England and that of Scotland in the matter of wills should be noticed because of the important results which may flow from it. Under English Law a will is revoked automatically by the subsequent *marriage* of the testator; therefore, a domiciled Englishman, if he makes his will and then some time later gets married, should remember on his marriage to make a new will, because the marriage has, so to speak, killed his previous one. This rule does not apply in Scotland, but instead Scots Law provides that a will, or at any rate a will which contains no provision for children who may be born to the testator after he has made the will, shall be revoked by the *subsequent birth of a child* to the testator. Thus a domiciled Scotsman who, perhaps, has made a will in early life, need not (if he is content with its terms) make a new one on getting married, but if a child is thereafter born to him his will is revoked and if he wishes to provide for the distribution of his estate after his death he must make a new one.

Marriage

In Scotland, as in England, a young person must have reached the age of sixteen before he or she can get married. This age was fixed for both countries by the Age of Marriage Act, 1929; before that date a youth in Scotland could get married as soon as he became a minor—that is, when he reached his fourteenth birthday or, in the case of a girl, her twelfth birthday. The two forms of regular marriage in Scotland are marriage before a minister of religion and marriage in the presence of a registrar. Before either form of marriage can take place the parties must generally have resided in Scotland for a certain period and must have given public notice, either by proclamation of banns or in accordance with a special statutory procedure, of their intention to wed. Under the Marriage (Scotland) Act, 1939, the sheriff may, if it appears to him that, owing to the illness of one of the parties to an intended marriage or 'other unforeseen and exceptional circumstance', there is reasonable excuse for the failure of the parties to give the required public notice of their wedding, grant the parties a licence to get married, and such a licence—which is valid for ten days only—dispenses them from the necessity of going through the usual formalities of giving notice. This power of the sheriff is not often used, but it was found convenient during the late war, when members of the armed forces on leave frequently made up their minds to get married before returning to their units, but had not time to give the necessary public notice.

Apart from the forms of regular marriage, Scots Law recognized until 1940 three forms of 'irregular' marriage. These irregular marriages were valid marriages in every way, but they were constituted by unusual, or 'irregular', methods. They were marriage by declaration *de praesenti* (that is, marriage constituted by the parties' simply exchanging consent to immediate marriage), marriage by promise *subsequente copula* (which meant that if a man was allowed by a woman to have intercourse with her on the faith of his promise to marry her, he was in fact legally married to her as from the time when they had intercourse), and marriage by *cohabitation with habit and repute*. The last-mentioned is the only form of irregular marriage now in existence, the first two forms having been abolished in 1940. What it means, briefly, is that if a man and a woman live together over a number of years and are generally reputed to be husband and wife, the law of Scotland will presume that they have consented to marry each other and are in fact married, although they have never gone through a ceremony of marriage.

Though it finds its origin in the pre-Reformation canon law, marriage by cohabitation with habit and repute is by no means unknown even today. As recently as 1957 a man successfully petitioned the Court of Session for a declaration that he and the defender were lawfully married, the circumstances being that the parties had gone through what proved to be an invalid marriage ceremony, had thereafter lived together as man and wife for more than six years in the innocent though mistaken belief that the ceremony had been a valid one, and had during all that period been generally reputed to be married. The Court held that the fact that they had cohabited openly as man and wife and had publicly acquiesced in that relationship meant that their consent to marry each other must be inferred and that accordingly they were validly married persons. And in 1951 there was a much publicized litigation in the High Court in England in which the petitioner asked the Court to declare that he had from the date of his birth been the legitimate child of his parents, his object being to claim certain rights which could not by law devolve on a person of illegitimate birth. In fact, his parents had been validly married after his birth, but he sought to show that, before the formal ceremony and before his birth, his parents had contracted an irregular marriage by cohabitation with habit and repute in Scotland. The Court, however, held that the evidence brought by the petitioner was not sufficient to establish this.

Although marriage by declaration has now disappeared, it retains a modest claim to fame in that it was responsible for originating the famous 'Gretna marriages'. The history of these runaway marriages goes back a long way and originally there were two reasons for them. The first was that by Scots Law a young man or woman under twenty-one did not need the consent of his or her parents before getting married, whereas by English Law such parental consent was necessary. As a result, a young English couple who could not obtain, say, the consent of the girl's parents to her marriage naturally took the road to Scotland in order to attain their dream of connubial bliss without the tedious delay forced on them by English Law. The second reason lay in the fact of the elopement and the strong possibility of pursuit by an outraged father. The lovers had to get married quickly before father caught up, and here again Scots Law came to aid the cause of true love. Once across the border they stopped at the first convenient village—Gretna—where without delay or formalities of any kind, they exchanged their consent to marriage there and then, and a valid marriage by declaration was thus immediately constituted. (The 'ceremony' of exchanging consent traditionally took place before the local blacksmith, but this was not necessary to the validity of the marriage.) In other words, Gretna owes its fame to its geographical position alone, and not to any other peculiarity attaching to it.

Eventually, the number of hasty and ill-considered marriages taking place at Gretna became something of a scandal, and Parliament found it necessary to intervene. By Lord Brougham's Act, 1856, it was provided that no irregular marriage contracted by declaration in Scotland should be valid unless one of the parties had his or her usual place of residence in Scotland or had lived in Scotland for three weeks immediately before the marriage. In the end marriage by declaration was abolished by the Marriage (Scotland) Act, 1939. Youthful couples from England still travel to Scotland in order to get married, their

"Youthful couples from England still travel to Scotland to get married"

purpose generally being to circumvent their parents' refusal to allow them to marry. In this they are frequently successful, for parental consent to a marriage is still not necessary under Scots Law, but nowadays the parties to the intended marriage must normally reside in Scotland for several weeks before the marriage and must enter into an ordinary regular marriage of which public notice has to be given.

The obligations arising from marriage

The principal obligation which falls on a man as a result of entering into the contract of marriage is that of cohabiting with his wife and maintaining her at bed and board; other duties also arise, but this is his primary obligation. The husband must maintain his wife (so far as he is able to) on a standard appropriate to their position in life. On the other hand, Scots Law also imposes a certain duty on the wife in these matters; if her husband is, to use the words of the Married Women's Property (Scotland) Act, 1920, 'indigent' and cannot maintain himself, and if the wife has means of her own, then she comes under an obligation to 'aliment' her husband—that is, to provide him with the necessaries of life and keep him, so far as she can, in reasonable comfort. (To 'aliment', in Scottish legal parlance, means to maintain, and maintenance is known in Scotland as 'aliment'.)

If a husband should fail in his duty to live with his wife and maintain her, the wife's remedy is to raise against him what is called an action of 'adherence and aliment'. In this action—which is generally, though by no means always, raised in the Sheriff Court—the wife asks the court to order her husband to 'adhere' to her and (since no court can in practice compel a husband to live with his wife) to order him also to pay her aliment at a specified rate so long as he refuses to cohabit with her.

Where one of the parties to a marriage is guilty of adultery or cruelty, the other is relieved of the obligation to cohabit with the offender and may (if he or she does not want a divorce) raise an action for judicial separation. To the plea for separation, if it is raised by the wife, there is generally added a claim for aliment. If decree of judicial separation is granted, the successful party is relieved of the duty of adhering to the other. Such a decree does not dissolve the marriage; it merely separates the parties *a mensa et thoro* (from bed and board). Because the marriage remains intact it has been decided in Scotland (differing in this respect from the law of England) that a husband who obtains a judicial separation from his wife on the ground of the latter's adultery or cruelty is nevertheless bound to continue to aliment her, since the obligation to aliment arises from the marriage and subsists so long as the parties remain husband and wife.

The development of the law governing the relationship of husband and wife has in both England and Scotland been in the direction of greater freedom for the wife. The old conception of husband and wife being 'one flesh', so dear to the hearts of English lawyers, has almost disappeared, leaving only a few traces. A wife still takes her husband's domicil. In Scotland (though not in England) the husband has the right to choose the matrimonial home, and if his wife refuses to follow him there, she is in desertion. Nor has Scots Law so far adopted the various doctrines which have sprung up in England in recent years whereby a husband is apparently forbidden to exclude his wife from his house. But in matters of property the development has been similar in both countries. A hundred years ago a woman who married in Scotland automatically ceased to be the owner of her moveable property; at the moment of her marriage all of it—money, stocks and shares, jewellery, etc.—became her husband's property, to deal with as he wished. Moreover, any moveable property acquired by the wife during the marriage also passed automatically to her husband. Any land or houses which she owned—her heritable property—remained her own, but she could administer it only under her husband's supervision, and subject to his consent. As a result of a series of Acts of Parliament, however, a Scottish married woman is today as free to hold, administer, and dispose of her own property, heritable and moveable, as if she were a single woman and, unless in very special circumstances, her husband has no rights in relation to it.

In Scotland, a husband may sue his wife in connection with a matter arising out of a contract, but, like English Law, Scots Law does not allow one party to a marriage to sue the other for damages in respect of a wrong done to him or her by the other. Thus, if a husband is slandered by his wife he cannot, however great the loss he has suffered in consequence of the slander, sue his wife for damages. Similarly, a wife who is injured in a road accident while being driven by her husband in his car is unable to raise an action for damages against him, though the accident may clearly be due to his negligence. This bar on proceedings between husband and wife has been traced in England to the old principle, already mentioned, that husband and wife are one person in the eyes of the law; Scots Law, on the other hand, has preferred to base its refusal to allow the parties to a marriage to sue each other for wrongs done on the principle that it would be contrary to the public interest to allow domestic peace to be shattered by actions of this nature between husband and wife.

Divorce

Divorce has a much longer history in Scotland than in England. Until comparatively recently a person in England who wished a divorce had to obtain a private Act of Parliament to achieve his object—a proceeding whose expense effectively restricted divorce to the wealthy few. Scots Law, however, has recognized divorce for adultery since the Reformation, and divorce for desertion since shortly after that time—1573, to be exact. In 1938 the Divorce (Scotland) Act added to these grounds incurable insanity, cruelty, sodomy and bestiality. The Act also provides for the dissolution of a marriage on the ground of the presumed death of one of the parties, if reasonable grounds exist for supposing that party to be dead. (Seven years' continuous absence coupled with the fact that the petitioner has no reason to believe that the missing party has been living within that time is evidence that he or she is dead, unless the contrary is proved.)

It will be seen that the grounds for divorce in Scotland are today apparently almost identical to those laid down in English Law. But it would be a mistake to conclude on this account that the laws of Scotland and England are the same in questions of divorce. Apart from procedural differences (many of which are of very considerable importance) conceptions such as cruelty and desertion have in some ways received quite different treatment in the Scottish courts from the English, so much so that an eminent Scottish Judge was prompted to declare in one case involving desertion that, "The history of desertion in English Law has proceeded on such different lines and with so different an outlook that English conceptions are no certain guide in this chapter of the law." One difference between the two laws is that the modern English doctrine of 'constructive desertion', by virtue of which a wife (for example) who is

843

forced by her husband's conduct to leave the matrimonial home may sue him for divorce on the ground of desertion, is not accepted in Scots Law. Cruelty also has probably been more widely interpreted by the English courts. So far as adultery is concerned, there is admittedly not much room for difference as to meaning, but nevertheless there is one important matter on which the laws of the two countries do not agree. In England a person who sues for divorce on the ground of adultery is not entitled as of right to obtain a divorce if he has himself committed adultery. He must make a statement to the court admitting his offence and the court may in its discretion (but need not) overlook his adultery and grant him a divorce. Under Scots Law, however, a husband or wife whose partner has committed adultery has a right to a divorce even if he or she has also committed adultery: in such cases cross-actions of divorce are quite common.

In procedural matters, as has been said, there are several important differences between the two laws. In England a husband or wife cannot, as a general rule, bring an action of divorce within the first three years after the date of the marriage: in Scotland there is no such restriction. The Scottish courts do not grant a 'decree nisi' or a 'decree absolute'; in Scotland there is only one kind of decree of divorce and, apart from the possibility of an appeal, it is final. Significantly, that sinister English figure, the Queen's Proctor, has no part to play on the Scottish stage. There is no corresponding Scottish official, though the Lord Advocate may appear in an action of divorce as representing the public interest if he has grounds for believing that the case is being brought by collusion.

The effect of divorce on the property of the parties is yet another aspect of the law of husband and wife on which Scots and English Law diverge widely. Suppose, for example, the case of a wife who succeeds in obtaining a decree of divorce against her husband. If the action is in an English court the petitioner may ask the court to award her maintenance, and in all probability the court will do so and will order the divorced husband to pay to his former wife a suitable sum by way of maintenance at regular intervals. Such an order could not be made in Scotland where, except in the one case mentioned below, the court has no power to order a divorced man to pay aliment to his former wife. Instead, Scots Law provides that the successful pursuer in an action of divorce shall be entitled to exact from the defender's estate the legal rights in that estate to which the pursuer would have been entitled had the defender died on the date on which decree of divorce was granted. Put simply, the defender is supposed to have died at the date of the divorce and the pursuer (if the wife) is allowed to claim her legal rights of terce and *jus relictae* out of her former husband's property in exactly the same way as if he had really died on that date. Similarly, a husband who obtains decree of divorce against his wife may at once exact courtesy from her estate, though by a curious anomaly he cannot obtain *jus relicti*. Thus in the example mentioned above, the innocent wife would be entitled, on decree of divorce being granted, to exact her legal rights out of her former husband's estate, but she could not ask for an award of aliment against him. The only case in which the court has power to order payment of aliment by one ex-spouse to another is where the ground for divorce is incurable insanity; in such a case the court may order the successful pursuer to pay 'a capital sum or an annual or periodical allowance to or for behoof of the defender'. A decree of divorce on the ground of incurable insanity has no effect on property rights.

Criminal Law

In the field of criminal law one very great difference between the Scottish and English systems is that the former depends to a great degree on the Common Law—that is, on a body of rules and principles long accepted and applied by the courts but nowhere laid down by Act of Parliament, whereas in England the criminal law is today almost entirely statutory. One result of this is that in Scotland the law of crime has tended to be more flexible and, in the hands of the courts, more capable of development to meet the changing needs of society than has the English Law. An interesting example of this is found in the law of murder, and concerns what is called in Scotland the doctrine of 'diminished responsibility'.

The plea of diminished responsibility is most often put forward on behalf of the accused in a trial for murder, and in making it the defence seek to prove that, even if the accused really committed the crime, he was so affected by mental weakness or aberration of mind as not to be completely responsible for his actions. In such a case the defence does not go so far as to maintain that the accused was completely insane and consequently in no way responsible for his actions; some responsibility for the crime is admitted, but due to the accused's abnormal state of mind the responsibility is said to be 'diminished'. If a plea of diminished responsibility succeeds the accused will be found guilty of culpable homicide (known in England as manslaughter) and may be sentenced to imprisonment for any term of years—even, in the most serious cases, for life. The defence of diminished responsibility has been developed by the Scottish courts over a period of more than three centuries and has proved a most useful means of mitigating the severity of the law (and, incidentally, avoiding the extremity of the death penalty) in cases where a plea of insanity would be bound to fail. The doctrine, however, formed no part of the law of England until the passing of the Homicide Act, 1957, which for the first time introduced the conception into English Law.

The administration of the criminal law in Scotland is centred on the Lord Advocate, who is the chief law officer of the Crown in Scotland and who controls, directly or through his assistants, the whole system of criminal prosecutions throughout the country. (Minor prosecutions in Justice of the Peace and Burgh Courts are a partial exception to this.) Ultimately it is he who decides whether or not to prosecute in any case, what crime is to be charged, in what court proceedings are to be taken and how the prosecution is to be conducted. In more serious cases he may even conduct the case himself—thus, in 1953, Lord Advocate Clyde conducted the prosecution in the High Court of Justiciary in Edinburgh of a number of young men charged with conspiring with the intention of overthrowing Her Majesty's government in Scotland. Obviously no one man could deal with every single prosecution himself, and the Lord Advocate is assisted by the Solicitor-General for Scotland (who is empowered by statute to deputize for the Lord Advocate in certain circumstances) and by several 'advocates depute', members of the Bar appointed by the Lord Advocate to assist in the work of criminal administration, and who themselves conduct most of the prosecutions in the High Court of Justiciary. There is also the Crown Agent, a permanent civil servant who heads a small staff in the Crown Office in Edinburgh, and who, under the direction of the Lord Advocate, plays a central part in co-ordinating and directing the administration of the criminal law.

The officers who have been mentioned are all centred on Edinburgh and represent, as it were, the higher direction of criminal justice in Scotland. The great burden of day-to-day work in this field, however, is carried by an officer called the Procurator Fiscal. Procurators fiscal are appointed by the Lord Advocate in every district in Scotland, and their functions are of the highest importance to the administration of criminal justice. In the first place, there being no coroners in Scotland and nothing resembling a coroner's inquest, the duty of investigating cases of sudden and unexplained death falls upon the procurator fiscal—a duty which he carries out thoroughly but in discreet privacy, without the glare of publicity which so often surrounds proceedings in the Coroner's Court. Secondly, with the aid of the police (who in this matter are subject to his instructions) the procurator fiscal investigates cases of suspected crime and decides whether the evidence available justifies the bringing of proceedings against any person. In the case of the more serious crimes, such as murder, rape, etc., or where questions of doubt or difficulty have arisen, the procurator fiscal will report the matter to the Crown Office and obtain the instructions of the Crown Agent or of the Lord Advocate himself. Should it be decided to raise a prosecution against any person then, if the prosecution is to be brought in the Sheriff Court, the proceedings are normally conducted by the procurator fiscal himself. More serious offences are tried in the High Court of Justiciary, but even in those cases the procurator fiscal, though he does not himself prosecute, conducts the preliminary investigation into the crime and prepares and collates the Crown case.

It is obvious that the procurator fiscal plays a vital part in administering the criminal law in Scotland. There is no comparable official in England, where very much more power in the field of investigating crime and prosecuting criminals is exercised by the police; in such matters in Scotland the police act under the direction of the procurator fiscal and the Crown Office; they do not decide whether a prosecution is to be brought in any particular case and they do not themselves conduct prosecutions. Another remarkable difference between the Scottish and the English systems which touches on the duties of the procurator fiscal is that after a man has been charged with a serious crime in Scotland he does not have to face a preliminary hearing in public before magistrates, as in England. Instead, the pre-trial investigation is carried out in private by the procurator fiscal, and only if there is very clear evidence of guilt will an accused person even be brought to trial.

Private prosecutions are practically unknown in Scotland. Except for a few very minor exceptions provided by Act of Parliament, a private prosecution in Scotland can be brought only with the concurrence of the Lord Advocate or, if he refuses to concur, with the leave of the High Court of Justiciary. The High Court will grant such leave only if the complainer can show that he has some substantial and peculiar personal interest (otherwise than as a member of the general public) in the alleged offence. That such an interest is not easily

THE LAW OF SCOTLAND

established is shown by a case in 1961 (*McBain* v. *Crichton*) which involved the sale of the book *Lady Chatterley's Lover* in Scotland. A certain Mr McBain wished to institute a prosecution against a bookseller in Glasgow for selling that book, on the ground that the book was obscene. He applied to the Lord Advocate for permission to raise a private prosecution, but permission was refused. He then asked the High Court for a 'bill for criminal letters' which, if granted, would have allowed him to raise the prosecution in spite of the Lord Advocate's refusal. The court, however, rejected his application, holding that Mr McBain had not that 'particular and special interest' in the matter which alone would have justified them in acceding to his request.

Apart from the differences which have been mentioned, Scots and English criminal procedure show a number of interesting divergencies. Thus, the jury in a Scottish criminal trial has fifteen members, not twelve as in England. In Scotland there is no opening speech for the prosecution as there is in England; and the defence counsel always delivers his closing speech after that of the prosecutor, so that the prosecutor in Scotland never has the last word, as he generally has under the English procedure. A Scottish jury need not be unanimous in their verdict—majority verdicts are quite common—and there is, in addition to the two verdicts of 'guilty' and 'not guilty', a third possible verdict, namely, that of 'not proven'. The verdict of 'not proven' has exactly the same effect as a verdict of 'not guilty'; it is a verdict of acquittal and the accused person can never be tried again for the same offence, but its merits have been much debated over the years. A person in whose case a 'not proven' verdict has been returned may feel that his name has not been altogether cleared, but on the other hand there have been cases in which such a verdict was returned and where it was difficult to say whether, if the verdict had not existed, the jury would have returned a verdict of 'not guilty' or one of 'guilty'. In one of the most famous cases where a 'not proven' verdict was given—the trial of Madeleine Smith for the murder of her lover in the nineteenth century—it is by no means certain that she would have been acquitted had the verdict of 'not proven' not been available to the jury.

One last point on the criminal law may be noted, namely, that while in England a man may be convicted on the evidence of only one witness, in Scotland this is not possible. Under Scots Law a man cannot (except in certain special cases provided for by statute) be convicted by the uncorroborated evidence of a single person. Some corroboration, either by another witness or from the circumstances of the case, is necessary.

Influence of Scots Law on the Law of England

Scots Law has been responsible for many important developments in legal principle. One of the most famous arose out of the case of Donoghue v. Stevenson —the famous 'snail in the bottle' case. One day in 1928 a certain Mrs Donoghue and a friend of hers went into a café in Paisley and sat down at a table, where the friend ordered a bottle of ginger beer for Mrs Donoghue. The proprietor of the café opened a bottle and brought it to her along with a tumbler. He poured some of the ginger beer out of the bottle into the tumbler and she drank it. As commonly happens, the bottle was made of dark opaque glass, so that Mrs Donoghue could not see what was inside it and, when the remainder of the contents was poured into the tumbler, there floated out on the ginger beer a snail in an advanced state of decomposition. Mrs Donoghue alleged that as a result of this she suffered a severe shock and was taken ill with acute gastro-enteritis.

The result of the incident was that Mrs Donoghue raised an action, not against the proprietor of the café (who could have had no better idea than she as to the contents of the bottle), but against the manufacturer of the ginger beer. She alleged that, although the manufacturer sold his ginger beer to the café proprietor and had no direct relationship with her, nevertheless, in the particular circumstances of the case, since no one could have had any opportunity of inspecting the contents of the bottle between the time when it left the factory and the time it was sold to her by the café proprietor, the manufacturer owed her a duty to see that there was nothing harmful in the ginger beer which he manufactured and she drank. Strange as it may seem, the question whether the manufacturer of an article might in any circumstances owe a duty of care to the ultimate consumer had never been authoritatively decided by the courts, and there was a good deal of difference of judicial opinion before Mrs Donoghue eventually won her case in the House of Lords.

The case of *Donoghue* v. *Stevenson* has become one of the leading cases in the law both of Scotland and of England relating to the recovery of damages for personal injuries and, indeed, it is cited all over the world in countries whose laws derive from the British tradition.

CONCLUSION

This article has attempted to set out some of the more important features of the law of Scotland and to draw attention to some of the more important divergencies which exist between that law and the law of England—especially such as may affect people in their everyday lives. The attempt is necessarily incomplete. There are, for instance, many other fields of law in which the two countries go their separate ways: thus, for example, the ancient—almost sacred— writ of *habeas corpus*, on which English liberties have so greatly depended through the centuries, is unknown in Scotland. There the subject is protected against unlawful imprisonment by a different procedure laid down in the Criminal Procedure (Scotland) Act, 1887. The law relating to the ownership of land is also entirely different in Scotland, where a feudal system of holding (though in a modern form) still largely obtains. And the law concerning illegitimate children, and the circumstances in which they may be legitimated, also differs as between the two countries.

It has not been possible within the compass of this article to treat exhaustively of all these matters, but the main purpose has been to give a broad portrait of Scots Law as an independent system and to emphasize that differences do exist between the two systems, that they can be of importance to ordinary people and that, as a consequence, the reader should not accept without question what is contained in other articles in this volume as being necessarily valid in Scotland but should, if he is personally concerned in any of these matters, at once take legal advice. Lastly, a caution should be given that this article is on very general lines and that legal advice on any particular case should always be sought.

THE CIVIL COURTS

INTRODUCTION

OUR LEGAL SYSTEM is roughly divided into the 'criminal' side and what is called the 'civil' side; and the Courts of Law are similarly divided. In the Criminal Law section of this encyclopaedia you will find a description of the criminal courts; this section describes the more important civil courts and says something about the procedure connected with them.

Definition of 'Civil' side

Civil proceedings means roughly legal proceedings between private persons as opposed to those where (as in the case of crime) the State has an interest. Of course the same facts may lead to both criminal and civil proceedings: if somebody has swindled you, he may be prosecuted criminally for the fraud, but you may have to bring a civil action against him as well in order to recover the property he got from you as the result of the swindle. Most civil proceedings, however, have no connection with crime: they concern such things as misunderstandings over contracts, trespass to property, difficulties about wills, perhaps even libel or slander, or divorce. They are primarily disputes between private individuals in which the State does not desire to intervene—at any rate from a criminal point of view. There are, however, some civil cases where the State has an interest: divorce, for example, which involves public morality and the welfare of children; and cases under the Rent Acts, where the State has sometimes given protection to tenants to which they are not entitled under their contract.

Courts for all purposes

As in the case of the criminal courts, different courts have been provided so that there is an appropriate tribunal for all sorts of proceedings according to their subject-matter, the amount of money involved, the degree of specialized knowledge required, and so on.

COUNTY COURTS

Introduction

Some cases have to be tried in the High Court, either because of their importance from a legal point of view, or because of the amount of money involved, or because they are of a kind which only the High Court is allowed to try. But in addition to the High Court there are what are called County Courts where less important cases can be tried more quickly, more easily, and more cheaply than in the High Court. As these are the courts into which most people are likely to go (if they go at all) they are described here more fully than the other kinds of court.

Description

There are over four hundred County Courts, and they cover the whole of England and Wales. For this purpose they are divided into fifty-eight 'circuits' (or districts) and each circuit has a judge (sometimes two) who must visit each court in the circuit at least once a month.

These judges have to be barristers of at least seven years' standing; but, of course, they have always been in practice a great deal longer than that and are very experienced. They are known as 'His Honour Judge ——' and are addressed in court as 'Your Honour'.

In addition to the judges each County Court has a Registrar. He looks after the administration of the court, but he also acts as a judge—for example, in cases where the amount involved is not more than £10.

Registrars have to be solicitors of at least seven years' standing; but again, of course, they are likely to have been solicitors for far longer than that, and they are persons of great experience.

Jurisdiction

Jurisdiction means, 'What cases can a Court try?' Almost any kind of case can be tried in a County Court. Indeed, if a case is brought in the High Court which could have been brought in a County Court it may be remitted (that is, transferred) to a County Court; and in some cases, if it is not remitted but is tried in the High Court, the plaintiff, even though he is successful, may not be allowed all his costs—because he should have saved expense and brought his case in the County Court.

The main limit to the jurisdiction of County Courts is a financial one. They can try almost all cases involving contract or tort, but only if the claim is for not more than £400—or both parties agree to have it tried in a County Court. Sometimes a plaintiff deliberately limits his claim to £400 so as to have the advantages of having it tried in a County Court; but, on the other hand, if the defendant (the person against whom the claim is being made) objects to its being tried there the judge must transfer it to the High Court if the claim is for more than £100.

The only cases of contract or tort which a County Court cannot try are actions for libel or slander, seduction, or breach of promise of marriage. The main reasons for these exclusions are largely historical; but there are some good practical reasons. One is that the damages in such cases may go far beyond any £400 limit; another is that such cases usually involve a jury, and these are seldom found in County Courts.

Another important type of case which comes within the jurisdiction of County Courts is actions for the recovery of land. Here the limit is that the 'net annual value for rating' of the land in question must not exceed £100.

In particular, of course, County Courts deal with questions arising out of the Rent Acts, where a landlord cannot recover possession of a 'controlled' dwelling-house unless he can satisfy the judge that suitable alternative accommodation is or will be available for the tenant, or that he can establish one or other of the grounds laid down in the Rent Acts (see the section on the Rent Acts). Rent Act cases have for many years formed a substantial part of the County Courts' work.

Other matters which are dealt with in County Courts include the adoption of children, bankruptcy, and the administration of the estates of deceased persons.

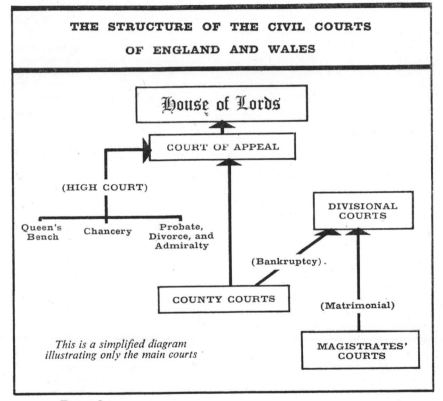

THE STRUCTURE OF THE CIVIL COURTS OF ENGLAND AND WALES

House of Lords

COURT OF APPEAL

(HIGH COURT)

Queen's Bench — Chancery — Probate, Divorce, and Admiralty

DIVISIONAL COURTS

(Bankruptcy)

COUNTY COURTS

(Matrimonial)

This is a simplified diagram illustrating only the main courts

MAGISTRATES' COURTS

Procedure

If you want to bring an action against somebody in a County Court you must usually do it in the district in which he lives or carries on business.

The normal way to start an action (or 'enter a plaint', as it is called) is to fill in a form (known as a *Praecipe*) which you file at the Court office. This form contains the names and addresses of the parties concerned and sets out shortly the nature and amount of the claim you are making. At the same time you file *Particulars of Claim*. For example, the *Praecipe* might say quite shortly that it was a claim for £84 3*s* 6*d* for goods supplied, but the *Particulars* would set out a complete list of the debt—*e.g.* 'January 14th, 1962, sports jacket, £10 10*s*; February 3rd, pair of brown shoes, £5 10*s*', and so on, the total adding up to the £84 3*s* 6*d* on the *Praecipe*.

When these two documents have been filed the clerk will hand you what is called a *Plaint Note*. This gives the date on which the action will be heard.

Next a summons has to be served on the other party to appear on the date mentioned. You can do this yourself or it can be done by the court bailiff. With this summons the defendant also gets a copy of your particulars of claim together with forms on which he can either admit the claim, defend it, or make a counter-claim, as he sees fit. He must return one of these within eight days.

If the defendant admits the claim, then he has only to say so on the form and also to indicate how he proposes to pay—*e.g.* by instalments.

If he wishes to defend he must give the grounds of his defence on the form —*e.g.* that some of the goods were not supplied, or were returned.

If he wishes to make a counter-claim, this is really like a separate action, and it can accompany either an admission or a defence. The plaintiff may have broken some agreement with the defendant: the defendant might therefore admit the claim for the goods sold, but counter-claim for damages for breach of contract.

Default summons. If your claim is for a definite sum of money (*e.g.* a debt) quite a useful alternative to an ordinary action in the County Court is by what is called a 'default summons'. The major difference is that there is a special form of *Praecipe* and that no date is at first fixed for the hearing. Under this procedure, if the defendant does not deliver a defence within eight days, you can 'sign judgment', as it is called, without further proof. This means that the defendant has now been ordered by the court to pay the amount of your claim plus your costs.

Trial. If the person against whom you are making the claim puts in a defence or counter-claim or both, then of course the case has to be heard so that the court can decide who is right and what ought to be done about it. This will usually be done by the County Court Judge, but in some cases it may be by the Registrar.

If the defendant does not turn up you can sometimes get judgment in his absence. If he does, the case starts by the claimant (the plaintiff) or his advocate opening the case and calling his witnesses, who are examined by him and then cross-examined by the other side. Then the defendant or his advocate replies and, if he calls any witnesses, they too are examined and cross-examined. Finally the plaintiff usually has a chance to reply to what the defence have said.

Professional help. Whether you are the plaintiff or the defendant you are entitled to conduct your own case in the County Court, or indeed in any other court; but in any but the simplest case you will be well-advised to consult a solicitor. He 'knows the ropes'—and they are tricky. Furthermore, if it comes to a trial, your opponent may be represented by solicitor or barrister, and you will be at a disadvantage if you are not represented.

Even before the case is heard a professional man is a great help. Apart from knowing the procedure and how and when the various documents have to be filed, he will be able to advise you about the evidence that will be required, what witnesses you ought to call, and how you can make sure they turn up.

Obviously it is not enough to have only your word against that of your opponent. Although the judge may be able to form a fairly accurate opinion about who is telling the truth, in a way both of you may be telling the truth as you see it, and what will count in the long run will be the evidence you can bring to corroborate what you say.

Judgment. After both sides have been heard there comes the judgment. If the court decides that the plaintiff has not proved his case, that is the end of the matter and judgment is given for the defendant. If, however, the plaintiff has made out his case, the judgment obviously will depend on what kind of case it is. If it is for the recovery of goods or land the judgment may simply order their return; but there may be other matters to be decided, such as when the return shall be made. In Rent Restriction cases the judge has to consider whether, although the case has been made out, it is 'reasonable' to make an order for possession. In hire-purchase cases he may have to decide whether some or all of the goods are to be returned. In ordinary cases of debt he may have to make some order about payment by instalments.

Enforcement of Judgment. Even though you have got a judgment the defendant may not obey it. There are a number of ways of enforcing judgments or orders.

In the case of recovery of land or goods it can be done by a 'warrant of possession' or a 'warrant of delivery', as the case may be. These are carried out by the court bailiff.

In the case of money claims there are various methods. One is called 'execution'. This means that the plaintiff fills in a form at the office of the court, and a warrant will then be issued authorizing the bailiff to seize sufficient of the defendant's goods for sale by auction to satisfy the judgment and the plaintiff's costs. A few difficulties may arise over this: for example, certain goods cannot be seized by law; or there may be trouble because goods are seized which do not belong to the defendant—e.g. because they are on hire purchase.

Another method is called a 'judgment summons'. This requires much the same formality as the original hearing. The purpose is to discover what means the defendant has to pay the debt: consequently, it is not much use unless the plaintiff is in a position to produce some evidence that he can in fact pay something, even if not the whole of the debt. In order to get the defendant to court you must have paid him 'conduct money'—i.e. a reasonable sum in cash to cover his journey—and no order will be made unless the judge or registrar is satisfied that it was at least offered to him. It is only if it is proved to the court that the defendant could have paid that there is any question of sending him to prison: there is (apart from a very few special exceptions) no longer any question of imprisonment for debt as such. Usually what happens is that the court makes a new order to fit the defendant's ability to pay—and it is often so small that it is very unsatisfactory from the plaintiff's point of view.

A third method of enforcing a judgment for a money claim is by what are called 'garnishee' proceedings. If the person who owes you money is himself owed money by a third person, these proceedings enable you to get that money (or enough of it to satisfy your debt and costs) passed over directly from the third person to you. This is particularly useful where your debtor has a bank account in credit—provided you get your garnishee order before he has managed to take his money out of the bank.

Appeals

Either party who is dissatisfied with the decision of a County Court has a right of appeal. These appeals go to the Court of Appeal, which is described below. As, in the event of appeal, professional help is certainly indispensable, there is little point in describing the technicalities involved. In many cases you need leave to appeal; in others you have an unfettered right, but you would be wise to take advice on whether to exercise it. In all cases there is a time limit within which the appeal must be brought.

HIGH COURT OF JUSTICE

Introduction

If a civil case is outside the jurisdiction of the County Courts it must usually be tried in one of the divisions of what is called the High Court of Justice. This sits at the Royal Courts of Justice in London, in a vast building on the north side of the division between the Strand and Fleet Street. Further north, just behind the Royal Courts, are the Bankruptcy Courts and also Lincoln's Inn, where barristers who practise in the Chancery Division tend to have their chambers; further south, just across the street, is the Temple, where other barristers practise.

Description

The High Court is divided into three divisions—for the sake of convenience. Each division is adapted to try particular types of case, and the way in which cases are assigned to particular divisions is explained below.
The divisions are called:

> Queen's Bench,
> Chancery, and
> Probate, Divorce, and Admiralty.

There are a number of Courts within each division, ranging from a dozen or more downwards. Each of these Courts is presided over by a High Court Judge, who is known as 'The Hon. Mr Justice ——' and is addressed in Court as 'My Lord'. In the Divorce division the Judge is sometimes a County Court Judge or a Queen's Counsel who is given a special 'commission' to sit as a High Court Judge.

Queen's Bench Division

Description. This is the largest division, and the one which tries the greatest variety of cases. The President is the Lord Chief Justice of England. He is also the President of the Court of Criminal Appeal and rarely sits as an ordinary Judge of the Queen's Bench except in criminal trials at the Old Bailey. There are thirty-one other Queen's Bench Judges.

The cases tried in the Queen's Bench include such matters as breach of contract, torts such as trespass, or road or factory accidents, libel, slander, malicious prosecution, false imprisonment, seduction, and breach of promise of marriage. Apart from the last six cases, where either side may demand a Jury, they are usually heard before a Judge sitting alone.

Procedure. Proceedings are started in the Queen's Bench by a 'writ of summons' (which corresponds with the *Praecipe* in the County Court). This is a document which is issued by the plaintiff or his solicitor and calls on the defendant to 'enter an appearance' within eight days, failing which judgment may be given in his absence. It also contains a short statement of what is claimed.

In some cases the writ can be 'specially endorsed'. This means that the details as well as the outline of the claim appear on the writ, so that the plaintiff has stated his whole case and therefore can get judgment much more speedily if the defendant fails to appear.

In more complicated cases, in addition to the writ there is a 'statement of claim' (corresponding to the 'particulars of claim' in the County Court). This statement of claim can be delivered at the same time as the writ, or at latest within ten days of the defendant entering an appearance.

When the defendant has the statement of claim he must answer it within fourteen days by a document which sets out which parts of the claim he admits and which parts he denies, and he can also make a counter-claim as in the County Court. If there is a counter-claim the plaintiff has to reply to it, but he need not reply to a mere defence.

By this stage both sides have a fair idea of the issues which will have to be fought; but in order further to save time and expense it is open to either side to ask for 'particulars' of anything the other side has said in his pleadings. For example, if the claim is for the price of goods sold and the defendant alleges that the goods were defective, the plaintiff could ask for particulars of the nature of the defects alleged.

There are, of course, many other arrangements which have to be made before trial, and these are controlled by a Queen's Bench Master. He decides such things as the method of trial (*e.g.* whether there shall be a jury); and if there is a dispute about the time for delivering the pleadings, about answering requests for particulars, or about what documents ought to be produced by either side, he makes the necessary orders.

Briefing Counsel. Although you can appear in person in the Queen's Bench you would be very unwise to attempt to conduct your case on a do-it-yourself basis. All the steps leading up to the trial, as well as the trial itself, are highly technical, and your solicitor will brief counsel (employ a barrister) to deal with them. Apart from litigants in person, only barristers have the right of audience in the High Court.

Trial. The trial and methods of enforcing judgment are very like those in the County Court.

Chancery Division

Jurisdiction. In practice there is never a jury in the Chancery Division. The cases tried are not suitable for this method of trial, because they involve primarily questions of law rather than of fact. They include the administration of estates, trusts, mortgages, interpretation of wills, partnership, companies, and the guardianship of infants.

Procedure. The procedure varies slightly from that in the Queen's Bench;

but, as in this court perhaps more than any other, it would be sheer folly for a layman to attempt to conduct his own case, only the broad differences will be mentioned here.

The first is that, although actions can be started by a writ, they can also be started in other ways—principally by what is known as an 'originating summons'.

The second is that in many cases there are no witnesses: the evidence is taken on 'affidavit'—that is, by written documents, sworn to on oath.

The third is that you cannot get judgment in default of appearance of the defendant quite so simply as in the Queen's Bench: it is left to the judge to decide what you appear to be entitled to.

Very often in Chancery cases, unlike those in other courts, the parties are not really opposed to each other: they merely want to discover what they ought to do. For example, trustees may want to know whether the powers given to them authorize them to put the money in a particular kind of invest-ment, or whether a will allows them to advance money to a beneficiary for some particular purpose. The 'originating summons' mentioned above is very suitable for this because no 'pleadings' are necessary (*i.e.* there need be no statement of claim, defence, reply, and so on, as described under Queen's Bench above), nor is it necessary to call witnesses for examination and cross-examination.

Probate, Divorce, and Admiralty

Jurisdiction. This division covers a curious mixture of types of case not covered by the other two divisions. It is largely the result of historical accident, culminating in the reorganization of the Supreme Court of Judicature toward the end of the nineteenth century.

Probate. The Probate side deals with wills—for example, where there is doubt whether it has been properly 'executed', whether the testator was of sound mind when he made it, who is entitled to probate of the will (that is, entitled to administer it). It does *not* deal with the construction or meaning of a will: this, as we have seen above, is a matter for the Chancery Division.

Divorce. The Divorce side deals not only with divorce in the popular sense (dissolution of marriage) but also with judicial separation (where the parties remain married but no longer bound to live together), restitution of conjugal rights (where one of the parties is ordered to return to the other) and nullity (where the marriage is declared void).

In the divorce Courts proceedings are brought by 'petition' and the defence is called an 'answer'. In some cases the other side may not only answer but bring a 'cross-petition'—*i.e.* himself (or herself) 'pray' for a divorce. For example, my wife might seek to divorce me on the grounds of cruelty. I might not wish to defend it, in which case it would go into the 'undefended' list. On the other hand, I might wish not only to 'answer' by denying the cruelty but also to 'cross-petition' for divorce on the grounds of my wife's adultery. Such a case would be contested and would therefore go into the 'defended' list; and the Judge, after hearing the evidence, would have to decide which (if either of us) was entitled to judgment in his favour.

The judgment is called a 'decree'. At first it is a 'decree nisi'—*nisi* being the

Latin for 'unless'—unless some reason is discovered why it should not have been granted. After a certain period (three months at present) the decree is made 'absolute', though in certain cases the time may be shorter, at the Judge's discretion.

Admiralty. The Admiralty side deals with collisions at sea, salvage claims, and other matters concerning ships, cargoes, and seamen. To help the Judge there sit with him two 'Elder Brethren of Trinity House' who are experts in maritime technicalities and practice: they advise the Judge but play no actual part in the final judgment.

APPEALS

Although there are other Courts of appeal, such as Divisional Courts, the major Courts of appeal in civil cases are the Court of Appeal and above it the House of Lords. Appeals from the High Court (Queen's Bench, Chancery, and Probate, Divorce, and Admiralty) go first to the Court of Appeal. So do appeals from County Courts.

Court of Appeal

Description. There are usually four Courts of Appeal sitting at the same time, and each Court is composed of three Judges.

The Judges are the Master of the Rolls and eleven others who are called Lords Justices of Appeal (called 'The Rt. Hon. Lord Justice Blank' and addressed in Court as 'My Lord'). Occasionally 'puisne' Judges of the High Court (*i.e.* Judges below the rank of Judges of the Court of Appeal) may sit to make up numbers—for example, if there is illness or the pressure of business requires an extra Court.

County Court Appeals. In the case of County Courts any party has a right of appeal on a question of law or on the admission or rejection of evidence. In some cases the leave of the Judge is required if the sum under dispute does not exceed £20. There is also a right of appeal on a question of fact; but usually the amount claimed must exceed £200 or, if the claim concerns land, the rateable value must exceed £60. The notice of intention to appeal must be given within three weeks.

High Court appeals. There is a similar right of appeal from the Queen's Bench, Chancery, or Probate, Divorce, and Admiralty divisions. The notice of intention to appeal must usually be given within six weeks.

Procedure. At the appeal the case is argued on the facts which were considered in the court below or on the judgment which was given there. It is only in very rare cases that additional evidence can be given: if it is allowed, it must be evidence that was not available at the time of the original trial or could not have been discovered with reasonable diligence. No further evidence can be given where the appeal is simply on a question of law.

Consequently it is very rare to find witnesses in the Court of Appeal. In the case of an appeal from the High Court all the evidence and the judgment will have been taken down in shorthand, and a transcript of this will be available. The proceedings are mostly confined to reading out the relevant passages, followed by argument about them by counsel on either side.

Judgment. Finally the court gives its decision—which may or may not be unanimous. Each judge delivers his own judgment. The result may be either that the result reached in the lower court is confirmed or that the decision is reversed and the judgment of the Court of Appeal substituted for it. Very rarely a new trial may be ordered, but this will be done only if there was a substantial miscarriage of justice at the original trial—as by the judge misdirecting the jury or not leaving to them a question which it was for them to decide.

HOUSE OF LORDS

The House of Lords is the supreme Court of Appeal in civil as in criminal cases. The composition of the House of Lords when sitting as a Court of Appeal is described in the Criminal Law section of this encyclopaedia. It takes not less than five judges to form a court.

As the supreme Court of Appeal it is the only court which is not bound by the decisions of any other court, though like other courts it will, except in certain well-defined circumstances, follow its own previous decisions; and indeed it will pay regard to the decisions even of inferior courts. Consequently, if a decision of the House of Lords is to be changed, the only way it can be done, there being no higher court, is by Act of Parliament. The Royal prerogative in connection with criminal cases does not extend to judgments in civil cases.

There is an appeal to the House of Lords only by leave. This leave has to be sought first from the Court of Appeal; if they refuse it it can be sought from the House of Lords. The application for leave must be made within one month, and the appeal itself must be lodged within six months.

ADDENDUM

Law Reform (Husband and Wife) Act 1962

IT IS STATED in more than one section of this book (*e.g.* in the sections on Marriage, Road Traffic, Insurance, the Law Relating to Scotland), that as a general rule, husbands and wives cannot sue each other for wrongful acts committed by one against the other, *e.g.* trespass, libel or slander, negligence and so on, wrongful acts which are known in English Law as 'torts', a technical word which is described in the section dealing with the general law on torts.

This very ancient rule of our law has been completely changed by a new Act of Parliament—the Law Reform (Husband and Wife) Act, 1962. Very briefly, this provides that from August 1st, 1962, a husband and wife can sue each other just as if they were not married.

The same Act provides that the law in Scotland is also to be changed to the same effect from the same date.

The passing of this Act is not likely to lead to a spate of litigation between husbands and wives. It has, however, one consequence of considerable practical importance. If, for example, a husband causes injury to his wife through his negligence and the husband has an insurance policy—either a personal liability policy, or some other, such as a comprehensive motor car policy, his insurers will now be liable to pay her proper claims just as they would if she were a stranger. Hitherto, many a wife who has been injured in a motor accident as a result of her husband's negligence has been unable to claim anything under her husband's policy unless that policy contained some special clause in her favour. Even then her rights were limited. Now, the fact that she can sue means that she is covered by the policy. The same principle applies to a husband injured by his wife's negligence.

Transport Act, 1962

This Act provides for the reorganization of the National Transport undertakings. The function of the former British Transport Commission is now divided among a Railways Board, a London Board (which is responsible for London Transport), a Docks Board, and a Waterways Board. The Boards are independent of each other. But, in addition to this reorganization, the Act makes a substantial change by permitting the Boards to act much more as commercial concerns and to have much greater freedom with regard to fixing their rates and charges.

Landlord and Tenant Act, 1962

This Act came into force on November 1st, 1962. It provides that all weekly tenants, whose rent includes no payment in respect of board, shall be provided with rent books by their landlords, and specifies the particulars which have to be given in those rent books. One of the most important is that the name and address of the landlord shall be included. In fact, one of the main reasons for the passing of this small but important Act was because so many weekly tenants do not know who their landlord is. Where the premises are protected by the Rent Acts it is already an obligation of the landlord to provide a rent book. This Act gives a similar right to all weekly tenants whose rent does not include anything in respect of board.

INDEX

A

'A' ordinary shares, 273.
636
'A' (Public Carriers)
Licence, 411-13
Abatement notice, 108
Abduction, 585
Abortion, defined, 581
Absolute bars to divorce,
188-9
Absolute bills of sale, 460,
461
unregistered, 463
Absolute discharge, 615
Absolute privilege, 548-9,
551
Acceptance of bills of
exchange, 425
Acceptance of offer (con-
tract), 274-7
Acceptance of risk in tort,
473-4, 485
Acceptor of bill of exchange,
421, 425
'Access' to children, 196
Accessory before and after
the fact, 566
Accident and illness insurance, types of, 664-6
'Accident' as defence in
tort, 472-3
Accidents:
fatal, see Fatal accidents
'foreseeability' of cause
of, 482-3, 505
more than one cause of,
480-1
motor car, see Motor-car
accidents
railway, 479-80, 484
road, see Road accidents
'Account payee' on cheques,
426
'Accounts' (Stock Ex-
change), 633
'Acknowledgement of Ser-
vice', 193
Acquisition of Land
(Authorization Pro-
cedure) Act (1946), 63
'Act of God', 411, 473
Actions:
breach of contract, 296
limitations on right of
bringing, 375-6

Actions—*continued*
motoring, procedure in,
508-9
right of, 466
see also legal proceedings
Acts of bankruptcy, 377-9
bankruptcy starts with
earliest of, 383
'Actuarial' basis, premium
fixed by, 641
'*Actus non facet reum nisi
mens sit rea*', 568
Adjudication of bank-
ruptcy, 380-2
annulment of, 381
Administration, Letters of.
See Letters of Adminis-
tration
Administration of Justice
Act (1960), 609, 611
leave to appeal to House
of Lords under, 622
publication of certain
matters no longer con-
tempt of Court, 609-10
Administrator:
of estate, right of action
passing to, 490, 495
Admiralty Court, 443
contributory negligence
dealt with by, 475
fatal accident cases before,
495
Adopted Children Register,
220, 224-5
Adopted persons, fatal
accidents to, 495
Adoption, 220-5, 228
infant's qualifications, 221
meaning and effect of, 220
probationary period for,
222-3
Adoption Act (1960), 236
Adoption certificates, 236
Adoption of Children Act
(1926), 220
Adoption order, 220
application to Court for,
220-1, 223-4
applicants' qualifications,
221
conditions essential to
granting, 221, 224
illegitimate child, 236
provisional, 221, 223
revocation of, 236

Adoption Societies, 220
Adultery, 184, 583
claims for damages for,
491
conduct conducing to,
191, 212
divorce petitioner's own,
188, 190, 197
Magistrates' order regarding, 211, 212
proof of, 184
'revival' of condoned, 18ɔ
wife's departure caused
by, 184
Advance Payments Code,
39, 40
Advertisement:
change of name, 248
display of outdoor, 52, 61
Advertisements (Hire Pur-
chase) Act (1957), 309
Aeroplanes, noise from, 530
Affairs of State, absolute
privilege for, 549
Affidavit:
Chancery Division evi-
dence taken on, 856
debtor's, 380
definition, 856
Inland Revenue, see
Inland Revenue affidavit
Affiliation order, 234
application for, 237-9
legal aid and, 515
revocation or variation
of, 239
Affinity:
as bar to marriage, 178
fatal accidents to rela-
tions by, 495
Affreightment, contract of,
414, 416
Age of Marriage Act (1929),
839
Age of marrying, 177
Scotland, 839
Agency, 443-8
termination of, 444, 447
Agents:
authority of, 447
classes of, 448
del credere, 429, 448
dealers are not finance
company's, 304
effects of contracts made
by, 446-7

861

F

Factories Acts, 395
Factors, 448
lien of, 442, 448
Factors Act (1889), 292
Factory, statutory definition of, 396
Facts and opinions in 'fair comment', 555
Faculty of Advocates, 832
Faculty Office, Westminster, 179
'Fair comment on matter of public interest', 553–6
'fair' in, 555–6
justification distinguished from, 552
False document defined for purposes of forgery, 605
False imprisonment, juries can still try, 557
False pretences, 595–7
by 'Ring Trick', 596
False representation, 467
False statements, 297
birth registration, 219
Legal Advice application, 517
Fatal accidents, 489–98
air travel, 726
new statutory rule, 490–1
old Common Law rule, 489–90
Fatal Accidents Act (1846), 490
air travel under, 726
dependants' rights under, 494–8
Fatal Accidents Act (1959), dependants under, 495–8
Fatal Accidents Acts, 234
Fatal and non-fatal 'offences against the person', 575–83
Father:
control of child by, 503–4
custody of children, 225–6
illegitimate child and, 235
putative, 237
Feeble-minded, the, see Mental disorder
Fees:
auctioneer's, 22
executors not entitled to, 695
mortgage deed, 14
solicitors', 14, 679
Felonies:
definition of, 565
misdemeanours distinguished from, 565

Fences, boundary, 520–2, 534
Fidelity bonds, 432
'Fi. fa.', see Fieri facias
Fieri facias, writ of, 373
Films, see Cinematograph
Finance:
home ownership, 26–48
house-buying, 6–9
Finance Act (1949), 29
Finance Act (1956), annuities under, 360–1
Finance Act (1960), Estate duty five-year rule under, 688
Finance Act (1961), 428
Finance Acts (1960 & 1961), 362
Finance Act (1962), 30
Finance Act (1963), 14, 29
Finance companies (hire purchase), 302, 304, 630–1
dealer not their agent, 304
Finance Houses Association, 630
Finding, rights of finder, 624
Fines:
business names offences, 261
caravan site licence offences, 59
enforcement notice defiance, 57
excessive rent or demand of premium, 157
failure to execute repairs, 33
lodgings offences, 161
misrepresentation re patent, 313
slum clearance, 67, 68
Fire, damage by, 89, 91
Fire insurance, 654–5
house—purchases not completed, 10–11
leasehold property, 89
Firearms, assault with, 583
Firms (partnership), 262–6
Fish Royal, ownership of, 826
Fishing, 807–12
close season, 812
high seas, 807
inland rivers, 809–12
licence fee, 812
licences from River Boards, 812

Fishing—continued
rights of fishery owner, 809
territorial water, 808–9
tidal rivers, 809
Fixed Term Insurance.
See 'Term' Life policy
Fixtures, 114–17
agricultural holdings, 115–17, 164, 169–70
Flats:
notice to quit, 87
rent control and, 144
repairs to, 113
Flint v. Lovell (1935), 491–2
'Floating charge', 273, 462
Flying clubs, 781
Foreclosure, 375
Forenames:
change of, 250
Christian names distinguished from, 244
Forgery, 604–7
negotiable instrument, 424
Forgery Act (1913):
definition of forgery, 605
documents which it is a crime to forge, 606
penalties, 606
Fornication, 583
Founders' shares, 273
Fox's Libel Act (1792), 558
Fraud:
limitation period for action in, 376
obtaining credit by, 597
Frauds and cheats, 597
'Fraudulent', meanings of, 377
Fraudulent conversion, definition and examples of, 594–5
Fraudulent conveyance, 377–8
Fraudulent misrepresentation, 299–300
Fraudulent preference for one creditor, 378, 384
Fraudulent trading by director, 274
Freehold property, 16
Freight, 414
Friendly Societies, 407–9
benefits from, 498, 513
officer of, 408
rules of, 409
working-men's clubs as, 781